Let's Go:

ITALY

is the best book for anyone traveling on a budget. Here's why:

▓ No other guidebook has as many budget listings.

In Italy we list over 6,000 budget travel bargains. We tell you the cheapest way to get around, and where to get an inexpensive and satisfying meal once you've arrived. We give hundreds of money-saving tips that anyone can use, plus invaluable advice on discounts and deals for students, children, families, and senior travelers.

▓ Let's Go researchers have to make it on their own.

Our Harvard-Radcliffe researcher-writers travel on budgets as tight as your own—no expense accounts, no free hotel rooms.

▓ Let's Go is completely revised each year.

We don't just update the prices, we go back to the place. If a charming café has become an overpriced tourist trap, we'll replace the listing with a new and better one.

▓ No other guidebook includes all this:

Honest, engaging coverage of both the cities and the countryside; up-to-the-minute prices, directions, addresses, phone numbers, and opening hours; in-depth essays on local culture, history, and politics; comprehensive listings on transportation between and within regions and cities; straight advice on work and study, budget accommodations, sights, nightlife, and food; detailed city and regional maps; and much more.

▓ Let's Go is for anyone who wants to see Italy on a budget.

LET'S GO PUBLICATIONS

Let's Go: Alaska & The Pacific Northwest
Let's Go: Britain & Ireland
Let's Go: California
Let's Go: Central America
Let's Go: Eastern Europe
Let's Go: Europe
Let's Go: France
Let's Go: Germany
Let's Go: Greece & Turkey
Let's Go: Ireland
Let's Go: Israel & Egypt
Let's Go: Italy
Let's Go: London
Let's Go: Mexico
Let's Go: New York City
Let's Go: Paris
Let's Go: Rome
Let's Go: Southeast Asia
Let's Go: Spain & Portugal
Let's Go: Switzerland & Austria
Let's Go: USA
Let's Go: Washington, D.C.

Map Guides (coming March 1996)

Let's Go: Boston
Let's Go: London
Let's Go: New York City
Let's Go: Paris
Let's Go: San Francisco
Let's Go: Washington, D.C.

LET'S GO

The Budget Guide to

ITALY

1996

Celeste Raina Young
Editor

Lisa Ann Halliday
Associate Editor

Amy E. Yeager
Assistant Editor

Macmillan

HELPING LET'S GO

If you want to share your discoveries, suggestions, or corrections, please drop us
a line. We read every piece of correspondence, whether a postcard, a 10-page
e-mail, or a coconut. All suggestions are passed along to our researcher-writers.
Please note that mail received after May 1996 may be too late for the 1997 book,
but will be retained for the following edition.

Address mail to:

Let's Go: Italy
Let's Go, Inc.
One Story Street
Cambridge, MA 02138
USA

Send e-mail to:

LetsGo@delphi.com
Subject: "Let's Go: Italy"

Visit Let's Go in the travel section of:

http://www.americanexpress.com/
student/

In addition to the invaluable travel advice our readers share with us, many are
kind enough to offer their services as researchers or editors. Unfortunately, the
charter of Let's Go, Inc. enables us to employ only currently enrolled Harvard-
Radcliffe students.

Published in Great Britain 1996 by Macmillan Reference Books, a division of
Macmillan Publishers Limited, 25 Eccleston Place, London SW1W 9NF and
Basingstoke

10 9 8 7 6 5 4 3 2 1

Maps by David Lindroth, copyright © 1996, 1995, 1994, 1993, 1992, 1991,
1990, 1989, 1986 by St. Martin's Press, Inc.

Map revisions pp. 2-3, 497, 557 by Let's Go, Inc.

Published in the United States of America by St. Martin's Press, Inc.

ISBN: 0 333 65288 6

Let's Go: Italy is written by Let's Go Publications, 1
Story Street, Cambridge, MA 02138, USA.

About Let's Go

THIRTY-SIX YEARS OF WISDOM

Back in 1960, a few students at Harvard University banded together to produce a 20-page pamphlet offering a collection of tips on budget travel in Europe. This modest, mimeographed packet was offered to passengers as an extra on their student charter flights to Europe. The following year, students traveling to Europe researched the first full-fledged edition of *Let's Go: Europe*, a pocket-sized book featuring irreverent write-ups of sights and a decidedly youthful slant. Throughout the 60s, our guides reflected the times; one section of the 1968 *Let's Go: Europe* discussed "Street Singing in Europe on No Dollars a Day," which we said "has very little to do with music." The 1969 guide to America led off with sound advice on San Francisco's Haight-Ashbury ("dig the scene"). During the 70s and 80s, we gradually added regional and city guides, and expanded coverage into the Middle East, Central America, and Asia.

We've seen a lot in 36 years. *Let's Go: Europe* is now the world's best-selling international guide, translated into seven languages. And our guides are still researched, written, and produced entirely by students who know first-hand how to see the world on the cheap. As the budget travel world expands, so does Let's Go. The first editions of *Let's Go: Central America* and *Let's Go: Southeast Asia* hit the shelves this year, and *Let's Go: India & Nepal* is right on their heels. Our useful new series of map guides combine concise city coverage with vivid foldout maps. Our new guides bring our total number of titles, with their spirit of adventure and their honesty, accuracy, and editorial integrity, to 28.

HOW WE DO IT

Each guide is completely revised and updated every year by a well-traveled set of 200 students, who work on all aspects of each guide's development. Every winter, we recruit over 110 researchers and 50 editors to write our books anew. After several months of training, Researcher-Writers hit the road for seven weeks of exploration, from Anchorage to Ankara, Estonia to El Salvador, Iceland to Indonesia. Those hired possess a rare combination of budget travel sense, writing ability, stamina, and courage. Train strikes, stolen luggage, food poisoning, and irate tourist officials are all part of a day's work. Editors work from spring to fall, massaging copy written on Himalayan bus rides into witty yet informative prose. A student staff of typesetters, cartographers, publicists, and managers keeps our lively and sophisticated team together. In September, the collected efforts of the summer are delivered to our printer, who turns them into books in record time. And even as you read this, work on next year's editions is well underway.

WHY WE DO IT

At Let's Go, our goal is to give you a great vacation. We don't think of budget travel as the last recourse of the destitute; we believe that it's the only way to travel. Living cheaply and simply brings you closer to the real people and places you've been saving up to visit. Our book will ease your anxieties and answer your questions about the basics—to help you get off the beaten track and explore. Once you learn the ropes, we encourage you to put Let's Go away now and then to strike out on your own. As any seasoned traveler will tell you, the best discoveries are often those you make yourself. When you find something worth sharing, drop us a line. We're Let's Go Publications, One Story Street, Cambridge, MA 02138, USA (e-mail: LetsGo@delphi.com).

HAPPY TRAVELS!

Contents

Maps

Color Maps

Researcher-Writers

Katrina Berkow Barnett   *Liguria, Piedmont, Lombardy, Emilia-Romagna*
We love Katrina, but not as much as the policeman who found her stolen backpack in the train station and subsequently took her out to dinner, or the Turinese-*cum*-hostel resident who threatened to throw himself in front of a train when he heard about Bachelor #1. In spite of these distractions, the Riviera sun, and her pilgrimage to Umberto Eco's monastery (see page 289), Katrina sent us beautiful copy.

A. Omiyinka Doris   *Trentino-Alto Adige, Friuli-Venezia Giulia,*
Veneto, Emilia-Romagna, Le Marche
Omiyinka thought she'd seen it all in New York City, but that was nothing compared to northeast Italy. Spacious rooms and lovely views gave way to prostitute roommates, halfway-house hostels, drug deals *in piazza*, and Rimini's scope scene à la McDonalds. But Omi rose above the situation with her impressive language skills, and withstood that most Italian of pickup lines, "Would you like to get a coffee with me?" She'll be living in Padua with even more friendly *Italiani* this year.

Sandrine S. Goffard   *Calabria, Sicily*
No woman had researched Sicily since the first edition of the guide. That is, until SANDRINE. Sandrine went out, and three train strikes later, Sandrine came back. She may have wanted to use her black-belt martial art skills on each and every one of the slimy men in Sicily; she may bemoan her acquired "*gelato* butt"; she may even lament our inability to spell her last name correctly—but we're just glad she didn't disappear down one of Etna's craters or amongst the Aeolian Islands.

Corey M. O'Hara   *Abruzzo, Apulia, Basilicata, Campania*
Corey is the man. Corey rewrote southern Italy. Corey called almost every day. Twice. Corey solved the Capri Hotel Mystery. Corey drew multi-colored, alternative pictures of gnome life. Corey cared enough to send the very best. Corey braved bats, spiders, imminent death, and the wrath of the *pensione* owner to retrieve his copybatch from the edge of a ravine. But most of all, Corey just is.

Maria Alexandra Ordoñez   *Sardinia, Tuscany, Umbria*
Last year, Ali went to Switzerland; this year she went back in time. From the backroads of Sardinia to the *duomo* of Florence, from misplacing a contact lens to replacing all of our information, Ali stomped through her itinerary clad in a miniskirt (to avoid attention) and hiking boots (to avoid blisters). Her tan lines (not that *we* know anything about tans) would wow the most decorated of zebra. Congratulations, Ali the phone numbers were all there from the start.

Jonathan Caverley   *Tunisia (and Morocco, but that's another book)*
Third-year trooper for the *Let's Go* series, "Old Reliable" sent us museum-quality prose and expertly avoided numerous offers of love, marriage, and carpet business. He had enormous patience with us Tunisia-impaired types back at home, put the country code back in the book, and would like everyone to know that he neither lived on cockroaches nor inhaled (except maybe a little *chicha*).

Elisabetta Anna Coletti   *Rome*
Betta is the loudest, wackiest person we know. She's chillin' in Bologna now, and you wish you were there too so you could be her friend. We do. *Buon anno, cara!*

William G. Ferullo   *Rome*
Bill, like Ali, researched for this book. (Unlike Ali, he didn't wear skirts.) He did this job, two other jobs, and a great job overall. You should feel lazy compared to him.

Emily Tucker   *Editor, Let's Go: Rome 1996*
While no R-W (due to circumstances beyond her control), Em contributed as much to this book as the rest of us, and darn well deserves three lines on this page. Heck, make it four. Any misspelled Italian words should be brought to her attention.

Acknowledgments

Team ITA Thanks: Sammy our shiny, happy **ME**; **Mike and Yoonice** for tolerating our endless questions; intern **Karlene**; **Em** 'cause she's *great*; **Jen** for being strong; and everyone within hearing distance (that's you, **Romance Room, SEAS, & Eur**).

CY Thanks: Lis with all of my well-formatted heart (hyphen!) for your patience and pluck. Scampi. **Ames** for salmon cream cheese, dedication, and a conscience. **Lala, Donella,** e **'Milia** per l'aiuto e l'amicizia. **Mom** for the Italian genes, **Dad** for the Italian experience, and **Cliff** for feeding me and caring. **Natly** and **Thos,** the backrubs saved me. **Nathan,** remember you *are* the top. **Schmiz, Cat, Schmyn, Smich, MEM,** & the **6 dwarves** for believing me when I said I would call, and still being my friends when I didn't. **RJ** for food 'n' fun; **SiRelli** for being a freak too; **APS** for ever; **Haneen** for asking; **Pat** for knowing; and **AnneC** for believing. And of course, **DF.**

Lisa: Thank you: Celeste, for a wonderful summer of laughs, Pooh, and 'sauce. **Amy,** for being pulchritudinous in every way. **Blaine,** for his help (and for teaching me *Addio!*). **Rita,** for being art savvy; **Tony,** for his mandolin; **Ron,** for *La Dolce Vita;* **Stacey,** *(sogni d'oro);* **Pinsky,** for dancing out of the supermarket; **Mimi,** the Italian whom I love the most; **Peepa,** for my blond hair; **Mom, Andrea, Dad, Ralph and Donna,** because I love you; and ***butter*,** for an incredible summer. **LAH**

Ames thanks: all who kept me laughing & sane(?): ;-)**Celeste & Lisa**—scampi and toodles. Mmmm. Team Italy. I'll miss you:-(; music & rumblebumble of **Jesse, Andy,** and **Pai; TimmygirlfriendlivesLet'sGosoIdotooYu; Mom** and **Dad** (yes, I'm still at work, but I love you alot!); **Nana, Grampy,** & **Nonnie** for Italian in my blood; gnomes; **Eric Goldstein** for fast, crucial Tunisia info; and **all my roommates. AY**

Editor	Celeste Raina Young
Associate Editor	Lisa Ann Halliday
Assistant Editor	Amy E. Yeager
Managing Editor	Samuel P. Trumbull
Publishing Director	Sean Fitzpatrick
Production Manager	Michael L. Cisneros
Associate Production Manager	Eunice C. Park
Cartography Manager	Samuel P. Trumbull
Associate Cartography Manager	Amanda K. Bean
Editorial Manager	Timothy S. Perlstein
Editorial Manager	Haneen M. Rabie
Financial Manager	Katarzyna Drozd
Personnel Manager	Sean K. Desmond
Publicity Manager	Timur Okay Harry Hiçyılmaz
Associate Publicity Manager	Eleni N. Gage
General Manager	Richard Olken
Assistant General Manager	Anne E. Chisholm
Office Coordinator	Jennifer L. Schuberth
Director of Advertising and Sales	Jean C. Anderson
Sales Assistant Manager	Sammy Lai
Sales Representatives	Matthew S. Abramson
	Delphine Gabbay, Godffrey Williams

How To Use This Book

Everything You Ever Wanted to Know About Italy and Tunisia? Doubt it. The Bible of the Budget Traveler? Maybe. *Let's Go: Italy '96* tries to be a comprehensive, useful, and somewhat entertaining guide to one of the most beautiful and culture-rich regions in the world. This book not only provides you with Ventimiglia's telephone code and Trapani's ferry schedules, but also attempts to help *you* decide where you want to go for your dream Italy itinerary.

Essentials. The name says it all. Granted, it is somewhat more important to know how to obtain a passport than how to import a BMW, but we try to provide for all your vacationing needs. Pay particular attention to the little **white boxes**—they contain warnings and other vital information. ATMS, ziti, and everything in between is covered in the **Planning Your Trip** and **Life and Times** sections; take to heart the advice offered regarding documents and formalities, accommodations reservations, emergency telephone numbers, and health requirements listed in the former, and wile away a seemingly endless train ride thumbing through the 4000-year historical survey, food description, and literature and art summary contained in the latter.

La bella Italia is easily divided in to **six regions:** Rome, northern Italy, central Italy, southern Italy, Sardinia, and Sicily. The book begins with Rome and radiates from there; this makes it easier for you to plan a route between towns and regions. **Tunisia** is its own chapter, with information on ferry and air connections from the continent. Towns close to each other in the book will be nearby geographically as well; even so, remember that Italy is much smaller than the U.S.: you can go to sleep on the train in Palermo and wake up the next morning in Rome. Heck, you could go to sleep on the train in *Paris* and wake up the next morning in Rome.

Each city and town listing provides information on transportation to and from nearby cities or larger transportation hubs. Orient yourself with the help of **country, regional, and city maps;** some even have gridlines and listing coordinates. The **Orientation and Practical Information** listings are standardized in order of their relative importance, beginning with the area's tourist office, police station, post office, and telephone prefix (usually listed just once, so please don't panic).

Your Italian's rusty? The Appendix contains sections on **pronunciation,** helpful Italian **phrases,** and a **glossary** of the Italian, French, and Arabic terms that are sprinkled throughout the book. Some **French** and **Arabic phrases** appear in the Tunisia Essentials. If you get really desperate or bored, check out the **index.** Seriously.

Remember that Italy offers a little of everything, and that Tunisia is a whole different world. Visit Tuscany (with everyone else), or escape from the tourist track by venturing south to towns that haven't seen a foreigner since our researcher left. Hike or ski in the Sila Massif, Abruzzo, or the Alps, and sunbathe topless in the Riviera. Sleep in Luke Skywalker's home on the edge of the Sahara. But wherever your travels take you, *Let's Go: Italy '96* wishes you *buon viaggio.*

A NOTE TO OUR READERS

The information for this book is gathered by Let's Go researchers during the summer months. Each listing is derived from the assigned researcher's opinion based upon his or her visit at a particular time. The opinions are expressed in a candid and forthright manner. Other travelers might disagree. Those traveling at a different time may have different experiences since prices, dates, hours, and conditions are always subject to change. You are urged to check beforehand to avoid inconvenience and surprises. Travel always involves a certain degree of risk, especially in low-cost areas. When traveling, especially on a budget, you should always take particular care to ensure your safety.

ESSENTIALS

GEOGRAPHY

Italy is more than just your average boot. Its landscape ranges from rocky promontories to plains, lakes, and valleys, often all in close proximity. Mountains play a particularly important role; the Alps define Italy's northern border, the Apennines run its length, and the Gargano and Sila Massifs cross the spur and foot of the boot respectively. With hill towns so prevalent, it's hardly surprising that the average Italian grandmother carrying home the groceries can beat the average American teenager up a hill, or that the country has bred a form of human being capable of simultaneously negotiating three-inch heels, 13th-century cobblestone paving, and a 60° incline. Though the largest Italian cities (e.g., Rome, Milan, Turin, Naples) now feature urban sprawl, the vast majority of the landscape remains a symbiotic mixture of countryside and enclosed cities.

The motley landscape is broken up by three substantial regions of plain: the largest area is the valley of the Po River, which stretches from Piedmont through a collection of low-lying Lombard cities and across the farmlands of Emilia Romagna. Also, a coastal plain runs along the Tyrrhenian Sea from southern Tuscany through Lazio, culminating in Apulia, a rich farming region, on the heel. A similar situation exists on the islands. Most of the smaller islands are mountains rising from the ocean. Sicily and Sardinia have mountainous interiors, though many of the major cities are located along the flatter coast.

Outlining a peninsula roughly 1000km long and 150-250km across, the Italian coastline seems endless. Much of the coast will surprise only with its dullness, but the long wastelands set off the astonishingly beautiful Amalfi coast (south of Naples), the crescent of Liguria (the Italian Riviera), and the Gargano Massif (the spur jutting into the Adriatic). Other attractive mainland seashores include Calabria's Tyrrhenian coast, the wee southern coast of Lazio (near Gaeta), and the Monte Conero cliffs (just south of Ancona). Sicily and Sardinia boast Greek ruins in romantic settings, as well as lots more sand. For the best swimming in Sardinia, venture beyond the more touristed areas. In Sicily, try the smaller islands, such as the Aeolians, but be aware that when the currents change, they often bring refuse.

Italian wilderness has been whittled away over the millennia, but is selectively preserved in the great national parks: Abruzzo National Park in the Apennines and the Alpine Gran Paradiso National Park set between Valle D'Aosta and Piedmont.

PLANNING YOUR TRIP

The best time to start your vacation is beforehand. Creating a basic itinerary without setting it in stone enables you to call ahead for reservations without sacrificing spontaneity. A flexible game plan is required in Italy since offices, hotels, and entire towns tend to close on a whim. Despite broad stereotypes, Italy is multiregional and multifaceted, with as many different accents, tastes, and cuisines as the United States or United Kingdom. Above all, remember that small towns can be just as interesting as the large cities, and are usually less congested. "Doing" Florence, Venice, and Rome may be a time-honored tradition, but it is also one of the most expensive of all possible Italian vacations. Visiting one of these cities and then exploring the region around it will give you a far better sense of the area and the diversity of Italian life. You will also be able to avoid spending all of your time amid other tourists.

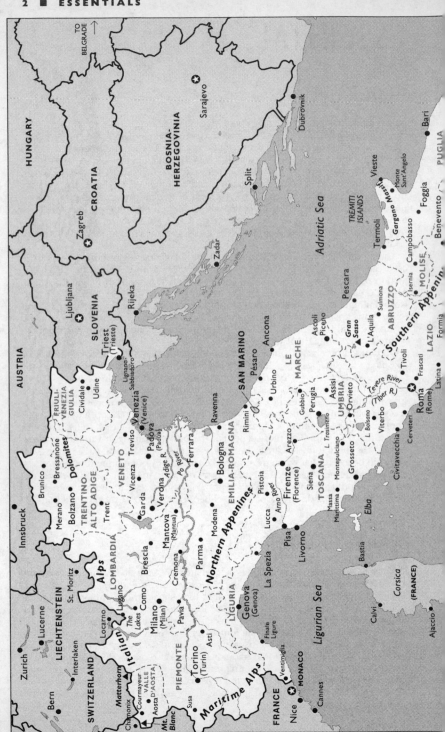

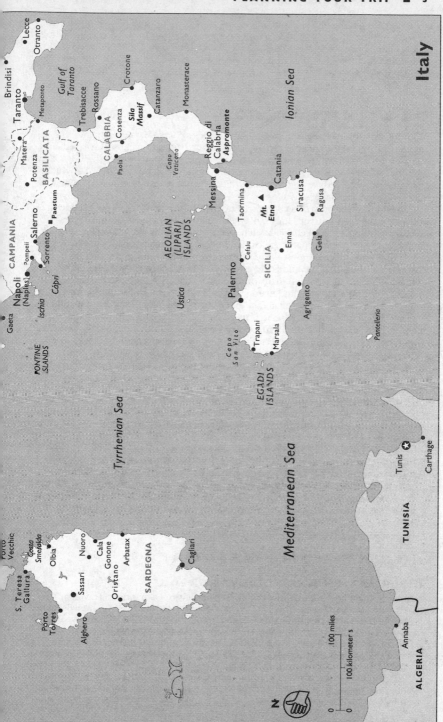

Italy

In order to get the most out of your experience, allow for leisure time in your itinerary—zipping through all of Italy in two weeks will sap both your sight-seeing energy and your social time. Also make an effort to be polite and friendly; if you do, you'll find that most of the people you meet will respond in kind. It's even worth attempting to speak a few words of Italian—any effort, however mangled, will be enthusiastically received.

■■■ WHEN TO GO

Without a doubt, the best time to see Italy is in either late May-June or late August-September, when the summer crowds have not arrived or have just dispersed, and the weather is pleasant. Whenever you go, try to plan a rough itinerary based on the season: weather, festivals, and tourist congestion should all be considered. A winter camping plan would face endless rain, while a February visit that doesn't include a *Carnevale* celebration seems a loss.

Unfortunately for most of us, summertime travel is the only option. Consequently, the tourist invasion overruns Italy in July and August. At this time, tourism goes into overdrive: hotels are booked solid, Michelangelo's *David* has hour-long lines, Elba is inundated with Germans, and the ocean view is perpetually obstructed by seven levels of lounge chairs. Almost without exception, hotel rates go up and trains are extremely crowded; reservations are a must (see box below). There are, however, summertime benefits: though many of the best restaurants are closed for holiday in August, some youth hostels and many campgrounds open *just* for the summer, and museums and tourist offices maintain extended hours. The best way to avoid the summer blues is by making reservations at least a few days in advance (unless you want to visit Siena during the Palio, or sleep on Cápri, Elba, or the Amalfi Coast; in which case you should make reservations six months in advance).

Be aware that some areas have an *additional* high season. The Dolomites and Alps are popular skiing destinations for Europe's wealthy: high season includes the two weeks after Christmas, mid-February to mid-March, and Easter. Easter week in Rome gets a little tight, as does Christmas in Venice. In general, though, visiting Italy between September and May means enjoying the benefits of the off-season. You'll not only avoid the odoriferous waters of Venice, but you'll also be able to attend Italy's fall wine harvests, the first olive pressings of early winter, and Holy Week processions in April.

Italy in August. A final word of warning: if you choose to travel in August, reservations are a matter of necessity; most Italians take their own vacations in August and close up their businesses and restaurants. Some of the industrial cities of the north become complete ghost towns (scarcely one in a hundred establishments in Milan remains open) and many other cities remain alive only as tourist-infested infernos.

■■■ AT-HOME RESOURCES

INFORMATION AND TOURIST BUREAUS

Animal and Plant Health Inspection Service, Attn: Quarantines/Travelers Tips, P.O. Box 96464, Washington, D.C. 20090-6464 (tel. (301) 734-8645). A division of the USDA, APHIS publishes the *Traveler's Tips* pamphlet, which provides information on which plant and animal products you can safely bring home from other countries. Consult your local Blue Pages for the number of the nearest branch.

Federation of International Youth Travel Organizations (FIYTO), Bredgade 25H, DK-1260, Copenhagen K, Denmark (tel. +45 (33) 33 96 00; fax (33) 93 96 76). International organization promoting educational, cultural, and social travel for young people. Member organizations include language schools, educational travel companies, national tourist boards, accommodation centers, and other suppliers of travel services to youth and students. FIYTO sponsors the GO25 Card (US$10, with travel insurance US$16; prices subject to change).

Italian Government Travel Office (ENIT), 630 Fifth Ave., #1565, Rockefeller Center, **New York,** NY 10111 (tel. (212) 245-4822; fax 586-9249). Write for their detailed (and indispensable) guide *Italia: General Information for Travelers to Italy* (containing everything from train and ferry schedules to where to yacht), and for regional information. Branch offices: 12400 Wilshire Blvd., #550, **Los Angeles,** CA 90025 (tel. (310) 820-0098; fax 820-6357); 1 Pl. Ville Marie, #1914, **Montréal,** Qué. H3B 3M9 (tel. (514) 866-7667; fax 392-1429); 1 Princes St., **London,** England WIR 8AY (tel. ±44 (0171) 408 12 54; fax 493 66 95).

International Student Travel Confederation, Store Kongensgade 40H, 1264 Copenhagen K, Denmark (tel. ±45 (33) 93 93 03; fax 93 73 77). A nonprofit confederation of student travel organizations. Sponsors the International Student Identity Card (ISIC). Member organizations include International Student Rail Association (ISRA), Student Air Travel Association (SATA), ISIS Travel Insurance, and the International Association for Educational and Work Exchange Programs (IAEWEP).

Superintendent of Documents, U.S. Government Printing Office, P.O. Box 371954, Pittsburgh, PA 15250-7954 (tel. (202) 512-1800; fax 512-2250). Open Mon.-Fri. 8am-4pm. Publishes *Your Trip Abroad* (US$1.25), *Health Information for International Travel* (US$7), and "Background Notes" on all countries (US$1 each). Postage is included in the prices.

Travel CUTS (Canadian University Travel Services, Ltd.), 187 College St., Toronto, Ont. M5T 1P7 (tel. (416) 798-CUTS (798-2887), fax 979-8167). Offices across Canada. Also, in the **U.K.,** 295-A Regent St., London W1R 7YA (tel. (0171) 637 31 61). Discounted European, South Pacific, and domestic flights; ISIC, GO 25, and HI hostel cards; and discount travel passes. Special fares with valid ISIC or FIYTO cards. Offers free *Student Traveller* magazine and info on Student Work Abroad Program (SWAP).

READING UP

Bon Voyage!, 2069 W. Bullard Ave., Fresno, CA 93711-1200 (tel. (800) 995 9716, from abroad 209-447-8441, email 70754.3311@compuserve.com). Annual mailorder catalog offers a range of products for everyone from the luxury traveler to the diehard trekker. Books, travel accessories, luggage, electrical converters, maps, videos, and more. All merchandise may be returned for exchange or refund within 30 days of purchase, and prices are guaranteed (lower advertised prices will be matched and merchandise shipped free).

The College Connection, Inc., 1295 Prospect St., La Jolla, CA 92037 (tel. (619) 551-9770). Publishes *The Passport*, a booklet listing hints about every aspect of traveling and studying abroad. The College Rail Connection, a division of the College Connection, sells railpasses with student discounts.

The European Association of Music Festivals, 120B, rue de Lausanne, 1202 Geneva, Switzerland (tel. ±41 (22) 732 28 03; fax 738 40 12). Publishes the free booklet *Festivals,* which lists dates and programs of many major European festivals, including music and theater events.

Forsyth Travel Library, P.O. Box 2975, Shawnee Mission, KS 66201 (tel. (800) 367-7984). A mail-order service that stocks a wide range of city, area, and country maps, as well as guides for rail and ferry travel in Europe; also sells rail tickets and passes. Sells the *Thomas Cook European Timetable* for trains, a complete guide to European train departures and arrivals (US$25.95, or $35.95 with full map of European train routes; postage $4). Write for free catalog and newsletter.

Hippocrene Books, Inc., 171 Madison Ave., New York, NY 10016 (tel. (212) 685-4371; orders: tel. (718) 454-2366; fax 454-1391). Free catalog. Publishes travel reference books, travel guides, maps, foreign language dictionaries, and language learning guides that cover over 100 languages.

Hunter Publishing, 300 Raritan Center Parkway, Edison, NJ 08818 (tel. (908) 225-1900; fax 417-0482). Has an extensive catalog of travel books, guides, language learning tapes, and quality maps, among them *Charming Small Hotel Guides* to Italy, France, England, Germany, and Greece (each US$12.95).

John Muir Publications, PO Box 613, Santa Fe, NM 87504 (tel. (800) 888-7504; fax (505) 988-1680). In addition to many travel guides, publishes an excellent series of books by veteran traveler Rick Steves. This includes *Europe though the Back Door,* offering great advice on the dos and don'ts of budget travel (US$17.95) and *Mona Winks: Self-Guided Tours of Europe's Top Museums* (US$16.95). Also available in bookstores.

Michelin Travel Publications, Michelin Tire Corporation, P.O. Box 19001, Greenville, SC 29602-9001 (tel. (800) 423-0485; fax (803) 458-5665). Publishes three major lines of travel-related material: *Green Guides,* for sight-seeing, maps, and driving itineraries; *Red Guides,* which rate hotels and restaurants; and detailed, reliable road maps and atlases. All three are available at bookstores and distributors throughout the world.

Specialty Travel Index, 305 San Anselmo Avenue, Suite 313, San Anselmo, CA 94960 (tel. (415) 459-4900; fax 459-4974). Publishes a bi-yearly listing of "off the beaten track" and specialty tour operators (US$6 for one copy; US$10 for 2).

Superintendent of Documents, see above: Information and Tourist Bureaus.

Transitions Abroad, 18 Hulst Rd., P.O. Box 1300, Amherst, MA 01004-1300 (tel. (413) 256-3414; fax 256-0373). Invaluable magazine listing publications and resources for overseas study, work, and volunteering. Also publishes *The Alternative Travel Directory,* a comprehensive guide to living, learning, and working overseas (US$19.95; postage $3).

Travel Books & Language Center, 4931 Cordell Ave., Bethesda, MD 20814 (tel. (800) 220-2665; fax (301) 951-8546). Sells over 70,000 items, including books, cassettes, atlases, dictionaries, and a wide range of specialty travel maps, including wine and cheese maps of France, Michelin maps, and beer maps of the U.S.

Ten Speed Press, P.O. Box 7123, Berkeley, CA 94707 (tel. (800) 841-2665). *The Packing Book* (US $7.95) provides various checklists, suggests wardrobes, addresses safety concerns, and more.

U.S. Customs Service, 1301 Constitution Avenue, N.W., Washington, D.C. 20229 (tel. (202) 927-5580). Publishes 35 books, booklets, leaflets, and flyers on various aspects of customs. *Know Before You Go* (KBYG) tells everything the international traveler needs to know about customs requirements; *Pockets Hints* summarizes the most important data from KBYG.

Wide World Books and Maps, 1911 N. 45th St., Seattle, WA 98103 (tel. (206) 634-3453; fax 634-0558; email travelbk@nwlink.com). A good selection of travel guides, travel accessories, and hard-to-find maps.

GETTING IT ON-LINE

As you research your trip, be aware that there is a vast amount of information available through the international computer network: the **Internet.** Some commercial providers, such as **America Online, CompuServe,** and **Prodigy,** offer sophisticated services like **on-line airline reservations.** Even the most basic mode of access, though, can provide the moderately skilled user with more information than s/he could possibly ever use. Most universities and many businesses offer students and employees access to the Internet; if you are unsure about your own situation, contact your system manager or ask a computer-savvy friend. If you own a modem, you can also gain access through one of the many commercial providers such as **Netcom On-Line Communication Services,** 3131 Tisch Way, San Jose, CA 95128 (tel. (800) 501-8649; fax (408) 556-3155; e-mail info@netcom.com). Individual accounts cost US$17.50-19.50 per month; Netcom has access numbers in many U.S. cities.

One primary means of transmission and discussion of information across the Internet are forums known as **"newsgroups."** Newsgroups are accessible by users all over the world; you can use them to do everything from reading articles to communicating directly with people in Italy. New groups are always sprouting up, and not all groups are available from all systems, so the list that follows may not be exhaustive. One of the most common news-reading programs can be accessed on many systems by typing "rn" for "read news." Some systems and programs provide a tutorial for new users; for others, consult a system manager. Be warned that, since most newsgroups are unmoderated and unsupervised, the quality of conversation and the reliability of information posted within them is not always certain. Before posting messages yourself, you should also try to familiarize yourself with the standards of "netiquette" that help keep discussion polite and coordinated; again, ask someone in the know for advice.

There are several hierarchies of newsgroups. One, the "soc" groups, primarily addresses social issues and socializing; of interest to travelers to Italy are **soc.culture.italian** and **soc.culture.europe.** The "alt" groups are a less formalized collection of newsgroups, among them **alt.politics.italy** and **alt.politics.ec.** "Rec" groups, such as **rec.travel.air** and **rec.travel.europe,** are oriented toward the arts, hobbies, and recreation. Some computer services also provide access to the "ClariNet" newsgroups, read-only groups that compile and present the latest news from Reuters, the Associated Press, and other sources; travelers to Italy should take a look at **clari.world.europe.italy** and **clari.news.europe.**

Three of the other services available on the Internet are **FTP** (file transfer protocol), **gopher,** and **world wide web;** each can be used to obtain files and other information stored in areas of other computer systems accessible to the public. Thousands of such archives exist, including many with information on travel and Italy. A particularly useful archive is **rec-travel** at ftp.cc.umanitoba.ca; it includes travelogues, U.S. State Department Advisories, and other useful information. Learning how to navigate the Internet to these sites is not extraordinarily complex, but somewhat beyond the scope of this book. Again, ask a system manager or computer-using friend, or check out any one of the many comprehensive guides to the Internet now available in most bookstores.

■■■ RED TAPE

It is strongly recommended that you file applications for all necessary documents well in advance of your planned departure date. Some offices even suggest that you apply in the winter off-season (Aug.-Dec.) for faster service, regardless of when you actually plan to leave. Once you have acquired the documents, it is a good idea to photocopy them all (as well as credit cards), and leave copies at home with someone you can easily contact.

When you travel, *always carry on your person two or more forms of identification, including at least one photo ID.* Never carry all identification, traveler's checks, and credit cards together. If you plan an extended stay, you might want to register your passport with the nearest embassy or consulate. Consulates also recommend that you carry an expired passport or official copy of your birth certificate in a separate part of your baggage, as well as an extra passport photo or two; these measures will facilitate replacement of your passport. If you do find that your passport has been lost or stolen, contact the local police and your embassy or consulate immediately.

PASSPORTS

Citizens of the U.S., Canada, the U.K., Ireland, Australia, New Zealand, and South Africa all need valid passports to enter both Italy and Tunisia and to re-enter their own countries. Some countries will not allow entrance if the holder's passport will expire in less than six months, and returning to the U.S. with an expired passport may result in a fine. Some countries require that a child under 16 carry his or her own passport whether traveling with a parent or not.

Your passport is a public document that belongs to your government and may not be withheld without your consent. Although you may be asked to surrender it to an Italian government official, if you don't get it back in a reasonable amount of time, you should inform the nearest mission of your country. In Italy and Tunisia, hotel proprietors are apt to ask you to leave your passport with them overnight as collateral. Even though this is an accepted custom, you are not required to leave it for any extended period of time (i.e., beyond the time it takes them to simply note the number). Offering to pay the full price up front is one way of avoiding this practice.

RED TAPE

U.S. citizens obtain a passport (US$65, under 18 $40) by applying at any Passport Agency or a courthouse or post office that accepts applications. **In 1986, more American citizens than ever before applied for passports; this means that in 1996 the same people will most likely be re-applying, and that you should be prepared to wait in long lines.** All travelers to Italy, including infants, must have a passport in their name. You can renew your passport by mail for US$55, but you must apply in person for your first passport, or if your current passport is more than 12 years old or was issued before your 18th birthday. The passport office normally requires three to four weeks to process an application, but it is wise to apply several months in advance. Rush service is available for travelers who are willing to pay for express mail and can prove that they are departing within five working days. If you need to replace your passport abroad, the nearest U.S. embassy or consulate can usually do so (given proof of citizenship). For more information, call the U.S. Passport Information's helpful 24-hr. recorded message at (202) 647-0518.

Canadian citizens residing in Canada may apply in person at a regional office or at the Passport Office, Promenade du Portage, Place du Centre, Hull, Ottawa; mailing address: Department of Foreign Affairs, Ottawa, Ont. K1A 0G3, or, outside Canada, at the nearest Canadian embassy or consulate. (Citizens residing outside Canada may apply by mail, enclosing the CDN$35 fee, to the above mailing address.) All requirements are listed on the application. Citizens under 16 traveling with a parent may be included on the parent's passport. If a passport is lost abroad, Canadians must be able to present alternative proof of citizenship. For additional information, call (800) 567-6868 (in Canada only, 24 hrs.).

British citizens: British Dependent Territories citizens and British Overseas citizens may apply for a full passport (£18) in person or by mail to a passport office (located in Liverpool, Newport, Peterborough, Glasgow, and Belfast). Processing by mail normally takes 4 to 6 weeks. A full passport is valid for 10 years, 5 years for children under 16; children under 16 can also be included on a parent's passport. Residents of the U.K., the Channel Islands, and the Isle of Man also have the option of applying for a more restricted British Visitor's Passport (UK£12). The Visitor's Passport, valid for 1 year in some Western European countries and Bermuda only, is available from main post offices in England, Scotland, and Wales, and from passport offices in Northern Ireland, the Channel Islands, and the Isle of Man.

Irish citizens can apply for a passport by mail to one of the following two passport offices: Department of Foreign Affairs, Passport Office, Setanta Centre, Molesworth St., Dublin 2 (tel. ±353 (01) 671 16 33), or Passport Office, 1A South Mall, Cork (tel. (021) 27 25 25). Passports cost IR£45 and are valid for 10 years. Citizens younger than 18 and older than 65 can request a 3-year passport that costs IR£10.

Australian citizens must apply in person at a local post office, a passport office, or an Australian diplomatic mission overseas. A parent may file an application for a child who is under 18 and unmarried. Fees are adjusted every three months.

New Zealand citizens can apply for a passport by contacting a Link Centre, travel agent, or Representative for an application to be mailed to the Passport Office, Documents of National Identity Division, Dept. of Internal Affairs, Box 10-526, Wellington (tel. ±64 (04) 474 81 00). The fee is NZ$80.00 if submitted in New Zealand, NZ$130.00 if from abroad (if under age 16, NZ$40.00 and NZ$65.00 respectively). Standard processing time is 10 working days.

South African citizens can apply for a passport (R38) at any Department of Home Affairs Office.

ITALIAN EMBASSIES AND CONSULATES

U.S.: Embassy of Italy, 1601 Fuller St. NW, **Washington, DC** 20009 (tel. (202) 328-5500; fax (202) 462-3605) and Italian Consulate General, 12400 Wilshire Blvd., #300, **Los Angeles,** CA 90025 (tel. (310) 820-0622; fax (310) 820-0727). Other consulates of Italy at 2590 Webster St., **San Francisco,** CA 94115 (tel. (415) 931-4924); 500 N. Michigan Ave., #1850, **Chicago,** IL 60611 (tel. (312) 467-1335); 630 Camp St., **New Orleans,** LA 70130 (tel. (504) 524-2271; fax 581-4590); 100

Boylston St., #900, **Boston,** MA 02116 (tel. (617) 542-0483); 535 Griswold St., #1840, **Detroit,** MI 48226 (tel. (313) 963-8560; fax 963-8180); 690 Park Ave., **New York,** NY 10021 (tel. (212) 737-9100); Public Ledger Building, 100 S. Sixth St., #1026, **Philadelphia,** PA 19106 (tel. (215) 592-7329; fax 592-9808); 1300 Post Oak Blvd., #660, **Houston,** TX 77056 (tel. (713) 850-7520).

Canada: Embassy of Italy, 275 Slater St., 21st floor, **Ottawa,** Ont. K1P 5H9 (tel. (613) 232-2401/2/3; fax (613) 233-1484); Consulate of Italy, 3489 Drummond Ave., **Montréal,** Qué. H3G 1X6 (tel. (514) 849-7113).

U.K., Embassy of Italy, 14 Three Kings Yard, **London,** W1Y 2EH (tel. ±44 (0171) 312 22 00); Consulate General of Italy, 38 Eaton Place, London, SW1 8AN (tel. (0171) 235 9371); Italian Consulate in Manchester, 111 Piccadilly, **Manchester,** M1 2HY (tel. (0161) 236 90 24); Consulate General of Italy in Scotland and Northern Ireland, 32 Melville St., **Edinburgh,** EH3 7HA (tel. (0131) 220 36 95).

Australia, Embassy of Italy, 12 Grey St., Deakin, Canberra City A.C.T. 2600 (tel. ±61 273 33 33).

New Zealand, Embassy of Italy, P.O. Box 463, 36 Grant Rd., Wellington (tel. (644) 473 53 39 or 472 93 02; fax 472 72 55).

South Africa, Embassy of Italy, 796 George Ave., Arcadia, Pretoria (tel. ±27 (2712) 43 55 41/2/3; fax 43 55 47).

VISAS

A **visa** is a stamp that permits you to visit that country; it is placed on your passport by a foreign government. Tourists from the United States, Canada, Great Britain, Australia, New Zealand, and South Africa do not need a visa to visit Italy for three months or less. If you wish to remain longer as a bona fide tourist with means of support, you may obtain a one-time, three-month extension from any local police station *(questura)*. The Bureau of Consular Affairs warns that extensions are granted infrequently. If you intend to travel for more than three months, consider obtaining a long-term visa before departure. You may do so either by applying directly to the nearest Italian consulate or through the **Center for International Business and Travel (CIBT),** 25 West 43rd St., Suite 1420, New York, NY 10036 (tel. (800) 925-2428 or (212) 575-2811 from NYC). The CIBT secures visas for travel to and from all possible countries for a fee, usually around US$50 per visa (for a U.S. citizen). Travelers from countries other than those listed above should be sure to check with an Italian Government Travel Office or Italian Embassy or consulate; Italy does require visas from citizens of many countries.

Entrance to Italy as a tourist does not include permission to study or work there. There are special requirements for **student and work visas,** which can be obtained from the nearest Italian consulate. For student visas, the U.S. consulate requires a valid passport, an official letter of acceptance from the school or program, a photograph, a notarized declaration of financial responsibility, and a letter from your medical insurance company accepting responsibility for you while you're in Italy. Working visas require a passport, a contract of hire from your place of work (which needs to be signed by the Italian Minister of Labor and the police station near your prospective place of work), and a photograph.

Italy requires foreigners to register at a local police station within three days of arrival in the country. Hotels are responsible for registering their guests, but if you aren't staying in a hotel, the responsibility is yours.

CUSTOMS: COMING...

Unless you plan to import a BMW, you will probably pass right over the customs barrier and forge onward in the direction of the nearest *cannoli.* Most countries restrict the importation of firearms, explosives, ammunition, fireworks, controlled drugs, most plants and animals, lottery tickets, and obscene literature and films. To avoid problems when you transport prescription drugs, ensure that the bottles are clearly marked, and carry a copy of the prescription. Officials may seize articles made from protected species, such as certain reptiles and big cats that roar.

RED TAPE

TOP 5 Ways to Save Money While Traveling

5. Ship yourself in a crate marked "Livestock." Remember to poke holes in the crate.

4. Board a train dressed as Elvis and sneer and say "The King rides for free."

3. Ask if you can walk through the Channel Tunnel.

2. Board the plane dressed as an airline pilot, nod to the flight attendants, and hide in the rest room until the plane lands.

1. Bring a balloon to the airline ticket counter, kneel, breathe in the helium, and ask for the kiddie fare.

But if you're serious about saving money while you're traveling abroad, just get an ISIC--the International Student Identity Card. Discounts for students on international airfares, hotels and motels, car rentals, international phone calls, financial services, and more.

The International Student Identity Card

For more information call:

1-800-GET-AN-ID

Available at Council Travel offices (see ad in this book) and universities nationwide.

Council

CIEE: Council on International Educational Exchange
205 East 42nd Street, New York, NY 10017-5706

...AND GOING

United States citizens returning home may bring US$400 worth of goods for personal use duty-free and must pay a tax on the next $1000. You must declare all merchandise acquired abroad; keeping sales slips handy will probably help you sort things out. To be eligible for the allowance, you must have remained abroad for at least 48 hours and cannot have used this exemption within the preceding 30 days. You can mail unsolicited gifts duty-free if they are worth less than $50, though you may not mail liquor, tobacco, or perfume. Mark the price and nature of the gift and the words "Unsolicited Gift" on the package. If you mail home personal goods of U.S. origin, you can avoid duty charges by marking the package "American goods returned." For more information, consult *Know Before You Go*, available from the U.S. Customs Service, P.O. Box 7407, Washington, DC 20044 (tel. (202) 927-6724), or call them with questions. Somewhat different regulations apply to foreign nationals living in the U.S. These individuals should get a copy of *Customs Hints for Visitors (Nonresidents)* by writing the address or calling the phone number above.

Canadians abroad for at least a week may bring back up to CDN$300 worth of goods duty-free once every calendar year. You are permitted to ship articles home under this exemption as long as you declare them when you arrive. For more information, write to Canadian Customs, 2265 St. Laurent Blvd., Ottawa, Ontario K1G 4K3 (tel. (613) 993 0534); or, from within Canada, call (800) 461-9999.

EU nationals who travel between EU countries no longer need to declare the goods they purchase abroad. Goods for personal use are not taxed further, provided that duty and tax are paid in the other country.

British citizens are allowed up to £136 of goods (not including cigarettes/cigars/tobacco, liquor, perfume, and toilet water; contact the organization listed below for specific quantities) from outside the EU (this does not apply to Italy but is relevant to **Tunisia**). You must be over 17 to import liquor or tobacco. For more information, contact H.M. Customs and Excise, Custom House, Heathrow Airport North, Hounslow, Middlesex TW6 2LA (tel. +44 (081) 910 37 44; fax 910 37 65).

Irish citizens must declare everything in excess of IR£34 (IR£17 under 15) of goods (not including cigarettes/cigars/tobacco, liquor, perfume, and toilet water; contact the organization listed below for specific quantities) purchased either outside the EU or duty and tax free in the EU. For more information, contact the Revenue Commissioners, Dublin Castle (tel. +353 (01) 679 27 77; fax 671 20 21) or the Collector of Customs and Excise, The Custom House, Dublin 1.

Australian citizens may bring into or take out of Australia an unlimited amount of Australian and/or foreign cash; however amounts of AUS$5000 or more, or the equivalent in foreign currency, must be reported. A duty/tax free allowance of AUS$400 (AUS$200 under 18) is available for goods (excluding cigarettes/cigars/tobacco and liquor; contact organization below for specific quantities) intended as gifts. For further information, contact the Australian Customs Service, 5 Constitution Ave., Canberra, ACT 2601 (tel. +61 (616) 275 62 55; fax 275 69 89).

New Zealand citizens may bring home up to NZ$700 worth of goods (not including cigarettes/cigars/tobacco, liquor, and perfume; contact the organization listed below for specific quantities) duty-free if they are for personal use or are unsolicited gifts. You must be over 17 to import liquor and tobacco. Consult the *New Zealand Customs Guide for Travelers*, available from customs offices, or contact New Zealand Customs, 50 Anzac Avenue, Box 29, Auckland (tel. +64 (09) 377 35 20; fax 309 29 78).

South African citizens may import duty-free up to R500 worth of goods (not including cigarettes/cigars/tobacco, liquor, perfume, and toilet water; contact the organization listed below for specific quantities). Goods acquired abroad and sent home as unaccompanied baggage do not qualify for any allowances. You may not export or import South African bank notes in excess of R500. For information and the pamphlet *South African Customs Information*, write to: The Commissioner for Customs and Excise, Private Bag X47, Pretoria, 0001. South Africans in the U.S.

should contact: South African Mission to the IMF/World Bank, 3201 New Mexico Ave. #380, NW, Washington, DC 20016 (tel. (202) 364-8320/1; fax 364-6008).

YOUTH, STUDENT, & TEACHER IDENTIFICATION

The **International Student Identity Card (ISIC)** is the most widely accepted form of student identification. Flashing this card earns you discounts for sights, theaters, museums, accommodations, train, ferry, and airplane travel, and other services throughout Europe. Make a habit of presenting it and asking about student discounts wherever you go (*c'è uno sconto studentesco?*) Don't be surprised, though, if they look at your ID and laugh or give you a puzzled look. Student discounts are rare and often exclusively for Italian or EU students. It never hurts to try, but don't expect much. ISIC also provides repatriation insurance up to $7500, medical/accident insurance of up to US$2000 with no daily limit. In addition, cardholders have access to a toll-free Traveler's Assistance hotline whose multilingual staff can provide help in medical, legal, and financial emergencies overseas.

ISICs are issued by many travel offices, including Council Travel, Let's Go Travel, and STA Travel in the U.S.; Travel CUTS in Canada; and any of the organizations under the auspices of the International Student Travel Confederation (ISTC) around the world (see Budget Travel Services, page 41). When you apply for the card, request a copy of the International Student Identity Card Handbook, which lists by country some of the available discounts. The card is valid from September to December of the following year. The fee is US$18. Applicants must be at least 12 years old and must be a degree-seeking student of a secondary or post-secondary school. Because of the proliferation of phony ISICs, many airlines and some other services now require other proof of student identity: have a signed letter from the registrar attesting to your student status and stamped with the school seal, and carry your school ID card. To obtain a card by using a credit card, please call (800) 255-1000, extension 425. The new, US$19 **International Teacher Identity Card (ITIC)** offers similar but limited discounts, as well as medical insurance coverage.

Federation of International Youth Travel Organisations (FIYTO) issues a discount card to travelers who are not students but are under 26. Also known as the **International Youth Discount Travel Card,** the one-year **GO 25 Card,** offers many of the same benefits as the ISIC, and most organizations that sell the ISIC also sell the Go 25 Card. A brochure that lists discounts is free when you purchase the card. To apply, bring: (1) proof of birthdate (copy of birth certificate, passport, or valid driver's license); and (2) a passport-sized photo (with your name printed on the back). The fee is US$18. (See Information and Tourist Bureaus, page 4.)

HOSTELLING ORGANIZATIONS

A one-year **Hostelling International (HI)** membership permits you to stay at youth hostels all over Italy and Tunisia at unbeatable prices: $5-22. You can save yourself potential trouble by procuring a membership card, available at most budget travel organizations (Council Travel, STA), before you leave home. (For details on the Italian hostel network, see Accommodations, page 55.) Also, the Internet Guide to Hostelling is an Internet-based publication that provides travelers with information on hostels around the world, as well as other budget travel-related info. The guide currently includes: frequently asked questions, the worldwide hostel guide, what's "new" in hostelling, the Backpacker's Guide to budget guidebooks, and the Backpacker's Transportation Guide. To access, you'll need a Web browser. You can find the guide at these URLs: http://hostels.com/rec-travel/hostels/ or http://www.crl.com/-overby/, or you can write to them at info@hostels.com for more info.

Hostelling International (HI), headquarters (and info) at 9 Guessens Rd., Welwyn Garden City, Herts AL8 6QW, England (tel. 44 (01707) 33 24 87). The "head honcho" of the domestic and international hostelling scene, HI is a worldwide federation of youth hostels (more than 6000 total) and of individual national hos-

RED TAPE

telling associations. One extremely good option is the **International Booking Network (IBN),** which allows you to make confirmed reservations at any of almost 200 HI hostels in the U.S. and abroad for only US$2 (in addition to the regular overnight fee). Credit card (MC or Visa) guarantee required. To make reservations, call or visit the HI-American Youth Hostels (HI-AYH) headquarters at 733 15th St. NW, Suite 840, Washington, DC 20005 (tel. (202) 783-6161), or the travel stores of their Golden Gate, Potomac Area, and Greater Boston Councils. Reservations can also be made at any participating hostel.

The following are national HI affiliates in English-speaking countries. In many cases, **membership must be acquired through the HI affiliate in one's own country,** not abroad; check with your local organization before you go.

American Youth Hostels (HI-AYH), 733 15th St. NW, Suite 840, Washington, DC 20005 (tel. (202) 783-616, (800) 444-6111; fax (202) 783-6171). HI-AYH is comprised of 38 local councils which, in addition to licensing hostels, provide local members and visitors with special programs, events, trips, and activities, including those for the physically challenged, disadvantaged youth, and senior citizens. HI-AYH membership cards cost US$25, renewals $20, under 18 $10, over 54 $15, family cards $35. Membership is valid for 12 months from date of issue. Make reservations by letter, phone, or fax, or through the IBN.

Canadian Hostelling Association (HI-Canada), 400-205 Catherine Street, Ottawa, Ontario, Canada K2P 1C3 (tel. (613) 237-7884; fax (613) 237-7868). One-year membership fee CDN$26.75, under 18 CDN$12.84; 2-year CDN$37.45.

Youth Hostels Association of England and Wales (YHA),YHA Adventure Shop, 14 Southampton St., Covent Garden, London WC2E 7HY (tel. ±44 (0171) 836 1036; fax 836 6372). Enrollment fees are UK£9, under 18 UK£3.

An Óige (Irish Youth Hostel Association), 61 Mountjoy St., Dublin 7 (tel. ±353 (01) 830 45 55; fax 830 58 08). One-year membership is IR£7.50, under 18 IR£4, and family IR£7.50 per adult, children under 16 free.

Youth Hostels Association of Northern Ireland (YHANI), 22-32 Donegall Rd., Belfast BT17 5JN, Northern Ireland (tel. ±353 (0232) 32 47 33; fax 43 96 99).

Scottish Youth Hostels Association (SYHA), 7 Glebe Crescent, Sterling FK8 2JA (tel. ±44 (0786) 45 11 81; fax 45 01 98). Membership UK£6, under 18 UK£2.50.

Australian Youth Hostels Association (AYHA), Level 3, 10 Mallett St., Camperdown, NSW, 2050 (tel. ±61 (25) 65 16 99; fax 565 12 35). Fee AUS$40 when purchased by Australians for use overseas, renewal AUS$24. Under 18 AUS$12. Visitors travelling to Australia and not YHA members from their own country can join YHA in Australia for AUS$24 and will receive a Hostelling International card.

Youth Hostels Association of New Zealand (YHANZ), P.O. Box 436, 173 Gloucester St., Christchurch 1 (tel. ±64 (33) 79 99 70; fax 365 44 76). Annual memberships NZ$24.

Hostel Association of South Africa, P.O. Box 4402, Cape Town 8000 (tel. ±27 419 18 53). Membership good for one year.

INTERNATIONAL DRIVER'S PERMIT

Italy honors the IDP, although it is unclear whether it is mandatory. Even if it is not explicitly required, it is probably a good idea to get one in case you're in a town where the police do not read or speak English.

American Automobile Association (AAA), 1000 AAA Drive (mail stop 28), Heathrow, FL 32746-5080 (tel. (407) 444-4245; fax (407) 444-7823). The IDP is available on the spot from any AAA branch in the U.S., or by mail from the address above (valid for 1 year). You must submit (1) a completed application; (2) two recent passport-sized photos; (3) a valid U.S. driver's license (which must always accompany the IDP abroad). The fee is US$10, and you must be 18 or over.

American Automobile Touring Alliance, Bayside Plaza, 188 The Embarcadero, San Francisco, CA 94105 (tel. (415) 777-4000; fax (415) 882-2141).

Canadian Automobile Association, CAA Ottawa, 2525 Carling Ave., Lincoln Hts., Ottawa ON K2B 7Z2 (tel. (613) 820-1890). Canadian citizens 18 or over with valid Canadian Provincial or Territory driver's licenses are eligible to purchase the IDP through any CAA Member club office. They must complete a CAA application form (available either in person or from the above address) in triplicate, provide 2 passport-type photographs, present a valid driver's license, and pay a fee of CDN$10. CAA club membership not required for purchase.

■■■ MONEY MATTERS

> **A note on prices and currency:** This book's prices and exchange rates were compiled in the summer of 1995. Since rates fluctuate considerably (and tend to favor the *lire* in the summer), be sure to confirm them before you go. **Prices may have changed as well; you will fare better if you are financially flexible.**

There are lots of options on how to manage money while traveling. Generally speaking, if you go on the assumption that 10,000 lire equals about six bucks (at the current exchange rate, it's actually worth a little more), you should be able to estimate your current financial status safely. Check and compare prices with caution, and beware of commission rates. As always, a little common sense goes a long way.

CURRENCY AND EXCHANGE

US$1 = 1621lire (L)	L1000 = US$0.62
CDN$1 = L1199	L1000 = CDN$0.83
UK£1 = L2496	L1000 = UK£0.40
IR£1 = L2561	L1000 = IR£0.39
AUS$1 = L1186	L1000 = AUS$0.84
NZ$1 = L1053	L1000 = NZ$0.95
SAR1 = L443	L1000 = SAR2.26

The Italian currency unit is the *lira* (plural: *lire*). The smallest denomination of Italian currency is the L10 coin (though you will probably never see one), and the smallest note is the L1000 bill. We recommended that, before you leave home, you buy enough *lire* to last for the first 24-72 hours of your trip in order to avoid a frenzied exchange (at terrible rates) at the airport when you arrive. When exchanging money in Italy, look for *"cambio"* signs and shop around. Try to avoid exchanging at luxury hotels, train stations, and airports; the best rates are usually found at banks (although you still pay a commission of 1-2%). Changing currency is best done in the morning; banking hours are usually Monday through Friday 8:30am-1:30pm, with an extra hour in the afternoon (often 3-4pm). Remember that unless a percentage rate is charged, you will lose a fixed chunk of money each time. To minimize such losses, exchange large sums at once, but never more than you can safely carry around. It also helps to plan ahead: you don't want to get caught without *lire* at night or on a Sunday.

TRAVELER'S CHECKS

Traveler's checks are the safest way to carry large sums of money. They are refundable if lost or stolen, and many issuing agencies offer additional services such as refund hotlines, message relaying, travel insurance, and emergency assistance. Although not all Italian establishments accept traveler's checks, your peace of mind will far outweigh the occasional inconvenience. Be sure to bring your passport with you when you plan to use traveler's checks; some places won't accept them otherwise.

None of the major companies listed below supply traveler's checks in *lire*, so buy checks in your home currency. Aussies and New Zealanders may be better off buy-

MONEY MATTERS

You can't eat pasta without bread.

When in Rome, it's not a problem if your cash supply runs dry. Because with Western Union, you can receive money from the States within minutes, in case the situation arises. Plus, it's already converted into lire.

Just call our number in Italy, 039 6 16701 6840, or in the United States, 1 800 325 6000,* and then hop on a gondola to the nearest Western Union location.

Oh, and enjoy your dinner.

WESTERN UNION | MONEY TRANSFER®

*The fastest way to send money worldwide.*SM

ing U.S. dollar or British pound traveler's checks; the teller at the bank in the small town may not know where New Zealand is, let alone its exchange rate. **Refunds** on lost or stolen checks can be time-consuming. To accelerate the process and avoid red tape, *keep check receipts and a record of which checks you've cashed in a separate place from the checks themselves.* Leave a photocopy of check serial numbers with someone at home as back-up in case you lose your copy. Never countersign checks until you're prepared to cash them. To protect yourself from clever thieves who take just one or two checks from the middle of the pile to escape detection, record the number of each check as you cash it.

American Express (tel. (800) 221-7282 in the U.S. and Canada; (0800) 52 13 13 in the U.K.; (008) 25 19 02 in Australia; (0800) 44 10 68 in New Zealand with questions or to report lost or stolen checks. **In Italy, call (1678) 72 00 00.** AmEx traveler's checks are the most widely recognized worldwide and easiest to replace if lost or stolen—just call the information number or the AmEx Travel Office nearest you. AmEx offices cash their own checks commission-free (except where prohibited by law) and sell checks that can be signed by either of 2 people traveling together ("Cheque for Two"). Checks are available in 9 currencies and can be purchased at American Express Travel Services offices, banks, and American Automobile Association (AAA) offices. Call and ask for AmEx's *Traveler's Companion,* which gives office addresses and stolen check hotlines for each European country, call well in advance of your trip, as it is extremely popular and can be difficult to get. Cardmembers can also purchase checks at American Express Dispensers at Travel Service Office at airports, or by ordering them by phone (tel. (800) ORDER-TC (673-3782)). Soon, traveler's checks will be available over America OnLine. Call (800) 673-3782 to find out more about this service, or check ExpressNet or America OnLine.

Citicorp sells both Citicorp and **Citicorp Visa** traveler's checks (tel. (800) 645-6556 in the U.S. and Canada, (0171) 982 40 40 in London; from elsewhere call the U.S. collect (813) 623-1709). Commission is 1-2% on check purchases. Citicorp's World Courier Service guarantees hand-delivery of traveler's checks anywhere in the world. (Note, too, that any kind of Visa Traveler's Checks can also be reported lost at the general Visa number below).

Thomas Cook MasterCard: Call (800) 223-9920 in the U.S. and Canada; elsewhere call the U.S. collect (609) 987-7300; from the U.K. call (0800) 62 21 01 free or (1733) 502 995 collect. Commission ranges from 1-2% for purchases. Try buying the checks at a Thomas Cook office for potentially lower commissions. You can buy Mastercard traveler's checks from Thomas Cook at any bank displaying a Mastercard sign.

Visa (tel. (800) 227-6811 in the U.S. and Canada; from abroad, call New York collect (212) 858-8500 or London (0171) 937 80 91.) Sells its traveler's checks by mail; call (800) 235-7366 to order them. Any kind of Visa traveler's checks (Barclay's or Citicorp) can be reported lost at the Visa number.

CREDIT CARDS

Credit cards for the budget traveler can be a blessing, a curse, or both. On the dark side, many smaller establishments will not accept them, while those enticing, pricier, big-city establishments accept them all too willingly. Relying exclusively— or extensively—on credit cards while abroad could be a big mistake, especially if doing so leads you to spend more than you would otherwise. However, used sparingly, credit cards can be a great boon even to the careful spenders. Perhaps the most important benefit is that holders of most major credit cards can now get cash advances around the clock at automated teller machines (ATMs) throughout Europe (increasingly common in Italy, especially in the larger cities). Often, the fee charged by the credit card company will be less than the commission you would pay in exchanging traveler's checks, and, because you make your withdrawal in foreign currency, you benefit from the wholesale exchange rate. In order to use this service, you must have a PIN number, available from your issuing bank (check with them about charges, interest rates, and ATM locations as well). Unfortunately, in most

cases you will pay mortifying interest rates for such advances, but if you only with-draw what you can pay back immediately (or have someone at home take care of it while you're away), you can avoid paying anything other than the fee for the trans-action. You can also reduce conversion fees by charging purchases instead of chang-ing traveler's checks.

Lost or stolen cards should be reported *immediately,* or you may be held respon-sible for forged charges. Write down the card-cancellation telephone numbers and keep them in a safe place separate from your cards. Always be sure that the carbon has been torn into pieces, and ask to watch as your card is being imprinted; an imprint onto a blank slip can be used later to charge merchandise in your name.

CASH CARDS AND ATMS

Cash cards (ATM cards) function throughout Italy at varying rates of success. You will probably want to access your own personal bank account whenever you're in need of funds, so check to see what network (Cirrus and Plus are two of the most common) your bank belongs to and how much they'll charge you for each transac-tion. Happily, ATMs get the same wholesale exchange rate as credit cards and often offer menus in English. It is advisable to exchange as much as you can handle safely in order to minimize fees, but there is usually a limit to the amount of money you can withdraw per day, and computer network failures are not uncommon. (Some networks stop transactions for a short period each day for maintenance reasons, so try again later.) Be sure to memorize your PIN code since machines abroad often don't have letters on the keys. Also, if your PIN is longer than four dig-its, ask your bank whether the first four digits will work, or whether you need a shorter number. As always, most ATMs are outdoors; don't let anyone distract you while you are at the machine, and use discretion when you walk away from it.

> **ATM fraud** is not uncommon; in the event that you should not receive the cor-rect amount of cash, remember to **keep your receipt.**

MONEY FROM HOME

Sending money overseas is a complicated, expensive, and often extremely frustrat-ing adventure. Do your best to avoid it by carrying a credit card or a separate stash of emergency traveler's checks.

The easiest way to get money from home is to bring an **American Express Card.** American Express allows green card holders to draw cash from their checking accounts at any of its major offices and many of its representatives' offices (up to $1000 every 21 days, no service charge, no interest). AmEx also offers Express Cash, which allows green card holders to withdraw up to $1000 in a seven day period. There is a 2% transaction fee for each cash withdrawal with a $2.50 minimum. To enroll in Express Cash, cardmembers may call 1-800-CASH NOW.

Another approach is to wire money through the instant **international money transfer services** operated by **Western Union** (tel. in the U.S. and Canada (800) 325-6000; in Europe, call the London office at (0181) 741 36 39). Also, American Express offers **moneygrams** (tel. (800) 543-4080, in Canada (800) 933-3278). The money is usually available within the hour in the country to which you are sending it. Rates are US$29 to send US$250, US$40 to send US$500, and US$50 to send US$1000. To pick up the money, you'll need to show ID.

The least expensive but often cumbersome route is to **cable money** from bank to bank. Usually, both sender and receiver must have accounts at the respective insti-tutions. Transfer can take up to a few days; the fee is usually a flat US$20-30. Outside AmEx, avoid trying to cash checks in foreign currencies as they usually require weeks and a US$30 fee to clear.

Finally, if you are an American in a life-or-death situation, you can have money sent to you via the **State Department's Citizens Emergency Center,** 2201 C St. NW, Washington, DC 20520 (tel. (202) 647-5225; after hours and holidays, (202)

647-4000). For a fee of about US$25, the State Department will forward money within hours to the nearest consular office, which will then pass it on according to instructions. The agency prefers not to send sums greater than $500, and will enclose a message upon request. In an emergency, cable the State Department through Western Union or leave cash, a certified check, a bank draft, or a money order at the department itself. Up-to-the-minute travel advisories and general information are also available from the numbers listed above.

VALUE-ADDED TAX

The **Value-Added Tax (VAT,** in Italian, *imposto sul valore aggiunta*, or **IVA**) is a form of sales tax levied in the European Union. VAT is generally part of the price paid on goods and services. In Italy there are two main VAT rates: IVA 16% (13.8% of sale price), applied to fashion, textiles, and shoes, and IVA 19% (16% of sale price) on all other items. Non-residents of EU countries have a legal right to a refund of the VAT, subject to the following conditions: (1) total value of goods purchased in a store must be over L300,000 net (without the VAT added), (2) an invoice, including the passport number of the purchaser, must be issued in the store, (3) when leaving the EU, the invoice, purchases, and purchaser's passport must be presented to and stamped by the Customs Office, and (4) the invoice is then returned to the store within 90 days of the date of issue. Some of the more upscale stores offer another service, called Tax-Free Shopping for Tourists, which enables you to get your VAT refund in cash when leaving from the airport or crossing road borders. For more info on rules and rights, contact **Italy Tax-Free Shopping,** Via C. Battisti, 3, 21045 Gazzada (Varese) (tel. (0332) 87 07 70; fax (0332) 87 07 71).

BARGAINING

Bargaining is common in Italy, but use discretion: it is appropriate and warranted in dealings at markets, with street vendors, and over unmetered taxi fares (always settle your price *before* getting into the cab). But haggling over prices is out of place almost everywhere else, especially in large stores. Hotel haggling is most often done in uncrowded, smaller *pensioni* or for *affitta camere* (*Let's Go* mentions when such activity is common). If you don't speak Italian, at least memorize the numbers. Let the merchant make the first offer and counter with one-half to two-thirds of his or her bid. You can expect the merchant to act extremely offended by your offer, but stand firm. Never offer anything you are unwilling to pay—you are expected to buy if the merchant accepts your price.

■■■ SAFETY AND SECURITY

If you are ever in a potentially dangerous situation anywhere in Italy, call the **Emergency Assistance Number:** 113 or 112. 113 is the Public Emergency Assistance number for the State Police, and usually has an English interpreter on hand; 112, the Immediate Action Service of the Carabinieri, should be your second choice. 115 is the nationwide telephone number for the fire department, and 116 will bring the *Soccorso Stradale* or ACI (Italian Automobile Club).

Tourists are particularly vulnerable to crime for two reasons: they carry large amounts of cash and are not as savvy as locals. To avoid unwanted attention, blend in as much as possible. (Though it's counterintuitive, women in shorts will receive more attention than women in skirts.) This is often harder than it sounds; even so, time spent learning local style will be well worth it. If you do feel nervous, walking purposefully into a *caffè* or shop and checking your map there is better than checking it on a street corner. Muggings are more often impromptu than planned. Try to look assured and confident; walking with nervous glances can be a tip that you have something valuable to protect. Carry all your valuables (including your passport, railpass, traveler's checks, and airline ticket) either in a **money belt** or **neckpouch** stashed securely inside your clothing. These will protect you from skilled thieves who use razors to slash open backpacks and fanny packs. Making **photocopies** of important documents and credit cards will allow you to recover them; carry one copy separate from the documents and leave another at home.

If you carry a purse, buy a sturdy leather one with a secure clasp, and carry it crosswise on the side away from the street with the clasp against you. (Even these precautions do not always suffice: moped riders who snatch purses and backpacks often tote knives to cut the straps.) As far as packs are concerned, buy some small combination padlocks which slip through two zippers, securing a pack shut. Be particularly watchful of your belongings on buses or in thick crowds (never, for example, carry your backpack on your back, but always in front of you where you can see it), don't check baggage on trains, especially if you're switching lines, and don't trust *anyone* to "watch your bag for a second." Ask the manager of your hotel or hostel for advice on areas to avoid, and if you feel unsafe, look for places with either a curfew or a night attendant. Keep your valuables on you in low-budget hotels where someone else may have a passkey, and always in dormitory-style surroundings— otherwise a trip to the shower could cost you a passport or wallet.

When you explore a new city, extra vigilance may be wise, but don't let fear inhibit your ability to experience another culture. At night, daytime precautions should become mandates. In particular, stay near crowded and well-lit areas and do not attempt to traverse parks, parking lots, or any other large, deserted areas.

Among the more colorful aspects of Italian cities are the **con artists.** Hustlers often work in groups, and children, unfortunately, are among the most effective at the game. Tricks are many and adaptable. Be aware of certain classics: sob stories that require money, or mud spilled (or saliva spit) onto your shoulder, distracting you for enough time to snatch your bag. Another common one, especially with small children, is to shove a newspaper or other large item directly under your face, allowing the children to clean you out while you can't see what they're doing. (Some unfortunate souls have had gypsy mothers literally throw their babies at them, and then, with arms outstretched to catch the baby in mid-air, been pickpocketed by the baby's siblings!) Be especially alert in these situations: among the tactics you can employ are simply not responding or making eye contact, walking quickly and purposefully away, and keeping a solid grip on your belongings. Do your best to keep them far from your person; shouting or making large, threatening gestures often sends them toward a quieter, more passive person. Contact the police if a hustler is particularly insistent or aggressive.

Trains are notoriously easy spots for thieving. Professionals wait for tourists to fall asleep and then carry off everything they can. When traveling in pairs, sleep in alternating shifts, close the door securely, and pull the blinds shut. When alone use good judgment in selecting a train compartment: never stay in an empty one. Keep important documents, etc. on your person, and try to sleep on "top bunks" with your luggage stored above you (if not in bed with you). Sleeping in an auto is one of the most dangerous ways to rest; it is more advisable to park in a well-lit area as close to a police station or 24-hr. service station as possible. Sleeping outside can be even more dangerous; camping is recommended only in official, supervised campsites.

There is no sure-fire set of precautions that will protect you from all situations you might encounter when you travel. A good self-defense course will give you more concrete ways to react to different types of aggression, but it might cost you more money than your trip. **Model Mugging** (East Coast tel. (617) 232-7900; Midwest tel. (312) 338-4545; West Coast tel. (415) 592-7300) teaches a comprehensive course on self-defense (course prices vary from US$400-500). Community colleges frequently offer self-defense courses at more affordable prices. **Travel Assistance International by Worldwide Assistance Services, Inc.** provides its members with a 24-hr. hotline for emergencies and referrals. Their year-long frequent traveler package ($226) includes medical and travel insurance, financial assistance, and help in replacing lost documents. Call (800) 821-2828 or (202) 828-5894, fax (202) 331-1530, or write them at 1133 15th St. NW, Suite 400, Washington, D.C. 20005-2710.

DRUGS

Travelers should avoid drugs altogether. Italy enacted a "zero-tolerance" law in 1991; although this law is apparently no longer intact, possession of any amount of narcotics or even "soft drugs" (i.e. marijuana) is illegal. Your home government is powerless to interfere with the judicial system of a foreign country, and all foreigners are subject to Italian law. Even if you don't use drugs, beware of the person who asks you to carry a package or drive a car across the border. For more info, write for the pamphlet *Travel Warning on Drugs Abroad* from the **Bureau of Consular Affairs,** #6831, Department of State, Washington, DC 20520 (tel. (202) 647-1488).

■■■ HEALTH

For **medical emergencies** in Italy, dial 113 (112 for police). **First Aid Service** (*Pronto Soccorso*) is available in airports, ports, and train stations. Every **pharmacy** (*farmacia*) in Italy has a list of pharmacies open all night and on Sundays.

BEFORE YOU GO

Prior to embarking on your trip, certain precautionary measures should be taken. A little foresight (and an apple a day) will help you maintain good health on the road.

For minor health problems on the road, a compact **first-aid kit** should suffice. Some hardware stores carry ready-made kits, but it's just as easy to assemble your own. Items you might want to include are bandages, aspirin, antiseptic soap or antibiotic cream (some brands even contain an anaesthetic), a thermometer in a sturdy case, a Swiss Army knife with tweezers, moleskin, a decongestant, a motion sickness remedy, medicine for diarrhea and stomach problems, sunscreen (see On the Road: heatstroke, page 24) insect repellent, burn ointment, and an elastic bandage.

People with asthma or allergies should be aware that larger Italian cities often have visibly high levels of air pollution, particularly during the summer, and that, as elsewhere in Europe, "non-smoking" areas or sections are almost nonexistent. Take **antihistamines, decongestants, inhalers,** etc. (be it prescription or over-the-counter); Italian equivalents are often unreliable and in different dosages.

If you wear **glasses** or **contact lenses,** take an extra prescription with you and arrange for someone at home to send you a replacement in an emergency. If you wear contacts, you should take along a pair of glasses to rest tired eyes. Bring extra contact equipment; it's often expensive abroad. And, if you use a heat disinfection system, you may want to switch over to a "cold" or chemical system for the duration of your travels; you'll be less likely to fry your lenses on weird electric currents.

Reliable *and* familiar **contraception** may be difficult to come by while traveling. See the sections on AIDS and Gynecology, Contraception, and Abortion for information concerning availability, page 25.

Travelers with chronic medical conditions should consult their physicians before leaving. Always go prepared with any **medication** you may need while away, as well as a copy of the prescription and/or a statement from your doctor, especially if you will be bringing insulin, syringes, or any narcotics into Italy (some drugs legal at home may not be legal there).

In your passport, write the names of people you wish to be contacted in case of a medical emergency, and also list any allergies or medical conditions of which you would want doctors to be aware. Any traveler with an important medical condition that cannot be easily recognized may want to obtain a **Medic Alert Identification Tag.** The internationally recognized tag indicates the nature of the bearer's problem, as well as the number of a 24-hr. hotline. Medical personnel can call this number to obtain info about the member's medical history. Lifetime membership begins at US$35. Contact Medic Alert Foundation, P.O. Box 1009, Turlock, CA 95381-1009 (tel. (800) 432-5378). The **American Diabetes Association,** 1660 Duke St., Alexandria, VA 22314 (tel. (800) 232-3472) provides copies of an article "Travel and Diabetes" and 18-language ID cards. In the U.S., contact your local ADA office for info.

Let's Go should not be your only information source on common health problems while traveling, hiking, or camping in Italy. Complete **health information** for travelers is available from a variety of published sources. Consult your local bookstore for books on staying healthy at home or on the road or write the **Superintendent of Documents**, U.S. Government Printing Office, Washington D.C. 20402 (tel. (202) 783-3238). Check with the organizations and publications listed below for more info, and send for the **American Red Cross'** *First-Aid and Safety Handbook* (US$14.95); contact the American Red Cross, 61 Medford St., Somerville, MA 02143 (tel. (800) 564-1234). In the U.S., the American Red Cross also offers many first-aid and CPR courses; these are well-taught and relatively inexpensive, so contact your local American Red Cross office.

The **United States Center for Disease Control** (based in Atlanta, Georgia) is an excellent source of general info on health for travelers around the world, and maintains an international travelers hotline (tel. (404) 332-4559). If you have access to a fax, you can request printed info from the CDC fax info service; call the hotline from a phone and follow the prompts. (You will need the document code for the "disease directory," which provides the codes for info on a variety of diseases (including HIV/AIDS) and on travelers' health; it is 000004.) Or write directly to the Centers for Disease Control and Prevention, CDC, 1600 Clifton Rd. NE, Atlanta, GA 30333. If you want to talk to a person, call the public inquiry number at (404) 639-3311. The CDC publishes the booklet *Health Information for International Travelers* (publication # HHS-CDC 90-8280, US$6), an annual global rundown of disease, immunization, and general health advice, including risks in particular countries. Request the booklet by calling the CDC's hotline, or writing the Superintendent of Documents, U.S. Government Printing Office, Washington, DC 20402.

One organization that you may find extremely useful is the **International Association for Medical Assistance to Travelers (IAMAT).** Membership is free, and IAMAT offers a membership ID card, a directory of English-speaking doctors around the world (in over 125 countries and territories) who have agreed to treat members for a set fee schedule, and a series of detailed brochures and charts on immunization requirements, various tropical diseases, and climate and sanitation. Contact chapters in the U.S., 417 Center St., Lewiston, NY 14092 (tel. (716) 754-4883), Canada, 40 Regal Road, Guelph, Ontario, N1K 1B5 (tel. (519) 836-0102) or 1287 St. Clair Avenue West, Toronto, M6E 1B8 (tel. (416) 652-0137; fax (519) 836-3412), New Zealand, P.O. Box 5049, Christchurch 5, or Switzerland, 57 Voirets, 1212 Grand-Lancy-Geneva. IAMAT is likely to respond much more quickly in the mail than government agencies like the CDC might.

Second to the CDC or IAMAT in usefulness for travelers (and not just United States citizens) is the **United States State Department,** which compiles Consular Information Sheets on health, entry requirements, and other issues for all countries of the world. This info can be heard by calling the Overseas Citizens Services (tel. (202) 647-5225). If you have access to a fax, you can request those sheets by dialing (202) 647-3000 directly from the fax and following the recorded instructions. You can also request copies of the information from the State Department's regional passport agencies in the U.S., from the field offices of the U.S. Chamber of Commerce, from U.S. embassies and consulates abroad; or you can send a self-addressed, stamped envelope to the Overseas Citizens Services, Bureau of Consular Affairs, Room 4811, U.S. Department of State, Washington, DC 20520. If you are HIV-positive, call (202) 647-1488 for country-specific entry restrictions or write to the Bureau of Consular Affairs, #6831, Department of State, Washington, DC 20520.

Travelers' very specific questions are probably best answered by calling the U.S. Public Health Quarantine Station: Chicago (312) 894-2961/8; Hawaii (808) 861-8531; Los Angeles (310) 215-2365/6; Miami (305) 526-2910; New York: (718) 553-1685; San Francisco (415) 876-2872; or Seattle (206) 553-4519; or try the fax service in Atlanta (404) 332-4565.

HEALTH

ON THE ROAD

Common sense is the simplest prescription for good health while you travel: eat well, drink plenty of liquids, get enough sleep, and don't overexert yourself. While traveling, pay attention to signals of pain and discomfort that your body may send you; while you are on the road you are more susceptible to illness, and some of the milder symptoms that you may safely ignore at home may be signs of more serious problems. The following paragraphs list some health problems commonly experienced by travelers.

Italy, especially the south, scorches in the summer. When traveling during this season, protect yourself against the dangers of sun and heat, especially **heatstroke.** If you are prone to sunburn, be sure to take a potent sunscreen with you (it can be expensive abroad) and keep reapplying it as you sweat. Wear a hat as much as possible and—if you can stand it—cover up with long pants and/or sleeves. Heatstroke can cause death within a few hours if not treated. It results from continuous heat stress, lack of fitness, or overactivity following heat exhaustion. In the early stages of heatstroke, sweating stops, body temperature rises, and headache develops, soon followed by confusion. To treat heatstroke, cool the victim off *immediately* with fruit juice or salted water, wet towels, and shade. Rush the victim to the hospital as soon as possible.

Extreme cold is no less dangerous—it brings risks of hypothermia and frostbite. **Hypothermia** is a result of overexposure to cold and can occur *in the middle of the summer,* especially in rainy or windy conditions. Body temperature drops rapidly, resulting in the failure to produce body heat. Other symptoms are uncontrollable shivering, poor coordination, and exhaustion followed by slurred speech, sleepiness, hallucinations, and amnesia. *Do not* let the victim fall asleep if he or she is in advanced stages—if s/he loses consciousness, it can result in death. To avoid hypothermia while traveling, always keep dry. Wear wool, *especially* in soggy weather. Dress in layers, and stay out of the wind, which carries heat away from the body. Remember that loss of body heat is primarily through your head, so always carry a wool hat with you. **Frostbite** occurs in freezing temperatures. The affected skin will turn white, then waxy. To counteract the problem, drink warm beverages and gently and slowly warm the frostbitten area in dry fabric or with steady body contact. *Never rub frostbite.*

If you're going to be doing a lot of walking, remember to treat your most valuable resource well: **lavish your feet with attention.** Wear good walking shoes, change your socks often, use talcum powder to keep your feet dry, and use moleskin to pad hotspots before they become excruciating blisters. Also, take along some quick-energy foods. You will need plenty of protein (for sustained energy) and fluids (to prevent dehydration and constipation). Carry a water bottle, and drink from it even when you don't feel thirsty. Italian water is generally safe to drink unless marked *"non potabile,"* or unless it is running water on public transportation (ferries, trains, etc.). Relying on bottled mineral water for a while at the start of your trip minimizes chances of a bad reaction to the few unfamiliar microbes in Italian water.

Food poisoning can spoil any trip. Some of the cheapest and most convenient eating options are also the biggest culprits: street vendors, tap water, and perishable food carried for hours in a hot backpack. One of the most common symptoms associated with eating and drinking in another country is **diarrhea.** Many people take with them over-the-counter remedies (such as Imodium AD or Pepto-Bismol), but such remedies can complicate serious infections; don't use them if you suspect you have been exposed to contaminated food or water, which puts you at risk for cholera, typhoid fever, and other diseases. Since dehydration is the most common side effect of diarrhea, those suffering should drink plenty of fruit juice and pure water. Rest, and let the dastardly disease run its course.

Women traveling in unsanitary conditions are vulnerable to **bladder infection,** a very common and severely uncomfortable bacterial disease which causes its victim to suffer a burning sensation during urination. A strong antibiotic (available without a prescription in some countries) usually gets rid of the symptoms within a couple of days. Other recommendations: drink enormous amounts of cranberry or another vitamin C-rich juice and plenty of water, and urinate frequently. Untreated bladder infections can lead to even more serious kidney infections. Treat an infection as best you can while on the road; if it persists, take time out to see a doctor and definitely check with one when you get home.

If you plan to **romp in the forest,** learn of any regional hazards. Any three-leaved plant might be poison ivy, poison oak, or poison sumac—pernicious plants whose oily surface causes insufferable itchiness if touched. Many areas have indigenous snakes, spiders, insects, and creepy-crawlies. In general, insect repellent is a must in overgrown or forested areas. Also, if you will be hiking in such areas, aim to maximize clothing coverage; long sleeves and pants tucked into boots make it that much harder for those biting insects to get at you, and also reduce your chances of getting scratched by the brambles, nettles, etc. that grow all over the Mediterranean.

Travelers in **high altitudes** should allow their bodies a couple of days to adjust to the lower atmospheric oxygen levels before engaging in any strenuous activity. Those new to high-altitude areas may feel drowsy, and one alcoholic beverage may have the same effect as three at a lower altitude.

AIDS

On or off the road, you should be concerned about **Acquired Immune Deficiency Syndrome (AIDS),** transmitted through the exchange of body fluids with an infected individual (HIV-positive). Remember that there is no assurance that someone is not infected: HIV tests only show antibodies after a six-month lapse. Do not have sex without using a condom or share intravenous needles or syringes with anyone. The Center for Disease Control's **AIDS Hotline** provides information on AIDS in the U.S. and can refer you to other organizations with information on Italy (tel. (800) 342-2437; Spanish (800) 344-7332, daily 8am-2pm; TTY (800) 243-7889, 10am-10pm). Call the **U.S. State Department** for country-specific restrictions for HIV-positive travelers (tel. (202) 647-1488; fax (202) 647-3000; modem-users may consult the electronic bulletin board at (202) 647-9225; or write to the Bureau of Consular Affairs, Rm. #6831, Dept. of State, Washington, D.C. 20520). In Europe, call (022) 791 46 73 (Switzerland) or write to the **World Health Organization,** Attn.: Global Program on AIDS, 20 Avenue Appia, 1211 Geneva 27, Switzerland.

There are no restrictions on travelers with HIV or AIDS entering Italy, nor is there any obligation to report an infection on arrival in the country or if you find you have it once there. Italians are generally very sensible about medical treatment, and the medical professionals will not pry if you get tested; do double-check that your test is confidential, or even done anonymously if need be. AIDS education is becoming more prevalent throughout the country, and you will not have any problems finding condoms *(preservativi)* at any pharmacy. The **toll-free AIDS number** for Italy is 167 86 10 61 (call Mon.-Fri. 1-6pm).

AIDS tests can be performed at any **Analisi Cliniche** (a private lab that handles all sorts of tests, from allergies to pregnancy). Simply ask for the "AIDS test" or "HIV test"—there isn't an Italian word. (AIDS is pronounced AH-eeds in Italian; HIV is AH-ka-ee-voo.) Tests can be expensive (up to L150,000). Look in the Yellow Pages under *Analisi* for private labs or refer to one of the following Analisi Cliniche located in Rome:

Unione Sanitaria Internazionale, Via V. Orsini, 18 (tel. (06) 321 50 53), north of the Vatican, off Piazza della Libertà; or Via Machiavelli, 22 (tel. 70 45 35 44), Metro Linea A, Vittorio Emanuele stop. Open for info. 7am-7:30pm. Open for tests 7am-11am.

Analisi Cliniche Luisa, Via Padova, 96 (tel. (06) 44 29 14 06), take Metro Linea B to Piazza Bologna. Open Mon.-Fri. 7:30am-4:30pm, Sat. 8am-1:30pm. HIV test costs L110,000 for a result within 4 days, L150,000 for same-day results.

Alessandrini, Viale Mazzini, 33 (tel. (06) 321 79 99 or 323 05 04), take Metro Linea A to LePanto. Open Mon.-Fri. 7:30am-1:30pm and 4-7pm.

Cavour, Via Cavour, 238 (tel./fax (06) 474 39 48), at the Metro Linea B Cavour. Open Mon.-Fri. 7:30-11am and 4-6pm, Sat. 7:30-11am.

GYNECOLOGY, CONTRACEPTION, AND ABORTIONS

If you are straight and sexually active, you will need to worry about contraception. Reliable devices may be difficult to come by while traveling. Women on the Pill should bring enough to allow for possible loss or extended stays, and should bring a prescription, since forms of the Pill vary a good deal. The sponge is probably too bulky to be worthwhile on the road; if you use a diaphragm, be sure that you have enough contraceptive jelly on hand. In Italy, **condoms** (*profilattici,* or in common parlance, *preservativi*) can be bought over the counter at pharmacies and in some supermarkets. A packet of six costs around L15,000.

Analisi Cliniche will perform tests for venereal disease (*malattia venerea*) as well as pregnancy tests, or you can buy home tests over the counter at pharmacies throughout the city. These labs also do pap smears and cryotherapy.

Abortion is legal in Italy, although not as a means of birth control. Local health units called *consultori* advise women on rights and procedures. The U.S. **National Abortion Federation's hotline** (tel. (800) 772-9100, Mon.-Fri. 9:30am-5:30pm) can direct you to organizations that provide info on abortion in other countries. Another source of general info on contraception and abortion worldwide is the **International Planned Parenthood Federation,** European Regional Office, Regent's College Inner Circle, Regent's Park, London NW1 4NS (tel. (0171) 486 07 41, fax (0171) 487 79 50). The Vatican surrendered its right to interfere in Italian politics in the Lateran Treaty of 1929, and the anti-choice movement is fairly low-key. Being a Catholic country, however, Italy isn't the easiest place to get an abortion.

International Medical Center, Via Amendola, 7 (1 block from Termini), 2nd floor (tel. 488 23 71; nights and Sundays (06) 488 40 51). On call 24 hrs.; English spoken. Referrals to English-speaking doctors. Open Mon.-Sat. 8am-9pm.

Ospedale San Camillo in Monteverde, Circonvallazione Gianicolense, 87 in Gianicolo (tel. 587 01). Abortion on demand is not available; women must have a gynecological exam, discussion with a doctor, and possibly counseling. Simple abortion about L500,000-600,000. Open Mon.-Sat. 8-11am.

■■■ INSURANCE

Beware of unnecessary coverage: your current policies might well extend to many travel-related accidents. **Medical insurance** (especially university policies) often covers costs incurred abroad, although **Medicare's** coverage is usually only valid in Mexico and Canada. Canadians are protected by their home province's health insurance plan up to 90 days after leaving the country; check with the provincial Ministry of Health or Health Plan Headquarters. Australians are covered by Medicare when traveling in Italy; consult Medicare's brochure "Health Care for Australians Traveling Overseas" to find out the extent of coverage and how to obtain benefits.

Your **homeowners' insurance** (or your family's coverage) often covers theft during travel. Homeowners are generally covered against loss of travel documents (passport, plane ticket, railpass, etc.) up to US$500.

ISIC and **ITIC** provide US$3000 worth of accident and illness insurance and US$100 per day up to 60 days of hospitalization. The cards also give access to a toll-free Traveler's Assistance hotline (in the US and Canada (800) 626-2427; elsewhere call collect to the US (713) 267-2525) whose multilingual staff can provide help in emergencies overseas. **Council** offers the inexpensive Trip-Safe plan with options covering medical treatment and hospitalization, accidents, baggage loss, and even charter flights missed due to illness; **STA** offers a more expensive, more comprehensive plan. **American Express** cardholders receive automatic car-rental and flight insurance on purchases made with the card.

Insurance companies usually require a copy of the police report for thefts, or evidence of having paid medical expenses (doctor's statements, receipts) before they will honor a claim, and may have time limits on filing. Have documents written in English to avoid fees for translation. Always carry policy numbers and proof of insurance. Note that some of the plans listed below offer cash advances or guaranteed bills. Check with each insurance carrier for specific restrictions.

ARM Coverage, Inc./Carefree Travel Insurance, 100 Garden City Plaza, P.O. Box 9366, Garden City, NY 11530-9366 (tel. (800) 323-3149 or (516) 294-0220; fax (516) 294-1821). Offers two comprehensive packages including coverage for trip delay, accident and sickness, medical, baggage loss, bag delay, accidental death and dismemberment, and travel supplier insolvency. Trip cancellation/interruption may be purchased separately at a rate of US$5.50 per US$100 of coverage. 24-hour hotline.

Globalcare Travel Insurance, 220 Broadway, Lynnfield, MA 01940 (tel. (800) 821-2488; fax (617) 592-7720). Complete medical, legal, emergency, and travel-related services. On-the-spot payments and special student programs.

Travel Assistance International, by Worldwide Assistance Services, Inc., 1133 15th St. NW, Suite 400, Washington, DC 20005-2710 (tel. (800) 821-2828 or (202) 828-5894; fax 331-1530). TAI provides members with a 24-hr. emergency and referral hotline. The year-long frequent traveler package ($226) includes medical and travel insurance, financial assistance, and help in replacing lost documents.

■■■ ALTERNATIVES TO TOURISM

VOLUNTEERING

Volunteering is a good way to immerse yourself in a foreign culture. Besides the personal satisfaction, you may even receive room and board for your work; many people whom you meet will invite you into their home. *Volunteer! The Comprehensive Guide to Voluntary Service in the U.S. and Abroad,* (US$13, postage US$1.50) offering advice and listings, is available from **Council Travel** (see page 41).

Volunteers for Peace, 43 Tiffany Rd., Belmont, VT 05730 (tel. (802) 259-2759; fax 259-2922). A non-profit organization that arranges for speedy placement in over 800 10-15 people workcamps in over 50 countries, primarily in Europe. Gives the most complete and up-to-date listings in the annual *International Workcamp Directory* (US$12 postpaid). Registration fee US$150. Some workcamps are open to 16 and 17 year-olds for a slightly higher fee (US$175). Free newsletter.

Service Civil International/International Voluntary Service (SCI-VS), 5479 Walnut Level Road, Crozet, VA 22932 (tel. (804) 823-1826). Arranges placement in workcamps; there are 200 opportunities in Europe (ages 18 and over). Registration fees for the placement service range from US$50-250. Call or write for a summer listing (US$5).

ARCHAEOLOGICAL DIGS

The **Archaeological Institute of America,** 656 Beacon St., Boston, MA 02215-2010 (tel. (617) 353-9361; fax 353-6550) puts out the *Archaeological Fieldwork Opportunities Bulletin.* The 1995 edition (US$11 for non-members) lists over 250 field sites throughout the world, and is available from Kendall/Hunt Publishing 4050 Westmark Drive, Dubuque, IA 52002 (tel. (800) 228-0810). For other questions, contact the AIA directly at the first address. For information on anthropology, archaeological digs, and art history in Italy, write to the **Centro Comune di Studi Preistorici,** 25044 Capo di Ponte, Valcmonica (Brescia) (tel. (0364) 420 91; fax 425 72). This research center is involved with the management of cultural property and the organization of congresses, research projects, exhibitions, parks, and museums. They offer volunteer work, grants, tutoring, research assistant positions, and training and apprenticeship in prehistoric and primitive art, research methods, and editing (they publish *BCSP,* the world journal of prehistoric and tribal art).

Local colleges and universities in your home country are another excellent source of information on archaeological digs in Italy and elsewhere. Check with the

perCorsi I T A L I A N I

CENTRO FIORENZA
via S. Spirito, 14
50125 FIRENZE
tel : 055/2398274
fax : 055/287148

A GUARANTEE OF QUALITY

ITALIAN LANGUAGE COURSES IN ITALY
Florence ● Rome ● Siena ● Milan ● Elba

Scuola LINGUAVIVA
via Fiume, 17
50123 FIRENZE
tel : 055/294359-280016
fax : 055/28366

The five schools which make up our group are located in Florence, Rome, Siena, Milan, and the Island of Elba. They are among the most prominent in Italy and all offer the same high quality of standards in the organization of courses and in the services provided for their students.

Courses

- Group courses offered throughout the year at all levels from beginner to advanced. Average class size: 10 students.
- Preparation courses for students interested in studying fashion and design
- Individual executive courses tailored to meet the needs of people working in business, industry, and the professions.
- Courses in Italian art, music, and cooking.

CENTRO INTERNAZIONALE
DANTE ALIGHIERI
piazza La Lizza, 10
53100 SIENA
tel : 0577/49533
fax : 0577/270646

DILIT - International House
via Marghera, 22
00185 ROMA
tel : 06/4462592-4462602
fax : 06/44440888

Accommodations

- Homestay: single or double rooms with breakfast or half-board.
- Shared flats with other students.
- Independent flats.

Scuola LINGUADUE
Corso Buenos Aires, 43
20124 MILANO
tel : 02/29519972
fax : 02/29519973

Social Activities

- Visits to museums and churches, excursions, film showings, evening entertainment and sports.

Departments of Classics, Archaeology, Anthropology, Fine Arts, and/or other relevant area studies; many excavations send information and applications directly to individual professors or departments rather than to the general public.

STUDY

Foreign study seems a fail-proof good time, but programs vary tremendously in expense, academic quality, living conditions, and exposure to local students and culture. Most American undergraduates enroll in programs sponsored by domestic universities, and many colleges' staff offices give advice on study abroad. Take advantage of these resources and put in some hours in their libraries. Ask for the names of recent participants, and talk to them. You may also want to check with the **United States Information Service** at the American Embassy in Rome, which publishes a list of all American schools in Italy.

Publications

Council publishes *Work, Study, Travel Abroad: The Whole World Handbook,* which covers all continents and includes summer and long-term work abroad. Includes a list of specific programs. Published by St. Martin's Press (US$13.95). Write to CIEE-Pubs. Dept., 205 E. 42nd St., New York, NY 10017-5706.

Institute of International Education (IIE), 809 United Nations Plaza, New York, NY 10017-3580 (tel. (212) 984-5413 for recorded info; fax 984-5358). Nonprofit international and cultural exchange agency. Their library of study abroad resources is open to the public Tues.-Thurs. 11am-3:45pm. Publishes *Academic Year Abroad* (US$43 with US$4 s&h) detailing semester and year-long programs worldwide and *Vacation Study Abroad* ($37 with $4 s&h) which lists over 1600 short-term, summer and language school programs. Write for a publications list.

Transitions Abroad Publishing, Inc., 18 Hulst Rd., P.O. Box 1300, Amherst, MA 01004 (tel. (800) 293-0873), publishes a bimonthly magazine listing all kinds of opportunities and printed resources for those seeking to study, work, or travel abroad. They also publish an *Alternative Travel Planner,* a truly exhaustive listing of information for the "active international traveler." For subscriptions (USA US$19.95 for 6 issues, Canada US$26, other countries US$38), contact them at *Transitions Abroad,* Dept. TRA, Box 3000, Denville, NJ 07834.

Organizations

Centro Turistico Studentesco e Giovanile (CTS) is connected with the Italian Ministries of Foreign Affairs and of Education, and provides information on study in Italy. For contact info, below, page 41.

Youth For Understanding International Exchange (YFU), 3501 Newark St., NW Washington, DC 20016 (tel. (800) TEENAGE or (202) 966-6800; fax (202) 895-1104). One of the oldest, most respected exchange programs; it places U.S. high school students worldwide for a year, semester, summer, and homestays.

World Learning, Inc., Summer Abroad, Kipling Rd., P.O. Box 676, Brattleboro, VT 05302 (tel. (802) 257-7751 or (800) 345-2929). Conducts several programs for students in high school, college, and beyond. The Summer Abroad program is for high school students, but also offers tour group leader positions to people over 24 with appropriate travel and language experience. Programs run 4-6 weeks.

Italian Universities

If your Italian is fluent, consider enrolling directly in an Italian university. Universities are overcrowded, but you will probably have a blast and develop a real feel for the culture. For an application, write to the nearest Italian consulate. In Rome, contact the **Segretaria Stranieri,** Città Universitaria, Piazzale delle Scienze, 2 (tel. 499 91; open Mon., Wed., Fri. 8:30am-1pm). For more advice, contact **Ufficio Centrale Studenti Esteri in Italia (UCSEI),** Via Lungotevere dei Vallati, 14, 00186 Roma (tel. (06) 880 40 62; fax 880 40 63), a national organization for foreign students who have already started their course of study in Italy.

ALTERNATIVES TO TOURISM

Another option is studying at an institute designed for foreigners but run by an Italian university. The following schools and organizations offer a variety of classes in Italian language, art, and culture; contact them directly for more information.

ABC Centro di Lingua e Cultura Italiana, Language Dept.: Via Dei Rustici, 7 - 50122 Florence (tel. (39-55) 21 20 01; fax 21 21 12). Six levels offered. Extra-curricular activities. Classes of no more than 10 students.

Centro di Cultura per Stranieri (University of Florence), The Secretary: Via Vittorio Emanuele, 64-50134 Firenze (tel. (055) 47 21 39; fax (055) 47 16 20). Offers lectures on anything and everything Italian—in Italian.

Centro Fiorenza—Corsi di Lingua e Cultura Italiana per Stranieri, Via S. Spirito 14 - I -50125 Firenze. Contact Augusto Merlini (tel. (055) 239 82 74; fax 28 71 48). Offers Italian language courses in small groups or individual tuition. Accommodates six levels of Italian proficiency. Intensive business courses and complementary courses offered. Fees include text books and other instructional materials. The Centro is open year-round and offers an accommodation service. Summer courses available on the island of Elba.

Centro Internazionale Dante Alighieri (SienaLingue), La Lizza, 10, 53100 Siena (tel. (0577) 495 33 or 464 21; fax. 27 06 46). Offers month- and two-week-long group language and culture courses year-round, as well as extracurricular activities, sports (Oct.-May), and accommodation services. Proof of health insurance required. Say hi to Giancarla while you're there.

Instituto per l'Arte e il Restauro, Palazzo Spinelli, Borgo Santa Croce, 10, 50122 Firenze (tel. (055) 234 58 98; fax 24 07 09). A private school with training courses for restoration of various art media. Also offers courses in antique trade, painting, goldsmithery, advertising graphics, and interior and fashion design. Language courses are held for foreign students wishing to take the art courses.

Italiaidea, Piazza della Cancelleria, 85, 00186 Rome (tel. 68 30 76 20; fax 689 29 97). Offers every level of Italian study from an intensive short-term "survival Italian course" to more advanced, semester-long courses meeting once or twice a week. Offers on-site lectures and visits to historic sites, Italian conversation, and flexible scheduling. College credit courses offered at some U.S. college and university programs in Italy. Italiaidea offers academic assistance and travel study assistance to its client institutions. Homestays (food and lodging with Italian families) are offered as well.

John Cabot University, Via della Lungara 233, Rome 00165 (tel. 687 88 81; fax 638 20 88; e-mail rspit/mi§nexus.it). Located in Trastevere, this American international university offers undergraduate degrees in Art History, Business Administration, English Literature, and International Affairs. Foreign students can enroll for summer-, quarter-, and year-long sessions. Qualifying students can obtain academic internships in business and international organizations in Rome. Apply directly to the Admissions Office.

Koinè, Centro Koinè, Via de' Pandolfini, 27, 50122 Firenze (tel. (055) 21 38 81; fax 21 69 49). Contact Andrea Koradei.

Finally, be aware that study in Italy for longer than three months requires a **student visa.** For info on how to get one, see the section on visas in Red Tape, page 9.

WORK

The employment situation in Italy is grim for natives (especially in the South) and even worse for foreigners. Openings are coveted by herds of would-be expatriates, so competition is fierce. Foreigners are most successful at securing harvest, restaurant, bar, and domestic work, or jobs in the tourism industry, where English-speakers are needed.

Officially, you can hold a job in European countries only with a **work permit,** applied for by your prospective employer (or by you, with supporting papers from your employer). An employer must demonstrate that a potential employee has skills that locals lack. You will also need a **working visa,** obtainable from your local consulate (for requirements, see the section on visas, page 9). On the other hand, there is the cash-based, untaxable **underground economy**—*economia sommersa* or *economia nera*—which makes up as much as one-third of Italy's economy. Many permitless agricultural workers go untroubled by local authorities, who recognize the need for seasonal labor. **European Union** citizens can work in any other EU country without working papers, and if your parents or grandparents were born in an EU country, you may be able to claim dual citizenship or at least the right to a work permit. Students can check with their university's foreign language departments, which may have official or unofficial access to job openings abroad.

Teaching English, one of the few long-term job possibilities, can be particularly lucrative. Local language schools are listed in the phone book. You may be able to secure a teaching position with an American school in Italy through one of these organizations: **U.S. Department of State,** Office of Overseas Schools, Room 245 SA-29, Department of State, Washington, DC 20522-2902 (tel. (703) 875-7800), which can send you a list of English-language schools abroad to contact directly; the **U.S. Department of Defense,** Dependant Schools, 4040 North Fairfax Dr., Arlington, VA 22203-1634 (tel. (703) 696-3058); and **International Schools Services,** P.O. Box 5910, 15 Roszel Rd., Princeton, NJ 08543 (tel. (609) 452-0990). **Amicizia di Maria de Angelis,** Via XX Settembre 21/7 - 16121 Geneva GE (tel. (010) 553 10 96; fax (010) 553 11 52) is an international student organization for work and study in Italy and abroad.

Publications

Start with Council's free *Work Abroad,* then graduate to the books put out by the following publishers:

Vacation Work Publications, 9 Park End St., Oxford OX1 1HJ (tel. ±44 (01865) 24 19 78; fax 79 08 85). Publishes a number of guides and directories with job listings, including *Live & Work in Italy, Directory of Summer Jobs Abroad,* and *Travellers Survival Kit Europe.* Many of their books are available in bookstores, or from Peterson's, P.O. Box 2123, Attn.: Customer Service, Princeton, NJ 08543 (tel. (800) 338-3282 or (609) 243-9111).

InterExchange Program, 161 6th Ave., New York, NY 10013 (tel. (212) 924-0446; fax 924-0575). Offers pamphlets on work programs and *au pair* positions.

Addison-Wesley, Jacob Way, Reading, MA 01867 (tel. (800) 322-1377 for college, (800) 552-2259 for high school). Publishes *International Jobs: Where They Are, How to Get Them* (US$14.95).

Childcare International, Ltd., Trafalgar House, Grenville Place, London NW7 3SA (tel. ±44 (0181) 959 36 11 or 906 31 16; fax 906 34 61) offers *au pair* positions in Italy and many other European countries. UK£60 application fee. Provides info on qualifications required and local language schools. The organization prefers a long placement but does arrange summer work.

Remember that many of the organizations listed in books like these have very few jobs available and have very specific requirements.

Once in Italy, check out community bulletin boards, as well as the help-wanted columns in the English-language papers *Daily American* and the *International Daily News.* In Rome, *Wanted in Rome* and *Metropolitan* are available in English-language bookstores (and from the *Wanted in Rome* office at Via dei Delfini, 17, 00185 Roma (tel. (06) 679 01 90)). In Milan, you can place a free ad in the weekly *Secondamano* (also good for finding rides); in Rome, contact *Porta Portese,* Via di Porta Maggiore, 95 (tel. 73 37 48). To obtain the magazine *AAM Terra Nuova,* good for agricultural jobs and other opportunities, contact AAM Terra Nuova, cp 199, 50032 Borgo S. Lorenzo (Fi) (tel./fax (055) 845 61 16; L5000 per issue).

■■■ WOMEN TRAVELERS

Italy and other southern European and North African countries have long been viewed as particularly difficult areas for women traveling in groups or on their own. Although women travelers do face additional safety concerns, excessive caution can also make it difficult to experience the safe—and rewarding—aspects of a foreign culture. The best recipe for traveling safely is to inform yourself as much as possible about the conditions and customs of the area you'll be visiting. The following paragraphs are meant to be an introduction to, rather than an exhaustive survey of, problems and possible means of avoiding them. When in doubt, trust your instincts and err on the side of caution.

Italian culture, friendly in general, often overwhelms foreigners. While the constant barrage (and we mean *constant*) of queries and catcalls can become annoying, most comments should not be taken as a precursor to violence. Women, whether alone or in groups, can avoid most harassment by adopting the attitude of Roman women: walk like you know where you are going, avoid eye contact (sunglasses are indispensable), meet advances with silence and dignity, and, if still troubled, walk or stand near older women or couples until you feel safe. Many experienced travelers also recommend wearing a fake (or real, if you've got one) wedding or engagement ring; in a Catholic country like Italy, this token can carry weight, even with would-be harassers. Wearing tight or suggestive clothing can attract unwanted attention, but so can attire that is perfectly modest but obviously American (sweatshirts, college t-shirts, sneakers, hiking shorts). Finally, if you're blonde and want to avoid continual outcries of "*bionda*" (or worse) as you pass, keeping your hair pulled back and covered with a hat or scarf may save you a lot of hassle.

All travelers to Italy (especially from countries like the U.S.) should be aware that the Italian conception of **personal space** is different from what you're probably used to. The guy crowded next to you on the bus or the woman gesticulating madly in your face is not necessarily threatening you or being rude; it is acceptable and normal in Italian culture to stand close to the person you're addressing, to gesture wildly, and to shout. Beyond this, if you feel at all uncomfortable, don't hesitate to seek out a police officer or a passerby. Memorize the **emergency numbers** in Italy

(112 and 113) and always carry change for the phone and enough extra money for a bus or taxi. Self-defense courses suggest carrying a whistle or an airhorn on your keychain—a series of short blasts can call nearby passersby to your help. If you are physically harassed on the bus or in some other crowded space, don't talk to the person directly (this often encourages him). Rather, use body language, like a well-aimed knee or elbow, to make your point. Stepping hard on toes works admirably. Again, if you sense real trouble ask the people around you for help. When traveling on Italian trains, avoid empty compartments, especially at night. Look for compartments with nuns for maximum safety.

Budget **accommodations** can sometimes mean more risk than savings. Avoid small dives and city outskirts; go for university dormitories or youth hostels instead. Centrally located accommodations are usually safest and easiest to return to after dark. Some religious organizations also offer rooms for women only. For a list of these institutions, contact the city's archdiocese or write to the provincial tourist office. Also helpful is the **Associazione Cattolica Internazionale al Servizio della Giovane,** which runs hostels for women throughout Italy. Their main offices are at Via Urbana, 158, 00184 Roma (tel. (06) 488 00 56), and Corso Garibaldi, 123, 20121 Milano (tel. (02) 29 00 01 64; fax 29 00 42 52).

For additional information, see the following **publications:** *The Handbook for Women Travelers* (£8.99), by Maggie and Gemma Moss, is published by Piatkus Books, 5 Windmill St., London W1P 1HF (tel. +44 (0171) 631 0710). *Women Going Places,* a new women's guide, is geared toward lesbians but offers advice appropriate for all women (US$14). It's available from Inland Book Company, P.O. Box 12061, East Haven, CT 06512 (tel. (203) 467-4257).

■■■ OLDER TRAVELERS

Senior travelers are entitled to a number of travel-related discounts—always ask about these (and be aware that proof of senior status is often required). The following organizations and publications provide information on discounts, tours, and health and travel tips.

AARP (American Association of Retired Persons), 601 E St. NW, Washington, DC 20049 (tel. (202) 434-2277). U.S. residents over 50 and their spouses receive benefits including the AARP Motoring Plan from Amoco (tel. (800) 334-3300) and discounts on lodging, car rental, and sight-seeing. US$8 per couple annual fee; US$75 for lifetime membership.

Elderhostel, 75 Federal St., 3rd floor, Boston, MA 02110-1941 (tel. (617) 426-7788; fax (617) 426-8351). You must be 60 or over, and may bring a spouse of any age. Programs at colleges and universities in over 50 countries focus on varied subjects and generally last 1 week.

Gateway Books, 2023 Clemens Rd., Oakland, CA 94602 (tel. (510) 530-0299; fax (510) 530-0497). Publishes Gene and Adele Malott's *Get Up and Go: A Guide for the Mature Traveler* (US$10.95, postage US$1.90), and *Adventures Abroad* (US$12.95), which offer general hints for the budget-conscious senior considering a long stay or even retiring abroad. Call (800) 669-0773 for credit card orders.

■■■ BISEXUAL, GAY, AND LESBIAN TRAVELERS

Gay and lesbian travelers may find Italians unwelcoming, particularly in the south. Holding hands or walking arm in arm with someone of the same sex, however, is common in Italy, especially for women, and sexual acts between members of the same sex are legal for those above the age of consent (16). People in large cities—Bologna, Milan, and Turin—tend to be more tolerant: two years ago, Italians elected their first openly gay candidate to Parliament. Gay bars are a part of the nightclub scene in most cities (they also provide a refuge for women of all persuasions who want nightlife without incessant ogling), and a few gay beaches (*spiagge gay*) dot the shores.

The Italian national gay organization, **ARCI-GAY/LESBICA,** has its headquarters at P. di Porta Saragozza, 2, P.O. Box 691, 40123 Bologna (tel. (051) 644 70 54; fax 644 67 22). *Babilonia,* a national gay magazine, is published monthly. Call and ask for Roberto; he'll give you the info on the ARCI-GAY/LESBICA near you.

Are You Two...Together?, published by Random House and available at bookstores. A gay and lesbian guide to spots in Europe, including overviews of regional laws and lists of organizations abroad. Written by a lesbian couple; covers Western European capitals and gay resorts.

Gay Europe, published by Perigee Books. A gay guide geared toward travel in Europe. Provides a series of quick looks at gay life in countries throughout Eastern and Western Europe, including restaurants, clubs, and beaches (where applicable). Available in bookstores (US$14).

Gayellow Pages, P.O. Box 533, Village Station, New York, NY 10014 (tel. (212) 674-0120). An annually updated list of accommodations, resorts, and hotlines of interest to the gay traveler. USA/Canada edition US$12; Northeastern USA US$5; New York and New Jersey US$55; Southern USA US$5.

Giovanni's Room, 345 S. 12th St., Philadelphia, PA 19107 (tel. (215) 923-2960; fax 923-0813). International feminist, lesbian, and gay bookstore. Carries many useful publications; call or write for a free mail-order catalogue.

Spartacus International Gay Guides, published by Bruno Gmunder, Postfach 1107295, D-10837 Berlin, Germany (tel. ±49 (30) 615 00 30); also available from Giovanni's Room (see above). Extensive list of gay bars, restaurants, hotels, bookstores, and hotlines throughout the world. Very specifically for men (US$29.95).

Women Going Places, (US$14) a new women's travel and resource guide emphasizing women-owned enterprises. Geared towards lesbians, but offers advice appropriate for all women. Available from Inland Book Company, P.O. Box 12061, East Haven, CT 06512 (tel. (203) 467-4257).

■■■ TRAVELERS WITH DISABILITIES

Italians are making an increased effort to meet the needs of people with disabilities. The **Italian Government Travel Office (ENIT)** will let you know whether a certain hotel or other building is handicapped-accessible. When making arrangements with airlines or hotels, specify exactly what you need and allow time for preparation and confirmation of arrangements. Many **train stations** have "Reception Centres" for disabled travelers in the info office, the ticket office, or the stationmaster's office, where they offer a number of services and types of assistance. Look for the awkwardly titled pamphlet *Servicing for Disabled People,* available in most train stations. Major train stations will provide aid as long as you make reservations by telephone 24 hours in advance. You can generally find a *portiere* to assist you for L500 to L1000 per bag. Italy's rail system is modernized, so most trains are wheelchair-accessible. For more info, call the **Italian State Railway Representative** in New York (tel. (212) 697-1482) or **Rail Europe** in the U.S. (tel. (800) 438-7245).

If you plan to bring a seeing-eye dog to Italy, contact your veterinarian and the nearest Italian consulate. You will need an import license, a current certificate of your dog's inoculations, and a letter from your veterinarian certifying your dog's health (see Pets, page 37).

American Foundation for the Blind, 11 Penn Plaza, New York, NY 10011 (tel. (212) 502-7600). Open Mon.-Fri. 8:30am-4:30pm. Provides info and services for the visually impaired. For a catalogue of products contact **Lighthouse Low-Vision Products** at (800) 829-0500.

Facts on File, 460 Park Ave. S., New York, NY 10016 (tel. (212) 683-2244). Publishers of *Access to the World*, a guide to accessible accommodations and sights. Available in bookstores or by mail order.

Graphic Language Press, P.O. Box 270, Cardiff by the Sea, CA 92007 (tel. (619) 944-9594). Publishers of *Wheelchair Through Europe* (US$12.95, postage included). Comprehensive advice for the wheelchair-bound traveler, including planning advice and specifics on wheelchair-related resources in various cities throughout Europe—accessible hotels, museums, etc.

The Guided Tour, Inc., Elkins Park House, Suite 114B, 7900 Old York Road, Elkins Park, PA 19117-2339 (tel. (215) 635-2637 or (800) 738-5841). Year-round travel programs for people with developmental and physical challenges as well as persons requiring renal dialysis. Trips and vacations planned both domestically and internationally. Call or write for a free brochure.

Mobility International, USA (MIUSA), P.O. Box 10767, Eugene, OR 97440 (tel. (503) 343-1284 voice and TDD; fax (503) 343-6812). International headquarters in Britain, 228 Borough High St., London SE1 1JX (tel. (0171) 403 56 88). Contacts in 30 countries. Info on travel programs, international work camps, accommodations, access guides, and organized tours. Membership US$20 per year, newsletter US$10. Sells updated and expanded *A World of Options: A Guide to International Educational Exchange, Community Service, and Travel for Persons with Disabilities* (US$14 for members, US$16 for nonmembers, postpaid). MIUSA also offers a series of courses that teach strategies to disabled travelers.

Society for the Advancement of Travel for the Handicapped, 347 Fifth Ave., Suite 610, New York, NY 10016 (tel. (212) 447-7284; fax (212) 725-8253). Publishes quarterly travel newsletter *SATH News* and information booklets (free for members, US$3 each for nonmembers). Offers advice on trip planning for people with disabilities. Annual membership US$45, students and seniors US$25, agents and corporations US$100.

■■■ TRAVELING WITH CHILDREN

Italians are well-known for their love of children, and you will probably encounter more cooing than complications. Most hotels will put a cot in your room for a percentage price increase, and even picky children tend to enjoy the simplest (and cheapest) of Italian foods: pizza, spaghetti, and *gelato*. In addition, train systems in Italy sometimes offer discounts for groups or families. There are **discount Eurailpasses** for groups and children (those under 25 get a flat discount, those under 12 travel at half-price, and those under four travel free), and an Italian kilometric ticket can be used by up to five at once. Still, planning ahead and drawing up a detailed itinerary are especially useful for those traveling with small children. Remember that you may have to slow your pace considerably, and that all the new sights and experiences are especially exhausting for kids—you may want to leave room for a mid-afternoon nap for everyone (remember: most businesses and tourist attractions in Italy are closed from around noon to 3pm anyway). For some families, it may be more convenient to travel by rental car, but train travel will often be cheaper, reduce the fidgets, and provide a novel, absorbing experience for children. Finally, make sure that your children have some sort of ID on their person in case they get lost and/or are faced with an emergency.

For more information, see the following publications: **Wilderness Press,** 2440 Bancroft Way, Berkeley, CA 94704 (tel. (800) 443-7227 or (510) 843-8080), distributes *Backpacking with Babies and Small Children* (US$9.95) and *Sharing Nature with Children,* which present useful tips for the outward-bound family. **Lonely Planet Publications,** Embarcadero West, 155 Filbert St., Suite 251, Oakland, CA 94607 (tel. (510) 893-8555 or (800) 275-8555; fax (510) 893-8563), or P.O. Box 617, Hawthorn, Victoria, 3122, Australia, publishes *Travel With Children* (US$10.95, US$1.50 postage in the U.S.), a book packed with user-friendly tips and anecdotes, as well as a free quarterly newsletter full of general travel advice. **Mason-Grant Publications,** P.O. Box 6547, Portsmouth, NH 03802 (tel. (603) 436-1608; fax (603) 427-

0015 publishes *Take Your Kids to Europe* by Cynthia W. Harriman (US$14) a budget guide geared toward family travel.

■■■ DIETARY CONCERNS

Jewish travelers who keep **kosher** should consult local tourist boards for a list of kosher restaurants. Also useful is *The Jewish Travel Guide* (US$11.95, US$1.75 postage) from Ballantine-Mitchell Publishers, Newbury House 890-900, Eastern Ave., Newbury Park, Ilford, Essex 1G2 7HH (tel. (0181) 599-8866; fax 599-0984).

Let's Go includes some **vegetarian** restaurants and you can always request a dish *senza carne* (without meat), though you may elicit a puzzled or hostile reaction from the chef. Vegetarians should contact the **Associazione Culturale Vegetariana,** Via Treviglio, 9, 20123 Milano (tel. (02) 27 20 27 60), for information on vegetarian restaurants, foods, and stores. Also, the **Vegetarian Society of the U.K.,** Parkdale, Dunham Rd., Altrincham, Cheshire WA14 4QG (tel. ±44 (0161) 928 07 93), publishes the *Vegetarian Times* and *The European Vegetarian Guide to Restaurants and Hotels:* orders only tel. (201) 783-1129.

■■■ MINORITY TRAVELERS

We have been hard-pressed to find any resources that advise members of visible minorities on specific travel concerns; if you have knowledge of any such institution, please write to us and let us know.

In certain regions, tourists of color or members of certain religious groups may feel unwelcome. Furthermore, either historical or newly developed discrimination against established minority residents may surface against travelers who are members of those minority groups. *Let's Go* asks that our researchers not include known discriminatory establishments in our guide. If, in your travels, you encounter discriminatory treatment, please let us know so that we can check out the establishment and, if appropriate, warn other travelers.

In terms of safety, we don't have any easy answers. Keep abreast of the particular cultural attitudes of the regions that you're planning to visit. Although immigrants of color do experience discrimination in Italy, tourists of color from the West, who are easily distinguishable by clothes and language, are not the usual targets of racism. In Rome, women of color, such as Asians, Indians, or African-Americans, may find themselves being referred to as *"giapponese"* (a reference to a woman of any Asian heritage), *"indiana,"* or merely *"bellissima."* Women of color may be seen as exotic, but not unwelcome. Traveling in groups and taking a taxi whenever you are uncomfortable are always good ideas. The best answer to xenophobic comments and other verbal harassment is often no answer at all. But above all, keep in mind that your own ethnicity will not necessarily be problematic; you may well find your vacation trouble-free and your hosts open-minded.

■■■ TRAVELING WITH PETS

If you must bring an animal with you to Italy, know that there are a number of restrictions depending on the kind of beastie; contact the Italian Government Travel Office (see page 5) or a nearby Italian embassy (page 8). Bring a leash or muzzle if you have a dog; one or the other is always required in public.

■■■ PACKING

Pack light. Set out everything you think you'll need, eliminate half, and take more money. Once you're on the road you'll be thankful; remember, everything you pack *you* have to carry. If you find yourself packing "just in case," remember that almost all supplies are readily found in Italy (though not necessarily in Tunisia; see Health,

PACKING

page 22, for tips on medical and hygienic supplies you may want to bring from home). For more exhaustive advice on packing, consult *The Packing Book* by Judith Gilford (see Ten Speed Press, page 6).

LUGGAGE

Backpack: Ideal if you're planning to hike over a lot of ground or camp; get one with several external compartments. Some convert into a more normal-looking suitcase. In general, **internal-frame** packs are easier to carry and more efficient for general traveling purposes. If you'll be doing extensive camping or hiking, you may want to consider an **external-frame** pack, which offers added support, distributes weight better, and allows for a sleeping bag and other handy items to be strapped on. External-frame packs have been known to get caught and mangled in baggage conveyors; tie down loose parts to minimize risk. In any case, get a pack with a strong, padded hip belt to transfer weight from your shoulders to your hips. Quality packs cost anywhere from US$125 to US$300.

Suitcase/trunk/other large or heavy luggage: OK if you plan to live in one city and explore from there, but a bad idea if you're going to be moving around a lot. Features to consider: wheels on suitcases, PVC frame for soft luggage, weight, durability, and maneuverability. Remember: you bring it, you carry it.

Daypack or courier bag: Bringing a smaller bag in addition to your pack or suitcase allows you to leave your big bag in the hotel while you carry a picnic to that beautiful spot by the river outside town. Make sure it's big enough to hold lunch, camera, water bottle, and *Let's Go*. Get one with secure zippers and closures.

Moneybelt or neck pouch: Guard your money, passport, railpass, and other important articles in either one of these, and keep it with you *at all times*. Moneybelts should sit *inside* the waist of your pants or skirt, and neck pouches should be worn under at least one layer of your clothing. Avoid the oh-so-popular "fanny pack": it's an invitation to thieves, even worn in front.

CLOTHING AND FOOTWEAR

No nation outdresses Italy. Although attempts to compete or blend in will prove difficult, do bring clothes appropriate for visits to cathedrals and churches, where shorts, skirts above the knees, and sleeveless or cut-off shirts are usually forbidden. Some more athletic travelers have been seen slipping jogging suits over a T-shirt and shorts before entering sacred grounds. In general, bring few but comfortable clothes, and keep accessories to a minimum. Climate and convenience should determine your wardrobe. Dark colors will not show the dirt they're bound to accumulate, but light colors will be cooler in hot weather. Natural fibers are also good choices; synthetics trap heat. Laundry facilities are expensive in Italy and nonexistent in Tunisia: bring non-wrinkling, quick-drying clothes that you can wash in a sink. Above all, shorts, university t-shirts, and running shoes brand you as a tourist and may be the cause of increased attention in Italy.

Women: During the summer, light cotton pants are the most appropriate travelwear and are the only option besides long dresses for getting by cathedral dress codes. A lightweight drape or shawl can also be used to cover the shoulders. Your favorite pair of jeans may cause you problems on the road—they're hot, and hard to dry after a downpour. Shorts will definitely make you stand out and garner unwanted attention from men. Surprisingly enough, you might be just as comfortable and attract fewer stares in a knee-length skirt. Really.

Men: Again, cotton pants will be more comfortable than jeans and less likely to brand you as a tourist. Shorts are more acceptable on men than on women and provide a break from the heat, but remember that they will not pass in cathedrals.

Walking shoes: Not a place to cut corners. For **city** walking, lace-up leather shoes with firm grips provide better support and social acceptability than athletic shoes. If you plan to travel in the **rainy** fall or spring, waterproof your shoes. For alpine forays, a good pair of **hiking boots** is essential. Teva **sandals** are excellent for resting and airing out your feet after a long day, or buy a pair of Italian leather sandals once you get there. *Break in your shoes before you plan to wear them.*

Don't forget: Raingear (ponchos are good) and a light sweater or jacket, even in summer. Gloves and thermal underwear are handy, perhaps even necessary, in winter.

MISCELLANEOUS

The following is not an exhaustive list. For a **first-aid kit** see Health, page 22.

Washing clothes: Laundry facilities in Italy are expensive and inconvenient. Washing clothes in your hotel sink is a better option. Bring a small bar or tube of detergent soap, a rubber squash ball to stop up the sink, and a travel clothes line (available at camping stores) for drying.

Electric Current: Voltage is generally 220v in Italy, although some hotels offer 110v. Check before plugging in or you could fry your appliance into oblivion. Visit a hardware store for an adapter (which changes the shape of the plug) and a converter (which changes the voltage). Don't make the mistake of using only an adapter (unless appliance instructions explicitly state otherwise, as with some portable computers), or you'll melt your Clapper. If you don't feel like going to the hardware store, order a converter or the free pamphlet *Foreign Electricity Is No Deep Dark Secret* by mail from the Franzus Co., Murtha Industrial Park, P.O. Box 142, Beacon Falls, CT 06403 (tel. (203) 723-6664; fax 723-6666).

Film: Expensive in Europe, and Italy is no exception. In short, bring lots of film from home and, if you will be seriously upset if the pictures are ruined, develop it at home. If you're not a serious photographer, you might want to consider bringing a **disposable camera** or two rather than an expensive permanent one. They come in everything from outdoor to underwater and panoramic, and generally cost around US$10 (not including developing). Whatever kind of camera you use, be aware that, despite disclaimers, airport security X-rays *can* fog film. A lead-lined pouch, sold at camera stores, protects film. Pack it in your carry-on luggage, since higher-intensity X-rays are used on checked luggage.

Also valuable: insect repellent, travel alarm clock, plastic bags that seal shut (for damp clothes, soap, food), sun hat, needle and thread, clothespins/-line, sleep-sack (if you intend to stay in youth hostels, they're required), safety pins, sun glasses, Walkman, pocketknife, tweezers, plastic water bottle, small flashlight, padlock, towel, and moleskin (for blisters).

CAMPING

Purchase **equipment** before you leave. As a rule, prices drop in the fall when stores clear out their old merchandise. For **backpacks,** see Luggage, page 38.

Sleeping bag: either down (space-conserving, lightweight and warm, but useless if it gets wet) or synthetic (cheaper, heavier, more durable, lower maintenance, and warmer when wet). Bags are rated according to the lowest outdoor temperature at which they will still keep you warm. A 3-season or 20°F bag (US$135-180 for synthetic, US$170-225 for down) keeps you warm even below the freezing point.

Pads: A cushion between your soft body and the hard, hard ground. Closed-cell foam pads start at $13; open-cell foam pads: $25 and up; and an air mattress will cushion your back and neck for $25-50. A **Thermarest air mattress** (US$50-90) is a deluxe ensolite pad and self-inflating air mattress; like sleeping on air.

Tents: Last year's models are often drastically reduced. The best models are free-standing, with their own frames and suspension systems. Low profile dome tents tend to be the best all-around, entailing very little unnecessary bulk. Also be sure your tent has a rain fly and that you have a **tarpaulin** or **plastic groundcloth** to put under the tent.

Campstoves: Don't rely on campfire cooking; some regions restrict fires. Simple stoves (US$30-85) burn butane or white gas. Also bring a **mess kit** and a **battery-operated lantern**.

Other: Waterproof matches, calamine lotion, and water-purification pills.

PACKING

The following **organizations** provide advice and/or supplies:

Family Campers and RVers (NCHA), 4804 Transit Rd., Bldg. 2, Depew, NY 14043-4906 (tel./fax (716) 668-6242). Sells the International Camping Carnet, required at some European campgrounds (US$30 includes membership in their association). Issues a short bibliography of camping travel guides and a list of camping stores in major European cities.

Recreational Equipment, Inc. (REI), P.O. Box 1700, Sumner, WA 98352-0001 (tel. (800) 426-4840). Long-time outdoor equipment cooperative. Stocks a wide range of the latest in camping gear and holds great seasonal sales. Huge selection, and many items are guaranteed for life. Lifetime membership available US$15.

L.L. Bean, Casco St., Freeport, ME 04033-0001 (ordering: U.S. and Canada (800) 221-4221, International, (207) 865-3111; customer service: U.S. and Canada (800) 341-4341, International (207) 865-3161; fax: U.S. (207) 797-8867, Canada and International (207) 878-2104). Equipment and preppy outdoor clothing favored by northeastern Americans; high quality and chock-full of info. Call or write for their free catalog. The customer is guaranteed 100% satisfaction on all purchases; if it doesn't meet your expectations, they'll replace or refund it. Open 24 hrs. per day, 7 days per week, 52 weeks per year. They don't even lock their doors.

GETTING THERE

■■■ BUDGET TRAVEL SERVICES

Campus Travel, 52 Grosvenor Gardens, London SW1 OAG. A large supplier of student travel products in the U.K., with 37 branches throughout the country. Supplies student cards, flights, trains, boats, and a full range of related products and services. In London, telesales and bookings for Europe (tel. ±44 (0171) 730 34 02); for North America (tel. 730 21 01); worldwide (tel. 730 81 11). In Manchester (tel. (0161) 273 17 21). In Scotland (tel. ±44 (0131) 668 33 03).

Centro Turistico Studentesco e Giovanile (CTS), Via Genova, 16, 00184 Roma (tel. (06) 467 91; fax 467 92 05). With 90 offices throughout Italy, CTS provides travel, accommodation, and sight-seeing discounts, as well as currency exchange and information for students and young people. Sells the *Carta Verde* for discounts on train fares, the International Student Identity Card (ISIC), the International Youth Cards (FIYTO card), and the Euro Youth Card. Branch offices also in **London** and **Paris.** Open Mon.-Fri. 9am-1pm and 3:30-7pm, Sat. 9am-1pm.

CIT Tours, 342 Madison Ave., #207, **New York,** NY 10173 (tel. (212) 697-2100); 6033 West Century Blvd., #980, **Los Angeles,** CA 90045 (tel. (310) 338-8616); 1450 City Councillors St., #1450, **Montréal,** Qué. H3A 2E6 (tel./fax (800) 361-7799 or (514) 845-9137); **Toronto,** Ont. (tel. (416) 415-1060). Over 100 offices worldwide, most in Italy. The official representative of the Italian state railways in the US; also sells Eurail.

Council Travel, the travel division of Council, is a full-service travel agency specializing in student, youth, and budget travel with over 50 offices worldwide. Offers discount airfares on scheduled airlines, railpasses, hostelling cards, low-cost accommodations, budget tours, travel gear, and international student (ISIC), youth (GO25) and teacher (ITIC) identity cards. Forty-one offices in the U.S. include: 729 Boylston St., Suite #201, **Boston,** MA 02116 (tel. (617) 266-1926); 1153 N. Dearborn, **Chicago,** IL 60610 (tel. (312) 951-0585); 10904 Lindbrook Dr., **Los Angeles,** CA 90024 (tel. (310) 208-3551); 205 E. 42nd St., **New York,** NY 10017 (tel. (212) 661-1450). Council Travel also has offices in Europe, including 28A Poland St. (Oxford Circus), **London** WIV 3DB, England (tel. (0171) 437 77 67).

Educational Travel Centre (ETC), 438 North Frances St., Madison, WI 53703 (tel. (800) 747-5551; fax (608) 256-2042). Flights, HI-AYH cards, Eurail and regional railpasses. Call or write for their free pamphlet *Taking Off.*

Let's Go Travel, Harvard Student Agencies, 53A Church St., Cambridge, MA 02138 (tel. (800) 5-LETS GO (553-8746), or (617) 495-9649). Offers railpasses, HI-AYH memberships, ISICs, International Teacher ID cards, Go 25 cards, guidebooks (including every *Let's Go*), maps, bargain flights, and a complete line of budget travel gear. All items available by mail; call or write for a catalog.

Rail Europe Inc., 226 Westchester Ave., White Plains, NY 10604 (tel. (800) 438-7245; fax (800) 432-1329). Sells all Eurail products and passes, national railpasses, and point-to-point tickets. Up-to-date information on all rail travel in Europe, including Eurostar, the English Chunnel train.

STA Travel, 6560 North Scottsdale Rd. #F100, Scottsdale, AZ 85253 (tel. (800) 777-0112). A student and youth travel organization with over 100 offices around the world and 14 U.S. locations offering discount airfares (for travelers under 26 and full-time students under 32), railpasses, accommodations, tours, insurance, and ISICs. In the UK: Priory House, 6 Wrights Lane, **London** W8 6TA (tel. ±44 (071) 938 4711). In New Zealand: 10 High St., **Auckland** (tel. ±64 (09) 309 9723). In Australia: 224 Faraday St., Carlton, **Melbourne** VIC 3050 (tel. ±61 (03) 347 6911). U.S. offices include 297 Newbury Street, **Boston,** MA 02116 (tel. (617) 266-6014); 48 E. 11th St., **New York,** NY 10003 (tel. (212) 477-7166); and 51 Grant Ave., **San Francisco,** CA 94108 (tel. (415) 391-8407).

Travel CUTS (Canadian University Travel Services, Ltd.), 187 College St., Toronto, Ont. M5T 1P7 (tel. (416) 798-CUTS (798-2887); fax 979-8167). Offices across Canada. Also, in the **U.K.,** 295-A Regent St., London W1R 7YA (tel. ±44 (0171) 637 31 61). Discounted European, South Pacific, and domestic flights; ISIC, GO 25, and HI hostel cards; and discount travel passes. Special fares with valid ISIC or FIYTO cards. Offers free *Student Traveller* magazine, and info on Student Work Abroad Program (SWAP).

Unitravel, 117 North Warson Rd., St. Louis, MO 63132 (tel. (800) 325-2222; fax (314) 569-2503). Offers discounted airfares on major scheduled airlines from the U.S. to Europe, Africa, and Asia.

Usit, 19-21 Aston Quay, O'Connell Bridge, Dublin 2 (tel. ±353 (01) 679 88 33; fax 677 88 43). Sells ISIC, HI hostel cards and *Let's Go*. In addition to selling discounted student fares on scheduled flights, Usit books its own charter flights in the summer for some of the best flight deals going.

■■■ FROM NORTH AMERICA

Constantly fluctuating prices make estimating airfares impossible, but a few general rules do apply. Most airlines maintain a fare structure that peaks between mid-June and early September. Midweek (Mon.-Thurs.) flights run about US$30-40 cheaper each way than on weekends. If you plan on traveling elsewhere in Europe, consider beginning your trip outside Italy; a flight to Brussels or Frankfurt could cost considerably less than one to Milan or Rome. Round-trip tickets from New York or Boston to major cities such as Florence or Rome will cost anywhere from US$400 to 800 (stays in Italy limited to one year).

Have a knowledgable travel agent (or better yet, several) guide you through the options. Remember that travel agents might not want to do the legwork to find the cheapest fares (for which they receive the lowest commissions). Travel sections in newspapers often list bargain fares from the local airport. You might be able to outfox airline reps with the phone-book-sized *Official Airline Guide* (at large libraries). This monthly guide lists every scheduled flight in the world (including prices).

Since inexpensive flights from Canada cost substantially more than the lowest fares from the U.S., Canadians may want to consider leaving from the States. Also check with Travel CUTS for information on special charters (see above).

COMMERCIAL CARRIERS

If you decide to make your transatlantic crossing with a commercial airline, you'll be purchasing greater reliability, security, and flexibility—usually at a higher price. The commercial airlines' lowest regular offer is the **APEX (Advance Purchase Excursion Fare).** Specials advertised in newspapers may be cheaper, but have more restrictions and fewer available seats. APEX fares provide you with confirmed reservations and allow "open-jaw" tickets (landing in and returning from different cities). Reservations must usually be made at least 21 days in advance, with minimum and maximum stay limitations, and hefty cancellation and change fees. For summer travel, book early. **Alitalia,** Italy's national airline, is geared primarily to executives and well-heeled travelers, but does offer APEX and off-season youth fares. Main address in the U.S. is 666 Fifth Avenue, New York, NY 10103 (tel. (800) 223-5730 or (800) 442-5860 in the U.S., (800) 361-8336 in Canada).

A few airlines offer other miscellaneous discounts. Look into flights to less popular destinations or on smaller carriers. Call **Icelandair** (tel. (800) 223-5500) or **Virgin Atlantic Airways** (tel. (800) 862-8621) for info on last-minute offers.

STUDENT TRAVEL AGENCIES

Students and people under 26 with proper ID qualify for deliciously reduced airfares. These are available from student travel agencies like **Council Travel, STA,** and **Travel CUTS** (see Budget Travel Services, page 41). In 1995, peak season round-trip rates from the east coast of North America to even the offbeat corners of Europe rarely topped US$800, and off-season fares were considerably lower.

CHARTER FLIGHTS AND TICKET CONSOLIDATORS

The theory behind a charter is that a tour operator contracts with an airline (usually a fairly obscure one that specializes in charters) to use planes to fly extra loads of passengers to peak-season destinations. Charter flights thus fly less frequently than major airlines and have correspondingly more restrictions. They are also almost always fully booked, schedules and itineraries may change at the last moment, and flights may be traumatically cancelled. Shoot for a scheduled air ticket if you can, and pay with a credit card. Consider traveler's insurance against trip interruption.

Ticket consolidators resell unsold tickets on commercial and charter airlines that might otherwise have gone begging. Look for their tiny ads in weekend papers and start calling. There is rarely a maximum age, tickets are heavily discounted, and they may offer extra flexibility or bypass advance purchase requirements since you are not tangled in airline bureaucracy. Yet, unlike tickets bought through an airline, you won't be able to use your tickets on another flight if you miss yours, and you will have to go back to the consolidator to get a refund. Pay with a credit card—you can't stop a cash payment if you never receive your tickets. Find out everything you can about the agency you're considering and get a copy of their refund policy *in writing*. Insist on a receipt that gives full details about the tickets, refunds and restrictions, and if they don't want to give you one or just generally seem clueless, use a different company. Consult Kelly Monaghan's *Consolidators: Air Travel's Bargain Basement* (US$5 plus US$3.50 shipping) from the Intrepid Traveler, P.O. Box 438, New York, NY 10034, for more info and a list of consolidators.

It's best to buy from a major organization that has experience in placing individuals on charter flights. One organization is **Unitravel** (for contact info see Budget Travel Services, page 42). You should also try **Interworld Travel** (in Florida tel. (305) 443-4929 or (800) 331-4456; from the New England area (800) 468-3796), **Rebel** (tel. (800) 227-3235), and **Travac** ((800) 872-8800).

If budget travel inspires your utmost bravery and patience, **Airhitch,** 2646 Broadway (3rd floor), Suite 200, New York, NY 10025 (tel. (800) 326-2009 or (212) 864-2000) and Santa Monica, CA (tel. (310) 394-0550), will add a certain thrill to the prospects of how you will get to Europe and exactly where you will end up. The Better Business Bureau of New York and *Let's Go* have received complaints about Airhitch; the company has recently changed hands, but consumers should make careful inquiries. A very similar service is offered by **Air-Tech, Ltd.,** 584 Broadway #1007, New York, N.Y. 10012 (tel. (212) 219-7000; fax 219-0066), 1A York Mansion, Earl Court Rd., London 5W5 9AF, England (tel. ±44 (0171) 373 77 96), and 1A York Mansion, Earls Court Rd., London 5W5 9A5 (tel. ±44 (0171) 373 77 96). *Let's Go* has received multiple complaints about Air-Tech delays, inaccurate information, and poor service. Patrons of both companies have reported delays of up to several days in length—a delay could incur costs that outweigh initial savings.

Eleventh-hour **discount clubs** and **fare brokers** offer members savings on European travel, including charter flights and tour packages. Research your options carefully. **Last Minute Travel Club,** 1249 Boylston St., Boston, MA 02215 (tel. (800) 527-8646 or (617) 267-9800), and **Discount Travel International** (tel. (212) 362-3636) are among the few travel clubs that don't charge a membership fee. Others include **Moment's Notice** (tel. (212) 486-0500; US$25 annual fee) and **Traveler's Advantage** (tel. (800) 835-8747; US$49 annual fee). For a processing fee, depending on the number of travelers and the itinerary, **Travel Avenue** (tel. (800) 333-3335) will search for the lowest international airfare available and even give you a rebate on fares over US$300. Study these organizations' contracts closely; you don't want to end up with an unwanted overnight layover.

COURIER FLIGHTS AND FREIGHTERS

Those who travel light should consider flying to Europe as a **courier.** The company hiring you will use your checked luggage space for freight; you may only bring carry-ons. Restrictions to watch for: you must be over 18 and have a valid passport, most flights are round-trip only with short fixed-length stays (usually one week); you may not be able to travel with a companion (single tickets only); and most flights are from New York. Round-trip fares to Western Europe from the U.S. range from US$250-400 (during the off-season) to US$400-550 (during the summer). **NOW Voyager,** 74 Varick St. #307, New York, NY 10013 (tel. (212) 431-1616), acts as an agent for many courier flights worldwide primarily from New York. It offers special last-minute deals to such cities as London, Paris, Rome, and Frankfurt for as little as US$200 round-trip plus a US$50 registration fee. Other agents are **Halbart Express,**

147-05 176th St., Jamaica, NY 11434 (tel. (718) 656-5000), **Courier Travel Service,** (tel. (516) 763-6898), and **Discount Travel International,** (tel. (212) 362-3636).

You can also go directly through courier companies in New York, or check your bookstore or library for handbooks such as *Air Courier Bargains* (US$15 plus $3.50 shipping from the Intrepid Traveler, P.O. Box 438, New York, NY 10034. *The Courier Air Travel Handbook* (US$10 plus US$3.50 shipping) explains how to travel as an air courier and contains names, phone numbers, and contact points of courier companies. It can be ordered directly from Bookmasters, Inc., P.O. Box 2039, Mansfield, OH 44905 (tel. (800) 507-2665).

If you really have travel time to spare, **Ford's Travel Guides,** 19448 Londelius St., Northridge, CA 91324 (tel. (818) 701-7414) lists **freighter companies** that will take passengers worldwide. Ask for their *Freighter Travel Guide and Waterways of the World* (US$15, plus US$2.50 postage if mailed outside the U.S.).

A final caveat for the budget conscious: don't get so caught up in the seemingly great deals. Always read the fine print; check for restrictions and hidden fees. There are amazingly cheap fares waiting to be unearthed, but you can't get something for nothing.

■■■ FROM EUROPE

■ BY PLANE

Budget fares are available on high-volume flights between northern Europe and Italy, but usually only in the spring and summer. Carriers within Europe often offer student discounts. There are many good charter flights from London.

Air Travel Group Ltd., 227 Shepherds Bush Rd., **London** W6 7AS (tel. +44 (0181) 748 4999; fax 748 6381), acts as an umbrella organization for services including **Italy Sky Shuttle,** which programs flight assignments from U.K. hubs to Italian cities. **Campus Travel,** 52 Grosvenor Gardens, London SW1W 0AG (tel. +44 (0171) 730 88 32, fax 730 57 39), offers competitive fares all over the continent. Also check **Magic Bus** (see By Bus, page 46), which operates inexpensive flights within Europe.

■ BY TRAIN

The great majority of budget travelers in Europe use the economical and efficient train system. Purchasing a railpass or special ticket may help to make the experience even more economical and efficient; be aware, though, that not all passes and tickets are created equal, and some may end up costing you more than you actually need to pay. Shop around, and compare ticket and pass plans. Add up the second-class fares for your planned routes and deduct 5% (listed prices automatically include commission) for comparison. And be aware that having a pass doesn't mean you don't have to stand in line for things like reservations and initial validation.

Eurailpasses may be used to get to Italy from a number of European countries and are also valid for travel within Italy (but if you're only traveling in Italy, they aren't worth it). They should be bought before arrival in Europe, but if you're stuck, they can be obtained from some travel agencies in Europe as well (despite what travel agents in the U.S. may try to tell you). Keep in mind that Eurailpasses are not refundable once validated, and replacements can be issued only if you have purchased insurance from Eurail.

For travelers under 26, **BIJ tickets** *(Billets Internationals de Jeunesse),* sold under the names **Wasteels, Eurotrain,** and **Route 26,** are a good alternative to rail-passes. Available for international trips within Europe, interior travel within France, and some ferry routes, they knock 30-45% off regular second-class fares. Tickets are good for 60 days and allow an unlimited number of stopovers along the normal direct route of the train journey. Issued for a specific international route between two points, they must be used in the direction and order of the designated route without side- or back-tracking. You must buy BIJ tickets in Europe, at Wasteels or Eurotrain offices (usually in or near train stations). However, detailed information on tickets for international journeys originating in the U.K., France, and Germany is given in the U.S. by **Wasteels Travel,** 7041 Grand National Dr. #207, Orlando, FL 32819 (tel.(407) 351-2537; fax (407) 363-1041). For departures from other countries, tickets can be purchased from European travel agents and from ticket counters in many countries.

Lenore Blaken's *Camp Europe by Train* (US$15.95) covers all aspects of train travel. The two annual Eurail Guides: the Eurail Guide to Train Travel in the New Europe (US$14.95) and the Eurail Guide to World Train Travel (US$18.95), are published by Houghton Mifflin and are available in most bookstores. The ultimate reference is the *Thomas Cook European Timetable* (US$25.95, US$35.95 includes a map of Europe highlighting all train and ferry routes; add US$4 for postage). In the U.S., order it from **Forsyth Travel Library** (see Reading Up, page 5).

■ BY BUS

Few people think of buses when planning travel to Italy, but they are available and cheap. **Magic Bus** runs direct service between many major cities in Europe. Their main magic office is located at 20 Filellinon, Syntagma, Athens, Greece (tel. ±30 (01) 323 74 71/4), but info is available from cooperating offices in many other cities. **Euroline Buses** at 52 Grosvenor Gardens, London SW1W 0AW (tel. ±44 (0171) 730 82 35), operates express buses from London to destinations in Italy.

■ BY FERRY

Ferry services in the port towns of Bari, Brindisi, and Otranto connect Italy to Greece. Unless you have a Eurail pass (only honored at the Brindisi port), Bari and Otranto services are cheaper, and they don't involve Brindisi's chaotic hordes of tourists. There are also connections from Genoa, Sardinia, and Trapani to Tunisia. (For more info on ferries, see Getting Around: By Ferry, page 51.)

ONCE THERE

■■■ TOURIST OFFICES IN ITALY

The **Ente Nazionale Italiano di Turismo (ENIT)** is a national tourist office with bureaus in Rome (on Via Marghera, 2) and abroad. In provincial capitals, look for a branch of the **Ente Provinciale per il Turismo (EPT),** which provides info on the entire province. Many towns also have an **Azienda Autonoma di Soggiorno e Turismo (AST),** the city tourist board. The Azienda tends to be the most useful and approachable. The smallest towns sometimes sport a privately run **Pro Loco** office. Recently, a new brand of tourist office, the **Azienda di Promozione Turismo (APT)** has popped up. Watch out for these, because they are allowed to present you with a list of only those hotels that have paid to be listed and some of the hotels we recommend may not be on the list. Keep an eye out for the student-oriented **Centro Turistico Studentesco e Giovanile (CTS)** and **Compagnia Italiana Turismo (CIT)** (see Budget Travel Services, page 41), the government-subsidized travel agency that specializes in outdoor activities such as camping and boating. Local offices are listed in the Practical Information section of each town.

■■■ EMBASSIES AND CONSULATES

Embassies in Rome have a tendency to close on holidays even the Romans don't know about. Call in advance to make sure your embassy is actually open before you wander over. All embassies answer the phone around the clock in case of emergencies and have lists of English-speaking doctors and lawyers.

United States: Via Veneto, 121 (tel. (06) 467 41). Passport and consular services open Mon.-Fri. 8:30-11:30am and 1:30-3pm. Report stolen passports here; new passports can be issued in about an hour for a US$65 fee (US$40 for minors. Closed on U.S. and Italian holidays).
Canada: Consulate, Via Zara, 30 (tel. (06) 440 30 28). Near the corner with Via Nomentana, on the 5th floor. Consular and passport services here open Mon.-Fri. 10am-noon and 2-4pm. A passport issued here costs CDN$35. English and French spoken. Embassy, Via G.B. De Rossi, 27 (tel. (06) 44 59 81).
Britain: Via XX Settembre 80A (tel. (06) 482 54 41; fax 487 33 24), near the Porta Pia and the corner with Via Palestro. Consular and passport services open Mon.-Fri. 9:30am-12:30pm and 2-4pm; mid-July-Aug. open Mon.-Fri. 8am-1pm.
Australia: Via Alessandria, 215 (tel. (06) 85 27 21; fax 85 27 23 00). Consular and passport services around the corner at Corso Trieste 25, open Mon.-Thurs. 9am-noon and 1:30-4pm, Fri. 9am-noon. They have lots of useful information for Australians (or any English-speakers) staying in Rome. Passport costs AUS$100.
New Zealand: Via Zara, 28 (tel. (06) 440 29 28/29/30; fax 440 29 84). Consular and passport services Mon.-Fri. 8:30am-12:45pm and 1:45-5pm. Passport L104,000. If you need the passport after hours or during the weekend, a whopping L224,000 surcharge is added.

Often, there are restrictions on travel from other countries, so it is a good idea to contact your embassy before leaving to find out what these are. Some other embassies in Rome are: **Austria,** Via Pergolesi, 3 (tel. (06) 855 82 41); **Belgium,** Via Monti Parioli, 49 (tel. (06) 32 24 441/2/3/4/5); **Czech Republic,** Via dei Colli della Farnesina, 144 (tel. (06) 36 30 87 41); **Egypt,** Via Salaria, 265 (tel. (06) 855 53 61); **France,** Piazza Farnese, 67 (tel. (06) 68 60 11); **India,** Via XX Settembre, 5 (tel. (06) 48 84 642); **Ireland,** Piazza Campitelli, 3 (tel. (06) 69 79 121); **Israel,** Via M. Mercati, 12 (tel. (06) 36 19 81); **Spain,** *(Embassy)* Largo Fontanella Borghese, 19 (tel. (06) 68 78 172), *(Consulate)* Via Campo Marzio, 34 (tel. (06) 686 43 92).

■■■ EMERGENCIES

Few legal systems are as convoluted and ambiguous as Italy's. Interpretations of the law are as varied as the dialects of the land. Your consulate will provide an attorney and advice, but after that you are on your own; you will be subject to Italian law.

If you can't avoid the police system, at least know with whom you are dealing. The **Polizia Urbana,** or **Pubblica Sicurezza** (emergency tel. 113), are the non-military police who deal with local crime. Try to contact them first if you are robbed or attacked. The **carabinieri** (emergency tel. 112) are actually a part of the Italian Army. They usually deal with the most serious crimes, such as terrorism (hence their intimidating, well-armed presence at airports). They are also a source of endless stupid Italian jokes, or *barzellette,* such as the one that claims that *i Carabinieri* travel in pairs because one can read and one can write. The **Vigili Urbani** manage less violent, less serious offenses, such as traffic violations. They also give directions to lost tourists. This book provides listings of police offices and medical emergency numbers in the Practical Information section of individual cities. Consult the Safety and Security section (page 20) for further guidelines.

■■■ GETTING AROUND

■ BY PLANE

Italy's train system is so efficient and airline prices so high that it makes little sense to fly Italy's three domestic airlines, **ATI, Alitalia,** or **Alisarda,** unless you need to

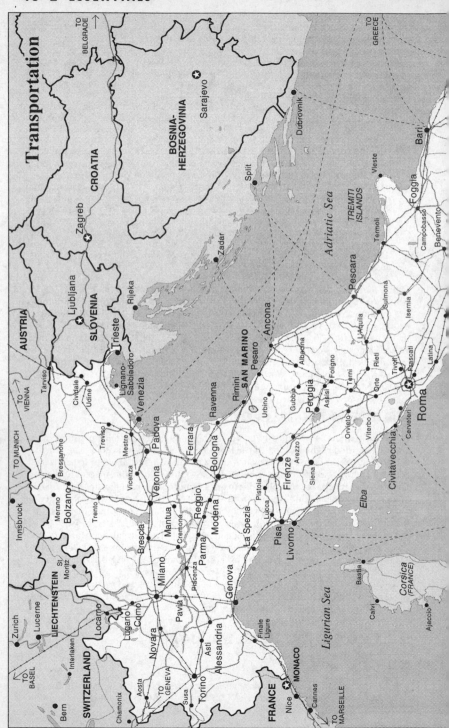

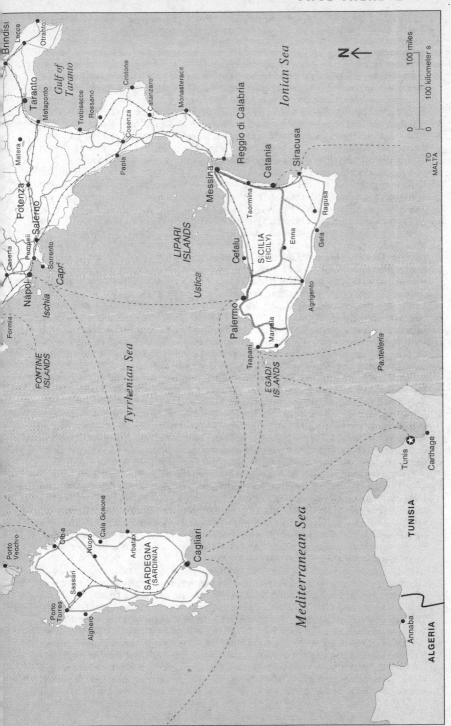

go a long distance in speed-of-light time. Ask about discounts on domestic travel at one of their many offices.

■ BY TRAIN

Ferrovie dello Stato (FS), the Italian State Railway, is one of the last European train systems to offer really inexpensive service. The fare between Rome and Venice, one of the longer trips in Italy, is about US$30 one way, second-class. Moreover, passengers between the ages of 12 and 25 are eligible for reduced rates (see below).

Italian trains retain the romance and convenience American railways have lost. Unfortunately, **they are not always safe.** While passengers sleep deeply, they may be molested, robbed, or attacked. Sleep wearing your money belt or neck pouch and, if you are traveling with a companion, try to sleep in shifts. Rumor has it that compartments are sometimes gassed (common on overnight runs to the southern departure points for Greece, according to what our researcher was told)—be sure you open a window to thoroughly ventilate your compartment. (For more tips, see Safety and Security, page 20.)

If you didn't purchase a Eurailpass or BIJ tickets, the Italian State Railway offers its own passes, valid on all train routes within Italy. They are seldom worthwhile costwise (with regular fares so cheap), but there are a few exceptions. The **Italian Kilometric Ticket** is good for 20 trips or 3000km (1875 mi.) of travel, whichever comes first, and can be used for two months by up to five people, who *must* travel together at all times. Three thousand kilometers is a long way in Italy, so it's virtually impossible for one person to break even on the Kilometric Ticket. For a couple or a family traveling reasonably widely, however, it can pay off. Ticket holders may travel on Intercity, Eurocity, Rapido, and ETR450 (Italy's newest and fastest train providing express service to major cities), but must pay a supplemental fare. When used by more than one person, mileage per trip is calculated by multiplying the distance by the number of users. Children under 12 are charged half of the distance traveled, and those under four travel free. A first-class kilometric ticket is US$264, second-class US$156, plus a US$15-per-person fee. When buying the ticket, be sure the sales agent stamps the date on it, or you may find yourself with a useless pass. Either pass may be bought from the **Italian State Railway** representative, 342 Madison Ave., Suite 207, New York, NY 10113 (tel. (212) 697-2100), or in Italy (where purchase price is slightly lower) at major train stations and offices of the **Compagnia Italiana Turismo (CIT).** Be aware that while using this pass, you must go to the ticket booth and have your mileage stamped; otherwise, you will pay hefty fines assessed for buying a ticket on the train.

The **cartaverde** is available to anyone between the ages of 12 and 26. The card costs L40,000, is valid for one year, and entitles you to a discount of 20% on any state train fare. They can be purchased only in Italy and if you're under 26 and plan to travel extensively in Italy, it should be your *first* purchase upon arrival. Families of four or more, or a group of up to five adults traveling together, qualify for discounts on Italian railways. Anyone over 60 with proof of age can get a 20% discount on tickets for travel on the Italian State Railway if they buy a **carta d'argento** ("silver card")— good for a year—for L40,000.

The Italian train system involves four kinds of regular trains. The *accelerato,* more commonly (and appropriately) referred to as a *locale,* usually stops at every station along a particular line, sometimes taking twice as long as a faster train. The *diretto* makes fewer stops than the *locale,* and the *espresso* only stops in major stations. The air-conditioned *rapido,* or *intercity (IC)* trains stop only in the largest cities. You will be charged more for a *rapido* ticket (waived for Eurail or BTLC holders), but it's often worth the money on long hauls (but check your train schedules; sometimes an *espresso* train is just as fast). Some *rapido* trains do not have second-class compartments, rocketing the cost of a ticket just out of a budget traveler's range, and a few require reservations. The cost of a *pendolino* (a direct train with first-class seats only, meals, bowling alleys, tennis courts, etc.) ticket is well out of a budget traveler's range. On overnight trips, consider paying extra for a *cuccetta*, a fold-down bunk which typically comes six to a compartment (the cost will vary depending on the length of the journey—usually around US$15). If you're not willing to spend the money on a *cuccetta*, consider taking an *espresso* train for overnight travel—they usually have compartments with fold-out seats. Finally, *freccie* trains run directly between cities that are normally connected only through other cities. There are 14 *freccie* that cover Italy, each running once per day.

■ BY BUS

Buses in Italy are neither faster nor cheaper than *diretto* trains. On the other hand, they are more punctual, comfortable, frequent, and they serve many points in the countryside that are inaccessible by train. Buses are also often crowded, so buy tickets in advance. Italy's bumpy terrain requires a strong stomach. As a reward for your possible sufferings, the scenery along the way often outshines the beauty of any final destination. Bus rides in the southern Tuscan hills and along the route from Bolzano to Cortina D'Ampezzo in the Dolomites are among the most incredible.

■ BY FERRY

The islands of Sicily, Sardinia, and Corsica, as well as the smaller islands along the coasts, are connected to the mainland by ferries *(traghetti)* and hydrofoils *(aliscafi;* motor boats with metal fins that lift the hull out of the water as speed is attained). Italy's largest private ferry service is **Tirrenia;** for info, contact the Rome office at Via Bissolati, 41 (tel. (06) 67 54 62 04). Tirrenia and other major companies (including **Moby Lines, Siremar, Caremar,** and hydrofoil services **SNAV** and **Alilauro**) make departures and arrivals in major port towns such as Ancona, Bari, Brindisi, Genoa, Livorno, La Spezia, Naples, and Trapani. Not only do ferry services allow tourists to visit the Tremiti, Pontine, and Lipari Islands, but they also give tourists a reason to spend time in a port town to which they otherwise would not have given a second thought. While away the time prior to your departure by enjoying the "Stop-Over in Bari" program, exploring the medieval Tuscan town of Pontremoli (near La Spezia), or simply indulging in the coast's fresh seafood.

Reserve ferry tickets at least two weeks ahead of time, especially if you are traveling with a bicycle, motorcycle, or car. When planning your itinerary, keep in mind that ferry schedules change unpredictably, and that you should confirm your departure a day in advance. Some stations require that you check in two hours before your departure, or your reservation will be cancelled. The cheapest option is *posta ponte* (deck class; preferable in the warm summer months); however, it is often only available when the *poltrone* (reclining cabin seats) are taken. Port taxes often apply. Student, Eurail pass, and round-trip (10-20%) discounts are usually available.

■ BY CAR

If you're pressed for time, or touring with friends or a large family, traveling by car may prove the most enjoyable and practical way to see Italy. Keep in mind, however, that much of Italy's infrastructure was constructed before the age of the automobile. Some towns will prove virtually unnavigable; consider parking on the outskirts and walking to town centers. (On the other hand, the Italian *Autostrade* are worthy successors to the Roman roads, barreling through mountains and soaring over valleys.) Reckless drivers are not uncommon in Italy, and the convoluted street system often inflames tempers.

A car can cut severely into your budget. The *Autostrade* charge stunning tolls: the ride from Rome to Bologna will run you about L40,000 in booth stops alone. Gas *(benzina)* computes to about L1500 per liter (about a quart) and renting a four-seater for one week will be at least US$200. **Automobile Club d' Italia (ACI)** has border offices and branch offices nationwide. The ACI is located at Via Marsala, 8, 00185 Rome (tel. (06) 499 81; fax 49 98 22 34). David Shore and Patty Campbell's

Europe by Van and Motorhome (US$13.95, US$2 postage, US$4 to Canada, US$8 overseas) guides you through the entire process of renting, leasing, buying, and selling vehicles (vans are their specialty) in Britain and the Continent, including buyback options, insurance, and dealer listings. To order, write to 1842 Santa Margarita Dr., Fallbrook, CA 92028 (tel./fax (619) 723-6184 or (800) 659-5222).There's also a brand-new comprehensive guide, *Moto-Europa* (US$17.95 plus $3 s&h), which details everything from itinerary suggestions to a motorist's phrasebook. It's available from **Seven Publishing,** P.O. Box 1212, Dubuque, IA 52004 (tel. (800) EUROPA-8 (387-6728)).

If renting a car, always check if prices quoted include tax and collision insurance. (Some credit card companies will cover this automatically. This may be a substantial savings, but ask if a credit hold will be put on your account and if so, how much.) Ask about student and other discounts and be flexible in your itinerary; it can be cheaper to pick up your car in some places than in others. Ask your airline about special packages. Minimum age restrictions vary by country; rarely is it below 21. If you are a student or faculty member, inquire about special discounts or contact Council Travel or CTS. Reserving in the U.S. is usually much cheaper than renting once you've arrived. Many agencies require advance reservation made in the U.S.

The major firms renting in Italy are **Auto-Europe,** #10 Sharp's Wharf, P.O. Box 1097, Camden, ME 04843 (tel. (800) 223-5555); **Avis Rent-A-Car,** 900 Old Country Rd., Garden City, NY 11530-9795 (tel. (800) 331-1084); **Budget Rent-a-Car,** (tel. (800) 472-3325); **Foremost Euro-car, Inc.,** (tel. (800) 272-3299; in Canada (800) 253-3976); **Hertz Rent-A-Car,** (tel. (800) 654-3001); **Kemwel Group, Inc.,** (tel. (800) 678-0678); and **Maiellano Tours,** (tel. (718) 727-0044).

If you need a car for three weeks or more, **leasing** will be less expensive than renting. Most firms lease to drivers over 17 and rent to those over 20. Many companies also require a major credit card, and some offer discounts to foreigners.

Caravanning, usually involving a **campervan or motorhome,** gives the advantages of car rental without the hassle of finding lodgings or cramming six friends into a Renault. You'll need those six friends to split the gasoline bills, however. Prices vary greatly, but for the outdoor-oriented group trip, caravanning can be a dream. Contact the car rental firms listed above for more info.

Foreign drivers in Italy need both an international driver's permit (or, if it's your own car, your license accompanied by a translation (see International Driver's Permit, page 14) and an international insurance certificate (or "green card"). Remember that all *Autostrada* direction signs are marked in green, all secondary roads in blue. Maps are essential, or you may find yourself confounded by Italy's labyrinth of small roads. It's good to have more than one map, as each emphasizes different roads. For any serious driving emergency, call the 24-hr. **nationwide auto service** at 116 (charges apply).

■ BY MOPED AND SCOOTER

Mopeds and scooters, an enduring (if not always endearing) feature of Italian life, provide an enjoyable way to tour the country, especially in coastal areas where the view demands frequent attention. They are, however, dangerous in the rain and on rough roads or gravel. Always wear a helmet and never ride wearing a large backpack. If you've never been on a moped before, Italy is not the place to start. The Vespa-style motorbikes with small wheels and a center platform for your feet are particularly hazardous. Ask about rentals at bicycle and motorcycle shops. Rates are between L50,000 and L80,000 per day.

■ BY BICYCLE

A bicycle's pace allows you to see everything that Italy has to offer. Anywhere outside the flat Po Valley, Italy's hills require a purpose-built touring or mountain bike with very low gears for any sustained expedition, along with an excellent set of lungs and legs. For info about touring routes, consult national tourist offices or any of the numerous books available. *Europe By Bike*, by Karen and Terry Whitehill (US$14.95), offers specific area tours (available from **The Mountaineers Books,** 1001 Klickitat Way #201, Seattle, WA 98134; tel. (800) 553-4453 or (206) 223-6303, fax 223-6306). *Cycling Europe: Budget Bike Touring in the Old World* is by N. Slavinski (US$12.95). Michelin road maps are clear and detailed guides. For more info, you may also want to contact the **European Cyclists' Federation,** (tel. (88) 32 32 88; fax 75 15 50), or the **Federazione Italiana Amici della Bicicletta (FIAB), Federazione Italiana Amici della Bicicletta (FIAB),** contact the FIAB c/o Gianni Catania, C. Regina Margherita 152, 10152 Torino (tel./fax (11) 521 23 66; fax (11) 888 981).

Be aware that touring involves pedaling both yourself and whatever you store in the panniers (bags that strap to your bike). Take some reasonably challenging day-long rides to prepare before you leave. Have your bike tuned up by a reputable shop. Learn the international signals for turns and use them. Before leaving, learn how to fix a modern derailleur-equipped mount and change a tire, and practice on your own bike before you have to do it overseas. A few simple tools and a good bike manual will be invaluable.

If you're nervous about two-wheeling alone, contact **Worldwide Rocky Mountain Cycle Tours,** which offers coed bike tours of European countries for all ages, including two itineraries in Italy (Tuscany and Umbria) for about US$2000 each. For more information, write to them at Box 1978 Canmore, Alberta, Canada T0L OM0 (tel. (800) 661-2453 or (403) 678-6770; fax 678-4451). You may also want to check with **AYH** (listed above, page 14; their Program Department phone number is (202) 783-6161); they offer a variety of cycle, hiking, and backpacking tours in Italy and elsewhere at relatively inexpensive prices. **I Bike Italy** provides you a bike, lunch, helmet, and bilingual leaders who keep an easy pace for L75,000 per day (in Firenze, tel. (055) 66 75 29).

Most airlines will count your bicycle as your second free piece of luggage; check with the airline before buying your ticket. The safest way to send your bike is in a box, with the handlebars, pedals and front wheel detached. Within Europe, many ferries let you take your bike for free. You can always ship your bike on trains, though the cost varies from a small fixed fee to a substantial fraction of the ticket price. You may also be able to purchase an appropriate bike in Italy. Long- and short-term rentals are also readily available.

Getting all the necessary equipment together may be your biggest hassle. It is definitely worthwhile to buy proper equipment for touring; riding a bike with a frame pack strapped on it or your back is about as safe as pedaling blindfolded over ice. Bicycle accessories—panniers and other touring bags, lighting equipment, racks—are cheaper and of better quality in the U.S. Don't spend a penny before you scan *Bicycling* magazine and the *Performance* bicycling catalog for the lowest sale prices. **Bike Nashbar,** 4111 Simon Rd., Youngstown, OH 44512 (tel. (800) 627-4227), almost always offers the lowest prices, but when they don't, they cheerfully subtract 5¢ from the best price you can find. The first thing you should buy is a **bike helmet.** At about US$40, it's a lot cheaper and more pleasant than neurosurgery.

To increase the odds of finding your bike where you left it, buy a U-shaped lock made by **Citadel** or **Kryptonite.** They may seem expensive (US$20-40) until you compare them to the price of buying a new bike in Italy.

■ BY THUMB

> **Let's Go** does not recommend hitching as a means of travel in Italy or anywhere else. Be sure to consider the risks involved before you hitch.

Not everyone can be a brain surgeon, but most every bozo can drive a car. Hitching means entrusting your life to a randomly selected person who happens to stop beside you on the road, risking theft, assault, sexual harassment, and unsafe driving.

GETTING AROUND

In spite of this, the gains are many: favorable hitching experiences allow you to meet local people and get where you're going. The choice remains yours.

If you're a woman traveling alone in Italy, don't hitch. It's just too dangerous. Those who choose to hitch usually do so with a companion—a man and a woman are a safer combination, two men will have a harder time finding a ride, and three will go nowhere. Bulletin boards at hostels are often cited as a good place to start looking. Likewise, newspapers and university message boards sometimes carry ads seeking passengers to share driving and costs.

Hitchhiking pros usually refuse rides in the back seat of a two-door car, insure that the inside door handle operates before getting in, and keep the door unlocked and their belongings close at hand—in case a quick escape becomes necessary, luggage locked in the trunk will probably stay that way. They also take care never to fall asleep in cars—some drivers may consider it tantamount to a wholesale sexual invitation. If a situation becomes uncomfortable for any reason, hitchers firmly ask to be let out, regardless of how unfavorable the spot seems for finding another ride. Hitching for women reportedly becomes more dangerous the farther south or off the mainland one goes, and anywhere near a large city poses a particular risk.

■■■ ACCOMMODATIONS

HOTELS

A note on the use of *piano*: The floor-system of hotels and other buildings in Italy can be rather confusing. *Piano terra* means ground floor, *1° piano* means 2nd floor, *2° piano* means 3rd floor, and *pianissimo* means play softly.

A provincial board inspects, classifies, and registers all hotels. No hotel can legally charge more than the maximum permitted by inspection, but some proprietors double their prices at the sound of a foreign voice—remember that an official rate card must adorn the inside of the door of each room, and that you should ask to look at the room (and the card) before committing to anything. Keep in mind that bathrooms and breakfast often cost extra, and prices rise from year to year. In general, the most charming places are near the historic town center, while cheaper, nastier joints reside near the train and bus stations.

Hotels in Italy have been classified on a five-star system. Under this system, all accommodations should be called *hotels;* however, a number of establishments retain their old classifications as *pensioni* (small one-to-three star hotels) or *locande* (the cheapest, usually one star, if any). *Albergo* is synonymous with hotel.

Prices fluctuate regionally; expect higher prices in the north and in Rome and Florence. The cheapest non-institutional singles generally start at about L25,000 and doubles at L50,000. Rates tend to be lower per person in a shared room. A room with a double bed is called a *matrimoniale* (though marriage is no longer a prerequisite). A double with separate beds is called a *camera doppia*, and a single is a *camera singola*. Rooms with a private bath cost 30-50% more. Some places offer only **full pension,** meaning room and board (3 meals per day), or **half-pension,** meaning room, breakfast, and one other meal.

Italian law establishes a high and low season for areas popular with tourists. Remember that off-season months are different for alpine regions and seaside resort areas. **When there is a difference in high and low season prices, Let's Go indicates in which order they are listed.** Except in summer tourist spots such as Florence, Venice, the Riviera, and Cápri, you usually needn't write for reservations. Without reservations, start looking for a room in the morning during high season, or call a day in advance. Pick up a list of hotels and their prices from the local tourist office (they'll also quote rates over the phone). If you plan to arrive late, call and ask a hotel to hold a room for you. However, few hotels accept phone reservations more than a day in advance. Many small places don't have an English speaker, but this shouldn't dissuade a non-Italian-speaker from calling. Instructions on making a room reservation in Italian are included at the back of this book, and most *pensione* pro-

ACCOMMODATIONS

prietors are used to receiving this type of call. **If you do make a reservation, keep it.** Proprietors have recently become disgruntled with travelers who make reservations and don't show; for this reason many hotels no longer accept reservations. As a courtesy to hotel owners and fellow travelers (who may get turned away when a hotel is "reserved" to capacity), be sure to either keep your reservation or cancel it as soon as you know that you are not going to keep it.

HOSTELS

Hostels are great places to meet travelers from all over the world. If you are alone, there is no better place to find a temporary traveling companion. Italian youth hostels are inexpensive and open to travelers of all ages; many are situated in historic buildings and areas of great natural beauty. They offer inexpensive meals and often provide services unavailable at hotels, including kitchen privileges, laundry facilities, and bike rental. On the other hand, you must adapt to curfews, daytime lockouts, and separate quarters for men and women (some hostels do have doubles). You should also be warned that many hostels close in late fall and winter. Hostels are not as abundant in Italy as in northern Europe, and their locations are often inconvenient. Security is also less certain than in a hotel room, so keep your valuables with you, or check them at the office.

Hostel accommodations usually consist of bunk beds, each with a mattress and blanket, in dormitory rooms. You may be required to use a **sleep sack,** a special sheet (you can purchase them from a number of travel and camping stores, but most hostels that require them also provide them for a small surcharge). The curfew is usually midnight in summer and 11pm in winter; some hostels turn off lights and hot water after this time. Rates vary by hostel, but you can expect to pay around L18,000 per person including breakfast; dinners cost between L5000 and L13,000 (less for just a pasta course).

To stay in youth hostels affiliated with **Hostelling International (HI),** you must usually be an HI member. (For more info on membership, see Hostelling Organizations, page 13.) The Italian HI affiliate organization, **Associazione Italiana Alberghi per la Gioventù (AIG),** is at Via Cavour 44, 00184 Roma (tel. (06) 487 11 52; fax (06) 488 04 92). They offer (among other things) a free fax booking service between Florence, Naples, Rome, and Venice.

STUDENT ACCOMMODATIONS

Student residences in Italy are inexpensive and are theoretically open to foreign students during vacations and whenever there is room. In reality, these accommodations are often nearly impossible to arrange. All university towns operate a *Casa dello Studente* to which you can apply. These towns' tourist offices can provide specific info. The **Centro Turistico Studentesco e Giovanile (CTS)** can help you find and book accommodations in *pensioni* or dormitories. The London, Paris, and Athens offices can reserve a room for you in Italy for the first few nights. (See listing on page 41 for complete info.)

CAMPING

Lakes, rivers, the ocean, and the Alps are common backdrops for Italian campgrounds. Though there's often little space between sites, peaceful seclusion is usually only steps away. In August, arrive early—well before 11am—or you may find yourself without a spot. Rates average L8000 per person and another L7000 for the car. Many of the campgrounds are downright luxurious, boasting everything from swimming pools to bars, while others may be more primitive—you may want to shop around. The **Touring Club Italiano,** Corso Italia, 10, 20122 Milano (tel. (02) 85 26 12; fax 852 63 62), publishes an annual directory of all camping sites in Italy, *Campeggi in Italia,* available in bookstores throughout Italy. A free map and list of sites is available from the Italian Government Travel Office or directly from **Federcampeggio,** Via V. Emanuele, 11, Casella Postale 23, 50041 Calenzano (Firenze) (fax (055) 88 23 91).

An **International Camping Carnet** (membership card) is required by some European campgrounds but can usually be bought on the spot. The card entitles you to a discount at some campgrounds, and often may be substituted for your passport as a security deposit. In the U.S., it's available through a US$30 membership fee to **Family Campers & RVers/NCHA** (see page 41).

When you're out in the **wilderness,** the first thing to preserve is *you*—health, safety, and food should be your primary concerns when you camp. See Health (page 22) for info about basic medical concerns and first-aid. A comprehensive guide to outdoor survival is *How to Stay Alive in the Woods*, by Bradford Angier (Simon and Schuster, US$8). A few words of general advice: *never go camping or hiking by yourself for any significant time or distance.* If you're going into an area that is not well-traveled or well-marked, let someone know where you're hiking and how long you intend to be out. If you fail to return on schedule or if you need to be reached, searchers will at least know where to look for you.

The second thing to protect while you are outdoors is the wilderness. The thousands of outdoor enthusiasts that pour into the parks every year threaten to trample the land to death. Don't cut vegetation, and don't clear campsites. Check ahead to see if the park prohibits campfires. Even if not, firewood is scarce in popular parks; campers are asked to make small fires using only dead branches or brush, and to use a campstove to cook. To avoid digging a rain trench for your tent, pitch it on high, dry ground. If there are no toilet facilities, bury human waste at least four inches deep and 100 feet or more from any water supplies and campsites. *Biosafe* soap or detergents may be used in streams or lakes; otherwise, don't use soaps in or near bodies of water. Always pack up your trash and carry it with you until you reach the next trash can; burning and burying pollute the environment. In more civilized camping circumstances, respect fellow campers: keep light and noise to a minimum, especially if you arrive after dark.

ALTERNATIVE ACCOMMODATIONS

Italian history comes alive when you stay in the guest house of a Roman Catholic **monastery.** Guests need not attend services but are expected to make their own beds and, often, to clean up after meals. Found in rural settings, monasteries are usually peaceful, and you shouldn't stay in one unless you want a quiet and contemplative experience. Carrying an introduction on letterhead from your own priest, pastor, or rabbi may facilitate matters, although many monasteries will accept only Catholic guests. For more info about specific regions and a list of convents, monasteries and other religious institutions offering accommodations, write to the archdiocese *(arcivescovado)* of the nearest large town. Many regional tourist boards also maintain a list of monasteries with guest houses.

For a quiet, non-religious atmosphere, choose the *agriturismo* option and stay in a **rural cottage** or **farmhouse.** Usually, you will be given a small room and asked to clean up after yourself, but you will have freedom to come and go as you please. For more info, write to the main office of **Agriturist,** Corso V. Emanuele II, 101, 00186 Roma (tel. (06) 685 23 42) or contact their office in the region that you will be visiting. Also, if you plan to hike in the Alps or the Dolomites, contact the **Touring Club Italiano** (see entry under Camping in this section), which publishes a number of books with detailed hiking itineraries including stopovers in mountain refuges.

The **Associazione Cattolica Internazionale al Servizio della Giovane—Protezione della Giovane (PDG)** is a religious organization that helps women find inexpensive accommodations in its own hostels, convents, and *pensioni* throughout Italy. If you don't mind the occasional 10:30pm curfew, this service is extremely convenient. The PDG staffs offices in train stations of major cities and maintains centrally located bureaus in many towns. (For more info, see above, page 33.)

In many smaller towns (and some larger ones), householders rent rooms in their homes to passing travelers, sometimes with the blessing of the tourist authorities, sometimes without. Look for **affitta camera** signs posted around town or notes in store windows. Rates vary wildly; be prepared to bargain, but don't expect to pay much less than what a reasonable one-star *pensione* in town would cost. Call, write, or fax the new organization **Intranet,** P.O. Box 31703, 6503 CB Nijmegen, Netherlands (tel. (806) 014 10; fax (806) 535 99), a network of private homeowners in Europe, the Middle East, and the U.S. Subscriptions will be free until April 1997, and the standard charges for bed and breakfast in a subscriber's home is US$10. **Sleeping in European train stations** is a romanticized, time-honored tradition, but while free and often tolerated by local authorities, it is neither fun, nor comfortable, nor safe (particularly dangerous for women and solo travelers).

■■■ KEEPING IN TOUCH

■ MAIL

The postal system in Italy has justly drawn snickers from the rest of Western Europe, and now ranges from barely decent to deplorable. Aerograms and airmail letters from Italy take anywhere from one to three weeks to arrive in the U.S., while surface mail—much less expensive—takes approximately three months. Since postcards are low-priority mail, send important messages by airmail letter. Letters and small parcels rarely get lost if sent *raccomandata* (registered), *espresso* (express), or *via aerea* (air mail). Stamps *(francobolli)* are available at face value in *tabacchi* (tobacco shops), but you should mail your letters from a post office to be sure they are stamped correctly. Letters and postcards sent overseas cost L1300; within the EU L750; outside the EU (but not overseas) L900.

Make sure anyone sending you mail from North America allows at least two weeks for it to reach you. Mail from home can be sent to a hotel where you have reservations, or you can collect mail from most **American Express** offices if you have an American Express card or carry their traveler's checks. Have the sender write "Client Mail" on the envelope with the office's complete address. Letters addressed to the post office with your name and the phrase **fermo posta** (general delivery) will be held at the post office of any city or town. You must claim your mail in person with your passport as identification, and you may have to pay L300 per piece of mail. In major cities like Rome, the post office handling *fermo posta* is usually efficient and has long hours (though they close at noon on Sat. and the last day of the month, and are also closed on Sun.). Since a city may have more than one post office, write the address of the receiving office if possible. It's also a good idea to have the sender capitalize and underline your last name to ensure proper sorting. Before writing off a letter as lost, check under your first name, too.

Regarding sending or receiving something to or from Italy with celerity, **Federal Express** (U.S. & Canada tel. (800) 238-5355) operates in Italy, as do several Italian competitors. Express mail is available as well, but involves much higher rates.

■ TELEPHONES

Country code for Italy (39); **city code** for Rome from: within Italy (06); elsewhere (6). **Directory assistance** for: Italy (tel. 12; free); Europe and the Mediterranean (tel. 176; L1200), and intercontinental (tel. 17 90; L1200). For an **English-speaking operator,** dial 170. The country from which you are dialing determines whether or not a country code (preceded by ± in *Let's Go: Italy '96* international listings) is applicable.

Telecom recently replaced SIP and other smaller companies as Italy's primary telephone service; this should explain any discrepancies between the name provided in a *Let's Go* listing and the corresponding name used by an office or resource at the time of your visit. (It should also explain a potential future monopoly.) Many small towns may have not yet made the changeover at this time either.

Italian phone numbers range from four to eight digits in length. *Let's Go* makes every effort to get up-to-date phone numbers, but everyone is at the mercy of the Italian phone system. Everywhere, phone numbers change with bothersome frequency; in Rome they change as quickly as traffic lights. If you call an old number, you may hear a recording of the new number in Italian, possibly even in English. Phone books often list two numbers: the first is the number at the time of printing, the second (marked by the word *prenderà*) is what the number will be at some future, unspecified time.

There are four types of telephones in Italy. Hold-outs from the dark ages of telecommunications take only coins. Deposit more than you think you'll need, even if your call is local. If you underestimate, you may be cut off in the middle of your conversation. At the end of your call, press the return button for unused coins. To place long-distance calls, initially deposit at least L2000, and watch the display carefully to make sure you don't run out of money. For intercity calls, deposit eight or more. When using them, be sure to dial slowly as they sometimes misdial and disconnect if you treat them roughly. Expect a couple of tries to get through.

Scatti calls are made from a phone run by an operator (who may simply be the proprietor in a bar). Every town has at least one bar with a *telefono a scatti,* which can be used for international calls. A meter records the cost of your call, and you pay when you finish. Check with the operator before you lift the receiver, and remember that he or she may tack on a substantial service fee.

The third type of phone is most common, and accepts either coins (L100, 200 or 500) or **phone cards.** Cards can be bought for L5000, L10,000, or L15,000 from vending machines (near the phone), *tabacchi,* bars, or the post office. When you insert the card, a meter subtracts lire from it as you speak and displays the remaining value. Partially used cards can be removed and re-used. If you happen to run out in the middle of a call, you must insert another card, so buy more than one if you're planning a long conversation. The fourth type of phone accepts only phone cards, and will leer at you if you are without one.

For the most part, it is not difficult to make **long-distance calls within Europe.** A person to person call is *con preavviso,* and a collect call is *contassa a carico del destinatario* or *chiamata collect.* Intercontinental calls can be made from phonecard pay phones. In some small towns, however, international calls must be made from telephone company offices, generally found near the main post office and sometimes in major train stations, or from a *telefono a scatti.* To place a call at a telephone office, fill out a form at the counter. You will be assigned to a specific booth. Some offices ask for a deposit. When direct-dialing is possible, you can dial two zeros and then the **country codes** (U.S. and Canada 1, Ireland 353, Great Britain 44, Australia 61, New Zealand 64, South Africa 27), followed by the area code and number. Perhaps the simplest way to call long-distance is to use **AT&T, MCI, or Sprint Direct Service;** dialing a single number will connect you to an overseas, English-speaking operator who will then dial your collect call for you (you can also use a calling card). When calling the U.S. from most major cities in Italy, you can reach an AT&T operator by dialing 172 10 11, an MCI operator with 172 10 22, or Sprint with 172 18 77. To reach Canada easily, call **Canada Direct** at 172 10 01. **British Telecom** also has direct service from Italy at 172 00 44; **Ireland Direct** is at 172 03 53; **New Zealand Direct,** at 172 10 64; **South Africa Direct,** at 172 10 27; **Australia Direct,** at 172 10 61. You may want to consider getting a calling card if you plan to make a lot of international calls; the cost is significantly lower. To receive a little card with the AT&T Direct numbers for most European countries, call AT&T (from the U.S.) at (800) 545-3117; for MCI info, call (800) 444-3333. Getting through often takes several tries. For more info, call **AT&T** about its **USADirect** and **World Connect** services (tel. (800) 331-1140, from abroad (412) 553-7458); **Sprint** (tel. (800) 877-4646); or **MCI World Phone** and **World Reach** (tel. (800) 996-7535).

Calls to Italy must be preceded by the country code *and* the city code. When direct-dialing, the zero should be dropped from the beginning of each city code. Italians usually yell into the phone when calling long-distance, but that's more due to the omnipresent loud street traffic (and the fact that Italians *always* yell when they talk) than to a bad connection.

■ TELEGRAMS AND FAX MACHINES

The surest way to get an important message across the ocean is by wire service. **Telegrams** are sent from the post office and cost L1242 per word, including the address. **Faxes** may be sent from an increasing number of private enterprises (the larger the city, the greater the availability). If you're desperate, ask at the tourist office for the nearest fax service; sometimes you can use the fax at an upscale hotel for exorbitant fees. (We have found that faxing to and from the U.S. is impossible.)

■■■ CLIMATE

Due to the cooling waters of the ocean and the protective Alps encircling the north, Italy's climate is for the most part temperate. In the summer, the north grows fairly warm (and, in some places, very rainy), the central region wallows in stifling humidity, and the south bakes in arid heat. A breeze off the sea, however, cools both coasts. Winter in the Alps is very cold, while Milan, Turin, and Venice turn chilly, damp, and foggy. Tuscany fares similarly, with temperatures in the 30s Fahrenheit, although rain is a sure bet. Southern temperatures usually remain in the 50s and 60s during the winter.

LIFE AND TIMES

■■■ HISTORY AND POLITICS

Italian history is a complex tapestry of events, personalities, and political parties with which no brief overview could aspire to keep pace. Duchies, kingdoms, republics, and empires have washed over the Italian peninsula, a region united only twice: once under the Roman Empire, and more recently by 19th-century nationalism.

THE PENINSULA BEFORE ROME

The 1979 discovery of a million-year-old village in Isernia dated the earliest human settlement in Italy to the beginning of the Paleolithic era (1,000,000-70,000 BC). Starting around 2000 BC, *Italic tribes* inhabited scattered areas of the peninsula. Around 900 BC, the **Etruscans** arrived in central Italy and subjugated many of these tribes. The Etruscans, practical workers and intuitive futurists, primed the land for farming, mining, and engineering by building sewers and draining the swampy area that is now the center of Rome. They also predicted the future by gauging the direction of lightning bolts and examining the livers of sacrificed animals. Scholars still debate the tribes' origin; combined with evidence of a complex written language based on the Greek alphabet, recent archaeological theories seem to support Herodotus' ancient opinion that they came from Asia Minor. At Tarquinia and Cerveteri, you can see the remains of two of their largest cities.

Beginning in the 8th century BC, the **Greeks,** who had already been trading and exploring around the boot for more than a millennium, began to settle in southern Italy. They first stopped along the Apulian coast and later founded city-states in Campania, Calabria, and Sicily, collectively known as *Magna Graecia* (Great Greece). The Greek city-states bickered amongst themselves, but effectively survived until the 6th and 5th centuries BC. The Etruscan federation, which by that time ruled most of northern Italy, eventually succumbed to the invading barbarian Gauls in the north and to the increasingly powerful Romans in the south.

ANCIENT ROME

The Monarchy: 753-509 BC

Even the ancient Romans couldn't agree on how their civilization was founded. One mythological tradition has it that the twins **Romulus and Remus** established a settlement on the Palatine Hill in Rome in 753 BC. Romulus eventually slew his brother, and thus became the sole first king of Rome.

Another foundation story relates that the Trojan hero **Aeneas,** having escaped the destruction of Troy, made his way to Italy sometime around the 12th century BC (after a doomed affair with Queen Dido of Carthage), married the local king's daughter, and, after a few struggles with jealous locals, founded the Roman race; Romulus came along only later. In any case, most traditions agree that Rome had seven successive kings, some of whom were Etruscan conquerors. One Etruscan dynasty, comprised of the Tarquins, was particularly successful, until the son of the seventh and last king, **King Tarquinius Superbus** (Tarquin the Proud), raped the virtuous Roman maiden Lucretia. Lucretia committed public suicide, and the enraged Roman populace expelled him (and the monarchy) in 509 BC.

La Lupa

Legend claims that one of Rome's Vestal Virgins (priestesses and protectors of the Eternal Flame) lost her virginity to Mars, the Roman God of War, thereupon losing her vestality as well. In a fury over her losing her honorable Vestal Virginity and in turn shaming the family name, her father killed her, and—in proper mythological form—left the twins whom she had borne to die on a mountaintop. However, the defenseless babes (Romulus and Remus) were found and nursed by a she-wolf *(La Lupa),* whom tourists can now see represented in sculptures and paintings throughout Italy. Interestingly, the word *lupa* in Italian also translates into a slang word for prostitute.

The Republic: 509-27 BC

The monarchy gave way to an aristocratic republic, and Rome spent the next 250 years torn by conflict. In addition to waging campaigns of conquest, the republic suffered from internal struggle between the upper-class **patricians** and the middle- and lower-class **plebeians,** as well as campaigns of conquest against their neighbors. These difficulties had two important long term results: the establishment of the **Roman code of law,** which would provide the underpinnings of administration for millennia and civilizations to come, and the almost completely unified control of the Italian peninsula (except for the Greek cities) by Rome.

Having conquered Italy, the republic waged its most important battles, the three **Punic Wars** (264-146 BC), against Carthage for control of the Mediterranean. The first war brought Sicily under Roman control; the second won for Rome the ex-Carthaginian territory in Spain and modern Tunisia, but lost the rest of Africa; and the third resulted in the complete destruction of Carthage. The Romans sowed the land around Carthage with salt so that it would never yield crops again. It was during the Punic Wars that Rome moved towards world power, consolidating its control over the Mediterranean and wiping out piracy in order to protect supply routes.

Under the umbrella of Roman military power, trade and shipping flourished. The spoils of war and taxes enriched Rome and its upper classes, creating an environment ripe for corruption. Two tribunes, **Tiberius and Gaius Gracchus,** tried to combat this corruption by promoting legislation more favorable to the plebeians, and both died in the process. Despite their efforts, social upheaval quickly ensued; by 131 BC, slave, farmer, and plebeian demands for land redistribution led to popular riots against the patrician class. Shortly thereafter the **Social War** erupted (91-87 BC), in which Latins and other Roman allies throughout the peninsula successfully fought for the extension of Roman citizenship. **Sulla,** the general who had com-

HISTORY AND POLITICS

manded Rome's troops during the conflict, then led the Roman army into Rome (an unprecedented and taboo move), taking control in a bloody military coup.

In the wake of this latest upheaval, **Spartacus,** an escaped gladiatorial slave, led an army of 70,000 slaves and farmers in a two-year rampage down the peninsula. (See the movie of the same name starring Kirk Douglas for a mind-boggling re-creation.) When the dust cleared, **Pompey the Great,** a close associate of Sulla, had taken effective control of the city, but he soon found himself in conflict with his periodic co-ruler **Julius Caesar,** the charismatic conqueror of Gaul. Caesar finally emerged victorious, but a small faction, fearful of his growing power, assassinated him on the Ides (15th) of March, 44 BC. Power eluded several would-be heirs (among them **Marcus Antonius,** a.k.a. Mark Antony) before falling to Caesar's nephew, Octavian, who assumed the title of **Augustus** and instated an imperial government in 27 BC.

The Empire: 27 BC-476 AD

Augustus, the first emperor of Rome, was also the founder of the **Julio-Claudian dynasty** (27 BC-68 AD). His reign (27 BC-14 AD), generally considered the golden age of Rome, initiated the **Pax Romana** (200 years of peace). With the aid of a professional army and imperial bureaucracy, Augustus and his successors were able to maintain the empire. Roman law and civic culture were also extended out to the frontiers. The imperial urban centers, with their Romanized upper classes and standardized civic systems, enabled the emperor to rule over a vast empire with fewer officials and troops.

Nero, the last of the Julio-Claudian emperors, committed suicide in 68 AD. The following year, in which three would-be rulers seized and lost power in succession, is generically known as the Year of the Four Emperors. Finally, the general **Vespasian** triumphed and initiated the **Flavian** dynasty (69-117 AD). Rome reached its maximum geographical expansion under the Flavian emperor **Trajan** (98-117 AD). At his death, his adopted successor **Hadrian** became the first emperor of the **Antonine** dynasty (117-193 AD). Antonine Emperor **Marcus Aurelius** (161-180 AD) is better known to posterity for his philosophical writings than for his reign, which he was forced to spend fending off barbarian invasions. The last of the Antonine emperors, **Commodus,** was a self-centered madman who wanted to rename Rome after himself; he was assassinated in 193 AD, and **Septimius Severus,** a general from Lepcis Magna in northern Africa, took over the principate and founded the **Severan** dynasty (193-235 AD). With the death of the last of the Severans, Alexander Severus, in 235 AD, the era of smooth dynastic succession came to an end.

Weak leadership and the southward invasions of Germanic tribes combined to create a state of anarchy in the 3rd century AD. **Diocletian** was one of the few major figures to secure control of the fragmented empire (284 AD). He divided the empire into eastern and western halves, and escalated the persecution of Christians in a period that became known as the "age of martyrs." The Roman people were entertained by the sight of Christians dressed in the hides of animals and torn to shreds by savage beasts, or set on fire as lamps so law-abiding citizens could do a little reading before bed. Despite this hazardous environment, by the end of Diocletian's violent reign approximately 30,000 Christians remained in Rome.

The fortunes of the Christians took a turn for the better when **Constantine,** Diocletian's successor, claimed to have seen a huge cross in the wartime sky along with the words, *"In hoc signo vinces"* (By this sign you shall conquer). Sure enough, victory followed the vision. Combining military strategy with spiritual conversion, Constantine declared Christianity the state religion in 315 AD. But soon provincial capitals decayed while armies of barbarian mercenaries patrolled the frontiers. In 410 AD, **Alaric,** king of the Visigoths, deposed the last of Rome's western emperors and sacked the city. The ensuing scramble for power wasn't fully resolved until 476 AD, when **Odoacer,** an Ostrogoth chieftain, was crowned King of Italy.

THE DARK AGES: C.500-1300 AD

With the weakening of imperial authority in the Latin West, the church and the papacy grew in power. Italian city-states dissipated their political energy and military strength in constant bickering, leaving themselves vulnerable to Hungarian attacks from the north and Saracen assaults on Sicily, Sardinia, and the western coast. Italy's relapse into near-chaos paved the way for increased papal authority. In 1054 AD, three legates of the pope went to the Church of the Holy Wisdom (Agia Sophia) in Constantinople and placed a **Bull of Excommunication** at the altar. Some scholars say that this marked the schism between the Latin West and the East Orthodox Churches. Although he was unable to repel the Normans in 1084, **Pope Gregory VII** (1073-1085) did much to free Italy from outside rule, and Rome subsequently grew as the administrative center of the Roman Catholic Church.

THE RENAISSANCE

Although the papacy eventually reasserted itself, the leaders who clasped the fallen scepter in the 14th through 16th centuries were secular politicos ruling the individual city-states. Left to their own devices, the leaders of these *communi* concentrated on extending their own economic and territorial power. To this end, they established a political fragmentation that would describe Italian history for centuries. Ironically, such instability planted the seeds of the greatest intellectual and artistic flowering of history—the **Renaissance.** Great ruling families like the Gonzaga in Mantua, the d'Este in Ferrara, and the Medici in Florence instituted important reforms in commerce and law, and accelerated the already rapid cultural and artistic flourishing of their respective cities. Princes, bankers, and merchants channeled their increasing wealth into patronage for the artists and scholars whose work defined the era. Unfortunately, power-hungry princes also cultivated the dark side of the Renaissance—constant warfare, usually among mercenaries. The weakened cities yielded easily to the Spanish invasions of the 16th century under Charles V and, by 1556, both Naples and Milan had fallen to King Ferdinand of Aragon.

As if the frequently warring factions of the Renaissance weren't enough, Italians also had to contend with natural disasters. In 1348 the **Black Death** killed over one half of Florence's population. Over a century later, another contagion struck: syphilis. The disease was most likely imported to the continent in 1494 from Africa, the West Indies, or from America by Christopher Columbus' crew. French soldiers who contracted syphilis from prostitutes in Naples nicknamed it the "Neapolitan disease", the Italians, in turn, called it *morbo gallico* (Gallic disease). In Rome the disease spread wildly, infecting seventeen members of the pope's family and court, including Cesare Borgia. To add to the city's horrors, the Tiber produced a violent flood in 1495. Water gushed into the streets and surged through churches and homes. The ascetic Florentine friar **Girolamo Savonarola** proclaimed these calamities a punishment for sin and inaugurated a war on the excesses of Rome. The pope tried to silence the pesky friar, and subsequently excommunicated him, but Savonarola persevered until the Florentines themselves got sick of his continual haranguing and tortured, burned, and hanged him.

AFTER THE RENAISSANCE: FOREIGN DOMINATION

Sixteenth-century Spaniards extended the **Inquisition** into Italy and, with invading armies, suppressed the Protestants and Jesuits and rolled back the Reformation. The end of the 16th century brought the depletion of Spanish control over the Italian states and a corresponding rise in the temporal power of the papacy. At the same time the Duke of Savoy, Victor Amadeus II, extended his territorial control in Piedmont, leaving Italy a patchwork of political regimes.

The rise of **Napoleon** ushered in the century. He united Italy for the first time since antiquity by bringing the southern provinces together with the Kingdom of Naples and the Roman Republic in 1798. Napoleon further stimulated Italian patriotism by arousing national resentment against the Austrian presence. After Napoleon's fall in 1815, the **Congress of Vienna** carved up Italy anew, shuffling kingdoms and granting considerable control to Austria.

THE ITALIAN NATION

Unification

In subsequent decades, strong sentiment against foreign rule prompted a movement of nationalist resurgence called the **Risorgimento,** ultimately culminating in national unification in 1870. The success of the *Risorgimento* is attributed primarily to three Italian heroes: **Giuseppe Mazzini,** the movement's intellectual leader, **Giuseppe Garibaldi,** the military leader and commander of the "red-shirts," and **Camillo di Cavour,** the political and diplomatic mastermind. Although the much-revered Garibaldi and his army of 1000 defeated the Bourbons in the south, the credit for Italy's birth as a nation belongs to Cavour. Throughout Italy, streets and *piazze* bear the names of these heroes.

The new Kingdom of Italy, under **Vittorio Emanuele** (also commemorated by a *via* or *piazza* in seemingly every town), went on to annex Romagna, Parma, Modena, and Tuscany. France ultimately relinquished Rome on September 20, 1870, *the* pivotal date in modern Italian history. Once the elation of unification wore off, however, age-old provincial differences reasserted themselves. Northern regions wanted to shield their relative prosperity from the economic stagnation of the agrarian south; central city-states were wary of surrendering too much power to a central administration; and the pope, whose Roman Empire had been seized by the new kingdom, threatened Italian Catholics (98% of the population) with excommunication for participating in politics. Disillusionment increased as Italy became involved in World War I, fighting to gain territory and vanquish Austria.

The chaotic aftermath of World War I paved the way for the rise of **fascism,** with its promise of order and stability. The Bolsheviks had recently gained control in Russia, and **Benito Mussolini** politically milked a "red scare" to destroy his strongest domestic opponents. In 1940, Italy entered World War II and joined the Axis. Success came quickly, but was short-lived; when the Allies landed in Sicily three years later, Mussolini fell from his pinnacle of power. As a final indignity, he and his mistress, Claretta Petacci, were captured, executed, and strung up by their heels by infuriated citizens.

By the end of 1943 the government had changed direction and declared war on Germany, which promptly invaded and occupied its former ally. Skirmishes between supporters of the deposed fascist government and its democratic replacement further ravaged Italy.

Mussolini's Assassination

There has been much recent speculation regarding the events leading up to the actual assassination. Supposedly, angry partisans captured the couple as they were fleeing to Switzerland. Mussolini's feisty mistress attempted an escape, but was accidentally shot and killed in the process; Mussolini was killed in the brawl as well. Having promised Italy's citizens a firing-squad-style execution, those responsible for the accidental shootings staged a fake execution, and duped the citizens into believing that they had witnessed the actual assassination. In reality, if the speculations are valid, the public watched as hours-old corpses were shot and strung up by their heels.

Post-War Politics

The constitution adopted in 1948 established a new Italian Republic with a president, a bicameral parliament, and an independent judiciary. The president, elected for a seven-year term by an electoral college, is the head of state and appoints the prime minister. Chief executive authority rests with the prime minister and his Council of Ministers. Within this framework, the **Christian Democratic Party**

(DC), bolstered by American money and military aid (and, as has been recently suggested, Mafia collusion), bested the Socialists and surfaced as the consistent ruling party in the new republic. But domination by a single party has not given the country stability: continual political turmoil has reigned with more than fifty different governments since World War II. (For a political-party breakdown, see below.)

The instability of the postwar era, in which the Italian economy sped through industrialization at an unprecedented rate, gave way to violence and near-anarchy in the 1970s. The *autunno caldo* (hot autumn) of 1969, a season of strikes, demonstrations, and riots, came on the heels of the international mayhem of 1968 and foreshadowed the violence of the 70s, to which the Italian government was at a loss to respond. Perhaps most shocking was the 1978 kidnapping and murder of ex-Prime Minister **Aldo Moro** by the leftist, terrorist *Brigate Rosse* (Red Brigades).

The well-known **Mafia** are much more of a cultural element of Italian society than their well-dressed, gun-toting image implies. Leaders of the nebulous organization still command great and unseen control over Italy's society, politics, and economy, especially in Sicily. Manipulation of Italy's black market has made the Mafia one of the (crooked) pillars of the Italian economy. Some of the *mafiosi's* success stems from the cultural acceptance of their activities, but today's Mafia—with its heightened passion for drug-running and violence—inspires near-universal fear and resentment among Italians. The Italian Parliament passed an unprecedented anti-Mafia law in 1982, followed by the Palermo *maxi processi* (maxi-trials), the largest series of Mafia trials in history. (See page 498 for more information on the Mafia.)

Divisions in Italy are not just between frightened citizens and organized criminals. Because the nation is still very young, city and regional bonds often prove stronger than nationalist sentiment. The most pronounced split exists between the north's highly industrialized European areas and the south's agrarian Mediterranean territories. (Native Italians will often treat foreigners better than their co-nationals from the other side of Rome.) Despite the many obstacles, Italy has nonetheless expanded with astonishing rapidity, becoming the world's fifth largest economy.

The chaos of Italian politics disillusions even its leaders. After three long years, Socialist **Bettino Craxi,** lamenting his inability to work with the Christian Democratic majority, resigned from the prime minister's chair in March 1987 (He was convicted of fraud in August 1994 and sentenced to 8½ years in prison, but refuses to return from Tunisia to face the sentence.) After Craxi's fall, three Christian Democrats took office in quick succession. Then, following a rare period of relative stability, the musical chairs of Italian politics resumed in April 1992, when Prime Minister **Giulio Andreotti** resigned and President **Francesco Cossiga** announced his retirement. On May 27, 1992, after disputes over voting procedures, a fist-fight between the neo-Fascists and Christian Democrats, and ten days and fifteen rounds of voting, **Oscar Luigi Scalfaro** was finally elected Italy's new president. He pledged his support for significant institutional reform of government, including a streamlining of the cabinet.

Since that time the slow and painful process of reforming electoral laws has resulted in "Tangentopoli" ("Kickback City"), an unprecedented political crisis in which over 2600 politicians have been implicated in scandals. Reaction to continued exposure and prosecution of mass corruption has included the May 1993 bombing of the Uffizi, Florence's premier art museum, and the "suicides" of ten vindicated officials over the past three years, not to mention the unleashing of open Mafia retaliation against judges. Until the winter of '94, right-wing **Prime Minister Silvio Berlusconi** (who moonlights as a billionaire publishing tycoon and owns three national TV channels and the ubiquitous STANDA supermarket chain), presided over a tenuous **"Freedom Alliance"** of three parties: his **Forza Italia** (who claim to be right-center but are in fact more extreme than the Fascists), the **Northern League** (conservative federalists), and the neo-fascist, extreme right **National Alliance.** When the National League pulled out of the Alliance last winter, Berlusconi lost his parliamentary majority and was forced to resign. In January of '95, **Lamberto Dini** was appointed the new Italian premier and acting prime minister over a temporary government of non-politicians *(tecnici)* who are currently running the country. Though the next national elections are not due to take place until March 1999, they are expected to take place in October or November of '95. Much campaigning is going on and Berlusconi prefers that the elections happen sooner rather than later, before his popularity declines. Others, of course, are hoping to have the elections *rimandati (*postponed) for exactly that reason.

Asini ed Elefanti

The Italian party system traditionally follows a pattern of "polarized centrism"— a multi-party system with most voters belonging either to the right-leaning Christian Democrats, who recently split into the **Italian People's Party** (PPI) and the **New Christian Democrats** (CCD); or to one of the left-leaning parties: the **Socialist Unity Party** (PSU, though usually referred to by its old name, the PSI) or the **Democratic Party of the Left** (PDS, a much less radical version of the old Communist Party, the PCI). The PDS, in conjunction with the PPI and the **Rifondazione Comunista** (RC; a radical left party) constitutes the Progressives. Since no party can claim a majority of the voters, Italian governments are formed with volatile and tenuous party coalitions.

■■■ ART AND ARCHITECTURE

Any understanding of Italian art must begin with ancient Greece. Through trade and cultural exchange, the **Etruscans** incorporated into their art and architecture many Greek elements which later found their way into the Roman repertoire: column types, wall frescoes, vaults, and even certain divinities are only a few examples. The quintessential feature of Roman architecture, however, is the **arch,** a deceptively simple innovation that dominated the famous Roman aqueducts, bridges, and triumphal monuments. The arch was also incorporated into building types, including: the semicircular **theater** (where plays were staged), the oval **amphitheater** (for gladiatorial and military displays, of which the Colosseum (80 AD) in Rome is the most famous example), and the **basilica** (a type of multi-purpose building created in the second century BC). Not all Roman construction, however, used the arch; the Romans also built *insulae* (similar to tenement housing), as well as large private villas based on a range of plans and techniques.

The interior walls of houses and shops were often extensively painted, usually in the **fresco** technique of paint on wet plaster. Sometimes a wall was painted to look like a beautiful outdoor scene (as in the Villa of the Empress Livia at Prima Porta), or *trompe-l'oeil* doors or columns were painted in to make the house look bigger. In other cases, mythological or still-life scenes were painted on walls or executed in **mosaic,** a popular genre in Roman art from the Hellenistic period on.

The collapse of the Roman Empire and the rise of Christianity marked the beginning of a search for new aesthetic forms. The most pressing concern was the accommodation of the Christian mass; hence the adaptation of the *basilica* for this purpose. New trends in painting emerged more slowly; as early as the 5th century, however, Pope Gregory the Great was calling for art which would edify the illiterate masses and exalt the afterlife. The Christian art that emerged in the Middle Ages was thus crafted by artists with an eye fixed firmly on heaven. These paintings combined a disregard for the physical world with a diminution of the individual in a larger hierarchy of symbols and belief.

Following these early years of the millennium, two great styles emerged to dominate art and architecture. From 500-1200 AD **Romanesque** flooded Europe with churches easily identified by small, rounded arches resting on massive stone piers. Great Italian Romanesque churches include the cathedral of Pisa, San Ambrogio in Milan, the cathedral of Massa Marittima, and San Miniato in Florence.

The **Gothic** style of the 12th to 14th centuries resulted from the combination of the pointed arch and the flying buttress—together, they supported the heavy roof and allowed the Romanesque wall to be replaced by the glorious Gothic window. For some unknown reason, Italian Gothic never adopted the flying buttress and thus the incredible light-filled churches of France and Germany are absent in Italy. San Petronio in Bologna and the cathedrals of Milan and Siena are lovely examples of this style, incorporating the pointed arch and high ceiling without the buttresses and glass walls. Great Gothic artists include **Simone Martini** and **Pietro Lorenzetti** (especially his Crucifixion in San Francesco, Siena).

In late 13th and 14th centuries, artists gradually grew more inclined to realism. The initiator of the great aesthetic achievements of the **Renaissance, Giotto di Bondone** (1267-1337), ushered in the "new naturalism" with his use of lifelike, fluid figures. He also replaced the bland backgrounds of his predecessors with landscapes of trees and mountains. His successor **Masaccio** (1401-1428) is worth noting for his work with light, shadow and color. His painting *The Crucifixion* was the first ever to use one-point perspective. These new techniques revolutionized painting, sculpture, and architecture in Italy. One of the most prominent early Renaissance sculptors was **Lorenzo Ghiberti** (1378-1455). **Donatello** (1386-1466) revered the Roman style while producing some of the most original work of his time. His close study of anatomy not only informed his sculpting, but made his statues an inspiration for anatomical accuracy and realism among later Renaissance painters. The two most important architects of the early Renaissance are **Filippo Brunelleschi** (1377-1446) and **Leon Alberti** (1404-1472). Brunelleschi was an extraordinary engineer, often credited with the "discovery" of linear perspective in painting; it was he who raised the first great dome of the Renaissance over Santa Maria del Fiore in Florence. Alberti, whose style was less grandiose but more practical, was the first to confront architecture in the context of town-planning. In the high Renaissance, their mantle would be taken up by **Donato Bramante** (1444-1514).

There is no doubt, however, that the peak of the Renaissance (1450-1520) was dominated by three men known as the Triumvirate of the High Renaissance: **Leonardo da Vinci** (1452-1519), **Michelangelo Buonarroti** (1475 1564), and **Raphael** (1483-1520). Leonardo was the original Renaissance man—artist, scientist, architect, engineer, musician, weapons designer—and although he seldom finished what he started, his achievements were extraordinary. His monumental painting *The Last Supper* (in Santa Maria delle Grazie in Milan) is a veritable handbook of Renaissance individualism in a religious theme. He also perfected the use of aerial perspective, defined standards of human proportional perfection, and stylized the use of *sfumato*, a technique that revolutionized painting throughout Europe. That another genius of Leonardo's caliber existed at the same time—and in the same place—is stupefying. Michelangelo painted and sculpted with as much skill as his contemporary—and perhaps with even greater results. The ceiling of the Sistine Chapel remains his greatest achievement in painting (after completing the project, he didn't paint again for 25 years). His architectural achievements are equally noteworthy—the master's designs for St. Peter's elevated Italian architecture to new heights. But sculpture is where Michelangelo's true genius lay. Classic examples are the formal, tranquil *Pietà* in St. Peter's, its half-finished, anguished counterpart in the Castello Sforzesco in Milan, the majestic, virile *David* in Florence's Academy, and the powerful *Moses* in Rome's San Pietro in Vincoli. Raphael is notable for his prolificacy and his technical perfection. He invented the seated three-quarter-length portrait and the group portrait, and his frescoes in the papal apartments in the Vatican are a must for lovers of Renaissance art.

When Rome was pillaged in 1527 by German and Spanish mercenaries, instability and conflict brought an end to the golden age of the Renaissance. The widespread disillusionment that followed was reflected in the emerging style of **Mannerism**, a short-lived link between the Renaissance and Baroque periods. Mannerism was concerned with solving abstract artistic problems rather than with the idealism of the High Renaissance or any kind of "realism." Its figures are oddly and unreally elongated, its perspective flattened, and its color schemes unusual and not particularly harmonious. A non-Mannerist precursor to the Baroque was the great architect

Andrea Palladio (1508-1580), originator of Palladian architecture (known for its classical, centralized proportions); his most important works were the Villa Capra at Vicenza and Il Redentore in Venice. His most lasting contribution, however, may have been the *Four Books of Architecture,* which influenced countless architects. The **Baroque** period that followed lasted into the 18th century. Born of the counter-Reformation and of absolute monarchy, Baroque art and architecture was intended to inspire passion, faith, and awe. It is generally grandiose, vivid, and dynamic, and often (especially with sculpture) meant to be viewed from a single point. At the beginning of this era, **Michelangelo de Caravaggio** (1573-1610) urged a return to naturalism—a commitment to portraying nature as is, whether ugly or beautiful. **Gianlorenzo Bernini** (1598-1680), the most prolific artist of the high Baroque, designed the ornate colonnades of St. Peter's, but the façade and nave of the church are the work of **Carlo Maderno** (1607). **Tiepolo** (1696-1770) was the last of the great Italian decorative painters, and his sunny palate and strong frescoes marked the end of the tradition begun with Giotto.

Through French influence, the decorative **rococo** style (of which the most conspicuous example is the Spanish Steps in Rome) and the sterner formalities of **Neoclassicism** succeeded the Italian Baroque, to be succeeded themselves by the major trends of the 20th century. Two of Italy's greatest artists of this period were expatriates **Amadeo Modigliani** (1884-1920), who drew inspiration from sources ranging from Mannerism to African primitivism, and **Giorgio de Chirico** (1888-1978), originator of **metaphysical painting,** a precursor of surrealism. Other modern Italian artists include **Sandro Chio** and **Enzo Cucci,** both neo-expressionists. **Marcello Piacentini's** monstrous fascist architecture looms at EUR in Rome. To trace the current path of Italian art, you can visit modern art galleries in most major cities, as well as at the Canova Museum at Passagno.

■■■ LITERATURE

GREEK AND ROMAN MYTHOLOGY

Ovid's work is a principal source for our knowledge of Roman mythology. Usually disguised as animals or humans, the gods and goddesses often descended to earth to intervene romantically or combatively in human affairs. The 14 major deities are: **Jupiter,** king of gods, his wife **Juno,** who watches over child-bearing and marriage, **Neptune,** god of the sea, **Vulcan,** god of smiths and fire, **Venus,** goddess of love and beauty, **Mars,** god of war, **Minerva,** goddess of wisdom, **Apollo** (or Phoebus), god of light and music, **Diana,** goddess of the hunt, **Mercury,** the messenger god and patron of thieves and tricksters, **Pluto,** god of the underworld, **Ceres,** goddess of the harvest, **Bacchus,** god of wine, and **Vesta,** goddess of the hearth.

LITERATURE OF THE REPUBLIC AND EMPIRE

Roman literature exists in many forms, including plays, historical writings, philosophical treatises, and satires. **Plautus** (c.220-184 BC) wrote popular farces which entertained the masses much as sitcoms do today. The lyric poetry of **Catullus** (84-54 BC), on the other hand, set a high standard for passion. **Livy** (c.59 BC-17 AD) recorded the authorized history of Rome from the city's founding to his own time, while **Julius Caesar** (100-44 BC) gave a first-hand account of the final shredding of the Republic; his *Commentaries* recount his experiences on the front lines of the Gallic wars. Caesar's close contemporary **Cicero** (106-43BC) penned several works noteworthy for their ideas and use of carefully crafted Latin, including the speech *In Catilinam* ("O tempora, O mores!"), *De Republica,* and a collection of letters to his family and friends.

Despite a government prone to banishing the impolitic, Augustan Rome produced some of the greatest Latin authors of antiquity. **Virgil** (70-19 BC), revered by posterity as the only Roman poet worthy of comparison with Homer, wrote the *Aeneid,* an epic recounting the adventures of the Trojan hero Aeneas. **Horace's** (65-8 BC) verse derives more from his personal experiences, which he worked into his pro-lific *Odes, Epodes, Satires,* and *Epistles.* An acquaintance of Horace, **Ovid** (43 BC-17 AD) had quite an experience of his own. His poems, among them the *Amores* (per-haps more accurately titled "lusts"), the mythological *Metamorphoses,* and the *Ars Amatoria* (a guide to scamming on Roman women), earned him banishment at the hands of Augustus. (He blamed Ovid for his daughter Julia's lewd behavior.)

From the post-Augustan empire, **Petronius'** (1st century AD) *Satyricon* is a bawdy, blunt look at the decadence of the age of Nero (and a movie by Fellini), while **Suetonius'** (c.69 AD) *De Vita Caesarum* was the gossipy version of imperial history. **Tacitus'** (c.56 AD) *Histories* summarize Roman war, diplomacy, scandal, and rumor in the years after Nero's death. His *Annals* look down from the upright Rome of Trajan's reign onto the scandalous activities of the Julio-Claudian emperors (Tiberius is a favorite target). Finally, **Marcus Aurelius'** (121-180 AD) *Meditations* bring us the musings of a philosopher-king on the edge of a precipice—it was all downhill after him.

EARLY RENAISSANCE

Italy had no *Beowulf* to brighten the Dark Ages, but the silence of a millennium was broken by a quite characteristic Italian cultural formation: a triumvirate. Although scholars do not agree on the precise dates of the Renaissance, many argue that **Dante Alighieri** (1265-1321) marked its inception. One of the first Italian poets to write in the *volgare* (common Italian) instead of Latin, Dante is considered the father of modern Italian language and literature. In his epic poem *The Divine Com-edy,* Dante fills the afterlife with famous figures from throughout history. Among the *Commedia*'s chief themes are Dante's call for social reform and his scathing indict-ment of those contributing to civic strife.

While Dante is described as a man with one foot in the Middle Ages and one in the Renaissance, **Petrarch** (Francesco Petrarca, 1304-74) tried to extricate himself com-pletely from the Middle Ages. The third member of the medieval literary triumvirate was a close friend of Petrarch's, but the style of **Giovanni Boccaccio** owes little to his sonnet-writing friend. The *Decameron,* Boccaccio's collection of 100 stories supposedly told by ten young Florentines fleeing their plague-ridden city, ranges in tone from suggestive to downright bawdy; in one story, a hard-working gardener has his way with an entire convent!

THE RENAISSANCE AND ITS AFTERMATH

Fifteenth- and sixteenth-century Italian authors branched out from the genres of their predecessors. **Leon Battista Alberti** and **Palladio** (Andrea di Pietro) wrote treatises on architecture and art theory; **Baldassare Castiglione's** *The Courtier* instructed the inquiring Renaissance man on deportment, etiquette, and other fine points of behavior. **Vasari** took time off from redecorating Florence's churches to produce a primer on art history and criticism (*The Lives of the Artists*). The most lasting work of the Renaissance, **Niccolò Machiavelli's** *Il Principe* (*The Prince*), is a sophisticated assessment of what it takes to gain and hold political power. Although Machiavelli did not make many friends with his candid and brutal sugges-tions, he is now regarded as the father of modern political theory. Less well-known but of great literary significance was Machiavelli's comedy *La Mandragola,* part of the tradition of the **commedia dell'arte.**

In attempts at living up to the title of "Renaissance men," non-professional writers often tried their hands at multiple media, including writing. Among Renaissance art-ists, **Benvenuto Cellini** wrote about the most interesting of all subjects, himself, in *The Autobiography;* **Michelangelo** wrote enough sonnets to fuel a fire, while **Leonardo da Vinci** wrote about anything and everything (*The Notebook*). The scathing and brilliant **Pietro Aretino** created new possibilities for literature when he began accepting payment from notable targets for *not* writing about them.

As Italy slid into international inconsequence, literary production floundered. However, the prolific 18th-century dramatist **Carlo Goldoni** (1709-1793) trans-

LITERATURE

formed the traditional theater of the *commedia dell'arte* by replacing its stock figures with original, unpredictable characters in such works as *Il Ventaglio*. Also an evolutionary event, the publication of **Alessandro Manzoni's** (1785-1873) epic *I promessi sposi* (*The Betrothed*) marked the birth of the modern novel in Italy.

19TH AND 20TH-CENTURY LITERATURE

Twentieth-century exposure to communism, socialism, and fascism gave rise to anti-traditional literary achievements among Italian writers. Nobel Prize-winning playwright **Luigi Pirandello** (1867-1936) became the father of modern experimental theater with his exploration of the relativity of truth in works including *Six Characters in Search of an Author, Henry IV,* and *Right You Are (It Is So If You Think It Is So)*. Another unconventional writer, **Italo Svevo,** has three great works on the bourgeois mind: *A Life, The Confessions of Zeno,* and *Senility*.

Italy was a center of Modernist innovation in poetry. The most flamboyant and controversial of the early poets is **Gabriele d'Annunzio,** whose cavalier heroics and sexual escapades earned him as much fame as his eccentric, over-the-top verse. D'Annunzio was a true child of pleasure, or *Il Piacere,* the title of his novel set in Rome. In the mid- and late-20th century, **Giuseppe Ungaretti,** and Nobel Prize-winners **Salvatore Quasimodo** and **Eugenio Montale** dominated the scene. Montale and Quasimodo founded the "hermetic movement," but both became more accessible and politically committed after the Second World War. Ungaretti brought to Italy many of the innovations of the French Symbolists; his collection *L'allegria* set a trend toward increased purity of language and clarity of meaning in Italian poetry. Ungaretti was drawn to Rome to study Keats and Shelley, and during his stay he disseminated his ideas to hundreds of admiring college students.

The 1930s and '40s heralded the heyday of a group of young Italian writers greatly influenced by the experimental narratives and themes of social alienation in the works of certain U.S. writers: Ernest Hemingway, John Dos Passos, and John Steinbeck. This school included **Cesare Pavese, Ignazio Silone, Vasco Pratolini,** and **Elio Vittorini.** One of the most representative works of 1930s Italian literature is Silone's *Bread and Wine,* written while the left-wing intellectual and political-activist author was in exile. The most prolific of these writers, **Alberto Moravia,** wrote the ground-breaking *Time of Indifference* which launched an attack on the fascist regime and was promptly censored. To evade the stiff government censors, Moravia

---

Hit the Books

Italian life has also inspired many American and British writers, including Henry James, Thomas Mann, and Morris West. Toby Cole's *Venice: A Portable Reader* and *Florence: A Traveler's Anthology* are collections of insightful passages from an array of literary figures. And don't forget Shakespeare, who, despite never having set foot in Italy, wrote the highly relevant *Romeo and Juliet, The Merchant of Venice,* and *Julius Caesar.* In addition to the books mentioned above, the following are also worth a read.

–Clark, Eleanor. **Rome and a Villa.** Beautiful essays about the eternal city.
–Dibdin, Michael. **Cabal.** Murder mystery set in ancient Rome.
–Graves, Robert. **I, Claudius** and **Claudius the God.** A hysterical work narrated by the clumsy Claudius. The BBC made an excellent TV movie of the books.
–Hoffman, Paul. **That Fine Italian Hand.** Articles and essays.
–Levi, Carlo. **Christ Stopped at Eboli.** An anti-fascist work. There is also a movie of the same name.
–Sterling, Claire. **The Mafia.** A fascinating exposure of the institution.
–Vidal, Gore. **Julian.** Just about everything, including the Constantinian era.
–Walston, James. **The Mafia and Clientelism: Roads to Rome in Postwar Calabria.** More on the modern and "slick" clientelism in southern Italy.
–**Let's Go: Italy '96.** We couldn't put it down.

employed experimental, surreal forms in his subsequent works. His later works use sex to symbolize the violence and spiritual impotence of modern Italy.

Particularly appealing prose works for travelers include **Giorgio Bassani's** *The Garden of the Finzi-Continis*, **Cesare Pavese's** *The Moon and the Haystacks,* and **Elio Vittorini's** *Conversation in Sicily.* The works of the greatest modern Italian author, **Italo Calvino,** are (not surprisingly) those most widely available in English. Calvino's writing—full of intellectual play and magical realism—is exemplified in *Invisible Cities,* a collection of cities described by Marco Polo to Kubla Kahn. His work includes the trilogy *Our Ancestors,* and the more traditional narrative *If on a winter's night a traveler...* a boisterous romp about authors, readers, and the insatiable urge to read, but perhaps most enjoyable for the traveler is *Italian Folktales,* Calvino's collection of traditional regional fairytales.

More recently, **Umberto Eco's** wildly popular *The Name of the Rose,* an intricate mystery set in a 14th-century monastery (see the Sacra of S Michele page 289 for more info), somehow managed to keep readers on edge while making the history of the revolutionary crisis in medieval Catholicism vaguely intelligible. His *Foucault's Pendulum* becomes rather precious in its complications, but wraps the story of the Knights Templar and half-a-millennium of conspiracy theories into a neat pocket-size package for transport. The hype surrounding the publication of Eco's latest novel, *L'isola del giorno primo,* reflects not only his tremendous popularity and literary influence, but also his symbiotic relationship with the Italian media.

■■■ MUSIC

Musically, Italians are responsible for a number of "famous firsts": the musical scale, the piano, the Stradivarius violin, and the invention of the system of musical notation still used today, are only a few. Even so, for Italians, vocal music has always occupied a position of undisputed preeminence. Born in Florence, nurtured in Venice, and revered in Milan, **opera** is Italy's most cherished art form Invented by the **Camerata,** an art *coterie* of Florentine writers, noblemen, and musicians, opera began as an attempt to recreate the dramas of ancient Greece by setting their lengthy poems to music. After several years of effort with only dubious success, Jacobo Peri composed *Dafne,* the world's first complete opera, in 1597. As opera spread from Florence to Venice, Milan, and Rome, the forms of the genre grew more distinct. The first successful opera composer, **Monteverdi,** drew freely from history, juxtaposing high drama, love scenes, and bawdy humor. His masterpiece *L'Orfeo* (1607) assured the survival of the genre and is still performed today.

The history of Italian vocal and instrumental music dates back several centuries prior to the advent of opera. Sacred music of the Medieval and Renaissance periods can still be heard in many of the ancient cathedrals and *basiliche* (churches). The composers who wrote *musica da chiesa* (music for the church), also frequently wrote pieces for performance in the home or at court. The latter were more often than not rather naughty love songs. Early performers were generally gifted amateurs, but one can now hear the *da camera* (literally "in room") repertoire performed at the various music academies and summer festivals of Italy. *Virtuoso* instrumental music began to establish itself as a legitimate genre in 17th-century Rome. **Vivaldi** wrote over 400 concertos while teaching at a home for orphaned girls in Venice. Under Vivaldi the concerto assumed its present form, in which the soloist is accompanied by a full orchestra.

Eighteenth-century Italy exported its music. At mid-century, operatic overtures began to be performed separately, resulting in the creation of a new genre of music. The **sinfonia,** modeled after the melody of operatic overtures, was simply opera detached from its setting. Thus began the symphonic art form, which later received its highest expression in the hands of Italy's northern neighbors. In opera, baroque virtuosity and detail yielded to classical standards of moderation, structural balance, and elegance. To many of today's opera buffs, Italian opera is epitomized by 19th- and 20th-century composers Verdi, Puccini, Bellini, Donizetti, and Rossini. Rossini,

MUSIC

Donizetti, and Bellini are the preeminent creators of the *bel canto* school of opera in the early 19th century. *Bel canto* literally means "beautifully sung" and defines operas in which the drama is conveyed through beautifully conceived melodies.

With plots relying on wild coincidence and strong, dramatic music, 19th-century Italian opera continues to dominate modern stages. Late in the 19th century came **Puccini,** the great master of *verismo* opera, which deals largely with everyday people caught in powerful and often tragic emotional dilemmas. Above all, *verismo* should ring with dramatic honesty. Puccini, creator of *Madame Butterfly, La Bohème,* and *Tosca* is noted for the beauty of his music and for the strength, assurance, and compassion of his female characters. The great *bel canto* master **Rossini** boasted that he could produce music faster than copyists could reproduce it, but he proved such a procrastinator that his agents resorted to locking him in a room until he completed his now-renowned masterpieces. The transcendent musical and operatic figure of 19th-century Italy is **Giuseppe Verdi.** His development of operatic style through his lengthy career virtually defines the history of 19th-century opera. From early Verdi we have *Nabucco,* a pointed and powerful *bel canto* work. The chorus "*Va pensiero*" from *Nabucco* became the hymn of Italian freedom and unity. From Verdi's middle period we have the touchingly personal drama and memorable melodies of *Rigoletto, La Traviata,* and *Il Trovatore.* From the last third of the century, Verdi gives us the grand and heroic conflicts of *Aida,* the drama thrust of *Othello,* and the mercurial comedy of *Falstaff.* Verdi became such a national icon that "*Viva Verdi*" was a battle cry of the *Risorgimento.* Much of Verdi's work promoted Italian unity; his operas include frequent allusions to political assassinations, exhortations against tyranny, and jibes at French and Austrian monarchs.

Italian music continues to grow in the 20th century. **Ottorino Respighi,** composer of the popular *Pines of Rome* and *Fountains of Rome,* experimented with rapidly shifting orchestral textures. **Giancarlo Menotti,** now a U.S. resident, has written short opera-like works such as *Amahl and the Night Visitors,* but is probably best known as creator of the Two Worlds Art Festival in Spoleto (see page 169). Known for his work with meta-languages, **Luciano Berio** defied traditional instrumentation with his *Sequence V* for solo trombone and mime. **Luigi Dallapiccola** worked with serialism, achieving success with choral works including *Songs of Prison* and *Songs of Liberation*—two pieces that protest fascist rule in Italy. And that *pagliaccio* **Luciano Pavarotti** remains universally adored.

Opera season runs from December to June. The productions at the Teatro alla Scala in Milan, the Teatro San Carlo in Naples, the Teatro dell'Opera in Rome, and La Fenice in Venice are especially spectacular, but those in Bari, Bergamo, Genoa, Modena, Trieste, and Turin are also quite prestigious. Tickets are surprisingly cheap for standing room or day-of-purchase. Don't despair if you miss the season; throughout the summer, you can enjoy open-air opera at the Roman Arena in Verona, and at many major music festivals including the *Maggio Musicale Fiorentino* in Florence from May to June.

Rock music (ah!) came to Italy in the 1960s, a reflection of musical trends set in U.S. and Britain, but endowed with a unique, indigenous character that blended Italian folk songs and Mediterranean rhythms with pop beats. Light rock singers **Pino Daniele, Vasco Rossi, Lucio Battisti** and others no longer play live to university audiences; they have been replaced by pop stars **Laura Pausini, Eros Ramazotti,** and **883** (Otto Otto Tre). Pausini's "Non C'è" and "La Solitudine" express the angst felt by all 15-year olds, while 883's ballad "Come Mai" was suggested by some as the new Italian national anthem. Slightly more radical groups like **Gang** and **Mau Mau** mix African drums and Euro-pop. Believe it or not, Italian rap exists, and it isn't that bad: **99 Posse**'s hybrid of reggae and rap was featured in the controversial film *Sud,* while rapper **Jovanotti** has risen from TV-variety-show pop star to semi-alternative, goatee-sporting singer-songwriter. Although Italian discos often rely on English and U.S. bands (**U2** is a big favorite), they also pump the sounds of techno remixes and groups like **Ace of Base.** But Italian popular music is not all frivolous. In fact, Italian popular music, much more so than American music, often has a political agenda.

Lucio Dalla was one of the first to use pop music as a vehicle for political protest. Today, many socially conscious bands from southern Italy promote improving relations between the industrial North and the impoverished South, while others address issues such as corruption in the government and the Mafia.

■■■ THE MEDIA

PRINT

Throughout the larger cities in Italy, you'll be able to find some representative newspaper of your home country (*The Herald Tribune* in the American case) at the numerous **edicole** (newsstands). These stands are compact stations of printed information (not to mention fire hazards); you can find newspapers, magazines, train schedules, comic books, coloring books, and sometimes even postcards amongst the sheafs of colorful paper. Often, sandwich boards with the front pages from the day's newspapers will be set up nearby, where locals gather to discuss the news. In small towns, natives are likely to purchase one of the many local papers rather than one of national import. The ones you'll see the most of will be the **Corriere Della Sera,** a conservative publication from Milan, and **La Repubblica,** a liberal paper from Rome. Other big papers include **La Stampa** (conservative, published in Torino and owned 100% by Fiat) and **Il Messaggero** (liberal, published in Rome as well). There is also an amazing breed of daily sports newspapers, **La Gazzetta Dello Sport** and the **Corriere Dello Sport** being the two largest. Italian men will cluster around them in the morning; it's certainly more important to some of them than the state of the nation.

TELEVISION

If you thought American television was sexist, then you haven't seen Italian television. Game shows, commentary, and even children's programs are overwhelmingly populated by buxom (often topless), leggy bombshells in flashy clothes. More generally, Italian television comes in two varieties: three vaguely educational state-owned **RAI** channels and the shamelessly insipid networks owned by former Prime Minster Silvio Berlusconi. **Italia 1, Rete 4,** and **Canale 5** transmit all your favorite American trash, including "Beverly Hills 90210" and "Saved by the Bell" (called "Bayside School"), as well as a few indigenous crimes against humanity. Eight-year-old girls and adolescent boys rush home every day at two o'clock to watch "Non È La RAI," a variety show featuring scantily clad high-school girls dancing and lip-synching to all your favorite tunes. Similarly, "Karaoke" features lip-synching fools—but it may help your Italian if you too throw caution to the winds and sing along with the bouncing ball. One last word of warning about *la tivvù* if your name is Brooke, Carolyn, Ridge, or Thorn, don't be too flattered if Italians exclaim "Beautiful!" when they meet you—it's likely to be the name of their favorite soap opera character; (The Bold and The) **Beautiful** U.S. soap opera hit Italy five years ago with full force, and every Italian (housewife, student, and businessman alike) now spends a portion of his/her afternoon break following the lives of big-haired blondes and hunky heartthrobs dressed in Gitanos.

■■■ FILM

For Italy's contributions to the arts in this century, don't go to the museum—go to the movies. Years before Hollywood existed, the **Cines** studios thrived in Rome. *Cines* constructed in 1905-6 created the so-called Italian "super-spectacle," extravagant, larger-than-life re-creations of momentous historical events. One of these, Enrico Guzzani's incredible *Quo Vadis,* enjoyed international success as the first "blockbuster" hit in film history.

Immediately before World War I, Italy's star system (*divismo*) emerged, and the public appeal and economic success of films became increasingly dependent upon

FILM

the presence of celebrities—particularly *dive* ("goddesses") like Lyda Borelli and Francesca Bertini, who epitomized the destructive yet suffering Italian *femme fatale*. With the advent of World War I and the rise of fascism, government leaders and supporters became more and more visible in the film scene. Mussolini recognized the power of popular cinema and created the *Centro Sperimentale della Cinematografia*, a national film school, and the gargantuan **Cinecittà studios**. The famous director and covert Marxist **Luigi Chiarini** attracted many students—including **Roberto Rossellini** and **Michelangelo Antonioni**—who rose to directorial fame after the war. Mussolini avoided most aesthetic questions of film, but enforced a few "imperial edicts," one of which forbade laughing at the Marx Brothers' *Duck Soup*.

When fascism fell, a generation of young filmmakers enjoyed freedom from the constraints of the discredited regime. Mussolini's nationalized film industry produced no great films, but sparked the subsequent explosion of **neo-realist cinema** (1943-50). This new style rejected sets and professional actors and emphasized location shooting and authentic drama. Low budget productions, partly necessitated by postwar economic circumstances, soon shaped a revolution in film. Neo-realists first gained attention in Italy with **Lucino Visconti's** 1942 *Ossessione,* based on James Cain's pulp-novel *The Postman Always Rings Twice*. Roberto Rossellini's widely acclaimed *Roma, Città Aperta* (Open City), a 1946 movie of a Resistance leader trying to escape the Gestapo, was filmed mostly on the streets of Rome. Because of its neo-realist documentary style and authentic setting, the movie appears to be actual newsreel footage. **Vittorio de Sica's** *The Bicycle Thief* (1948) was perhaps the most famous and commercially-successful neo-realist film.

When neo-realism turned its wobbly camera from the Resistance to social critique, it lost its popularity and, after 1950, gave way to individual expressions of Italian genius. Post-neo-realist directors **Federico Fellini** and Antonioni rejected the mechanics of plots and characters to portray a world of moments and witnesses. In Fellini's autobiographical *Roma*, a gorgeous stand-in for the director encounters an otherwise grotesque cast of characters. *La Dolce Vita* (1960), banned by the pope but widely regarded as *the* representative Italian film, scrutinizes the stylish, vapid Rome of the 1950s. Antonioni's films include *L'Eclisse* (1962), *Deserto Rosso* (1964), and *Blow-Up*, a 1966 English-language hit about mime, murder, and mod London. Antonioni's *L'Avventura*, a story of bored young aristocrats, has been hailed the second-greatest film of all time (the idea was still original back then).

Pier Paolo Pasolini—who spent as much time on trial for his politics and atheism as he did making films—was both a successful poet and one of the greatest and most controversial Italian directors. An ardent Marxist, he set his first films in Italian shanty neighborhoods and in the Roman underworld of poverty and prostitution. His masterpiece, *Hawks and Sparrows,* investigates the philosophical and poetic possibilities of film.

Time, aging old-boy directors, and the lack of money for Italian films led to another era in directing: in 1974, **Lina Wertmuller's** *Swept Away*—which portrays a rich Milanese woman stranded on a desert island with a chauvinist provincial sailor—left many feminists fuming. Those familiar with **Bernardo Bertolucci's** *Last Tango in Paris* and *Last Emperor* should see his 1970 *Il Conformista* (The Conformist), about a man hired to assassinate his former teacher. Other major modern Italian films include Vittorio De Sica's *Il giardino dei Finzi-Contini* (Garden of the Finzi-Continis) and **Francesco Rosi's** *Cristo si è fermato a Eboli* (Christ Stopped at Eboli). In the 1980s, the **Taviani** brothers catapulted to fame with *Kaos,* a film based on stories by Pirandello, and *La Notte di San Lorenzo* (Night of the Shooting Stars), which depicts an Italian village during the ludicrous and tragic final days of World War II. Recently, Oscar-winners **Giuseppe Tornatore** (*Cinema Paradiso*) and **Gabriele Salvatore** (*Mediterraneo)* have won the affection of U.S. audiences.

Those seeking a change from "serious" films should not ignore Italy's rich comic film tradition. Actor **Totò**, the bastard son of a Neapolitan duke, was Italy's challenge to Charlie Chaplin (known as "Charlot" in Italy). Totò's genius lay in his dignified antics and clever language, which took the Italian's minds away from their post-

WWI misery. More recent star **Roberto Begnini** is featured in many Italian comedies, as well as the American *Son of the Pink Panther* and Jim Jarmusch's *Down by Law*. If you want to sample the Italian film scene during your trip, try one of Italy's **film festivals:** the International Festival of New Cinema in Pesaro (June), the International Film Festivals in Taormina and Messina (July) and in Venice (Sept.), or the Festival Dei Popoli International Review of Documentary Film in Florence (Dec.).

■■■ FOOD AND WINE: LA DOLCE VITA

Don't plan to lose weight in Italy. Any ground gained in health through monounsaturated olive oil and complex-carbohydrate-rich pasta will be lost to waves of *gelato* and pizza, coffee pit-stops, and the cholesterol haven Italians call a dessert tray.

Italian cuisine differs radically by region. The north offers creamy sauces, exotic mushroom dishes, stuffed pasta, and flat, handmade egg noodles. **Piedmont** and its southern neighbor **Umbria** are best known for their delectable (but pricey) truffles; **Lombardy** specializes in cheeses and *biscotti* (sweet, shortcake-like biscuits). The coastal region of **Liguria** is noted for its seafood, *pesto,* and olive oil, while German and Austrian influences on the **Trentino-Alto Adige** and **Veneto** regions have popularized *gnocchi,* dumplings typically made of potatoes and flour. Central Italy serves richer, spicier dishes. The **Emilia-Romagna** region is the world's pasta palace, its dishes loaded with meat, cream, cheese, and butter. **Tuscany** draws justifiable acclaim for its pricey olive oil and bean dishes, and **Abruzzo** is known for spicy, peppery food and a wealth of game. The food of the south is a bit coarser, but far less expensive. Tomato sauces and tubular pasta originated in **Campania,** also the birthplace of that most renowned "Italian" food: pizza. Greek influence can be detected in **Calabria**'s cuisine, with its figs, honey, strong spices, and eggplant. **Sicily** produces luscious deserts, such as *cannoli,* pastry stuffed with sweet cheeses and chocolate, and *cassata,* a rich ice cream.

While breakfast often goes unnoticed (coffee and a *cornetto* (croissant) at most), **lunch** is the main meal of the day in Italy. If you don't want a big meal, grab lunch at an inexpensive *tavola calda* ("hot table"), *rosticceria* (grill), or *gastronomia* (serving hot prepared dishes). A new breed of fast food joints springing up around the country, painful to see in a place that prides itself on homemade food. **Burghy** is a McDonald's-like chain, while others feature pasta-to-go (cooked *al dente,* of course). The Italian McDonalds, however, features a salad bar that's actually **decent veggie food.** For more authentic and less carcinogenic eats, buy picnic materials at a *salumeria* or *alimentari,* both grocery stores. STANDA and COOP are two large supermarket chains, though political activists avoid the Berlusconi-owned STANDA. Fresh fruits and vegetables are best purchased at the open markets.

Italian **dinners** begin considerably later and last much longer than their American counterparts. The farther south you travel, the later dinner is served. A full supper begins with an *antipasto* (appetizer), which can be as simple as *bruschetta,* a type of garlic bread, or as fancy as *prosciutto* (cured ham) with melon. Next comes the *primo piatto* (the first course, usually pasta or soup), followed by the *secondo,* consisting of meat or fish, and accompanied by a *contorno* (small vegetable side dish). Most restaurants offer a fixed-priced tourist *menù* that includes *primo, secondo,* bread, water, and wine. As far as **coffee** is concerned, ordering a *caffè* will get you strong Italian espresso (quaff it in two sips like natives do); ask for *caffè macchiato* (literally "spotted coffee") if you would like a drop of milk in it. *Cappuccino,* which the Italians drink only before noon, has frothy scalded milk (whipped cream is *not* authentic), while *caffè latte* is heavier on the milk, lighter on the coffee. But the key to Italian coffee is *caffè corretto* ("correct"): an espresso with a drop of some strong liqueur, usually *grappa.*

A **bar** is an excellent place to grab a coffee or have a quick and inexpensive bite (take care to avoid bars on major tourist thoroughfares; prices go through the roof).

Bars offer any number of hot and cold sandwiches, drinks both alcoholic and non-, and *gelato*. **Tramezzini** come with an assortment of fillings, smothered in mayo, and surrounded by soft, de-crusted white bread, just like Mom used to make. Try the rolls and pizza bread stuffed with *prosciutto crudo* or *cotto* (ham either smoked or cooked), *formaggio* (cheese), or even *frittate* (omelettes); ask for them *scaldato* (heated). In smaller towns or close-knit neighborhoods, bars are both social and gastronomical centers. Children come for *gelato*, (see page 349 for more info) old men come for wine and conversation. When you buy something, pay for it at the cashier's desk first and take the receipt to the bartender, who will take your order.

The billing at Italian restaurants can also be a bit confusing. Most restaurants add a *pane e coperto* (cover charge) of about L2000 to the price of your meal, as well as a *servizio* (service charge) of 10-15%. In city restaurants, you may want to tip if the bill does not include service, but in family-run establishments without hired servers, tipping may give offense. In a bar, look for a sign stating either *servizio compreso* (service included) or *servizio non compreso* (not included). In the latter case, drop some cash into the kitty on the bar. *Caffè* prices are lower if you don't sit down. Proprietors at all shops will force you to take a *scontrino* or *ricevuta fiscale* (receipt) when you leave; they aren't being rude—it's required by law—so smile and dump it in the nearest *cestino* (trash can) once you leave.

Italy's rocky soil, warm climate, and hilly landscape have proven themselves ideal for growing grapes, and Italy produces more **wine** than any other country in the world. Wines from the north tend to be heavy and full-bodied; most touted (and expensive) are Piedmont's *barolo* and *barbera,* but the equally famous and more affordable *Asti spumante* deserves a swig. (The Piedmontese also claim to have invented vermouth.) Tuscany is regarded as Italy's wine-making capital; its rich *chianti,* similar to French burgundy, is a universal favorite. Other good heavy red wines include *salerno* from Naples and *valpolicella* from the Venetian district. White wine connoisseurs should sample *soave* from Verona, *frascati* from Rome, *orvieto* from Umbria, *lacrima Christi* (Christ's Tear) from Naples, and *tocai* and *pinot grigio* from Friuli. The hotter climate of southern Italy and the islands produces stronger, fruitier wines than the north. Try the Sicilian *marsala,* which resembles a light sherry, or *cannonau* from Sardinia.

You can usually order by the glass, carafe, or half-carafe, although bars rarely serve wine by the glass. *Secco* means "dry" and *abboccato* means "sweet." *Superiore* usually implies a higher alcohol content. When in doubt, request the local wine—it will be cheaper (typically around L3500 a liter) and best suited to the regional cuisine.

Don't ask, just drink (Italian wines explained)

Ever wondered just what, exactly, those wine names meant? Here's a quick guide: The Veneto region produces the sweet **Soave** ("gentle," "delicate") while Le Marche features a strangely-colored **Verdicchio** ("greenish-yellow") with an alcohol content to make up for the stomach-turning hue. Lombardy wins the contest, however, with the **Cortese** ("well-behaved") wine, the **Sangue di Giuda** ("blood of Judas"), and finally, the **Buttafuoco** (pronounced BOO-tah-foo-OH-koh and meaning "fire-thrower"). Some things just don't translate.

■■■ SPORTS AND RECREATION

In Italy, **il calcio** ("soccer" in the United States or "football" to those who can play it) far surpasses all other sports in popularity. Some claim that Italy's victory in the 1982 World Cup did more for national unity than any political movement; their near win in 1994 sparked a wave of excitement that crested with every victory and ultimately crashed with their defeat by Brazil. Every city and town has its own team, and major cities like Milan have more than one. Teams in the premier league pay huge sums to import the best players from around the world and pack their stadiums every Sunday. Italian football fans are called *tifosi*—that is, "typhoid-fevered."

Inter-urban rivalries—especially that between Naples and Rome—can easily become overheated. Catch a game in person if you have time; the fans are raucous and energetic, and make even the noisiest of American crowds seem tame.

Bicycling has long been popular in Italy. Besides manufacturing some of the best bikes in the world, Italians host the **Giro d'Italia,** a 25-day cross-country race in May. Professional **basketball** has also become a popular sport, importing players from the United States and other countries. As the only country to encompass the entire 1400-km arc of the Alps (and a comparable stretch of the Apennines), Italy attracts thousands of **skiers** from December to April. Summer skiing is available on glaciers, as is **hiking** and **mountain climbing** throughout the north and in the Sila Massif in Calabria. As Mediterranean pollution worsens, **swimming** has become rarer and riskier. Try the beaches in the less-populated deep south or on any of the Italian islands. Sardinia, for example, features crystal-blue waters with visibility as far down as 30m. For **horseback riding** information, contact the Federazione Italiana Sport Equestri, V. Tiziano, 70, Roma.

Every day of good weather from roughly 6 to 8pm in every medium-sized (i.e., not metropolitan) city, you can participate in one long-standing Italian tradition: the **passeggiata** (the promenade). It's nothing more than it sounds like—a walk—yet the whole town will dress up, come out, window shop, and mutually ogle. This open interaction continues at a lesser level through the night as most people spend their evening in the *piazza* talking, scoping, and eating *gelato.* It's a great, inexpensive way to pass the time and meet people.

■■■ FESTIVALS AND HOLIDAYS

Despite a dearth of national holidays, Italy suffers no shortage of town festivals. The most common excuse for a local festival is the celebration of a religious event—a patron saint's day, a miracle or two—all of which are enthusiastically celebrated. An unbelievable number of festivals occur Easter weekend. Most bizarre is Coculla's May celebration of *Festi di San Domenico Abate,* where people march through the city carrying a likeness of the saint draped with live snakes.

Less reptilian, though perhaps equally stomach-wrenching, is Italy's glut of jousting festivals—check out Arezzo, Ascoli Piceno, and Oristano (among others) during the late summer. Another medieval legacy, the Sienese *Palio,* features a bareback horse race in the town square, once in July and once in August. Other towns feature similar, less famous *Palii* (see index for page listings). On the third Sunday in July, Venetians commemorate the end of the plague epidemic of 1575 with a gondola procession and celebrate *Carnevale* in February with masks and some discreet street revelry. Carnevale action is much better in Ivrea, where anyone not wearing a red hat is likely to get dyed orange in the *Battle of Oranges.* Every June, Florence stages a soccer match with its players in 16th-century costume to commemorate Charles V's siege of the city.

Italy also hosts plenty of equally delicious food and art festivals. While food festivals and religious celebrations often end at nightfall, art festivals may span weeks or months. The month-long *Festival dei Due Mondi* (Festival of Two Worlds) in Spoleto, a delightful hodge-podge of classical art and cultural events, follows this trend. For a list of festivals, write to the **Italian Government Travel Office** (see page 5).

Take into account holidays, both legal and religious, when planning your itinerary. Banks, shops, and almost everything else shut down, but merriment abounds. Italy officially closes on the following dates: **January 1** (New Year's Day); **January 6** (Epiphany); **Easter Monday; April 25** (Liberation Day); **May 1** (Labor Day); **August 15** (Assumption of the Virgin); **November 1** (All Saints' Day); **December 8** (Immaculate Conception); **December 25** (Christmas Day); and **December 26** (Santo Stefano). Offices and shops in the following cities also shut down for feast days in honor of their respective patron saints: Venice (April 25, St. Mark); Florence, Genoa, and Turin (June 24, St. John the Baptist); Rome (June 29, SS. Peter and Paul); Palermo (July 15, Santa Rosalia); Naples (Sept. 19, St. Gennaro); Bologna (Oct. 4, St.

Petronio); Cagliari (Oct. 30, St. Saturnino); Trieste (Nov. 3, San Giusto); Bari (Dec. 6, St. Nicola); and Milan (Dec. 7, St. Ambrose). Be prepared for other surprises as well.

■■■ THE ITALIAN LANGUAGE

One of the six Romance languages, Italian has seduced lovers for centuries. It is not only a beautiful language, but also relatively easy to learn—especially if you already have some background in Spanish or French. Since Italians usually greet even a butchered attempt at pronunciation with appreciation and good-natured humor, it's worth the effort to learn a few simple phrases before you go. Be aware that in some particularly remote areas such as southern Italy, English is not spoken at all.

Modern Italian is a descendant of vulgar (spoken) Latin and was standardized in the late Middle Ages thanks to the literary triumvirate of Dante, Petrarch, and Boccaccio. All three wrote in the Tuscan dialect which, through its popularity with the educated classes, subsequently became the basis for today's **Italiano standard di lingua.** (In your travels, however, you should be entertained by every native's claim that his dialect is the "true" Italian.)

As a result of the country's past internal strife and fragmented history (Italy's wasn't united until 1861), the variations in **dialect** are particularly strong. The throaty Neapolitan can be extremely difficult for a northerner to understand; Ligurians use a mix of Italian, Catalàn, and French; Sardinian is considered a dialect related to but separate from Italian; and Sicilian ("mìtzica!") is more or less its own language. Some inhabitants of the northern border regions don't speak Italian at all: the population of Val d'Aosta speaks mainly French, and the people of Trentino-Alto-Adige harbor a German-speaking minority. In the southern regions of Calabria and Sicily, entire villages speak Albanian and Greek. The differences in speech are so significant that even native Italians are often confused when traveling around the country. Today, although most Italians still converse in local dialects at home, they also communicate in *Italiano standard.* This is taught and spoken at school and pervades the wonderful world of Italian television; listen to newscasters for the best version of accent-less, dialect-free standard Italian. In order to facilitate a conversation, natives often employ standard Italian when speaking with a foreigner.

Knowing a few basic terms will make your trip much easier. In the Appendices of your *Let's Go* you'll find a glossary of useful terms and phrases, as well as guidelines for pronunciation and stress. (See page 636.) Don't forget that **hand gestures** are a large part of the Italian conversation; some positions (like the tips of the fingers of one hand together pointing up; hand waved emphatically) punctuate conversations, while others (like the pointer finger on cheek, rotated back and forth) convey meaning ("yum!"). *"Boh"* is Italian for "I have no idea"; you'll hear it a lot in your travels. Also, take a more extensive phrase book with you (the *Barron's* book is fairly useful, and *Berlitz* has some handy phrases, though the vocabulary is geared toward business travelers) and practice before you leave.

Il Cornuto

Be sure **never** to make the sign of the *cornuto* ("the horn": pinkie and pointer finger extended, thumb and remaining fingers tucked under). Pointing it at someone is equivalent to insulting him/her and every mother figure he/she has ever had, and will cause you big trouble. Literally it means that he/she has been cheated on; culturally it means much, much more.

■■■ RECENT POLITICS

The chaos of Italian politics disillusions even its leaders. After three long years, Socialist **Bettino Craxi,** lamenting his inability to work with the Christian Democratic majority, resigned from the prime minister's chair in March 1987. After Craxi's fall, three Christian Democrats took office in quick succession. Then, following a rare period of relative stability, the musical chairs of Italian politics resumed in April 1992, when Prime Minister **Giulio Andreotti** resigned and President **Francesco Cossiga** announced his retirement. On May 27, 1992, after disputes over voting procedures, a fist-fight between the neo-fascists and Christian Democrats and ten days and fifteen rounds of voting that produced no majority, **Oscar Luigi Scalfaro** was finally elected Italy's new president, pledging his support for significant institutional reform of government, including a streamlining of the cabinet.

Since that time the slow and painful process of reforming electoral laws has resulted in "Tangentopoli" ("Kickback City"), an unprecedented political crisis in which over 2600 politicians have been implicated in corruption scandals. Reaction to the continued uncovering and prosecution of mass corruption has included such acts of violence as the May 1993 bombing of the Uffizi, Florence's premier art museum, and the "suicides" of ten indicted officials over the past three years, not to mention the unleashing of open Mafia retaliation against judges. Until the winter of 1994, right-wing **Prime Minister Silvio Berlusconi** (who moonlights as a billionaire publishing tycoon and owner of three national TV channels as well as of the ubiquitous STANDA supermarket chain), presided over a tenuous "Freedom Alliance" of three parties: his Forza Italia (the traditional rally cry for the Italian soccer team), the Northern League (Lega Nord), and the neo-fascist National Alliance. When the Northern League pulled out of the Alliance, Berlusconi lost his Parliamentary majority and was forced to resign. A temporary government of non-politicians runs the country, awaiting the October elections. By the time this book goes to print, anything may have happened.

Extra! Extra! Italian sports officials voted to cancel February 5 events in a protest of the **murder of a soccer fan** outside a Genoa stadium. The murder—a testament to the escalating soccer-related violence thought to be correlated with Italy's many so-called "ultras," militant neo–Nazis and Fascists—was the first incident of its kind in Italy since World War II.

ROME

Everything that can be said about Rome has already been said. Rather than be subjected to some pompous, overworked, purple prose that is plagued with the pretentiousness of charming *trattorie,* winding *vicoli,* friendly proprietors, the glory of the Roman Empire, airy *piazze,* sweeping panoramas, picturesque cityscapes, the *chic* of modern Italian culture, and baroque-Romanesque-rococo-bas-relief-terra-cotta *basiliche* with the pulchritudinous chapel on the left that you just can't miss, you are simply advised to visit Rome whenever you can, for as long as you possibly can—the Eternal City sure as hell ain't going anywhere.

■■■ GETTING THERE

BY PLANE
All roads lead to Rome, but you can fly there too.

Fiumicino (Leonardo da Vinci International Airport)
International, most domestic, and non-charter flights touch down at **Leonardo da Vinci International Airport** (tel. 659 51), referred to as **Fiumicino** for the coastal village in which it is located. Rome provides train service directly from Fiumicino to Rome's main train station, **Termini;** follow signs for *Treni* after leaving customs. The pedestrian bridge to the airport train station will be two floors up. Trains run to and from the airport from about 7am to 10pm; times are subject to change, but these trains generally leave once an hour. As of 1995, the last train leaving from Termini to Fiumicino is at 9:15pm, while the last leaving from Fiumicino to Termini leaves at 10:05pm. The price of a one way ticket is L13,000, and the trains leave from track #22 at Termini. At Fiumicino, tickets may be bought at the *tabaccaio* or the ticket booth, both on the right as you enter the airport train station. At Termini, tickets may be bought in the **Alitalia** office right next to the track (there's a sign that says, *"biglietti per Fiumicino"*). Vending machines on Via Marsala also sell tickets.

The **Tiburtina-Fiumicino** train line also goes to the airport from Rome, but do not get the two lines confused: the Tiburtina line does not stop at Termini. Most of the stops on this line are not particularly helpful to tourists, since they are not near the city center. The advantages to the Tiburtina-Fiumicino line are that it's less expensive (L7000 one way) and that it leaves more often—every 20 minutes from 6am until 10pm. Unless you know exactly what you're doing, you will probably find the Termini line more convenient. If you do take the Tiburtina line and need to reach Termini, get off at **Ostiense;** it is only steps away from the Piramide stop on the Metro Linea B, which you can take in the direction of Rebibbia to arrive at Termini. You can also get off at the last stop, Tiburtina, and then transfer to Metro Linea B to get to Termini.

Early/Late Flights
Don't fly into Rome late at night or early in the morning if you can help it. If you do arrive at the airport during the time in which no trains run to Termini (10pm-7am), don't panic. You can take a **COTRAL bus** from **Fiumicino** (one leaves each hour from 11:30pm-6am) to **Tiburtina station** where you then take the **42N bus** to **Termini.** Follow these directions in reverse if you need to go to the airport from Termini after hours. Or, take a cab; despite the expense, it's worth avoiding the hassle.

Ciampino
Most charter and a few domestic flights arrive at **Ciampino** airport (tel. 79 49 41). From here take the blue COTRAL bus to the Anagnina stop on Metro Linea A of the

Metropolitana (L1500; departures every 30min. from 6am-11:30pm). Linea A takes you to Termini, the Spanish Steps, or the Vatican. Ciampino is inside Rome's city limits; do not allow a taxi driver to charge you the long-distance supplement.

BY TRAIN

Stazione Termini, the transportation hub of Rome, is the focal point of most train and both subway lines. The various stations on the fringes of town (**Tiburtina, Trastevere, Ostiense, San Lorenzo, Roma Nord, Prenestina**), where you may but probably won't end up, are connected by bus and/or subway to Termini. Be particularly wary of pickpockets in and around the train stations. For more tips on how to avoid theft, see the section on Safety And Security, page 20.

In Termini, the crowded **railway information** and **Eurail offices** are at the opposite end of the trains in the station, facing the buses, near Piazza del Cinquecento. Train reservations must be made in person. The EPT **tourist information** booth (tel. 482 04 78 or 482 12 70) is inside between tracks #2 and 3 (open daily 8:15am-7:15pm). For items lost or stolen on the train try the **Oggetti Smarriti** office far down track #22 (tel. 473 06 02) or find the **police** on the same track (tel. 481 95 61 or 488 25 88; open 24 hrs.). For theft inside the station, find the **carabinieri** to the right of the tourist office (between tracks 1 and 2). Improve the odds against theft by using the **waiting room** along track #1 when you can. **Luggage storage** is available along tracks #1 and 22 (open daily 5am-1am; L1500 per piece per day). If you need to freshen up between journeys, the **Albergo Diurno** (tel. 48 48 19), downstairs, provides showers (L10,000), baths (L12,000), and a barber, manicurist, and pedicurist (L11,000-18,000). Sheets, towels, and soap are available for modest fees.

Second class seats to/from: **Florence** (2-3 hrs., L24,400, sup. L18,000); from: **Venice** (5 hrs., L44,100, sup. L17,600), **Naples** (2¼ hrs., L17,200, sup. L9700), **Milan** (5 hrs., L47,700, sup. L18,500), **Bologna** (3¼-4 hrs., L33,400, sup. L13,400), **Brindisi** (7-8hrs., L47,700, sup. L18,500), and **Palermo** (12hrs., L68,900, sup. L23,700).

BY CAR

To drive in Italy, you need to get an International Driver's Permit or an official translation of your driver's license before you leave home. See page 14 for more info. Those entering Rome by car approach the city center by way of the **Grande Raccordo Anulare (GRA)**, the beltway that encircles Rome. You can take any of several exits into the city. If you are coming from the north, enter on **Via Flaminia, Via Salaria**, or **Via Nomentana**. At all costs, avoid **Via Cassia;** the ancient two-chariot lanes weren't intended for modern-day traffic. **Via Tiburtina**, to the east, is even worse. Follow the Grande Raccordo around to **Via del Mare** to the south, which connects Rome with **Lido di Ostia**. When leaving the city, don't try to follow the green **Autostrada per Firenze** signs; get on the Grande Raccordo instead and follow it around; it's longer but faster. From the south, **Via del Mare** and **Via Pontina** are the most direct leads to the coastal road from Naples. From the Adriatic coast, take **Via Appia Nuova** or **Via Tuscolana** off the southeastern quadrant of the Raccordo.

■■■ GETTING AROUND

BY BUS AND TRAM

Rome's extensive bus system is a surprisingly efficient means of traversing the city. Though the network of routes may seem daunting at first, the **ATAC** (Aziende Tramvie Autobus Comunali) intra-city bus company (tel. 469 51) has ubiquitous booths and a friendly staff who can help you find your way. The more independent may want to buy the in-depth Roma Metro-Bus map, published by Lozzi and available at almost all newsstands for L7000. Each bus stop (*fermata*) is marked by yellow signs listing all routes that stop there, key streets/stops on those routes, and routes with nighttime service (*servizio notturno*). Regular service route numbers are marked by red shields. Some buses run only on weekdays (*feriali*) or weekends

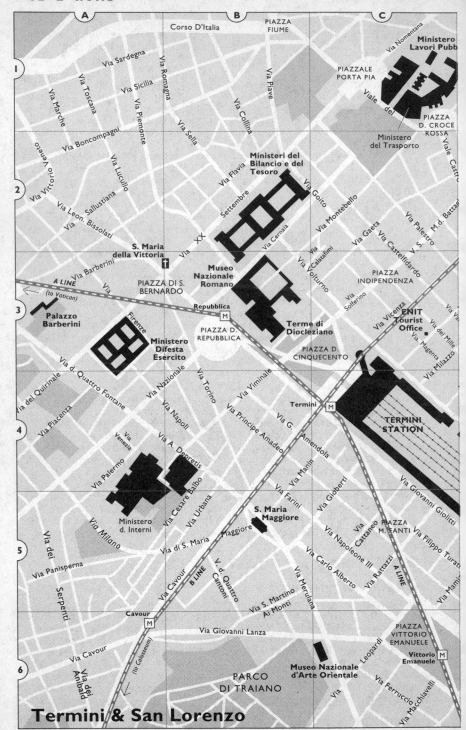

Termini & San Lorenzo

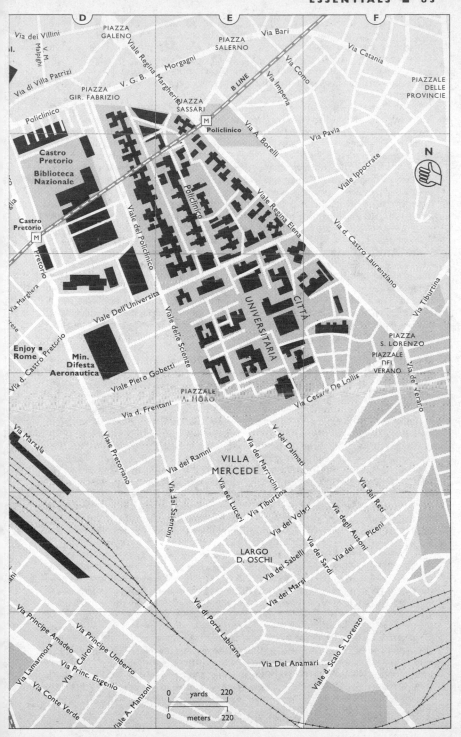

(festivi), while others may have different routes, depending on the day of the week. Hours of service vary, but most begin around 5 or 6am and end at midnight.

Night routes (notturno) are indicated by black shields on the newer signs, by the letter N following the number, or both. Signal a night bus to stop by standing right under its sign and motioning with your arm. Don't depend too heavily on *notturno* buses; they run infrequently and you may have to transfer several times to get where you want to go.

Tickets are available at newsstands, *tabacchi,* and kiosks for L1500 each. **Board from the back door of the bus (not from the middle or front) then immediately stamp the ticket in the orange machine at the back;** the ticket is then good for any number of transfers over the next 90 minutes. If you exceed 90 minutes during your last ride, stamp the other end of the ticket. Many people take advantage of ATAC's honor system and ride the bus without a validated ticket or bus pass. This is against the law and inadvisable; Roman transportation officials arbitrarily board buses and issue L50,000 fines to passengers not carrying a validated ticket or pass. If you don't have the cash on you, the inspectors will take you to a police station until you can arrange to pay. Playing dumb tourist will make things worse. Buy a number of tickets during the day, since they are difficult to come by at night and on weekends. After midnight, ticket salesmen ride the buses and will sell you a ticket on board.

COTRAL bus service between Rome and the province of **Lazio** (tel. 591 55 51) has moved its departure points outside of the city proper to facilitate traffic; you need to take the subway to an outlying area and catch the bus from there. Take **Anagnina** (last stop on Linea A Metro) for Frascati and the Colli Albani; **Rebibbia** (last stop on Linea B Metro) for Tivoli and Subiaco; **Lepanto** (last stop on Linea A before Ottaviano) for Cerveteri, Tarquinia, Bracciano, Lago Vico, and Civitavecchia. *Let's Go* lists specific transportation information in the Lazio section. For information, call CTS (tel. 467 91) or any travel agency where English is spoken.

BY SUBWAY

The two lines of the subway (*Metropolitana*) intersect at Termini and can be reached by the stairway inside the station, as well as by numerous entrances around the station. Entrances to all stations are marked on the street by a white "M" on a red square. **Linea A** runs from Ottaviano, near the Vatican, through P. di Spagna, P. Barberini, P. della Repubblica, and Termini, before heading to Anagnina and intervening stops in the southeastern suburbs of the city. **Linea B** runs from Rebibbia in the northeastern suburbs, through the university area around P. Bologna, to Termini, then on to the Colosseum, the Testaccio area at the Piramide stop, and Magliana (change here for trains to Ostia and the beach) before terminating at Laurentina in EUR. The subway is fairly safe, but guard your valuables. The stops on the city's outskirts are often deserted, even in the middle of the day, so use caution. Though many of Rome's sights are a trek from the nearest subway stop, the subway beats the bus when you need to cover large distances quickly, especially during the day, during protests, and during rush hour. Remember that the subway does not run after 11:30pm.

Tickets are L1500 and can be bought in newsstands, *tabacchi,* at coin-operated machines, and some machines that accept bills in the stations. Not all Metropolitana stations have open ticket booths, so keep an extra ticket or two handy. Unlike on the bus, it is often impossible to board the subway without a ticket. Trains to Ostia and the Lido beach, as well as many of the outlying suburbs not on the A and B lines, are not part of the subway and require a separate ticket.

Bus and Subway Passes

If you will be in Rome for more than a few weeks, consider purchasing the *abbonamento mensile,* which allows one month (beginning the first of that month) of unlimited transport on the buses and subways for L50,000. Ask for a *tessera* (pass), anywhere bus and subway tickets are sold. Student bus passes are cheaper, but are only for Italian students or foreign students at Italian university who hold a special document from ATAC stating their financial need for such a pass. Non-Italian students can buy the pass and may get by the bus ticket patrol with the student pass, but if officials are in a bad mood, those carrying the student pass without the proper documentation will have to pay a hefty fine. **Weekly bus/metro passes** are also available at the ATAC booth in Piazza del Cinquecento in front of Termini (on the left, near the cab stand, with your back to the station) for L24,000. The BIG **daily bus/subway ticket,** also on sale at this booth, costs L6000.

BY TAXI

Taxis are a viable but expensive option. On call 24 hrs., they can be flagged down en route, but are more easily found at taxi stands. Stands can be found in Piazza Sonnino on Viale Trastevere (right near the Ponte Garibaldi and next-door to McDonald's), at Piazza Venezia, Piazza della Repubblica, Via Nazionale, and at Piazza del Popolo, as well as many other places throughout the city. Ride only in yellow or white taxis, and make sure your taxi has a meter; that way you'll know that you're being legally robbed. Official rates are L7500 for the first 3km or a waiting period of 9 minutes, then L1500 per km. Night surcharge L3000; Sunday surcharge L1000; luggage L500 per piece—small parcels and lap dogs excluded. Radio taxis (tel. 35 70 or 66 45 or 49 94 or 881 77). Taxis between the city center and the airport cost around L70,000. Despite what the meter reads, most taxi drivers claim a minimum charge of L60,000 for trips to and from the airport.

BY CAR

We hesitate to comment on the sanity of any traveler wishing to get around Rome by car. But if the thought of aggressive drivers, weaving antics of moped maniacs, and suicide squads of pedestrians fails to unnerve you, you'll learn. Parking is expensive and difficult to find, and if you don't keep your eyes peeled for the little signs, you may drive into a car-free zone and incur a fine. Gas (*benzina*) costs four times as much in Italy as in the U.S. (approximately L1600-1700 per liter). Contact **TCI (Touring Club Italiano),** Via Marsala, 14 (tel. 491 17 41), inside the shopping arcade, for regional maps, guides, and books (in Italian) of Italy. (Open Mon.-Fri. 9am-1pm and 4-7pm.) There's a branch office at Via Ovidio, 7/A (tel. 687 44 32; open 9am-1pm and 2:30-5:30pm).

If you're still game to rent, Avis, Hertz, Maggiore, and Europcar all operate booths on the east side of Termini. Arrangements can be made with the firms' booths or their city headquarters (over the phone or in person). By calling the central reservation numbers you can arrange to rent a car in Rome or in any part of Italy. English is spoken at all locations.

Maggiore, Main office (tel. 22 93 51), info only; Termini (tel. 488 37 15), open Mon.-Sat. 7am-7pm; Fiumicino (tel. 65 01 06 78), open 8am-11pm; toll-free national number (tel. (167) 86 70 67), open Mon.-Fri. 8:30am-6:30pm.
Avis, Termini (tel. 470 12 19), open Mon.-Fri. 7am-8pm, Sat. 8am-6pm, Sun. 8am-1pm; main office, P. Esquilino 1C, by phone only (tel. 470 14 00); Fiumicino office (tel. 65 01 15 31), open 7am-midnight.
Hertz, Termini (tel. 474 03 89; fax 474 67 05); Fiumicino (tel. 65 01 14 48 or 65 01 15 53); toll-free national number (tel. (167) 82 20 99).
Europcar, Termini (tel. 488 28 54), open Mon.-Fri. 7am-8pm, Sat. 8am-6pm; Fiumicino (tel. 65 01 09 77), open 7am-11pm; toll-free number (tel. (167) 01 44 10).

BY BIKE OR MOPED

Rome's many hills, cobblestone streets, dense traffic, and lunatic drivers make most areas of the city less than ideal for bikes and mopeds. In some sections, however, bikes can be a perfect way to explore; bike rides around Rome's parks are a welcome relief from a city of stone. A ride down the Appian Way, though quite dangerous, may be the best way to see the many monuments and the long stretches of countryside between them. Bike rental costs around L5000 per hour or around

L15,000 per day, but the length of a "day" varies according to the shop's hours. In summer, try the unmarked stands at P. di San Lorenzo at Via del Corso or Via di Pontifici at Via del Corso. Both are located near P. di Spagna (and are open from 10am-1am). Also look for *"Noleggio Bicicletta"* signs around the city, at P. di Spagna metro stop, at P. Sidney Sonnino off Viale Trastevere, and in Villa Borghese. Rome is definitely not the place to take your first moped or scooter ride, but moped aficionados can rent mopeds and scooters for between L50,000 and L85,000 a day. You need to be at least 16 years old, but you don't need a driver's license. **Practice safe cycling and always wear a helmet.**

I Bike Rome, Via Veneto, 156 (tel. 322 52 40), rents from the Villa Borghese's underground parking garage. The subterranean entrance is near the intersection of Via di S. Paolo del Brasile and Via della Magnolie. Bikes L5000 per hour, L13,000 per day, L38,000 per week. Tandems, too. Mopeds L30,000 per 4 hrs., L45,000 per day. Open daily 9am-8pm.

Scooters for Rent, Via della Purificazione, 84 (tel. 488 54 85), off P. Barberini. Bicycles L15,000 per day, L80,000 per week. Mopeds L50,000 per day. Vespas L60,000 per day. You can get cheaper gas elsewhere. Open Mon.-Sat. 9am-7pm, Sun. 9am-6pm. AmEx, MC, Visa.

■■■ ORIENTATION

In his *Early History of Rome,* Livy concluded that "the layout of Rome is more like a squatter's settlement than a properly planned city." Two thousand years of city-planning later, Rome is still a splendid, unnavigable sea of one-way streets, dead-ends, clandestine *piazze,* incongruous monuments, and incurable traffic. Getting lost is inevitable, but it is also the best way to get a sense of the city.

No longer defined by the Seven Hills, modern Rome sprawls over a large area between the hills of the **Castelli Romani** and the beach at **Ostia.** The central sights, however, lie within a much smaller compass. Rome was initially built to be traversed on foot. From Termini Station, the arrival point for most visitors to Rome, the **Città Universitaria** and the student area of **San Lorenzo** are to the east and northeast, respectively, while to the south are S. Giovanni and the seedy but historic Esquiline hill, home to some of the oldest, biggest, and most beautiful churches in the city. Many of the major tourist sights slope down between the hills to the west and southwest toward the Tiber. **Via Nazionale** is the central artery connecting Termini with the city center. At one end is Piazza della Repubblica; the other end of Via Nazionale is connected by Via IV Novembre and Via C. Battisti to the immense **Piazza Venezia,** crowned by the conspicuous white marble pile of the **Vittorio Emanuele II Monument.** From Piazza Venezia, Via dei Fori Imperiale leads southeast to the **Forum** and **Colosseum,** south of which are the ruins of the **Circus Maximus, the Baths of Caracalla,** and **the Appian Way. Via del Corso** stretches north from Piazza Venezia to **Piazza del Popolo** and the neighboring **Pincio.** East of the Corso, fashionable streets border the **Piazza di Spagna** and, beyond that, the lush **Villa Borghese.** South and east are the **Trevi Fountain, Piazza Barberini,** and the churches of the Quirinal Hill. From Piazza Venezia to the west, **Largo Argentina** marks the start of the Corso Vittorio Emanuele II, which leads into the *centro storico,* the medieval and Renaissance tangle of alleys, towers, churches, and fountains around the **Pantheon, Piazza Navona, Campo de' Fiori,** and **Piazza Farnese,** before crossing the Tiber to gargantuan **Castel Sant'Angelo** and the **Vatican City.** Also across the Tiber from the *centro storico* is the **Trastevere** quarter, home to countless *trattorie* and the best streets through which one can wander. Back across the Tiber from Trastevere, via the Tiber Island, is the old **Jewish Ghetto.** To the south of the Ghetto and the Ancient City are the peaceful **Aventine Hill,** crowned with rose gardens and churches, and the earthy, working-class **Testaccio** district.

■■■ PRACTICAL INFORMATION

TOURIST OFFICES

In addition to the tourist offices listed below, you may also take advantage of the **Info-Tourism Boxes,** kiosks conveniently set up in the historic center. (Open Tues.-Sat. 10am-6pm and Sun. 10am-1pm.) Locations include those at Largo Carlo Goldoni (tel. 687 50 27), off Via del Corso, across from Via dei Condotti; Largo Corrado Ricci (tel. 678 09 92) near the Colosseum; and on Via Nazionale (tel. 474 59 29), near the Palazzo delle Esposizioni.

Enjoy Rome, Via Varese, 39, 00185 Roma (tel. 445 18 43; fax 445 07 34). From Termini station, cross Via Marsala (adjacent to the station to the right as you exit the train terminal), and head 3 blocks up to Via Varese. The hip and friendly English-speaking owners, Fulvia and Pierluigi, will handle your questions and concerns with kindness and care. They'll aid with hotel accommodations, short and long-term apartment rentals (for the price of 1 week's rent surcharge for long-term accommodations), as well as walking, cycling, and bus tours throughout the city. Very warm and solicitous, they'll even book you a cab back to the airport. In summer open Mon.-Fri. 8:30am-7pm, Sat. 8:30am-1:30pm; in winter Mon.-Fri. 8:30am-1:30pm and 3:30-6:30pm, Sat. 8:30am-1:30pm. Emergency calls taken Mon.-Sat. until 10pm.

EPT Tourist Office (tel. 487 12 70 or 48 89 92 53), at the Termini Station in front of track #2. Lines can be horrendous. **Central Office,** Via Parigi, 5 (tel. 48 89 91 or 48 89 92 53; fax 481 93 16). Walk left from the station diagonally across P. Cinquecento (filled with buses) and cross P. della Repubblica. Via Parigi originates on the other side of the *basilica,* at the Grand Hotel. English spoken. Open Mon.-Sat. 8:15am-7:15pm. At any office, pick up a map and copies of *Romamor.* If you will be traveling in the region around Rome, also ask for *Alberghi di Roma e Provincia,* which lists all accommodations registered with the EPT.

ENIT, Via Marghera, 3 (tel. 497 12 82); as you exit the tracks at Termini, head to your right—turn right onto Via Marsala, and take your first left onto Via Marghera; it's 2 blocks down on the left, across the street from the right hand end of the shopping arcade. Some info on Rome, but mostly brochures and hotel listings for the rest of Lazio, Italy's provinces, and major cities. Open Mon.-Fri. 9am-5:30pm.

BUDGET TRAVEL ORGANIZATIONS

Centro Turistico Studentesco (CTS), Via Genova, 16 (tel. 467 91), off Via Nazionale, about halfway between P. della Repubblica and P. Venezia. Open Mon.-Fri. 9am-1pm and 4-7pm, Sat. 9am-1pm. Another office at Via degli Ausoni, 5 (tel. 445 01 41), open Mon.-Fri. 10am-6:30pm, Sat. 10am-1pm. Branch offices at Termini at track #22 (tel. 467 92 54; open 8:30am-8:30pm); at Via Appia Nuova, 434 (tel. 780 84 49; open 9:30am-1pm, 3-7pm); at Corso Vittorio Emanuele II, 297 (tel. 687 26 72); and at Terminal Ostiense (tel. 574 79 50; open 9am-1pm, 2-6pm). ISIC and YIEE cards L20,000 each. (Bring ID photo and proof of student status.) *Cartaverde,* available to those under 26, offers a year of 30% discounts on trains within or originating in Italy (L40,000). Discount travel reservations and tickets, a free map, and currency exchange. Accommodations service, including out-of-town reservations, arranged for free. Bulletin boards post info on rides, companionship, special services, etc. Lines can be veerrry slow; if info is all you need, it's better to phone (info tel. 467 91). Excellent English spoken at all locations.

Compagnia Italiana di Turismo (CIT), P. della Repubblica, 64 (tel. 474 65 55; fax 481 82 77). A national travel agency that books discount train tickets and tours. Open Mon.-Fri. 9am-1pm and 2-5:30pm.

Italian Youth Hostels Association (Associazione Italiana Alberghi per la Gioventù), HI-IYHA, Via Cavour, 44 (tel. 487 11 52; fax 488 04 92). Provides plenty of advice and a list of hostels throughout Italy. IYHA cards L30,000. Open Mon.-Thurs. 7:30am-5pm, Fri. 7:30am-3pm, Sat. 8am-noon.

OTHER SERVICES

Police: tel. 113.**Carabinieri:** tel. 112. **Ufficio Stranieri** (Foreigner's Office), Via Genova, 2 (tel. 46 86 29 28). English spoken. Report thefts here in person. Open 24 hrs. **Police Headquarters (Questura),** Via San Vitale, 15 (tel. 468 61). **Railway Police,** on track #1 in Termini (tel. 481 95 61).

Post Office: P. San Silvestro, 19, 00186 Roma (tel. 67 71), between P. di Spagna and the Corso. Stamps are at booths #31-33, *fermo posta* at #65. Currency exchange (*cambio;* no checks) is at booths #25-28. (Open Mon.-Fri. 8:25am-7:40pm, Sat. 8:20-11:50am. Exchange open Mon.-Fri. 8:25am-5:30pm, Sat. 8:20-11:50am.) Branch offices dot the city but most are open only in the morning. **Vatican City** is said to run a more efficient post office. The generic **postal code** for Rome is 00100; other codes are variations on the 001XX theme.

Telephones: Telecom (SIP), in the Villa Borghese parking lot, accessible from Via Veneto. Open daily 8am-9:30pm. Booths throughout the city. Phone cards, or *carte telefoniche,* are on sale in *tabbacai,* newsstands, and post offices.

Currency Exchange: Large banks including **Banco d'Italia, Banca Nazionale del Lavoro,** and **Banca di Roma** operate throughout the city. **Termini** has many *cambi,* usually with low rates and/or high commissions. Avoid the machines that trade *lire* for your foreign banknotes. To get a cash advance on a credit card, try Banca Nazionale del Lavoro on Via Veneto or any of the **ATMs** on Via Arenula, near the Pantheon, and on Via del Tritone. To use your PLUS or Cirrus cash card, cross your fingers and head to Banca Nazionale del Lavoro.

American Express: P. di Spagna, 38, Roma 00187 (tel. 722 82; lost or stolen cards: toll-free 24 hrs. tel. (167) 86 40 46; lost or stolen traveler's checks: toll-free 24 hrs. tel. (167) 87 20 00). Chaotic at times, but fairly efficient, and perfect English is spoken. Mail held free for 30 days for traveler's check- and cardholders. Mail can be forwarded for a L7000 fee on arrival, or by airmail with prepaid postage. Messages can be left in the office in a stamped envelope for L2000. Excellent maps of Rome are free. Open Mon.-Fri. 9am-5:30pm, Sat. 9am-12:30pm.

Lost Property: Oggetti Rinvenuti, Via Nicolò Bettoni, 1 (tel. 581 60 40), near the Trastevere train station. Open Mon.-Fri. 8:30-4pm, Sat. 8:30-11:30am. **Termini,** at track #22 (tel. 473 06 02). Open daily 7am-11pm. **ATAC,** Via Volturno, 65 (tel. 469 51). Open Mon.-Fri. 9am-noon and 2-5pm. Also check at your **embassy** and with the police (listed below).

Laundromat: OndaBlu, Via Principe Amedeo, 70/b, off Via Cavour 2 blocks south of Termini. Also Via Milazzo, 8, off Via Marsala. Wash L6000 per 6½kg load (40 min.). Dry L6000 for 20 min.

Athletic Club: Roman Sport Center, Via del Galoppatoio, 33 (tel. 361 43 58) in Villa Borghese. Also at Largo Somalia, 60 (tel. 86 21 24 11). One-day use of weight room, pool, sauna, Turkish baths, aerobics classes, and squash courts costs L25,000 per person. Open Mon.-Sat. 9am-10pm.

Bookstores: Economy Book and Video Center, Via Torino, 136 (tel. 474 68 77), off Via Nazionale. Open Mon.-Fri. 9am-8pm, Sat. 9am-2pm; Oct.-May Mon. 2-8pm, Tues.-Sat. 9am-8pm. **Anglo-American Bookshop,** Via della Vite, 102 (tel. 679 52 52). Steps from P. di Spagna. Open Mon.-Fri. 9am-1pm and 4-8pm, Sat. 9am-1pm. **Open Door Bookshop,** Via della Lungaretta, 25 (tel. 271 69 00), off Viale Trastevere. Paperbacks of all languages and a fax machine, too (L4000 1st page, L2000 per additional page, plus phone charges). Also rents videos (L8000 per day with L50,000 deposit). Open Mon. 4-8pm, Tues.-Sat. 10am-1pm and 4-8pm.

Women's Bookstore: Al Tempo Ritrovato, Piazza Farnese, 103 (tel. 68 80 37 49), off Campo dei Fiori. There is a small section of English books about Italian and European feminism and politics, as well as American women's writing and lesbian literature. Bookstore open Mon.-Sat. 10am-1pm and 4-8pm; Oct.- May Mon.-Sat. 10am-8pm.

Feminist Center: Via San Francesco di Sales, 1a (tel. 686 42 01), off Via della Lunghera in Trastevere. Seminars, cultural events, and lesbian archives.

Community Bulletin Boards: Lion Bookshop, Via del Babuino, 181. **Cinema Pasquino,** Vicolo del Piede in Trastevere. **All Saints Anglican Church,** Via del Babuino, 153. Also check the area around the **university** for apartment listings, English-tutoring jobs, Italian tutors, and other services.

Late-Night Pharmacies: (tel. 19 21 for recorded listings in Italian). *La Repubblica* and *Il Messaggero* newspapers publish a list of pharmacies open in Aug., and the closed pharmacies usually post a list. In Aug., try the following: **Farmacia Grieco,** Piazza della Repubblica, 67 (tel. 488 04 10 or 48 38 61), steps from Termini. Open 24 hrs. **Farmacia Piram,** Via Nazionale, 228 (tel. 488 07 54). Open 24 hrs. **Farmacia Risorgimento,** P. Risorgimento, 44 (tel. 37 22 157).
Hospitals: Rome-American Hospital, Via Emilio Longoni, 69 (tel. 225 51 or 225 33 33). Private emergency and laboratory services. English-speaking physician on call 24 hrs. **Policlinico Umberto I,** Viale di Policlinico, 255 (tel. 499 71), near Termini. Take Metro Linea B to the Policlinico stop. A free public facility. Open 24 hrs. **Dental Hospital: G. Eastman,** Viale Regina Elena, 287/B (tel. 445 01 66). On call 24 hrs. every day. Call in the morning for an appointment in the afternoon. Check *Wanted in Rome* or *Metropolitan* for English-speaking dentists in private practices. **Red Cross:** Via Antonio Pacinotti, 18 (tel. 55 10), in Piazza della Radio. Offers **ambulance** service and a refreshment stand.
Emergency Lines: First Aid (Pronto Soccorso): 118. **Fire:** tel. 115. **Road Assistance:** tel. 116. **Anti-Violence Hotline:** tel. 683 26 90 or 683 28 20, Mon.-Fri. 10am-1pm and 4-7pm. Italian only.

TOURING TIPS

Getting lost in the streets of Rome can be either the most frustrating or enjoyable part of your stay. Rome's greatest treasures often lie hidden in the perplexing tangle of streets: the Pantheon emerges quite suddenly as you wind your way through the narrow *vie* and Bramante's Tempietto sits in the small courtyard of a lonely church.

Travel schedules and timetables are often unreliable, so it's best to call ahead whenever possible. Don't forget that much of the city will shut down during the Italian lunch "hour" from about 1pm to 3:30 or 4pm. Most shops and offices are open weekdays and Saturdays from approximately 9am-1pm and 4-8pm (in winter 3:30-7:30pm). Most shops, businesses, and some *caffè* shut down on Sundays and Monday mornings, while restaurants, tourist organizations, some department stores, supermarkets, and nearly everything on Via del Corso remain open for business. In the summer, some shops may also close on Saturday afternoon. Don't forget that **food stores** (*alimentari*) are usually closed on Thursday afternoons. Plan your day strategically; important business (money changing, travel plans) should be dealt with first thing in the morning, museums and sights until the afternoon, and then, if you haven't drifted off to sleep yourself, sights that don't observe *siesta*, such as the Forum, Colosseum, and the seven major *basiliche* (including Santa Maria Maggiore, San Giovanni in Laterano, and St. Peter's).

Numerous companies organize bus and walking tours in the city. Try **Carrani Tours** (tel. 474 25 01), **Appian Line** (tel. 488 41 51), and **American Express** (tel. 676 41) for bus tours and tour packages that include Papal encounters, dinner, and entertainment. For walking tours call **Secret Walks in Rome** (tel. 39 72 87 28) or Enjoy Rome (tel. 445 18 43). Rome's beloved transportation authority, **ATAC**, also offers a no-frills, 3-hour circuit of the city, leaving from P. dei Cinquecento (Bus #110, daily at 3:30pm, winter and holidays at 2:30pm; L15,000). You can also take bus #119 for an orienting glance at some of the city's more visible monuments.

Finally, a note on **safety:** Rome is congested day and night with lost, bewildered, and distracted tourists, each loaded with cash and valuables. The thieving hordes are especially thick around the Forum and the Colosseum and on crowded buses like the #64 and 492. At night, women and men will generally feel safe walking through the center of town during all but the darkest hours. Outside the *centro storico* (historic center), however, use caution. The areas around Termini and to its south (especially near Piazza Vittorio Emanuele II and the Oppian Hill, notorious drug areas) and around Testaccio deserve special care; the area north of the city center near the Olympic Village also requires extra vigilance. Women should consult the section on women travelers in Essentials, page 33.

■■■ ACCOMMODATIONS

In July and August, Rome swells with tourists. A huge quantity of rooms meets this demand, but quality ranges significantly and hotel prices are often astronomical. Though reservations help, they do not always guarantee that a room awaits you for the full length of your intended stay or at the agreed price; some proprietors give precedence to large groups. Make sure the hotel charges you no more than the price posted on the back of your room's door; it's the law.

The **tourist offices** in Rome will scrounge (sometimes reluctantly in peak season) to find you a room. They offer a list of hotels and their prices, and also quote rates over the phone. The main office, at Via Parigi, 5, is the most helpful. They can also provide a booklet of current official prices for all of the hotels and *pensioni* in Rome—the maximum rates allowed by law. The **Centro Turistico Studentesco e Giovanile (CTS)** will be of some help, and the **Enjoy Rome** agency will be both helpful and informative all the time. **Associazione Cattolica Internazionale al Servizio della Giovane,** Via Urbana, 158 (tel. 488 14 19), assists women age 25 or younger in finding lodging in religious institutions.

Termini is full of "officials" swarming around to find you a place. Many of them are the real thing and have photo IDs issued by the tourist office. Some sneaky impostors issue themselves fake badges and cards, and they will likely direct you to a rundown location charging significantly more than the going rate. Ask the officials for maps and directions, but exercise caution.

If you're too timid to call and bargain for rooms yourself, employ Enjoy Rome's help. **Always insist on seeing a room first,** though some proprietors are not always amenable. Check the mattresses, the bathroom, and the water pressure. Check the security; test the locks, ask about the curfew, check how accessible the room-keys are to other guests or passers-by, and find out whether someone monitors the front desk at all times. Inquire about additional costs. Some hotels charge for hot showers, heat (if they have it; check in winter), private bathrooms, and breakfast; if you don't want a certain feature, make this clear.

It is illegal and just plain stupid to "camp out" in the public places of Rome. Though violent crime is infrequent, dozing tourists beg for trouble. If you must, sleep in groups with designated sentry watches in Termini (check your bags at the station's luggage storage room or risk serious material loss). Ask at the tourist office for a list of day-hotels. **Women, whether alone or in a group, should never sleep outdoors.** Be careful, even at designated campgrounds.

NORTH OF TERMINI

There are plenty of clean and reasonable *pensioni* and hotels awaiting the weary traveler within five to 15 minutes of Termini. Although once somewhat run-down, the area has recently experienced a renaissance of sorts, making it a trendy haven for budget travelers, cheaper than the historic center to the west and safer than the seedy Esquiline area south of Termini. The area's grid-like layout makes it more navigable than the older parts of the city. The big blue BNL (Banca Nazionale del Lavoro) sign outside the station indicates north. Small **alimentari** line Via Marghera and Via Marsala. A convenient laundromat, **Ondablu,** at Via Milazzo, 8, is equipped with English instructions; wash and dry 6kg for L12,000 (open daily 8am-10pm).

> **Pensione Papa Germano,** Via Calatafimi, 14A (tel. 48 69 19). With the trains behind you, exit the station to your right and turn left on Via Marsala, which shortly becomes Via Volturno; Via Calatafimi will be on your right. Though their last name might indicate otherwise, Papà Gino and Mamma Pina run this place with pure Italian warmth. Deservedly popular with backpackers and students. Reservations are encouraged during summer. Gino speaks English and will help you find a place if he's booked; he may also try to match lone travelers with others to fill a room. Cheerful flowered walls and bedspreads. No curfew. Singles L35,000. Doubles L60,000, with bath L75,000. Triples with bath L90,000. Quads L23,000 per person. 10% reduction Nov.-March. AmEx, MC, Visa.

Pensione Fawlty Towers (formerly Il Nido), Via Magenta, 39 (tel. 445 03 74). Turn right off Via Marghera, which crosses Via Marsala near the station's exit. You won't find Polly running around trying to cover for Manuel who has lost "Basil, the rat." Instead, an enthusiastic English-speaking staff runs this hostel-like backpacker's haven with genuine affection. The communal porch/terrace is so peacefully detached from the chaos of Roman life that you might forget you're only a block away from Termini. A satellite TV in the living room provides cable. The bathrooms are newly renovated and meticulously maintained. People are put together in rooms of three or four, but doubles and singles are available at slightly higher rates. No curfew. In summer L22,000 per person, L25,000 in room with private shower. In winter L18,000 per person, L21,000 with shower. International staff, including the personable owners of Enjoy Rome. Linen included.

✓ **Hotel Matilde,** Via Villafranca, 20 (tel./fax 445 43 65), off Via S. Martino della Battaglia (what Via Solferino becomes when it crosses P. Indipendenza). Newly opened by the Riccioni brothers of Pensione Jonella, this young, energetic, freshly painted establishment is decorated with frescoes and has a safe in each of its spotless rooms. Staff will help find restaurants, nightlife, and even discounts for parking. No curfew. Singles L50,000. Doubles L80,000. AmEx, MC, Visa.

Sant'Andrea, Via XX Settembre, 89 (tel./fax 481 47 75), near the British Embassy and the intersection with Via Palestro. If you brush the long-striped curtains aside, there's a view of Michelangelo's nearby Porta Pia. Flowers and incense add a pleasant smell to the pleasant view, especially if you ignore the '70s carpet. Bar, TV room, beautiful marble foyer. Twenty-four rooms with showers. Discounts for extended stays; 20% discount Nov.-March; the prices below reflect another discount for *Let's Go* readers. Singles L35,000, with bath L50,000. Doubles L50,000, with bath, L70,000. Triples L70,000, with bath L90,000. AmEx.

✓ **Hotel Romae,** Via Palestro, 49 (tel. 446 35 54; fax 446 39 14). Exit the station on the right and head up Via Marghera, until it hits Via Palestro. Recently renovated, each of these pink rooms has a safe and an antiseptic bath. Francesco and Lucy are young, enthusiastic, helpful hosts. Breakfast is included; a 3rd bed is free for children under 12. Excellent English spoken. Prices listed represent a 20% discount for *Let's Go* adherents. Singles L80,000. Doubles L120,000. Triples L150,000. AmEx., MC, Visa.

Pensione Tizi, Via Collina, 48 (tel. 482 01 28; fax 474 32 66). A 15-min. walk from the station. Take Via Goito from P. dell'Indipendenza, cross Via XX Settembre onto Via Piave, then take the first left onto Via Flavia, which leads to Via Collina. In a safer location than many other hotels around Termini, this family pensione has welcomed students for years. The upper floor has sinfully comfortable singles (L45,000) and doubles (L60,000, with bath L75,000). Triples L80,000-90,000.

✓ **Pensione Piave,** Via Piave, 14 (tel. 474 34 47; fax 487 33 60). Off Via XX Settembre. A step up from the garden variety budget accommodation, and worth the extra *lire*. All rooms have private bath, telephone, and carpeted floors. The singles have double beds and one room even has a little fireplace. English spoken. Check-out at 10:30am, but luggage can be left all day. Singles L45,000, with bath L62,000. Doubles with bath L80,000. Triples with bath L109,000. Quads L120,000. No curfew.

Pensione Alessandro, Via Vicenza, 42 (tel. 446 19 58). Across the street from a *pizzeria rustica*, near the corner with Via Palestro. Buzz #6 to get in. Thirty beds in occasionally co-ed dorm rooms. Almost identical establishment in an annex of **Hotel Positano.** The rooms aren't much to look at, but it's close to the station, the price is right, and the inimitable owner, Alessandro, is loved by locals and travelers alike. Backpacker bonding is inevitable in the close-knit (i.e. bunk-bed furnished) quarters. Check-in 8am-midnight. No curfew; they'll give you a key. L20,000 per person at both hotels. Showers, tiny lockers, communal mini-fridge (occasionally stocked with goodies from the owner), maps, advice, and even coffee included. Visa accepted when no banks are open to exchange money.

Pensione Monaco, Via Flavia, 84 (tel. 474 43 35 or 481 56 49), around the corner from Tizi and Ercoli. Dim, but bathrooms and beds are sparkling clean. Curfew midnight. One shower per day included, L2500 per extra one. Singles L40,000. Doubles L55,000. Triples and quads L25,000 per person.

M&J Place, Via Solferino, 9 (tel. 446 28 02), just off Via Marsala. Dorm-style accommodations for young people. TV, radio, fridge, and pub, all under one roof. Ceiling fans will keep you cool. L20,000 per night, per person.

Pensione Rubino, Via Milazzo, 3 (tel. 445 23 23) and **Pensione Alvisini,** Via Milazzo, 3 (tel. 495 23 23; fax 495 82 32). Sister establishments run by a family that speaks some English. Immaculate hallways with blue walls and plain rooms. Same prices for both places. Singles L50,000, with bath L60,000. Doubles L65,000, with bath L70,000-80,000. Triples L90,000. AmEx, MC, Visa.

✓ **Hotel Continentale,** Via Palestro, 49 (tel. 445 03 82; fax 445 26 29). Exit the station to the right and head up Via Marghera until it hits Via Palestro. Rooms renovated in a tasteful navy blue have phones and TVs; some have balconies. Breakfast included during the winter. Some English spoken. Prices listed represent a 20% discount for *Let's Go* readers. Singles with shower L75,000. Doubles with shower and toilet L100,000. Quads with shower L160,000. AmEx, MC, Visa.

Pensione Ercoli, Via Collina, 48 (tel. 474 54 54; fax 487 33 60), above the Pensione Tizi on the third floor. The young, English-speaking, Sardinian management is eager to house students and families. Friendly dorm atmosphere. Rooms and large common bathrooms are in perfect order. Singles L40,000. Doubles L55,000. Triples L70,000-90,000.

✓ **Pensione Lachea,** Via San Martino della Battaglia, 11 (tel. 495 72 56), off P. dell'Indipendenza. *Let's Go's* biggest fan, the warm-hearted owner will ensure readers every comfort. Recently renovated, the place is absolutely gleaming. Each room has a different theme: the Colosseum, the Spanish Steps, etc. Doubles L55,000, with bath, L75,000. Triples L65,000-70,000, with bath, L90,000-95,000.

Hotel Bolognese, Via Palestro, 15 (tel. 49 00 45). In a land of *pensioni* filled with campy artwork, this place stands out with fruit still-lifes (painted by the owner) and terraces, a luxury in Termini. The view isn't spectacular, but the idea is liberating. Suites with sitting rooms are available for families and larger groups. Singles L40,000, with bath L50,000. Doubles L65,000, with bath L75,000. Triples and suites L100,000, with bath L130,000.

Hotel Gexim, Via Palestro, 34 (tel./fax 444 13 11 or tel. 446 02 11). A 9-room pensione on the third floor, run by a young English-speaking couple. The sumptuous, placid peach rooms are adorned with elegant artwork. Singles L38,000-42,000. Doubles L55,000-65,000, with shower, L70,000-85,000. Triples with bath L99,000-115,000. Laundry L18,000 for 5kg. Breakfast L10,000.

Hotel Fenicia, Via Milazzo, 20 (tel. 49 03 42), on first floor. Friendly, English-speaking management. Rooms are small but clean. Singles L40,000. Doubles L50,000. Triples and quads L30,000 per person.

Hotel Positano, Via Palestro, 49 (tel. 49 03 60; fax 446 91 01). Comfortable, family-style place, on the 5th floor. Singles L50,000-60,000, with bath L70,000. Doubles L60,000, with bath L80,000. Triples L90,000. L20,000 per person for dorm-style annex; up to 8 beds per room. MC, Visa.

Hotel Galli, Via Milazzo, 20 (tel. 445 68 59), off Via Marsala. Clean and close to Termini. A haven for garage-sale knickknack aficionados. Many of the rooms were very recently renovated, with brand new bathrooms. Singles L45,000. Doubles L60,000, with bath L80,000. Crowded triples with bath L75,000.

Locanda Marini, Via Palestro, 35 (tel. 444 00 58), across the hall from and in cahoots with Pensione Katty. The interior is warmed by the sprightly proprietress. Very clean. Singles L30,000. Doubles L60,000. Triples L70,000.

Hotel Pensione Catherine, Via Volturno, 27 (tel. 48 36 34). A hop, skip, and a jump from Termini. Mint-green decor with big single beds. Prices listed are for *Let's Go* readers. Singles L40,000-45,000. Doubles L60,000. Triples L80,000.

SOUTH OF TERMINI

The area south of the station is generally busier, noisier, and seedier than the one to the north. Many places overcharge the hapless and exhausted tourist. With a little perseverance, however, one can find decent places at great bargains. Prices tend to be very flexible in this area and depend on the season, length of stay, how many people are in your group, and how busy the establishment is. As a result, a double which may cost L80,000 in August could drop to L40,000 a few weeks later. Don't

be afraid to haggle, but do realize that bargaining is rather futile during the peak season, particularly if you're looking for a single or double for just a few nights. **Many of the prices listed below are in the form of ranges; expect to pay near or above the maximum during high season and closer to the minimum during low season.**
Via Principe Amedeo runs parallel to the southwest side of the station two blocks down. It can be reached by taking any of the side streets that intersect with Via Giolitti outside the southwest exit of the station. The closer you get to P. Vittorio Emanuele, the more unsafe and disreputable the area becomes at night; it's known for harboring prostitution and drug dealers. Via Giolitti, Via Filippo Turati, and Via Principe Amedeo can also become intimidating at night so use appropriate caution and watch your pockets. Southwest of Santa Maria Maggiore (heading down Via Cavour or towards Via Nazionale) the area becomes less foreboding.

Hotel San Paolo, Via Panisperna, 95 (tel. 474 52 13; fax 474 52 18), at Via Caprareccia, just off Via Cavour to your right after S. Maria Maggiore. Recently renovated with sparkling white wall tiles and colorful art, San Paolo's modestly sized rooms provide ample atmosphere for quality relaxation. Some rooms have terraces and most are decorated with huge puzzles assembled by the proprietor. Singles L40,000, with bath L50,000. Two-bed doubles L55,000, *matrimoniale* with bath L65,000. Triples L75,000. English spoken, reservations accepted.

Pensione Sandy, Via Cavour, 136 (tel. 488 45 85), near Santa Maria Maggiore. No sign; look for the Hotel Valle next door. Managed by young Australians bursting with energy. At prices like these, it's well worth the 4-flight trek to the top. Hostel-style rooms, usually for 4-6 people, in a great central location. L20,000 per person during the summer, L18,000 per person in winter (no heat, but lots of blankets). Showers included. Lockers available.

Hotel Giugiu, Via del Viminale, 8 (tel./fax 482 77 34). A warm, pleasant family runs Giugiu as an extension of their own house. Recently expanded with a breakfast area and 12 airy rooms with high frescoed ceilings. Great *espresso.* Singles L40,000-L55,000. Doubles L60,000-L70,000, with bath L70,000-L85,000.

Pensione di Rienzo, Via Principe Amedeo, 79A (tel. 446 71 31). A tranquil family-run retreat with moderately priced rooms, including many newly renovated with baths. Most are spacious with balconies overlooking a peaceful courtyard. Hall baths usually shared by only 2-3 people. Kind manager speaks English. Singles L40,000-55,000, with bath L50,000-64,000. Doubles L50,000-70,000, with bath L70,000-85,000. Triples up to L100,000, with bath up to L120,000.

Hotel Kennedy, Via Filippo Turati, 62 (tel. 446 53 73). Trendy rooms with the works. Private bath, color TV, phone, and A/C. Hearty breakfast includes cornflakes, croissant, all-you-can-drink *cappuccino,* and endless varieties of jams and tea, served on biscuit-shaped placemats. Everyone speaks some form of English. The hip, helpful manager takes pride in the youth and vitality of the staff and offers a 10% discount to people "under 29, like us." Singles L70,000-99,000. Doubles L85,000-145,000. Triples L110,000-150,000. AmEx, MC, Visa.

Pensione Cortorillo, Via Principe Amedeo, 79A (tel. 446 69 34), at Via Gioberti. Charming rooms with wooden beds. Continental breakfast included. The proprietress will cook dinner for L10,000-15,000. Singles with bath L35,000-40,000. Doubles L60,000-70,000. Negotiate.

Hotel Orlanda, Via Principe Amedeo, 76 (tel./fax 488 06 37), at Via Gioberti. Sparse, clean rooms. One anomalous room with a charming wooden floor; the rest are the usual tile. Tentative midnight curfew. Singles with bath L70,000. Doubles L80,000, with bath L100,000-120,000. AmEx, MC, Visa.

Albergo Teti, Via Principe Amedeo, 76 (tel./fax 48 90 40 88). Exceedingly comfortable, though a bit pricey for the neighborhood. Tastefully decorated. The singles and doubles with bathrooms also have TVs. Singles L40,000-60,000. Doubles L90,000-120,000. Breakfast L6000. AmEx, MC, Visa.

Hotel Scott House and **Hotel Eliana,** Via Gioberti, 30 (tel. 446 53 92 or 446 53 79; fax 446 49 86). Inexpensive, relatively standard, tidy, and clean. Rooms have TVs and baths. English spoken. Singles L50,000-70,000. Doubles L70-000-90,000. Special discount for *Let's Go* users. Again, negotiate.

YWCA, Via Cesare Balbo, 4 (tel. 488 04 60 or 488 39 17; fax 487 10 28), off Via Torino, south of Termini. Say "EEV-kah." A fantastic place for women travelers who enjoy safety in numbers. It lacks the authenticity of the family-run *pensione,* but has an pleasant, cheerful atmosphere with a garden terrace and large TV room. Services include fax and photocopying. Curfew midnight. No men allowed, except Al Pacino. Singles L45,000. Doubles L35,000 per person. Triples and quads L30,000 per person. Showers and breakfast (7:30-8:15am) included. Inform reception by 10am same day if you want lunch (1-2:15pm, L15,000).

PIAZZA NAVONA AND CAMPO DEI FIORI

Il centro storico (the historic center) is the ideal, though expensive, base for living as the Romans do. By day, its winding cobblestone streets, hidden *piazze,* and many *caffè* will enchant and mesmerize you; by night, the area swarms with boisterous Romans and tourists alike. Most major sights are within walking distance and the day market at nearby Campo dei Fiori yields bounties of cheap fruit, vegetables, and, of course, flowers. Unfortunately, hotel proprietors (mostly English-speaking) successfully exploit this desirable location; you can expect to pay about 10-15% more to finance the charm and the deeper sense of Roman history absent from Termini accommodations. Also watch out for hotels that hide standard budget rooms behind that thin marble veneer in the lobby. Reservations are strongly recommended.

Piazza Navona lies to the north of Corso Vittorio Emanuele II, the avenue that cuts through the historic center; Campo dei Fiori is to the south. From Stazione Termini, take bus #64 (70 at night). Also originating near Termini, #75 and 170 stop in Largo Argentina, the transportation hub of the historic center. Bus #62 and 60 travel along Via XX Settembre and Via del Tritone and stop at Largo Argentina.

Hotel Mimosa, Via Santa Chiara, 61 (tel. 68 80 17 53; fax 683 35 57), off P. di Minerva behind the Pantheon. Haphazard decoration, but cozy with a fantastic location. A matronly woman and her kindly husband preside over this kitschy abode, with puppy wall calendars and red-checkered tablecloths in the breakfast room. English spoken. Drunkenness not tolerated. Singles L65,000. Doubles L85,000, with bath L120,000. Triples L125,000. Breakfast L5000.

Albergo della Lunetta, P. del Paradiso, 68 (tel. 686 10 80 or 686 36 87; fax 689 20 28), near the Church of Sant'Andrea della Valle. Take Via Chiavari off Corso Vittorio Emanuele II, then the first right off Via Chiavari. An economical Eden in the heart of Old Rome, this is the best value in the Campo dei Fiori area. Flowered wallpaper, tidy rooms with armoires, desks, and phones. Muse in the central garden or the TV lounge, but definitely not in the somewhat cramped common baths. English spoken. Singles L45,000, with bath L65,000. Doubles L85,000, with bath L120,000. Triples L115,000, with bath L150,000. Reservations accepted with payment by check or bank draft, since credit cards are not accepted.

Albergo Pomezia, Via dei Chiavari, 12 (tel./fax 686 13 71). The renovated section on the 1st floor is far nicer than the old one; all of the redone rooms have baths. Phones, matching furniture, heat in the winter, and stylish bathrooms (on the 2nd and 3rd floors). Bar on the 1st floor (*caffè,* L1000). Don't let the hall mirrors fool you—the two owners really are twins. Singles L60,000, with bath L100,000. Doubles L90,000, with bath L140,000. Triples L110,000, with bath L180,000. Prices drop Nov.-Feb., except at Christmas. Breakfast included. AmEx, MC, Visa.

Pensione Navona, Via dei Sediari, 8 (tel. 686 42 03; fax 680 38 02; call before faxing). Take Via dei Canestrari off P. Navona, cross over Corso del Rinascimento, and continue straight. A very helpful Italo-Australian family runs a tight ship in this 16th-century Borromini building, which has served as a *pensione* for over 150 years. During World War II, Jews hid in the extensive network of tunnels leading to the Teatro Marcellus. The renovated section, peach with matching wood fixtures, puts the older section to shame, but all of the rooms are quiet and clean and most have bathrooms; ask for a room facing the courtyard. Cheery breakfast area. Call weeks in advance and send a US$100 deposit to secure a room. If full, they can refer you to other hotels in the area. Checkout 11am. They also organize bus tours to Tivoli and Pompeii. Singles L65,000, with bath L75,000. Doubles L105,000, with bath L115,000. Breakfast included.

Albergo Abruzzi, P. della Rotonda, 69 (tel. 679 20 21). Here the humble can contemplate the great; this *albergo* is located smack dab in front of the Pantheon and its noisy admirers. While cleaner than the Pantheon, it could use some of the Pantheon's overhead lighting. English spoken. Singles L60,000-75,000. Doubles L82,000-100,000. Triples L135,000. Reservations recommended in summer.

Hotel Piccolo, Via dei Chiavari, 32 (tel. 689 23 30 or 68 80 25 60), off Corso Vittorio Emanuele II, behind Sant'Andrea della Valle. Next to a bustling grocery but off the beaten path. Clean, quiet, and comfortable, with pleasant wood trimming in the bathrooms. Spacious singles in a mellow atmosphere. No elevator. Curfew 1:30am. Breakfast L5,000. English spoken. Singles L60,000 with bath L80,000. Doubles L80,000-90,000, with bath L100,000. Triples with shower L120,000, with bath L420,000. Reservations recommended in summer. AmEx, MC, Visa.

Pensione Campo Marzio, Piazza Campo Marzio, 7 (tel. 68 80 14 86). Take Corso del Rinascimento over to Via della Scrofa. The hotel due north of the Pantheon, near Via Stelletta and the government buildings. Stay here for the location, not the faux brick wallpaper. The rooms are big and have heavy wood armoires. Proprietor's young sidekick speaks some English. Singles L60,000, doubles L90,000.

NEAR THE SPANISH STEPS

Marxist ideologues, budget travelers, and quiet Amish types be warned: this section of Rome will not be sympathetic to your lifestyle. In this area, where designer silk suits, leather loafers, mini-skirts, and face-lifts abound, inexpensive accommodations are scarce. However, it may be worthwhile to spend a few extra bucks to sleep in the hippest part of town. For fashion victims who find themselves lingering in front of Fendi after the buses stop running, the following havens are worth a try:

✔ **Pensione Parlamento,** Via delle Convertite, 5 (tel./fax 679 20 82, for reservations tel. 69 94 16 97), off Via del Corso, one block before the post office, on the street leading up to P. San Silvestro. Plant-crowded landing, glamorous rooftop terrace with flowers; safes, hairdryers, and TVs in every room. High ceilings, balconies, and plush velvet chair lounge with magazines galore. Living room with color TV and bar. English spoken. Breakfast included. Lone single L75,000, with bath L110,000. Doubles L106,000, with shower L122,000, with shower and bath L132,000. Each additional person L35,000. Reservations recommended.

✔ **Pensione Panda,** Via della Croce, 35 (tel. 678 01 79 or 69 94 21 51), between P. di Spagna and Via del Corso. Repainted annually to retain a fresh Tom Sawyer decor, this light, airy place may be just the refuge you need from the chic mayhem below. Large single beds. No curfew, but you'll need a key. Single L60,000. Doubles L95,000. Triples L120,000. Reservations recommended. Discount for *Let's Go* readers. AmEx, MC, Visa.

Pensione Jonella, Via delle Croce, 41 (tel. 679 79 66), between P. di Spagna and Via del Corso. A marble stairway becomes steeper and narrower on the ascent to 5 effervescent rooms with high ceilings. Luckily, prices aren't as steep. Owned by friendly Carlo and his brothers, who also run Hotel Matilde. Singles L50,000. Doubles and triples L35,000 per person.

Pensione Fiorella, Via del Babuino, 196 (tel. 361 05 97), just off P. del Popolo. The charming management asks only that you respect the 1am curfew. Airy, comfortable breakfast room. Happening location can mean motorcycle wake up calls. Singles L55,000. Doubles L85,000. Breakfast included. No reservations; arrive early.

Hotel Boccaccio, Via del Boccaccio, 25 (tel. 488 59 62), off Via del Tritone down from P. Barberini. Patrizia runs this peaceful little establishment with her very own sense of familial comfort. Paisley comforters blend with old wooden heirlooms passed down from Grandma. The single costs L48,000. Doubles L60,000, with bath L80,000. Triples L82,000, with bath L100,000.

Hotel Marcus, Via del Clementino, 94 (tel. 68 30 03 20; fax 68 30 03 12). Off Via di Ripetta, Via Clementino is an extension of Via Condotti and Via della Fontanella di Borghese. Situated on the second floor, this homey hotel is filled with eloquent tile-work, a chandelier, and matching wood furniture. All rooms have telephones, heaters in the winter, secure double doors, small baths, and lots of mirrors. Singles L110,000. Doubles L140,000. Triples L189,000. AmEx, MC, Visa.

Hotel Pensione Suisse S.A.S., Via Gregoriana, 54 (tel. 678 36 49; fax 678 12 58), off P. di Trinità dei Monti; turn right at the top of the Spanish Steps. In the Swiss tradition of pricey perfection and a neutral, quaint location. TV lounge, phones, and tidy bathrooms. Singles L85,000, with bath L100,000. Doubles L115,000, with bath L150,000. Triples L195,000. Cold drinks and fans (on request) during the summer. Breakfast included. MC, Visa (can be applied to half of bill only).

PRATI (NEAR THE VATICAN)

The *pensioni* on the other side of the Tiber aren't the cheapest in Rome, but they do tend to be comfortable, clean, and friendly. Many have plans for—or are in the process of—renovation, which may raise prices. Those in **Prati,** near the Vatican, are attractive for their proximity to popular sights and a safer residential area. Bus #64 from Termini ends right near St. Peter's and Metro Linea A runs to Ottaviano, the metro stop in the area.

Pensione Ottaviano, Via Ottaviano, 6 (tel. 39 73 72 53 or 39 73 81 38), off P. del Risorgimento north of P. San Pietro. Minutes from St. Peter's, this is the only hostel-style *pensione* in the area—3 to 6 beds per room. Doubles are available for L70,000 in summer and L45,000 in winter. A backpackers' haven, including satellite TV and individual lockers. Energetic, English-speaking staff. L18,000-23,000 per person (depending on the season) for a bed in a shared room. No curfew.

✓ **Residence Giuggioli,** Via Germanico, 198 (tel. 324 36 97). At Via Paolo Emilia, 1st floor. Five of the best rooms in Rome. Beautiful antiques adorn pristine rooms and the common bath is gleaming and newly refurnished. Ask for room #6: it's huge and filled with antiques. The wonderful proprietress will chat with you in Italian. Doubles L90,000; matrimonial suite with private bath L120,000.

✓ **Hotel Alimandi,** Via Tunisi, 8 (tel. 39 72 39 48 or 39 72 39 41 or 39 72 63 00; fax 39 72 39 43). Take the steps off Viale Vaticano near the Vatican museums and go straight. A gorgeous place with a beautiful garden terrace on the roof, the site of Friday night BBQ and the usual nighttime socializing. Telephones, hairdryers, and radios in every room. Air-conditioned TV lounge and bar. Singles L69,000, with bath L89,000. Doubles L85,000, with bath L120,000. Triples with bath L133,000. Buffet breakfast L12,000. L10,000 per extra bed. Better reserve. AmEx, MC, Visa.

Pensione Nautilus, Via Germanico, 198 (tel. 324 21 18), same building as the more charming Guiggioli; reception on the 2nd floor. Spacious with clean bathrooms. English spoken. Curfew 1:30am, but they occasionally give out keys. Doubles L90,000, with bath L120,000. Triples L120,000, with bath L150,000.

✓ **Hotel Florida,** Via Cola di Rienzo, 243 (tel. 324 18 72; fax 324 18 57). On the 2nd and 3rd floor, below Hotel Joli. Charming, modern rooms flaunt their recent renovation: new wallpaper, floral carpeting, and ceiling fans. Bathrooms are delightfully clean with every imaginable amenity. Phones in each room. Friendly management. Singles L70,000-75,000, with bath L90,000-100,000. Doubles L85,000-100,000, with bath L115,000-130,000. AmEx, MC, Visa.

Hotel Pensione Joli, Via Cola di Rienzo, 243, 6th floor (tel. 324 18 54 or 324 18 93; fax 324 18 93). At Via Tibullo. It's comfortable, but somber with polished upholstered chairs. A few views of Roman rooftops and St. Peter's cupola. Breakfast in the TV sitting corner for L7500. Singles L60,000, with bath L75,000. Doubles with bath L105,000. Triples with bath L140,000. MC, Visa.

TRASTEVERE

Hedonists and bohemians flock to **Trastevere,** scene of much nighttime revelry and home to many young expatriates. Bus #75 from P. Indipendenza and #170 from P. del Cinquecento run from near Termini to Trastevere. Bus #56 and #60 to Trastevere leave from Via Claudio at Piazza San Silvestro, south of the Spanish Steps.

Pensione Manara, Via Luciano Manara, 25 (tel. 581 47 13). Take a right off Viale di Trastevere onto Via delle Fratte di Trastevere to Via Luciano Manaro. Friendly management runs this homey establishment overlooking colorful P. San Cosimato in the heart of Trastevere. Undergoing reconstruction in summer 1995 to brighten up the somber interior. English spoken. Singles L50,000. Doubles L68,000, with bath L85,000. Triples L85,000.

Pensione Esty, Viale Trastevere, 108 (tel. 588 12 01), about 1km down Viale di Trastevere from the Ponte Garibaldi. You're almost there when you pass the towering stone municipal building on your right. It's easy to miss; make sure you ring the buzzer on the right, labelled "*pensione.*" This uncommonly clean, airy hotel sits somewhat removed from the rowdy heart of Trastevere. Some rooms have balconies overlooking busy Viale di Trastevere. Singles L55,000. Doubles L75,000.

STUDENT AND INSTITUTIONAL ACCOMMODATIONS

If you are looking for a raucous time in Rome, avoid institutions. While providing affordable accommodations, most of them are inconveniently located and difficult to arrange; not to mention that curfews at the HI hostel and various religious organizations hinder indulgence in *la dolce vita.* Consider other comparably priced accommodations that are less contingent on the whims of public transportation.

Ostello del Foro Italico (HI), Viale delle Olimpiadi, 61, 00194 Roma (tel. 323 62 67; fax 324 26 13). Take Metro Linea A to Ottaviano (last stop) and then exit onto Via Barletta and take bus #32 (in the middle of the street) to Cadorna. If you pass the Stadio del Nuoto, you've gone too far. The hostel is across the street, on the corner. Inconvenient location is redeemed by a bus- and metro- ticket vending machine. French school groups and the street outside can be noisy. Three-day max. stay when full. Reception noon-midnight. Lockout 9am-2pm. Sizeable but not superlative lunch or dinner. Bar downstairs open 7:30am-11pm. Curfew midnight. L20,000 per person; L25,000 without HI/IYHF card (buy one at the desk for L30,000). Breakfast and curtain-less showers included. Wheelchair accessible.

CAMPING

You probably won't catch the malaria that killed Daisy Miller, but there are still many mosquitoes menacing tourists in campgrounds near the city. There's often little space between sites, but peaceful seclusion is usually steps away. In August, arrive well before 11am for a spot. Rates average L9000 per person and another L5000 per car. Many of the campgrounds are downright luxurious, with everything from swimming pools to campground bars, while others may be more primitive. (See Accommodations: Camping, page 56 for informative organizations.)

Camping on beaches, roads, or any flat, inconspicuous plot is not uncommon, but it is illegal. Respect for property rights is extremely important—always ask permission before bedding down. Campers who don't make fires or litter will lessen their chances of being booted.

Seven Hills, Via Cassia, 1216 (tel. 30 36 27 51, 303 31 08 26; fax 303 31 00 39), 8km north of Rome. Take bus #907 from P. Risorgimento to Via Cassia. A camping commune in the hills that harkens back to the '60s. Strutting ostriches, clucking chickens, bragging peacocks, promenading swans, bucking goats, bounding deer, and hopping rabbits. Young international campers play volleyball on the manicured grounds. Laze by the poolside and dance the night away in the **discoteca** (9:30pm-1am). Completely self-sufficient, it houses a bar, market, BBQ, restaurant, convenience store, and *pizzeria.* Laundry service L15,000. Free medical service. Daily shuttle to the Vatican leaves at 9:30am, returns at 1:30 and 5:30pm (L2500 one way, L5000 round-trip). Ask about direct bus service from Termini. L10,000 per person, L8000 per tent. Bungalows L70,000 (2-person), L110,000 (4-person with bath). L5000 per car. Open March 15-Oct. 30.

Flaminio, Via Flaminia Nuova, 821 (tel. 333 14 31), about 7km outside of Rome. Take bus #910 from Termini to Piazza Mancini, then transfer to #200. Get off when you see the "Philips" or EUCLID building on Via Flaminia Nuova (open 9am-5pm; Via Flaminia Nuova is crowded; keep your eyes peeled) on your right. Shaded grass strewn with closely knit enclaves of tents, campers, and bungalows.

The landscaping is a little rough around the edges, but there is a pool, market, restaurant, bar, and *discoteca* that rages long into the night. Coin-operated washing machines L500. L10,000 per person, L5700 per tent. Bungalows L33,000; singles and doubles L56,000, triples L89,000, quads L120,000. Open March-Oct.

Capitol Campground, Via di Castel Fusano, 195 (tel. 565 73 44), in Ostia Antica, is 3km from the beach and ruins and has a swimming pool, tennis courts, markets and bar. From Magliana or Metro line B, take the Ostia Lido-Centro bus to its Capolinea. Then take #05 bus to Casal Palocco. L13,000 per person, 10,000 per tent, L6000 per car. Hot showers L1000.

Nomentano, on Via della Cesarina (tel. 41 40 02 96), at Via Nomentana. Eight km from Rome. Take bus #36 from Termini and transfer to bus #337 at P. Sempione. Ask the bus driver where to get off on Via Nomentana. A smaller campsite with market, bar, cafeteria, and access to tennis courts and a pool at the private club next door (L8000 per day). But, alas, no grass. Instead, there's a view of the flat, dry countryside on the side opposite street traffic. L9500 per person, L4800 per tent, bungalows L18,000 per person. Open March-Oct. AmEx, MC, Visa.

■■■ FOOD

Alimentari are your best bet for grocery staples. Food stores are open roughly Mon.-Wed. and Fri.-Sat. 8am-1pm and 3:30-7:30pm (4pm-8pm in summer), Thurs. 8am-1pm. *Alimentari* may also close on Saturday afternoons in the summer. Outdoor **markets** can be found at P. Campo dei Fiori, P. Vittorio Emanuele II, and Piazza San Cosimato in Trastevere. They generally operate Mon.-Sat. 6am-2pm, and sell a variety of goods from food and housewares to clothing and antiques. Supermarket **STANDA** offers an array of food, toiletries, clothing, and other necessities. There is one on Viale Trastevere, a few blocks down from Piazza Sidney Sonnino, and one on Via Cola di Rienzo, several blocks down from the Ottaviano Metro stop.

For an authentic Roman culinary experience, hop on a bus to reach the university district of **San Lorenzo** or the working-class neighborhood **Testaccio.** These are the last truly untouristed restaurant districts in Rome. The areas around **Piazza Navona** and **Campo dei Fiori** harbor inviting *trattorie,* and **Trastevere** has the liveliest *pizzerie.* Don't forget that Thursday night in Rome is *gnocchi* night. Romans generally eat late—at around 8 or 9pm; set out early to avoid the rush. Most restaurants close for at least two weeks in August.

CENTRO STORICO: PIAZZA NAVONA

Authentic, inexpensive *trattorie* are easy to find in the Piazza Navona area, but steer clear of the main *piazze* where the restaurants entice tourists with English menus and then shamelessly overcharge them. Some of the best restaurants in the city hide along Via Governo Vecchio and the alleys emerging from it; head here for authentic Italian restaurants that cater to Italians. Often, lunchtime favorites are unmarked; look for doorways with bead curtains or follow an Italian worker on lunchbreak. There is no shortage of *alimentari* (grocery stores), *tavole calde* (self-service cafeterias that serve hot dishes), and *pizzerie rustiche* lining Via di Ripetta and around the Pantheon. The best *gelato* places surround the Pantheon and its *piazza.* A **market** sells fruit in Via della Pace (off Via del Governo Vecchio) Mon.-Sat. 7am-2pm.

Palladini, Via del Governo Vecchio, 29 (tel. 686 12 37). Essentially a *salumeria* (deli) rather than a bona fide restaurant. No sign or place to sit, but bustling with a Roman lunch crowd eating seconds-old *panini.* Point to the fillings of your choice and eat outside. Favorites include *prosciutto e fiche* (ham and figs) or *bresaola e rughetta* (smoked meat with arugula) sprinkled with parmesan cheese and lemon juice. A plethora of vegetable options—artichoke, peppers, mushrooms, tomatoes, and more—make anything possible. Hearty sandwich L2500-5000. Open Sept.-July Mon.-Sat. 8am-2:30pm and 5-8:30pm.

Pizzeria Baffetto, Via del Governo Vecchio, 114 (tel. 686 16 17), on the corner of Via Sora. Once a meeting place for 60s radicals, Baffetto now overflows with

Romans of all political persuasions. The *pizza gigante* could feed almost the entire Forza Italia party, Berlusconi included. Outdoor seating. Harried service. Pizzas L5000-9000. Wine L6000. Cover L1000. Open Mon.-Sat. 7:30pm-1am.

Trattoria Gino e Pietro, Via del Governo Vecchio, 106 (tel. 686 15 76), at Vicolo Savelli. Keep your eyes peeled for the reddish wood sign that marks the location of this cozy place, teetering on the line between *trattoria* and *osteria*. The main menu is always in an exciting state of flux. Delve into the back room for a huge homemade array of *antipasti vegetali* (L7000). *Secondi* L8500-14,000. Cover L2000. Open Fri.-Wed. noon-3pm and 6:30pm-11pm. Closed mid-July to early August. Reservations accepted.

L'Insalata Ricca 2, P. Pasquino, 73, at beginning of Governo Vecchio. Who ever said sequels are inferior? This spin-off of the original is just as good. Omelettes cooked to order (L6000). The *gnocchi verdi alla gorgonzola* L9000 are astounding. *Secondi* L8000-12,000. Cover L2000. Open Tues.-Sun. noon-3pm and 7:30-11:30pm. Reservations recommended on Sat.

Il Giardinetto, Via del Governo Vecchio, 125 (tel. 686 86 93). Escape the hard, dusty cobblestones of the area, and dine beneath the leaf-lined ceiling of this Tunisian-run oasis. Edith Piaf's *La Vie en Rose* and soothing Barry Manilow lilt through this pastel heaven. Take your time over the well-seasoned pastas—try the *gnocchetti* (L9000) or the *pennette alla gorgonzola* (L9000) and house wine (L8000 per liter). Portions generous enough to skip the *secondi* (L13,000-15,000). Open Tues.-Sun. 12:30-3pm and 7:30pm-1am. AmEx, MC, Visa.

CENTRO STORICO: CAMPO DEI FIORI

For many Romans, this neighborhood is the authentic, pre-commercial Rome of years gone by. Its cobblestone streets and miniature *piazze* are equally enticing to the uninitiated seeking spirited meals and romantic wine bars. The only time the crowd bustles is during the lively market at the Campo, overflowing with flowers, fruit vendors, cheese sellers, oversized swordfish, and screaming Italian housewives (open Mon.-Sat. 6am-2pm). There are innumerable restaurants hidden away in these streets; try Via Monserrato and to the south and west of the *piazza*. *Caffè*, bars, pastry shops, and *alimentari* tantalize along Via dei Giubbonari.

L'Insalata Ricca, Largo di Chiavari, 85 (tel. 68 80 36 56), off Corso Vittorio Emanuele near P. Sant'Andrea della Valle. Modern art, innovative dishes, and an off-beat ambience are successfully combined here with neighborly service and savory, traditional *trattoria* food. New, expanded seating downstairs and outside accommodates the devoted masses. Try the *gnocchi al sardi* (L8000) or request their title dish *insalata ricca,* a robust salad with everything on it (L7000). Whole wheat pasta *integrale* L7000. Cover L2000. Summer open noon-3:15pm and 6:45-11:15pm. Closed Wednesday in winter.

Hostaria Grappolo d'Oro, Piazza della Cancelleria, 80-81 (tel. 686 41 18), on Via Cancelleria off Corso Vittorio Emanuele II. The owner is the subject of a 1988 *New Yorker* article praising his cuisine, but he has never read it. Instead, he concentrates on turning his neighborhood *trattoria* into a stellar (but still inexpensive) gastronomic ecstasy. Words are too cheap for his *antipasti* (L8000) and *penne all'arrabbiata* (L9000; see appendix for proper pronunciation). House white wine L6000. Cover L2500. Open Mon.-Sat. noon-4pm and 7pm-midnight.

Arnaldo ai Satiri, Via di Grotta Pinta, 8 (tel. 686 19 15), near Via Baullari. Unusual dishes include spicy *fusilli con melanzane* (pasta with eggplant; L10,000), fresh *gazpacho* (L9000), and the specialty of the house, pasta with cabbage cream sauce (L10,000). Alight with red lightbulbs and candles, the interior is a cross between a bordello and a darkroom. At night you can opt for the L35,000 *menù*. Outdoor dining in summer. Open Wed.-Mon. 12:30-3pm and 7:30pm-1am. AmEx, MC, Visa.

Filetti di Baccalà, Largo dei Librari, 88 (tel. 686 40 18). Take Via dei Giubbonari off P. Campo dei Fiori; Largo dei Librari will be on your left. Be sure not to miss this busy, unpretentious little establishment located in a tiny *piazza* beneath a quaint church. The ideal spot for informal *antipasti* and wine, this self-service

favorite makes an unforgettable *filetto di baccalà* (deep-fried cod filet, L4000).
Wine L6000 per liter. Cover L1500. Open Sept.-July. Mon.-Sat. 5:30-10:30pm.
L'Oasi della Pizza, Via della Corda, 5 (tel. 68 80 27 46). Off the southern side of
Campo dei Fiori. The brick oven in the center of the room is not a mirage. Quiet,
simple, yummy. Pizzas L6500-13,500; wine L6000 per liter; pasta (L8000-11,000).
Cover L2000. Open Thurs.-Tues. noon-3pm and 7-11:30pm.
Da Sergio, Vicolo delle Grotte, 27 (tel. 654 66 69). Go left out of P. Farnese to P.
della Quercia; Vicolo delle Grotte leads left back up to Via dei Giubbonari. Da Sergio is legendary for its pasta plates, so much so that they occasionally run out. Fortunately, their pizzas are excellent too (L7000-15,000). On summer nights,
romantic Romans throng the tables in the cobbled alley outside. Service ranges
from Parisian to personal, depending on how often you eat here. Cover L2000.
Open Mon.-Sat. noon-3:30pm and 6:30pm-midnight.

THE JEWISH GHETTO

To the west of the roaring Via Arenula, the former Jewish Ghetto has endured centuries of anti-Semitism, modernization, and tourism to remain a proud community.
This neighborhood is now becoming an extremely chic locale, with all kinds of
Romans trekking there to sample the home cooking. Many traditional Roman dishes
actually originated in the neighborhood, like *carciofi alla giudia* (fried artichokes,
also known as *carciofi alla romana*) and *fiori di zucca* (cheese-filled zucchini blossoms that are lightly fried). Keep an eye out for kosher groceries and bakeries.

Margarita, Via di S. Maria de' Calderari, 30, next to the S. Maria del Pianto church,
off Piazza Cenci. Behind the green rope door (don't look for a sign), locals and
RISD European Honors Program students fight over politics in a basement filled
with the smoke. Daily specials are scrawled on the single paper menu—on Thursday, you might be able to experience homemade *gnocchi* for L9000. *Fettuccine*
L9000. *Baccalà* (fried cod) L11,000. Cover L2000. Open Mon.-Fri. noon-3pm.
Ristorante Il Portico, Via del Portico d'Ottavio, 1E (tel. 68 30 79 37), around the
corner from the Teatro di Marcello. Wonderful fresh anchovies with green beans,
delicious and unusual kosher pastries in a comfortable outdoor setting. Kosher
meat, wine, and marinated vegetables served along with non-kosher food. *Pasta e
ceci* (chickpeas; L10,000). *Spaghetti cacio e pepe* (grated cheese and pepper)
L10,000. Cover L3000. Open Mon. and Wed.-Sat. 12:30-3pm and 8pm-1am.
Ristorante da Giggetto, Via del Portico Ottavio, 21-22 (tel. 686 11 05). Swallow a
lot of the *carciofi alla giudia* (fried artichoke, L8000 each) as you sit at arms
length from the ancient ruins of the Portico d'Ottavio. *Supplì* (a deep-fried rice
ball with mozzarella, tomato sauce, and meat) L2000. *Buccatini all'amatriciana*
L12,000. Cover L3000. Open Tues.-Sun. 12:30pm-3pm and 7:30-11pm.

NEAR THE SPANISH STEPS

Caveat edax (let the diner beware): the high prices in this flashy district are no guarantee of quality. Although looking for inexpensive meals around Piazza di Spagna is
like looking for a bargain at Armani, there are a few places that don't check for gold
cards at the door. Skip McDonald's and opt for a hot *panino* with mozzarella and
prosciutto, a salad, or a piece of *pizza rustica* at one of the many bars in this area.
There are *alimentari* at Via Laurina, 36 and Via di Ripetta, 233. Look for outdoor
markets on Via del Lavatore, near the Trevi Fountain, and halfway down Via Tomacelli between the fountain and Via dell'Arancio.

La Capricciosa, Largo dei Lombardi, 8 (tel. 687 86 36), right off Via del Corso and
across from the intersection of Via del Corso and Via della Croce. This is the home
of the famous *capricciosa* pizza, divided into 4 sections of ham, egg, artichoke,
and, um, we forget. The venerable waiters are attentive, serving up perfect pies
on the outdoor terrace. *Primi* (L8000-11,000), including *ravioli di ricotta e
spinaci*. Desserts L6000. Cover L2000. Open Wed.-Mon. 12:30-3pm and 7pm-
1am. Closed last week in Aug. Reservations accepted. AmEx, MC, Visa.

Trattoria da Settimio all'Arancio, Via dell'Arancio, 50 (tel. 687 61 19). Take Via dei Condotti from P. di Spagna, cross Via del Corso, continue on Via della Fontanella Borghese, take your 1st right and then your 1st left. A favorite among savvy Romans. Excellent 3-course meals L26,000-30,000. Try the *ossobuco* (braised veal shank in sauce, L12,000) or the *ravioli all'arancia* (with orange), L10,000. Huge portions of fresh vegetables (L4000-8000) and delicious *antipasti*. Cover L2000. Fresh fish Tue. and Fri. Open Mon.-Sat. 1-3:30pm and 7pm-midnight. Closed 1 week in Aug. Reservations accepted. AmEx, MC, Visa.

Al Piccolo Arancio, Vicolo Scanderberg, 112 (tel. 678 61 39), near the Trevi Fountain in a quaint alley off of Via del Lavatore, which is on the right as you face the fountain. The sign says *"Hosteria."* Delicious pasta and appetizers. Try the *fiori di zucca* (fried zucchini flowers stuffed with mozzarella, L7000) or the *carciofi alla giudia* (fried artichoke, L5000). If you're lucky enough to hit this place the same day the fish merchants do (Tues. and Fri.), order the homemade *gnocchi al salmone* (L7000) or the *linguine all'aragosta* (lobster linguini). Cover L2500. Arrive early. Open Sept.-July Tues.-Sun. 12:30-3pm and 7-11:30pm. AmEx, MC, Visa.

Pizzeria al Leoncino, Via del Leoncino, 28 (tel. 687 63 06). Take Via Condotti from P. di Spagna, cross Via del Corso, continue on Via della Fontana Borghese, then take your first right onto Via del Leoncino. Quick, inexpensive, and informal. Traditional, hand-prepared pizzas (L6000-9000) baked in front of you and the hordes of Romans who love the place. Wine L4000 per liter. Open Thurs.-Tues. 7pm-midnight and Mon., Tues., Thurs., and Fri. also 1-2:30pm.

Ristorante Vegetariano Margutta, Via Margutta 119 (tel. 36 00 18 05), off Via del Babuino. A bastion of rich vegetarians. Unclassifiable music plays in the background as well-dressed waitresses rush by, leaving you to drift into oil paint oblivion while your lettuce is prepared. Greek or arugula and parmesan salad (L12,000), *radicchio and provola risotto* (L12,000). Bottle of slightly alcoholic apple cider L12,000. Lunch *menù* L18,000. Open Sept.-July Mon.-Sat. 12:30-3pm and 7:45-11pm. AmEx, MC, Visa.

Er Buco, Via del Lavatore, 91 (tel. 678 11 54), steps from P. di Trevi. Possibly the oldest pizza oven in the city. It's tiny, so get there early and avoid the crowds. Their pizza *"Er Buco"* (tomatoes, cheese, parmesan, and basil; L8000) is edible perfection. *Bruschetta alla crema di carciofi* (toast with artichoke paste) L3000. Salmon calzone L10,000. Open Mon.-Sat. noon-2:30pm and 7:30-11:30pm.

Centro Macrobiotico Italiano-Naturalist Club, Via della Vite, 14 (tel. 679 25 09), on the 3rd floor, just off Via del Corso. A different menu is made each day; lunch items and sweets are usually gone by 3pm, but the tea room remains open. They also sell New Age books and natural cosmetics, host guest speakers lecturing (often in English) about macrobiotic cooking, and conduct classes in yoga, tai chi, and shiatzu. Membership costs L30,000 per year (which reduces as the year progresses; in the summer months, membership is only about L13,000). Tourists are allowed one meal with a L2000 surcharge and a passport. A full meal comes to about L15,000. *Cous-cous vegetale* L6800. Open Mon.-Fri. 10am-6:30pm.

Hostaria al Vantaggio, Via del Vantaggio, 34 (tel. 323 68 48), off Via del Corso, a few blocks south of Piazza del Popolo. Lovely outdoor dining in summer. Don't confuse the peach tablecloths and massive canvas umbrellas with those of its overpriced neighbors. Filling, elegant meals. *Pizza gorgonzola* L10,000. Roast chicken L9000. *Saltimbocca alla romana* (L8000). *Menù* L20,000. Cover L2500. Open Mon.-Sat. noon-3pm and 7-11pm. Closed 2 weeks in Aug. AmEx, MC, Visa.

NEAR THE COLOSSEUM AND FORUM

Despite its past glory, this area has yet to discover the noble concept of the affordable restaurant. Flanked on all sides by wide, traffic-ridden streets, you may want to head straight out to the many bars and *tavole calde* on Via Cavour. If you need immediate relief, head to one of the following locales.

Taverna dei Quaranta, Via Claudia, 24 (tel. 700 05 50). This is the best food you can afford in the shade of the mighty amphitheater. Its cool, tree-shaded outdoor dining provides the ultimate respite from baking in the sun. The ever-changing menu features an outstanding *bruschetta al pomodoro* (toasted bread topped with chopped tomatoes, olive oil, and basil, L3500) and such creations as *linguini alla crema di zucchini* (L9000). Beer from the tap L5000. No cover. Open daily noon-3pm and 8pm-midnight. Open August. AmEx.

Trattoria di Priscilla, Via Appia Antica, 68 (tel. 513 63 79), across from the Domine Quo Vadis, it can be reached from the parking lot of the S. Calisto catacombs. Its sign says simply *Trattoria,* so look for the street number. A cozy, family-run establishment hidden in an area where overpriced, tourist-oriented restaurants abound. Takes its name from an upper-class contemporary of Nero, whose tomb is visible in an exposed segment of the back wall. Pasta dishes L8500. *Pollo alla romana* L13,500. Open daily noon-3pm and 7:30-11pm. AmEx.

Pizzeria Imperiale, Largo C. Ricci, 37 (tel. 678 68 71), at the start of Via Cavour opposite the Roman Forum entrance gate. Recover from the ruins under one of the many umbrellas. Good pizzas; try the *peccato del frate* (red peppers, zucchini, spicy sausage, olives, and artichokes) for L11,000. Check out the *calzone gigante.* Pasta L8000-12,000. Wine L10,000 per liter. Cover L1500. Open daily noon-5pm and 7pm-midnight.

TRASTEVERE

You can't justifiably claim that you've been to Rome without having savored a pizza and swilled some house wine in a rowdy outdoor *pizzeria* of Trastevere. Just down the river from the Vatican and on the opposite bank of the historic center, Trastevere contains the city's most raucous beer parlors, hopping *pizzerie,* and a loud bohemian population. By day, the laundry-filled streets buzz only with the sounds of children and the occasional Vespa, but by night, the Piazza di Santa Maria di Trastevere is packed with expatriate hippies and their dogs, who howl along with the out-of-tune folk guitars while the monied patrons of costly establishments stroll by.

Pizzeria Ivo, Via di San Francesca a Ripa, 158 (tel. 581 70 82). Take a right on Via delle Fratte di Trastevere off Viale Trastevere as you're coming from the river. Alas, the tourists have finally discovered this Trastevere legend, but the mouthwatering pizza is still well worth the long wait and chaotic atmosphere. Dining *al fresco* is the only summertime option. Pizza L9500-13,000. Crisp, delicious wine with the restaurant's own label, L9000. Cover L1500. Open Sept.-July Wed.-Mon. 1:30-3:30pm, 6pm-2am.

Taverna della Scala, P. della Scala, 19 (tel. 65 87 41 00). A *trattoria* with quiet outdoor dining, or cool, air-conditioned dining in a cave-like interior downstairs. Pasta L6000-9000, pizza L5500-11,000, wine L6000 per ¾liter. Cover L2500. Look for the *consiglio dello chef* (chef's special) written on the board outside. Open Wed.-Mon. 12:30-3pm and 7pm-midnight.

Pizzeria Sonnino, Viale di Trastevere, 23, two doors down from the big movie theater. A hectic, popular *pizza a taglio* joint. Potato with rosemary and *margherita* slices cost L1500 per *etto,* and their *supplì* (vegetarian) and *crochette* are out of this world (L1000 each). Roast chicken. Open late. Closed Mon.

Taverno del Moro, Via del Moro, 43 (tel. 580 91 65), off Via Lungaretta in Trastevere. A large, airy restaurant with outdoor dining. Beautiful *antipasto* spread (L7000). *Pizza con verdura* L12,000. Cheesecake L4000. Cover L2000. *Menù* L18,000. Open Tues.-Sun. 5:30pm-12:30am. Credit cards accepted.

Hostaria da Augusto, P. de Renzi, 15 (tel. 580 37 98). Take Via Fonte Olio out the northern end of P. Santa Maria in Trastevere, to Vicolo del Piede. Neighborhood crowds spill from this no-frills restaurant into its tiny *piazza. Fettuccine all'amatriciana* L6500. Open Mon.-Sat. noon-3pm, Mon.-Fri. 8-11pm. Closed Aug.

Il Tulipano Nero, Via Roma Libera, 15 (tel. 581 83 09), in P. San Cosimato. A friendly, rowdy *pizzeria*—dine outdoors in the summer. Iron palates can attempt the *rigatoni all'elettroshock* (very hot indeed; L9000), or try the innovative pizza combos. *Pizza tonno, mais, e rughetta* (with tuna, corn, and arugula, L10,000) tastes far better than it sounds. All plates served in small or gigantic portions. Wine L9000 per liter. Cover L1500. Open Thurs.-Tues. 5pm-1:30am.

Il Duca, Vicolo del Cinque, 56 (tel. 581 77 06). Off Via del Moro on the left as you head toward the river. A classic Roman *trattoria* on a lively nighttime street. Divine *bruschetta* (try it *al carciofo*—with artichoke paste—L2500), *lasagne,* and other pastas (L8000-12,000). *Risotto alla crema di scampi* L12,000. Wine L6000 per liter. Open Tues.-Sun. 12:30-2pm and 7:30pm-midnight.

Mario's, Via del Moro, 53 (tel. 580 38 09). Take Via della Lungaretta off Viale di Trastevere and turn right after the church. Pasta is consistently phenomenal for only L5500-7000. *Fettuccine ai funghi porcini* (with *porcini* mushrooms) is L7000. *Menù* L17,000. Wine L4400. Cover L1000. English menus. Open Sept.-mid Aug. Mon.-Sat. noon-4pm and 7pm-midnight. AmEx, MC, Visa.

Hostaria er Belli, Piazza Sant'Apollonia, 11 (tel. 580 37 82). Off Via di Lungaretta right before P. Santa Maria in Trastevere. A friendly *trattoria* specializing in Sardinian cooking. *Ravioli sardi* (in tomato-cream sauce, L11,000), *fettuccine alla sarda* (with ham and mushrooms, L11,000), wine L8000 per liter. Cover L2500. Open Tues.-Sun. 11:30-2pm and 7:30-midnight.

India House, Via di Santa Cecilia, 8 (tel. 581 85 05). Turn left (east) off Viale Trastevere at McDonald's, continue down Via dei Genovesi, and turn right at its end. Up the street on the left. Perfume of a curry sort wafts through the stillness of this perfectly beautiful, quiet, and authentically Italian section of Trastevere. Fine *menù* L20,000. No ordering; just sit and let it happen. Open Tues.-Sun. 7-11pm. Call ahead to find out what the day's *menù* is.

Mister George, Via del Moro, 17 (tel. 58 82 88 11). Recently opened American burger grill with "American food." Guacamole with chips L6000. Bagels (with tuna salad, lox, etc. L2500-5000). Pita pockets (L5000). Homemade waffles with ice cream or fresh fruit L1500. BLT L5000 A tiny place with a tiny cover for sit down meals: L1000. Open Thurs.-Tues. 8am-3pm and 6pm-2am.

Ocak Başi, Via del Moro, 24. A Turkish restaurant brimming with the smells and sounds of Istanbul. Good choices include fried eggplant with yogurt (L8000), kebabs with vegetables (L8000), and baklava (L8000). Cover L1000, service included. Open Mon.-Sat. 8-11:30pm. AmEx, MC, Visa.

THE BORGO AND PRATI (NEAR THE VATICAN)

At night, the streets of Prati and the Borgo fill with Romans heading to various restaurants, *birrerie*, and clubs. The residential district around Via Cola di Rienzo hides some of the best bargains in town, as well as an immense indoor food market.

L'Archetto, Via Germanico, 105 (tel. 323 11 63). The friendly staff will bring traditional *pizzeria* fare to you as you sit in your comfy green chair. Pizzas (L7000-9000), *filetti di baccalà* (fried fish, L3000), and *fiori di zucca* (fried zucchini flowers, L1500). Open Tues.-Sun. 7pm-midnight. Also open Mon. in July.

Hostaria dei Bastioni, Via Leone IV, 29 (tel. 39 72 30 34), off P. del Risorgimento near the Vatican Museums. A miraculous subterranean restaurant which rightly boasts of its seafood specialties. Vegetarians need not be deterred; one of the house specialties is *fettuccine alla bastione* which is smothered in a creamy tomato and orange sauce. *Risotto al pescatore* (rice with seafood sauce) L9000. Fresh fish dishes L13,000-18,000. The buzz of traffic means noisy dining *al fresco*. Cover L2000. Service 10%. Open Mon.-Sat. noon-3pm and 7pm-1:30am.

Pizzeria Il Bersagliere, Via Candia, 24 (tel. 372 45 11), near Via Tolemaide. A squadron of peach tablecloths call the weary traveler to mouth-watering pizzas (L8500-10,500); try the *fiori di zucca* pizza (L10,500). The *bruschetta al pomodoro* (L2500) tingles the tongue. Cover L2000. Open Tues.-Sun. 7pm-midnight.

Cucina Abruzzese, Via dei Gracchi, 27 (tel. 39 73 32 90), on the corner of Via Catone. The apricot-colored exterior hides some of the area's best home-cooking. A pretty arbor on the street shields you from the sun. Pasta L6000-8000. Cover L2500. Ravenous? Order the L20,000 *menù*. Open Tues.-Sun. noon-midnight.

Armando, Via Plauto, 38-39 (tel. 68 30 70 62), off Borgo Angelico. Delicious *lasagne* is the house specialty at L8500; the *vino bianco* is a delight after a day of museum-trudging at L7000 per liter. Don't pass up the *antipasto* (L7500). Cover L2500. Open Thurs.-Tues. 12:30-3pm and 7-11pm.

Non Solo Pizza, Via degli Scipioni, 95 (tel. 372 58 20). O.K., so maybe there isn't just pizza here, but once you smell how wonderful it is, you might forget about the pasta. A giant slab of pizza is folded in half and ingested right from a greasy napkin. Simple decor, but there are plenty of bargain-hunting Italians bumping elbows with you. Pizza sold by weight. Open Tues.-Sun. 8:30am-9:30pm.

Trattoria La Caravella, Via degli Scipioni, 32 (tel. 39 72 61 61). Near entrance to Vatican Museums. Pasta L5000-10,000. *Menù* L15,000. Pizza, too. Cover L2000. Open Fri.-Wed. noon-4pm and 7-11pm. AmEx, MC, Visa.

Hostaria l'Etrusco, Via dei Gracchi, 12-14 (tel. 31 21 24). A simple wooden room located compellingly near the Vatican for museum dwellers. Unbelievable pasta, L6500-13,000. Cover L3000. Open Thurs.-Tues. noon-3pm and 6:30pm-midnight.

TESTACCIO

One of the oldest areas of Rome, yet still unassailed by tourism, Testaccio remains a stronghold of Roman tradition. The food here is for people who want to get a true taste of Rome, or at least a taste of local animal parts. In the Mattatoio neighborhood around the old slaughterhouses, you can dare to eat as the Romans do at restaurants that serve authentic local delicacies, such as *animelle alla griglia* (grilled sweetbreads) and *fegato* (liver). The hippest **nightclubs** are located here as well, particularly around Monte Testaccio, so you can boogie your oxtail-intake away. Take Metro Linea B to Piramide, bus #27 from Termini or bus #92 from P. Venezia to reach this area south of the historic center.

Pizzeria Ficini, Via Luca della Robbia, 23 (tel. 574 30 17). Take Via Vanvitelli off Via Marmorata, then take your 1st left. For those who've lost their carnivorous nerve, a friendly, no-nonsense *pizzeria.* Pizzas L6000-8000, calzone L8000, wine L6000 per liter. Don't miss the *bruschetta con fagioli* (with beans, L2500). No cover. Open Sept.-July Tues.-Sun. 6pm-11:30pm.

Trattoria da Bucantino, Via Luca della Robbia, 84/86 (tel. 574 68 86). Take Via Vanvitelli off Via Marmorata, then take the first left. A Testaccio tavern with fabulous *antipasti.* Indigenous pasta delights like *bucatini all'amatriciana* (L9000) and *coda alla vaccinara* (stewed oxtail, L10,000). Wine L5000 per liter. Cover L3000. Open Tues.-Sun. noon-3pm and 7:30-11pm. Closed most of August.

Il Caffè del Seme e la Foglia, Via Galvani, 18 (tel. 574 30 08), on the corner of Via Nicola Zabaglia. A friendly bar/sandwich place that specializes in all possible permutations of salad. The lively pastoral scene painted on the wall matches the temperament of the locals squashed around the tables. Salads L7000, creative sandwiches (try the *Indiano* with turkey and curry) L4000 and up. Open daily 7am-2am, lunch served 1-3:30pm, dinner served 8pm-midnight.

Trattoria Turiddo, Via Galvani, 64 (tel. 575 04 47), in the Mattatoio district of Testaccio (take bus #27 from Termini or the Colosseum). Locals come here for the food that they grew up on, like *rigatoni con pagliata* (with tomato and lamb intestine, L9000), *coda alla vaccinara* (stewed oxtail, L15,000), and *animelle alla griglia* (grilled sweetbreads, L11,000). Standard Roman specialties available for the weak of stomach. Vegetarians and the queasy are strongly cautioned. Cover L2000. Open mid-Sept. to mid-Aug. Mon.-Tues. and Thurs.-Sat. 12:30-2:30pm and 7-10:30pm, Sun. 1-2:30pm.

SAN LORENZO

A five-minute bus ride east of Termini on bus #71 or 492 (get off when the bus turns onto Via Tiburtina by the old city walls), San Lorenzo sits at the edge of the Città Universitaria. This trendy, tourist-free zone is home to Marxist students and cutting-edge artists. Many unpretentious *trattorie* and *pizzerie* offer grand cuisine for the university students and the traveler who dares to leave the historic center.

Il Pulcino Ballerino, Via degli Equi, 66/68 (tel. 49 03 01), off Via Tiburtina. Artsy atmosphere, artsy cuisine. English and American rock music plays in the background while the cook stirs up unusual dishes like their *tagliolini del pulcino* (pasta in a lemon cream sauce, L9000), *trofie* with rosemary, spinach, and *mascarpone* (L10,000), or *risotto Mirò* (with arugula, radicchio, and *parmigiano*, L10,000). Cover L2000. Open Mon.-Sat. 8pm-midnight. Closed 1st 2 weeks of August. AmEx, MC, Visa.

Super Pizza Rustica a Taglio, Largo degli Oschi, 67, off Via degli Umbri. Wonderful pizza by the slice at non-tourist prices. Pizza with peppers (L1500 per *etto*) and potato with rosemary (L2000 per *etto*). Try the *fiori di zucca* (L1600 per *etto*). Open Mon.-Sat. 8am-9pm.

La Tana Sarda, Via Tiburtina, 116 (tel. 49 35 50). Personable Sardinians rush from table to table, piling plates with delicacies. Romans rave about the *gnocchetti sardi* (L8000) and the *penne alla gorgonzola* (L8000). For dessert, try the *dolcetti sardi* for L5000. Pizza L8000-10,000. Cover L2000. Open Mon.-Sat. noon-2:30pm, 5-11pm. Closed mid-Aug. through mid-Sept.

Pizzeria la Pappardella, Via degli Equi, 56 (tel. 446 93 49), off Via Tiburtina at the Largo dei Falisci. Exquisitely inexpensive, offering a variety of authentic Roman cuisine in a relatively tourist-free atmosphere. Try their *pappardelle alla burina* (pasta with sausage, peas, and cream sauce, L6000), with the *bruschetta al pomodoro* (crisp bread with tomatoes and olive oil, L1500). Open Tues.-Sat. noon-3:30pm, 6pm-midnight.

Trattoria Colli Emiliani, Via Tiburtina, 104, at the corner of Via dei Latini. Charming, with homestyle cooking at tables with checkered tablecloths. The grilled *scamorza* (L7000) and *penne all'arrabbiata* (L7500) are especially good. Open Mon.-Sat. noon-3pm and 7:30-11pm.

Pizzeria Formula I, Via degli Equi, 13 (tel. 445 38 66), in San Lorenzo, off Via Tiburtina. Romans know their pizza, so when it's as good and cheap as this, expect to wait. Pizza of all varieties L6000-8500; *alla melanzane* L7,500. The owner recommends *filetti di baccalà* (fried fish fillet, L12,500). Very crowded. Open Mon.-Sat. 6:30pm-12:30am.

Pizzeria il Maratoneta, Via dei Sardi, 20 (tel. 49 00 27), off Via Tiburtina. Four young marathoners bake pizza on the run (L6000-10,000). Tomatoes and marinated seafood cover half of their gorgeous *pizza mare e monte* (sea and mountain pizza), while tomatoes, *mozzarella,* mushrooms, eggplant, onion, zucchini, and peppers bury the other half (L8000). Crowded. No cover. Throngs at outdoor tables. Open Mon.-Sat. 5:30pm-12:30am.

Pizzeria l'Economica, Via Tiburtina, 46 (tel. 445 66 69), after Largo dei Falisci. Eating here is like eating at a United Nations Pizza Convention, since the name and outdoor dining seem to attract more tourists than Italians. It doesn't bother the family that owns it; they just serve delicious, cheap pizza and hope they serve you what you ordered. *Antipasto* salad L6000. *Pizza con funghi* L6000. Crowded. Go early or late to avoid a wait. Open Sept.-July Mon.-Sat. 6:30-11pm.

NEAR THE STATION

There is no reason to subject yourself to the gastronomic nightmare of the tourist-trapping restaurants around Termini; a 20-minute stroll from the station can take you to virtually any historic district this side of the Tiber—with quieter streets, tastier viands, and a more relaxing atmosphere. Still, when you've got blisters on your feet and hunger pangs in your belly, the following establishments provide excellent service for a largely local clientele.

North of Termini

La Cantinola da Livio, Via Calabria, 26 (tel. 482 05 19 or 474 39 62). Take Via Piave off Via XX Settembre, then take the 4th left onto Via Calabria. This cozy establishment specializes in *frutti di mare;* live lobsters wait nervously in tanks by the door. Stellar cuisine; impeccable service. Seafood fresh from Sardinia daily. *Spaghetti alla Cantinola* L9000. *Scampi* L16,000. *Antipasto di mare* L10,000. Cover L2500. Open Mon.-Sat. 12:30-3pm and 7:30-11:30pm. AmEx, MC, Visa.

Da Giggetto, Via Alessandria, 43 (tel. 854 34 90), near the Porta Pia. This place claims to be "the king of pizza"—you'll have a festive and satisfying meal deciding if it's true. The savory *bruschetta* with tomatoes and mozzarella (L3500) is just a prelude to the pizza (L7000-10,000). Open Mon.-Sat. 7pm-1am. Open in August.

Restaurant Monte Arci, Via Castelfidardo, 33 (tel. 474 48 90). Take Via Solferino past P. dell'Indipendenza and then take the first left past the piazza. Boisterous waiters serve delectable *paglia e fieno al Monte Arci* (a pasta and spinach dish,

L10,000) and *gnocchetti* (L7000). Wood-oven pizzas in the evening. Cover L2500. Open Mon.-Sat. 12:30-2:30pm and 7-11:30pm. AmEx, Visa.

Hosteria la Capitale, Via Goito, 50 (tel. 48 62 91), off Piazza Indipendenza. Perfect for those times when your *lire* just can't stretch any farther. Tasty and friendly. Pastas and rice dishes L6000; pizzas around L7000. Open Tues.-Sat.

South of Termini

Osteria con Cucina de Andreis Luciano, Via Giovanni Amendola, 73/75 (tel. 488 16 40). Take Via Cavour west from P. del Cinquecento; Via Giovanni Amendola is the 1st intersecting street. A green beaded curtain screens the entrance to this haven for the hungry. International crowd does not make this place any less Italian. Pasta L3900-4700. Huge marinated half-chicken L6500. Wine L3300 per liter. Cover L1000. Service 10%. Open Mon.-Fri. 11:30am-9pm, Sat. 11:30am-5pm.

Ristorante Due Colonne, Via dei Serpenti, 91 (tel. 488 08 52), 2nd right off Via Nazionale from Largo Magnanapoli (behind Trajan's Forum). Don't let the touristy-looking cover of the menu fool you. Here you'll find Roman standards served up to Italians on their lunch breaks from offices on nearby Via Nazionale. *Pasta e fagioli* L6500. *Penne con gorgonzola e rucola* L9000. *Pizza Margherita* L8000. Open Mon-Sat. noon-3:30pm and 7pm-midnight. AmEx, MC, Visa.

Est!!! Est!!! Est!!!, Via Genova, 32 (tel. 488 11 07), to the right of Via Nazionale from the station. Named for the wine (L6000 per liter). Colorful and campy interior, with great *insalata caprese* (L9000) and pizzas (L9500). No cover. Open Tues.-Sun. 6:30-11:30pm.

Trattoria Fulvimari, Via Principe Amedeo, 7 (tel. 474 06 26). As rustic as the area gets. Expansive wall murals show off famous sights. Pasta L6000-9000. Omelettes L8000. Steak L13,000. Cover L1500. Open daily noon-3pm and 6-11pm.

DOLCI (DESSERTS)

✓ **Palazzo del Freddo Giovanni Fassi,** Via Principe Eugenio, 65/67 (tel. 446 47 40), off P. Emanuele, west of Termini. This century-old *gelato* factory is a confectionery altar duly worshiped by many. Try *riso* (rice), try *coco* (coconut), try them all. Some argue that the *gelato* here beats Giolitti's hands down, and we agree. Try both and argue your calories away. Cones L2000-3000. Open Tues.-Sun. noon-midnight; in summer also open Mon. 6pm-midnight.

Giolitti, Via degli Uffici del Vicario, 40 (tel. 699 12 43). From the Pantheon, follow Via del Pantheon (at the north end of the *piazza*) to its end and then take Via della Maddelena (in front of you) to *its* end; Via degli Uffici del Vicario is on the right. A Roman institution as venerable as the Vatican, Giolitti is revered by many as the home of Rome's greatest *gelato*. Indulge yourself with their gargantuan 10-scoop "Olimpico" sundae for L11,000, and don't forget the homemade *panna*. It's futile to make flavor suggestions. You'll just have to try them all yourself. Open Tues.-Sun. 7am-2am.

Sweet Sweet Way, Via del Corso, 70 (tel. 36 00 18 88), near intersection with Via Vittoria. A bright, colorful candy smorgasbord and perfect remedy for a sudden drop in blood-sugar, perhaps induced by the prices of the clothing in the swanky boutiques near the Spanish Steps. Gargantuan assortment of chewy, sugary morsels for L2000-3500 per 100g, chocolate morsels L4000 per 100g. Open every day, 10am-8pm. AmEx, MC, Visa.

Tre Scalini, Piazza Navona, 30 (tel. 68 80 19 96). This classy, old-fashioned spot is famous for its perfect *tartufo,* a menacing hunk of chocolate ice cream rolled in chocolate shavings, but fame has brought tourists and boosted the prices. *Tartufo* at the bar is L5000; still a splurge, but *so* worth it. Open Thurs.-Tues. 8am-1am.

Gelateria Trevi di A. Cercere, Via del Lavatore, 84/85 (tel. 679 20 60), near the Trevi Fountain. A small *gelateria* of yesteryear whose famous *zabaglione* (L2000) puts the glitzy *gelaterie* down the street to shame. Open daily 10am-2am.

Il Fornaio, Via dei Baullari, 5-7 (tel. 68 80 39 47), across from P. San Pantaleo, south of Piazza Navona. The smell of goods baking makes it impossible to walk on by. Every cookie possibility imaginable (*biscottini*, L1900 per *etto*); desserts (*mele in gabbia* L1300 per *etto*). Open Mon.-Sat. 7:30am-8pm.

Grattachecca (di Ponte Cestio), at the end of the Trastevere side. Rightfully the most popular booth in town. Watch a butterfly tattoo come to life, as the bulging bicep of the man shaving the ice pumps life into your *granita*. Ask for a few syrups on your slush—*amarena* (sour cherry) and *mirtillo* (blueberry) are great choices. The house specialty is lemon and coconut. Regular L3500. Open daily in summer, 11am until around 2am.

Selarum, Via dei Fienaroli, 12 (tel. 581 91 30), off Via d. Fratte di Trastevere. A lusciously leafy garden terrace where heftily priced gourmet desserts are served to the lilting tones of live jazz. Dessert wines (L8000-13,000). Try one of the specialties like the *mandorlita* (chocolate, *amaretto,* and whipped cream, L15,000). Open May-Oct. 9pm-1:30am (music usually starts around 10:30pm).

Da Quinto (*frullateria*), Via di Tor Millina, 15 (tel. 686 56 57) off Piazza Navona. Talk about refreshing. Every combination of ice, milk, fruit, cream, and *gelato* imaginable. Possibilities are endless. Prices range from L3000-6000. Open daily noon-2am. Closed Wed. in winter. Hours may vary.

CAFFÈ

In most *caffè* and *bar,* you pay one price to stand and drink at the bar, and a higher price (as much as double) if you sit down at a table. There should be a menu on the wall of the bar listing the prices *at bar* (standing up) and *a tavola* (at a table). Check the prices before you settle in: around the historic center and the major *piazze,* the price of a *cappuccino* can jump from L1500 to L5000 when your tush hits the chair.

Caffè Sant'Eustachio, P. Sant'Eustachio, 82 (tel. 686 13 09), in the *piazza* southwest of the Pantheon. Take Via Monterone off Corso Vittorio Emanuele II. Rome's "coffee empire." Once a favorite haunt of Stendhal and other literary expatriates, now bursting with Romans. Neither the recipe nor the decor has changed since it opened in 1938. Sit in the *piazza* and nurse a steaming *cappuccino* (L4000, L2000 at the bar). *Granita di caffè* with the works (L8000, L6000 at the bar), or try their very own *gran caffè speciale* (L5000, L3000 at the bar) for a sweet, frothy, and powerful zap of climactic delight. Buy some beans to take home (½kg L15,000). Open Sept.-July Tues.-Sun. 8:30am-1am.

Bar S. Calisto, P. S. Calisto, 4, in Trastevere (tel. 583 58 69). *Il preferito* across the river, where Trasteverean youth, expatriates, and Roman elders socialize over truly incredible yet inexpensive *cappuccino* (L1200 sitting or standing) and *granita di limone* (L2000). Open Mon.-Sat. 6am-1:30am, Sun. 4pm-1:30am; winter Sun. closed. Crowded.

Caffè della Pace, Via della Pace, 3/7 (tel. 686 12 16), off P. Navona. Not just a L4000 cup of *cappuccino,* but an entire lifestyle. Come prepared with newspapers, books, letters to write, and clever conversations to start up; get the most out of the *a tavola* price hike at the dark wood tables. Chic, expensive, and beneath vines and church façades. *Cappuccino:* daytime L2000 at bar, L4000 at table; nighttime L4000 at bar, L8000 at table. Red wine L7000 at bar, L10,000 at table. Open 5pm-midnight.

Tazza d'Oro, Via degli Orfani, 84/86 (tel. 679 27 68), off the northeast corner of P. della Rotonda. No place to sit down, but a great brew at fantastic prices (*caffè* L1100). Superlative *granita di caffè* (L1300) after a hot day of sight-seeing. Extensive coffee bean selection at L32,000-34,000 per kg. Chamomile tea L2000. Open Mon.-Sat. 7am-8pm.

■ ■ ■ SIGHTS

Rome wasn't built in a day, and it's not likely that you'll see much of the city in 24 hours either. The city practically implodes with monuments—ancient temples, medieval fortresses, baroque confections of marble and rushing water—crowding next to and on top of each other on every street. No other city in the world can lay claim to so many masterpieces of architecture from so many different eras, not to mention the treasures of painting and sculpture hidden inside. Use this guide to get an idea of the possibilities, decide what appeals to you, and set out to see what you can, remembering that the city is a hot and dusty place in summer (and a crowded and chaotic one year-round), likely to sap the energy of even the most experienced sight-seer. Pace yourself, make time for a stop in a bar or *caffè*, and carry a bottle of water refillable at any of Rome's corner water-spouts; you'll see Romans bending to drink from the more than potable streams.

THE ANCIENT CITY CENTER

The Capitoline Hill (Campidoglio)

The original capitol and one of the most sacred parts of the ancient Roman city, the **Capitoline Hill** still serves as the seat of the city's government and is crowned by a spectacular *piazza* of Michelangelo's design. In ancient times the hill was dominated by a gilded temple to Jupiter, chief god of the Roman pantheon, along with the state mint and senatorial archives.

The north face of the hill, facing Piazza Venezia, has been completely swallowed by the gargantuan **Vittorio Emanuele II Monument** (1885), a colossal structure of gleaming white marble commemorating the short-lived House of Savoy, whose kings briefly ruled the newly unified Italy. A monstrosity of epic proportions, it is often dubbed "the wedding cake" or "Mussolini's typewriter." Around the right of the monument as you face it, a cluster of staircases rises to the top of the hill. The left-hand staircase has 124 steep medieval steps climbing to the unadorned façade of the 7th-century Church of Santa Maria in Aracoeli (see below). The right-hand staircase, the curving Via delle Tre Pile (1692), climbs toward a small park. In the center rises Michelangelo's magnificent staircase, **la cordonata,** a stepped ramp built in 1536 so that the Emperor Charles V, apparently penitent over his sack of the city a decade before, could ride his horse right up the hill to meet Pope Paul III during a triumphal visit. On your way up *la cordonata,* pause to note the **statue of Cola di Rienzo** (on your left), leader of a popular revolt in 1347 which attempted to reestablish a Roman Republic. The statue marks the spot where the disgruntled populace tore the demagogue limb from limb, when only a short while before they had elected him first consul.

To the left and right of Michelangelo's spacious **Piazza di Campidoglio** stand the twin **Palazzo dei Conservatori** and **Palazzo Nuovo,** while at the far end, opposite the stairs, is the turreted **Palazzo dei Senatori.** Paul III had the famous equestrian **statue of Marcus Aurelius** brought here from the Lateran Palace, but both man and steed proved too delicate to combat the assault of modern pollution and were removed for restoration ten years ago. The emperor now resides in climate-controlled comfort in the courtyard of the Palazzo dei Conservatori. Michelangelo also set up the imposing statues of the twin warriors Castor and Pollux and, at the base of his ingenious split staircase, the two reclining river gods and the statue of the goddess Roma. The twin *palazzi* are not exactly parallel to each other, nor do they meet the Palazzo dei Senatori at an exact 90° angle; the ground slopes gently toward the great staircase, drawing the visitor into the open space.

The **Musei Capitolini** are housed in the twin *palazzi* on either side of the *piazza*. The museums' collection of ancient sculpture is among the largest in the world. In the **Palazzo Nuovo** (on the left as you enter the *piazza*), look for the colossal statue of Marcus Aurelius on his horse, the morbid *Dying Gaul,* his chest pierced with wounds, and the *Satyr Rising* on the windowed wall nearby (the "Marble Faun" that inspired Hawthorne's book of the same title). Across the *piazza*, the **Palazzo dei Conservatori** houses four museums: the **Museo Nuovo** on the ground floor, the **Sale dei Conservatori** and the **Museo del Palazzo dei Conservatori** on the first floor, and the **Pinacoteca** on the second floor. In the courtyard, check out the assorted gigantic body parts of what was once a colossus of Constantine. Among the statues in the halls above are the Etruscan *Capitoline Wolf* (Romulus and Remus included and suckling) and the *Spinario,* a sculpture of a young lad extracting a thorn from his foot. The Pinacoteca houses Bellini's *Portrait of a Young Man,* Titian's *Baptism of Christ,* Rubens's *Romulus and Remus Fed by the Wolf,* and Caravaggio's *Gypsy Fortune-Teller.* (Museums open winter Tues. and Sat. 9am-1:30pm and 5-8pm, Wed.-Fri. and Sun. 9am-1:30pm; summer Tues. 9am-1:30pm and 5-8pm, Wed.-Fri. 9am-1:30pm, Sat. 9am-1:30pm and 8-11pm, Sun. 9am-1pm. Admission L10,000, with student ID L5000, under 18 and over 60 free. Free on last Sun. of each month. One ticket entitles entrance to both buildings.)

Flanking the Palazzo dei Senatori, paths lead downward to promontories with panoramic **views of the Forum and the Colosseum.** Stairs lead up from the left of the Palazzo dei Senatori to the rear entrance of the **Church of Santa Maria in Aracoeli,** a 7th-century church filled with a jumble of monuments from every century since. Cross the pavement, studded with worn medieval tombs, to the stunning **Bufalini Chapel,** considered among the finest works of Pinturicchio. (Open daily 7am-noon and 4-7pm.) Down the hill from the back stairs of the Aracoeli squats the gloomy **Mamertine Prison,** later consecrated as the **Church of Saint Pietro in Carcere** in commemoration of St. Peter's incarceration here. Other famous inmates include Vercingetorix, chieftain of the Gauls, and the accomplices of would-be dictator Catiline. (Open daily 9am-noon and 2:30-5pm. Free but donation requested.)

Near the Campidoglio, two parks provide great spots for picnicking. Walk around Via delle Tre Pile to reach the first; climb up the stairs by the Museo Nuovo (passing through a *loggia*) to reach the wilder second and its views of the Palatine.

The Case of the Burgled Bambino

In a small chapel behind the Bufalini's altar complex, the *Santo Bambino*—a relic supposedly carved from an olive tree in the Garden of Gethsemane—reposes in swaddled majesty and bears a disturbing resemblance to a Cabbage Patch Kid. Around the Bambino's cradle lie stacks of letters sent from around the world, often simply addressed to "Bambino. Roma." The blessed Bambino was traditionally carried to the houses of sick children. In recent years, these trips have become less frequent, and now they are usually made by taxi. According to one legend, a Roman woman who stole the Bambino promptly fell gravely ill; upon returning the relic on the advice of her confessor, she was miraculously healed. Unfortunately, a contemporary thief, apparently lacking such sound advice, absconded with the Bambino on February 1, 1994 and has not returned. For now, a Holy Copy takes the Holy Baby's place among the piles of mail.

The Roman Forum

The Forum was originally a marshy valley prone to being flooded by the Tiber. Rome's earliest Iron Age inhabitants (1000-900 BC) eschewed its low, unhealthy swampiness in favor of the Palatine Hill, descending only to bury their dead. In the 8th and 7th centuries BC, Etruscans and Greeks used Tiber Island as a crossing point for their trade; they brought prosperity to the area, which soon became a weekly marketplace. The early Romans came down from the Palatine, paved the site, drained it with a covered sewer (the **Cloaca Maxima**), and built their first shrines to the vital forces of fire and water. By the end of the 6th century BC the Romans, boosted by commercial success, had overthrown their Etruscan overlords and established a republic. The Curia (the meeting place of the Senate), the Comitium Well (or assembly place), and the Rostra (or speaker's platform) were built to serve the infant democracy, along with the earliest temples (to Saturn and to Castor and Pollux) dedicated in thanks for the civic revolution.

The conquest of Greece in the 2nd century BC brought new architectural forms to the city, including the *basilica,* which was first used as a center for business and judicial activities. The wealthiest Roman families (including Julius Caesar's) lined the town square in front of the Curia with *basiliche,* for the good of the public and for their own reputations. The Vestal Virgins built their house over a street full of prostitutes, priests sacrificed in the temples, victorious generals led triumphal processions up the Capitoline, and pickpockets cased the tourists (some things never change). (Forum and Palatine open Mon.-Sat. 9am-7pm, Sun. 9am-2pm; winter

Mon.-Sat. 9am-3pm, Sun. 9am-1pm. Admission L10,000 and last admittance 1 hour before closing.)

Before entering the Forum proper, you may want to invest in a map to help you make more sense of the chaotic and frequently overlapping ruins. From the entrance gate in Via dei Fori Imperiali (across from the end of Via Cavour), a ramp descends, past the Temple of Antoninus and Faustina on the left and the remains of the Basilica Aemilia on the right, to the basalt stones of the **Via Sacra,** the main thoroughfare of the Forum and the oldest street in Rome. The Via Sacra leads right to the slopes of the Capitoline Hill.

Turn right at the end of the entrance ramp; you will be on the Via Sacra facing the Capitoline Hill and the Arch of Septimius Severus. The Via Sacra cuts through the old market square and civic center of Republican Rome, bordered by the **Basilica Aemilia** (to your immediate right) and the intact brick **Curia** building (to your right after the Basilica Aemilia as you walk down to the arch). The Basilica Aemilia, built in 179 BC, housed the guild of the *argentarii,* or money-changers, who operated the first *cambi* in the city, providing Roman *denarii* for traders and tourists. The broad space in front of the Basilica is the **Forum** itself. The Curia was one of the oldest buildings in the Forum, although the present structure dates from the time of Diocletian (303 AD); it was converted to a church in 630 AD and only restored this century. Occasionally the interior is open; you can see an intricate well-preserved inlaid marble pavement and the steps where the Senators brought their own portable chairs to their meetings. The broad space in front of the Curia was the **Comitium Well,** where male citizens came to vote. The brick platform to the left of the Curia (as you face the arch) was the **Rostra,** named for the beak-shaped prows of ships which were mounted here after a Roman naval victory at the Battle of Anzio in 338 BC. Senators and consuls orated to the Roman plebes from here, and any citizen could mount to voice his opinion. The hefty **Arch of Septimius Severus** at the end of Via Sacra is in this Republican square; dedicated in 203 AD to celebrate that emperor's victories in the Middle East, the arch reliefs depict the imperial family. Severus's son and successor, Caracalla, grabbed the throne, knocking off his brother Geta and scraping his portrait off the arch. Halfway up the Capitoline Hill, the grey tufa walls of the **Tabularium,** once the repository of senate archives, now serve as the basement to the Renaissance **Palazzo dei Senatori** (closed for renovation). Across the square to the left of the Temple of Saturn, the **Basilica Julia,** built on the site of an earlier *basilica* by Julius Caesar in 54 BC, followed the same plan as the Basilica Aemilia but on a grander scale. It was used for judicial tribunals; look for inscribed grids and circles in the steps where anxious Romans, waiting their turns to go before the judge, played an ancient version of tic-tac-toe.

This part of the Forum, the original market square, was graced by a number of shrines and sacred precincts. Between the Curia and the Rostra, a flat gray stone — the **Lapis Niger** (meaning "black stone")—marks the supposed burial place of Romulus, the legendary founder of the city. Closer to the Basilica Julia, the **Three Sacred Trees** of Rome—olive, fig, and grapevine—have been replanted. On the other side, right across from the Basilica Julia, a circular tufa basin commemorates the **Lacus Curtius,** an ancient spring where, legend says, a gaping chasm opened in 362 BC, into which the Roman patrician Marcus Curtius threw himself in order to save the city. A relief records his sacrifice.

The three great temples of the lower Forum (dedicated to Saturn, the Emperor Vespasian, and Concord) have been closed off during excavations, although the eight recently restored columns of the **Temple of Saturn** have finally been freed of their scaffolding. This was the site of the public treasury and an underground stash of sacred treasures. At the far end of the Basilica Julia, three white marble columns and a shred of architrave mark the massive podium of the **Temple of Castor and Pollux,** dedicated in 484 BC in celebration of the Roman rebellion against their Etruscan king, Tarquinius Superbus (see page 61). Legend says that immediately after the battle the twin gods Castor and Pollux appeared in the Forum to water their horses at the adjacent **Basin of Juturna** (*Lacus Juturnae*), now marked by a reconstructed marble aedicule to the left of the gods' own temple. Across the street from the Temple of Castor and Pollux is the rectangular base of the **Temple of the Deified Julius,** which Augustus built in 29 BC to honor his murdered adoptive father and to proclaim himself the son of a god. The circular pile of rocks inside probably marks the spot where Caesar's body was cremated in 44 BC (he was assassinated near Largo Argentina); pious Romans still leave flowers here on the Ides of March. For himself, Augustus built the **Arch of Augustus,** marked by a marble slab next to the temple, which framed the Via Sacra and commemorated his triumphs. The circular building behind the temple is the restored **Temple of Vesta,** which sits on a foundation dating back to the Etruscan period. Built in imitation of an archaic round Latin hut, this is where the Vestal Virgins tended the sacred fire of the city. Behind the temple lay the triangular **Regia,** the palace of Numa Pompilius, the second king of Rome, and later the office of the Pontifex Maximus, Rome's highest priest.

The **House of the Vestal Virgins** occupied the sprawling complex of rooms and courtyards to the right and rear of the temple of Vesta, in the shade of the Palatine Hill. The six virgins who officiated over Vesta's rites, each ordained at the age of seven, lived in spacious and celibate seclusion here for thirty years above the din of the Forum. A tour through the storerooms and lower rooms of the house brings you back to Via Sacra and the **Temple of Antoninus and Faustina** (to the immediate right as you face the entrance ramp), whose columns and frieze were incorporated into the **Church of San Lorenzo in Miranda** before the 12th century (its façade dates from the Baroque period). Antoninus, one of the "good emperors" of the 2nd century AD, had the temple built in honor of his wife Faustina, who died in 141; the Roman people returned the favor after his own death, and the temple now stands to commemorate both of them. In the shadow of the temple (to the right as you face it), the archaic **necropolis,** with Iron Age graves from the 8th century BC, was excavated earlier in this century, lending credence to Rome's own legendary foundation date of 753 BC. Bodies were found in two types of burials: *tombe a fossa* (hollowed-out tree trunk-coffins buried in ditches) and *tombe a pozzo* (cremation urns in the shape of little village huts, visible in museums all over Rome). Here the Via Sacra runs over the **Cloaca Maxima,** the ancient sewer that still drains water from the marshy valley. The street then passes what is called the **Temple of Romulus,** a round building that still retains its ancient bronze doors from the 4th century AD. Not a temple at all, it probably served as the office of the urban praetor during the Empire (no admittance).

The Velia

The street now leads out of the Forum proper to the gigantic **Basilica of Maxentius** (also known as the Basilica of Constantine). The three gaping arches you'll see are actually only the side chapels of an enormous central hall whose coffered ceiling covered the entire gravel court, as well as another three chapels on the other side. Michelangelo studied its architecture before constructing St. Peter's Cathedral.

The baroque façade of the **Church of S. Francesca Romana** (built over Hadrian's Temple to Venus and Rome) hides the entrance of the **Forum Antiquarium** (open daily 9am-1pm). Most of the rooms have been closed for years, but a few on the ground floor display funerary urns and skeletons from the necropolis. On the summit of the Velia (the shoulder running down from the Palatine) is the **Arch of Titus,** built by the emperor Domitian to celebrate his brother Titus's destruction of Jerusalem in 70 AD. The reliefs inside the arch depict the Roman sack of the great Jewish temple, including the pillage of a giant menorah. The Via Sacra leads to an exit on the other side of the hill, an easy route to the Colosseum.

The Palatine Hill

The flowering sculptured gardens and broad grassy expanses of the **Palatine Hill** are a refreshing change from the dusty Forum; the hill is an ideal place to picnic after a morning in the ruins. Though there are lots of ancient remnants to see here, the cool breezes and sweeping views of Rome are the real reason to make the steep

THE ANCIENT CITY CENTER

climb from below. The best way to begin is from the stairs (to the right after the street turns at the Arch of Titus) which ascend past the Villa Farnese to the **Farnese Gardens.** Go through the gardens and past a *nymphaeum,* or enclosed fountain room, to a series of terraces with views of the city. From the top, head through the avenues of roses and orange trees until you reach another terrace, with a breathtaking view of the Forum, the Imperial Fora, and the Quirinal Hill. The gardens continue along the western side of the hill, where an octagonal boxhedge maze in the center follows the layout of a real maze excavated from the Palace of Tiberius underneath (excavated early in this century, but the Romans decided the gardens were nicer, and filled the dig back in). At the southwest corner (at the extreme top right of the gardens), another terrace looks out over Capitoline Hill, the Republican temples of the Forum Boarium, and the Farnese Gardens to the long, spooky **Cryptoporticus,** a tunnel which connected Tiberius' palace with the later buildings on this side of the hill (closed for renovation in 1996). Used by slaves and imperial couriers, it may have been built by Nero as a secret passage. The short end of the tunnel brings you up to the vast ruins of the solemn **Domus Augustana,** the imperial palace built by Domitian (81-96 AD) and used by most of the subsequent emperors as the headquarters of the empire. The exterior walls, even in their ruined state, are so high that archaeologists are still unsure how the roof that once covered them was constructed. The easternmost wing of the palace contains the curious so-called **Stadium,** a sunken oval space that was once thought to have been a private racetrack; it now seems that it was a garden.

Imperial Fora

The **Imperial Fora** sprawl across the street from the Roman Forum; they are a vast conglomeration of temples, *basiliche,* and public squares constructed by the emperors of the first and 2nd centuries AD, partly in response to increasing congestion in the old Forum and partly for their own greater glory. With imperial aspirations of his own, Mussolini cleared the area of medieval constructions in 1930s and built the Via dei Fori Imperiali to pass among (and over) the newly excavated remains. The fora were only partially excavated, and the broad, barren thoroughfare cuts across the old foundations at an awkward angle. All of the fora remain closed for renovation in 1995, with the exception of the Markets of Trajan (see below). The rest are all at least partially visible (except for the Forum of Vespasian) from street level.

The **Forum of Trajan,** the largest and most impressive of the lot, spreads across Via dei Fori Imperiali below two baroque churches at the eastern end of Piazza Venezia. The complex was built between 107 and 113 AD to celebrate the emperor's victorious Dacian campaign (fought in modern Romania). Eight years of restoration helped reveal the nearly perfectly preserved spiral of the **Column of Trajan,** one of the greatest specimens of Roman relief-sculpture ever carved. The 200-meter-long continuous frieze wrapped around the column is one of the most dense and ambitious artistic endeavors of the ancient world. A statue of the emperor once crowned the column, but was destroyed in the Middle Ages and replaced by a statue of St. Peter; Trajan's ashes, however, are kept in the base. Down the street (but with the entrance on Via IV Novembre, 94, up the steps in Via Magnanapoli behind the baroque churches), the **Markets of Trajan** provide a glimpse of daily life in the ancient city. The semicircular complex, built into the side of the Quirinal Hill, sheltered several levels of *tabernae,* or single-room stores, along cobbled streets. You can stroll along the basalt paving stones and climb to a spectacular view of Trajan's Forum and the Capitoline Hill. (Tel. 679 00 40. Open in summer Tues., Thurs., and Sat. 9am-6pm, Wed. and Fri. 9am-1:30pm, Sun. 9am-1pm; in winter Tues.-Sat. 9am-1:30pm, Sun. 9am-1pm. Admission L3750, EU members under 18 and over 60 free.)

Across the Via dei Fori Imperiali, in the shade of the Vittorio Emanuele II Monument, lie the paltry remains of the **Forum of Caesar.** A few reconstructed columns are all that remain of Caesar's **temple to Venus Genetrix** (Mother Venus, from whom he claimed descent), but the stone façades of the arcades he built for Roman shops are better preserved.

Adjacent to the Markets of Trajan across Via dei Fori Imperiali, the gray tufa wall of the **Forum of Augustus** backs up against the side of the Quirinal Hill. Dedicated by the Emperor in 2 BC in honor of Mars Ultor (Mars the Avenger), the huge complex commemorated Augustus's victory over Julius Caesar's murderers at the Battle of Philippi and the founding of his new imperial dynasty. The wall, built to protect the new forum from the seamy Subura slums that once spread up the hill behind it, isn't exactly straight; legend says that when the land was being prepared for construction, the ever-democratic Augustus couldn't convince one stubborn homeowner to give up his land, so the wall was built at an angle around it.

The Colosseum and the Arch of Constantine

The **Colosseum,** accessible from the Metro stop of the same name (Linea B; head for the plastic statue vendors across the street), stands as the enduring symbol of the Eternal City—a hollowed-out ghost of somber travertine marble that dwarfs every other ruin in the city. At its inauguration in 80 AD it could hold as many as 50,000 spectators; the first 100 days of operation saw some 5000 wild beasts perish in the bloody arena, and the slaughter didn't stop for three centuries. Gladiators fought each other here, and it is said the elliptical interior could be flooded for mock sea battles (we'll let you figure out how it was possible). The outside of the arena, still well preserved around three-quarters of its circumference, provided the inspiration for countless Renaissance and Baroque architectural confections, the triple stories of Doric, Ionic, and Corinthian columns being considered the ideal orchestration of classical orders. Almost all the marble stands and seats that once lined the now-raw interior were quarried by Renaissance popes for use in their own grandiose constructions, including St. Peter's Basilica and the Palazzo Barberini. The floor (now gone) lay over a labyrinth of brick cells, corridors, ramps, and elevators used for transporting wild animals from their cages up to the level of the arena. (Ground level of the Colosseum is open Mon.-Tues. and Thurs.-Sat. 9am-7pm, Wed. and Sun. 9am-1pm; June-Aug. until 6pm; free.) An ascent to the upper floors provides better views of the whole city and the nearby Forum. (Upper decks open Mon.-Tues. and Thurs.-Sat. 9am-6pm, Wed. and Sun. 9am-1pm; in winter Mon.-Tues. and Thurs. 9am 3pm. Admission to upper decks L8000; free for EU citizens under 18 and accompanied by an adult.)

Between the Colosseum and the Palatine Hill lies the remarkably intact **Arch of Constantine.** After his conversion to Christianity by a vision of a cross in the sky, Constantine built the arch to commemorate his victory over Maxentius at the Battle of the Milvian Bridge in 312. The triple arch, though well proportioned, is constructed almost entirely from sculptural fragments pillaged from older Roman monuments. The medallions were originally part of a monument to Hadrian and include depictions of his lover Antonius; the rectangular reliefs were taken from Trajan's Forum and show incongruous scenes of that emperor's defeat of the Dacians.

CENTRO STORICO (NORTHWEST OF THE ANCIENT CITY)

Campo dei Fiori and Via Giulia

Across Corso Vittorio Emanuele II from Piazza Navona (down Via della Cancelleria) is **Campo dei Fiori.** During Papal rule, the area was the site of countless executions. In the middle of the Campo, a statue marking the death site of one victim, Giordano Bruno (1548-1600), rises above the bustle, arms folded over his book. Scientifically and philosophically ahead of his time, Bruno sizzled at the stake in 1600 for taking Copernicus one step further: he argued that the universe had no center at all. Now the only carcasses that litter the *piazza* are those of the fish in the colorful market that springs up with fruit, fish, and flowers (open Mon.-Sat. 7am-2pm). The streets around the Campo are among the most picturesque in Rome and merit a few hours of exploration. The winding alleys may take you to a cloistered fountain, a secluded *piazza,* or a hidden church, or perhaps spill you back onto noisy Corso Vittorio Emanuele II. To get to the *centro storico,* take any bus to Largo Argentina, including the #75, 170, and 64 from Termini and Via Nazionale or the #56 and 60 from Piazza San Silvestro (south of the Spanish Steps) and Via del Tritone. From Piazza Venezia, take Via del Plebiscito at the north end of the *piazza* to Corso Vittorio Emanuele II.

Several streets lead south from Campo dei Fiori into **Piazza Farnese.** The square is dominated by the huge, stately **Palazzo Farnese,** considered the greatest of Rome's Renaissance *palazzi.* The Farnese, an obscure noble family from the backwoods of Lazio, parlayed Pope Alexander VI's affair with Giulia Farnese into a clutch of bishoprics for her son Alessandro, a fling at the Papal throne, and eventual dukedoms in Parma and Piacenza. Alessandro Farnese refounded the Inquisition as Paul III, the first Counter-Reformation pope (1534-1549), and commissioned the best architects of his day—Antonio da Sangallo, Michelangelo, and Giacomo della Porta—to design his dream abode. Since 1635, the French Embassy has rented the *palazzo* for one *lira* per 99 years in exchange for the Grand Opera House in Paris, home of the Italian Embassy. (Palace definitely *not* open to the public.) In the 16th and early 17th centuries, the Farnese family hosted great spectacles in the square and had two huge tubs (later converted into the present-day fountains) dug up from the Baths of Caracalla to serve as "royal boxes" for members of the self-made patrician family. Go around the back of the Palazzo Farnese for a glance at the gardens and Michelangelo's beautiful vine-covered bridge over Via Giulia.

Behind the elaborate baroque façade of the **Palazzo Spada,** in Piazza della Quercia to the left (east) of the Palazzo Farnese, you'll find the jewel-like picture collection of the **Galleria Spada** (tel. 686 11 58). In the 17th century, Cardinal Bernardino Spada bought up a grandiose assortment of paintings and sculpture, then commissioned an even more opulent set of great rooms to house them. The collection includes Titian's early *Portrait of a Musician* and Pietro Testa's *Allegory of the Massacre of the Innocents.* (Open Tues.-Sat. 9am-7pm, Sun. 9am-12:30pm; admission L4000, under 18 and over 60 free.)

As part of his campaign in the early 1500s to clean up Rome after the "Babylonian Captivity," Pope Julius II commissioned Bramante to construct the long street leading directly to the Vatican. The result was **Via Giulia,** an elegant and revolutionary contrast to the narrow and winding medieval streets. Today, the street remains one of the most peaceful and exclusive in Rome, with well-maintained *palazzi*, antique stores, and art galleries.

Piazza Navona

Despite popular belief, Emperor Domitian never used his 30,000-person stadium to shred naughty Christians; later emperors can take credit for that. Instead, he used the site of modern day **Piazza Navona** as a racetrack. From its opening day in 86 AD, the stadium witnessed daily contests of strength and agility: wrestling matches, javelin- and discus-tosses, foot- and chariot-races, and even mock naval battles (where the stadium was flooded and then floated with fleets of convicts). As the empire fell, real-life battles with marauding Goths replaced staged contests, and the stadium was used less and less. Resourceful Romans used its crumbling outer walls as foundations for new houses, thus preserving the original outline of the stadium. Large crowds returned to the *piazza* with the Renaissance, and from 1477 to 1869 the space hosted the city's general market. Festivals and jousts were commonplace, as was the contest of the *cuccagna,* in which contestants shimmied up a greased pole to win fabulous prizes. Nowadays, caricaturists, painters, and tourists mingle and people-watch from the benches and *caffè* tables. Female travelers will have no problem getting lights for cigarettes or company for strolls, as prowling Romeos vie to test their virility as well as their English.

Bernini's exuberant **Fountain of the Four Rivers** *(Fontana dei Quattro Fiumi),* commands the center of the *piazza.* Each of the four male river gods represents one of the globe's four continents (as they were then envisioned): the Ganges for Asia, the Danube for Europe, the Nile for Africa (veiled since the source of the river was unknown), and the Rio della Plata for the Americas. An old story holds that Bernini designed the Nile and Plata statues to shield their eyes from the sight of his archrival

Borromini's **Church of Sant'Agnese in Agone.** The story is cute but unlikely; the fountain was finished before the church was started. According to Christian legend, Saint Agnes was stripped naked in Domitian's stadium for saying no to the lascivious son of a low-ranking magistrate. When her hair miraculously grew and covered her sinful nudity, the powers-that-were tried to burn her at the stake. When the flames didn't even singe her, efficient Diocletian decided to cut her head clean off. This time it worked. The church marks the spot where she was exposed and houses her severed skull (the *sacra testa,* or "holy head") in its sacristy.

South of the church, **Palazzo Pamphili** was also built by the Rainaldis and Borromini. The façade of the **Church of San Giacomo degli Spagnoli** (a.k.a. **Madonna del Sacro Cuore**), on the southeast side of the *piazza,* hides a pristine Gothic interior (1450), restored in 1879. At the southern end of the *piazza,* the **Fontana del Moro** attracts pigeons and small children alike. Originally designed by Giacomo Della Porta in the 16th century, Bernini renovated it in 1653 and added *Il Moro,* the central figure perched on a mollusk (actually carved by Antonion Mari, one of Bernini's pupils). The tritons around the edge of the fountain were moved to the Giardino del Lago in the Villa Borghese in 1874 and replaced by copies.

Adding balance to the whole scene is the **Fountain of Neptune,** flowing in the north end of the *piazza.* It too was designed by Della Porta in the 16th century and spruced up by Bernini, but was without a central figure until 1878. Antonio Della Bitta then added the Neptune from which the fountain takes its name. The ruler of the sea frolics with Nereids, sea horses, and a cockeyed octopus.

From Piazza Navona, make your way west to the Vatican along narrow **Via del Governo Vecchio,** an ancient street now lined with offbeat art and antique galleries, vintage clothing stores, and cheap *trattorie.* The narrow passage used to be a Papal thoroughfare, lined with the townhouses of prosperous bankers and merchants. Though you probably won't be bumping into His Holiness anytime soon, you can still gawk at the medieval mansions overhanging the street, now filled with trendy boutiques. Via del Governo Vecchio meanders into **Piazza dell'Orologio,** where Borromini's baroque clock-tower stands guard (when not under scaffolding).

The Pantheon

The majestic **Pantheon** (tel. 36 98 31) has stood here for nearly 2000 years; its marble columns and pediment, bronze doors, and soaring domed interior (save superficial decorative changes) are all unchanged from the day it was erected. The temple has drawn visitors for centuries, in large part because it's one of the few Roman ruins that doesn't force you to rely too much on your imagination; the vast, serene interior not only preserves its perfect architectural proportions, but also retains the power to mystify and inspire, as it must have done for the ancients.

The building as it stands today is the product of the Emperor Hadrian's fertile architectural imagination. Though it's unclear whether the emperor actually drew up the plans himself, it's certain that the 2nd-century AD philosopher-king, for whom architecture was a favorite hobby, had a hand in its design. The temple, dedicated to "all the gods," was conceived as a celebration of the abstract spatial harmonies and celestial order bestowed on the universe by the divine powers. The classically proportioned façade, with its traditional triangular pediment, dedicatory inscription, and Corinthian columns, was designed to deceive the first-time visitor into expecting an equally traditional interior. Deceptive too is the inscription across the architrave and the façade: "Marcus Agrippa made it in his third consulship" (27 BC). Agrippa did build a "pantheon" here, but Hadrian tore it down and started over; Hadrian kept the inscription to avoid accusations of overweening pride.

Inside, the effects of light and shadow on the recessed coffers endow the vast space with an awesome, dizzying power. The dome itself, some 43m across, was constructed entirely out of poured concrete, without the support of vaults, arches, or ribs. Archaeologists and architects have puzzled for centuries over how the thing was actually erected, and it wasn't until the present century that a larger concrete dome could be built. The central oculus, which provided the only source of light for the entire building, also supports the weight of the dome, as all the inward forces of the sloping concrete are trapped in a ring of tension around the hole. The sunlight falling through the hole was used as a sundial to indicate not only the passing of the hours but also the dates of equinoxes and solstices.

Converted to the Church of Santa Maria ad Martyres (which title it retains to this day), the temple weathered the Middle Ages with few losses, though it sometimes did double-duty as a fortress and even a fishmarket. Later artists and architects adored and imitated the building, which served as the inspiration for countless Renaissance and neoclassical edifices, including Bramante's Tempietto, Palladio's Villa Rotonda, and America's own Jefferson Memorial. Michelangelo, using the dome as a model for his designs in St. Peter's Basilica, is said to have made his own dome 1m shorter in diameter than the Pantheon's, out of respect for his ancient model. (Pantheon open June Mon.-Sat. 9am-6pm, Sun. 9am-1pm; July-Aug. Mon.-Sat. 9am-6:30pm, Sun. 9am-1pm; Oct.-May Mon.-Sat. 9am-4pm, Sun. 9am-1pm, Sun. Mass 9:45-11:15am; free.)

In the *piazza* before the temple, Giacomo della Porta's playful, recently restored late-Renaissance fountain supports an **Egyptian obelisk,** added in the 18th century when obelisks, popular among ancient Romans, were once again in fashion. Around the left side of the Pantheon another obelisk marks the center of tiny **Piazza Minerva,** supported by Bernini's curious elephant statue. Behind the Pantheon, the unassuming façade of the **Church of Santa Maria Sopra Minerva** hides some of Renaissance Rome's artistic masterpieces. To the right of the entrance, six plaques mark the high-water level of floodings of the Tiber over the centuries. Inside the church, stained-glass windows cast a soft radiance on the Gothic interior and celestial ceiling. The chapels in the right-hand aisle (on the south side) house a number of treasures, including a panel of the *Annunciation* by Antoniazzo Romano and a statue of *St. Sebastian* recently attributed to Michelangelo. The south transept houses the famous **Carafa Chapel,** with a brilliant fresco cycle by Filippino Lippi. The altar of every Catholic church must house a holy relic or body part, and Santa Maria Sopra Minerva has a great one—the body of St. Catherine of Siena, the 14th-century ascetic and church reformer, who died in a nearby house. Another medieval master, the painter Fra Angelico, lies under a tomb surrounded by a bronze-leaved fence to the left of the altar. Between the tombs, Michelangelo's *Christ Bearing the Cross* stands guard. (Open daily 7am-noon and 4-7pm.)

Standing in Piazza delle Rotonda with your back toward the Pantheon, head northwest to Via Giustiniani, in the upper left corner of the *piazza.* Take it to its intersection with Via della Scrofa and Via della Dogana Vecchia, halfway to the Corso del Rinascimento. Here stands the simple white façade of the **Church of San Luigi dei Francesi,** the French National Church in Rome and home to three of Caravaggio's most famous ecclesiastical paintings, including the *Calling of St. Matthew.* (Church open daily 7:30am-12:30pm and 3:30-7pm; closed Thurs. afternoon.) Continuing past the intersection onto Via Salvatore, turn left at Corso del Rinascimento. On the left, the celestial **Church of Sant'Ivo** parades its corkscrew cupola over the **Palazzo della Sapienza,** the original home of the University of Rome, founded by Pope Sixtus IV in the 15th century. The entrance to the **cloister** on Corso del Rinascimento (#40) provides the best view of Borromini's intricate façade and cupola, designed in 1660 and recently restored. (Open Sept.-May daily 9am-noon.)

Continue down Corso del Rinascimento, then turn left on Corso Vittorio Emanuele II, where a short walk will lead to the **Piazza del Gesù** and **Il Gesù,** the mother church of the Jesuit Order (on your left as Via del Plebiscito meets Corso Vittorio Emanuele II). The nave remains relatively dark, while the large windows on the Eastern side of the church (in the drum of the dome) spotlight the altar with sunbeams. The Gesù became the prototype for innumerable churches built or rebuilt during the Counter-Reformation. Toward the front of the church, look to the left of the dome for the **Chapel of Sant'Ignazio di Loyola,** dedicated to the founder of the order, who lies buried under the altar. (Open daily 6am-12:30pm and 4-7pm.)

NORTH AND NORTHEAST OF THE ANCIENT CITY

Via del Corso

Originally the Broad Street (Via Lata) of the Roman Republic, Via del Corso became a prestigious address when the popes widened the street in the 15th century to accommodate the wild antics of Carnival. The storm of riderless horses and the hunchback races of the 18th century have been replaced by streams of crazed shoppers and the apocalyptic onslaught of buses and scooters. The nearby **Galleria Doria Pamphili** (at P. del Collegio Romano, 1A; tel. 679 43 65; in the *palazzo* of the same name) houses treasures from the 15th through 18th centuries, including Caravaggio's *Flight into Egypt* and *Mary Magdalene*, Bellini's *Madonna*, and Velázquez's *Portrait of Innocent X*. The private apartments contain some of the best paintings: Fra Filippo Lippi's *Annunciation* and Memling's *Deposition*. (Open Fri.-Tues. 10am-1pm. Admission L10,000.)

Ara Pacis and Mausoleum of Augustus

Heading north on Via del Corso, if you take a left at Largo Carlo Goldoni onto Via Tomacelli and a right onto Via di Ripetta, you will come to the **Piazza Augusto Imperatore**. The circular brick mound of the **Mausoleum of Augustus** (opening to the public in 1996) once housed the funerary urns of the Imperial Roman family. Next door stands the (now) glass-encased **Ara Pacis**, an elaborate piece of propaganda designed to commemorate the *Pax Romana*, or Great Peace, achieved by the Emperor Augustus in the last decades of the first century BC. Covered in some of the most impressive sculpture of the Augustan age, the decorative program mixes images of Augustus and his family with heroes and figures of Roman mythology such as Aeneas, Romulus and Remus, and the she-wolf. (Open Tues.-Sat. 9am-4pm; Sun. 9am-1pm. Admission L4000.)

Piazza del Popolo

Piazza del Popolo was the first sight to greet 19th-century visitors entering the city from the north through the Porta del Popolo. The "people's square" has always been a popular gathering place. Masked revelers once filled the square for the torch-lit festivities of the Roman carnival, and today the *piazza* remains a favorite arena for communal antics. After a soccer victory or the latest government collapse, the *piazza* resounds with music and celebration. The south end of the square marks the start of three streets: the central Via del Corso, which runs straight for over a mile to Piazza Venezia (you can see the gleaming white Vittorio Emanuele II Monument at the end), the Via di Ripetta, built by Leo X for service to the Vatican, and the Via del Babuino, cleared in 1525 by Clement VII, which leads to the Spanish Steps.

Nineteenth-century architect Giuseppe Valadier spruced up the once-scruffy *piazza* in 1814, adding the two travertine fountains on the western and eastern sides. Each fountain is accentuated by a triad of marble figures. To the west, a beefy Neptune splashes in his element with two of his Tritons; the opposite figures represent Rome flanked by the Aniene and the Tiber. Behind its simple early Renaissance façade, the **Church of Santa Maria del Popolo**, tucked away on the north side of the *piazza* near the Porta del Popolo, contains some of the most important Renaissance and baroque art in Rome. Immediately to the right as you enter, the **della Rovere Chapel** harbors Pinturicchio's *Adoration*. Bramante designed the **apse** behind the altar. The **Cerasi Chapel**, immediately to the left of the main altar, houses two superb Caravaggio paintings, *The Conversion of St. Paul* and *The Crucifixion of St. Peter*. The **Chigi Chapel**, second on the left, was designed by Raphael for the wealthy Sienese banker Agostino Chigi. (Open daily 7am-12:30pm and 4-7:30pm.)

The great **Obelisk of Pharaoh Ramses II**, restored in 1984, stands in the center of the *piazza*. The obelisk, some 3200 years old, was already an antique when Augustus brought it back as a souvenir from Egypt in the first century BC. The symmetry of the oval *piazza*, centered by the obelisk, is reinforced on the south side by Carlo Rainaldi's **Churches of Santa Maria di Montesanto** (open April-June Mon.-Fri. 5-

8pm; Nov.-March 4-7pm) and **Santa Maria dei Miracoli** (open Mon.-Sat. 6am-1pm and 5-7:30pm, Sun. and holidays 8am-1pm and 5-7:30pm; Sunday mass at 7pm and daily mass at 7:30am, noon, and 7pm). Outside the Porta del Popolo, opposite these fraternal twin churches, is an entrance to the Villa Borghese. You can also reach the Pincio and the Villa Borghese from the *piazza* itself by climbing up the wooden steps that cut across the switch-back road on the left as you face the churches.

Villa Borghese

Take Metro Linea A to **Flaminia,** four stops past Termini heading toward Ottaviano, to reach Rome's largest patch of public green, the park around the **Villa Borghese.** The cool, shady paths, overgrown gardens, scenic terraces, and numerous fountains and statues are a refreshing break from the fumes and noise of daytime Rome.

Abutting the gardens of Villa Borghese to the southwest is the **Pincio Hill,** first known as the "hill of gardens" *(Collis Hortulorum)* for the monumental gardens of the Roman Republic aristocracy built on it. The north and east boundaries of the Pincio are formed by the **Muro Torto,** or crooked wall, known for its irregular lines and centuries-old dilapidation. When the Goths failed to break through this precarious pile of rocks in the 6th century, the Romans decided Saint Peter was protecting it and refused to strengthen or to fortify it.

The park contains three major museums: Museo Borghese, the Galleria Nazionale d'Arte Moderna, and Museo di Villa Giulia. Unfortunately, the **Museo Borghese** has been undergoing extensive repairs since 1984, and there's no end in sight. The ground floor and its remarkable sculpture collection remain open, but the gallery's first-floor (and first-rate) painting collection (a cache of Titian, Caravaggio, Raphael, and Cranach) has been shipped off for the interim to the Chiesa Grande di San Michele a Ripa in Trastevere (see below, page 106). Keep an eye out for some of Bernini's most famous works—*Apollo and Daphne* (Room 3), *The Rape of Persephone* (Room 4), and *David* (Room 11). (Open Tues.-Sat. 9am-7pm, Sun. 9am-1pm. Admission L4000.)

The **Galleria Nazionale d'Arte Moderna** (tel. 322 41 54) is housed in the forbidding **Palazzo delle Belle Arti,** designed by Cesare Bazzani. The white marble façade incorporates four sets of double pillars, and several large pieces of sculpture sit in the foreground, including Guerrini's primitive *Personaggi* (1974) and Colla's stark *Grande Spirale* (1952). Inside, the museum's rooms are filled with the best Italian art of the 19th and 20th centuries. The most striking works, however, are by foreigners—Degas, Klimt, Monet, and Pollock. (Open Tues.-Sat. 9am-7pm, Sun. and holidays 9am-1pm. Admission L8000, under 18 or over 60 free.)

A short walk towards the river along Viale delle Belle Arti takes you to the other temporal extreme: the **Museo Nazionale di Villa Giulia,** which houses a huge and impressive collection of things Etruscan. (Villa Giulia itself was built under Pope Julius III, who reigned 1550-55.) Check out the prodigious collection of Greek vases, the reconstructed Etruscan tomb of the 6th century BC, the small but amazingly intricate bronzes, and even a pair of ancient Roman dentures (Room 33). (Museo Villa Giulia open Tues.-Sun. 9am-7pm; Sept.-May Tues.-Sun. 9am-1pm. Admission L8000.) The villa hosts **evening concerts** by the Santa Cecilia Music Society from mid-June to late August; tickets are L15,000-30,000. For concert information and schedules, call 678 07 42/3/4/5. (Tickets available at the museum Tues.-Sun. 9am-2pm, 9am-5pm on performance days, or at Via Vittoria, 6, Mon.-Tues. 9am-2pm and 4-7pm, Wed.-Fri. 9am-2pm.)

If all the museums are closed, don't lose hope; art is rampant even along the paths. In the **Giardino del Lago** (Garden of the Lake), find Jacopo della Porta's Tritons, looking suspiciously like the ones in Piazza Navona. These are the real thing, moved here in 1984—the ones in Piazza Navona are copies. In the lake itself is a **Temple of Aesculapius.** Get a close-up from a rowboat. (Rentals 9am-sunset; L4000 per person per 20min., with a 2-person minimum.)

The Spanish Steps and Piazza di Spagna

Designed by an Italian, paid for by the French, named for the Spaniards, occupied by the British, and currently under the sway of American ambassador-at-large Ronald McDonald, the **Spanish Steps** (*Scalinata di Spagna*, in the aptly named *piazza di Spagna*) exude a truly international air. When the 137 steps were built in 1725, Romans hoping to earn extra *scudi* as artist's models flocked to them dressed as the Madonna or Julius Caesar. Today, posers of a different sort abound; women beware—every eligible man in Rome (usually a self-awarded title) prowls here at night, along with drunken foreigners imitating their Italian counterparts.

The **Fontana della Barcaccia,** at the foot of the steps, was designed by Gianlorenzo Bernini's less-famous father Pietro. The fountain was built below ground level to compensate for the meagerness of the water pressure. The water from the spout is cool, refreshing, and potable. The rosy neoclassical façade of the **Church of Santa Trinità dei Monti** provides a worthy climax to the grand curves of the Spanish Steps, not to mention a sweeping view of the city. The interior is open daily from 9:30am to 12:30pm and 4 to 7pm, but the upper half is usually blocked by a gate. The whole church opens up only on Tuesdays and Thursdays from 4-6pm.

In its day, the *piazza* has attracted many a creative spirit. Stendhal, Balzac, Wagner, and Liszt all stayed near here; at Caffè Greco, the well-known establishment on swanky Via Condotti, Goethe, Gogol, Berlioz, and Baudelaire used to linger over cups of *espresso*. Henry James and the Brownings lived at different times on Via Bocca di Leone, a small side street in the area, while Rubens and Poussin took flats on Via Babuino. A small plaque on the side of the pink house (P. di Spagna, 26) to the right of the Spanish Steps marks the home where Keats died in 1821. The second floor now houses the charming **Keats-Shelley Memorial Museum** (tel. 679 01 41). You can scrutinize a lock of Keats's hair, his deathbed correspondence, an urn containing Shelley's bones, and even some of Keats's curious drawings. (Open Mon.-Fri. 9am-1pm and 2:30-5:30pm. Admission L5000.)

Along Viale Trinità dei Monti on the other side of Santa Trinità, the **Villa Medici** houses the **Accademia di Francia** (tel. 676 11). Founded in 1666 to give young French artists an opportunity to live in Rome (Berlioz and Debussy were among the scheme's beneficiaries), the organization now keeps the building in mint condition and arranges excellent exhibits, primarily of French art. (Academy closed to the public for restoration in 1995. Opening and exhibition times vary.) To the left of the Church of Santa Trinità dei Monti as you face it a road climbs to the Pincio, a public park neighboring the Villa Borghese (see above).

Trevi Fountain

From Via del Corso, turn onto Via delle Muratte (across from Piazza Colonna), which leads right to the Piazza di Trevi. Taking up most of the tiny *piazza*, the rocks and figures of Nicola Salvi's (1697-1751) famed and now sparkling clean **Fontana di Trevi** emerge from the back of **Palazzo Poli.** The water for the fountain flows from the Acqua Vergine aqueduct, whose name derives from the maiden who allegedly pointed out the spring to thirsty Roman soldiers. She is immortalized in one of the bas-reliefs above the fountain; the other presents Augustus's right-hand man Agrippa giving the go-ahead for the aqueduct in 19 BC. In the foreground is Neptune's winged chariot, guided by two burly Tritons. In Fellini's *La Dolce Vita,* Anita Ekberg takes a midnight dip in the fountain with Marcello Mastroanni and a kitten, but the watchful *carabinieri* that sit in the *piazza* all night will prevent you from reenacting the famous scene. Tradition claims that travelers who throw a coin into the fountain will return to Rome, but we urge you to refrain from the practice; the fountain is eroding (despite recent renovation) because of rust from the coins. Opposite the fountain is the baroque **Church of Santi Vincenzo ed Anastasio,** rebuilt in 1630. The crypt preserves the hearts and lungs of popes from 1590-1903.

Piazza del Quirinale and Via XX Settembre

Piazza del Quirinale, at the southern end of Via del Quirinale, occupies the summit of the tallest of Rome's seven hills. From the belvedere (reached by stairs leading from Via Scanderberg, just east of Piazza di Trevi), the view takes in a sea of Roman domes, with St. Peter's in the far distance. In the middle of the *piazza* the heroic **statues of Castor and Pollux** (twin demigods whom ancient Romans embraced as their special protectors) flank yet another of Rome's many obelisks. The President of the Republic officially resides in the **Palazzo del Quirinale,** a baroque architectural collaboration by Bernini, Carlo Moderno, and Domenico Fontana.

Via del Quirinale leaves the *piazza* to the north, passing the modest façade of the **Church of Sant'Andrea al Quirinale** (tel. 48 90 31 87) on the right. Bernini's theatrical orchestration of the central altar is extraordinary. (Open Wed.-Mon. 8am-noon and 4-7pm.) Farther along the street, the marvelous undulating façade of Borromini's **Church of San Carlo alle Quattro Fontane** (often called **San Carlino**) provides a sharp contrast to Bernini's neighboring work. It also has the distinction of being Borromini's first and last work: though he designed the interior early in his career, he finished the façade just before his suicide. (Open Mon.-Fri. 9am-12:30pm and 4-6pm, Sat. 9am-12:30pm.)

Farther down Via del Quirinale, the intersection with **Via delle Quattro Fontane** showcases one of Pope Sixtus V's more gracious additions to the city. In the corner of each of the four buildings is a fountain with a reclining figure. In an effort to ease traffic and to offer greater definition to the city's regions, the 16th-century pontiff straightened many of Rome's major streets and erected obelisks at important junctions. From the crossroads here, you can catch sight of the obelisks at Piazza del Quirinale, at the top of the Spanish Steps, and at Santa Maria Maggiore, as well as (in the distance) Michelangelo's famous Porta Pia.

Via del Quirinale becomes Via XX Settembre at this point, which, after a few more blocks, opens into the Baroque **Piazza Bernardo,** site of Domenico Fontana's colossal **Moses Fountain.** The fountain, recently cleaned but already showing signs of new pollution, was built in 1587 at the point where the Acqua Felice aqueduct enters the city. The beefy statue of Moses was carved by Prospero Antichi, who nearly died of disappointment after seeing the finished product. Across the way the **Church of Santa Maria Della Vittoria** harbors Bernini's *Ecstasy of St. Theresa of Avila* (1652) in the Cornaro Chapel, the last on the left. As the saint put it: "The pain was so great that I cried aloud but at the same time I experienced such infinite sweetness that I wished the pain would last forever. . . It was the sweet caressing of the soul by God." (Open daily 7am-noon and 4:30-6:30pm; dress code touted but sporadically enforced.) The **Church of Santa Susanna** (1603) to the left has a distinctive Counter-Reformation façade by Carlo Maderno. Inside, Maderno's frescoes of the biblical life of Susanna cover the walls, as do his four large statues of the prophets who stand atop 9th-century pillars. (Mass Sun. 10:30am.)

Piazza Barberini

Down Via Barberini from Largo S. Susanna, Bernini's **Triton Fountain** spouts a stream of water high into the air over the bustling traffic cirle of Piazza Barberini. This cascade marks the fulcrum of baroque Rome, as well as five major traffic-ways. Twisting north is the opulent stretch of **Via Veneto,** which has seen its *dolce vita* replaced by a flood of tourists, embassies, and airline offices. In the north end of the *piazza* is Bernini's **Fontana delle Api** (Bee Fountain); intended for the "use of the public and their animals," the fountain buzzes with the same motif that graces the Barberini family's coat of arms. In stern rejection of Baroque hedonism, the 1626 Counter-Reformation **Church of Santa Maria della Concezione,** farther up Via Veneto, is a mausoleum housing the tomb of Cardinal Antonio Barberomo, who also founded the church; the tomb's inscription reads "Here lies dust, ashes, nothing." In the **Capuchin Crypt** downstairs, the artfully arranged bones of 4000 Capuchin friars keep him company, making this one of the most bizarre and elaborately macabre settings in Rome. (Open daily 9am-noon and 3-6pm. Donation requested.)

In the other direction from the church, up Via delle Quattro Fontane, the sumptuous **Palazzo Barberini**, at Via delle Quattro Fontane, 13, houses the **Galleria Nazionale d'Arte Antica** (tel. 481 44 30), a collection of paintings dating from the 11th to 18th centuries. Consider purchasing the informative English guide (L9000) at the entrance, as the descriptions in the museum are in Italian. Maderno, Borromini, and Bernini all had a hand in the architecture. Of the earlier works, note Filippo Lippi's *Annunciation and Donors*, Piero di Cosimo's *La Maddalena*, Holbein's *Portrait of Henry VIII*, and the superb canvases by Titian, Tintoretto, Caravaggio, El Greco, and Poussin. Most startling, however, is the entrance hall, whose ceiling glows with Pietro da Cortona's *Triumph of Divine Providence*, a glorification of the papacy of Urban VIII and his family, the Barberini. The family apartments on the second story definitely merit a visit for the period memorabilia. (Open Tues.-Sat. 9am-1:30pm; Sun. 9am-12:30pm. Admission to both galleries and apartments L6000.)

Baths of Diocletian

From Piazza di San Bernardo, head down Via E. Orlando to **Piazza della Repubblica**, home to the **Fountain of Naiads** and the ruins of the **Baths of Diocletian**. Forty thousand Christian slaves took almost ten years—298-306 AD—to build what must have been the grandest community center of the age. The public baths, which could accommodate 3000 Romans at once, contained gymnasia, art galleries, gardens, libraries, and a 30-person public toilet, in addition to pools of various temperatures. In 1561, Pope Pius IV ordered Michelangelo, then 86, to convert the ruins into a church as a posthumous thank you to the 40,000 Christians, but both Michelangelo and the Pope died three years later. The eventual result is the **Church of Santa Maria degli Angeli**. Despite the departure from Michelangelo's plan and years of design screw-ups, the vast interior gives a sense of the magnitude and elegance of the ancient baths. The church was constructed in the ancient tepidarium (lukewarm baths). A door marked "Sacristy" leads to ruins of the frigidarium and an exhibit on the stages of the church's construction. (Open daily 7:30am-12:30pm and 4-6.30pm. Free.)

Exiting the church to the right, on Via Giuseppe Romita, the Museo Nazionale Romano delle Terme (see below) has a separate exhibit on the baths. Statues on display include the 3rd-century BC *Hellenistic Prince*, and the first-century BC *Pugilist at Rest*. (Exhibit open daily 10am-1pm and 3-6pm. Free.)

Around the corner on Viale Enrico de Nicola (across the street from the buses lined up in front of Termini Station), the **Museo Nazionale Romano delle Terme** (tel. 488 05 30) combines several important patrician collections with sculptures and antiquities found in Rome since 1870. The museum, located in the charterhouse built with Santa Maria degli Angeli, makes use of some of the rooms from the ancient baths. Don't miss the **Sala dei Capolavori** (Room of Masterpieces) and the so-called **Ludovisi Throne**, a Greek sculpture dating from the 5th century BC depicting the birth of Aphrodite from the sea. (Museum open Tues.-Sat. 9am-1:30pm, Sun. 9am-12:30pm. Admission L12,000, free for EU citizens under 18 or over 60.)

EAST OF THE ANCIENT CITY

Esquiline Hill

The **Basilica of Santa Maria Maggiore** (4 blocks down Via Cavour from Termini) occupies the summit of the Esquiline Hill. As one of the seven major *basiliche* of the city, it is officially a part of Vatican City. Both its front and rear façades are rococo works, but its interior, built in 352 AD, is the best-preserved example of a Paleo-Christian *basilica* in the city. The coffered ceiling is believed to have been gilded with the first gold sent back from America by Columbus. To the right of the altar, a simple marble slab marks the **tomb of Bernini**. (Church open daily 7am-8pm; dress code enforced.) The 14th-century mosaics in the church's *loggia* tell the story of the miraculous August snowfall that prompted Pope Liberius to build the church (*loggia* tickets available at the souvenir stand just inside the entrance, L4000).

From Piazza Santa Maria Maggiore, Via Santa Prassede leads, by an alley on the right of the *piazza,* to the **Church of Santa Prassede,** built in 822 AD. The tiny **chapel of Saint Zeno** (lit by a coin-operated machine outside the door, L600) in the right aisle is the only chapel in Rome lined entirely in mosaic. The chapel also holds a portion of a column retrieved from Jerusalem in 1228, on which Christ was reputedly strapped and flagellated. (Open daily 7am-noon and 4-6:30pm.)

Down Via Carlo Alberto from Piazza Sta. Maria Maggiore lurks the shabby **Piazza Vittorio Emanuele II,** home to Rome's biggest daily outdoor market, which vends fresh fish, fruits, and non-edibles such as clothes, shoes, and luggage. (At night, prostitutes and drug dealers do the only selling.) Down Via Cavour (away from the station from Santa Maria Maggiore), steps on the left lead you up to and under the narrow archway of Via San Francesco di Paola to the *piazza* and **Church of San Pietro in Vincoli,** home to Michelangelo's unfinished Tomb of Julius II. The imposing **statue of Moses,** at the center, is a vivid masterpiece in itself. (Open daily 7am-12:30pm and 3:30-7pm.)

The Caelian Hill

Though the **Caelian Hill** is adjacent to the south side of the Esquiline Hill, perhaps the easiest way to begin an ascent is from the valley of the Colosseum. Via di S. Giovanni in Laterano leads away from the Piazza del Colosseo (on the opposite side of the amphitheater from the entrance) to the multiple **Churches of San Clemente** (about 1 block down on the left). True to Roman building traditions, the complex incorporates architecture and handiwork from the first through 12th centuries. (Open Mon.-Sat. 9am-12:30pm and 3:30-6:30pm, Sun. and holidays 10am-12:30pm and 3:30-6:30pm.) Up the street, on the hill of Via dei Querceti (take your first right off S. Giovanni in Laterano after the Church of San Clemente, and head up Via SS. Quattro), the solemn **Church of Santi Quattro Coronati** lies fortified behind medieval battlements. The church itself is remarkable more for its strange shape and overly wide apse than for any decoration, but the little **Chapel of San Silvestro** off the entrance courtyard (to the right before the church entrance) contains an extraordinary fresco cycle of the life of the Emperor Constantine (ring the bell of the convent; the cloistered nuns will send you a key on a lazy susan; admission L1000).

Via SS. Quattro leads up the hill past the auto-mechanics and left onto Via S. Stefano Rotondo. In the hectic *piazza* before you lies the grandiose **Church of San Giovanni in Laterano,** the cathedral of the diocese of Rome. The church is actually the oldest Christian *basilica* in the city, founded by Constantine in 314 AD. The traditional pilgrimage route from St. Peter's ends here, and the Pope still celebrates festival masses here on occasion. The giant Gothic *baldacchino* over the altar houses two golden reliquaries containing the heads of Saints Peter and Paul. Unfortunately, a terrorist bomb heavily damaged the *basilica* in 1993. Most of the damage was to the façade, and some frescoes were left in danger of collapsing. The building reopened in 1994, though restoration is ongoing. (Open daily 7am-6pm.)

As you exit the church, across the street and to the left you'll see the **Scala Santa,** marked by an Egyptian obelisk from the 5th century BC. The Scala Santa houses what are believed to be the marble steps used by Jesus outside Pontius Pilate's house in Jerusalem. Pilgrims earn an indulgence for ascending the covered steps on their knees; if you prefer to walk up to the chapel at the top, use the secular stairs on either side. (Scala Santa open 6:15am-12:15pm and 3:30-7pm, in winter 6:15am-12:15pm and 3-6:30pm.)

SOUTH OF THE ANCIENT CITY

Circus Maximus, Baths of Caracalla, and the Appian Way

Cradled in the valley between the Palatine and Aventine Hills (a short walk down Via S. Gregorio from the west side of the Colosseum), the **Circus Maximus** today offers only a grassy shadow of its former glory. After its construction in about 600 BC, more than 300,000 Romans gathered to watch the riotous, breakneck careening of chariots round the quarter-mile track. The turning points of the track, now marked by a raised hump, were perilously sharp by design, to ensure enough thrills and spills to keep the crowds happy.

At the east end of the Circus, down Via dei Cerchi, **Piazza di Porta Capena** marks the beginning of the **Via Appia Antica (the Appian Way),** built in 312 BC and rightly called the queen of roads ever since. The *via* once traversed the whole peninsula, providing a straight and narrow path for legions heading to Brindisi and conquests in the East. Some of Italy's modern *autostrade* still follow the ancient path, but a sizable portion leading out of the city remains in its antique state, with basalt paving stones, avenues of cypress trees, views of the Roman countryside, and crumbling necropoleis of tombs both pagan and Christian.

From the Piazza di Porta Capena at the east end of Circus Maximus (near the Metro Station), Via delle Terme di Caracalla passes the remains of the **Baths of Caracalla,** the largest and best preserved of their kind in the city. Some 1600 heat-soaked Romans could sponge themselves off here at the same time. While the occasional mosaic floor (particularly in the *apodyteria,* or dressing rooms) is beautiful, it's the sheer magnitude of this ancient after-work hangout that boggles the mind. (Open Tues.-Sat. 9am-3pm, Sun.-Mon. 9am-1pm; in summer Tues.-Sat. 9am-6pm. Admission L6000, EU citizens under 18 and over 60 free.)

Bad news for fans of early Imperial Rome: service on the #118 bus, which used to run from the Colosseum, past the Baths of Caracalla, and down Via Appia Antica to the catacombs, has been temporarily suspended. To get to the catacombs, take bus #90b or #714 from the baths (and on the same side of the street as the baths) to Piazza di S. Giovanni in Laterano. From here, take bus #218 from its capolinea at Piazza di S. Giovanni in Laterano (a short walk from the Metro Linea A stop, S. Giovanni) or pick it up joins Via Appia Antica, just outside the Porta di S. Sebastiano. If you're coming from near the train station, it may be easier to take Metro Linea A in the direction of Anagnina to Colli Albani, where you can switch to bus #660. Bus #218 proceeds down Via Appia Antica to the Church of Santa Maria in Palmis, also known as **Domine Quo Vadis;** two stops later, it branches off to the right at Domine Quo Vadis and stops at the San Calisto catacombs, near the gates of Santa Domitilla. Bus #660, which continues down Via Appia Antica from Domine Quo Vadis, stops at the gates of San Sebastiano and San Calisto. You can also walk down the tree-lined path that begins across the street from Domine Quo Vadis, between Via Appia Antica and Via Ardeatina, and leads to the entrance to the S. Calisto catacombs.

Catacombs

Outside the city proper lie the catacombs, multi story condos for the dead, stretching tunnel after tunnel for up to 25km and on as many as five levels. Of the 60 around Rome, five are open to the public; the most notable are those of **San Sebastiano, San Calisto,** and **Santa Domitilla,** next door to one another on Via Appia Antica south of the city. The Roman catacombs lie shrouded in mystery; no one can adequately explain how persecuted Christians found the time and means to construct these elaborate structures. Try to visit the catacombs between Friday and Monday, when the standard three are open. Get off bus #218 or 660 at Domine Quo Vadis, where Via Ardeatina meets Via Appia, and you'll be at the tree-lined path that leads to the entrance to **San Calisto,** Via Appia Antica, 110 (tel. 513 67 25 or 513 67 27), the largest catacomb in Rome (almost 22km of winding, subterranean paths). Its four serpentine levels once held 16 popes, 7 bishops, Santa Cecilia (the patron saint of music—her remains are now in the Church of Santa Cecilia in Trastevere, see page 129), and some 500,000 other early Christians interred in the first public Christian cemetery. (Open Thurs.-Tues. 8:30am-noon and 2:30-5:30pm, until 5pm in winter. Admission L8000.) **Santa Domitilla,** Via delle Sette Chiese, 283 (tel. 511 03 42), can be reached by exiting S. Calisto at the far gates (where the #218 bus stops), crossing Via Ardeatina, and taking a right on Via delle Sette Chiese. Santa Domitilla enjoys acclaim for its paintings and for its collection of inscriptions from tombstones and sarcophagi. (Open Fri.-Wed. 8:30am-noon and 2:30-5:30pm, until 5pm in winter. Admission L8000, under 10 free.)

Perhaps the most impressive is **San Sebastiano,** Via Appia Antica, 136 (tel. 788 70 35; fax 784 37 45), accessible from the entrance to San Calisto. This structure served as the temporary home for the bodies of Peter and Paul (or so ancient graffiti on its walls suggest). Running for 7 mi. on three levels and accommodating 174,000 dead, the tunnels here are eerily decorated with animal mosaics, disintegrating skulls, and fantastic symbols from early Christian iconography. In the church above stands Bernini's statue to St. Peter. (Open Wed.-Mon. 8:30am-noon and 2:30-5:30pm, until 5pm in winter. Admission L8000, under 10 free.)

In all three catacombs, visitors follow a guided tour in the language of their choice; non-English tours are significantly less crowded (every 20min., included in admission). Santa Domitilla receives few visitors, so you're almost assured a personalized tour. Because the catacombs have winding, uneven paths and the tours move briskly, they are not recommended for people who are claustrophobic or have difficulty walking.

Testaccio

South of the Aventine Hill, the working-class district of Testaccio is known for its *trattorie* with cheap and delicious food, raucous nightclubs, and an eclectic collection of monuments. Bus #27 runs from Termini down Via Cavour and across the river, entering Testaccio along Via Zabaglia. Metro Linea B also goes to Testaccio; get off at the Piramide stop. In ancient times the area served as the docklands of Rome, where grain, oil, wine, and marble were unloaded from river barges into giant warehouses. After the goods had been transferred to storage, Roman merchants tossed the leftover terra-cotta urns into a vacant lot. The pile grew and grew, and today the bulbous **Monte Testaccio** (from *testae,* or pot shards) rises 150 ft. over the drab surrounding streets (to the right on Via Zabaglia). Though overgrown with grass, the hill is punctured everywhere by fragments of orange clay amphorae. The park is no longer open to the public, and pilfering of pot shards is illegal.

Via Zabaglia turns left onto Via Caio Cestio, which runs along the length of the peaceful **Protestant Cemetery,** final resting place for many English visitors to the city, including Keats, Shelley, and Goethe's son Julius. Henry James buried his fictional heroine Daisy Miller here after she died of malaria. (Open April-Sept. 9am-6pm; Oct.-March 9am-5pm. Ring the bell for admission at number 6. Free, but donation requested.) Outside the cemetery, past the well-preserved **Porta San Paolo,** the colossal **Pyramid of Caius Cestius** shares a burial plot with the Protestants. Like the collection of Egyptian statuary in the Vatican and most of the obelisks in the city, there's nothing Egyptian about this pyramid except its inspiration. When the Goths were marauding in the 3rd century, the emperor Aurelian had the pyramid built into his city walls as a bastion; nowadays it's the favored hangout of Rome's impeccably modish transvestite population.

Basilica San Paolo

From the pyramid, take Metro Linea B or grab bus #673, 23, or 170 down Via Ostiense to the eerie **Basilica San Paolo** (in the Ostiense neighborhood, Metro Linea B stop Basilica San Paolo), one of Rome's extraterritorial *basiliche* (with S. Giovanni and Sta. Maria Maggiore) and the largest church in the city after St. Peter's. St. Paul, who was martyred near the modern EUR (see below), is believed to be buried under the altar (his body, that is; his head is in S. Giovanni). Until the construction of the new St. Peter's, San Paolo was the largest and most beautiful in Rome. It was completely destroyed by fire in 1823; the present church is a modern reconstruction. (Open daily 7am-6:30pm.) The **cloister** is a peaceful remnant of the original construction, lined with twisted pairs of Cosmatesque columns and enveloping a rose garden. (Open daily 9am-1pm and 3-6:30pm.)

EUR

Rome is famous for monuments that harken back to ancient empires. South of the city stands a monument to a Roman empire that, fortunately, never was. The zone is called **EUR** (pronounced EH-oor), an Italian acronym for Universal Exposition of Rome, the 1942 World's Fair that Mussolini intended to be a showcase of fascist achievements. The outbreak of World War II led to the cancellation of the fair, and wartime demands on manpower and material ensured that EUR would never complete its mission of extending Rome to the sea, but the completed buildings house some of Rome's enormous museum overflow. Visit the area only to see the cavernous museums, or to see where the Cleavers would have lived if Wally had been a strapping young Fascist. EUR lies at the EUR-Palasport stop on Metro Linea B, or take bus #714 from Termini to Piazza G. Marconi. **Via Cristoforo Colombo,** EUR's main street, runs roughly north to south. From the metro stop, walk north up Via Cristoforo Colombo to **Piazza Guglielmo Marconi,** which sprouts a 1959 modernist **obelisk** (the first of many bad takes on Classical Roman architecture).

Located to the right of Piazza Marconi, the **Museo Preistorico ed Etnografico Luigi Pigorini,** at Viale Lincoln, 14 (tel. 592 30 57), features objects from various parts of the Italian peninsula from the Stone, Bronze, and Iron Ages. (Open Mon.-Sat. 9am-7pm, Sun. 9am-1pm. Admission L6000.) In the same building, through the entrance at Viale Lincoln, 1 (walk to the end of the building and up the stairs to the right of the snack bar), is the **Museo del Alto Medioevo** (tel. 592 58 06). (Open Mon.-Sat. 9am-2pm, Sun. 9am-1pm; admission L2000.)

Beyond Via della Civiltà Romana, oddball museum buffs should check out the **Museo della Civiltà Romana,** a museum consisting entirely of fake stuff. There's not a genuine artifact in the place, despite the fact that many of the pieces imitated are so commonplace that obtaining them would be no problem. Don't miss the famous *Plastico,* a scale model of the city of Rome in the 4th century AD. (Hours are erratic; stop by if you're in the area.)

Continuing north, you will reach the **Viale della Civiltà del Lavoro.** To the east (right) stands the **Palace of Congress,** but the awkward **Palace of the Civilization of Labor,** at the west (left) end of the street, serves as EUR's definitive symbol; it wraps arch-like windows around the "Square Colosseum" building, in an effort to evoke Roman ruins. Nearby **Piazzale delle Nazioni Unite** embodies the EUR that Mussolini had intended: imposing modern buildings decorated with spare columns attempt to meld the ancient empire with an empire to come.

Heading east from EUR, take Viale dell'Industria (on the right of Via C. Colombo) down to Via delle Tre Fontane. The **LUNEUR** park (tel. 592 59 33), an old-fashioned amusement center on Via delle Tre Fontane, features cheap thrills like the "Himalaya Railroad" for L3000. (Open Mon.-Sat. 5pm-midnight. No charge to enter the park, but you must pay for each ride.) Farther down the road, at the intersection of Via delle Tre Fontane and Via Laurentina, stands the **Abbazia delle Tre Fontane** (Abbey of the Three Fountains), where St. Paul lost his head (literally). The legend says that Saint Paul's head bounced on the ground three times, creating a fountain with each bounce—hence the name. A millennium later, Saint Bernard, not yet in his dog days, stayed here during his 12th-century visit to Rome. The monks living here today sell the monastery's own eucalyptus liquor and special chocolate. (Store open Mon.-Sat. 11am-5pm, Sun. noon-5pm.) South of EUR, across the lake (known simply as *il lago,* or "the lake"), looms the **Palazzo dello Sport,** designed for the 1960 Olympic Games.

WEST OF THE ANCIENT CITY TO THE TIBER

Piazza Mattei and the Jewish Ghetto

In **Piazza Mattei,** the graceful 16th-century **Fontana delle Tartarughe** (Tortoise Fountain) designed by della Porta, executed by Taddeo Landini, and blessed with turtles by Bernini, marks the center of the **Ghetto,** the lowland quarter where Jews were confined from the 16th to the 19th century. The 16th-century ghetto was only

WEST OF THE ANCIENT CITY TO THE TIBER

270m long and 150m wide, extending from the Ponte Fabricius to the Portico d'Ottavia, across the Piazza Giudea to the Vicolo Cenci (excluding the fish market and the Teatro Marcello); this small region was home to 3500 Jews. While Dickens declared the area a "miserable place, densely populated, and reeking with bad odors," today's Jewish Ghetto is one of Rome's most picturesque and eclectic (even chic) neighborhoods, with family businesses dating back centuries and restaurants serving some of the tastiest food in Rome. Although Jews have fared better (and certainly longer) in Rome than in almost any other place in Europe, even here they have endured centuries of hostility, prejudice, and segregation.

In the area surrounding the Ghetto are five *palazzi* belonging to the Mattei family, who made much of their money collecting tolls over the bridges to Trastevere and, later, serving as sentinels for the Ghetto. Leaving Piazza Mattei on the east along Via dei Funari brings you past the **Palazzo Mattei** (on the left), one of the many Mattei properties that stretch over several blocks. The Mattei constructed their huge expanse of *palazzi*, often called the Island of Mattei, over a period of two centuries (1400-1600). A Papal housing decree in 1574 required all new buildings to be attached by courtyard or wall to another; thus the Mattei *palazzi* are actually separated only by styles of architecture, and are not freestanding structures.

On the next block of Via Funari, the austere **Church of Santa Caterina dei Funari,** a rare late-Renaissance specimen in Rome, towers above the street of the same name (entitled for the rope makers who worked here). The bell tower is a sorry addition to the church, and adding insult to injury, recent restoration attempts have made the top look like a wedding-cake decoration, now called "the sacrilege of St. Catherine."

Down to the right is **Piazza di Campitelli,** a harmonious example of the Counter-Reformation Church's extreme efforts to demonstrate the superiority of the Vatican by beautifying Rome above all other cities. To create the perfect space for the *piazza,* the **Church of Santa Maria in Campitelli** had to be moved and rebuilt. Carlo Rainaldi designed the church, which is arguably his best work. Similar to his Church of Sant'Andrea della Valle, it exemplifies the theatrics of baroque architecture by creating a grand sense of space. (Open Mon.-Sat. 7am-noon and 4-7:15pm.) From Via dei Funari, take Via Sant'Angelo in Pescheria (off Piazza Lovatelli) toward the river to **Via Portico d'Ottavia.** Several houses on this street, notably #13, 17, and 19 (part of the Portico d'Ottavia), date from medieval times. Note in particular the inscription on the building at Via Portico d'Ottavia, 1; after the patriotic invocation *Ave Roma,* it praises the owner for beautifying Rome. At the end of Via Portico d'Ottavia near the Tiber, facing the synagogue on the south, the façade of the **Church of San Gregorio a Ponte Quattro Capi** carries a Hebrew and Latin inscription admonishing Jews to convert to Catholicism. (Open Mon.-Sat. 7:30am-11:30am and 4-7pm.)

Across the street from San Gregorio, the **Sinagoga Ashkenazita** (Synagogue of Rome; tel. 687 50 51), at Via Catalana and Lungotevere de' Cenci, defiantly proclaims its divergent heritage in a city of Catholic iconography and classical designs. There were originally five different *scuole* (synagogues) in the Ghetto, reflecting the diversity of the Jewish settlers (of Spanish, Italian, Sicilian, and other origins), but they were destroyed in 1910. Built between 1874 and 1904, Sinagoga Ashkenazita incorporated Persian and Babylonian architectural devices, purposely avoiding any resemblance to a Christian church. The building is topped by an exuberant rainbow-colored dome, which, along with the Pantheon's, is visible from the top of the Gianicolo. Inside, the temple has a strictly Orthodox seating plan, with women seated upstairs, apart from men. The massive marble columns are quintessentially Roman, in contrast to the seven huge gold menorahs at the front. Services, to which anyone is welcome, are performed entirely in Hebrew. Since a 1982 attack on the synagogue, *carabinieri* and video devices keep terrorists at bay, and all visitors must be searched and questioned before entering.

The synagogue also houses the **Jewish Museum,** which displays ceremonial objects from the 17th-century Jewish community as well as the original plan of the

Ghetto. Several objects, like the green morocco leather prayer book from 1325 AD, attest to the tenaciousness of the Jewish Sephardic community over the centuries. The collection was hidden in a *mikvah* (Jewish ritual bath) during the nine-month Nazi occupation of Rome. The director of the museum, herself a Holocaust survivor, shares her knowledge of Ghetto history in enthusiastic English. (No cameras. Synagogue open only for services. Museum open June-Aug. Mon.-Fri. 9:30am-6pm, Sun. 9:30am-noon; in winter Mon.-Thurs. 9:30am-1pm and 3-5pm, Fri. 9:30am-1:30pm, Sun. 9:30am-12:30pm. Hours fluctuate wildly; check ahead for changes. Museum admission L8000.)

Also note the **Palazzo Cenci** on a slight rise (Monte Cenci) at the end of Via Catalana. The *palazzo* was the scene of a September 9, 1598 scandal when Beatrice Cenci, aided by her brother and her stepmother, had her father, Francesco Cenci, murdered. The whole clan was beheaded a year and two days later at the command of Pope Clement VIII, but the public sympathized with the group's plea of self-defense against the incestuous drug addict Francesco. Some things never change.

The Theater of Marcellus and the Velabrum

Back at the end of Via Portico d'Ottavia, a shattered pediment and a few ivy-covered columns are all that remain of the once magnificent **Portico d'Ottavia,** one of Augustus's grandest contributions to the architecture of the ancient city. The pediment crowned the side entrance to a long, rectangular enclosure whose 300 columns formed a sacred precinct around two important temples to Jupiter and Juno. Medieval Romans built around, inside, and on top of the marble portico, then filled the remaining space with a fish market, which functioned until this century. The market lent its name to the **Church of Sant'Angelo in Pescheria** (still called the **Foro Piscario**), installed inside the portico in 755 AD. It was here that the Jews of the Ghetto were forced to attend mass every Sunday from 1584 until the 18th century—an act of aggressive evangelism which they quietly resisted by stuffing their ears with wax. The church is rarely open. At #28 Via Portico d'Ottavia, to the right of the old fish market, there is a plaque in memory of the 2091 Roman Jews who died in the Holocaust.

If you think the stocky **Theater of Marcellus** (Teatro di Marcello) next door looks like a Colosseum wanna-be, think again. The pattern of arches and pilasters on the theater's exterior, completed in 11 BC, actually served as a model for the great amphitheater across town. You can still make out the classic arrangement of architectural orders, which grows—in accordance with ancient principles—more complex from the ground up. Normally closed to the public, the park around the theater hosts classical concerts on summer nights (call 481 48 00 for more information).

Farther down Via di Teatro di Marcello towards the Tiber, the remains of three more Roman temples jut out from the walls of the **Church of San Nicola in Carcere** (tel. 686 99 72). Originally the buildings were dedicated to the gods Juno, Janus, and Spes (Hope). The most complete temple lies to the right of the church, its Ionic columns littering the tiny lawn and embedded in the church's wall. The left wall of the church preserves the Doric columns of another of the temples; the third lies buried below the church. (Open Sept.-July 7am-noon and 4-7pm, Sun. mass at noon.)

The Velabrum

The Velabrum lies to the south of the Ghetto, in a flat floodplain between the Capitoline and Palatine Hills. This was a sacred area for the ancient Romans, who believed it was the site where the she-wolf rescued Romulus and Remus. During the Republic, the area held the city's vegetable and cattle markets, and it remained a busy market center through the Middle Ages.

One block farther south along Via Luigi Petroselli lies the **Piazza della Bocca della Verità,** the site of the ancient **Forum Boarium,** or cattle market. The boarium's weedy paths and lawns could use some cattle today. The two ancient **temples** in the Forum Boarium are among the best-preserved in Rome. The rectangular **Temple of Portunus,** once known as the Temple of Fortuna Virilis, shows both Greek and native Etruscan influences in its design. The present construction dates from the late 2nd century BC, though there seems to have been a temple on the site for some years before. The **circular temple** next door, presently cloaked in scaffolding for restoration, was also built in the late second century BC, making it one of the oldest marble structures in Rome. Though similar to the Temple of Vesta in the Forum, the temple was probably dedicated to Hercules Victor.

Across the *piazza* from the temples, Via del Velabro climbs a short way toward the Capitoline Hill. Behind the hulking **Arch of Janus,** built in the 4th century as a covered market for cattle traders, the little **Church of San Giorgio in Velabro** was once a beautiful medieval edifice. A terrorist car-bombing on July 27, 1993 reduced the church's famed portico to a single arch and part of a stone beam. To the left, the **Arch of the Argentarii** was erected by the *argentarii* and cattle merchants who used the *piazza* as a market in the 3rd century AD, in honor of Emperor Septimius Severus and his family.

Closer to the river, past Piazza della Bocca della Verità, the exquisite **Church of Santa Maria in Cosmedin** (also called Church of S. Maria de Scuola Greca) harbors some of Rome's most beautiful medieval decoration. The front porch and bell tower, dating from the 12th century, welcome daily mobs of bus-borne tourists, all on their way to see the famous **Bocca della Verità** in the portico. Originally a drain cover carved as a river god's face, the circular relief was credited with supernatural powers in the Middle Ages. It was said the hoary face would close shut on the hand of a liar, severing his fingers; the caretaker-priest used to stick a scorpion in the back to bite the fingers of those little-white-liars. Clay replicas of the Bocca sell for L2000-65,000 (for big fat liars) in the shop inside the church. (Portico open daily 9am-5pm. Church open daily 9am-noon and 3-5pm. Byzantine mass Sun. 10:30am.)

From the Bocca della Verità, the hazardous Lungotevere Aventino leads a short way to the Clivio di Rocca Savella, a lonely, foliage-lined ramp (on the right side of the street) that climbs between crumbling walls to the spacious gardens of the **Aventine Hill.** The ramp leads through an iron gate to a park on the same site, where orange trees frame a sweeping view of the Tiber and the south part of the city—an ideal spot for picnicking. Across the park, another gate opens onto the courtyard of the **Church of Santa Sabina,** with a porch of ancient columns and a towering campanile. Via di Santa Sabina continues along the crest of the hill past the **Church of Sant'Alessio** to the **Piazza dei Cavalieri di Malta,** home of the crusading order of the Knights of Malta. The keyhole in the pale yellow gate on the right offers a perfectly framed view of the dome of St. Peter's. From Santa Sabina, Via di Valle Murcia descends past a public garden (where a rose show blooms in June and early July) to the **Circus Maximus,** where you can catch a stunning view of the ruined Palatine palaces and the churches of the Caelian Hill.

ACROSS THE TIBER

Halfway across the river, the elegant **Isola Tiberina,** lounging in the Tiber between Trastevere and the historical center, splits the river's unsavory yellow-green flow with banks swathed in marble and brick. Its history is closely bound up with, of all things, medicine; originally it was a dumping-ground for sick slaves, and the Romans established a cult to Aesculapius, god of healing, here in the early 3rd century BC. Look for the travertine relief of a serpent, symbol of Aesculapius, carved on the southeast side near the "prow" of the boat-shaped island. Nowadays, the island is the site of a hospital originally established in 154 AD. One of the bridges to the mainland, the **Ponte Fabricio,** is the oldest in all of Rome, dating to 62 BC.

Trastevere

Trastevere, which only became a part of Rome when Augustus insisted on incorporating it, has a proud, independent vitality. The *Trasteverini* claim to be descendants of the purest Roman stock *(Romani di Roma)*—from Horatius, Scaevola, and others who defended the city from the Tarquinian invasion; some residents boast of never having crossed the river. Trastevere's dark maze and medieval quarters, with webs of laundry strung across the buildings, may give you a better sense of a traditional Roman community than any other part of the city—hordes of expatriates, bohemians, and artists notwithstanding. Take bus #170 or 75 from Termini or #56 or 60 from Via Claudio in front of Piazza San Silvestro and Rome's main post office to Viale Trastevere.

Just past the Ponte Garibaldi stands the statue of the famous dialect poet, Giacchino Belli, in the middle of his own *piazza*, which spills onto Viale di Trastevere, a busy thoroughfare. On the left, the **Torre degli Anguillara,** dating back to the 13th century, stands over a *palazzo* of the same name. Across the street, the **Church of San Crisogno** perpetuates yet another well-known Roman name, Cardinal Borghese, etched into the façade. The visible church reflects many rebuildings, but the original 5th-century AD structure hides away in the basement. Turn left at McDonald's and head down Via dei Genovesi until it ends at Via dei Vascellari and Via di Santa Cecilia. Turn right and head through the *piazza*/parking lot and past the iron gate to the rose garden in front of the **Church of Santa Cecilia in Trastevere,** dedicated to the patron saint of music. Don't miss the famous **statue of Santa Cecilia** under the high altar, Stefano Maderno's marble representation of what the saint looked like when she was exhumed from her tomb in 1599.

Via di S. Cecilia merges here with Via di S. Michele, at the end of which is Porta Portese, home to the city's largest flea market, every Sunday morning. The **Chiesa Grande** (tel. 581 67 32), before Porta Portese at Via di S. Michele, 22, is the temporary home of the **Museo Borghese painting collection,** while the museum undergoes extensive renovations. The exciting collection of 16th- to 19th-century works is crammed along the apse walls of a disused chapel. (Open Tues.-Sat. 9am-7pm, Sun.-Mon. 9am-1pm. Last entrance 30min. before closing. Admission L4000.)

Scurry back up Via di S. Michele and turn left on Via della Madonna dell'Orto. Vignola designed a quirky façade for the **Church of Santa Maria dell'Orto** at the street's end. Via Anicia runs left from the church to Piazza San Francesco d'Assisi to the **Church of San Francesco a Ripa,** one of the first Franciscan churches in Rome. Inside, you'll find Bernini's *Beata Lodovica Albertoni,* depicting her ecstasy at her moment of death. (Open daily 7am-1pm and 4-7:30pm.)

From the church, take Via di San Francesco a Ripa across Viale Trastevere to Piazza San Calisto which spills into Piazza di Santa Maria in Trastevere, home to numerous dogs and expatriates—not to mention the grandiose **Church of Santa Maria in Trastevere** (open daily 7am-1pm and 3:30-7pm; Sun. mass at noon and 5:30pm). The church, built between 337 and 352 by Pope Julius II, has the distinction of being the first of Rome's hundreds of churches dedicated to the Virgin. The mosaics of the Virgin and the ten saintly women lining the exterior are only a warm-up for the ones inside.

From P. di Santa Maria in Trastevere, Via della Scala leads past a church of the same name, with a melon-colored 16th-century façade, to the **Porta Settimania.** The gateway is part of the Aurelian Wall, which incorporated Trastevere in its grasp and fended off invasions in the 3rd century. Today you can pass freely through it, where Via Lungara leads north to the **Galleria Corsini,** on the first floor of the Rococo Palazzo Corsini. Sprawling across northern Trastevere from the Tiber to the foot of the Janiculan Hill, the gallery houses one half of the **Museo Nazionale dell'Arte Antica;** the other half hangs in the Palazzo Barberini. The gallery's seven rooms (numbered clockwise) feature no fewer than 41 portrayals of the Virgin Mother, with 17 in one room alone, but despite the consistency of theme the collection's haphazard arrangement is uninspiring. If you do visit, concentrate on **Room 2,** with its eclectic assortment of 14th- to 17th-century masters. (Open Tues.-Sat. 9am-2pm, Sun. 9am-1pm. Admission L8000.)

Via Corsini skirts the side of the palace to meet Rome's breezy and umbrageous **Botanical Gardens.** This impressive and well-maintained assemblage of worldly flora stretches from valleys of ferns, through groves of bamboo, to a hilltop Japanese garden. (Entrance off Via della Lungara. Grounds open Mon.-Sat. 9am-5:30pm,

ACROSS THE TIBER

greenhouse open 9am-12:30pm; winter Mon.-Sat. 9am-5pm, greenhouse 9am-12:30pm. Closed Aug. Admission L4000, children under 6 free.)

Across the street from the Galleria Corsini the magnificent Renaissance **Villa Farnesina** houses several rooms frescoed by Raphael, Peruzzi, Il Sodoma, and Giulio Romano. The villa was home to the Renaissance millionaire Agostino Chigi, who bankrolled the Vatican and hosted elaborate, dish-tossing parties. Check out the *Fables of Psyche,* which ring the ceiling of the Loggia of Cupid and Psyche (under construction in 1995), and Raphael's *Galatea,* in the Sala of Galatea, which depicts the astrological position of the stars on the night of Chigi's birth. Il Sodoma's *Marriage of Alexander and Roxana* on the first floor and Peruzzi's *trompe l'oeil* perspective room next to it complete the highlights.

Adorned with busts of obscure 19th-century Italian heroes, the **Janiculan Hill (Gianicolo)** overlooks Trastevere from the northwest. To get to the summit take Via della Scala from Santa Maria in Trastevere to Via Garibaldi. Atop the hill sits the **Church of San Pietro in Montorio,** on the spot once believed to be the site of St. Peter's upside-down crucifixion. The church itself is nothing spectacular, but in the courtyard next door sits the *real* site where St. Peter was martyred. In this spot sits Bramante's tiny, perfect **Tempietto** (1499-1502), a brilliant combination of Renaissance theory and ancient architecture. Its site is the precise spot where St. Peter was martyred. From the front of the Tempietto you can gaze at all of Rome; the roof of the Pantheon rises straight ahead. Up the road from San Pietro splashes the lovely **Acqua Paola** fountain, a sore temptation to would-be waders; the hordes of *carabinieri* who hang out there, though, should be enough to dissuade anyone. From the fountain, follow Via Garibaldi over Porta San Pancrazio to the gravel road that leads to the large and gorgeous **Villa Doria-Pamphili Park,** filled with Roman kids and assorted canines at play.

■■■ ENTERTAINMENT

Ever since the days of bread and circuses, Roman entertainment has been a public affair—concerts under the stars, street fairs with acrobats and fire-eaters, Felliniesque crowds of slick Romeos, modern-day minstrels and maestros, yapping dachshunds, and enchanted foreigners flooding *piazze* and *caffè.* Clubs are not necessarily an integral part of nightlife, especially during the summer when the social scene spills out-of-doors. You're more likely to find Romans sipping beer or coffee in a bar, eating *gelato* near a fountain, munching on *cornetti* outside an all-night bakery, or contemplating an alternative lifestyle in a *centro sociale.* By night, the monuments of Rome, including the Forum, the Colosseum, St. Peter's, and Trevi Fountain, are flooded with light, making a walk, drive, or even a bus ride past these sights a spectacular finish to a day of touring. If you must have organized entertainment, however, look no farther than Thursday's edition of **La Repubblica,** which includes *Trovaroma,* a comprehensive list of concerts, plays, clubs, movies, and special events in the city and the surrounding area.

PUBS

If you're craving a Guinness, you should have no problem finding one. There are numerous pubs in Rome, many with some sort of Irish theme. Most of the pubs cater to tourists and expatriates, though there's no shortage of Italian patrons. Often drinks go up in price after 9pm, so imbibe accordingly. If you want to meet Italians (the kind that don't come to foreign bars to pick up the American clientele), avoid the pubs and head to a nightclub or jazz bar. The pubs and *birrerie* in Trastevere offer the best mix of foreigners and Romans.

Jonathan's Angels, Via della Fossa, 16 (tel. 689 34 26). West of P. Navona. Take Vicolo Savelli Parione Pace off Via Governo Vecchio. Jonathan is one wild and cuh-ray-zee guy, covered in tattoos and sporting a huge gold-like medallion around his neck. There's live music and a hip, young crowd, enjoying the campy, candlelit ambience. Medium beer on tap L10,000, cocktails/long drinks L15,000. Open Tues.-Sun. 5pm-2:30am.

Druid's Den, Via San Martino ai Monti, 28. Traveling south on Via Merulana from Via Santa Maria Maggiore, take your second right. An Irish hangout where Romans get to be tourists. Pints of Guinness L5000. Open 8pm-1am.

The Drunken Ship, Campo de' Fiori, 20/21 (tel. 68 30 05 35). Hipper than it was in its pre-renovation frat-house days, this slick establishment warmly welcomes backpackers with special reduced prices on drinks and jello shots (normally L1000). The DJ spins mostly American favorites and the staff speaks English. Buffet lunch featuring *panini,* nachos, and more (L10,000) and happy hour 6-9pm. Beer L5000. Plate of nachos and salsa L5000. Open 9am-2am.

Pigmalione, Via di Porta Labicana, 29 (tel. 445 77 40). Mellow rock and blues play under the watchful gaze of a massive one-eyed Buddha painted on the wall. An eclectic mix of Indian, Egyptian, and astrological decor; it's a bit cheaper than its Irish counterparts. Open 8pm-2am.

MUSIC CLUBS

Rome's music clubs attract a much hipper Italian crowd than the pubs; some even have dancing and they're usually much cheaper than discos. Most are officially *associazione culturali* (i.e., they're private); some require *tessera* (membership) which means you pay a one-time fee (often around L1000, sometimes including a drink) for a card. Memberships are usually not exclusive, but on the weekends some of these clubs only allow members to enter (depending on how crowded the place is) and won't sell you a card. Call before setting out; opening hours tend to change seasonally and/or at the manager's whim.

Yes Brasil, Via San Francesco a Ripa, 103 (tel. 581 62 67), in Trastevere, off Viale di Trastevere on the left as you come from the river. Foot-stomping live Brazilian music in crowded quarters. A favorite hang-out of young Romans. Drinks L8000-10,000. Open Mon.-Sat. 7:30pm-2am. Music 10pm-midnight.

Alexanderplatz, Via Ostia, 9 (tel. 37 29 398), north of Vatican City. Take Metro Linea A to Ottaviano. From here, head west on Viale Giulio Cesare (in the direction of the cars parked by the side of the island in the middle of the street), take the second right onto Via Leone IV and then your first left onto Via Ostia. Night buses to Piazza Venezia and Termini leave from Piazzale Clodio; to get there from the club, just keep going north on Via Leone IV, which becomes Via della Giuliana. This is, without a doubt, *the* place to hear jazz in Rome and the only jazz-only club. Read the messages left all over the walls by the greats who have played here, from old pros like Art Farmer and Cedar Walton to young stars like Christian McBride and Josh Redman. You must buy a *tessera* the first time you go, but it is good for three months. Watch for their free outdoor summer concerts at the Villa Celimontana. Open Sept.-June 10pm-1:15am. Shows start at 10:30pm.

Big Mama, Vicolo San Francesco a Ripa, 18 (tel. 581 25 51), around the corner from Yes Brasil in Trastevere. Excellent jazz and blues for the diehard fan. Weekend cover (L20,000) makes it more of a commitment; weeknights are just as fun, although less crowded. Open Oct.-June daily 9pm-1:30am (sporadically closed Sundays and Mondays).

Down Town, Via dei Marsi, 17 (tel. 445 62 70). Take bus #11 or 71 to Piazzale Tiburtina or #492 from Termini to Via Tiburtina. From Piazzale Tiburtino, head down Via di Porta Labicana to Via dei Marsi. An Irish pub with very non-Irish decor. Post-modern black, white, and yellow walls covered with collages of pretty faces and pop culture icons. Live music by Irish bands, local and folk groups on Fri., Sat., and Sun. No cover. Lots of Irish beer. Open daily 9pm-2am; in winter 8pm-3am. Closed part of July and Aug. Happy hour midnight-3am.

DISCOS AND DANCING

Italians are really not great dancers, but they still pay over L20,000 to get into embarrassingly flashy *discoteche* circa 1984. The really cool club scene changes as fast as Romans change outfits, so check under "Dolci Notti" in *Trovaroma,* which lists a day-by-day, play-by-play account of discos and happy hours. Many clubs are in the area near the notoriously unsafe Olympic Village, so think twice before heading out alone. The bigger clubs survive Rome's sultry, steaming summer by closing up shop and bounding beachward to **Fregene, Ostia,** or **San Felice Circeo.** Call ahead.

La Makumba, Via degli Olimpionici, 19 (tel. 396 43 92), up Via Flaminia in the north of the city, across the Tiber from the Stadio Olimpico. One of the funkiest places. Hot Brazilian and African music, an old-fashioned mirrored ballroom with palm trees, a thatched roof, and Hawaiian drinks served in Kon-Tiki bowls. Prices vary. Open daily 11pm-3am.

The Groove, Vicolo Savelli, 10 (tel. 68 72 427). Take your second left as you walk down Via del Governo Vecchio from Piazza Pasquino. Look for the black door and the small, probably unlit, neon sign. This cozy joint with pale yellow walls and vaulted ceilings serves up some of the grooviest dance music in Rome. Sip drinks (L10,000) at the bar then boogie down to acid jazz, funk, soul, and disco downstairs. No cover. Open Tues.-Sun. 10pm-2am and later. Closed most of August.

Gilda, Via Mario de Fiori, 97 (tel. 67 84 838 or 66 56 06 49), near the Spanish Steps. Dubbed by foot-stompin' Romans as "the best" in 1994. Gilda becomes **Gilda on the Beach,** Lungomare di Ponte, 1, in the summer. It remains an exhilarating, hip disco in Fregene, a beach that hosts its share of hedonistic Roman commuters. Tues. Sat. 11pm-4:30am. Step aerobics and beach volleyball during the week.

RadioLondra, Via di Monte Testaccio, 67 (tel. 57 50 04), just down the street from L'Alibi. Funky, lively, and friendly club for straight, gay, striped, and wild types. Caffè Londra, upstairs, offers more intimate encounters in the air-raid-shelter atmosphere, complete with sandbags. In the summer, there's an outdoor terrace with umbrellas. First drink required. Mixed drinks L15,000. Beer from the tap, L6000. Crowded. *Caffè* and club open daily 11:30pm-4am.

Gay Clubs

Pick up a *Pianta Gay di Roma* at any bar or disco for a detailed map with complete listings of cruising spots, bars, and baths in Rome. Check the gay magazine *Babilonia*, *La Repubblica*'s *TrovaRoma*, or the *Rome Gay News* for more information.

L'Alibi, Via Monte di Testaccio, 18 (tel. 574 34 48), in the Testaccio district (Piramide metro stop). Large, elegant, and diverse, the club's rooms spread over three levels, including an expansive, beautiful rooftop terrace. Especially during the summer, this is *the* gay club in Rome. Mostly men, but popular with women too. Mainstream-looking types not welcome. Wednesday is '70s night. The #20N and 30N night buses pass nearby Piramide all night long. On Wed. and Fri.-Sun. nights there is a steep L20,000 cover; Tues. and Thurs. the first drink is required (L10,000). Open Tues.-Sun. 11pm-5am.

Hangar, Via in Selci, 69 (tel. 488 13 97; fax 68 30 90 81). Centrally located (off Via Cavour where it bends near the Colosseum; take Metro B to Cavour, or any bus down Via Cavour from Termini, or up from the Colosseum). Though it is usually packed from wall to wall with men, the atmosphere is cool and laid back. Women are welcome (except on Monday, dirty movie night) but might feel out-of-place. Blaring music and a cheery crowd. Located on a well-lit street. No cover; drinks are the cheapest in Rome. Open Wed.-Mon. 10:30pm-2am. Closed most of Aug.

Joli Coeur, Via Sirte, 5 (tel. 839 35 23), off Viale Eritrea. Rome's primary lesbian bar is located a little out of the city center, east of Villa Ada. Kind of a seedy neighborhood; go with another woman and split the cab fare. L15,000 mandatory first drink. Open Sat.-Sun. 10:30pm-2am.

Angelo Azzurro, Via Cardinal Merry del Val, 13 (tel. 580 04 72), off Viale di Trastevere, in Trastevere. Subterranean bar with a crowded dance floor and *gelato*. Black lights illuminate a vast collection of trippy statuettes, nouveau art, mirrors, and plenty of dance space. Friday is women only. A little slow in getting started. Cover: Fri. and Sun. L10,000, Sat. L20,000. Open Fri.-Sun. 11pm-4am.

RadioLondra, Via di Monte Testaccio, 67 (tel. 57 50 04). See above.

MUSIC AND THEATER

Check with the tourist office for upcoming events—consult their free publication *Carnet di Roma*, keep your eyes peeled for posters, and scan the newspaper to keep up with the incessant barrage of events. Also, **Il Messaggero** features a monthly arts supplement that includes a daily account of events. Annual festivals, particularly during the summer, feature everything from jazz to video art. Concerts are held at the **Foro Italico**, the **Palazzo dello Sport**, and the **Palazzo della Civiltà del Lavoro** (the last two in EUR).

OPERA

The spectacular stage of the **Terme di Caracalla** used to host summertime opera performances, but this lively tradition was halted once it was discovered that performers' barreling voices brought the ancient house down, literally. Instead, look for performances and tickets (students L20,000) at the aptly-named **Teatro dell'Opera** in P. Beniamino Gigli (tel. 48 16 01). You can buy tickets weeks in advance. Performances may be staged in Piazza di Spagna in 1996. Occasionally, **Teatro Valle** also presents opera (tel. 687 90 28) as do the **Teatro Manzoni** (tel. 322 36 34) and the **Loggia della Villa Medici** (tel. 372 02 16).

CLASSICAL MUSIC

The **Accademia Nazionale di Santa Cecilia** (tel. 36 12 873) performs symphonies and chamber music in its auditorium at Via di Conciliazione, 4 (the street leading up to the Vatican). In summer, the company moves outdoors to the *nymphaeum* in the Villa Giulia. Special concerts are sometimes also held in Piazza di Campidoglio. Tickets cost L15,000 to L30,000. Call (tel. 32 26 571 or 36 11 072) for more information about the Villa Giulia concerts.

L'Ippocampo puts on an array of musical events, from Gregorian chants to Bartok, in the ancient Auditorium of Maecenas (tel. 780 76 95). The **Amici di Castel Sant'Angelo** (tel. 854 61 92) liven up Hadrian's mausoleum with classical music concerts on Saturdays at 9pm (tickets L15,000). **La Risonanza** performs sacred masses in the Basilica di S. Eustachio near the Pantheon Wednesdays at 9pm (tickets at the door). The **International Chamber Ensemble** plays classical music in June and July at the Chiostro del Bramante in the courtyard of Santa Maria della Pace (on Via dei Coronari near Piazza Navona; tel./ fax 86 80 01 25 or 68 68 441).

Also check with the **Accademia Filarmonica Romana** (tel. 320 17 52), the **Coro Polifonico Romano** (tel. 68 75 95 20), and the **Associazione Musicale Claudio Monteverdi** (tel. 481 48 00) for periodic performances. An annual international classical concert festival sails through Rome Aug. 27-Sept. 17. Though the concerts are costly (L30,000-100,000), student discounts are available. Call the **Palazzo dei Congressi** (tel. (03 23) 310 95), where the concerts are held, for more details. **Euromusica** (tel. 637 22 94), features performances from September to mid-June at the Teatro Ghione, Via delle Fornaci, 37, near Piazza San Pietro (tickets L10,000-25,000).

In summer, the association for the **Concerti del Tempietto** performs symphonic and chamber music pieces at night in the shadow of the magnificent Theater of Marcellus, at Via Teatro di Marcello, 44 (tel. 481 48 00). Concerts run from June 21 to Sep. 30 every night at 9pm (tickets about L20,000). The **Villa Doria Pamphili** hosts a series of nighttime concerts in the summer months. Though tickets are on sale, you can sit on an umbrella-pine covered hill above the seats and hear just fine. To get to the park, take bus #41 from the Vatican or #44, 75, or 710 from Largo Argentina and Trastevere to the Janiculan Hill. The entrance to the park (where tickets are sold) is 200m down from the Porta San Pancrazio. From mid-June through the first week in August, the **Cortile della Basilica di San Clemente** features the **Rome Festival,** a highly acclaimed orchestra and opera series in the Piazza di S. Alessio. Call (tel. 561 15 19) 10am to noon and 4 to 6pm for more info.

JAZZ

The **Alexanderplatz Jazz Club** (tel. 372 93 98) features *free* open-air jazz concerts at the lush **Villa Celimontana**, between the Colosseum and the Terme di Caracalla. Jazz greats jam away here, from mid-June to mid-August; when the most famous names play, there is sometimes a small fee. For info on pop, rock, and jazz clubs and gigs around Rome, check under "music box" in *TrovaRoma*.

ROCK N' ROLL

Tickets for rock concerts, held primarily at **Palazzo dello Sport,** start at L12,000. It's always packed, but excellent groups perform. For tickets to and info on contemporary music events, visit the **ORBIS** agency at P. d'Esquilino, 37 (tel. 474 47 76 or 482 74 03; open Mon.-Sat. 9:30am-1pm and 4-7:30pm), near Santa Maria Maggiore. Check Music Clubs, page 131, for lower-scale happenings. *Rockerilla* is a popular music magazine that prints concert and ticket info; also check in record stores, *Wanted in Rome, Metropolitana*, and the "music box" section of *TrovaRoma*.

THEATER AND BALLET

The **Rome Opera Ballet** shares the stage and ticket office with **Teatro dell'Opera** (tel. 48 16 01 or 481 70 03). Tickets cost L16,000-250,000. For **theater** listings check again with the tourist office or call the information number at **Teatro delle Arti,** (tel. 474 35 64); **Teatro delle Muse,** Via Forli, 43 (tel. 44 23 13 00); or **Teatro Ghione,** Via delle Fornaci, 37 (fax 637 22 94), which has both music and theater performances; **Teatro Argentina,** Largo Torre Argentina, 52 (tel. 687 54 45; tickets 68 80 46 01), and **Teatro Sistina,** Via Sistina, 129 (tel. 482 68 41), feature musicals and plays from September to May.

CINEMA

First-run cinemas in Rome tend to charge about L10,000 and, though the movies are often American, they're generally dubbed into Italian. *Cineclubs* show the best and most recent foreign films, old goodies, and an assortment of favorites in the original language. **Cinema Pasquino** (tel. 580 36 22) tucked away at Vicolo del Piede, 19/A off Piazza Santa Maria in Trastevere, features undubbed American films daily (the only such theater in Rome). Take Via della Lungaretta from P. Sonnino to P. Santa Maria in Trastevere and turn right at the end of the *piazza*. Their program changes quite often and they have a community bulletin board. (Closed August. Admission L7000.) **Alcazar,** Via Merry Del Val, 14 (tel. 588 00 99), also in Trastevere, shows American films *in lingua originale* on some Mondays (admission L10,000). On Monday nights from October to June, **The Majestic,** Via SS. Apostoli, 20 (tel. 679 49 08), shows new releases in English. You'll find English-language movies Monday and Tuesday at **Nuovo Sacher,** Largo Ascianghi, 1 (tel. 581 81 16), near Porta Portese in Trastevere. Check out the agenda section in the English-language magazine *Metropolitana,* available at the newsstand next to Largo Torre Argentina, 11. The **Economy Book and Video Center,** Via Torino, 136, rents English-language videos. Open 9am-8pm, closed Sun. and Mon. morning. Look to **Bookshelf,** Via Due Macelli, 23, for a list of what's showing at Pasquino, as well as special showings at other theaters (art films, outdoor shows, etc.).

SPORTS

The best sources for sporting info (either to watch or to participate) are the tourist office and two magazines sold at newsstands, *Corriere dello Sport* and *Gazzetta dello Sport*. If you are in Rome between September and May, take in a **soccer** (**calcio;** KAHL-choh) game at the **Stadio Olimpico.** Of Rome's two teams, Roma and Lazio, Roma is the favorite, playing in the most competitive *serie A* league. If one of the teams is playing *in casa* (at home), you'll witness a violent enthusiasm reminiscent of the Colosseum spectacles of yesterempire. The **Foro Italico,** at the Stadio, hosts the games (tel. 368 51). Each team sets its own price, which can be as much as L30,000 or L40,000. You can purchase Lazio tickets at Lazio Point, Via Farina, 24 (tel. 482 66 88), and Roma tickets at Enjoy Rome, Via Varese, 39 (tel. 445 18 43).

■■■ VATICAN CITY

Occupying 108½ independent urban acres entirely within Italy's capital, the Vatican City is the last toehold of the Church that once wheeled and dealed as a mighty European power. Under the Lateran Treaty of 1929, the Pope exercises all legislative, judicial, and executive powers over his tiny theocracy, but must remain neutral in Italian national politics and Roman municipal administration. As spiritual leader for hundreds of millions of Catholics around the world, however, the Pope extends his influence far beyond the walls of his city. The nation manages to preserve its independence by minting coins (in Italian *lire* but with the Pope's face), running an independent postal system, and maintaining its own army in the form of the Swiss Guards, who continue to wear flamboyant uniforms designed by Michelangelo.

Located on the west bank of the Tiber, the Vatican City can be reached from Rome's center by Metro Linea A to Ottaviano (from the station, walk south on Via Ottaviano toward the distant colonnade) or by buses #64 and 492 from Termini, bus #62 from P. Barberini, #19 from San Lorenzo, or #23 from Testaccio and anywhere along the Lungotevere north of Testaccio. A bus connects St. Peter's to the Vatican museums (L2000; buy ticket on the bus), but the walk is only five to ten minutes. The country also has a train station, San Pietro—for official use only.

ORIENTATION AND PRACTICAL INFORMATION

Tourist: Pilgrim Tourist Information (tel. 69 88 44 66 or 69 88 48 66; fax 69 88 51 00), in P. San Pietro, to the left of the *piazza* as you face the *basilica*. Expect to pay for English pamphlets on history and towns, but you can still ask questions for free. Money exchange with no commission. Tours of the otherwise inaccessible **Vatican Gardens** (Mon.-Sat. at 10am, 2hr., except Wed. when the Pope's in town; L16,000; you can see them free from St. Peter's cupola); book in advance. Open daily 8:30am-7pm.

Post Office: P. San Pietro, on the left as you face St. Peter's. Service from Vatican City is somewhat more reliable than from its Italian counterpart. Open Mon.-Fri. 8:30am-7pm, Sat. 8:30am-6pm. **Branch office** on the 2nd floor of the Vatican Museum (open during museum hours). No *fermo posta*. Packages up to 2kg and 90cm, tied with string, can also be sent from here. Mail rates are the same as Italian rates. Express mail to North America takes 4-5 days and costs L4350 per letter.

To attend a **Papal Audience,** apply in writing to the **Prefettura della Casa Pontificia,** 00120 Città del Vaticano, or go to the office by the bronze door of St. Peter's (to the right of the *basilica*, often indoors when it's hot or raining) the Monday or Tuesday before the audience you wish to attend (tel. 69 88 30 17; open 9am-1pm; free). The Papal Audiences are held Wednesday, usually at 10:30am, in the Audience Hall behind the colonnade to the left of the *basilica*. During an audience, the Pope gives a message in several languages (Italian, English, French, Spanish, German, and Polish) to about 2000-3000 people, greets the groups by name and country, and gives his blessing to all. Prepare yourself for crowds of grouchy tourists who realize how far general seating is from the white spot on the stage. Seating is limited, so arrive early. Wear subdued colors; women should wear dresses with sleeves, and men should wear a tie and somewhat formal clothing. **Multi-lingual confession** is available inside St. Peter's. Languages spoken are printed outside the confessionals toward the main altar.

A hospital, **Ospedale Santo Spirito,** awaits the sick at Via Borgo Spirito, and **First Aid** is available at Via S. Uffizio, to the left of the *basilica* (open Wed. 8:30am-1pm, Sun. 9:30am-12:30pm). **Public toilets** are located next to the info office, to the left of the *basilica*.

SIGHTS

The pontiff's incomparable collection of architecture, painting, sculpture, decorative arts, tapestries, books, carriages, and cultural artifacts from around the globe merits enormous amounts of your time and energy. The official guidebook thoughtfully offers suggested itineraries for the flagging and the faint of heart, available at the Vatican Museum and tourist office (L12,000).

St. Peter's Basilica

Appropriate dress is always required in the *basilica*. No shorts, miniskirts, sleeveless shirts, or even sundresses are allowed, but jeans and a t-shirt are fine for both men and women.

As you enter the Piazza San Pietro, Bernini's colonnades draw you toward the colossal church in a sweeping embrace. Mussolini's broad Via della Conciliazione, built in the 1930s to connect the Vatican with the rest of the city, opened up a view of St. Peter's that Bernini never intended; he had wanted the spacious marble *piazza* to greet pilgrims as a surprise after their wanderings through the medieval Borgo. The obelisk in the center, originally erected in Alexandria by the Emperor Augustus, is framed by two fountains; round porphyry disks set in the pavement between each fountain and the obelisk mark the spots from where the quadruple rows of Bernini's colonnades visually resolve into one perfectly aligned row. One hundred and forty statues perch above on the colonnade; those on the *basilica* represent Christ (at center), John the Baptist, and the Apostles (except for Peter).

The *basilica* itself rests on the reputed site of its eponym's tomb, and a Christian structure of some kind has stood here since the Emperor Constantine made Christianity the state religion in the 4th century AD. As you ascend past the Swiss Guards to the porch of the *basilica*, gaze into the courtyard they protect. Here, in the first century AD, thousands of Christians were slaughtered (probably St. Peter among them). The **Porta Sancta** (holy door), the last door on the right, can only be opened by the pope, who knocks in its bricked-up center every 25 years with a silver hammer (next knocking will be in 2000).

The overwhelming interior of St. Peter's measures 186 by 137 meters along the transepts. (Metal lines in the floor mark the puny-by-comparison lengths of other major world churches.) To the right, Michelangelo's sorrowful **Pietà** is protected by bullet-proof glass, since an axe-wielding fiend attacked the famous sculpture in 1972, smashing the nose and breaking the hand off the Madonna.

The crossing of the vault is anchored by four niches with statues of saints, among them, in the northeast niche, Bernini's **St. Longinus.** In the center of the crossing, the **baldacchino** (also by Bernini) rises on spiraling solomonic columns over the plain marble altar, which only the Pope may use. The canopy, cast out of bronze pillaged from the porch of the Pantheon, was unveiled on June 28, 1633 by Pope Urban VIII Barberini. Note, among the vines and *putti,* a good number of fair-sized bronze bees crawling around; the bee was the symbol of the Barberini family, and Urban VIII, with characteristic modesty, had it plastered all over the baldacchino.

In the apse, more Bernini treasures gleam in marble and bronze. The convoluted **Cathedra Petri** is a baroque reliquary that houses the original throne of St. Peter in a riot of bronze and gilt. On either side, the **tombs** of Popes Paul III and Urban VIII slumber in mixed-media splendor. To the left of the altar, in the left aisle, and behind the statue of St. Veronica in the crossing, lurks Bernini's last work in St. Peter's; the gruesome **monument to Alexander VII** is enlivened by the skeletal figure of Death raising an hourglass from among amazingly fluid pink marble drapery.

Steps at the crossing, below the statue of St. Longinus, lead down to the **Vatican Grottoes,** the final resting place of innumerable popes and saints. The passages are lined with tombs both ancient and modern, and though the space is modernized and well-lit, it's still creepy. The grottoes lead you out to the entrance to the cupola. You can go up by stairs or elevator to the walkway around the interior of the dome, or ascend some fairly taxing stairs (350 of them) to the outdoor top ledge of the cupola. From here there's an excellent view of the roof of the *basilica*, the *piazza*, the Vatican Gardens, and the hazy Roman skyline. Mass is given several times per day in the church, with a particularly beautiful vespers service Sunday at 5pm. (St. Peter's Basilica open April-Sept. 7am-6pm; Oct.-March 7am-7pm. Free. Dome closes 1hr. earlier and may be closed when the Pope is in the *basilica*, often Wed. morning. Admission on foot L5000, by elevator (part of the way) L6000. It's worth going up, even at L6000, and if the remaining steps are too much for you, at least walk along the interior rim of the dome and enjoy the view of the colorful floor below.)

On the left side of the *piazza*, through a gate protected by Swiss Guards, stairs descend to the **necropolis**, one level below the grottoes. A double row of mausoleums dating from the first century AD lies here. Multi-lingual guides remind you that the center of the Catholic Church used to be a pagan burial ground and tell the entrancing tale of the discovery of **St. Peter's tomb** here (tours L10,000). Only small, prearranged tours may enter. Apply a few days in advance to the *Ufficio Scavi* (excavation office) beneath the Arco della Campana to the left of the *basilica* (Mon.-Sat. 9am-noon and 2-5pm). You can also request an application before your arrival in Rome from the Delegate of the Fabbrica di San Pietro, Excavations Office, 00120 Vatican City.

Vatican Museums

A 10-minute walk around the Vatican City walls (or the bus that drives from the *piazza* through the Vatican Gardens) brings you to the **Vatican Museums** (tel. 698 33 33). The major galleries are open Mon.-Sat. 8:45am-1pm. Easter week, April, May, Sept., and Oct. the museums are open Mon.-Fri. 8:45am-4pm, Sat. 8:45am-1pm. Last entrance is 45min. before closing. The museums are closed on major religious holidays, but the last Sunday of every month they're open 8:45am-1pm and **free.** Otherwise admission is L15,000, with an ISIC card L10,000, children under 1m tall free.

The Vatican Museums constitute one of the world's great collections of art, a vast storehouse of ancient, Renaissance, and modern statuary, painting, decorative arts, and sundry Papal odds and ends. The galleries stretch over some four miles of the old Papal palace and are stuffed with many more treasures than you could possibly see in one day. Though the entrance price is steep, consider making more than one visit. If you've only got a morning, invest some time planning your tour before you go—the galleries are so crowded and poorly labeled, and the distances between them so long, that simply wandering will leave you more frustrated and exhausted than enlightened. The best known and most noteworthy attractions in the collection are the **Pio-Clementino Museum** with its celebrated masterpieces of ancient sculpture, the brilliantly frescoed **Borgia Apartments** and **Raphael Stanze,** Michelangelo's incomparable **Sistine Chapel,** and the eclectic **Pinacoteca,** or picture gallery. Collections off the beaten track include specialized galleries of Egyptian, Etruscan, Greek, and Roman art, each housing world-class collections of antiquities, the more esoteric **Pio-Christian Museum** (with early Christian sarcophagi), the exhibition rooms of the **Vatican Library,** and the intermittently-open **Ethnological Museum** (with artifacts from Third World cultures) and **Historical Museum** (with furnishings and carriages from Papal households of the past). The remaining collections (of tapestries, maps, and modern religious art) are housed in long corridors leading to the Sistine Chapel.

The galleries function as a conduit for taking visitors from the entrance and the Belvedere Courtyard down to the Papal apartments and the Sistine Chapel and back again. Two long, parallel corridors funnel the crowds through; the specialized galleries mentioned above cluster at either end. The museum management has laid out four color-coded tours and tries to make visitors follow one. Tour A hits only the barest essentials, making a swift trip to the Sistine Chapel and back, while tour D hits **absolutely everything.** Tour C will take clock-conscious art buffs to the magnificent Roman sculptures and Raphael rooms that A and B ignore. It's possible to pick and choose your way through, but remember that once you have passed a room or gallery, it's difficult to retrace your steps.

The entrance in Viale Vaticano leads to a strange bronze double-helix ramp (like the one in the Guggenheim in New York) that climbs to the ticket office, where there is also a money exchange, post office, cloakroom (large bags only), telephones, first aid station, and a booth selling a guidebook (L12,000) that's well worth the price. After the turnstiles you'll reach a courtyard, with the intricately carved base of Antoninus Pius's column, and be faced with a choice of itineraries. A good place to start is the stellar **Pio-Clementino Museum,** the world's greatest collection of antique sculpture. Amongst other gems, it features the sublime **Apollo Belvedere** and the tortured **Laocoön** group. There's also an entire room of marble animals, ranging from slobbering Molossian hounds to green porphyry crustaceans. The last room of the gallery contains the enormous red porphyry **sarcophagus of St. Helen,** mother of Constantine. Statues of Egyptian demigods hold up the ceiling.

The next flight of the Simonetti Stairway climbs to the **Etruscan Museum,** filled with artifacts from the necropoleis of Tuscany and northern Lazio. Back on the landing of the Simonetti Staircase is the usually closed **Room of the Biga** (an ancient marble chariot outfitted with recent wheels and horses) and the entrance to the **Gallery of the Candelabra,** named for the ancient marble candleholders housed here, along with yet more examples of Roman statuary and decorative arts. Here begins the long trudge to the Sistine Chapel, through the **Gallery of the Tapestries,** the **Gallery of the Maps,** the **Apartment of Pius V** (here there is a shortcut stair to the Sistine Chapel), the **Sobieski Room,** and the **Room of the Immaculate Conception.** From the Room of the Immaculate Conception, a door leads into the first of the four **Raphael Rooms,** the sumptuous Papal apartments built by Pope Julius II in the first decade of the 16th century. Raphael painted the astonishing **School of Athens** as a trial piece for Pope Julius, who was so impressed he fired his other painters, had their frescoes destroyed, and handed the entire suite of rooms over to Raphael. The commission marked the beginning of Raphael's brilliant Roman career, and on his untimely death in 1520, his students completed the decoration according to his designs. The **Stanza della Segnatura** (which features the *School of Athens,* covered for restoration in 1995) was painted entirely by Raphael and is considered his masterpiece. The four walls represent four branches of learning—theology, law, philosophy, and poetry. Depending on your itinerary, a staircase leads down to the Borgia Apartments and the horrid Museum of Modern Religious Art or, more directly, to the Sistine Chapel. The staircase descends into the **Room of the Sibyls,** where, legend has it, Cesare Borgia allegedly had his brother-in-law Alfonso D'Aragone murdered in order to free up his sister Lucrezia for marriage to the future Duke of Ferrara.

The Sistine Chapel

Ever since its completion in the 16th century, the Sistine Chapel (named after its founder, Pope Sixtus IV) has served as the chamber in which the College of Cardinals meet to elect a new pope. Its inclusion in the museum tour is somewhat deceiving, since the chapel is really part of St. Peter's Basilica. The door through which you enter is the west entrance, in the altar wall; the opposite wall forms the proper entrance, opening onto the official state rooms of the Vatican Palace and the second-story *loggia* of the *basilica.*

The barrel vault of the ceiling, some 70 ft. above the floor, gleams with the results of its recent, celebrated, and hotly debated restoration. Before craning your neck, prepare yourself by taking in the frescoes on the side walls which predate Michelangelo's ceiling work. On the right wall, scenes from the life of Moses prefigure parallel scenes of the life of Christ on the left wall. The cycle, frescoed between 1481 and 1483, was completed under the direction of Perugino by a team of artists that included Botticelli, Ghirlandaio, Roselli, Pinturicchio, Signorelli, and della Gatta. Down the right wall are the *Journey of Moses* (Perugino), *Flight from Egypt* (Botticelli), *Crossing the Red Sea, Tablets of the Law, Punishment of Korah, Dathan,*

The Sistine Chapel Ceiling

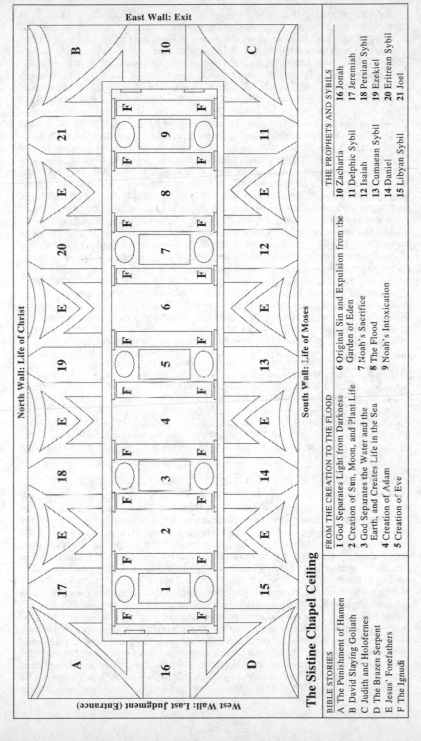

East Wall: Exit

North Wall: Life of Christ

South Wall: Life of Moses

West Wall: Last Judgment (Entrance)

A
B
C
D
E
F

1 2 3 4 5 6 7 8 9
10 11 12 13 14 15 16 17 18 19 20 21

BIBLE STORIES
A The Punishment of Hamen
B David Slaying Goliath
C Judith and Holofernes
D The Brazen Serpent
E Jesus' Forefathers
F The Ignudi

FROM THE CREATION TO THE FLOOD
1 God Separates Light from Darkness
2 Creation of Sun, Moon, and Plant Life
3 God Separates the Water and the
   Earth, and Creates Life in the Sea
4 Creation of Adam
5 Creation of Eve
6 Original Sin and Expulsion from the
   Garden of Eden
7 Noah's Sacrifice
8 The Flood
9 Noah's Intoxication

THE PROPHETS AND SYBILS
10 Zacharia
11 Delphic Sybil
12 Isaiah
13 Cumaean Sybil
14 Daniel
15 Libyan Sybil
16 Jonah
17 Jeremiah
18 Persian Sybil
19 Ezekiel
20 Eritrean Sybil
21 Joel

Abiram (Botticelli), and the *Testament of Moses* (Signorelli); on the left wall, *Baptism of Christ* (Perugino), *Temptation of Christ* (Botticelli), *Calling of the First Apostles* (Ghirlandaio), *Sermon on the Mount, Consignment of the Keys to Peter* (Perugino), and the *Last Supper*. Botticelli, Ghirlandaio, and Fra Damante painted the series of 26 early popes who stand in the niches between the high windows. On the right side of the far wall (the east entrance) is the *Disputation Over the Body of Moses*, by Matteo de Lecce, which replaces a lost work by Signorelli. On the left side of the wall is Arrigo Paludano's *Resurrection*, which fills the place once occupied by a Ghirlandaio piece.

Above stretches the undaunted genius, brave simplicity, and brilliant coloring of Michelangelo's unquestioned masterpiece; some have called these powerful frescoes the greatest works of Western art ever created. The fledgling painter divided the vault into a monumental architectural scheme, each section enclosing a separate scene from Genesis. These are, from west to east, *Separation of Light from Darkness, Creation of the Sun, Moon and Planets, Separation of Land and Sea and the Creation of Fishes and Birds, Creation of Adam, Creation of Eve, Temptation and Expulsion from Paradise, Sacrifice of Noah, Flood,* and the *Drunkenness of Noah*. The scenes are framed by the famous *ignudi*, contorted naked male youths who cavort among the decorative vaulting. In the four spandrels are depictions of *David and Goliath, Judith and Holofernes,* the *Brazen Serpent,* and the *Punishment of Hanan*. Surrounding the spandrels are monumental figures of Old Testament prophets and classical sibyls, some pondering the events of Christian history to come, and some holding aloft books of revealed wisdom. The altar wall, covered by Michelangelo's *The Last Judgement,* was revealed in 1994 after a lengthy restoration. As angels pull the blessed to heaven on the left, Charon, on the right, carts an unfortunate load of evil-doers across the river. The figure of Christ as Judge hovers in the upper center, surrounded by Mary and his saintly entourage. It's ironic that the altar, the holiest region of the chapel, lies smack in the mouth of hell.

The Pinacoteca

Although the Sistine Chapel is a hard act to follow, the **Pinacoteca,** near the snack bar and the exit, holds the best painting collection in Rome, including Filippo Lippi's *Coronation of the Virgin,* Perugino's *Madonna and Child,* Titian's *Madonna of San Nicoletta dei Frari,* and Raphael's *Transfiguration*. On your way to the Pinacoteca from the Sistine Chapel, among all the Renaissance splendor, don't forget to take a look at the **Room of the Aldobrandini Marriage,** which contains a series of rare and famous ancient Roman frescoes. For more info on the Vatican, see *Let's Go: Rome*.

NEAR VATICAN CITY: CASTEL SANT'ANGELO

A short walk down Via d. Conciliazione from St. Peter's (and across from the angel-lined Ponte Sant'Angelo) stands the hulking mass of brick and stone known as **Castel Sant'Angelo.** Built by the Emperor Hadrian (117-138 AD) as a mausoleum for himself and his family, the edifice has served the popes of Rome in the centuries since as a convenient (and forbidding) fortress, prison, and palace. The complex, towering over a bend in the Tiber, consists of the original mausoleum, a suite of palatial Renaissance apartments built on top, and concentric rings of fortifications including the Ponte Sant'Angelo across the river and the Leonine Wall extending to the Vatican Palace. Hadrian, a dilettante architect as well as emperor, designed the mausoleum in imitation of his predecessor Augustus's more modest tomb across the river. He had the surviving round marble base crowned with an earthen tumulus and planted with cypress trees. But as the city fell to barbarian depredations, panicked Romans quickly converted the imposing structure for defensive purposes. When the city was wracked with plague in 590 AD, it is said, Pope Gregory the Great saw an angel sheathing his sword at the top of the citadel; the plague then abated, and since that time the edifice has been dedicated to the angel. The fortress now contains a museum of arms and artillery, but the real reasons to visit are the

Papal apartments and the incomparable views of Rome. (Open daily 9am-2pm; closed the 2nd and 4th Tues. of each month. Admission L8000, EU citizens under 18 or over 60 free. Occasional guided tours (in English) Sun. at 10am; meet inside the gates). Outside, the outer walls of the fort enclose a large park. The marble **Ponte Sant'Angelo,** lined with statues of angels designed by Bernini, leads back across the river and is the starting point for the traditional pilgrimage route from St. Peter's to the Basilica of San Giovanni in Laterano on the other side of Rome.

DAYTRIPS FROM ROME (LAZIO)

The cradle of Roman civilization, Lazio (originally *Latium*) stretches from the low Tyrrhenian coastline through volcanic hills to the foothills of the Abruzzese Apennines. Latium has always been a rich area. Volcanic soil feeds farms and vineyards, and marble quarried from the Latin hills built the Colosseum, St. Peter's, and nearly every other Roman monument standing between them. With such resources, the territory attracted the notice of the Etruscans, who sent out colonies to Tarquinia, Cerveteri, and Veio in the 9th century BC; meanwhile, the Latin tribes in the hills around Lake Albano quickly rose to prominence in the south. While Rome was still a collection of mud huts on the Palatine hill, Etruscan and Latin towns enjoyed a sophisticated religious, political, and artistic culture. After centuries of war, Rome emerged as anchor of an empire, and the Latian towns settled down to a peaceful, wealthy existence, providing—as they did in the Renaissance and do even today— vacation retreats for Romans seeking some R&R. Most of the region's famous sights can be seen in a series of day excursions from the capital—few demand a night's stay. Trains for Lazio locations leave from the Laziale section of Termini, and one private line serves Viterbo from the Roma Nord Station in P. Flaminio (outside P. del Popolo). COTRAL buses also serve the area.

■■■ TIVOLI

In Tivoli, water is the inspiration and principal attraction. Ancient Roman glitterati enjoyed the delicious cool of the cascades. Horace, Catullus, Propertius, Maecenas, and many others retreated to villas lining the ravine where the River Aniene falls; some remains of these villas are still visible. In addition, some of the best-preserved imperial architecture near Rome lies here, amidst gardens and pools of Anio water.

To get to Tivoli, take Metro Linea B to Rebibbia (L1500), then exit the station from the COTRAL terminal above. Tickets to Tivoli (L3000) are on sale here; the **buses** leave from Capolinea 1 (30min., 5am-midnight). After passing through factory areas and travertine quarries, the bus climbs to Tivoli and stops at Largo Garibaldi. Here a **tourist office** (tel. (0774) 212 49 or 33 45 22; fax 33 12 94) gives out maps and info on sights, restaurants, and hotels. (Open Mon.-Sat. 9am-6pm, Sun. 9am-2pm.)

SIGHTS

From Largo Garibaldi, the gardens of the **Villa d'Este** spill over watery terraces from the entrance in Piazza Trento. Cardinal Ippolito d'Este (son of Lucrezia Borgia) shaped the property to recreate the limpid sumptuousness of ancient Roman *nymphaea* and pleasure palaces. You may want to pick up a map at the gift shop before you explore; the maze of pathways can be confusing and frustrating unless you literally and figuratively "go with the flow." Immediately below the terrace outside the shop is the **Fontane del Bicchierone,** a shell-shaped goblet of Bernini's design. To the left, a path leads down to the stuccoed **Grotto of Diana,** a popular shelter from the burning summer heat. Take another path (right) to the **Rometta,** or Little Rome, a series of fountains including one symbolizing the Tiber (the boat with the obelisk being Tiber Island).

The **Viale delle Cento Fontane** runs the width of the garden. At the other end from the Rometta, the **Fontana dell'Ovato** spurts one great sheet of water 15 ft. into the air. Hidden to the right of the fountain is a papyrus museum with a paper-making laboratory and book relics. Down the semicircular steps from the center of the Viale delle Cento Fontane is the Fontana dei Draghi. Two great fishponds spread out from this point, stagnating amidst cypress and orange plantations. Nearby lurks the **Fontana della Civetta e degli Uccelli,** a waterwork said to emit bird chirps. Across the ponds, the architectural behemoth **Fontana dell'Organo Idraulico** once powered a water organ. Don't miss the **Fontana della Natura** with its colossal statue of Diana of Ephesus and her multiple, egg-shaped breasts at the bottom of the garden.

Follow Via di Sibilla across town to two exemplary Republican temples, the **Temple of Vesta** and the **Temple of the Sibyl,** which overlook the cascades of the Anio. Archaeologists have been scratching their heads for centuries over which gods were worshipped here, but it's pretty clear that the deities have long since taken their leave. Back down Via di Sibilla and through Piazza Rivarola, take Ponte Garibaldi to the entrance of the **Villa Gregoriana**—actually not a villa at all, but a natural park with paths descending through scattered ancient ruins to a series of lookouts over the cascades. From the opening of Gregory XVI's tunnel, the Anio plunges 110m in the startling **Great Cascade.**

From the Great Cascade, it's a short trip to the intriguing remains of the **Villa Adriana.** Either return to Largo Garibaldi and take the orange #4 bus (tickets L800, available at the news kiosk; avoid #4/, which does not go to the villa), or take the COTRAL bus headed for Giudonia from Largo S. Angelo (every hr., 10min.; L1500). The villa is the largest and costliest ever built in the Roman Empire and was apparently designed by the Emperor Hadrian in the 2nd century in the style of monuments he had seen in his travels. Although Romans resented him for keeping his distance, it's easy to see why he chose this serene, flat expanse for his personal retreats. The entrance gate leads to the **Pecile,** built to recall the famous Painted Porch (*Stoa Poikile*) at Athens where Hadrian's heroes, the classical Greek philosophers, met to debate. At the northeast corner of the Pecile, Philosopher's Hall leads to the **Maritime Theater,** the emperor's private study and bedroom protected by its own moat. Underneath the broad **Court of the Libraries,** a shadowy **Cryptoporticus** concealed the emperor's army of slaves as they ran the enormous complex. The rest of the **Imperial Palace** sprawls nearby in well-labeled enclaves. South of the Pecile, beyond the main buildings, you'll find the **Canopus,** a murky expanse of water surrounded by plasters of the original architecture and sculpture found here; it replicates a canal near Alexandria in Egypt (hence the crocodile). The **Serapeum,** a semicircular dining hall, anchors the far end of the canal. On the walk back to the entrance, note the **Small Thermae** and **Great Thermae** (baths), which house the remains of a dome suspiciously similar to the Pantheon. (Villa open May-Aug. 9am-7:30pm; Sept.-April 9am-dusk. Last entrance 1hr. before closing. Admission L8000.)

■■■ SUBIACO

From Tivoli you can trace the Aniene back to its source in the stunning, untouched valley of **Subiaco,** a rocky town that dominates one of Lazio's emptier up-country quarters. As the road climbs inland, the sheer, forested crags of the Monti Simbruni rise above lush pastures and scattered vineyards. The town owes its origins to Nero, but its real fame is due to Benedetto di Norcia, a rich 6th-century wastrel who gave up everything to live a life of contemplation; after three years of seclusion he founded a monastery, giving rise to the Benedictine Order. The nearby hills have housed a great number of monasteries and convents, among them two that survive today: the Convent of Santa Scholastica and the Convent of San Benedetto.

COTRAL buses shuttle between Rome and Subiaco (about every 45min., on Sun. every 1-3hr.); buses to Subiaco leave from Rebibbia at the end of Metro Linea B (Mon.-Fri. 5:50am-10:10pm, Sat. 6:20am-10:10pm, Sun. and holidays 7:10am-9:40pm; 1-1½hr.); buses returning to Rome leave from Piazza del Campo Mon.-Sat.

4:30am-8:30pm, Sun. 5am-7:30pm. CORTRAL buses also leave for Subiaco from Viale Mazzini in Tivoli about every 45min. (buy tickets at the capolinea in Largo Massimo, L1800; buses leave Mon.-Sat. 6:10am-10:50pm, Sun. (6 buses only) 9am-10:10pm.). After passing through the **Arco Trionfale,** the buses stop at Piazza Sant'Andrea (across from the Church of Sant'Andrea). Get off here and head down Via Cadorna to #59, home of the **tourist office** (tel. (0774) 82 20 13; open Mon. 8am-2pm, Tues.-Sat. 8am-2pm and 3:30-7:30pm, Sun. 9am-noon). If you're feeling adventurous, you can take the bus past the tourist office all the way to the capolinea at **Piazza della Resistenza.** From there, catch the TRL bus labeled Ienne/Vallepietra, which stops near the entrances to the monasteries (departs Tues.-Sun. 6, 10am, 2, and 6:30pm, Mon. 6, 10am, 2, 4, and 6:30pm; L1000).

To the right rises the **Convento di Santa Scolastica** (tel. 855 25), which housed Italy's first printing press in 1465. The complex, a huge architectural hodgepodge, encompasses three different cloisters, each built around a well and a garden. In the first, look for the words **Ave Maria planted in artichokes.** The second features an intricately carved Gothic arch and faded frescoes. The third and earliest court is the work of the 13th-century Cosmati family, whose twisted columns and bright mosaics found their way into most Roman churches. Off this court reposes a Neoclassical church by Quarenghi (the Italian architect who designed much of Moscow's St. Petersburg). The library shelters the first two books printed in Italy. (Convent open daily 9am-12:30pm and 4-7pm; free monk-led tours every 30min.)

The **Convento di San Benedetto** (tel. 850 39), another 500m up the hill, occupies one of the most spectacular hilltop sites in central Italy; from its terraces the peaks and valleys of the Monti Simbruni recede as far as the eye can see. The sights inside the church complex, carved entirely out of its limestone cliff, aren't bad either. The convent was founded on the site of the **Sacro Speco,** the rocky grotto where St. Benedict spent three years of penitential solitude. Each generation of monks carved new chapels out of the rock and plastered them with precious frescoes. The *loggia* at the entrance to the upper church is decorated with the monastery's newest art, a series of late 15th-century frescoes of the Madonna and Child and the Evangelists by the school of Perugino. Inside, the first section of the upper church features an elaborate cycle of 14th-century frescoes by a member of the Sienese school, depicting the Biblical events surrounding the Crucifixion. Below the altar, the lower church glows with the colorful paintings of Conxolus, a late 13th-century painter. The walls and vaults depict the many miracles of St. Benedict and other scenes from his life; to the right, the Sacro Speco itself holds a 17th-century marble statue of the monk. The next staircase down is lined with 14th-century Sienese frescoes of the *Triumph of Death* (including a grucsome skeleton on horseback). On the lowest level sits the **Grotto dei Pastori,** where Benedict taught catechism to local shepherds. Fragments remain of an 8th-century Byzantine fresco of the *Madonna and Child,* the oldest painting in this speluncular treasure-house. (Convent open daily 9am-12:30pm and 3-6pm. Free.)

As you leave Subiaco, head through the Arco Trionfale to Corso Cesare Battisti. The small stone **Ponte di San Francesco** (1358), leads to the **Chiesa di San Francesco,** at the summit of a small hill. The somber interior of the church is filled with notable paintings, including frescoes in the third chapel on the left by Il Sodoma, and an altarpiece of the Nativity by Pinturicchio.

■■■ OSTIA ANTICA

The romantic remains of ancient Ostia (tel. 565 14 05 for the central office at the park) offer a cooler, cheaper alternative to the more famous ruins at Pompeii and Herculaneum. The ruins are so sparsely visited you'll have no trouble finding a secluded spot for a picnic—and you'll need to bring one, since doing the site justice requires the better part of a day. (Bring a water bottle as well.) The settlement at Ostia, the first Roman colony, was developed as a commercial port and naval base during the 3rd and 2nd centuries BC. The ruins that remain—warehouses, shipping

OSTIA ANTICA

offices, hotels, bars, and shrines—all speak of the thriving activity that the port once saw. Ostia's fortunes declined as Rome's did; the port fell into disuse during the onslaught of the Goths, and the silty Tiber eventually moved the coastline a mile or so to the west. Happily, though, the mud effected a remarkable archaeological preservation, and the brick site was quarried and pillaged far less than the monumental marble precincts of Rome. Walking through Ostia's main streets and narrow alleyways, you can easily imagine the din and flow of ancient city life.

To reach Ostia Antica from Rome, take the Metro Linea B to the Magliana stop (L1200), change to the Lido train and get off (25min.) at the Ostia Antica stop (buy another ticket for this leg). The bar outside the train station has the only food and drink before the site. Cross the overpass, go left when the road ends, and follow the signs to the entrance. The **Via Ostiensis** leads through a **necropolis** of brick and marble tombs to the low remains of the **Porta Romana,** one of the city's three gates; the road then becomes the **Decumanus Maximus,** the main street, and leads into the city center. A few hundred yards inside, the **Baths of Neptune** rise on the right, paved with a mosaic of Neptune driving his chariot, surrounded by marine creatures. Via dei Vigili leads off to the right of the baths to the **Caserma dei Vigili** (Firemen's Barracks). Evidently, the firemen kept an imperial cult; their main meeting hall is lined with statue bases inscribed to various emperors. Off the Decumanus on the left of the Baths of Neptune, the well-preserved **Via della Fontana** leads back to a **Fullonica,** or ancient laundry shop.

The well-preserved but much-restored **Theater** rises next on the right. Beyond the theater lies the expansive **Piazzale delle Corporazioni** (Forum of the Corporations), which held offices of importers and shipping agents from all over the Roman world. The sidewalk is lined with mosaic inscriptions proclaiming their businesses, the ancient precursors of modern welcome mats. In the center of the *piazza* are the remains of a **temple to Ceres,** the goddess of grain, Ostia's lifeblood. Several dozen meters from the Piazzale delle Corporazioni, on the theater side of the Decumanus, Via dei Molini leads to the **Casa di Diana,** the best-preserved Roman house at Ostia, and among the most complete in the world. Buildings like this, known as *insulae* (apartment blocks), once filled Rome and every city of the Roman empire. These, rather than the expansive (and expensive) villas of Pompeii, are where most ancient Romans lived. Behind the House of Diana is the **museum,** where a diverse collection of artifacts, both monumental and quotidian, are displayed. (Open daily 9:30am-1:30pm. Entrance included in admission to site.)

Back on the Decumanus, past the House of Diana, the street opens onto the **Forum of Ostia,** anchored, as at Rome, by the imposing **Temple to Jupiter, Juno,** and **Minerva** (called the **Capitolium;** climb to the top for an excellent panoramic view of town). Across the Forum a street leads to a **public latrine** (on the first left), and the vast **Terme del Foro** (Forum Baths). The Via del Tempio Rotondo runs parallel to the Decumanus and passes the 3rd-century **Round Temple,** a miniature Pantheon dedicated to the cult of all emperors. At the fork in the Decumanus, the **Via della Foce** leads right to the sumptuous **House of Cupid and Psyche** (on the right), where a statue of the two lovers (now in the museum) was found. The house, amazingly intact and paneled in elaborate polychrome marble, was home to one of Ostia's wealthier merchants. Farther down the street, a staircase descends to another eerie subterranean **Mithraeum,** from where an endless maze of sewers and cisterns spreads beneath the city.

Across the Via della Foce, the two-story **Casa di Serapide** has a central atrium with paintings and a relief of the god himself. The house opens into the **Baths of the Seven Wise Men,** named for a fresco cycle found in one of the rooms. The circular mosaic hall was once heated by a system of hot air ducts and served as an exercise area for the bath. Take a left down Via degli Aurighi to reach the **Porta Marina.** Beyond it, on Via Severiana near the ancient river bank, the entrance to the **Synagogue** is marked by two steps leading into a vestibule. Two architraves bearing Jewish symbols led to the discovery that these remains, including a mikvah (ritual bath), an oven, and a podium for religious services, were indeed an ancient synagogue.

The site is open in summer daily 9am-6pm, in winter 9am-4pm; admission L8000. The Bureau of Archaeological Digs (tel. 565 00 22) offers free tours in Italian at the excavations (July-Oct. every Sun. morning). Look for the schedule in the Sunday edition of Rome's *Il Messaggero.*

■■■ VITERBO

Imposing tinctured walls surround Viterbo, sheltering vestiges of a medieval eminence partially destroyed by Allied bombing. The city began as an Etruscan center, but earned prominence as a papal refuge from Frederick Barbarossa's siege in the 12th century. It was here that the (literally) torturous process of papal elections first took shape. The *capitano* (city dictator) locked the cardinals in their palace until they chose a new pope. Threats to cut off food and remove the roof from the conference room (so the cold could creep in more easily) were added incentives for a quick decision. Today Viterbo's streets brim with boys in uniform, the occasional punks, window shoppers, and senior citizens. The city also draws many to its sulphurous hot Bulicane spring (3km from the center), famous for its curative powers.

Orientation And Practical Information   Viterbo is easily accessible via the **Rome-Viterbo line** from Termini (trains run 6:30am-7:35pm). Alternatively, take Metro Linea A to the Flaminio station and follow the signs to the Roma Nord station. There, buy a combination train/bus ticket to Viterbo (one-way L5900, round-trip L11,800). The train stops at Saxa Rubra (15min.; deserted at night); then you board a COTRAL bus to Viterbo (1½hr.). The last bus to Rome leaves Viterbo at 7pm. To confirm prices and times, call the Saxa Rubra Station (tel. 332 83 33). Buy **bus tickets** at the theater/snack bar at Viale Trento or at the COTRAL (tel. 22 65 92) on Via Sauro (1 block east). Board all buses across from the theater. Buses to: Orvieto (1½hr., L5000); Civitavecchia (1¾hr., L5600); and Tarquinia (1hr., L4300).

The town is easily navigated: its walls form a trapezoid, with the wide parallel side along the east. **San Francesco** and **Santa Rosa** are in the northeast region (inside the **Porta Fiorentina**), **San Sisto** and **San Pellegrino** (the historical center) in the southeast, and **San Lorenzo** west of center. **Piazza dei Caduti** is just north of **Piazza del Plebiscito** (which is practically dead center). The **bus station** is just outside the northeast corner. South of P. del Plebiscito, at Via Cavour, 31, you'll find **telephones (SIP).** More phones are located at Via Calabresi, 7. (Open Mon.-Fri. 8.10am-7:50pm, Sat. 9am-12:30pm.) **Telephone code:** 0761. North of P. del Plebiscito, Via Cavour becomes Via Ascenzi and converges with Via Marconi at the **tourist offices.** Between P. Plebiscito and the tourist offices lies the **post office,** Via Ascenzi (tel. 23 48 06; open Mon.-Fri. 8am-1:25pm, Sat. 8am-12:25pm.) **Postal code:** 01100.

When you arrive at the bus or train terminal, turn right on Viale Trieste, walk along the city wall to the first opening, Porta Fiorentina (on the left), and descend along Via Mattcotti to P. Verdi at the base of the hill. Via Marconi on the right takes you to the tourist offices. The **EPT** at P. dei Caduti, 16 (tel. 34 63 63; fax 32 62 06). The staff is terse but informed; a large map is displayed outside. (Open Mon.-Fri. 8:30am-2pm and 3:30-6pm, Sat. 8:30am-2pm.) To the left is the **Azienda di Turismo,** P. Verdi, 4 (tel. 22 66 66; fax 34 60 29), with a helpful wall map. (Open Mon.-Sat. 8am-2pm). (In summer, the EPT **Tourist Office** at P. della Morte (tel. 34 52 29), in the southwest of town, is open Sat.-Sun. 3-7pm.) Corso Italia, sloping up to the right, leads to the medieval San Pellegrino district.

In an **emergency,** call 113. The **police** station (Polizia Stradale) is at Via Palmanova, 4 (tel. 34 31 07). The **hospital, Belcolle,** is 2km from the center, at Strada Sammartinese (tel. 30 58 73). In a **medical emergency,** call 30 40 33 or 112.

Accommodations and Camping   Only two *alberghi* within the old city walls are accommodating to the budget traveler, but they are beautiful; reserve in advance. **Albergo Roma,** Via della Cava, 26 (tel. 22 64 87; fax 22 72 74), has comfy, old-fashioned quarters, some with fridge and TV. Some English spoken. (Sin-

VITERBO

gles L39,000, with bath L59,000. Doubles L59,000, with bath L85,000. Triples with bath L115,000. Quads with bath L140,000. Rates may drop if they're not busy. AmEx, MC, Visa.) **Albergo Antico Angela,** Via dell'Orologio Vecchio, 1 (tel. 30 75 55), lies off Piazza d'Erbe. Although it no longer hosts the Queen of England, its cavernous, stone-lined walls still hold clean, comfortable rooms, all with bath. Coffee bar and TV lounge. (Singles L55,000. Doubles L75,000. Triples L98,000.) The nearest **campgrounds** are on the immaculate beach of **Lago di Bolsena,** 30km north. Most accessible by public transport are those in Bolsena (COTRAL bus, L3000). **Il Lago,** Viale Cadorna (tel. 79 91 91), is L7500 per person, L11,000 for tent and car; open March-mid-Oct. Prettier campgrounds are near Bolsena off the Cassia in the towns of Capodimonte and Montefiascone. The tourist office (tel. 79 91 52) has a list of Viterbo's campgrounds.

Food   Local specialties include *lombriche* (earthworm-shaped) pasta and a chestnut soup, *zuppa di mosciarelle*. Try Viterbo's native *sambuca,* a sweet anise-flavored liqueur. According to Dante, Pope Martin IV experienced the sufferings of purgatory for his weakness for a local dish, roasted eel from Bolsena. *Alimentari* can be found along Via dell'Orologio, or check out the huge **outdoor market** (Sat. 7am-2pm) in P. Martiri d'Ungheria, next to the EPT. There is a **Supervivo supermarket** on Via Marconi, 40, before P. dei Caduti (open daily 8am-1pm and 4:30-8pm, closed Thurs. afternoon).

Dine under the eyes of the patron saint of travel beneath a charming medieval arch at the **Trattoria del'Archetto,** Via Cristoforo, 1 (tel. 32 57 69). (*Primi* L6000. L20,000 *menù* includes ¼ liter of wine. Closed Sun.) In the southeast of town, near the Porta Romana gate, is **Porta Romana,** Via della Bontà, 12 (tel. 30 71 18). You decide how much you're willing to pay, and they'll tell you how much you're entitled to eat. The provincial specialties are lauded by locals. (Full meals about L25,000. Cover L2000. Open Mon.-Sat. 12:30-2:30pm and 7:30-11:30pm.) The tasty pizzas and lively atmosphere of **Taverna del Padrino,** Via della Cava, 22, are popular with locals. (Pizzas average L7000. Cover L2000. Open noon-2:30pm and 7pm-3am.)

Sights   At the south end of town is the medieval quarter's administrative center, **Piazza del Plebiscito.** The medallion-decked building with the tall clock tower is the **Palazzo del Popolo,** across from the **Palazzo della Prefettura.** Large stone lions, the symbol of Viterbo, guard both. Between them lies the **Palazzo Comunale,** in full Renaissance sprawl (open 8am-2pm; free). Odd frescoes in the **Sala Regia,** painted in 1592, depict the history of Viterbo, mixing Etruscan, Classical, Christian, and medieval legends. Ask at the office upstairs to have the Royal Room opened.

Curious *palazzi* line **Via San Lorenzo,** which winds from P. del Plebiscito into Viterbo's medieval heart, P. San Lorenzo. As you walk down the *via,* enter **Piazza del Gesù,** on the right, crowned by the medieval **Borgogne Tower.** A plaque on the seemingly peaceful 1000-year-old stone façade of the **Chiesa del Gesù** recounts family murders that took place during a morning mass in 1271. At the bend of Via San Lorenzo is the tree-lined, unfortunately named **Piazza delle Morte** (Square of Death), whose center contains a vibrant fountain and the 13th-century **Palazzetto di San Tomaso.** Note the medieval balcony next to the **Church of Santa Giacinta,** also on the square. Just north of P. della Morte, Via Cardinale La Fontaine leads to Via San Pellegrino, which extends through the medieval quarter of **San Pellegrino.** Churches and towers block the path completely, whittling the sky to a scant strip of blue between the dark *peperino* walls of the volcanic rock. At the end of Via San Lorenzo (in Piazza San Lorenzo) stands the Siena-influenced bell tower of the **cathedral;** its slender, arched windows climb to a sharp peak. The **Loggia dei Papi** (open Mon.-Sat. 10am-12:30pm), topped by toothlike merlons, fills the far end of the *piazza.* From the *loggia,* enjoy a bird's-eye view of early Christian churches.

Via Cavour and Via Giuseppe Garibaldi converge near the Porte Romana at the **Piazza Fontana Grande,** the appropriately named home to the city's largest, most luxurious fountain. Steps surround the Great Fountain, which is crowned by a magnificent Gothic spire.

Back near the bus station at the north end of town, the solemn **Basilica of San Francesco** contains the tombs of two popes who died in Viterbo: Adrian V (1276, whom Dante put in hell with the misers) and Clement IV (1265-68). (Open daily 3:30pm-7pm.) At the **Church of Santa Rosa** (near the *basilica*), the 700-year-old corpse of Viterbo's celebrated saint is preserved in a glass case. The people of Viterbo honor the saint every September 3 at 9pm, when one hundred burly bearers carry the *Macchina di Santa Rosa,* a towering construction of iron, wood, and *papier-mâché,* through the illuminated streets. Several days of frenzied celebration surround this event.

Directly inside the Porta Fiorentina, the **National Archaeological Museum,** P. della Roca, 21 (tel. 32 59 29), contains exhibits on Viterbo's Etruscan heritage. (Open Tues.-Sat. 9am-2pm, Sun. 9am-1pm. Admission L4000.) The **Festival Barocco** brings excellent classical music to Viterbo's churches in June. Ask at the tourist office about tickets (L12,000) and schedules.

■ NEAR VITERBO

Villa Lante (tel. (0761) 28 80 08), located in the town of **Bagnaia,** is a particularly enjoyable example of the grandiose villas that were *en vogue* among 16th-century church bigwigs. The villa is framed by a verdant park once used as a hunting reserve for popes and cardinals, now open to the public. Local (orange) bus #6 leaves Viterbo from P. Martiri d'Ungheria every 30 minutes for Bagnaia (15min., L1300; last bus back leaves Bagnaia at 8:30pm). From the *piazza* where the bus drops you off, walk uphill and enter the villa's right-hand gate. To enter the gardens next to the villa, you must ring at the gatehouse (on the left as you enter) and wait for a keeper to give you a tour. (Villa Lante open Tues.-Sun. 9am-7:30pm; March-April and Sept.-Feb. 9am-5:30pm. Tours of the inner gardens every 30min., L4000.)

■ ■ ■ THE PONTINE ISLANDS

A weekend playground for city-weary Romans, the Pontine Islands are Lazio's most splendid marine assets. In ancient times, Nero and Agrippina (Caligula's sister) were exiled to the island of **Ventotene;** and more recently, Mussolini was imprisoned on **Ponza.** Now, Italians flock to the turquoise-framed islands all too willingly, making the stunning archipelago very busy in July and August. **Ponza** and **Ventotene** are the only two inhabited islands. Both offer several options for staying over and connections to various ports for day trips. They are geared mainly toward Italians—a welcome change from the rampaging Germans on Elba and the international mayhem of Cápri. You can reach the islands by ferry from Anzio, Terracina, Fiumicino, and Formia. **Formia,** located between Rome and Naples, is the main jumping-off point for ferries (which are the most exciting things there). Ferry schedules change from season to season and even day to day; call before starting out.

GETTING THERE

Ferry companies run *aliscafi* (hydrofoils) and the slower, less expensive *traghetti* (large ferries that also transport cars). **CAREMAR** has offices in Anzio (tel. (06) 983 08 04; fax 984 62 91), Formia (tel. (0771) 227 10; fax 210 00), and Ponza (tel. (0771) 80 98 75; fax 851 82). **Linee Vetor** uses *aliscafi* only and has offices in Anzio (tel. (06) 984 50 85; fax 984 50 97), Formia (tel. (0771) 70 07 10; fax 70 07 11), Ponza (tel. (0771) 805 49), and Ventotene (tel. (0771) 851 95).

Smaller companies, such as **Mazzela** (in Ponza, tel./ fax (0771) 80 99 65; in Terracina, tel. (0773) 74 02 36), run less frequently than CAREMAR and Vetor but often more cheaply (Terracina to Ponza L10,000; to Ventotene L12,000). From Rome the best option is the train to Anzio (L5000) and then the CAREMAR ferry (L19,000).

CAREMAR: Anzio-Ponza: 2 ferries daily each way, L19,000 (8:10am and 2pm from Anzio; 11am and 5pm from Ponza). **Formia-Ponza:** *traghetti* departures 9am and 4:30pm, 2¼hr., L18,900. Returns 5:30am and 1:30pm. **Formia-Ventotene:** departures Fri.-Wed. 8:45am, Thurs. 1pm, 2¼hr.; returns 5:30pm. L14,000 each way. If no one is at the Ventonene port info booth, ask at the bar next door. **Ponza-Ventotene:** *aliscafi* departure 6:10pm, 35min., L18,900. Return 7pm. **Linee Vetor: Anzio-Ponza:** 4 departures daily June-Sept. (1¼, L35,000). One hydrofoil daily continues to Ventotene (L42,000). **Formia-Ponza:** one hydrofoil daily in each direction in the early afternoon (L35,000). **Formia-Ventotene:** one hydrofoil daily in each direction (L35,000). **Med Mar: Ponza-Ventotene:** depart 11am and 6pm, ½hr., L18,000. Return 11am.

PONZA

Practical Information   The **tourist office** (Pro Loco; tel. (0771) 800 31) awaits at Piazza Carlo Pisacane, 5, at the far left of the port (looking from the ocean). Walk up the steps under the "Ponza Municipio" sign on the long yellow building with arched entrances. (Useful brochure with hotel listings. Open daily 9am-1pm; July-Aug. also 4-8pm.) Three doors to the left, at P. Pisacane, 32, is the **post office.** (Open Mon.-Fri. 8:15am-1:30pm, Sat. 8:15am-noon.) **Postal code:** 04027. To **exchange money,** try Banco di Napoli, also in P. Pisacane (open Mon.-Fri. 8:30am-1:30pm). Autolinee Ponzesi (tel. 804 47) **buses** leave from Via Dante. (Follow Corso Pisacane until it becomes Via Dante; the bus station will be to your left.) Buses depart to Le Forna 8am-10:30pm every 20min. (L3000 round-trip). Since there are no official stops, on the way back, flag down buses anywhere along Via Panoramica. In case of **emergencies,** dial 113. The **police** are at Molo Musco (tel. 801 30); for **first aid** and **medical care,** contact Poliambulatorio at Via Panoramica (tel. 806 87).

Accommodations   Unfortunately, prices have skyrocketed over the past few years due to increased tourism; and unauthorized **camping** was outlawed years ago due to fire hazards. There are two helpful agencies to help you find a room: **Agenzia Immobiliare "Arcipelago Pontino,"** Corso Piscane, 49 (tel. 806 78), and **Agenzia Afari "Magi,"** Via Branchina Nuova, 22 (tel. 80 98 41). If you plan to stay more than one night, they'll help you find a room in **affitta camere** (private homes) for L70,000 per night for two people in July and August; L40,000 in off-season.

Hotels are spread out across the island and many are atop steep hills; consider taking a taxi (usually L10,000). **Pensione-Ristorante "Arcobaleno,"** Via Scotti D. Basso, 6 (tel. 803 15), is worth the haul. Go up the ramp, follow the street until it ends, then veer right until you pass the Bellavista Hotel. Turn left and follow the signs up, up, up. As you ascend the stairs, you'll curse the writer who sent you here, but when you reach the summit, you'll understand why you came: wonderful people, the best views in Ponza, and excellent food. (Half pension mandatory. L70,000 per person; L80,000 in July and August. Call ahead in summer.) **Casa Vitiello,** Via Madonna, 28 (tel. 801 17), is in the historic part of town (to the left when facing away from the port). Walk up the ramp from Piazza Pisacane, take a left at the top, then a right. Follow the signs to La Torre dei Borbini; it's across the street. The comfortable, tidy rooms have splendid views. (Doubles L110,000; off-season L80,000.)

Food   The Pontine Islands are known for their *zuppa di lenticchie* (lentil soup), fish, and lobster. Several restaurants and bars line the port and spark the island's nightlife. They set up tables along the boardwalk, and the fun lasts past 1am. For grocery and fruit stores, take a stroll along Corso Pisacane and Via Dante. One cheap restaurant option is **Pizzeria del Ponte,** Via Dante, 2 (tel. 803 87), next door to the bus station. With pizza at L2000 per piece, you can save up for your hotel and a boat tour. You'll think eggplant was invented especially for their vegetarian pizza. (Open Tues.-Sat. noon-1am.) **Ristorante Lello,** Via Dante, 10 (tel. 803 95), on the other side of the bus station, specializes in regional dishes. The *zuppa di lenticchie* is especially tasty. (*Secondi* L12,000.) For cool jazz and cool drinks, try **L'Airone,** Via

Banchina T. di Fazio (tel. 805 07). Located right on the waterfront, this "piano bar" features live music nightly. (First drink L5000. Open 10:30pm-5am depending on the crowd.)

Sights Ponza is full of grottoes and hidden beaches. Explore on foot or rent a boat (L70,000 plus gas). Guided boat tours are L30,000 per person. At the port ask for *una gita* (JEE-tah) *a Palmarola* to get a tour of Ponza's coastlines and a neighboring island, **Palmarola.** The water is clear and green, and the white cliffs are tinted red by iron deposits and yellow by sulphur. As you approach Palmarola, you will see Dala Brigantina, a natural amphitheater of limestone. Most trips also motor through the **Pilatus Caves,** an ancient Roman breeding ground for fish.

On Ponza the spectacular beach and surrounding white cliffs at **Chiai di Luna** are a 10-minute walk up Via Panoramica (off Via Roma). The **Piscine Naturali** (natural swimming pools) provide excellent views of the whitewashed houses of Le Forna while you bronze in the sun. You can rent paddle-boats, scuba equipment, and more (**kayaks** L25,000 per day, L35,000 for a 2-person model). Check **Ponza Mare** (tel. 80 679; via Banchina Nuova) for rentals, and **Scuola Sub "Nautilus"** (tel. 80 87 01) for scuba lessons. There are numerous **scooter rental** companies near the port.

VENTOTENE

If the crowds of Campania drive you mad, tiny, tranquil Ventotene, though barren, provides a refuge to rejuvenate your travel-weary bones. The pace of life is much slower on this island; bicycles replace mopeds and most of the shopkeepers work "when they feel like it." The tiny **tourist office** is located right on the port (follow the signs with the "*i*") and is managed by an affable English-speaking staff. **Centro Servizio Ventotene,** Via Pozzo di S. Candida, 13 (tel. (0771) 852 73; fax available), will help you find a room in a hotel or in an *affitta camera* (private home) for L30,000 per person, less in off-season. (Open Feb.-Nov. daily 9:30am-7:30pm.)

At **Albergo Isolabella,** Via Calarossano, 5 (tel. 850 27), Signora Santomano and her family pamper the weary with large, clean rooms and terrific sunset views. (Singles L50,000, in Aug. L55,000.) Although you might feel at home, don't stay for lunch (the increase to half pension costs L35,000). To reach the hotel, walk up the ramps from the port to **Piazza Alcide de Gasperi** and the yellow church. Go right, pass Caffè Fredo, take another right, then a left. This road is poorly lit, so take a flashlight For an elegant meal, walk to Via Olivi, 45 from Piazza dei Castello; **Ristorante Il Giardino** (tel. 850 20) serves a wonderful *zuppa di lenticchie* (lentil soup) for L10,000 and *fusili con zucchini* (pasta with zucchini, L8000), along with a variety of seafood selections. For basic staples, head to the grocery store in the *piazza.* Another rewarding option is **Le Grotte di Mast'Agnello** on the Via Calanone (tel. 852 27).

The somewhat dry **Archaeological Museum** is also in P. Castello. (Open daily 10am-1pm and 7pm-midnight. Admission L3000. During the winter call 85 14 20 to open the museum.) Here you can inquire about Italian-language guided tours of archaeological sites: **Villa Giulia** (2½hr., L6000), and **Cisterna Romana di Villa Stefania** (L5000). Coraggio on the Porto Romano rents **rowboats** (L10,000 per day), **motorboats** (L50,000 per day), and **scuba diving equipment** (L35,000 per day). Two splendid **beaches,** Cala Rossano and Cala Nave, flank the port.

For the week and a half leading up to September 20, the day of their patron saint, Santa Candida, the residents of Ventotene celebrate with hot air balloons, dancing, and rowboat races. Look out!

■■■ ETRURIA

The Etruscans, a tribe whose origins and language are still shrouded in mystery, dominated north-central Italy from the 9th through 4th centuries BC. In the shadow of expanding Roman power to the south, most traces of the Etruscans' culture disappeared. What remains, excavated from their necropoleis, is fascinating. Etruscan tomb paintings celebrate life, love, eating, drinking, sport, and the rough country-

ETRURIA

side. Their tombs, inside large earth mounds called *tumuli,* are carved out of rock in the shape of houses. Vandalism has forced the government to close many tombs, and the artifacts that have been excavated now reside in the Villa Giulia and Vatican Museums at Rome and in the national museums in Tarquinia and Cerveteri. Still, a visit to Etruria conjures up plenty of ghosts, and the deserted tombs have a quiet, shadowy appeal quite different from the pomp and grandeur of Rome.

CERVETERI

Blue COTRAL **buses** run to Cerveteri (ancient Caere) from Rome at Via Lepanto (every 30min., 1hr., L3900; take Metro Linea A to Lepanto, or bus #70 from Sta. Maria Maggiore or Largo Argentina). The last return bus to Rome leaves at 9:30pm. There's a small **tourist office,** Caere Viaggi, at Piazza Moro, 17 (tel. (06) 994 28 60), across from the bus stop. (No maps, but they answer questions. Open daily 9am-1pm and 4:30-9:30pm.) From the village, it's another 2km to the necropolis along a tree-lined country road; follow the signs downhill and then to the right. Whenever you see a fork in the road without a sign to guide you, choose the fork on the right. Bring a flashlight and a picnic lunch. Bring courage, too; few sounds chill the heart like the flapping of the **giant grasshoppers** that lurk in the abandoned tombs.

The bulbous earthen tombs of the **Etruscan necropolis** (tel. 995 00 03) slumber in the tufa bedrock from which they were carved. (Open Tues.-Sun. 9am-7pm; Oct.-April Tues.-Sat. 9am-4pm, Sun. 11am-4pm; admission L8000; maps L1000; fossilized grasshopper fangs L7000.) Don't miss the **Tomb of the Shields and the Chairs,** the smaller **Tomb of the Alcove** (with a carved-out matrimonial bed), and the row-houses where less well-to-do Etruscans rested in peace. Look for the colored stucco reliefs in the spectacular **Tomba dei Rilievi.** Also worthwhile is the **Museo Nazionale di Cerveteri,** P. Santa Maria Maggiore (tel. 994 13 54), located in **Ruspoli Castle,** displaying Etruscan artifacts found in the Caere necropolis in the last 10 years. (Open Tues.-Sun. 9am-7pm; free.) The last bus for Rome leaves at 9:30pm; if you're stuck, try the **Albergo El Paso,** Via Settevene Palo, 293 (tel. 994 30 33; fax 995 35 82), 500m out the bottom left side of the main *piazza.* (Singles L65,000. Doubles L90,000. Triples L105,000. Breakfast L8500. Shower included. AmEx, MC, Visa.)

Navigating the Necropolis

Several aspects of the tombs provide clues about the bodies they contain. *Cippi* (stone markers) signify the gender of each individual within: some are little houses and others erect rods—you guess which one is which. The chambers inside are carved to resemble the houses of living Etruscans, and locations of graves are indicators of status. Small rooms off the antechamber held the remains of slaves and household servants; the central room housed the rest of the family, and the small chambers is the back were reserved for the most prominent men and women. A triangular headboard on a couch marks a woman's grave; a circular one indicates a man's.

TARQUINIA

When Rome was simply a village of mud huts on the Palatine hill, Tarquin kings held the fledgling metropolis under their sway. The tables turned, of course, and today little remains of the once-thriving Etruscan city. But the subterranean **necropolis** of tombs on the ridge opposite the city and the vibrant frescoes housed within are an enticing testimony to a fascinating culture. The town gracefully drapes itself over a hill above the Etrurian plains, a pleasant change from the hustle and bustle of Rome.

Buses arrive in the Barriera San Giusto outside the medieval ramparts. The **tourist office** (tel. 85 63 84; open Mon.-Sat. 8am-2pm and 4-7pm) provides a wealth of information and bus schedules. In adjoining P. Cavour stands the **Museo Nazionale** (tel. 85 60 36), one of the best collections of Etruscan art outside of Rome. Look for the famous **Winged Horses** on the second floor. Don't pass up the second-floor ramparts of the building, where you can sun yourself and catch great views of the sea.

(Open Tues.-Sun. 9am-7pm; winter 9am-2pm. Guided evening tours in summer Tues.-Fri.; inquire at the tourist office. Admission L8000.)

The same ticket admits you to the **necropolis** (tel. 85 63 08). Take the bus from Barriera San Giusto (any that go to the "Cimitero" stop) or walk (15min. from the museum). Head up Corso Vittorio Emanuele from P. Cavour and turn right down Via Porta. Then take Via Ripagretta to Via delle Croci, which leads to the tombs. Because of the tombs' sensitivity to air and moisture, only 6 to 8 may be seen on a given day (and even then only peered at from behind a metal railing in the doorway). All of the tombs are splendidly decorated with scenes of Etruscan life, including banquets, sacrifices, and portraits, as well as animals and geometric designs. (Open Tues.-Sun. 9am-7pm, winter 9am-2pm.)

Trip over Tarquinia by day. The site is a local stop on the Rome-Grosseto **train** line, and buses run from the station and beaches into town every 30 minutes until 9:10pm (5min., L1000). (Trains leave from Termini in Rome starting at 7:20am; the last train back leaves Tarquinia at 10:48pm; 1hr., L9500 one-way, L15,000 roundtrip.) **Buses** also link the town with Viterbo (1hr., L7500), Civitavecchia (½hr., L3200), and Rome (8 per day, 2hr., L6500). The bus from Rome leaves from Via Lepanto, and requires a switch in Civitavecchia. From the Lepanto metro stop, walk down to the end of the column of blue buses and purchase your ticket in the bar on the left corner. For information on southern Etruria (Provincia di Viterbo), try the **Azienda Autonoma di Turismo** at P. Cavour, 1 (tel. (0766) 85 63 84), or at the **EPT** in Viterbo, P. dei Caduti, 16 (tel. 22 61 61). The sole "budget" hotel in Tarquinia is **Hotel San Marco,** P. Cavour, 18 (tel. 84 08 13; singles L70,000, doubles L110,000).

CENTRAL ITALY

■ Abruzzo and Molise

Only a short distance from Rome (about 3 hours by train), but a long stretch from the frenzy of tourism, the highlands of Abruzzo offer the traveler a tranquil retreat. The well-preserved medieval towns of L'Aquila and Sulmona are surrounded by easily accessible natural areas: to the south of Sulmona is the **Abruzzo National Park** in its unspoiled beauty: wild animals, hidden mountain lakes, and spectacular vistas of miles of uninterrupted wilderness. To the north of L'Aquila looms the *Gran Sasso d'Italia* (Big Rock of Italy), the highest peak of the Apennines. In summer its sheer wall attracts climbers and hikers, and in winter the mountain hosts three ski resorts. Unfortunately, the coastal region has been reduced to shapeless cultural shambles by "progress." Pescara and the surrounding coast are a tumble of *pizzerie,* discos, and beach blankets, completely alien to the rugged and unspoiled interior highland. Music lovers looking for a little regional sustenance shouldn't miss *maccheroni alla chitarra* (square-shaped pasta that has been squeezed through parallel wires), or *zafferano* (saffron), the famous spice exported to "gild" the dishes of Milan (it turns rice yellow). Fun food fact: Over 100,000 stigmas of the *zafferano* flower go into one kilogram of the spice.

The nation's second smallest region, **Molise,** is deservedly the least known Italian corner, lacking any cities of distinction. Nevertheless, its mountainous areas abutting the Abruzzo National Park offer more unspoiled wilderness, where roaming bears, wolves, and boars try to avoid assimilation into the local cuisine. Also scattered through the region are ancient Roman and medieval towns, and some ruins dating back to the Golden Age of Greece. Keep in mind that much of unspoiled Molise is beyond the scope of public transportation, so a car is almost essential.

In both regions, where train lines are painfully circuitous and inaccessible at some points, the **ARPA** bus service proves very useful. For bus information call the ARPA office in Avezzano (tel. (0863) 26 561). Avoid traveling on Sundays, when bus service is sharply reduced.

■■■ L'AQUILA

L'Aquila (The Eagle) seems a fitting name for this busy commercial city perched in the highest segment of the Apennines. Unfortunately, prices here are as lofty as the town's name, making budget travel nearly impossible.

Orientation and Practical Information Corso Vittorio Emanuele II, the main artery of the northern half of the city, stretches between the **Castello Cinquecentesimo** and surrounding park to the north and the **Piazza del Duomo,** the heart of the city's historic district. Beyond the Piazza del Duomo, the street continues as **Corso Federico II** until it reaches the plush gardens of the **Villa Comunale** and **Via XX Settembre,** which circumscribes the southern half of the city. Be sure to pick up a map; navigating the small streets can be aggravating, and street names change every few blocks.

The **train station** (on the Sulmona-Termi line) is at Piazzale delle Stazione, on the outskirts of town. Take bus #1, 3, or 3/5 (L1200) to the center of town, or turn right and follow the signs to the *Fontana delle 99 Cannelle* and hike up the hill from there. Buses arrive near the *castello,* and tickets are available in the ticket booth there. To obtain maps and tourist information, go to the **EPT** (tel. 41 08 08 or 41 03

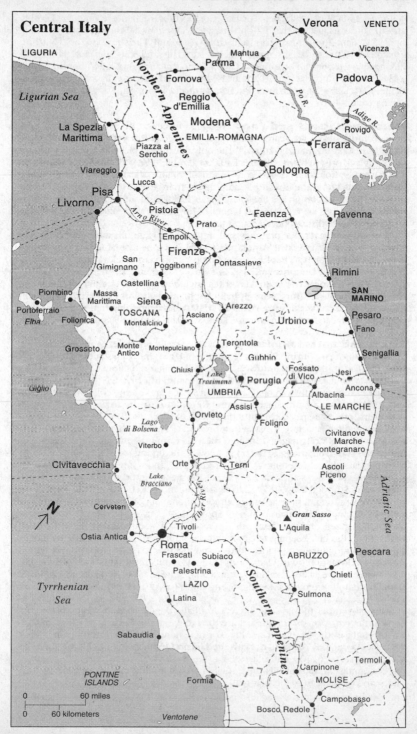

Central Italy

LIGURIA

Ligurian Sea

VENETO

Verona

Vicenza

Mantua

Parma

Fornova

Padova

Reggio d'Emilia

Modena

EMILIA-ROMAGNA

Po R.

Adige R.

Rovigo

Ferrara

La Spezia Marittima

Piazza al Serchio

Northern Appenines

Viareggio

Lucca

Bologna

Pisa

Pistoia

Faenza

Ravenna

Livorno

Arno River

Prato

Empoli

Firenze

Pontassieve

Rimini

San Gimignano

Poggibonsi

SAN MARINO

Piombino

Castellina

Pesaro

Portoferraio

Massa Marittima

Siena

Asciano

Arezzo

Urbino

Fano

Elba

Follonica

TOSCANA

Montalcino

Terontola

Senigallia

Grosseto

Monte Antico

Montepulciano

Chiusi

Gubbio

Fossato di Vico

Jesi

Ancona

Giglio

Lake Trasimeno

Perugia

UMBRIA

Albacina

LE MARCHE

Assisi

Lago di Bolsena

Orvieto

Foligno

Civitanove Marche-Montegranaro

Viterbo

Civitavecchia

Orte

Terni

Ascoli Piceno

Lake Bracciano

Cerveteri

Tiber River

Adriatic Sea

▲ *Gran Sasso*

Tivoli

L'Aquila

Ostia Antica

Roma

Frascati

Subiaco

ABRUZZO

Pescara

Palestrina

Chieti

LAZIO

Tyrrhenian Sea

Latina

Sulmona

Southern Appenines

Sabaudia

Carpinone

Termoli

PONTINE ISLANDS

Formia

MOLISE

0   60 miles

Campobasso

0   60 kilometers

Bosco Redole

Ventotene

40) in P. Santa Maria Paganica. Turn off Corso Vittorio Emanuele onto Via Leosini, and the office is just up the hill on the right. (Open Mon.-Fri. 8am-2pm and 3:30-6pm, Sat. 8am-2pm). Also stop in at the **Azienda di Turismo,** at Corso Vittorio Emanuele, 49 (tel 41 08 59; open Mon.-Fri. 9am-1pm and 3:30-7pm, Sat. 9am-1pm). **Hiking information** can be found at **Club Alpino Italiano,** Via XX Settembre, 15 (tel. 243 42; open Mon.-Sat. 9am-1pm and 4-8pm), or Libreria Colacchi, Via Andrea Bafile, 17 (tel. 253 10; open Mon.-Fri. 9am-1pm and 4-8pm, Sat. 9am-1pm). The **telephone code** is 0862.

Accommodations and Food Although three-star hotels are plentiful, budget accommodations are scarce in L'Aquila. **Albergo Aurora** at Via Cimino, 21 (tel. 220 53), just off Piazza del Duomo, is the only reasonable place in town. Rooms are large but lack private baths. (Singles L40,000, doubles L52,000.) **Lo Shaly** (tel. 44 15 21) is a more affordable but less convenient alternative, located in Bazzano, a block down the road from the bus stop. Catch the #6 train (every 30min., 10min., L1500) in front of the *castello* on Via Castello. Singles L29,000. Doubles L42,000, with bath L55,000. All prices are L3000-5000 higher in July and August, and half and full pension are available throughout the summer.

Torrone, a nougat made of honey and almonds, is to L'Aquila what chocolate is to Perugia. Manufactured in L'Aquila, this local sweet is available in many stores throughout the city; try **Tappirullan** on Corso Vittorio Emanuele. For more substantial fare, **Trattoria Da Lincorta,** at P. S. Pietro di Coppito, 19 (tel. 286 62) off Via Roma, offers a variety of regional favorites, including *agnello ai ferri* (grilled lamb, L11,000). (Open Sat.-Thurs. noon-3pm and 6pm-midnight. AmEx.) Tired of sitting in crowded restaurants? **Supermercato STANDA** has everything that you need for a complete picnic. (Open Mon. 4-8pm, Tues.-Sat. 9am-1pm and 4-8pm.)

Sights and Entertainment L'Aquila's **castello** dominates the pleasant park at the end of Corso Vittorio Emanuele, up the hill from the train station. The Spanish built this fort in the 16th century as a defense against rebellious townspeople. Its intimidating walls now house the **National Museum of Abruzzo** (tel. 63 31), which showcases (among other things) the region's early art, a large collection of sacred medieval works, and a fossilized mammoth found near the town in 1954. (Open daily 9am-2pm, holidays 9am-1pm. Admission L8000.)

From the intersection of V. XX Settembre and C. Federico II, take Viale Francesco Crispi to Viale di Collemaggio, through the Villa Comunale, to reach the **Basilica of Santa Maria di Collemaggio,** begun in 1287 at the urging of local hermit Pietro da Marrone (later Pope Celestine V). The striking pink and white checked façade with its elaborate doorways and windows belies the austere interior; Baroque embellishments were stripped away in 1972 to restore the more medieval look inside.

The oldest monument in L'Aquila, almost an emblem of the city, is the **Fontana delle 99 Cannelle** (Fountain of the 99 Spouts, 1292); take Via Sallustio from Corso Vittorio Emanuele and bear left until you reach Via XX Settembre. Follow the small roads down the hill, keeping to the left at the bottom. The fountain is a symbol of the city's founding, when 99 local lords came together to build a fortress that would protect the local hill towns; each of the unique spouts represents a different town. The source of the water remains unknown, in spite of an earthquake in 1703 that partially demolished the medieval city and more recent renovations to the fountain itself.

From November to May, the Società Aquilana dei Concerti holds classical concerts in the *castello*. Also of interest are the recitals at the **Festival of Classical Guitar** throughout the last week in May. For ticket and schedule information, check with the Azienda di Turismo, or with the **Ufficio Organizzativo dell'Ente Castello Cinquecentesco,** 67100, L'Aquila (tel. 242 62 or 41 41 61, fax 616 66). Every morning but Sunday, a **market** fills the P. del Duomo with artisan's booths, local handicrafts, and clothing from local stores.

■ NEAR L'AQUILA

The craggy terrain around L'Aquila conceals isolated medieval towns, ancient churches and monasteries, and abandoned fortresses. East of the city lies the 15th-century **Rocca Calascio**, one of the world's most sophisticated works of military architecture. It's surrounded by the medieval towns of **Santo Stefano di Sessanio** and **Castel del Monte**, as well as the 9th-century **Oratorio di San Pellegrino** in the town of Bominaco. To the west of L'Aquila lie extensive Roman ruins at **Amiternum** and the enormous **Lago di Campotosto**, the largest man-made lake in Italy, which supplies electricity to the Abruzzo and surrounding regions. ARPA buses service these sights from both L'Aquila and Sulmona (2-3 departures daily, 1½hr.-2½hr., L4300-7600). North of L'Aquila, the town of **Assergi** contains a beautiful 12th-century abbey, **Santa Maria Assunta**, with well-preserved frescoes reminiscent of Byzantine art. To get there, take one of the hourly #6 municipal buses (1hr., L1500) from Porta Paganica.

The **Grottoes of Stiffe** at San Demetrio ne' Vestini, 21km from L'Aquila, afford visitors glimpses of the land *below* Abruzzo. Here, an underground river has carved out striking rock formations, lakes, caverns, and waterfalls. A recent cave collapse has restricted access, but it's still stunning. Guided tours are available weekends 9am-1pm and 3pm-sunset every day. Daily tours in July and August, and special tours available for groups of 20 or more. Closed Dec.-Feb. (For more information, contact the EPT of L'Aquila; for reservations call or write the Gruppo Speleologico Aquilano, Svolte della Misericordia #2, 67100, L'Aquila. Tel./fax (0862) 41 42 73.)

GRAN SASSO D'ITALIA (BIG ROCK OF ITALY)

Twelve km above L'Aquila rises the snowcapped **Gran Sasso d'Italia**, the highest peak entirely within Italy and a mountaineer's delight. First procure a map marked *carta topografica per escursionisti* or *Wanderkarte*. Make sure it includes *sentieri* (trails marked by difficulty) and *rifugi* (hikers' huts charging L9000-16,000 per night). Always call these refuges before setting out, and bring food, as prices rise with the altitude. **Club Alpino Italiano** in L'Aquila (tel. 243 42) has the most up-to-date Apennine advice. The accommodations booklet available at L'Aquila's **EPT** contains a list of Abruzzo refuges. From L'Aquila, take bus #6 (about 5 daily, 1hr., L1500 from a local bar or *tabacchi*) from Porta Paganico, on Via Castello; make sure it's going all the way to the *funivia* (gondola). Get off at the base of the cableway. If you don't feel like hiking to the top, you can take the *funivia* halfway up (prices vary depending on the season, day of the week, whether you're going up or down or round trip, and your astrological sign; the price range is from L7,000-15,000). The *funivia* runs every half-hour in high season (July-Aug.) and every hour in low season from 8:30am-4:45pm, except at 1:30pm. Camp and munch at **Camping Funivia del Gran Sasso** (tel. 60 61 63), an immaculate, grassy area down the hill from the cableway. (L7000/person, L6000/tent.)

The area around the *funivia* offers several scenic hikes. Trail #10 (about 500m down the road) will take you up to **Monte Della Scindarella** and offers a stupendous view of the Gran Sasso and L'Aquila. The upper *funivia* station provides access to several trails; to tackle the mountain itself, take trail #3 to trail #4. For useful information on Alpine guides, inquire at the tourist office or write to **Collegio Regionale Guide Alpine,** Via Serafino, 2, 66100 Chieti (tel. (0871) 693 38). In the winter, the Gran Sasso teems with skiers. Weekly passes are available at **Camp Imperatore** (tel. 60 61 43 or 41 05 57) and **Campo Felice** (tel. 91 78 03), and lessons are available from the Gran Sasso **ski school** (tel. 41 13 44).

■ ■ ■ SULMONA

Sulmona's most famous son and greatest pride, the poet Ovid (43 BC-17 AD), stands immortalized in bronze in **Piazza XX Settembre,** the city's main meeting space. Although seemingly preoccupied with its ancient past, Sulmona owes much of its beauty to the late Middle Ages, when prosperity spurred the construction of innumerable churches and palaces. Sulmona's intimate size and noteworthy architecture make it the perfect town in which to relax for a day or a weekend. It maintains a distinct sweetness, thanks not only to the residents' friendliness but also to the proliferation of candy stores—Sulmona has been the primary home of *confetti* candy, its second greatest pride, since the 15th century. These flower-shaped candies made from sugar-coated almonds are traditionally thrown at weddings worldwide.

Orientation and Practical Information Sulmona is easily reached by ARPA **bus** from L'Aquila (9 daily, 1½hr., L7300), and Pescara (5 daily, 1½hr., L7300). For more bus info call 21 04 69. Buy tickets on the bus. Located on the Rome-Pescara line, the city is more accessible by **train;** there are 12 daily trains in each direction (Rome, 3hr., L13,700; Pescara, 1¼hr., L5700). To get to the town center from the station, take bus A (every ½hr., buy tickets from the driver, L1500), or walk the two km uphill, to the right upon leaving the station. The **tourist office** is at Corso Ovidio, 208 (tel. 532 76), on the third floor. (Open Mon.-Sat. 8am-2pm.) **Telecom (SIP)** phones are located behind the **Church of the SS. Annunziata** on Largo San Tommasi. (Open daily 8am-10pm.) **Telephone code:** 0864.

Accommodations and Food The friendly and helpful proprietors of **Albergo Italia,** P. Tommasi, 3 (tel. 523 08), off P. XX Settembre, go out of their way to make guests feel welcome. Elegant rooms overlook the dome of the church of the SS. Annunziata and the mountains. (Singles L35,000; doubles L60,000, with bath L70,000.) **Albergo Stella,** Via Panfila Mazara, 16 (tel. 526 53), is conveniently located off Corso Ovidio near the aqueduct. Rooms are clean and well-maintained. (Singles L30,000, with bath L35,000. Doubles L50,000, with bath L56,000. Breakfast L5000.) **Ristorante Stella** (downstairs) offers regional specialties at reasonable prices. *Primi* L7000, *secondi* L8000-12,000. Cover L2000. (Open daily noon-2pm and 7:15-9pm.) **Ristorante Cesidio,** P. Solimo (tel. 527 24) is a family-run escape from busy Corso Ovidio and the main *piazze. Primi* L6000-8000, *secondi* L7000-10,000. Cover L2500. (Open Sat.-Thurs. noon-3pm and 7pm-midnight, Fri. noon-3pm. AmEx, MC, Visa.) **Ristorante Italia** (tel. 330 70), has an enchanting dining room and offers great food with friendly service. Located to Ovid's left in Piazza XX Settembre. Menu changes daily. *Primi* L8000, *secondi* L8000-11,000. (Open Tues.-Sun. noon-3pm and 7-11pm. AmEx, Eurocard, MC, Visa.) For a light meal, try **Pizzeria Ernano,** Corso Ovidio, 263 (tel. 505 93). Inexpensive pizzas (L7500) and beer (L2500) are great for a tight budget. (Open Fri.-Wed. 10am-2pm and 5pm-1am.) Those with a sweet tooth will not want to miss **G. Di Carlo e Figlio,** Corso Ovidio, 185, and its famous *confetti.* (Open daily 9:30am-1pm and 3-8pm.) **Supermercato STANDA,** Corso Ovidio, 15, is just past the arch at the end of the street. (Open Mon.-Sat. 9am-1pm and 4-8pm.)

Sights At one end of Corso Ovidio is the Romanesque-Gothic **Cathedral of San Panfilo,** the first nucleus of which was built a thousand years ago on the ruins of a temple to Apollo and Vesta. The **gardens** of Sulmona offer shade to the weary. Down Corso Ovidio from the gardens rests the **Church and Palace of SS. Annunziata,** an extravagant baroque church façade which abuts a delicate Gothic-Renaissance **palazzo.** The *palazzo* now houses a small museum featuring Renaissance Sulmonese goldwork. (Closed for restoration in 1995.) The colossal **Piazza Garibaldi,** just beyond the church, is marked by the Renaissance-era **Fontana del Vecchio** gushing clear mountain water from the nearby medieval aqueduct (1256). A **market** takes place here daily, and is expanded on Wednesdays and Saturdays.

■■■ ABRUZZO NATIONAL PARK (PARCO NAZIONALE D'ABRUZZO)

Zoned to preserve parts of the area for human habitation while remaining pristine, the National Park occupies a huge tract of land in the mountainous wilderness of southwest Abruzzo. The mountains offer visitors spectacular views of lush woodlands, crystal-clear lakes, and flora and fauna protected from human molestation for over 70 years. Lynx have recently been reintroduced near Civitella Alfedena, and the park is home to the Marsican Brown Bear, Apennine Wolf, and Abruzzo Chamois. Pescasseroli, the park's administrative center, provides a base for exploration.

ORIENTATION AND PRACTICAL INFORMATION

Enter the park from **Avezzano** (on the Rome-Pescara train line, 1½hr. from Rome (L9800) and 2½hr. from **Pescara** (L11,700)). You can also catch an ARPA bus from L'Aquila to Avezzano (40min., L7100). ARPA buses also take you from Avezzano to the park and between the cities within the park. (Avezzano to Pescasseroli, Mon.-Sat. 6 daily, Sun. at 9am; last return 6pm; 1½hr.; L5700.) From June 12 to mid-September an ARPA bus leaves from Rome Tiburtina for Pescasseroli daily at 7:30am and returns for Rome at 6:30pm (3hr., L17,000 one way). For more information call ARPA at tel. (0863) 265 61 or 229 21.

In Pescasseroli, go to the **Ufficio di Zona** (tel. 919 55) off P. Sant'Antonio (where the bus stops), with hiking questions and for the essential park map (L10,000—it's expensive, but profits go toward maintaining the park). Office staff are very friendly and willing to answer questions or direct you to a campsite. (Open daily 9am-noon and 3-7pm.) For all your accommodation and restaurant questions, drop by the helpful **tourist office** (tel. 91 00 97; fax 91 04 61), on Via Piave off Piazza Sant'Antonio (open daily 9am-1pm and 4:30-6:30pm). In Opi, 6km to the west of town at the turnoff to Camosciara, there's an **Information center** (tel. 891 70) for foreign visitors. (Open July 10-Aug. Mon.-Sat. 9am-1pm and 2-5pm.) A **museum** dedicated to the Abruzzo Chamois is located here. (Open 9am-noon and 3-6pm.)

The town of **Alfedena**, 1km from its train station and 33km from Pescasseroli, showcases picturesque archaeological sites. Its **tourist office** (tel. 873 94), in the main square, stocks information on the Roman **acropolis** and the pre-Roman **necropolis** dating from the 10th century BC.

The **telephone code** for Pescasseroli, Opi, and Avezzano is 0863; for Civitella Alfedena, Castel di Sangro, and Pescocostanzo: 0864.

ACCOMMODATIONS, CAMPING, AND FOOD

Avezzano

Avezzano is notable mainly for its location on both the Rome-Pescara train line (train station tel. 41 56 31) and the main bus route though the park. Although decent, affordable lodging is rare, **Creati,** Via XX Settembre, 208 (tel. 41 33 47), has clean, modern rooms (all with private bath). (Singles L30,000. Doubles L60,000.) From the train station, walk left for 10min. and turn right at the street's end onto Via de Fiori; the hotel is another 10-min. walk to the left at the end of the street. The bus to Pescasseroli makes a stop across Via XX Settembre from the hotel. Restaurants in Avezzano are few, hard to find, and generally very expensive.

Pescasseroli

Most reasonably priced accommodations in Pescasseroli do not offer single rooms, but solo travelers can often finagle a double or quad to themselves for the price of a single during the off-season. **Pensione al Castello** (tel. 91 07 57), across from the park office, has large, modern rooms with private bath, and is convenient to the bus stop and trails. (L30,000 per person, half pension offered during peak season; all prices higher in Aug.) The spectacular views are definitely worth the 2-km walk uphill to **Albergo Valle del Lupo,** Via Collachi (tel. 91 05 34). Walk down Viale S. Lucia off P. S. Antonio and turn right along Viale Colle dell'Oro; follow the signs from there. Rooms are quiet, homey, and most have a balcony overlooking the mountains. (Singles L30,000 with bath L35,000, doubles with bath L60,000.) There are four campgrounds within 21km of town; the best is **Campeggio dell'Orso** (tel. 919 55), by the river on the Opi road (L6000 per person, L6000 per tent).

For pizza or regular restaurant fare, **Il Cerbiatto,** Via Napoli, 19 (tel. 91 04 65) offers a wide selection. A hearty bowl of *gnochetti e fagioli* (potato pasta and beans, L8000) coupled with the *maiale ai ferri* (possibly the best grilled pork chops you've ever tasted, L8000) will satisfy the hungriest of mountain-climbers. Pizzas L8000-12,000. Cover L3000. (Open Thurs.-Tues. noon-3pm and 7:30-11pm.) The nearby pastry shop, **Pasticceria Alpina,** Traversa Sangro, 6 (tel. 91 05 61), serves a full array of award-winning goodies. (Open daily 8am-midnight; in winter closed Mon.) **Supermercato Delfino A&O** is on Via S. Lucia, the main highway, just past the zoo and the park office. (Open daily 8:30am-1pm and 4-8pm; AmEx, MC, Visa.)

Opi

ARPA buses follow the winding road through the park to the village of **Opi** (5km), named for the pagan goddess of abundance (there was a temple here in ancient times). Two km past the village on the bus route lies the campground **Vecchio Mulino** (tel. 91 22 32; L7500 per person, L8000 per tent). In August, Opi hosts the **Sagra degli Gnocchi** (Gnocchifest), a nationally renowned eat-along where thousands converge to consume *gnocchi*, sausages, and cheese. (*Gnocchi* are potato-flour dumplings whose consistency ranges from delicate puffs that melt in your mouth to lumps of dough that hit your stomach with a thud.)

Civitella Alfedena

Ten km past Opi, the bus reaches the village of **Villetta Barrea;** 200m down, the turnoff to Civitella Alfedena leads to the **Pinas Nigra Campground** (L6000 per person, L7000 per tent.) The site is large and pleasant, bordered by the River Sangro. In Civitella Alfedena, make yourself at home at the **Alberghetto La Torre,** Via La Torre (tel. 89 01 21; doubles L60,000, extra bed L30,000). Museo Lupo has information on the habits and history of the Apennine Wolf and the lynx. (Admission L5000.) Ice-cold **Barrea Lake** cuts majestically into the mountains, stretching 7km between Villetta Barrea and the next village of **Barrea.** The **Colle Ciglio campground** (tel. 881 97), on the banks of the lake, is 500m above town on the way to Alfedena. (Open June 15 through August.)

Alfedena

Stay at **Leon D'Oro** (tel. 871 21; singles L30,000, with bath L40,000; doubles L60,000, with bath L75,000). A track leads from Alfedena to **Lago Montagna Spaccata** (3km away), where the intrepid and insulated can brave the freezing waters.

EXCURSIONS

You don't really enter the park until you begin the scenic ascent on the bus ride from Avezzano to Pescasseroli. Fields of poppies, rocky outcrops, dazzling valleys, and dizzying views will delight you. To avoid gastronomical *déjà vu,* don't eat too much before this twisting climb. If you don't see any wildlife in the park, compensate in Pescasseroli by checking out the **museum** and **zoo** on Via S. Lucia, which include animals indigenous to the park, colorful gardens, and exhibits showing the park's natural history. (Open daily 10am-noon and 3-6pm. Admission L10,000.)

Once you get off the bus, you'll find the region undeveloped and its trails poorly marked. Look for red and orange signs; the other colors are used by naturalists to mark off trees of interest. Begin by purchasing a trail map (L10,000) from the Ufficio di Zona in Pescasseroli. The clear, detailed map points out where the different animals protected in the preserve—brown bears, chamois, deer, wolves, and eagles— are most likely to be found. The trails are arranged so that all paths that begin with

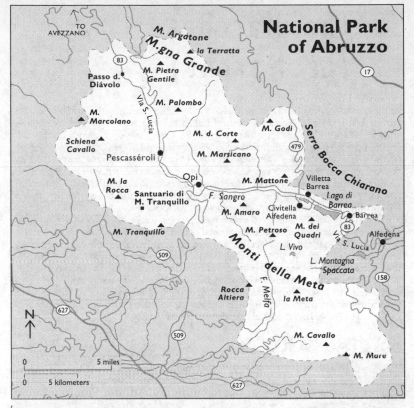

the same letter start from the same point. Some of the best trails are within walking distance of Pescasseroli. For a short hike, take **trail B1** up to ancient castle ruins (50min. round-trip). To really stretch those legs, make the beautiful five-hour (round-trip) hike to **Valico (Pass) di Monte Tranquillo** (1673m). Take **trail C3,** which starts at the southern end of town, up through the green Valle Mancina past the Rifugio Della Difesa. Keep climbing and you'll eventually reach the pass and its impressive view of the mountain peaks to the north.

If you can tune your hiking timetable to that of the ARPA bus line, venture further afield. From Civitella Alfedena (15km from Pescasseroli) take **trails I1 to K6** through the sublimely beautiful **Valle di Rose** and by the park's largest herd of chamois (more than 200). From approximately July 15-Sept. 5, this area can only be explored with a guide (L10,000 per person). Call **Museo del Lupo** (89 01 41) to reserve or to get more info about the trails. From Barrea (20km from Pescasseroli) you can take **trail K5** to the refreshing (i.e., cold) lake **Lago Vivo** (3½hr. round-trip; lake dries up late June). The adventurous may want to rent **mountain bikes** (about L5000/hr.); call **Sport House** in Pescasseroli (tel. 91 07 96), or turn left from the tourist office and cross the river, then turn right. Sport House is at the end of the street, less than a 5-min. walk. Several paths, including C3, can be covered by bike.

In winter, this area has excellent skiing, with challenging slopes and plentiful snowfall. Package deals on **settimane bianche** (white weeks) provide room, lift tickets, and half pension (full pension optional). For more info, contact the tourist office in Pescasseroli. For a regional snow bulletin, call (0862) 665 10.

The Marches (Le Marche)

As the mountain peaks and rolling hills of the Marches taper into the Adriatic Sea the farther east you go, picturesque central Italian hill towns are replaced by endless seaside resorts and tourist traps. Away from the water, however, are numerous valleys and coastal plains, a patchwork of wheat, maize, and olives. Originally inhabited by the Gauls and Picenes, the area later fell under Roman control. It received its present name in the 10th century, when it was a border province of the Byzantine Empire; in the 12th and 13th centuries the powerful Montefeltro family of Urbino and the Malatesta clan of Rimini ruled the area, altering the faces of many towns with a number of extraordinary churches and palaces.

Since World War II, summer tourism has emerged as the mainstay of the region's economy. A crowded strip of international beach resorts has sprung up beside the ancient cities that dot the Marches' once-serene shoreline. Each summer sees a migration of Germans to the area, making the coast appear more like the North Sea than the Adriatic. The region's two gems are actually not on the sea but 90 minutes inland; Renaissance Urbino and medieval Ascoli Piceno are easily accessible and should not be missed. Direct trains roll from Rome to Ancona (4½hr., L26,200), and vacation buses cross to Urbino, Ascoli Piceno, and the coast from Tuscany and Umbria. The Milan-Lecce coastal line also serves the region.

■■■ PESARO

Though Pesaro is on the beach, it is not an entirely beach-oriented town. Instead, the beach and the city coexist, allowing tourism to flourish alongside a vital historic center where buildings date from over 1000 years ago. Even in modern times Pesaro provides hospitable urban spaces, such as the Piazza Lazzarini at the entrance to the old town, and the Piazza della Libertà on the sea at the far end of the main street. Pesaro is also appealing due to its proximity to magnificent Urbino.

ORIENTATION AND PRACTICAL INFORMATION

Pesaro lies on the main Bologna-Lecce route along the Adriatic coast. From Rome, take a train toward Ancona (6 or 7 per day), then change at Falconara to one of the frequent *locali* to Pesaro (4½hr., L26,200). The center of the old city is **Piazza del Popolo.** From the train station, walk across the small *piazza* onto Viale del Risorgimento and continue on Via Branca (5min.). From the Piazza del Popolo, the beach and Piazza della Libertà are only 5-10min. away. Walk straight along Via Rossini (which becomes V.le della Repubblica) away from Piazza del Popolo to get there.

> **Tourist Office: APT,** 3 offices. At the train station (tel. 68 78), open erratically in summer, Mon.-Sat. 9:30am-1pm and 4-6:30pm. At Via Rossini, 41 (tel. 693 41), in the town center, open daily 9am-noon and 4-6:30pm. At Piazzale della Libertà (tel. 636 90), on the beach, open Mon.-Sat. 8am-8pm, Sun. (in summer only) Mon.-Sat. 8am-1pm and 3:30-7:30pm. Both Via Rossini and the Piazzale offices have friendly and helpful English-speaking staff.
> **Police:** Main station and foreigners' office (tel. 692 41).
> **Post Office:** P. del Popolo (tel. 691 55), at the beginning of Via Rossini. *Fermo posta* at #1. Open Mon.-Sat. 8:15am-7:40pm. **Postal Code:** 61100.
> **Telephones: Telecom,** P. Matteotti, 23/24, across the street from the bus station (AMANUP). Open Mon.-Fri. 9am-1pm and 4-7pm. Booths open 7am-11pm. **Telephone Code:** 0721.

Buses: P. Matteotti, down Via S. Francesco from P. del Popolo. Buses #1, 2, 4, 5, 6, 7, 9, and 11 stop at P. Matteotti. To: Fano (frequent buses, 15min., L1400), Ancona (5 per day except Sun., 1½hr., L5000), and Urbino (8 per day, 1hr., L3500). Two express buses per day to Rome Tiburtina station (4½hr., L32,800). **Emergencies:** tel 113 or 115. **Hospital:** P. Cinelli (tel. 36 11). **Medical Assistance:** tel. 314 44. **Night and holiday Medical Service:** Via Nitti, 36 (tel. 45 53 79). **Emergency: Pronto Soccorso,** tel. 329 57.

ACCOMMODATIONS AND CAMPING

Except in July and August, you should have no trouble finding a bed.

Ostello Ardizio (HI) (tel. 557 98), at Fosso Sejore 6km from town. Take the **AMANUP** bus toward Fano from P. Matteotti (6am-9pm, every 30min., L1000; to arrive at P. Matteotti from the station take bus #3 (L1000) or walk along Via 24 Maggio from the station (which becomes Via Manzoni). Get off when you see the "Camping Norina" sign on the beach to your left; you will be dropped off at a hotel/bar. Walk back (away from the bar) and take the road that separates from the highway to a grassy area and a yellow sign pointing toward the hostel. Quality hostel with 88 beds, in a serene area close to the beach. Fastidiously kept. Free tennis courts. L14,000 per person. Breakfast included. Meals L12,000. Reservations essential in July and Aug. Open May-Oct.

Pensione Ristorante Arianna, Via Mascagni, 84 (tel./fax 319 27), 100m from the beach. Spotless rooms, excellent food. All rooms with bath. Singles L40,000-50,000. Doubles L55,000-72,000. Breakfast L8000. Full pension required in Aug., L68,000 per person. Reservations help. MC, Visa.

Hotel Riviera, Via Ninchi, 4 (tel. 302 28). Old but well-kept hotel. Freshly painted and thoroughly scrubbed. Prime location on the beach. Singles L25,000-30,000, with bath L37,000. Doubles L40,000-45,000, with bath L55,000. Breakfast L6000. Full pension required in August, L43,000-55,000 per person. Open April-Sept.

Camping Panorama (tel. 20 81 45), 7km north of Pesaro on the *strada panoramica* to Gabicce Mare. Take bus #1 to the end; from there it's a 20-min. uphill walk. A path leads to a quiet beach. L7500 per adult, L5500 per child, L9500 per tent. Hot showers included. 2 swimming pools. Open May-Sept.

Campo Norina (tel./fax 557 92), 5km south of the city center on the beach at Fossoseiore. Take the bus for Fano from P. Matteotti (L1000). L11,000-14,700 per person, L8500 per tent or site. 4-person bungalows L90,000. Open April-mid-Oct.

FOOD

Pesaro's **public market** is at Via Branca, 5, off P. del Popolo behind the post office (open Mon.-Sat. 7:30am-1:30pm). **Pizzerie** line the beach, while **alimentari** crowd the sidewalks on Corso XI Settembre. Best of all is the **STANDA supermarket** upstairs at Via Branca, 52, off P. del Popolo. (Open Tues.-Sat. 8:30am-12:30pm and 4-8pm, Mon. 4-8pm.)

Mensa Arco della Ginevra, Via della Ginevra, 3 (tel. 343 08), near Musei Civici. Enter through the door in the arch. A self-service cafeteria and bargain-hunter's delight with elephantine portions. This place has both selection and price. Hearty complete meal with wine or water L10,000. Open Mon.-Fri. noon-2pm.

Harnold's, P. Lazzarini, 34 (tel. 687 86), close to Teatro Rossini. Outdoor seating in the *piazza*. Fresh, cheap, and delicious with a wide range of eccentrically named, satisfying *panini* (L2500-6000). Open Thurs.-Tues. 11:30am-2am.

Trattoria Pinocchio, Via Venturini on P. Antaldi, 12 (tel. 347 71). Hip crowd. *Primi* L9000, *secondi* L16,000-18,000. Open daily noon-2pm and 8-10pm.

Trattoria da Maria, Via Mazzini, 73 (tel. 687 64). The place to go for a large home-cooked meal. Lots of locals. *Primi* L6000-9000. *Secondi* L10,000-16,000. Try the fresh *zuppa di pesce* (fish soup, L15,000). Cover L2500. Open Fri.-Wed. noon-3pm and 7-11pm.

SIGHTS AND ENTERTAINMENT

The robust arcade and *putti*-weighted window frames of the 15th-century **Ducal Palace,** home of Pesaro's ruling della Rovere clan, preside over the **Piazza del Popolo,** Pesaro's main square. On **Corso XI Settembre** and its side streets, narrow passages pass open arcades and sculptured doorways. Off the *corso* on Via Toschi Mosca, the **Musei Civici** (tel. 312 13) house a superb collection of Italian ceramics and primitives. (Open Tues.-Sat. 9am-8pm, Sun. 9am-1pm; Oct.-March Tues.-Sat. 8:30am-1:30pm, Sun. 9:30am-12:30pm. Admission L5000.) An extensive collection of photographs, portraits, theatrical memorabilia, letters, and scores pertinent to the composer's life awaits at the **Rossini Birthplace and Museum,** Via Rossini, 34 (Casa Rossini). (July-Sept. open Tues.-Sun. 10am-7pm; winter open Tues.-Sun. from 10am-1pm, but call ahead to be sure. Admission L3000.)

Most of Pesaro's modest Gothic churches hide behind lavish Baroque portals. Among them are the **Chiesa di San Domenico** on Via Branca and the **Chiesa di Sant'Agostino** on Corso XI Settembre. Enter the latter to see its beautiful late 15th- and early 16th-century wooden choir stalls inlaid with still-lifes, landscapes, and city scenes. (Open 9am-12:30pm and 3:30-8pm.) Outside of town is the **Villa Imperiale** (4th- to 15th-centuries), a mansion currently owned by a duke. The lavish villa and gardens can be visited July 19-Sept. 21 on Wed. at 4pm by making arrangements with the APT (tel. 636 90). Tours depart from P. della Libertà (L5000).

The evening *passeggiata* (high style and *gelato* are musts) cruises along Viale Trieste and P. della Libertà. Older folk meander through P. del Popolo, window-shopping in ritzy stores. For a great view of the **sunset,** head up to **Parco Ortigiuli,** Via Belvedere, near the River Foglia (6:30-8pm; free). Popular nightspots for the youthful are **The Bistro,** Viale Trieste, 281, under Hotel Cruiser, and **Big Ben,** Via Sabbatini, 14, between the Palazzo Ducale and the Conservatorio Rossini.

Pesaro hosts the **Mostra Internazionale del Nuovo Cinema** (International Festival of New Films) during the second and third weeks of June. Organizers make an effort to show interesting and rarely screened films. Movies new and old, commercially and independently produced, are shown in the buildings along Via Rossini and at the Teatro Comunale Sperimentale off P. del Popolo. Check at the tourist office for more info. The fortune of native opera composer Rossini endowed a music school, the **Conservatorio di Musica G. Rossini,** which sponsors events throughout the year; contact the conservatory at P. Olivieri for a schedule. The annual **Rossini Opera Festival** begins in early August, but opera performances and orchestral concerts continue until September. Contact the tourist office for exact dates and prices, or reserve tickets through the information office at Via Rossini, 37 (tel. 301 61).

■ NEAR PESARO: FANO

The 12km between Pesaro and Fano are home to the quietest retreats on this stretch of the Adriatic. The sandy beach on the north side of Fano is much less crowded than its Adriatic neighbors and is a good choice for those seeking a more secluded seaside vacation. The best way to reach Fano is by **train** (south of Pesaro on the Bologna-Lecce line). Walk right from the train station and turn right over the tracks onto Viale Battisti to reach the **tourist office** at #10 (tel. (0721) 80 35 34; fax 82 42 92). Pick up a map of the city and a list of local events here. (Open Mon.-Sat. 8am-2pm and 4-7pm, holidays 8:30am-1:30pm.)

Two of Fano's best budget hotels are on the quiet north-side beach. **Hotel Amelia,** Viale Cairoli, 80 (tel. 82 40 40), a 10-15-min. walk from the train station, offers sparkling, newly remodelled rooms only 15m from the water. Turn right out of the station, take the bridge across the train tracks, turn left after the bridge (onto Via da Fabriano, the street that runs along the tracks), and turn right on Via Fabriano. Continue under an overpass and over a canal until you reach Viale Cairoli, and turn right. The hotel and beach are at the end of this tree-lined street. (All rooms with bath. Singles L45,000-65,000. Doubles L50,000-95,000. Full pension L56,000-90,000 per person. Open May-Sept.) **Albergo Fortuna,** Viale Cairoli, 74/76 (tel. 80 35 23), next door to Amelia, offers clean, basic rooms at good prices. (One single L35,000. Doubles with bath L60,000. Breakfast included. Reserve one week ahead in summer.) Several reasonably priced *trattorie* cluster along the beach here. **Food** staples and picnic supplies can be found at the small corner grocery store/fruit stand just inland from the hotels. (Open Mon.-Sat. 8:15am-7:30pm, Sun. 8:15am-1pm.)

Even in summer, the beaches to Fano's north are only lightly sprinkled with vacationers. To get to the quietest spots, walk left along the water and watch the crowds thin out. American tourists are a real novelty here, and the beach is the main attraction—bask in the sunshine and solitude!

■■■ URBINO

If you want to visit the epitome of the Italian town, make it Urbino. Under the leadership of philosopher and warrior Federico da Montefeltro (1444-1482), the city exemplified the finest in Renaissance style and tradition, which can be best seen in Urbino's stunning Palazzo Ducale. Urbino's fairy tale skyline has changed little in the last 500 years. And while tourists shape the character of many cities, Urbino owes its flair to its university students.

ORIENTATION AND PRACTICAL INFORMATION

The **SAPUM bus** from Pesaro's P. Matteotti or train station is cheap, frequent, and direct (10 per day, 1hr., L3500). After winding up steep hills, the bus will deposit you at Borgo Mercatale, which lies below the beautiful city center. A short uphill walk, or a ride in the elevator takes you to **Piazza della Repubblica,** the city's hub.

Tourist Office: P. Rinascimento, 1 (tel. 26 13; fax 24 41), across from the Palazzo Ducale. Distributes a list of hotels and an unnecessarily large map. Open Mon.-Sat. 9am-1pm and 3-6pm, Sun. 9am-1pm; off-season Mon.-Sat. 8:30am-2pm.
Police: P. della Repubblica, 1 (tel. 26 45 or 32 04 91).
Post Office: Via Bramante, 22 (tel. 25 75), right off Via Raffaello. Open Mon.-Fri. 8:30am-7:40pm, Sat. 8:30am-1pm. **Postal Code:** 61029.
Telephones: Telecom, P. Rinascimento, 4, off P. Duca Federico. Open daily 8am-10pm. **Telephone Code:** 0722.
Buses: Information (tel. 97 05 02). Departures from Borgo Mercatale. Timetable posted at the beginning of Corso Garibaldi, under the portico at the corner bar on P. della Repubblica. To Pesaro (10 per day, 4 on Sun., 1hr., L3500).
Public Toilets: Via San Domenico, off P. Duca Federico next to the APT office, L500. Open daily 7am-noon and 2-7:30pm.
Emergencies: tel. 113. **Hospital:** Via B. da Montefeltro (tel. 32 93 51, 32 81 21, or 32 81 22), to the north of the city out of P. Roma.

ACCOMMODATIONS AND CAMPING

Cheap lodging is rare in Urbino, and reservations are essential. You might want to consider staying in the youth hostel in Pesaro and taking a day trip to Urbino. For longer stays, write to the Università degli Studi, Calle dei Cappuccini.

Albergo Italia, Corso Garibaldi, 52 (tel. 27 01), off P. della Repubblica, near the Palazzo Ducale. A truly elegant (yet affordable) hotel with affable management. Patio, great view, and elevator. Singles L37,000, with bath L48,000. Doubles L50,000, with bath L70,000.
Pensione Fosca, Via Raffaello, 67 (tel. 32 96 22 or 25 42). Top floor. Signora Rosina takes good care of her guests. Large, charming rooms with high ceilings. Singles L32,000-35,000. Doubles L45,000-49,000.
Hotel San Giovanni, Via Barocci, 13 (tel. 28 27). A relatively modern hotel with a helpful manager. Restaurant downstairs. Singles L35,000, with bath L48,000. Doubles L50,000, with bath L70,000. Triples with bath L80,000. Closed July.

Camping Pineta, Via San Donato (tel. 47 10), in the *località* of Cesane, 2km from the city walls. L8000 per person (L6000 per child), L16,000 per tent. Open April-mid-Sept.

FOOD

Many *paninoteche, gelaterie,* and burger joints are located around P. della Repubblica. Shop for supplies at **Supermarket Margherita,** Via Raffaello, 37. (Open Mon.-Wed. and Fri.-Sat. 7:45am-12:45pm and 5-7:45pm, Thurs. 7:45am-12:45pm.)

Pizza Evoé, P. S. Franceso, 3 (tel. 48 94). A very popular *pizzeria* with a young crowd. Outdoor seating in a secluded *piazza,* around the corner from P. della Repubblica. Pizza L6000-10,000. *Primi* L5000-7000, *secondi* L7000-10,000. Cover L2000. Open Mon.-Sat. noon-3pm and 8pm-2am.

Morgana, Via Nuova, 3 (tel. 25 28), across from Club 83. Traditional atmosphere, excellent food. Pizza L7500-8000. *Primi* L6000-10,000, *secondi* L6000-18,000. No cover charge. Open Thurs.-Tues. noon-3pm and 7pm-1am; closed July 5-25.

Pizzeria Le Tre Piante, Via Foro Posterula, 1 (tel. 48 63), off Via Budassi. Spectacular view from the outside tables, in addition to the delicious food. Very popular. Pizza L5000-10,000. *Primi* L10,000, *secondi* L8000-16,000. Cover L2000. Open Tues.-Sun. noon-3pm and 7pm-2am.

Bar del Teatro, Corso Garibaldi, 88 (tel. 62 92 84), at the base of the Palazzo Ducale. Not exactly cheap, but it's got the best view in town (P. Ducale on one side, a vista overlooking the valley on the other). A cool, shady place to spend the afternoon. *Cappuccino* or tea outside L2500. Open Mon.-Sat. 7:30am-2am.

SIGHTS AND ENTERTAINMENT

Urbino's most remarkable monument is the Renaissance **Palazzo Ducale** (Ducal Palace). The façade, which overlooks the edge of town, boasts a unique design attributed to Ambrogio Barocchi: two tall, slender towers enclose three stacked balconies. Most of the palace, celebrated in Italy as "the most beautiful in the world," was designed by Luciano Laurana. Enter the palace from P. Duca Federico. The interior **courtyard** is the essence of Renaissance harmony and proportion. To the left, a monumental staircase takes you to the private apartments of the Duke, which now house the **National Gallery of the Marches.** Federico was one of the great patrons of the early-middle Renaissance (the Quattrocento—1400s). Works here reflect the transition into the age of Humanism; fledgling attempts at perspective in painting appear in Piero della Francesca's *Flagellation of Christ.* Also among the works here are Berruguete's famous portrait of Duke Federico, Raphael's *Portrait of a Lady,* and Paolo Uccello's tiny, strange *Profanation of the Host.* The most intriguing room of the palace is the Duke's study on the second floor, where stunning inlaid wooden panels give the illusion of real books and shelves covered with astronomical and musical instruments. Nearby, a circular stairway descends to the **Cappella del Perdono** and the **Tempietto delle Muse,** where the Christian and pagan components of the Renaissance are commingled. At one time, eleven wooden panels representing Apollo, Minerva, and the nine Muses covered the walls of the temple, but all have been removed (eight of them are currently in Florence's Galleria Corsini). Don't leave the palace without heading underground to see the well-documented "works" of the Palazzo. Here the meandering maze includes the Duke's bath (both hot and cold tubs), kitchen, washroom, freezer, and lavatory for the staff (an ingenious underground cistern system provided water to these rooms). (Open daily 9am-2pm. Admission L8000.)

At the end of Via Barocci lies the 14th-century **Oratorio di San Giovanni Battista,** decorated with brightly colored Gothic fresco-work representing events from the life of St. John. If you speak Italian, the *custode* can give you a wonderful explanation of how fresco painters used lamb's blood as ink for their sketches. (Open Mon.-Sat. 10am-noon and 3-5pm, Sun. 10am-12:30pm. Admission L3000, but you will be obliged to see S. Giuseppe next door for another L2000.) **Raphael's house,** Via Raffaello, 57, is now a vast and delightful museum with period furnishings. His earliest work, a fresco entitled *Madonna e Bambino,* hangs in the *sala.* (Open Mon.-Sat. 9am-1pm and 3-7pm, Sun. 9am-1pm. Admission L5000.) The hike up to the **Fortezza Albornoz** (turn left at the end of Via Raffaello) ends with an awe-inspiring view of the Ducal Palace and the rest of the city: the perfect spot for a picnic. (Closed for restoration in 1995, but check out the beautiful view anyway. Free.)

Urbino's P. della Repubblica serves as a modeling runway for local youth in their chic threads. Take a walk down this fashion ramp and then stroll (or climb) the serpentine streets at dusk. If you seek more active entertainment, dance the night away at **Club 83** on Via Nuova (opens late, go around midnight). Throughout July you can attend the **Antique Music Festival** in the Church of S. Domenico. A cheaper alternative, and more popular with students, is the **University ACLI,** on Via Santa Chiona, a bar with music and small crowds. All this begins in August, when the Italian university summer session convenes. August also brings the ceremony of the **Revocation of the Duke's Court,** replete with Renaissance costumes. Check at the tourist office for the exact date.

■■■ ANCONA

Ancona is the archetype of a port city. The old town is tough and gritty, like an old, weathered seaman. Buildings are high, streets dark and sooty. Unlike most historic centers, commerce exists only around the periphery, and the core is quiet and dilapidated. While the Roman Emperor Trajan might have recognized the city's value as a trade center in the first century AD, today's cargo consists of tired, ferry-borne tourists. The old town and its Romanesque cathedral warrant a half-day tour. Be warned: the buildings in Ancona are occasionally deserted and the town does not have many street lights, so exercise caution when walking at night.

Orientation and Practical Information Ferry schedules, in excruciating detail, are available at the **Stazione Marittima** on the waterfront just off P. Kennedy. Take bus #1 to and from the station (L1000). All ferry lines operate ticket and info booths. The **information office** at the entrance of the station gives free guided tours of Ancona twice a day in summer. (English spoken. Open daily 8am-2pm and 3:30-8:30pm.) Make reservations if you're traveling during July or August. For ferry service, be at the station at least two hours before departure. Main ferry lines are:

> **Marlines** (tel. 20 25 66; fax 411 77 80; 542 68 (for Greece); 549 00 (for Turkey))
> **Minoan/Strintzis** (tel. 207 39 92; fax 56 00 09 or 56 03 46)
> **Adriatica** (tel. 20 49 15; fax 56 01 73 (for Albania); 56 00 22 (for Croatia))
> **ANEK** (tel. 207 32 22; fax 56 10 24)
> **Egnatia Ferries** (tel. 20 10 80; fax 20 63 31)
> **Jadrolinija** (tel. 20 45 16; fax 562 56)
> **SEM Maritime Co.** (tel. 552 18; fax 20 26 18 or 552 62)
> **Superfast** (tel. 20 20 33; fax 20 22 19)
> **TOPAS** (tel. 20 23 91; fax 20 31 67)

Ancona is an important junction on the Bologna-Lecce train line and is also served by trains from Rome. The **train station** (tel. 439 33) at P. Rosselli, houses a **tourist office** (tel. 417 03). (Open Mon.-Sat. 8am-noon and 5-7pm.) **Telephone code:** 071. *Fermo posta* and stamps are available at the **post office,** Viale della Vittoria, 2 (tel. 20 13 20 or 517 28), off P. Cavour. (Open Mon.-Fri. 8:15am-7:40pm and Sat. 8:15-1pm.) **Postal code:** 60100. For **emergencies,** tel. 288 88 (police), 113 or 116. The center of town, **Piazza Cavour,** is a 10-minute ride from the train station on bus #1 (L1000). **Corso Garibaldi** and **Corso Mazzini** connect Piazza Cavour to the port.

Accommodations and Food In summer, people waiting for ferries often spend the night at the Stazione Marittima, but you'll find lots of reasonably priced hotels in the town center. Avoid the overpriced lodgings in the area by the train station. Make reservations or arrive early—rooms fill quickly in the summer. A 10-minute stroll from the Stazione Marittima will take you to **Pensione Centrale,** at Via Marsala, 10 (tel. 543 88), 1 block from P. Roma, on the 4th floor. Fine rooms with high ceilings. (Singles L30,000. Doubles L40,000, with bath L60,000.) Or take bus #1 to Viale della Vittoria, and head to **Hotel Cavour,** V.le della Vittoria, 7 (tel. 20 03 74), 1 block from P. Cavour. The fragile-looking elevator will take you to large rooms on the 3rd floor. (Singles L30,000-38,000. Doubles L55,000-65,000.) Pack a meal for your ferry ride at the old-fashioned **Mercato Pubblico** (across from Corso Mazzini, 130). (Open Mon.-Wed. and Fri. 7:30am-12:45pm and 5:15-7:30pm, Thurs. and Sat. 7:30am-12:45pm.) **Supermarket SIDIS,** at Via Matteotti, 115, offers the best grocery deals around. (Open Mon.-Wed. and Fri.-Sat. 8:15am-12:45pm and 5-7:30pm, Thurs. 8:15am-12:45pm.) For hearty Italian fare in a cheery sky-blue-and-white decor, try **Trattoria Vittoria,** Via Calatafimi, 2/B (tel. 20 27 33), on the corner of P. Cavour and Corso Mazzini. *Primi* L7000, *secondi* L8000-18,000. *Menù* L16,000. Cover L2000. (Open Tues.-Sun. noon-3pm and 7:30-10:30pm.) If you prefer dining *al fresco,* head to **Trattoria 13 Cannelle,** Corso Mazzini, 108 (tel. 20 60 12), off P. Roma opposite the fountain in the wall. *Primi* L8000, *secondi* L10,000-23,000. (Open Mon.-Sat. 12:15-2:45pm and 8-11pm. Cover L2000. AmEx, MC, Visa.)

Sights and Entertainment   Survey the Anconan sea and sky from **Piazzale del Duomo,** atop **Monte Guasco.** Climb up Via Papa Giovanni XXIII, or take bus #11 from P. Cavour. If you decide to walk, you'll enjoy the beautiful **Scalone Nappi,** a verdant stairway street. (Follow the left-hand steps at the point where the street forks; there are only 244 steps, and the view is magnificent.) In P. del Duomo sits the **Cathedral of San Ciriaco,** erected in the 11th century on the site of a Roman temple to Venus. Its stolid Romanesque design reflects the influences of the Apulian Romanesque from the south and the remnants of the Byzantine from the north. (Cathedral open daily 9-10:30am and noon-6pm.)

After decades of restoration (World War II bombings and a 1972 earthquake among its trials), the **Museo Archeologico Nazionale delle Marche** is open for business on Via Ferretti above Via Pizzecolli. The impressive collection includes the Ionian *Dinos of Amandola,* some wonderful Greek vases, and two life-size equestrian bronzes of Roman emperors. (Open Mon.-Sat. 9am-1:30pm, Sun. 2:30-7:30pm.) Ancona's painting gallery, the **Galleria Comunale Francesco Podesti,** is housed in the 16th-century **Palazzo Bosdari** at Via Pizzecolli, 17. Carlo Crivelli's tiny, flawless *Madonna col Bambino* completely shows up Titian's *Apparition of the Virgin,* recently restored to the full glory of its original colors. (Open Tues.-Sat. 10am-7pm, Sun. 9am-1pm. Admission L4000, Sun. free for everyone.) Join the evening *passeggiata* on the tree-lined esplanade from Corso Garibaldi past P. Cavour to Viale della Vittoria. In mid-July, the **Festa della Birra e del Rock** (Rock 'n' Beer Fest) features sex, drugs, and rock 'n' roll (well, one out of three ain't bad).

■■■ ASCOLI PICENO

Ascoli Piceno, a medieval hill town not unlike Urbino, offers the architecture, museums, and history without the blight of tourism. As a result, prices are downright reasonable and the near-empty hostel, housed in a 13th-century *palazzo,* completes the picture of Ascoli as an attractive place to stay if you're in or near San Benedetto.

According to legend, Ascoli was settled by Greeks who were guided westward by a woodpecker—a *picchio*—which gave the city its surname and provided a symbol for the Marches. In another account, Ascoli was the metropolis of the Piceno people, a quiet Latin tribe that controlled much of the coastal Marches and had the woodpecker as its clan totem. Whatever its origins, Ascoli has always been fiercely independent, from its role as a center of anti-Roman power during the Social Wars to its successful resistance to Nazi occupation. In the late 13th century, this independence produced a splendid architecture that remains unspoiled today. Ascoli is celebrated for its lovely, well-preserved historic center and romantic medieval streets that make the town seem untouched by modernity. Stroll through the historic center and avoid the new town; Ascoli is a place to visit to recollect the past.

ORIENTATION AND PRACTICAL INFORMATION

Ascoli is about one hour by bus or train from San Benedetto del Tronto, which is itself one hour from Ancona on the Bologna-Lecce train line. **Cotravat** buses, cheaper, less crowded, and more frequent than the trains, leave San Benedetto del Tronto for Ascoli about every 45 minutes (L3100; buy tickets at Bar Massimo across from the S. Benedetto train station). If you do take the train, you'll still need to hop a city bus (L1000) once you arrive. Walk straight out of the station, one block to Viale Indipendenza, take a right, and then walk half a block to the stop. Catch bus #2 or 3 to arrive at the historic center. Get off at the bus station behind the *duomo*, where the Cotravat buses stop as well. Take Via XX Settembre to your left off P. Arringo in front of the *duomo* to Via del Trivio, which connects to Corso Mazzini and P. del Popolo.

Tourist Office: Ufficio Informazioni, P. del Popolo, 17 (tel. 25 52 50). Very helpful. Open Sun.-Fri. 8am-1:30pm and 3-7pm, Sat. 8:30am-12:30pm and 3-7pm.

Post Office: Via Crispi, off Corso Mazzini. Open Mon.-Sat. 8:15am-7:40pm. *Fermo posta* (at window #3) open Mon.-Sat. 8:30am-1pm and 4-7:40pm. Stamps at #4 and 5. **Postal Code:** 63100.

Telephones: Telecom, Via Dino Argelini Patriota 145/147 off Via del Trivio. Office open Mon.-Fri. 9am-1pm and 3:30-7:30pm, Sat. 9am-1pm. Public phones next door open daily 8am-10pm. **Telephone Code:** 0736.

Buses: all leave from Viale de' Gasperi (behind the *duomo)* except Amadio, which runs from Viale Indipendenza. Timetable outside on the wall at **Agenzia Viaggi Brunozzi,** Corso Trento e Trieste, 54/56 (tel. 25 94 60). Buy train and bus tickets here. Open Mon.-Fri. 9am-1pm and 4-7pm. **ARPA** (tel. (0861) 24 83 43) to Pescara: 5 per day, 2hr., L6000. If the Agenzia is closed, you can get tickets to S. Benedetto in a *tabacchi*.

Emergencies: tel. 113.

ACCOMMODATIONS

There are a few quiet and well-kept hotels in Ascoli Piceno, but the best choice for the budget traveler is clearly the city's relaxed youth hostel.

Ostello de Longobardi, Via Soderini, 26, Palazzetto Longobardo (tel. 25 90 07). From P. del Popolo take Via del Trivio 3 blocks past S. Francesco until it forks into 2 streets. Take Via Cairoli going left to P. San Pietro Martire and continue past a church for a few short blocks. The hostel is on the street marked Via dei Longobardi to your right (there is also a yellow sign). Close to the historic center and run by an endearing owner who takes pride in the 11th-century origin of the hostel's site. No lockout and no curfew; you get the keys. L13,000 per person. Showers L1000. He gives free guided tours of the city.

Albergo Piceno, Via Minucia, 10 (tel. 25 25 53), near the cathedral and the bus stop. Close to the center of things, and so clean you could eat off the floor. Rooms without baths mean no access to a shower. Singles L40,000, with bath L50,000. Doubles L60,000, with bath L70,000. Triples with bath L90,000.

Cantina Dell'Arte, Via della Lupa, 8 (tel. 25 57 44 or 25 56 20), behind the post office. Take the street to the left of the ugly concrete building (there are no street signs or hotel/restaurant signs). Gorgeous modern rooms in the medieval heart of town. TVs and private baths included. Friendly manager. Singles L45,000. Doubles L65,000. Triples L90,000. Quads L100,000. Breakfast L3000.

Hotel Pavoni, Via Navilella, 135/B (tel. 34 25 75 or 34 25 87), 3km ahead on the road to San Benedetto. Take bus #3 from P. Arringo (L1000). Quiet hotel near the beach. Singles L32,000, with bath L44,000. Doubles L54,000, with bath L66,000.

FOOD

Fill your tummy without emptying your pockets—an excellent meal should run around L12,000. There's also an **open-air market** in P. San Francesco, behind P. del Popolo (Mon.-Sat. mornings). In P. Santa Maria Inter Vineas, you can find the small **Supermarket Gierre** (open Mon.-Fri. 9am-1pm and 5-8pm, Sat. 9am-1:30pm).

Trattoria Lino Cavucci, P. della Viola, 13 (tel. 503 58). An excellent choice. *Primi* L4500-5000, *secondi* L7500-9000. Cover L2500. Open Sat.-Thurs. noon-3pm and 5-11pm.

Cantina dell'Arte, Via della Lupa, 5 (tel. 25 11 35), across from the hotel (no sign). Family-run restaurant with long communal tables. Delicious daily specials. *Primi* L6000-8000, *secondi* L10,000. *Menù* L13,000. Cover included in prices. Open daily noon-2:30pm and 7-9:30pm.

L'Assaggino, Via Minucia, 24 (tel. 25 55 43), at the end of Via Civo del Duca (2 blocks from P. del Popolo). A self-service *pizzeria* with indoor and outdoor seating. *Primi* and *secondi* about L5000. Pizza L1000-2000 per slice. Open Mon.-Sat. 9am-9pm.

Pizzeria Italia, Corso Mazzini, 205. Near the post office. Standing only. Pizza L1000-3500 per slice. Open Mon.-Sat. 9am-9pm.

SIGHTS AND ENTERTAINMENT

Museum hours in Ascoli are constantly changing. Confirm your sightseeing plans with the tourist office in P. del Popolo.

Piazza del Popolo, the historic center of town, is a calm oasis in this busy city. The 16th-century *portici* lining two sides of the square recall the Piazza San Marco in Venice. The third side houses the 13th-century **Palazzo dei Capitani del Popolo,** whose massive portal and statue of Pope Paul III date from 1548. The history of the edifice is full of Renaissance (and later) intrigue. Originally erected as the palace of the city's hierarch, or captain, the building was burned on Christmas Day 1535 in an inter-familial squabble; the *piazza* smoldered for two days. A decade later the palace was refurbished and dedicated to the pope, who brought peace to Ascoli. In 1938 the palace was the seat of the principal Fascist party, only to be wrested away for partisan use in early 1945. Through the entrance to the left of the main portal, an excavated area beneath the presumed foundation of the *palazzo* is exposed. Remains from the Roman era were revealed here in 1982. This discovery legitimated the view that the *piazza* was originally the forum in the Roman town known as "Asculum." Works from both the Republican and Augustan eras can be viewed here, via a serpentine wooden pathway weaving down and under the structure of the *palazzo.* The **museum** on-site is very handsome and worth a visit, especially since it's free. (Open July-mid-Sept. daily 9am-1pm.) The *piazza* is the forecourt for the elegant eastern end of the **Church of St. Francis** (13th-16th centuries). Its spacious three-aisled interior houses a 14th-century wooden crucifix, the only art object saved from the 1535 fire. At dusk Ascoli's youths gather here for a lively *passeggiata.* (Open 8am-noon and 3-7pm.) Abutting the church to the south, the gracious **Loggia dei Mercanti** (Merchant's Gallery, 1509-1513), now a favorite meeting place for the town elders, leads to Corso Mazzini and the austere 14th-century **Church of St. Augustine.** (Open 9am-noon and 3-7pm.)

Via delle Torri, off P. Sant'Agostino, runs past the stone houses of the old quarter to the 13th-century **Church of St. Peter the Martyr** and tiny **Via di Solestà.** This street, one of the oldest in the city, leads to the single-arched **Ponte di Solestà,** one of Europe's tallest Roman bridges. Cross this bridge (or the Ponte Nuovo) and walk to the edge of town (turning on Viale Marcello, right or left respectively) to find the **Church of St. Emidio alle Grotte,** a baroque façade grafted onto the natural rock wall. Inside, the walls are formed by a series of catacombs. The first Ascoli Christians are buried here.

On the other side of town, **Piazza Arringo** ("orate") derives its name from the speeches delivered there by local leaders. The massive, travertine **duomo** is a blend of art and architecture from the 5th through the 20th centuries. A Roman *basilica* forms the transept, topped by an irregular octagonal dome from the 8th century. The two towers were built in the 11th and 12th centuries, respectively, while the lateral naves and central apse were constructed in the 1400s. In the *duomo's* **Cappella del Sacramento,** an intricately framed polyptych of the *Virgin and Saints* (Carlo Crivelli, 1473) surmounts a 14th-century silver altar. (Open daily 9am-noon and 4-7pm.) Next to the cathedral stands the compact 12th-century **baptistery,** decorated with a *loggia* of blind arches. Works by Crivelli, Titian, van Dyck, and Ribera hang amid red velvet curtains and pink walls in the **Pinacoteca Civica** (tel. 29 82 13), inside the **Palazzo Comunale** (southern flank of the *piazza*). (Open Mon.-Fri. 9am-12:30pm and 3-7pm, Sat. 9am-12:30pm, Sun. 3-7pm. Mid-Sept.-June Mon.-Sat. 9am-1pm, Sun. 9am-12:30pm. Admission L2500, students and seniors free.) Visit the **Museo Archeologico** (tel. 25 35 62), also on the *piazza,* for its hall of mosaics. (Open daily 2-7:30pm. Mid-Sept.-June Mon.-Sat. 9:30am-1:30pm, Sun. 9:30am-1:30pm and 3:30-5:30pm. Admission L4000, students free.)

On the first Sunday in August, Ascoli holds the **Tournament of Quintana,** a medieval pageant in which over 1000 people deck themselves out in traditional costume. The tournament, which features armed (man-on-dummy) jousting and a torchlight procession to P. del Popolo, is the culmination of the four-day festival of Sant'Emidio, the city's patron. The **carnival** in February is one of Italy's best. Insanity reigns on the Tuesday, Thursday, and especially the Sunday preceding Ash Wednesday. Residents don costumes, and folk dancers perform in P. del Popolo. Happily, the event is not mobbed by tourists, but you should still make hotel reservations a week ahead. If you have already seen all the historical points of interest you can handle, simply indulge instead in the intrinsically entertaining **passeggiate** of Ascoli. Try the one in the Piazza del Popolo; it's loaded with young people-watching fodder.

■ Umbria

Known as the "Green Heart of Italy," Umbria has enjoyed renown for its rivers, valleys, and wooded hills since ancient times. This region inspired its sons, the Latin poets Plautus and Propertius, as well as Dante and Giosuè Carducci. Often shrouded in an ethereal silvery haze, the landscape also nurtured a spiritual tradition that stretches from prehistory to St. Benedict, who preached the doctrine of the marriage of work and worship, and to Umbria's most famous visionary, the nature-adoring ascetic St. Francis. Generations of visual artists also clambered about these hills, among them Giotto, Signorelli, Perugino, and Pinturicchio.

Umbria's earliest inhabitants may have been the Umbrii, an ancient and reclusive tribe that withdrew to the east as the Etruscans and then the aggressive Romans expanded their frontiers. Barbarian invasions in the 5th and 6th centuries provoked the inhabitants to retreat to Etruscan hill towns, setting the stage for the rise of medieval city-states. More than half a millennium of constant Guelph-Ghibelline warfare followed, finally allowing Pope Paul III to seize the weakened region in the 1530s. Although the yoke of papal government was lifted during the *Risorgimento,* its legacy of stagnation lingered well into this century. Umbria has now achieved a measure of prosperity by cultivating interest in its beautifully situated medieval cities and by promoting itself as a cultural center through such summer festivities as the pioneering Two Worlds Festival of Spoleto and the Umbrian Jazz Festival.

Umbrian cuisine draws heavily from the region's lakes and woods. Trout, carp, and squirmy little eels are big favorites, as are all manner of grilled meats. More refined palates indulge in Umbria's most famous contribution to the gourmet world: truffles. Both black and white, they are most often put into pasta. Umbria's best-known wine is the distinctive Orvieto.

PERUGIA

While trains link most major towns, buses provide the most convenient access, especially as they drop you off in the center of town rather than at the bottom of a steep hill. Thermal springs, clear streams, Etruscan ruins, and verdant ravines make the valleys nearly as appealing as the numerous hill towns.

■■■ PERUGIA

Perugians may be the most polite people you'll meet in Italy, which is somewhat odd considering that Perugia was the country's most violent and disreputable town for centuries. From its roots as an Etruscan *polis* through Roman domination, Perugia was a chronic troublemaker. Perugians found time (between attacks on neighbors) for a friendly annual festival called the *Battaglia de' Sassi* (Battle of Stones), during which two teams threw rocks at each other until a sufficient number of casualties or fatalities left a winner. In addition to being celebrated as the town that once imprisoned St. Francis of Assisi (albeit during his dissolute, pre-preaching days), independent Perugia gets bonus religious points as the birthplace of the Flagellants, who wandered Europe whipping themselves in public, and as the deathbed of three popes (two were poisoned). But the good times eventually ended, and Perugia found itself crushed underneath the papal heel when it fell to Paul III in 1538.

Three centuries of economic misery as part of the Papal States apparently taught the Perugians some manners (though not subservience—they were rebelling against the Pope as late as 1859). The present-day capital of Umbria claims a delightfully civilized atmosphere seasoned by the motley international crowd drawn to its universities and art academies. Perugia also attracts huge crowds to its world-renowned jazz festival every July; apart from jazz, many visitors are lured by steep medieval streets filled with shops and spectacular views of the countryside. The *palazzi* that crowd Corso Vannucci, Perugia's main street, shelter the city's impressive collection of medieval and Renaissance art; interspersed are bars offering the city's contemporary masterpieces, the infamous chocolate *baci* (kisses).

ORIENTATION AND PRACTICAL INFORMATION

Perugia lies on the Foligno-Terontola line, with frequent trains to these hub stations. To get to Rome, change at Foligno to get on the Rome-Ancona line or change at Terontola to get on the Florence-Rome line. Several direct trains depart for Florence and Rome. Local buses (#26, 27, and 36) from the station will leave you in P. Matteotti (L1000). Otherwise, it's a treacherous 4-km uphill trek. From the bus station in P. dei Partigiani, follow the signs to the **escalator** (*scala mobile*) which takes you underneath the old city to Piazza Italia. Straight ahead, **Corso Vannucci,** the main shopping thoroughfare, leads to **Piazza IV Novembre** and the *duomo;* behind the *duomo* lies the university area. One block to the right of Corso Vannucci you'll find P. Matteotti, the municipal center. The new **Digiplan** machines in the train station are extremely helpful, providing instant printout information (in Italian) on sights, museums, stores, restaurants, and more. Of course, they don't always work. Train information machines provide info in English.

> **Tourist Office:** P. IV Novembre (tel. 572 53 41 or 572 33 27). Extremely friendly, patient, and knowledgeable staff gives info on accommodations and travel. Artistic but misleading city map. Ask for the detailed walking guide, the *Umbria Informazione* brochure, and the map of Umbria. Open Mon.-Sat. 8:30am-1:30pm and 4-7pm, Sun. 9am-1pm; in winter Mon.-Sat. 3:30-6:30pm.
>
> **Police:** tel. 112. **Questura,** P. dei Partigiani.
>
> **Post Office:** P. Matteotti. Open Mon.-Sat. 8:10am-7:25pm. **Postal Code:** 06100.
>
> **Telephones: Telecom (SIP),** next to the post office in P. Matteotti. Open daily 7am-9:45pm. Also at Corso Vannucci, 76. Open daily 8am-10pm. Also at the train station, open 8am-10pm. **Telephone Code:** 075.
>
> **Budget Travel: CTS,** Via del Roscetto, 21 (tel. 572 02 84), off Via Pinturicchio toward the bottom of the street. Student center with travel and accommodations

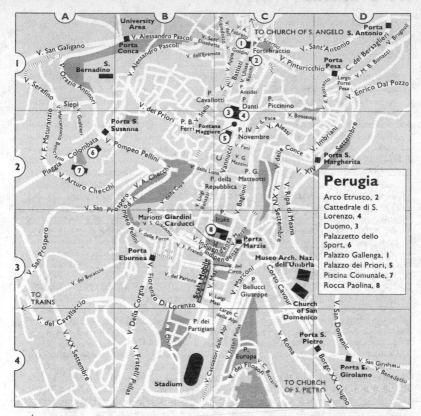

Perugia

Arco Etrusco, 2
Cattedrale di S.
Lorenzo, 4
Duomo, 3
Palazzetto dello
Sport, 6
Palazzo Gallenga, 1
Palazzo dei Priori, 5
Piscina Comunale, 7
Rocca Paolina, 8

offices. Open Mon.-Fri. 9am-12:15pm and 4-7pm, Sat. 9am-noon. **CIT:** Corso Vannucci, 2 (tel. 572 60 61), by the fountain. Open Mon.-Fri 9am-1pm and 3:30-7pm.

Currency Exchange: Best rates are found at the banks in town. At the train station, no commission for exchanges of less than L80,000, but rates are worse. **Banca di Roma**, in P. IV Novembre, has an ATM that takes Cirrus.

Trains: Fontivegge, P. Veneto. **F.S.** south to: Assisi (25min., L2700); Foligno (40min., L3400); Spoleto (1hr., L5700); Orvieto (1¾hr., L9800); Rome via Terontola (3hr., L26,900). North to: Passignano sul Trasimeno (30min., L2700); Arezzo (1½hr., L6900); Florence (2½hr., L21,800); Siena (L21,800). **Sant'Anna** station in P. Bellucci serves Città di Castello and Sansepolcro to the north and Todi to the south. **Information: F.S.**, P. Veneto (tel. 500 10 91). Open 8am-noon and 3-7pm. **Ferrovia Centrale Umbra,** Largo Cacciatori delle Alpi, 8 (tel. 291 21), near the bottom of the escalator on the 1st floor. The **ticket window** in the F.S. station is open 6am-9pm. **Luggage Storage:** L1500, open daily 6:20am-8:20pm.

Buses: P. dei Partigiani, down the *scala mobile* from P. Italia. City bus #28, 29, 36, or CD (L1000) from the train station. **ASP buses,** P. dei Partigiani (tel. 573 17 07), to most Umbrian towns, along with Urbino, Rome, and Florence.

Taxis: tel. 500 48 88.

Public Toilets, Showers, and Baths: Viale Indipendenza, 7 (enter through the *scala mobile* under P. Italia). Open daily 8am-10:45pm. Toilet L500, shower L5000, bath L5500, towel and soap L1500.

English Bookstore: Libreria, Via Rocchi, 1. English books L12,000-16,000. Open Mon.-Sat. 10am-1pm and 5-8pm.

Higher Education: Università per gli Stranieri, Palazzo Gallenga, P. Fortebraccio, 4 (tel. 57 46 21). The university offers courses in Italian language and culture

PERUGIA

for foreigners. The student *caffè*, replete with pinball machines, is frequented by the young and the restless. A good place to meet other travelers. Check university bulletin board for cultural events and free concerts. Check with the registrar for rooms for rent (only for longer stays).

Laundromat: Lava e Lava, Via Annibale Vecchi, 5 and Via Mario Angeloni, 32. Wash L6000 per 8kg. Dry L500 for 3min. Open daily 8am-10pm.

Swimming Pool: Piscina Comunale, Via Pompeo Pellini (tel. 573 51 60), near Santa Colombata. Open daily 1-7:30pm; off-season Mon.-Fri. 6:30am-8:30pm, Sat. 3-8pm. Admission L7000.

Emergencies: tel. 113. **Medical Emergency:** tel. 444 44. **Hospital: Ospedali Riuniti-Policlinico,** Via Bonacci Brunamonti (tel. 57 81).

ACCOMMODATIONS AND CAMPING

Reservations are absolutely necessary during the Umbria Jazz Festival in July.

Centro Internazionale di Accoglienza per la Gioventù, Via Bontempi, 13 (tel. 572 28 80). From P. Matteotti walk up Via de' Fari, take a right on Corso Vannucci, and go until you hit P. IV Novembre. Then take the road off P. Dante away from the *duomo* past P. Piccinino (a parking lot), and take the right fork (Via Bontempi). This clean hostel offers many amenities: the 4-bed rooms have high ceilings, night tables, and firm bunks. The spacious kitchen is a great meeting spot. Three-wk. max. stay. Lockout 9:30am-4pm. Curfew midnight. L14,000; showers and kitchen use included. Sheets L1000. Open mid-Jan. to mid-Dec.

Albergo Anna, Via dei Priori, 48 (tel. 573 63 04), off Corso Vannucci. Walk up 4 flights to clean and cool 17th-century rooms, with daunting ceilings and lovely views. Friendly owners recently renovated. Singles L34,000, with bath L50,000. Doubles L50,000, with bath L68,000. Triples L88,000, with bath L90,000.

Albergo Etruria, Via della Luna, 21 (tel. 572 37 30), down the passageway by Corso Vannucci, 55. As central as it gets. This *pensione* sits at the end of an alleyway. Immense 12th-century sitting room. Singles L38,000. Doubles L59,000. Showers L3500.

Pensione Paola, Via della Canapina, 5 (tel. 572 38 16). From the train station, take bus #26 or 27 and get off on Viale Pellini, once the bus passes a large municipal parking lot on the left. Walk up the stairs; the *pensione* is on the right. A comfortable place with big rooms and plenty of homey touches. Buoyant owner. Singles L38,000. Doubles L58,000. Breakfast L5500. Lower rates for people who stay 1 month or more.

Camping: Paradis d'Ete, 5km away in Colle della Trinità (tel. 517 21 17). Take bus #36 from the station and ask the driver to leave you in Colle della Trinità. Hot showers and pool at no extra charge. L7000 per person, L6000 per tent, L3000 per car. Open year-round.

FOOD

Though renowned for chocolate, Perugia also serves up a variety of delectable breads and pastries; be sure to sample the *torta di formaggio* (cheese bread) and the *mele al cartoccio* (the Italian version of apple pie). Both are available at **Ceccarani,** P. Matteotti, 16, or at the **Co.Fa.Pa.** bakery two doors down at #12 (both open Mon.-Sat. 7:30am-1pm and 5-7:45pm). For such local confections as sweet bread in the shape of a snake and *baci* (chocolate-hazelnut kisses), don't miss the old-world elegance of **Pasticerria Sandri,** Corso Vannucci, 32. This gorgeous bakery/candy shop also doubles as a bar and *caffè*. It's a great place for morning coffee (open Tues.-Sun. 8am-10pm). If you prefer your chocolate cold and creamy, head to the student-infested **Gelateria 2000,** Via Luigi Bonazzi, 3, off P. della Repubblica (open Mon.-Sat. 8am-midnight), where the *gelato* is excellent (cones L1500-3000).

On Tuesday and Saturday mornings you can salivate over the **open-air market** in P. Europa; on other days, try the covered market in P. Matteotti for plenty of fruit, vegetables, and nuts (open Tues.-Sat. 8am-1pm). The entrance is below street level. On summer nights the market becomes an outdoor *caffè.* Buy essentials at the small markets in Piazza Matteotti (open during regular business hours, Mon.-Fri. 8am-1pm and 4-7pm, Sat. 8am-1pm). Complement your meal with the reasonably priced regional wines: *Sagrantino Secco,* a dry, full-bodied red, or *Grechetto,* a light, dry white. There is a **STANDA** with the grocery store downstairs in P. Della Repubblica (open Mon-Sat. 9am-1pm and 4-8pm).

Trattoria Dal Micocco, Corso Garibaldi, 12 (tel. 625 11), up from the University for Foreigners. Gives the weirdest names to its food, but enjoys well-deserved popularity. The L20,000 *menù* includes a pasta that changes daily, an entree, side dish, and dessert. Open Tues.-Sun. 12:30-2:30pm and 7:30pm-midnight.

L'Oca Nera, Via dei Priori, 78-82 (tel. 572 18 89). Hidden in the caverns below the north-central quarter, this joint draws a crowd for its delicious food, hip atmosphere, and quick, pleasant service. Massive selection ranges from würstel to *gnocchi* to hamburgers (average L6000 per dish). Open 7:30pm-1am.

The Australian Pub, Via de Verzaro, 39 (tel. 572 02 06). A neighborhood joint for Italians, but also a great place to munch on burgers and have a Fosters with other Anglophiles. Have a quiet dinner on the terrace and come back for the late-night crowd. (Pizzas and burgers L6000-9000.) Open daily for dinner noon-2pm and 7-11pm, for drinks until 3am or whenever the last person leaves.

Tavola Calda, P. Danti, 16 (tel. 572 19 76). Wide selection of meat and vegetables available cafeteria-style, outdoor seating. Pizza L1500 per slice, sandwiches from L3500, and a decent *rosticceria.* Baked *ziti* L4000. Rambunctious late-night crowd. Open Mon.-Fri. 10am-3pm and 8-10pm, Sun. 10am-3pm.

SIGHTS

Piazza IV Novembre

The city's most interesting sights frame Piazza IV Novembre; all other monuments of distinction lie within a 20-minute walk of this spot. In the town center (the middle of the *piazza*) sits the **Fontana Maggiore,** designed by native son Fra' Bevignate and decorated by Nicolà and Giovanni Pisano. The bas-reliefs covering the majestic double basin depict scenes from religious and Roman history, the allegories of the months and sciences (lower basin), and the saints and other historical figures (upper basin). Sadly, the beautiful fountain is now undergoing lengthy restoration.

The 13th-century **Palazzo dei Priori** presides over the *piazza*; its long rows of mullioned windows and toothlike crenelation embody archetypal Perugian bellicosity. This building, one of the finest examples of Gothic communal architecture, shelters the impressive **Galleria Nazionale dell'Umbria,** Corso Vanucci, 19 (tel. 572 03 16). The immense collection contains fine works by Tuscans Duccio, Fra Angelico, Taddeo di Bartolo, Guido da Siena, and Piero della Francesca, but look for its Umbrian art. Viewing Perugian Pinturicchio's *Miracles of San Bernardino of Siena* is the visual equivalent of eating a *bacio.* Perhaps too sweet for some tastes are the colors and dazzling subjects of Pietro Vannucci, alias Perugino, the town's most celebrated artist. His newly restored *Adoration of the Magi* is the gallery's premier piece. (Open Mon.-Sat. 9am-1:45pm and 3-7pm, Sun. 9am-1pm. Admission L8000.)

Next door in the **Collegio del Cambio** (Banker's Guild; tel. 572 85 99), Perugino demonstrated what a talented artist could do with even a mundane commission. In his frescoes, he suffuses each piece with the gentle softness that he later passed on to his greatest pupil, Raphael. The latter is said to have collaborated on the *Prophets and Sibyls.* Notice also Perugino's self-portrait *(autoritratto)* on the left wall. In the small chapel adjacent to the chamber hang paintings of scenes from the life of John the Baptist by Giannicola di Paolo (1519), including an especially grisly decapitation scene with a grinning Salomé. Farther toward the *piazza,* at #15, visit the **Collegio della Mercanzia.** This richly paneled room is the meeting room for Perugia's merchant guild; from 1390 to this day, the guild's 88 members have met here to debate tax law and local commerce. (Cambio and Mercanzia open Tues.-Sat. 9am-12:30pm and 2:30-5:30pm, Sun. 9am-12:30pm. Admission L6000, good for both.) You can visit the **Sala dei Notari,** containing interesting 13th-century frescoes, up the flight of steps across the fountain, for free.

PERUGIA

At the end of the *piazza* rises Perugia's austere Gothic **duomo.** Though it was built in the 14th and 15th centuries, the façade was never finished. (Initially, the *Perugini* were going to use some marble they stole from Arezzo's cathedral-building supply during a battle, but the *Aretini* made them give it back when they won the next round.) Fifteenth- to 18th-century embellishments of varying quality adorn the Gothic interior, but the town is most excited by the **Virgin Mary's wedding ring,** a relic they snagged from Chiusi in the Middle Ages. The ring is kept securely under lock and key—15 locks and keys, in fact.

Via dei Priori

Stroll along Via delle Volte della Pace (off Via Bontempi), which follows the city's old Etruscan walls; or follow Via dei Priori (which begins behind the palace) and Via San Francesco past the church of the same name, to the spartan **Oratory of San Bernadino,** near the end of Via dei Priori. Agostino de Duccio built it between 1457 and 1461 in the early Renaissance style, embellishing its façade with finely carved reliefs and sculpture. Inside, a 3rd-century Roman sarcophagus forms the altar. A walk down medieval Via Ulisse Rocchi, the city's oldest street, will take you through the north city gate to the **Arco di Augusto,** a perfectly preserved Roman arch built on Etruscan pedestals and topped by a 16th-century portico. Past the newly cleaned **Palazzo Gallenga,** at the end of a little byway off medieval Corso Garibaldi, lies the jewel-like **Church of Sant'Angelo.** The 5th-century church, built upon an ancient Roman temple, is the oldest in Perugia; the circular interior incorporates 16 columns appropriated from various ancient buildings. The small park in front of it makes for an alluring picnic spot.

The East Side

At the end of town opposite the Porta Sant'Angelo, near Via Cavour, towers the imposing **Church of San Domenico,** the largest in Umbria. The church's huge Gothic rose window contrasts dramatically with the sobriety of its Renaissance interior. Don't miss the magnificently carved **Tomb of Pope Benedict XI,** finished in 1325—in the chapel to the right of the high altar; his bones lie in a box tied with a red ribbon on the wall. Next to the church, the **Museo Archeologico Nazionale dell'Umbria** occupies the old Dominican convent and showcases Etruscan and Roman artifacts. (Open Mon.-Sat. 9am-1:30pm and 2:30-7pm, Sun. 9am-1pm. Admission L4000.) Continue on Corso Cavour, past the Porta San Pietro, and you'll come to the **Church of San Pietro.** It maintains its original 10th-century *basilica* form: a double arcade of closely spaced columns leads to the choir. Inside, the walls (and visitors) are overwhelmed by paintings and frescoes depicting scenes of saints and soldiers; amidst the mass of paint, look for Perugino's *Pietà* along the north aisle. (Churches open 8am-noon and 3:30pm-sunset.)

At the far end of Corso Vannucci, the main street leading from P. IV Novembre, lie the **Giardini Carducci.** These well-maintained public gardens are named after the 19th-century poet Giosuè Carducci, who wrote a stirring ode to Italy inspired by Perugia's historic zeal for independence. From the garden wall you can enjoy a panorama of the Umbrian countryside: a castle or an ancient church crowns each hill. On the corner of the street below the gardens, a semi-circular lookout point shows you which direction you're gazing and names the monuments in view. Go around the gardens and down Via Marzia to see the **Rocca Paolina,** the 16th-century fortress built by Sangallo—and long a symbol of papal oppression; its interior juxtaposes Italian antiquity and dubious modern art. Pope Paul III had Sangallo demolish this section of the city in the 1500s in order to create the prison. In 1860, when Perugia was liberated from the rule of the Papal States and became part of the now-unified Italy, the *Perugini* spontaneously began hacking it to pieces. The **Porta Marzia,** the Etruscan gate in the city wall, opens onto **Via Bagliona Sotterranea.** This street within the fortress is lined with 15th-century houses that were buried when the gardens were built above them. (Gate open Tues.-Sat. 8am-2pm, Sun. 9am-1pm.) The Rocca is also accessible by the escalator, which runs from 6am until 1am.

ENTERTAINMENT

Perugia's biggest annual event is the glorious **Umbria Jazz Festival,** which draws performers of international renown for 10 days in July. (Admission L15,000-35,000. Some events free.) For more information, contact the tourist office.

July and August bring **Estate a Perugia,** a series of musical, cinematic, and dance performances. In September a **Festival of Sacred Music** features concerts in various churches. Check Palazzo Gallenga for listings of English films and other events. If you miss the jazz festival, you can still take in some fusion or dixieland at **Il Contrappunto,** next to the University for Foreigners. Free buses depart Piazza Grimana at 9pm, 10pm, and 11pm for the **disco Turchia,** on the outskirts of town. In town, hang with the locals at the lively **Pozzo Entrare,** Via della Volte Pace.

■ NEAR PERUGIA: LAKE TRASIMENO

This placid and somewhat marshy lake, 30km west of Perugia, is an ideal spot to enjoy some tranquility while watching fishermen mend their nets in the hamlets along the shore. While hazy and peaceful today, Lake Trasimeno witnessed some violent battles in the second Punic War: in 217 BC, Hannibal's elephant-riding army, fresh from the Alps, routed the Romans on the plain north of the lake. The names of the villages of Ossaia ("place of bones") and Sanguineto ("bloody") recall the carnage of 16,000 Roman troops.

In the summer, landlocked Umbria's permanent haze and stifling heat make splashing in the waters of Trasimeno quite refreshing. The two main towns girding the lake, Passignano sul Trasimeno and Castiglione del Lago, are easily accessible by bus (from Perugia's P. Partigiani for both lakeside towns L9500 round-trip), and train (Passignano sul Trasimeno lies on the Foligno-Terontola line, with frequent connections to Perugia, while Castiglione lies on the Florence-Rome train line; from Perugia, change at Terontola). The **Pro Loco** (tourist office), at Via Roma, 38 (tel. (075) 82 76 35), overlooks the peaceful town park (coming from the dock, turn left; coming from the station, go across the tracks and take a left). Here you'll find maps, hotel listings, and boat schedules. (Open Mon.-Tues. and Thurs.-Sat, 9am-noon and 4-7pm.) **Hotel Aviazione,** Via Roma, 54 (tel. 82 71 62), has doubles for L50,000, with bath L65,000. It also offers **bike rental** (1hr. L5000, half-day L10,000, full day L15,000). Boats leave from the dock for Isola Maggiore (14 per day, 20min., L5000, round-trip L9000). Food is expensive in both towns; plan a picnic on the lakeshore.

Follow in St. Francis's footsteps and spend a delightful day on **Isola Maggiore,** Lake Trasimeno's only inhabited island. An erratically opened and staffed **tourist information booth** is by the dock. If no one's there, just take a good look at the large map of the island. As you leave the dock, turn right and follow the path to the tip of the island (being careful not to squish the green-brown salamanders who will accompany you) to the ruined **Guglielmi castle.** A bit further on sits a tiny chapel enclosing the hard rock where St. Francis spent 40 days in 1211. From here, hike five minutes up to the **Chiesa di San Michele Arcangelo** for a wonderful view of the island. (Open Sun. 10:30am-noon and 3-6pm.) **Castiglione del Lago,** a quiet town that takes its name from the castle that towers above it, is accessible by bus, boat, and train (on the Florence-Rome train line, leave from Perugia and change at Terontola). The **tourist office** in P. Mazzini, 10 (tel. (075) 96 52 484), will help you find a hotel (singles from L40,000, doubles from L52,000), a room in a private home, or a private apartment (from L190,000 per week). You can also **change money** and get boat schedules here. (Open Mon. 8am-1:30pm, Tues.-Fri. 8am-1:30pm and 3-7:30pm, Sat. 8:30am-1pm and 3-7:30pm, Sun. 9am-1pm.) The clear choice among the hotels is the **Albergo Santa Lucia,** Via Buozzi, 84 (tel. 965 24 92) complete with a private garden and immaculate rooms, all with bath. (Doubles L80,000.) For food, try the shops lining Via Vittorio Emanuele, or hop into **Paprika,** Via Vittorio Emanuele, 107, whose local specialties include *spaghetti al sugo d'anguilla* (spaghetti with eel sauce). (Open Fri.-Wed. noon-2:30pm and 7:30-10pm.) Take Viale Garibaldi

A S S I S I

down to the dock, where 8 boats daily make the 30-min. trip to Isola Maggiore, the largest of the lake's three islands (L3500, round-trip L6800).

■■■ ASSISI

Oh Lord, make me an instrument of your peace.

—*St. Francis of Assisi*

Assisi's serenity originates from the legacy of St. Francis, a 12th-century monk who generated a revolution in the Catholic church. He founded the Franciscan order, devoted to a then unusual combination of asceticism, poverty, and chastity, while promulgating what he described as the "abundance of the divine" in this world. Today, young Franciscan nuns and monks—the primary inhabitants of this city—carry on his legacy with spiritual vigor. Assisi is still a major pilgrimage site, especially for Italian youths, who converge here for conferences, festivals, and other religious activities. You need not be particularly religious, however, to adore Assisi; the (always generous) resources of the Church ensured that St. Francis would be remembered with particularly spectacular works of art. Moreover, the town is beautifully preserved, the accommodations are terrific, and the restaurants are some of the best in Umbria (though somewhat expensive).

ORIENTATION AND PRACTICAL INFORMATION

Towering above the city to the north, the **Rocca Maggiore** can help you re-orient yourself with a glance should you become lost among Assisi's winding streets. The center of town is **Piazza del Comune**, with Via Portica and Via Seminario connecting it to the **Basilica di San Francesco** toward the west end, and Corso Mazzini leading to the **Chiesa of Santa Chiara** in the opposite direction. **Buses** from the train station run every half-hour (L1000), stopping at P. de Italia near the *basilica*, Largo Properzio near the Church of St. Claire, and P. Matteotti above P. del Comune.

Tourist Office: P. del Comune, 12 (tel. 81 25 34), 1 doorway left of Telecom. Information and accommodations service. Unenthusiastic staff and a street-name-deficient map. Ask about upcoming musical events. Open Mon.-Fri. 8am-2pm and 3:30-6:30pm, Sat. 9am-1pm and 3:30-6:30pm, Sun. 9am-1pm. Train and bus schedules outside. Beware: the "tourist office" on Corso Mazzini is a travel agency.
Police: Carabinieri, P. Matteotti, 3 (tel. 81 22 39).
Post Office: P. del Comune. Open Mon.-Fri. 8:10am-5:25pm, Sat. 8:10am-1pm. **Postal Code:** 06081.
Telephones: Telecom (SIP), P. del Comune, 11. The most beautifully frescoed phone building in the world. Open daily 8am-10pm; off-season 8am-7pm. **Telephone Code:** 075.
Currency Exchange: Cassa di Risparmio, P. del Comune. Automatic currency exchange machine.
Trains: Assisi lies on the Foligno-Terontola train line, 30min. (L2700) from Perugia. Change for Florence at Terontola (L16,400); change at Foligno for Rome (L14,500) or Ancona (L12,000). **Luggage Storage:** L1500 per day. Open daily 6:30am-7pm.
Buses: ASP buses to Perugia (8 per day, L4700), Foligno (8 per day, L2500), and other surrounding hamlets, leaving from P. Matteotti. From P. del Comune, walk up Via San Rufino to P. Matteotti. Buses run from the station, below the town near the Basilica of Santa Maria degli Angeli, to the town (every 30min., L1000).
Car Rental: Agenzia Assisiorganizza, Borgo Aretino, 11 (tel. 81 52 80). Prices begin at L90,000 per day, L500,000 per week. Minimum age 21.
Taxis: P. del Comune (tel. 81 31 93).
Swimming Pool: Centro Turistico Sportivo, Via San Benedetto (tel. 81 29 91). Take the bus from P. del Comune. Open late July-Aug. daily 9:30am-7pm. Admission L6000.

Emergencies: tel. 113. **Hospital:** tel. 813 91, on the outskirts. Take a city bus from P. del Comune. **First Aid:** tel. 81 28 24.

ACCOMMODATIONS AND CAMPING

Reservations are crucial around Easter, and strongly recommended for the *Festa Calendimaggio* (early May) and in August. If you prefer to be in town, ask the tourist office for a list of **religious institutions.** These are peaceful and cheap, but they shut down around 11pm. The tourist office also has a long list of *affitta camere.*

Ostello della Pace, Via San Pietro Campagna (tel. 81 67 67). Turn right out of the train station and then left at the light onto Via San Pietro (1km), or take the bus to P. Unità and head down. A tremendous hostel with big rooms and spotless bathrooms. Impressive views of the town from 3 sides. Laundry facilities. Open daily 7-9:15am and 5-11pm. L17,000 per person, breakfast and hot shower included.

Ostello Fontemaggio, Via per l'Eremo delle Carceri (tel. 81 36 36). Via Eremo begins at the top of P. Matteotti and leads out the Porta Cappuccini—follow it 1km or so up the road, then veer right at the sign. Rooms are a bit crowded (10 beds each) but well maintained and sunny. There's a **campground** next door with a market attached. Hostel L15,000, breakfast L4000; campground L6500 per person, L5000 per tent, L2500 per car.

Albergo La Rocca, Via di Porta Perlici, 27 (tel. 81 64 67). From P. del Comune, follow Via S. Rufino up the hill, cross the *piazza*, and go straight up Via Porta Perlicia until you hit the old arches—La Rocca is on the left. A great choice away from the crowds. Commodious, attractive rooms, some with views. Singles L30,000, with bath L40,000. Doubles L46,000, with bath L61,000. In summer, may require full pension at L49,000 per person, L54,000 with bath. Breakfast L7000.

Albergo Italia, Vicolo della Fortezza (tel. 81 26 25), just off P. del Comune. A small but well-kept hotel in the center of town. Friendly staff keeps the comfortable rooms spotless and welcomes younger guests. English spoken. Singles L28,000, with bath L36,500. Doubles L47,000, with bath L69,000. Triples with bath L90,000. Quad with bath L100,000. Breakfast on request L5000.

Albergo Anfiteatro Romano, Via Anfiteatro Romano, 4 (tel. 81 30 25), off P. Matteotti. Built into the old Roman amphitheater. Comfortable, clean rooms, some with views of the Rocca. Singles L29,000. Doubles L43,000, with bath L65,000. Restaurant downstairs. AmEx, MC, Visa.

St. Anthony's Guesthouse of the Franciscan Sisters of the Atonement, Via Alessi, 10 (tel. 81 25 42). The sisters treat you like family. No room for asceticism here—the rooms are far too comfy. Gorgeous views, a library full of English-language books, a garden, an orchard, and a relaxing terrace. Two-night minimum stay. Curfew 11pm. Singles L40,000. Doubles with bath L70,000. Breakfast included, served in a delightful stone-walled dining room. Open March-Nov. 1.

FOOD

Assisi tempts you with a sinful array of nut breads and pastries; *bricciata umbria,* a strudel-like pastry with a hint of cherries, is particularly divine. **Pasticceria Santa Monica,** at Via Portica, 4, right off P. del Comune, boasts the best quality/selection/ price ratio (open daily 7am-1:15pm and 4-8pm). On Saturday mornings there's a market on Via San Gabriele and Via Alessi. For well-made *panini* and picnic staples, try **Micromarket Baldoni,** Via Fortabella, 61, near P. Unità and San Francesco. (Open Mon.-Sat. 8am-1pm and 3:30-8pm; closed Thurs. afternoon.)

Pizzeria Otello: Via Sant'Antonio 1. No-nonsense *pizzeria* on a side street off P. del Comune. *Primi* L7000-10,000. Pizza L5000-10,000. Also serves *focaccia* sandwiches and big salads. Open for *pizza al taglio* 7:30am-noon and 4-7pm, *pizza al piatto* and lunch noon-4pm, and dinner 7-11pm. AmEx, MC, Visa (except for *pizza al taglio).*

Trattoria Erminio, Via Monte Cavallo, off Via Porta Perlici. A good place to enjoy such dishes as spaghetti with butter and arugula (L5000) or fresh grilled trout (L9000). *Menù* L19,000. Open Tues.-Sun. noon-2:30pm and 7:30-10pm.

Trattoria Spadini, Piazza Chiara (tel. 81 30 05). Dine under low, white arches in a medieval Tuscan space now occupied by a single *trattoria. Menù* L18,500. Open Mon.-Sat. noon-3pm and 7-10pm.

Pallotta, Via San Rufino, 4 (tel. 81 23 07), near P. del Comune. A medieval atmosphere overseen by a graceful proprietor. Try their specialty, *strangozzi alla pallotta* (pasta with mushrooms and olives, L9500). *Menù,* including wine and dessert, L21,000. Open Wed.-Mon. noon-2:30pm and 7-9:30pm. AmEx, MC, Visa.

SIGHTS

St. Francis, born in 1182, abandoned military ambitions at age 19 and rejected his father's wealth to embrace asceticism. His repudiation of the worldliness of the church, his love of nature, and his devoted humility earned him a huge following throughout Europe, posing an unprecedented challenge to the decadent papacy and corrupt monastic orders. He continued to preach chastity and poverty until his death in 1226, whereupon the order he founded was gradually co-opted by the Catholic hierarchy. The result was the paradoxical glorification of the modest saint in churches named for him and for his follower St. Clare, founder of the Poor Clares, the female order of the Franciscan movement.

The enormous and lavishly frescoed **Basilica di San Francesco** bears witness to this conflict of integrity and bureaucracy. When construction began in the mid-13th century, the Franciscan order protested: Francis had adhered to a stark asceticism, and the elaborate church seemed an impious monument to wealth. As a solution, Brother Elia, then vicar of the order, insisted that a double church be erected—the lower level built around the saint's crypt, the upper as a church for services. The subdued art in the lower church commemorates Francis's modest life, while the upper church pays tribute to his sainthood and consecration. This two-fold structure subsequently inspired a new type of Franciscan architecture.

The walls of the church are almost completely covered with Giotto's *Life of St. Francis* fresco cycle, dramatically lit from the windows above. Giotto's early genius is evident in his illustration of Francis's turbulent path to sainthood, which starts on the right wall near the altar and runs clockwise, beginning with a teen-aged Francis in courtly dress, surprised by a prophecy of his future greatness. The cycle closes with an image of the saint passing through the mystical agony of the "Dark Night." The final stage of his approach to God occurs in the 19th frame, where St. Francis receives the stigmata. Sadly, Cimabue's frescoes in the transepts and apse have so deteriorated that they look like photographic negatives. Most frescoes and sculptures have "History Tell" machines; it costs L1000 to view the history of each work.

Pietro Lorenzetti adorned the left transept with an outstanding *Crucifixion, Last Supper,* and *Madonna and Saints.* Above the altar, four sumptuous allegorical frescoes formerly attributed to Giotto are now thought to be the work of the so-called "Maestro delle Vele." Cimabue's magnificent *Madonna and Child, Angels,* and *St. Francis* grace the right transept. Best of all are Simone Martini's frescoes in the first chapel off the left wall, based on the life of St. Martin. Descend through a door in the right side of the apse to a room that houses some of St. Francis' possessions: his tunic, his sandals, and sundry flesh-mortifying instruments.

The precious piece that inspired the entire edifice, St. Francis' tomb, lies below the lower church (the steps to it are marked by a sign in the middle of the right aisle). St. Francis' coffin was hidden in the 15th century for fear that the war-mongering Perugians would desecrate it; it was only rediscovered in 1818. The stone coffin sits above the altar in the crypt, surrounded by the sarcophagi of four of his friends. (Mass in English in the upper church Sun. 8:30am. Tours in English of the whole structure Mon.-Sat. 10am and 3pm; meet in front of the lower church. Both churches open daily from sunrise to sunset—in summer, about 6:30am-7pm, closed on Holy Days. **Dress codes** here are very strictly enforced. No photography, no miniskirts, no short shorts, and no revealing shirts allowed. Fashion police screen visitors at the door and circulate through the *basilica.*)

While here, don't bypass the modern, well-lit **Museo Tesoro della Basilica,** with its graceful 13th-century French ivory *Madonna and Child,* 17th-century Murano glass work, and a fragment of the Holy Cross. (Open April-Oct. daily 9:30am-noon and 2-6pm. Closed Sundays Nov.-March. Admission L3000.)

Via San Francesco leads away from the front of the upper church between medieval buildings interspersed with 16th-century additions—note especially the **Sala del Pelegrino** (Pilgrim Oratory), frescoed inside and out. Via San Francesco boasts Italy's first public **asylum,** a 13th-century building at the corner of Via Fortebella. At the end of the street P. del Comune marks the old **Roman forum.** Here, bits of Roman Assisi alternate with buildings of the 13th-century commune. (Open daily 10am-1pm and 3-7pm. Admission L4000. A good deal is the *biglietto cumulativo,* which allows entry into the forum, Rocca Maggiore, and Pinacoteca for L10,000, students L7000.) The **Palazzo del Comune,** on the downhill side, contains the **Pinacoteca,** housing Umbrian Renaissance art. (Open daily 10am-1pm and 3-7pm, in winter daily 10am-1:30pm and 2:30-5pm. See above for ticket info.)

Via San Rufino climbs steeply up from P. del Comune between closely packed old houses, opening onto P. San Rufino to reveal the squat **duomo** with its massive bell tower. The restored interior may be a disappointment after the decorative façade. (Open daily 9:30am-noon and 2:30-6pm.) Continue uphill on the cobblestone street to the left of the *duomo* as you face it, and take the steps that branch off to the left. At the top is the towering, dramatic **Rocca Maggiore,** an essential sight to visit if you're here just for the day. The keep has been recently restored, and views from the top are unparalleled. You can walk (or grope) around the old corridors; most of the fortress is poorly lit, if at all. (Open daily 10am-dusk; in winter 10am-4pm. Closed in very windy or rainy weather. Admission L5000. Cumulative ticket L10,000, students L7000.) In one of the courtyards of the Rocca Maggiore sits the **Museum of Martyrs and Torture.** Come visit wax figures of martyrs and models of various instruments of torture. (Same hours as the Rocca. Admission L5000.)

The pink-and-white **Basilica of Santa Chiara** stands at the other end of Assisi, on the site of the ancient *basilica* where St. Francis attended school. The church shelters not only the tomb (and hair) of Santa Chiara, the founder of the Poor Clares, but also the tunic and shoes of St. Francis, along with the crucifix that spoke to him and revealed God's message. The nuns are sworn to seclusion (therefore they wear veils), but if you're lucky one might give you a tour of the church. (Open Mon.-Sat. 6:30am-noon and 2-7pm; in winter until 6pm.)

ENTERTAINMENT

All of Assisi's religious festivals involve feasts and processions. An especially long dramatic performance marks **Easter Week.** On Holy Thursday, a mystery play based on the Deposition from the Cross is acted out, and traditional processions trail through town on Good Friday and Easter Sunday. Assisi welcomes May with the **Festa di Calendimaggio** on May Day. A queen is chosen and dubbed *Primavera* (spring), and the various neighborhoods compete in a noisy musical tournament. Classical concerts and organ recitals occur once or twice per week from April to October in the various churches. October 4 is the **Festival of St. Francis,** in which one region of Italy (a different one each year) offers oil for the cathedral's votive lamp; that region's traditional dances and songs are performed in local costumes. During July and the beginning of August, the **Festa Pro Musica** features internationally known musicians and opera singers. For details, look for posters or ask at the tourist office. On any given evening you can join the many youth groups who flood P. del Comune and sing every folk song you can think of, from "Blowing in the Wind" to "Kumbaya," all to the accompaniment of guitar-strumming monks.

■ NEAR ASSISI

Several churches associated with St. Francis and St. Clare stand in the immediate vicinity of town. If you travel to Assisi by train, you'll see the huge **Basilica di Santa**

Maria degli Angeli. The *basilica* itself shelters the **Porziuncola,** the first center of the Franciscan order, and is actually owned by the Benedictines; the Franciscans pay them a basket of carp every year for rent. In order to overcome temptation, St. Francis supposedly flung himself on thorny rosebushes in the garden just outside the *basilica,* thus staining the leaves forever red. Now, in deference to the saint, the bushes grow no thorns. The site grew popular when St. Francis instituted the annual **Festa del Perdono** (Aug. 2), during which an indulgence was (and is) awarded to all who come to the church. When he died in the adjacent infirmary, now **Cappella del Transito,** the chapel began to attract throngs of pilgrims, and a whole ring of supporting chapels sprang up. (Open daily 7am-noon and 2:30-7pm.)

A pleasant but steep hour-long hike through the forest above the town leads to the most memorable and inspiring sight near Assisi, the **Eremo delle Carceri** (Hermitage of Cells). Pass through the Porta San Francesco below the *basilica* and follow Via Marconi. At the crossroads take the left road, which passes by the Seminario Regionale Umbro. The site of St. Francis's retreats, this placid area conveys the spirit of St. Francis better than the opulent *basilica.* Inside the hermitage you can see the small cell where he slept, and back outside is the stone altar where he preached. (Hermitage open daily 8am to dusk.)

A 15-minute stroll down the steep road outside Porta Nuova takes you to the **Convent of St. Damian,** where St. Francis received his calling and later wrote the *Canticle of the Creatures.* The chapel contains fine 14th-century frescoes as well as a riveting woodcarving of Christ. (Open daily 10am-noon and 3-6pm.)

■■■ GUBBIO

Gubbio was founded under the name *Iuvium* by ancient Umbrians, and for many years drew pilgrims to the temple of a mountain god associated with Jupiter; the town later became a strategic checkpoint on the Roman transapennine road, Via Flaminia. Today, the National Board of Ancient Towns, situated in Gubbio, acts to preserve and restore Umbria's historic hamlets. The results of their efforts can be seen locally in the winding cobblestone streets, Roman portals, medieval houses, and stunning *palazzi* with incredible views of the countryside. Gubbio boasts its own school of painting and ceramic tradition, and claims Italy's first novelist, Bosone Novello Raffaelli.

ORIENTATION AND PRACTICAL INFORMATION

Gubbio is a tangle of twisting streets and medieval alleyways that lead to sweeping *piazze.* Of these, **Piazza della Signoria** remains the civic headquarters, set on a ledge of the hill. Buses will leave you in P. Quaranta Martiri. A short uphill walk on Via della Repubblica, the street directly ahead as you get off the bus, will connect you with Corso Garibaldi, where you can find the tourist office.

Tourist Office: Piazza Oderisi, 6 (tel. 922 06 93), off Corso Garibaldi next door to the local Communist Party headquarters. Extremely helpful; English spoken. Open Mon.-Fri. 8am-1:25pm and 3:30-6:30pm, Sat. 9am-1pm and 3:30-6:30pm, Sun. 9:30am-12:30pm; off-season, Mon.-Sat. afternoon hours are 3-6pm. Also try **Easy Gubbio,** Via della Repubblica, 13 (tel. 922 00 66), on your way up the hill. The friendly English-speaking staff also sells bus tickets, rents cars, has telephones and changes money—one-stop shopping for all your tourism needs. Open in summer daily 8am-midnight; 8am-10pm in off-season.

Police: Carabinieri, Via Matteotti (tel. 927 37 31).

Post Office: Via Cairoli, 11 (tel. 927 39 25). Open Mon.-Sat. 8:10am-1:25pm. **Postal Code:** 06024.

Telephones: Easy Gubbio, Via della Repubblica, 13 (see above). **Telephone Code:** 075.

Trains: There are no trains to Gubbio itself; the nearest station is at Fossato di Vico, 19km away on the Rome-Ancona line (L6500 from Ancona, L15,000 from Rome). Buses connect Gubbio and the station (Mon.-Sat. 9 per day, 6 on Sun., L2000). For

tickets, go to **Clipper Viaggi,** in P. San Giovanni, 15 (tel. 37 17 48), the *piazza* up the hill from P. Quaranta Martiri. Open daily 9:30am-1pm and 3:30-7pm.
Buses: Via della Repubblica, 13-15 (tel. 927 15 44). Ticket office open daily 7:15am-1:45pm. To Perugia (4 per day, 1hr., L7400). In summer buses also run to Urbino once a week.
Taxis: P. Quaranta Martiri (tel. 927 38 00).
Emergencies: tel. 113. **Medical Emergency:** tel. 923 91. **Hospital:** P. Quaranta Martiri, 14 (tel. 923 91).

ACCOMMODATIONS

Gubbio is an easy day trip from Perugia. The town can be seen in a few hours, and an overnight stay will drain your wallet unnecessarily. If you must stay, but can't find a hotel room, look for *affitta camere.*

Albergo dei Consoli, Via dei Consoli, 59 (tel. 927 33 35), 100m from P. della Signoria toward P. Bruno. Stone-walled dining room downstairs. Curving wood staircase leads up to simple, neat rooms, all with bath. Doubles with bath L70,000. Triples with bath L90,000. Breakfast L5000. AmEx, MC, Visa. Closed Jan.
Albergo Galletti, Via Piccardi, 3 (tel. 927 42 47), off P. Quaranta Martiri. Small and photogenic, on the edge of medieval Gubbio. Hospitable proprietor. Singles L47,000. Doubles L58,000, with bath from L70,000. Closed mid-June-mid-July.
Pensione Grotta dell'Angelo, Via Gioia, 47 (tel. 927 34 38), off Via Cairoli. Cotton-candy-pink spreads and wicker chairs remove this *pensione* from the ranks of run-of-the-mill budget accommodations. TV in most rooms. Singles with bath L45,000. Doubles with bath L70,000. Half and full pension available. Closed Jan.
Hotel Gattapone, Via Ansidei, 6 (tel. 927 24 89), off Via della Repubblica. Carpeted, furnished rooms. Ask for a room on the top floor—the ceilings are beamed and the views stupendous. Singles L60,000 with bath. Doubles L85,000 with bath. One family room—4 beds and crib L125,000. Closed Jan. AmEx, MC, Visa.

FOOD

Guard against expensive meals. Go for the *salumeria* at P. Quaranta Martiri, 36, across from the bus station, which makes great sandwiches for around L2500. (Open daily 7:15am-1:15pm and 3:15-8pm). Tuesday morning, there's a **market** under the *loggie* of P. Quaranta Martiri. Local delicacies await you at **Prodotti Tipici e Tartufati Eugubbini,** Via Piccardi, 17. Here you can sample *salumi di cinghiale o cervo* (boar or deer sausage) and *pecorino* cheese, or pick up some truffle oil (so your truffles don't get sunburned; open daily 8:30am-1pm and 3:30-8pm.)

Taverna del Buchetto, Via Dante, 30 (tel. 927 70 34), near the Porta Romana. *Primi* L5000-8000, tasty pizzas L6000-9000, unless your refined palate demands one with truffles (L15,000). You can afford to try the spicy *pollo alla diavola* (L10,000), since they have the air-conditioning to cool you off. Open Tues.-Sun. noon-2:30pm and 7:30-10pm. AmEx, MC, Visa.
Ristorante Il Bargello, Via dei Consoli, 37 (tel. 927 37 24), in a little *piazza* down the road from P. della Signoria. Vaulted 14th-century ceiling, wine bottles lining the walls, and pleasant management. Outstanding pizza L4000-8000; full meals from L25,000. Cover L2500. Open Tues.-Sun. noon-2:30pm and 7-10:30pm; open for pizza noon-3pm and 7-10:30pm. AmEx, MC, Visa.
San Francesco e il Lupo (tel. 927 23 44), at the corner of Via Cairoli and Corso Garibaldi, near the Azienda. A homey place despite all the neon. *Primi* L6000-12,000, *secondi* L10,000-16,000. *Menù* L22,000. Open mid-July through mid-June daily noon-2:30pm and 7-9:30pm. MC, Visa.

SIGHTS

As you descend from the bus, the **Giardino dei Quaranta Martiri** (Garden of the 40 Martyrs) lies to your left, a memorial to those shot in reprisal for the assassination of two officials during WWII. Across the way is the **weaver's loggia,** where 14th-century weavers stretched their cloth so it would shrink evenly. Today it shades a handful of outdoor *caffè* and a fruit and vegetable market.

In **Piazza della Signoria** stands the **Palazzo dei Consoli,** one of Italy's most graceful public buildings. The white stone palace (1332) was built for the high magistrate of Gubbio by local boy Matteo di Giovanello (also known as Gattapone) who went on to knock 'em dead in Bologna and Perugia. Enter to examine the **Museo Civico's** idiosyncratic mix of stone sculpture and old coins, featuring the puzzling **Tavole Eugubine.** Discovered in 1444 near the Roman theater outside the city walls, these seven bronze tablets (300-100 BC) provide the main source of our knowledge of the ancient Umbrian language. Their ritual text spells out the social and political organization of early Umbrian society, while providing the novice with good hints on how to take auguries from animal livers. Upstairs visit the stately rooms of the **Pinacoteca Comunale,** an eclectic collection of paintings, wooden crucifixes, and 14th-century furniture. (Open daily 9am-12:30pm and 3:30-6pm; Oct.-mid-March daily 9am-1pm and 3-5pm. Admission L4000 for both; students, under 18, and over 60 L2000.) Across the *piazza* stands the **Palazzo Pretorio,** also designed by Gattapone.

Via dei Consoli will take you to the **Bargello** and its fountain. This 13th-century edifice is one of many medieval buildings still in use; others nearby include the 13th-century **Palazzo del Capitano del Popolo,** on the street of the same name, and the 15th-century **Palazzo Beni** on Via Cavour. Besides wool, Gubbio's main industry in the Middle Ages was ceramics. Some particularly fine examples lie in the Palazzo dei Consoli Museum. To get your own, try the **Antica Fabbrica Artigiana,** Via San Giuliano, 3 (near the Bargello), a cavernous old palace. Walk down the narrow streets that run parallel to the Camignano stream. When you arrive in P. Quaranta Martiri, the **Church of San Francesco** stands to the right. The church was built on the site of the house of the Spadalonga family, friends of St. Francis who gave him the tunic that became the prototype for today's Franciscan frock. The central apse holds the splendid *Vita della Madonna* (Life of the Madonna), a partially destroyed 15th-century fresco series by Ottaviano Nelli, Gubbio's most famous painter.

Climb to the top of the town where the 15th-century **Palazzo Ducale** and the 13th-century **duomo** face off. (*Palazzo* open daily 9am-1:30pm. Admission L4000.) Federico da Montefeltro commissioned Luciano Laurana, designer of his larger palace in Urbino, to build a miniature version here. The *duomo,* an unassuming, pink Gothic building, boasts fine stained-glass windows (late 12th century) and Pinturicchio's *Adoration of the Shepherds,* temporarily closed for restoration. Check at the tourist office for details. (And don't miss the actual, decaying corpses of several of Gubbio's prominent medieval bishops).

During lunch, when the museums close, take the seven-minute bird-cage chairlift *(funivia)* to the peak of **Monte Ingino** for a splendid view and prime picnicking. (Round-trip L6500. Open July-Aug. Mon.-Sat. 8:30am-7:30pm, Sun. 8:30am-8pm; Sept. Mon.-Sat. 9:30am-7pm, Sun. 9am-7:30pm; Oct.-Feb. Thurs.-Tues. 10am-1:15pm and 2:30-5pm; June Mon.-Sat. 9:30am-1:15pm and 2:30-7pm, Sun. 9am-7:30pm.) While you're there, visit the **basilica and monastery of Sant'Ubaldo,** Gubbio's patron saint. The *basilica* houses the three *ceri,* the large wooden candles carried in the Corsa dei Ceri procession each May, as well as Saint Ubaldo's poor pickled body in a glass case. On your way back to the town center, stop at the **Church of Santa Maria Nuova,** near the funicular station, which contains the lyrical *Madonna del Belvedere* by Ottaviano Nelli. Ask the custodian at Via Dante, 66 to let you in, but avoid going during midday.

Let's Go Crazy

The Fontana del Bargello (Bargello Fountain) has the unique power of bestowing honorary Gubbian citizenship upon anyone who runs around it three times (either direction works). Since Gubbians are considered *matti* (crazy) by other Italians, this means that you too can become certifiably insane. After your run, just pick up a tacky certificate from any of the nearby souvenir shops.

ENTERTAINMENT

The **Corsa dei Ceri** (May 15), a 900-year-old tradition and one of Italy's most noted processions, brings out the three *ceri*. These are supposedly candles, but actually huge wooden blocks carved like hourglasses and topped with little saints, each one representing a distinct faction of the populace—the Masons, the artisans and merchants, and the peasants. After 12 hours of furious flag-twirling and elaborate preparations, squads of husky runners *(ceraioli)* clad in Renaissance-style tights heave the heavy objects onto their shoulders and race up Monte Ingino. Making occasional pit stops for alcoholic encouragement, they eventually reach the *basilica* of Sant'Ubaldo, and plop down the *ceri* for safe keeping until the following May.

During the **Palio della Balestra**, held on the last Sunday in May, archers from Gubbio and nearby Sansepolcro gather in P. della Signoria for the latest installment of a fierce crossbow contest dating back to 1461. If Gubbio wins, an animated parade ensues. (Gubbio's major industry these days is the production of toy crossbows—*balestre*—for tourists.) The **Bulldog Pub**, Via Ansidei, 3, is a good place for a beer. (Open Tues.-Sun. 9:30pm-2:30am.)

■■■ SPOLETO

Like its peers in Umbria and southern Tuscany, Spoleto offers a beautiful hilltop setting and almost unbearably charming medieval streets. The town's biggest draw is its summer arts festival, the *Festival dei Due Mondi* (of the Two Worlds). The composer Gian Carlo Menotti selected Spoleto in 1958 to be the test site for his claim that art need not be merely the *dolce* after *cena* (sweet after dinner), but could become a community's bread and butter. His optimism was not unfounded: Spoleto's transformation into an internationally renowned center for the arts has brought prosperity to the town. Prices run as high as the pretentiousness that has spawned expressionist pizza parlors and chi-chi boutiques. Art of all sorts explodes around the town in late June and usually lingers through the summer. If you wish to rub shoulders with the artistically inclined, remember to reserve tickets and rooms. But don't stay away even if you can't make the festival; the precious little shops stay open year-round and there's a magnificent gorge to stroll along beyond town.

ORIENTATION AND PRACTICAL INFORMATION

Spoleto is typically Umbrian in that its narrow, cobblestoned streets make it difficult to navigate. **Plazza del Mercato** is the social center of the city, and many shop-lined streets radiate from it. Via Brignone connects P. Mercato with **Piazza della Libertà**, home of the tourist office and city bus stop. The adjacent **Piazza del Municipio** and **Piazza del Duomo**, which contain most of the city sights, are close to P. Mercato as well. From the train station, walk straight up Viale Trento e Trieste, take a right through P. Garibaldi and continue straight along Corso Garibaldi as it curves along and eventually ends at Corso Mazzini, which terminates in P. della Libertà (20min.). Or, take the ATAF bus from the station (L1200).

Tourist Office: P. della Libertà, 7 (tel. 22 03 11). A warm and savvy office with an excellent if unwieldy map. Be prepared to wait. English spoken. Open daily during the festival 9am-1pm and 3-9pm; in off-season Mon.-Fri. 10am-1pm and 4:30-7:30pm, Sat. 10am-1pm.
Police: Carabinieri, Via dei Filosofi, 57 (tel. 490 44). English speaker available.
Post Office: P. della Libertà, 12 (tel. 403 73). Open Mon.-Sat. 8:10am-7:30pm. **Postal Code:** 06049.
Telephones: During the festival, a **Telecom** office appears on Via Brignone between P. Mercato and P. Libertà (open daily 10am-midnight). At other times, forage for phones in bars and hotels. **Telephone Code:** 0743.
Trains: (tel. 485 16) in P. Polvani. From: Rome via Orte (2hr., L12,200); Ancona (2½hr., L14,000); Perugia (10 per day, 1hr., L5400); and Assisi (16 per day, 20min., L4100). From the station, take any orange bus to **Piazza della Libertà**

and the tourist office (L1200); otherwise it's a 30-min. uphill trek. Ask for a free city map at the newsstand in the station. **Luggage Storage:** L1500 per day; open 6:30am-8:20pm. **Buses:** Two buses per day run to Perugia from P. della Libertà and P. Garibaldi. Service to Urbino and Rimini runs Mon.-Sat. mornings in summer, from Via Flaminia (near the API gas station). Check at the tourist office for current schedules. **Taxis:** P. della Libertà (tel. 445 48). **Box Office:** buy advance tickets at Teatro Nuovo (tel. 440 97). Open Tues.-Sun. 10am-1pm and 4-7pm. **Emergencies:** tel. 113. **Hospital:** Via Loreto, 3 (tel. 21 01), outside Porta Loreto. **24-hr. pharmacy: Farmacia Scoccianti,** Via Marconi, 11.

ACCOMMODATIONS AND CAMPING

Finding accommodations is almost impossible during the summer music festival (end of June-mid-July). If you're organized enough to make reservations, do so as early as possible. The tourist office keeps a list of *affitta camere.* Otherwise, the youth hostel in **Foligno** is an easy commute. Performances take place during the day, so getting back before curfew shouldn't infringe on your festival experience.

Ostello "Fulginium" (HI), P. San Giacomo, 11 (tel. (0742) 35 28 82), in Foligno, 26km away. Curfew 11pm. L15,000 per person. Hot showers and breakfast included. Open March-Aug.

Hotel Panciolle, Via del Duomo, 3-5 (tel. 455 98), near the *duomo.* Bright, airy rooms with nondescript, modern furnishings. **Restaurant** downstairs. Singles with bath L55,000. Doubles with bath L80,000.

Albergo Anfiteatro, Via Anfiteatro, 14 (tel. 498 53). Don't let the spooky staircase put you off. Whitewashed rooms with modern furnishings. Singles L50,000, with bath L65,000. Doubles L65,000, with bath L85,000.

Fracassa, Via Focaroli, 15 (tel. 22 11 77). Head toward the Roman Theatre, off Via dei Gesuiti. Seven tidy rooms on the small, slightly worn side. Singles L30,000. Doubles L40,000.

Camping Monteluco (tel. 22 03 58), behind the church of San Pietro, a 15-min. walk from P. della Libertà. Take Viale Matteotti out to the tennis courts, say hi to Buffy, cross the highway, take Via San Pietro left to the church, and go up the hill. Beyond the church a dirt path branches to the right and leads directly to the campground. Pleasant and shaded, with a *bocce* court. Mmm. *Bocce.* L7000 per person, L6000 per tent, L2500 per car. Open April-Sept.

Camping Il Girasole (tel. 513 35), next to a vast sunflower field (hence the name; no relation to the Cápri hotel), 10km from Spoleto, near the small town of Petragnano. Hourly buses connect it with the train station. Quiet, with plenty of shade and hot showers, and a swimming pool. L8000 per person, L7000 per tent, L3000 per car. Price lower for longer stays. Open March 25-Sept.

FOOD

An open-air market enlivens **Piazza del Mercato** Monday through Saturday from 8:30am to 1pm. At other times, try the **Lo Sfizioso** market at P. Mercato, 26 (open Fri.-Wed. 7:30am-1:30pm and 4:30-7:30pm). or the **STANDA** supermarket at Corso Garibaldi, 11 (open Mon.-Sat. 9am-1pm and 4:30-8pm). During the festival, you'll need reservations to get into most restaurants, even during lunch.

Trattoria Del Panciolle, Via del Duomo, 3-4 (tel. 455 98), right below the hotel of the same name. Simple country fare skillfully prepared. *Stringozzi* (a local stringlike pasta) with mushrooms L8000, most *secondi* L9000. Also has outdoor tables on a shaded porch. Open Thurs.-Tues. noon-2:30pm and 7:30-10pm.

Ristorante Pentagramma, Via Tommaso Martini, 4 (tel. 372 33), off P. della Libertà. Despite the decor, this is a fine traditional restaurant which cooks up Umbrian specialties. *Zuppa di ceci* (chickpea soup) L9000. Open Tues.-Sun. noon-2:30pm and 7-10pm.

Osteria dell'Enoteca, Via Saffi, 9, is a cozy place to sample local wines (L2000 per glass) and snack on light dishes like *bruschetta al tartufo* (L4000) and asparagus *frittata* (L8000). Open Tues.-Sun. 9am-2am.

Casa del Frulatto, Via Mazzini, 75. Whips up all manner of fresh fruit shakes right before your eyes. Try the exotic mango-blueberry-kiwi mix (L4000). *Gelato* and sandwiches too. Open Tues.-Sun. 8am-1am.

SIGHTS

Tucked on a ledge midway between the great papal fortress above and the Roman Anfiteatro below rests Spoleto's monumental Romanesque **duomo.** It was built in the 12th century and then augmented by a portico (1491) and 17th-century interior redecoration. An amalgam of styles and materials, its soaring bell tower was cobbled together from fragments of Roman structures and is held up by incongruous flying buttresses. Eight rose windows animate the façade, and the largest one bears the four symbols of the evangelists. Inside, brilliantly colored scenes from the life of the Virgin by Fra Filippo Lippi fill the domed apse. Lippi died here while working on these frescoes. Lorenzo the Magnificent asked the *Spoletini* to send his body back, but with tourism waning from lack of noble corpses, Spoleto insisted on keeping it. Lorenzo could only commission Lippi's tomb, which lies in the right transept and was decorated by the artist's son, Filippino. Don't miss the gilding and ornate frescoes of the beautiful Renaissance reliquary to the left of the altar. (*Duomo* open daily 8am-1pm and 3-6:30pm; in winter 8am-1pm and 3-5:30pm.)

Santa Eufemia, across the *piazza* to the side of the *duomo*, lacks both the stature and the frescoes of the latter; poor Eufemia never amounted to much in the eyes of the Vatican. The beautiful Romanesque church named for her, however, was built with Umbria's first *matronea* or "women's balconies." (Open daily 7am-8pm.)

Spoleto's many classical ruins testify to its prominence in Roman times. The first-century **theater** stands just outside the Roman walls, visible from P. della Libertà. Walk through the theater to the *loggia* next to it and then to the **Museo Archeologico,** which has ceramic and statuary finds from the area. (Open Mon.-Sat. 9am-1:30pm and 2:30-7pm, Sun. 9am-1pm. Admission L4000.) The **Arco Romano** at the top of Via Bronzino marked the entrance to the town, and farther along, the **Arco di Druso** marked the entrance to the forum (now P. del Mercato). On nearby Via de Visiale you can enter a restored **Roman house.** (Open April-Sept. Tues.-Sun. 10am-1pm and 3-6pm. Admission L5000, students L3000; includes admission to the Pinacoteca and Museum of Modern Art. Hours the same for all three museums.)

The **papal fortress,** or Rocca, sits on the hillside above Spoleto. This fortress, until recently a prison, was used during the war to confine Slavic and Italian political prisoners; in 1943 the prisoners staged a dramatic escape to join the partisans in the Umbrian hills. Unfortunately, the Rocca is closed for renovations, though it opens to host some events of the festival. Follow the walk that curves around the fortress for panoramic views of Spoleto and the countryside. Farther on, you'll reach one of the region's most stunning architectural achievements, the 14th-century **Ponte delle Torri.** The 80m bridge and aqueduct span the channel of the river Tessino. On the far bank rise the craggy medieval towers for which the bridge was named.

On the far side of the bridge, take the left fork past elegant villas and ancient churches to **Monteluco,** Spoleto's "mountain of the sacred grove." An invigorating 1½-hr. climb through a forest leaves you at the tiny Franciscan **Sanctuary of Monteluco,** once the refuge of St. Francis and San Bernadino of Siena. (Open May-Sept. daily 8am-1pm and 4-8pm. Buses leave P. della Libertà for Monteluco approximately every 1½hr. when it's open. Ask at the newsstand for schedules and tickets; the bus costs L2000.) A five-minute stroll down the right fork brings you to the Romanesque **Church of San Pietro,** on whose tan façade appears a menagerie of bas-relief beasties, cavorting among cosmological diagrams and scenes from popular fables. Note the wolf wearing a monk's cowl and holding a book to the right of the door. Beyond the bestiary, you'll spot the remains of mosaics laid in the 5th century.

The **Museum of Modern Art** hosts exhibits of art displayed during the summer arts festival. From Corso Mazzini, turn left on Via Sant'Agata, then right on Via delle Terme. The museum lies ahead on your right. (Open April-Sept. Tues.-Sun. 10am-1pm and 3-6pm. Admission with cumulative ticket (see above) L5000.)

ENTERTAINMENT

The **Festival dei Due Mondi,** held from mid-June through mid-July, has become one of Italy's most important cultural events. The festival features numerous concerts, operas, and ballets with performances by well-known Italian and international artists. Film screenings, modern art shows, and local craft displays abound. (Tickets L15,000-200,000; a few events are free. Purchase well in advance from travel agents in most large cities or send a bank check covering the cost of the tickets plus 10% commission to: Associazione Festival dei Due Mondi, Biglietteria Festival, c/o Teatro Nuovo, 06049, Spoleto.) The opera season, which includes a number of modern and experimental works, runs from late August to September. For cultural entertainment of a different sort, check out **Pub La Fenice,** Via Porta Fuga, 43 (tel. 22 23 98; open 7pm-2am) or **The American Bar,** P. del Duomo (open until 2am).

■ NEAR SPOLETO: TREVI

Trevi, perched on a hilltop of olive trees about 30 minutes north of Spoleto by train, is a delightful place to spend an afternoon. The town is a spectacular sight, splaying along a hillside in almost complete verticality. In **Piazza del Comune,** the city center, you'll find the **Palazzo del Comune,** home to the **Pinacoteca Comunale.** The museum contains a replica by Pinturicchio of his *Madonna e Bambino,* now in London's National Gallery, as well as archaeological finds from the area. Two km from train station (toward the center of Trevi) is the **Chiesa della Madonna delle Lacrime.** The church is on the site of a house on whose wall a Mother and Child with St. Francis had been painted in 1483. Two years later blood-colored tears were seen on the image, inspiring the construction of first a chapel, then a temple, then finally a church on the site. Perugino's frescoed *Adoration of the Magi, Saints Peter and Paul,* and *Annunciation,* from 1521, decorate the interior. The **Illumination Procession,** a candle-lit parade through town in honor of St. Emiliano, is held on January 27 in Trevi, and during the first three weeks in August the town celebrates "Trevi in Piazza," with musical and theatrical performances in P. del Comune.

Trevi is easily reached by train from Foligno (L1500) or Spoleto (L1700). From the station, it's 4km uphill to town. Ten city buses per day run to town (L1200), the last at 7:50pm; nine buses per day run to the station, the last at 7:30pm. Buy tickets at the *tabacchi* (50m uphill from the stop). The bus leaves you at P. Garibaldi; from there, take Via Roma to P. del Comune. **Pro Trevi,** the information office, is at the far end of the *piazza* at #16 (open daily 10am-1pm). Unless you've got plenty of dough, there's really no place to stay in Trevi itself. **La Casarecchia,** P. Garibaldi, 19 (tel. (0742) 98 03 43), fixes up pizza and rents a few rooms (about L45,000 per person). (*Pizzeria* open Tues.-Fri. 9am-1:30pm and 3pm-midnight, Sat. 9am-midnight, Sun. 5pm-midnight.) **La Cerquetta** (tel. 783 66) lies outside town on Flaminia, km 144. (Singles with bath L45,000. Doubles with bath L70,000.)

■■■ TODI

According to legend, an eagle led the founders of Todi to this site when it absconded with a tablecloth to a rocky crag. Reclaiming it, the intrepid ancestors celebrated the recovery of their picnic-set by establishing Todi in this aerial setting. History seems to have bypassed the steep, narrow streets of this isolated town; as a result, it retains visible traces of its Etruscan, Roman, and medieval past. But Todi has certainly not been bypassed by the modern world—the town figures prominently a recent TV commercial for Visa.

ORIENTATION AND PRACTICAL INFORMATION

In the Todi of today, there's barely room for cars, let alone eagles with tablecloths. All areas in the city that don't house an important sight (and some that do) seem to have been transformed into parking lots. **Piazza del Popolo,** the center of town, houses the *duomo* and sundry *palazzi;* P. Jacopone and P. Umberto lie around the corner. Corso Cavour, Via Roma, Via Matteotti, and Viale Cortesi form one street leading steeply downtown and out the ancient city walls to the hotels.

Tourist Office: APT, P. Umberto, 1 (tel. 894 26 86). Buy the map for L3000; the photocopy they'll hand you is illegible. Open Mon.-Sat. 9am-1pm and 4-7pm, Sun. 9:30am-12:30pm and occasionally 4-6:30pm; in winter closed Sun. afternoon.
Police: Carabinieri, Via Angelo Cortese (tel. 894 23 23).
Post Office: P. Garibaldi (tel. 894 22 02). Open Mon.-Sat. 8:10am-7pm. **Postal Code:** 06059.
Telephones: at the tourist office. **Telephone Code:** 075.
Trains: The private **Ferrovia Centrale Umbria** (Central Umbrian Railway) provides infrequent service to Todi from Perugia, via Spoleto and Terni. City bus B runs to the station 15min. before every train; it'll carry you the 4km up to the town center (L1100).
Buses: ASP runs 4 buses per day to P. Jacopone or P. Consolazione from Perugia (1½hr., L5700). The last bus for Perugia departs at 5pm from the Church of Santa Maria della Consolazione, a pleasant 1km walk from the town's center.
Emergencies: tel. 113. **Hospital: Ospedale degli Infermi,** Via Matteotti (tel. 88 34 47).

ACCOMMODATIONS AND FOOD

Unless you've got gold versions of major credit cards, hotels in Todi are pretty much out of reach, not to mention out of the way. **Hotel Tuder,** Via Maestà dei Lombardi, 13, off Via Cortesi (tel. 894 21 84), has luxurious singles with bath for L85,000, and doubles with bath for L100,000. The hotel lies along a busy highway; be careful walking there at night.

Pick up provisions at the **alimentari** at Via Cavour, 150. (Open Mon.-Sat. 7.45am-1:30pm and 5:30-8pm, closed Wed. afternoon.) Fresh fruit and veggies are at the **Frutta e Verdura market** on the corner of P. Jacopone (open Mon.-Wed. and Fri.-Sat. 7am-1:30pm and 4-8pm, Thurs. 7am-1:30pm).

AgriTodi, Via San Lorenzo, 1 (tel. 894 23 96). Facing the *duomo* in P. del Popolo, take the small street to the right under the portico. Not content to simply offer an interesting menu, this place also has low prices. *Bruschette* L3000-8000, *primi* L7000-8000, *secondi* L7000-10,000. Lots of local wines for sale. Open Dec.-Oct. Wed.-Mon. 12:30-2:30pm and 4:30-10pm.
Ristorante Cavour, Via Cavour, 21-23 (tel. 894 24 91). Excellent, filling meals L22,000. Pizza around L7500. Specialty is *tortellini al tartufo nero* (with black truffles, L13,000). Try to get a seat in the cool medieval dungeon. Open Feb.-Dec. Thurs.-Tues. noon-3pm and 7:30-9:30pm for meals, until 2am for pizza. AmEx.
Bar 'Icopertio, Via G. Matteotti, 120 (tel. 894 39 57). For those who wish to avoid the exorbitant expense of full-fledged restaurant dining. It's a trip downhill from P. Jacopone to a *tavola calda* with delicious pizza, lasagna, *bruschette,* fried vegetables, etc. L12,000 for a healthy portion of 2 items.

SIGHTS

Piazza del Popolo is a stately ensemble of glowering *palazzi* and a somber *duomo;* the square's air of authority is only slightly diminished by the cars whizzing around its edge. This *piazza* has been Todi's focal point since Roman times and remains its high point in altitude and architectural achievement. The **Palazzo del Capitano** (1290) stretches its cavernous portico across the east end of the *piazza* with peaked Gothic windows on the second floor, lending relief to the imposing façade. (Open daily 10am-12:30pm and 4-8pm.) The **Pinacoteca Civica** occupies the fourth floor; keep climbing for the fascinating frescoes in the **Sala del Capitano del Popolo** at the top of the exterior marble staircase. Huge wooden arches soar across the immense hall. The adjoining **Palazzo del Popolo** with its distinctive crenelated profile was begun in 1213. Across the *piazza* from the *duomo,* the tower and façade of the **Palazzo dei Priori** (1297-1337) retain visages of medieval gloom, despite the rows of Renaissance windows carved out in the early 16th century.

Directly across the *piazza* the rosy-faced **duomo** rests solidly atop a flight of broad stone steps. The central rose window and arched doorway command attention with their intricate decoration. Inside, Romanesque columns with Corinthian capitals support a plain wall punctuated by slender windows. The delicate Gothic side arcade, added in the 1300s, shelters an unusual altarpiece: the Madonna's head emerges in high relief from the flat surface of a painting. A strangely subdued scene of the Last Judgment (16th century) occupies the church's back wall. The 8th-century crypt hides some intricate inlaid wooden stalls in the chancel. (*Duomo* open daily 8:30am-12:30pm and 2:30-6pm.)

Neighboring **Piazza Garibaldi** opens to a superb vista. From the *piazza,* follow the signs leading off Corso Cavour to the remaining walls of the **Foro Romano** and the nearby 12th-century **Chiesa di S. Ilario.** From here, it's a brief jaunt to the **Fonti Scarnabecco,** whose 13th-century porticoes still house one solitary working tap. Return to P. del Popolo and take Via Mazzini to the majestically angular **Church of San Fortunato.** Built by the Franciscans between the 13th and 15th centuries, the church features Romanesque portals and a Gothic interior. The story of the sacrifice of Isaac decorates the space between the first and second columns to the right of the door. Note Masolino's fresco of the Madonna and angels. To the right of San Fortunato, a path bends uphill toward **La Rocca,** a ruined 14th-century castle. Next to the castle, follow a sinuous path, appropriately named **Viale della Serpentina,** to a breathtaking *belvedere* constructed on the remains of an old Roman wall. Farther down stands the isolated Renaissance **Church of Santa Maria della Consolazione.**

The **Mostra Nazionale dell'Artigianato** (National Exhibit of Crafts) takes place in August and September. For some years there has also been a national exhibit of antique and modern **woodwork** in April, since Todi is, after all, home to some of the finest woodcarvers in Italy. The city's most colorful festival is the **Mongolfieristico,** a three-day hot-air-balloon show which occurs in mid-July. In August and September, Todi hosts its own arts festival with classical and jazz concerts, ballet performances, and film screenings. For more festival info and tickets, contact the tourist office.

■■■ ORVIETO

The town of Orvieto lies atop a volcanic plateau hidden from the rolling farmlands of southern Umbria. Although it originated as one of the cities of the Etruscan *Dodecapolis,* it is the city's medieval legacy that colors it more strongly today. While Thomas Aquinas lectured in the local academies in the 13th century, crusades were planned within the city walls. A well-preserved medieval center provides the backdrop for the stunning 13th-century *duomo,* which has rewarded Orvieto's piety with touristic fame and wealth. Though Orvieto is a popular tourist stop, its residents are far from embittered by aimless wanderers. They are proud to share their rich history, their justifiably famous white *Orvieto Classico* wine, and their equally famous handcrafted ceramics.

ORIENTATION AND PRACTICAL INFORMATION

Orvieto lies midway on the Rome-Florence train line. From the train station, cross the street to take the funicular up the volcano. When you reach the top you can walk up **Corso Cavour** to the city center (10min.) or take a **shuttle** to Piazza del Duomo. (Funicular departs every 15min.; L1300, with shuttle L1500.) **Corso Cavour** is the town's backbone, site of most of the city's restaurants, hotels, and shops. Via Duomo branches to the left off C. Cavour and ends at P. del Duomo.

Tourist Office: P. del Duomo, 24 (tel. 417 72). The shuttle drops you at the door. Friendly and patient staff, but the office is often crowded. Get the incredibly complete pamphlet on hotels, restaurants, sights, and practical information. Complete info on trains and buses; **city bus tickets** for sale. Open Mon.-Fri. 8am-2pm and 4-7pm, Sat. 10am-1pm and 4-7pm, Sun. 9am-7pm. Also has a public phone.
Police: P. della Repubblica (tel. 400 88).
Post Office: Via Cesare Nebbia, which begins after the Teatro Mancinelli, next to Corso Cavour, 114 (tel. 412 43). Stamps are available at *tabacchi,* and mail drops dot the town. Open Mon.-Sat. 8:15am-6:40pm. **Postal Code:** 05018.
Telephone Code: 0763.
Trains: To Florence (2hr., L15,000), Rome (1½hr., L11,500), and Perugia (L8800). **Luggage Storage:** L1500.
Buses: COTRAL, P. Cahen. Seven per day to Viterbo. **ACT,** P. Cahen, 10 (tel. 419 21). To: Perugia (L10,700) and Todi (L7700). Buy tickets at the *tabacchi* up Corso Cavour or on the bus.
Emergencies: tel. 113. **Hospital:** P. del Duomo (tel. 30 91).

ACCOMMODATIONS AND CAMPING

Da Fiora, Via Magalotti, 22 (tel. 410 83 or 411 19), just off P. della Repubblica through small P. dell'Erba (take minibus B to Erba). The best deal in town. The proprietress rents private rooms in her home. Filled with spotless antique furniture. Prices lower in winter. L20,000 per person.
Hotel Duomo, Vicolo di Maurizio, 7 (tel. 418 87), off Via Duomo, the first right once you leave the *piazza.* Spacious, light, well ventilated, and steps away from the towering cathedral. Singles L34,000, with bath L48,000. Doubles L50,000, with bath L76,000. Triples L60,000, with bath L95,000. Breakfast L8000.
Camping Orvieto (tel. 95 02 40), on Lake Corbara 14km from the center of town. From the station, take the local Oriveto-Baschi bus and ask to be dropped off at the site (the stop is 200m from the entrance). Swimming pool and hot showers included. L9000 per person, L7500 per tent, L3500 per car. Open Easter-Sept.

FOOD

Although the food here is expensive, you'll probably find yourself saying, "At least the wine's cheap." An excellent *alimentari* sits below P. della Repubblica at Via Filippucchi, 39 (open Mon.-Tues. and Thurs.-Sat. 7:30am-1:30pm and 5-8pm, Wed. 7:30am-1:30pm).

Cooperativa al San Francesco (tel. 433 02), on Via Bonaventura Cerretti, off Via Lorenzo Maitani (off the front side of P. del Duomo). Follow the large signs, your nose, or the crowd. Extremely popular with locals. A huge restaurant, self-service cafeteria, and *pizzeria* all rolled into one. Pizza (at night only) and wine L11,000. Pasta L8000-10,500. Open daily 12:30-3pm and 7-10:30pm. MC, Visa.
Da Fiora, Via Magalotti, 24 (tel. 411 19). Just below her rent-a-room residence, Signora Fiora has established a bustling restaurant enterprise with the best deals in town. *Menù* (L14,000) will fill you up as you take in a spaghetti Western on TV.

SIGHTS AND ENTERTAINMENT

The shuttle bus takes you from the train to P. del Duomo. A first glance at the **duomo** (1209), Orvieto's fervor and pride, promises to be overwhelming: the duomo's fanciful façade, intricately designed by Lorenzo Maitani, dazzles and enraptures the admirer with intertwining spires, mosaics, and sculptures. The bottom level features exquisitely carved bas-reliefs of the Creation and Old Testament prophecies, and a final panel of Maitani's realistic *Last Judgment*; the bronze and marble sculptures, set in niches surrounding the rose window by Andrea Orcagna (1325-1964), emphasize the Christian canon. Thirty-three architects, 90 mosaic artisans, 152 sculptors, and 68 painters worked over six centuries to bring the *duomo* this far, and the work continues; the bronze doors were only installed in 1970. The **Cappella della Madonna di San Brizio** (sometimes called the **Cappella Nuova**) is off the right transept; although it is undergoing lengthy restoration, the tourist office offers free tours (in Italian) of the parts being restored. Inside are Luca Signorelli's dramatic **Apocalypse frescoes,** considered to be his *chef d'oeuvre.* Begun by Fra Angelico in 1447, they were supposed to be completed by Perugino, but the city grew tired of waiting and enlisted Signorelli to finish the project. His mastery of human anatomy, dramatic compositions, and vigorous draftsmanship paved the way for the genius of Michelangelo. On the left wall hangs the *Preaching of the AntiChrist.* On the opposite wall, muscular humans and skeletons pull themselves out of the earth in the uncanny *Resurrection of the Dead.* Beside it is the *Inferno,* with Signorelli (a blue devil) and his mistress embracing beneath the fiery display. Rumor has it that the Whore of Babylon, being carried on the back of a devil above the masses, was modeled after a woman from Orvieto who rejected Signorelli's advances. In the **Cappella del Corporale** off the left transept, Lippo Memmi's *Madonna dei Raccomandati* hangs with abashed pride. This chapel also holds the gold-encrusted **Reliquary of the Corporale** (chalice-cloth), the *raison d'être* of the whole structure. The cloth inside the box caught the blood of Christ, which dripped from a consecrated host in Bolsena in 1263, thereby substantiating the doctrine of transubstantiation. (The *duomo* is open all year 7am-1pm, but the afternoon hours vary each month—2:30-5:30pm is a safe bet. Free.)

The austere 13th-century **Palazzo dei Papi** (Palace of the Popes) sits to the right of the *duomo.* Here, in 1527, Pope Clement VII rejected King Henry VIII's petition to annul his marriage with Catherine of Aragon, condemning both Catherine and English Catholicism to a dim prospect. Set back in the *palazzo* is the **Museo Archeologico Nazionale,** where you can examine Etruscan artifacts from the area and even walk into a full-sized tomb. (Open Mon.-Sat. 9am-1:30pm and 3-7pm, Sun. 9am-1pm. Admission L4000, under 18 and over 60 free.)

Return to Corso Cavour and continue to P. della Repubblica, where the **Church of Sant'Andrea** marks the beginning of Orvieto's **medieval quarter.** The church, founded over the ruins of an Etruscan temple, served as a meeting place or *comune* in the medieval republic of Orvieto. Inside, the crypt, at the beginning of the right aisle, contains recently excavated remains from the Etruscan temple.

From P. della Repubblica, take Viale dei Mercanti down into the medieval quarter and turn right onto Via Ripa di Serancia. The **Church of San Giovanni** at the end of the road sits just inside the ancient city walls and offers a truly stunning view of the countryside below. The soils of the verdant slope below P. San Giovanni are enriched by the graves of thousands who perished in the Black Death of 1348.

On the east edge of town, down Via Sangallo off P. Cahen (to the left of the train station; you can take the shuttle back), descend into the **Pozzo di San Patrizio** (St. Patrick's Well). Having fled freshly sacked Rome, Pope Clement VII wanted to ensure that the town did not run out of water during a siege, and in 1527 commissioned Antonio da Sangallo the Younger to design the well. (Open daily 9:30am-7pm; in winter daily 10am-6pm. Admission L6000; L10,000 includes the Museo Greco.) After cooling off in the clammy well shaft, enter the **Fortezza,** where a fragrant sculpture garden and lofty trees crown battlements overlooking the Umbrian landscape. (Open daily 7am-8pm; Oct.-March 9am-7pm.)

For the most complete tour of Etruscan Orvieto, consider the **Underground City Excursions** departing from the tourist office. Speleological guides lead groups on a labyrinthine path through tunnels, quarries, cellars, wells and cisterns that were dug from the *tufa* 3000 years ago. (Tour lasts 1½hrs., L10,000.)

On Pentecost (42 days after Easter), Orvieto celebrates the **Festa della Palombella.** Small wooden structures filled with fireworks and connected by a metal wire are set up in front of the *duomo* and the Church of San Francesco. At the stroke of noon, the San Francesco fireworks are set off, and a white metal dove shoots across the wire to ignite the explosives. **Concerts** are held in the *duomo* on August evenings. In June, the **Procession of Corpus Domini** celebrates the Miracle of Bolsena.

Tuscany (Toscana)

Tuscany is the stuff Italian dreams (and more than one romantic Brits-in-Italy movie) are made of. With rolling hills covered with olives and grapevines, bright yellow fields of sunflowers, and inviting cobblestone streets, it's hard not to wax poetic. Tuscany's Renaissance culture, an unprecedented explosion of art, architecture, and humanist scholarship, became the culture of Italy, while Tuscan, the language of Dante, Petrarch, and Machiavelli, is today's textbook Italian.

Despite its appearance of eternal eminence, everything of importance in this region occurred within one outstanding half-millennium. A backwater in both Etruscan and Roman times, the region was far from the center of the barbarian kingdoms. Toward the end of the 10th century, increasingly powerful local aristocrats wrested away control of towns, creating the free *comuni,* independent city-states. Many of the walls that surround Tuscan towns today first sprang up during this period of upheaval. In the 1100s, the free *comuni* of Tuscany began to engage in their two most characteristic activities: inter-city warfare and artistic production, with the Renaissance emerging out of the mayhem. The bubble burst in the early 16th century, when the rich, leisured Tuscans, who had long since left their warfare to hired hands *(condottiere),* fell to the invading armies of the French and the Hapsburgs. The entire region was then placed under the rule of the Medici, a family of bankers. They presided over Tuscany's descent from the summit of the High Renaissance to a cultural and political non-entity. Protected by a few centuries of relative serenity, the cities and towns of Tuscany remain almost unchanged.

An extensive and convenient transportation system makes it easy to tour Tuscany's countryside. The state railroad serves all major towns and many smaller ones, though the hill towns are better reached by bus. Given the ease of transportation and the inevitable crowds of sightseers, plan your itinerary wisely. Florence and Pisa are not to be missed; consequently, no tourist misses them. Once you've seen them, consider devoting a little time to four of the most hospitable and beautiful of Tuscan cities: Siena, Montepulciano, Cortona, and Lucca. The only area to avoid is the unattractive coast. To list all of the Tuscan hill-towns worth visiting would take a book twice this size, so the following are only the larger and more historically and culturally significant places; if you plan an extended stay in the region, exploring on your own will lead you to innumerable towns crowning hills and clustered in valleys. If you ask in almost any restaurant, they'll tell you who lets rooms.

Youth hostels abound in Tuscany, but hotels are on the expensive side. Reservations are advisable all summer, especially in Florence, Siena, and Pisa. Camping is possible at the many lakes, mountains, and coastal resorts.

As familiar as Tuscany seems visually, its cuisine may surprise you: neither southern pasta and tomatoes nor northern *risotto* and *polenta* are staples of the Tuscan table. White beans *(fagioli)* are a regional obsession, so join locals and enjoy them in everything; tasteless Tuscan bread, however, is best eaten when hidden in such local concoctions as *crostini* (roasted bread topped with liver pâté or cheese). Other local specialties include *ribollita* (bean and cabbage stew) and *fiori di zucca fritti* (fried zucchini flowers). Meat dishes include *coniglio* (rabbit), *trippa* (tripe), *lepre* (wild hare), *cinghiale* (wild boar), *salsicce* (grilled sausages), and the famous and costly beef steak *bistecca alla fiorentina.* Tuscany's gastronomic triumph, however, is its wine. The region's most popular type of wine is the red *chianti,* from the area around Florence and Siena, while the premier red is the expensive *brunello di Montalcino.* Another unique Tuscan indulgence is *vin santo,* a sweet dessert wine made from grapes hung in lofts to dry for several months before being crushed. Drink it as Tuscans do—with a plateful of *cantuccini di Prato* (crispy almond cookies) for dipping.

■■■ CORTONA

The ancient town of Cortona (it's older than Troy) arrogantly surveys both Tuscany and Umbria from its mountaintop. This now-quiet city once rivalled Perugia, Arezzo, and even Florence in power and belligerence. But the 15th-century Florentine take-over was, artistically speaking, in Cortona's best interest; artist Fra Angelico sojourned here for a decade and painted an *Annunciation* that rivals the one in Florence's San Marco. Not much in the town has changed since it succumbed to Florentine rule; Cortona's high roost leaves little room for expansion. Serpentine cobblestone streets traverse the city, leading to marvelous medieval *palazzi* and breathtaking views of the Tuscan hills.

ORIENTATION AND PRACTICAL INFORMATION

The easiest way to reach Cortona is by **bus** from Arezzo (30min., L4900). If you *have* to take the train from Rome (L16,000), or Florence (L10,500), get off at either Terontola-Cortona or Camucia-Cortona. From there catch the LFI bus to Piazza Garibaldi in Cortona (every 30min.-1hr., L2200 and L1900 respectively). Buses leave you at **Piazza Garibaldi** just outside the main gate of the city's wall. Enter through this gate and follow **Via Nazionale,** passing the tourist office almost immediately on your left, to the town's center at **Piazza della Repubblica.** From there, cross the *piazza* diagonally to the left to reach the other main square, **Piazza Signorelli.**

Tourist Office: Via Nazionale, 42 (tel. 63 03 52). Friendly and helpful, with lots of maps and brochures. Open Mon.-Sat. 8am-1pm and 3-6pm.
Police: Via Dardano, 9 (tel. 60 30 06).
Post Office: off P. della Repubblica. Open Mon.-Fri. 8:30am-7pm, Sat. 8:30am-12:30pm. **Postal Code:** 52044.
Telephones: Telecom (SIP), Via Guelfa, off P. della Repubblica. Open daily 8am-midnight. **Telephone Code:** 0575.
Currency Exchange: Banca Populare, Via Guelfa, 4. Open Mon.-Fri. 8:20am-1:20pm.
Bike Rental: Rent a Bike, Piazza della Repubblica, 12A (tel. (0368) 45 01 91). Rents bikes with delivery service and offers guided tours of Cortona and environs.
Swimming Pool: (tel. 60 13 74), 7km away at Sodo. Take the bus for Arezzo and ask the driver to let you off at the *piscina*. Water slides! Open daily 8am-midnight. Admission L8000.
Pharmacy: Farmacia Centrale, Via Nazionale, 38 (tel. 60 32 06). Open Mon.-Fri. 9am-1:30pm and 4-7pm; Sat. 9am-1pm.
Emergency: tel. 113. **Medical Assistance: Servizio Guardia Medica Turistica,** Via Roma, 3 (tel. 60 18 17). Open 8am-8pm. **Ambulance: Misericordia,** tel. 60 30 83. **Hospital:** Via Maffei (tel. 63 91).

ACCOMMODATIONS

Cheap hotels are scarce in Cortona, but institutional arrangements take up the slack. The hostel, one of Italy's best, is a converted 13th-century house with exceptionally friendly management, and the nuns down the hill welcome any weary traveler.

Ostello San Marco (HI), Via Maffei, 57 (tel. 60 13 92). From the bus stop, walk up steep Via S. Margarita and follow the signs to the hostel (about 5min.). Clean and cozy with a cavernous, stone-walled dining room. 8-10 bunks per room; 1 double. Laundry facilities available. Open 7-10am and 6:30-11:30pm. L14,000 per person. Breakfast, sheets, and showers included, but no hot water late at night. Dinner L12,000; reserve ahead. Open mid-March-mid-Oct.; year-round for groups.
Istituto Santa Margherita, Viale Cesare Battisti, 15 (tel. 63 03 36). Walk down Via Severini from P. Garibaldi; the *istituto* is at the corner of Via Battisti, on the left. Echoing marble hallways take you to spacious rooms, all with bath. Curfew midnight. Singles L28,000. Doubles (no unmarried, mixed-sex couples) L48,000. Dormitory-style rooms L18,000 per person.

Albergo Italia, Via Ghibellina, 5 (tel. 63 02 54), off P. Repubblica. High, beamed ceilings, firm beds, and whitewashed rooms in a huge 16th-century *palazzo*. Pristine bathrooms, downstairs bar, and a wonderful upstairs terrace for breathtaking views. Singles L40,000, with bath L65,000. Doubles L60,000, with bath L85,000.

Albergo Athens, Via San Antonio, 12 (tel. 63 05 08). Head up Via Dardano and take a right. Usually filled with University of Georgia students, who use it as (and make it feel like) a college dorm, but if there's room, they'll fit you in. It's cheap, and you get what you pay for. Singles L26,000. Doubles L43,000.

FOOD

With several *trattorie* featuring immense pasta dishes and an abundance of grocery, fruit, and *rosticcerie* (prepared food) stores, even the budget traveler won't starve in Cortona. The best local wine is the smooth *bianco vergine di Valdichiana*. True penny-pinchers can pick up a bottle (L3000) at the **Despar Market,** in Piazza della Repubblica, 23, which also makes *panini* (L3000-5000) to order. (Open Mon.-Tues. and Thurs.-Sat. 7:30am-1:30pm and 4-8pm; Wed. 7:30am-1:30pm. MC, Visa.) On Saturday the same *piazza* metamorphoses into a great **open-air market.**

Trattoria La Grotta, P. Baldelli, 3 (tel. 63 02 71), off P. della Repubblica. Truly delectable fare at outdoor tables in a secluded courtyard. Sample the homemade *gnocchi alla ricotta e spinaci* (ricotta and spinach balls in tomato and meat sauce, L8000). *Menù* L22,000. Open daily Aug.-Sept. (Oct.-July Wed.-Mon.) noon-3pm and 7-11pm.

Trattoria Etrusca, Via Dardano, 35. Specializes in *primi,* serving up marvelously unique (and huge!) pasta creations inside or outside along the old city walls. Try the house specialty, *tagliatelle colle zucchine* (pasta with zucchini, L8000). Full meals for under L12,000. Kitchen open daily 12:30-2:30pm and 7:30pm-1am; Oct.-May closed Thurs. *Bar* and *birreria* open 9am-2am. MC, Visa.

SIGHTS

The most stunning sights in Cortona are the incredible views of the surrounding valleys and hills. From the ancient **Fortezza** on the summit of Cortona's rugged hill (Mont. S. Egidio), you can gaze out over Tuscany with the entire town spread out below. On the walk to the *Fortezza,* you pass several small meadows with beautiful views and no people. On the other side of town, at P. Garibaldi, tourists lean over the iron fence to peer down the jagged cliff to the floor of the valley below; Hannibal's beloved Lake Trasimeno and Umbria can be seen in the distance.

In P. della Repubblica stands the 13th-century **Palazzo del Comune,** with a clock tower and monumental staircase. **Palazzo Casali,** to the right and behind the Palazzo del Comune, dominates P. Signorelli. Only the courtyard walls with their coats-of-arms and the outside right wall remain from the original 13th-century structure—the façade and interlocking staircase were added in the 17th century. Inside the courtyard, steps lead to the **Museo dell'Accademia Etrusca,** which cherishes many treasures and artifacts from the Etruscan period, as well as an overflow of carvings, coins, paintings, and furniture from the first through 18th centuries. In the first gallery is a circular bronze chandelier from the 5th century BC, mounted in a glass case suspended from the ceiling. With 16 voluminous oil reservoirs, it weighs 58kg when empty. A rare example of intricate Etruscan metalwork, the *lampadario* was discovered by a local farmer plowing his field. The same room contains a two-faced *Janus,* depicted as a full figure rather than the usual bust. In the third gallery you'll find 12th- and 13th-century Tuscan art, including works by Taddeo Gaddi, Cenni di Francesco, and Bici di Lorenzo. The museum wraps up with the 20th-century work of local boy Gino Severini, including lithographs, collages, and an intriguing *Maternità.* (Open Tues.-Sun. 10am-1pm and 4-7pm; Oct.-March Tues.-Sun. 9am-1pm and 3-5pm. Admission L5000.)

To the right of and downhill from the Palazzo Casali is **Piazza del Duomo.** Note the brick entry of the original Church of S. Maria on the façade of the *duomo,* poking out like a sore thumb from the stone fronting. During renovations, enter the

AREZZO

church from the side door, near the Palazzo Vescovile. Inside, you'll find an impressive Baroque-canopied high altar, completed in 1664 by Francesco Mattioli. The two-floored **Museo Diocesano** across from the *duomo* houses the stunning *Annunciation* by Fra Angelico in the upstairs gallery on the right. Across the corridor on the left, Christ's pain-wrenched face confronts you in Pietro Lorenzetti's fresco of *The Way to Calvary*. Vasari's staircase leads to a frescoed oratory on the lower level containing a painted cross by Lorenzetti. (Open April-Sept. Tues.-Sun. 9am-1pm and 3-6:30pm; Oct.-March 9am-1pm and 3-5pm. Admission L5000.) Perhaps the best example of Luca Signorelli's work is *The Deposition,* which resides in the 16th-century **Church of San Niccolò,** up the hill beyond the youth hostel. Ring the bell if the church isn't open, and, after the kind woman shows you the painting, ask her to activate the nifty James Bond mechanism that turns the panel around so you can see Signorelli's *Madonna and Saints* on the other side. (Church generally open 9am-12:30pm and sporadically in the afternoon, but be sure to go after 2 or 3pm.)

When afternoon sedates Cortona, head up to the **Fortezza Medicea** for a splendid view and a refreshing breeze. Take Via San Cristoforo, which winds up the hill between tall cypresses from the small church of the same name. At the top enter the tree-filled fortress, built on the remains of an Etruscan fortification. (Open mid-July to Aug. Tues.-Sun. 10am-1pm and 4-7pm.) On the way down, take **Via Crucis,** which leads away from the church of Santa Margherita. The futurist Severini designed the mosaic stations of the cross that line the path as a war memorial in 1947. Speaking of war monuments, don't miss the beautiful, heart-breaking memorial to the dead of WWI that guards the entrance to the **Giardino Pubblico.**

The Renaissance **Church of Santa Maria delle Grazie al Calcinaio,** designed by Francesco di Giorgio Martini, awaits visitors about 2km down the road near Camucia. The soft gray *pietra serena* stone is beautifully carved in the interior, and combined with the white walls to create a cool tonality. Paintings of the Signorelli school hover near the altar and a Marcillat stained-glass window energizes the opposite wall. (Open daily 8:30am-noon and 4-7pm.) Ask at the tourist office for information about the **Meloni del Sodo,** recently discovered Etruscan tombs near Sodo.

ENTERTAINMENT

Of the numerous gastronomic festivals throughout the year, the most important is the **Sagra della Bistecca** of August 14-15, when the whole town pours in to feast upon the superb local steak. Various musical and theatrical events take place throughout the year, clustering in the summer months when Cortona absorbs the spillover from the Perugia Jazz Festival. The Azienda's informative *Cortona '96* will give you the lowdown. Relax in the **public gardens** or join in the evening *passeggiata* in the park. Italian movies are screened here in summer (L6000). If you like your entertainment a bit more lively, check out **Tuchuleha** (tel. 60 18 82), in P. Garibaldi. It's a popular place with American students who come to drink and dance away their homesickness. (Open Tues.-Sat. 9pm-2am.)

■■■ AREZZO

Pause in Arezzo before continuing to other Tuscan destinations and muse about the others who found inspiration here: your illustrious predecessors include the poet Petrarch, the humanist Leonardo Bruni, the artist and historian Giorgio Vasari, and the inventor of the musical scale, Guido d'Arezzo. Michelangelo, born in the surrounding countryside, attributed some of his genius to Arezzo's surrounding hills and valleys. Today's Arezzo blends the old, the new, and the ancient, as Medieval and Renaissance structures give way to shopping arcades. Even the massive monthly antique fair allows tourists of the '90s to sift through tangible history.

ORIENTATION AND PRACTICAL INFORMATION

Arezzo lies on the Florence-Rome train line. Arezzo's train station and modern quarter lie at the bottom of a hill that ascends through the historic center and peaks at the *duomo*. Follow **Via Guido Monaco,** which begins directly across from the station in Piazza della Repubblica, to the park and traffic circle at P. Guido Monaco. Turn right on Via Roma and then left onto the pedestrian walkway, **Corso Italia.** The Corso leads up to the old city; **P. Grande,** its center, will be off to the right.

Tourist Office: P. della Repubblica, 22 (tel. 37 76 78), to the right as you leave the station. More than happy to give out free maps and other information. Some English spoken. Open April-Sept. daily 8:15am-8pm; Oct.-March Mon.-Fri. 8:15am-8pm, Sat. 8:15am-1pm; during antique fairs (1st Sat. & Sun. of every month) 8:15am-1pm.

Police: off Via Fra' Guittone, near the train station.

Post Office: Via Monaco, 34, to the left of P. Monaco when facing uphill. Open Mon.-Fri. 8:15am-7pm, Sat. 8am-12:30pm. **Postal Code:** 52100.

Telephones: Telecom (booths only), P. Monaco, 2, in the shopping arcade. Open 24 hrs. Assisted service at Via Margaritone, off Via Niccolò Aretino near the Archaeological Museum. Open Mon.-Sat. 8:30am-12:30pm and 3:30-6:30pm. **Telephone Code:** 0575.

Currency Exchange: Banca di Roma on Via Petrarca has an ATM that takes Cirrus cards. Bank open Mon.-Fri. 8:20am-1:20pm and 2:45-3:45pm.

Trains: Information open Mon.-Fri. 9am-noon and 3-5:30pm, Sat. 9am-noon. From Florence (1hr., L7800) and Rome (2hr., from L21,400, not inter-city). **Luggage storage** to the left as you exit the tracks (L1500), open daily 8am-7pm.

Buses: (tel. 38 26 44), TRA-IN, SITA, and LFI buses all stop at P. della Repubblica, to the left as you exit the train station. To: Siena (4 per day, 1½hr., L7500), San Sepolcro, Cortona. Buses connect Arezzo with nearby hilltowns, including Cortona (LFI, 1½hr., L4900) and Sansepolcro (CAT, 1hr., L4800). Four buses run daily to Siena (1½hr., L9000), returning to Arezzo in the afternoon. Buy tickets at the office on the left. Open daily 6:20am-7:40pm.

Emergencies: tel. 113. **Guardia Medica:** tel. 30 04 44. **Hospital:** on Via Fonte Veneziana (tel. 35 67 57; at night and Sun. 35 18 00).

ACCOMMODATIONS

The hotels of Arezzo fill to capacity during the Fiera Antiquaria (Antique Fair) on the first weekend of every month. Reservations are also necessary in the last four days of August during the Concorso Polifonico Guido d'Arezzo, a vocal competition. Otherwise, you should have little trouble finding a room.

Ostello Villa Severi, Via Redi, 13 (tel. 290 47). Take bus #4 (L1000) from the righthand-side of Via Guido Monaco (100m up Via G. Monaco from the train station), and get off at the stop after the Ospedale Civile (about 7min.). A beautiful 16th-century villa in the countryside overlooking hills and vineyards, but a bit of a hike from town. 6 beds per room. Plenty of hot water. Open 8am-4:30pm and 6:30pm-midnight. L20,000 per person, breakfast included. Dinner L14,000. Half-pension L34,000; full pension L45,000. Reserve ahead for meals.

Hotel Astoria, Via Guido Monaco, 54 (tel. 24 361). From the station, walk straight up Via G. Monaco, through the *piazza*, and to the hotel on the left. Most rooms are quiet, with towering ceilings and formerly mod furniture. Singles L43,000, with bath L53,000. Doubles L78,000, with bath L88,000. Triples L92,000, with bath L119,000. MC, Visa.

Albergo Cecco, Corso Italia, 215 (tel. 209 86). Follow Via G. Monaco from the station; take a right on Via Roma and another right 2 blocks down, on the Corso (5min. from the train station). Big, clean rooms trapped in the '60s: Age of Formica. Singles L45,000, with bath L58,000. Doubles L70,000, with bath L85,000. Breakfast included. Decent restaurant downstairs.

FOOD

Arezzo has some wonderful, inexpensive restaurants, but if you'd rather do it your way, check out the **supermarket Santa Prisca** at Via Monaco, 56 (open Mon.-Sat. 8am-1pm and 4:30-8pm). Or try the **open-air market** held Tues., Thurs., and Sat. in

P. Sant'Agostino. For excellent cheese, the best bet is **La Mozzarella,** Via Spinello, 25 (open 8am-1pm and 4:30-7:30pm, Wed. 8am-1pm). Eat in the park behind the *duomo,* with an impressive view of the Tuscan countryside.

Vecchia Suizzera, Corso Italia, 57 (tel. 21 26 70). When you can't face another plate of pasta, come here to revive your faith in Italian cooking. Wonderful, innovative delights like zucchini crepes (L8900), or ravioli in a herb-specked saffron sauce (L10,900). Open Mon.-Sat. noon-2:30pm and 7:30-10:30pm. AmEx, Visa.

Antica Osteria L'Agania, Via Guiseppe Mazzini, 10 (tel. 253 81), off Corso Italia. Serves good-old-fashioned food the way Mom would cook (if she were Italian). Locals pack the place to feast on homemade *gnocchi* and their famous *ribollita. Primi* L8000, *secondi* from L10,000. Open Tues.-Sun. noon-2pm and 7:30-9:30pm. AmEx, MC, Visa.

SIGHTS AND ENTERTAINMENT

The **Church of San Francesco** at P. S. Francesco forms the spiritual and physical center of Arezzo. This 14th-century structure guards Piero della Francesca's famous fresco cycle *Legend of the Cross,* the story of the wood used for Christ's cross from seed to crucifix. The city planned to have finished the restoration for 1992, the 500th anniversary of Piero's birth, but like the Energizer Bunny, restorations are still going... Now that the 500th has passed, the urgency seems to have evaporated. It's anybody's guess as to when the restoration will be completed. In the meantime, the frescoes to the right of the altar, including the wonderful "Constantine's Dream," are visible, and there's an interesting exhibit documenting the restoration process. (Open daily in summer 8am-noon and 1:30-6pm.)

Contrast this Franciscan art with the decoration of the rival Dominican order on the other side of town. The **Church of San Domenico** contains a superb Cimabue crucifix (1265), Spinello Aretino's *Annunciation* in the chapel to the right of the altar, and the Marcillat rose window over the door. (Open daily 7am-noon and 3-7pm.) Beyond the church on Via XX Settembre, 55, is **Vasari's house,** filled with heroic frescoes. (Open daily 9am-7pm.)

The massive **duomo,** on Via Ricasoli, encloses Piero della Francesca's *Mary Magdalene* just to the right of Bishop Guido Tarlati's tomb. Light filters into the cathedral through a series of 20-ft. stained-glass windows by Marcillat onto the altar, a wildly complex assemblage of 14th-century local carvings. The Lady Chapel (to the left near the entrance), covered by an ornate wrought-iron screen, is home to a terra-cotta *Assumption* by Andrea della Robbia. (Open 7am-noon and 3-6:30pm.) Between the *duomo* and the fortress, a leafy park gives magnificent views of the countryside beyond its edge.

If you backtrack down Corso Italia, on the left you'll see the Pisan-Romanesque **Church of Santa Maria della Pieve,** Arezzo's most important architectural monument and something of a city emblem, (though some of it is masked by temporary restoration work). Its tower is nicknamed "the tower of a hundred holes" for the Romanesque windows that pierce the structure on all sides. A brilliantly restored polyptych, *Il Politico* by Pietro Lorenzetti, sits on the elevated presbytery, depicting the Annunciation and the Madonna and Child. (Open Mon.-Sat. 8am-noon and 3-7pm, Sun. 8:30am-noon and 4-7pm.) Behind the Pieve is **Piazza Grande,** surrounded by a chronological succession of Arezzo's best architecture. Next to the arches of the Pieve's rear elevation, the **Palazzo della Fraternità dei Laici** mixes Renaissance and Gothic styles. A reconstruction of the **Petrone,** a column where criminals were exhibited and proclamations read, rises at the *piazza's* high point.

Arezzo's famous **antique fair** takes place on the first weekend of every month in P. Grande, but if you miss it, you can entertain yourself by browsing through the innumerable antique shops that dot the old town. The **Giostra del Saraceno** is a medieval joust performed on the last Sunday of August and the first Sunday in September. "Knights" representing the four quarters of the town charge with lowered lances at a wooden effigy of a Saracen. Feasting and processions accompany the event, and the winning region carries off a golden lance.

■ NEAR AREZZO: SANSEPOLCRO

Lost in a valley among Tuscany's densely forested hills, medieval Sansepolcro is the **birthplace of Piero della Francesca,** and hosts some of his finest works. The town is most easily accessible by the hourly CAT line bus from Arezzo (1hr., L4700), with the last bus returning to Arezzo at 7:30pm (weekend service is less frequent). This bus ride is not for the weak of stomach, though the incredible views of the countryside are worth the punishment. The bus drops you off on **Via Vittorio Veneto.** To get to the museum, take a left from the bus station, then turn left again at the next street, Via Firenzuola, and walk three minutes until you come to the street light; the museum will be on your right.

The **Museo Civico,** Via Aggiunti, 65 (tel. 73 22 18), houses some of Piero della Francesca's most famous works. The *Resurrection,* his masterpiece, features a triumphant Jesus wearing a red and white banner. Also by della Francesca is the *Madonna della Misericordia,* a polyptych with a huge Madonna protecting a confraternity under her cloak. Don't miss Antonio and Remigio Cantagallina's *Ultima Cena* (Last Supper), with Judas in the foreground holding his money bag and looking nonplussed while a devil on the floor spits blood on him. (Open daily 9:30am-1pm and 2:30-6pm; in summer 9:30am-1pm and 2:30-7:30pm. Admission L7000.)

The **Palio della Balestra** takes place the second Sunday in September. Stay overnight and join in the revelry generated by this competition between archers of Gubbio and Sansepolcro. To reach Sansepolcro's **tourist office** on Via della Fonte (tel. (0575) 73 02 31 or 74 05 36) from the museum, turn right on Via Firenzuola and then take the first left on P. Garibaldi; the tourist office is one block ahead on the left. (Open daily 9am-1pm and 4-7pm.) Maps and guidebooks of the region are available. Should night fall or hunger strike, try the comfortable **Albergo Fiorentino,** Via Luca Pacioli, 60 (tel. 74 03 50; fax 74 03 70), two blocks from the Museo Civico (singles L35,000, with bath and TV L47,000; doubles L55,000, with bath and TV L78,000; triples with bath and TV L108,000; breakfast L6000), or the **Ristorante Da Ventura,** Via Aggiunti, 30 (tel. 74 25 60), which serves outstanding homemade pasta dishes. The house specialties include ravioli with spinach and *ricotta* filling, and *tagliatelle* with *porcini* mushrooms. Whole roasts are carved right at the table. (*Primi* L7000, *secondi* L10,000; open Sun.-Fri. 12:30-2:30pm and 7:30-9:30pm.)

Another important stop on any Piero della Francesca odyssey is the tiny chapel halfway between Arezzo and Sansepolcro, outside the town of **Monterchi.** Twenty-four km outside Arezzo on Highway 73, there is a fork in the road; take the right branch (Highway 221) to the chapel. Within, marvel at the unusual *Madonna del Parto,* Piero's rendition of a proud, earthy Madonna immaculately pregnant with *bambino.* (Open Tues.-Sun. 10am-12:30pm and 3-7pm. Admission L5000.) The Arezzo-Sansepolcro bus stops nearby in Le Ville, where you can follow the signs to the chapel (about a 20-min. walk).

■ ■ ■ SIENA

Most tourists stampede directly from Rome to Florence and bypass Siena; due to their oversight, Siena remains a gorgeous medieval city that has fewer tourists than its larger cousins to the north and south. During the 13th century, Siena's flourishing wool trade, crafty bankers, and sophisticated civil administration marked it as one of the principal cities of Europe—easily Florence's equal. In 1230, the belligerent (and jealous?) Florentines catapulted excrement over Siena's walls, attempting to trigger a rampant plague. The ploy failed, and in 1260 Siena routed the Florentines at the Battle of Montaperti. The century of grandiose construction that followed this brief ascendancy endowed the city with its flamboyant Gothic cathedral, the Piazza del Campo, and a multitude of *palazzi.* However, in 1348, half of Siena's citizens succumbed to the first of three outbreaks of plague (none of which involved donkeys), and the weakened city bid *adieu* to its glory days.

Today, the Sienese are determined to maintain their identity as more than just a Florentine satellite. They boast their own painting tradition, led by Duccio, Simone Martini, and the Lorenzetti brothers, who expanded upon decorative elements of Gothic art. Siena also claims the mystic tradition that produced the 15th-century Saint Catherine, an ecstatic illiterate who brought the papacy back from Avignon, and Saint Bernadine, who roamed the Italian peninsula reviving the teachings of St. Francis. But there's nothing mystical about the pageantry and bravado of the most characteristic of Senese rituals, the wild *Palio* and the *contrade* (neighborhood) competition that swirls around it. The *Palio* is the main attraction of Siena's tourist industry, but the event is no mere show; modern-day Sienese still identify strongly with their local *contrada* and throw a year's worth of pent-up excitement, rivalry, and revelry into the races.

ORIENTATION AND PRACTICAL INFORMATION

Siena once lay on the main road between Rome and Paris; modernity finds it on a secondary train line off the Rome-Florence route. Change at Chiusi from Rome and the south, at Empoli from Florence and the north. To reach the town proper from the train station, take any bus from the stop across the street (buy tickets from the vending machines by the station entrance or at the *biglietteria* window for bus tickets, L1300). **The easiest and most convenient way to get to Siena is by bus.** Frequent buses link Siena to Florence and the rest of Tuscany, making this an ideal base for exploring the smaller Tuscan hill towns. Buses stop just outside the city's historic center at P. San Domenico, at the top of Siena's hills, which makes life a lot easier. Follow the signs to **Piazza del Campo** (also called *Il Campo*). Walking to the center from the train station can be a pleasant if strenuous way to orient yourself with the city, but be prepared to spend at least 45 minutes, and pick up a decent map before you set off.

Our map of Siena may be *piccolo*, but we've tried to help you by including the **map grid coordinates** of our Siena listings whenever possible. At times, two adjacent squares are listed.

Tourist Office: APT, Il Campo, 56 (C2; tel. 28 05 51), provides info on local sights and hotels, restaurants, and other Tuscan towns. The agency also has a **travel agency** that sells bus, train, and boat tickets. (Tourist office open Mon.-Sat. 8:30am-7:30pm; in winter 8:30am-1:30pm and 3:30-7pm. Travel agency open Mon.-Fri. 9am-1pm and 3:30-7pm, Sat. 9am-1pm.) **APT main office,** Via di Città, 43 (tel. 422 09). Down a long hallway across the street from the Libreria Senese. Harried, but has a list of *affitta camere*. (Three-day minimum stay.) Open Mon.-Fri. 9am-1pm and 4-7pm. There is also a **tourist info booth** in the train station that will help with hotels and general orientation. Open Mon.-Sat. 9am-1pm and 4-7pm. The **Prenotazioni Alberghiere** counter (A2; tel. 28 80 84) in P. San Domenico can also help you find lodging for a L3000 fee. Open in summer Mon.-Sat. 9am-8pm, winter 9am-7pm.

Police: Questura (C3; tel. 112), Via del Castoro, near the *duomo*.

Post Office: P. Matteotti, 36 (B1). *Fermo posta* at window #12. Open Mon.-Sat. 8:15am-7pm; last day of each month 8:15am-noon. **Postal Code:** 53100.

Telephones: Telecom (SIP), Via dei Termini, 40 (C2). You can make assisted calls (Mon.-Fri. 9am-1pm and 4-7pm); self-service pay phones are accessible daily 7am-midnight, in winter 7am-9pm. **Telephone Code:** 0577.

Budget Travel: CTS, Via Cecco Angiolieri, 49 (C2; tel. 28 50 08), off P. Tolomei. Student travel services. Open Mon.-Fri. 9:30am-12:30pm and 4-7pm.

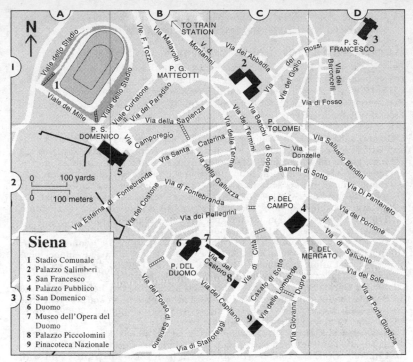

Siena

1 Stadio Comunale
2 Palazzo Salimbeni
3 San Francesco
4 Palazzo Pubblico
5 San Domenico
6 Duomo
7 Museo dell'Opera del Duomo
8 Palazzo Piccolomini
9 Pinacoteca Nazionale

Currency Exchange: The **Banca di Roma** at Via dei Termini, 37 (C2), has an ATM that accepts Cirrus cards, even though it doesn't say so. Open 24 hrs. There are also ATMs at the **Monte dei Paschi di Siena** (C1), along Via Banchi di Sopra.

Trains: P. Rosselli. Hourly departures to Florence (via Empoli, L7800) and Rome (via Chiusi, L19,900). Ticket office open daily 6:30am-9pm. **Train information** (tel. 28 01 15) open Tues.-Sat. 12:30-7:40pm in summer; 8:30am-1:30pm and 2:30-4:40pm in winter. **Luggage Storage:** L1500 per day, per piece. Open 24hrs.

Buses: TRA-IN/SITA, P. San Domenico, 1 (A2; tel. 20 42 45). Service to all of Tuscany, including Florence (express bus, every hr., L10,000), San Gimignano (every 1-2 hr., change at Poggibonsi, L7600), Volterra (4 per day, L8000), Montepulciano (3 per day, L8000), Pienza (4 per day, L7000), Arezzo (4 per day, L8500), and Montalcino (5 per day, L6000). Open daily 5:50am-8:15pm.

Car Rental: Hertz and **Intercar,** Via S. Marco, 96 (tel. 411 48). You must have a driver's license. Fiat Panda L150,000 per day, L625,000 per week. (Min. age 21.) Vespas L80,000 per day. (Min. age 18.) Open daily 8:30am-1pm and 3-7:30pm.

Taxis: Stands in P. Matteotti (B1) and P. Stazione (tel. 492 22).

Lost and Found: Casato di Sotto, 23 (C2-3). Open Mon.-Sat. 9am-12:30pm.

Laundromat: Onda BW, Casato di Sotto, 17 (C2-3; toll-free tel. (167) 86 13 46). Wash and dry L12,000 per 6.5kg. Open daily 8am-10pm. Last wash 9pm.

Public Toilets: Via Beccharia (C2; L500). Open daily 8am-7pm.

English Bookstore: Messagerie Bassi, Via di Città, 6/8 (C2; tel. 28 92 31). Excellent selection, reasonable prices. Open Mon.-Fri. 9am-8pm, Sat. 9am-1pm and 4-8pm. **Libreria Senese,** Via di Città, 62/66 (C2-3; tel. 28 08 45). Open Mon.-Sat. 9am-8pm. Both take AmEx, MC, Visa.

Pharmacy: Farmacia Centrale, Banchi di Soporti, 2. Open 24 hrs. in summer.

Emergencies: tel. 113. **Hospital:** P. del Duomo, 1 (B3; tel. 29 01 11). **Ambulance: Misericordia,** Via del Porrione, 49 (D2; tel. 28 08 28).

ACCOMMODATIONS AND CAMPING

Finding a room in Siena is usually easy enough, but in late June, July, and August, rooms become scarce. Try to call as far ahead as possible; book months ahead for either *Palio*. For stays of a week or more, rooms in private homes provide an attractive alternative, with singles for L40,000-70,000. The tourist office (see above) has a list and will phone for you.

Ostello della Gioventù "Guidoriccio" (HI), Via Fiorentina, 89 (tel. 522 12; fax 561 72), in Località Lo Stellino, a 20-min. bus ride from the *centro*. Take bus #15 across from the station at P. Gramsci or from P. Matteotti. If coming from Florence by bus, get off at the stop after you see the large black-and-white sign announcing entry into Siena. Considering the availability of inexpensive rooms in the *centro* and the extra cost and inconvenience of bus tickets to the hostel, you might try searching for a spot inside the city's walls before making the journey. 110 beds. Curfew 11:30pm. L18,000 per person. Breakfast included.

La Casa del Pellegrino, Via Camporegio, 31 (B2; tel. 441 77), behind San Domenico. A hotel run by nuns—enjoy stunning views of the *duomo* from the spotless and secure rooms. Free discourse on the state of sin and salvation. Opens at 7:30am. Curfew 11pm. Singles L40,000, with bath L50,000. Doubles with bath L75,000. Triples with bath L90,000. Quads with bath L120,000.

Locanda Garibaldi, Via Giovanni Dupré, 18 (C3; tel. 28 42 04), behind the Palazzo Pubblico and P. del Campo. A homey establishment with an equally home-style restaurant downstairs. Off-season singles L35,000. Doubles L65,000. Triples L85,000. Curfew midnight. Fills early.

Piccolo Hotel Etruria, Via Donzelle, 3 (C2; tel. 28 80 88). Renovated, modern, and sparklingly clean. All rooms with TV and phone. Curfew 12:30am. Singles L50,000, with bath L60,000. Doubles with bath L90,000. Triples with bath L121,500. Quads (on request) L153,000. Breakfast L6000. Outdoor parking L10,000, indoor parking L15,000.

Albergo La Perla, Via delle Terme, 25 (C2; tel. 471 44), on P. dell'Indipendenza off Via Banchi di Sopra. Two floors of nondescript rooms, all with tiny bathrooms. The walls are scuffed, but the pictures of guys in their *contrade* outfits help distract the eye. Singles L50,000. Doubles L80,000. Triples L110,000.

Albergo Tre Donzelle, Via Donzelle, 5 (C2; tel. 28 03 58). Just 1 door up from the Etruria. Airy rooms around a light-flooded stairwell. English spoken. Curfew 12:30am. Singles L34,500. Doubles L56,500, with bath L71,000. Triples L76,000, with bath L95,500. AmEx, MC, Visa.

Albergo Cannon d'Oro, Via Montanini, 28 (C1; tel. 443 21), near P. Matteotti. A genteel place, with tastefully decorated rooms and lovely views over gardens and hills. Singles L70,000. Doubles L90,000. Triples L115,000. Quads L150,000. Breakfast L7000. Handicapped accessible.

Camping: Colleverde, Strada di Scacciapensieri, 47 (tel. 28 00 44). Take bus #8 or 12 from P. Gramsci. L10,000-14,000 per adult (car and tent or camper included), L5500 per child. Pool L3000, children L1500. Open mid-March to mid-Nov.

FOOD

Siena specializes in rich pastries, the most famous being *panforte*, a dense concoction of honey, almonds, and citron. For a lighter snack try *ricciarelli*, soft almond cookies with powdered vanilla on top. Both are technically Christmas sweets, but you can sample either one year-round at the **Bar/Pasticceria Nannini,** the oldest *pasticceria* in Siena, with branches at Via Banchi di Sopra, 22-24 (C1-2), and elsewhere in town. **Enoteca Italiana,** in the Fortezza Medicea near the entrance off Via Cesare Maccari, sells the finest of the regional wines in Italy, from Brunello to Barolo, Asti Spumante to Vernaccia, at the lowest prices around. You can sample for only L2000 per glass. (Open daily 3pm-midnight.) Siena's **open-air market** fills Piazza La Lizza each Wednesday (8am-1pm). Shoestringers can pick up supplies at the **Consortio Agrario supermarket,** Via Pianigiani, 5 (C1), off P. Salimberi (open Mon.-Fri. 7:45am-1pm and 5-8pm, Sat. 7:45am-1pm), **COOP,** close to the train station (take bus #1; open Mon.-Tues. and Thurs.-Fri. 8:30am-1pm and 4-7pm, Wed. and Sat. 8:30am-1pm), or the **Simpatica/Crai** supermarket at Via di Città, on the way to the *duomo* (open Mon.-Sat. 7:30am-1:30pm and 5-8pm).

Grotta del Gallo Nero, Via Porrione, 65-67 (D2; tel. 28 43 46), behind P. del Campo. One of the most popular places in town. Italian rock blares as a young staff serves excellent Tuscan specialties at unbeatable prices. Hearty dish of homemade *pici* (plump, hand-rolled spaghetti) with *porcini* and sausage L8000. Juicy *vitello arrosto* (roast veal) L10,000. Open Tues.-Sun. noon-3pm and 7pm-1:30am, Mon. noon-3pm.

Ristorante Guidoriccio, Via Dupré, 2 (C3; tel. 443 50), right off Il Campo. A pleasant atmosphere, with vaulted ceilings and intimate lighting. Try the *tagliatelle* with asparagus cream sauce (L8000). A/C. *Menù* L21,000. Cover L3000. Open Mon.-Sat. noon-2:30pm and 7:30-10:30pm. AmEx, MC, Visa.

Osteria San Martino, Via Porrione, 31 (D2). Delicious Tuscan dishes served at outside tables or a second-floor dining room. *Antipasti* L4000. *Primi* L7000. *Secondi* L9000. Cover L2000. Open Mon.-Sat. noon-3:30pm and 7-10:30pm.

Osteria Le Logge, Via Porrione, 33 (D2; tel. 480 13), off P. del Campo. Reputedly one of Siena's very best, this charming dark wood- and marble-filled restaurant also has reasonable prices. *Primi* offerings include their specialty, *malfatti osteria* (spinach and *ricotta* in egg pasta, coated with meat sauce and baked, L9000). *Secondi* average L18,000. Cover L2000. Service 10%. Open Mon.-Sat. noon-3pm and 7-10:30pm. Very popular; make reservations. MC, Visa.

Bibo, Via Banchi di Sotto, 61-63 (C-D2). Come here for generous sandwiches (L3500) and beer (L3000). Homemade *gelato* starting at L2000. Open Tues.-Sun. 7:30pm-1am.

SIGHTS

Siena now offers a combined ticket to most religious monuments and museums, valid for three days and providing entry to the baptistery, the Piccolomini library, the Museo de l'Opera del Duomo, and the Oratory of St. Bernadino (L8500; offered in summer only).

Il Campo

Where other Italian towns center on their respective *duomi,* Siena radiates from the **Piazza del Campo,** the shell-shaped brick square designed expressly for civic events. The paving stones of the *piazza* are allegedly divided into nine sections representing the city's medieval "Government of Nine," though many observers count 11. The *campo* has always been the center stage of Siena; Dante described the real-life drama of Provenzan Salvani, the heroic Senese *condottiere* who panhandled around Il Campo in order to ransom a friend (these days, you'll just see Italian teenagers, overfriendly tourists, and souvenir carts). Later, Sienese mystics like San Bernadino found the *piazza* a natural auditorium. *Il Palio* reduces Il Campo to splendid mayhem twice each summer as horses race around its outer edge.

At the highest point in Il Campo's central axis, you'll find the **Fonte Gaia,** a pool surrounded by reproductions of native son Jacopo della Quercia's famous carvings (1408-1419; the originals can be found in the Museo Civico). The water here courses through the same 15-mile aqueduct that has refreshed Siena since the 14th century. Closing the bottom of the shell is the **Palazzo Pubblico,** a graceful Gothic palace. A gluttonous bell-ringer nicknamed "Mangiaguadagni" (literally, "eat the profits") bestowed his moniker on the **Torre del Mangia,** the clock tower that rises like a scepter to the left. Siena's Council of Nine commissioned a tower whose republican might would overshadow any other skyscraper the nobility or clergy could erect; a pair of Perugian architects gave them the second-tallest structure raised in medieval Italy with, surprisingly, no subterranean foundations (102m; Cremona has the tallest). In front of the *palazzo* is the **Cappella di Piazza,** built in 1348 in gratitude for the end of an outbreak of Black Death that claimed half the population. It took Siena 100 years to complete the Cappella; you can trace the transition from Gothic to Renaissance architecture as pointed arches give way to gracefully rounded ones halfway up the walls.

The Museo Civico

The Palazzo Pubblico holds masterpieces of Sienese art in the **Museo Civico.** While the museum's collection ranges from medieval triptychs to 18th-century landscapes and tributes to 19th-century generals, its treasure is its extensive collection of Sienese art. The two rooms that provide the best introduction to both Sienese art and the spirit of the city are the **Sala del Mappamondo** and the **Sala della Pace.** In the first, named for a lost series of astronomical frescoes, lies Simone Martini's *Maestà* (Enthroned Virgin) and *Guidoriccio da Fogliano.* These two frescoes, facing each other across the vast room, illustrate the contradictions of Siena's medieval government. On the one hand, Siena looked to the Virgin, the town's patron saint, for justification and legitimacy; on the other hand, it hired mercenary soldiers (*condottiere*) like Guidoriccio to defend the city. In the next room, the Sala della Pace, Sienese civic pride shines through in Pietro and Ambrogio Lorenzetti's famous frescoes of the **Allegories of Good and Bad Government and their Effects on Town and Country.** On the right side, Good Government embraces utopia: people dance in the streets, artisans toil happily, and contented farmers labor on vast stretches of fertile land that unfold to the horizon. On the left side, the Pride, Wrath, and Avarice of Bad Government wield their evil rule: a gloomy, desolate landscape is populated only by thieves, sinners, devils, sundry lost souls, and plenty of trash. The frescoes, in what was once the deliberating chamber of the Council of Nine, might well have shamed the Sienese government into civic decency, but the rule of the Nine came to an end shortly after the frescoes were completed. The Allegory of Good Government is remarkably well preserved, while the Allegory of Bad Government is chipping its way into oblivion—read into this what you will. Upstairs, on the Loggia dei Nove, you'll find the original della Quercia sculptures from the Fonte Gaia, now sadly debilitated. Step into the next room to witness Matteo di Giovanni's particularly ghastly rendition of the *Slaughter of the Innocents.* Head back downstairs to the entrance, cross the courtyard, and climb the tower's 300-odd narrow steps to bask in the spectacular view of the *duomo* and the entire city. (*Palazzo* and museum open Mon.-Sat. 9:30am-6:15pm, Sun. 9:30am-12:45pm; Nov.-March daily 9am-12:45pm. Admission L6000, students L3000. Torre del Mangia open daily 10am-6pm, mid-March to mid-April and mid-Oct. to mid-Nov. 10am-5pm, mid-Nov. to mid-March 10am-1pm. Admission L5000.)

Il Duomo

The zebra-striped **duomo,** perched atop one of Siena's three hills, took so long to build that it spanned two architectural eras, incorporating Gothic pinnacles and Romanesque arches. Civic pride demanded both enormous scale and prominent position, but the limited size of the hill posed a design problem. The apse would have hung in mid-air over the edge of the hill had the Sienese not built the **baptistery** below it to support the structure. Because of its obscure placement, the baptistery is missed by many travelers, and those who do visit are further challenged by the miserly lighting. However, those who concentrate are doubly rewarded. First, the delicate and intricate frescoes that decorate all the walls of the baptistery are fine examples of Sienese artistry. Second is the **baptismal font** (1417-30), which deftly incorporates Gothic and Renaissance styles. In the bronze panels that decorate the lower part of the font, compare Ghiberti's *Baptism of Christ* to the adjacent *Herod's Feast* by his contemporary Donatello. Ghiberti's Gothic panel is a supremely crafted and finished celebration of tactile pleasures, while Donatello's Renaissance work is a more reserved, intellectual study of perspective and movement. Other panels are by della Quercia (*Birth of John the Baptist*), and the six bronze angels are by Donatello. (Open mid-March-Sept. 7:30am-7:30pm, Oct.-early Nov. 7:30am-6:30pm, Nov.-mid-March 10am-1pm and 3-5pm. Admission L3000.)

Climb the stairs to the left of the baptistery to reach the Piazza del Duomo. On the way you'll pass through a huge arch that's part of a striped wall; this is the sole remnant of Siena's early 14th-century plan to rebuild the cathedral in response to Florence's commencement of its great domed Duomo. Siena's was to be the largest in the world, but building was halted forever by the bubonic plague and the fact that the hill would never have supported such an enormous cathedral. As you see Siena's present building, you'll hardly mind that they were halted in their ambitions—it would be hard to imagine a more wonderful cathedral than the present one. Giovanni Pisano carved the lower part of the façade; the statues of prophets, sybils, and philosophers you see are copies of his ground-breaking works, whose interacting postures and oddly proportioned figures were sculpted with the idea of the upward-looking viewer in mind. (The originals are in the Museo dell'Opera Metropolitana, where you can see the rough-cut, deeply grooved chiseling that created the effect.)

If you're overwhelmed and not quite sure where to direct your attention upon entering, simply look down; the floor, whose inlaid **pavement** is mostly covered (in a rotating cycle) to help preserve the marble masterpieces, depicts a variety of intriguing themes like "Alchemy" and "The Massacre of the Innocents." The ideal time to visit is August 15 through September 15, when the best works, by the Marchese d'Adamo, are visible. To the right of the altar, pause at the Chapel of Madonna del Voto, which holds a stunning icon (well loved by the Senese) of the Madonna and child resting on a gilded altarpiece (sometimes moved into the cathedral for better viewing). Halfway up the left aisle you'll find the **Piccolomini altar,** a complete architectural structure designed by Andrea Bregno in 1503. At the bottom on either side are statues of St. Peter and St. Paul, two oft-forgotten works executed by Michelangelo during the same years as his *David*. A bit farther down this aisle is the lavish **Libreria Piccolomini,** commissioned by Pope Pius III to house the elaborately illustrated books of his uncle Pius II, whose collection still lines the walls. The library also contains the Roman statue *The Three Graces*, some 15th-century illuminated lyrical scores, and an amazingly vibrant 360° fresco. (Library open mid-March Oct. 9am-7:15pm, Nov. mid-March 10am-1pm and 2:30-5pm. Admission L2000.) The cathedral's **pulpit** is one of Andrea Pisano's best, with allegorical and Biblical reliefs wrapping around the barrel (though you may be startled by the children-suckling she-wolves). (*Duomo* open mid-March Oct. 7:30am-7:30pm, Nov.-mid-March 7:30am-5pm. No tank tops, shorts, or skirts above the knee.)

The **Museo dell'Opera Metropolitana** (cathedral museum), located beneath the arches of P. Jacopo della Quercia, which adjoins P. del Duomo, houses all the extra art that formerly graced the cathedral. The first floor contains some of the foremost Gothic statuary in Italy, all by Giovanni Pisano. Upstairs is the *Maestà*, by Duccio di Buoninsegna, originally the screen of the cathedral's altar. But to enjoy the museum's greatest find, drag yourself away from the brilliant paintings and statues. At the top of the second flight of stairs, cross the room to the right, and take a flight of stairs leading down to another set of steps. There you can climb the tower for a **stunning view of Siena and Tuscany.** Climb an even smaller staircase at the end of the terrace, for an even *better* view. (Open mid-March to early Nov. 9am-7:30pm, Nov. to mid-March 9am-1pm. Admission L7000, student groups L5000.)

Around the City

Siena's **Pinacoteca Nazionale,** in the Palazzo Buonsignori down the street from the cathedral museum at Via San Pietro, 29, features works by every major artist of the highly stylized Sienese school: the seven magnificent followers of Onccio, Simone Martini, the Lorenzetti brothers, Bartolo di Fredi, Sano di Pietro, Il Sodoma, and many others. (Open Tues.-Sat. 8:30am-1:30pm, Sun. 8am-1pm; in winter Tues.-Sun. 8am-1pm. Admission L8000.)

The **Sanctuary of St. Catherine** on Via del Tiratoio honors the most renowned daughter of Siena, a simple girl who had a vision in which she became the bride of

Christ, who went on to influence popes, found a religious order, and be proclaimed patron saint of Italy by Pope Pius XII in 1939. The building offers a pleasant sojourn among roses and geraniums. (Open daily 9am-12:30pm and 3:30-6pm.)

As in other Italian towns, the Franciscans and the Dominicans have set up rival *basiliche* at opposite ends of town. The **Church of San Domenico** contains Andrea Vanni's portrait of St. Catherine and dramatic frescoes by Il Sodoma (1477-1549). The *cappella* also contains the requisite relic, this one the delightfully preserved head of Catherine herself. (Church open daily 8:30am-1pm and 4-7pm.) The **Church of San Francesco** houses two mournful frescoes by Pietro and Ambrogio Lorenzetti. The huge, stark space offers a sharp contrast to the *duomo*. (Open daily 9am-1pm and 4-7pm.) The adjacent **Oratory of San Bernardino** contains several more works by Il Sodomas. (Open in summer, same hours as the church; closed in winter. Admission L2000.)

The *Palio*-obsessed may enjoy Siena's *contrade* museums. Each neighborhood organization maintains its own collection of costumes, artifacts, banners, and icons. Most require an appointment—check at the tourist office for information.

ENTERTAINMENT

The Accademia Chigiana sponsors an excellent music festival, the **Settimana Musicale Senese,** Siena's Musical Week (late July). Siena also hosts a **jazz festival** in July, which features internationally known bopsters. During the summer evenings, everyone congregates in the *campo* after a long *passeggiata* along Via Banchi de Sopra; look out for the festivals sponsored by individual *contrade* or the wide range of concerts in Piazza del Campo. Check the posters or the tourist office for details.

Palio di Siena

Siena's Palio takes place on July 2 and August 16. As the bare-backed horse race approaches, Siena's emotional temperature steadily rises. Ten of the 17 *contrade* (chosen by lot—there's limited space in Il Campo) make elaborate traditional preparations. Young partisans sporting the colors of their *contrada* chant in packs on the street. Five trial races take place over the three days leading up to the race, and a final trial is run the same morning. On the eve of the race everyone revels until 3am or so, strutting and chanting around the city, pausing only to eat and drink. Just before the race, each horse is brought into the church of its respective *contrada* to be baptized. A two-hour parade of heralds and flag-bearers prefaces anarchy with regal pomp—the last piece in the procession is the *palio* itself, a banner depicting

And the Contestants are...		
The Contrada	**The Mascot**	**The Colors**
Aquila	two-headed eagle	yellow, black, lt. blue
Bruco	silkworm	yellow, green, navy
Chiocciola	snail	red, yellow, lt. blue
Civetta	owl	burgundy, black, white
Drago	dragon	lt. green, yellow, magenta
Giraffa	giraffe	red, white
Istrice	porcupine	white, red, black, navy
Leocorno	unicorn	lt. blue, orange, white
Lupa	she-wolf	black, orange, white
Montone	ram	yellow, red, white
Nicchio	shell	navy, yellow, red
Oca	goose	green, white, red
Onda (Wave)	dolphin	white, celeste (lt. blue)
Pantera	panther	red, navy, white
Selva (Forest)	rhinoceros	green, orange, white
Tartuca	turtle	blue, yellow
Torre (Tower)	elephant	burgundy, blue, yellow

the Madonna and Child, drawn in a cart by white oxen. Officials pad the buildings of the *piazza* with mattresses, for many a rider has careened off the track. The race begins at 7pm, and it takes the jockeys about 70 seconds to tear three times around Il Campo (after a few false starts that allow them to make deals with each other).

To stay in Siena during the *Palio*, book rooms at least four months in advance—especially for budget accommodations. Write the APT in March or April for a list of individuals and companies that rent rooms, or to reserve a seat in the stands. You can stand in the "infield" of the *piazza* for free. Access to the *piazza* closes early, so stake out a spot early in the day. For the full scoop on *Il Palio,* ask at the tourist office and pick up their excellent program (available in English). To witness a less-touristed event of *Il Palio,* attend *La Tratta* (the choosing of the horses), which takes place on June 29 and August 13 at 10am.

■ NEAR SIENA

SAN GALGANO

Only slightly removed from a winding country pass between Siena and Massa Marit-tima, the ruined **13th-century Cistercian abbey** of **San Galgano** was once one of the richest and most powerful in Tuscany. Its monks served as treasurers and judges for the communes of Siena and Volterra, helped construct the duomo in Siena, and became bishops and even saints. Their vast fortune permitted the monks to con-struct an abbey of noble proportions, but by the mid-16th century, most of the church had crumbled to dust due to their corruption. Its very dilapidation makes San Galgano an unforgettable sight. Nature has been kind to the massive old build-ing, the foremost specimen of Cistercian Gothic architecture in Italy; it has removed the roof completely without harming the majestic columns within. Gothic windows and rosettes frame Tuscan landscapes, and nests of birds chirp from its corners. To reach San Galgano, take the TRA-IN **bus** that runs between Siena and Massa Marit-tima, and get off at the San Galgano stop. Two buses leave daily from Siena (8:30am and 5:15pm) and two return from Massa Marittima (L5200).

MONTALCINO

Montalcino has changed little since medieval times when it was a Sienese strong-hold. With few historic monuments to attend to, Montalcino has concentrated on looking quaint and making the heavenly *brunello di Montalcino,* a smooth, full-bod-ied wine that is widely acknowledged as Italy's finest red.

With its nearly impregnable walls, Montalcino sheltered a band of republicans escaping from the Florentine siege of Siena in 1555. The city walls still stand, along with the remains of the town's original 19 fortified towers. Montalcino's **fortezza** (fortress) watches over the southeast corner of town. Two courtyards beckon inside the fortress, one sunny and cheered by tiger lilies, the other sylvan and shaded by foliage. You can explore the 14th-century walls, chambers, and turrets, which offer a stunning view of the exquisite landscape. (Open July 15-Sept. 15 daily 9am-1pm and 2:30-8pm; Sept. 16-July 14 Tues.-Sat. 9am-1pm and 2-6pm. Admission to ramparts L3500, inside fortress free.) The museum-starved might enjoy the **Museo del Vetro (Museum of Glass),** at the Castello di Poggio, in the town walls. Luminescent works of antique glass mingle with displays showing how the stuff was made. (Open Sat.-Sun. 11am-1pm and 3:30-7pm; in winter 10am-1pm and 2:30-5:30pm. Admission L3000.) On the way down, stop at the small *enoteca* in the *fortezza's* cavernous main room; try the tasty sandwiches (L3500) as you sample the local wines (L4500 per glass). Montalcino's most inspiring sight lies 9km away down a serpentine country road. Built in the 12th century on the remains of a 9th-century church allegedly founded by Charlemagne, the well-touristed **Abbazia di Sant'Antimo** (tel. (0577) 83 56 69) rates as one of Tuscany's most beautiful Romanesque churches, with its rounded apse and individually carved alabaster cap-itals. Inside, monks still give mass in Gregorian chant. (Open April-Sept. daily 10:30am-12:30pm and 3-5pm; buses run Mon.-Sat. 4 per day, Sun. 2 per day; L1200.)

The best deals on *brunello* are found at the **COOP Supermarket** off P. del Popolo. To gain a real appreciation for the local vineyards, head 5km down the road to the **Fattoria dei Barbi** in Sant'Antimo (tel. (0577) 84 82 77). You can also visit the **Azienda Agricola Greppo,** which produced the first *brunello* in 1888, and lies 3km away from Montalcino on the road to Sant'Antimo. Call before heading out in order to arrange a tour of the cellars (tel. (0572) 84 80 87). Contact the tourist office for information about guided tours of the local vineyards. To sample some of the exotic **honey products** made in Montalcino buzz over to **Apicoltura Ciacci** on Via Ricasoli, 26, up the street from the Chiesa di S. Agostino, where you'll discover every honey product imaginable, including honey soap, honey biscuits, honey *grappa,* honey milk, and honey candies. (Open daily 10am-12:30pm and 4-7pm, honey.)

Not only do local products tickle the wine-lover's throat, but the superb *trattoria* **Il Moro,** Via Mazzini, 46 (tel. 84 93 84), is itself reason enough to visit Montalcino .Sample the local catch of *cinghiale* (wild boar) with *pappardelle* (broad, home-made ribbons of pasta) for L5000, or the mixed grill for L10,000. (Open Fri.-Wed. noon-2:30pm and 7:30-10:30pm.) There's a **market** for picnics on Fridays (7:30am-1pm) on Viale della Libertà. Rooms are expensive and few in Montalcino; try to find a bed in a private home. The **tourist office,** Costa del Municipio, 8 (tel./fax (0577) 84 93 21), can help you find lodging. (Open Tues.-Sun. 9:30am-1pm and 3:30-7pm.) You might also try **Affitacamere Casali,** Via Sagna, 3 (tel. 84 82 79 or 84 71 50), which lends adequate doubles with bath (L55,000). More refined, the **Albergo Il Giardino,** Via Cavour, 4 (tel. 84 82 57) has doubles for L70,000, with bath L85,000.

Ten **TRA-IN** buses make the one-hour trip daily from Siena to Montalcino (L5200). If coming from Pienza or Montepulciano, change buses at Torrenieri. In June, the old town comes alive for a *teatro* festival. Contact the tourist office for information and tickets (about L10,000).

■■■ MONTEPULCIANO

This small medieval town, stretched along the crest of a hill, is one of the finest locations in Italy for enjoying the beautiful countryside and fine wine. Though the smooth, garnet-colored *vino nobile* has earned the town notoriety, the landscape and museums alone make the town an excellent choice for a daytrip from Siena.

ORIENTATION AND PRACTICAL INFORMATION

Buses drop you at the bottom of the hill outside the town. From there it's a short, steep climb to reach the **Corso,** the town's main street, and a long, steeper one to **P. Grande,** the main square. Orange ATAF **buses** make the trip easier (L1200).

Tourist Office: Via Ricci, 9 (tel. 75 86 87), off P. Grande. Pick up the helpful booklet *Montepulciano—Perla del Cinquecento,* in English and French, which includes a list of *affitta camere.* Check before you trek, however, as such information is subject to change. Open Tues.-Sun. 9am-noon and 3-6pm.

Police: P. Savonarola, 16 (tel. 112).

Postal Code: 53045.

Telephone Code: 0578.

Currency Exchange: Banca Toscana, P. Michelozzo, 2. Open Mon.-Fri. 8:20am-1:20pm and 2:45-3:45pm.

Trains: Hourly trains to Chiusi make Montepulciano a convenient stopover on the Florence-Rome line; take the bus from there (45min., L4200).

Buses: TRA-IN buses run to Montepulciano from Siena, Florence, Pienza, and Chiusi. Montepulciano is an easy trip from Siena (Mon.-Sat. 6 per day, 2hr., L7200; change at Buonconvento). Service is very limited on Sundays, so plan accordingly.

Bike Rental: A. S. Cicloposse, Via dell'Opio nel Corso, 16 (tel. 71 63 92).

Pharmacy: Farmacia Franceschi, Via di Voltaia nel Corso, 47 (tel. 75 73 24). Open Mon.-Sat. 9am-1pm and 4-7pm.

Emergencies: tel.113.

ACCOMMODATIONS

The mild trauma of hotel prices in Montepulciano makes the town more attractive as a daytrip; *Let's Go* recommends that you buy your wine and head back to home-base in Siena or Florence.

Affitta Camere Bella Vista, Via Ricci, 25 (tel. 75 73 48), down the hill from the tourist office, rents small but adequate rooms. The logical choice at L40,000 for a single, L55,000 for a double with bath (L60,000 for double with a bath and balcony). Call before you head up there.

Albergo La Terazza, Via Piè al Sasso, 16 (tel./fax 75 74 40), off the Corso. Pretty, antique-filled rooms marshalled by a friendly, gregarious proprietor. Breakfast is served in a garden downstairs, and there's a lovely flower-bedecked terrace from which to watch the Montepulcian sunset. Doubles L75,000-80,000, with bath L78,000-85,000. Mini-apartments with fully equipped kitchens L85,000.

Ristorante Cittino, Vicolo della via Nuova, 2 (tel. 75 73 35), off Via di Voltaia nel Corso. Clean and homey with the smell of Mom's cooking wafting up from the kitchen downstairs. Each of their 4 doubles (L50,000) may also serve as a family's triple or quad. The popular restaurant serves superb home-cooked food. Full meals around L25,000. Open July to mid-June. Restaurant and hotel closed Wed., but you can check in Wed. night if you call ahead.

FOOD

Montepulciano offers a smorgasbord of excellent, affordable restaurants. Ristorante Cittino is one of the best deals (see above). There are **minimarkets** all along the Corso (try **Eurospar,** at #46, open Thurs.-Tues. 7:30am-1pm and 5-8pm) and a larger **supermarket** in P. Savonarola at the bottom of the Corso, as well as an **open-air market** in P. Sant'Agnese (Thurs. 8am-1pm).

Osteria dell'Acquaccheta, Via del Teatro, 24, off the Corso as you head further up the hill. Run by a group of friends. Simple, tasty dishes and great wine. *Bruschetta,* made with the greenest olive oil you've ever seen, L3500. Salads L3500-7000. Ravioli in tomato sauce L4500. Open Tues.-Sun. noon-2:30pm and 6-11pm.

Trattoria Diva e Maceo, Via Gracciano nel Corso, 92 (tel. 71 69 51). Where locals go to socialize over *cannelloni* stuffed with *ricotta* and spinach or a divine *ossobuco.* Open Wed.-Mon. noon-4pm and 7-11pm. Closed 1st 2 weeks in July.

SIGHTS AND ENTERTAINMENT

Montepulciano boasts an impressive assemblage of 16th- and 17th-century Renaissance and Baroque *palazzi.* The town's main drag, the **Corso,** divides nominally into four parts: Via di Gracciano nel Corso, Via di Voltaia nel Corso, Via dell'Opio nel Corso, and Via del Poliziano nel Corso. It winds languorously up the hill, passing near the summit where the Piazza Grande and the *duomo* are located. Impressive *palazzi* line the lowest quarter of the Corso, Via di Gracciano. On your right at #91 is **Palazzo Avignonesi** (1507-1575), attributed to Vignola. The elegant windows of the second floor are in sharp contrast to the bold protruding windows of the ground floor, marking different stages of construction. The lions' heads on either side of the door belong to the same pride as the lion on top of the **Marzocco Column,** in front of the *palazzo.* The lion, the heraldic symbol of Florence, replaced the she-wolf of Siena in this spot when Florence took the city in 1511. The original lion now rests in the Museo Civico. Farther up on the other side of the street at #70 rises the asymmetrical façade of **Palazzo Cocconi,** attributed to Antonio da Sangallo the Elder (1455-1534). Cross the street to #73, the **Palazzo Bucelli,** whose base is inset with Roman and Etruscan reliefs, urn slabs, and inscriptions collected by the 18th-century proprietor, Pietro Bucelli.

The **Church of Sant'Agostino** dominates P. Michelozzo, farther up the street. The lower part of the façade demonstrates Michelozzo's masterful classicism, while the second level "quotes" the Gothic style. Just in front of the Church of Madonna di Fatima looms the **Torre di Pucinella,** constructed in 1524 of wood and metal plating. The Pucinella gongs the bell punctually on the hour, keeping time for the surrounding neighborhood. Back on the Corso, which becomes Via di Voltaia nel Corso at #21, stop at the U-shaped **Palazzo Cervini.** This *palazzo's* external courtyard is typical of country villas but rare in urban residences.

To reach **Piazza Grande** and the **duomo** at the top of the hill you can either meander around and up Il Corso, or scale the steep alleys to the right. The unfinished *duomo,* the Palazzo Tarugi, the Palazzo Cantucci, and the 14th-century Palazzo Comunale ring the *piazza.* The unpretentious *duomo,* with its simple stone and brick exterior and unfinished façade, clothes an even sparser interior. It houses a poignant *Assumption of the Virgin* by Taddeo di Bartolo in a triptych above the altar. (Open 9am-1pm and 3:30-7:30pm.) The austere **Palazzo Comunale** took nearly a century to build, and was finally completed in the mid-1400s by Michelozzo. From the *palazzo's* tower you can take in a view that ranges from Siena's towers in the north to the snow-capped Gran Sasso massif in the south. (Open Mon.-Sat. 8am-1pm. Admission to tower L2000.) The remaining two *palazzi* were both designed by Antonio Sangallo the Elder. The elegant white façade of **Palazzo de' Nobili-Tarugi** faces the *duomo;* two arches on the bottom left allow you to enter a deep-vaulted *loggia* that cuts through the entire corner of the building.

The Palazzo Neri-Orselli, Via Ricci, 10, houses the **Museo Civico,** one of Montepulciano's foremost attractions. The museum contains a collection of enameled terracotta by della Robbia, Etruscan cinerary urns, and over 200 paintings. (Open Wed.-Sat. 9:30am-1pm and 3-6pm; Sun. 9:30am-1pm. Admission L5000.) The **Church of San Biagio,** outside the town walls, is Sangallo's masterpiece. The steep 500m walk down the hill is well worth the effort. The church is a wonder of Renaissance architecture—well balanced, filled with graceful details, and gleaming on an emerald green plot of grass overlooking the hills. (Open daily 9am-6pm.) The **Caffè Poliziano,** Via di Voltaia nel Corso, 27 (tel. 75 86 15), offers some of the most stunning views in Montepulciano from its marble tables. This thoroughly art nouveau *caffè* hosts concerts (including a jazz festival in July) and is a wonderful place for a drink. Otherwise, the main form of entertainment for tourists in this town consists of traipsing from one **wine store** to the next. All of them offer free samples of the wines they sell, and many don't seem overly concerned with whether you're buying or not. Try the one at Porta di Bacco, on the left immediately after you enter the city gates. (Open daily 9am-8pm.)

Around August 15, the **Bruscello** (a series of amateur theatrical productions) takes place on the steps of the *duomo.* To buy tickets (around L10,000), contact the tourist office. Visit Montepulciano the last Sunday in August to see the raucous **Bravio** (Barrel Race), held to commemorate the eight neighborhood militias who fended off the Florentines and Sienese. Pairs of youths, dressed in costumes bearing their team markings, roll barrels up the steep incline of the Corso, exchanging insults and blows as they battle their way to the Piazza Grande.

■■■ VOLTERRA

When you finally find Volterra, you'll think you've reached the edge of the world. Perched atop a huge bluff, the town broods over the surrounding checkerboard of green and yellow fields. The Etruscans were drawn here by the cliffs' impregnability and established Velathri, which by the 4th century BC had become one of the most powerful cities of the Dodecapolis. Medieval Volterra shrank to one-third the size of its ancestor, leaving a still-palpable sense of decline and desolation. It is this melancholic air that gives Volterra its ineffable appeal, but its many alabaster workshops and it's impressive Etruscan museum don't hurt either.

ORIENTATION AND PRACTICAL INFORMATION

Although nearer to San Gimignano and Siena, Volterra is linked administratively to Pisa, from which **TRA-IN** bus service is most frequent (change at Pontederra, L8200). There is a small train station 9km west of town at Saline di Volterra, with trains from Pisa (L7100) and the coastal line. **APT** buses synchronized with the trains run between Saline and Volterra (7 per day, L2200). All buses arrive and depart from **Piazza della Libertà,** where you can buy tickets from the vending machine or in the bars down the street. From P. della Libertà, take the only street leading out of the *piazza*, and turn left onto central **Piazza dei Priori.** From October to May bus service is less direct and you will have to change buses at intermediate stops. Ask at the bus station.

Tourist Office: Via Turazza, 2 (tel. 861 50), just before P. dei Priori. Sells tickets and provides info on buses, trains, and accommodations. Some pamphlets about the city and environs. Open daily 9am-1pm and 2-7pm. Closed Sun. in winter.
Police: tel. 860 50.
Post Office: P. dei Priori, 14 (tel. 869 69). Open Mon.-Fri. 8am-7pm, Sat. 8am-noon. **Postal Code:** 56048.
Telephone Code: 0588.
Train Information: tel. 441 16.
Buses: SITA buses run from Florence (4 per day, 2½hr., L11,200), Siena (5 per day, 2hr., L7600), and San Gimignano (4 per day, 1½hr., L6500; change twice, at Poggibonsi and Colle Val d'Elsa).
Public Baths: Via delle Prigioni, 3, off P. dei Priori. Toilets L300. Showers L2000. Open Fri.-Wed. 8am-7pm.
Emergencies: tel. 113. **Medical Assistance:** P. San Giovanni (tel. 861 64)

ACCOMMODATIONS AND CAMPING

The spacious youth hostel, convent, and campgrounds provide the only cheap beds in Volterra. Signs for *affitta camere* frequently appear in shop windows.

Youth Hostel (tel. 855 77), Via Firenzuola, across from Porta a Selci. A squeaky clean hostel with a lush garden out back. Small rooms with terrific views of the valley below. Reception open 8-10am and 6-11pm. Curfew 11:30pm. L18,000; no membership required, sheets and showers included. Breakfast L3000.
Conventa Sant'Andrea (tel. 860 23), P. S. Andrea, next door to the church, about a 5-min. walk exiting the city from Porta A Marcoli. Quiet, private rooms off frescoed hallways, and some gorgeous views. L22,000 per person, L30,000 per person in rooms with bath.
Albergo Etruria, Via Matteotti, 32 (tel. 873 77). As you exit P. Libertà, take a right before P. dei Priori; the Etruria is a few blocks down. The best prices in town for a "real" hotel. Rooms are big and nicely decorated and there's a garden lounge. Singles L55,000. Doubles L80,000, with bath L97,000. Visa.
Le Balze, Via Mandringa, 15 (tel. 878 80). Exit through the Porta San Francesco, and bear right on Strada Provincial Pisana; Via Mandringa will veer off to the left. This attractive campground has a restaurant and a pool, plus tennis, volleyball, *bocce*, fishing, horseback riding (all for additional fees), and a view over Le Balze. L8000 per person, L7000 per tent, L3000 per car. Showers and use of the pool included. Open March-late Oct. Reservations accepted.

FOOD

An excellent selection of Volterra's game dishes and local cheeses is available at **alimentari** on Via Guarnacci and Via Gramsci. Sample *salsiccia di cinghiale* (wild boar sausage) and *pecorino* (sheep's milk) cheese. You can pick up a tasty challenge for your dentalwork at any of the local *pasticcerie*. Try *Ossi di Morto* (singular *osso*), a rock-hard local confection made of egg whites, sugar, hazelnuts, and a hint of lemon. Do your bulk shopping at the **COOP supermarket** on Via delle Casine outside the city walls. (Open Mon.-Tues. and Thurs.-Sat. 7:30am-12:30pm and 4:30-7:30pm, Wed. 7:30am-12:30pm.)

L'Ombra della Sera, Via Gramsci, 70 (tel. 866 63), off P. XX Settembre. Wild boars' heads on the wall jealously watch diners as they feast on copious portions of homemade pasta. *Secondi* L12,000-14,000 for entrees such as *coniglio alla*

VOLTERRA

contadina (rabbit with tomatoes and vegetables). *Menù* L18,000. Cover L2700. Service 10%. Open Tues.-Sun. noon-3pm and 7-10pm. AmEx, MC, Visa.

Pizzeria/Birreria Ombra della Sera, Via Guarnacci, 16. Great pizza, great prices. Pizzas L6000-8000. Open Tues.-Sun. noon-3pm and 7pm-midnight.

Il Pozzo degli Etruschi, Via dei Prigioni, 30. Hearty Tuscan fare served in a private garden Open Fri.-Wed. 12:30-2pm and 7:30-10pm. AmEx, MC, Visa.

SIGHTS AND ENTERTAINMENT

Volterra's **Fortezza Medicea,** an elegant remnant from the period of Florentine domination used as a jail since its completion in 1472, is the first structure you'll see as you approach the town. Volterra revolves around **Piazza dei Priori,** a medieval center surrounded by sober, dignified *palazzi.* The **Palazzo dei Priori,** the oldest governmental palace in Tuscany (1208-1254), presides over the square. (Open Mon.-Sat. 9am-1pm and 3-6pm.) Across the *piazza* sits the **Palazzo Pretorio,** a series of 13th-century buildings and towers.

Behind the Palazzo dei Priori, admire the **duomo's** haphazard construction. Initiated in Pisan-Romanesque style in the 1200s, desultory work continued for three centuries without reaching completion. Inside, on the left, the **oratory** houses a series of wooden statues depicting the life of Jesus from nativity to crucifixion. The chapel off the transept holds frescoes by Rosselli, including the brilliant *Mission per Damasco.* Over the main altar stands the huge 12th-century polychrome wood sculpture group *Deposition from the Cross,* above which is an intricate alabaster tabernacle by Mino da Fiesole. (*Duomo* open daily 7:30am-12:30pm and 2-7pm.)

Across the *piazza* down Via dell'Arco is the massive, 3rd-century BC **Etruscan arch,** one of the city's oldest gates. The black lumps of stone on the outside were once sculpted human heads that symbolized, according to your preferred interpretation, Etruscan gods or beheaded enemy prisoners. On the other side of P. dei Priori, on Via dei Sarti, the **Pinacoteca Comunale** occupies the **Palazzo Minucci-Solaini** (tel. 875 80), an elegant building with an arcaded courtyard. Inside, Taddeo di Bartolo's graceful *Madonna and Saints* altarpiece will surprise anyone who has seen his gruesome *Last Judgement* in San Gimignano. But the art professors and students come to Volterra for the treasure in the last room on the first floor. In his frenetic *Deposition* (1520), Rosso Fiorentino eschewed High Renaissance conventions of order and restraint with a cacophony of colors swirling towards a shockingly green body of Christ. Volterra's other major attraction is the **Museo Etrusco Guarnacci,** at Via Minzoni, 15 (tel. 863 47). It displays over 600 finely carved Etruscan funerary urns from the 8th and 7th centuries BC. Each is topped by a stylized figure representing the deceased; below are dramatic bas-reliefs recreating various episodes from classical mythology. (The museum helpfully groups together scenes from a single story and provides English interpretations.) On the first floor you can find the museum's most famous piece, the oddly elongated bronze figure dubbed *L'Ombra della Sera* (Shadow of the Evening), unearthed by a farmer in the 19th century and used as a fireplace poker until someone realized it was a masterpiece of Etruscan art. (*Pinacoteca* and *museo* open daily 9am-7pm. Admission (includes *pinacoteca, museo,* and the sacred art museum near the *duomo*) L10,000.)

Take a left on Via Lunga le Mura del Mandorlo (before Porta Marcoli) for a spectacular view of the surprisingly intact **Teatro Romano** (free). Continue past the *teatro* to the **Church of San Francesco** on the edge of town. Inside, the **Cappella della Croce,** off the right aisle, encloses frescoes by Cenno Cenni that relate the story of the True Cross. (Open daily 7:30am-12:30pm and 2-7pm.)

Volterra's most spectacular natural sight lies a half-hour's walk outside of town at **Le Balze.** Exit the city through the Porta San Francesco and keep going. Erosion has carved cliffs that tower over the valley floor. These gullies have been growing over the millennia, swallowing churches in the Middle Ages and uncovering an Etruscan necropolis in the 18th century.

■■■ SAN GIMIGNANO

From the road approaching San Gimignano, the hilltop village looks like a collection of skyscrapers in some great, distant city. Only upon arrival does one see that the "skyscrapers" are actually the ancient crenelated towers of a tiny but perfectly preserved medieval town. The 14 towers, survivors of the original 72, recall a tumultuous period when warring families fought battles within the city walls, using their towers for grain storage during sieges. (The towers were also convenient for dumping boiling oil on passing enemies.) With the rise of the commoners in the 14th century, however, most towers were demolished. The ones that remain are relics of San Gimignano's medieval vitality. San Gimignano then stagnated in poverty for six centuries until its towered horizon proved a sure lure to postwar tourists, whose tastes and wallets resuscitated production of the golden *vernaccia* wine. With its hordes of daytrippers, piles of souvenir shops, and innumerable restaurants, San Gimignano today feels a bit like some Disneyland executive's idea of MedievalLand. An overnight stay, however, promises blissful tranquility.

ORIENTATION AND PRACTICAL INFORMATION

TRA-IN buses run to Florence and Siena every 1-2 hours, and less frequently to Volterra. Change buses at Poggibonsi, also the nearest train station (20min., L2500). Buses arrive at Porta San Giovanni just outside the town. To get to the center, enter through the *porta* and follow the crowd up the hill to **Piazza della Cisterna** and **Piazza del Duomo,** which are linked. The tourist office is in Piazza del Duomo, to the left of the church.

> **Tourist Office: Pro Loco,** P. del Duomo, 1 (tel. 94 00 08). Reams of pamphlets. No accommodations service, but a list of hotels and rooms in private homes. Organizes tours in English, depending on the crowd; call ahead. (Sun. at 9:30am; L10,000, children free.) Also **exchanges currency** and sells bus tickets. English spoken. Open daily 9am-1pm and 3-7pm **Ufficio Informazioni Turistiche (UIT),** Via S. Giovanni, 125 (tel. 94 08 09), on your right as you enter the city gates, will reserve hotel rooms Open Mon.-Sat. 9:30am 1pm and 3-7.30pm.
>
> **Police: Carabinieri,** Piazzale Martiri di Montemaggio (tel. 94 03 13).
>
> **Post Office:** P. delle Erbe, 8, behind the *duomo.* Open Mon.-Fri. 8:15am-7pm, Sat. 8:15am-12:30pm. **Postal Code:** 53037.
>
> **Telephones:** at the tourist (APL) office Also at **Telecom (SIP),** Via San Matteo, 13. Open daily 8am-midnight. **Telephone Code:** 0577.
>
> **Buses: TRA-IN** buses leave from P. Martiri outside Porta San Giovanni. Schedules and tickets available in the UIT office or the bar across the street. Change at Poggibonsi for Florence (1½hr., L9500), Siena (1hr., L7600), Volterra (1½hr., L6800).
>
> **Pharmacy:** Via San Matteo, 13 (tel. 94 20 29). All-night availability to fill urgent prescriptions. Open Mon.-Sat. 9am-1pm and 4-7pm.
>
> **Emergencies:** tel. 112. **Hospital:** Via Folgore da San Gimignano (tel. 94 03 12). **Ambulance: Misericordia,** tel. 94 02 63.

ACCOMMODATIONS AND CAMPING

San Gimignano caters to wealthy tourists, making most accommodations well beyond budget price range. A peaceful convent saves the day if you arrive early. **Affitta camere** provide another alternative to overpriced hotels, with singles for about L45,000 and doubles about L75,000. Get a list from either the tourist office or **Associazione Extra Alberghiere,** Piazza delle Erbe (tel. 94 21 94), near the Piazza Popolo, which can also find you a room for a small fee. (Open 9am-1pm and 3-6pm.)

> **Convento di Sant'Agostino** (tel. 94 03 83), in P. Sant'Agostino. Refreshingly spartan rooms (some with views) set around a rose- and poppy-filled courtyard. Singles L25,000. Doubles L35,000. Triples L55,000. Write 1 month in advance for summer reservations.
>
> **Ostello del Chianti (HI),** Via Roma, 137 (tel. (055) 807 70 09), in **Tavernelle Val di Pesa.** It's not really anywhere near San Gimignano, but it's a nice place any-

SAN GIMIGNANO

way. Take the SITA bus to Tavernelle, changing at Poggibonsi (1hr., L3700). Connections are poor, so check the schedule before you go. A superb 54-bed hostel in a beautiful setting. Membership required. Reception open 6:30-10:30pm, but you may get a key. L14,000 per person. Showers and breakfast included.

Albergo/Ristorante Il Pino, Via S. Matteo, 102 (tel. 94 04 15). Rustic simplicity in the quiet quarter near the convent. Rustic beamed ceiling, but red plastic bed frames. Doubles L60,000, with bath L80,000. Breakfast included. Reservations recommended.

Camping: Il Boschetto, at Santa Lucia (tel. 94 03 52), 2½km downhill from Porta San Giovanni. Buses run from town (L1000), but it's not a bad hike. Bar, market, and *pizzeria*. Office open 8am-1pm, 3-8pm, and 9-11pm. L7000 per person, L7000 per small tent (and 1st car). Hot showers included. Open April-Oct. 15.

FOOD

Boar and other wild game are San Gimignano's specialities, but the town caters to less-daring palates with mainstream Tuscan fare at fairly high prices. Whether you're looking to save or simply to savor, try the **open-air market** in P. del Duomo (Thurs. morning). A small **market** sells cheap, filling sandwiches and take-out pasta, salads, and drinks at Via S. Matteo, 19. (Open Mon.-Sat. 8am-1:30pm and 4-8pm.) A good place to purchase the famous *Vernaccia di San Gimignano*, a light white wine with a hint of sweetness, is **La Buca**, Via San Giovanni, 16 (tel. 94 04 07)—look for the stuffed boar. This cooperative also specializes in terrific sausages and meats, all made at its own farm. The boar sausage *al pignoli* is especially delicious (L3000 per *etto*) and the store plays a highly educational video that depicts all the stages of its production, from little piglet to luncheon meat. (Open Mon.-Sat. 9:30am-1pm and 3-7:30pm; Sun. 2-7:30pm.)

Gustavo Enoteca, Via San Matteo, 29, down the hill from P. del Duomo. A great place to sample a glass of *vernaccia* (L2000) and a heavenly tomato *bruschetta* (L3500). The *panini* (L4000), like the one with fennel and locally made salami, are equally terrific. Open daily 8am-8pm.

La Stella, Via Matteo, 75 (tel. 94 04 44). Tasty and reasonably priced. *Gnocchi all'etrusca* (with tomatoes, cream, and cheese) L7000. *Menù* includes a pasta dish, a hearty *bistecca di morales*, potatoes, L23,500. Open Thurs.-Tues. noon-2:30pm and 7-9:30pm. AmEx, MC, Visa.

Pizzeria Perucà, Via Capassi, 16 (tel. 94 31 36). Great food, hidden in a small side street behind Via Matteo. *Menù* L22,000. Pizza from L6500. Open Fri.-Wed. 12:15-2:30pm and 7-10:30pm.

SIGHTS AND ENTERTAINMENT

Famous as the *Città delle belle torri* (City of Beautiful Towers), San Gimignano always had enough tourist appeal that no artist could turn down a commission. They came in droves, and the resulting collection of 14th- and 15th-century works luminously (and sometimes ludicrously) complements San Gimignano's asymmetric cityscape. The city rightly treats itself as a unified work of art—one ticket (L16,000; available at any museum or tourist sight) allows entry to almost all of San Gimignano's sights.

Via San Giovanni, the principal street, runs from the city gate to **Piazza della Cisterna.** The triangular *piazza*, surrounded by towers and *palazzi*, adjoins **Piazza del Duomo,** site of the impressive tower of the **Palazzo del Podestà.** To its left is the **Palazzo del Popolo,** riddled with tunnels and intricate *loggie*. (Open Tues.-Sun. 9am-7:30pm.) To the right of the *palazzo* rises its **Torre Grossa,** the highest tower in town and the only one you can ascend; it's well worth the climb. But beware—the huge bell rings every day at noon. (Open April-Sept. daily 9:30am-7:30pm; Oct.-March Tues.-Sun. 9:30am-1:30pm and 2:30-4:30pm. Admission L7000.) On the left stand the twin towers of the Ardinghelli, truncated thanks to a zoning ordinance that prohibited the building of structures higher than the Torre Grossa.

Within the Palazzo del Popolo, the frescoed medieval courtyard leads to the **Sala di Dante.** The poet spoke here in 1299 as the ambassador from Florence, hoping to convince the city to join the Guelph league. On the walls, Lippo Memmi's sparkling *Maestà* blesses the accompanying 14th-century scenes of hunting and tournament pageantry. In the **Museo Civico** Taddeo di Bartolo's altarpiece, *The Story of San Gimignano,* teaches proper respect for this bishop of Modena. San Gimignano calmed oceans, exorcised demons, saved the city from the Goths, and even fought the devil himself with his trusty cross. The museum maintains an excellent collection of other Sienese and Florentine works, most notably Filippino Lippi's *Annunciation,* crafted in two circular panels, and Pinturicchio's serene *Madonna in Glory.* The best part of the museum is the room of wedding frescoes off the stairs, a unique series of 14th-century scenes that take a couple from initial courtship to a shared bath and their wedding bed. (Open April-Sept. daily 9:30am-7:30pm; Oct.-March Tues.-Sun. 9:30am-1:30pm and 2:30-4:30pm. Museum admission L7000. Museum and tower L12,000.)

The **Piazza del Duomo** shelters the **Collegiata,** whose bare façade hides a Romanesque interior covered with exceptional Renaissance frescoes. Start with the **Chapel of Santa Fina** off the right aisle (open same hours as Museo Civico), a marvel of Renaissance harmony designed by Giuliano and Benedetto Maiano and adorned by Ghirlandaio's splendid frescoes. (Chapel open April-Sept. 9:30am-12:30pm and 3-6pm; Oct.-March 9:30am-12:30pm and 3-5:30pm. Admission L3000.) In the main church, Bartolo di Fredi painted jewel-like frescoes depicting Old Testament scenes along the north aisle, while Barna da Siena provided the appropriate, if less enthusiastic, New Testament counterparts along the south aisle. Taddeo di Bartolo's *Last Judgement* frescoes over the entrance are unfortunately a bit faded. At the back wall, laugh and cry at sight of St. Bartholomew, decked out in his BVDs and legions of piercing arrows. (Open daily 9am-12:30pm and 3-6pm.)

Next to the *duomo,* in Piazza delle Erbe, sits the **Museum of Etruscan Art and Sacred Art.** Here you'll find a variety of displays with local origins, including artifacts found in the area, Etruscan religious art from the *duomo,* and other paintings. (Open daily 9:30am-8pm; in winter Tues.-Sun. 9:30am-12:30pm and 2:30-5:30pm. Admission L7000.) One cheery addition to the San Gimignano museum scene is the **Museo di Criminologia Medioevale,** (tel. 94 22 43) Via del Castello, home to an inventive collection of antique instruments of torture. (Open daily 10am-1pm and 2-7pm. Admission L8000, students L5000.)

Dinner finishes early in the hills, and the *passeggiata* along Via San Giovanni and Via San Matteo (passing by the towers of the Salvucci clan) provides the principal entertainment. During the summer, pass the evening under the stars at the **rocca** (fortress), where you can enjoy movies at San Gimignano's outdoor theater (L7000; weekly showings during July and Aug.; check with the tourist office for info).

■■■ FLORENCE (FIRENZE)

Florence's greatest native son, Dante Alighieri, bitterly bemoaned his hometown's greed and penchant for warfare. But Dante died before the High Renaissance began; since then, nearly every visitor to walk Florence's cobblestone streets has fallen in love with the city. Henry James, Stendhal, Albert Camus, and even cranky Mark Twain were all won over by Florence's immense beauty. The city drapes itself languidly along the Arno, with picture-perfect bridges connecting the older *centro* to the Oltrarno district. Streets weave and wind past churches, medieval fortresses, and *palazzi.* While Florence carefully maintains its Renaissance architecture and culture, it is not locked in time; the city still pulses with life, from scurrying students in the university quarter to the businessmen who whiz by on Vespas.

Fueled by an innovative banking system, the city evolved from a booming 13th century wool- and silk-trading town into the archetype of political experimentation and artistic rebirth. Periodic civil wars disrupted Florentine civic life until the ascendancy of the Medici clan and the establishment of peace in the 15th century under

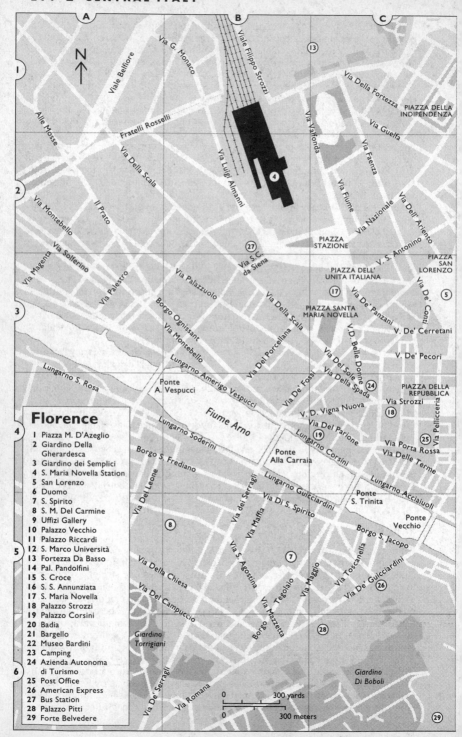

N

A　　　　　B　　　　　C

Via G. Monaco
Viale Belfiore
Viale Filippo Strozzi
Via Della Fortezza
PIAZZA DELLA
INDIPENDENZA
13
Fratelli Rosselli
Alle Mosse
Via Guelfa
Via Vallonda
Via Della Scala
Via Faenza
Via Luigi Alamanni
Via Fiume
4
Il Prato
Via Montebello
Via Solferino
Via Magenta
Via Palestro
Via Nazionale
Via Dell' Ariento
PIAZZA
STAZIONE
27
Via S.C.
da Siena
V. S. Antonino
PIAZZA
SAN
LORENZO
PIAZZA DELL'
UNITA ITALIANA
17
Via De' Conti
5
Via Palazzuolo
Via Del Porcellana
Via Della Scala
Via De' Panzani
PIAZZA SANTA
MARIA NOVELLA
V.D. Belle Donne
V. De' Cerretani
Borgo Ognissant
Via Montebello
Via Del Sole
V. De' Pecori
Lungarno Amerigo Vespucci
Lungarno S. Rosa
Via Del Sole
Via Della Spada
Via De' Fossi
24
PIAZZA DELLA
REPUBBLICA
Ponte
A. Vespucci
Via Strozzi
Via Pellicceria
Fiume Arno
V. D. Vigna Nuova
18
Lungarno Soderini
Via Del Parione
19
Via Porta Rossa
25
Borgo S. Frediano
Lungarno Corsini
Via Delle Terme
Ponte
Alla Carraia
Lungarno Acciaiuoli
Via Del Leone
Lungarno Guicciardini
Ponte
S. Trinita
Via Dei Serragli
Via Di S. Spirito
8
Ponte
Vecchio
Via Maffia
Borgo S. Jacopo
Via Della Chiesa
Via S. Agostina
7
Via Toscanella
Via Maggio
Via De' Guicciardini
26
Via Del Campuccio
Via Tegolaio
Borgo Mazzetta
Giardino
Torrigiani
28
Via De' Serragli
Giardino
Di Boboli
Via Romana
29

Florence

0 ___ 300 yards
0 ___ 300 meters

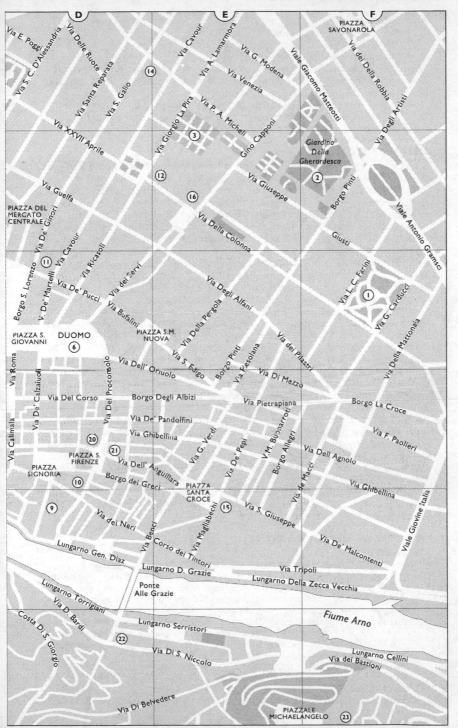

FLORENCE

Lorenzo the Magnificent. At this time, Renaissance culture began its most splendid years of production. At its apex in the mid-15th century, Florence was the unchallenged European capital of painting, sculpture, architecture, medicine, astronomy, physics, commerce, and political thought.

Since the Renaissance, Florentines have taken great care to preserve the cultural heritage of their city. When the Arno flooded in 1966, swamping Santa Croce and the Uffizi, Florentines left their sinking apartments to rescue paintings, sculptures, and books. Today, Florence is overrun by tourists clamoring for a glimpse of the David, but the locals don't seem to mind. They, of all people, understand the allure of one of the world's most beautiful cities.

ORIENTATION

Florence is easily accessible by train from Milan, Bologna, Venice, Rome, and just about any city in Italy. From Stazione Santa Maria Novella, it's a short walk on Via de' Panzani and then left on Via de Cerrentari to the center of Florence. This area, the heart of the city, is bordered by the *duomo* on the north, the Arno River on the south, and the Bargello and Palazzo Strozzi on the east and west.

Major arteries radiate from the *duomo* and its two *piazze:* **Piazza San Giovanni** encircling the baptistery and **Piazza del Duomo** around the cathedral. A lively pedestrian walkway, **Via dei Calzaiuoli**, runs from the *duomo* to **Piazza Signoria** in the direction of the Arno. Parallel to Via dei Calzaiuoli on the west (the baptistery end of the square), **Via Roma** leads from Piazza S. Giovanni through **Piazza della Repubblica** (the city's largest open space) to the **Ponte Vecchio**, which spans the Arno to the **Oltrarno** district. Parallel to Via dei Calzaiuoli on the east, Via del Proconsolo runs to the **Badia** and the **Bargello**. Heading north (away from the river) from P. S. Giovanni, Borgo San Lorenzo runs to **Piazza San Lorenzo** and Via dei Servi leads to **Piazza SS. Annunziata**.

For guidance through Florence's tangled center, grab a **free map** (ask for the one with the street index) from one of the tourist offices (see Practical Information below for locations). Artistic and historical sights are scattered throughout Florence, but few sights are out of walking distance; weary sightseers can take orange ATAF city buses almost anywhere. **Florence's streets are numbered in red and black sequences.** Red numbers are for commercial establishments and black numbers (occasionally blue) denote residential addresses (including most sights and hotels). Black addresses appear here as a numeral only, while red addresses are indicated by a number followed by an "r." The two sequences rarely coincide; if you get to an address and it's not what you're looking for, you've probably got the wrong color.

As in the rest of Italy, most establishments close for two to four hours in the afternoon. On major holidays, including the festival of Florence's patron saint San Giovanni (June 24), everything but the occasional bar closes.

Let's Go: Italy tries to help you by including the **map grid coordinates** of our Florence listings whenever possible.

PRACTICAL INFORMATION

Tourist Offices:

Consorzio I.T.A. (B2; tel. 28 28 93 and 21 95 37), in the train station by track #16, next to the pharmacy. Give them a price range and they'll find you a room, though probably near the station and perhaps not the best value. No booking by phone. L3000-10,000 commission. They also have a bulletin board for travelers trying to contact each other. No train info, though. Open daily 8:30am-9pm.

Informazione Turistica, inside the squat, round, glass-and-concrete building outside the train station (exit by track #16). No booking service, but plenty of up-to-date info on entertainment and cultural events. Open April-Oct. daily 9am-7pm; Nov.-March 9am-2pm.

APT at Via Cavour, 1r (D3; tel. 29 08 32). Open Mon.-Sat. 8am-7pm. Other offices at Piazzetta Guelfa, 3 (tel. 28 40 15) and Via Martelli, 6 (D3; tel. 21 38 93). Open Mon.-Sat. 9am-3pm, Sun. (summer only) 8:15am-1:15pm.

Consortium Italian Tourist Association, Viale Gramsci, 9a (tel. 247 82 31).

Police: Questura (headquarters), Via Zara, 2 (D0-1; tel. 497 71). On weekends or after hours go around the corner to Via Duca D'Aosta. English-speaking personnel usually available. **Ufficio Stranieri** (for visa, work-permit, or passport problems), at the same address and phone number.

Post Office: (C4; tel. 21 61 22) on Via Pellicceria off P. della Repubblica. Stamps at windows #21 and 22, or from the vending machines as you enter; *fermo posta* at windows #23 and 24. To send packages, go to the back of the building to Via dei Sassetti, 4 (C4). Open Mon.-Fri. 8:15am-6pm, Sat. 8:15am-12:30pm. **Telegram** office in front open 24 hrs. **Postal Code:** 50100.

Telephones: Telecom (SIP) phones, at the post office. For assisted or metered calls, try the **Telecom Office,** at Via Cavour, 21r (D2-3), open daily 8am-9:45pm. **Telephone Code:** 055.

Budget Travel: S.T.S.-Student Travel Service, Via Zanetti, 18r (C3; tel. 28 41 83). Student-discounted train, plane, and bus tickets. Open Mon.-Fri. 9:30am-12:30pm and 3:30-6:30pm, Sat. 9:30am-12:30pm. **CTS,** Via Ginori, 25r (D2; tel. 28 95 70). No Eurail passes, but just about everything else, including Transalpino tickets, discount airfares, car rentals, organized trips, and ISICs. Get there *early* or expect to wait. Open Mon.-Fri. 9am-1pm and 2:30-6pm, Sat. 9am-noon.

Tour Guides: Ufficio Guide Turistiche, Viale Gramsci, 9/A (tel. 247 81 88). English-speaking guides. Three-hr. tour (no shipwreck with Gilligan, though) L120,000 for any group up to 18 people.

Consulates: U.S., Lungarno Vespucci, 38 (A3; tel. 239 82 76), at Via Palestro near the station. Open Mon.-Fri. 8:30am-noon and 2-4pm. **U.K.,** Lungarno Corsini, 2 (B-C4; tel. 28 41 33). Open Mon.-Fri. 9:30am-12:30pm and 2:30-4:30pm. Call the U.K. Embassy in Rome for after-hours emergencies (tel. (06) 475 55 51). Canadians, Australians, and New Zealanders should contact their consulates in Rome and Milan.

Currency Exchange: Local banks have the best exchange rates. Most open Mon.-Fri. 8:20am-1:20pm and 2:45-3:45pm. Some banks open Sat. mornings. **Cassa di Risparmio di Firenze** now has automatic tellers that exchange money at: Via de' Bardi, 73r (D5-6); Via de' Tornabuoni, 23r (C4); Via degli Speziali, 16r (D4); and Via dei Servi, 40r (D3-E2). Open 24 hrs. There are **Banca di Roma ATMs,** which accept Cirrus, at Piazza Gaetano Salvemini (E4) and on the corner of Via de' Serragli and Lungarno Guicciardini (B4).

American Express: Via Dante Alighieri, 20-22r (D4; tel. 50 981). From the *duomo*, walk down Via dei Calzaiuoli; turn left onto Via dei Tavolini. AmEx is on the little *piazza* at its end. Cashes personal checks for cardholders. They also hold mail (free for card- and checkholders, L3000 per inquiry for everyone else, whether you have mail or not). L3000 to leave messages. L10,000 to forward mail. Does not accept wired money. Open Mon.-Fri. 9am-5:30pm, Sat. 9am-12:30pm.

Flights: Amerigo Vespucci Airport, in the Florentine suburb of **Peretola** (tel. 33 34 90). Largely domestic and charter flights. SITA runs regular buses (L6000) to the airport from their station at Via S. Caterina da Siena, 157 (tel. 48 36 51). **Galileo Galilei Airport** (tel. (050) 50 07 07), in Pisa. Take the airport express from the Florence train station (every hr., 5:55am-8pm, 1hr., L6500). In Florence, call for flight information (tel. 27 88) or ask at the "air terminal" (tel. 21 60 73) at platform #5 in the Florence train station, where you can also check in, register baggage, and get an embarkation card for L3000 (open daily 7am-8pm). Direct train service to Rome's Fiumicino airport departs from track #16.

Trains: Santa Maria Novella Station, (B2) near the center of town. Info office (tel. 27 87 85) open daily 7am-9pm. The wait can be long, and you need to take a number from the machine on the left as you enter. You can also use the bright-yellow (English-speaking) computers to plan your trip. Every hr. to: Bologna (1hr., L13,200); Siena (1½hr, L8500); Venice (3hr., L31,600); Milan (3½hr., L36,600); and Rome (2½hr., L36,200; prices for IC trains). **Trains to and from Rome arrive/depart from the Campo di Marte station** on the east side of town. Bus #19 connects the 2 stations about every 20min. around the clock (25min.). **Luggage Storage:** by track #16. Open daily 4:30am-1:30am. L1500. **Lost Property:** For objects left on a train, go to the **Ufficio Oggetti Rinvenuti** (tel. 235 21 90), next to the baggage deposit.

FLORENCE

Buses: SITA, Via Santa Caterina da Siena, 15r (B3; Mon.-Fri. tel. 48 36 51; Sat.-Sun. tel. 21 14 87). Frequent buses to: Siena (2hr., L10,000), San Gimignano (13 per day, L9000), Poggibonsi (L6300), Arezzo (5 per day, L10,000), and Volterra (6 per day, L11,000). **CAP,** Via Nazionale, 4 (tel. 21 46 37), to Prato (L2700). **LAZZI,** P. Via Stazione, 4-6r (tel. 21 51 54), to Pisa (L9500), Prato (L2700), Lucca (L7600), and Pistoia (L5700). Also services to Rome and Naples.

Metropolitan Transport: Orange ATAF city buses traverse all of Florence, generally between 6am and 1am, although schedules vary by line. Tickets: L1400 for 1hr., no matter how many buses you take, L2000 for 2hr., and L5400 for 4 tickets. A 7-day pass costs L27,000. Tickets must be bought *before boarding* and validated by the punch-machine on board; if you're caught without one, it's a L50,000 fine, no excuses; many bus stops are equipped with ticket-vending machines, but these take coins only. **ATAF information and ticket office** is outside the train station (B2; tel. 58 05 28), open daily 7am-3pm; otherwise, you can buy tickets at most kiosks and *tabacchi*. Ask at the office for a **bus map.** City bus #7 goes to Fiesole, #10 to Settignano.

Taxis: tel. 43 90, or 47 98, or 42 42. Taxi stands are outside the train station.

Car Rental: Hertz, Via Finiguerra, 17 (B3; tel. 239 82 05). Must be 23 or older. Open Mon.-Fri. 8am-7pm, Sat. 8am-1pm and 2-7pm., Sun. 8am-1pm. Prices start around L110,000 per day. **Avis** (tel. 31 55 88) and **Maggiore** (tel. 31 12 56) are both at the airport and offer similar rates.

Parking: Most hotels in the city center do not offer parking, and leaving your car in the street is a sure way to get it towed. Many small garages (look for a blue sign with a "P") dot the city, but these keep sporadic hours. One underground lot at the train station, and one beneath Piazza della Libertà, open daily 6:30am-1am.

Towed-Car Retrieval: Via Circondaria, 16 (tel. 35 52 31).

Hitchhiking: Hitchers take the A-1 north to Bologna and Milan or the A-11 northwest to the Riviera and Genoa, or take bus #29, 30, or 35 from the station to the feeder near Peretola. For the A-1 south to Rome and the extension to Siena, they take bus #31 or 32 from the station to exit #23, Firenze Sud. As always, **hitchhiking is extremely risky.** The **International Lift Center,** Corso Tintori, 39 (E5; tel. 28 06 21), matches passengers with drivers for a fee. Open Mon.-Sat. 9am-7:30pm, Sun. noon-3pm.

Bike and Moped Rental: I Bike Italy (tel. 66 75 29). Take a tour of the Tuscan hills on a bike. (See Alternatives to Tourism, page 27.) **Promotourist,** Via B. Bandinelli, 43 (tel. 70 18 63). **Program,** Borgo Ognissanti, 135r (B3-4; tel. 28 29 16). **Ciao and Basta,** Via Alamanni (B2), under the Central Station (tel. 21 33 07). **MotoRent,** Via S. Zanobi, 9r (C-D2; tel. 49 01 13). Bikes start at L9000 per 3hr., L20,000 per day. Mountain bikes run about L35,000 per day. Mopeds begin at L9000 per hr., L40,000 per day, L210,000 per week. No license necessary, but bring ID indicating you are at least 16.

Laundry: Wash and Dry Lavarapido, Via dei Servi, 105 (D3-E2), two blocks from the *duomo*, Via della Scala 52/54 (B2), Via dei Serragli 87r (B5), and Viale Morgagni 21r. Self-service L13,000 for wash, dry, and detergent. Open daily 8am-10pm, last wash 9pm. **Elensec,** Via dei Neri, 46r (D5; tel. 28 37 47), near P. San Remigio. L4000 per kg (3kg. min.). Open Mon.-Fri. 8:30am-1pm and 3:30-7:30pm.

Public Toilets: in the Mercato Centrale (upstairs; D2), Palazzo Vecchio (D4), Palazzo Pitti (C6), and the train stations. L500 includes a lovely paper towel.

Public Baths: Bagno S. Agostino, Via S. Agostino, 8 (B5; tel. 28 44 82), off P. Santo Spirito. Bath L3500. Soap and towel L2000. Open Tues. and Thurs. 3-6pm, Fri.-Sat. 8am-12:30pm.

Gym: Gymnasium, Via Palazzuolo, 49r (A2-B3; tel. 29 33 08). Latest in workout equipment, daily step aerobics, body building, and stretching classes. L20,000 per day. L160,000 per month.

Swimming Pools: Bellariva, Lungarno Colombo, 6 (tel. 67 75 21). Bus #14 from the station or a 15min. walk upstream along the Arno. Open June-Sept. daily 10am-6pm. Free. **Costoli,** Viale Paoli (tel. 67 57 44), in a huge sports complex at Campo di Marte. Take bus #17 from P. Unità toward the *duomo*. Arrive early. Open daily 10am-6pm. Admission June-Sept. L6000, children L2000, over 60 free.

Libraries: Biblioteca Marucelliana, Via Cavour, 43 (D2), a communal library 2min. from the Duomo. Open Mon.-Fri. 9am-7pm, Sat. 9am-1pm. **Biblioteca Nazionale,** P. D. Cavalleggeri (E5), the largest library in Florence, requires you to go through a time-consuming bureaucratic process, but the reading rooms are beautiful and you can request books from the extensive collection. Open Mon.-Fri. 9am-7:30pm and Sat. 9am-1pm. **Biblioteca Storia dell'Arte,** Via della Pergora, 37, a beautiful library focusing on art history. Open Mon.-Fri. 8am-2pm.
English Bookstores: After Dark, Via Ginori, 37r (D2; tel. 29 42 03). New English books and magazines. Open Mon.-Fri. 10am-1:30pm and 3-7pm, Sat. 10am-1:30pm. **BM Bookstore,** Borgo Ognissanti, 4r (B3-4; tel. 29 45 75). No used books, but great selection. Stocks textbooks for American study-abroad programs. Open Mon.-Sat. 9am-1pm and 3:30-7:30pm, Sun. 9am-1pm; Nov.-Feb. closed Sun. **Paperback Exchange,** Via Fiesolana, 31r (E3-4; tel. 247 81 54). Open Mon.-Sat. 9am-1pm and 3:30-7:30pm; mid-Nov. to mid-March closed Mon. MC, Visa.
Bulletin Boards: Listings of people seeking Anglophone roommates, English teachers, baby-sitters and notices of Anglophone religious, musical, and theatrical activities (see also The Paperback Exchange under Bookstores above): **The American Church,** Via Rucellai, 16 (A-B2; tel. 29 44 17), near the train station off Via della Scala. Open Mon., Wed., Fri. 9am-12:30pm and Sun. 9-11am. **The British Institute,** Via Tornabuoni, 2 (C3-4), between P. Santa Novella and P. della Repubblica. **CarLie's American Bakery,** Via Brache, 12r (D5; tel. 12 51 37), near Via dei Neri. Open Sept.-July 15 Mon.-Sat. 8am-noon and 4-7pm. **La Raccolta,** Via Leopardi 10 (tel. 247 90 68). A center for alternative activities with listings for roommates, apartments, activities, and classes.
Religious Services:
 Anglican: St. Mark's Church of England, Via Maggio, 16 (tel. 29 47 64). Sun. 9am and 10:30am.
 Catholic: In English at the *duomo* (D3), Sat. 5pm.
 Episcopal: The American Church, Via Bernardo Rucellai, 9 (A-B2; tel. 29 44 17). Services Sun. 9am and 11am.
 Jewish: Tempio Israelito, Via Farini, 4 (F3; tel. 24 52 52). Sabbath services Fri. at sunset, Sat. 8am, some Fridays 8pm.
 Muslim: Centro Culturale Islamico, P. degli Scarlatti, 1 (tel. 238 14 11).
Ticket Agency: Box office at Via della Pergola, 10r (E3; tel. 24 23 61; fax 234 02 57). Advance booking service. Open Mon.-Sat. 10am-8pm.
Late-Night Pharmacies: Farmacia Comunale (B2; tel. 28 94 35), at the train station by track #16, **Molteni,** Via dei Calzaiuoli, 7r (D3-4; tel. 28 94 90). **Taverna,** P. S. Giovanni, 20r (tel. 28 40 13). All open 24 hrs.
Legal Assistance: SOS Turista, Via Cavour, 1r (D3; tel. 276 03 82). Open April-Oct. 9:30am-12:30pm and 3-6pm.
Medical Assistance: Misericordia, P. del Duomo, 20 (D3; tel. 21 22 22 or 21 95 55). Call for ambulance. **Tourist Medical Service,** Via Lorenzo il Magnifico, 59 (tel. 47 54 11). A group of general practitioners and specialists with someone on call 24 hrs. Housecalls about L80,000. **Medical First Aid:** tel. 47 48 91. **Drug Addiction Service:** tel. 48 30 10. A list of French- and English-speaking doctors is available from the U.S. consulate.
Emergency: tel. 113.

ACCOMMODATIONS

Florence abounds with one-star *pensione* and private *affitta camere*. If you arrive late in the afternoon, check with the accommodations service at the train station to find out who still has room and at what prices. (Sleeping in the train stations, streets, or parks is a poor idea—police strongly discourage it.) The best places go early, so make reservations (*prenotazioni*) far in advance, especially if you plan to visit at Easter or in summer. The vast majority of *pensioni* prefer to take written reservations with at least one night's deposit in the form of a postal money order.

Some warnings about hotels in Florence: If you do make a reservation, keep it. Hotel owners have recently become disgruntled with travelers who make reservations and don't show, and no longer accept reservations for this reason. As a courtesy to hotel owners and fellow travelers (who get turned away when a hotel is "reserved" to capacity), either be sure to keep the reservation or cancel as soon as you know you're not going to take it. Also, **expect higher rates than those listed here.** Don't embarrass hotel owners or yourself by insisting on the infallibility of *Let's Go* or any other guide.

If you have any complaints, talk first to the proprietor, and then to the **Ufficio Controllo Alberghi,** Via Cavour, 37 (D2; tel. 276 01). Hotel prices are strictly regulated by the municipal government; proprietors can charge neither more nor less than the approved range for their category. Prices are uniformly raised by 5% or so every year, with the increase taking effect in March or April.

The city's best budget lodgings can be found at the **Ostello Archi Rossi** near the train station and at **Pensionato Pio X** and **Istituto Gould** in the Oltrarno, but clean and inexpensive lodgings are dispersed throughout the city. **Long-term housing** can be secured easily in Florence. If you plan on staying a month or more, check the classified ads in *Le Pulce,* a bi-weekly paper (L3500) that has apartment, sublet, and roommate listings or **Grillo Fiorentino,** a free monthly local paper (call 48 77 10 for more info). Prices range from L350,000 to L800,000 per month. If you only want to stay a month, try to strike a bargain with someone who's looking for a roommate; he/she might be willing to take you short-term while seeking a permanent roomie. Also check the **bulletin boards** (see Practical Information above).

Hostels

Ostello Archi Rossi, Via Faenza, 94r (C2; tel. 29 08 04; fax 230 26 01), only 2 blocks from the train station. Exit left from the station onto Via Nazionale and turn left at Via Faenza. Look for the blue neon *"ostello"* sign. A new hostel with a TV room and a courtyard patio. The walls of the lobby are decorated floor-to-ceiling with colorful graffiti. Lockout 9:30am-2:30pm. Curfew 12:30am. No breakfast. L20,000 per person in a room with 5-6 beds; L23,000 in a room with bath. Very popular. Management doesn't accept phone reservations, so arrive by noon to get a bed in summer. Wheelchair accessible.

Istituto Gould, Via dei Serragli, 49 (B5; tel. 21 25 76), in the Oltrarno. Leave the station by track #16, turn right and walk to P. della Stazione. Go straight down Via degli Avelli, with the church Santa Maria Novella on your immediate right. Cross P. Sta. Maria Novella and continue straight down Via dei Fossi, over the Ponte alla Carraia, and down Via dei Serragli (15min.). Or take bus #36 or 37 from the station to the 1st stop across the river. One of the best lodgings in Florence: staff is happy to answer questions and the sunny rooms are spotless. All the profits support a local orphanage. The *palazzo* itself is cool and cavernous, with a large courtyard. There are only two drawbacks: it's impossible to check in or out on Saturday afternoons and Sundays (the office is closed) and the rooms overlooking the street are often noisy. No curfew, no lock-out, and no charge for showers. Office open Mon.-Fri. 9am-1pm and 3-7pm, Sat. 9am-1pm. **Prices are charged per person.** Singles with bath L44,000. Doubles L30,000, with bath L32,000. Triples with bath L29,000. Quads with bath L26,000. Quints with bath L23,000.

Pensionato Pio X, Via dei Serragli, 106 (B5; tel. 22 50 44). Follow the directions to the Istituto Gould (above) then walk a few more blocks down the street. Quiet, no daytime lock-out, gregarious management, and only 4 or 5 beds per room. Clean rooms and bathrooms. Guests can use the nearby Instituto Artigianelli, V. dei Serragli, 104, to get in a quick aerobics or *aikido* class. Two-day min. stay, 5-day max. stay. Check-out 9am. Curfew midnight. L20,000 per person; showers included, but L3000 more for a room with bath. No reservations. Usually full in summertime, but turnover is high. On weekends, arrive before 9am.

Ostello della Gioventù Europa Villa Camerata (HI), Viale Augusto Righi, 2-4 (tel. 60 14 51), northeast of town. Leave the station by track #5, then take bus #17B (20-30min.). You can also catch this bus from P. del Duomo. In a gorgeous villa with *loggia* and gardens. Tidy and popular, though far away. Reception open Mon.-Fri. 9am-1pm and 3-7pm. Check-out 9am. Curfew midnight. L20,000 per person. L15,000 to stay in beds in tents outside without breakfast, L5000 extra per night for those without hostel card. Sheets and breakfast included. Dinner L12,000. Open 2-11:30pm; off-season 3-10:30pm. Reserve by letter only.

Suore Oblate dello Spirito Santo, Via Nazionale, 8 (C2; tel. 239 82 02), near the station. Numbers on Via Nazionale are tricky; ask along the street for help. The nuns take in women, married couples, and families; the atmosphere is almost oppressively peaceful. Thirty beds in huge rooms with modern bathrooms and good security. Curfew 11pm. Doubles with bath L76,000. Triples and quads L28,000 per person. Breakfast included. Phone reservations accepted; written are preferred. Open July-Oct. 15.

Ostello Santa Monaca, Via S. Monaca, 6 (B5; tel. 26 83 38), off Via dei Serragli near Istituto Gould in the Oltrarno. This hostel tends to crowd many beds (about 10) into high-ceilinged rooms, but it's away from the masses on the other side of the river. Curfew 1am. Shower included. Sign-up sheet posted 9:30am-1pm, with as many spaces as there are beds open. No reservations. Kitchen facilities, but no utensils. No meals in-house, but sells inexpensive tickets to a nearby restaurant. Self-service laundry, L12,000 per 5kg. Seven-day max. stay. L18,000 per person, shower included. Open 6-9:30am and 4pm-12:30am.

Piazza Santa Maria Novella and Environs

Standing in front of the station, you will see the back of the Basilica of Santa Maria Novella. Beyond the church and in the immediate vicinity you'll find budget accommodations galore. Ask for rooms overlooking the *piazza.* In this area you'll be close to the *duomo* and *centro,* and it's a short walk from the station.

Pensione La Mia Casa, P. Santa Maria Novella, 23 (C3; tel. 21 30 61). A 17th-century *palazzo* with clean rooms, fabric-covered walls, and stunning frescoes on some ceilings. Three hundred years and innumerable American backpackers have worn it down a bit. Every night, the personable proprietor screens a documentary in English on Florence (8pm; free) and a relatively recent American film (9pm). Curfew midnight. Singles L33,000. Doubles L47,000, with bath L50,000. Triples L63,000, with bath L78,000. Quads L80,000, with bath L98,000. Breakfast L6000. Reservations taken, but you must arrive before 1pm.

Locanda La Romagnola and **Soggiorno Gigliola,** Via della Scala, 40 (B2; tel. 21 15 97 and 28 79 81). Leave the station by track #5, walk across the street to V. S. Caterina da Siena, and turn right onto Via della Scala after a block. Simple rooms with plenty of space. Some rooms have frescoed ceilings or ornately carved beds. Curfew midnight. Singles L38,000, with bath L46,000. Doubles L60,000, with bath L70,000. Triples L87,000, with bath L96,000. May be closed Jan.-Feb.

Albergo Montreal, Via della Scala, 43 (B2; tel. 238 23 31). Clean and friendly, with a little lounge and TV. Wood-beamed ceilings and clean white walls. Ample rooms get plenty of light and noise. Curfew 1:30am. Singles L45,000. Doubles L70,000, with bath L75,000. Triples with bath L100,000. Quads with bath L120,000.

Hotel Visconti, P. Ottaviani, 1 (C3; tel. 21 38 77). Attempted neo-classical decor, with huge Grecian nudes. Friendly management serves breakfast (included) in the flowery courtyard. Open 24 hrs. Singles L50,000. Doubles L80,000, with bath L94,000. Triples L108,000, with bath L127,000.

Soggiorno Abaco, Via dei Banchi, 1 (C3; tel./fax 23 81 919). With S. Mara Novella behind you, walk to the end of the *piazza* onto Via dei Banchi. Six well-kept rooms have a medieval feel, with polished wood-beamed ceilings. All rooms have fans. Singles L60,000. Doubles L80,000, with bath L120,000. Triples with bath L100,000. Quads available on request. Laundry L5000 per load. Kitchen facilities 6000. No curfew. AmEx, MC, Visa.

Hotel Elite, Via della Scala, 12 (B3; tel. 21 53 95). Polished wood and brass edges enhance the carefully maintained rooms. Welcoming management speaks some

FLORENCE

English. Single with shower L80,000, with full bath L90,000. Doubles with shower L90,000, with full bath L110,000. Breakfast included.

Hotel Universo, P. Santa Maria Novella, 20 (C3; tel. 28 19 51). Central, clean, with TV lounge. Modern rooms done in soothing colors; Michelangelo sketches and funky armoires add flair. Singles L70,000, with bath L100,000. Doubles L90,000, with bath L110,000. Triples with bath L140,000. Quad on request L180,000. Breakfast L10,000. Prices drop 15-20% off-season. AmEx, MC, Visa.

Old City (Near the Duomo)

Though tourists flood the area, budget accommodations are available. Many offer great views of Florence's monuments, and others lie hidden in Renaissance *palazzi*.

Locanda Orchidea, Borgo degli Albizi, 11 (E4; tel. 248 03 46). Take a left off Via Proconsolo, which begins behind the Duomo. Dante's wife was born in this 12th-century *palazzo* built around a still-intact tower. Maria and Miranda preside over 7 cozy rooms, 4 of which open onto garden views. Closed 2 weeks in Aug.; reservations *strongly* recommended for the rest of the summer. Singles L45,000. Doubles L68,000. Triples L92,000.

Hotel Il Perseo, Via Cerretani, 1 (C3; tel. 21 25 04), one block from the *duomo* as you head toward P. Santa Maria Novella. Enthusiastic Australian owners welcome travelers to their bright, immaculate rooms, many of which have absolutely breathtaking views. Ample breakfast included. If they're full, they'll call around to find you a place to stay. Singles L55,000, with bath L65,000. Doubles L85,000, with bath L99,000. Triples L115,000, with bath L129,000. Quads L125,000, with bath L160,000. AmEx, MC, Visa with 3% surcharge.

Soggiorno Panerai, Via dei Servi, 36 (D3; tel./fax 26 41 03). Face the *duomo*'s entrance; Via dei Servi radiates out from the cathedral's left-hand corner. Serene, whitewashed rooms, each with a few antiques and wood beams. Every 2 rooms share a bath. Coffee machine and refrigerator available to guests. Doubles L55,000. Triples L70,000. Quads L85,000.

Soggiorno Bavaria, Borgo Albizi, 26 (E4; tel./fax 234 03 13). Clean, neat, newly renovated rooms on two floors of a cool, quiet 15th-century *palazzo*. Cavernous lounge on the second floor available to guests. Singles L40,000. Doubles L60,000, with bath L85,000. Triples L75,000, with bath L90,000. Breakfast L5000.

Soggiorno Brunori, Via del Proconsolo, 5 (D3; tel. 28 96 48), off P. del Duomo. Simple rooms with parquet floors, some with balconies looking onto Via del Proconsolo. Friendly management speaks English. Singles L34,000 (available in winter only). Doubles L72,000, with bath L78,000. Triples L87,000, with bath L110,000. Quads with bath L138,000.

Albergo Firenze, P. Donati, 4 (D4; tel. 21 42 03 and 26 83 01; fax 21 30 70), off Via del Corso. Modern, bright rooms fill this beautiful ancient *palazzo*. Central, but no tourist masses. Singles L50,000, with bath L60,000. Doubles L74,000, with bath L86,000. Triples L100,000, with bath L115,000. Breakfast included.

Albergo Costantini, Via dei Calzaiuoli, 13 (D4; tel./fax 21 51 28). A 14th-century *palazzo* with big, clean rooms and elegant frescoes. Singles L55,000, with bath L70,000. Doubles L74,000, with bath L100,000. Triples L135,000. Quads L170,000. Breakfast L15,000.

Hotel Maxim, Via dei Medici, 4 (D4; tel. 21 74 74; fax 28 37 29). Another entrance (with elevator) at Via dei Calzaiuoli, 11. Cheerful proprietor lets clean, sunny rooms filled with old-fashioned furniture. Single L75,000. Doubles L85,000, with bath L98,000. Triples L120,000, with bath L135,000. Laundry L18,000 per 4½kg. Some English spoken. Breakfast included. AmEx, MC, Visa.

Via Nazionale and Environs

As you leave the station, a left onto Via Nazionale will plunge you into a neighborhood swarming with travelers. If you can't avoid this quarter, at least walk away from its heart. Cheap establishments abound along **Via Nazionale, Via Faenza, Via Fiume, Via Guelfa,** and nearby streets—often there are several to a building.

Via Faenza, 56 (C2) houses 6 separate *pensioni*, all among the best budget lodgings in the city. From the station, follow the directions to Via Nazionale, on which Via Faenza is the 2nd intersection.

Pensione Azzi (tel. 21 38 06) styles itself as the *locanda degli artisti* (the artists' inn). Even the art-inept will enjoy the friendly management, large, immaculate rooms, and elegant dining room and terrace. Curfew 2am. Singles L55,000. Doubles L75,000, with bath L95,000. Triples L90,000, with bath L120,000. Quads L115,000, with bath L150,000. Breakfast L5000. AmEx, MC, Visa.

Albergo Merlini (tel. 21 28 48; fax 28 39 39). Light and airy with careful furnishings (the owner handpaints the designs on the bed frames). Some rooms have views of the *duomo*. Curfew 1am. Singles L45,000. Doubles L65,000, with bath L75,000. Triples/quads L25,000 *per person;* with bath L28,000-30,000 *per person*. Breakfast L8000-10,000.

Albergo Marini (tel. 28 48 24). Polished wood hallway leads to simple white rooms with brass beds. Curfew 12:40am. Singles L50,000, with bath L60,000. Doubles L70,000, with bath L90,000. Triples L90,000, with bath L110,000. Quads L110,000, with bath L130,000. Breakfast L7000. Coffee machine.

Albergo Anna (tel. 239 83 22). Lovely rooms—some with ceilings with frescoes, others with fans. Management and prices the same as the Albergo Azzi.

Albergo Armonia (tel. 21 11 46). Clean, with decoratively tiled walls. Pay in advance. Singles L55,000, with bath L60,000. Doubles L85,000, with bath L95,000. Triples L100,000. Quads L120,000.

Locanda Paola (tel. 21 36 82). Standard rooms, some with views of Florence. All rooms with bath. Doubles L90,000. Triples L129,000.

Hotel Nazionale, Via Nazionale, 22 (C1-2; tel. 238 22 03), near P. Indipendenza. Sunny, carpeted rooms and comfy beds with quilted spreads. Breakfast included. Door locks at midnight, but ask for the key. Singles L52,000, with bath L63,000. Doubles L79,000, with bath L92,000. Triples L105,000, with bath L124,000.

Pensione Daniel, Via Nazionale, 22 (C1-2; tel. 21 12 93), above the Hotel Nazionale. Basic, whitewashed rooms; recently renovated bathrooms. No curfew. Breakfast included. Doubles L55,000.

Via Faenza, 69 (C2):

Hotel Soggiorno d'Erico, 4th floor (tel./fax 21 33 31). Small rooms have nice views of the hills around Florence. Free kitchen use. Laundry L6000 per load (no dryer). Singles L40,000. Doubles L60,000. Triples L75,000. Quads L100,000.

Locanda Giovanna. Seven basic, well-kept rooms, some with garden views. Singles L40,000. Doubles L65,000.

Locanda Pino and **Albergo Nella,** on the 1st and 2nd floors. These twin establishments offer basic rooms at a good price. Singles L35,000. Doubles L55,000. Quads L25,000 per person. Free kitchen use. Laundry L5000 per load; no dryer.

Ausonia e Rimini, Via Nazionale, 24 (C2; tel. 49 65 47). Welcoming owners. The spotless rooms are nicely decorated and well-lit. Curfew 1am. Singles L55,000, with bath L65,000. Doubles L75,000, with bath L98,000. Triples L102,000, with bath L133,000. Breakfast included. AmEx, MC, Visa.

Kursaal, Via Nazionale, 24 (C2; tel. 49 63 24), downstairs from the Ausonia—same charming owners. A 2-star; take advantage of its lovingly decorated rooms while they're still affordable. Floral designs and Impressionist prints everywhere. Rooms toward the back are quieter. Singles L70,000, with bath L85,000. Doubles 98,000, with bath L108,000. Triples 126,000, with bath L164,000. Breakfast included. Handicapped accessible. AmEx, MC, Visa.

Near Piazza San Marco and the University Quarter

This area is considerably calmer and less tourist-ridden than its proximity to the center might suggest. Follow Via Nazionale from the station and take a right on Via Guelfa, which intersects with Via San Gallo and Via Cavour.

Hotel Tina, Via San Gallo, 31 (D2; tel. 48 35 19 or 48 35 93). Small *pensione* with high ceilings, artsy posters, new furniture, and bright bedspreads. Friendly owners who will find you another place if they're full. Gargantuan breakfast (conti-

FLORENCE

nentally speaking) included. Singles L45,000. Doubles L80,000, with bath L90,000. Triples with bath L100,000. Quads L125,000.

La Colomba, Via Cavour, 21 (D2-3; tel. 28 43 23). Sunny, white modernity. Windows peer across the Florentine roofscape. Italo-Australian proprietor Rosanna is helpful and friendly, and her husband often goes to the train station to recruit guests. Negotiable curfew 1:30am. Singles L65,000. Doubles L90,000, with bath L110,000. A *real* continental breakfast is included. MC, Visa.

Albergo Sampaoli, Via San Gallo, 14 (D2; tel. 28 48 34). A peaceful hotel with a proprietress who strives to make her *pensione* an American backpacker's "home away from home." A little faded, but expected renovations should brighten things up. Refrigerators on each floor. Singles L40,000. Doubles L50,000, with bath L70,000. Triples L90,000, with bath L105,000. Quads L100,000, with bath L140,000. No written reservations; call the night before you arrive.

Hotel Sofia, Via Cavour, 21 (D2-3; tel. 28 39 30), just upstairs from La Colomba. New furniture fills somewhat worn-out rooms. Curfew 1am. Singles L38,000. Doubles L55,000. Triples and quads L25,000 *per person.*

✹ **Hotel Globus,** Via Sant'Antonio, 24 (C2-3; tel. 21 10 62; fax 239 62 55). The sun shoots through rooms filled with bright bedspreads and wicker furniture. Young but professional, outgoing staff. Reception open 24 hrs. Singles L50,000, with bath L75,000. Doubles L80,000, with bath, L110,000. Triples L100,000, with bath L140,000. Rates much lower in the off-season. Breakfast L7000. Arrive before 2pm to keep a phone reservation. AmEx, MC, Visa.

Hotel San Marco, Via Cavour, 50 (D2; tel. 28 42 35). Three floors of modern, bright, airy rooms, highlighted by lively bedspreads. Curfew midnight, but you can negotiate for the key. Singles L50,000, with bath L65,000. Doubles L70,000, with bath L90,000. Triples with bath L115,000. Breakfast included. MC, Visa.

Hotel Enza, Via S. Zanobi, 45 (D2; tel. 49 09 90). From Via Nazionale, turn right on Via Guelfa—Via Zanobi is the first cross-street. Neat albeit mismatched rooms and clean sea-blue bathrooms, all tended by a friendly owner and her tiny dog. Singles L55,000. Doubles L75,000, with bath L90,000. Prices lower in winter.

In the Oltrarno

Only a 10-minute walk away from the *duomo,* but literally "outside the Arno," *pensioni* here offer a respite from the bustle of Florence's hub. Rooms are generally quiet and airy, and some overlook the Arno, tranquil *piazze,* or well-kept gardens.

Pensione Sorelle Bandini, P. Santo Spirito, 9 (B5; tel. 21 53 08). Old-world elegance and happy staff on the top floor of a large *palazzo.* Beautiful views of the Boboli gardens and the *duomo* from the sun-drenched *loggia.* Doubles L110,000, with bath L140,000. Triples L153,000, with bath L193,000. Quads L196,000, with bath L243,000. Some singles available in the off-season. Breakfast included. Often books to groups, who can organize half-pension.

Hotel La Scaletta, Via Guicciardini, 13 (C5; tel. 28 30 28), across the Ponte Vecchio towards the Pitti Palace. Rooftop terraces with spectacular views of the Boboli gardens and the city. Rooms with an English touch. Singles L70,000, with bath L80,000. Doubles L100,000, with bath L130,000. Breakfast included. MC, Visa.

Camping

Michelangelo, Viale Michelangelo, 80 (tel. 681 19 77), near P. Michelangelo. Take red or black bus #13 from the station (15min., last bus 11:55pm). Extremely crowded, but offers a spectacular panorama of Florence. Fantastic facilities, including a well-stocked food store and bar. They may post a *completo* sign or tell you the same by phone, but if you show up without a vehicle they will often let you in. L7000 per person, L7000 per tent, L5000 per car, L3500 per motorcycle. Open mid-March to Nov. 6am-midnight.

Villa Camerata, Viale A. Righi, 2/4 (tel. 60 03 15), outside the HI youth hostel on the #17B bus route. Catch the bus at the train station or at P. del Duomo. L6000 per person, L8000 per small tent. Open April-Oct. 7:30am-1pm and 3-9pm; if the office is closed, stake your site and come back later to register and pay.

Camping Panoramico, Via Peramonda, 1 (tel. 59 90 69), outside the city near Fiesole. Take bus #7 from the station to Fiesole (last buses 11:25pm and 12:30am, L1100). L9000 per person, L15,000 per tent, car included.

Villa Favard, Via Rocca Tedalda. Take bus #14. Free campsite. A fenced-in area with a security guard, though you should keep an eye on your valuables just the same. No hot water, but running cold water and toilets. Open in summer only.

FOOD

Florence's hearty Tuscan cuisine is rooted in the peasant fare of the surrounding countryside. Yet Tuscan food, typified by fresh ingredients and simple preparations, ranks among the world's best. White beans and olive oil are the two main staples of Florentine food, and most regional dishes come loaded with one or the other, if not both. Specialties include such *antipasti* as *bruschetta* (grilled Tuscan bread doused with olive oil and garlic, and sometimes topped with tomatoes and basil). For *primi* Florentines have perfected the Tuscan classics *minestra di fagioli* (a delicious white bean and garlic soup) and *ribollita* (a hearty bean, bread, and black cabbage concoction). Florence's classic *secondo* is *bistecca alla Fiorentina*, thick sirloin steak, each inch more succulent and expensive than the last. You will gain murmurs of admiration if you order it as Florentines do: *al sangue* (very rare—literally "bloody"). The best local cheese is *pecorino,* made from sheep's milk. Wine is another Florentine staple, and the local *chianti* is superb. Genuine *chianti classico,* the highest quality, commands a premium price. Hannibal Lecter recommends *chianti* with a meal of liver and fava beans. A liter of house wine typically costs L6000-7000 in Florence's *trattorie,* while stores sell bottles of delicious wine, even *chianti classico,* for as little as L4000. Florentine refinement shines through in the local dessert, *cantuccini di prato* (almond cookies made with tons of egg yolks) dipped in *vinsanto* (a rich dessert wine made from raisins).

For lunch, visit one of the many *rosticcerie gastronomie,* stop by the **students' mensa** at Via dei Servi, 52, or browse over pushcarts throughout the city. Buy your own fresh produce, tripe, and meats at the **Mercato Centrale,** between Via Nazionale and the back of San Lorenzo. (Open Mon.-Sat. 8am-1pm; Oct.-May Mon.-Sat. 6:30am-1pm and 4-8:30pm.) For staples, head to **Supermercato STANDA,** Via Pietrapiana, 1r (open Tues.-Sat. 8:30am-8pm, Mon. 3-8pm), or to any of the small markets throughout the city.

Vegetarians and health-conscious travelers will find several health-food markets operating throughout the city. The best are two stores named after the American book, **Sugar Blues.** The first is a 5-min. walk from the *duomo* at Via XXVII Aprile, 46r (tel. 48 36 66). (Open Mon.-Fri. 9am-1pm and 5-7pm, Sat. 9am-1pm.) The second is in the Oltrarno, next to the Institute Gould at Via dei Serragli, 57r (tel. 26 83 78). (Open Mon.-Fri. 8:30am-1:30pm and 4:30-8pm.) Both stock vitamins, algae, homemade take-out vegetable tarts, organic vegetables, and more, all with an Italian touch. Also try **La Raccolta,** at Via Leopardi, 10 (tel. 247 90 68), downstairs—a health food center and a meeting place for an alternative community in Florence. (Open Tues.-Fri. 10am-2pm and 4-7:30pm.)

A **kosher** restaurant sits on the second floor of the building to the right of the synagogue, at Via Farini, 2. **Il Cuscussú** (F3) serves kosher meals Sun.-Thurs. 12:30-2:30pm and 7:30-9:30pm. Friday dinner and Saturday lunch are served by reservation only. No Sunday dinner Oct.-March; no Saturday dinner March 16-Sept. 30. For information on **halal** vendors, ring the Centro Culturale Islamico. (Addresses and phone numbers under Religious Services page 219 above.)

Santa Maria Novella and Environs

Trattoria Contadino, Via Palazzuolo, 71r (B3; tel. 238 26 73). Filling, home-style meals; perfect for the working man and the weary traveler. Lunch and dinner *menù* (L14,000 and L15,000). Open Mon.-Sat. 11am-3pm and 7pm-midnight.

Trattoria da Giorgio, Via Palazzuolo, 100r (B3). Same deal as Contadino (L14,000 *menù,* same fixins). Short on atmosphere, long on quantity. Menu changes daily. Expect to wait. Open Mon.-Sat. 11am-3pm and 7-midnight.

Il Giardino, Via della Scala, 67 (B2; tel. 21 31 41). Enjoy a hearty portion of *penne* with eggplant (L6500) under the vines of the garden inside. The roast veal is enough to coax anyone on to a *secondo* (L9000). *Menù* L18,000. Cover L2000. Open Wed.-Mon. noon-3pm and 7-10pm. MC, Visa with 12% service charge.

Amon, Via Palazzuolo, 26-28r (B3; tel. 29 31 46). Cheerful, English-speaking Egyptian owner serves up scrumptious Middle Eastern food. Try the *moussaka,* a homemade, heated pita filled with baked eggplant and hot sauces, or the *foul,* which despite its name is a delicious concoction of beans and spices. English menu. Falafel L3500, shish kebab L4500. Stand-up or take-out only. Open Mon.-Sat. noon-3pm and 7-11pm.

La Scogliera, Via Palazzuolo, 80r (B3; tel. 21 02 57). Good pizza in an authentic Italian environment, heightened by the Italian cadences of the proprietor's English and the Italian folk music playing in the background. Try the pizza with spicy sausage (L8000). *Menù* L14,000. Dine in the small terrace outside and do some star-gazing. Open Mon.-Fri. noon-3pm and 6pm-midnight. AmEx, MC, Visa.

The Station and University Quarter

✓**Trattoria da Garibaldi,** P. del Mercato Centrale, 38r (D2; tel. 21 22 67). Local butchers from the nearby market crowd this place, and for good reason. The food is fresh, tasty, and totally cheap. Menu changes daily, but the *penne ai quattro formaggi* is a treat, and the huge, crisp salads are a marked improvement over the wilted lettuce served elsewhere. *Menù* L14,000. Don't worry, vegetarians; they have meatless *secondi.* Cover L2000 for meals outside the *menù.* Open Mon.-Sat. noon-3:30pm and 7-11pm.

Trattoria Mario, Via Rosina, 2r (D2), right around the corner from P. Mercato Centrale. Share huge wooden tables with the crowds of locals that flock here for lunch. Menu changes daily. *Primi* L4000-7000, *secondi* L7000-12,000. Open Mon.-Sat. noon-3:30pm; in July 8am-3:30pm.

Trattoria da Zà-Zà, P. Mercato Centrale, 26r (D2; tel. 21 54 11). Soups are a specialty in this hopping *trattoria;* try the *tris* ("mix of 3") bean, tomato, and vegetable soup for L8000, the *tagliatelle al pesto* made fresh every morning (L8000), or an *insalate giganti* (niçoise, greek, etc., L9000). Cover L2000. Open Mon.-Sat. noon-3pm and 7pm-midnight. Reservations suggested. AmEx, MC, Visa.

✓**Trattoria Antichi Cancelli,** Via Faenza, 73r (C2; tel. 21 89 27). Home-style and hearty. They ladle out a great bowl of vegetable soup (L5500). *Menù* L18,000. Open Tues.-Sun. noon-2:30pm and 7-10:30pm. AmEx, MC, Visa.

Ristorante Il Vegetariano, V. Ruote, 30 (D1; tel. 47 50 30), off V. San Gallo. Pretty landscape scenes surround you in this meat-free zone as you dine on fresh, healthy cuisine. *Primi* L6000-7000, *secondi* L9000-11,000. Cover L2000. Open Tues.-Fri. 11am-3pm and 8pm-midnight, Sat.-Sun. 8pm-midnight.

Ristorante Miro, V. San Gallo 57/59 (D2). A huge, inventive interior in which to enjoy inventive food. Dishes include *risotto* with radish and a mouth-watering broccoli tart. Lunch *primi* L5000; *secondi* L8000-10,000; cover L1500. Dinner *primi* L7000-12,000; *secondi* with *contorno* L10,000-16,000; cover L3500. Open Mon.-Sat. 11am-3pm and 7pm-midnight.

✓**Caffè Carocal-Mexican Restaurant,** Via de Ginori, 10r (D2). Bar atmosphere in which hordes of homesick Americans munch on decent nachos (L8000), burritos (L14,000), tostadas (L14,000), and combination dinners (L10,000-20,000). Happy hour 6-7pm. Open Thurs.-Tues. 5pm-1am.

Old City (The Center)

I Latini, Via Palchetti, 6r (D2). From the Ponte alla Carraia, walk up Via del Moro; V. Palchetti is on the right. Be prepared to wait. Patrons dine on delicious Tuscan classics beneath dangling hams. *Primi* L8000-12,000; *secondi* L15,000-20,000. Cover L2500. Open Tues.-Sun. noon-3:30pm and 7pm-midnight.

Trattoria da Benvenuto, Via dei Neri, 47r (D5; tel. 21 48 33). Skillfully-made portions of *gnocchi* L6000. L9000 for grilled *braciola* (veal chop). Open Mon.-Tues. and Thurs.-Sat. noon-3pm and 7:15-10pm.

Acqua al Due, Via Vegna Vecchia, 40r (D4; tel. 28 41 70), behind the Bargello. Florentine specialties in a cozy, air-conditioned place popular with young Italians.

The *assaggio*, a dish of 5 types of pasta, demands a taste (L11,900); getting a table, however, usually demands a reservation. *Primi* L8000-11,000, *secondi* L10,000-20,000. Open Tues.-Sun. 7:30pm-1am. AmEx, MC, Visa.

Aquerello, Via Ghibbelina, 156r (D-E4; tel. 234 05 54). Pseudo-Memphis decor and superb, offbeat food. Duck when your *spaghetti flambé all' Aquerello* (L8500) arrives, or have your duck *à l'orange* (*anitra all'arancia*, L16,000). Cover L3000. *Menù* L26,000. Open Fri.-Wed. 11am-3pm and 7pm-1am. AmEx.

✓ **La Maremmana,** Via dei Macci, 77r (F4; tel. 24 12 26), near the Mercato Sant'Ambrogio. A rare combination: simple, well-prepared, generous, and affordable. *Menù* starting at L20,000. Tablecloths, cut flowers, pasta, *secondo*, side dishes, a fruit dessert, and wine included. Justifiably busy. A/C. Open Sept.-July Mon.-Sat. 12:30-3pm and 7:30-10:30pm. MC, Visa.

✓ **Trattoria l'che c'è c'è,** Via de Mangalotti, 11r (D5; tel. 21 65 89). The chef cares about his food, as you'll taste. *Topini (gnocchi) al gorgonzola*, L8000. Try a Tuscan *secondo* like *salsicce e faglioli* (sausage and beans, L10,000). *Menù* L19,000. *Primi* L6000-14,000, *secondi* L13,000-20,000. Cover L2000. Open Tues.-Sun. 12:30am-2:30pm and 7:30-10:30pm; in summer 11am-3pm and 7pm-midnight.

Acquacotta, Via dei Pilastri, 51r (F3; tel. 24 29 07), between Borgo Pinti and P. Sant'Ambrogio. Florentines hop on over for their crispy fried *coniglio* with zucchini flowers (L16,000). Bunny-lovers can munch on a delicious *risotto alla fiorentina* (L8000) instead. Cover L1000. Open Thurs.-Mon.11am-3pm and 7-1am, Tues. noon-3pm.

The Oltrarno

Oltrarno Trattoria Casalinga, Via Michelozzi, 9r (B5), near P. Santo Spirito. Delicious Tuscan specialties in relaxed, if crowded, atmosphere. Ravioli made with spinach and *ricotta*, L6000. *Primi* L4500-7000, *secondi* L7000-12,000. Menu changes daily. Cover L1500. Open Mon.-Sat. 11am-3pm and 7pm-midnight.

Il Borgo Antico, P. Santa Spirito, 61 (B5; tel. 21 04 37). A jammin' restaurant with an impressive array of slightly offbeat, but tasty, dishes. Enormous, flamboyant salads (L10,000). Try the *ravioli alla crema di salvia*, in a sweet cream and sage sauce (L10,000). *Primi* L4500-7000, *secondi* L6500-13,000. Pizzas L10,000-12,000. Cover L3000. Reservations recommended. Open Mon.-Sat. 12:30-2:30pm and 7:30-11pm. (*Pizzeria* open until 12:30am.)

Osteria del Cinghiale Bianco, Borgo San Jacopo, 43r (C5; tel. 21 57 06). The White Boar may be one of the most romantic restaurants in Florence, with stone

---

Eat Your Heart Out, Chef Boyardee

We all know the deepest, darkest challenge to the traveler in Italy. It's not the Tuscan hills, the hairy men, or the train strikes, but—the pasta. How do you slurp your strings of Italian heaven without 1) the whiplash, and 2) the sauce stain? Lucky for you, Marco Polo's souvenir has fostered generations of pasta derivatives designed to suit every picky *mamma's* needs. And don't even think of belittling the dazzling array of doughy delights; selecting the correct pasta for the dish and cooking it up right (*al dente*—literally "to the teeth" and slightly crunchy) is as close to Italian hearts as the Madonna herself. *Lasagna* comes in at least two forms: flat or *ricce* (one edge crimped). The familiar *spaghetti* has larger, hollow cousins: *bucatini* and *maccheroni* (not the Yankee Doodle kind); as well as smaller, more delicate relatives like *capellini*. Flat pastas include the familiar *linguine* and *fettuccine*, with *taglierini* and *tagliatelle* filling in the size gaps. Short, roughly two-inch pasta tubes include *ziti*, *penne* (cut diagonally and occasionally *rigate* or ribbed), *sedani* (curved), *rigatoni* (bigger), and *cannelloni* (biggest and usually stuffed). Funny-shaped and good for entertaining the stimulation-deprived/Renaissance-art-overwhelmed include *fusilli* (corkscrews), *farfalle* (butterflies or bow-ties), and *ruote* (wheels). Don't be alarmed if you see pastry displays with the label "pasta"; the Italian word refers to anything made of dough and vaguely edible. What we refer to as pasta is actually *pasta asciutta* or "dry" pasta; anything else means it comes in soup. *Buon appetito!*

FLORENCE

walls, cozy tables, and candles everywhere. Their namesake shows up in a number of delicious guises; try the boar *prosciutto* (L7000) or the stewed boar with *polenta* (L16,000). Open Thurs.-Tues. afternoon noon-2:30pm and 7-11pm. Closed for vacation in July. Call ahead.

Gelaterie and Bakeries

No dinner in this *gelato* capital would be complete without a luscious lick from one of the many *gelaterie*. Set off on your own odyssey, but before plopping down L3000-4000 for a cone, assess the quality of any establishment by checking out the banana *gelato*. If it's bright yellow, it's been made from a mix—keep on walking. You know you've found a true Florentine *gelateria* when the banana is slightly off-gray, indicating that only real live bananas are inside. Vegans can find soy-milk *gelato* at many *gelaterie*, so don't make any excuses!

Gelateria Dei Neri, Via dei Neri, 20-22r (D5; tel. 21 00 34). A popular upstart with scrumptious *gelato*, including a mythical *"mitica"* (chocolate ice cream with just about everything mixed in). Soy-milk *gelato* in several flavors. For a rich and creamy experience, close to American ice cream, try their *semi-freddo*. Cones L3000-7000. Open daily 10:30am-midnight.

Il Granduca, Via dei Calzaiuoli, 57r (D4; tel. 239 81 12). They do one thing, but oh, do they do it well. Delicious *gelato* with fresh fruit and sweets (L2500-7000).

Vivoli, Via della Stinche, 7 (E4; tel. 29 23 34), behind the Bargello. The most renowned of Florentine *gelaterie*, with a huge selection. No cones, only cups (from L2500). Open Sept.-July Tues.-Sun. 8am-midnight.

Perché No?, Via Tavolini, 19r (D4; tel. 239 89 69), off Via dei Calzaiuoli. Though the decor doesn't show it, this is the oldest *gelateria* in Florence—it opened in 1939. Cones L3000-8000. Open Wed.-Mon. 8am-12:30am.

Gelateria Triangolo delle Bermuda, Via Nazionale, 61r (C2; tel. 28 74 90). With *gelato* this good, you may never leave. Ananas flavor has real chiquita chunks and the *baci* oozes with hazelnuts. Oreo *semi-freddo*. Cones L2500-8000.

CarLie's Bakery, Via Brache, 12r (D5; tel. 29 26 64). Behind Via de' Benci, near the river. From P. Signoria, walk between the Palazzo Vecchio and the Uffizi. Head along Via dei Neri and turn left onto Via Brache. Even non-Americans will enjoy the fudge brownies and gooey chocolate-chip cookies. Open 11am-7:30pm; in summer Mon.-Fri. 10am-1:30pm and 3:30-6:30pm.

SIGHTS

Florence! One of the only places in Europe where I understood that underneath my revolt, a consent was lying dormant.

—Albert Camus

It takes quite a city to reduce an existentialist to acquiescence. The same secret spell that Florence has cast over intellectuals from Goethe to Camus can overwhelm the first-time visitor. Beware the "Stendhal Syndrome"—dizziness and palpitations of the heart that result from aesthetic overload (named for the famed French author who first described this ailment). In past years visitors have had to battle the crowds to see the most popular museums—the Uffizi, the Accademia, the Bargello. This is less true today, but the explanation for this phenomenon is unfortunate for the budget traveler: all Florentine museums (and most Italian museums) recently doubled their admission price, making art-viewing an extremely costly endeavor—6000-12,000 at most major venues. Florence merits budget-bending for its museums, but choose what you want to see carefully, and plan to spend a healthy chunk of your day at each museum. Before writing off the Uffizi (L12,000) or the Bargello (L8000), remember that they house the best collections of Renaissance painting and sculpture in the world. Fill in gaps left by budget strictures by exploring Florence's churches, most of which double as treasuries of great works of art. Also, in summer, look for the *Sera al Museo*, when certain museums are open in the evening (8-11pm) and are free. Each museum has one night a month during the season.

Piazza del Duomo

Florentines often refer to their cathedral as "Santa Maria del Fiore"; you'll see the famous brick *duomo* the minute you step out of the train station. In 1296 the city fathers commissioned Arnolfo di Cambio to erect a cathedral and carry out the project "with the most high and sumptuous magnificence so that it is impossible to make it either better or more beautiful with the industry and power of man." Filippo Brunelleschi won the inevitable competition to direct the construction of the largest dome since the Roman Pantheon. To accomplish the task, Brunelleschi came up with the revolutionary idea of building a **double-shelled dome** with interlocking bricks that would support itself during construction. He also supervised every step of the building process, personally designing the system of pulleys and constructing kitchens between the two walls of the cupola so that the masons would not have to descend for lunch. Alberti described the dome as "large enough to shelter all of Tuscany within its shadow...and of a construction that perhaps not even the ancients knew or understood"—the ultimate compliment in a period awed by the genius of Greece and Rome. The cupola was finished in 1436, but the half-completed Gothic Renaissance façade was taken down by an overly ambitious 16th-century Medici rebuilding campaign and not replaced until 1871, when Emilio de Fabris, a Florentine architect influenced by the Gothic style, received a commission to put it back.

Inside, the nave's sheer immensity overwhelms the art, though restoration of the dome's frescoes has added some scaffolding. In the form of a Latin cross, the church claims the **world's third-longest nave,** behind St. Peter's in Rome and St. Paul's in London. A fresco in the left aisle (painted by a student of Fra Angelico, illustrates the *Divine Comedy;* the divine author Dante was forced to flee to Florence after backing the losing side (white) in the struggle between the black and white Guelphs. Check out the back wall of the cathedral, above the entrance—no one will give you the time of day here, because the **orologio,** a 24-hour clock designed by Paolo Uccello, runs backwards. (*Duomo* open daily 10am-5:30pm. Masses 7-10am and 5-7pm.)

Climb up the 463 steps around the inside of the dome (at 110m, the tallest structure ever built in medieval Italy) to the **lantern** (tel. 230 28 85), where you'll have a great view of the city from the external gallery. (Lantern open Mon.-Sat. 10am-4:45pm. Admission L8000.) You can also visit the **crypt** to see the tomb of Brunelleschi, some 13th-century tombs, and bits of mosaic. (Open Mon.-Sat. 10am-5pm. Admission L3000.)

Most of the *duomo's* art has been placed in the **Museo dell'Opera di S. Maria del Fiore** (tel. 230 28 85), behind the *duomo* at P. del Duomo, 9. Up the first flight of stairs is a late *Pietà* by Michelangelo. Frustrated by his own work, he intentionally damaged the figure by taking a hammer to it and severing Christ's left arm. Soon thereafter a pupil touched up the work, leaving parts of Mary Magdalene's head with visible "scars." There are other masterpieces here as well: Donatello and Luca della Robbia's wonderful *cantorie* (choir balconies with bas-reliefs of cavorting children and *putti*), Donatello's *St. Mary Magdalene* (1555), and a silver altar by Michelozzo, Pollaiuolo, and Verrocchio. The art that once covered the *campanile's* exterior includes Donatello's prophets and Andrea Pisano's *Progress of Man* cycle of small reliefs. The museum now houses four of the frames from the baptistery's *Gates of Paradise* (see below), and after the usual interminable restoration will house the entire collection. (Open Mon.-Sat. 9am-7:30pm; in winter, Mon.-Sat. 9am-6pm. Admission L8000. Look for the tours in English: they're given twice a week.)

Though it was built sometime between the 7th and 9th centuries, by Dante's time Florentines thought their **baptistery** had originally been a Roman temple. The interior contains 13th- to 15th-century Byzantine-style mosaics, whose stylized, cartoonlike execution seem more modern than medieval. The lowest circle is thought to be the work of Cimabue. Along the wall rests the elegant, typical early Renaissance *Tomb of the Anti-Pope John XXIII,* by Donatello and Michelozzo, faithfully arranged so that the sculpted figure lies directly in the line of Christ's blessing.

The commission to execute the famous **bronze doors** of the baptistery was among the most coveted in Florence. In 1330, Andrea Pisano was lured away from Pisa, and Venetian foundry-workers were brought in to cast the first set of doors, which now guard the south side (toward the river). In 1401, the cloth guild announced a new competition to determine who would forge the remaining doors. The original field of eight contestants narrowed to two, Brunelleschi (then 23 years old) and Ghiberti (20). Each was given a year to complete a panel, and Ghiberti, whose entry more elegantly molded its subject to the quatrefoil Gothic frame, was awarded the commission. (The competition panels depict the sacrifice of Abraham; they now hang in the Bargello.)

Ghiberti's doors, on the north side away from the river, start with Pisano's frame-work, but add detail, movement, and classical draperies. His work was so admired that the last set of doors was commissioned from him as soon as he finished the first in 1425. The **"Gates of Paradise,"** as Michelangelo reportedly called them, are nothing like the two earlier portals, abandoning the quatrefoil framing and the 28-panel design for 10 large, entirely gilded squares, each incorporating mathematical perspectives to recess the scenes into startlingly deep space. Originally intended to stand as the third set of doors on the north side, they so impressed the Florentines that they were switched with the second doors and placed in their current honored position facing the cathedral. The doors were finished in 1452, after 24 years of labor. (The panels have been under restoration since the 1966 flood and will eventually reside in the Museo del Duomo.) Be sure to examine the mosaics in the baptistery's interior; the scenes from hell are accurate portrayals of Dante's *Inferno*. The author was baptized here. (Open Mon.-Sat. 1-6pm, Sun. 9am-1pm.)

Next to the *duomo* rises the 82m-high **campanile,** the "lily of Florence blossoming in stone." Giotto, then the official city architect, drew up the design and laid the foundation, but died soon after construction began. Andrea Pisano added two stories, and Francesco Talenti completed the tower in 1359, but only after doubling the thickness of the walls to support the weight. The original exterior decoration now resides in the **Museo del Duomo.** The 414-step endurance test is worth the effort—the views are magnificent. (Open daily 8:30am-6:50pm; Nov.-March 9am-5:30pm. Admission L7000.)

Palazzo Vecchio and Piazza della Signoria

From P. del Duomo, **Via dei Calzaiuoli,** one of the city's oldest streets, leads to P. Signoria. Laid out as part of the original Roman *castrum* (camp), today Via dei Calzaiuoli bustles with crowds, chic stores, *gelateria,* and vendors peddling their wares. At the far end, the area around the **Palazzo Vecchio** (tel. 276 84 65) forms the civic center of Florence.

The fortress-like *palazzo* was built between 1298 and 1314 according to the plans of Arnolfo di Cambio, who intended it to replace the Bargello as the seat of the *comune's* government; its interior apartments served as living quarters for the seven members of the *signoria* (council) during their rotating one-month terms in office. By the time of Cosimo di Medici's autocratic rule, however, the building's role as a symbol of communal government was simply ironic.

The courtyard, rebuilt by Michelozzo in 1444 and ruined by Vasari in 1565 to please a Medici bride, contains a copy of Verrocchio's charming 15th-century *putto* fountain and several stone lions (the heraldic symbol of the city). Michelangelo and Leonardo da Vinci were commissioned to paint opposite walls of the **Salone dei Cinquecento,** the meeting room of the Grand Council of the Republic. Although they did not get around to executing the frescoes, their preliminary cartoons, the *Battle of Cascina* and the *Battle of Anghiari,* were studied by all young Florentine artists and copied for mass production by engravers. The tiny, windowless **Studio of Francesco I,** built by Vasari, is a treasure trove of Mannerist art, with paintings by Bronzino, Allori, and Vasari, and bronze statuettes by Giambologna and Ammannati. The best of the art waits in the **Mezzanino.** Look for Bronzino's portrait of the poet

FLORENCE

Laura Battiferi and Giambologna's *Hercules and the Hydra*. (Open Mon.-Wed., Fri. 9am-7pm, Sun. 8am-1pm. Admission L8000.)

A vast space by medieval standards, **Piazza della Signoria** was created in the 13th century by the destruction of the house-towers belonging to the Uberti clan. For a long time, no one of means wanted to own or build on the site. In 1497, Savonarola convinced Florentines to light off the **Bonfire of the Vanities** in the square, a grand roast that consumed some of Florence's best art. A year later, disillusioned Florence sent Savonarola up in smoke on the same spot. Massive symbolic sculptures cluster in front of the *palazzo:* Donatello's *Judith and Holofernes,* Michelangelo's *David* (only a copy is displayed; the original stood here over a century ago), Giambologna's *Equestrian Monument to Cosimo I,* and Bandinelli's *Hercules.* The awkward Neptune statue to the left of the Palazzo Vecchio occasioned a quip by Michelangelo: "Oh Ammannato, Ammannato, what lovely marble you have ruined!"

Built as a space for civic speakers, the graceful 14th-century **Loggia dei Lanzi** gradually became a misogynist sculpture gallery under the Medici dukes. Here you can see Benvenuto Cellini's *Perseus Slaying Medusa,* which Cellini signed on Perseus' sash; Giambologna's *Rape of the Sabines,* whose spiral quality invites viewing from any angle; and the dynamic and violent *Rape of Polyxena* by Pio Fedi.

The Uffizi

In May of 1993, a bomb was detonated in the Uffizi, killing five people in nearby buildings and destroying priceless works of art. The bombing came as a terrible shock to Florentines and other Italians, who cherish the Uffizi as a symbol of their precious Renaissance heritage. The political disruptions caused by these bombings are matched by the cultural losses: many of the rooms in the Uffizi remain closed to the public and will not open for several years as reconstruction of the bombed-out rooms carefully goes ahead. A list of the several works destroyed and the almost 40 works seriously damaged can be obtained from the tourist office. Rooms 25-35 and 41-45 remain closed to the public, but three important works, Michelangelo's *Doni Tondo,* Caravaggio's *Bacchus,* and Titian's *Flora* have been moved to a room near the entrance so that visitors may still have access to them as reconstruction continues. Other rooms may be closed for regular restoration work; check the list at the head of the line near the ticket window. Do not skip the Uffizi because of the closed rooms; it continues to display an unparalleled collection of Renaissance works.

The Rooms

The **Uffizi** (offices, tel. 21 83 41) form a double row behind the *loggia.* Vasari designed the Uffizi in 1554, when Duke Cosimo demanded housing for his consolidated administration of the Duchy of Tuscany. The street makes a strong political statement, framing the tower of Palazzo Vecchio at one end and the Medici Forte Belvedere across the Arno at the other. Giambologna's bust of Cosimo oversees the entire complex at the Arno end. Vasari included a **secret corridor** in the structure, between Palazzo Vecchio and the Medici's Palazzo Pitti; it runs through the Uffizi and over the Ponte Vecchio and houses more art, including a special collection of artists' self-portraits. The city can thank the Medici for the most stunning collection of Renaissance art in the world: the last Medici, Anna Maria Ludovica (1667-1743), bequeathed the entire clan's hoard of art to the people of Tuscany, provided that it never be moved from Florence.

Before heading up to the main gallery on the second floor, stop at the first floor to see the exhibits of the Cabinet of Drawings and Prints. The few drawings displayed here only hint at the much larger collection squirreled away for scholars. Upstairs, the long main corridor wrapping around the building holds an impressive collection of Hellenistic and Roman marbles, the inspirations for many Renaissance works.

The collection is arranged chronologically, and provides a complete education on Florentine painting in the Renaissance, with detours into a select collection from the German and Venetian Renaissances. Despite the hefty admission, it would be artistic overload to try to see everything in the Uffizi in one day.

Room 2 starts you off in the late 13th and early 14th centuries with three great *Maestà* (huge panels of the enthroned Madonna) by three great artists: Cimabue, Florence's first remembered genius, Sienese Duccio di Buoninsegna, whose riot of color clearly marks him as a foreigner, and Giotto, whose vastly informed use of perspective and naturalistic flesh foreshadows the onset of the High Renaissance (still 100 years away). Room 3 moves to Siena to fill out the 14th century with the delightful Gothic works of Simone Martini and the Lorenzetti brothers, because, as Room 4 shows, the Florentines weren't very busy then. Rooms 5 and 6 contain some examples of International Courtly Gothic, but in no way prepares you for the explosion of the early Renaissance in the next room.

Perhaps the most charming room in the museum, Room 7 houses two minor Fra Angelicos, an over-painted *Masolino Madonna and Child* (whose central figures are by Masaccio), and three masterpieces. The softly colored, innovative *Sacra Conversazione* by Domenico Veneziano is one of the master's few known works, and one of the first paintings to incorporate the Madonna and Saints into a unified space. Piero della Francesca's double portrait of Duke Federico and his wife Battista Sforza glows in translucent color and intricate detail. Rounding out the room, Paolo Uccello's famed *Rout of San Romano* is an absurd and disturbing perspective-play where rabbits hop behind huge, toy-like fighting warhorses (this is only the central panel of a triptych—the Louvre and London's National Gallery each have a side). Room 8 contains earthy, brown works by Filippo Lippi; the Pollaiuolo brothers share space with a (probably) forged Filippino Lippi in Room 9.

Rooms 10-14 are a vast Botticelli shrine: *Primavera, Birth of Venus, Madonna della Melagrana,* and *Pallas and the Centaur* glow with luminous color after their restoration; the recently installed glass and difficult lighting go largely unappreciated. Room 15 moves into High Renaissance gear with Leonardo da Vinci's remarkable *Annunciation* and the perhaps more remarkable, unfinished *Adoration of the Magi.* Room 18, designed by Buontalenti to hold the Medici treasures, is more impressive for its collection of portraits, many by Bronzino. Room 19 features Piero della Francesca's students Perugino (the *Portrait of a Young Man* is thought to be of his student Raphael) and Signorelli. Rooms 20 and 22 make an incongruous detour into German territory, and Room 21 sandwiches the major Venetians between them. Ponder Bellini's famous *Sacred Allegory,* an inexplicably moving work, before examining Mantegna's little *Triptych* in Room 24.

As you cross to the gallery's other side, glance out the windows of the south corridor over Florence—the Medici commissioned an impressive view. The second half of the Uffizi rounds out the Florentines in Rooms 25-27 with Michelangelo's only oil painting, the proto-mannerist *Doni Tondo,* a string of Raphaels unaccountably accompanied by Andrea del Sarto's *Madonna of the Harpies,* and Pontormo's odd *Supper at Emmaus.* Florence cares less for the museum after this, and you'll find rooms sporadically closed. If they're open, the best bits are Titian's influential *Venus of Urbino* and Parmigianino's completely preposterous *Madonna of the Long Neck,* an apparent cross between Mary and a giraffe, both found in Room 30; a clutch of Caravaggios, including his *Sacrifice of Isaac* and *Bacchus,* in Room 43; and Room 44's two Rembrandt self-portraits, one young, one old. (Open Tues.-Sat. 9am-7pm, Sun. 9am-2pm. Admission L12,000.)

The Ponte Vecchio

From the Uffizi, turn left onto V. Georgofili, then right when you reach the water. The nearby **Ponte Vecchio** has spanned the Arno at its narrowest point since Roman times. Until 1218 this was Florence's only bridge over the Arno. The Medici, in an effort to "improve" the area, kicked out the butchers and tanners, whose shops lined the bridge in the 1500s, and installed the goldsmiths and diamond-carvers whose descendants remain today. The commander leading the German army's retreat across the river in 1944 could not bear to blow up the bridge, and instead destroyed the medieval towers and nearby buildings on either side to make the bridge impassable. Today, the peddlers and artisans who line the bridge by day make way for tourists at sunset and street musicians at night.

Around the Bargello

The heart of medieval Florence lies between the *duomo* and the Signoria around the 13th-century **Bargello**, in Piazza San Firenze. The Bargello fortress was once the residence of the chief magistrate and later the police headquarters. Now it houses the **Museo Nazionale** (tel. 21 08 01), a treasury of Florentine sculpture. Upstairs on the first floor in the Salone del Consiglio Generale, Donatello's remarkably effeminate bronze *David*, the first free-standing nude since antiquity, exemplifies the early period of Renaissance sculpture. Compare it with the marble *David*, also by Donatello, along the wall to the left. Completed about thirty years earlier (1408), this statue appears more of a Roman patrician than a shy young boy. Along the wall to the right hang two beautiful bronze panels of the *Sacrifice of Isaac*, submitted by Ghiberti and Brunelleschi for the baptistery door competition (see Piazza del Duomo, page 229). Toward the other end of the room resides a series of della Robbia terra-cotta Madonnas. In the *Loggia* (also upstairs on the first floor), one finds a menagerie of bronze animals created by Giambologna for a Medici garden grotto. Downstairs on the ground floor, Michelangelo's early works dominate the first room, including a debauched *Bacchus*, a handsome bust of *Brutus*, an early unfinished *Apollo* or *David*, and a *tondo* of the *Madonna und Child*. Devote your attention to Cellini's work on the other side of the room, especially the models for Perseus and the *Bust of Cosimo I*. Giambologna's *Oceanus* reigns in the Gothic *cortile* outside, while his *Mercury* twirls off his pedestal back in the Michelangelo room. (Open Tues.-Sun. 9am-2pm. Admission L8000.)

The **Badia**, across Via del Proconsolo from the Bargello, was the seat of medieval Florence's richest monastery. Filippino Lippi's *Apparition of the Virgin to St. Bernard*, one of the most famous paintings of the late 15th century, greets you on the left as you enter. (Open 9am-noon and 4-6pm.) Around the corner in Via S. Margherita you can visit the **Casa di Dante** (tel. 28 33 43), the reconstructed house of the great poet. (Open Mon.-Wed. and Sat. 10am-6pm, Sun. 10am-2pm. Admission L5000, groups over 15 L3000 per person.) The small museum outlines Dante's life, but you'll get a better idea of a characteristic 14th-century dwelling at **Palazzo Salviati,** a few blocks away on Via della Vigna Vecchia at Via dell'Isola delle Stinche.

Equidistant from the *duomo* and the Signoria is the intriguing **Orsanmichele,** Via dei Calzaiuoli (tel. 28 47 15). Built in 1337, it is the only surviving example of the Florentine Gothic architectural style. Originally built as a granary and *loggia*, and only later partially converted into a church, Orsanmichele today mixes secular and spiritual concerns in the statues along its façade: they represent the patron saints of the major craft guilds. These niched figures make up another gallery of Florentine art: look for Ghiberti's *St. John the Baptist* and *St. Stephen*, Donatello's *St. Peter* and *St. Mark*, and Giambologna's *St. Luke*. Inside, Bernardo Daddi's miraculous *Virgin* is encased in a Gothic tabernacle designed by Andrea Orcagna. Temporary exhibits are shown in the *saloni* on the top floor; it's worth the climb just for the view of the city. (Open daily 8am-noon and 3-6:30pm. Free.)

Markets, Palazzi, and Santa Maria Novella

After hours of contemplating great Florentine art, visit the area that financed it all. In the early 1420s, 72 banks operated in Florence, most in the area around the **Mercato Nuovo** and **Via Tornabuoni**. Trade generated profits that were then reinvested in land and the manufacture of wool and silk. The Mercato Nuovo arcades, constructed in 1547, housed the gold and silk trades. Pietro Tacca's ferocious statue *Il Porcellino* (The Little Pig), actually a wild boar, was added some 50 years later. Its snout remains brightly polished—rubbing it supposedly brings good luck. The starkly neoclassical **Piazza della Repubblica** replaced the Mercato Vecchio, the old market, in 1890. Today, the inscription *"Antico centro della città, da secolare squalore, a vita nuova restituito"* ("The ancient center of the city, squalid for centuries, restored to new life"), seems emblematic of a more determinedly progressive age. The statue in the center, on the corner near the Upim store, is a facsimile of Donatello's statue of *Abundance,* which once presided over the square. Here you'll find several of the city's most popular *caffè;* the Gilli, perhaps Florence's most famous, was founded in 1733.

As Florence's 15th-century economy expanded, its bankers and merchants showed off their new wealth by erecting palaces grander than any seen before. The great Quattrocento boom commenced with the construction of the **Palazzo Davanzati,** Via Porta Rossa, 13. Today the *palazzo* has been reincarnated as the **Museo della Casa Fiorentina Antica** (tel. 21 65 18), and illustrates the lives of affluent 15th-century merchants. The building houses furniture, tapestries, utensils, and paintings typical of a wealthy family during the Renaissance. See a video on the history of the building at 10am, 11am, and noon on the fourth floor (about 40min., either in Italian or English, depending on the crowd). (Open Tues.-Sun. 9am-2pm. Admission L5000.)

The relative modesty of the Palazzo Davanzati soon gave way to more elegant and extravagant *palazzi.* The **Palazzo Strozzi** (tel. 21 59 90), on Via Tornabuoni at Via Strozzi, begun in 1489, may be the grandest of its kind. With its regal proportions and carefully rusticated façade, it is the best example of the Florentine *palazzo* type, which has spawned endless permutations the world over. (Open Mon., Wed., and Fri. 4-7pm. Free.) Alberti's architectural triumph of half a millennium ago, the **Palazzo Rucellai,** Via della Vigna Nuova, 16, is renowned for its delicate classical façade. Its newly renovated interior now houses the **Alinari Museum of Photographic History** (tel. 21 33 70), with temporary exhibits from the vast Alinari photo archives. (Open Thurs.-Tues. 10am-7:30pm. Admission L5000.)

Many owners of the earlier *palazzi* also commissioned family chapels in the **Church of Santa Trinità** (tel. 21 69 12), on Via Tornabuoni, so as to spend eternity in the best possible company. Restoration has added scaffolding to the façade, but you can still see the splendid interior. The fourth chapel on the right houses remains of a fresco cycle of the life of the Virgin and, on the altar, a magnificent *Annunciation* by Lorenzo Monaco. Scenes from Ghirlandaio's *Life of St. Francis* illuminate the Sassetti chapel in the right arm of the transept. The famous altarpiece of the *Adoration of the Shepherds,* also by Ghirlandaio, rests in the Uffizi; the one you see here is a copy. (Open Mon.-Sat. 7am-noon and 4-7pm.)

The wealthiest merchants built their chapels in the **Church of Santa Maria Novella** (tel. 21 01 13), near the train station. The nave is undergoing restoration, but this in no way detracts from the altar's beauty. Built from 1246 to 1360, the church boasts a green and white Romanesque-Gothic lower façade. Giovanni Rucellai commissioned Alberti to design the top half, then had a chapel built inside. Frescoes covered the interior until the Medici commissioned Vasari to paint others in their honor; they ordered most of the other walls whitewashed so their rivals would not be remembered. Fortunately, Vasari respected Masaccio's powerful (but misnamed) *Trinity,* the first painting to use geometric perspective. About halfway down the left side of the nave, Masaccio's fresco creates a tabernacle in the wall; its use of perspective and space includes the worshipper in a vision of the mercy seat. The **Cappella di Filippo Strozzi,** just to the right of the high altar, contains frescoes by Filippo Lippi, including portrayals of a rather green Adam, a woolly Abraham, and an excruciatingly accurate *Torture of St. John the Evangelist.* The tomb of Filippo Strozzi, by Benedetto da Mareno, lies behind the altar. After making a bet with Donatello over who could create a better crucifix, Brunelleschi made the realistic wooden crucifix in the **Gondi Chapel,** to the left of the high altar. The **Sanctuary** is covered by a fantastic series of Ghirlandaio frescoes. (Church open Mon.-Sat. 7-11:30am and 3:30-6pm, Sun. 3:30-6pm. Sanctuary open Mon., Wed., Fri., and Sat.10-11:45am; Tues. and Thurs. 4-5:45pm.) Next door, visit the cloister to see Paolo Uccello's frescoes, including *The Flood* and *The Sacrifice of Noah.* Even more fascinating, the adjoining so-called **Spanish Chapel** (tel. 28 21 87) harbors the important

14th-century frescoes of Andrea di Bonaiuto. (Open Mon.-Thurs. and Sat. 9am-2pm, Sun. 8am-1pm. Admission L5000.)

Around San Lorenzo

The Medici staked out an entire portion of the city north of the *duomo* in which to build their own church, the spacious **Basilica of San Lorenzo** (tel. 234 27 31), and the Palazzo Medici. San Lorenzo was begun in 1419 following Brunelleschi's plans. The Medici loaned the city the necessary funds to build the church, and in return were given control over its design. Their coat of arms, with its six red balls, is carved all over the nave; their tombs fill the two sacristies and the Cappella dei Principi behind the altar. (Cosimo's is cunningly placed in front of the high altar, thus making the entire church his personal mausoleum.) Michelangelo designed the church's exterior, but the profligate Medici ran out of money to build it, so it stands bare. (At least it is consistent with the rusticated Palazzo Medici—officially called Palazzo Medici Riccardi—diagonally across the *piazza;* see below.) Inside the *basilica*, two massive bronze pulpits by Donatello command the nave. (Open daily 7am-noon and 3:30-5:30pm.) Next door, the **Biblioteca Mediceo-Laurenziana** (tel. 21 07 60) illustrates Michelangelo's architectural virtuosity with his recasting of the vocabulary of classical architecture in a Mannerist mode. Inside is one of the largest and most valuable collections of codices and manuscripts in the world. Changing exhibitions on themes such as Dante or Virgil can be seen in the library from April to June and September to October. At other times of year, atmospheric conditions would damage the collection. (Open Mon.-Sat. 9am-1pm. Free.)

To reach the **Cappelle Medicee** (tel. 21 32 06), go out the front entrance and walk around the church through the market to the back entrance on P. Madonna degli Aldobrandini. Intended as a grand mausoleum, Matteo Nigetti's **Cappella dei Principi** (Princes' Chapel) emulates the baptistery. Except for the operatic gilded portraits of the Medici dukes, the decor is oppressive—a rare moment of the Baroque in Florence. Michelangelo's **New Sacristy** (1524) is a welcome contrast, its starkly simple architectural design reflecting the master's study of Brunelleschi. Michelangelo sculpted two impressive tombs for Lorenzo and Guiliano de' Medici, representing the four stages of the day. On Guiliano's tomb recline the figures of Night (the sleeping woman) and Day (the alert man). In contrast, Lorenzo's tomb supports Dawn (the woman who refuses to wake up) and Dusk (the man tired from a hard day's work). The woman's physique is especially intriguing; her unnatural look may derive from Michelangelo's refusal to work from female models. (Open Tues.-Sun. 9am-2pm. Admission a steep L10,000.) In the basement of the New Sacristy, you can view some Michelangelo sketches (ask for a free ticket).

According to art historians, Brunelleschi proposed a sumptuous design for the **Palazzo Medici** (tel. 276 01), but was rejected. With its arched window frames and Michelangelo's "kneeling" windows on the southwest corner, Michelozzo's *palazzo* set the trend in palace styles. The private chapel inside features Benozzo Gozzoli's ornate 15th-century tapestry-like murals of the three Magi and portraits of the Medici family. The *palazzo* also hosts exhibits ranging from Fellini memorabilia to architectural sketches. Check with the tourist office. (Open Mon.-Tues. and Thurs.-Sat. 9am-12:45pm and 3-5:45pm, Sun. 9am-12:45pm. Admission L6000.)

Around Piazza Santissima Annunziata

The complex of religious buildings encircling P. Santissima Annunziata emanates serenity. The *loggia* of the **Spedale degli Innocenti** (tel. 24 36 70) on the right, designed by Brunelleschi and built in the 1420s, was copied on the other side by Antonio da Sangallo a century later. The visual unity so pleased contemporary tastes that the *loggia* was continued across the façade of the church in 1601. The statue of Ferdinando de' Medici stands over the *piazza* in a position intentionally reminiscent of that of Marcus Aurelius in Rome's Campidoglio. The **Galleria dello Spedale degli Innocenti** contains Botticelli's *Madonna e Angelo* and Ghirlandaio's *Epiphany*. (Open Thurs.-Tues. 8:30am-2pm. Admission L3000.)

The miraculous works of Fra Angelico adorn the **museum** of the **Church of San Marco** (tel. 21 07 41), one of the most peaceful and deeply spiritual spots in Florence. A large room to the right contains some of the painter's major works, including the altarpiece used in the church. Mount the stairs to see Angelico's most famous *Annunciation,* a rainbow celebration that greets you at the top. In the dormitory each cell contains its own Fra Angelico fresco, painted in flatter colors and sparser forms to facilitate the monks' meditation. Michelozzo's library is one of the most successful examples of Brunelleschian serenity. On the whole, you might feel like following in the footsteps of Cosimo I, the patron of the convent, who retired here. His cell, unsurprisingly, is the largest. Look for Savonarola's cell as well. (Open Tues.-Sun. 9am-2pm. Admission L8000.)

The **Accademia** (tel. 21 43 75) lies between the two churches at Via Ricasoli, 60. Most of the museum is off-limits, but the collection itself remains on display. Michelangelo's triumphant *David* stands in self-assured perfection under the rotunda designed just for him. He was brought here from P. della Signoria in 1873 after a stone hurled during a riot broke his left wrist in two places. Note the opaque finish—the original polish was inadvertently removed during a cleaning. Leading up to *David* are Michelangelo's *Prisoners,* a series of five sculptures. The master left these statues intentionally "unfinished"; envisioning a prisoner inside the stone, he sculpted each block only enough to "liberate" it. Don't miss the impressive collection of Gothic triptychs on the second floor, or the back room filled with an astounding collection of Russian icons. (Most areas of the museum are handicapped accessible. Open Tues.-Sat. 9am-7pm, Sun. 9am-2pm. Admission L12,000.)

From P. S.S. Annunziata, take bus #6 (get off at Via Andrea del Sarto) to Sarto's **Cenacolo di San Salvi,** Via di San Salvi, 16 (tel. 67 75 70). This abbey refectory houses Sarto's stupendous *Last Supper* (1519) alongside other 16th-century Florentine paintings. (Open Tues.-Sun. 9am-2pm. Admission L5000.) The **Cenacolo di Sant'Apollonia,** in the **Museo di Andrea del Castagno,** Via 27 Aprile, 1 (tel. 28 70 74), is just as impressive. This mid-15th-century fresco of the Last Supper takes up an entire wall, and is del Castagno's masterpiece. (Open Tues.-Sun. 9am-2pm. Admission L2200.)

Around Santa Croce

The Franciscans built the **Church of Santa Croce** (tel. 24 46 19) as far away as possible from Santa Maria Novella and their Dominican rivals. Despite the ascetic ideals of the Franciscans, it is quite possibly the most splendid church in the city. Construction began in 1294 on a design by di Cambio, but the façade and Gothic bell tower were not added until the 19th century. Originally the nave was covered by Andrea Orcagna's master fresco cycle. Never heard of Orcagna? Maybe it's through the good offices of Vasari, who not only destroyed the entire cycle, but left Orcagna out of his famous *Lives of the Artists.* On the right of the altar, the tempera murals of the **Peruzzi Chapel** vie with the frescoes of the **Bardi Chapel;** Giotto and his school painted both. Among the famous Florentines buried here are Michelangelo, who rests at the beginning of the right aisle in a tomb designed by Vasari, and humanist Leonardo Bruni, shown holding his precious *History of Florence* on a tomb designed by Bernardo Rossellino. Between the two sits Donatello's gilded limestone *Annunciation.* The Florentines, who banished the living Dante, decided that his corpse would not make much trouble and eventually got a tomb all ready; Dante died in Ravenna, however, and the literary necrophiliacs there have never sent him back, leaving the tomb empty. A bit closer to the altar lies Machiavelli, on whose sarcophagus no extravagance was lavished. In the right aisle is the tomb of the Pisan Galileo. (Open Mon.-Sat. 8am-12:30pm and 3-6:30pm, Sun. 3-6pm.)

The barn-like Gothic style of Santa Croce contrasts with the brittle delicacy of Brunelleschi's small **Pazzi Chapel,** at the end of the cloister next to the church. This is a perfect place to recover your energy, surrounded by cool *pietra serena* pilasters, Luca della Robbia tondos of the apostles, and rondels of the evangelists by Donatello. The second cloister, also by Brunelleschi, offers even more calm. The

Museo dell'Opera di Santa Croce (tel. 24 46 19; through the *loggia* in front of the Pazzi Chapel) is still recovering from the disastrous 1966 flood that left many works, including the great Cimabue *Crucifixion,* in a tragic state. The one-time refectory contains Taddeo Gaddi's imaginative fresco of *The Tree of the Cross,* and beneath it, the *Last Supper.* (Open Thurs.-Tues. 10am-12:30pm and 2:30-6:30pm; in winter 10am-12:30pm and 3-5pm.)

From Piazza St. Croce, follow Via de' Pepi, and make a right onto Via Ghibellina to reach the **Casa Buonarroti,** Via Ghibellina, 70 (tel. 24 17 52), which houses Michelangelo memorabilia and two of his important early works, *The Madonna of the Steps* and *The Battle of the Centaurs.* Both are in the first rooms to the left of the landing on the second floor. He completed these panels when he was about 16 years old; they show his transition from bas-relief to full sculpture. (Open Wed.-Mon. 9:30am-1:30pm. Admission L8000, students L6000.)

A few streets north of Via Ghibellina stands the **Synagogue of Florence,** also known as the **Museo del Tempio Israelitico,** Via Farini, 4 (tel. 24 52 52 or 24 52 53), at Via Pilastri. Said to be the most beautiful synagogue in Europe, and built between 1872 and 1874 by the architects Micheli and Treves, the Sephardic temple is decorated in a modified Moorish style, enhanced with elaborate geometrical designs. (Open Sun.-Thurs. 11am-1pm and 2-5pm, Fri. 10am-1pm. Admission L5000, students L4000. Frequent informative tours.)

In the Oltrarno

Historically disdained by downtown Florentines, the far side of the Arno remains a lively, unpretentious quarter, even in high season. Start your tour a few blocks west of P. Santa Spirito at the **Church of Santa Maria del Carmine.** Inside, the **Brancacci Chapel** houses a group of revolutionary 15th-century frescoes that were declared masterpieces in their time. In 1424 Felice Brancacci commissioned Masolino and his partner Masaccio to decorate his chapel with scenes from the life of St. Peter. While Masolino probably designed the series, applying perspective techniques not fully grasped by previous artists, it was Masaccio who executed these revolutionary frescoes before his death in 1428, imbuing his figures with a solidity and sober dignity that built upon the innovations of Giotto. Fifty years later a respectful Filippino Lippi completed the revered cycle. Note especially the *Expulsion from Paradise* and *The Tribute Money.* (Open Mon. and Wed.-Sat. 10am-4:30pm, Sun. 1-4:30pm. Admission L5000.)

As Brunelleschi designed it, the **Church of Santo Spirito** (tel. 21 00 30) would have been one of the most exciting pieces of sacred architecture ever. He envisioned a four-aisled nave encircled by hollow chapels, which the exterior would reveal as a series of bumps. Brunelleschi died when the project was only partially completed, and the plans were altered to make the building more conventional. Nonetheless, it remains a masterpiece of Renaissance harmony. (Open daily 8am-noon and 3:30-6:30pm, in winter 4-6pm.)

Luca Pitti, a *nouveau-riche* banker of the 15th century, built his *palazzo* east of Santo Spirito, against the Boboli hill. The Medici acquired the *palazzo* and the hill in 1550, and enlarged everything possible. The courtyard was redesigned by Ammannato; the columns captured in the rough blocks reflect the 16th-century preoccupation with the theme of nature versus art. The **Pitti Palace** (tel. 21 34 40) now houses no fewer than five museums. The **Museo degli Argenti** (tel. 21 25 57), on the ground floor, exhibits the Medici loot. Browse among cases of precious gems, ivories, and silver, then peruse Lorenzo the Magnificent's famous collection of vases. (Open Tues.-Sun. 9am-2pm. L8000 admission gets you into the costume museum as well.) The **Museum of Costumes** (tel. 21 25 57) and the **Porcelain Museum** (tel. 21 25 57) host more Medici debris. (Museum of Costumes open Tues.-Sat. 9am-2pm, Sun. 9am-1pm. Combined L8000 ticket with Museo degli Argenti. Porcelain Museum temporarily closed.) The **Royal Apartments** (tel. 28 70 96), on the main floor, preserve their furnishings from the residence of the Royal House of Savoy, together with a few treasures from the Medici period. (Open Tues.-

Sun. 9am-2pm. Admission L12,000.) The **Galleria Palatina** (tel. 21 03 23) was one of only a few public galleries when it opened in 1833. Today its collection includes a number of Raphaels (most, unfortunately, behind glass), and works by Titian, Andrea del Sarto, Rosso, Caravaggio, and Rubens. Note the neoclassical Music Room and the Putti Room, dominated by Flemish works. (Open Tues.-Sun. 9am-2pm. Admission L12,000.) The fifth and final museum, the **Galleria d'Arte Moderna** (tel. 28 70 96), houses one of the big surprises of Italian art: the early 19th-century proto-impressionist works of the Macchiaioli school. The collection also includes neoclassical and Romantic works. Look for Giovanni Dupré's sculptural group *Cain and Abel*. (Open Tues.-Sat. 9am-2pm and Sun. 9am-1pm. Admission L4000.)

The elaborately landscaped **Boboli Gardens** (tel. 21 34 40), behind the palace, stretch to the hilltop **Forte Belvedere** (tel. 234 24 25), once the Medici fortress and treasury. Ascend Via di Costa San Giorgio (off P. Santa Felicità, to the left after crossing Ponte Vecchio) to reach the villa, an unusual construction with a central *loggia* designed by Ammannati. Buontalenti built this star-shaped bastion for Grand Duke Ferdinand I; now the fortress hosts summer exhibitions and sun-tanning exhibitionism. (Gardens open Tues.-Sun. 9am-7:30pm; April-May and Sept. 9am-6:30pm; March and Oct. 9am-5:30pm; Nov.-Feb. 9am-4:30pm. Admission L4000. Fort open 9am-10pm; in winter 9am-5pm.)

The splendid view of Florence from the fort is matched only by the picture-perfect panorama from **Piazzale Michelangelo.** Go at sunset for the most spectacular vista of the city, from the Ponte Vecchio to Santa Croce and beyond. Above the *piazzale* is **San Miniato al Monte,** one of Florence's oldest churches, and one of the best examples of the early Romanesque. (Take bus #13 from the station or climb the stairs from P. Michelangelo.) The inlaid marble façade with its 13th-century mosaics is only a prelude to the incredible pavement inside, which is patterned with lions, doves, and astrological signs. Inside the Cardinal of Portugal's chapel you'll find a collection of superlative della Robbia terra-cottas (ask the sacristan to let you in. Church open Mon.-Sat. 8am-noon and 2-7pm., Sun. 2:30-5:30pm; in winter Mon.-Sat. 8am-noon and 2-6pm, Sun. 2:30-5:30pm.)

ENTERTAINMENT

For reliable information on what's hot and what's not, consult *Firenze Spettacolo* (L2500). The **passeggiata** promenades along Via dei Calzaiuoli; afterward Florentines frequent the ritzy *caffè* in P. della Repubblica. Street performers draw crowds to the steps of the *duomo*, the arcades of the Mercato Nuovo, and P. Michelangelo. Florence vies with England for the honor of having invented modern soccer, and every June the various *quartieri* of the city turn out in costume to play their own medieval version of the sport, known as **Calcio Storico.** Two teams of 27 players face off over a wooden ball in one of the city's *piazze*. The line between athletic contest and riot is often blurred in these games. Check newspapers or the tourist office for the dates and locations of either historic or modern *calcio*. Tickets (starting at about L15,000) are sold at the Chiosco degli Sportivi on Via dei Anselmi (tel. 29 23 63). To watch a real game, head for the **stadio,** north of the city center. You can buy tickets (starting at L20,000) from the bar across the street from the stadium.

Caffè **La Dolce Vita,** P. del Carmine, draws a respectable crowd, and is convenient to the budget lodgings in the Oltrarno. Just two blocks away, **P. Santo Spirito** hops with a good selection of bars and restaurants. A raucous crowd of beautiful people frequents **Lo Sfizzio,** on Lungarno Cellini, 1, where they carouse over enormous drinks on the outdoor terrace (open until 1am). For a quieter evening of wine tasting, **Fuori Porta,** Monte alle Croce, 10r, offers an impressive selection of *vino* by the glass from L4000. (Open Mon.-Sat. 10am-midnight.) If you prefer a little guitar-strumming with your *chianti*, check out **Chiodo Fisso,** V. Dante Alighieri, 16 (tel. 238 12 90); music begins at 10:30. **The Red Garter,** Via dei Benci, 33r, is a raucous mix of American students, Italians, flying peanut shells, and classic American rock. If you can rock they might even let you on stage. For an authentic Irish pub serving cider, Guinness, and other draught beers (L6000 a pint), try **The Fiddler's**

Elbow, P. Santa Maria Novella, 74. It's crowded and convivial but plagued by foreigners. (Open daily noon-12:15am.) A little mellower, the **Robin Hood** (also called the **English Pub**), Via dell'Oriuolo, 58r, has the requisite beer, cider, and dart boards. (Happy hour 8-9pm. Open 5pm-1am.) **Angie's Pub,** Via dei Neri, 35r (tel. 29 82 45), is an Italian place (despite the name) catering mostly to students, and therefore usually uncrowded in the summer months. Offers a selection of imported beer and cider on tap from L4000 per glass, and serves hamburgers on its own special rolls (L5000-6000; open Tues.-Sat. 12:30-3pm and 7pm-1am). For live jazz, **Jazz Club,** Via Nuova dei Caccini, 3, at Borgo Pinti, lives up to its billing. (Disregard the "members only" sign on the door. Open Sept. 21-July 14.) Or try **BeBop,** V. dei Servi, 76r (tel. 28 91 12), which also mixes in some blues. (Open 9pm-1am.) For entertainment Italian-style, why not—bowl? **Pin's Club Bowling,** Via Faenza, 71 (tel. 238 13 80), has 11 regulation lanes. (L6000 per person per game, Sat.-Sun. L7000. Shoes L1500.) There's also pool, ping-pong, and video games. Call ahead to reserve a lane, especially if you want to bowl in the evening. (Open daily 3pm-midnight.)

Dancing

Note that many of the discos listed below cater almost exclusively to tourists, with a sprinkling of Italians who have designs on foreigners. Near Santa Maria Novella, somewhat-cheesy **Space Electronic,** Via Palazzuolo, 37 (tel. 29 30 82), has a young international crowd multiplied by many mirrors. (Beer L7000, mixed drinks L8000. Free karaoke. Open Sun.-Fri. 10pm-2am, Sat. 10pm-3am. Sept.-Feb. closed Mon. Cover with 1 drink L20,000.) Or try **Yab Yum,** Via dei Sassetti, 5r (tel. 28 20 18), off P. della Repubblica, where you pay for all drinks on the way out. (Cover with first drink L15,000. Open nightly 11pm-4:30am.) In summer, Yab Yum's business moves to **Capitale** (tel. 35 67 23), in the Parco delle Cascinè, in front of the Hotel Michelangelo. Take bus #17C from the *duomo* or station. (Open daily.) The trendy spot for Italian students is **Rockafè,** Borgo degli Albizi, 66 (tel. 24 46 62), where American infiltration is not yet complete. (Cover L15,000. Open Sept.-June Tues.-Sun. 10pm-4am.) In a tiny alleyway across P. della Signoria from the Palazzo Vecchio is **Tabasco Gay Club,** P. S. Cecilia, 3r (tel. 21 30 00), Florence's most popular gay disco. (Minimum age 18. No cover, but 1 drink min. Open Tues.-Sun. 10pm-3am.)

Festivals

The most important of Florence's traditional festivals, that of St. John the Baptist on June 24, features a tremendous fireworks display from P. Michelangelo. Easily visible from the Arno, it starts at about 10pm. The summer swings with music festivals, starting in May with the classical **Maggio Musicale.** The **Estate Fiesolana** (June-Aug.) fills the Roman theater in nearby Fiesole with concerts, opera, theater, ballet, and movies. For info on tickets, contact the **Biglietteria Centrale** in the Teatro Comunale, Corso Italia, 16 (tel. 21 62 53 or 277 92 36), or Universalturismo, Via degli Speziali, 7r (tel. 21 72 41), off P. della Repubblica. In September, Florence hosts the **Festa dell'Unità,** with organized music and concerts at Campi Bisenzia (take bus #30). The **Florence Film Festival,** generally held in December, is justly famous. For more info contact the film festival office at Via Martiri del Popolo (tel. 24 07 20). The **Festa dei Porcini** is an annual festival celebrating and presenting a variety of mushrooms for three days in August. Contact the local tourist office for up-to-date info.

SHOPPING

The Florentine flair for design comes through as clearly in the window displays of its shops as in the wares themselves. Via Tornabuoni's **swanky boutiques** and the somewhat tacky and overpriced **goldsmiths** on the Ponte Vecchio proudly serve a sophisticated clientele. Florence makes its contribution to *alta moda* with the biannual **Pitti Uomo show** (mid-Jan. and July), Europe's most important exhibition of menswear, and its companion Pitti fashion shows. If you're looking for high-quality used and antique clothing, try **La Belle Epoque,** Volta di S. Piero, 8r (tel. 21 61 69), off P. S. Pier Maggiore, or **Lord Brummel Store,** Via del Purgatorio, 26r (tel. 28 75 40), off Via Tornabuoni. The city's artisan traditions continue to thrive at the open markets. **San Lorenzo,** the largest, cheapest, and most tourist-oriented, sprawls for several blocks around P. San Lorenzo, trafficking in anything made of leather, wool, cloth, or gold (and souvenirs as well). (Open Mon.-Sat.) High prices are rare, but so are quality and honesty. For everything from potholders to parakeets visit **Parco delle Cascinè,** a park that begins west of the city center at P. Vittorio Veneto and stretches along the Arno River. (At night the park transforms into a "strip" where transvestite prostitutes solicit customers from an endless stream of cars, driven mostly by curious onlookers). The market at the Cascinè also sells some clothing and shoes, but come here for the used clothing vendors. For a flea market specializing in old furniture, postcards, and bric-a-brac, visit **Piazza Ciompi,** off Via Pietrapiana (walk out Borgo degli Albizi); it's one of the city's best. (Open Tues.-Sat.) Florentines are not hagglers: bargaining usually won't get you far, but try it if you feel the price is truly outrageous.

Books and art reproductions are some of the best souvenirs you can carry away from Florence. Famed Alinari, Via della Vigna Nuova, 46-48r (tel. 21 89 75), stocks the world's largest selection of art prints and high-quality photographs. (L5000-8000 apiece. Open Mon.-Sat. 9am-1pm and 4-7pm.) Rizzoli's *Maestri del Colore* series of color reproductions is a bargain. Feltrinelli, Via Cerretoni, 34 (tel. 29 63 20), has an unbeatable selection of art books. (Open Mon.-Fri. 9am-7:30pm, Sat. 9am-1pm.) *Cartolerie* (stationery stores) and many gift shops carry samples of the famous **carta fiorentina,** paper covered in an intricate floral design. Florentine **leatherwork** is generally of high quality and frequently affordable. Leather shops fill the city, but P. Santa Croce and Via Porta Santa Maria are particularly good places to look. A number of smaller shops, such as **Bagman,** Via dell'Alberto, 19, off Via della Scala, let you peek in at the artists. Check for such opportunities in other stores too, especially in jewelry stores: many of them sell only goods made on the premises. One of the best leather deals in the city hides in one of its most beautiful churches. The **Santa Croce Leather School** (tel. 24 45 33/34 and 247 99 13), in the back of the church to the right, offers some of the best quality artisan products in the city, but has prices to match. (Open 9am-12:30pm, 3-6:30pm, and 7:30-10:30pm.)

■ NEAR FLORENCE: FIESOLE

Atop majestic hills just 8km to the northeast of Florence, Fiesole has long been a welcome escape from the sweltering summer heat of the Arno valley below. Built originally as a Roman outpost, the tiny village became a refuge for Etruscans fleeing the Romans. It has since led a quiet existence as a satellite of Florence and a source of inspiration for numerous famous figures—among them Alexandre Dumas, Anatole France, Marcel Proust, Gertrude Stein, Frank Lloyd Wright, and Paul Klee. Leonardo da Vinci even used the town as a testing ground for his flying machine. Fiesole's location provides **incomparable views** of both Florence and the rolling countryside to the north—it's a perfect place for a picnic or a day-long *passeggiata.* No trains run to Fiesole, but the town is easily accessible from Florence by bus. ATAF city bus #7 leaves from the train station, from P. del Duomo, and from P. San Marco during the day (less frequently at night) and drops passengers at Piazza Mino da Fiesole in the center of town. Fiesole features a number of churches and museums, but the best reason to come here by far is the unsurpassed view of Florence and the valley chiseled by the Arno into the surrounding hills. Take Via San Francesco up the steep hill from the main piazza.

■ ■ ■ PISTOIA

Pistoia came into its own in 1177 when it joined a handful of other Italian city-states and declared itself a free commune. Despite this bold debut, Pistoia's neighbors soon surpassed it in military, political, and economic sophistication. While Pistoia's claim to fame (or infamy) is the tool of war it perfected in the 16th century—the pistol, today the city is home to one of the world's leading train manufacturers. This city isn't all steel, however; Pistoia is also one of Europe's leading greenhouses— fields of bright flowers dot the hills. A handful of interesting monuments make Pistoia a good day trip from Florence (35min.), but if you're on a tight schedule, head to the less steel-edged towns of Tuscany first.

Orientation and Practical Information From the train station, the center is easily reached by walking up Via XX Settembre and straight on to Via Vanucci, Via Cino, and Via Buozzi, at the end of which you turn right for the *duomo* (15min.). You can also take bus #10, 12, 26, 27, or 28 to the *duomo* from the station (buy tickets at the COPIT office outside the station, L1100). Or take the Lazzi bus (tel. 251 32; L5700; last bus returns to Florence at 9pm). The **tourist office** (tel. 216 22) is in Palazzo dei Vescovi, P. del Duomo. The friendly staff is highly knowledgeable and has worked with *Let's Go* readers for years. (Open Mon.-Sat. 9:30am-12:30pm and 3-6pm, Sun. 9:30am-12:30pm and 3:30-6pm; off-season Mon.-Sat. 9:30am-12:30pm and 3:30-6pm.) The **post office** is at Via Roma, 5 (tel. 227 56), off P. del Duomo; the **postal code** is 51100. (Open Mon.-Fri. 8:15am-6pm, Sat. 8:15am-12:30pm.) **Telephone code:** 0573. There's a **pharmacy** in Piazza del Duomo (open Mon.-Fri. 9am-1pm and 4-7:30pm, Sat. 9am-1pm). In case of **emergencies,** dial 113. The **police** (Carabinieri) can be reached at tel. 212 12.

Accommodations and Food A reasonable room at a reasonable price is a rare find in Pistoia, so visit the town on a daytrip from Florence. If you do spend the night, your best bet is **Albergo Firenze,** Via Curtatone e Montanara, 42 (tel. 231 41; fax 216 60). The American owner is friendly, offers advice, and keeps the bright rooms perfectly clean. Many have TVs. Show your *Let's Go* in 1996 and you'll get the prices listed below, regardless of the hotel's price increases. (Singles L42,000, with bath L60,000. Doubles L75,000, with bath L85,000. Triples L97,000. Quads L120,000. Breakfast L6000. MC, Visa.)

Cruise side streets for grocery and inexpensive specialty shops. Market junkies should browse the slightly touristy **open-air market** held in P. della Sala every Wednesday and Saturday (7:30am-2pm). A daily fruit and vegetable **market** is also held on weekdays in P. della Sala, near the *duomo* (8am-2pm and 5-7pm). A wonderful meal awaits at **Trattoria Lo Storno,** Via Lastrone, 8. Pen-and-ink portraits line this long hall of a restaurant, which serves up simple and delicious fare. *Menù* L18,000. (Open daily noon-2pm, Wed. and Fri.-Sat. 7:30-9:30pm.) Another sit-down option is **Pizzeria Tonino,** Corso Gramsci, 159b (tel. 333 30), behind the Palazzo Marchetti. Try the wonderfully tasty and filling *gnocchi* (L8000), or a Tuscan favorite like the grilled *salsicce* (sausage, L8000). (Open Tues.-Sun. 10am-4pm and 6:30pm-midnight. AmEx, MC, Visa.)

Sights and Entertainment Geographically and culturally, Pistoia converges on the **Piazza del Duomo,** with the **Cattedrale di San Zeno** on the right. Originally erected in the 5th century, the church has been rebuilt three times. Inside the *duomo* you'll find an impressive store of early Renaissance art; look for the della Robbia lunette over the central door and several sculptures by Verrocchio. San Zeno's greatest treasure is the *Dossale di San Jacopo,* a tremendously ornate altarpiece that dominates a plain chapel along the right. Nearly every important Tuscan silversmith alive between 1287 and 1456 worked on the piece, including the young Brunelleschi. The church must never have paid off the altar, though—they charge L1500 to get close to it. (Cathedral open daily 8am-noon and 4-7pm.) Designed by Andrea Pisano, the octagonal 14th-century **baptistery** across from the *duomo* presents a modest interior enlivened by Nino and Tommaso Pisano's *Virgin and Child* in the tympanum. (Open Tues.-Sat. 9am-noon and 3-6pm, Sun.-Mon. 9am-noon.)

To the left of the *duomo* stands the **Palazzo Comunale.** Built in the 13th and 14th centuries, the *palazzo* has a curious detail on its façade: left of the central balcony an arm reaches out of the wall, brandishing a club above the black marble head below—a tribute to the 1115 Pistoian victory over the Moorish king Musetto.

One of Italy's most renowned 20th-century artists, native son Marino Marini, is celebrated at the center bearing his name in the **Palazzo dei Tau,** Corso Silvano Fedi, 72. Most of the collection consists of studies and paintings, but it also includes some of the primitively sensuous, highly-charged sculptures for which Marini is most famous. (Open Tues.-Sat. 9am-1pm and 3-7pm, Sun. 9am-12:30pm. Free.)

Exit P. del Duomo by Via del Duca and continue up Via dei Rossi; the typical Pisan-Romanesque façade of the **Church of Sant'Andrea** will appear on the left. Here Giovanni Pisano carved a pulpit that almost shows up his efforts in Pisa. The sculptor saved the most impressive scene, the *Massacre of the Innocents,* for the panel most clearly visible from the nave. (Open daily 8am-1pm and 4-7pm.)

At the southern end of the city, on Via Cavour at Via Crispi, don't miss the 12th-century **Church of San Giovanni Fuorcivitas.** The single-naved interior is a vast, box-like space. The church contains Luca della Robbia's vibrant *Visitation* and a font by Giovanni Pisano. (Open daily 8am-1pm and 4-7pm.)

If you missed out on Woodstock '94, don't despair; the thousand or so remaining flower children of western Europe converge annually on Pistoia for the **Pistoia Blues** concert series held during the last weekend of June or first few days of July. For information and tickets inquire at the tourist office or the *Comune di Pistoia* (tel. 37 11). The city allows free camping in specially designated sites near the stadium during the festival, which culminates with the **Giostra dell'Orso** (Joust of the Bear), held in P. del Duomo on July 25, the feast of St. James (the city's patron saint). (The *Giostra* began in the 14th century as a bloody contest between 12 mounted knights and a dressed-up bear.)

■■■ LUCCA

Encircled by tree-topped ramparts, peaceful Lucca lacks the two defining characteristics of many Tuscan hill towns: the tourists and the hill. There are no hordes to fight in order to get at Lucca's many interesting monuments; exquisite churches and yellow-toned medieval houses built around the Roman amphitheater provide lasting reminders of the city's heritage. The absence of the hill translates into happier hamstrings and a unique feel to the city. Because Lucca is flat, the vast majority of residents ride bicycles, creating a recreational, friendly atmosphere.

ORIENTATION AND PRACTICAL INFORMATION

Trains provide the most convenient form of transportation to Lucca, while **Lazzi** buses also run to Pisa and to Florence, stopping in many other towns in the immediate area. The station lies just outside the city walls; from the station, walk left on Viale Cavour and enter the first city gate on the right. Inside the walls, head left on Via Carrara; Via Vittorio Veneto on your right will lead you to **Piazza Napoleone** (also known as P. Grande), the hub of the city. To get to the tourist office, head to the far end of P. Napoleone (one big parking lot), turn left on Via Vittorio Emanuele II, and follow it until it (not you) hits the city wall. The white building to your right is the tourist office.

Tourist Office: Centro Accoglienza Turistica, P. Verdi (tel. 535 92). Located within a former city gate. The enthusiastic staff gives out brochures. Some English spoken. The *cambio* in the building has exorbitant rates. Office open daily 9am-7pm; Nov.-March 9am-1:30pm.

Police: Carabinieri, tel. 112.

Post Office: Via Vallisneri (tel. 456 90), off P. del Duomo. Open Mon.-Fri. 8:15am-7pm, Sat. 8:15am-noon. **Postal Code:** 55100.

Telephones: Via Cenami, 15-19 (tel. 553 66), off P. San Giusto. Open Mon.-Sat. 8:45am-12:30pm and 3:30-7pm. Or try Bar Casali, P. San Michele. Open 8am-10pm. **Telephone Code:** 0583.

Currency Exchange: Credito Italiano, P. S. Michele, 47 (tel. 475 46). Open Mon.-Fri. 8:20am-1:20pm and 2:45-4:15pm.
Trains: P. Ricasoli (tel. 470 13). From: Florence (Florence-Viareggio line, 1½hr., L6000) or Pisa (½hr., L2700). Information open Mon., Wed.-Fri. 6:50am-9pm, Tues., Sat., Sun. 9am-12:30pm and 2:20-6pm. **Luggage storage:** L1500.
Buses: Lazzi, Piazzale Verdi (tel. 58 78 97), next to the tourist office. To: Pisa (L3000), Florence (L7700), Prato (L5000), and Pistoia (L5000). Open before bus departures—ask for a schedule at the tourist office.
Bike rental: Cicli Barbetti, Via Anfiteatro, 23 (tel. 95 44 44). Bikes L15,000 per day. Open Tues.-Sun. 9am-1pm and 4-7pm.
English books: Libreria Baroni, V. San Paolino, 47. Good selection of on-the-road standards. Open Tues.-Sat. 9am-1pm and 4-8pm.
Pharmacy: Farmacia, P. San Michele, 42. Open Mon.-Sat. 9am-1pm and 4-8:30pm.
Emergencies: tel. 113. **Hospital:** Campo di Marte (tel. 97 01). **Medical Assistance: Misericordia,** tel. 49 23 33.

ACCOMMODATIONS

The **CIV-EX travel agency,** at Via Veneto, 28 (tel. 567 41), provides an accommodations service and a list of families in Lucca who rent rooms in private houses.

Ostello della Gioventù Il Serchio, Via Brennero, 673 (tel. 34 18 11). Take bus #1 or 11 from P. Giglio (last bus 8pm), or walk out Porta S. Maria. Turn right onto Via Batoni and then left onto Viale M. Civitali and follow the signs for the *ostello* (20min.). Charmless and cramped. Check-out 9am; office open 4:30-11pm. Curfew midnight. L14,000 for bunk bed, shower, and breakfast. There is also a bar which serves food (lunch or dinner, L12,000). Hostel card required, but they may slip you in if you don't have one.
Albergo Diana, Via del Molinetto, 11 (tel. 49 22 02), off P. San Martino. Large and appealing, with a central garden, cool marble floors, and a TV in every room. Singles L42,500. Doubles with bath L80-90,000.
Pensione Cinzia, Via della Dogana, 9 (tel. 49 13 23), also off P. San Martino, on a quiet side street. Sign is covered by ivy. The rooms are decent and filled with old-fashioned furniture. Singles L28,000. Doubles L45,000.

FOOD

You may have to search out Lucca's restaurants, but, once you find them, you'll be assured of good Tuscan food. The **central market** occupies the large building at the west side of P. del Carmine. (Open Mon.-Sat. 7am-1pm and 4-7:30pm.) An **open-air market** overruns P. Anfiteatro every Wednesday and Saturday (8am-1pm). The **Supermercato STANDA** stands at Via Emanuele, 50, off P. Napoleone.

Trattoria da Leo, V. Tegrimi, 1 (tel. 49 22 36), off P. del Salvatore; ask for the restaurant by name. A bustling, peach-colored hangout for locals who come for the *risotto* with zucchini. *Primi* L6000, *secondi* L9000-13,000. Open Mon.-Sat. noon-2:30pm and 7:30-10:30pm.
Ristorante Da Guido, Via Battisti, 28 (tel. 472 19), at Via degli Angeli. Filled with the sounds of the latest soccer match or cycling race on the television as locals enjoy the cheap and filling meals. *Gentile* proprietor welcomes tourists. *Menù* L17,000. *Penne all'arrabbiata* (spicy) L4500. Most *secondi* L7000, including roasted veal or rabbit. Open Mon.-Sat. noon-2:30pm and 8-10pm.
Pizzeria Rusticanella 2, Via San Paolino, 30, between P. Verdi and P. San Michele. Float indoors on the aroma of their mouth-watering pizzas. Slices from L1500. If you're not up for pizza, try the *salsicce* (sausage, L5000). Open Mon.-Sat. noon-3pm and 6-10:30pm.

SIGHTS AND ENTERTAINMENT

Piazza Napoleone, in the heart of Lucca, is the town's busy administrative center. The 16th-century **Palazzo Ducale** houses government offices. Head down Via del Duomo to the noble **Piazza San Martino,** where the ornate, asymmetrical **duomo**

San Martino leans against its bell tower on one side and the post office on the other (the architects designed the façade around the pre-existing bell tower, which had been constructed two centuries earlier). Thirteenth-century reliefs decorate the exterior, including Nicola Pisano's *Journey of the Magi* and *Deposition*. Matteo Civitali, Lucca's famous sculptor, designed the floor, contributed the statue of St. Martin to the right of the door, and carved two beautiful sculptures of angels for the altar. His prize piece is the **Tempietto** halfway up the left aisle, which houses the *Volto Santo*. Reputedly carved by Nicodemus at Calvary, this wooden crucifix is said to be the true image of Christ. Later, the statue passed into the hands of the Bishop of Lucca. Somewhat ignorant of navigational technique, the bishop set off in a boat without a crew or sails, but, miraculously, the boat landed safely at Luni. To settle the ownership dispute that arose between Lucca and Luni, the statue was placed on an ox-cart and the oxen were left to choose the rightful site; they turned immediately toward Lucca. (The *Volto* is taken for a ride through the town every Sept. 13 to commemorate the wise choice.) The sacristy contains the beautiful and well preserved *Madonna and Saints* by Ghirlandaio (unfortunately, the art is undergoing extensive restoration), and Tintoretto's *Last Supper* waits in the third chapel on the right. (Open daily 7am-noon and 3:30-6:30pm; Oct.-Feb. 7am-noon and 3-5:30pm.)

From the cathedral, return to P. Napoleone past the 12th-century Church of San Giovanni, turn right on Via Beccheria, and continue to **Piazza San Michele,** the old Roman forum, which is ringed by impressive brick *palazzi* typical of medieval Lucca. The annual **Palio della Balestra,** a crossbow competition dating back to 1443, takes place here. The participants appear in traditional costume on July 12 and Sept. 14 for the competition, which was revived as a tourist draw in the early 1970s. The **Church of San Michele in Foro,** again with multi-patterned columns, epitomizes Pisan-Lucchese architecture and has a Filippo Lippi painting of *Saints Helena, Jerome, Sebastian, and Roch*. (Open 8:30am-12:30pm and 3:30-7:30pm.)

From the *piazza*, stroll along nearby **Via Fillungo,** Lucca's best-preserved medieval street. Off P. Scalpellini rises the **Church of San Frediano,** an imposing Romanesque structure graced by a huge polychrome mosaic—*The Ascension* by Berlinghieri—on its façade. Within, the second chapel to the right holds the decaying (officially incorruptible) **mummy of Santa Zita,** the beloved Virgin of Lucca and patron saint of baked pasta dishes (just kidding). One chapel to the left are the frescoes of the *Legend of the Volto Santo* by Amico Aspertini. (Open 8:30am-12:30pm and 4-7:30pm.) From the church, head back across Via Fillungo to **Piazza Anfiteatro.** A perfect oval of medieval houses rings the site of a former Roman amphitheater. Cut across the *piazza* to Via A. Mordini. A right on Via Guinigi brings you to the **Palazzo Guinigi,** a splendidly preserved complex of medieval palaces alternating red brick with white marble columns. Climb the 230 steps to reach the **Torre Guinigi,** crowned by flowers and oak trees. From here you can see the Apuan Alps. (Open March-Nov. Mon.-Sat. 9am-7:30pm; Dec.-Feb. 10am-4:30pm. Admission L4500.)

Music lovers should not miss the birthplace of Giacomo Puccini (Corso San Covenzo, 9), the composer of *La Bohème* and *Madama Butterfly*, among other masterpieces. The set of rooms exhibit the piano on which he composed several of his scores, letters, and manuscripts, while the strains of his operas filter through the apartment. (Open April-Sept. 10am-1pm and 3-6pm, Oct.-March 11am-1pm and 3-5pm. Free.)

Conclude your tour of Lucca with a walk or bike ride around the perfectly intact city walls. The shaded, breezy 4-km path (closed to cars) meets grassy parks and cool fountains along the *baluardi* (battlements), from which you can appreciate both the layout of the city and the beautiful countryside high above the moat. The **Caffè di Simo,** V. Fillungo, 58, is an elegant place to refresh yourself, complete with chandeliers, marble tables, and a zinc bar. In the 19th century, artists, writers, and *risorgimento*-plotters gathered here, but they probably didn't have to pay L4500 (L1500 at the bar) for their coffee.

Lucca's calendar bulges with dance and classical music events. The musical delights of the **Estate Musicale Lucchese** linger from July to September. The **Teatro Comunale del Giglio's** opera season is September. During the summer, you can take in an Italian **film** under the stars in Piazza Guidiccioni. (June-Aug. nightly at 9pm, L7000; students, children, and those over 60, L4000.) The **Settembre Lucchese** is a lively jumble of artistic, athletic, and folkloric presentations. Pick up a calendar of events from the tourist office.

■■■ PISA

It's hard to believe that a wobbly tower could prove so popular. Yet, every year millions of tourists descend on Pisa, turning its famed Campo dei Miracoli into a seething, t-shirt-buying, ice-cream-licking, photo-taking wasteland with a couple of white buildings sulking nearby. Not that the Leaning Tower isn't worth seeing; it's a prime example of the innovative architecture of the Pisan Romanesque period, whose instantly recognizable stripes and blind arcades are featured on churches from Sardinia to Apulia. In the Middle Ages when the unclogged Arno still flowed to the sea, Pisa was a major port city whose Mediterranean empire extended to Corsica, Sardinia, and the Balearics, and whose international contacts led to a cultural revolution at home. Unfortunately, when the Arno silted up, Pisa's fortunes dried up; Pisans now thrive on the international contact of tourism. Be a typical tourist and take that photo of yourself holding up the tower, but also try to branch out into the city; its quieter squares, renowned university, and lovely riverwalks are the stuff of a beautiful Italian city.

ORIENTATION AND PRACTICAL INFORMATION

Pisa lies on the Tyrrhenian coast of Italy at the mouth of the Arno, directly west of Florence. **APT** runs both intra- and intercity buses, connecting Pisa with other towns along the coast, including Livorno. The town's focus is not on the *duomo*, but the Arno. Most of Pisa's important sights lie to the north of the Arno; the main train station unaccountably rests far to the south. To get to the **Campo dei Miracoli** ("Field of Miracles"; also known as the **Piazza del Duomo**) from the station, take bus #1 (buy tickets to the left outside the station, L1100), or walk straight up Viale Gramsci, turn left at P. Vittorio Emanuele onto P. Sant'Antonio, and take V. Crispi across the river. On the other side, it turns into V. Roma, which leads to P. del Duomo (1.5km).

Tourist Office: P. della Stazione, 11 (tel. 422 91). Friendly staff hands out detailed maps. No accommodations service, but will call around to see who has space. Open Mon.-Sat. 8am-8pm, Sun. 9am-noon. A **branch** office at P. del Duomo (tel. 56 04 64), behind the leaning thing. Open Mon. and Fri. 8:30am-3pm and 3:30-6:30pm, Tues.-Thurs. 9:30am-3pm, and Sat. 9:30am-noon and 3-6pm.

Police: tel. 50 15 13.

Post Office: P. Emanuele, 8 (tel. 242 97), near the station. Go to the windows on your left. Open Mon.-Fri. 8:15am-7pm, Sat. 8:15am-noon. **Postal Code:** 56100.

Telephones: Telecom, Via Carducci, 15 has a room full of phones; also use the phones at the train station. **Telephone Code:** 050.

Budget Travel: CTS, Via Santa Maria, 45/B (tel. 45 431). Daytrips, international tickets, and boats to nearby islands. Be prepared to wait at least 30min. English spoken. Open Mon.-Fri. 9:30am-12:30pm and 4-7pm, Sat. 9:30am-12:30pm.

Currency Exchange: Your best bet is a bank near the center of town, but the train station offers reasonable rates and is open 24hrs. **Banca di Roma** on V. Santa Maria has an ATM that takes Cirrus.

Airport: Galileo Galilei (information: tel. 50 07 07). Charter, domestic, and international flights. Trains make the 4-min. trip (L1000) from the train station, at times coinciding with departures.

Trains: P. della Stazione (tel. 413 85), in the southern end of town. Ticket and information office open 7am-8:30pm. Trains run between Pisa and Florence every hr. (1hr., L7200), stopping in Lucca on the way (20min., L2700). The main coastal line links Pisa to Livorno (L2000), Genoa (L15,000), and Rome (L27,000). Local or regional trains often stop at Pisa's other station, **S. Rossore,** which is much closer to the *duomo* and youth hostel.

Buses: Lazzi, P. Emanuele, 11 (tel. 462 88). Frequent service to Lucca, Pistoia, Prato, and Florence. **APT,** P. Sant'Antonio (tel. 233 84), near the station. Frequent service to Livorno and Volterra.

Taxis: tel. 54 16 00.

Car Rental: Avis (tel. 420 28), **Budget** (tel. 454 90), **Eurodollar** (tel. 462 09), **Hertz** (tel. 491 87), and **Maggiore** (tel. 425 74) all have offices at Pisa's airport. Prices start around L180,000 per day. Minimum age 23yr.

Bike Rental: Bici Bike, Via della Spina, 28 (tel. 202 00). Rents bikes (L3000 per hr., L15,000 per day), mountain bikes (L5000 per hr., L30,000 per day), and mopeds (L10,000 per hr., L55,000 per day). Drop-off office in Florence.

English Bookstore: Librerie Reunite, Corso Italia, 95. The right-hand wall as you enter is stocked with classics and lots of trashy novels. Great prices—about what you'd pay in the U.S. Open daily 9am-1pm and 4-8pm.

Late Night Pharmacy: Farmacia, P. del Duomo. Open all night.

Emergencies: tel. 113. **Hospital:** (tel. 59 21 11) on Via Bonanno near P. del Duomo. **Medical Assistance:** P. San Fredino, 6 (tel. 50 11 00).

ACCOMMODATIONS AND CAMPING

Pisa has plenty of cheap *pensioni* and *locande,* but demand is always high and the new hostel is a bit of a hike. Call ahead and make reservations, or pick up the hotel map at the station, take the bus to the *duomo,* and start looking.

Centro Turistico Madonna dell'Acqua, Via Pietrasantina, 15 (tel. 89 06 22). Take bus #3 from the station and ask the driver to let you off at the *ostello.* A relatively new hostel beneath an old sanctuary. Check-out 9am. Office open 6-11pm. Singles L30,000. L20,000 per person for beds in double or triple rooms. Sells cold drinks and bottled water.

Albergo Gronchi, P. Archivescovado, 1 (tel. 56 18 23), adjacent to P. del Duomo. Pisa's top pick has a cool, welcoming entryway replete with stained glass and a fluffy white cat, plus rooms with frescoed ceilings and patterned tile floors. Garden in back puts you just beyond the range of the Tower, should it topple. Curfew midnight. Singles L28,000. Doubles L44,000. Triples L62,000. Come early or reserve ahead of time; rooms fill quickly.

Casa della Giovane (ACISJF), Via F. Corridoni, 29 (tel. 430 61), 10min. from the station (turn right as you leave). This women's hostel is a great place to stay if you're the right gender. Bright, clean rooms include bath. Curfew 10pm. L20,000 per person in doubles or triples. Breakfast L2000. Reception open 7am-10pm.

Hotel Galileo, Via Santa Maria, 12 (tel. 406 21). Spacious rooms with tiled floors and frescoed ceilings converge on a lounge with a soft sofa and an ebullient proprietress. Don't be put off by the dark entryway. Singles L34,000. Doubles L45,000. Triples L60,000. Quads L80,000.

Locanda Serena, Via D. Cavalca, 45 (tel. 244 91), near P. Dante. A new coat of paint has brightened this small pension in the heart of the *centro storico.* Curfew midnight. Singles L32,000. Doubles L46,000. Triples L62,000. Breakfast L4500.

Albergo Helvetia, Via Don G. Boschi, 31 (tel. 55 30 84), off P. Archivescovado, 2min. from the *duomo.* Large, clean rooms contain beds covered with wild spreads and walls hung with brightly painted tribal masks. Go figure. Singles L34,000. Doubles L46,000, with bath L62,000.

Camping: The 3 campgrounds near Pisa can be dreadfully hot and crowded in summer. For information call 56 17 94. **Campeggio Torre Pendente,** Viale delle Cascine, 86 (tel. 56 06 65), 1km away, is the closest to town. Follow the signs from P. Manin. At least L12,000 per person, tent included. Open March 15-Sept. 30. **Camping Internazionale** (tel. 365 53), on Via Litoranea in Marina di Pisa, is 14km away, on a private beach with a bar and restaurant. Take an ACIT bus to San Marina di Pisa. L10,000 per person. Open April 15-Oct. **Camping**

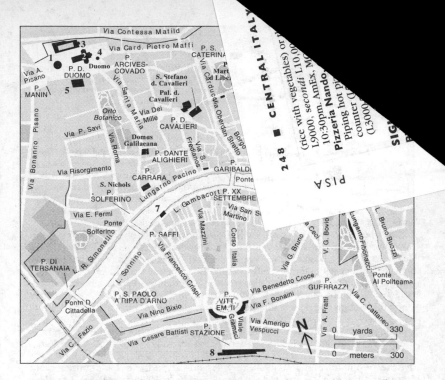

(rice with vegetables) or p...
L9000, *secondi* L10,00...
10:30pm. AmEx, M...
Pizzeria Nando...
Piping hot piz...
counter (L...
(L3000...
SIG...

Mare e Sole (tel. 327 57), on Viale del Tirreno, in nearby Calambrone. Bungalows on the beach. L7000 per person, L8000 per tent. Open April-Sept.

FOOD

For a more authentic ambience than that manufactured by the touristy *trattorie*
near the *duomo,* head toward the river. Cheap restaurants are plentiful around the
university area. You'll find an **open-air market** in P. Vettovaglie (take Via Vigina off
Lungarno Pacinotti), at the heart of the residential quarter preferred by Pisans. Bakeries and *salumerie* also abound. Buy staples at the **COOP supermarket** at P. Don
Minzoni and Via S. Agostino (open daily 8am-8pm). The local specialty is *torta di
ceci* (or *cecina*) a delicious pizza made with chick peas, available at most *bar-pizze-
rie* for L2000 per slice.

Trattoria da Matteo, Via l'Aroncio, 46 (tel. 410 57), off Via S. Maria, near Hotel
Galileo. Friendly proprietor and a wide range of culinary treats. Start with *gnocchi
al pomodoro* (L6000) and continue with *scaloppina in umido con i funghi* (veal
with mushrooms, L9000). Pizza from L6000. *Menù* L15,000. Beer and a slice at
the bar L5000. Open Sun.-Fri. noon-3pm and 7-10:30pm.

Il Paiolo, Via Curtatone e Montanara, 9 (tel. 425 28), near the university. A pub that
draws a lively crowd. Offers several *menù:* pasta and *panino* (L11,000), *primo*
and *secondo* (L13,000). Open Mon.-Fri. noon-3pm and 7pm-1am, Sat. 7pm-1am.

Ristoro al Vecchio Teatro, V. Collegio Ricci, 2 (tel. 202 10), off P. Dante. Delicious, innovative food with an emphasis on fresh vegetables, served in a cool, gar-
den-like room. Menu changes daily, but, if they have it, try the *risotto d'ortolana*

...he buttery *sfogliata di zucchine* (zucchini tart). *Primi*
...0, desserts L4000. Open Mon.-Fri. 12:30-2:30pm and 8-
..., Visa.
...Corso Italia, 103, between P. Vittorio Emanuele and the river.
...zas fly to the customers straight from the blazing oven behind the
...5500-7000). Fantastic *panini* created from bread that's baked to order
...000). Open Mon.-Sat. 10am-2:30pm and 4-10pm.

...TS AND ENTERTAINMENT

...iazza del Duomo, also known as the **Campo dei Miracoli** (Field of Miracles),
contains the **cathedral, baptistery, Camposanto,** and the **Leaning Tower,** which
all rise from a plush blanket of green grass. The city offers an all-inclusive ticket to
the *duomo,* the baptistery, Camposanto, the Museo delle Sinopie, and the Museo
del Duomo for L15,000; ticket for the *duomo* and another monument L10,000; the
duomo and 3 other monuments L12,000; *or* the *duomo* and what's behind Door #2
just $9.99! Admission to the cathedral is L2000 (unless you're there to attend mass,
and you have to look *extremely* pious to get past the guards).

The black-and-white façade of the **duomo** is the archetype of the Pisan
Romanesque period (and the interior definitely warrants the L2000 admission).
Begun in 1063 by Boschetto (whose dedication to his work was so great that he
actually had himself entombed in the wall), the cathedral was the first structure of
the Campo. Enter the five-aisled nave through Bonanno Pisano's bronze doors
(1180). Though most of the interior was destroyed by fire in 1595, paintings by
Ghirlandaio along the right wall, Cimabue's mosaic *Christ Pantocrator* in the apse,
and the bits of the Cosmati pavement remain in good condition. Giovanni Pisano's
last and greatest **pulpit,** no doubt designed to outdo his father's in the baptistery, is
the *duomo's* highlight. Relief panels depict classical and biblical subjects; the *Nativity,* the *Last Judgment,* and the *Massacre of the Innocents* are among the most striking. Never one to resist a good allegory, Pisano carved the pulpit's supports into
figures symbolizing the arts and virtues. (Open daily 10:45am-5:40pm; in winter
10:45am-12:45pm and 3-4:45pm. Closed for mass 10-10:45am; mass also at 8am.)

The **baptistery,** an enormous barrel of a building begun in 1152, measures
107.24 meters in girth and reaches 54.86 meters into the Pisan sky. The building's
architecture mixes the Tuscan Romanesque and Gothic styles—the lower half in
typical Tuscan stripes, but the upper half in a stunning Gothic ensemble of gables,
pinnacles, and statuary set in lacy tracery. Nicola Pisano's **pulpit** (1260) is to the left
of the baptismal font; it recaptures the sobriety and dignity of classical antiquity and
is considered one of the harbingers of Renaissance art in Italy. Astoundingly, the
dome's acoustics are such that an unamplified choir singing in the baptistery can be
heard 20km away. (Open daily 9am-5:40pm. In winter daily 9am-4:40pm.)

The **Camposanto,** a long, white-cloistered cemetery filled with earth brought
back from Mt. Calvary by the Crusaders, holds, among other things, the Roman sarcophagi whose reliefs inspired Nicola Pisano's pulpit. Fragments of frescoes shattered by Allied bombs during World War II line the galleries. Enter the Cappella
Ammannati for a reprieve from the screaming hordes of tourists, but don't expect
peace from the haunting frescoes of an unidentified 14th-century artist known for
these works as the "Master of the Triumph of Death." (Open daily 9am-5:40pm; off-
season 9am-4:40pm.)

The last and greatest miracle in the Campo dei Miracoli is the **Leaning Tower.**
Intended as the *il campanile del duomo,* it was begun by Bonanno Pisano in 1173
and had reached the height of 10m when the soil beneath it unexpectedly subsided.
The belfry contains seven bells, each corresponding to a note on the diatonic scale.
Because the ground below is none too firm, all the structures in the *campo* tilt, but
none so dramatically and famously as the tower. The tilt intensified as post-World
War II tourists ascended in ever-increasing numbers, and the tower continues to slip

1-2mm every year. The Tower has been **closed** indefinitely, to the dismay of thousands of visitors. More drastic measures are being taken to halt its slow collapse— for instance, steel cables were wrapped around the bottom story, the walls of which were thought to be in danger of fracturing. The possible construction of an aqueduct to Pisa might solve the problem, allowing the closure of all wells in the surrounding area. (Groundwater depletion by thirsty Pisans and shower-mad American tourists is thought to cause the Tower's settling.)

Cross the square from the Camposanto to the **Museo delle Sinopie,** which displays preliminary fresco sketches by Traini, Veneziano, Gaddi, and others discovered during restoration after World War II. (Open daily 8am-7:40pm; off-season 9am-12:40pm and 3-4:40pm.) The new **Museo dell'Opera del Duomo,** located behind the Leaning Tower, displays artwork from the three buildings of P. del Duomo, including the ivory *Madonna and Crucifix* and *Madonna and Child* by Giovanni Pisano. (Open daily 9am-5:20pm; off-season 9am-12:30pm and 3-4:30pm.)

Beyond the Campo dei Miracoli, museums, Romanesque churches, and *piazze* dot the city. The **Museo Nazionale di San Matteo,** on the Arno not far from P. Mazzini, includes panels by Masaccio, Fra Angelico, and Pietro Lorenzetti, and sculpture by the Pisano clan. (Open Tues.-Sat. 9am-7:30pm, Sun. 9am-1:30pm. L6000.)

Piazza dei Cavalieri, designed by Vasari during Medici rule, on the site of the Roman forum, held Pisa's town hall during the Middle Ages. Today it is the seat of the **Scuola Normale Superiore,** one of Italy's premier universities, thanks to the Medici who transferred Florence's university here in the 16th century. The administrative offices of the Scuola occupy the beautiful **Palazzo dei Cavalieri,** its façade decorated with busts of the Grand Dukes of Tuscany and with *graffiti* (the etched, not the spray-painted, kind).

Of Pisa's numerous churches, two merit special attention. Don't miss the **Chiesa di Santa Maria della Spina,** a spectacle of Gothic art, which faces Lungarno Gambacorti against the river. From the Campo, walk down Via Santa Maria and over the bridge. Originally an oratory, the church was enlarged in 1323 and renamed Chiesa della Spina (Church of the Thorn) because it claims to house one of the thorns from Christ's crown. (Open daily 8am-noon and 3:30-7pm.) Another worthy sidetrack from P. del Duomo is the **Church of San Nicola,** between Via S. Maria and P. Carrara, dedicated to Pisa's patron saint. See him in the famous altarpiece of the fourth chapel on the right, breaking and deflecting the arrows a wrathful God aims at Pisa. The bell tower of the church inclines slightly, not unlike its more famous cousin. (Open daily 8am-noon and 4-6:30pm.)

Occasional **concerts** are given in the *duomo,* where the acoustics are astounding. A former church on **Via San Zeno** holds performances of experimental music, and on the last Sunday in June, the annual tug-of-war, the **Gioco del Ponto,** revives Pisa's medieval color and pageantry. On the second weekend of every month, an antique fair fills the Ponte di Mezzo.

■■■ LIVORNO

Overwhelmed by the monstrous liners awaiting departure for Sardinia, Corsica, Greece, and Spain, Livorno is something of a rough-and-ready port town that lives happily in industrial oblivion. Livorno first enjoyed prominence as a port under Cosimo I starting in 1571 when Pisa became landlocked, and in 1608 became a free port, open for business to Jews, Greeks, and, unfortunately, a flourishing slave trade. Nevertheless, a tradition of liberal thinking continues in Livorno; in 1921 the PCI (Partito Comunista Italiano) was established here. The main draws to Livorno are its ferries into or out of the town, but if you do happen to be here with time on your hands, there are a few interesting monuments to see and some excellent seafood to enjoy. Join the locals for a sunset stroll along the waterfront.

LIVORNO

ORIENTATION AND PRACTICAL INFORMATION

Take bus #1, 2, or 8 from the train station (buy tickets outside at machines or inside at the *tabacchi* for L1100) to reach **Piazza Grande**, the center of town. Or cross the park in front of the station and walk straight down Viale Carducci, which becomes Via dei Larderel, to Piazza Repubblica. Cross the *piazza* and take Via delle Galere to Piazza Grande.

Tourist Office: P. Cavour, 6 (tel. 89 81 11), up Via Cairoli from P. Grande, on the 3rd floor. Friendly and helpful. Open Mon.-Sat. 8:30am-2pm, Tues. and Thurs. also 3-6pm. **Branch** office at Calata Carrara, near the Corsica departure site (tel. 21 03 31). Open June 15-Sept. 30 Mon.-Sat. 9am-noon, and some afternoons.

Post Office: Via Cairoli, 12-16 (tel. 89 76 02). Open Mon.-Fri. 8:15am-7pm, Sat. 8:15am-1pm. **Postal Code:** 57100.

Telephones: Telecom (ASST), P. Grande, 14. Open Mon.-Sat. 7:30am-11:30pm. **Telephone Code:** 0586.

Currency exchange: at the train station. Fair rates. Open daily 8-11:45am and 3-5:45pm. Also at Stazione Marittima, or one of the many banks on Via Cairoli.

Trains: From: Pisa (15min., L2000), Florence (1hr., L9000), Rome (3hr., L24,500), and Piombino (1hr., L7000).

Buses: ATL (tel. 896 11) buses to Pisa (frequent, L2600) and Piombino (8 per day, L6700) leave from Piazza Grande. **Cazzi** makes trips to Florence, Pisa, Lucca, and Empoli, and is located at P. Manin, along Scali Manzoni. Office open Mon.-Fri. 8:30am-12:30pm.

Ferries: at the Stazione Marittima. From P. Grande, walk down Via Logorano, across P. Municipio to Via Porticciolo, which becomes Via Venezia, which in turn leads to the port and the Stazione Marittima. Reserve tickets about 2 weeks in advance in July and August, especially if you're traveling with a bicycle, motorcycle, or car. Be sure to check where and when your boat leaves; schedules change unpredictably with little advance notice. Prices are higher in high season and on weekends. At the Stazione Marittima, there are offices for **currency exchange, luggage storage, restaurant,** and **nursery.** All are open before and after arrivals and departures, but generally closed at midday.

Corsica Marittima (tel. 89 78 51 or 89 89 52 or 21 05 07), sails to **Bastia (Corsica):** April-mid-Sept. always on Sat. afternoons and occasionally other days—check for the current schedule (3¼hr., L34,000-38,000).

Moby Lines (tel. 89 03 25) sails to **Bastia:** April-Oct., 2 per day (June-Sept. 19 always at 8:30am); 4hr.; L34,000-39,000. To **Olbia (Sardinia):** mid-June-early Sept., (2 per day, 10am and 10pm). Spottier schedule at other times (10hr., L34,000-80,000, higher in high season and on weekends).

Corsica and Sardinia Ferries (tel. 88 13 80 or 88 63 28). To **Bastia:** June-mid-Sept. 1-3 per day (always at 8:30am), mid-Sept.-May, 2-6 boats per week. (4hr., L32,000-L44,000.) To **Olbia:** April-early Oct. (mid-June-early Oct. at 9:30am and 9:30pm, 10hr., L39,000-80,000). Slightly cheaper stand-by fares on some journeys—just show up at the port before a departure.

Taxis: tel. 40 12 94.

Luggage storage: in train station. L1500 per day. Open daily 8am-1pm and 4-8pm.

All-night pharmacy: Farmacia Comunale, V. Fiume, 1, up from P. Grande.

Emergencies: tel. 113. **Hospital: Pronto Soccorso,** tel. 40 33 51 or 42 13 98.

ACCOMMODATIONS

Finding a room is easy even in summer since most people stay here only one night before catching a boat.

Pensione Dante, Scali D'Azeglio, 28 (tel. 89 34 61). Take a right as you leave the port and walk straight along the waterfront until you come to a canal on the left. The *pensione* is up a few blocks. The paisley bedspreads and orange formica furnishings are not exactly fashionable, but rooms are clean and ample; many have views of the canal. Singles L40,000. Doubles L50,000, with bath L55,000.

Hotel Goldoni, Via Enrico Mayer, 42 (tel. 89 87 05). Take Via Rossi 1 block out of P. Cavour. Centrally located, with compact garden. The oddly shaped rooms are clean and modern. Friendly, helpful staff. Singles with bath L48,000. Doubles L55,000, with bath L65,000/75,000. Triples L75,000, with bath L95,000.

FOOD

Livorno owes its culinary specialties, like its livelihood, to the sea. The city has its own interpretation of the classic bouillabaise—a fiery, tomato-based seafood stew called "*cacciucco.*" An **open-air market** sprawls along Via Buontalenti, behind the APT station (Mon.-Sat. 8am-1pm). Fill your brown bag at the **STANDA supermarket** off P. Grande at Via Grande, 174. (Open daily 8:30am-1pm and 4-8pm.)

Hostaria della Crema, Scala Ciadini, 39 (tel. 88 14 87). Just plain pretty, with pink walls, pink tile floors, and little potted plants on all the tables. Order the *menù* and try the *cacciucco* (L22,000). Or choose your own fish from the fresh selection. Open Sun.-Tues. noon-2:30pm and 7-10pm. AmEx.

La Cantonata, Corso Mazzini, 222 (tel. 88 14 42). Smiling owner dishes out huge plates of *spaghetti ai frutti di mare* (seafood spaghetti, L7000), the freshest fish, and brimming glasses of *chianti*. Other-worldly *riso nero* (rice turned black from squid ink) only L8000. *Secondi* L9000. Cover L2000. Service 10%. Open Tues.-Sun. noon-2:30pm and 7-11pm.

Trattoria Il Sottomarino, Via dei Terrazzini, 48 (tel. 237 71), off P. della Repubblica at the end of Via Pina d'Oro. Not cheap, but people come from all over to taste the *cacciucco*. Open Aug.-June Fri.-Wed. 12:30-2:30pm and 7:30-10pm.

SIGHTS AND ENTERTAINMENT

Located in the heart of the quarter known as **Piccola Venezia** for the canals that course through the neighborhood, the **Fortezza Nuova** is protected by a complete moat. The fortress was completed in the early 1600s by the Medici family and now houses a well maintained public garden and park; compare this fortress to the massive, sprawling **Fortezza Vecchia** (from the new fortress, walk to P. Municipio, and then down Via S. Giovanni). Built by the powerful Marquises of Tuscany in the 9th century, the portly tower in the middle was the first fortification on the site. When Pisans conquered Livorno, they built a fort around the tower (out of fear it would lean over and put them out of business). In the 16th century the Medici surrounded the ensemble with robust brick walls to consolidate their hold on Livorno, by then the chief Tuscan port. Piazza Micheli, across from the port, is home to the **Monumento del Quattro Mori.** This marble figure of Duke Ferdinand I was carved by Bandini in 1595, but the four miserable, manacled bronze slaves were added by Pietro Tacca in 1626.

Livorno has inspired two important contributions to painting. Foremost is the group of 19th-century painters "I Macchiaioli" (literally, "the blotters"), led by Giovanni Fattori. In the **Museo Civico Giovanni Fattori** (tel. 80 80 01) in Villa Fabbricotti at Via della Libertà, 20, you can see their proto-impressionist work. (Open Tues.-Sun. 10am-1pm, Thurs. and Sat. also 4:30-7:30pm; admission L4000.) Livorno's second gift to art history was 20th-century painter Amadeo Modigliani.

Livorno's chief festival, the **Palio Marinaro,** takes place just off this stretch of coast. In mid-July, rowers from the various neighborhoods of the city race traditional crafts toward the old port, spurred on by the spectators who line the banks.

▪▪▪ ELBA

"Lucky Napoleon!" Dylan Thomas exclaimed in a letter written from Elba to his friends. Once you've witnessed the island's deep turquoise waters, dramatically poised mountains, and velvety beaches, you'll share the sentiment. A surviving fragment of the giant peninsula that once joined Corsica to the Tuscan shore, Elba first drew Etruscan settlers, who mined its hills for iron. Jason and his Argonauts made a stop here, but it was the jeering Greeks who named it Aethalia (Soot Island). Roman patricians saw the island's beauty through the smoke and built their summer villas here. Of course, Elba derives its greatest fame from its association with Napoleon; the Little Emperor was sent into exile (the first time) here in 1814. Elba hardly seems like much of an exile; in summer, it is overrun with vacationing Germans. Fortunately, the best parts of the island lie off the beaten track, and if you come in the off-season you will have virtually the whole place to yourself.

In July and August, vacationing Italians flock to Elba, making it impossible to find lodging on the island without a reservation made several months ahead. During June and September the weather is perfect and the beds plentiful. Camping may be the best way to go on Elba, but beware—camping space comes as dear as a hotel on the island and often requires a reservation. There are also about 100 **affitta camere** on the island and about 30-40 **agriturismo** locations, depending on the month.

Getting There The best way to reach Elba is by **ferry** from Piombino Marittima (also called Piombino Porto) to Portoferraio, Elba's largest city. **Trains** on the Genoa-Rome line stop at Campiglia Marittima, from which a tiny commuter train leaves for the ferries in Piombino Marittima (wait for the *porto* stop). From Florence change at Pisa to arrive at Campiglia Marittima. Both Toremar (1hr., L9000-13,000 depending on season and day of the week; **hydrofoil** 30min., L16,000) and Navarma (1hr., same prices as Toremar) run frequent boats to Elba, a total of about 18 per day during the summer months. Talk directly to Toremar (tel. (0565) 91 80 80) or Navarma (tel. 22 12 12) at Piazzale Premuda, 13, in Piombino. You can also buy tickets for the next departing ferry at the **FS** booth in the train station. Elba's only **airport** (tel. 97 79 30) is in Marina di Campo, with flights to Florence, Pisa, Bologna, and Monaco. Should you get stuck in Piombino, take a train from the port to the city (every 30 min., 5min., L1500). In town, **Albergo Il Piave** sits right across from the train station at Piazza F. Niccolini, 2 (tel. 22 60 50) and has standard rooms, with bath and stained carpet. (Singles L40,000. Doubles L50,000.) There is also a **tourist office,** open in summer only, at the port.

Transportation On Elba, **ATL** buses constitute the only form of public transportation between the major cities of Portoferraio, Marina di Campo, Marciana Marina, and Porto Azzurro (all L2700 from Portoferraio). Popular **boat excursions** cover various parts of the coast; contact **Etruria** in Portoferraio (tel. 90 42 73) for details. Renting a **moped** (L25,000-50,000 per day) allows you to see the more isolated parts of the island.

Orientation Each of the different zones of the island attracts a distinct variety of loyal visitor, from families in **Marina di Campo** and **Marciana Marina,** to party-hard beach fanatics in **Capo Civeri,** to the private-yacht set in **Porto Azzurro.** The coast is mostly sandy from Procchio, around Portoferraio, down the east coast and around to Marina di Campo. Elba's western shore, with its stone-slab waterfront, remains relatively unfrequented. Wherever you decide to go, bypass Portoferraio, a chaotic port-city with the most overcrowded beach on the island. Head over to the **tourist office** as soon as you land to pick up the essential *"notizie Utili per il Turista,"* which gives information for the entire island on beaches, hotels, restaurants, entertainment of any kind, and a decent map of Elba.

PORTOFERRAIO

Tourist Offices: APT, Calata Italia, 26 (tel. 91 46 71), on the 1st floor, across from the Toremar boat landing. Info galore: accommodations, a map, bus schedule, and brochures. They have info on **agriturismo** and **affitta camere** in the cities and countryside of Elba (open summer Mon.-Sat. 8am-8pm, in winter Mon.-Sat. 8am-1pm and 4-7pm,). There's also a **tourist info booth** at the bus station, Viale Elba, 20, which provides brochures, reserves rooms, holds luggage (L1500), and sells bus tickets. Open June 15-Sept. 15 Mon.-Sat. 8am-8pm. **Associazione**

Albergatori, Calata Italia, 21 (tel. 91 47 54). Offers free room-finding. Open Mon.-Sat. 9am-12:30pm and 3:30-7pm. **Police:** tel. 92 006, on Via Garibaldi.
Post Office: P. Hutre, off P. della Repubblica. Open Mon.-Fri. 8:15am-7pm, Sat. 8:15am-1pm. There is another **branch,** nearer the port, on Via Carducci. Open Mon.-Fri. 8:15am-1:30pm, Sat. 8:15am-12:30pm. **Postal code:** 57037.
Telephones: Telecom (SIP), Calata Italia, across Viale Elba from Hotel Massimo. Open daily 8am-10pm. In Marina di Campo, try **Pietre Bigiotteria,** Via Roma, 41. Open Mon.-Sat. 8am-10pm, Sun. 10am-noon. **Telephone code:** 0565.
Currency Exchange: There are a zillion places in the port willing to rip you off, but hold onto your cash and walk up to V. Manganaro, where there are several banks, including **Banca di Roma** (tel. 91 84 59). Open Mon.-Fri. 8:20am-1pm.
Buses: ATL, Viale Elba, 20 (tel. 91 43 92). Open June-Sept. Mon.-Sat. 8am-8pm, Oct.-May 8am-1pm and 5-7pm. A list of places to buy tickets on Sun. is posted on the door. **Luggage storage** L1500 per piece. Open daily 8am-8pm.
Ferries: Toremar, Calata Italia, 22 (tel. 91 80 80). Hydrofoil tickets available at the **Toremar Aliscafi booth** on the waterfront in front of the main Toremar office. **Navarma,** Viale Elba, 4 (tel. 91 81 01). **Elba Ferries** (tel. 93 06 76). Calata Italia, 30 (tel. 71 82 70).
Car Rental: Rent Chiappi, Calata Italia, 30 (tel. 71 82 70). Rents small Fiats, Renaults, Clios and Moke starting at L50,000. Friendly staff helps you get gas and get around. Also rents **mountain bikes** (L18,000/20,000 per day) and mopeds (starting at L25,000). Insurance included.
Bike/Moped Rental: Rent Ghiaie, Via Cairoli, 26 (tel. 91 46 66), in front of the Ghiaie beach. Easily the best place to rent mopeds and bikes on the island. Rent a well-maintained bike (L17,000 for 9am-7:30pm, L22,000 per 24hrs.) or moped (L36,000 per day, less in Sept.-July). You can also rent from or drop off at any of their other branches around the island (at Marciana Marina, Porto Azzurro, Lacona, or Marina Di Campo; L10,000 fee for returning to a different branch). Auto driver's license required. MC and Visa accepted at the Portoferraio office only. Open 9am-1pm and 3:30-7:30pm. Also see **Rent Chiappi,** above.
Emergencies: tel. 113. **Hospital: Ospedale Civile Elbano** (tel. 91 74 21), off Via Carducci. **Ambulance:** P. Repubblica, 37 (tel. 91 40 09).

Accommodations and Food If you want to be centrally located on the island, your best bet for clean, economical accommodations in this town is the **Nobel Hotel,** Via Manganaro, 72 (tel. 91 52 17). Walk up Viale Elba from the port, and turn left when it intersects Manganaro—a 5-minute walk. (Big, bright rooms behind green shutters. Singles L30,000/50,000, with bath L35,000/60,000. Doubles L35,000/65,000, with bath L50,000/85,000.) If you can't do without a view of the sea, **Albergo Bagni Elba,** Loc. Le Ghiale (tel. 91 51 78), offers light and breezy quarters, all with private bath and many with balconies over the beach. (Singles L50,000/70,000. Doubles L70,000/80,000.)
Infested with overpriced tourist restaurants, Portoferraio is not the best place to indulge the appetite. If you select carefully at the **Osteria del Ponticello,** Via Carducci, 33, though, you probably won't blow your budget. Try their garlicky *farfalle alle pesce spado* (bow-ties with swordfish, L9000). (*Primi* L6000-9000, *secondi* L8000-14,000; cover L1500. Open noon-3pm and 7-11pm.) You can also sustain yourself at the **Enoteca al Solito Posto,** a charming wine bar that also dishes out some delicious meals. They have a *menù degustazione* that includes one dish (like *ravioli di pesce alle erbe*) plus *contorno*, a glass of wine, and coffee. (L16,000). They also serve brunch. Across from the port, basic picnic fare can be found at **Margherita Supermarket,** Calata Italia, 6. (Open 7:30am-1:30pm and 4:30-8:30pm.)

Sights If you are caught in Portoferraio with some time to spare, you won't want to miss the **Napoleon Museum,** located at his one-time residence, the Villa dei Mulini (tel. 91 58 46). Inside, you'll find furniture graced by the imperial derrière, his own library, and a good many of his letters from exile. (Open Mon.-Fri. 9am-5pm, Sat. Sun. 9am-12:30pm. Admission L5000.) Also consider stopping by the **Archaeology Museum,** Fortezza dell Lingrella (tel. 91 73 98), which guides you through the history of Elba from prehistoric times to the present. (Open Mon.-Sat. 9:30am-12:30pm and 6-9pm, Sun. 6-9pm. Admission L4000, children L2000.)

MARINA DI CAMPO

Marina di Campo's fine sandy beaches, winding their way for miles along the coast, attract masses of vacationing families with strollers and countless boxes of diapers. The numerous campgrounds around Marina di Campo are popular with young people. You can either bake in the sun or rent sporting equipment like **windsurfers** at **Tropical Bagni** during the day (starting at L15,000 per hour; no office or phone, just go to the beach and you'll see them). **Biko's Bikes** in P. Torino (tel. 71 05 36) rents cycles for L7000 per hour or L20,000 per day, and mopeds for L30,000 per day. **Hotel Lido,** Via Mascagni, 29 (tel. 97 60 40), is near the center of town (turn left from P. Torino). It's only a minute from the beach, with clean and comfortable rooms, some with balconies. (Doubles L40,000/60,000, with bath L50,000/70,000.) Limited parking available for guests. You must reserve by Easter for July and August. For camping, try **La Foce** (tel. 97 64 56), a well-equipped place right on the beach, or the nearby **Del Mare** (tel. 97 62 37; open Apr. 1-Oct. 30). Both lie to the left of Marina di Campo's waterfront. The **Minimarket** in P. Torino, half a block up from the bus stop, stocks all the essentials (open daily 7:30am-8pm). The **Canabis Restaurant,** Via Roma, 41-43 (tel. 97 75 55), bakes the best food around, including killer crêpes stuffed with cheese and *prosciutto* for around L6000. No brownies, though. (Open daily 7am-2am.) Via Roma, along the waterfront, is also chock full of *alimentari,* where you can provision yourself for next to nothing. In summer, the party moves to **Marina 2000** at night for dancing and carousing.

PORTO AZZURRO

If you intend to stay in Porto Azzurro, brace yourself for impressive financial outlay. Sunspot of the too-thin and too-rich, Porto Azzurro naturally shelters some of the finest beaches on the island, but the beauty doesn't come cheap. **La Lanterna,** an *affitta camera* located above the restaurant of the same name, offers doubles, sometimes requiring half pension. Ask at the restaurant for prices (circa L50,000). **Albergo Barbarossa,** (tel. 950 87), at Loc. Barbarossa a bit outside of town is actually affordable. (Singles L35,000, with bath L40,000. Doubles L50,000, with bath L55,000.) Even cheaper, although decidedly more crowded and dusty, is **Camping Roclan's** (tel. 95 78 03), also at Loc. Barbarossa. For food, **The Grill,** Via Marconi, 26, near the Blumarine Hotel, offers copious portions of *penne* with a choice of tomatoes or clams for L8500. (Open daily 8:30am-2:30pm and 6pm-1am.)

MARCIANA MARINA

The strip of pebble beach that borders Marciana Marina's waterfront is just one of the countless beaches that hide in isolated coves along this part of the island. **Casa Lupi,** Via Amedeo (tel. 99 143), is your best bet here. It's a bit of a hike (5-10min. uphill from the beach), but it sports clean rooms behind green shutters and a terrace that looks out over a vineyard to the sea below. (Singles L50,000. Doubles L80,000. All rooms with bath. Half pension 75,000.) Marciana Marina is also the perfect base to explore the less developed western half of Elba. You can reach the numerous beaches along the western coast by boat; rentals are available in Capo Sant'Andrea for about L100,000 per day. If you bring a few friends with you, the mission to secure your own beach doesn't really cost that much. From Marciana Marina, partiers head to the **Claxon** in nearby **Procchio** to hear live music at night. Marciana Marina's **post office** is at Viale Loyd (open Mon.-Sat. 8:30am-1pm). For **medical emergencies,** contact the Guardia Medica Turistica, Viale Regina Margherita (tel. 90 44 36).

From Marciana Marina, a possible side excursion is a visit to **Monte Capanne.** From the top of this 1019m mountain you can see the entire island, and even as far as Corsica on a clear day. The strenuous uphill trek takes two hours, but a cable car will carry you up for L7500, round-trip L12,000 (open 10am-12:15pm and 2:30-

6pm). To get to Monte Capanne take the bus from Marciana Marina to Marciana, and get off at the Monte Capanne stop (15min.). From Marciana one can also walk to the **Romitorio di San Cerbone** and the **Santuario della Madonna del Monte,** two sanctuaries described by one Italian writer as "dense with mysticism." If you're interested in **guided hikes** to explore Elba's natural beauty contact **Il Genio del Bosco, Centro Trekking Isola d'Elba in Antiche Saline,** near Portoferraio (tel. (0565) 93 03 35).

NORTHERN ITALY

■ Liguria

The crescent-shaped coastal strip of Liguria (the Italian Riviera) stretches 350km along the Mediterranean between France and Tuscany. Genoa, in the center, divides the coast into the *Riviera di Levante* (rising sun) to the east, and the *Riviera di Ponente* (setting sun) to the west. Ligurians are known for their cultural isolation; they claim Nordic, not Latin, ancestry, and have their own vocabulary and accent incomprehensible to other Italians, let alone foreigners. The distinctive character of Ligurians, however, does not make them any less Italian, nor did it prevent them from playing a leading role in the unification of the Italian peninsula. Giuseppe Mazzini, known as the father of the *Risorgimento,* and Giuseppe Garibaldi, its most popular hero, were both Ligurians.

Protected by the Alps from the severe weather to the north, Liguria cultivates its crops and a lively tourist trade all year long, making it one of Italy's most prosperous regions. In summer the landscape comes ablaze with deep reds and purples, while lemon and almond blossoms scent the air. In winter, olive trees shade the robust flower beds and produce what may be Italy's best oil (a title contested by Tuscany).

The character of the Italian Riviera differs from that of its French neighbor. Here you'll find neither the arrogance nor the cultural sterility of Cannes or St. Tropez. (See *Let's Go: France 1996* for more details.) The palm-lined boulevards and clear turquoise water are the same, but above these rise *città vecchie* or *alte* (old or upper cities)—distinctly Italian mazes of narrow cobblestoned streets and tiny *piazze.* Unless you're coming from France, you will do best by starting at the eastern edge of Liguria and working your way only as far as Genoa. Although slightly more expensive, the eastern (Levante) coast is the more inviting of the two: it's less congested than Ponente, and the dramatic juxtaposition of Appenine mountains and Ligurian Sea creates a landscape where pine forests hover thousands of feet above the water, and tiny pebble beaches are wedged between rugged escarpments. Santa Margherita Ligure and the Cinque Terre offer picturesque havens of relaxation. But if your taste runs instead towards long stretches of sand and seemingly infinite boardwalks, head for Ponente in the west. A short hop from the French border, the western towns offer plenty of sunbathing tempered by cool, clear waters and enlivened by Italian techno music. For an affordable base, try Finale Ligure—a resort town that combines Hollywood palm trees with a medieval ambience.

All the coastal towns are linked by frequent trains on either the Genoa-La Spezia or Genoa-Ventimiglia line and frequent intercity buses pass through all major towns. Boats also connect the resort towns, and local buses run to the hill towns inland.

■■■ GENOA (GENOVA)

Genoa's name comes from the Latin word *janua,* meaning gate, appropriate for a town that is one of Italy's busiest ports. Genoa's delightfully narrow, shop-filled streets lie between the lofty peaks of the Ligurian coast and the now semi-polluted waters of the Ligurian Sea. Starting in the 13th century, Genoa's leading families were able to furnish the city with parks, palaces, and a generous store of art, almost all of which can be seen today. Christopher Columbus, Giuseppe Mazzini (the Risorgimento idealogue), and Nicolò Paganini (the virtuoso violinist) are only a few of Genoa's famous men. While still a bustling port, today's Genova is defined by its

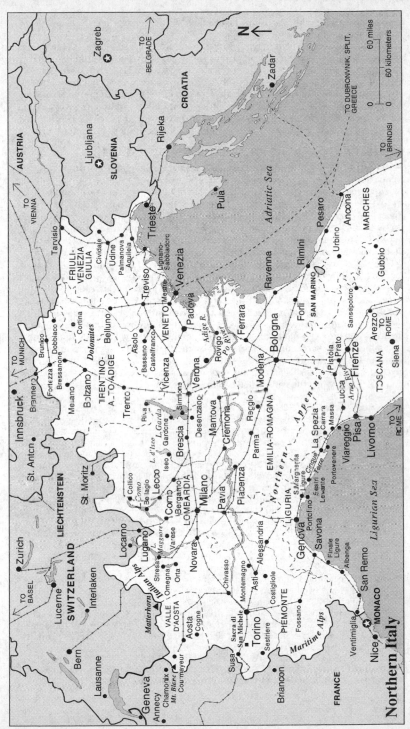

GENOA

Northern Italy

industrialists, who lend a sense of fashion and an understanding of international business to the modern city.

Built on mountains which extend almost to the water itself, Genoa's tall buildings are packed tightly together. In addition to the buses which snake uphill on narrow switchbacks, Genoa's public transportation includes public elevators and rapidly ascending funiculars, cog-rail trolleys that provide quick access to higher altitudes. For a peaceful respite from the chaotic modern city, stick to the *creuze* (narrow footpaths), and winding *vicoli* that meander upwards among houses, overhanging gardens, and ubiquitous cats. These trails offer spectacular views of the bustling city below, which, from a distance, takes on an unexpected air of cheerful tranquility.

ORIENTATION AND PRACTICAL INFORMATION

Most visitors arrive at one of Genoa's two train stations, **Genova Principe**, in Piazza Acquaverde, or **Genova Brignole**, in Piazza Verdi. Buses #40 and 37 connect the two stations (25min., L1300). From Brignole take bus #40 and from Principe take #41 to the center of town. The city stretches along the coast; from the central **Piazza de Ferrari** to Stazione Principe take **Via XXV Aprile** to **Via Garibaldi** to **Via Balbi**. **Via XX Settembre** runs east from P. de Ferrari towards Stazione Brignole. Avoid the free tourist office map—procure a decent one at the *edicola* (newsstand) in the train station for about L8000; Genoa's tangled streets can stump even a native.

Genoa's double sequence of **street numbers** (red for commercial establishments, black for residential or office buildings) is confusing, especially since dirty red numerals often appear black. Don't get discouraged if you come to the supposed address of a place and it's not there; chances are you've simply come to the number of the wrong color. **We list red addresses with an "r" after the number.**

The *centro storico* preserves many of Genoa's most important monuments; unfortunately, it is the city's most dangerous quarter and riddled with drugs and prostitution at night. The problem is complicated by the labyrinthine streets; you'll need a sixth sense of navigation here, even with a map, and it's an extremely bad place to get lost. Don't wander the area after dark or on shop-closed Sundays, and be cautious in August when the natives leave. But do visit: the sights are well worth seeing.

Tourist Office: EPT, Via Roma, 11r (tel. 54 15 41; fax 58 14 08), up 2 flights off P. Corvetto. From Stazione Brignole, go right on Via de Amicis to P. Brignole, then continue up Via Serra to P. Corvetto. Friendly to tourists and generous with its little store of useful info. Some English spoken. Open Mon.-Fri. 8am-1:15pm and 2-6:30pm, Sat. 8am-1:30pm. There are **branches** at both the Principe train station (tel. 246 26 33) and the C. Colombo airport (tel. 241 52 47). Both open Mon.-Fri. 8am-8pm. You can also head to the **Informegiovani** in the Palazzo Ducale at P. Matteotti, 5, for a better map and information geared towards young people. Open Mon.-Fri. 10am-1pm and 3-6pm (July and Aug. 9am-12:30pm).

Police: Via Diaz (tel. 536 61). Ask for the *ufficio stranieri* (office for foreigners).

Post Office: Many offices all over the city, in both train stations and the airport. Try the office at P. Dante, 4 (tel. 259 46 87), for *fermo posta* or express mail service, 2 blocks from P. de Ferrari down Via Dante. Another office at Via Rela, 8 (tel. 64 67 71). Both open Mon.-Sat. 8:10am-7:40pm. **Postal Code:** 16100.

Telephones: Telecom, office at Stazione Brignole, just to the right as you exit the station. Pay phones, directories, and real, live employees! Open Mon.-Sat. 8am-9:30pm. Plenty of phones in the **train stations** as well. **Telephone Code:** 010.

Budget Travel: CTS, Via San Vincenzo, 117r (tel. 56 43 66 or 53 27 48), off Via XX Settembre. Just before the road curves, it's off to the right, up a flight of stairs. Student fares to all destinations. Open Mon.-Fri. 9am-1pm, 2:30-6pm. **Associazione Albergatori per la Gioventù,** Via Cairoli, 2 (tel. 29 82 84), near P. Nunziata. HI cards. Open Mon.-Fri. 9:30-11:30am and 3-6pm. Closed Wed. afternoons.

Consulates: U.S.: Try the consulate at Via Dante, 2 (tel. 58 44 92), or contact the consulate in Milan (tel. (02) 29 00 18 41). Open Mon. 4:30-5:30pm. **U.K.,** Via XII Ottobre, 2 (tel. 56 48 33). Open Tues.-Thurs. 9am-noon.

Currency Exchange: Banks abound; Sat.-Sun., when banks are closed, head to either train station. Both give slightly lower rates but only take L500 (and sometimes no) commission. Open daily 7:15am-1pm and 2:30-7:30pm.

American Express: Viatur, P. Fontane Marose, 3 (tel. 56 12 41), inside a travel agency. Doesn't handle money, but will authorize **check cashing** for cardmembers (they give you an authorization, which you take to a bank to get your *lire*). Open Mon.-Fri. 9am-1:30pm and 3:30-7pm.

Flights: C. Colombo Internazionale (tel. 24 11), in Sestiere Ponente. European destinations. You can take a bus from Stazione Principe to the airport.

Trains: Stazione Principe in P. Acquaverde, **Stazione Brignole** in P. Verdi (for train info tel. 28 40 81, 7am-11pm). Trains run from both stations to points along the Ligurian Riviera and to major Italian cities. To Turin (15 per day, 2hr., L13,600) and Rome (15 per day, 6hr., L37,000).

Buses: AMT, Via D'Annunzio, 8r (tel. 499 74 14). One-way fares within the city L1300; good for 1½hr. All-day tourist passes L4000 (foreign passport necessary). Tickets and passes can also be used for *funicolare* and elevator rides also.

Ferries: Stazione Marittima, (tel. 25 66 82). Major destinations are Porto Torres (Sardinia) and Palermo (each more cheaply and easily reached from elsewhere). Listed fares are 1-way deck class. **Grandi Traghetti** (tel. 58 93 31). To Palermo (Mon., Tues., Thurs., 20hr., L142,000). **Tirrenia** (tel. 275 80 41). To Porto Torres (daily, 14hr., L70,000). **Corsica Ferries** (tel. 59 33 01 or 25 54 24). To Corsica (2 per day, 6hr., L44,000-61,000). Check with the tourist office for specific info.

Boat Excursions: Cooperativa Battellieri del Porto di Genova (tel. 26 57 12). Guided boat tours of Genoa's port from the aquarium (daily at about 11:30am and 3:15pm, 40min., L10,000). Trips to the Cinque Terre (L18,000, round-trip L33,000) and Portofino (L12,000, round-trip L20,000).

Hitchhiking: Let's Go does not recommend hitchhiking for anyone. Remember that hitchhiking is very risky; women in particular should exercise extreme caution, and should never hitch alone. Hitchers take bus #17, 18, 19, or 20 from Stazione Brignole to the Genoa West entrance, where highways lead to points north and south. It is illegal to hitchhike on the highway itself.

Public Baths: Diurno, Sottopassaggio de Ferrari, 67r (tel. 56 49 80), in the underpass in front of the bombed-out Teatro Carlo Felice in P. de Ferrari. Showers L6700, bath L8500. Towels included. Shampoo L1150, soap L650. Other bathroom facilities run from urinals (L300) to bathrooms complete with bidet (L2500). Open Tues.-Sat. 8am-7pm, Sun. 8am-noon.

Swimming Pool: Stadio del Nuoto (Albaro), P. Dunant (tel. 362 84 09). Open 8am-8pm.

English Bookstore: Bozzi, Via Cairoli, 2r (tel. 29 87 42; fax 29 44 21). Open Mon.-Fri. 8:30am-7pm, Sat. 8:30am-12:30pm. Closed 1 wk. around the 10th of Aug.

Pharmacies: (tel. 192 for the name of an all-night pharmacy). **Pescetto,** Via Balbi, 185r (tel. 26 26 97), **Ghersi,** Corte Lambruschini, 16 (tel. 54 16 61), **Europa,** Corso Europa, 576 (tel. 38 02 39) are open all night.

Emergencies: tel. 112 for medical concerns. **Hospital: Ospedale San Martino,** Viale Benedetto XV, 10 (tel. 353 51). **Ambulance:** tel. 651 12 36.

ACCOMMODATIONS AND CAMPING

Genoa may have more one-star hotels *per capita* than any other city in Italy, so finding cheap shelter isn't a problem. Unfortunately, finding someplace you *want* to stay *is*. Almost without exception, budget lodgings in the *centro storico* and near the port prefer to rent rooms by the hour, and no one should stay there at night. Head for the hostel, or stick to the area around Stazione Brignole; the establishments are substantially nicer and more secure. Rooms get scarce only in October, when Genoa hosts nautical conventions.

Ostello Per La Gioventù (HI), Via Costanzi, 120 (tel./fax 242 24 57). From Stazione Principe, take bus #35 for 5 stops to Via Ambrogio Spinda, then transfer to bus #40 (which you can take direct from Brignole). Ride #40 to the end of the line, just uphill from the hostel. Everything you want in a hostel: bar, cafeteria (pasta starts at L4500), elevators, free lockers, info on Genoa, laundry (L12,000/

GENOA

8kg), new facilities, parking, patios, *scampi*, TV, wheelchair access, and panoramic views. Bus #40 goes back to the *centro* every 10min. Open 7-9am and 3:30-11:30pm. Checkout 9:30am. Curfew 11:30pm. HI card required. L19,000 per night, L22,000 for a family room; sheets, breakfast, and hot showers included. Multi-lingual staff is extremely friendly and helpful.

Pensione Mirella, Via Gropallo, 4/4 (tel. 839 37 22). From Stazione Brignole, turn right on Via de Amicis to P. Brignole and right again onto Via Gropallo. In a beautifully maintained and secure building. Large, clean, elegantly furnished rooms and pleasant proprietor. Singles L37,000. Doubles L60,000.

Albergo Carola, Via Gropallo, 4/12 (tel. 839 13 40), 2 flights up from Mirella. An excellent alternative. Singles L45,000. Doubles L70,000.

Pensione Barone, Via XX Settembre, 2/23 (tel. 58 75 78), off Via Fiume, near Stazione Brignole, on the 3rd floor. Delightful, family-run hotel, complete with baroque designs on the ceilings and very clean facilities. Ask for towels. Singles L45,000, with bath L60,000. Doubles L65,000, with bath L75,000. Large rooms sleep up to 4 people, L80,000-90,000, with bath. Self-serve coffee L1000. Desk open 9am-midnight. Call ahead, especially around Oct.15-25. MC, Visa.

Camping: The area around Genoa teems with campgrounds, but many are booked solid during July and Aug. Options in the city are scarce and some unsavory; try for something on the beach. **Villa Doria,** Via al Campeggio, Villa Doria, 15 (tel. 696 96 00), in Pegli. Take the train or bus #1, 2, or 3 from P. Caricamento to Pegli, then walk or transfer to bus #93 up Via Vespucci. The closest campground west of the city. Beautiful location and hospitable hosts. English spoken. L6000 per person, L9000-15,000 per tent. Also try **Genova Est,** Via Marcon–Loc Cassa (tel. 347 20 53). Take the train to Bogliasco. L7000 per person, L7000 per tent.

FOOD

Partaking of the culinary offerings of Genoa may expand your waistline, but your wallet and tastebuds will thank you. *Trattorie* and their local specialties are innumerable. *Pesto,* the Genovese pride and joy, is an incomparable pasta sauce made from ground basil, pine nuts, garlic, *parmigiano* (parmesan cheese), and olive oil. Other Genovese specialties include *pansotti,* ravioli stuffed with spinach and *ricotta* and served with a creamy walnut sauce, *farinata,* a fried bread made from chick-pea flour, and *polpettone,* a baked composite of mashed potatoes and beans sprinkled with bread crumbs. Enhance any meal with loads of olive oil-soaked *focaccia,* a delicious flat bread topped with herbs, olives, onions, or cheese (a specialty of nearby Recco). The *centro storico* offers the best *trattorie* at the best prices. (Head there for lunch, because you don't want to be here at night.) Wander around Borgo Incrociati and look for small, family-run restaurants with daily specials.

Trattoria Colombo, Borgo degli Incrociati, 44r (tel. 87 72 24), behind the Stazione Brignole. A traditional *trattoria* frequented at lunch by local workers. *Menù* L14,000. Open Sept.-July Mon.-Sat. 12:30-2:30pm and 7:30-10pm.

Trattoria da Maria, Vico Testadoro, 14r (tel. 58 10 80), off Via XXV Aprile near P. Marose. Fresh selection changes daily. Wonderful staff helps translate the *menù* L12,000. Open Sun.-Thurs. noon-2pm and 4:30-10pm, Fri. noon-2pm.

Brera Express, on Via di Brera, 11r (tel. 54 32 80), just off Via XX Settembre, near Stazione Brignole. *Pizzeria* and full-service; the best deal is the *menù* (L15,000). Open daily 11:30am-2pm and 7pm-midnight (self-service closes at 10pm).

Sa Pesta, Via dei Giustiniani, 16r (tel. 20 86 36), south of P. Matteotti, in the *centro storico.* Sa Pesta knows *pesto;* everyone from doctors to dockworkers converges here to wolf down incomparable Genovese specialties like *farinata* (fried chickpeas, L7000) and *minestrone alla genovese* (with *pesto*). *Primi* L5500-8000; *secondi* L10,000. *Focaccia* and *pizzato* for takeout. Open Sept.-July Mon.-Sat. noon-2:30pm. During the winter serves dinner from 6-10pm; call for reservations.

Bakari, Vico del Fieno, 16r (tel. 29 19 36), to the northwest of P. San Matteo in the *centro storico.* Packs 'em in at lunch. Six different *menùs* (including 3 different vegetarian dinners) from L18,000 for a beggar's banquet to L25,000 for a regal feast. Open Mon.-Fri. noon-2:30pm and Mon.-Tues., Thurs. also 6-9pm.

Kilt 2 Self Service, Vico Doria, 1r (tel. 20 27 98), in the shade of P. San Matteo in the *centro storico.* A cafeteria set-up that dishes out otherworldly gourmet meals for L14,000. Menus change daily. Open Mon.-Sat. 1:45-2:30pm.

Moody, Via XII Ottobre, 8 (tel. 570 54 31). Self-Service. *Primi* L4000-L5500, *secondi* L7500, great *menù* L14,500. As busy and bustling as the street surrounding it. Open Mon.-Sat. 12:30-2:30pm and 7-9:30pm. Bar open 7:30am-9:30pm.

Focacceria San Vincenzo, Via San Vincenzo, 185r (tel. 58 83 68), off Via XX Settembre. Bakes up a wide variety of tasty *focaccie* (L1800 per *etto*), plus a selection of pizza and pastries. Open Mon.-Sat. 7am-7:30pm.

Antico Forno, Via di Porta Soprana, 15 (tel. 29 99 86), on the corner of Vico dei Notari. The smell will draw you in for a piece of fresh bread, sweet bread, *focaccia*, or pizza, all L1000-5000. Open Mon.-Sat. 7:30am-1:30pm and 4:30-7:30pm.

Il Fornaio, Via San Luca, 97r (tel. 28 15 80), off Via Lomellini. The place to come for the tastiest *biscotti,* bread, pastries, *focaccie,* and pizza. Open Mon.-Sat. 7:30am-1pm and 4-7:30pm. Closed Wed. afternoons.

Gelateria Biza, Via San Vincenzo, 65 (tel. 58 11 30). Thirty different kinds of scrumptious *gelato* are sure to please anyone's palate. If you can't decide on a flavor, go for the strawberry—you won't be sorry. Also try *crema di riso* or the fresh fruit *granite:* lemon and blackberry are divine! Open daily 11am-7:30pm.

SIGHTS

From Principe to the Centro Storico

Because of its long-standing commercial strength, Genoa has managed to collect some of the finest 16th- and 17th-century works of Flemish and Italian art. It is also well endowed with the *palazzi* and *ville* of its famous merchant families. Start your tour at the airy *piazza* in front of Stazione Principe, graced by a statue of Christopher Columbus. In the distance is the port; nearby, just before the *palazzo*-lined **Via Balbi** on Salita S. Giovanni, lies one of Genoa's oldest monuments, the Romanesque church **San Giovanni di Pre'.** The stone vaulted roof and the feeble light filtering into the church add to its Romanesque weight and cavernous feel. Next door, the 12th-century **La Commenda** quartered the Knight Commanders of St. John.

Via Balbi, the heart of Genoa's university quarter, preserves some of the most lavish *palazzi* in Genoa. At #10, the fine courtyard of the 18th-century **Palazzo Reale** (Royal Palace) once opened onto a beautiful seaside garden; now it looks out on a major road and city sprawl. Upstairs, the **Galleria d'Arte** (tel. 247 06 40) provides a glimpse into the lifestyles of 18th-century Genovese nobility, with paintings by Tintoretto, van Dyck, and Bassano. (Open Mon., Tues., and Sun. 9am-1:30pm, Wed.-Sat. 9am-6:30pm. Admission L8000; under 18 and over 60 free.) Across the street is the **Palazzo Balbi,** home to many of the departments of the **Università di Genova.** The street runs into P. della Nunziata, formerly called "Guastato" (broken) for the large number of ruins in the square. Today it typifies the Genovese square: small, irregular, and distinguished by formal *palazzi.* The severe neoclassical façade (1843) of the **Church of SS. Annunziata del Vestato** (1591-1620), P. Nunziata, 4 (tel. 29 76 62), conceals an incongruously rococo interior which resembles King Midas' personal residence. The gold-washed interior was almost entirely reconstructed after suffering heavy damage during World War II bombing raids. Although the chapels that line the aisles do not preserve any great masterpieces, they form an impressive gallery of 17th-century art. (Open daily 6:30-11:30am and 4-7pm. Free.)

Bookstores line Via Cairoli on its way to **Via Garibaldi,** the most impressive street in Genoa and bedecked with elegant *palazzi.* A glance inside their courtyards reveals impressive frescoes, fountains, and leafy gardens complete with goldfish pools. The **Palazzo Bianco** (1548, rebuilt 1712) at Via Garibaldi, 11 (tel. 29 18 03), is now home to one of the city's most important collections of Ligurian art, as well as its best Dutch and Flemish paintings. **Palazzo Rosso,** Via Garibaldi, 18, built in the 17th century, houses magnificent furnishings and a lavishly frescoed interior. Today it plays host to the **Galleria di Palazzo Rosso** (tel. 28 26 41). On the second floor, you'll see several full-length van Dyck portraits and Bernardo Strozzi's masterpiece,

La Cuoca. (Due to lack of funding, the *palazzi* alternate staff, so one will be open in the morning, the other in the afternoon. Admission L6000, under 18 and EU citizens free.) Next door to the Palazzo Bianco at Via Garibaldi, 9, **Palazzo Tursi (Palazzion Municipale),** now the city hall, showcases Nicolò Paganini's violin, the *Guarneri del Gesù.* The sounds of this instrument broke the hearts of many, drove others to suicide, and convinced the rest that they were hearing angels sing. The violin is still used on rare occasions to perform Paganini's works, but with less extreme consequences. (Open Mon.-Fri. 8:30am-noon and 1-4:30pm. Free.)

The *galleria* faces the vigorous Renaissance façade of the **Palazzo Municipale** (1564-70) and its beautiful roof gardens. Peer into the courtyard of the **Palazzo Podestà** (1565), Via Garibaldi, 7, to glimpse an unusual *grotto* fountain and an intriguing stucco decoration of a merman. **Palazzo Parodi** (1578), Via Garibaldi, 3, boasts an elegant doorway with noseless telamons—a freakish tribute to the owner's ancestor, Megollo Lecari, who took revenge on his enemies by chopping off their noses and ears. Via Garibaldi spills into P. Fontane Marose, from which you take Via Interiano to P. del Portello, the base for a public elevator (runs 6:50am-10:30pm; L400) that whisks you up to **P. Castelletto.** The *piazza* maintains an extraordinary vista over the entire city and port. From P. del Portello you must take the *funicolare* (L1300) to reach the **Chiesa di Sant'Anna.** A harmonious Renaissance work, Sant'Anna is also notable for its location, peeking out precariously from the steep hillside among leafy gardens. One of Genoa's most beautiful and peaceful *creuze* descends from the church among trees, *palazzi,* and stray cats.

From P. Fontane Marose, Salita di Santa Caterina takes you to Piazza Corvetto. The **Villetta Di Negro** spreads out along the hill to your left, inviting you to relax amid waterfalls, grottos, and terraced gardens. Its summit houses a real treasure, the **Museo d'Arte Orientale E. Chiossone** (the Museum of Oriental Art, tel. 54 22 85). Check out the impressive sculptures on the first floor houses, particularly the diminutive dog-dragon. (Open Tues., Thurs.-Sat. 9am-1pm, every 1st and 3rd Sun. of the month 9am-1pm. Admission L6000.) From P. Corvetto, Via Roma leads to **Piazza de Ferrari,** the city's bustling center, home to a monstrous fountain resembling, naturally, a raised hubcap. Off P. de Ferrari lie P. Matteotti and the **Palazzo Ducale,** once the home of the city's rulers. Inside, visit the two beautiful courtyards, one punctuated by an elegant 17th-century fountain. On the corner opposite to this imposing palace stands the ornate **Church of the Gesù** (also known as SS. Ambrogio e Andrea; 1549-1606). This baroque edifice features *trompe l'oeil* effects, double cupolas, and two important Rubens canvases, *The Circumcision* and *St. Ignatius Healing a Woman Possessed of the Devil.*

The Centro Storico

The unkempt and often dangerous historical center is a mass of confusing streets bordered by the port, Via Garibaldi, and P. de Ferrari. Due to its crime, prostitution, and drugs, the historic center is a safe spot for tourists only during weekdays when stores are open; at night the quarter's underground elements crawl out and not even the police venture in. But the *centro storico* is also home to Genoa's most memorable monuments: the *duomo* S. Lorenzo, the Church of San Luca, and the medieval Torre Embraici. As you walk, look up for the numerous sculpted and painted tabernacles, or *"Madonette,"* that adorn the corners of buildings.

Off P. Matteotti resides the **duomo San Lorenzo.** Already in existence in the 9th century, the church was enlarged and reconstructed in the 12th through 16th centuries, resulting in the characteristically striped Gothic façade and uncharacteristically lopsided appearance—only one of the two planned bell towers was completed. The carved central portal decorated with lions, sirens, and vines opens to a severe and simple interior with a checkered floor. Along the left wall, the chapel of St. John the Baptist is decorated with statues of Adam and Eve by Matteo Civitali. A vintage American bomb adorns the right wall of the church, miraculously unexploded after having crashed through the roof during World War II. (Open Mon.-Sat. 8am-noon and 3-6:30pm, Sun. noon-6:30pm. Free.) Behind the *duomo* Sal-

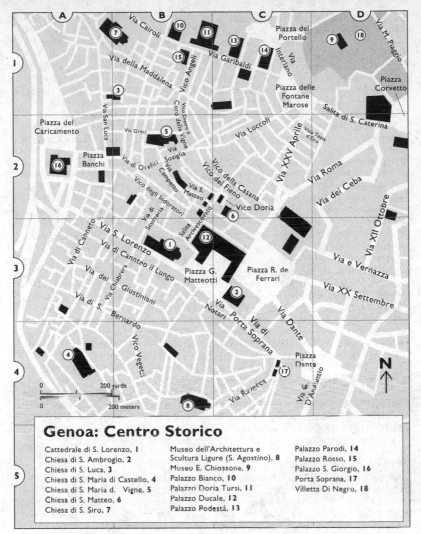

Genoa: Centro Storico

Cattedrale di S. Lorenzo, 1
Chiesa di S. Ambrogio, 2
Chiesa di S. Luca, 3
Chiesa di S. Maria di Castello, 4
Chiesa di S. Maria d. Vigne, 5
Chiesa di S. Matteo, 6
Chiesa di S. Siro, 7

Museo dell'Architettura e
Scultura Ligure (S. Agostino), 8
Museo E. Chiossone, 9
Palazzo Bianco, 10
Palazzo Doria Tursi, 11
Palazzo Ducale, 12
Palazzo Podestà, 13

Palazzo Parodi, 14
Palazzo Rosso, 15
Palazzo S. Giorgio, 16
Porta Soprana, 17
Villetta Di Negro, 18

ita all'Arrivescovato leads to Genoa's most characteristic and charming square, **Piazza San Matteo**. It contains the houses and chapel of the Doria family, members of the medieval oligarchy that ruled Genoa. The animal reliefs above the first floor are the trademarks of the masons who built the houses. Chiseled into the façade of the small but elaborately decorated **Church of San Matteo** (1125) are descriptions of the Dorias' great deeds, and to the left a small door protects a lovely 14th-century cloister. If the gate is closed, slip the caretaker a cigarette and he might let you in. (Open Mon.-Sat. 7:30am-noon and 4-6:30pm, Sun. 9am-noon and 4-6:30pm.) A short walk down Via S. Matteo and Via Lampetto, resides one of Genoa's oldest churches, **Chiesa Santa Maria delle Vigne**, a highly ornate building with gold working in the ceiling and large paintings on the walls. Dating from the 10th century, it still maintains its Romanesque arc-spired bell tower. (Open 8am-noon and 3:30-7pm. Free.)

From here head down Via Greci to **Via San Luca**, the main artery of the old quarter, where you'll find many of Genoa's most important monuments. The **Church of**

San Siro was Genoa's first cathedral (rebuilt 1588-1613). A dome crowns the little yellow and gray **Church of San Luca,** a 12th-century treasure in the shape of a Greek cross. (Both open Mon.-Fri. 4-6pm. Free.) **Palazzo Spinola,** in P. di Pellicceria, 1 (follow the yellow signs), exemplifies Genoa's mercantile wealth from the 16th through 18th centuries. Its rooms retain most of their original furnishings and are adorned by works of art donated by the Spinola family as well as later additions. This is the **Galleria Nazionale di Palazzo Spinola** (tel. 29 46 61). Don't miss the portraits of the four evangelists by van Dyck in the Sala da Pranzo. (Open Mon. 9am-1pm, Tues.-Sat. 10am-7pm, Sun. 2-7pm. Admission L8000. Under 18 and over 60 free.)

Medieval arcades (Portici di Sottoripa) border one side of P. Caricamento, by the port on the other side of P. Banchi. Across the *piazza,* the **Palazzo San Giorgio,** a part-Gothic, part-Renaissance structure, once housed the famous Genovese bank of St. George. Intense World War II bombing left much of the area in need of reconstruction, but some interesting churches remain scattered among the old tenements and medieval ruins. Follow the waterfront to the **Church of Santa Maria di Castello,** whose foundations date back to the Greeks and Etruscans, later served as a crusaders' church and hostel. It's now a labyrinth of chapels, courtyards, cloisters, and gardens. In the chapel to the left of the high altar, check out the *Crocifisso MiraColoso.* According to legend, it moved its head to attest to the truth of a young lady betrayed by her lover; supposedly, Jesus' beard grows longer every time crisis hits the city. If you enjoy the gruesomely morbid, look for the painting of San Pietro Martire di Verona above the door in the room to the left of the sacristy; he's shown complete with a halo and the means of his martyrdom—a large cleaver in his skull. Nearby, the medieval **Torre Embraici** (Hebrew Towers) loom over Santa Maria di Castello, with Guelph battlements jutting out from the rough stone surface.

The old city's newest addition, the **Museo dell'Architettura e Scultura Ligure,** occupies the former monastery of Sant'Agostino at P. di Sarzano (tel. 20 16 61). This museum surveys Genoa's history through its surviving art. Giovanni Pisano carved the museum's most outstanding piece, the funerary monument of Margherita di Brabant, in 1312. Fragments of this monument have been scattered across the continent, but the museum hopes to eventually reassemble it. (Open Tues.-Sat. 9am-7pm, Sun. 9am-12:30pm. Admission L6000.) From P. di Sarzano, Via Ravecca leads to the medieval **Porta Soprana,** which flaunts its enormous twin towers and noble arched entryway, the emblem of this district. Walk past the reputed boyhood home of Christopher Columbus *(Casa di Cristoforo Colombo;* his father was the gatekeeper of Soprana) and the ruins of the 12th-century **Cloister of Sant'Andrea.**

ENTERTAINMENT

Like any large city, Genoa has a number of interesting if somewhat unpredictable exhibitions and concerts. Ask at the tourist office for the latest information.

As for nightlife, there are many options. Those seeking the bar scene should explore the area around P. Matteotti and P. delle Erbe, which is inhabited by many lively little pubs and cafes. Try **Caffè degli Specchi,** Salita Pollaiuoli, 43r (tel. 28 12 93), one block from both P. Matteotti and P. delle Erbe. A beautiful *caffè* with seats outside in the summer and upstairs in the winter. Drinks are a bit expensive (glass of wine L4000-5000) but are usually accompanied by typical Genovese appetizers. In the summer the action moves to **Nervi,** only minutes away by train or bus, where people can barhop or stroll along the *lungomare* lapping *gelato.*

If you're in the mood for **jazz,** try **Charlie Christian,** Via S. Donato, 20r (tel. 29 83 93), a smoky live jazz and blues bar named for the father of the jazz guitar. For more active evenings, Genoa has numerous *discoteche* that open around 10:30-11pm and close around 3am. Cover charges are usually between L15,000 and L20,000. Near Via XX Settembre, off Via Fieschi is **Nessundorma Caffè** ("no one sleeps" caffè), Via alla Porta degli Archi, 74r (tel. 56 17 63), a favorite with the student crowd. In the area around Stazione Brignole are **Temptatiane** at P. Tommaseo, 17r (tel. 36 86 52) and **Cézanne** at Via Cecchi, 7r (tel. 56 10 21). **Makò,** Corso Italia, 28r (tel. 36 76 52), down by the water, is slightly more elegant and expensive.

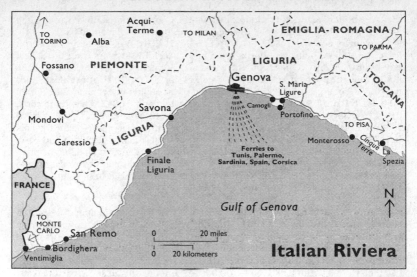

Italian Riviera

RIVIERA DI LEVANTE

■■■ CAMOGLI

Camogli takes great pride in its ancient maritime traditions. Old peach and yellow houses crowd the hilltop, vibrant red and green boats bob in the water, and piles of fishing nets lie heaped over the docks along the waterfront. Camogli is a family town where everyone seems to know everyone else; the town takes its name from the wives who ran the town while their husbands manned its once-huge fishing fleet ("Camogli" is a contraction of "Casa Mogli"—"Wives' House"). The husbands are back now, and what Dickens once called a "piratical little place" has mellowed into a small, peaceful resort of 6,000, with a picturesque and very friendly boardwalk scene. Those seeking a budget version of the more glamorous Portofino might find Camogli to be the right place for fun and relaxation.

Orientation and Practical Information The town climbs uphill from the sea into pine and olive groves separated by a promontory from the pebble beach and fishing harbor below. To get to the **boardwalk**, go right as you exit the Camogli-San Fruttuoso station. After you pass a pea soup-colored *palazzo* about 100m from the station, turn left and go down the steep stairs that lead to **Via Garibaldi**. From Via Garibaldi, turn right into a little alley which will lead you to great, free beaches.

Camogli can be reached by *locale* **train** on the Genoa-La Spezia line. From: Genoa (30 per day, 20min., L2000), La Spezia (10 per day, 1½hr., L5700), Sestri Levante (20 per day, 30min., L2700), Santa Margherita (20 per day, 10min., L1500). Tigullio (tel. 513 06 or 77 44 24) **buses** depart from P. Schiaffino to nearby towns. Buy tickets at Bar Aldo across from the tourist office or at the *tabacchi* on Via Repubblica, 25. To: Santa Margherita, (14 per day, L2000), Portofino Vetta—*not* Portofino Mare, the port—(4 per day, L1700). **Ferries** are more expensive, but offer incredible views of the peninsula's cliffs. From Camogli, take Golfo Paradiso, Via Scala, 2 (tel. 77 20 91), ferries around the rugged headland to San Fruttuoso (May-Sept. 8-11 per day, L6000, round-trip L11,000). They also run a nighttime trip to Portofino (Sat. leaving 9:30pm and returning 11:20pm, Sun.-Mon. leaving 3:15pm and returning 6pm, one-way L10,000, round-trip L17,000); buy tickets on the boat. Or you may prefer to make the three-hour **hike** to San Fruttuoso; pick up the Camogli tourist office's useful trail map if you do, or just follow the double blue dots on the well-marked path.

The **tourist office** at Via XX Settembre, 33 (tel. 77 10 66), to your right as you leave the station, helps you find a room and cheerfully answers even the silliest questions in English. (Open Mon.-Sat. 8:30am-12:30pm and 3:30-6pm, Sun. 9:30am-noon.) Find the **police** at Via Cuneo, 30F (tel. 113 or 77 00 00). The **post office** holds mail at Via Cuneo, 1 (tel. 77 43 32), to the left of the station under an arcade. (Open Mon.-Fri. 8:10am-5:30pm, Sat. 8:10am-noon.) **Postal code:** 16032. **Telephone code:** 0185. **Exchange** your money at the Banco di Chiavari della Riviera Ligure, Via XX Settembre, 19 (tel. 77 25 76 or 77 00 33). You'll find a **pharmacy,** Machi Dr. Enzi (tel. 77 10 81), at Via Repubblica, 4 (open Tues.-Sat. 8:30am-12:30pm and 3:30-7:30pm), with a sign outside that tells you where you can find an all-night pharmacy. For **medical emergencies,** dial 112. There is a **hospital** at Corso Mazzini, 96 (tel. 741 02). The **Red Cross** is located at Via XX Settembre, 58 (tel. 77 00 85 or 77 14 51), and the **police** at Via Cuneo, 30F (tel. 77 00 00).

Accommodations and Food

Your best bet is unquestionably **Albergo La Camogliese,** Via Garibaldi, 55 (tel. 77 14 02; fax 77 40 24). Walk down the long stairway near the train station to #55, near the seafront. The large, clean rooms are a joy, and the proprietors have definitely found their calling. They refer to *Let's Go* readers as "Let's Go *amici"* and offer them a 10% discount. (Singles with bath L50,000. Doubles with bath L75,000-90,000, depending on size and view. Breakfast L5000. Phone and TV in every room. Reservations strongly recommended. AmEx, MC, Visa, traveler's checks.) The pleasant **Pensione Augusta,** Via Schiaffino, 100 (tel. 77 05 92), at the other end of town, has clean and simple rooms enlivened by the ceaseless rumbling of nearby trains. (Singles L50,000. Doubles L65,000-90,000. All rooms with bath. AmEx, MC, Visa.) If these are full, walk left from the station past the post office to **Albergo Selene,** dark but affordable, on Via Cuneo, 16 (tel. 77 01 49; fax 77 20 38). (Singles L50,000. Doubles L80,000. Triples 110,000. Breakfast L8000. Some rooms with balcony. AmEx, MC, Visa.) If you still can't find anything, talk to the owner of La Camogliese and he'll try to find you a room in town.

For a do-it-yourself meal, the scores of shops on Via Repubblica should suffice, or try the **Picaso Supermercato** next to the tourist office at Via XX Settembre, 35. (Open Mon.-Sat. 8am-12:30pm and 4:30-7:30pm. Closed Wed. afternoons. **Revello,** Via Garibaldi, 183 (tel. 77 07 77), on the waterfront at the street's end, offers a huge array of snacks including the Riviera's best *focaccia,* but their secret treat is the *camogliese al rhum,* a chocolate-covered cream puff with a rum filling (both are L2900 per *etto*). (Open daily 8am-1pm and 3:30-7:30pm.) An open-air **market** in the main *piazza* is open Wednesdays 7am-1:30pm for food, clothes, and bargain fishhooks. For great pizza and a view of the ocean to boot, try **Pizzeria Il Lido** on the boardwalk at Via Garibaldi, 133 (tel. 77 50 09). Pizza from L8000-13,000, *primi* from L10,000. Cover L2500. A/C and modern dance music. (Open Wed.-Mon. 11am-6:30pm.) For wonderful *gelato* and a friendly smile, check out **Slurp,** also on the boardwalk, at Via Garibaldi, 105 (tel. 77 43 53). With a name like that, how can you go wrong? Lots of innovative flavors, and their *granite* (ices) are popular too. Cones L2000-3000. (Open daily 10am-midnight; closed Mon. in the winter.)

There are slim pickings when it comes to nightlife, but for live music ranging from *bossa nova* to jazz, try **Porto Prego,** Piazza Colombo, 32 (tel. 77 26 66), right after Via Garibaldi ends on the boardwalk. Cover L15,000 when there's live music (includes 1st drink). Call for scheduled concerts. (Open Thurs.-Tues. 5pm-3am.) One stop away on the train is the city of Recco, which has several *discoteche.* Ask at the tourist office for more info.

Sights and Festivals

Camogli is famous internationally for its enormous fishfry, the **Sagra del Pesce.** On the second Sunday in May, tourists descend on Camogli to partake of the free fish, fried up in a giant four-meter-across pan, which holds 2000 sardines at once and adorns a wall at the entrance to the town when not in use. Another magical event is the **Festa della Stella Maris** (Festival of Our Lady of the Sea), which takes place the first Sunday of August. A procession of boats, led by the town priest, sails out to the Punta Chiappa, a piece of land you can see jutting into the water a mile from the boardwalk in Camogli. About 10,000 floating candles are released from both shores. Lovers wait on the beach until the current carries all the candles together, signifying another year of unity.

Though best known for its pebble beach, Camogli has its share of sights to see on a cloudy day: start with the 12th-century **Basilica di Santa Maria Assunta** on the seashore next to Piazza Colombo. From the church, stone steps lead left to the **Acquario Tirrenico,** Castello della Dragonara (tel. 77 33 75). (Open summer daily 10am-noon and 3-7pm, winter Fri.-Sun. 10am-noon and 2-5:30pm. Admission L4000.) The maritime museum, **Gio Bono Ferrari,** across from the station at Via Gio Bono Ferrari, 41, honors sailors who traveled from Cape Horn to Rangoon. (Open Mon. and Thurs.-Fri. 9-11:40am, Wed. and Sat.-Sun. 9-11:40am and 3-5:40pm. Free.)

■ NEAR CAMOGLI

SAN FRUTTUOSO

The tiny fishing hamlet of San Fruttuoso, set in a natural amphitheater of pines, olive trees, and green oaks, is much too expensive for a prolonged stay or even a meal, but it's still worth a daytrip. The town is accessible by foot (1½hr. from Portofino Mare or Portofino Vetta) or by boat. Both **Golfo Paradiso** (tel. (0185) 77 20 91; around 12 boats per day from Camogli, L6000, round-trip L11,000) and **Servizio Marittimo del Tigullio** (tel. (0185) 28 46 70; every hr. from 10:30am-4:30pm from Portofino, L7000, round-trip L12,000) provide service.

For a great view, walk to the left of the bay to the medieval lookout tower, the **Torre Andrea Doria** (admission L5000, children L2000). Fifteen meters offshore and 18m underwater stands a bronze statue with upraised arms, the *Christ of the Depths,* which was erected in memory of casualties at sea. The statue now serves as protector of scuba divers, and, in late July, the townlet sponsors a **festival** commemorating those lost at sea. Be sure to visit the Benedictine **Abbazia di San Fruttuoso di Capo di Monte** (tel. (0185) 77 27 03), for which the town was named. Here nonswimmers can see an exact replica of the *Christ of the Depths.* (Open Dec.-Feb. Sat.-Sun. and holidays 10am-4pm; March-April, Oct. Tues.-Sun. 10am-4pm; May-Sept. Tues.-Sun. 10am-6pm. Admission L5000, children L2000.)

PORTOFINO

Gorgeous Portofino was discovered long ago by the well-to-do. Today the yachts of the wealthy fill the harbor and boutiques line the streets, but the curve of the shore and the tiny bay may be enjoyed by paupers and princes alike. A nature reserve surrounds Portofino; trek through it to San Fruttuoso (90min.) or Santa Margherita (2½hr.). If you choose to hang around town, you can escape to the cool interior of the **Chiesa di San Giorgio** by following the signs uphill from the *piazza* at the bay. A few more minutes up the road to the **castle** will set you in a fairy-tale garden with a view of the sea. The castle is also home to a museum (admission L3000). To reach *il faro* (lighthouse), look for the footpath marked "al faro" (20min.—watch out for the salamanders); there is a breathtaking coastline view. If you make it to the top, reward yourself with a *gelato* from **Il Faro.** (Open April-Sept. daily 9:30am-8pm.)

There's no train to Portofino, but Tigullio **buses** run along the coastline to and from Santa Margherita. (Every 20min., L1700; make sure you take the bus to Portofino Mare, not Portofino Vetta, and buy tickets at an *edicola* (newsstand) or in a *tabacchi*) Maps and English brochures are available at the **tourist office,** Via Roma, 35 (tel. 26 90 24), on the way to the waterfront from the bus stop. Some English spoken. A large signboard of the arrivals and departures from Santa Margherita is posted outside. (Open daily 9:30am-1pm and 1:30-6:30pm in the summer; 9:30am-12:30pm and 3-6pm in the winter.) Currency may be exchanged at the **bank** on Via Roma, 14 (tel. 26 91 64). The **post office** is at Via Roma, 32 (tel. 26 91 56).

Portofino's **telephone code** is 0185; use the **telephones** at the tourist office. For emergencies, the **police** are at Via del Fondaco, 8 (tel. 26 90 88), and there's a **pharmacy** at P. Martiri della Libertà, 6 (tel. 26 91 01). To fortify yourself for the hike to San Fruttuoso, buy fruit and cool drinks at **Alimentari Repetto,** at P. Martiri dell'Olivetta, 30 (open daily 7:30am-8pm).

■■■ SANTA MARGHERITA LIGURE

Santa Margherita Ligure evokes the elegance of a past era. It was once a vacation spot known for its whispers of glamour and a tourist industry geared toward the wealthy. It now possesses a serenity expressed by the soft hues of blue, orange, and pink of *trompe l'oeil* façades, and by the graceful old ladies who spend the summer here, taking their evening *passeggiate* through town in softly flowing dresses. Abandon other over-touristed destinations and come here to escape or just indulge in the fantasy of former elegance. Santa Margherita is one of the few remaining affordable Riviera towns, so stay here and explore the rest of the coast.

ORIENTATION AND PRACTICAL INFORMATION

Major inter-city trains along the Pisa-Genova line stop at Santa Margherita. The town spreads in an arc around its small port. From the station, turn right and follow **Via Roma** down towards the waterfront. (For a short cut, take the stairs to the right of the stop sign in front of the station and follow Via della Stazione directly to the water.) There are two main squares that cover the waterfront: the **Piazza Martiri della Libertà** and the smaller **Piazza Vittorio Veneto.** Both are lovely parks lined with palm trees. As you face the water, **Via Gramsci** winds around the port to your left, while **Via XXV Aprile** leads to the tourist office, continuing on to become **Corso Matteotti** alongside the other main square in town, the **Piazza Mazzini.**

Tourist Office: Via XXV Aprile, 2b (tel. 28 74 85). Turn right from the train station onto Via Roma, then right onto Via XXV Aprile. Information, town map, and accommodations service. An enthusiastic and helpful English-speaking bunch. Open Mon.-Sat. 9am-12:30pm and 3-7pm, Sun. 9am-12:30pm.
Police: (tel. 28 71 21), on Via Vignolo.
Post Office: Via Roma, 36 (tel. 28 88 40), to the right of the station. Open Mon.-Fri. 8:10am-5:30pm, Sat. 8:10am-noon. **Postal Code:** 16038.
Telephone Code: 0185.
Trains: (tel. 28 66 30), in P. Federico Raoul Nobili at the summit of Via Roma. To: Genoa (3 per hr., 5am-midnight, L2700); La Spezia (2 per hr., 6am-1am, L5700).
Luggage Storage: L1500 per piece (open daily 5:35am-7:50pm).
Buses: Tigullio buses depart from P. Vittorio Veneto at the small green kiosk on the waterfront. Ticket office open daily 7:10am-7:40pm. To: Camogli (every hr., 15km, L2000) and Portofino (every 20min., 5km, L1700).
Ferries: Tigullio, Via Palestro, 8/1/B (tel. 28 46 70). Boats leave from the docks at P. Martiri della Libertà. To: Portofino (every hr. from 10am-4pm, L5000; round-trip L8000); San Fruttuoso (every hr. from 10am-4pm, L10,000; round-trip L16,000); and Cinque Terre, Monterosso, or Riomaggiore (July-Sept. daily, during winter, Sat.-Sun. 2 per day, L18,000; round-trip L25,000).
Bike Rental: Noleggio P. Agrifoglio, Via Roma, 1 (tel. 28 70 45). Bikes L7000 per hr., L15,000 per 3 hr., or L34,000 per day. You can also rent a tandem or a motor-scooter for L15,000 per hr. or L70,000 per day. Must be over 14 and accompanied by an adult to rent a moped. Motorscooter driving license required for rental. Open sporadically off-season; Mar.-Sept. daily 9:30am-12:30pm and 2:30-6:30pm.
Emergency: tel. 113. **Hospital: Ospedale Civile di Rapallo,** P. Molfino, 10 (tel. 60 31), in Rapallo near the train station. For late-night and weekend medical attention, call **Guardia Medica** (tel. 603 33 or 27 33 82).

ACCOMMODATIONS

Stay away from the water. Your room won't have a view and you'll have to trek a bit, but the reward will be peace, quiet, and an extra L10,000 in your pocket.

Hotel Terminus, Piazzale Nobili, 4 (tel. 28 61 21; fax 28 25 46), to the left as you exit the station. Proprietor Angelo speaks perfect English and dedicates his days to re-creating the grace of the Italian Riviera's famed hotel culture. Clean, well-furnished rooms with new bathrooms and insulated windows with fantastic views of the water and hills. Singles L50,000, with bath L60,000. Doubles L80,000, with bath L100,000. Triples L120,000. AmEx, MC, Visa.

Hotel Conte Verde, Via Zara, 1 (tel. 28 71 39; fax 28 42 11), on your right as you come down Via Roma. Was once an 18th-century *villa.* Clean, modern rooms. Singles L45,000-70,000. Doubles L80,000-110,000. Bicycles lent out free to guests. **Restaurant** downstairs gives discount to *Let's Go*-ers. English spoken, and they get CNN. Breakfast included. Reservations encouraged. AmEx, MC, Visa.

Albergo Annabella, Via Costasecca, 10 (tel. 28 65 31), off P. Mazzini, not far from the beach. Spacious, clean, and modern rooms. Singles L40,000-45,000. Doubles L60,000-65,000. Triples L90,000. Breakfast L6000. During high season, you may be required to pay for half-pension at L65,000 per person.

Hotel Nuova Riviera, Via Belvedere, 10 (tel. 28 74 03). A beautiful old villa set in a garden near P. Mazzini. Large, elegant rooms. Singles L50,000-65,000. Doubles L70,000-80,000, with bath L95,000. Prices negotiable. Half-pension sometimes required in summer at L63,000-85,000 per person, depending on room size. Reservations recommended.

FOOD

Markets, bakeries, fruit vendors, and butcher shops line Corso Matteotti. On Fridays from 8am to 1pm, the shops oust cars and spill onto the *corso.* The **COOP Supermarket,** Corso Matteotti, 9C (tel. 28 43 15) off P. Mazzini stocks basics including soy products for vegetarians. (Open Mon.-Sat. 8:15am-1pm and 4-8pm. Visa.)

Trattoria Baicin, Via Algeria, 9 (tel. 28 67 63), off P. Martiri della Libertà near the water. Papà Piero is the master chef, and Mamma Carmela rolls the pasta and boils the sauces. Try Mamma's homemade *Trofie alla Genovese (gnocchi* mixed with potato, string beans, and *pesto,* L7500). *Primi* from L6000, *menù* L25,000. 10% service charge. Cover L2000. Open Tues.-Sun. noon-3pm and 7pm-midnight, but the kitchen closes at 10:30pm. AmEx, MC, Visa, traveler's checks.

Cutty Sark, Via Roma, 35 (tel. 28 70 09), on the right coming from the station. Furnished with dark wood and sailor's paraphernalia, this 2-story establishment has a big-screen TV and, occasionally, live music. *Primi* L7000-8000, 40 different types of *panini,* and a bar. Open Tues.-Sun. noon-2pm and 8pm-2am.

Rosticceria Revelant, Via Gramsci, 15 (tel. 28 65 00), east of P. Martiri della Libertà. Scrumptious take-out meals. Try the lasagna (L1500 per *etto).* Open daily during the summer 8am-noon and 4:30-8pm; in winter closed Sun. afternoon and Mon. AmEx, MC, Visa.

SIGHTS AND ENTERTAINMENT

Santa Margherita's attractions remain its tranquility and proximity to Camogli and Portofino. From 8am to 12:30pm, you can ogle the day's catch at the local **fish market** on Lungomare Marconi, or come between 4 and 6pm to watch the fleet bring in its haul. (Market closed Wed. afternoon.) More exalted sights include the rococo **Basilica di Santa Margherita** on P. Caprera, dripping with gold and crystal, which houses some good Flemish and Italian works. To reach the **Church of the Cappuccini,** Via San Francesco d'Assisi, a favorite feline hangout, walk along the waterfront past P. Martiri della Libertà and climb the stone ramp behind the castle. For human companionship, head to the **Old Inn Bar,** P. Mazzini, 40 (tel. 28 60 41 or 28 66 20), for pool tables and beer, or try **Salot American Bar** at P. Martiri della Libertà, 32, a gregarious place with music and drinks. Open for lunch, too. Open Wed.-Mon.

CINQUE TERRE

■■■ CINQUE TERRE

The Cinque Terre (Five Lands) are five connected fishing villages that cling precariously to a small stretch of cliff above the startlingly turquoise sea. The fish that once schooled in the Mediterranean have been replaced by swimming tourists, and with good reason. The Cinque Terre are justly famed for impressive vistas, beautiful clear waters, and a sweet white wine called *sciacchetrà*.

The five towns in order of proximity to Genoa are Monterosso, Vernazza, Corniglia, Manarola, and Riomaggiore; Monterosso is the biggest and least charming.

ORIENTATION AND PRACTICAL INFORMATION

The listings here are for **Monterosso,** which is easily accessible by local train from all the villages.

Tourist Office: Via Fegina, 38 (tel. 81 75 06), below the train station. The only tourist office in the Cinque Terre, well-stocked with info on boats, hikes, and hotels. Accommodations service for Monterosso and **currency exchange** (fair rates). Open April-Oct. Mon.-Sat. 10am-noon and 5-7:30pm, Sun. 10am-noon.

Police: Carabinieri, tel. 81 75 24.

Post Office: Via Loreto (tel. 81 75 27). Open Mon.-Fri. 8:30am-6pm, Sat. 8:30am-noon. **Postal Code:** 19016. **Telephone Code for all of Cinque Terre:** 0187.

Trains: V. Fegina, on the north end of town, to the right as you face the water. To Vernazza, Corniglia, Manarola, and Riomaggiore (every hr., 5-20min., L1400). The "Cinque Terre Tourist Ticket," is good for unlimited trips between towns in any 24-hr. period, at any of the five train stations—ask at the ticket window (L4500).

Boats: Navigazione Golfo dei Porto (tel. 96 76 76), at the port to the right of the beach in the south end of town. Trips to Manarola and Riomaggiore (5 per day, L9000, round-trip L15,000). **Motobarca Vernazza** makes the trip to Vernazza every hour (15min., L5000 one way, L8000 round-trip).

Boat Rental: on the beach. Pedal boats L12,000 per hour, L60,000 per day. Motorboats L30,000 per hour, L150,000 per day.

Taxis: tel. 75 57 30.

Beaches: There are only two public beaches in the Cinque Terre, one on the south side of Monterosso (to the left as you face the harbor), and the other a long strip of pebbles between Corniglia and Manarola. You can also swim off the rocky outcroppings between Manarola and Riomaggiore, and in the inlet formed by Vernazza's harbor. Most of the beach in Monterosso is reserved, with only small, unappealing patches open to the public. If sand is what you want, it's probably worth the L2000 to get your own patch for the day. Deck chairs with umbrellas L13,000. Changing rooms at the beach.

Pharmacy: V. Roma, 2, in the old section of Monterosso. Open Mon.-Sat. 8:30am-12:30pm and 4-7:30pm. Closed Thurs. afternoons and Sun.

Emergencies: tel. 113. **Medical Emergency: Guardia Medica,** tel. 80 04 09.

ACCOMMODATIONS

With the exception of Monterosso, most of the five towns' accommodations hide in private homes. These *affitta camere* are plentiful, but can often be difficult to locate; try the tourist office in Monterosso, or just show up in town and ask around—bars are good places to start. Find a place to sleep as soon as possible; accommodations fill up as early as noon.

Hostel Mamma Rosa, P. Unità, 2 (tel. 92 00 50), in **Riomaggiore.** No sign, but it's across from the train station, or ask a local and he'll send Mamma running to meet you. Fun central: co-ed dorms, outdoor showers, and cooking facilities, all presided over by ebullient, lovable Mamma Rosa herself. She'll try to find room for a latecomer. No curfew. Bunk beds, 4-10 per room, L20,000 per person.

Albergo Barbara, P. Marconi, 21 (tel. 81 22 01), at the port in **Vernazza.** Ask about the hotel in Trattoria Capitano downstairs. Bright, airy rooms with fantastic views of Vernazza's colorful port. Singles L45,000. Doubles L60,000-80,000.

Cecio (tel. 81 20 43), in **Corniglia**. On the small road that leads from Corniglia to Vernazza; follow the signs at the top of the stairs that lead to town from the train station. This wonderful restaurant (see Food below) hides equally wonderful rooms, all with bath and the sort of view postcards are made of. Doubles only, L70,000 (less for longer stays).

Hotel Souvenir, Via Gioberti, 24 (tel. 81 75 95) in **Monterosso**. Quiet, family-run hotel with bright rooms and friendly staff. Good breakfast included. Singles L45,000. Doubles L65,000.

Marina Piccola (tel. 92 01 03), near the water in **Manarola**. An upscale place with cream-colored walls, tasteful prints, and little lamps. Many rooms with mind-blowing views. All rooms with bath. Singles and doubles from L70,000.

FOOD

The uniformly overpriced seafood restaurants that crowd the five towns attest to Cinque Terre's growing tourism savvy. However, the seafood is always swimmingly fresh, and the locally-produced sweet wine, called *sciacchetrà,* is a delicious complement. If you've got your heart set on a picnic by the beach, stock up at **Conce Sta. Margherita,** P. Matteotti, 9, in **Monterosso**. (Open Mon.-Sat. 8am-1pm and 5-7:30pm; closed Wed. afternoons.)

Ristorante Cecio, in **Corniglia**. See listing under Accommodations for directions. A small restaurant overlooking the hills and water, with absolutely fantastic food. *Primi* L7000-8000; get the *gnocchi al pesto* for an out-of-body experience. If you eat too much to make it home again you could spend the night here!

Focacceria Il Frontoio, Via Gioberti, 1, in **Monterosso**. The wood-burning oven fires up every kind of mouth-watering *focaccia* imaginable: with olives, onions, or herbs, or stuffed with different fillings. Slices L1500-2500. A great place to stock up before heading out on a hike. Open Fri.-Wed. 9am-1:30pm and 4-8pm.

Il Baretto, Via Roma, 31 (tel. 81 23 81), in **Vernazza**. One of the more reasonably priced of Vernazza's many outdoor restaurants. *Menù,* including freshly caught mussels steamed in wine and herbs, L25,000. *Primi* L8000-10,000, *secondi from* L10,000. Open daily noon-2pm and 7:30-9:30pm.

SIGHTS

Nature created Cinque Terre's best sights: savage cliffs and lush tropical vegetation surround the stone sea villages. Enjoy the best views from the narrow goat paths that link the towns, winding through vineyards, streams, and dense foliage clotted with cacti and lemon trees. Come with a good pair of walking shoes, and you can cover the distance between Monterosso and Riomaggiore in one day; or take strolls between frolics in the water. The best hikes lie between Monterosso and Vernazza (1½hr.), Vernazza and Corniglia (1½hr.), and Corniglia and Manarola (1hr.). The "Via Dell'Amore" that links Manarola and Riomaggiore is more notable for its easy access to the water than for its view.

In Monterosso visit the **Convento dei Cappuccini,** perched on a hill in the center of town. The convent preserves an impressive *Crucifixion* by Flemish master van Dyck, who sojourned in this area during his most productive years. (Open daily 9am-noon and 4-7pm.) In Vernazza, the remains of a **castle** (facing the port, up a steep staircase to your left) offer another spectacular view. (Open daily 9am-8pm.)

■■■ LA SPEZIA

A major commercial and naval port, La Spezia serves as a departure point to Corsica and an unavoidable transfer station on the way to and from Cinque Terre. Enjoy the relatively few merits of the city by following locals in their evening *passeggiate* along the portside Morin promenade.

Orientation and Practical Information Sadly, La Spezia's tourist office is no longer with us; pick up brochures in the train station. The **post office** is a few blocks from the port at P. Verde (tel. (0187) 284 76). (Open Mon.-Sat. 8am-2pm.) **Telephones** can be found at the nearby **Telecom (SIP)** office, Via da Passano, 30 (open daily 8am-10pm). **Taxis** answer at tel. 361 79 or 220 40. In an **emergency,** call 361 30 for city **police,** and 51 10 45 or 51 15 11 for **medical assistance.**

La Spezia is a convenient Italian port for Bastia (Corsica). Two lines service the route, both at the Molo Italia dock. **Corsica Ferries** (tel. 212 82), in the round ticket booth, sails daily at 8:15am and on Fri.-Sat. in summer at 7:30pm (5hr., L34,000-38,000). **Navarma Lines** (tel. 218 44) is next door and embarks daily at 8:30am, plus Fri.-Sat. in summer at 8pm (times/prices same).

Accommodations and Food Only stay in La Spezia if you can't find a room in nearby Cinque Terre (only a few minutes away by train or bus). Try **Albergo Terminus,** Via Paleocapa, 21 (tel. 71 49 35), to the left as you exit the train station. The eccentric, *loggia*-style lobby foreshadows the large rooms within. (Singles L30,000-35,000, with bath L40,000. Doubles L47,000, with bath L58,000.) **Albergo Spezia** lies on V. Cavalloti, 31 (off V. Prione, near the port end), and houses ample rooms with squishy mattresses. (Singles L24,000-30,000, with bath L32,000-39,000. Doubles L34,000-42,000, with bath L45,000-56,000.)

While in La Spezia, try the local specialty, *mescuia,* a thick soup of beans, cornmeal, olive oil, and pepper. Sample at **Trattoria da Sandro,** V. del Prione, 268 (tel. 372 03), where pizzas go for L6000-8000, and the house specialty is *trittico della casa,* a combo plate of seafood pastas (L9500). (Open Sat.-Thurs. noon-2pm and 7:30-10pm.) Directly across the street, **Trattoria da Vito** draws a more down-to-earth crowd and pleases them with hearty food and a TV always tuned in to sports events. (Pastas L6000-8000, and a tasty eggplant *parmigiana* L6000. No cover.)

■ NEAR LA SPEZIA: PONTREMOLI

Situated on the banks of the Magra and Verde rivers, the enchanting medieval Tuscan village of **Pontremoli** stands majestically amidst hills of cypress and olive trees in the ancient Lunigiana Valley. Terra-cotta rooftops, 15th-century stone bridges, and labyrinthine cobblestone alleyways from the Middle Ages dot the countryside of this magnificent town, known in Italy as the *Città del Libro* (city of the book). Every year, usually during the third weekend of July, Pontremoli plays host to the international **Premio Bancarella,** a festival characterized by numerous book vendors selling their wares at *bancarelle* (open-air booths), large outdoor antique markets in the central town squares, **Piazza della Repubblica** and **Piazza Duomo,** and, finally, the awards ceremony for Italy's finest book of the year. (Umberto Eco won the prestigious award for *Foucault's Pendulum* a few years back.)

Porn in Parliament

In 1987, the Radical Party's candidate Ilona Staller, commonly known as the ex-porn star "La Cicciolina," was elected to the house of deputies in Viareggio. The buxom blonde celebrated her win by baring her breasts to the eternally grateful city in a victory parade. In 1991, Staller married American kitsch artiste Jeff Koons, whose major works include an enormous sculpture of himself and Ilona as Adam and Eve in the Garden of Eden. She also made an innovative attempt at a peace plan during the Gulf War, offering Saddam Hussein her body if he would agree to pull out early. She has since retired from the house of deputies and has divorced Koons.

Orientation and Practical Information Pontremoli is located on the Parma-La Spezia train line, or you can catch the twice-daily train headed from Milan to Livorno, with stops at Pontremoli. From the **train station,** head right on **Via dei Mille** until you reach a bridge. Turn left here, and cross the river onto **Via Cairoli.** The *centro storico* lies to your right as you head down Via Generale Armani to

Piazza della Repubblica, with the impressive 14th-century **campanone** (bell tower), known as Il Campanone. Behind the Campanone lies **Piazza Duomo.** From here, follow the signs up the twisting alleys to the **Castello del Piagnaro,** built by Cealberti and the Longobards during the 10th century, now home to the **Museo dell Statue-Stele,** housing pre-Etruscan (around 6000 BC) tombstones. (Museum open in summer Tues.-Sun. 9am-noon and 4-7pm; in winter 9am-noon and 2-5pm. Admission L3000, under 12 free.) The **tourist office** (Pro Loco) holds irregular hours, but can be reached off P. della Repubblica, next to the Municipio (tel. (0187) 83 11 80). The **post office** lies on Via Pirandello, tel. 83 00 57. **Taxis:** tel. 83 04 67 (train station) or 83 00 54 (P. della Repubblica). There is a **pharmacy** on P. Italia (tel. 83 01 78). The **police** can be reached at tel. 83 00 22; **ambulance:** tel. 83 00 49.

Accommodations and Food Accommodations in Pontremoli can be costly; it is best seen as a day trip from La Spezia. If you decide to stay, try **Hotel Napoleon** on P. Italia, 2 (tel. 83 05 44), an elegant hotel with marble floors and rooms decorated with antiques. (Singles L75,000 with bath. Doubles L105,000 with bath. AmEx, MC, Visa.) At mealtime, head to one of the typical *trattorie* in the *centro storico.* Pontremoli's claims to fame are their *testaroli:* large, pancake-like flatbread oven-cooked in special pots called *testi,* then boiled quickly, and topped with *pesto,* grated *parmigiano* cheese, and *pignoli* (pine nuts). Try them at **Trattoria da Tonino,** known to locals as La Gravagnotti, off P. Duomo on Via Garibaldi, 16 (tel. 83 05 48). Literally a "hole in the wall," it lies at the end of a cool stone corridor. (*Primi* L6000, *secondi* L10,000. Cover L2000.) A few doors down at Via Garibaldi, 22, to the right in the tiny Piazzetta di San Geminiano, is **Trattoria da Fernando** (tel. 83 06 53), where *primi* run L5000-L6000 and *secondi* go for L10,000-13,000. Try the *risotto ai funghi* (L8000). (Reservations recommended.) For some of the best *gelato* you'll lick in Italy, go to **Bar Moderno** on Via IV Novembre, 2.

RIVIERA DI PONENTE

■■■ FINALE LIGURE

A prime spot to take a vacation from your vacation, Finale Ligure is the antidote for any weary traveler fed up with train schedules and tourist attractions. Popular with the twenty-something crowd, this Riviera town is blessed with a sparkling emerald sea, a long sand beach, a boardwalk lined with palm trees and kiddie rides, and tons of *gelaterie.* Medieval turrets emerge out of the rocky hillsides that attract rock climbers from all over the world.

ORIENTATION AND PRACTICAL INFORMATION

The city divides into three sections: **Finalpia** to the east, **Finalmarina** in the center, and **Finalborgo,** the old city, to the west. Most of the places listed below, including the **train station,** are located in Finalmarina. The main street in town changes names several times between the main station and the main *piazza,* from **Via de Raimondi** to **Via Pertica** to **Via Garibaldi,** which opens into **Piazza Vittorio Emanuele II,** also known as **Piazza di Spagna.** From this central *piazza* along the water are **Via della Concezione** to the west and **Via S. Pietro** to the east. To reach the old city, take a left out of the station and go under the tracks to pick up **Via Domenico Bruneghi.**

Tourist Office: IAT, Via San Pietro, 14 (tel. 69 25 81 or 69 25 82), on the main street overlooking the sea (as opposed to the *lungomare,* which is really more of a promenade than a street). Luisa has been here for over 30 years and knows her stuff. She will gladly offer maternal advice for all of your problems, as well as a great map. Open Mon.-Sat. 9am-1pm and 3-7pm, Sun. 9am-noon. The **Associazi-**

FINALE LIGURE

one **Alberghi e Turismo,** Via de Raimondi, 29 (tel. 69 42 52), across from the station on the corner of Via de Raimondi and Via Saccone, helps you find rooms in the summer. Open May-Oct. Tues.-Sun. 10am-1pm and 2:30-6:30pm.

Police: Via Brunanghi, 68 (tel. 113 or 69 26 66).

Currency Exchange: Banca Carige, Via Garibaldi, 4, across from the *Casa del Formaggio.* A 24-hr. Cambiomat will exchange foreign currency into *lire.* Open Mon.-Fri. 8:20am-1:20pm and 2:30-4pm. On Sat., head to the post office.

Post Office: Via della Concezione, 27 (tel. 69 28 38). Open Mon.-Fri. 8:10am-5:30pm, Sat. 8:10am-noon. Fax services available. **Postal code: 17024.**

Telephones: Telecom, Via Roma, 33. Pay phones, directories, and vending machines selling tokens and phone cards. Open June-Sept. 8am-11pm; Oct.-May 8am-8pm. If it's late, there's a phone in the train station, as well as an automatic telephone card machine. **Telephone code: 019.**

Trains: P. Vittorio Veneto (tel. 69 27 77). Frequent service to: Genoa (L5700), Ventimiglia (L7200), and Santa Margherita Ligure (L8000).

Buses: SAR, Via Aurelia, 28 (tel. 69 22 75) outside and to the left of the train station. Ticket office (and currency exchange) open Mon.-Sat. 8am-12:30pm and 3-7pm. If this ticket office is closed, try **Bar Rino,** at the corner of Via Mazzini and Via Bruneghi. To: Borgo Verezzi (L1300), Savona (L3100), Finalborgo (L1100), and other towns. No round-trip discounts.

Bike Rental: Oddone, Via Colombo, 20 (tel. 69 42 15), on the street behind the tourist office. Bikes: L3500 per hr., L10,000 per day. Mountain bikes: L10,000 per hr., L35,000 per day. You must leave a passport (ask them to make you a photocopy). Open in summer daily 9am-12:30pm and 3:30-7:30pm; in winter closed Mon. morning and Sun. MC, Visa.

Pharmacy: Comunale Via Ghiglieri, 6 (tel. 69 26 70), off Via Pertica. Open Mon.-Fri. 8:30am-12:30pm and 3:30-7:30pm. Closed Mon. mornings and Fri. afternoons. A posted sign shows which pharmacies are open when this one isn't.

Medical emergencies: tel. 112. **Guardia Medica:** (tel. 62 77 77) 8pm-8am and Sat. 2pm until Mon. 8am. **Hospital: Ospedale Santa Corona,** Via XXV Aprile, 28 (tel. 623 01), in nearby Pietra Ligure. **First Aid: P. A. Croce Bianca,** Via Torino, 16 (tel. 69 82 32 in Varigotti or 69 23 33 in Finalmarina). In Finalborgo call the **Croce Verde** (tel. 69 13 25) directly through the hospital.

ACCOMMODATIONS AND CAMPING

A visit to the Associazione Alberghi prior to seeking shelter could save you time and legwork. In July and August the youth hostel is always your best bet, not to mention the best view. Rooms in private homes can be arranged through the tourist office.

Youth Hostel: Castello Wuillerman (HI) (tel./fax 69 05 15), on Via Generale Caviglia in a red brick castle overlooking the sea. From the station (15min.), take a left onto Via Mazzini, which becomes Via Torino. Turn left onto tiny Via degli Ulivi when you hit the *Esso* gas station, and start your hellish climb up the Gradinata delle Rose. A small sign and, yes, another set of steps marks the way up to the castle on your left (318 steps altogether). The view makes the climb worthwhile. *Really* crowded in summer, but cheap and convivial. Cristina fixes great meals (L12,000). No phone reservations. Limited showers and crazy barking German Shepherd are overshadowed by enthusiastic staff, beautiful courtyard, and plenty of activities. Reception open 7-9:30am and 5-11pm. Check-in 5pm, but you can leave your bags 7-9:30am. Doors locked 11:30pm-7am. Curfew 11:30pm. L16,000 per person for HI cardholders (without card add L5000), sheets and breakfast included. Family rooms available on a very limited basis. Open March 15-Oct. 15.

Albergo San Marco, Via della Concezione, 22 (tel. 69 25 33), on the street facing the beach, down from the station. Enter through a restaurant with purple and lavender tablecloths. Friendly proprietors keep spotless rooms, all with bath and phone. Singles L40,000. Doubles L65,000-73,000. Hearty, full-spread breakfast included. Minimal English spoken. Full pension prices range from L60,000 to L78,000 depending on the season. Closed Oct.-Nov.

Albergo Marita, Via Saccone, 17 (tel. 69 29 04 or 69 34 15 at home), the street directly in front of the station. This small hotel is set back from the street on the left. Attractive, functional rooms, some with balconies. Singles L25,000-35,000, with bath L30,000-40,000. Doubles L50,000-70,000, with bath L60,000-80,000. Prices vary according to season (more expensive in July-Aug.). Breakfast L5000. Reservations required in the summer.

Camping: Del Mulino (tel. 60 16 69), on Via Piemonte. To get here from the station, take the bus for Calvisio from the stop in the Piazza Vittorio Veneto and get off at the Boncardo Hotel, Corso Europa, 4, right on the waterfront (in the Finalpia district). From here, turn left at the Piazza Guglielmo Oberdan, then right onto Via Porra, go left under an arch onto Via Castelli, and follow it uphill. On your left, just after an olive grove ends, there will be stairs leading up to a footpath. Follow these until you see a yellow sign for the entrance to the campsite. About a 20-min. walk from the station, and 300m from the seashore. Bar, restaurant, and mini-market on the premises, but no laundry. L9000 per person, L7000 per small tent, L12,000 per large tent; less if it's not July. Open April-Sept.

Camping Tahiti (tel. 60 06 00), is slightly farther away on Via Varese. Same directions as Del Mulino, but from Via Porra turn left onto Via Orione which becomes Via Molinetti. Via Varese is on the left. L8000 per person (L9000 during July-Aug.), L7000 per tent (L8000 during July-Aug.). Hot showers L1000. Open Easter-Sept.

FOOD

Trattorie and *pizzerie* line the streets closest to the beach. Pay less for comparable fare farther inland along Via Rossi and Via Roma.

Spaghetteria Il Posto, Via Porro, 24 (tel. 60 00 95). An elegant and creative pasta house with an unusual menu. Forebearing staff endures all foreign foibles with a smile. Try the *penne quattro stagioni* (tube pasta with bacon, mushrooms, tomatoes, artichokes, and mozzarella, L9000) or the *penne pirata* (with shrimp and salmon, L10,000). Plenty of options for vegetarians as well. Cover L1500. Open Tues.-Sun. 7-10:30pm. Closed for the first 2 weeks in March.

La Grotta, Vico Massaferro, 17, off Via San Pietro (along the waterfront), right across the alley from the tourist office. A restaurant originally built in the '40s to resemble a cave. A busy local hangout. Excellent, very filling pizzas from L5500. 10% service charge. Open Wed.-Mon. 7pm-midnight, Sun. noon-3pm.

Salumeria Chiesa, Via Pertica, 13 (tel. 69 25 16), 30m from the *Palazzo Comunale* (town hall), is the perfect place to pack a picnic lunch for the beach. *Insalata di mare* (seafood salad) L4000 per *etto*. Lasagna L1800 per *etto*. (The average serving is about 3 *etti*.) Open daily 7:30am-1pm and 4-7:30pm Oct.-May, closed Thurs. and Sun. afternoons. Sit-down restaurant open Mon.-Fri. noon-2pm.

Panetteria Ghigo Maria, Via G. Rossi, 32, off Via Garibaldi. In this locals' favorite bakery, an award hangs from the wall: "Panino Più Lungo Del Mondo" ("Longest Sandwich in the World"). Come here for low-priced *focaccia* slices (plain L1000, cheese L1200, and olive L1300), pizza (L1500), and authentic cookies including the popular *brutti ma buoni* ("ugly but yummy"). Open daily 7am-1pm and 4-8pm, closed Sun. afternoons; off-season, closed Thurs. and Sun. afternoons.

Paninoteca Pilade, Via Garibaldi, 67 (tel. 69 22 20), off P. Vittorio Emanuele. If you're jonesing for Americana, this is the place—MTV, old Coke posters, banana splits. Right out of *Happy Days.* Fabulous *panini* ranging from L3500-5000. Pizza by the slice (L2000-3500). Beer on tap (L2500-7500). Open daily 10am-3am.

SIGHTS AND ENTERTAINMENT

Finalborgo, enclosed within solid ancient walls, is just a one-km walk up Via Bruneghi from the station. The baroque **Basilica di San Biagio,** inside the city walls through the elegant Porta Reale, features a 13th-century octagonal belfry, while the **Chiostro di Santa Caterina,** (tel. 69 00 20) is a five-minute walk across town. The **Civico Museo del Finale,** dedicated to Ligurian history, is housed in this 14th-century edifice. (Open Tues.-Sat. 9am-noon and 2:30-4:30pm, Sun. 9am-noon. Admission L5000, children L2500.) You can climb a tough, rocky trail up to the 13th-century **Castel Govone** (closed to the public) for a spectacular view of Finale. If you're interested in more rock-climbing fun, get the lowdown on routes in Finale at

Rock Store, Piazza Garibaldi, 14 (tel. 69 02 08), where you can obtain maps and all necessary gear. (Open Tue.-Sun. 9am-12:30pm and 4-7:30pm.)

At the waterfront in **Finalmarina,** you can climb the steps at the intersection of Via Colombo and Via Torino to the lofty 14th-century **Castelfranco.** World War II ravaged much of this structure, but it has recently been restored, and the view is tremendous. Ask at the tourist office for hours and admission charge. Make sure to head to the Genovese baroque **Basilica di San Giovanni Battista** in the *piazza* of the same name. (Follow your nose—the whole square is decorated with gardenias!)

The towns surrounding Finale Ligure invite discovery. Take an SAR bus (L1300) to tiny **Borgo Verezzi.** Get off at the first stop in the town of Borgio. From here, five buses leave daily for Verezzi. From mid-July through August, performances animate **Teatro di Verrezzi,** the town's outdoor theater in the main *piazza.* The performing company is one of Italy's most renowned. (About L35,000. Call the Borgo Verezzi tourist office at (019) 61 04 12 for details.)

If you don't mind a meat-market atmosphere, try **Il Covo,** Capo San Donato (tel. 60 12 84). It's a small disco right next to the best free beach in Finale, right after the tunnel near the waterfront on Via Aurelia. (Open Tue.-Sun. 11pm-4am; cover L20,000, Sat. L25,000.) Other options include **Mirò** (tel. 60 02 14) on Via Santuario, a live discobar (Thurs.-Fri. free), or try the **Scotch Club** on Via San Pietro near the tourist office (tel. 69 24 81). (Open Thurs.-Sat. 11pm-3am.) Go down San Pietro and turn left past the Mironi Hotel. A local favorite is **Il Patio,** at the end of the promenade to the east: left along the beach, on the right.

■■■ SANREMO AND DOLCEDO

SANREMO

Once a glamorous retreat for Russian nobles, czars, *literati,* and artists, Sanremo is still first and foremost the largest resort on the Italian Riviera. Overlooking an expansive bay, the palm-lined **promenade** and the casino are the main attractions of this *very* expensive, *very* "V.I.P.," and *very* entertaining city. You can take the bus or train from Ventimiglia or Imperia. The terminally nostalgic can relive Sanremo's glory days at the city's whitewashed Edwardian **Casino,** a dazzling example of Art Nouveau architecture, located at Corso Inglesi, 18 (tel. 53 40 01). The entrance fee is "only" L15,000, although you must be 18 to enter, and guys have to wear a coat and tie. Blackjack begins at 8:30pm, but early gamblers can start spinning the roulette wheel at 2:30pm. The "American Room" of one-armed bandits has neither dress code nor entrance fee and lures early risers with its 10am opening. Depending on how the games are going, the casino fun stops around 3am.

Also worth seeing in Sanremo are the old **Pigna** quarter, with its medieval splendor, and the Russian Orthodox **Church of Santa Caterina Martire and San Serafino,** with intricate onion-domes reminiscent of St. Basil's in Moscow. In August, Sanremo hosts its traditional festival, **Nostra Signora della Costa,** with a procession in medieval garb and a "Sailors' Mass." In February, floral carpets and an exciting parade of floats can be seen throughout the month. In late July and August, Sanremo holds the **Humor Festival,** an international event with performances and exhibits. Check with the tourist office for specifics. Sanremo's **tourist office** is located at Largo Nuvolini, 1 (tel. 57 15 71; fax 50 76 49). (Open Mon.-Sat. 8am-7pm, Sun. 9am-1pm.) Sanremo's **postal code** is 18038; the **telephone code** is 0184. The **museum hotline** can be reached at tel. 53 19 42.

DOLCEDO

A short bus ride into a valley dotted with farmhouses and the sunny groves that produce Liguria's finest olive oil leads to the medieval village of **Dolcedo.** There, bridges cross the river Prino, ancient oil mills grind, and the 15th-century chapel of Santa Brigida still stands. The bridge on which the Knights of Malta carved "*mcclxxxxii die 3 juli hoc opus perfectum fuit*" ("on July 3, 1292 this work was finished") leads to the old market square, an area that seems utterly unchanged since the Middle Ages. Make a right on Via de Amicis to the **Church of San Tommaso,** a parochial church with 17th-century arcades. Its striking pink-and-green exterior seems to have partially inspired the peculiar half pink-and-green, half blue-and-gold interior. At the moderately priced **Ristorante Da Tunu,** Piazza Dovia, 2 (tel. 28 00 13), a full meal costs around L16,000. (Wine L7000-20,000 per liter.) *Cinghiale* (wild boar) is an autumn specialty. (Cover about L1500—depends on food. Open Tues.-Sun. noon-2:30pm and 7:30-9pm.) Launch your excursion to Dolcedo from **Imperia,** where Riviera Trasporti buses (the blue ones) leave from in front of the Hotel Italia up to the left of the train station. Buy tickets from any *tabacchi* (L2000). About 7 buses per day, labeled either Dolcedo or Lecchiore; ask the driver for specifics.

The medieval hillside village of **Cervo** is a picturesque retreat from the larger beach towns of the Riviera. Its white houses, red roofs, stone archways, and tiny *piazze* are well worth the simple excursion: take the *locale* along the Ventimiglia-Genoa line, or take a bus from Imperia. Cervo hosts an international **chamber music festival** in July and August, held in front of the baroque Church of San Giovanni Battista. Call the tourist office at Piazza Castello, 1 (tel. (0183) 40 81 97) for details.

■■■ BORDIGHERA

Bordighera is known as the "City of Palms." Legend has it that Sant'Ampelio brought the original palm seeds from Egypt and planted them in the town's fertile soil. The town's green thumb persists: it proudly supplies the Vatican with palm leaves for Holy Week. Even Claude Monet fled his gardens at Giverny for relaxing winters by the sea and the lush flower-lined parks of Bordighera. Bordighera provides an oasis of small-town tranquility in the overly touristed Riviera di Ponente.

ORIENTATION AND PRACTICAL INFORMATION

The bus from Ventimiglia (15min., L2000) drops you off on the main street, **Via Vittorio Emanuele II,** which runs west from the city's train station in **Piazza Eroi della Libertà.** Behind the station is the scenic **Lungomare Argentina,** a 2-km promenade along the beach. In the **città moderna** (new town), most offices and shops sit on Via Vittorio Emanuele; most residential neighborhoods are in the **città alta,** the historic center. Built on a hill, the 15th-century *città alta* is accessible by three gates, of which the **Porta Sottana** is the most convenient.

> **Tourist Office:** Via Roberto, 1 (tel. 26 23 23; fax 26 44 55), just past the small park. From the train station, go left on Via Vittorio Emanuele, and take the 1st right onto Via Roberto. Marvelous Marisa doles out maps, hotel listings and info in English. She doesn't book rooms, but makes good suggestions. Open Mon.-Sat. 8am-7pm, Sun. 9am-1pm.
> **Post Office:** (tel. 26 23 74), just to the left of the station in P. Eroi della Libertà. Open Mon.-Fri. 8am-6:30pm, Sat. 8am-noon. **Postal Code:** 18012.
> **Telephones: Telecom (SIP),** Via Roberto, 18, across from the tourist office. Pay phones only. Open 24 hrs. **Telephone Code:** 0184.
> **Currency Exchange:** Via Vittorio Emanuele II, 165 (tel. 26 36 54).
> **Trains: Stazione F.S.** in P. Eroi della Libertà (tel. 26 32 09). Bordighera lies on the Genova-Ventimiglia line.
> **Pharmacy: Farmacia Centrale,** Vittorio Emanuele, 145 (tel. 26 12 46). Open Sun.-Fri. 8:30am-12:30pm and 3:30-7:30pm.
> **Emergencies:** tel. 113. **Medical services** can be obtained at Via Aurelia, 66 (tel. 29 10 25). For an **ambulance** dial 27 51.

ACCOMMODATIONS

In summer, most hotels want clients to stay several days, and require that they accept full or half-pension.

Pensione Miki, Via Lagazzi, 14 (tel. 26 18 44), off Via Vittorio Emanuele II, about 500m from the station as you exit to the left. Small rooms, but a serene setting, firm beds, and balconies overlooking the town and valleys. L30,000 per person. Showers and breakfast included. Full or half-pension required during summer and Easter, L55,000-60,000 per person.

Villa Loreto, Via Giulio Cesare, 37 (tel. 29 43 32). Take Via Vittorio Emanuele left from the station for 200m, then go right on orange-tree-lined Via Rossi and left on Via Aldo Moro, which leads into Via Cesare. Though it's a bit of a hike to get there, the nuns provide the lowest prices and best company around in their palatial, tranquil residence graced by palm and lemon trees. Women and married couples only. Curfew 9pm; July-Aug. 10:30pm. Mandatory full pension includes meals L60,000-62,000 per person. Open Dec.-Sept.

Albergo Nagos, P. Eroi della Libertà, 7 (tel. 26 04 57), right next to the train station and the post office. Basic new furniture, nice views, private showers, and a warm reception make up for smallness of rooms. Singles L35,000. Doubles L55,000. Full pension (L60,000) required July-Aug., half-pension (L50,000) required May-June and Sept.

FOOD

As Bordighera is a rather trendy vacation spot, affordable restaurants are few and far between. The *trattorie* in the *città alta*, however, are pretty reasonable and offer the traditional flavors of Ligurian cuisine. While in Bordighera, make sure to sample the local dessert, *cubaite* (elaborately decorated wafers filled with caramel cream), and the local *Rossese* wine from Dolceaqua. **Trattoria degli Amici,** at Via Lunga, 2 (tel. 26 05 91), in the *città alta,* serves *spaghetti al pesto* for L10,000. Cover L4000. (Open Jan.-Oct. Tues.-Sun. 7-11pm, Sat.-Sun. noon-2pm. AmEx, MC, Visa.) Or try the **Trattoria dei Merinai di Costa Bianca,** at Via dei Merinai, 2 (tel. 26 15 11), an attractive place with additional outdoor seating in the tiny Piazza del Popolo. *Primi* from L9000, pizza from L7000. They even have an "I love you" pizza *dolce* (sweet) with chocolate, bananas, and cream. (Open Thurs.-Tues. noon-3pm and 7:30-11:30pm. AmEx, MC, Visa.) For picnics and more affordable fare, try the **mercato coperto,** P. Garibaldi (open daily except Wed. afternoons 7am-1pm; in winter closed Sun.), or the **Supermercato STANDA,** Via Libertà, 32 (open daily 8:30am-12:30pm and 3:30-7:30pm; in winter closed Mon. mornings).

SIGHTS AND ENTERTAINMENT

If you're up for a long but worthwhile walk, head east along Via Romana. Fork off onto Via Rossi, where cannons still stand guard above an awesome expanse of deep blue sea. Take the steps down to the **Church of Sant'Ampeglio,** built around the grotto where Ampeglio the hermit holed up. (Open Sun. at 9am, or knock on the door until someone lets you in.) The church is also open on May 14 for the **Festival of Sant'Ampeglio,** complete with an impressive procession, pomp and circumstance. The **Giardino Esotico Pallanca** ("exotic garden") at Via Madonna della Ruota, 1 (tel. 26 63 47), contains over 3000 species of cacti and other rare South American flora. (Open Tues.-Sun. 9am-noon and 3:30-7:30pm.) For inspiration of a more melodic nature ask at the tourist offices about concerts during May-Sept. given at the **Paviliano** down on the boardwalk. If you want to catch the latest film (dubbed in delayed Italian, of course), head to the **Cinema Olimpia** at Via Cadorna, 3 (tel. 26 19 55), just off the main drag, Via Vittorio Emanuele II. Look at the list posted outside for the movies of the month. Showings at 8:30 and 10:30pm. They offer reduced prices for youth and students.

■■■ VENTIMIGLIA

The quiet town of Ventimiglia (ven-tee-MEEL-yah) lies at the mouth of the Roya river and on the shores of the Mediterranean. With its numerous promontories and rocky crags, it is perfect for sitting and indulging in what the Italians call *il dolce di far niente* (the joy of doing nothing). While a former Roman municipality, Ventimiglia has long lost all vestiges of the splendor of its ancient and medieval past. For the historical-minded, however, the remains of a Roman theater remain to the east of town, and the city is filled with winding 11th-century streets. Just minutes form the French border, Ventimiglia bustles with international energy, yet maintains its small-town cleanliness and friendliness. While seen primarily as a point of departure for the French Côte d'Azur, Ventimiglia's affordability, proximity to all the famous Riviera oases, and pebble beaches make it an attractive base from which to explore.

ORIENTATION AND PRACTICAL INFORMATION

As the "western door of Italy" on the French-Italian border, Ventimiglia is an important gateway in and out of the country. Frequent buses link it to the rest of the Riviera dei Fiori and parts of France while trains run to the Italian and French Riviera. From the train station, cross the street and walk down **Via della Stazione.** The second crossroad is **Via Cavour,** and the third is **Via Roma.** Most of what you'll need can be found on these two streets. Via della Stazione eventually becomes **Corso Repubblica,** which leads to the waterfront at the **Lungo Roya G. Rossi.**

Tourist Office: Via Cavour, 61 (tel. 35 11 83). City maps and lots of brochures. English spoken. Open Mon.-Sat. 8am-7pm, Sun. 9am-1pm.

Police: P. della Libertà, 1 (tel. 35 75 75).

Post Office: Via della Repubblica, 8 (tel. 35 13 12), toward the water. Open Mon.-Fri. 8:10am-5:30pm, Sat. 8:10am-noon. Closes at noon on the last working day of each month. **Postal Code:** 18039.

Telephones: At the restaurant in the train station (tel. 35 19 35). Open 24 hrs. **Telephone Code:** 0184.

Currency Exchange: Inside the train station (tcl. 35 11 54). Open 7am-11:30pm. Also right outside at Via Stazione, 3/A (tel. 35 12 15). Open Mon.-Sat. 8am-12:30pm and 2:30-7pm. Neither charge commission.

Trains: Piazzale Stazione. To: Nice (26 per day, 40min., L11,800); Genoa (23 per day, 3hr., L13,700); Cannes (25 per day, 1½hr., L17,600); Marseille (5 per day, L52,600). Buy tickets early in the day, as the *biglietteria* has irregular hours.

Buses: Riviera Trasporti, Via Cavour, 61 (tel. 35 12 51), next to the tourist office. Open Mon.-Sat. 7:20am-7:30pm. On Sun., get tickets at **Pasticceria Viale,** Via Cavour, 626 (open daily 8am-noon and 3-8pm). To: Sanremo (L3000), Bordighera (L2000), Imperia-Porto Maurizio (L6000, change in Sanremo), as well as other local towns No round-trip discount.

Bike Rental: Eurocicli, Via Cavour, 70/B (tel. 35 18 79). L3000 per hour, L5000 per day. Open Mon.-Sat. 8:30am-noon and 3-7:30pm, Sun. 9am-12:30pm. MC.

Emergencies: tel. 113 for **Pronto Intervento. Ambulance: Croce Rossa Italiana,** Via Dante, 12 (tel. 25 07 22), or **Croce Verde Intemelia,** Piazza XX Settembre (tel. 35 11 75). **Hospital: Ospedale Santo Spirito,** Via Basso, 2 (tel. 27 51).

ACCOMMODATIONS AND CAMPING

Ventimiglia is one of the Riviera's most inexpensive places to stay, but it fills up in July and August, so reserve in advance. Consider crossing the border and staying in the **youth hostel** (tel. (033) 93 35 93 14; from Italy, dial another 0 first) in the nearby French town of **Menton** (15 min. by train, L3100). **Bring your passport.**

Hotel XX Settembre, Via Roma, 16 (tel. 35 12 22). Price-wise, possibly the best deal in town. Friendly owners and clean rooms decorated with jigsaw puzzle masterpieces on the walls. Singles L20,000. Doubles L34,000. Triples L50,000. Full pension L54,000, half-pension L40,000. Breakfast L6000. The **restaurant** serves a good meal for L20,000. Restaurant open Fri.-Wed. noon-3pm and 7:30-9:30pm. May be closed for vacation in May or June—call ahead.

Pensione Villa Franca, Corso Repubblica, 12 (tel. 35 18 71), right next to the waterfront and the public park. Rooms are clean, if somewhat small. Friendly management and lots of exotic pet birds. They'll bring you your own pot of coffee and pitcher of hot milk for *caffè latte* in volume. Singles L41,000. Doubles around L60,000 with bath L77,000. Breakfast and showers included. MC, Visa.

Albergo Al Mare, Vico Pescatori, 7 (tel. 29 90 55), like the name says, it's at the sea—about a half-block from the beach. Small, clean rooms brightened by flower boxes outside every window. Friendly staff works 24 hrs. Singles L30,000, with bath L41,000. Doubles L51,000, with bath L62,000. Half pension L46,000-50,000. Full pension L56,000-62,000. Breakfast L4000. MC, Visa.

Camping Roma, Via Peglia, 5 (tel. 23 90 07), 400m from the waterfront, across the river. From the station, follow Via della Stazione and turn right on Via Roma. Follow Via Roma until you reach the river at Lungo Roya G. Rossi. Turn right, and about 100m later turn left onto a bridge and cross the river. Make an immediate right on Corso Francia, and about 100m later turn right onto Via Peglia. Nice campsites with great hillside panoramas. Market and bar nearby. L10,000 per person, L10,000 per tent. Free showers. Open 8am-midnight May-Sept.

FOOD

You will pay dearly for quality, sit-down meals. The two restaurants in the *pensioni* above serve good meals. The covered **open-air market,** which sprawls every morning along Via della Repubblica, Via Libertà, Via Aprosio, and Via Roma, is the best place to grab fresh produce. Many of the *pizzerie* lining the beach prepare personal-sized take-out pizzas for about L7000. **Supermercato STANDA,** at the corner of Via Roma and Via Ruffini, is well stocked with staples. (Open Mon.-Sat. 8:30am-7:30pm; July-Aug. Sun. 8:30am-1pm.) The **Buffet Stazione,** inside the train station (tel. 35 12 36) is a fastidiously clean, modern option. Stand or sit. Slices of pizza and *focaccia* L1500, *panini* under L7500. Prices are lower if you don't sit at a table. Restaurant open daily noon-3pm; bar open 5am-midnight.

SIGHTS AND ENTERTAINMENT

Most visitors to Ventimiglia never venture beyond the beach, but for those willing to sacrifice a day of tanning there are a number of worthwhile sights. The Gothic **Cathedral,** with its intricate portal and adjoining 11th-century baptistery, is easy to find in the old town. Take Via Banchieri after the bridge, and from there take Via Falerina. **San Michele,** a Romanesque church of the same vintage, is on the other side of town. Follow the signs off Via Garibaldi to P. Colleta (open Sun. 10:30am-noon). The well-preserved **Roman theater** anchors the **archaeological zone** (tel. 25 23 20 or (010) 241 73 18 in Genoa) off Corso Genova to the east of the town. Turn left on Via Cavour, and continue about 1km to find it between gas stations and railroad tracks. (The zone is now "closed," but clearly visible from Corso Genova.)

A trip to the **Balzi Rossi** (Red Cliffs, tel. 381 13), 9km from Ventimiglia toward France, offers you a glimpse of an even earlier civilization. The blue Riveria Trasporti bus from the corner of Via Cavour and Via Ruffini in Ventimiglia (3 per day, 20min., L2000) takes you to a series of **caves** where you can view the remains of Cro-Magnon cave-dwellers. The most spectacular artifacts are housed in Balzi Rossi's **Prehistoric Museum** near the seaside. (Open Tues.-Sun. 9am-7pm. Admission L4000, under 18 and over 60 free.) Or try the **Museo Archeologico** at Via Verdi, 41. (Tel. 35 11 81 or 26 36 01. Open Tues.-Fri. 9:30am-12:30pm and 5-9pm in summer, 3-7pm in winter; Sat.-Sun. 10am-noon. Admission L4000.) The world-famous botanical **Hanbury Gardens** (tel. 22 95 07) stretch from the summit of Cape Mortola down to the sea and contain some of the world's most exotic flora, taken from three continents. Take the blue Riveria Trasporti bus (20min., L2000) from Via Cavour and Via Martiri della Libertà to La Mortola. (Open daily 9am-6pm; off-season Thurs.-Tues. 10am-4pm. Admission L8500, ages 6-12 L4500, under 6 free.) The **weekly market** in Ventimiglia takes place every Friday along the Lungo Roya G. Rossi.

■ NEAR VENTIMIGLIA

Of the many beautiful valleys fanning inland from Ventimiglia, **Val di Nervia** is the most accessible. On foot, pass the Roman theater to the Val di Nervia road on your left. Alternatively, take the blue **Riviera Trasporti** bus from the train station in Ventimiglia (10 per day, 15min., L2000). Riviera Trasporti also runs buses to the surrounding castle-topped hills.

Dolceacqua, 9km from Ventimiglia, is crowned by a medieval castle and an old city whose narrow, winding stone streets still bustle with activity (L2000 by bus from the Ventimiglia train station, 10 per day). Turn right at the bottom of the new city and cross the arched Roman bridge to the orange, pink, and green rococo **cathedral** at the bottom of the old city, then continue up the narrow streets to the wonderful **Castello dei Doria** (tel. 20 66 38). (Open Sept.-June daily 9am-noon and 3-7pm; July-Aug. daily 10am-noon and 3-5:30pm. Admission L2000.) Visitors and locals alike come from miles around for the region's biggest and tastiest pizza at **Pizzeria La Rampa,** Via Barberis, 11 (tel. 20 61 98), on the left side of the new town's main *piazza* (overlooking the bridge and old city). (Open Tues.-Sun. 7pm-midnight.) Dolceacqua is world-famous for its passion for ballet. Check with the **tourist office (IAT)** at Via Patrioti Martiri, 22 (tel. (0184) 20 66 66) or the Comune at Via Roma, 50 (tel. 20 64 44) for more info. In August, the village celebrates **Ferragosto** with swirling regional dances, traditional costumes, and mouth-watering pastries.

■ Piedmont (Piemonte)

The fertile Piedmont region is not only the source of the mighty Po River, but has also long been a fountainhead of fine food, wine, and nobility. The area falls into three zones. The **Alpine,** with the two stellar peaks of Monviso and Gran Paradiso, contains a string of ski resorts and a huge national park that spills across the regional border into Valle D'Aosta. The **Pianura,** the beginning of the fecund Po valley, encompasses industrial Turin, the wineries of the Asti region, and Italy's only rice paddies. Finally, many of the region's isolated castles survey the **hills** north and south of the Po. Piedmont has also been an influential region in Italy; Turin was the capital between 1861 and 1865. It was the savoy King Vittorio Emanuele II (whose family had dominated in Piedmont since the 11th century) and Minister Camillo Cavour who ushered in the *Risorgimento,* uniting Italy in 1859. But the region's political activity didn't end with the removal of the capital; both the latter-day monarchists and the Red Brigades were based here. Today, medieval towns throughout the region attempt to re-create the festivals and pageantry of the middle ages, inviting the traveler to explore Piedmonte's beautiful geography and rich history.

■■■ TURIN (TORINO)

Turin's peaceful, baroque elegance is the direct result of years of urban planning, and the more recent influence of the locally based Fiat auto company. Just beyond the train station, cars circle neatly around the putting-green grass of Piazza Carlo Felice, where only the occasional jogger disturbs well-rooted cosmopolitans perusing their morning *La Stampa.* Piazza Castello, the city center, pulses with university students and Armani-clad businessmen. The Turin you're likely to encounter is cultured, courteous, and rather well-educated. Graceful, arcaded avenues reveal Turin's bookstores, from those specializing in rare, prized volumes to the many sidewalk *bancarelle* (secondhand book stalls) lining the Via Po.

The fact that Turin is also the capital of Italian extremism, however, is something you may not suspect and probably won't experience. But Turin is also known for its counter-culture, from its claim to fame as Europe's center of the occult, to the chaos of the old-fashioned **Gran Balôn** flea market (held every second Sun. in the Piazza della Repubblica), to the gypsies dancing through the streets. As the birthplace of the radical Red Brigades of the 1970s, and the stomping-ground of leftist intellectu-

TURIN

als like Pavese and Natalia Ginzburg, Turin maintains its reputation as a cradle of revolutionary thought and the fountainhead of the *Risorgimento*..

ORIENTATION AND PRACTICAL INFORMATION

Turin lies on a broad plain on the north bank of the Po River, flanked by the Alps on three sides. **Stazione Porta Nuova,** in the heart of the city, is the best place to disembark. The city itself is an Italian rarity in that its streets meet at right angles, making it easy to get around either by bus or on foot. Of the four main streets, **Corso Vittorio Emanuele II** runs past the station to the river, and the elegant **Via Roma,** housing the principal sights, runs north through P. San Carlo and P. Castello. The other two main streets, **Via Po** and **Via Garibaldi,** extend from P. Castello. Via Po continues diagonally though the **Piazza Vittorio Veneto** (the university center) to the Po River. Via Garibaldi stretches from **Piazza Castello** to **Piazza Statuto** and the **Stazione Porta Susa.**

Let's Go: Italy helps you navigate by including the **map grid coordinates** of our Turin listings whenever possible.

Tourist Office: APT, Via Roma, 226 (B3; tel. 53 59 01; fax 53 00 70), under the left arcade on the small, divided Piazza C.L.N., just before P. San Carlo. English spoken. Extensive literature on Turin and its province. Open Mon.-Sat. 9am-7:30pm. Smaller office at the Porta Nuova **train station** (B3; tel. 53 13 27; open Mon.-Sat. 7:15am-7pm), next to the info office and exchange. Both offices will help you find a room. **Informa Giovani,** Via Assarotti, 2 (A2; tel. 442 49 76; fax 442 49 77), off Via Garibaldi between P. Castello and Porta Susa. This place is a gold mine: from feminist groups to fortune tellers, for info on renting bikes, getting a job, or finding an apartment, they'll have the scoop. Ask for the pocket-sized, *"Torino Giovani:* A Young Visitor's Tourist Guide," available free in English or Italian. Open Mon. and Wed.-Sat. 10:30am-6:30pm.

Police: Corso Vinzaglio, 10 (A3; tel. 558 81).

Post Office: Via Alfieri, 10 (B3; tel. 53 58 91 or 562 81 00), off P. San Carlo. Telex, fax, and telegram service. Open Mon.-Fri. 8:15am-5:30pm, Sat. 8:15am-1pm, last day of the month 8:15am-noon. *Fermo posta* open 9am-noon and 3-7pm, Sun. 9am-noon. **Postal code:** 10100.

Telephones: Telecom (SIP), Via Arsenale, 13 (B3), off Via S. Teresa, around the corner from the post office. Open Mon.-Fri. 8:30am-12:30pm and 3-7pm. Coin- and card-operated phones also available at Telecom, Via Roma, 18. Open daily 8am-10pm. Plenty of phones at the **Stazione Porta Nuova** (B3) as well (open 7am-9pm). **Telephone Code:** 011.

Currency Exchange: The exchange in the Porta Nuova Station (B3) is the easiest and offers a decent rate (open daily 7:30am-10pm). Also try the banks along Via Roma and Via Alfieri, and the automatic exchange machine by the APT office.

Flights: Caselle Airport (tel. 567 63 61 or 567 63 62). European destinations. Take a bus from the main **Autostazione Terminal Bus,** Corso Inghilterra, 3.

Trains: Porta Nuova (B3-4; tel. 561 33 33). To: Milan (every hr., 1¾hr., L13,600); Venice (10 per day with change at Milan, 3 per day direct, 4½hr., L33,400); Genoa (every hr., 2hr., L13,600); Rome (9 per day, 9-11hr., L51,200); Paris (4 per day, change at Lyon, 8hr., L125,000). AmEx. **Luggage Storage:** L1500 per piece. Open 24 hrs.

Buses: Autostazione Terminal Bus, Corso Inghilterra, 3 (tel. 33 25 25). Take tram #9 or 15 west from Porta Nuova to the station. Serves ski resorts, the Riviera, and the western valleys of Susa and Pinerolo. To: Courmayeur (9 per day, 4hr., L13,200); Aosta (every hr., 3hr., L10,300); Milan (15 per day, 2hr., L15,700); Chamonix (6 per day, 3½hr., L37,000). Buy tickets daily 7am-noon and 3-7pm.

Metropolitan Transit: City buses cost L1200. Tickets can be bought at *tabacchi* (there's one in Porta Nuova) before boarding. The system is easy to navigate and a helpful map is available at most terminal offices. Buses run 5am-1am.

Taxis: tel. 57 37 or 57 30 or 33 99. L4200 plus L1200 per km. L4000 surcharge at night, and L2000 Sun. and holidays. Baggage L1000.

TURIN

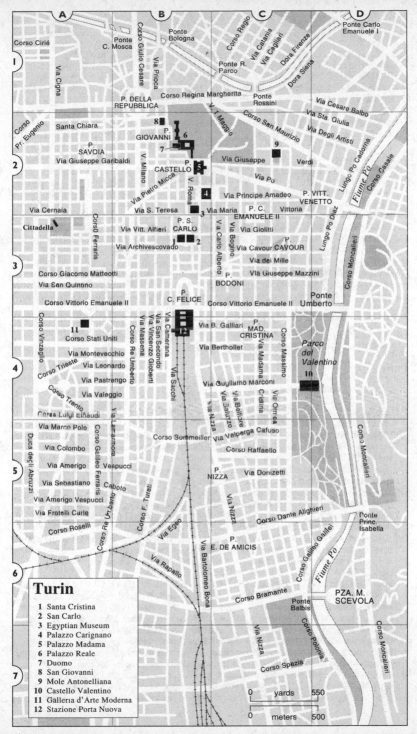

Turin

1 Santa Cristina
2 San Carlo
3 Egyptian Museum
4 Palazzo Carignano
5 Palazzo Madama
6 Palazzo Reale
7 Duomo
8 San Giovanni
9 Mole Antonelliana
10 Castello Valentino
11 Galleria d'Arte Moderna
12 Stazione Porta Nuova

Bike Rental: Parco Valentino (C4) on Viale Mattioli in Parco Valentino, a 15-min. walk down Corso Vittorio Emanuele as you exit Porta Nuova to the right. Open Tues.-Fri. 2:30-7pm, Sat.-Sun. 9am-12:30pm and 2:30-7pm. L2000 per hr., L4000 per half-day, L7000 per day. No age restrictions, but you must leave ID.

Lost Property: Ufficio Oggetti Smarriti, Porta Nuova (tel. 665 33 15), open 8am-noon and 2-5pm.

Laundromat: Lavanderia Vizzini, Via San Secondo, 30 (B4; tel. 54 58 82). Wash and dry: 4kg L15,000; 6kg L20,000. Open Mon.-Fri. 8am-1pm and 3-7:30pm, Sat. 9am-1pm.

Public Baths: Albergo Diurno (B3; tel. 54 78 34), just outside Porta Nuova near the Via Sacchi entrance, in the train station. Go down the spiral stairs. Clean and efficient. Showers L8000. Towels included. Soap L200, shampoo L800. Toilets L1500. Open Mon.-Sat. 7am-7pm, Sun. 7am-noon.

Swimming Pool: Piscina Comunale Stadio Civile, Corso G. Ferraris, 294 (tel. 36 75 50). Take bus #41 south from Corso Vittorio Emanuele near the station. Huge and clean. Open June-Sept. Tues.-Sat. noon-7pm, L7000, Sun. 12:30-6:30pm, L9000. Changing room included. Swim caps required (available at pool, L1500).

English Bookstore: Libreria Internazionale Luxembourg, British Bookstore, Via Accademia delle Scienze, 3 (B2; tel. 561 38 96), across from Piazza Carignano. A wide and worldly selection, with a strong Judaica section, and a very helpful English-speaking staff. Open Mon. 3-7:30pm, Tues.-Sat. 7am-7:30pm, Sun. 10am-1pm and 3-7pm. MC, Visa.

Late-Night Pharmacies: Farmacia Boniscontro, Corso Vittorio Emanuele II, 66 (B3; tel. 54 12 71 or 53 82 71), or try the **Farmacia Nizza** at Via Nizza, 65 (B3-4; tel. 669 92 59), down the street just to the right of Stazione Porta Nuova. Both close for lunch 12:30-3pm. After dark, ring to summon the pharmacist.

Emergencies: tel. 113. **Medical Assistance:** tel. 57 47. **Hospital: Mauriziano Umberto,** L. Turati, 62 (B6; tel. 508 01). **Ambulance: Red Cross:** tel. 28 03 33.

ACCOMMODATIONS AND CAMPING

Hotels abound but prices can be steep, even for the most basic rooms. Accommodations are easier to find in summer than during the rest of the year, and more easily uncovered on weekends than during the week.

Ostello Torino (HI), Via Alby, 1 (D4; tel. 660 29 39; fax 66 04 45), a small street off Via Gatti. Take bus #52 from Stazione Porta Nuova (on Sun. take bus #64). Get off at the 3rd stop after crossing the Po River, and follow the road uphill immediately to your right through Piazzale Luserna. Via Alba branches off Viale Thovez at the top of the *piazzale;* the hostel is at the corner of Via Gatti. Contemporary, clean, and comfortable with somewhat brusque service. Desk open 7-9am and 3:30-11pm. Curfew 11pm, but request a key if you want to stay out later. L17,000 per person. Extra L5000 per night for non-HI members. Dinner L12,000. Bring your own towel. Lockers available for a L20,000 deposit. Breakfast and sheets included. Laundry (wash and dry) L10,000 per load. **Bike rental** L8000 per day.

Albergo Magenta, Corso Emanuele, 67 (B3; tel. 54 26 49; fax 54 47 55), left of the train station. Very chic, with high, baroque ceilings and fresh flowers in the hallway. Centrally located. Prices are negotiable if rooms aren't full. All rooms have TV and firm beds. Singles L45,000, with bath L65,000. Doubles L54,000, with bath L70,000. Triples L100,000. Breakfast L7000. AmEx, MC, Visa.

Hotel Bellavista, Via B. Galliari, 15 (B-C4; tel. 669 81 39; fax 66 87 89), on a street slightly behind and to the right of Porta Nuova as you exit. Large, airy rooms and a sunny hallway full of plants. TVs and phones in the rooms. Communal patio/balcony. Very nice folks here. Singles L55,000. Doubles L90,000, with bath L110,000. Triple with bath L140,000-145,000. Breakfast L2000-8000.

Albergo San Carlo, P. San Carlo, 197 (B3; tel. 56 27 46 or 53 86 53), on the 4th floor. In the midst of the action, yet set back from the noisy *piazza*. High-class, ski-lodge style rooms, all with TV, fridge, and phone. Singles L60,000, with bath L70,000. Doubles L70,000, with bath L90,000. Triples L120,000.

Camping: Campeggio Villa Rey, Strada Superiore Val S. Martino, 27 (tel. 819 01 17). Take bus #61 north from the right side of the Porta Nuova across Emanuele bridge. Get off when you see the Porta Margherita bridge on your left. Then take bus #54 or walk up Corso Gabetti away from the river to the right. Quiet location in the hills above the city. L6000 per person, L3000 per small tent, L6000 per large tent. Light L2000, showers L1000. Bar, restaurant, and small supermarket on the premises. Open March 1-Oct. 30.

FOOD

Piemontese cuisine is a sophisticated blend of northern Italian peasant staples and elegant French garnishes. Butter replaces olive oil in cooking; cheese, mushrooms, and white truffles are used instead of tomatoes, peppers, and spices. *Agnolotti* (ravioli stuffed with lamb and cabbage) are the local pasta specialty, but *polenta,* a cornmeal mush often topped with *fontina* cheese, is the more common starch. Many *secondi* involve meat simmered in wine sauces, not surprising in a region with an abundance of excellent wine. Three outstanding red wines (Barolo, Barbaresco, and Barbera) are available in Turin's markets and restaurants, and are worth the extra price. The cheapest supplies are found on Via Mazzina, where fruit, cheese, and bread shops abound. There's also a supermarket, **Metà,** at Via Montebello, 21/a (C2; tel. 812 59 59; open Mon.-Sat. 8:45am-noon and 3:30-7:30pm; closed Wed. afternoons).

Turin serves delectable local pastries, including the remarkably rich *bocca di leone,* a doughnut filled with whipped cream, fruit, or chocolate (about L3000). You can sample it at **Cossolo il Pasticciere,** Via Gramsci, 1 (B3; tel. 53 95 62), and Via Garibaldi, 9 (A-B2; tel. 54 08 17). Their *viennesi alla crema* (L1200) are definitely worth a try as well. (Via Garibaldi location open Tues.-Sun. 7am-8pm. Via Gramsci location open Tues.-Sun. 7am-1am.)

Several trendy *gelaterie* line the near side of P. Castello coming from the station. Try the spiffy **Bar Blù** (tel. 53 14 24; open Tues.-Sun. 7am-1am) or **Paradice Gelateria,** Via Roma, 307 (tel. 53 08 48; open daily 7:30am-2am), where you can sample the exotic flower flavors *rosa* and *viola.* The **open-air market** at P. della Repubblica (B1) runs Mon.-Fri. 8am-1pm. (On Sat. (8am-6pm), an assortment of non-edibles are also sold here—everything from baskets to underwear.) There is also the **Market Rossini** (cheerfully named *Simpatia* on the sign), Via Rossini, 1 (C1-2; tel. 817 06 86; open Mon.-Tues. and Thurs.-Sat. 8:30am-1pm and 4-7:30pm, Wed. and Sun. 8:30am-1pm). To mingle with the fashion nobility, try **Caffè Torino,** Via Roma, 204 (B2-3; tel. 54 51 18), on P. San Carlo, a Turin institution. If you're in an extravagant mood, sit down and savor the solicitous service provided by tuxedo-clad waiters. (*Cappuccino* L6000 if you sit, L2500 if you stand. Open Wed.-Mon. 7:30am-1am.)

Porto di Savona, Piazza Vittorio Veneto, 2 (D2; tel. 817 35 00). This place is an institution in Turin, revered as serving the best in traditional Piemontese fare. Frescoed walls are adorned with black and white pictures of Turin at the turn of the century. Best bets are the *gnocchi al gorgonzola* (L8000) and the *fusilli alla diavola,* a delight made with tomato, *pesto,* and cream sauce (L8000). Huge portions. Open Tues. 7:30-10:30pm, Wed.-Sun. 12:30-2:30pm and 7:30-10:30pm.

Ristorante Taverna Fiorentina, Via Palazzo di Città, 6 (B2; tel. 53 72 89), off P. Castello. A small restaurant run by the Cicerale family. If you're tired of pasta, try the *Spiedino alla Fiorentina* (L9000). Plate of the day L7500-20,000. Cover L2500. Open Aug.-June Sun.-Fri. noon-3pm and 7-10pm. MC, Visa.

Ristorante da Michele, P. Vittorio Veneto, 4 (D2; tel. 88 88 36). Friendly service in a homey atmosphere including old "Coke" posters and a Derby mirror. Popular—get there early. Brick-oven pizza from L7000; *primi* L10,000-18,000. Cover L3000. Open Wed.-Mon. noon-2:30pm and 7:30-11:30pm.

Trattoria Messico, Via B. Galliari, 8 (B-C4; tel. 650 87 98), 2 streets south of Via Vittorio Emanuele, near Porta Nuova. No sombreros here, just tourists afraid to stray too far from the station and a smattering of locals. Terrific pasta and *fettuccine messico* (L7000). On Fri. and Sat. evenings, they serve Mexican food—real enchiladas 'n' stuff. Wine L8000 per liter. Cover L3000. Open Mon.-Sat. 11am-3pm and 7-10pm.

Trattoria Toscana, Via Vanchiglia, 2 (D2; tel. 812 29 14), off P. Vittorio Veneto near the university. This hit with locals rewards those who undertake the walk. Don't miss the *bistecca di cinghiale* (boar steak), which clashes with the rose-covered tables. Open Sept.-July Sun.-Fri. noon-2pm and 7-10pm. Closed Fri. night.

Café Gran Corso, C. Vittorio Emanuele, 63 (B3; tel. 562 93 49). A 5-min. walk to the left of Stazione Porto Nuova. The Regoni family is sure to please with fresh *panini* (L3000) made to order; eat in or take out. Open Mon.-Sat. 5:30am-8pm.

Seven-Up, Via Andrea Doria, 4 (B3; tel. 54 35 82). Crepes or silky *risotto* (both L8000) in a crisp, clean, no-caffeine atmosphere. Pizza from L6000. Open Aug.-June Tues.-Sun. noon-2:30pm and 6:30-11pm. AmEx, MC, Visa.

Brek, P. Carlo Felice, 22 (B3; tel. 54 96 11), in the center of the action off Via Roma. Chic and delicious self-serve fare, including beautiful salads, soups, and desserts. *Primi* around L5000, *secondi* around L7000. Open Mon.-Sat.11:30am-3pm and 6:30-10:30pm.

Il Punto Verde (Vegetarian), Via San Massimo, 17 (C2-3; tel. 88 55 43) off Via Po near Piazza C. Emanuele II. Friendly, pink tablecloths. A good place for lunch. *Primi* L6000-8000, *secondi* L6000-12,000, *menù* L15,000. Cover L2000. Open Mon.-Sat. noon-3pm and 6-10pm. Closed in Aug. MC, Visa.

SIGHTS

It's hard to say which the Turinese revere more: their successful auto industry or the (now somewhat less holy) Holy Shroud. Whatever the preference of locals, the city has a great deal to offer those who are neither religious pilgrims nor auto buffs. Turin's museums, architectural sights, and serene gardens are on par with some of the great capitals of Europe, and its manageable size and relative safety make it an excellent city to explore for visitors of all interests and budgets.

From Piazza Carlo Felice at the Porta Nuova station, **Via Roma,** flanked by arcades and stores, leads to the heart of the city. Just ahead, **Piazza San Carlo** displays all the formality and grandeur the 17th-century Baroque era was capable of inspiring. In the center of this perfect rectangle, the statue of Duke Filiberto Emanuele stands proudly above the crowds (and cars) on his horse. In addition to the elegant baroque buildings, the *piazza* features the twin churches of **Santa Cristina** and **San Carlo,** both the work of Filippo Juvarra, architect to King Vittorio Amadeo II.

Beyond P. San Carlo, Via Roma ends in **Piazza Castello,** the historic center of the city, dominated by the imposing **Madama Palace** (tel. 54 38 23), so called because the widow of Vittorio Amadeo I, "Madama Reale," Marie Christine of France, lived here. (Natives often refer to it as the Palazzo Reale, however, which is a bit confusing as there is another royal palace in Turin.) The colossal two-story pilasters and columns are set against Juvarra's richly decorated façade, which hides a jumble of fragments—including a Roman gate and a 13th-century castle. Inside, the **Museo Civico di Arte Antica** contains a fine collection of medieval and Renaissance objects. The **Armeria Reale** (Royal Armory) of the House of Savoy (tel. 54 38 89) is located just across P. Castello at #191, and contains the world's best collection of medieval and Renaissance tools of war. Upstairs in the library you'll find Leonardo da Vinci's self-portrait *(autoritratto)* in red ink. (Open Tues. and Thurs.-Fri. 2:30-7:30pm, Wed. and Sat. 9am-2pm. Admission L8000, under 18 and over 60 free.)

Though the city owes its glory to political rather than ecclesiastical leadership, unadulterated splendor blesses the interior of the **Church of San Lorenzo** in P. Castello. Constructed between 1668 and 1680, it is Guarini's most original creation—follow the moldings as they weave in and out of side chapels, or count the myriad columns of every color, shape, size, and texture imaginable. The highlight is the **dome,** a multi-layered kaleidoscope of wishbones and starfish with ribs in a dynamic, swirling composition. (Open 8:30am-noon and 4-7pm.) Cross the courtyard to see the **Palazzo Reale** (tel. 436 14 55), a plain apricot building that the Princes of Savoy called home from 1645 to 1865. Its red-and-gold interior houses an outstanding collection of Chinese porcelain vases. The small but sumptuous garden was designed by Louis le Nôtre (1697), who is more famous for his work on the *jar-*

dins of Versailles. (Palace open Tues.-Sat. 9am-7pm. Admission L8000, under 18 and over 60 free. Gardens open daily 9am-6pm. Free.)

The **Cathedral of San Giovanni,** behind the Palazzo Reale where Via XX Settembre crosses P. San Giovanni, is also a must-see. Guarini's remarkable creation, the **Cappella della Santa Sindone** (Chapel of the Holy Shroud, 1668-1694), lies within. His unrestrained, whirling black marble dome caps a somber rotunda that houses a silver vessel containing one of the strangest relics of Christianity, the **Holy Shroud of Turin.** This is the piece of linen in which it was thought that Christ was wrapped for burial after his crucifixion. Although radiocarbon dating places the piece in the 12th century AD, no one has been able to account for the unique front and back impressions of a crucified body. Before leaving the cathedral, don't miss Luigi Gagna's oil reproduction of Leonardo's *Last Supper* above the front door, considered the world's best copy of the Renaissance masterpiece. (Tel. 436 15 40. Chapel open Tues.-Sat. 9am-noon and 3:30-5pm. *Duomo* closed for restoration in 1995; ask the tourist office for updated info.)

The **Palazzo dell'Accademia delle Scienze,** at #6 of the Via of the same name, houses two of Turin's best museums. Crammed into two floors of this Guarini masterpiece, the **Egyptian Museum** (tel. 561 77 76) is one of the finest collections of Egyptian artifacts in the world this side of Cairo. Here you will find several copies of the Egyptian *Book of the Dead* and an intact sarcophagus of Vizier Ghemenef-Har-Bak, which stands out among the large sculptures and architectural fragments on the ground floor. Upstairs is the fascinating and well-furnished tomb of 14th-century BC architect Kha and his wife, one of the few tombs spared by thieves. (Open Tues.-Fri. 9am-7pm, Sat.-Sun. 9am-2pm. Admission L12,000, under 18 and over 60 free.) The third and fourth floors hold the **Galleria Sabauda** (tel. 54 74 40). With masterpieces from the House of Savoy, the gallery is renowned for its paintings by Flemish and Dutch artists: van Eyck's *St. Francis Receiving the Stigmata,* Memling's *Passion,* van Dyck's *Children of Charles I of England,* and Rembrandt's *Old Man Sleeping.* The Sabauda is also home to several Mannerist and Baroque paintings, including a noteworthy Poussin, several Strozzis, and Volture's *Decapitation of John the Baptist.* (Open Tues.-Sun. 9am-2pm. Admission L8000, under 18 and over 60 free.)

The **Museum of Antiquities** at Corso Regina Margherita, 105 (tel. 521 22 51), houses several beautiful Greek and Roman busts, a collection of Greek and Cypriot ceramics, and pieces from the treasury of Marengo. There are also several pre- and proto-historic artifacts from the Piedmont and Valle d'Aosta regions. (Open Tues.-Sat 9am-7pm. Admission L8000, under 18 and over 60 free.) The **Galleria d'Arte Moderna,** Via Magenta, 31 (tel. 562 99 11), off Largo Emanuele, contains representative works of late 19th- and 20th-century masters, including Chagall, Picasso, Courbet, and Renoir. (Open Tues.-Sun. 9am-7pm. Admission L8000.)

The **National Cinematographic Museum,** P. San Giovanni, 2 (tel. 436 11 48), occupies the Palazzo Chiablese. The museum contains an excellent collection of pre-cinematic and cinema stills, and maintains a library. Turin was the birthplace of Italian cinema; the seminal silent film *Cabiria* was filmed along the banks of the Po. (Closed for renovations in 1995; check with tourist office for updated info.)

The Palazzo Carignano contains the **Museo Nazionale del Risorgimento Italiano** at Via Accademia delle Scienze, 5 (tel. 562 11 47); enter from P. Carlo Alberto on the other side. One of the great Baroque palaces of Europe, its façade is a masterpiece of white marble relief and elegant statuary. In the 19th century, this palace housed the first Italian parliament and the cradle of Prince Vittorio Emanuele II. Today, the museum contains historic documents and other paraphernalia of national interest. On Sundays from 10:30am-noon there is a free guided tour of the exhibits. (Open Tues.-Sat. 9am-6:30pm, Sun. 9am-12:30pm. Admission L8000.)

For the culture-weary, a *siesta* in the shady **park** at P. Cavour is ideal, as is an amble through gorgeous gardens along the banks of the Po to the **Valentino Castle** (tel. 669 93 72). A "medieval" castle built in 1884 for a world exposition, it looks like something from *Alice in Wonderland.* The guide takes you through room after room of objects and oddities—a sink in the shape of a castle, a throne that converts to a potty. Unfortunately, both the dungeons and towers are inaccessible (as is the rest of the castle at the monument—closed for renovations in 1995.)

No Italian city would be complete without its expression of civic virility; in modern Turin, you can skip prowess-testing stairs and take a glass elevator to the top. The **Mole Antonelliana**, Via Montebello, 20 (tel. 817 04 96), a few blocks east of P. Castello, began as a synagogue in a flurry of political intrigue, but ended up as a Victorian eccentricity. The view inside the dome as you ascend to the top is dizzying. (Open Tues.-Sun. 9am-7pm. Admission L4000.)

ENTERTAINMENT

Turin's newspaper **La Stampa** publishes an excellent section on current events, music, cinema, and theater, as well as annual festivals. The sound of music, theater, and dance bring Turin alive from the beginning of June through July 6, when the city invites international companies to the **Sere d'Estate** festival. For info and programs, contact the **Assessorato per la Cultura**, P. San Carlo, 159. (Tel. 442 37 40. Open Mon. 3-7pm, Wed.-Sat. 9am-1pm and 3-7pm. Events L5,000-30,000.) **Settembre Musica** is a month-long extravaganza of classical concerts performed all over the city. Contact the Assessorato or the tourist office for a program. **Cinemas** are prevalent in Turin, offering the latest in both big-budget blockbusters and more obscure art films. During the academic year, a number of foreign films are shown in their original languages. For a list of the titles, times, and locations, contact the Informa Giovani office. Find a listing of summer films in *Arena Metropolismi.*

During his time as a student in Turin, Erasmus said that magic pervaded the city, and Turin has since extended its reputation as a center of **the occult.** Get your palm read at the Porta Pila, or flirt with the world of black garb and magenta walls at **Inferno,** Via Carlo Alberto, 55 (tel. 88 95 33), and Via Po, 14 (tel. 88 91 45). Local punks come to chat more than to shop. (Both open Mon.-Sat. 10am-noon and 3:30-7pm; closed Mon. morning and Sat. afternoon.) If you seek more traditional attire, but can't afford the chic shops lining Via Roma, try the **department store** at Via Lagrange and Via Teofilo Rossi.

As for nightlife, Turin has a number of *discoteche.* A young crowd gathers at the one in Parco Valentino (follow the loud music). **Hiroshima Mon Amour** is a centrally located club near Stazione Porta Nuova on Via Belfiore, off Via Bethedet. Both **El Patio,** Corso Moncalieri, 346/14 (tel. 661 51 66), and **Doctor Sax** are on the river, though in different directions. For El Patio, make a right on Corso Moncalieri after you cross the river on C. Emanuele II. Walk past a couple of bridges. As for Doctor Sax, make a right on Corso Cairoli from C. Emanuele II just before the river. Stay along the river and aim for Lungo Po Machiavelli. If you happen to have a car, the **parks** to the east of the river (like Parco Europa and Parco di Rimembranza) provide romantic, breathtaking views of the city below.

■ NEAR TURIN

When Turin was besieged by the French on September 6, 1706, King Vittorio Amadeo II made a pact with the Virgin Mary to build a magnificent cathedral in her honor if the city could withstand the invasion. Turin went unconquered, and the result was the magnificent **Basilica of Superga** (tel. 898 00 83), erected on the summit of a 672-m hill. The *basilica's* neoclassical deep porch and high drum support a magnificent dome. From the terrace you can survey the city, the Po Valley, and the Alps. Half the fun is getting there. Take tram #15 (L1200) from Via XX Settembre to Stazione Sassi and then board a small cable railway for a 20-minute ride through the countryside. (Closed for restoration in 1995; normally open daily 8:30am-noon and 3-6pm. Free.) The funicular departs on the hour (L4000). The tourist office also has info about boat trips on the Po, which normally run from mid-June to mid-September (L3000-10,000).

Turin is about two hours from **many excellent hiking areas and ski slopes in the Alps.** An hour up to the nearest mountain, alpine refuges begin appearing on the way to **Sestriere** (2035m). Only an hour and a quarter from Turin, it boasts a comprehensive resort with four cableways, 20 ski lifts, excellent runs, and a skating rink. Bus service connects the area with Oulx (on the Turin-Paris train line) and Turin. The **Venini,** a *rifugio alpino* (alpine hut) on the town's outskirts, supplements the town's conventional lodgings. Although Turin's tourist office has the latest on snow conditions, for specifics call **Sestiere's tourist office,** Piazzale Agnelli, 11 (tel. (0122) 760 45 or 768 65). **Alagna Valsesia** (1200m), 156km from Turin and 138km from Milan, boasts the second-longest lift in the area. Farther north looms **Macugnaga** (1327m), 183km from Turin and 141km from Milan, with its own enormous ski lift (1540m). The ski season runs November through May; ask in Turin about snow conditions before boarding a bus. All areas are linked with Turin by bus and train. For more info and a list of accommodations, write to the tourist office in Turin and request a booklet on *settimane bianche* ("white weeks," cheaper weekly skiing deals), as well as an *Annuario Alberghi* and their booklet *Orizzonte Piemonte: Dove la Neve è "Più Neve."*

■■■ SACRA DI SAN MICHELE

Perched on a bluff 1000m above the town of Avigliana, the massive stone **Sacra di San Michele** (tel. 93 91 30) looms in evocative splendor over the approaching traveler, seeming to grow out of the very rock that it is built on. *The Name of the Rose* was not filmed here, but that was the filmmaker's poor judgement; Umberto Eco did base the monastery of the book on this edifice here, and even in the summer it's easy to imagine monks plummeting to snowy deaths from the high windows, or turning up in a vat of pig's blood stowed in some creepy corner. Although it's easier going by car, the 12-km hike from nearby **Avigliana** (easily reached by train—15 per day, L2500 from Turin) will make you feel like a proper pilgrim. From Piazza del Popolo in Avigliana follow the main road, Corso Laghi, around Lago Grande and make a right on the street called Sacra di S. Michele, which winds its way up the mountainside. The way is clearly marked with signs. **Buses** to the top leave from Piazza Carlo Felice in Turin on Sundays during July and August at 8am. (Montaglio bus line, tel. 937 65 72; round-trip L8000.) The Sacra, a monastery founded in 1000 AD, perches atop Mt. Pirchiriano, making the place notable for both its interior and the views its location offers. Upon entering the structure, the impressive Stairway of the Dead, an immense set of steps helping to buttress the building leads outside to the beautifully carved wooden doors depicting the arms of St. Michael with the Serpent of Eden. As you enter the vast Romanesque-Gothic interior, the fresco to your left depicts the *Burial of Jesus, the Death of the Virgin,* and the *Assumption,* by Secondo del Bosco (1505). Peek into **the shrine of St. Michael,** down the small steps into the middle of the nave. As your eyes get accustomed to the dark, you'll see three tiny chapels. The largest one, to your left, with the back wall of solid rock, was built in 966 AD by St. John Vincent and supposedly consecrated by angels—and is the most sacred spot in the Sacra. In this crypt you'll find the tombs of medieval scions of the Savoy family. (Sacra open Tues.-Sun. 9am-noon and 3-5pm.) There are **public toilets** outside the entrance, but bring your own paper. There is also a **restaurant** just before the homestretch of the climb. While restoration on the building continues, it is still open to the public. For more info, contact Avigliana's **Informazione Turistico,** Piazza del Popolo, 6 (tel. (011) 93 86 50), where cordial workers will supply you with maps. (Open Mon.-Sat. 9am-noon and 3-6pm.)

■■■ SUSA

Though far from the capital, Susa never lets visitors forget its Roman origins. Surrounded by mountains and divided by a river, this tiny hamlet of 7,000 was once the seat of the Gaul Cottius, a prefect of the Empire. With its Roman artifacts and beautiful cathedral, Susa is the perfect escape from Turin's sometimes oppressive elegance, and a pleasant stopover on the way to the ski resorts of the Susa Valley.

To get to Susa from Turin, take the **train** to Bussoleno (every hr.) and change for Susa (1hr., L5000). From the station, walk up Corso Stati Uniti 50m to your right. The white stand on the park's corner is Susa's Pro Loco **tourist office,** with maps, brochures, and a money exchange. (Open Mon.-Sat. 8:30am-7:30pm, Sun. 8amnoon; in winter daily 8:30am-noon.) The **SAPAV bus** line (tel. 62 20 15) serves Susa, with departures to Turin (1 per day), and Sestriere (4 per day with change in Oulx), the most fashionable of the Piedmont ski resorts. Buses leave from the train station at Corso Stati Uniti, 33. **First aid/ambulance** (*pronto soccorso,* tel. 62 93 00) is across the street from the train station, up toward the tourist office, or try the hospital next door (tel. 62 12 12). **Telephone code:** 0122.

If you plan to stay, try **Hotel Stazione,** C. Stati Uniti, 2 (tel. 62 22 26), across from the station. Marco and Loris will fill you in on Susa's history, and give you spotless rooms as well. (Singles L31,000, with bath L42,000. Doubles L65,000, with bath L75,000. Breakfast L9000. Showers included. MC, Visa.) On Tuesday mornings from 8am-12:30pm a **market** offering everything from clothes to fresh cheese fills the length of Via Palazzo di Città and Via Martiri della Libertà. Tasty, fresh *focaccia* (L1200) is available at **Piazza al Taglio,** Via Mazzini, 2, next to the bridge. (Open Tues.-Sat. 9am-1pm and 4-7:30pm.)

A typically Italian historical jumble, Susa's cultural wealth centers on its collection of antique Roman remnants and operational medieval constructions. Medieval Susa centers on the **Cathedral of San Giusto,** a structure dating to 1029 AD that houses the 14th-century *Triptych of Rocciamelone,* a Flemish portrayal of the Virgin and saints in brass, and a fine 10th-century baptismal font, carved in serpentine. Beside the cathedral, the 5th-century **Porta Romana** hints with many-windowed splendor at the Roman remains around the town. The complete Roman tour takes in the **Amphitheater** and the **Baths** (follow the ubiquitous yellow signs), while the medievalist can continue on to the Romanesque church of **Santa Maria Maggiore,** with its handsome *campanile.*

■■■ ASTI

Located in the foothills of the Alps, Asti derives its name, not surprisingly, from the ancient Ligurian word for "high hill." Asti has bustled with activity since Roman times; BMWs and Armani suits pervade the city and attest to its success in the modern world. Although Asti did not fare well during the 13th-18th centuries (the house of Savoy struggled with local princes and the city was repeatedly destroyed by war), 120 13th-century towers have survived. The towers lend the city a medieval air, which is enhanced by the winding streets. Today, Asti is known not only for its poet Vittorio Alfieri (for whom both the central *piazza* and the main *corso* are named) and his cousin Count Benedetto (who designed much of the city), but also for its prestigious wine. Enthusiastic and friendly, the people of Asti do their part in making their city extremely pleasant to visit.

ORIENTATION AND PRACTICAL INFORMATION

The heart of the town lies in the triangular **Piazza Vittorio Alfieri.** Most of the historical sights lie slightly to the west of the *piazza,* off **Corso Alfieri.**

> **Tourist Office:** P. Alfieri, 34 (tel. 53 03 57). Assists in finding accommodations (no reservations made) and provides information on daytrips to wineries and castles. Ask about the *agriturismo* options. Pick up the *Guide to Asti and its Province* and the indispensable map of the town. English spoken. Open Mon.-Fri. 9am-12:30pm and 3-6pm, Sat. 9am-12:30pm.
>
> **Police:** Corso XXV Aprile, 5 (tel. 41 81 11).
>
> **Post Office:** Corso Dante, 55 (tel. 59 28 51), off P. Alfieri. Open Mon.-Fri. 8:15am-7pm, Sat. 8:15-noon. **Postal Code:** 14100.

Telephones: Telecom (SIP), P. Alfieri, 10 (tel. 39 11). Office open Mon. 3-7pm, Tues.-Fri. 9am-12:30 pm and 3-7pm. Automatic phones next door (open Mon.-Fri. 9am-12:30pm and 3-5:30pm) or around the corner on Via Ospedale (open daily 7am-10pm). **Telephone Code:** 0141.
Currency Exchange: Instituto Bancario di San Paolo di Torino, Corso Dante, 22 (tel. 43 42 11), at P. Alfieri and Corso Dante. Change located on the second floor. Open Mon.-Fri. 8:25am-1:25pm and 2:40-4:10pm. Also try the post office.
Trains: P. Marconi (tel. 53 54 00), a few blocks south of P. Alfieri. To: Turin (every ½hr., 40min., L5000); Alessandria (every 30min., 30min., L3400); Milan (you will have to change trains; 2hr., L11,900).
Buses: P. Medaglie d'Oro, across from the train station. To: Costigliole (5 per day, Mon.-Sat., ½hr., L2500), Isola d'Asti (every hour, 15min., L2000), Canelli (8 per day, 1hr., L3500), Castagnole (5 per day, 20min., L2500). Buy tickets on the bus. Ask at the tourist office for more scheduling information.
Taxis: tel. 53 26 05 (P. Alfieri) or 59 27 22 (P. Marconi).
Emergencies: tel. 113. **Hospital: Ospedale Civile,** Via Botallo, 4 (tel. 39 21 11). **Red Cross: (Ambulance)** tel. 41 77 41 or 41 77 11.

ACCOMMODATIONS AND CAMPING

Hotel Cavour, P. Marconi, 3 (tel. 53 02 22), across from the strain station, offers modern, clean singles for L46,000 (with bath L56,000). Doubles are L65,000 (with bath L86,000). (Open Sept.-July; desk open 6am-1am. AmEx, MC, Visa.)
Antico Paradiso, Corso Torino, 329 (tel. 21 43 85). A good hike from the action; take bus #3 (the one marked Canova) to the corner of Corso Torino and Corso XXV Aprile (L1200). Religious motifs adorn its white-washed walls. (Singles L35,000, with bath L45,000. Doubles L60,000. Closed Mon.).
Campeggio Umberto Cagni, Via Valmanera, 152 (tel. 27 12 38). From P. Alfieri, turn onto Via Aro, which becomes Corso Volta, take a left on Via Valmanera, and keep going (and going, and going...) (L5000 per person, L5000-6000 per tent, electricity L2300, showers free. Open April-Sept.)

FOOD

Astigiano cuisine is famous for its simplicity, its ability to create a *chof d'œuvre* with only a few crucial ingredients, delicious, pungent cheeses, and, of course, wine, wine, wine! This region creates the celebrated *bagna calda* (hot bath), that miraculous combination of raw vegetables dipped in a sizzling pot of olive oil infused with garlic and anchovies. Among the most cherished cheeses produced in the surrounding area are *robiole* and *tome*. For sweet tooths, the typical *dolce* is the *bunet al cioccolato,* a hedonistic treat of peaches stuffed with a chocolate mixture. An opportunity to discover the fabulous flavors of the local cuisine comes every year from late September through October during the *Sette Giorni* festival. The festival falls during the season of the sacred and prized *tartufo* (truffle), and is for the sole purpose of eating *really* well.

For snacking well, check out the extensive **fruit and vegetable market** in the Campo del Palio (open Wed. and Sat. 7:30am-1pm; afternoons primarily offer clothes and material goods), or the **market** in P. Catera, off Via Carducci in the heart of town. The **Super Gulliver Market,** Via Cavour, 81, could feed an army of Lilliputians. (Open Mon.-Sat. 8:30am-7:30pm, Thurs. 8:30am-12:30pm.) **Mercato Coperto Alimentari,** at P. della Libertà (between P. Alfieri and Campo del Palio) carries raw meats, cheeses, vegetables, and pastas—each merchant has a separate kiosk. (Open Mon.-Sat. 8am-1pm and 3:30-7:30pm. Thurs. 8am-1pm.)

Leon d'Oro, Via Cavour, 95 (tel. 59 20 30). Relaxed, elegant atmosphere—pink tablecloths, mirrored walls, cherry wood, and a pink marble bar. Filling meals, including some veggie entrees and veggie pizza. Pizza L7000-10,000, *primi* L7500. Open Thurs.-Tues. 10:30am-3pm and 6pm-1am. MC, Visa.
Ristorante Porta Torino, Viale Partigiani, 114 (tel. 21 68 83). Take a right at Corso Alfieri where the Torre Rosa lies. Pasta just L4500; try the *penne picante* if

you like hot stuff. Salad L2500. Restaurant open Sat.-Thurs. noon-2:30pm and 7-10pm, bar open all day.

Trattoria del Mercato, Corso Einaudi, 50 (tel. 59 21 42), at Campo del Palio. Serves typical *risotto* and *tortellini* for about L5000. *Primi* from L4500, *secondi* L7500, cover L2000. Groups (from 8 to 50) get a discount. Open Mon-Sat. noon-2:30pm and 7:30-9:30pm.

Gran Caffè Italia, Via Cavour, 125 (tel. 59 42 22), is on the corner of the rotary opposite the train station. Fresh *panini* (L2500) and a *menù* (L10,000). Open Oct.-Aug. Mon.-Sat. noon-2:30pm; bar open 6:30am-8:30pm.

Pizzeria Palio, P. Alfieri, 28 (tel. 59 24 74), on the corner of P. Alfieri, across from the park. Friendly staff serves pizza, pasta, and *gelato*—all in the same restaurant. Pizza around L7000, *primi* L7000, *secondi* L10,000. Cover L2000. Open Tues.-Sun. noon-2:30pm and 7pm-midnight. MC, Visa.

Ice Cream/Bar, Via della Valle, 2 (tel. 35 55 73), between P. Medici and Corso Alfieri. Lauded by locals as the best *gelato* in town. Open Mon.-Sat. 7am-8pm.

SIGHTS

From **Piazza Vittorio Alfieri,** a short walk west on Via Garibaldi to P. San Secondo will take you to the 18th-century **Palazzo di Città** (City Hall) and the medieval **Collegiata di San Secondo.** The Romanesque-Gothic church was built on the very spot where San Secondo, Asti's patron saint, was decapitated. Outside is red brick; inside the decor recalls the medieval period with banners and wall hangings. (Open daily 7am-noon and 3:30-7pm.) At the end of Corso Alfieri stands Asti's oldest tower, the 16-sided **Torre Rossa** (Red Tower; yep, it's brick), where the saint was imprisoned prior to his execution. The tower, with foundations dating back to the time of Augustus, adjoins the elliptical 18th-century **Church of Santa Caterina.**

North of Corso Alfieri, several medieval streets lead to P. Cattedrale, dominated by the eclectic **Cathedral of Asti,** whose size and grandeur make it one of the most noteworthy Gothic cathedrals in Piedmont. The outside is, again, done in the traditional red brick, contrasted with white around the doors to give it an intriguing checkered effect. The cathedral was begun in 1309; in the 16th and 17th centuries local artists, including native son Gandolfino d'Asti, covered every inch of the walls with frescoes. Even the columns are painted to appear as though there are vines climbing up them. Decaying 11th-century mosaics blanket the floor of the altar. If you wander about for a few minutes, the caretaker might come out and give you an exhaustive private tour. (Open daily 7:30am-noon and 3-7pm.) Up Via delle Valle from Corso Alfieri, off P. Medici, is the 13th-century **Torre de Troya.** Watch out for the circling swallows. They're not aiming for you, just the spaces in the brick that start about eight feet up. The **Giardini Pubblici,** between P. Alfieri and Campo del Palio, provide refreshing flora for picnickers. On the far end of the Corso is the 15th-century **Church of S. Pietro** with a 12th-century octagonal baptistery. (Open Tues.-Sat. 9am-noon and 4-7pm, Sun. 10am-noon; in winter Tues.-Sat. 9am-noon and 3-6pm, Sun. 10am-noon.) Exhibits of local artists are often shown in the baptistery, and the complex stays open later. The church served in WWII as an army hospital; Romans, friars, and war dead all share the space beneath the courtyard.

SEASONAL EVENTS

The series **Asti Teatro,** held during the last two weeks of June and the first week of July, offers theatrical productions from the medieval to the modern. The venue varies, so call for information; reservations are suggested. (Teatro Alfieri, Via al Teatro, 2; tel./fax 55 76 67 for tickets, tel. 35 39 88 for information. During Asti Teatro open Mon.-Fri. 9am-2pm, ticket office open 3:30-7pm. Admission L25,000, students and under 12 L18,000.) On the third Sunday of September, the theater takes to the streets with the **Palio di Asti.** The *Palio* recalls the town's liberation in 1200 with man and mare alike draped in medieval garb. A procession leaves from the cathedral at 2pm, passes through town, and ends at P. Alfieri, where the horses are relieved of their costumes for the festival's finale, one of the oldest horse races in Italy. While Siena's *Palio* may be more famous, Asti's hardly lacks in color and excitement.

Astian winemakers have made a tradition of courting prospective buyers with annual Bacchanalias, each dedicated to a different fruit of the vine. In spring you can celebrate the exposition **Vindimaggio** throughout May, in the *camera del commercio*, P. Medici (tel. 53 52 11). In June and July the **Asti Teatro Festival** incorporates jazz, drama, and dance at the Collegio and Michelerio Palaces. The popular **donkey races and amaretto-throwing festivities** take place at the end of June in Mombaruzzo. For two or three weeks in September, agricultural Asti revels in the **Douja d'Or**, a week-long festival celebrating the splendor of the grape. (After tasting the local wines, you too will want to offer homage.)

■ NEAR ASTI

Vineyards predominate around Asti, providing it with both an economic base and widespread renown: the sparkling *Asti Cinzano* and *Asti Spumante*, among others, begin their effervescing here. Many of these wineries remain under family control, and a warm reception awaits visitors who take time to explore less-trafficked areas. To make an appointment, call **Valleadona** (tel. 59 20 91) which can also provide information on **Cinaglio** and **Villafranca d'Asti**, other sites nearby. For those with paleontological interests, the Astian period (an actual paleontologic epoch) was named after the discovery of mastodon, rhinoceros, and other remains of other animals in the area. **Costigliole**, a brief bus ride away, is home to a medieval castle complete with drawbridge. Costigliole's **tourist office** can be reached at (0141) 96 60 31. Also a short distance from Asti and accessible by bus are **Isola d'Asti**, with its two medieval churches, and **Canelli**, surrounded by the muscat vineyards that produce the fruity *Asti spumante*. (Ask at Asti's tourist office for the *Carta dei Vini a D.O.C. Della Provincia di Asti*, a map of vineyards in the region offering wine tastings.) Phone the **Distilleria Bocchino**, Via G. B. Giulani, 88 (tel. 81 01, fax 83 25 46) to make an appointment at the wine factory. (Closed weekends.) The same holds true for the **Distelleria Beccaris**, Via Alba, 5 (tel. 96 81 27), in Costigliole. On weekdays, for wine tasting and a gastronomical tour call the **Cantina Sociale**, Via L. Bosca, 30 (tel. 82 33 47 or 83 18 28) to set up an appointment in Canelli, or while in Costigliole try the **Associazione Produttori Viticoli**, Fraz. Bionzo, 54 (tel. 96 83 59 or 96 84 58). Tours are free and open to those of all ages.

■ ■ ■ ACQUITERMI

If it were located on the coast, Acquitermi could easily be mistaken for a scaled-down Miami. Though tucked away in the green countryside, and sporting intermittent evidence of past greatness (such as the Roman aqueduct), Acquitermi's most noticeable feature is the number of people "taking the cure." Every year people arrive in droves to receive natural treatment for their afflictions with the help of *fangi* (mud baths), thermal springs heating up to a steamy and sulphuric 75° C, and treatment centers for everything from rheumatism to poor circulation. Don't despair if you're healthy and in good shape, however, for there are still parks, museums, and sights to be seen in this peaceful little town.

Orientation and Practical Information Acquitermi is located about 34km from Alessandria, in the province of the same name. From Milan, take any train en route to Alessandria; from Genoa, go by way of Ovada (trains run every hour, 1½hr., about L5700) to the **station** at P. V. Veneto in Acquitermi (tel. 32 25 83). To reach the **tourist office (APT)**, Corso Bagni, 8 (tel. (0144) 32 21 42), from the station, take a left on Via Alessandria, and another onto Via Monteverde, which leads to Corso Bagni. Very helpful English-speaking staff gives out a free map and great information about where to rent bikes, ride horses, eat, or stay. (Open Mon.-Fri. 8am-2pm and 3:30-6:30pm, Sat. 9am-noon.) Via Truco holds the **post office** (tel. 35 64 10; **postal code:** 15011), while **telephones** are found at Telecom, P. Matteotti, 31; **telephone code:** 0144. **Currency exchange** is at Cassa di Risparmio di Torino,

Corso Dante, 26 (tel. 570 01). **Emergencies:** tel. 122. **Police:** tel. 32 22 88. **Ambulance:** tel. 32 23 00 or 32 33 33.

Accommodations and Food The best places to stay are located across the Bormida river. From the tourist office, take Corso Bagni across the river to Viale Einaudi, the first left (notice the huge pool on the right). **Albergo Piemonte,** Via Einaudi, 19 (tel. 32 23 82), is run by a talkative young proprietor and her husband who wish to bring more youth to the town. (Singles L40,000, with bath L45,000. Doubles L55,000, with bath L65,000. You must have a reservation.) **Albergo Giaccobe,** Via Einaudi, 15 (tel. 32 25 37), has gloriously furnished rooms, some with balconies. (Singles L50,000, with bath L60,000. Doubles L60,000, with bath L70,000.) **Hotel Belvedere,** Via Einaudi, 8 (tel. 32 27 48), a former private villa with back and front patios, is now enclosed by a white picket fence and geraniums. (Singles L35,000, with bath L60,000. Doubles L55,000, with bath L65,000.) When you get hungry, head to **Vecchio Borgo,** P. della Bollente, 3 (tel. 32 26 15). Pizzas run from L5000-12,000, *primi* and *antipasti* from L8000-10,000. (Cover L2000. Open Tues.-Sun. 10:30am-3pm and 6:30pm-2am. MC, Visa.) **Bue Rosso,** Corso Cavour, 62 (tel. 32 27 29), will serve up a home-cooked meal at a reasonable price. Pasta L8000, *primi* L8000, *secondi* L9000. (Bar open 9am-10pm.)

Sights and Entertainment If you like archaeology, head up the hill to the **Museo Civico Archeologico Castello dei Paleogi** (tel. 575 55). The *palazzo* was constructed in the 11th century, partially destroyed in 1646, and restored in 1815. The museum inside focuses on the Roman history of the region, and tombs, *sarcophagi,* and mosaics abound. (Open Wed.-Sat. 9am-noon and 3-6pm, Sun. 3-6pm. Admission L2000, under 18 L1000.) The Romanesque **Duomo of San Guido** is adorned with multiple ceiling frescoes and painted purple columns. It houses the famous *Trittico* of Reubens (Madonna and Child) in the sacristy—ask to see it. As you cross the river, the **Acquedotto Romano** provides a beautiful backdrop. Certainly don't miss feeling the steamy, bubbling sulphuric water from P. Bollente. At 75°C, it's the hottest thing this side of boiling. For those looking for some excitement at night, the area around the pool is full of *discoteche,* but they are a bit expensive. Try **Clipper,** Via Acquedotto Romano (tel. 32 21 65) for dancing and Karaoke, or across the street at **Bar La Rotonda,** Via Aquedotto Romano, 98 (tel. 564 42). Both are open Tues. and Thurs.-Sun. from around 10pm until around 3am; both charge a cover of about L20,000.

■ Valle D'Aosta

Welcome to Valle D'Aosta, land of slate roofs, overhanging eaves, and the Italian Alps. Valleys lush with vegetation give way to pine forests reaching up to craggy peaks that are laced with snow even during the summer. Towns nestle in the rich valleys, terraced wineries and cattle dot the forests. While the most spectacular entrance is indisputably the international cable car connection over the mountains from Chamonix (about L87,000), the area is also accessible by combined train-bus routes that wind their way through the Alps. Gran Paradiso National Park is truly a "big paradise": waterfalls gush around boulders and tumble down cliffs, and the views are a traveler's dream. Remember that it can be cold up here even in the summer months, so pack long pants and a sweater if you plan to visit.

The majestic grandeur of the mountains attracts a year-round flood of tourists. Tourism (with a capital T) has become the primary basis for Valle D'Aosta's economy now that the region's mining and commercial farming have become obsolete. Many visitors come over the mountains from France, and the French influence here is reflected in the street names and the mixture of spoken languages. A warning to the budget traveler, however: Valle D'Aosta's attraction is well known and the region enjoys a year-round bustle of tourists that keeps the prices high.

HIKING

The Valle d'Aosta is a paradise for hikers. Each valley's tourist office provides information on routes (usually very well marked) and the comprehensive network of huts and refuges, which allows the bold to stay high for days at a time. Trails often bring you above 10,000 ft., so dress and pack carefully. You'll need a sweater, a windbreaker, a pair of gloves, heavy wool socks with polypropylene liners, a compass, and a first-aid kit. Because even the easiest trails have tricky stretches, you'll need a pair of good hiking boots. Don't forget that the strength of the sun intensifies with altitude—wear plenty of sunscreen even on cloudy or chilly days.

The best time of the year to hike is in July, August, and the first week of September, when all the snow has melted. In April and May, thawing snow often causes avalanches. Obtain a reliable map—*Kompass* maps (available at kiosks and hiking stores in the area) are the most accurate. Also beware of poisonous snakes, which have flourished as the birds that normally gobble them fall victim to illegal hunting.

The tourist offices in Aosta and in each smaller valley give out a list of campgrounds, bag-lunch *(al sacco)* vendors, and mountain huts and bivouacs (ask for the *elenco rifugi bivacchi*). Most regional offices also carry the booklet *Alte Vie* (High Roads) with maps, photographs, and helpful advice pertaining to the two serpentine mountain trails that link many of the region's most dramatic peaks. Long stretches require virtually no expertise and offer panoramic views and a taste of Alpine adventure. Both trails are subdivided into shorter hikes and assessed with regard to difficulty, availability of food, and accommodations.

Rifugi alpini (mountain huts) make convenient abodes for veteran mountaineers and novices alike. Some are only a cable-car ride or a half-hour walk from main roads, and many offer half-pension (L45,000). Public refuges, or *bivacchi*, tend to be empty and free, while those run by caretakers cost about L20,000 per night. For more detailed info, contact **Interguide**, Via Monte Emilius, 13 (tel. 409 39; fax 144 48), in Aosta, or the **Club Alpino Italiano**, P. Chanoux, 8 (tel. 401 94; fax 36 32 44), open Mon., Wed. Thurs. 5-7pm, Tues. and Fri. 8-10pm, above Aosta's tourist office. They offer insurance and membership deals with discounts on refuges.

SKIING

Skiing in Valle D'Aosta is sublime, but it's not the bargain it used to be. **Settimane bianca,** "white-week" packages for skiers, are one source of discount rates that may keep you from spending your *après-ski* hours contemplating financial woes In the off-season, one-star full pension runs about L400,000 per week, half pension L350,000, and bed and breakfast L280,000, while weekly lift passes average L75,000-80,000. In high season, prices jump by as much as 20%. Winter reservations should be made by writing directly to the hotels. For more specific information, write to the **Ufficio Informazioni Turistiche,** P. Chanoux, 8, 11100 Aosta, and request the pamphlet **White Weeks: Winter Season, Aosta Valley,** in English.

Courmayeur and **Cervinia** are the best-known ski resorts in the 11 otherwise tranquil valleys, basking in the glory of Mont Blanc and the Matterhorn. **Val d'Ayas** and **Val di Gressoney** offer equally challenging terrain for lower rates. If cross-country is more to your taste, head to **Cogne,** or to **Brusson** half-way down Val d'Ayas. In Cervinia (and Courmayeur, possibly, next summer) tank tops sometimes replace parkas for **summer skiing** (play it safe and bring both), and in June and late September it's possible to find a room without reservations. Arrange summer package deals, similar to those available in winter, through the tourist office in either Cervinia or Courmayeur (they're still quite expensive).

OTHER SPORTS

Kayaking, rafting, and swimming in the rivers of Valle d'Aosta provide cheaper adrenaline fixes than skiing. The most navigable rivers are: the **Dora Baltea,** which runs through the valley; the **Dora di Veny,** which branches south from Courmayeur; the **Dora di Ferre,** which wanders north from Courmayeur; the **Dora di Rhêmes,** which flows through the Val di Rhêmes; and the **Grand Eyvia,** which courses through the Val di Cogne. Contact the **Scuola di Canoa di Courmayeur,** Emanuele Pernasconi, Casella Postale, 11013 Courmayeur, or **Rafting Adventure** in Villeneuve for info on kayaking lessons, camping, and rafting adventures. The Aosta tourist office distributes a list of **mountain bike** rentals throughout the valleys.

■■■ AOSTA

Aosta is the hub of a region whose economy is increasingly dependent upon tourism. While Aosta itself sits in the flatlands, its prices have more in common with the nearby peaks of Monte Emilius (3559m) and Becca di Nona (3142m). On the positive side, remains of bridges, triumphal arches, and theaters recall Aosta's importance as a Roman center, and a medley of towers and churches provides architectural diversity from the Middle Ages and modern-day photo opportunities. Daytrips to the *real* alpine valleys from Aosta are tricky to schedule if you want to return before night falls, so plan ahead.

ORIENTATION AND PRACTICAL INFORMATION

Aosta sits approximately in the center of the region bearing its name, and is most easily reached by train from Turin (13 per day, 2hr.-4hr., L11,700). Alps-bound visitors from the east should change trains at Chivasso. Trains stop at **Piazza Manzetti,** which lies at the end of the Avenue du Conseil des Commis opposite **Piazza Chanoux,** Aosta's central *piazza.* Buses to surrounding valleys stop at the bus station to your right as you exit the train station, on Via Carrel.

> **Tourist Office:** P. Chanoux, 8 (tel. 23 66 27; fax 34 657), straight ahead and down Avenue du Conseil des Commis from the train station. Ask for the booklets *Aosta: Architecture, Art, Archaeology* and *Aosta Valley* and pick up copies of the regional listings of hotels, campgrounds, and *rifugi.* The compact yearly *Orari* contains comprehensive schedules of Val d'Aosta's transportation, including cable cars. English spoken. Open Mon.-Sat. 9am-1pm and 3-8pm, Sun. 9am-1pm.
> **Police:** Corso Battaglione Aosta (tel. 322 96).
> **Post Office:** P. Narbonne (tel. 26 22 87 or 36 35 61), the huge semi-circular building. Open Mon.-Fri. 8:15am-7pm, Sat. 8:15am-4pm. **Postal Code:** 11100.
> **Telephones: Telecom (SIP),** Viale Pace, 9 (tel. 439 97), off Via Chanoux. Open Mon.-Fri. 8:15am-12:15pm and 2:30-5pm. **Telephone Code:** 0165.
> **Currency Exchange: Banco Valdostano Berard,** P. Chanoux, 51 (tel. 23 56 56). Efficient and friendly. Accepts Visa for cash advances. Open Mon.-Fri. 8:20am-1:20pm and 2:40-4pm. **Banco Comerciale Italia,** next door, has similar hours.
> **Trains:** P. Manzetti (tel. 20 36 57). Frequent service to Chivasso and the intermediate stations at Chatillon, Verrès, and Pont-St-Martin which offer access, respectively, to the valleys of Valtournenche, Ayas, and Gressoney. To: Chivasso (17 per day, 1½hr., L8000) with stops at Chatillon (L2700); Verrès (L3400); Pont-St-Martin (L5000). To: Turin (13 per day, 2hr., L11,700) and Milan (15 per day with change at Chivasso, 4hr., L17,200). **Luggage Storage:** L1500. Open 7:30am-2:30pm.
> **Buses: SAVDA,** Via Carrel (tel. 26 20 27), off P. Manzetti, near the train station. To: Cogne (6 per day, 1hr., L3200, round-trip L5800); Courmayeur (12 per day, 1hr., L3600, round-trip L6100); Great St. Bernard Pass (2 per day, 2¼hr., L7400, round-trip L12,000); Fenis (7 per day, 30min., L1700); Valtournenche (2 per day, 2¼ hr., L5800, round-trip L10,100).
> **Taxi:** tel. 26 20 10, 318 31, or 356 56.

Alpine Information: Club Alpino Italiano, P. Chanoux, 8 (tel. 401 94), upstairs from the tourist office. Open Mon., Wed., and Thurs. 5-7pm, Tues. and Fri. 8-10pm. At other times, try the **Società Guide,** Via Monte Emilius, 13 (tel. 444 48). **Snow Conditions:** contact tourist office. **Pharmacy: Farmacia Chenal,** Via Croix-de-Ville, 1 (tel. 26 21 33), right at the corner of Via Aubert. Well-stocked with the basics, plus herbs and a wide selection of feminine hygiene products. Open Thurs.-Tues. 9am-12:30pm and 3-7:30pm. A digital sign in the window designates the nighttime pharmacy. **Emergencies:** tel. 113. **Hospital: Ospedale Regionale,** Viale Ginevra, 3 (tel. 30 41). **Ambulance:** tel. 30 42 11. **Alpine Emergency: Società Guide,** tel. 444 48 or 23 82 22.

ACCOMMODATIONS AND CAMPING

High season in Aosta Valley is generally considered to be from late December to mid-January, all of February and March, and the second and third weeks of April. In high season, most hotels will not accept reservations for fewer than three nights. Tradition decrees that all advance reservations be done by mail with a 30% deposit.

La Belle Epoque, Via d'Avise, 18 (tel. 26 22 76), centrally located off Via Aubert. Good-sized clean rooms, balconies, and palatial hall bathroom. Restaurant downstairs crowded with locals. Singles L30,000, with bath L40,000. Doubles L55,000, with bath L65,000. Triples L75,000, with bath L85,000. Half pension L52,000-55,000 per person. MC, Visa.

Mancuso, Via Voison, 32 (tel./fax 345 26). From the station, hang a left on Via Carducci, and another left under the tracks. Peaceful, family atmosphere, with a **restaurant** downstairs (*menù* about L20,000). All rooms with bath, some with terraces. Singles L30,000-40,000. Doubles L55,000-60,000.

Monte Emilius, Via Carrel, 9 (tel. 356 92), a skip and a jump to the right from the train station, upstairs from Ristorante Le Ramoneur. Newly renovated. Friendly management and a nightly serenade by passing traffic. Singles L50,000. Doubles L80,000. Breakfast L10,000. Reserve ahead. AmEx.

Camping: Camping Milleluci, Via Porossan, 15 (tel. 442 74 or 423 74; fax 23 52 84), in Roppoz, also 1km from Aosta. L6700 per person, L3700 per tent, L5900 per car. Open year-round. Check with the tourist office for other nearby options.

FOOD

Supplement a hearty one-dish meal with a sampling of local cheeses, especially *fontina,* the jewel of Valdostan gastronomy. Typical dishes are influenced by nearby Switzerland, and include *fonduta,* a creamy cheese fondue ladled over meat and vegetables, and *polenta valdostana,* sizzling with melted *fontina.* Prospective picknickers feast their eyes and imaginations on the food shops lining Via de Tillier and Via Pretoriane. Here, the siren song of pastries might entice you to hurl yourself upon the local bakeries. The most divine divas are *tegole,* wafer-thin cookies containing ground nuts, though the generous *krapfen* at **La Corbeille à Pain,** Via P. Pretoriane, 22 (open Mon.-Sat 6:30am-12:30pm and 3-6:30pm; closed Thurs. afternoons), are worth a try (L1100), as are the L1200 *brioches d'Aosta* at the bakery at Via de Tillier, 24. The **STANDA supermarket,** Via Festaz, 10 (tel. 357 57), sells more generic merchandise. (Open Mon.-Sat. 8:30am-12:30pm and 3:30-7:30pm.) The chic **Café Roma,** Via E. Aubert, 28 (tel. 26 24 22), serves *cappuccino* to those who want to see and be seen, while **Gelateria Linus,** to the left of Café Roma, spoons out the best *gelato* around (about L2000). Make sure you try the native *coppa,* also known as *caffè valdostano* and *caffè à la cogneintze,* a drink made with coffee, *grappa,* red wine, sugar, and the juice and peel of lemons and oranges.

Trattoria Praetoria, Via S. Anselmo, 9 (tel. 443 56), just past the Port Pretoriane. An intimate dining room where Valdostan chatter flows as freely as the wine. Try the standard Valdostan dish of *salsiccette in umido* (L9000), locally made sausages braised in tomato sauce, with a side dish of hearty *polenta*—a bargain at

L4000. *Primi* L7000-10,000, *secondi* L9000-18,000. Cover L3000. Open Fri.-Wed. 12:15-2:30pm and 7:15-9:30pm. MC, Visa.

Grotta Azzurra, Via Croce di Città, 97 (tel. 26 24 74), uphill from where Via de Tillier becomes Via Aubert. Fake wood paneling and delicious fare. Locals come for the fish specialties. Try the *gnocchi alla gorgonzola* (L9000). Pizza from L6000; *primi* from L5000. Cover L2000. Service 15%. Open Thurs.-Tues. noon-2:30pm and 6-10:30pm. Closed July 10-27.

SIGHTS AND ENTERTAINMENT

Ruins dating from the time of Augustus (the town's original name was "Augusta Praetoria") have given Aosta the nickname "Rome of the Alps." The virtually intact **Arco d'Augusta** marks the entrance to the ancient town. Within the Roman bounds, active excavation continues to unearth a growing number of historical monuments. The sprawling remains of the **Roman Theater** are the most spectacular. Follow the signs left from Rue Porte Pretorienne. (Open Mon.-Fri. 9am-6:30pm, Sat.-Sun. 9am-noon and 2-5pm. Free.) The forum's present incarnation is a tiny, subground-level park, the **Criptoportico Forense.** (Hours contingent on custodian's whim.) Jump ahead 400 years to the 5th century AD and round off the archaeological tour with a visit to the dig sites at the **Church of San Lorenzo.** (Dig sites open same hours as Roman Theater. Church open in summer daily 9am-8pm; in winter when exhibits are shown.) The **Fiera di Sant'Orso,** the region's most prestigious crafts fair, is held in late January and mid-August. Aosta's weekly **outdoor market** is held every Tuesday in P. Cavalieri di Vittorio Veneto.

No-bull Festivities

Only in Aosta cud you witness an annual, legendairy ritual with a rousing bovine finale. A series of concerts, exhibits, and feasts throughout spring and summer culminates on the third Sunday of October with the **Bataille des Reines** (Battle of the Queens), a head-butting bash in which about 200 well-trained Bessies engage in elimination rounds of brain-battering. Moo.

■ NEAR AOSTA

Turreted fortresses adorn the valley. You can get a preview by flipping through the photo-strewn pages of *Castelli della Valle d'Aosta* at a local bookstore or the free booklets at the tourist office. **Fenis** (tel. (0165) 76 42 63) comes with turrets of all shapes and sizes. The interior of the castle is equally noteworthy for its 14th-century Gothic paintings. (Easily reached by **bus** from Aosta: 7 per day, 30min., L1700). Farther down the valley, 1km from Verrès (17 trains per day, 35min., L3400), rests the artistic treasure trove of the **Issogne fortress** (tel. (0125) 92 93 73). (Both open March-Nov. 9am-7pm; Dec.-Feb. 10am-5pm. Admission L4000, under 6 free.) The first of the spectacular bus rides departs from Aosta at 8am, and the last return bus leaves at 4:15pm (2 per day, 1¼hr., L7400, round-trip L12,000). L29,600 will take you from Aosta to Martigny in Switzerland (2 per day, 2hr.).

VALLE DEL GRAN SAN BERNARDO

This sparsely populated valley links Aosta to Switzerland via the Great St. Bernard Pass. Napoleon trekked through here with 40,000 soldiers in 1800, but the pass is better known for the **Hospice of St. Bernard,** founded in 1505, home base for the patron saint of man's best friend. The legendary life-saver, Barry, was stuffed for posterity and can still be seen as you drive through the pass. The hospice (just across the Swiss border—don't forget your passport) offers amazing views of international peaks just a brisk walk past the dog museum to the summit of a crag. **Mont Velan** (tel. 782 07) in Saint-Oyen charges L60,000 per person, and **Des Alpes** (tel. 78 09 16) in Saint-Rhémy has singles for L40,000 and doubles for L80,000 in off-season. **Camping Pineta** (tel. 781 14) in Saint-Oyen lends riverside spots for L6000 per person and L4500 per tent. The smaller, more serene branch of the valley leading to

Ollomont and Oyace offers longer hikes. **Mont Gelé** (tel. 732 20) in Ollomont charges L60,000 per single, L100,000 per double (L10,000 less for each in off-season). For more info, contact the tourist office in Aosta or the **ski-lift office** at St. Remy (tel. 78 00 46) or St. Oyen (tel. 781 28). The valley's **telephone code** is 0165.

VALTOURNENCHE

The **Matterhorn** ("Cervino" in Italian) is a wonder to behold as it looms majestically over the less-wonderful town of **Cervinia-Breuil**. The nondescript buildings differ only in purpose: some serve expensive food, others offer expensive accommodations, and the rest rent expensive sports equipment. Many fresh-air fiends, however, consider these man-made deterrents a small price to pay for the opportunity to climb up or glide down one of the world's most famous glaciers. A cable car provides year-round service to **Plateau Rosa** (round-trip L36,000), where summer skiers frequently tackle the slopes in swimming gear. Don't forget your passport; a number of the trails spill over into Switzerland. Hikers can forgo the lift tickets and attempt the three-hour ascent to **Colle Superiore delle Cime Bianche** (2982m), with tremendous views of Val d'Ayas to the east. A 90-minute trek on the same trail leads to the emerald waters of **Lake Goillet**.

Hotel Lac Bleu (tel. 94 91 03; fax 94 99 02), 2km downhill from Cervinia, offers singles at L40,000 and doubles at L90,000 (off-season L35,000 and L80,000). Also quite reasonable is **Leonardo Carrel** (tel. 94 90 77), in the locality of Avouil. (Singles L37,000. Doubles L55,000. Open year-round.) Camp year-round at **Glair Lago di Maen** (tel. 920 77), 39km from Aosta (L7000 per person, L7200 per tent). There are two *rifugi* in the area, and both charge about L20,000 per night or L50,000 for half pension: **Guide del Cervino** (tel. 94 83 69) can be reached by 3½ hours of hiking or by cable car to Plateau Rosà; **Theodule** (tel. 94 94 00), a half hour walk or 10-minute ski from Plateau Rosà, has the odd distinction of holding summer yoga classes. For outdoor escapades complete with a fearless leader, contact the **Società Guide** (tel. 94 81 69), which organizes group outings. Restaurant prices are as steep as the Matterhorn itself, so consider stocking up at the **Despar supermarket** (open 8am-12:30pm and 3-8pm) by the bus stop. You can also save some dough by buying bread across the street and then heading for the nearest *Fontina* sign to purchase fillings. Try **Pizzeria Copa Pan** (tel. 94 91 40), a few doors past the tourist office— it's one of the only restaurants to serve dishes in the four-digit price range. Downhill in Valtournenche, an **outdoor market** is held on Friday mornings in summer.

The **tourist office** at Via Carrel, 29 (tel. 94 91 36 or 94 90 86), inundates visitors with info on "white weeks packages" and *settimane estive*, their summer equivalents. English spoken. (Open 9am-noon and 3-6:30pm.) If you plan to stick it out for a week during the summer months, look into the *Carta Estate*, a guest pass providing discounts on multitudes of post-ski activities. Six buses per day run to Cervinia-Breuil from Châtillon on the Aosta-Turin train line. Two direct buses also arrive daily from P. Castello in Milan. The **telephone code** for the valley is 0166.

VAL D'AYAS

Sports enthusiasts who value economy over impressive names should consider stopping here and bypassing the more ostentatious pleasure grounds to the west.

In Brusson, **Beau Site** (tel. 30 01 44) has the best deal on "white weeks": L350,000 for full board except at Easter and Christmas, when prices leap up to L65,000 per day. **Cai Casale** (tel. 30 76 68), a refuge in St. Jacques, 3km north of Champoluc, charges L20,000 per person, L50,000-55,000 with full pension. **Cre Fornè** (tel. 30 71 97) offers singles for L24,000 (high season L26,000) and doubles for an unbeatable L35,000 (high season L37,000). **Camping Deans** (tel. 30 02 97), also operates in Brusson. (L5000 per person, L5000 per tent. Open year-round.)

Mountain bikes and skis can be rented at **Agenzia Evançon,** Fraz Champoluc (tel. 30 76 48) and at many other spots. Contact the **Società Guide** (tel. 30 71 13) for hiking advice, or read through the list of itineraries on the map in Champoluc's central *piazza*. The *telecabina* (follow the signs) will take you up to the mountain community of **Crest,** a convenient base for excursions (lift operates daily 8am-5:50pm—ask tourist office for schedule; L10,000). Before setting off, you might want to buy supplies at the *salumeria* between the Champoluc bus stop and the cable car.

Six **buses** run daily to Champoluc from the train station at Verrès (1hr., L3200, round-trip L5500). Seventeen **trains** run to Verrès from Aosta (40min., L3400), and a comparable number cover the 90min. of track from Turin. If you can spare some time from outdoor pursuits, visit the **parish church** in Antagnod which has the most ornate baroque high altar in all of Val d'Aosta. The weekly **outdoor market** is held each Friday in the summer. The central **tourist office** in Brusson (tel. 30 02 40; fax 30 06 91), and smaller branches in Champoluc (tel. 30 71 13) and Antagnod (tel. 30 63 35), provide trail maps and hotel info. English spoken. (Open daily 9am-12:30pm and 3-7pm.) The **telephone code** for the valley is 0125.

VAL DI COGNE

When Cogne's mines ran dry in the 1970s, the townspeople resorted to more genteel pursuits—delicately parting cross-country skiers from their money. The quiet village has consequently become a harmonious blend of authentic and self-conscious rusticity for the entertainment of visitors; craftsmen sculpt wood in the open air and wildflowers abound in the surrounding meadows. In winter, **Cogne** functions as the head of a 50-km entanglement of cross-country trails, while a cable car transports Alpine addicts to the top of the modest downhill facilities (round-trip L10,000, L54,000 for a 7-day pass). In summer, however, the pastoral community is better known as the gateway to the **Gran Paradiso National Park** (tel. 741 25). In addition to offering a seemingly endless network of hiking trails and a population of 5000 ibex, the park hosts the highest glacier (4061m) fully contained within Italian borders, which sets it apart from the rest of Val d'Aosta's surrounding beauty.

For friendly, family-run accommodations, try the **Hotel Stambecco,** Via Clementine, 21. (Tel. 740 68. Singles L42,000. Doubles L84,000. Breakfast included. All rooms with bath.) **Du Soleil,** Via Cavagnet, 24 (tel. 740 33), on the main strip into town, charges L38,000 per person (L46,000 in high season) with breakfast, and has an economical *settimana bianca*—L250,000. (AmEx, MC, Visa.) Campers can choose between **Camping Gran Paradiso** (tel. 74 92 02 or 741 05; open June-Sept.; L5300 per person, L9000-10,500 for car, tent, and electricity), or the more popular **Lo Stambecco** (tel. 741 52; open June-Sept. 20) in the *località* of Valnontey (L6000 per person, L8000-10,500 for car, tent, and electricity). For pizza (L7000-15,000), try **Pizzeria Edelweiss,** Viale Cavagnet, 45 (tel. 74 92 44); open daily 7pm-midnight.

Valnontey is a wee hamlet in the midst of the national park, notable for its convenient *alimentari,* its cluster of two-star hotels, and the **Giardino Alpino Paradisia.** The inspiration for constructing a botanical garden amidst a barren scrubland at an altitude of 1700m struck during the Cogne Mountain Festival in 1955, no doubt aided by several bottles of wine. Practical complications notwithstanding, the thriving gardens boast a wide array of rare alpine vegetation, including everything you ever wanted to know about lichen. (Open June 10-Sept. 10 9:30am-12:30pm and 2:30-6:30pm. Admission L3000, groups L2000, under 10 free.) The **Mining Museum** in Cogne (tel. 74 92 64) is open daily 10am-8pm. (Off-season Tues.-Sun. 10am-12:30pm and 2:30-6pm. Admission L4000.) Those who find cross-country a little too staid can **brave the bungee:** contact **Jumping Club,** Via Chanoux, 94, Saint Vincent (tel. (0166) 53 73 88) or **Rafting Adventure** in Aosta (tel. (0165) 950 82), or contact the tourist office in Villeneuve (tel. 950 55).

Cogne's **tourist office,** P. Chanoux, 34 (tel. 740 40; fax 74 91 25), distributes maps of the park, and hiking and transport info. English spoken. The **post office** (tel. 740 61) is on P. Chanoux. There's a **bank** (tel. 740 20) on Via Dr. Grappein and a **pharmacy** (tel. 744 01) on Via Gran Paradis. Also on Via Dr. Grappein are the **police** (tel. 740 26). For other **emergencies** call the following: **ambulance** (tel. 74 91 02), **first aid** (tel. 74 91 07), or **alpine aid** (tel. 74 92 86, 742 04, or 740 26). For information on services call: **hotel info** (tel. 748 35; fax 740 50), **ski school** (tel. 743 00), **taxi** (tel.

740 00). Cogne is an easy **bus** ride from Aosta (6 per day, 1hr., L3200, round-trip L5800). The **telephone code** is 0165. Cogne's **outdoor market** is held each Sunday.

■■■ COURMAYEUR

Italy's oldest Alpine resort remains the jet-set's playground. **Monte Bianco** (Mont Blanc) is the main attraction: its jagged ridges and unmelting snowfields lure tourists with unsurpassed opportunities for hiking and skiing. Prices are astronomical and rooms are booked solid in summer and winter (reserve 6 months ahead), but the city shuts down in June while the shopkeepers take their own vacations.

Practical Information Buses access Courmayeur from: Aosta (11 per day, 1hr., L3600, round-trip L6100); Turin (6 per day, L13,200, round-trip L22,800); and Chamonix (8 per day, L15,000, round-trip L27,000). Pick up a schedule at the **tourist office** (tel. 84 20 60), on P. Monte Bianco at the base of the town by the main road. English spoken. (Open Mon.-Fri. 9am-12:30pm and 3-6:30pm, Sat.-Sun. 9am-7:30pm.) The same omnipotent office complex houses the **bus station** (tel. 84 13 97), **currency exchange** (open daily 7:30am-8:30pm), and **post office** (tel. 84 20 42; open Mon.-Fri. 8:15am-6:30pm, Sat. 8:15-11:40am); **postal code** 11013. A little wooden cabin in the parking lot houses **telephones**.

Accommodations and Food Budget accommodations in Courmayeur are few and difficult to reach. A safe bet is **Pensione Venezia,** Via delle Villete, 2 (tel. 84 24 61), up the hill to the left from P. Monte Bianco. Elegant singles for L35,000 and doubles for L52,000. Breakfast L8000. Signs in each room read "It is strictly forbidden to walk in clogs in rooms!" Pitch your tent at **CAI-Uget,** Mt. Bianco in Val Veny. (Tel. (0165) 892 15. L5100 per person, L4900 per tent. Hot showers L1000. Open June 15-Sept. and Dec.-1 week after Easter.) Keep in mind that this is quite a trek, and you must walk to arrive at the refuge, 1800m in altitude. Picnicking is the best option in this town of Michelin-starred eateries. At **Pastificio Gabriella,** Passaggio del Angelo, 94 (tel. 84 33 59), toward the *strada regionale* end of Via Roma, you'll find excellent cold cuts and pâté garnished with Alpine violets. (Closed for 2 weeks in July. MC, Visa.) **Il Fornaio,** at Via Monte Bianco, 17 (tel. 84 24 54), serves up scrumptious breads and pastries. Try the *bombolini* (L1500). (Open Thurs.-Wed. morning 7:30am-12:30pm and 4-7:30pm.) Wednesday is **market day** (8:30am-2pm) in nearby Dolonne (1km from Courmayeur). If you do choose to eat out, you have a few (somewhat) affordable options. **La Piazzetta** on Via Roma, 13 (tel. 84 41 45), has the advantage of serving pizzas (from L9000) and having no cover charge, but the *primi* and *secondi* are a tad overpriced. Salads are also served on the side (L4000-7000). (MC, Visa.) For crepes and pizza by the slice, try **Lady-Crêpe,** Via Marconi, 7 (tel. 84 41 44), off Via Roma. Particularly yummy and filling are the *crespelle alla valdostana,* hearty crepes wrapped with *prosciutto* and *fontina* and topped with a creamy *besciamella* sauce (L5500). Pizza and *focaccia* slices run L2500-3500. (Open daily 10am-7pm. June-Sept. and Dec.-April.)

Outdoor Activities Even "white-week specials" are exorbitant—bed-and-breakfast deals under L35,000 are a dream. Ski passes average L233,000 (ask tourist office for summer prices). Pick up the brochure *Courmayeur: Mont Blanc* for a complete list of athletics facilities and rental shops. For hiking excursions in Italy, catch the bus that departs every hour from Viale M. Bianco to La Visailli, near **Combal Lake** (L3000, round-trip L4800). A beautiful six-hour hike awaits you on the road up the valley past *Rifugio Elisabetta* to where the path (marked by a "2" in a triangle) branches off to the left and clambers up to the Chavannes Pass (2603m). The trail then runs along Mont Perce, beneath the crest, until it reaches Mont Fortin (2758m—"ooh" and "aah" at the view), where it descends once again to Lake Combal. The bus will deposit you back at Courmayeur. A map is crucial on these jaunts; arm yourself with tips at the **Ufficio delle Guide** (tel. 84 20 64) in P. Abbe-Heurl, facing the stone-steepled church, which also has a neat **mountaineering museum** featuring old equipment and some amazing photographs. (Open 9am-12:30pm and 3:30-7pm; in winter closes at 6:30pm. Admission L3500, under 10 L1500.)

Nineteenth-century English gentlemen brushed off the **Giro del Monte Bianco** as a two- or three-day tour for "less adventurous travelers." Today, more level-headed guides suggest that travelers take a week or more to complete the trip. The trail leads around Monte Bianco, past Chamonix and Courmayeur, and then into Switzerland. Refuges and hotel dormitories are spaced five or six hours apart all along the route (L20,000 per person, L30,000 bed and breakfast). You need not invest your whole vacation; one leg of the larger trail makes an ideal daytrip, and two sections can amply fill a weekend. This is serious mountaineering for which you should be thoroughly equipped and trained before you head out.

You can also pay a pretty penny to head in the same direction with the **Funivia del Monte Bianco,** a cable car heading to the Punto Helbronner (3462m) and then to Chamonix. From this point, see amazing views of the **Matterhorn, Mont Blanc,** and **Monta Rosa.** *Funivie* depart from La Palud near the Val Ferret. Depending on desired altitude, tickets range L13,000-45,000. Call 899 25 for more info. At the first stop of the *funivia,* Pavillion, there is a wonderful botanical garden, the **Giardino Alpino Saussurea** (2175m), open daily from July 15 to September 15. Call 899 25 for details. For other **nature excursions,** contact Cristina Gaggini and Claudia Marcello (tel. 86 21 40), who organize daytrips in places like Val Ferret and Val Veny.

The Lake Country

Some of Stendhal's most florid prose came while describing the Italian lakes, and most visitors find that even a simple postcard home suffers the same fate. After you've visited, you too can bore your friends with the sort of breathless, enchanted effusions 19th-century Romantics produced by the dozen.

There are distinct differences in the personalities of each of the lakes. Garda draws a younger crowd with sailboard-speckled waters by day and an assortment of nightclubs after sunset. Como hosts the sophisticates from nearby Milan, while Lago Maggiore doggedly retains a sleepy elegance with its elderly luxury hotels lining the shore. The cleaner waters of Garda and Orta are preferable for swimmers, but any lake will do if you prefer to contemplate placid ripples from *terra firma.*

Restaurant prices have soared to meet the mountains; pack picnic supplies at a small *alimentari.* Local cheeses include *robiola* (a cream cheese), *caprino* (goat cheese), the soft, tangy *taleggio,* and the spicy *fontale.* All cost about L1200 per *etto,* enough for several sandwiches. A specialty of the Como region is *agone,* sun-cured fish from the lake. *Brianza* is the trademark name of most local wines.

LAKE COMO (LAGO DI COMO)

A dreamy air of magnificence lingers over Lake Como's northern reaches. The shores combine the atmospheres of the Mediterranean and the mountains: lavish villas adorn a craggy backdrop, warmed by the heat of the Riviera sun and cooled by lakeside breezes. The lake itself is actually a forked amalgam of three long lakes joined in the Centro Lago area of Bellaggio, Tremezzo, Menaggio, and Varenna. The dense green slopes are peppered with villages—take the boat for Colico and get off at the first stop that strikes your fancy. Regular boat service connects towns in all three areas of the lake, as do convenient buses.

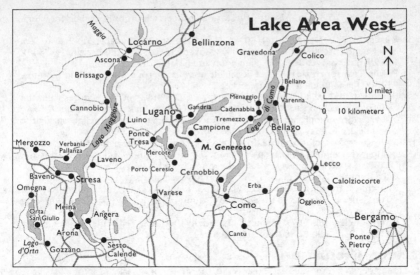

■■■ COMO

Situated on the southwest tip at the receiving end of the Milan rail line, Como is the lake's token industrial center. The city is famous for silk manufacturing, but has luckily maintained the slow, languorous atmosphere of smaller lake towns. While swimmers should head up the lake for cleaner waters, Como's little harbor permits boats to reach the shore. After dinner, the entire city migrates to the waterfront for a *passeggiata* among the wisteria and rows of 18th-century *ville*.

ORIENTATION AND PRACTICAL INFORMATION

Como is 40min. from Milan by train (every hr., L7700). As you leave the **Stazione San Giovanni** (tel. 26 14 94), the town is straight ahead and the lake is to your left. On the other side of town there is another train station, **Ferrovia Nord Milano** (tel. 30 48 00), on Via Manzoni off Lungo Lario Trieste, which serves only Milan (every 30min. morning and evening, every hr. 2-5pm, L5000).

The main square, **Piazza Cavour,** opens onto the waterfront and the **Lungo Lario Trento,** which winds its way around the mouth of the lake. From P. Cavour, take Via Plinio to **Piazza Duomo,** which becomes **Via Vittorio Emanuele.** This area is the commercial center of Como.

Tourist Office: P. Cavour, 16 (tel. 26 97 12), in the largest lakeside *piazza* near the ferry dock. From the train station, walk down to Via Gallio, which becomes Via Garibaldi and leads to the inland side of P. Cavour by way of P. Volta. Provides maps and extensive info in friendly English. Also reserves rooms and exchanges currency (see below). Open Mon.-Sat. 9am-12:30pm and 2:30-6pm.

Police: Viale Roosevelt, 7 (tel. 31 71).

Post Office: Via T. Gallio, 4 (tel. 26 93 36). Open Mon.-Fri. 8:15am-5:30pm, Sat. 8:15-11am. Also at Via V. Emanuele, 99 (tel. 26 02 10), in the center of town. Open Mon.-Fri. 8:10am-1:30pm, Sat. 8:10-11:40am. **Postal Code:** 22100.

Telephones: Telecom (SIP) has recently opened a new office on Via Albertolli. There are also telephones in Stazione San Giovanni and Piazza Cavour. **Telephone Code:** 031.

Currency Exchange: Banca Nazionale del Lavoro, P. Cavour, 34 (tel. 31 31), across from the tourist office. Dependable rates and cash advances on Visa. Open Mon.-Tues. and Thurs.-Fri. 8:20am-1:20pm and 2:30-4pm, Wed. 8:20am-5:50pm.

Mon.-Sat. 3-5:30pm. Also try the tourist office (which only cashes traveler's checks) or the train station.

Buses: SPT, P. Matteotti (tel. 30 47 44), at the bend in Lungo Lario Trieste. To: Menaggio (L4400), Bellaggio (L4100), Gravedona (L6500), and Bergamo (L7300). **Information** open Mon.-Fri. 8am-noon and 3-6pm, Sat. 8am-noon.

Public Transportation: Tickets available at *tabacchi* (or at the hostel for patrons). L1300 for an inter-city, one-use ticket.

Ferries: tel. 57 92 11. Daily to all lake towns, L2000-12,500. Departures from the piers along Lungo Lario Triest, in front of P. Cavour. Pick up the booklet *Orari e Tariffe* for a comprehensive listing of prices and departures. Hostel guests get the best deal: a full-day pass for only L15,000.

Swimming Pool: Lido Villa Olmo (tel. 57 09 68). Large lawn area for sunbathing, along with a sandy stretch down below. Tops not required, but bathing caps are. L7000, L4000 if you buy tickets at the youth hostel. Open daily 10am-6pm.

Bike Rental: The youth hostel rents them to guests for L6000 per day.

Pharmacy: Farmacia Centrale, Via Plinio, 1 (tel. 30 42 04), off P. Cavour. Open Tues.-Sun. 8:30am-12:30pm and 3:30-7:30pm. A listing of pharmacies offering evening services is posted outside.

Emergencies: tel. 113. **Hospital: Ospedale Valduce,** Via Dante, 11 (tel. 32 41 11), or **Ospedale Sant'Anna,** tel. 58 51 11.

ACCOMMODATIONS

Less expensive campsites and hostels line the shores of the lake (ask for a list at the tourist office).

Ostello Villa Olmo (HI), Via Bellinzona, 6 (tel./fax 57 38 00), on the inland side of Villa Olmo. From the station, walk for 20min. down Via Borgovico (on your left; it becomes Bellinzona), or take bus #1, 6, 11, or 14 (L1300). This hostel is very lively, fun, and down-to-earth. Run by a wonderful, multilingual couple, it offers bar facilities, English newspapers, homemade strawberry jam, incredible dinners, and discounts on assorted tickets. Slightly crowded rooms with your own locker and key. Self-service laundry L5000; ironing L1000. Curfew 11:30pm. L14,000 per person with breakfast. Full meals L13,000. Bag lunches L10,000. Open March-Nov. daily 7:30-10am and 4-11pm. Call ahead in summer. Off-season, groups by reservation only. MC, Visa accepted with 3% service charge.

Protozoon della Giovane, Via Borgovico, 182 (tel. 57 35 40), on the way to the youth hostel. Take bus #1, 6, 11, or 14 left. Run by nuns; women only. Not as lively as the hostel, but has only private rooms. Clean with crucifixes everywhere (it's a convent, all right). Big building with a central courtyard and garden. Free laundry and kitchen use. Curfew 10pm. L16,000 per person.

Albergo Sociale, Via Maestri Comacini, 8 (tel. 26 40 42), on the side of the *duomo*, upstairs from a restaurant. Central location. Singles L30,000, with bath L75,000. Doubles L55,000, with bath L75,000. Open year-round. Call ahead for reservations. AmEx, MC, Visa.

FOOD

Many of Como's residents eat lunch *alla Milanese,* downing a quick, satisfying meal in an inexpensive self-service joint. The food is wholesome, the atmosphere energetic, and cover charges rare. Unfortunately, finding an affordable *dinner* can be a challenge. Picnickers will appreciate the long hours of the **G.S. supermarket** (tel. 57 08 95) on the corner of Via Recchi and Viale Fratelli Rosselli, across from the park. (Open Mon. 2-8pm, Tues.-Sat. 8am-8pm.) Lakeside benches are great for free *al fresco* dining, although solo women should go prepared with *vai via* (go away) in their vocabulary. Mountainous loaves of *resta* (the typical Como sweet bread bursting with dried fruits) or the harder, cake-like *matalok* can be purchased at the **Franzi Bakery** (tel. 27 20 00), at the corner of Via Vitani and Via Francesco Muratto (open Tues.-Sun. 8:30am-12:30pm and 3:30-7:30pm). Another gem is the take-out haven **Gran Mercato,** P. Matteotti, 3 (tel. 30 47 50), near the bus station; great for

breads, cheeses, and meats. (Pizza L2000 per *etto.* Open Mon. 8:30am-1pm, Tues.-
Fri. 8:30am-1pm and 3-7:30pm, Sat. 8am-7:30pm.)

Gerald's, Via Bianchi Giovini, 10 (tel. 30 48 72), off P. Cavour. This green-tiled
feeding machine will suck you in and spit you out in less than half an hour, but
you'll eat well. *Primi* L5500-6000, *secondi* L6500-8500, with *contorno* L10,000.
Bar open Mon.-Sat. 7am-8pm; meals noon-2:15pm only.
Free Break Self-Service, Viale Innocenzo XI, 19 (tel. 26 14 49); walk down the
stairs from the train station, through the park, and turn right. Spiffy, modern joint
with Charlie Chaplin and Abbott and Costello on the walls. *Primi* L3000-6000,
secondi L6000-L12,000. Open Mon.-Fri. noon-2:30pm, bistro open Mon.-Sat. 7:30-
11pm. AmEx, MC, Visa.
Taverna Messicana, P. Mazzini, 5/6 (tel. 26 24 63). Inexpensive *primi* and *secondi* (both from L8500), and a million variations on the pizza (from L6000). Try
the *Ravioli di Magro* (L9000), in a delicate butter and sage sauce. Cover L2000.
Open Tues.-Sun. noon-2pm and 7pm-midnight.
Pasticceria Monti, Piazza Cavour, 21 (tel. 30 48 33 or 30 11 65), on the corner. For
divine *gelato,* go to the little window overlooking the Lungo Lago Trento, or sit
down at the tables for *primi* (L8000) and drinks. Open daily in summer 7am-2am.

SIGHTS AND ENTERTAINMENT

Near P. Cavour, Como's **duomo** harmoniously combines Gothic and Renaissance
elements. The vigorous sculptures that animate the exterior of the church are the
work of the Rodari brothers. Note especially Como residents Pliny the Elder and
Pliny the Younger on either side of the door. Against the *duomo* is the sturdy **Bro-
letto,** the former communal palace, with thick pillars, colonnaded windows, and
colorful marble balconies. The **Church of San Fedele,** two blocks from the *duomo,*
bears a resemblance to Ravenna's Byzantine churches, unsurprising since the oldest
parts of the church (notably the altar and the blind arcade) were built by the Lombards during the same period. A 20th-century version of the communal palace is
Giuseppe Terragni's **Casa del Fascio.** Built in 1939 to house the local fascist government, it has become an icon for modernist architecture—quite the antithesis of the
traditional heavy masonry and Roman imagery of "fascist architecture."

After visiting Como's monuments, take the *funicolare* up to **Brunate** for excellent hiking and views. The cars leave from the far end of Lungo Lario Triest every
half-hour (L3800; round-trip L6800, if purchased through the hostel L4500; children
L2400, round-trip L4200; open Thurs.-Sat., last return at midnight in summer,
10:30pm in winter). The other option is spending the night in one of the three
rough-and-ready *baite* (guesthouses) along the trail, which provide room and board
in either private or dorm-style rooms (about L29,500). Check with the tourist office
in the off-season to make sure they're open.

Across the lake from the *funicolare* is the **Tempio Voltano** (tel. 57 47 05), a
memorial museum dedicated to the inventor of the battery, Signor Volta.
(Volta...volts...get it? Open Tues.-Sun. 10am-noon and 3-6pm; in winter 10am-noon
and 2-4pm. Admission L4000, groups and under 6 L2500.) From there, you can take
a stroll among the villas lining the lake, namely the **Villa "La Rotonda"** and **Villa
Olmo** in the park of the same name. A couple of miles away in **Cernobbio** is the
world-famous **Villa d'Este,** once the luxury vacation spot of the Este family of Ferrara, now a decadent hotel with rooms starting at around US$900 a night!

The bustling **outdoor market** of Como is held every Tuesday and Thursday morning in Piazza Vittoria, and all day long on Sunday. The fabulous Como jazz festival,
Jazz & Co., holds about five concerts during a week in July in P. San Federale. Contact the tourist office for current details.

■■■ CENTRO LAGO

Explore the endless villas and towns of the Centro Lago at your leisure while staying
at one of the two excellent youth hostels in **Menaggio** (on the west shore) and

Domaso (on the north side). In Menaggio, Ty and Paola run the **Ostello La Prinula (HI),** Via IV Novembre, 86 (tel. (0344) 323 56), one of the jolliest and best-kept hostels around. It offers great cuisine (dinner L13,000, breakfast L2000), family suites, a washing machine (L5000, dryer L3500), and cooking equipment (L500). Bike rental L15,000 per day, and you can even do a little wine-tasting. (Lockout 10am-5pm. Curfew 11:30pm. L13,000 per person. Open mid-March to mid-Nov.) The **hostel (HI)** in Domaso is at Via Case Sparse, 12 (tel. (0344) 960 94). It lies 16km from Como by bus; also accessible by boat. Good windsurfing area. (L12,000 per person, L13,000 with breakfast. Open March-Oct.) The northwest lakeside hosts a plethora of **campsites;** Domaso itself has 12 of them. Near the hostel are **Europa** (tel./fax 960 44; L6500 per person, L13,000 per tent) and **Italia 90** (tel. 834 46; L4000 per person, L11,500 per tent). The Como tourist office has complete camping info.

Drop off your baggage, hop on a ferry, and hop off when a villa, castle, or village beckons you. Among the endless possibilities, stops at **Varenna,** on the western shore, offer a perfect cluster of houses below the castle Vezio, and at **Isola Comacina,** also on the western shore, provide a breathtaking **Oratory of San Giovanni.** Don't miss the magnificent **gardens of Villa Balbianello** in Leano. (Open April-Oct. Tues., Thurs., Sat.-Sun. 10am-12:30pm and 3:30-5:30pm. Admission L5000, ages 6-10 L3000.) Head to the **Villa Carlotta** in Tremizzo (tel. 404 05 or 410 11) for a stroll among manicured gardens, enormous azaleas, and sculpture. (Open March-Nov. Admission L9000, L5000 if you buy tickets through the hostel.)

LAKE MAGGIORE (LAGO MAGGIORE)

Lacking only the hustle of its easterly cousins, Lake Maggiore cradles the same temperate mountain waters and picture-perfect shores. A glaze of opulence coats the air here, and a stroll past any of the grandiose shore-side hotels reveals that Maggiore is the preferred watering hole of the elite. Modest *pensioni* tucked away in the shadows of their multi-storied superiors, however, enable travelers to partake of the lake's sedate pleasures for a surprisingly reasonable sum.

■■■ STRESA

Stresa retains much of the charm that brought visitors here in droves during the 19th and early 20th centuries. Splendid views of the lake and mountains appear at each turn of the cobblestone streets. Only an hour from Milan on the Milan-Domodossola train line (every hr., 1hr., L7200, L12,000 IC), the town is a convenient base for expeditions in the region. The **tourist office** (tel. 301 50 or 304 16) is at Via Principe Tommaso, 72. From the station, turn right on Via Carducci and follow the signs. English spoken. (Open Mon.-Sat. 8:30am-12:30pm and 3-6:15pm, Sun. 9am-noon; Oct.-April Mon.-Fri. 8:30am-12:30pm and 3-6:15pm, Sat. 8:30am-12:30pm.) The **post office** is at Via Roma, 5 (tel. 300 65), near P. Congressa. (Open Mon.-Fri. 8:15am-6:30pm, Sat. 8:15-11:40am. **Postal code:** 28049. **Telephone code:** 0323. For **emergency medical assistance,** tel. 318 44. If you have a medical problem, seek out the "Hopital" sign at Via De Martini, 20 (tel. 304 28). **Ambulance:** tel. 333 60.

Accommodations and Food **Albergo Luina,** Via Garibaldi, 21 (tel. 302 85), offers quiet comfort in the thick of the town's center. The kind, English-speaking proprietors request a 3-day min. stay during high season. (Singles L50,000. Doubles with bath L90,000. Breakfast L7000. AmEx, MC, Visa.) **Orsola Meublé,** Via Duchessa di Genova, 45 (tel. 310 87), awaits downhill from the station. Some rooms with terrace. (Singles L35,000, with bath L45,000. Doubles L50,000, with bath L65,000. Breakfast L8000. AmEx.) Pass under the tracks and go uphill to find the beautiful breezy rooms of **Hotel Mon Toc,** Via Duchessa di Genova, 67-69 (tel. 302 82; fax 93 38 60). (Singles L53,000. Doubles L81,000, including breakfast. All rooms with bath.

Occasional mandatory full pension L75,000 per person. Half-pension L65,000. MC, Visa.) **Taverna del Pappagallo**, Via Principessa Margherita, 46 (tel. 304 11), serves up appetizing and affordable meals in this area bereft of a supermarket. *Primi* L6000-10,000, *secondi* L13,000-18,000. Pizza from L7000. Cover L3000. (Open Thurs.-Mon. 11:30am-2:30pm and 6:30-10:30pm; open daily during high season.) Follow the diagonal continuation of Via de Amicis past Via P. Tommaso, and you'll stumble upon a number of appetizing dining possibilities. **Salumeria Bianchetti Augusto**, Via Mazzini, 1 (tel. 304 02), is great for a slice of pizza (L2000-2500) to munch on as you walk along the *lago*.

Entertainment From the last week in August to the third week in September, some of the finest orchestras and soloists in the world gather in Stresa for the internationally acclaimed **Settimane Musicali di Stresa.** (Tickets L30,000-100,000, students L15,000 for certain concerts.) For info, contact the ticket office (Palazzo dei Congressi, Via R. Bonghi, 4, 28049 Stresa; tel. 310 95; fax 325 61). Lake Maggiore also hosts a number of musical events that vary from year to year and month to month; check with the tourist office for current details.

■ NEAR STRESA: ISLANDS

The beauty of the **Borromean Isles, Isola Madre, Isola Bella,** and **Isola dei Pescatori,** has been amply touted over the past 300 years. Daily excursion tickets allow you to hop back and forth among the islands at liberty. L13,000 will buy a ticket to Pallanza and the intermediate islands (ticket office tel. 303 93). The L15,000 variety allows you to extend your itinerary even further to **Villa Taranto,** with its impressive botanical gardens. (Open April-Oct. daily 8:30am-7:30pm. Admission L9000, ages 6-14 L8000.) Enclosed gardens are a recurring theme in any tour of this end of the lake, and if you save your money by eschewing the flora, you will often find yourself with only a small plot of land to pace upon while waiting for the next ferry. **Isola dei Pescatori** is the only garden-free island, and vendors have capitalized on the unrestricted space by erecting souvenir stands on all sides. The tiny streets of this fisherman's island are full of eclectic shops and heavy daytime tourist traffic.

Isola Madre (tel./fax 312 61 for info) is the longest and quietest of the three islands. The elegant 16th-century villa, started in 1502 by Lancelotto Borromeo and finished by the Count Renato 100 years later, contains the Borromeo *bambini* doll collection as well as a number of portraits. Even if you decide to skip the house, the botanical garden is worth the entrance price, and is filled with a stupendous array of exotic trees, plants, and flowers. (Open March 27-Oct. 24 daily 9am-noon and 1:30-5:30pm. Admission L12,000, ages 6-15 L6000.) **Pallanza,** on the far side of Isola Madre, offers little of artistic interest, but lakeside dining is cheaper here and you might consider having a meal before cruising "home." Stresa's navigation offices are located in P. Marconi, and tickets are sold from 8:30am to 7pm. For additional info, contact the central office at **Arona,** Viale Barracco, 1 (tel. (0322) 466 51).

The sprawling opulence of the Palazzo e Giardini Borromeo has made **Isola Bella** (tel. (0323) 305 56; fax (02) 72 01 00 38 for info) the most famous of the islands. The palace, built in 1670 by Count Borromeo, is a monument to the Baroque era. The 10 terraces of the gardens, liberally punctuated with statues, rise up in true wedding-cake fashion to the Borromeo family emblem, the unicorn. By the way, the Borromeo family motto is "Humilitas." (Same hours and prices as Madre, above.)

LAKE ORTA (LAGO D'ORTA)

Lake Orta remains the Lake Country's unspoiled refuge, surrounded by hills and forests and graced by several small towns. Nietzsche retreated here from 1883 to 1885 to script his final work, *Thus Spoke Zarathustra*. Lake Orta lies on the Novara-

Domodossola **train** line (almost every hr., 1½hr., L4200). Get off at Orta Miasino, 3km above Orta, and then either walk down to the left or catch one of the four buses that travel to Orta. Connections from nearby Lago Maggiore are indirect, but possible. On weekdays, **buses** leave from Stresa (L3800) through Baveno to Orta. For bus and train schedules check with the tourist office. Train tickets out of Orta must be bought from the conductor.

Practical Information Orta's **tourist office** is at Via Olina, 9/11 (tel. 91 19 37; fax 90 56 78). (Open Tues.-Sat. 9am-noon and 3-5:30pm, Sun. 10am-noon and 3-5pm.) If you arrive on a Monday or are bound for a different town, check the office at Via Panoramica across the street and down from the Villa Crespi (with the mosque-like tower; tel. 90 56 14). (Open June 15-July 15 Wed.-Mon. 10am-1pm and 4-7pm.) The **post office** is at P. Ragazzoni (tel. 901 57; open Mon.-Fri. 8:30am-1:20pm, Sat. 8:30-11am). The **postal code** is 28016; the **telephone code** is 0322.

Accommodations and Food Restaurant prices (and the solicitous treatment given tourists) are a relief after those of the more commercialized lakes, but affordable accommodations await only a happy few. **Ristorante Olina,** Via Olina, 40 (tel. 90 56 56), across from the tourist office, offers beautiful doubles with private baths (L75,000-80,000, breakfast L10,000). Family rooms with kitchens are also available. (AmEx, MC, Visa.) The **Taverna Antico Angello,** Via Olina, 18 (tel. 902 59), provides central one-star economy. (Singles L35,000. Doubles L55,000-65,000. Breakfast L5000. MC, Visa.) For those with access to a car, the nearby lake towns of Alzo and Arola also have cheap options—contact the Orta tourist office for details. A good-sized **open-air market** sets up on Wednesday mornings in P. Motta. Good news for those lookin' for a piece of ass—Lago D'Orta is known as the home of *tapulon* (**donkey meat,** minced, well spiced, and cooked in red wine). For this and other warm comestible, hop on the boat to **Ristorante San Giulio,** Via Basilica, 4 (tel. 902 34), on the tiny island of the same name, with an 18th-century dining room and lakeside terrace. (*Primi* L7000-9000; *secondi* L10,000-15,000. Cover L2500. Opens at 7:30am and provides a return boat that runs after the public ones have quit. AmEx, MC, Visa.)

Sights Set high in the cool, verdant hills above town is the **Sacro Monte,** a monastic complex devoted to St. Francis of Assisi. The sanctuary was founded in 1591, and its 20 chapels boast some 376 life-sized statues and 900 frescoes whose combined forces tell the life story of Italy's patron saint (tel. 91 19 60; open daily 8am-6pm; free). **Isola di San Giulio,** across from Orta, has an interesting Romanesque **basilica** from the 12th century, built on 4th-century foundations. (Tel. 903 58. Open daily 9am-12:15pm and 2-6pm; closed Mon. mornings. Free.) A circular route around the island snakes through the narrow streets past ivy-covered walls and tiled roofs. Small motor boats weave back and forth every 10 minutes during the summer (round-trip L2500; tickets sold on board). Winter service is restricted to a couple of runs a day. There are also numerous music and sports events from May to December in the lake area. Ask at the tourist office for a schedule.

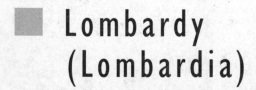

Lombardy (Lombardia)

Over the centuries Roman generals, German emperors, and French kings have vied for control of Lombardy's bounty. The agricultural riches of the region have since been augmented by industrial and financial resources, making it the cornerstone of the Italian economy. In many ways, Lombardy has more in common with its northern neighbors than with the rest of the peninsula, and Lombardians make periodic calls for an end to the subsidization of the Roman bureaucracy and the economically challenged South. Even so, since World War II, Lombardy's "new Italy" has attracted legions of ambitious southerners, and the province has recently become a magnet for immigrants from North Africa and the Middle East. Tension between long-time residents and immigrants persists, but thanks in part to this diversity, inhabitants of Lombardy are today among the least provincial Italians.

Cosmopolitan Milan, with its international reputation for high style and finance, looms large in foreigners' perceptions of the region, but Lombardy is much more than a metropolis and its countryside. Bergamo, Brescia, and Mantua, with their hints of Venetian influence, are culturally foreign to their western neighbor. The beginnings of the Alps are not far from the southern plain, merging the Italian climate with strains of Swiss and Austrian culture.

■■■ MILAN (MILANO)

Milan is built on Roman foundations, but has forged toward modernity with more force than any other major Italian city. Although the capital of the western half of the Roman Empire between 286 and 402 AD, Milan retains few reminders of that period; the *duomo* (1386), the city's emblem, is a rare remnant of its long history.

Milan's pace of life is quicker than that in most Italian cities. Even the *siesta* is shorter here, which means more precious hours for a frenetic pilgrimage to the glitzy boutiques. Once the style capital of Italy, Milan manages to preserve its reputation in the fashion world. Its wide, tree-lined boulevards and graceful architecture, more reminiscent of Austria than of Italy, are as elegant as ever, yet compete with more vibrant graffiti. Although petty crime, drug dealing, and prostitution are likely to strike your eye (especially in the area around the central station), Milan is an entertaining town with an active nightlife. If you arrive in August, however, you'll find the city "shut down" for the entire month and taken over by mosquitoes.

ORIENTATION

Milan is linked by train to all major cities in Italy and Western Europe. The layout of the city resembles a giant target, encircled by a series of concentric ancient city walls. In the outer rings lie suburbs built during the 1950s and 60s to house southern immigrants. The **duomo** and **Galleria Vittorio Emanuele II** comprise the bull's-eye, roughly at the center of the downtown circle. Within this inner circle are four central squares: **Piazza Cairoli**, near Castello Sforzesco, **Piazza Cordusio**, connected to Largo Cairoli by Via Dante, **Piazza Duomo**, at the end of Via Mercanti, and **Piazza San Babila**, the business and fashion district along Corso Vittorio Emanuele. Northeast and northwest lie two large parks, the **Giardini Pubblici** and the **Parco Sempione**. Farther northeast is the **Stazione Centrale**, Mussolini's colossal train station built in 1931. The area around the train station is a mishmash of skyscrapers dominated by the sleek **Pirelli Tower** (1959), still one of the tallest buildings in Europe. From the station, a scenic ride on bus #60 takes you to the downtown hub, as does the more efficient commute on subway line #3. The station is also connected to the downtown area by **Corso Buenos Aires,** where prices for clothing are actually reasonable.

The **subway** (*Metropolitana Milanese*, abbreviated "MM") is the most useful branch of Milan's extensive public transportation network. **Line #1** (red line) connects the *pensioni* district east of Stazione Centrale to the center of town and extends as far as the youth hostel (Molino Dorino fork). **Line #2** (green line) links Milan's three train stations and crosses MM1 at Cadorno and Loreto. **Line #3** (yellow line) runs from just north of the Stazione Centrale to the southern sprawl of the city, intersecting with line #2 at Stazione Centrale and #1 at the *duomo*. The subway operates from approximately 6am to midnight. Among the many useful train and

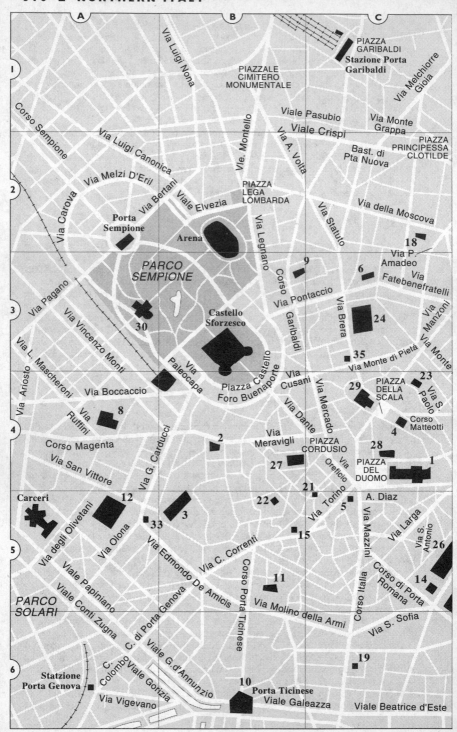

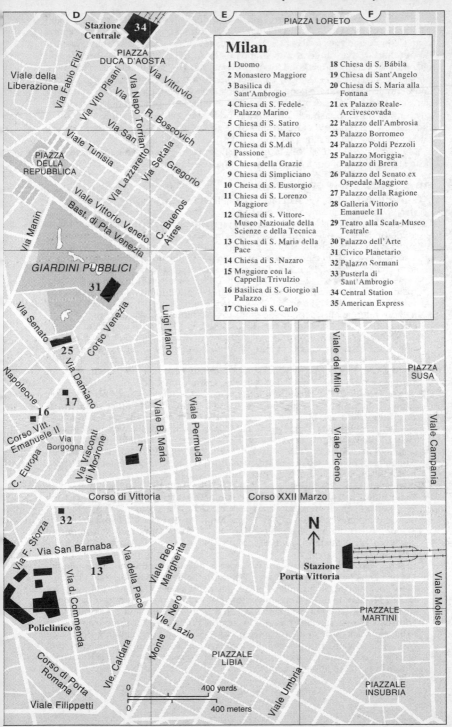

D Stazione Centrale 34

PIAZZA LORETO

E

F

Viale della Liberazione

Via Fabio Filzi

PIAZZA DUCA D'AOSTA

Via Vito Pisani

Via Napo Torriano

Via Vitruvio

R. Boscovich

PIAZZA DELLA REPUBBLICA

Viale Tunisia

Via San

Via Lazzaretto

Via Serbelloni

Gregorio

C. Buenos Aires

Viale Vittorio Veneto

Bast. di Pta Venezia

Via Manin

GIARDINI PUBBLICI

31

Corso Venezia

Via Senato

Napoleone

25

Via Damiano

17

16

Luigi Maino

Viale dei Mille

PIAZZA SUSA

Viale Piceno

Viale Campania

Corso Vitt. Emanuele II

C. Europa

Via Borgogna

Via Visconti di Modrone

7

Viale B. Maria

Viale Permuda

Corso di Vittoria

Corso XXII Marzo

N ↑

32

Via F. Storza

Via San Barnaba

Via della Pace

13

Viale Reg. Margherita

Monte Nero

Vle. Lazio

Stazione Porta Vittoria

PIAZZALE MARTINI

Viale Molise

Via d. Commenda

Policlinico

Corso di Porta Romana

Vle. Caldara

PIAZZALE LIBIA

Viale Umbria

PIAZZALE INSUBRIA

Viale Filippetti

0   400 yards

0   400 meters

Milan

1 Duomo
2 Monastero Maggiore
3 Basilica di Sant'Ambrogio
4 Chiesa di S. Fedele-Palazzo Marino
5 Chiesa di S. Satiro
6 Chiesa di S. Marco
7 Chiesa di S.M.di Passione
8 Chiesa della Grazie
9 Chiesa di Simpliciano
10 Cheisa di S. Eustorgio
11 Chiesa di S. Lorenzo Maggiore
12 Chiesa di s. Vittore-Museo Nazionale della Scienze e della Tecnica
13 Chiesa di S. Maria della Pace
14 Chiesa di S. Nazaro
15 Maggiore con la Cappella Trivulzio
16 Basilica di S. Giorgio al Palazzo
17 Chiesa di S. Carlo

18 Chiesa di S. Bábila
19 Chiesa di Sant'Angelo
20 Chiesa di S. Maria alla Fontana
21 ex Palazzo Reale-Arcivescovada
22 Palazzo dell'Ambrosia
23 Palazzo Borromeo
24 Palazzo Poldi Pezzoli
25 Palazzo Moriggia-Palazzo di Brera
26 Palazzo del Senato ex Ospedale Maggiore
27 Palazzo della Ragione
28 Galleria Vittorio Emanuele II
29 Teatro alla Scala-Museo Teatrale
30 Palazzo dell'Arte
31 Civico Planetario
32 Palazzo Sormani
33 Pusterla di Sant'Ambrogio
34 Central Station
35 American Express

bus routes, **trams #29** and **30** travel the city's outer ring road, while **buses #96** and **97** service the inner road. **Tram #1**, which runs during the wee hours, also departs from Centrale and runs to Piazza Scala. Tickets for buses, trams, and subways must be purchased in advance at newsstands or from ticket machines—bring small change. A ticket (L1400) is good for one subway ride or 75 minutes of surface transportation. All-day passes (L4800) are available from the **ATM** office at the Duomo and Centrale stops and are good from the first time you use them. Those planning a longer stay should consider the weekly pass (about L9000, photo required), valid for any form of public transportation. It is a good idea to have extra tickets on hand in the evening, as *tabacchi* close around 8pm and vending machines are unreliable (about L30,000 fine for riding without a ticket).

Whenever possible, *Let's Go: Italy 1996* includes the **map grid coordinates** and nearest MM station of our listings for your directional needs.

PRACTICAL INFORMATION

Tourist Office: APT, Via Marconi, 1 (C4; tel. 80 96 62/63/64; fax 72 02 29 99), in the "Palazzo di Turismo" in P. del Duomo, to the right as you face the *duomo*. Comprehensive local and regional info, and an especially useful map and museum guide (in Italian). Will not reserve rooms, but will phone to check for vacancies. Some English spoken. Be sure to pick up *Milano Mese* and *Youth in Milan* for info on activities and clubs, among other things. Open Mon.-Fri. 8:30am-8pm, Sat. 9am-1pm and 2-7pm, Sun. 9am-1pm and 2-5pm. Branch office at **Stazione Centrale** (D1; tel. 669 05 32 or 669 04 32; open Mon.-Sat. 8am-7pm); set back off the main hall on the 2nd floor. English spoken. For hotel info and reservations, call **Hotel Reservation Milano** (tel. 76 00 60 95; open Mon.-Fri.), which may request a deposit during busy periods and tends toward more expensive hotels.
Police: tel. 772 71."**SOS for Tourists**": tel. 545 65 51 for legal complaints.
Post Office: Via Cordusio, 4 (C4; tel. 869 20 69), near P. del Duomo in the direction of the castle. Stamps at #1 and 2. *Fermo posta* at the CAI-POST office to the left. Open Mon.-Fri. 8:15am-7:40pm, Sat. 8:15am-5:45pm. **Postal Code:** 20100.
Telephones: Telecom (SIP), in Galleria Vittorio Emanuele. Open 8am-9pm. In Stazione Centrale (D1), open 8am-7:45pm. **Telephone Code:** 02.
Budget Travel: CIT, Galleria Vittorio Emanuele (C4; tel. 86 37 01). Also **changes money.** Open Mon.-Fri. 9am-7pm, Sat. 9am-12:30pm. Another office at the **Stazione Centrale** (same hours). **Centro Turistico Studentesco,** Via S. Antonio, 2 (C5; tel. 58 30 41 21). Open Mon.-Fri. 9:30am-6pm, Sat. 9:30am-noon; Sept.-May closes Mon.-Fri. 1-2pm. **Transalpino Tickets:** Next to train info office in upper atrium of Stazione Centrale (D1; tel. 670 51 21). Open Mon.-Sat. 8am-9pm, Sun. 9am-8pm. When closed, go to **Italturismo** (D1), to the right from the station, under the grand drive-through. Open daily 6:45am-8pm.
Consulates: U.S., Via P. Amedeo, 2/10 (C2; tel. 29 00 18 41). Open Mon.-Fri. 9-11am and 2-4pm. **Canada,** Via Vittor Pisani, 19 (D1; tel. 675 81; emergencies tel. 66 98 06 00). Open Mon.-Fri. 9am-12:30pm. **U.K.,** Via S. Paolo, 7 (C5; tel. 72 30 01; emergencies tel. 87 24 90). Open Mon.-Fri. 9:15am-12:15pm and 2:30-4:30pm. **Australia,** Via Borgogna, 2 (D4; tel. 77 70 41). Open daily 9am-noon and 2-4:30pm. **New Zealand,** Via F. Sforza, 48 (tel. 58 31 44 43). Open daily 8:30am-12:45pm and 1:45-5pm.
Currency Exchange: All **Banca d'America e d'Italia** and **Banca Nazionale del Lavoro** branches eagerly await your Visa card. (Bank hours in Milan are generally Mon.-Fri. 8:30am-1:30pm and 3-4pm.) If you need money changed right away, try **Banca Nazionale delle Comunicazioni** (D1) at Stazione Centrale; it has pretty standard rates. (L6000 fee. Open Mon.-Sat. 8:30am-12:30pm and 2-7:30pm.)
American Express: Via Brera, 3 (C3; tel. 72 00 36 93), on the corner of Via dell'Orso. Walk through the Galleria, across P. Scala, and up Via Verdi. Holds mail free for American Express members, otherwise US$5 per inquiry. Receives (but does not send) wired money; fee of L2000 on transactions over US$100. Open Mon.-Thurs. 9am-5:30pm, Fri. 9am-5pm.

MILAN

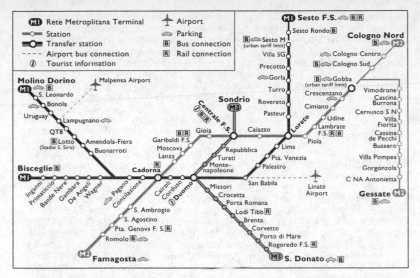

Flights: Malpensa Airport, 45km from town. Intercontinental flights. Buses (tel. 66 98 45 09) leave every 30min. in the mornings, every hr. in the afternoon from P. Luigi di Savoia, on the east side of Stazione Centrale (L12,000). **Linate Airport,** 7km from town. Domestic/European flights and intercontinental flights with European transfers. Much easier logistically. The bus to Linate leaves Stazione Centrale every 20min. 5:40am-7pm (L4000). It's cheaper (L1400) to take bus #73 from P. San Babila (MM1). **General Flight Info** for both airports, tel. 74 85 22 00.

Trains: Stazione Centrale, P. Duca d'Aosta (D1; tel. 67 50 01), on MM2, The primary station. To: Genoa and Turin (both every hr., 1½hr. and 2hr., L13,700); Venice (25 direct per day, 3hr., L20,800); Florence (every hr., 2½hr., L26,200); Rome (every hr., 4½hr., L47,700). Faster trains to Florence and Rome available for more money. Info office open daily 7am-9:30pm. Eurailpasses and *Cartaverde* available outside the building. **Luggage Storage:** L1500. Open 24 hrs. **Stazione Nord** (tel. 851 16 08) connects Milan with Como, Erba, and Varese. **Porta Genova** has lines to the west (Vigevano, Alessandria, Asti), and **Porta Garibaldi** (C1; tel. 63 71 61 06) links Milan to Lecco and Valtellina to the northwest.

Buses: ATM (C4; tel. 87 54 95 or 89 01 07 97), in the P. del Duomo MM station. Municipal buses require pre-purchased tickets (L1400). Day passes for non-residents L4800, L8000 for 2 days. Info office open Mon.-Sat. 8am-8pm; ticket office open 7:45am-7:15pm. Also at **Stazione Centrale** (same hours). **Intercity** buses are less convenient and more expensive than the trains, but **SAL, SIA, Autostradale,** and many others depart from P. Castello and the surrounding area (MM: Cairoli) for Turin, the lake country, Bergamo, Certosa di Pavia, and points as far away as Rimini and Triest.

Taxis: In P. Scala (C4), P. del Duomo (C4), P. S. Babila (D4), and Largo Cairoli (B4; tel. 67 67, 83 83, or 85 85). The official Milan taxis are yellow and uniformly expensive, starting at L5000, with a nighttime surcharge of L5000.

Car Rental: Hertz (D-E1; tel. 677 46, Galleria delle Carrozze office tel. 670 30 62). Outside the station, to the left as you exit. Open Mon.-Fri. 8am-7pm, Sat. 8am-2pm. Also check with **Europcar** (tel. 66 98 78 26 or 66 98 15 89) and **Avis** (tel. 669 02 80) at the same place: same rates, similar hours.

Lost and Found: (tel. 63 71 26 67) at baggage deposit in Stazione Centrale. Open daily 7:20am-8:45pm.

Laundromat: Minola, Via S. Vito, 5 (B5; tel. 58 11 12 71), on the corner with Papa Gregorio, near the *duomo*. Wash and dry 5kg L17,000, dry-clean 5kg L20,000. Open Mon.-Fri. 8:30am-6:30pm, Sat. 8am-12:30pm. **Onda Blu,** Via Scarlatti, 19

(E1; toll-free tel. 167 86 13 46) is self-service; 3 blocks from Stazione Centrale. Wash or dry 6.5kg for L6000, 16kg L10,000. Soap L1500. Open daily 8am-10pm. **Public Toilets, Showers, and Baths: Albergo Diurno** (D1; tel. 669 12 32), beneath P. Duca d'Aosta, reached by stairs underground as you leave the center of the Stazione Centrale. Toilets L500, with soap and towel L2500, with shower L9000, with bath L10,000. Open Thurs.-Tues. 7am-7pm.

Swimming Pool: Cozzi, Viale Tunisia, 35 (D-E2; tel. 659 97 03), off Corso Buenos Aires. Out of a dozen, the closest to Stazione Centrale. Open Sept.-June Mon. 10am-1:30pm and 6-10pm, Tues. and Thurs.-Fri. 10am-1:30pm, Wed. 10am-6pm, Sat.-Sun. 10am-4pm. Admission L6000. In summer, move outdoors to **Giulia Romano,** Via Ampere, 20 (tel. 70 63 08 25). Swimcap required (available for L2500). Admission L6000, under 12 and over 60 L3000. **Lido di Milano,** P. Lotto, 15 (tel. 39 26 61 00), near the youth hostel. Open daily 10am-7:30pm. Admission L7500, children L4000. Small indoor kids' pool. Swimcap required (L2000).

Library: United States Information Service, Via Bigli, 11 (C3-4; tel. 79 50 51), near P. S. Babila. Library with U.S. publications for perusal. Open Mon.-Thurs. 9:30am-12:30pm. **British Council Library,** Via Manzoni, 38 (C3-4; tel. 77 22 21), near USIS. Open Mon. 2-6pm, Tues.-Thurs. 10am-7:30pm, Fri. 10am-6pm.

English Bookstore: The American Bookstore, Via Camperio, 16 (B4; tel. 871 89 20; fax 72 02 00 30), at Largo Cairoli. The best selection in Milan. Open Mon. 1-7:30pm, Tues.-Fri. 10am-7:30pm, Sat. 10am-1pm and 2:30-7:30pm. Closed 2 wks. in Aug. **Hoepli Libreria Internazionale,** Via Hoepli, 5 (C4; tel. 86 48 71), off P. Media near P. Scala. Open Mon. 2-7pm, Tues.-Sat. 9am-7pm. MC, Visa. **Rizzoli's,** Galleria Vittorio Emanuele (C4; tel. 86 46 10 71) has only a small English collection, but is well stocked with *Let's Go.*

AIDS Hotline: Centralino Informazioni AIDS, (toll free *numero verde*: 1678 610 61). Also **Centri AIDS,** P. XXIV Maggio, Ex Casello (B6; tel. 89 40 24 06), Via Fantoli, 7 (tel. 506 19 31), and Via Masaniello, 23 (tel. 453 14 25).

Handicapped/Disabled Services: Direzione Servizi Sociali, Largo Treves, 1 (C2-3). For general info call 62 08 69 54; wheelchair info call Dr. Guarnieri 659 90 32.

Late-Night Pharmacy: Though nocturnal duty rotates among Milan's pharmacies, the one in Stazione Centrale never closes (D1; tel. 669 07 35 or 669 09 35). During the day, try the **Italo-English Chemist's Shop** on P. Duomo, 21 (C4; tel. 86 46 48 32) or at Via E. Lussu, 4 (D5; tel. 256 72 73).

Hospital: Ospedale Maggiore Policlinico, Via Francesco Sforza, 35 (tel. 550 31), 5min. from the *duomo* on the inner ring road.

Emergencies: tel. 113. **Medical Emergency: Pronto Soccorso,** tel. 38 83. **Ambulance:** tel. 77 33.

ACCOMMODATIONS AND CAMPING

There are over 50 "on-paper" bargains in Milan, but if you want a clean room in a safe and reasonably convenient location, only a few choices are worth your while. Every season is high season in Milan (except August), and a single room in a decent establishment for under L40,000 is a real find. For the best deals, make the trip from the station to the city's center or its southern periphery. Whenever possible, make reservations well ahead of time. The listings below are spread across the city; map grid coordinates and indicated MM stations are listed for your convenience.

Ostello Pietra Rotta (HI), Viale Salmoiraghi, 1 (tel. 39 26 70 95; MM1: QT8). In the leafy outskirts. Walk to the right from the metro (so that the round church is across the street on the left) for about 10min. The hostel will be on the right. Institutional hostel; modern facilities and 380 beds. Run on a strictly mechanized regimen. English spoken. HI card required, but available at the hostel for L30,000. Open 7-9am and 5pm-midnight, but no morning check-in. Unbending enforcement of daytime lockout. Depending on the management's whim, lights suddenly die between 11:20pm and midnight. Curfew 11:30pm. L20,000 per person. Breakfast, sheets, and lockers included. No individual reservations, but there is almost always room. Open Jan. 13-Dec. 20.

Due Giardini, Via Settala, 46 (D-E1-2; tel. 29 52 10 93 or 29 51 23 09; MM1: Lima). Go left on Via Vitruvio from the station and then right on Settala. "Feel-the-

springs" beds, but clean and neat. The main attraction is the big garden outside. Open all night. Singles L50,000. Doubles L70,000. Triples L90,000. MC, Visa.
Hotel San Marco, Via Piccinni, 25 (E-F1; tel. 29 51 64 14; fax 29 51 32 43; MM1-2: Loreto). From the station, head left to P. Caiazzo and turn onto Via Pergolesi, which becomes Via Piccinni. Comfortable rooms with TV and telephone compensate for unending street noise below. Friendly management speaks some English. Singles L55,000, with bath L70,000. Doubles L72,000, with bath L95,000. Triples with bath L125,000. Prices with bath include breakfast. AmEx, MC, Visa.
Albergo "Villa Mira," Via Sacchini, 19 (F1; tel. 29 52 56 18; MM1-2: Loreto), off Via Porpora 2 blocks from P. Loreto. Family-run, with rooms out of a Mr. Clean commercial. Bar downstairs. Singles L40,000. Doubles with bath L55,000. Call ahead if possible.
Hotel Ca' Grande, Via Porpora, 87 (F1; tel. 26 14 40 01; MM1-2: Loreto), about 7 blocks in from P. Loreto in a building protected by a spiked fence. Clean rooms with phones and hospital-style beds. Street below can be noisy. English spoken. Singles L45,000, with bath L65,000. Doubles L70,000, with bath L90,000. Desk closed 2-6am.
Viale Tunisia, 6 (D-E2; MM1: Porta Venezia). This building houses two budget hotels equidistant from the station and the city center. (Both deny having a curfew, but ask to be sure.)
Hotel Kennedy (tel. 29 40 09 34), 6th floor. Very tidy rooms, with dreamscape decor imported from the 60s. Some English spoken. Check-out 11am. Singles L50,000-65,000. Doubles L70,000-85,000, with bath L120,000-140,000. Breakfast L5000. Reservations recommended.
Hotel San Tommaso (tel. 29 51 47 47), on the 3rd floor. Orderly rooms with hardwood floors, some overlooking a courtyard. English spoken. Singles L35,000-45,000. Doubles L60,000-70,000. Prices may be a bit higher Sept.-Oct., a bit lower Dec.-Jan.
Hotel Aurora, Corso Buenos Aires, 18 (E2-F1; tel. 204 79 60; fax 204 92 80). Behind a grungy façade lies a spotless labyrinth of modern rooms, most with TV. The courtyard mutes street noise. English spoken. Open 24 hrs. Singles L60,000 with bath L65,000. Doubles with bath L90,000. Breakfast included. MC, Visa.
Hotel Julanda, Corso Magenta, 78 (A-B4; tel. 46 33 17; fax 48 01 90 12; MM1: Conciliazione), in a quiet neighborhood popular with university students, but becoming more tourist-oriented. Tasteful, wood-floored rooms, most with TV. No curfew. Singles L52,000. Doubles L80,000, with bath L115,000. AmEx.
Pensione Cantore, Corso di Porta Genova, 25 (A6-B5; tel. 835 75 65; MM2: Genova), a 15-min. walk southwest of the *duomo,* farther down Via Corso Correnti. A bit out of the way, but grand and immaculate rooms. Friendly atmosphere. Closes at 2am, 3:30am on weekends. Singles L40,000. Doubles L65,000. Triples 90,000. Reserve at least 1 week ahead.
Camping di Monza (tel. (039) 38 77 71), in the park of the Villa Reale in Monza. Take a train or bus from Stazione Centrale to Monza, then a city bus to the campground. L4500 per person and per tent, L2000 per child under 6. Hot showers L500. Restaurant/bar nearby. Open April-Sept.

FOOD

Like its fine *couture,* Milanese cuisine is sophisticated and overpriced. Specialties include *risotto giallo* (rice with saffron), *cotoletta alla milanese* (breaded veal cutlet with lemon), and *cazzouela* (a mixture of pork and cabbage). *Pasticcerie* and *gelaterie* crowd every block. Try the Milanese sweet bread *panettone,* an Italian fruitcake. The newspaper *Il Giornale Nuovo* lists all the restaurants and shops open in the city. The largest **markets** are around Via Fauché and Viale Papiniano on Saturday and sometimes Tuesday, and along P. Mirabello on Thursday. On Saturday, the **Fiera di Sinigallia**—a 400-year-old extravaganza of the commercial and the bizarre—occurs on Via Calatafimi.

Splurge on the local pastry at **Sant'Ambroeus** (C-D4; tel. 76 00 05 40), a Milanese culinary shrine, under the arcades at Corso Matteotti, 7 (open 8am-8pm). For supermarkets, try **Pam,** off Corso Buenos Aires at Via Piccinni, 2 (E-F1; tel. 29 51 27 15;

MILAN

open Mon. 2-9pm, Tues.-Sun. 8:30am-9pm). There's also a **Simpatia CRAI** at Via Casati, 21 (D-E2; tel. 29 40 58 21; open daily 8am-1pm and 4-7:30pm, closed Mon. afternoons). For a balanced meal at reasonable rates, sit down with the Milanese office workers at one of the countless self-service restaurants that now cater to professionals under time constraints. The strategically positioned **Ciao** (C4; tel. 86 42 67), on the 2nd floor of the Duomo Center in P. del Duomo, is very convenient. (*Primi* average L4500, *secondi* L7500. Open daily 11:30am-3pm and 6-11pm.)

Pizzeria da Sasa, Via Pergolesi, 21 (E1; tel. 669 26 74). Family-run with kids to prove it. Pizza and calzones L7500-11,000. *Primi* L8000-14,000. Cover L2500. Open Wed.-Tues. noon-3pm and 6pm-2am. AmEx, MC, Visa.

Ristorante "La Colubrina," Via Felice Casati, 5 (D-E2; tel. 29 51 84 27; MM1: Porta Venezia). Red tablecloths and mosaic-style stone floors. Pizza L5500-9000. Daily specials L10,000-18,000. Drinks L1000-10,000. Cover L2000. Open Tues. evening-Sun. noon-2:30pm and 7-11:30pm. Closed Aug.

Pizzeria del Nonno, Via Andrea Costa, 1 (F0-1; tel. 26 14 52 62; MM1-2: Loreto), off P. Loreto. Surprisingly genteel decor for a hungry, rowdy crowd. Enormous pizzas (L7000-12,000) keep their mouths full. Daily special L8000-15,000. Cover L2500. Open Mon.-Sat. noon-2:30pm and 7pm-midnight. (Closed Sat. for lunch.)

Tarantella, Viale Abruzzi, 35 (F2; tel. 29 40 02 18), just north of Via Plinio. Lively and leafy neighborhood place with sidewalk dining. Great *antipasti*. Immense specialty salads L10,000-13,000. Pizza L8000-20,000 (try the *gorgonzola*). *Primi* from L8000, *secondi* from L15,000. Open Sept.-July Sun. evening-Fri. noon-2:30pm and 7-11:30pm. AmEx, MC, Visa.

Isola del Panino, Via Felice Casati, 2 (D-E2; tel. 29 51 49 25), but enter from Corso Buenos Aires. Art Deco atmosphere serves up 47 different kinds of fresh *panini* for L3500-5000. (It's not uncommon to have two.) Open Tues.-Sun. 7am-12:30am.

Brek, Via Lepetit, 20 (D-E1; tel. 67 05 149), by the Stazione Centrale. Elegant self-service restaurant, becoming increasingly popular. A/C, a non-smoking room, and English-speaking staff. *Primi* average L5000, *secondi* L7500. Open Mon.-Sat. 11:30am-3pm and 6:30-10:30pm.

La Piccola Napoli, Viale Monza, 13 (tel 26 14 33 97; MM1-2: Loreto). A haunt for local night owls. A/C upstairs. Pizza L7000-11,000. Cover L2500 plus 10% service. Open late-Aug. to mid-July Tues.-Sun. 7pm-3am. MC, Visa.

Duomo Center, Piazza Duomo, 6 (C4), under the arcade on your right as you face the *duomo*. This mega-center houses a variety of fast-food and self-service establishments, including the rather good **Spizzico,** which sells pizza by the slice or by the pie (huge slice of cheese pizza L3000). Open daily 7am-2am.

Peck, Via Cantu, 3 (C4; tel. 869 30 17), off Via Orefici, 2 blocks from P. Duomo. Milan's premier *rosticceria*. Pizza and pastries by the kilo—L3000 will buy a large slice of either. You can't leave without trying the chocolate mousse (about L6000). Open Tues.-Fri. 8:45am-2:30pm and 4-7:30pm, Sat. 8am-1:15pm and 3:45-7:30pm, Sun. 8am-1pm. AmEx, MC, Visa.

Le Briciole, Via Camperio, 17 (B4; tel. 87 71 85), 1 street over from Via Dante. Lively and popular with young people. Pizza L8500-15,000. Spectacular *antipasto* buffet L12,000, *secondi* L10,000-18,000. Cover L3000. Open Tues.-Fri. and Sun. 12:15-2:30pm and 7:15-11:30pm. AmEx, MC, Visa.

Be Bop Caffè/Ristorante/Pizzeria, Viale Col di Lana, 4 (B6; tel. 837 69 72; MM2: Sant'Agostino or Genova), off the far side of P. XXIV Maggio. Elegant decor and background jazz, except after hours when the young staff pumps up the volume. Salads are generously proportioned (L14,000-18,000). Pizza L8000-16,000. There's even *soy* pizza! (Soy *pizza??*) Open Sept.-July Tues.-Sun. noon-2:30pm and 7:30pm-1am. Closed Sun. lunch. AmEx, MC, Visa.

La Crêperie, Via Corso Correnti, 24 (B5; tel. 837 57 08), the continuation of Via Torino. Fruit crepes L6000, liqueur dessert crepes L4000, and the "real food" variety L3000-6000. L9000 lunch special. Sip a lemon-and-celery juice to the non-stop music. Open daily 11am-1am.

Portnoy, Via de Amicis, 1 (B5-6; tel. 58 11 34 29), at Corso di Porta Ticinese. No complaints here. Young, socially conscious management presents new paintings and photographs every month. *Panini* L3000-5000. Open Mon.-Sat. 7am-8:30pm; fewer hours in winter. Poetry readings at 8pm the last Thurs. of every month. **Pizzeria Grand'Italia,** Via Palermo, 5 (B-C2; tel. 87 77 59). Pizza L6000-10,000, and a multitude of other selections. Open Wed.-Mon. 12:15-2:45pm and 7pm-1:15am; in August also open Tues. Very busy, but worth the wait.

Gelaterie

After World War II the Viel family (first the brother, then the cousins), began selling tutti-frutti *gelato* from a cart outside the *duomo*. The enterprise quickly took off and today the name Viel is synonymous with exotic, fresh fruit *gelati* (L1500-5000) and *frullati* (whipped fruit drinks, L4000-8000) all over Milan. At **Viel,** Via Marconi, 3E (C4), next to the tourist office, you can buy a cone packed with four scoops and take it to the outside tables, one of the cheapest places to sit near the *duomo* (L1500-5000 for a large cup). For more elegant and pricey fare, take your taste buds to the jolly **Viel Frutti Esotici Gelati** (B4), on the left as you face the Castello from Largo Cairoli (MM1: Cairoli). *Esotici frullati* from L8000 and *gelato* L7000-10,000. **Jack Frost Gelateria,** Via Felice Casati, 25 (D-E2; tel. 669 11 34; MM1: Porta Venezia), off Corso Buenos Aires at Via Lazzaretto, serves enormous helpings of creamy *gelato* in a fairy-tale decor packed to capacity. Try the *bacio* (chocolate and hazelnut). (Open Thurs.-Tues. 10:30am-1am.) Formerly Gelateria Pozzi, **Gelateria Milano Doc,** at P. Cantore, 4 (A6; tel. 89 40 98 30), has been renovated and offers an expanded menu, outside seating, and crazy-good *gelato* (cones L2500-3500). It's a household name in Milan. (Open Mon. 4pm-1am, Tues.-Sun. 8am-1am.)

SIGHTS

Around the Duomo

The **Piazza del Duomo** marks the geographical and conceptual focus of Milan, and makes a good starting point for a walking view of the city. The **duomo,** a radically vertical Gothic creation with vaguely classical proportions, presides over the *piazza.* Gian Galeazzo Visconti founded the cathedral in 1386, hoping to flatter the Virgin into granting him a male heir. Construction proceeded sporadically over the next four centuries and was finally completed at Napoleon's command in 1809. In the meantime, **2245 statues, 135 spires, 96 gargoyles, and kilometers of tracery** accumulated. The unusual triangular façade juxtaposes Italian Gothic and Baroque elements under a filigree crown. Inside, the 52 columns rise to canopied niches that shelter statues reaching almost the full height of the ceiling—48 meters. The church, a five-aisled cruciform, seats 40,000 worshipers. Narrow side aisles extend to the grand stained-glass windows, said to be the largest in the world. The imposing 16th-century **marble tomb of Giacomo de Medici** in the right transept was inspired by Michelangelo. From outside the north transept, you can climb to the top of the cathedral, where you will find yourself surrounded by florid outbursts of turrets and spires (admission L4000, with elevator L8000). This rooftop magical kingdom is crowned by a gold-plated Madonna. (Open daily 7am-5pm; Oct.-May 9am-4pm. No shorts, miniskirts, sleeveless shirts, or dresses.)

The **Museo del Duomo,** P. del Duomo, 14 (tel. 86 03 58), is across the *piazza* in the Palazzo Reale. The newly renovated museum hosts treasures from the cathedral. (Open Tues.-Sun. 9:30am-12:30pm and 3-6pm. Admission L7000.) It also houses the **Museo d'Arte Contemporanea.** Upstairs is a fine permanent collection of Italian Futurist art, though Picasso figures in as well. (Open Tues.-Sun. 9:30am-5:30pm. Free. Wheelchair accessible. All but one room closed for restoration in 1995.)

On the north side of the *piazza* is the monumental entrance to the **Galleria Vittorio Emanuele II.** The four-story arcade of *caffè,* shops, and offices is covered by a glass barrel vault and a beautiful glass cupola (48m). The gallery extends from the *duomo* to the **Piazza della Scala,** where you'll find the **Teatro alla Scala** (also known as **La Scala),** the world's premier opera house, a simple neoclassical building (1778), where Maria Callas became a legend. La Scala rests on the site of the

Church of Santa Maria alla Scala, from which it took its name. To see the lavish, multi-tiered hall, enter through the **Museo Teatrale alla Scala** (tel. 805 34 18). Here a succession of petite rooms are packed with opera memorabilia, including plaster casts of the hands of famous conductors and Verdi's top hat. (Open Mon.-Sat. 9am-noon and 2-6pm, Sun. 9am-noon; Oct.-April closed Sun. Admission L5000.)

Pass the 16th-century Palazzo Marino (opposite La Scala and now the mayor's office) and the side of the **Church of San Fedele** (1569); you will arrive at the curious **Casa degli Omenoni** (1565), embellished with eight giant figures of the worldly Atlas. The street ends at **Piazza Belgioioso,** a pleasant square of old Milan dominated by the 18th-century Belgioioso *palazzo* and the house of 19th-century novelist Alessandro Manzoni. The **Museo Manzoniano**, at Via Morone, 1 (tel. 87 10 19), is devoted to his life and works. Among the portraits of his friends is an autographed likeness of Goethe. (Open Tues.-Fri. 9:30am-noon and 2-4pm. Free.) Farther along down Via Morone you'll come to the entrance to Via Manzoni, the medieval **Porta Nuova**—it's a Roman tomb sculpture and a Gothic niche cradling statues of saints. The **Museo Poldi-Pezzoli,** Via Manzoni, 12 (tel. 79 48 89), contains an outstanding private collection of art bequeathed to the city in 1879. The museum's masterpieces are hung in the Golden Room, which overlooks a verdant garden. The paintings include a Byzantine *Virgin and Child* by Andrea Mantegna, Bellini's *Ecce Homo, St. Nicholas* by Piero della Francesca, the magical *Gray Lagoon* by Guardi; and the museum's signature piece, Antonio Pollaiolo's *Portrait of a Young Woman.* (Open Tues.-Fri. 9am-12:30pm and 2:30-6pm, Sat. 9:30am-12:30pm and 2:30-7:30pm, Sun. 9:30am-12:30pm. Admission L10,000.)

Near Castello Sforzesco

The enormous 15th-century **Castello Sforzesco** (tel. 62 36 39 47; MM1: Cairoli), restored after heavy bomb damage in 1943, is one of Milan's best-known monuments. The first interior court is so vast that architectural details seem to disappear, while the more enclosed, lesser courtyards are noted for their Renaissance arcades. On the ground floor is a sculpture collection renowned for Michelangelo's unfinished *Pietà Rondanini,* his last work. The picture gallery features paintings by Mantegna, Bellini, and other Renaissance masters, as well as *Madonna with Angels* by Fra Filippo Lippi. (Open Tues.-Sun. 9:30am-5:30pm. Free.)

Via Verdi, alongside La Scala, leads to **Via Brera,** another charming street lined with small, brightly colored palaces and art galleries just a few steps from the *duomo* (MM1: Cordusio; for doorstep service, catch bus #61 from MM1: Moscova). The **Pinacoteca di Brera** (Brera Art Gallery), Via Brera, 28 (tel. 72 26 31), presents an impressive collection of paintings in a 17th-century *palazzo.* Paintings include Bellini's *Pietà* (1460), Andrea Mantegna's brilliantly foreshortened *Dead Christ* (1480), Raphael's *Marriage of the Virgin* (1504), Caravaggio's *Supper at Emmaus* (1606), and Piero della Francesca's 15th-century *Madonna and Child with Saints* and *Duke Federico di Montefeltro.* The vibrant, animated frescoes by Bramante from the *Casa dei Panigarola* provide comic relief from the dramatic intensity of these works. A limited but well-chosen collection of works by modern masters including Modigliani and Carlo Carrà serves as an even more striking contrast. (Open Tues.-Sat. 9am-5:30pm, Sun. 9am-12:30pm. Admission L8000.)

The **Church of Santa Maria delle Grazie,** on P. di Sta. Maria delle Grazie and Corso Magenta off Via Carducci (MM1: Cairoli, or take bus #21 and 24), is renowned for the splendid tribune Bramante added in 1492. Inside, the Gothic nave with its tunnel-like vaults is juxtaposed with the airiness of the Bramante addition. To the left, a door leads to an elegant square cloister, the artist's other contribution to the church. Next to the church entrance in what was the monastery's refectory is the **Cenacolo Vinciano** (tel. 498 75 88), containing **Leonardo da Vinci's** *Last Supper* (closed for restoration through mid-1995). The fresco captures the apostles' reaction to Jesus' prophecy that "One of you will betray me." Scaffolding for an eternal restoration project covers only the bottom of the fresco, leaving the rest in full view. (Open Tues.-Sun. 8:15am-1:45pm. Admission to Cenacolo L12,000. Wheelchair accessible.) To further your study of da Vinci, explore the **Museo Nazionale della Scienza e della Tecnica "Leonardo da Vinci,"** Via San Vittore, 21 (tel. 48 01 00 40, MM1: San Ambrogio or bus #50 or 54), off Via Carducci. A large section is devoted to applied physics, and a huge room is filled with wooden models of Leonardo's most ingenious and visionary inventions. (Open Tues.-Sun. 9:30am-4:50pm. Admission L10,000.)

The **Church of Sant'Ambrogio** (MM1: San Ambrogio), which served as a prototype for Lombard-Romanesque churches throughout Italy, is the most influential medieval building in Milan. Ninth-century reliefs in brilliant silver and gold decorate the high altar. The crypt contains the gruesome skeletal remains of Sant'Ambrogio and two early Christian martyrs. The tiny 4th-century **Chapel of San Vittore,** with exquisite 5th-century mosaics adorning its cupola, is through the seventh chapel on the right. As you leave the church on the left, you will pass under the peculiar **Portico della Canonica** (1492) by Bramante, the end columns of which have notches resembling those of tree trunks. There's also a small museum housing a collection of works from the 4th century AD (tel. 86 45 08 95; open Mon.-Fri. 10am-noon and 3-5pm. Admission L3000).

Continue your spiritual pilgrimage to the land of the dead. The vast grounds of the **Cimitero Monumentale,** several blocks east of Stazione Porta Garibaldi, are a labyrinthine network of three-story mausoleums in architectural styles ranging from Egyptian pyramids to Art Deco jukeboxes.

From Corso di Porta Romana to the Navigli

The distances between sights are greater here—consider public transportation.

At the **Church of San Nazaro Maggiore,** on Corso di Porta Romana (MM3: Crocieta), a medieval Lombard-Romanesque structure conceals the remnants of a 4th-century *basilica*. The Renaissance funerary chapel of the Trivulzio in front is the work of Bramante's pupil Bramantino (1512-1547). The tomb bears the famous epigraph: *Qui numquam quivit quiescit: Tasc* (He who never knew quiet now reposes: Silence). (Open daily 8:30am-noon and 3 6:30pm.)

The **Church of San Lorenzo Maggiore,** on Corso Ticinese (MM2: Porta Genova, then tram #3 from Via Torino), is the oldest church in Milan, and testifies to the greatness of the city during the Paleo-Christian era. The building began as an early Christian church in the mid-4th century, and although it was rebuilt later (12th-century *campanile* and 16th-century dome), it retains its original octagonal plan. To the right of the church sits the 14th-century chapel of Sant'Aquilino. Inside is a 4th-century mosaic of a young, beardless Christ among his apostles. A staircase behind the altar leads to the remains of an early Roman amphitheater. (Church open Mon.-Sat. 8am-noon and 3-6pm, Sun. 10:30-11:15am and 3-5:30pm.) Near the front of the church is the 12th-century **Porta Ticinese.**

Farther down Corso Ticinese (bus #15) stands the **Church of Sant'Eustorgio** (tel. 835 15 83), founded in the 4th century to house the reputed bones of the Magi, spirited off to Cologne in 1164. The present building (erected in 1278) has a typical Lombard-Gothic interior of low vaults and brick ribs supported by heavy columns. The real gem of this church, and one of the great masterpieces of early Renaissance art, is the **Portinari Chapel** (1468), attributed to the Florentine Michelozzo (chapel closed for restoration in 1995). A *Dance of Angels* is carved around the base of the multicolored dome, and frescoes depict the life and death of Peter the Martyr. In the center of the chapel is the magnificent Gothic tomb of St. Eustorgius (1339), by Giovanni di Balduccio of Pisa. (Church open daily 8am-noon and 3-7pm.)

Through the Neoclassical Arco di Porta Ticinese (1801-1814), or outside the Porta Genova station (MM2), you will find the **navigli district,** the Venice of Lombardy: canals, small footbridges, open-air markets, alleys, and trolleys. This is the part of the medieval canal system (whose original locks were designed by Leonardo da Vinci) that linked northern cities and lakes.

MILAN

South and East of the Duomo

The long, arched 1456 **Ospedale Maggiore,** on Via Festa del Perdono near P. Santo Stefano, is one of the largest constructions of the early Renaissance. The "General Hospital"—now the University of Milan—contains nine courtyards. Inside is a magnificent 17th-century court and a gracious smaller one credited to Bramante. In 1479, Bramante designed the mystical **Church of San Satiro** on Via Torino, a few blocks (or a few minutes' ride on bus #15) from the *duomo.* Despite its modest proportions, the interior creates the illusion of wide spaces. Compare the imaginary and the real by standing at the back of the church and then behind the high altar. (Open daily 9am-noon and 2:30-6pm.)

Following Via Spadari off Via Torino and then making a right onto Via Cantù will deposit you at the tiny but lovely **Pinacoteca Ambrosiana,** P. Pio XI, 2 (tel. 86 45 14 36). The 14 rooms of the Ambrosiana house exquisite works from the 15th through 17th centuries, including Botticelli's *Madonna of the Canopy,* Leonardo's *Portrait of a Musician,* Raphael's cartoon for the *School of Athens,* Caravaggio's *Basket of Fruit,* the first example of still-life painting in Italy, and the two paintings of *Earth* and *Air* by Breughel. (Closed for renovation until 1996.)

East of the *duomo,* **Corso Vittorio Emanuele,** between P. del Duomo and P. San Babila, is the major shopping street of the city. The street was entirely rebuilt after the war. Off P. San Babila, **Via Monte Napoleon,** the most elegant street in Milan, is lined with early 19th-century *palazzi* and late 20th-century Armanis and Cardins. The part of **Corso Venezia** bordering the Giardini Pubblici is a broad boulevard lined with sumptuous palaces. Don't miss a stroll through the English-style **Giardini Pubblici** on a sunny afternoon. (Open roughly 7am-10pm.) A small **zoo** lies within the grounds (open 9:30am-5pm).

The **Galleria d'Arte Moderna,** Via Palestro, 16 (tel. 76 00 28 19), is next to the Giardini Pubblici in the Neoclassical Villa Comunale (MM2: Porta Venezia). Napoleon lived here with Josephine when Milan was capital of the Napoleonic Kingdom of Italy (1805-1814). Important modern Lombard art is displayed here, as well as works by Picasso, Matisse, Renoir, Gauguin, and Cézanne. (Open Tues.-Sun. 9:30am-5:30pm. Free.) Another worthwhile museum is the **Museo di Milano** (tel. 78 37 97) on Via Sant'Andrea, 6, which shows Italian art and shares an 18th-century mansion with the petite **Museo di Storia Contemporanea** (Museum of Contemporary History; MM2: San Babila). (Both open Tues.-Sun. 9:30am-5:30pm. Free.) Also check out the **Museo Civico di Storia Naturale** (Museum of Natural History) on Corso Venezia, 55 (tel. 62 08 54 05), in the Giardino Pubblico. It holds extensive geology and paleontology collections, including a room of complete dinosaur skeletons. (Closed for restoration until 1996.)

ENTERTAINMENT

Music, Theater, and Film

Emblematic of the blend of populism and posh that characterizes the arts scene in Milan is the **Musica in Metro** program, a series of summer concerts in subway stations performed by local music students dressed in their black-tie best. Those who turn professional await the chance of performing at **La Scala,** which traditionally opens its opera season on December 7 (though there are other productions year-round). Good tickets are usually sold out long in advance, but gallery seats (notorious for inducing altitude sickness) go for as little as L30,000. (Box office tel. 72 00 37 44, open daily noon-7pm. Two hundred gallery standing-room tickets go on sale 30min. before the show at the entrance of the *museo.*) The **Conservatorio,** Via del Conservatorio, 12 (tel. 76 00 17 55), near P. Tricolore, offers more classical music, while the **Teatro Lirico,** Via Larga, 14 (tel. 72 33 32 22), south of the *duomo,* is Milan's leading stage, offering everything from ballet to avant-garde plays. (Ticket office open Mon.-Fri. 10am-7pm; admission L50,000). Summer brings special programs of music and culture: **Milano d'Estate** (Milan in Summer) in July, and **Vacanze a Milano** (Vacation in Milan) in August.

The **Piccolo Teatro,** Via Rovello, 2, near Via Dante, began in the post-war years as a socialist theater and is now owned by the city. (Performances Tues.-Sun. 8:30pm.) **Ciak,** Via Sangallo, 33 (tel. 76 11 00 93), near P. Argonne east of the *duomo,* is a favorite haunt of young *Milanesi* for theater, films, and occasionally cabaret. Take train #5 from Stazione Centrale to Viale Argonne.

The **Teatro di Porta Romana,** Corso di Porta Romana, 124 (tel. 58 31 58 96; bus #13 from Via Marconi off P. del Duomo), is building a reputation for experimental productions and first-run mainstream plays (admission about L20,000). **Teatri d'Italia** (tel. 58 31 58 96) sponsors **Milan Oltre** in June and July, a festival of drama, dance, music and much more (call the City Coucil for Culture, tel. 86 46 40 94, for more info). For a different brand of street theater, the **Carnevale** in Milan is increasingly popular. As the crowds in Venice sport fewer costumes and more cameras each year, many come here instead for the friendlier atmosphere. Tickets for all performances are sold at the corresponding venue but can also be purchased through **La Biglietteria,** Corso Garibaldi, 81 (tel. 659 01 88).

Milan's cinematic scene thrives. Check any Milanese paper (especially the Thursday edition) for showings and general info, and remember that shows on Wednesdays are L7,000 (usually L10,000). In summer the **Cinema nel Parco** festival offers outdoor showings of recent films (L8000; at Villa Ghirlanda tel. 617 30 05 or 66 02 35 01). Old movies can be seen at the **Cineteca Italiana/Museo del Cinema,** Via Manin, 2/B (tel. 655 49 77; open Tues.-Fri. 3-6pm; admission L4000).

Clubs

Once again, check any Milanese paper on Wednesday or Thursday for info on clubs and events that weekend. *Corriere Della Sera* publishes an insert called *22 Milano* on Wednesday; *La Repubblica* produces *Tutto Milano* on Thursday. *Milano Magazine* comes out every two weeks with info on bars, films, and seasonal events. Although listings are in Italian, names and addresses of clubs will be helpful even for the Italiano-impaired. The APT tourist office also has helpful handouts (see above). In general, Milan parties Thursday-Sunday nights and rests up during the beginning of the week. Many of the clubs listed below have different "theme nights," and cover charges vary accordingly. Remember that everything shuts down in August, and clubs often reincarnate themselves in a totally different form in September.

When night falls, Milano's youth migrates to the areas around **Porta Ticinese** and **Piazza Vetra.** Hang out on the grass in the parks (soccer games and guitar players will entertain you), or grab a beer at one of the many *birrerie* (pubs). A safe, attractive, and chic district lies by **Via Brera;** here you'll find art galleries, small clubs, restaurants, and a thirtysomething crowd. If you do decide to head for the *discoteche,* though, expect a cover charge around L15,000 or a mandatory first drink.

Rock: Rolling Stone, Corso XXII Marzo, 32 (tel. 73 31 72), east of the *duomo.* Easy on hip and heavy on chic. Open Thurs.-Sun. until 3am. Cover L12,000-25,000. **Plastic,** Viale Umbria, 120 (tel. 73 39 96). Verging on disco, it swings between a punk/new wave and a fashionable New York crowd. Cover L15,000, Sat. L18,000. Open Tues.-Sun. until 3am. **New Magazine,** Strada Via Piceno, 3 (tel. 70 10 33 27). Close to Rolling Stone and Plastic. Crunchy atmosphere accentuated by peanut shells on the floor softens the orange and yellow neon paintings. Busier in winter. Open Tues.-Sun. evenings.

Jazz and Folk: Capolinea, Via Ludovico il Moro, 119 (tel. 89 12 20 24). Walk out Corso Italia toward the Navigli and Porta Ticinese, south of the *duomo.* A student crowd. Cover L15,000 (includes first drink). Open Tues.-Sun. until 1:30am. **Le Scimmie,** Via Ascanio Sforza, 49 (tel. 89 40 28 74), beyond the Capolinea. Milan's premier jazz spot. Open Wed.-Mon. 8pm-2am.

Discos: Madame Claude, Via Borgogna, 5 (tel. 76 01 10 62), decorated in Louis XIV and popular with local personalities. Cover L20,000-25,000. Open Thurs.-Sun. **Open House,** Via Carducci, 25 (tel. 869 26 25), popular with the university crowd. Theme nights. Cover L25,000, Sat. L30,000. Closed Sun.

Gay Bars and Clubs: Cicip e Ciciap, Via Gorani, 9 (tel. 87 75 55). Bar, also a restaurant in the evenings; women only. Open Tues.-Sun. **Nuova Idea,** Via de Castilla, 30 (MM2: Gioia), usually men only; women welcome Sat. and holidays. Open evenings Thurs.-Sun. **One Way,** Via Cavallotti Sesto San Giovanni, 204, in inner Milan. Disco and leather. Open Tues., and Fri.-Sun. **Sottomarino Giallo,** Via Donatello, 2, (tel. 29 40 10 47), women-only club. Open Tues.-Sun. **Towanda!,** Via Imonate, 3 (tel. 69 00 88 68), women-only bar. Open evenings Thurs.-Sun. **Uitibar,** Via Monvisa, 14 (tel. 331 59 96), mixed. Open Tues.-Sun. 8:30pm-2am.

Neither Fish nor Fowl: Ipotesi Latino Americana, Piazza XXIV Maggio, 8 (tel. 832 21 60), has—yes—Latin American music. Very popular. Cover L15,000. Open Wed.-Sun. **Leoncavallo,** Via Watteau, 7 (tel. 26 14 02 87). Dress as badly as you want. Cover rarely exceeds L5000. **New Zimba** ("lion" in Swahili), Via Natale Battaglia, 12 (tel. 26 14 42 65). Congo, rhythm and blues, and Caribbean music. Open Tues.-Sun. 10:30pm-3am.

No Cover Charge: Ebony Note, Via Bocconi (tel. 58 90 16 51), everything from Reggae to world music. Open Tues.-Fri. **Bataclan,** Piazzale Biancamano, 2 (tel. 657 28 12), plays different music every night. Drinks L8,000. Open Tues.-Sun.

SHOPPING

Milan's most elegant boutiques are found between the *duomo* and P. S. Babila, especially on the excessively chic **Via Monte Napoleone** and off **P. Babila** at **Via Spiga.** If you can tolerate the stigma of being an entire season behind the trends, purchase your famous designer duds from *blochisti* (wholesale clothing outlets). Try **Monitor** on Viale Monte Nero (MM2: Porta Genova, then bus #9), or **Il Salvagente,** on Via Bronzetti off Corso XXII Marzo (bus #60). More affordable, yet still well-designed, is the clothing sold along **Corso Buenos Aires,** and both **Via Torino,** near the *duomo,* and **Via Sarpi,** near Porta Garibaldi, are decked out in inexpensive department stores and boutiques catering to a younger crowd. Shop around the area of Corso di Porta Ticinese for *chic ma non snob* (hip) attire (MM2: Porta Genova, then bus #59). **Eliogabalo,** P. Sant'Eustorgio, 2 (tel. 837 82 93), named after a Roman emperor renowned for his preoccupation with aesthetics, offers the latest in *haute couture.* Reasonable prices for everything from clothes to groceries can be found at the **STANDA** department store at Via Torino, 45 (tel. 86 67 06), five blocks from the *duomo.* Photo booth, photocopy machine, and shoe repair are on the third floor. (Open daily 9am-7:30pm). True Milanese bargain hunters attack the giant street markets on Saturday and Tuesday to buy their threads. These are on **Via Fauché** (MM2: Garibaldi), **Viale Papinian** (MM2: Sant'Agostino) and the 400-year-old **Fiera di Sinigallia** on Via Calatafimi (Sat. only). For used clothing, try the Navigli district or Corso Garibaldi. Shop at the end of July for the pre-Ferragosto sale wars (20-50% off). (Clothing stores are generally open Mon. 10am-noon, Tues.-Sat. 10am-noon and 2-7:30pm.) Another fabulous option is the classy Italian department store **La Rinascente,** to the left of the *duomo* (as you face it). Keep in mind that shops in Milan close Monday mornings.

■■■ PAVIA

Once an important Roman outpost, Pavia weathered Attila the Hun in 452 before entering the limelight as the Lombard capital during the 7th and 8th centuries. Spanish, Austrian, and French forces governed Pavia in rapid succession from the 16th century until 1859, when Italy's independence movement liberated the city. With the help of agricultural and industrial development, today's Pavia has returned to a state of prosperity. Romanesque churches dating from Pavia's tranquil years as a Milanese satellite are scattered throughout the historic sector, and the 14th-century university continues to flourish. Though the center of town bustles with daily student activity, the city manages to retain the tranquility of a small town. The once-prominent city's status as an offbeat tourist locale is evident in the confidence with which non-Italians mispronounce its name (hint: emphasize the second syllable).

PAVIA

ORIENTATION AND PRACTICAL INFORMATION

Pavia is a mere 35km south of Milan, on the train line to Genoa (30min.). The city sits on the banks of the Ticino river not far from its intersection with the Po. The train station overlooks **Piazzale Stazionale** in the modern, west end of the town, which is linked to the historic center by a walk down **Viale Vittorio Emanuele II**, leading to **Piazzale Minerva**, and then to Pavia's main drag, **Corso Cavour**. This leads to the city's central square, **P. Vittorio**, which is connected to **P. Duomo**.

Tourist Office: Via F. Filzi, 2 (tel. 221 56; fax 322 21), in a characterless section of town. Take a left on Via Triest from station and then right on Filzi. Friendly staff speaks English and hands out a good map. Ask for the booklet *Pavia and its Province*. Open Mon.-Sat. 8:30am-12:30pm and 2-6pm.

Police: P. Italia, 5 (tel. 112).

Post Office: P. della Posta, 2 (tel. 212 51), off Via Mentana, 1 block over from Corso Mazzini. Stamps and *fermo posta* at #5. Open Mon.-Sat. 8am-7pm. **Postal Code:** 27100.

Telephones: Telecom, Via Galliano, 8 (tel. 38 21), around the corner from the post office. Open Mon.-Fri. 9am-12:30pm and 2:30-6pm. **Telephone Code:** 0382.

Trains: (tel. 230 00) at the head of Viale V. Emanuele II at the west end of town. To: Genoa (every 30min.-1hr., L9800); Milan (every 30min., L3400); Cremona (4 per day, L6500); Mantua (4 per day, L11,700); change at Codogno for Cremona and Mantua. **Luggage Storage:** L1500. Open 7am-7pm.

Buses: SGEA (tel. 30 20 20), departing from the space-age station on Via Triest (left from the train station). To Milan (every hr. 5am-10pm, 1hr., L4400) via the *certosa* (charterhouse, 15min., L2000).

Taxi: tel. 274 39.

English Bookstore: Libreria Ticinum, Corso Mazzini 2/C (tel. 30 39 16), off P. Vittoria. A small selection of classics and bestsellers. Open Tues.-Sun. 9am-12:30pm and 3-7:30pm. MC, Visa.

Pharmacy: Vilani, Via Bossolaro, 31 (tel. 223 15), at the corner of P. Duomo. Well-stocked with homeopathic supplies. List of pharmacies with night service. Open Mon.-Fri. 8:30am-12:30pm and 3:30-7:30pm.

Emergencies: tel. 113. **Hospital: Ospedale S. Matteo,** P. Golgi, 2 (tel. 50 11). **Medical Assistance/Ambulance:** tel. 52 77 77, nights and holidays tel. 52 76 00.

ACCOMMODATIONS AND CAMPING

A dearth of reasonably priced places to stay makes Pavia most appealing as a daytrip. Inquire at the tourist office about the current condition of the youth hostel at Vaghera. Another valuable option is to take advantage of the well-organized *agriturismo* program. Ask at the tourist office for a complete pamphlet.

Hotel Splendid, Via XX Settembre, 11 (tel. 247 03), off Corso Cavour near P. del Duomo. The Splendid is the last of Pavia's one-stars that has not been converted to student housing. Clean sheets and floors, whitewashed walls, and slightly mildewy showers. Singles L35,000. Doubles L60,000. Breakfast L6000-8000.

Camping: Ticino, Via Mascherpa, 10 (tel. 52 70 94). From the station, take bus #4 (toward Mascherpa) for about 10min.; get off at the Chiozzo stop. L6000 per person. L5000 for a small tent; L7000 for a large tent. Hot shower L500. Restaurant next door. Pool nearby about L7000; L10,000 on the weekends. Open March-Oct.

FOOD

Coniglio (rabbit) and *rana* (frog) are the local specialties, but if you don't eat things that hop and jump, stick to the local pastries on display in shop windows along Corso Cavour and Corso Mazzini. Another well-loved dish is *zuppa alla pavese,* piping hot chicken or beef broth with a poached egg floating on top and sprinkled with grated *grana* cheese. **Esselunga** (tel. 262 10) is a huge supermarket at the far end of the mall complex between Via Triest and Viale Battisti. (Open Mon. 1-9pm, Tues.-Sat. 8am-9pm).

Ristorante Pizzeria Marechiaro, P. Vittoria, 9 (tel. 237 39). Delicious pizza with exquisite crust, prepared before your eyes (L5000-15,000). Crowded, cozy atmosphere. Summertime diners overflow onto the *piazza.* Cover L3000. Open Tues.-Sun. 11am-3pm and 6pm-3am. AmEx, MC, Visa.

Pizzeria/Ristorante Regisole, P. Duomo, 4 (tel. 247 39), under the arcade facing the *duomo.* A/C and outdoor seating available. Reasonably-priced pizzas, including a *margherita* for L5000. *Primi* from L5000. *Secondi* from L10,000. Open Wed.-Mon. noon-3pm and 7pm-midnight. AmEx, MC, Visa.

Bar Pampanin, P. Vittoria 20/B (tel. 291 67). Ask anyone in Pavia where to get *gelato* and they'll pipe "Pampanin!" Interesting flavors, including the tart, thirst-quenching *pompelmo* (grapefruit), and a spaghetti sundae made with vanilla *gelato,* whipped cream and strawberry sauce. Cones L2500-3500. Open Thurs.-Tues. 10am-2am.

SIGHTS AND ENTERTAINMENT

For centuries the **Church of San Michele** (tel. 260 63) was the favored venue for coronations of Northern Italian kings, including Charlemagne in 774 and Frederick Barbarossa in 1155. Though it was rebuilt in the Romanesque style, this 7th-century church retains a heavy medieval feel. Decorating the chancel are a 1491 fresco of the *Coronation of the Virgin* and bas-reliefs from the 14th century. The 8th-century silver crucifix of Theodote graces the chapel to the right of the presbytery. To get to San Michele, go down Corso Garibaldi and turn right after Via della Rochetta. (Open daily 8am-noon and 3-6pm.)

From San Michele it's a short walk to what's left of Pavia's layered brick **duomo,** officially entitled the **Cattedrale Monumentale di Santo Stefano Martiro.** The **Torre Civica,** adjoining the *duomo,* collapsed in the spring of 1989, killing several people and taking with it a good portion of the *duomo's* left-hand chapel, as well as some nearby houses and shops. Disputes over what ought to be done with the rubble have led to a lackadaisical restoration, and the *piazza* is still garnished with barricades and scaffolding. The shaky brick exterior of the *duomo,* recently reinforced by concrete columns, conceals an impressive interior. Begun in 1488 and influenced by the designs of Bramante, Macaluso, and Leonardo, the *duomo* was one of the most ambitious undertakings of the Renaissance in Lombardy—naturally, much of it was not actually completed until 1895-1933. The huge interior space in the form of a Greek cross is typical of a Renaissance central-plan church.

The prestigious **University of Pavia,** founded in 1361 (tel. 50 41), sprawls along Strada Nuova. It claims such famous alumni as Petrarch, Columbus, and the Venetian playwright Goldoni. The university's most electrifying exponent, however, was the physicist Alessandro Volta (his experiments are on display at the university). And the patron of the university, Galeazzo II of Visconti, earned notoriety for his research into human torture. The three towers rising from the university's property on P. Leonardo da Vinci are the remnants of more than 100 medieval towers that once punctuated the city's skyline.

Strada Nuova ends at the **Castello Visconteo** (tel. 338 53), a colossal medieval castle (1360) set in a park that once extended to the Certosa di Pavia, the Visconti's private hunting ground 8km away. The castle's vast courtyard is bordered on three sides by richly colored windows and elegant terra-cotta decoration. The fourth wall was destroyed in 1527 during the Franco-Spanish Wars. Pavia's **Civic Museum** (tel. 338 53), located here, houses a picture gallery and an extensive Lombard-Romanesque sculpture collection. (Open June-Nov. Tues.-Sat. 9am-noon, Sun. 9am-12:30pm. Admission L5000, under 18 L2500.)

From the front grounds of the castle, you can see the low rounded forms of the Lombard-Romanesque **Church of San Pietro in Ciel d'Oro** (1132) (tel. 30 30 36). Inside on the high altar is a marble reliquary containing the remains of St. Augustine in an ornate Gothic ark. (Open daily 8am-noon and 3-6pm.)

■ NEAR PAVIA

Eight kilometers north of Pavia stands the **Certosa di Pavia** (Charterhouse of Pavia; tel. 92 56 13; ask to speak with Padre Tebreab). This Carthusian monastery and mausoleum was built for the Visconti who ruled the area from the 12th to 15th centuries, and summarizes four centuries of Italian art, from early Gothic to Baroque. The exuberant façade (late 1400s-1560) revels in sculpture and inlaid marble, representing the apex of the Lombard Renaissance. The Old Sacristy houses a Florentine triptych carved in ivory, with 99 sculptures and 66 bas-reliefs depicting the lives of Mary and Jesus. The monks lead delightful tours of the complex whenever a large enough group has gathered (usually every 45min.), leaving from inside the church. (Open Tues.-Sun. 9-11:30am and 2:30-6pm, March-April and Sept.-Oct. Tues.-Sun. 9-11:30am and 2:30-5pm, Nov.-Feb. Tues.-Sun. 9-11:30am and 2:30-4:30pm. Free.)

Both buses and trains can deposit you nearby. **Buses** leave Pavia from the Via Triest station (L2000) and Milan from P. Castello (L3300). From the bus stop, the *certosa* awaits you at the end of a long road lined with trees. From the **train station,** go left around the outside wall of the monastic complex and turn inside to the right at the first opening.

■■■ CREMONA

Cremona is best known for its music, which dates back to Andrea Amati, who created the violin in 1530 and established the Cremonese violin-making dynasty. Having learned the fundamentals as apprentices in the Amati workshop, Antonio Stradivari (1644-1737) and Giuseppe Guarneri (1687-1745) lifted the art of violin-making to unprecedented heights. Students from all over the world still come to learn the legendary craft at the International School for Violin-Making, ever hopeful of stumbling upon the formula of Stradivari's secret varnish. Though Cremona's earth-toned buildings create a somewhat sober atmosphere, an ever-active concert season at the Ponchielli Theater and some of the most remarkable architecture in all of Lombardy lend the city a more than compensatory dose of color and life.

ORIENTATION AND PRACTICAL INFORMATION

As you walk from the train station to the cluster of *piazze* at the city's historical core, **Via Palestro** becomes first **Via Campi** and then **Via Verdi,** right before **Piazza Cavour.** A left at Piazza Cavour or Piazza Pace leads to the **Piazza del Comune,** location of both the *duomo* and *torrazzo,* as well as the tourist office. If the 15-minute walk doesn't appeal to you, jump on bus #1 (L1300). Most Cremonese desert the city in July and August.

Tourist Office: P. del Duomo, 5 (tel. 232 33). Friendly staff. English spoken. Ask for the *Carnet Dell'Ospite* brochure for information on hotels, museums, and restaurants. Open Mon.-Sat. 9:30am-12:30pm and 3-6pm, Sun. 10am-noon.

Police, Viale T. Triest, 58 (tel. 48 81).

Post Office: Via Verdi, 21 (tel. 282 39). Open Mon.-Fri. 8am-5:30pm, Sat. 8am-1pm. **Postal Code:** 26100.

Telephones: Telecom (SIP), Via Cadorini, 3 (tel. 239 11). Open Mon.-Fri. 9am-12:30pm and 2:30-6pm. After hours, try the phone booths in P. Roma. **Telephone Code:** 0372.

Budget Travel: Centro Turistico Studentesco, Via Ingegneri, 7 (tel. 41 28 78). Open Mon.-Fri. 10am-noon and 3-5:30pm, Sat. 10am-noon.

Trains: Via Dante, 68 (tel. 222 37). Ask for P. Stazione. To: Milan (10 per day, 1¼hr., L7200); Pavia (2 per day, 1¾hr., L6500); Mantua (16 per day, 1hr., L5700); and Brescia (every hr., ¾hr., L5000).

Buses: Autostazione di Via Dante (tel. 292 12), to the left of the train station. To: Milan (8 per day, 2hr., L6700); Bergamo (4 per day, 1.8100); and Brescia (every hr., L7100). Tickets at the station (open 7:20am-1pm and 2:15-6:30pm) or across

CREMONA

the street at **La Pasticceria Mezzadri,** Via Dante, 105 (tel. 257 08; open daily 6am-8pm).
Taxi: tel. 213 00 or 267 40.
Emergencies: tel. 113. **Medical Assistance and Ambulance:** tel. 118. **Hospital: Ospedale** (tel. 40 51 11), in Largo Priori, past P. IV Novembre to the east.

ACCOMMODATIONS

While lodging runs cheap in Cremona, it can be difficult to find a room, especially during the week. If you want to stay in the summer, reserve ahead.

Albergo Touring, Via Palestro, 3 (tel. 369 76). From the station, walk across Via Dante and straight down Via Palestro. Singles L30,000. Doubles L50,000, with bath L70,000. Breakfast L5000.

Albergo Brescia, Via Brescia, 7 (tel. 43 46 15). A 20-min. walk to the left down Via Dante and a left at P. Libertà, or take bus #1, 3, 4, or 6 from the station. Nice management, clean bathrooms, and functional rooms that are booked solid during the week. Singles L45,000. Doubles L55,000. Triples L73,000. Half pension L50,000 per person; full pension L65,000. MC, Visa.

Albergo Bologna, P. Risorgimento, 8 (tel. 242 58), above a *pizzeria.* Very small singles only, L30,000. Reservations recommended. **Restaurant** Sat.-Thurs. noon-2:30pm and 7pm-midnight. Pizzas around L8000, *primi* (L8000-10,000) and *secondi* (L10,000-15,000). Cover L2000. MC, Visa.

Camping: Parco al Po (tel. 212 68), on Via Lungo Po Europa southwest of town. From P. Cavour, walk 20min. down Corso Vittorio Emanuele. L6000 per person, car and tent L11,000, camper L12,000. Showers and electricity included. Open May-Sept.

FOOD

First created in the 16th century, Cremona's bizarre *mostarda di Cremona* consists of a hodgepodge of fruits—cherries, figs, apricots, melons—preserved in a sweet mustard syrup and served on boiled meats. Bars of *torrone* (nougat with an egg, honey, and nut base) are less adventurous but equally steeped in Cremonese confectionery lore. *Mostarda* can be found in most local *trattorie,* while *torrone* can be purchased in the sweet shops on Via Solferino. **Spelari** (#25; tel. 223 46), has been keeping dentists in business since 1836. (*Torrone* L11,000. Open Mon. 8:30am-12:30pm, Tues.-Sat. 8:30am-12:30pm and 3:30-7:30pm.) For something a little less sweet, try the Grana Padono or the Provolone cheeses in the local *salumerie.* On Wednesday and Saturday from 8am-1pm, there is an **open-air market** in P. Marconi, past P. Cavour on Corso Verdi. For **supermarkets,** try either **CRAI** at P. Risorgimento, 30 (open Mon. 8am-12:30pm, Tues.-Sat. 8am-12:30pm and 4:30-7:30pm), or **GS** at Via San Tommaso, 9 (tel. 336 33; open Mon. 1-8pm, Tues.-Sat. 8am-8pm).

Ristorante Pizzeria Marechiano, Corso Campi, 49 (tel. 262 89). An attractive little place on the main window-shopping street. *Menù* L20,000, pizza from L6000. Cover L2500, L2000 for pizza. Open Wed.-Mon. noon-3pm and 6pm-1am. MC, Visa.

Ristorante Tonino, Via Antico Rodano, 9 (tel 286 87), a side street off the intersection between Via Palermo and Corso Garibaldi. *Primi* from L6000, *secondi* from L7000, pizza from L5000. Open Thurs.-Tues. noon-2:30pm and 7pm-1am.

La Bersagliera, P. Risorgimento, 12 (tel. 213 97), on the corner of Via Ghinaglia. Locals lavish praise on this family-owned establishment serving Neapolitan cuisine. Pizzas L6000-14,000. Try the *pizza Cremonese* (L11,000), with tomatoes, gorgonzola, and spinach. *Primi* L5000-10,000, *secondi* L7000-18,000. Cover L2500. Open Thurs.-Tues. noon-3pm and 7-10:30pm. AmEx, MC, Visa.

SIGHTS AND ENTERTAINMENT

Violins and their production are the primary attraction in Cremona. Closest to the train station, the small **Museo Stradivariano,** at Via Palestro, 17 (tel. 46 18 86), provides a fascinating introduction to the art of Stradivari and his contemporaries.

(Open Tues.-Sun. 8:30am-6pm. Admission L5000, groups L3000. Ticket is good for the Palazzo del Comune, the Museo Ala Ponzone, the Museo Stradivariano, the Museo Storia Naturale, and the Museo Civiltà Contadina. The ticket, good for five days, can be bought at any of the five museums.) On the second floor of the **Palazzo del Comune** in P. del Comune, decorated with 16th-century Renaissance terra-cottas, the **Saletta dei Violini (Violin Room)** showcases five masterpieces attributed to Andrea Amati, his grandson Nicolò Amati, Stradivari, and Guarneri. (Open June to mid-Aug. Tues.-Sat. 8:30am-6pm, Sun. 9:15am-12:15pm and 3-6pm.)

Directly facing the *palazzo* is the 12th-century pink marble **duomo** (officially known as **Santa Mari'Assunta**), a fine example of the Lombard-Romanesque style. The interior houses a cycle of 16th-century frescoes and, unfortunately, is undergoing restoration, though it is still open. (Open Mon.-Sat. 7am-noon and 3-7pm, Sun. 7am-1pm and 3:30-7pm.) To the left of the cathedral stands the late 13th-century **Torrazzo**, at 108m the tallest *campanile* in Italy. (Scale the heights in good weather, Easter-Nov. 1. Mon.-Sat. 10:30am-noon and 3-6pm, Sun. 10:30am-12:30pm and 3-7pm. Admission L5000.) The dome of the solid 1167 **baptistery** rises in a perfect, unadorned octagonal pattern. (Closed for renovations for at least a year; contact the tourist office for updated information.) The **Loggia dei Militi,** across from the baptistery, completes the square. Erected in 1292 in Gothic style, it functioned as a meeting place for the captains of the citizens' militia. The Gothic **Church of Sant'Agostino** (1345), near Via Plasio, contains Bonifacio Bembo frescoes and a *Madonna with Saints* by Perugino (1494).

Cremona is also endowed with fine Renaissance buildings, including the **Palazzo Fodri** (1499) at Corso Matteotti, 17. The columns in the courtyard bear French royal insignias in homage to Louis XII of France, who occupied the duchy of Milan in 1499. The **Palazzo Affaitati** (1561), Via Ugolani Dati, 4, flaunts an impressive grand marble staircase that leads to the **Museo Civico** (tel. 46 18 85), with Caravaggio's San Francesco contemplating a *memento mori* (skull), as well as 15th-century texts that recall Renaissance politics. (Hours and prices same as at Museo Stradivariano. Entrance included with admission to Museum.)

Cremona is alive with the sound of music all year long. **Cremona Jazz** in March and April eases the way into the summer season with a series of concerts throughout the city (tickets begin at L15,000). They'll be dancing in the streets with **Cremona Estate** (evenings from July to Aug.), when P. del Comune becomes an outdoor piano bar. On another note, **Luglio in Musica** is a series of free concerts of sacred works, held in the San Sigismondo Church during July. The May-June **Festival di Cremona** kicks off the Teatro Ponchielli season with a classical series heavy on the strings (tickets L20,000-25,000), and it all reaches a *crescendo* with the **opera season,** from mid-October through early December (tickets begin at L25,000). For ticket information on the Festival contact the Teatro Ponchielli ticket booth at Corso Vittorio Emanuele, 52 (tel. 40 72 73; open daily 4-7pm).

■■■ MANTUA (MANTOVA)

While Mantua first gained fame as Virgil's hometown, the monuments in the *centro storico* owe their existence to later rulers. Perhaps the most powerful of these was the Gonzaga family who, after ascending in 1328, zealously sought to change Mantua's small-town image by importing well-known artists and cultivating local talent. Evidence of the Gonzagas' successful efforts include the impressive churches of San Sebastiano and Sant'Andrea, and the carefully crafted frescoes of Mantegna and Pisanelli. While prosperous commercial agriculture and bustling industry attest to Mantua's place in the modern world, the historic center preserves much of the unhurried rustic flavor that its former rulers sought so fiercely to overcome.

ORIENTATION AND PRACTICAL INFORMATION

A few kilometers north of the Po, Mantua is girded on three sides by the calm waters of the Minro lagoons, producing a stubby, peninsular projection where most of the

MANTUA

historic center is concentrated. The unrestricted land at the far end has given way to modern expansion. To reach the center of town from the train station in **P. Don E. Leoni**, head left on Via Solferino, and right onto Via Bonomi until the main street **Corso Vittorio Emanuele II** on your left. Follow the *corso* and you will arrive at **P. Cavallotti**, connected by **Corso della Libertà** to **P. Martiri della Libertà**. From here, **Via Roma** leads to the *centro storico*, beginning at **P. Concordia**, with central **P. Marconi, P. Mantegna,** and **P. delle Erbe** clustered close by.

Tourist Office: P. Mantegna, 6 (tel. 32 82 54 or 32 82 53; fax 36 32 92), adjacent to the church of Sant'Andrea. From the train station take a left on Via Solferino through P. S. Francesco d'Assisi to Via Fratelli Bandiera, and turn right on Via Verdi. Ask for *Mantova e la Festa Padana* (a calendar of events in the province) and the invaluable *Mantova: Directions for Use*, which comes with a fabulous map. Open Mon.-Sat. 9am-noon and 3-6pm, Sun. 9am-noon.

Police: P. Sordello, 46 (tel. 20 51).

Post Office: P. Martiri Belfiore, 15 (tel. 32 64 03 for secretary, or 32 71 43 for telegrams), up Via Roma from the tourist office. Open Mon.-Fri. 8am-7pm, Sat. 8:20am-1:20pm. **Postal Code:** 46100.

Telephones: Telecom, Via XX Settembre, 29a (tel. 187 or 33 21). Open Mon.-Fri. 9am-12:30pm and 2:30-6pm. **Telephone Code:** 0376.

Currency Exchange: Banks are a dime a dozen. **Banca Nazionale del Lavoro,** P. Cavallotti, 3, where Corso Vittorio Emanuele II becomes Corso Umberto, has dependable rates and cash advances on Visa. (Don't be disturbed by the *Star Trek* entrance—the natives are friendly!) Open Mon.-Wed. and Fri. 8:20am-1:20pm and 3-4:30pm, Thurs. 8:20am-5:50pm.

Trains: P. Don Leoni (tel. 32 16 47), at the end of Via Solferino e S. Martino, southwest of town. To: Cremona (every hr., 1hr., L5700); Verona (every hr., 40min., L3400); and Milan (9 per day, 2hr., L36,600). **Luggage Storage** L1500, open 6:05am-9pm.

Buses: APAM, P. Mondadori (tel. 32 72 37), across and to the right as you leave the train station. Cross Corso Vittorio Emanuele II to Via Caduti. Buses to Brescia (17 per day, 1½hr., L8700). Tickets sold Mon.-Fri. 7am-1:15pm and 3-6:30pm, Sat. 7am-1:15pm. (L1200 for a ticket within the city.)

Taxis: train station (tel. 32 53 51), P. Cavallotti (32 44 07), P. Marconi (32 44 08), or hospital, Via Albertoni (36 24 91).

Bike Rental: La Rigola: Bici a Noleggio (tel. 32 74 87), an outdoor establishment next to the lake, on the Lungolago dei Gonzaga where it intersects with Largo Vigili del Fuoco. 1hr. L4000; all day L10,000; Sun. all day L15,000. Open Tues.-Sun. 9:30am-12:30pm and 3:30-7:30pm (additional summer hours 8:30pm-midnight).

Pharmacy: Via Roma, 24. Open Tues.-Sun. 8:30-11:30am and 3:30-7:30pm. List of pharmacies offering night service posted outside.

Emergencies: tel. 113. **Hospital: Ospedale Civile Poma,** Viale Albertoni, 1-3 (tel. 20 11). **Ambulance:** tel. 20 12 01 or 20 12 20.

ACCOMMODATIONS

The **Youth Hostel** in Mantova and the accompanying **campsite** Sparafucile remained closed during the summer of 1995, but are expected to re-open in 1996. Contact the tourist office for the current status of both. Also ask for an up-to-date **agriturismo** packet, listing possibilities for lodging and/or dining in a more rural setting (around L20,000 per person per night).

Albergo Bianchi Stazione, P. Don Leoni, 24 (tel. 32 64 65; fax 32 15 04), across from the train station. Chic, comfortable hotel with A/C; some rooms overlook a peaceful private garden. Singles L50,000, with bath L90,000. Doubles L90,000, with bath L125,000. Open 24 hrs. AmEx, MC, Visa.

Hotel ABC Moderno, P. Don Leoni, 25 (tel./fax 32 50 02), across from the station. Rooms in the renovated section are rather pricey (single L75,000 and double with bath L105,000), but less expensive rooms in the older section are available for groups of tourists and students. For tourist groups, doubles are L43,000; for students L38,000. Breakfast included. Extra bed can be added for L12,000. Ask at desk for details (open 6am-1am).

Albergo Maragò, Via Villanova De Bellis, 2-Loc Virgiliana. If you're looking for a bargain and you don't mind a small hike, this hotel/restaurant has quiet and clean rooms, and is about 2km from the center. Single L26,000. Double L38,000 with bath L60,000. Take bus 2M, which runs 6:30am-8pm every 30min., from P. Cavallotti into Virgiliana (10min.). The hotel is on the left, just past P. San Isidro.

FOOD

Antica Osteria ai Ranari, Via Triest, 11 (tel. 32 84 31), the continuation of Via Pomponazzo, near Porto Catena. A slightly more chic place specializing in regional dishes. *Primi* L7000-9000, *secondi* L9000-14,000. Don't leave without trying the Mantuan delight of *tortelli di zucca* (ravioli with pumpkin, L9000). Cover L2000. Open Tues.-Sun. noon-3pm and 7-midnight. Closed for about 3 weeks in July-Aug. Call ahead. AmEx, MC, and Visa.

Pizzeria Capri, Via Bettinelli, 8 (tel. 36 32 38), immediately on your right as you exit the train station. Specializes in Neapolitan cuisine—that means *real* pizza— and seafood. You can get a simple *margherita* (plain cheese) pizza for just L6000, or spring for one topped with fancy *porcini* mushrooms (L10,500). Open Fri.- Wed noon-3:30pm and 6:30-midnight. AmEx, MC, Visa.

Self-Service Nuvolari, Vicolo Varone, 11 (tel. 35 50 53), at the corner of P. Viterbi, off Via Pomponazzo. Follow the signs. A clean *mensa* with excellent values and A/C. *Primi* around L4500, *secondi* around L6700. Cover L1700. Open Mon.- Fri., 11:45am-1:45pm.

Self-Service Virgiliana, P. Virgiliana, 57 (tel. 32 23 77). From P. Sordello, take Via Fratelli Cairoli to P. Virgiliana. On the left corner of the *piazza*. Clean and inexpensive. Full meals around L11,000. Cover 1600. Open Mon.-Fri. 11:45am-2pm.

SIGHTS AND ENTERTAINMENT

Cobblestoned **Piazza Sordello** forms the center of a vast complex built by the Gonzaga. The **Palazzo Ducale** (tel. 32 02 83) towers over the *piazza*, a monument to Gonzagan "modesty." The 500 rooms and 15 courtyards, constructed over a period of 300 years (14th-17th centuries), now house an impressive collection of antique and Renaissance art. Within the palace itself, you can see several noteworthy sights. The **Magna Domus** (duomo) and the **Captain's Palace**, two 14th-century Gothic structures, constitute the main part of the palace. Look beyond the duomo's 18th century façade to its Romanesque *campanile* and the Gothic elements on its side. Its interior hails from the late Renaissance, but the baptistery below the *campanile* was frescoed in the 13th century. (Open daily 8:30am-12:30pm and 3:30-7:30pm.)

Near the entrance to the palace is the Hall of Dukes, where you'll find Antonio Pisanelli's frescoes (1439-44), discovered in 1969 under thick layers of plaster. The Gonzaga's Summer Room looks out onto a hanging garden (1579) bordered on three sides by a splendid portico. From the Paradise Chambers you enter the Dwarves' Apartments, tiny low rooms built as much to amuse the court as to house its substantial dwarf contingent. Formerly a fortress, the **Castello di San Giorgio** (1390-1406) is the most formidable structure in the palace complex, later converted into a wing of the palace. Andrea Mantegna's famed frescoes of the Gonzaga family (1474) in the **Camera degli Sposi** (Marriage Chamber) adorn the walls. (The entire *palazzo* can be seen for L12,000. Open Tues.-Sun. 9am-1pm and 2:30-6pm, Mon. 9am-1pm.)

Piazza delle Erbe, just south of P. Sordello, opens onto the **Rotonda di San Lorenzo.** The circular, 11th-century Romanesque rotunda (rebuilt early this century) is also known as "La Matildica" for the powerful noblewoman who left the rotunda to the pope. Opposite the rotunda rises Mantua's most important Renaissance creation, Leon Battista Alberti's **Church of Sant'Andrea** (1471-1594). This church contains a "holy relic," supposedly the blood of Christ, which is paraded through the streets in a religious procession on Good Friday. The façade combines the classical triumphal arch motif—barrel-vaulted portal and flanking pilasters—with an antique pedimented temple front. The gargantuan interior was the first monumental space constructed in the classical style since imperial Rome. The plan—a vaulted church with a single aisle, flanking side chapels, and a domed crossing—served as a prototype for ecclesiastical architecture for the next 200 years.

The **Palazzo d'Arco** (tel. 32 22 42), off Viale Ritentino, is blessed with an extraordinary zodiac chamber by Fontanello. From P. Mantegna, follow Via Verdi to the *palazzo*. (Open Tues.-Wed. and Fri. 9am-noon, Thurs. and Sat.-Sun. 9am-noon and 3-5pm; Nov.-Feb. Sat.-Sun. 9am-noon and 2:30-4pm. Admission L5000.)

A contrast to the luxurious palaces and academies can be found at the spartan home of **Andrea Mantegna** on Via Acerbi, 47 (tel. 36 05 06). Built in 1476, it frequently hosts traveling art exhibits. (During exhibitions open daily 10am-12:30pm and 3-6pm: when there's no exhibition, open Mon.-Sat. 10am-12:30pm and Mon. and Thurs. 2-5pm. Admission is always free.) Opposite the house stands Alberti's **Church of San Sebastiano** (1460), whose Greek cross layout initiated the Renaissance propensity for centrally-planned churches.

A trek through P. Veneto and down Largo Parri leads to the opulent **Palazzo del Te** (tel. 32 32 66 or 36 58 86). Built by Giulio Romano in 1534 as a suburban retreat for Francesco II Gonzaga, it is widely regarded as the finest building of the Mannerist period. The rooms inside demonstrate the late Renaissance fascination with the Roman villa type, along with a willingness to bend the rules of proportion. Idyllic murals of Psyche, remarkable for their vividness and eroticism, line Francesco's banquet hall. Another wing of the palace features regular shows of modern Italian artists alongside a collection of Egyptian art. (Open Tues.-Sun. 9am-6pm. Admission L12,000, students and those under 18 L8000.)

The **Teatro Sociale di Mantova**, P. Cavallotti (tel. 32 38 60), off Corso Vittorio Emanuele, stages operas in October and plays from November through May. (Seats from L20,000.) The **Spazio Aperto** series brings dance, music, and cinema events to various *piazze* and *palazzi* around town. Mantua also hosts a chamber music series in April and May. Most fun is the **Concorso di Madonnari** on August 15; the *madonnari*, street artists whose chalky madonnas wash away with the first rains, hold a competition in nearby Grazie di Curtatone.

Holy Relic, Batman!

Little did you know that every Catholic church must be consecrated by a holy relic. In fact, Italy features a gut-wrenching assortment of saints' remains and ghastly holy bits—here is just a small sample of the wonders that await you. In addition to the **blood of Christ** here in Mantua are: the **tooth** of San Matteo in Salerno; San Gimignano's **arm, encased in silver** in Modena; the **head** of Saint Catherine in Siena; the **tongue and jawbone** of St. Antonio in Padua; the **head and blood** of San Gennaro in Naples; and the **body, (minus half a head)** of St. Andrew in Amalfi—the other half is in Greece.

■ NEAR MANTUA: SABBIONETA

Sabbioneta, 33km southwest of Mantua, is well worth a visit. Founded by Vespasiano Gonzaga (1532-91) as the home for his feudal court, its importance as an artistic center in the late Renaissance earned it the title "Little Athens of the Gonzagas." Inside the well-preserved 16th-century city walls lie the **Ducal Palace,** the **Olympic Theater,** and the **Palazzo del Giardino,** all fascinating Renaissance structures. Only the guided walk enables you to visit the otherwise inaccessible interiors. The 45min. tour in Italian (L10,000) leaves roughly every 20min. from the **tourist office,** Via Vespasiano Gonzaga, 31 (tel. (0375) 520 39; open April-Sept. Mon.-Fri. 9am-noon and 2:30-6pm, Sat.-Sun. 9am-noon and 1:30-7pm; Oct.-March Tues.-Fri. 9am-noon and 2:30-5pm, Sat.-Sun. 9am-noon and 2:30-6pm.) In summer Sabbioneta stages a **Festival di Musica e Danza,** and from mid-March to mid-April antique aficionados come for the exhaustive **Mercato del Antiquariato.**

■■■ BERGAMO

Bergamo, like the *commedia dell'arte* it fostered, is endowed with a multitude of personalities. A bustling commercial and industrial center, an artistic hot-spot, and a focal point of both history and legend, the city is divided physically and spiritually into two parts. The hilltop *città alta* recalls its medieval origins with narrow, cobblestone streets shaded by solemn ecclesiastic façades. The rapid-paced *città bassa* below, however, is a modern metropolis.

ORIENTATION AND PRACTICAL INFORMATION

Poised at the juncture of the Brembana and Seriana valleys, Bergamo is an easy train ride from Milan, Brescia, and Cremona. The train station, bus station, and budget hotels are all in the *città bassa*. To get to the more interesting *città alta*, take bus #1 or 3 (L1200) to the funicular, which ascends from Viale Vittorio Emanuele II to the Mercato delle Scarpe (every 15min., L1200), or walk up the old footpath, starting from behind the funicular station on Viale Vittorio Emanuele II (10-20min.). Your bus tickets are good for 75 min. and can be used on the funicular (you don't have to buy two tickets).

Tourist Office: APT (*città bassa*), Viale Papa Giovanni XXIII, 106 (tel. 24 22 26), straight ahead through P. Marconi from the train station, on the left. The friendly staff can provide you with a *very* useful map. Open Mon.-Fri. 9am-12:30pm and 3-6:30pm. On weekends head to the *città alta:* **APT,** Vicolo Aquila Nera, 2 (tel. 23 27 30), off P. Vecchia. Open daily 9am-12:30pm and 3-6:30pm.

Police: Via T. Tasso, 1 (tel. 27 61 11).

Post Office: Via Masone, 2A (tel. 24 32 56), at Via Locatelli. Take Via Zelasco from Viale Vittorio Emanuele II. Stamps and *fermo posta* at #7. Open Mon.-Sat. 8:15am-8pm. **Postal Code:** 24122. Packages are handled at Via Pascoli, 6 (tel. 23 86 98). Same hours as main office.

Telephones: Telecom, Largo Porta Nuova, 1 (tel. 21 92 95), where Viale Papa Giovanni XXIII becomes Viale Vittorio Emanuele II. Open Mon.-Sat. 9am-12:30pm and 2:30-7pm., Sun. 9am-1pm. After hours try **Hotel Cappelle d'Oro,** Viale Papa Giovanni XXIII, 12 (tel. 78 25 03). In the *città alta,* try **Caffè Tasso,** P. Vecchia, 3 (tel. 23 79 66). Expect to pay a bit more in the hotels. **Telephone Code:** 035.

Telegrams and **telefax:** Via Pascoli, 6 (tel. 26 60 79). Open Mon.-Fri. 8:15am-7:40pm, Sat. 8:15am-1:40pm.

Currency Exchange: Banca Nazionale del Lavoro, Via Petrarca, 12 (tel. 39 81 11), off Viale Vittorio Emanuele II near P. della Libertà. Good rates. Open Mon.-Tues. and Thurs.-Fri. 8:20am-1:20pm and 3-4:30pm, Wed. 8:20am-5:50pm. Also in the office on the second floor of the **post office** (Mon. Fri. 8:15am-5:30pm, Sat. 8:15am-1pm.) After-hrs. money exchange at **Hotel Excelsior San Marco,** P. della Repubblica, 6 (tel. 36 61 11), off Viale Vittorio Emanuele II. **Cash only.**

Trains: P. Marconi (tel. 24 76 24). To: Milan (every hr., 1hr., L5000); Brescia (15 per day, 1hr., L4200); Cremona (6 per day, 1½hr., L7200). Round-trips are double the price. Reservation office open daily 7am-8:30pm. Information open daily 9am-5pm. **Luggage Storage:** L1500. Open 7am-9pm.

Buses: across from the train station (tel. 24 81 50). To: Milan (every 30min. 5:40am-10:30pm, L6700); Cremona (every 30min. 5:05am-7:30pm, L8900); Como (9 per day 6:55am-6:20pm, L7500); Brescia (8 per day 6:50am-6:45pm, L6300).

Emergencies: tel. 113. **Medical Emergency:** daytime tel. 26 91 11, at night or on Sun. tel. 25 02 46. **Hospital: Ospedale Riuniti,** Largo Barozzi, 1 (tel. 26 91 11). **Ambulance: Croce Bianca Città di Bergamo,** tel. 31 68 88.

ACCOMMODATIONS

The higher the altitude, the higher the price. The most affordable *alberghi* (hotels) are in the *città bassa*. Ask the tourist office about **Agriturismo** (for lodging in rural houses) as well as other alternatives.

Ostello Città di Bergamo (HI), Via G. Ferraris, 1 (tel./fax 36 17 24). Take bus #14 from Porta Nuova to Località Monterosso. The uphill hike is rewarded with an unparalleled view of an unattractive apartment complex. On the positive side, a well-stocked supermarket serves the community at the base of the hill. Open 7-9am and 3:30pm-midnight, but you can lounge around downstairs during the day. L20,000 per person, breakfast included. Meals L12,000. (Expected to re-open in the summer of 1995.)

Albergo S. Giorgio, Via S. Giorgio, 10 (tel. 21 20 43; fax 31 00 72), about a 15min. walk from the train station. Go left on Via Pietro Paleocopa, which becomes Via S. Giorgio after a few blocks; or take bus #7. The hotel is on the left. Near the train tracks, but quiet inside. Neat, modern rooms with TV, telephone, and a sink if there is no bathroom. 35 rooms, 2 are handicap accessible. English spoken. Singles L30,000, with bath L45,000. Doubles L55,000, with bath L70,000. Reservations helpful but not required. MC, Visa.

Locanda Caironi, Via Torretta, 6 (tel. 24 30 83), off Via Borgo Palazzo. A 20min. walk, or take bus #5, 7, or 8 out on Via Angelo Maj. A family-run affair in a quiet residential neighborhood. The *trattoria* downstairs is considered one of Bergamo's best-kept culinary secrets. Singles L20,000. Doubles L35,000. Closed Aug.

Antica Trattoria della Brianza, Via Brosetta, 611a (tel. 25 33 38). From Porta Nuova, take a left onto Via Tiraboschi (which becomes Via Zambonate). At Largo Cinquevie, take a right and then a left onto Via Brosetta. Or take bus #8a or 8b. This small hotel (7 rooms) is across from a supermarket, in a nice area chock full of antique shops. Singles L30,000. Doubles L60,000.

FOOD

Casonsei, a meat-filled ravioli dish, is a Bergamasco gastronomic delight, as are the *branzi* and *taleggio* cheeses. *Polenta,* made from yellow flour and water, should accompany any typical meal. *Valcalepio* red and white wines are made locally. Streets in the *città alta* are lined with *pasticcerie* selling yellow *polentina* confections topped with chocolate blobs intended to resemble birds. But beware of these sweet (and pricey) take-offs on Bergamo's culinary tradition: many natives never taste these for-tourists-only treats. For necessities, shop at **Roll Market,** on the right side of Viale Vittorio Emanuele II just before the hill to the *città alta* (open Mon. 8:30am-1pm, Tues.-Sat. 8:30am-1pm and 3:30-8pm).

Keep in mind that Bergamo's shops are closed on Monday.

Città Bassa

Capolinea, Via Giacomo Quarenghi, 29 (tel. 32 09 81), off Via Zambonate. Follow Via Tiraboschi from Porta Nuova. A favorite among Bergamo's young people, this modern establishment has both an energetic bar and quieter back rooms for the restaurant. Full meal from L15,000, but sandwiches start at L3500. Salads large enough to eat as a meal from L4500. Open Tues.-Sun. 11am-3pm and 6pm-2am.

Trattoria Casa Mia, Via S. Bernardino, 20 (tel. 22 06 76), off Via Zambonate. Follow Via Tiraboschi from Porta Nuova. An inviting, unpretentious place serving complete meals (including wine, coffee, bread, and service) for under L15,000. Open Sept.-July Mon.-Sat. 8am-3pm and 5:30-10:30pm.

Ristorante Self-Service Pastimbaldo, Via Taramelli, 23/B (tel. 22 07 55). From the station, walk down Viale Papa Giovanni XXIII, turn right on Via San Francesco d'Assisi, then turn left onto V. Taramelli. Affordable prices and appetizing dishes draw both students and business types. *Primi* from L3600, *secondi* from L6500. Pizza around L6000. Open Mon.-Fri. 11:45am-3pm, Sun. 11:45am-3pm and 6:30-11pm. MC, Visa.

Città Alta

Though you may withstand the temptations of the first bakery you pass on Via Colleoni or Via Gombito, be prepared to undergo the same trial at 20m intervals. Among the many *pasticcerie,* however, there are a number of well-priced restaurants with more substantial food.

Forno Tresoldi, Via Colleoni, 13 (tel. 24 39 60). Costs a little more than three coins, but the pizza is otherworldly (about L2500 per slice). Open Tues.-Sun. 8am-1:30pm and 4-8pm, except in Feb. when it's closed Sun. but open Mon. morning. Hours may be extended, especially in the summer.

Trattoria Bernabò, Via Colleoni, 31 (tel. 23 76 92), past P. Vecchia. One of the finest restaurants in Bergamo, with a *menù* from L15,000. A vast menagerie of *polenta* breads—enhanced with cheese, mushrooms, and sausage. For something more interesting, try the *brasato di asina* (donkey in vegetable sauce). Open Sept.-June Fri.-Wed. noon-2:30pm and 7-11:30 pm. MC, Visa.

Trattoria 3 Torri, P. Mercato del Fieno, 7/A (tel. 24 43 66), a left off Via Gombito when heading away from P. Vecchia. This corner establishment entertains with elegance and is always full (there are only about 6 tables, though there is outside seating May-Sept.). Try the *real* polenta (L15,000). *Menù* around L30,000, but *primi* begin at L8000. Cover L2000. Open Thurs.-Tues. 10am-3pm and 6pm-midnight. Reservations strongly recommended. MC, Visa.

Circolino Cooperativa Città Alta, Via S. Agata, 19 (tel. 21 85 68 or 22 58 76). This former prison is now a favorite of old and young alike. Offers sandwiches, pizzas, and salads for under L7000. Facilities for cards, swimming (L5000), and *bocce* (during the day L5000, night L6000), an Italian game similar to bowling (but taken much more seriously). Tennis shoes are required, and, weather permitting, you can practice for free on Wed. Restaurant open Thurs.-Tues. 9am-2am.

SIGHTS

Città Bassa

Begin a tour of the city at **P. Matteotti,** the heart of Bergamo Bassa and a favorite meeting place for the evening *passeggiata.* In the **Church of San Bartolomeo,** at the far right of the piazza, rests a superb altarpiece of the *Madonna and Child* by Lorenzo Lotto. On the right of San Bartolomeo, Via Tasso leads to the **Church of Santo Spirito,** with its strangely-sculptured façade. Its fine Renaissance interior (1521) houses paintings by Lotto, Previtali, and Bergognone. **Via Pignolo** connects the lower city with the upper, and winds past a succession of handsome palaces (16th to 18th centuries). Along the way is the tiny **Church of San Bernardino,** whose colorful interior is the humble backdrop to a splendid altarpiece by Lotto. A right on Via San Tommaso brings you to the astounding **Galleria dell'Accademia Carrara** (tel. 39 94 50), one of the most important art galleries in Italy. Housed in a glorious neoclassical palace, the 15 rooms of the second floor represent virtually all the Italian notables, joined by the canvases of Breughel, van Dyck, and El Greco. (Open Wed.-Mon. 9:30am-12:30pm and 2:30-5:30pm. Mon.-Sat. Admission L3000, students with ID L2000, under 18 and over 65 free; free for everyone on Sun.)

Città Alta

In contrast to the modern city below, the *città alta* is a wonderfully preserved medieval city, with a photo opportunity on every corner. It can be reached either by the funicular or on foot. From the Carrara gallery, the terraced Via Noca ascends from the lower city to **Porta Sant'Agostino,** a 16th-century gate built by the Venetians as fortification. Via Porta Dipinta leads to the heart of Bergamo Alta, passing first the Romanesque **Church of San Michele** (12th-13th centuries), decorated inside with colorful frescoes (open 8:30am-4:30pm), and then the neoclassical **Church of Sant'Andrea,** which contains an altarpiece by Moretto. The street continues as Via Gombito, passing by a massive 12th-century tower of the same name. The *città alta* can also be reached along the white marble **Porta San Giacomo,** which overlooks the *città bassa's* main thoroughfare.

Via Gambito ends in **Piazza Vecchia,** a majestic ensemble of medieval and Renaissance buildings flanked by restaurants and *caffè*—and a prime location for people watching. Rest your legs on the steps of the white marble **Biblioteca Civica** (1594), repository of Bergamo's rich collection of manuscripts and modeled after Venice's Sansovino Library. Across the piazza is the massive **Palazzo della Ragione** (1199), with its robust arcade. To the right, and connected to the *palazzo* by a 16th-century covered stairway, stands the 12th-century **Torre Civica** (Civic Tower). The view from the top is well worth the climb, but protect your eardrums: in addition to the traditional curfew sounded by the 15th-century clock at 10pm, the bells also ring on the hour.

A passage between (or under) the two buildings leads to **Piazza del Duomo.** Ahead is the awe-inspiring, multicolor marble façade of the masterful **Colleoni Chapel** (1476). It was designed by G. A. Amadeo (also responsible for the Charterhouse of Pavia) as a tomb and chapel for Bartolomeo Colleoni, a celebrated Venetian mercenary. (Open in summer daily 9am-noon and 2-6:30pm; in winter 9am-noon and 2:30-4:30pm.) To the right of the chapel is the octagonal **baptistery,** featuring a red marble gallery. It is actually a reconstruction of a 14th-century baptistery that once stood in the **Basilica of Santa Maria Maggiore.** This basilica, which adjoins the Colleoni Chapel to the left, was constructed in the second half of the 12th century. The understated Romanesque exterior contrasts sharply with the ornate Baroque interior. Other points of interest include the Victorian tomb of the composer Gaetano Donizetti (1797-1848). (Open Mon.-Sat. 8:30am-noon and 3-6pm, Sun. 10am-noon and 3-6pm.)

For a romantic conclusion to the tour, return to P. Mercato delle Scarpe and proceed left on Via alla Rocca. Sitting on a site occupied by fortifications since Roman times, the present Rocca is home to the **Risorgimento Museum** (tel. 24 71 16). The surrounding grounds have been dubbed the **Park of Remembrance** in honor of those soldiers who died for the Italian cause. (The museum is undergoing restoration, but the park is open.)

Bergamo is certainly a center for the arts; there is always something happening. The opera season lasts from Sept. to Nov., and is followed by the drama season, Nov.-April, featuring Italy's most prestigious companies at the Donizetti Theater. After April the spotlight shifts to the two-month-long, universally acclaimed **International Piano Festival,** co-hosted by Brescia. In September, Bergamo unabashedly celebrates its premier native-born composer with a festival of Gaetano Donizetti's lesser-known works. For further information, contact the tourist office or the theater itself at P. Cavour, 14 (tel. 24 96 31). During the summer the city council offers *Viva La Tua Città,* a program of free events. Ask at the tourist office for a pamphlet.

■■■ BRESCIA

Situated between bigger destinations, Brescia has long been overlooked by tourists. It is a city of surprises and a walker's paradise. The tiny winding streets of the *centro storico* open unexpectedly into spacious *piazze* overseen by towering churches. Balconies trail with flowers and even some alleyways have arched entrances. The ancient buildings have not faded into obscurity, but now house a plethora of stores and restaurants. Roman ruins and fascist *piazze* co-exist within the thoroughly urbanized center, and lest a single style of cathedral be thought undiplomatic, Brescia has not one *duomo* but two. Relative prosperity has been the one constant over the years. Today the city owes its place in the prosperous Lombardian economy to the production of weapons and sink fixtures, which gives Brescia the frenetic pace of a modern industrial center. (Or a public bathroom.)

ORIENTATION AND PRACTICAL INFORMATION

Brescia is between Milan (1hr.) and Verona (¾hr.) on the direct train line to Venice and is the main point of departure for buses to the western shores of Lake Garda. Most of the city's architectural gems are concentrated in the thoroughly rectangular, *piazza*-packed *centro storico,* linked to **P. della Repubblica** at the left-hand corner by **Corso Martiri della Libertà** and **Via Porcellaga.** Continuing diagonally through the center and out the other end, you will come to two aptly named streets, **Via del Castello** and **Via del Musei.** The first leads uphill to the castle; the latter slopes down to "museum row" and the Roman archaeological site.

Tourist Office: Corso Zanardelli, 34 (tel. 434 18; fax 29 32 84), across from the arcaded continuation of Corso Palestro, which branches to the right off Corso della Libertà/Via Porcellaga en route to the center. Set off slightly from the street, on the right. Helpful map and walking guides to the city available. Open Mon.-Fri. 9am-12:30pm and 3-6pm, Sat. 9am-12:30pm.
Police: on Via Botticelli (tel. 425 61).
Post Office: P. Vittoria, 1 (tel. 375 40 70). Stamps and *fermo posta* at #6 (in the room to the left). Open Mon.-Fri. 8:15am-5:30pm, Sat. 8:15am-1pm. **Postal Code:** 12001.
Telephones: Telecom (SIP), Via Moretto, 46 (tel. 375 12 74). Open Mon.-Fri. 9am-12:30pm and 2:30-6pm. **Telephone Code:** 030.
Currency Exchange: There are many banks in the area, such as **Banco San Paolo de Brescia,** located at Corso Martiri della Libertà. Open Mon.-Fri. 8:25am-1:25pm and 2:40-3:40pm. The *cambio* is inside to the right. Also, the **post office** has an exchange, inside to the right at #3.
Trains: connected to **P. della Repubblica** by the short Viale Stazione. To: Milan (every hr., 1hr., L7200); Verona (every hr., 45min., L5700); Venice (every hr., 2¼hr., L15,500); Bergamo (15 per day, 1hr., L4200); Padova (every hr., 1¾hr., L11,700); Vicenza (every hr., 1¼hr., L9800); Cremona (every 2 hr., 1¾hr., L5000). No round-trip discount. Information open 8am-noon and 3-6pm. **Luggage Storage:** L1500 for 24 hrs. Open 7am-8pm.
Buses: on Via Stazione (tel. 375 10 00 or 240 04 08). East-bound buses are opposite the train station in a bright orange building. West-bound buses leave from the **SIA** station just to the left of the train station. To: Verona (every hr. starting at 7:15am, 2¼hr., L9500); Mantua (every 2hr., 1½hr., L8700); Cremona (every hr., 1¼hr., L7100). Ticket office open Mon.-Sat. 6:30am-7pm. To Milan (7am, 9am and 5:50pm, 1¾hr., L11,100).
Emergencies: tel. 113. **Medical Assistance:** tel. 399 55 45. **Hospital: Ospedale Civile,** tel. 399 51. **Ambulance: Croce Bianca,** tel. 442 44.

ACCOMMODATIONS

Accommodations are reasonably priced in Brescia, but often fill during the week. Call a week ahead for reservations. You'll be fortunate to find any sort of bargain in the historic center. Inquire at the tourist office about **agriturismo** options.

Servizio della Giovane (ACISJF), Via Bronzetti, 17 (office in the train station; tel. 375 50 40). From the station, take Viale Stazione to P. della Repubblica and pick up Via dei Mille on the far side. Via Bronzetti is on the right after a couple of blocks. Women only. Run by friendly nuns. Spotless bathrooms off triples so newly furnished they look like promotional photos. Kitchen facilities. Curfew 10pm. L10,000 per person, sheets included. Call ahead for reservations.
Albergo Rigamonti, Via Mansione, 8 (tel. 481 52). From the station, follow Viale Stazione to P. della Repubblica. Take Corso G. Matteotti on the far side and turn right on Mansione. Modern, tidy, and respectable. TV room, bar, and car park. Singles L32,000, with bath L47,000. Doubles L55,000, with bath L65,000. Towels provided. Open 6:15am-midnight.
Albergo San Marco, Via Spalto S. Marco, 15 (tel. 455 41). From the station take Via Foppa, turn right on Via XX Settembre, make the next left, and turn right onto Via Vittorio Emanuele, which becomes Via Spalto S. Marco. Rooms are clean, but stuffy in the summer. Lots of noise from the traffic below. Towels provided. Singles L29,000. Doubles L49,000. Breakfast L3000.

FOOD

Open-air vendors do their thing in P. Rovetta and P. Vittoria (normally in P. Mercato, but it is under construction this year) Tues.-Fri. roughly 8:30am-6pm. The **Oviesse** clothing store off P. Rovetta at Corso Mameli, 23, conceals a grocery store called **SuperScontro** (tel. 29 54 98) in its basement (open Mon. 3-7:20pm, Tues.-Sat. 9am-12:25pm and 3-7:20pm). Similarly, the **COIN** department store on the corner of Corso Magenta and Via San Martiro della Battaglia also hides a large **PAM** supermarket downstairs. Whatever and wherever you choose to eat, or if you're not even eating at all, be sure to submerge yourself in one of the local wines. *Tocai di San Martino della Battaglia*, a dry white wine, *groppello*, a medium red, and *botticino*, a dry red of medium age, are all favorites in Brescia and beyond.

Ristorante/Pizzeria Cavour, Corso Cavour, 56 (tel. 240 09 00), off Corso Magenta. Great pizza and pasta dishes at reasonable prices. *Pizza margherita* L6500; *primi* L7500-13,000. Try the *gnocchi alla gorgonzola* (L8000), or, for macaroni-and-cheese-lovers, the *penne 4 formaggio*, which beats Kraft any day (L8000). Cover L3000. Open Wed-Mon. 10:30am-3pm and 6pm-midnight.

Ristorante San Marco, Via Spalto S. Marco, 15 (tel. 455 41). Follow Via Vittorio Emanuele II which becomes Spalto S. Marco. Filling meals in a cheerful atmosphere of wooden ceiling beams and whitewashed walls. *Primi* (from L8000) are large enough for a meal. *Secondi* from L12,500. Cover L3000.

Trattoria Al Frate, Via Musei, 25 (tel. 375 14 69), by the base of the ascent to the castle. Plentiful portions, and the ever-present drinkers who rise only for a refill are a living testament to the fine wines. *Primi* L10,000. Wine from L12,000 per liter. Cover L3500. Open Tues.-Sun. 12:30-2:30pm and 7:30pm-12:30am.

Vittoria Mix, Via XIV Novembre, 2, on the corner of Via XIV Novembre and Via delle X Giornati, under the arcade. A spankin' new fast food joint offering an array of delicacies from burgers to pizza (L3000-L4000). Up the spiral stairs is **Ciao**, which serves *primi* starting at L3900 and *secondi* from L6100. Open Tues.-Sun. 10am-11pm.

SIGHTS AND ENTERTAINMENT

Some of the museums of Brescia got together and settled on a standard museum admission (L5000; under 16, over 65, and organized student groups free), as well as a standard set of hours (June-Sept. Tues.-Fri. 10am-12:30pm and 3-6pm, Sat. and Sun. 10am-12:30pm and 3-7pm; Oct.-May Tues.-Sun. 9am-12:30pm and 3-5pm). They've also implemented a **museum "hotline,"** the *Centro Museale Bresciano* (tel. 443 27). All groups are *required* to call in advance. In this section, museums belonging to this *centro* will be marked with an asterisk.

Down from **Piazza della Vittoria** is the **Piazza della Loggia,** built when Venice ruled the city. On one side of this square stands the **Torre dell'Orologio,** modeled after the clock tower in Venice's Piazza San Marco, with an astronomic clock and two stone fellers that strike the hours. Across from the tower, the Renaissance **loggia,** the work of a gaggle of architects including Sansovino and Palladio, boasts intriguing carvings. An elaborate door underneath the portico leads to a monumental staircase and a room adorned with paintings from the 16th century. The **Piazza del Duomo,** across Via X Giornate, is dominated by its heavily manneristic **duomo nuovo** (1604-1825). Next door is the old *duomo,* or **Rotonda,** a refreshingly simple Romanesque building with endearing patchwork and uneven windows scattered over its two-story circular plan. (Open Apr.-Sept. Thurs.-Tues. 9am-noon and 3-7pm. Contribution desired, but not required.)

Down Via dei Musei from the center is Emperor Vespasian's vast **Tempio Capitolino*,** part of the ongoing archaeological efforts to unearth monuments from Brescia's classical roots as the Roman colony of Brixia. Upstairs is a small museum with mosaics, a medieval road map, and excellent bronzes. A few paces farther down the Via dei Musei you'll find the **Monastery of San Salvatore and Santa Giulia*,** the final retreat of Ermengarda, the ex-wife of Charlemagne. Its greatest treasure is the 8th-century **Cross of Desiderius,** encased in silver and encrusted with hundreds of jewels and cameos; note the 3rd-century portraits. Also look for the biblical carvings on a 4th-century ivory chest. From the Tempio Capitolino walk through P. Foro to Via Gallo, which becomes Via Crispi and leads to Brescia's principal attraction, the **Pinacoteca Tosio-Martinengo*.** The solemn 22-room *palazzo* displays a fine collection of works by Brescian masters (notably Moretto), but better still is Raphael's effeminate *Cristo benedicente*. There are also first-rate works by Veneziano, Tintoretto, Clouet, Vincenzo Foppa, and Lorenzo Lotto.

Rather than fret, strummers should check out the **Museo della Chitarra** (Guitar Museum), Via Triest, 34. (Open Mon.-Fri. 2:30-7:30pm. Free.) If you have more time, visit the **castello** hovering on the high ground behind Via dei Musei. This array of architectural styles houses an **observatory,** the **Risorgimento Museum,** and the **Luigi Marzoli Museum of Arms.** Down Via Piamarta is an intact **Roman gate.**

The bulk of Brescia's high-brow cultural events takes place in the splendor of the Teatro Grande. The annual **Stagione di Prosa,** a long-running series of dramatic performances, takes place from December to April. From April to June, the focus shifts to the **Festival Pianistico Internazionale,** co-hosted by nearby Bergamo. **Estate Aperta** includes an impressive series of concerts, theatrical performances, and films, held June through September in churches, courtyards, and *piazze*. Pick up a schedule at the tourist office, or call the coordinating forces at the **Centro Teatrale Bresciano** (tel. 377 11 11).

Veneto

The Veneto region stretches from the Austrian Alps down across the foothills of the Dolomites and the Venetian Alps to the fertile plain of the Po and its delta. The territory encompasses an extremely wide range of terrains, as well as a multitude of culturally independent towns and cities formerly linked by the Venetian Empire. While Venice's rule barely changed the characters of regions that had been firmly imprinted by Germany and Milan, today a certain unity is found in these regions' cuisine. Rice and *polenta*, a cornmeal concoction used with most local seafood dishes, provide the starch base. Wine is strictly regional, featuring the dry white *soave*, the sparkling *prosecco*, the light red *bardolino*, and the full-bodied *valpolicella*. The cities of the Veneto are also bound by a common claim of belonging to the most touristed region in Italy.

■■■ VENICE (VENEZIA)

> She is the Shakespeare of cities—unchallenged, incomparable, and beyond envy.
>
> —John Addington Symonds

It is with good reason that Venetians call their city *La Serenissima*—the most serene. Venice awakes each morning with a refreshing absence of the speeding cars and roaring mopeds that infest other Italian cities. Her citizens make their way on foot or by boat through an ancient maze of narrow streets and winding canals. Unfortunately, the serenity is now broken by swarms of tourists that collect in the *campi* (squares) and thoroughfares of the city, searching out its wealth of museums and landmarks. These visitors often overlook the real Venice, which lies hidden in the romantic back streets and residential quarters of the city. Venice cannot help but beckon visitors to her grand Renaissance architecture and stately legacy as queen of the Adriatic.

First driven by Attila's hordes, then by conquering Lombards, Roman refugees joined fishermen on the low barrier islands of the swampy lagoon. An unsuccessful attack by Charlemagne in 810 AD led to the settlement of the inner islands that underlie the modern city. In 828, two Venetian merchants stole St. Mark's remains from Alexandria, and established the city's eminence under a new patron saint. By the 11th century, ties to Constantinople and marine prowess had established Venice as the dominant middleman for trade with the Middle East. In 1204, Venice sent the

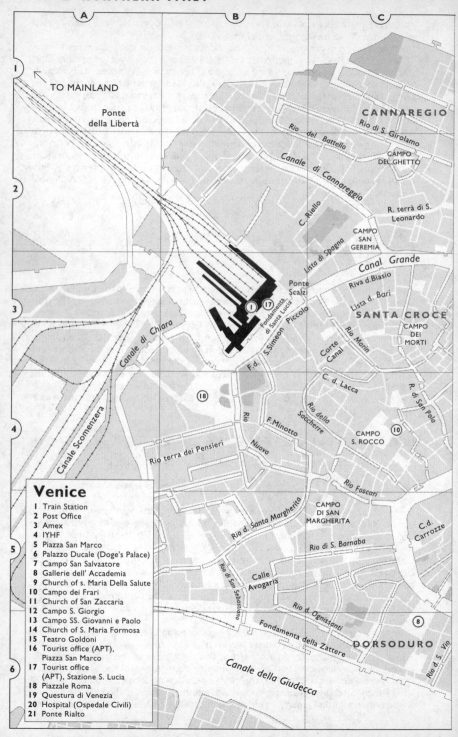

Venice

1 Train Station
2 Post Office
3 Amex
4 IYHF
5 Piazza San Marco
6 Palazzo Ducale (Doge's Palace)
7 Campo San Salvaatore
8 Gallerie dell' Accademia
9 Church of s. Maria Della Salute
10 Campo dei Frari
11 Church of San Zaccaria
12 Campo S. Giorgio
13 Campo SS. Giovanni e Paolo
14 Church of S. Maria Formosa
15 Teatro Goldoni
16 Tourist office (APT),
   Piazza San Marco
17 Tourist office
   (APT), Stazione S. Lucia
18 Piazzale Roma
19 Questura di Venezia
20 Hospital (Ospedale Civili)
21 Ponte Rialto

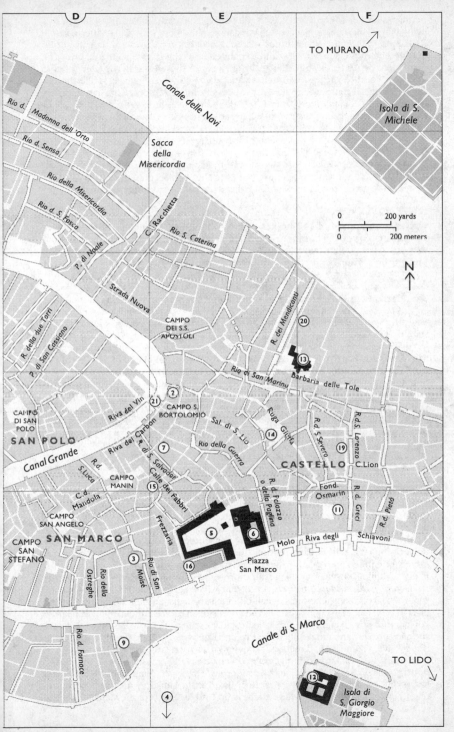

TO MURANO

Isola di S. Michele

Canale delle Navi

Rio d. Madonna dell'Orto

Rio d. Sensa

Rio della Misericordia

Rio d. S. Fosca

Sacca della Misericordia

C. Racchetta

Rio S. Caterina

0   200 yards

0   200 meters

N

P.di Noale

Strada Nuova

CAMPO DEI S.S. APOSTOLI

R. dei Mendicanti

20

R. della Aue Torri

P. di San Cassiano

Rio del Vin

21

2

13

Barbaria delle Tole

Rio di San Marina

CAI PO DI SAN POLO

SAN POLO

Riva del Vin

Riva del Carbon

CAMPO S. BORTOLOMIO

Sal. di S. Lio

Ruga Giuffa

R.d. S. Severo

R.d. S. Lorenzo

19

Canal Grande

R.d.

S. Luca

R.d. S. Salvador

Calle dei Fabbri

14

Rio della Guerra

CASTELLO

C. Lion

7

CAMPO MANIN

15

C. d. Mandola

R. d. Palazzo o della Paglina

Fond. Osmarin

R. d. Greci

R. d. Pietà

CAMPO SAN ANGELO

SAN MARCO

Frezzaria

5

6

11

CAMPO SAN STEFANO

3

Rio di San

16

Molo

Riva degli

Schiavoni

Ostreghe

Rio della

Moise

Piazza San Marco

Canale di S. Marco

TO LIDO

Rio d. Fornace

9

12

Isola di S. Giorgio Maggiore

4

VENICE

penniless armies of the Fourth Crusade to raid Constantinople; the spoils of this campaign filled Venetian squares and treasuries with new prosperity. After consolidating its oligarchic government in the 14th century, the Venetian Republic defeated its rival Genoa in 1380 and expanded onto the Italian mainland. Over the next three centuries, jealous European powers to the west and the unstoppable Ottoman Turks to the east whittled away *La Serenissima's* empire, while the discovery of ocean routes to the Far East robbed it of its monopoly on Asian trade. By the time Napoleon conquered it in 1797, idle Venice was little more than a decadent playground. French and Austrian rule capped off the glory days as the development of industry at Mestre drew away the archipelago's working population.

Today Venice is both a playground for tourists from all over the world and the home of loyal Venetians. The contrast of the two worlds is visible throughout: the flood of cameras in Piazza San Marco, and the sparsely populated back streets of Cannaregio and the Ghetto. Uniting both are the architectural gems of a glorious past and the green, serpentine canals eating away at the city's foundations.

ORIENTATION

Venice is composed of 117 bodies of land distributed throughout the Venetian lagoon, and is protected from the Adriatic by the Lido, an island which lies 2km farther out to sea. A 4km causeway links the urban center to the mainland. The **Santa Lucia train station** lies on the northwestern edge of the city, while the garages, car rentals, and bus terminals are across the Grand Canal in nearby **Piazzale Roma**— the last stop for all land-bound transportation. If you're in a rush to get to **Piazza San Marco** (and the central tourist office) from the station or Piazzale Roma, take *vaporetto* #82. For a splendid introduction to the *palazzi* along the Grand Canal, take #1. If you prefer to hoof it, the 40-min. walk to San Marco starts left from the station onto Lista di Spagna, and follows the signs (and the crowds).

Yellow signs placed around Venice guide you to the Rialto (the bridge connecting San Marco and San Polo), the Accademia (Dorsoduro), San Marco (at the border of San Marco and Castello), Piazzale Roma (Santa Croce), and the *ferrovia* (train station; Cannaregio). They can help you navigate the labyrinth of Venice from one end to the other, yet in doing so they can actually take you on the longer route, making you their prisoner. Moreover, these signs are the leading cause of the "pedestrian freeway" phenomenon. Liberate yourself with a real **map** (do not rely on the freebies at the tourist office, nor on the oversimplified maps given out at the AmEx office). The *Storti Edizioni* map-guide of Venice (L5000, available at newsstands and *tabacchi*) shows all the major streets, and is color-coded, in addition to having an invaluable street index. You *will* get lost in Venice, but with a map in hand you might not feel so helpless. And don't despair: wandering from the main pathways will reward you with cheaper prices, local hangouts, quiet *campi*, beautiful vistas, and friendly Venetians. It is true that many of the sights cluster around the Grand Canal, but it is easy enough to choose a route, find the site, and then return back to the tranquil waterways.

Orientation begins with a fundamental comprehension of the **sestieri,** the sections of the city. Within each section, there are no individual street numbers, but merely one long and haphazard sequence of numbers (roughly 6000 per *sestiere*). Every building, however, is also located on some type of a "street"—*fondamente, calli, campi, salizzade, canali, rii, ponti,* and *rii terrà,* (foundations, narrow streets, squares, paved roads, channels, small channels, bridges, and old channels that are now streets, respectively). To add to the confusion, it is often unclear which *sestiere* you are in at any given moment, as the boundaries are not clearly indicated. *Let's Go* supplies the *sestiere,* the number, the street name when possible, and supplements this by giving some basic directions—beyond that, try asking the locals.

The **Grand Canal,** the central artery of Venice, can be crossed on foot only at the **ponti** (bridges) **Scalzi, Rialto,** and **Accademia.** *Traghetti* (gondola-like ferry boats) may seem too picturesque for practical use, but in fact they are used fairly frequently for canal crossings where there is no bridge. North of the Canal, from the

1996 Catalog

LET'S GO®
T R A V E L

We give you the world...at a discount

Travel Gear

Supreme Convertible back-pack/carry-on suitcase with innovative hideaway suspension and parallel stay internal frame. Includes leather trim, lumbar support pad, torso and waist adjustments, and a dual pocket detachable daypack. Waterproof Cordura nylon, lifetime guarantee. 4400 cubic inches, 14" x 26" x 14". Black, Hunter, or Navy. *As seen on cover in Hunter.* $175

Backpack/Suitcase Hideaway suspension with an internal frame turns this backpack into a carry-on suitcase. Detachable daypack makes it three bags in one. Lightweight and versatile, Waterproof Cordura nylon, lifetime guarantee. 3750 cubic inches, 14" x 24" x 11". Black, Hunter, or Navy. *As seen on cover in Navy.* $130

Padded Toiletry Kit Large padded main compartment to protect contents. Mesh lid pocket with metal hook to hang kit on a towel rod or bathroom hook. Features two separate small outside pockets and detachable mirror. 9" x 4³/4" x 4¹/4". Black, Evergreen, or Blue. *As seen on cover in Blue.* $20

Departure Pouch Great for travel or everyday use. Features a multitude of inside pockets to store passport, tickets, and monies. Includes see-thru mesh pocket, pen slots, and gusseted compartment. Can be worn over shoulder, around neck, or cinched around the waist. 6" x 12". Black, Evergreen, or Blue. *As seen on cover in Black.* $16

Padded Travel Pouch Main zipper compartment is padded to protect a compact camera or mini binoculars. Carries as a belt pouch, or use 1" strap to convert into waist or shoulder pack. Front flap is secured by a quick release closure. 6" x 9" x 3". Black, Evergreen, or Blue. *As seen on cover in Evergreen.* $26

Undercover Neckpouch Ripstop nylon with a soft Cambrelle back. Three pockets. 5¹/4" x 6¹/2". Lifetime guarantee. Black or Tan. $9.95

Undercover Waistpouch Ripstop nylon with a soft Cambrelle back. Two pockets. 4³/4" x 12" with adjustable waistband. Lifetime guarantee. Black or Tan. $9.95

*Prices and availability of products are subject to change.

1-800-5-LETS GO

Discounted Airfares

Available on international flights all over the world. Domestic fares too! For prices and reservations, call 1-800-5-LETS GO.

1996 International ID Cards

Provides discounts on accommodations, airfares, tourist attractions, rental cars and more! Also includes basic accident and medical insurance. Instructions for ordering are located on the next page, at top of order form.

International Student ID Card (ISIC)......................$18
International Teacher ID Card (ITIC)......................$19
International Youth ID Card (GO25)..................$18

Hostelling Essentials

1996-97 Hostelling Membership: Often required at international hostels. Cardholders usually receive first preference and discounts. Must have a U.S. address to apply.
Adult (ages 18-55)..$25
Youth (under 18)..$10
Senior and family memberships also available.Please call.

Sleepsack: Required at all hostels. Two thin sheets sewn together (78" x 30") with 18" pillow pocket. Durable poly/cotton. Washable, folds into pouch size..$13.95

1996 International Youth Hostel Guide (IYHG): Contains essential information about the 4000 hostels located in Europe and the Mediterranean. $10.95

Travel Guides

Let's Go Travel Guides: The bible of the budget traveler! All 22 titles available.

Europe • USA & Canada................................$18.99

Regional & Country Guides (please specify)....$16.99
Alaska & The Pacific Northwest • Austria & Switzerland • Britain & Ireland • California & Hawaii • Central America • Eastern Europe • France • Germany • Greece & Turkey • Ireland • Israel & Egypt • Italy • Mexico • Southeast Asia • Spain & Portugal

City Guides (please specify)..........................$15.99
London • New York City • Paris • Rome • Washington, DC.

Let's Go Map Guides: New item for 1996! Includes fold-out maps and up to 40 pages of text!
City Maps (please specify) $7.95
Boston•London•NewYorkCity•Paris•San Francisco•Washington, DC

Eurail Passes

The most convenient and affordable way to travel in Europe. Save up to 70% off the cost of individual tickets.

Prices listed are 1995 prices. 1996 prices were not available at time of publishing; prices are expected to increase 5% to 6% and are subject to change. Please call before ordering to verify prices.

Eurailpass (First Class): Unlimited train travel for a specified duration of time. Accepted in 17 countries.
15 days...$498
21 days...$648
1 month...$798
2 months...$1098
3 months...$1398

Eurail Flexipass (First Class): Individual travel days that can be used at your convenience within a two month period.
Any 5 days in 2 months................................$348
Any 10 days in 2 months.............................$560
Any 15 days in 2 months.............................$740

Eurail Youthpass (Second Class): The same advantages of the Eurailpass but for those travelers who will be under 26 years old by the first date of the travel on the train.
15 days...$398
1 month...$578
2 months...$1078

Eurail Youth Flexipass (Second Class): The convenience of the Eurail Flexipass but for those travelers who will be under 26 years old by the first date of the travel on the train.
Any 5 days in 2 months................................$225
Any 10 days in 2 months.............................$398
Any 15 days in 2 months.............................$540

Europass: Offers the option of purchasing travel days within a two month period for 3, 4, or 5 country combinations for the following countries: France • Germany • Italy • Spain • Switzerland. Associate countries can also be added. Call for more details.

Regional and Country Passes and Point-to-Point Tickets also available. Call for more details.

1-800-5-LETS GO

Order Form

Please print or type. Incomplete applications will not be processed.

International Student/Teacher Identity Card (ISIC/ITIC) (ages 12 and up) enclose:

1. Proof of status (letter from registrar or administrator, proof of tuition payment, or copy of student/faculty ID card. FULL-TIME only.)
2. One picture (1 1/2" x 2") signed on the reverse side.
3. Proof of birthdate (copy of passport, birth certificate, or driver's license).

GO25 card (ages 12-25) enclose:

1. Proof of birthdate (copy of passport, birth certificate, or driver's license).
2. One picture (1 1/2" x 2") signed on the reverse side.

| Last Name | First Name | Date of Birth |

| Street | We do not ship to P.O. Boxes. | |

| City | State | Zip Code |

| Phone (very important!) | Citizenship (Country) |

| School/College | Date of Travel |

Description, Size	Color	Quantity	Unit Price	Total Price

Shipping & Handling

Domestic

If order totals ....add
up to $30.00........................$4
$30.01-100.00....................$6
over $100.00........................$8
add additional $5 for AK & HI

International

via Federal Express............$30

Total Merchandise Price	
Shipping and Handling (See box at left)	
Add $10 for Rush, $20 for Overnight	
MA Residents (Add 5% sales tax on gear & books)	
Total	
From which Let's Go Guide are you ordering?	

Master Card/Visa/Amex Order

cardholder name_____

card number_____

expiration date_____

Allow 2-3 weeks for delivery. Rush orders guaranteed within one week of our receipt.

Make check or money order payable to:

Let's Go Travel

53A Church Street • Cambridge, MA 02138 • USA

1-800-5-LETS GO

station to about the Rio dei Santi Apostoli, lies the *sestiere* **Cannaregio.** Continuing clockwise around the Canal, **Castello** is just south of the Rio di S. Giovanni Crisotomo, and **San Marco** extends from the Mercerie and P. San Marco to the Ponte Accademia. The easternmost extension of Venice is the **Santa Elena** *sestiere.* Cross the Rialto bridge from P. San Bartolomeo, and you will find yourself in the **San Polo** district. West of San Polo and encompassing Piazzale Roma is the *sestiere* of **Santa Croce.** Now trace an imaginary line from Cà Rezzonico on the Grand Canal to the church of Santa Maria Maggiore on the *rio* of the same name: the land south of this and hooking around to the Punta della Dogana is **Dorsoduro.**

High tides (usually November-April) cause *acque alte,* periodic floodings that swamp parts of the city (notably San Marco) under as much as three feet of water. If you don't like wet feet, check ahead with the tourist office and consult the signs posted at all ACTV landing stages. *Acque alte* usually last two to three hours, and planks or platforms are laid out across most major thoroughfares.

If you plan to drive to Venice, take the "Ponte della Libertà" causeway which ends in Piazzale Roma. Parking facilities can be found in P. Roma in the garages *comunale* and San Marco, with additional parking on the adjacent island of Tronchetto (follow the road signs). Parking on the Tronchetto "car park island" with 5000 parking spaces could cost you as much as L37,000 per day, while parking in the garages at the P. Roma runs up to L45,000 for a 24-hr. period. Motorists should consider leaving their cars in the parking lot at the Mestre train station on the mainland and taking a train into Venice (all trains into and out of Venice stop at Mestre).

Vaporetti

The alternative to walking is taking the **vaporetti** (motorboat buses), which cruise the Venetian waterways. (They're also an inexpensive, if less romantic, option to the *gondole.*) Most principal boats run 24 hrs., but frequencies are reduced after 11pm. A 24-hr. *biglietto turistico,* available at any ticket office, allows you unlimited travel on all boats (L15,000). You can also purchase a three-day ticket for L30,000. Neither is really worthwhile unless you're on a kamikaze tour. The ACTV office offers a special three day ticket for holders of the **Rolling Venice Card** (see tourist offices under Practical Information) for L20,000.

Not all stations sell tickets all the time—buy extras, but make sure to get the type that can be machine-validated (upon boarding) at any station. Tickets may be bought at the booths in front of the *vaporetti* stops and at various self-serve dispensers (located at the ACTV office at P. Roma and at the Rialto stop). Tickets may also be bought from the conductor after boarding (L800 surcharge). Be sure to count your change carefully when buying tickets at the station booths. Tourists dashing for a departing *vaporetto* sometimes find themselves short a few *lire* once the boat is on its way. The fine for riding the *vaporetti* without a ticket is L30,000. Enforcement can be lax, but tourists are much more prone to being checked (and fined) than locals..

Let's Go: Italy tries to help you by including the **map grid coordinates** of our Venice listings whenever possible. Due to the nightmarish complexity of Venetian streets we sometimes list two adjacent squares.

PRACTICAL INFORMATION

Tourist Offices: APT, Palazzetto Selva (E5; tel. 522 63 56). Exit P. S. Marco and turn right along the waterfront. The office is just past the park. Ask for *A Guest in Venice,* an indispensable booklet listing current exhibitions and shows. Open Tues.-Sun. 9:30am-12:30pm and 2-5pm. Also at the **train station** (B3; tel./fax 71 90 78). Usually mobbed; get in line at the left side of the booth. Open Tues.-Sun. 8am-7pm. In the **Lido** at Gran Viale 6/A (tel. 526 57 21). Open Mon.-Sat. 9am-2pm. **Hotel Information: AVA,** in the train station, just to the right of the tourist office (B3; tel. 71 50 16). Makes reservations in 1- and 2-star hotels with a deposit.

VENICE

Open daily 8am-10pm; Oct.-April 9am-9pm. Also an office at **P. Roma,** 540/D (B4; tel. 522 86 40). Open daily 9am-10pm; Oct.-Apr. 9am-9pm. **Youth Discount Card: Rolling Venice,** Comune di Venezia, Assessorato alla Gioventù, San Marco, 1529 (D-E5; tel. 270 76 50; fax 270 76 42), on Corte Contarina. Exit P. S. Marco opposite the *basilica* and turn right at the post office. Follow the road left and continue straight through the building (look for the yellow *Comune di Venezia* signs). Take a left, then a right, and go into the courtyard. For ages 14-29, discount card (L5000), valid at many hotels, restaurants, shops, and museums in Venice. Also gives a discounted price (L20,000, normally L30,000) for the 3-day *vaporetto* pass, valid on all lines. Comes with a guidebook featuring Venetian history and sight-seeing itineraries and a map listing the locations of participating establishments. Worth it if you're in Venice for more than a couple of days.

Police: Carabinieri, P. Roma (B4; tel. 523 53 33 or 112 in an emergency).

Post Office: San Marco, 5554 (E4; tel. 528 62 12), on Salizzada Fontego dei Tedeschi near the eastern end of the Rialto bridge off Campo San Bartolomeo. *Fermo posta* at #4, stamps at #12 or *tabacchi* all over town. Open Mon.-Sat. 8:15am-6:45pm. **Branch office** (E5) through the arcades at the end of P. San Marco. Open Mon.-Fri. 8:15am-1:30pm, Sat. 8:15am-12:10pm. **Postal Code:** 30124.

Telephones: Telecom, (B3) train station. Booths open 24 hrs. Also at San Marco, Fontego dei Tedeschi, 5550 (E4), next to the main post office (open Mon.-Sat. 8am-7:45pm), in P. Roma (B4), and along Viale Santa Maria Elisabetta on the Lido. Open daily 8am-9:30pm. **Telephone Code:** 041.

Budget Travel: CTS, Dorsoduro, 3252 (C4-5; tel. 520 56 60; fax 523 69 46) on Fondamenta Tagliapietra. Off the Dorsoduro-to-San Marco route, near Campo S. Margherita. Take Calle Piove to Calle Larga Foscari and turn right after crossing the bridge. Office on the bank of Rio Foscari. Open Mon.-Fri. 9am-12:30pm and 3:30-7pm. **Transalpino** (B3; tel/fax 71 66 00), for international train tickets, is to the right as you exit the train station. Open Tues.-Fri. 8:30am-12:30pm and 3-7pm, Sat. 8:30am-12:30pm, and Mon. 3-7pm.

Consulates: U.K., (C5) Dorsoduro, 1051 (E4-5; tel. 522 72 07). Cross the Accademia bridge from S. Marco and turn right. Open Mon.-Sat. 9am-noon and 2-4pm. The closest U.S., Canadian, and Australian consulates are in Milan; New Zealand and South African citizens should contact their embassy in Rome.

Currency Exchange: Banco Ambrosiano Veneto, San Marco, 4481 (E4-5; tel. 290 31 11) on Calle Goldoni off Campo S. Luca. Open Mon.-Fri. 8:20am-1:20pm and 2:35-4:05pm. Another **branch** in San Marco, 2378/A (D5) on Calle Larga XXII Marzo with the same hours. Some of the best rates you'll find in the region.

American Express: San Marco, Sal. S. Moise, 1471 (E5; tel. 520 08 44), between S. Marco and the Accademia (look for the AmEx directional mosaic underfoot). Mail service for those with a card or traveler's cheques only; no fees apply. No commission, but mediocre exchange rates. Office open Mon.-Fri. 9am-5:30pm, Sat. 9am-12:30pm. Exchange service open in summer Mon.-Sat. 8am-8pm.

Flights: Aeroporto Marco Polo (tel. 541 54 91). Take the ACTV (tel. 528 78 86) local bus #5 (every 1½hr., 30min., L1200), or take the ATVO coach (tel. 520 55 30) with luggage space for L5000.

Trains: Stazione di Santa Lucia (B3; tel. 71 55 55, lost and found 71 61 22). Info office in station across from tourist office. Open daily 7:15am-9:20pm. To: Padua (every 15min., 30min., L3400); Bologna (at least 20 per day, 1½hr., L13,600); Milan (18 per day, 3hr., L21,000); Florence (6 per day, 3hr., L21,000); Rome (6 per day, 5hr., L45,000). **Luggage Storage:** L1500 per day. Open 24 hrs.

Buses: ACTV, the local line for buses and boats (B4; tel. 528 78 86) in P. Roma. Open Mon.-Sat. 8am-2:30pm. Closed the last 2 weeks in Aug. **ATP** is the long-distance carrier. Buses roughly every 30min. to: the villas on the Riviera del Brenta (Malcontenta L1200, Mira L2700, Strà L3600), Padua (L4200), Mestre (L1200), Treviso (L3000). Ticket office open daily 6:40am-10pm. Information office open Mon.-Sat. 8am-6:30pm. Fine for riding without a ticket: L30,000.

Car Rental: Avis, Piazzale Roma, 496/G (B4; tel. 522 58 25). Open Mon.-Fri. 8am-7pm, Sat. 8am-1pm. **Budget,** P. Roma (B4; tel. 520 00 00; fax 522 30 00), just down from Avis. Open Mon.-Fri. 8:30am-noon and 3:30-6pm, Sat. 8:30am-noon.

Rates for both places approx. L150,000 per day, L180,000per weekend, L600,000 per week. Must be 21 or older with a credit card.

Laundromat: Lavaget, Cannaregio, 1269 (tel. 71 59 76), on Fondamenta Pescaria. Take a left from the station, cross 1 bridge, and turn left along the canal. 3 kilos L45,000, soap included. Open Mon.-Fri. 8:30am-12:30pm and 3-7pm.

Public Baths: Albergo Diurno (Day Hotel), San Marco, 1266 (E5), in the *ramo secondo* (2°), off the west end of P. San Marco. Toilets L500. Open daily 7am-8pm. Also in the **station** (B3)—next to *binario* (track) 1. Showers L4000. Soap and towel each L500. Open daily 7am-8pm. **Toilets** are scattered throughout town; look for "WC" signs where street signs are located. *Gabinetti* (also *toilette*) can be found on either side of the Rialto, on the waterfront near P. San Marco, under the Dorsoduro side of the Accademia bridge (L500), in P. Roma (B4) near Treponte, and in Castello on Calle Morosina, 4052/A (F5), to name but a few. Toilet L500, shower L3000, with towels L4000. Open daily 8am-7pm.

English Bookstores: Libreria Editrice Cafoscarina, Dorsoduro, 3246 (C5; tel. 523 89 69; fax 522 81 86) on Cà Foscari along the Rialto-to-Accademia route. The largest selection in Venice, including *Let's Go*. Rolling Venice: 10% discount. Open Mon.-Fri. 9am-7pm, Sat. 9am-12:30pm. Also try **Libreria Turcato**, Dorsoduro, 3214 (C5; tel. 523 18 64) on the corner at Calle del Cappeller, 2min. from the above along the same route. Smaller selection, but more contemporary books. Rolling Venice: 10% discount. Open Mon.-Fri. 9am-12:30pm and 3-7:30pm, Sat. 9am-12:30pm. MC, Visa.

Hotel Crises: Questura, on Fondamenta San Lorenzo in the Castello (F4; tel. 270 36 11). Contact them if you have a serious complaint about your hotel.

Late-Night Pharmacy: Check *A Guest in Venice* or call 192.

Emergencies: tel. 113. **Hospital: Ospedale Civili,** Campo SS. Giovanni e Paolo (E-F3; tel. 529 45 17). **Boat Ambulance/Medical Assistance:** tel. 523 00 00.

ACCOMMODATIONS

Plan to spend slightly more on rooms here than elsewhere in Italy. Reservations, preferably made as much as a month in advance, will preserve your sanity in summer. To avoid the crowds and expense of summertime stays in Venice, visit the city while based in a nearby town (Padua, 30min. away, is a good place to secure a room). In Venice, the **APT** at the train station and the **AVA** hotel service near the bus station will book rooms, but proprietors are more willing to bargain in person.

The singles listed below vanish in summer. If the situation becomes desperate, you can always resort to one of the campgrounds at Mestre (ask at the tourist office) or Padua's youth hostel (closes at 11pm, last train at 9:15pm). The police frown on impromptu crashing in parks or on beaches.

Dormitory-type accommodations are always available in Venice without reservations, even during August and September. Such accommodations often have irregular operating seasons, so check with the tourist offices to see which are open. In *pensioni*, look out for L12,000 breakfasts and other forms of bill-padding, and always agree on what you'll pay (and whether you want breakfast, etc.) before you hit the sack or surrender your passport. **Remember that prices are likely to have risen since this book's publication**; for better or for worse, the price quoted at the hotel is what you'll have to pay.

Institutional Accommodations

Ostello Venezia (HI), Fondamenta di Zitelle, 86 (E7; tel. 523 82 11; fax 523 56 89), on Giudecca. Take *vaporetto* #82 or #52 from the station (25min., L3500) from San Zaccaria near San Marco (5min., L2500). Get off at Zitelle and walk right. A recently renovated warehouse on the canal; you'll feel like you're in a *caffè*. English spoken. Check-in 1-10:30pm—the tourist office at the train station will let you know if they're already full. Lockout 9:30am-1pm. Curfew 11:30pm. L21,000 per person, small breakfast included, full meals L12,000. Membership required; HI cards available. No phone reservations.

Ostello Santa Fosca, Cannaregio, 2372 (D2; tel. 71 57 75), on Fondamenta Canal. From the train station, walk left along the main street over 3 bridges. Turn left

VENICE

over the bridge at the next *piazza* (S. Fosca), and left along the canal. Run by students. Dormitory-style rooms. Foosball and huge kitchen facilities. Check-in 10am-noon and 6-11:30pm. Check-out 9am. Lockout 9am-6pm. Curfew 11:30pm. Dorm L23,000 per person. Rolling Venice: L2000 discount. Open July 5-Sept 18.

Foresteria Valdese, Castello, 5170 (E4; tel. 528 67 97). Take the *vaporetto* to San Zaccharia, then walk to Campo Santa Maria Formosa (5min.). From the *campo*, take Calle Lunga S. M. Formosa, just over the 1st bridge. This is the 18th-century guesthouse of Venice's biggest Protestant church. Amiable management, frescoed ceilings in many rooms. Check-in 9am-1pm and 6-8pm. Lockout 10am-1pm. Dorms with bunk beds L25,000 per person, L23,000 each additional night. Breakfast included. Reserve 1 mo. ahead for their 2 beautiful doubles (L64,000). Two apartments with bath and kitchen; one L135,000 per day (4 beds), the other 150,000 per day (5 beds), breakfast not included. Phone reservations suggested. Closed 15 days in Nov.

Domus Civica, ACISJF, San Polo, 3082 (C4; tel. 72 11 03 or 52 40 46), across the street from a bar in both directions, on the corner of Calle Chiovere, Calle Campazzo, and S. Rocco, between the Frari Church and P. Roma. Along the road, follow the yellow arrows between P. Roma and the Rialto. Men and women welcome. Run by a church-affiliated organization. Everything the heart could desire: ping-pong tables, TV room, piano. Curfew 11:30pm. Singles L32,000. Doubles L54,000. Rolling Venice or ISIC: 20% discount. Open June to mid-Oct.

Suore Cannosiano, Fondamenta del Ponte Piccolo, 428 (C7; tel. 522 21 57), also on Giudecca. Take boat #82 to Giudecca stop and walk left just over the bridge. Women only. Nun-run. Arrive any time of day to leave your bags. Check-out 7:30-8:30am. Lockout 9am-3pm. Curfew 10:30pm. Large dorm-style rooms L17,000 per person.

Cannaregio (From the Station to the Rialto)

The area around the station on and near Lista di Spagna offers the best and most convenient selection in the city.

Hotel Calderan, Cannaregio, 283 (C2; tel. 71 55 62), in P. San Geremia at the end of Lista di Spagna. A short walk from the station. Large rooms with matching furniture; all without private bath. Some rooms overlook the square or the park behind. Friendly, family-run hotel. No English spoken. No curfew; you are given your own set of keys. Singles L35,000. Doubles L55,000-60,000. Triples L75,000. Quads L100,000. Breakfast L6000. Reserve ahead Aug.-Oct. MC, Visa.

Hotel Bernardi, Cannaregio, 4366, (D3; tel. 522 72 57; fax 522 24 24) on Calle dell'Oca. *Vaporetto* #1 to Cà d'Oro. Walk down Strada Nuova, turn left onto Calle dell'Oca. The hotel is in a small alleyway. Gorgeous, newly-renovated rooms. Owner is multi-lingual. Check-out 10:30am. Singles L35,000. Doubles L59,000, with bath L85,000. Breakfast L4000. Rolling Venice: 15% discount. MC, Visa.

Locanda Antica Casa Carettoni, Cannaregio, 130 (C2-3; tel. 71 62 31), along Rio Terrà Lista di Spagna, to the left of the station. Rooms steeped in antiquity described by the proud proprietor as "truly Venetian." Curfew midnight. Singles L35,000. Doubles L58,000. Triples L84,000. Closed either Aug. or Oct.

Hotel Minerva and Nettuno, Cannaregio, 230 (C2-3; tel. 71 59 68; fax 524 21 39), on your left on Lista di Spagna from the station. Large, remodeled rooms and convenient locale make this a prime choice. Singles L54,000, with bath L71,000. Doubles L78,000, with bath L114,000. Triples L102,000, with bath L147,000. Quads L126,000, with bath L180,000. Breakfast included. Rolling Venice: 15% discount. AmEx, MC, Visa.

Albergo Adua, Cannaregio, 233/A (C2-3; tel. 71 61 84), on Lista di Spagna. Tidy rooms with flowered wallpaper, most with wall-to-wall carpeting. Small, family-run, and quiet for the neighborhood. Singles L48,000. Doubles L65,000, with bath L105,000. Triples L90,000, with bath L142,000. Extra beds: 35% more per bed. Breakfast L8000. MC, Visa.

Dorsoduro and Santa Croce

Cà Foscari, Dorsoduro, 3887/B (C4-5; tel./fax 71 08 17), on Calle della Frescada. Take *vaporetto* #1 or #82 to San Tomà. Get off the boat, turn left over the bridge, and follow the road right, then left. Family-run with pride, in a quiet location. You'll want to take the elaborate furniture home with you. Singles 70,000. Doubles L85,000, with toilet or shower L120,000. Triples L115,000. Quads L140,000. Breakfast included. Closes at 1am. Rooms held until 2pm. Open Feb.-Nov.

Locanda Montin, Dorsoduro, 1147 (C5; tel. 522 71 51), near Accademia. Take boat #1 to Cà Rezzonico, walk straight ahead to Campo San Barnaba, go south through the passageway Casin dei Nobili, across the bridge, right on the Fondamenta Lombardo, and around the corner onto Fondamenta di Borgo. Modern paintings, restored antiques, and enthusiastic owners. Singles L55,000. Doubles L70,000, with bath L80,000. Breakfast included. Reserve with 1 night's deposit. Closed 20 days in Jan. and 10 days in Aug. AmEx, MC, Visa.

Hotel Messner, Rio Terrà Spizier, 217 (D6; tel. 522 72 66). Take bus #1 to the Chiesa della Salute stop. Walk past Chiesa della Salute, cross the white bridge, and continue straight ahead. Discounts available for large groups. Get a room in the annex, or face poverty: singles L65,000, with bath L100,000; doubles L90,000, with bath L130,000. Triples L117,000, with bath L169,000. Quads L147,000, with bath L200,000. Breakfast included. AmEx, MC, Visa.

San Marco (From the Basilica west to the Grand Canal)

Locanda San Salvador, San Marco, 5264 (E4; tel. 528 91 47), on Calle del Galliazzo, off Campo San Bartolomeo. Take *vaporetto* #1 or #82 to Rialto. Good views, large terrace. Right in the middle of the action. English spoken. Singles L55,000. Doubles L80-85,000, with bath L100,000. Triples L105,000, with bath L130,000. Extra bed: 35% more. Rolling Venice: 10% discount. Phone ahead. Proprietor may be able to find another room for you if they're booked.

Locande San Samuele, San Marco, 3358 (C5; tel. 522 80 45). Follow Calle delle Botteghe from Campo S. Stefano (near the Accademia) and go left on Salizzada S. Samuele. Large, attractive rooms with stone floors in a great part of town. Singles L45,000. Doubles L59,000, with bath L85,000. Breakfast L7000. Reserve ahead with 1 night's deposit.

Alloggi Alla Scala, San Marco, 4306 (D5; tel. 521 06 29). From Campo Manin take Calle della Vida o della Locande, then a left and a quick right on Corte Contarini del Bovolo. Located in a quiet and historic courtyard. Gorgeous, colorful rooms *alla carnevale*. Doubles L75-85,000. Extra bed: L30,000. Breakfast L7500. Reserve with 1 night's deposit. Closed Aug.

Locanda Casa Petrarca, San Marco, 4386 (D5; tel. 520 04 30). Take *vaporetto* #1 or #82 to the Rialto, walk inland and to the right until you reach Campo San Luca, then go south on Calle dei Fuseri, take the 2nd left and then turn right onto Calle Schiavone. English spoken. Singles L65,000. Doubles L88,000, with bath L110,000. Extra bed: 35% more. 5% discount with *Let's Go*. Phone ahead; rooms held until 3pm.

Hotel Riva, San Marco, 5310 (E4; tel. 522 70 34), on Ponte dell'Angelo. From P. S. Marco, walk under the clock tower and take a right on Calle Larga S. Marco. Turn left on Calle Angelo and go over the bridge. A brand-new hotel packed with Venetian antiques. All rooms overlook a canal. Prime location. Singles with bath L90,000. Doubles L95,000, with bath L120,000. Breakfast included. Closes at 1am. Reserve 2 weeks ahead with 1 night's deposit. Closed Nov.-Jan.

Castello (From San Marco to the Island of Sant'Elena)

Hotel Caneva, Castello, 5515 (E4; tel. 522 81 18), 2min. from the Rialto. Take Calle Stagneri from P. S. Bartolomeo, cross the bridge, and turn right after Campo della Fava. *The* find of this area. Most rooms overlook a canal and about half are carpeted. All include TV. Singles L50,000. Doubles L80,000, with shower L110,000. Triples L104,000, with bath L143,000. Quads L124,000, with bath L176,000. Breakfast included. Closed Nov. and Jan. AmEx, MC, Visa.

Locanda Sant'Anna, Castello, 269 (H5; tel. 528 64 66). Take Via Garibaldi, which becomes Fondamenta Santa Anna, turn left on Ponte Santa Anna, then right at

Corte del Bianco (*vaporetto*: #1 or 4 to Giardini). Worth the hike for the rooms and the neighborhood. Friendly family proprietors and a refreshing absence of tourists. TV downstairs. Curfew midnight. Singles L60,000. Doubles L86,000, with shower L96,000, with toilet L109,000. Triples L150,000. Quads 160,000-180,000. Breakfast included. Reserve with 1 night's deposit. MC, Visa.

Pensione Casa Verardo, Castello, 4765 (E4-5; tel. 528 61 27). Take Rimpetto la Sacrestia out of Campo SS. Filippo e Giacomo across the bridge. Large rooms with eclectic furnishings. No surface spared from decoration. Singles L55,000. Doubles L85,000 with shower, L95,000 with bathroom. Triples L130,000 with shower, L140,000 with bathroom. Quads L150,000 with shower, L160,000 with bathroom. Breakfast L7000. Reserve with 1 night's deposit. MC, Visa.

Locanda Corona, Castello, 4464 (F4; tel. 522 91 74; *vaporetto*: San Zaccharia). Head north on Sacrestia, from Campo SS. Filippo e Giacomo, take the first right, and then the first left onto Calle Corona. Fine rooms, limited hot water supply. Drop by the Fucina degli Angeli (Angel's Forge) next door for a look at glass-blowing. Singles L48,000. Doubles L72,000. Triples L107,000. Showers L3000. Closed late Jan.-early Feb.

Locanda Silva, Castello, 4423 (E4; tel. 522 76 43; fax 528 68 17). From S. Marco, walk under the Torre d'Orologio and take a right on C. Larga S. Marco, then a left on Calle d'Angelo. Turn right at Calle e Ramo Drio La Fara and cross the bridge. Walk down the street to the canal and turn left. Large and fastidiously kept. Singles L50,000. Doubles L80,000, with shower L95,000, with bath L105,000. Triples L115,000, with bath L150,000. Quads L130,000, with bath L180,000. Includes breakfast. Closed 2am. Open Feb.-Nov.

Camping

The **Litorale del Cavallino,** on the Adriatic side of the Lido east of Venice, is an endless row of campgrounds on the beach. From S. Marco, take *vaporetto* #14 to Punta Sabbioni (40min., L3500). You'll find **Camping Miramare,** Punta Sabbioni (tel. 96 61 50; fax 530 11 50), about 700m along the beach to your right from the Punta Sabbioni *vaporetto* stop. L7500 per person and L16,600 per tent in high season. Four-person bungalow L47,000, 5-person L68,000. Open Feb.-Nov. Take bus #5 to the Cà Pasquali stop (L2500). The bus passes Via Poerio (on your left). **Cà Pasquali,** Via Poerio, 33 (tel. 96 61 10; fax 530 07 97). In high season: L8000 per person, L10,000 per car. 4-person bungalow L83,500, 5-person, L116,000. Showers included. Open Mar.-Sept. Major credit cards accepted. Another option is **Campeggio Fusina,** Via Moranzani, in the locality of Malcontenta (tel. 547 00 55). L9500 per person, L7000 per tent, and L18,000 per tent and car. English spoken. Call ahead. From P. Roma, take bus #4 (L1100) to Mestre and change to bus #13 (across the street from Supermarket Pam). Ride to the last stop (1hr., last bus 9pm).

FOOD

It is becoming difficult to sit down to a good meal in Venice without emptying your wallet (assuming your wallet has some *lire* in it before the meal starts). To avoid paying a fortune, visit any *bar* or *osteria* in town and make a meal from the vast display of meat- and cheese-filled pastries, tidbits of seafood, rice, and meat, and *tramezzini,* triangular slices of soft white bread with every imaginable filling. (Venetians have long cultivated the tradition of this between-meal repast, known as the *cicchetto,* always washed down by *un'ombra,* a glass of local wine.) Good deals on tourist *menùs* abound along the broad **Via Garibaldi,** a lovely 15-min. walk along the waterfront from P. San Marco. Don't be afraid to walk the small alleyways, where you'll find less touristed eateries. If you're going to splurge, try one of the local seafood dishes. *Seppie in nero* is a tasty, soft squid-like creature coated with its own ink and usually served with *polenta,* Veneto's cornmeal mush staple. A plate of *pesce fritta mista* (mixed fried seafood, at least L12,000) usually includes *calamari* (squid), *polpo* (small octopus), shrimp, and the catch of the day. *Fegato alla veneziana* is the familiar but yummy liver and onions.

Kosher food is served in Europe's oldest Jewish quarter, the Ghetto Nuovo. Call or write ahead to reserve a space at the Casa Israelitica di Reposo, Cannaregio 2874 (C2; tel. 71 60 02), located across the Campo del Ghetto Nuovo from the Museo Ebraico. Take a left from the station, turn left after the first bridge and follow the yellow Hebrew signs to the *campo*. L35,000 per person, lunch served at 12:30pm, dinner at 7:30pm. Open daily year-round.

The Veneto and Friuli regions produce an abundance of excellent and inexpensive wines. A good local white wine is the sparkling, dry *prosecco della Marca,* or the *collio,* another dry white. In reds, try a *merlot* or *marzemino. Osterie* or *baccari,* simple and usually authentic wine and snack bars, can be found in alleys and streets throughout the city. Venetians drop by in the late afternoon, before dinner.

There are a few street markets in town. Located in the area surrounding the Rialto (San Polo side), the most famous market was once the center of trade and merchandise for the Venetian Republic. Fruit stands line the Ruga degli Orefici, and on the right are the *erberia* (vegetable) and *pescheria* (fish) markets. Another morning market appears in Cannaregio on Rio Terra S. Leonardo, just past Ponte Guglie.

Locals shop on the side streets near Campo Beccarie in San Polo near the Rialto. Less entertaining but more convenient are the *alimentari*. In Cannaregio, STANDA, on Strada Nuova, 3660 (D3), near Campo S. Felice, has groceries in the back (open daily 9am-7:20pm). In Castello near San Marco, there's Su. Ve., 5816, on Calle del Mondo Novo, off Campo Santa Maria Formosa. (Open Mon.-Tues., Thurs.-Fri. and Sat. 8:30am-1pm and 4-7:30pm, Wed. 8:30am-1pm.) In Dorsoduro, go to Mega I, at Campo Santa Margherita, 3019/B (C5), an unmarked entrance between a phone booth and a *caffè*. (Open Sun.-Fri. 9am-12:50pm and 5-7:45pm, Sat. 9am-8pm.) In Giudecca, try Vivo Supermarket, on Fondamenta delle Zitelle, 203A (E7), to the left of the *Redatore* church. (Closed Wed. afternoon and Sun.)

One word of caution: don't make the mistake of trying to rinse off your sticky *gelato*-smeared hands in the canal—those stairs leading into the water have been gathering slippery moss since Michelangelo was a boy.

Cannaregio

Caffè Puggi, Campo della Maddalena, 2103 (D2; tel. 524 07 58). On the main route, left from the station, across two bridges. A popular student hangout with loud music. *Panini* L3000-5000, wine L800-2500 per glass. Open Mon.-Sat. 7:30am-midnight.

I Quattro Rusteghi, Campo Ghetto Nuovo, 2888 (C2; tel. 524 06 35; fax 524 21 39). *Menù* including noodles, fried fish, potatoes, and bread costs L12,000. Decent food in an historic part of town. Owners discount 10% for *Let's Go* readers. Open Tues.-Sun. noon-3pm and 7-10pm. MC, Visa.

Ristorante Vegetariano, Cannaregio, 5401 (E3; tel. 523 81 53). On Calle Gallina, 2 bridges from Campo SS. Giovanni e Paolo. Organic dishes and brown rice. Indian food every Tues. *Primi* L8000-12,000. Combination dishes L13,000-19,000. *Menù* L22,000. No cover charge. Open Mon.-Fri. noon-2:30pm and 7-10:30pm, Sat 7-10:30pm. AmEx, MC, Visa.

Ristorante al Ponte, Cannaregio, 2352 (C2; tel. 72 07 44), quite literally *on* Ponte dell'Ancoretta, the 2nd bridge after you turn left from the station, just past P. San Geremia. The *menù* (L16,000) includes everything but beverage, and spotlights regional specialties. Worth the pricey cover charge. *Primi* L5000-9000, *secondi* and fish L8000-19,000. Cover L3000. Service 12%. Open Wed.-Mon. 11:30am-2:30pm and 6:30-9:30pm. AmEx, MC, Visa.

Ai Promessi Sposi, Cannaregio, 4367 (D-E3; tel. 522 86 09). From Strada Nuova, take a left on Calle del Duca just before Campo SS. Apostoli, then the first left. Mellow music and lots of locals. *Primi* L7000-10,000, *secondi* L12,000-18,000. Cover L1500. Open Thurs.-Tues. 10am-3:30pm and 5:30-10:30pm.

Trattoria Casa Mia, Cannaregio, 4430 (D-E3; tel. 528 55 90), in the same alley as Promessi Sposi. Popular with locals. Friendly owner. *Primi* L7000-10,000, *secondi* and fish L16,000-18,000. Cover L2000. Service 12%. Open Wed.-Mon. noon-3pm and 7-10pm. Closed Aug. MC, Visa.

San Polo and Santa Croce

Mensa Universitaria di Cà Foscari, S. Polo, 2480 (C5; tel. 71 80 69), on Calle del Magazen. From the main entrance of the Chiesa dei Frari, go over the bridge, turn left, over the next bridge, left again, followed by a quick right onto Calle del Magazen. Without a doubt the best meal deal in Venice. Full meals including drink L5500 with student ID (ISIC) or L7100 with Rolling Venice card. Open Mon.-Sat. 11:45am-2:30pm and 6:30-8:30pm, Sun. noon-2pm.

Trattoria/Pizzeria All'Anfora, Santa Croce, 1223 (C3; tel. 524 53 25), on Lista dei Bari. From the station, cross the Grand Canal, go straight, and then over the first bridge on your left. Walk around the Chiesa di S. Simeon onto Lista dei Bari. A hearty eatery populated by local folk. Vine-covered patio dining out back. *Primi* L4800-11,000, *secondi* L9000-17,000, pizza L5000-13,000. Cover L2000. Service 12%. Open Wed.-Mon. 7am-9pm. AmEx, MC, Visa.

Pizzeria alle Oche, Santa Croce, 1552 a/b (C3; tel. 524 11 61). Near Campo San Giacomo. Exit Campo San Polo on Calle Bernardo and follow the yellow *Ferrovia* signs over the *Parucheta* bridge. Rumor has it amongst the Venetian student population that it's the best *pizzeria* in town. *Primi* L5500-8500, *secondi* L8500-16,000, pizza L5000-13,500. Cover L2000. Service 12%. Open Tues.-Sun. noon-3pm and 7-11:00pm.

Trattoria alle Burchielle, Santa Croce, 393 (B4; tel. 71 03 42), on the Fondamenta Burchielle, off the corner of P. Roma over the bridge at Campazzo Tre Ponti, the 3-bridge intersection. A *trattoria* along the banks of a small canal since 1503. *Primi* L7000, *secondi* L10,000-15,000. Cover L1700. Service 10%. Open Tues.-Sun. noon-3pm and 7-10:30pm. AmEx, MC, Visa.

Osteria do Mori, San Polo, 429 (D3-4; tel. 522 54 01), from the Rialto, turn left at the end of the market on Ruga Orefici, then take the first right. Venetians have frequented this snack-and-wine bar since 1571. Standing room only. Wine L1500-7000 per glass. *Tramezzini* L1500. Open late Aug.-July Mon.-Tues. and Thurs.-Sat. 8:30am-1:30pm and 5-9pm, Wed. 8:30am-1:30pm.

Aliani Gastronomia, San Polo, 655 (D4; tel. 522 49 13), on Ruga Vecchia San Giovanni, after a left off Ruga Orefici, the street that leads to the Rialto bridge on the San Polo side. The best and most central take-out deli. Cheeses and cold cuts, lavish lasagna, roasted half chicken, and lots of vegetables. Open mid-Aug.-July Mon.-Sat. 8am-1pm and 5-8pm.

Dorsoduro

Ai Pugni, Dorsoduro, 2839 (C5; tel. 523 98 31), along the Rio di S. Barnaba and Fondamenta Gherardini off Campo S. Barnaba. Take *vaporetto* #1 to Cà Rezzonico. Huge, delicious pizzas, and waiters who will sing and dance for you. *Primi* L7000-8000, *secondi* L13,000, pizza L5500-8000. No cover charge. Open for drinks Wed.-Mon. 10am-1am, for eats 1:10-3:30pm and 7pm-1am.

Crepizza, Dorsoduro, 3760 (C4; tel. 522 62 80), on Calle San Pantalon. From Campo S. Margherita, walk across Rio di Cà Foscari and around the right side of Chiesa di S. Pantalon. Crepes (L5500-9000) and pizza (L6000-10,000) served with zeal. Cover L1500. Service 10%. Open Wed.-Mon. noon-2:30pm and 7-10:30pm. MC, Visa.

San Marco

Rosticceria San Bartolomeo, San Marco, 5424/A (E4; tel. 522 35 69), in Calle de la Bissa off Campo San Bartolomeo near the Rialto Bridge, under a sign for Rosticceria. Top-notch self-service. Venetian specialties such as *seppie con polenta* (squid with cornmeal pudding, L13,000). *Primi* L5500-6000, *secondi* L8000-13,000. Cover L2000. Open Feb.-Dec. Tues.-Sun. 9:30am-2:30pm and 4-9pm.

Vino, Vino, San Marco, 2007/A (D5; tel. 523 70 27), on Calle del Sartor da Veste, off Calle Larga XXII Marzo, which runs along the S. Marco to Accademia route. Good food, but you have to eat what they have available. A river of wines (L1000-6000 per glass) and a sea of tourists. *Primi* L7000, *secondi* L13,000. Cover L1000. Rolling Venice: 20% discount on food. Open for drinks Wed.-Mon. 10:30am-midnight; for eats noon-2:30pm and 7-11pm.

Leon Bianco, San Marco, 4153 (D4; tel. 522 11 80), on Sal. San Luca which runs between Campo San Luca and Campo Manin, northwest of P. San Marco. Highbrow interior and low prices make this a popular spot for the business crowd. *Tramezzini* L1600, *primi* L4500, *secondi* L6000. Open Mon.-Sat. 8am-8pm.

Alfredo, Alfredo, (E4) near the Rialto, across from the main post office. Venice's answer to McDonald's. Hamburgers L3000-4700, pizza L3000. Open Mon.-Fri. 11am-9:30pm, Sun. 11am-9pm, Sat. 11am-1am. AmEx, MC, Visa.

Castello

Trattoria Alla Rivetta, Castello, 9625 (E5; tel. 528 73 02), off Campo SS. Filippo e Giacomo. Walk on the left side of the Basilica from P. S. Marco—the restaurant is squeezed into a space right before the Ponte San Provolo. One of the only genuine and reasonable places in the area. *Primi* L7-8000, *secondi* L8000-16,000, excellent fish dishes L6000-15,000. Cover L2000. Service 12%. Open Tues.-Sun. 11am-10pm. Closed Aug.

Antiche Botteselle, Via Garibaldi, 1621 (G-H 5-6; tel. 523 72 92), a broad street that penetrates Castello near the Arsenale stop. A 15-min. waterfront walk from S. Marco. *Menù* L16,000. Cover L1500. Service 12%. There are 36 types of pizza (L5000-8000). *Primi* L6000-12,000. *Secondi* and fish L8000-19,000. Open Thurs.-Tues. 8:30am-3pm and 6-10pm (bar 'til midnight).

Cip Ciap, at Ponte del Mondo Novo, 5799/A (E4; tel. 523 66 21), off Fondamenta Santa Maria Formosa, southwest of the *campo,* deserves highest praise for its pizza (L3000-10,000, slices L1600 per *etto*); the *disco volante* (literally "flying saucer," stuffed with mushrooms, eggplant, ham, and salami, L11,500) is out of this world. Anyone for pizza at 6am? (Open Wed.-Mon. 6am-9pm.)

The Scoop on *Gelato*

Some tips to guide you through your quest for frozen, flavored perfection:

Singola (single) and *doppia* (double) portions are the most common, though some southern locales serve gelato in a *brioche* (sweet pastry bun). Some *gelateria* require you to pay before you eat, so head for the *cassa* (cashier) and present your receipt to the scooper. Saying *"con panna"* will add a mound of fresh whipped cream to your serving

Some flavorful vocabulary: *mela* (**apple**), *ananas* (**banana**), *mirtillo* (**blueberry**), *stracciatella* (**chocolate chip**), *cannella* (**cinnamon**), *noce/cocco* (**coconut**), *nocciola* (**hazelnut**), *miele* (**honey**), *latte/panna* (**milk/cream**), *arancia* (**orange**), *pesca* (PES-kah, **peach**—DON'T say *pesce* (PESH-ay); it means "fish"), *lampone* (**raspberry**), and *fragola* (**strawberry**). There are also some flavors that don't exist in America, like *baci* (chocolate and hazelnut, like the candy), *cassata* (fruity ice cream with nuts and candied fruits), riso (**rice**), and **tiramisu** (espresso, sweet cheese, and chocolate, like the dessert).

Many *gelaterie* also carry **soy-based gelato,** for the vegan and lactose-intolerant among us; another option is a flavored ice called *granita*. Don't knock the prepackaged *gelati* (you'll see signs everywhere you go); biting into **cornetti** is a national pastime, sure to cheer any weary wanderer.

Do not pig out. Let's Go does not recommend eating too much *gelato*.

Gelaterie and Pasticcerie

Idea Gelato, Castello 5727, (E4; tel. 522 32 83) on Sal. S. Lio, off Campo S. Lio. THE *gelateria* of Venice—you'll know by the tons of locals taking some home for the family, the big scoops for few *lire,* and the fact that you'll want seconds. Open daily 10am-8:30pm.

Gelateria Mille Voglie, San Polo, 3033 (C4; tel. 524 46 67), on Sal. S. Rocco. In the shadow of the Chiesa dei Frari on the way to the Chiesa di S. Rocco. One of the best and cheapest places in Venice. Cones L1000-3500. Plate-sized pizzas L2500. Open daily 9am-midnight.

Gelateria Santo Stefano, San Marco, 2962/A (C-D5; tel. 522 55 76), in the far corner of Campo Morosini San Stefano on the S. Marco side of the Accademia bridge.

Said to have the best *nocciola* (hazelnut) and *panna* (whipped cream) in the world. Cones L1500-3000. Open April-Sept. Tues.-Sun. 8am-11:30pm; Oct.-Nov. and Feb.-March 7:30am-9pm. Closed Dec.-Jan.

Gelati Nico, Fondamenta Zattere, 922 (C6; tel. 522 52 93), in Dorsoduro near the *vaporetto* stop of the same name, is the pride of Venice. *Gianduiotto,* a slice of dense chocolate hazelnut ice cream dunked in whipped cream, is their specialty (L3400). Cones L2000-4000. Open in summer Fri.-Wed. 7am-11pm; mid-Jan. to mid-Dec. 7am-9pm.

Panificio F. Paronuzzi, Cannaregio, 3843 D-E3, on Strada Nuova, the central street. Buy the dense *pane dei dogi* (L2800 per *etto*) and repent at your leisure. Open Mon.-Sat. 7am-8pm, Sun. 9:30-2pm.

A. Rosa Salva, San Marco, 5020 (E4; tel. 522 53 85), on Marzaria San Salvador, 5021, near the Rialto bridge. Locals claim that it is Venice's premier bakery, and the famous *budino di semolino* (rich pudding cake, L1200) affirms this. Open Mon.-Sat. 7:30am-9pm. Closed last week in July and first week in Aug.

SIGHTS

In Venetian churches a strict dress code applies. No shorts, sleeveless shirts or miniskirts allowed. Also, many of the sights in Venice have student, youth, senior, and group discounts, so be sure to ask.

The Grand Canal

The Grand Canal bisects the main islands which constitute the city of Venice, and is best seen by boat. Most important activity in the city happens on or near these shores. The façades of the opulent *palazzi* that crowd its banks testify to a history of immense wealth. From *vaporetto* #1 or #82 you will enjoy a tour of some of the greatest works of Renaissance architecture. The palaces share the same basic structure despite the external decorative features, which reflect the styles of various historical periods. From early on, cramped island life didn't permit the luxury of a central courtyard. Instead, Venetian *palazzi* were constructed with central halls running front to back, providing the necessary air circulation and light. The ground floor (*androne*) served as an entrance hall (from the canal), while the living quarters occupied the *piano nobile* (second floor). The overall effect, unlike that of the dense, massive urban palaces of the Florentine Renaissance, is one of delicate, inviting openness.

The oldest surviving palaces, some from the 13th century, were influenced by Byzantine and early Christian tastes. Look for rounded arches in low relief, like those on the **Cà da Mosto,** the *palazzo* on the S. Marco side of Grand Canal just past the Rialto bridge towards the train station. Further on toward the station on the same side of the canal is the **Cà d'Oro** ("house of gold"; *cà* is an archaic, dialect form of *casa,* or "house") whose name derives from the gold leaf that once adorned the tracery of its renowned façade. Built in 1440, the Cà d'Oro represents the pinnacle of the Venetian Gothic (see Cannaregio below).

Many of Venice's Renaissance edifices are the works of three major Venetian architects: Mauro Coducci, Jacopo Sansovino, and Michele Sanmicheli. Coducci's early **Palazzo Corner-Spinelli** (directly to the right of the S. Angelo stop between the Rialto and the Accademia Bridges, 1510) and **Cà Vendramin Calergi** (directly to the right of the S. Marcuola stop, near the station), both on the east bank, were the first *palazzi* to depart from the traditional Venetian style, infusing classical and Byzantine elements. Coducci's leadership inspired Sansovino's stately **Palazzo Corner della Cà Granda** (located on the San Marco side of the canal, directly left of S. Maria del Giglio stop, past the Accademia, 1550), and Sanmicheli's **Palazzo Grimani di San Luca** (the second *palazzo* to the left of the S. Angelo stop, just past the Rialto), also on the east bank.

San Marco and Castello

Piazza San Marco and Environs

Piazza San Marco is the city's nucleus. Water and land traffic merge at the Molo and Riva degli Schiavoni, from where Venice radiates in unsurpassed magnificence. The numerous domes and spires of the church of San Marco, along with the pink, Rococo decorations of the Doge's Palace, contrast with the classical façade of Sansovino's. Above the *piazza* soars the solid brick **campanile**. The campanile (96m high) originally served as a watchtower and lighthouse for the city. The most recent tower was rebuilt as an exact replica of the 16th-century campanile, after it collapsed during the earthquake of 1902. (Tel. 522 40 64; open daily 9am-7:30pm. Admission L5000). A fine photo spot, though cheaper admission, shorter lines, and better views are available at the **Campanile di San Giorgio** (tel. 528 99 00) across from P. San Marco on the small island of San Giorgio at the *vaporetto* stop of the same name (L2000 from S. Marco; open daily 9:30am-12:30pm and 2:30-6pm).

Construction of the **Basilica of San Marco** (tel. 522 52 05) began in the 9th century, when two Venetian merchants stole St. Mark's remains from Alexandria, and packed them in pork to hoodwink Arab officials. The caper is commemorated in a mosaic to the left of the three entrance arches. The *basilica*'s cruciform plan and five bulbous domes, a direct architectural reference to the Church of the Holy Apostles in Constantinople, suggest a prestige which was intended to rival both Byzantium and St. Peter's. Rebuilt after a fire in the 10th century and continually enlarged over the next half-millennium, San Marco is now a unique synthesis of Byzantine, Western European, and Islamic influences. (Open daily 9:45am-7:30pm. Free.) The church sparkles with mosaics of all ages—perhaps the best are those on the atrium's ceiling. Underfoot, 12th-century concoctions of marble, glass, and porphyry confuse the eyes with endless geometric intricacies. The *basilica*'s main treasure is the **Pala d'Oro** (tel. 522 56 97), a Veneto-Byzantine gold bas-relief encrusted with precious gems. In the area behind the screen are Sansovino's bronze reliefs and his sacristy door. The ticket to this area will also get you into the small **treasury,** a hoard of gold and relics left over from the spoils of the Fourth Crusade. (Open daily 9am-4:30pm. Admission L3000.) Through a door in the atrium is the **Galleria della Basilica** (tel. 522 52 05)—worth it for a better view of the mosaics on the walls and floors. The recently restored *Horses of St. Mark* (originals) are on display here. (Open daily 10am-6:30pm. Admission L3000.) Guided tours of the *basilica* are given April-June and Sept.-Oct. Mon.-Sat. at 11am. Call the **Curia Patriarcale** for further information (tel. 520 03 33. English spoken).

As you come out of San Marco you'll find Coducci's ornate **Torre dell'Orologio** (1499) on your right, a florid arrangement of sculpture and sundials. Two oxidizing bronze Moors strike the hours. The arch below marks the beginning of the **Mercerie,** Venice's main commercial street leading to the Rialto.

Between San Marco and the lagoon stands the **Palazzo Ducale** (Doge's Palace; tel. 522 49 51). The *palazzo*, built in the 14th century after the original was destroyed by a fire, is a magnificent example of Venetian Gothic. The exterior design is a combination of arcades and light-colored stone cladding which lends a light and delicate appearance to a massive structure. This clever design was also employed when the extension to the palace was added one century later. The sculpted Virtues of Temperance, Fortitude, Prudence, and Charity that adorn the **Porta della Carta** are attributed to the 15th-century duo of Giovanni and Bartolomeo Bon. At the side of San Marco stand the *Quattro Mori*, statues of four Roman emperors that crusaders "borrowed" from Constantinople in 1204. Rizzo's **Scala dei Giganti** ("giants' stairs"), sweeping up to the second floor in the left end of the courtyard, is crowned with Sansovino's *Mars and Neptune*. Up his famous **Golden Staircase** are the Senate Chamber and the Room of the Council of Ten (the much-feared secret police of the Republic), both shrouded in paintings. The route then returns to the second floor, where after passing some enormous globes, you can wander through the echoing **Grand Council Chamber.** The room contains the huge, resplendent *Paradiso* by Tintoretto as well as Veronese's *Apotheosis of Venus.* This room contains the portraits of all the doges of Venice except Marin Falier. An empty frame commemorates this over-ambitious doge, who was executed for treason after his unsuccessful coup attempt in 1355. Throughout the building are slits in the walls where secret denunciations were inserted to be investigated by the Ten. (Open daily 9am-7pm. Admission L10,000, students L6000.) For a **Secret Itineraries Tour** through the palace and then over the Bridge of Sighs through the prison, call 249 51. You must call ahead for reservations, since there is no tour info at the Palazzo Ducale. (Tours Thurs.-Tues. 10am and noon, 1hr. In Italian.)

From the Council Chamber, a series of secret passages leads across the **Ponte dei Sospiri** (Bridge of Sighs) from the back of the palace to the prisons. Casanova was among those condemned by the Ten to walk across into the hands of sadistic Inquisitors. The name of the bridge alludes to the bitter groans of prisoners pondering the slim prospects of ever regaining their freedom.

Facing the Palazzo Ducale across P. San Marco are Sansovino's greatest hits, the elegant **Libreria** (1536) and the **Zecca** (coin mint, 1547). The main reading room of the **Biblioteca Marciana** (tel. 520 87 88), on the second floor, is adorned with frescoes by Veronese and Tintoretto. (Entrance at #12. Open Mon.-Fri. 9am-7pm, Sat. 9am-1:30pm. Prior permission required.) Venetian artists received their quota of classical education from the sculptures in the **Museo Archeologico,** P. San Marco, 52 (tel. 522 59 78), next door. (Open daily 9am-2pm. Admission L4000.) Under the portico at the opposite end of the *piazza* from the church is the entrance to the **Museo Civico Correr** (tel. 522 56 25). It houses a couple of Bellinis and Carpaccio's *Courtesans,* not to mention such sundry curiosities of daily Venetian life as the foot-high platform shoes once worn by sequestered noblewomen. (Open Wed.-Mon. 10am-5pm. Admission L8000, students L5000.)

The Mercerie

Starting under the arch of the Torre dell'Orologio in San Marco, the shop-filled and tourist-clogged Mercerie leads up to the **Church of San Giuliano,** commissioned by the Venetian doctor Tommaso Ragone as a monument to himself. His portrait by Sansovino glowers over the door, framed by inscriptions and allegories. The Mercerie then passes by **Campo San Salvatore.** The church consists of three square crosses stuck together. The church was originally designed and built in the early 16th century, yet the façade was not completed until 1633; it contains Giovanni Bellini's *Supper in Emmaus* and Titian's *Annunciation* (1566). (Open daily 9:30am-noon and 4:30-7pm. Free.)

Around San Marco

North of P. San Marco stands the **Church of Santa Maria Formosa.** At the bottom of the *campanile* leers a hideous carved head, which to Ruskin, "embodied the type of evil spirit to which Venice was abandoned, the pestilence that came and breathed upon her beauty." Coducci's Greek-cross plan, a rebuilding of an ancient church, houses Palma il Vecchio's painting of St. Barbara, the exemplar of female beauty in Renaissance Venice. Across the bridge, a twisted alleyway leads to the haunting **Palazzo Querini-Stampalia** (tel. 522 52 35), whose intriguing aristocratic rooms contain paintings dating from the 14th through 18th centuries. (Open Tues.-Sun. 10am-12:30pm and 3:30-6pm. Off-season closed in the afternoon. Admission L5000.)

North of Campo Santa Maria Formosa, Calle Lunga and Calle Cicogna lead to Campo **SS. Giovanni e Paolo** and to the church of the same name (*San Zanipolo* in the Venetian dialect). This grandiose Gothic structure, built by the Dominican order over the course of two centuries (mid-13th to mid-15th), resembles a brick barn, and the monuments to various doges along the sides don't help. However, there is a wonderful polyptych by Giovanni Bellini hanging over the second altar of the right-hand nave. From the left transept you enter the **Cappella del Rosario** (Rosary Chapel) which, although damaged by a fire in 1867, still preserves four marvelous paintings by Veronese. If you cross the Ponte Rosso and go straight, you'll come to the Lombardos' masterpiece, the **Church of Santa Maria dei Miracoli.**

To the east of San Marco, off the Riva degli Schiavoni, stands the beautiful 15th-century **Church of San Zaccaria** (tel. 522 12 57). Coducci designed this striking façade, an enlarged version of his San Michele. Inside, the second altar on the left houses Bellini's masterpiece *The Madonna and Saints.* (Open daily 10am-noon and 4-6pm.) Around the corner, on the waterfront, is Massari's **Church of the Pietà** (built in 1475, façade in 1906), containing celebrated Tiepolo frescoes. Vivaldi was concertmaster here at the beginning of the 18th century, and concerts featuring his music are held in the church throughout the summer. (Open summers daily 9:30am-12:30pm and 3-6pm; off-season only for masses and concerts.)

For a real treat, make your way through the *calli* to the **Scuola di San Giorgio degli Schiavoni,** Ponte dei Greci, 3259 (tel. 522 88 28). Here, between 1502 and 1511, Carpaccio decorated the ground floor with some of his finest paintings, depicting episodes from the lives of St. George, St. Jerome, and St. Trifone. (Open Tues.-Sun. 10am-12:30pm and 3-6pm. Admission L5000.) The nearby **Museo dei Dipinti Sacri Bizantini** (tel. 522 65 81), at Ponte dei Greci, 3412, displays religious paintings from the Byzantine and post-Byzantine periods. (Open Mon.-Sat. 9am-1pm and 2-5pm. Admission L6000.) For the tale of *La Serenissima's* maritime supremacy, visit the **Museo Storico Navale** (tel. 520 02 76) on the waterfront of the Castello district where Via Giuseppe Garibaldi hits Riva dei Sette Martiri. (Open daily 9am-1pm and Thurs. 2:30-5pm. Admission L2000.)

Venice also has its own **Aquarium,** Calle Albanesi, 4259 (tel. 520 77 70), just off Campo SS. Filippo e Giacomo, which features examples of the local sea-life of the lagoon. (Open daily 9am-7pm. Admission L4000.) A bit farther down the waterfront lie the **Giardini** (gardens), which every two years plays host to the biennial International Exhibition of Modern Art, known as the **Biennale.**

Cannaregio From the Rialto to the Ghetto

Heading north from the Rialto bridge on Salizzada San Giovanni, you reach the last of Coducci's churches, **San Giovanni Crisostomo,** a refined Greek cross. The interior contains works by Giovanni Bellini and an altarpiece by Sebastiano del Piombo. Marco Polo supposedly lived under the arch in Corte Seconda del Milione.

From the Crisostomo church, head left toward the *rio* of the same name. Cross two bridges and two small squares to find the **Church of SS. Apostoli,** with an unassuming Tiepolo painting of Santa Lucia's first communion. Nearby is the **Cà d'Oro** (whose inaccessible front door taunts you from the Grand Canal), where the **Galleria Giorgio Franchetti** (tel. 523 87 90) opened in 1984. This formerly private collection displays works of minor Flemish painters and a few major pieces, including Titian's *Venus,* Mantegna's *St. Sebastian,* and Durer's *Deposition.* (Open Mon.-Sun. 9am-2pm. Admission L4000.) North of here the **Church of the Gesuiti** (tel. 523 06 25) boasts a florid green-and-white marble interior (rebuilt by Giorgio Massari in 1724), Titian's *Martyrdom of St. Lawrence,* and Tiepolo's altarpiece and ceiling fresco. In the northern corner of Cannaregio the **Church of Madonna dell'Orto** patiently awaits the venturesome. Take scenic *vaporetto* #52 (*destra*) to the Madonna dell'Orto stop (L4000). Several works by Tintoretto, notably the *Sacrifice of the Golden Calf, Last Judgement,* and *Presentation of the Virgin,* reside within. (Open daily 9:30am-noon and 3:30-5:30pm.)

Between the church and the train station lies the **Jewish Ghetto,** the first in Europe. The term *ghetto* itself originated in Venice; the quarter was named after the knife-grinders who once worked here. Established by ducal decree in 1516, the Ghetto Nuovo remained the enforced enclave of the Jews in Venice until Napoleon's victory over the Venetian Republic in 1797. Upon entering the ghetto through the underpass off Fondamenta di Cannaregio, you can still witness the grooves in the marble where the gate formerly stood, barring movement outside the ghetto at night. The area contains the tallest tenement buildings in Venice as well as five synagogues, of which three are open to the public. The **Sinagoga Grande**

Tedesca is less opulent but more intriguing than the **Sinagoghe Spagnola** and **Levantina.** Tedesca is also the oldest, dating back to 1528. Drop by the **Museo Ebraico** (tel. 71 53 59) in the Campo del Nuovo Ghetto for a fascinating exhibit documenting five centuries of Jewish presence in Venice. Inquire here about guided tours of the Old Ghetto (every ½hr. starting at 9:30am L10,000). (Museum open Sun.-Fri. 9am-5pm, holidays 10am-6pm. Admission L4000, students L3000.)

San Polo and Santa Croce

The **Ponte Rialto,** spanning the Grand Canal, is the entrance to this commercial district and an architectural gem in its own right. In the center of the **Erberia,** the grocery section of the open market, is the **Church of San Giacomo di Rialto,** the oldest in Venice. A stubby column with a staircase to the top stands in front of it, supported by a bent stone figure. The column served as a podium from which state proclamations were issued. The statue, called *il Gobbo* (the hunchback), has served as a bulletin board for public responses since Roman times.

From the **Rialto** bridge, drift with the crowd down the Ruga degli Orefici, then turn left and follow Ruga Vecchia San Giovanni to the **Church of San Polo** (*San Apponal* in the local dialect); the young Giandomenico Tiepolo completed the dramatic 14 stations of the Cross in the chancel. Nearby, in the great Gothic Franciscan **Basilica dei Frari** (1340-1443; tel. 522 26 37), Donatello's wooden *St. John the Baptist* keeps company with a later Florentine statue of the saint by Sansovino and three purely Venetian paintings: Giovanni Bellini's triptych of the *Madonna and Saints* over the sacristy, Titian's famous *Assumption of the Virgin,* and his *Madonna of Case Pesaro.* (Open Mon.-Sun. 9am-noon and 2:30-6pm. Admission L1000. Holidays free.)

The *scuole* of Venice were a combination of guilds and religious fraternities. Members paid annual dues for the support of their needy fellow members and for the decoration of the *scuola's* premises. Among the richest and most illustrious was the **Scuola Grande di San Rocco** (tel. 523 48 64), across the *campo* at the end of the Frari. Tintoretto, who set out to combine, in his words, "the color of Titian with the drawing of Michelangelo," covered the inside with 56 paintings. To see the paintings in chronological order, start on the second floor in the Sala dell'Albergo and follow the cycle downstairs. (Open daily 9am-5:30pm. Off-season Mon.-Fri. 10am-1pm, Sat. and Sun. 10am-4pm. Admission L8000, with Rolling Venice L6000.)

Dorsoduro

The Ponte dell'Accademia crosses the Grand Canal at the **Gallerie dell'Accademia** (tel. 522 22 47). This temple of Venetian-school art should top your list of things to see. Among the galleries, Room II stands out for Giovanni Bellini's *Pala di San Giobbe,* a sublime marriage of perspectival sense and Venetian sensibility. Room IV encloses more Bellinis (Giovanni and father Jacopo both) as well as an early Piero della Francesca, but Room V surpasses this, with a pair of certifiable Giorgione canvases, *La Tempesta* and *La Vecchia.* Rooms VI-IX build up High Renaissance anticipation, which receives its payoff in Room X. Displayed here, Veronese's huge rendition of the Last Supper enraged the leaders of the Inquisition with its indulgent improvisation—a Protestant German and a monkey figure among the guests—and Veronese was forced to change the name to *Supper in the House of Levi* to avoid having to make changes at his own expense. This room also contains several brilliant Tintorettos and Titian's last work, a brooding *Pietà.* Rounding off the collection are a number of works by Tiepolo, Canaletto, and Longhi, whose refined cityscapes are considered the height of early urban art. The wonderful cycle of *The Legend of St. Ursula* by Carpaccio (1490-95) in Room XXI boasts a scene of Ursula, 11,000 virgins in tow, trooping off to Cologne to meet martyrdom at the hands of the Huns. (Open Tues.-Sat. 9am-7pm, Sun.-Mon. 9am-2pm. Off-season Mon.-Sat. 9am-1pm. Admission L12,000, students: try an ID and see what happens.)

The **Cà Rezzonico** (*vaporetto* stop of the same name) is on the Fondamenta Rezzonico, across a bridge from Campo San Baranabà. Designed by Longhena, it's one of the great 18th-century Venetian palaces. Inside, learn about notorious intrigues and love affairs in the **Museo del Settecento Veneziano** (Museum of the 18th Century; tel. 522 45 43). The small bedrooms and boudoirs on the second floor house delightful works by Tiepolo, Guardi, and Longhi. (Open Sat.-Thurs. 10am-5pm. Admission L8000. Seniors and children under 12 L5000.)

The **Collezione Peggy Guggenheim,** Dorsoduro, 701 (tel. 520 62 88), housed in the late Ms. Guggenheim's Palazzo Venier dei Leoni, near the tip of Dorsoduro, is an small and eclectic collection of modern art. It has rapidly become one of Venice's most popular museums, and deservedly so. Tasteful presentation complements the diversity of the collection itself, which includes works by Brancusi, Marino Marini, Kandinsky, Rothko, Max Ernst, and Jackson Pollock. The grounds also feature a sculpture garden. (Open Wed.-Mon. 11am-6pm. Admission L10,000. Students with ISIC or Rolling Venice card, and seniors, L5000.) Just down the street from the Guggenheim Collection is a **Cenedesa Glass Blowing Factory** in Campo San Gregorio, 174. Witness the technique here without traveling to outer islands. (Open Mon. and Wed.-Sat. 10am-1pm and 2-5pm. Free.)

The **Church of Santa Maria della Salute** (tel. 522 55 58), standing at the tip of Dorsoduro, is the most theatrical piece of architecture in Venice. It was designed by Longhena as the site of the dramatic *Festa della Salute* (Nov. 21), which celebrates the deal struck by the church with God that purportedly saved Venice from the plague of 1630. In the sacristy are several Titians and a Tintoretto. (Open daily 9am-noon and 3-6:30pm. Admission to sacristy with donation.)

A bit north of Fondamenta Zattere, toward the western end of town, lies the 16th-century **Church of San Sebastiano.** It was here that Paolo Veronese took refuge in 1555 when he fled Verona, apparently after killing a man. By 1565 he had filled the church with some of his finest paintings and frescoes. On the ceiling, you'll marvel at his breathtaking *Stories of Queen Esther.* To get a closer look at the panels, climb to the nuns' choir. Here you'll also see the artist's evocative fresco *St. Sebastian in Front of Diocletian.* Ask the custodian to turn on the lights (tip L500). To get to the church by sea, take *vaporetto* #82 (L4000) to the San Basilio stop.

Outlying Sights

Many of Venice's most beautiful churches are a short boat ride away from San Marco. Two of Palladio's most famous churches are visible from the *piazza.* The **Church of San Giorgio Maggiore,** across the lagoon (take boat #52 or 82, L2500), graces the island of the same name. The church houses Tintoretto's famous *Last Supper.* Ascend the **campanile** (tel. 528 99 00) for a superb view of the main islands. (Open daily 9:30am-12:30pm and 2-6pm. Admission L2000.)

A bit farther out on the next island, Giudecca, is Palladio's famous **Church of Il Redentore** (the Redeemer). During the pestilence of 1576, the Venetian Senate swore that they would build a devotional church and make a yearly pilgrimage there if the plague would leave the city. Palladio accommodated the pilgrims by enlarging the church's tribune. (Open 2:30-6pm. Take *vaporetto* #82 (L4000) from S. Marco.)

The tiny **Church of San Michele in Isola,** on its own island on the far side of the lagoon, is a Venetian masterpiece and the final resting place of sometime madman (not to mention Fascist sympathizer), poet Ezra Pound. Begun by Coducci in 1469, the pristine marble façade was Venice's first Renaissance structure. The small hexagonal chapel to the left is a later addition. Take *vaporetto* #52 to the *cimitero* (cemetery) stop (L4000) from S. Marco.

The Islands of the Lagoon

Accessible by *vaporetto* #1, 6, 14, or 52, the **Lido** was the setting for Thomas Mann's *Death in Venice* and Visconti's boring film version, both of which give an unforgettable impression of the sensuality and mystery for which Venice is famous. Lovers of the *belle époque* will enjoy a visit to the fabled Grand Hôtel des Bains, though it's not as exciting nowadays. From the *vaporetto* stop, follow the crowd that troops daily down Gran Viale Santa Maria Elisabetta.

Boat #12 departs from Fondamente Nuove, near Campo dei Gesuiti, for the islands of Murano, Burano, and Torcello. (Murano is also serviced by the #52.) **Murano** has been famous for its glass since 1292, when Venice's artisans decided to transfer their operations there. Today, serious glass-making and tourist enterprises coexist, affording opportunities to witness the glass-blowing process. The **Museo Vetrario** (tel. 73 95 86) on Fondamenta Giustiniani, along the main canal, has a splendid glass collection dating from Roman times onward. (Open Thurs.-Tues. 10am-5pm. Admission L8000.) Also located on Murano is the exceptional **Basilica SS. Maria e Donato,** built in the 7th century but owing its exterior to a 12th-century renovation. **Burano,** P. Galuppi, a half-hour out of Venice by boat #12 (L4000), caters to tourists. It is famous for its lace, which is hawked all over Venice. The small **Scuola di Merletti di Burano** (tel. 73 00 34) documents the craft. (Open Tues.-Sat. 9am-6pm, Sun. 10am-4pm. Admission L3000.)

Today **Torcello,** the remaining island, is the most rural of the group. Of the first-time visitor to Venice, John Ruskin wrote, "let him not...look upon the pageantry of her palaces...but let him ascend the highest tier of the stern ledges that sweep round the altar of Torcello." The **cathedral** (tel. 73 00 84), founded in the 7th century and rebuilt in the 11th, has Byzantine mosaics inside so incredible that a 19th-century restorer took a few back to Wales with him. (Cathedral open daily 10am-12:30pm and 2-5pm. Admission L1500. Adjacent **museum** (tel. 73 07 61), Palazzo del Consiglio, open Tues.-Sun. 10am-12:30pm and 2-4pm. Admission L3000.)

Never too far from water, prosperous Venetians built their farming villas along the Brenta River which connects Venice and Padua. **Villa Malcontenta** (also called "Villa Foscari"), built by Palladio on a temple-like plan, is one of the most admired in the western world. (tel. (041) 547 00 12. Open May-Oct. Tues., Sat., and the first Sun. of the month 9am-noon. Admission L10,000.) **Mira** (also "Palazzo Foscari"), one of the most attractive villas on the Brenta, is now open for tours. (Tel. 42 35 52. Open Tues.-Sun. 9am-6pm. Admission including guided tour L7000, seniors L5000.) **Strà** (also "Villa Pisani"; tel. (049) 50 20 74) is renowned for its grand design by Figimelica and Preti and its interior decoration by Urbani and Tiepolo. (Open Tues.-Sun. 9am-6pm. Admission L6000.) To get to Villa Malcontenta, take bus #16 from P. Roma (L1200). To reach the other two villas, check the bus listings in the Practical Information section, page 342.

ENTERTAINMENT

The weekly booklet *A Guest in Venice* (free at tourist offices) lists current festivals, concerts, and gallery shows. Also ask for *Venice, 1996 Events.* There are concerts once or twice a week in the larger churches such as San Marco and the Frari. The **Teatro La Fenice** (tel. 521 01 61) has an excellent summer program, featuring mostly music, with many guest artists (Admission L10,000-30,000, half-price with the Rolling Venice card). The **Festival Vivaldi** takes place in early September. In summer, Vivaldi's music is also featured in a concert series in the church of **Santa Maria della Pietà,** where he was choirmaster.

For a historical introduction to the city, check out Steven Wolf's three-talk series *Venice in English: The Art and History of Venice,* an entertaining way to gain perspective on what's around. (Tel. 524 17 68. Mon.-Sat. 7pm at the Hotel San Cassiano at S. Croce, 2232. Admission L10,000, students L7000. The third talk is free, but one should be sufficiently enlightening.) Another option is *Venice for Venice in Venice,* a slide show in English on Venetian history. Proceeds benefit the S. Maria Formosa Church. (Call 526 23 79 or 526 92 61 for more info; fax 526 28 79. 3 lectures, Wed.-Fri. 7-8pm. May-June, Sept.-Oct. Admission L10,000, students L8000.)

Mark Twain called the **gondola** "an inky, rusty canoe," but only the gentry can really afford to ride one. The authorized rate starts at L80,000 for 50 minutes, which increases after sunset, but mercenary gondoliers will frequently quote prices in the six-digit range. Rides are most romantic if procured about 50 minutes before sunset, and almost affordable if shared with 5 people. Venice was built to be traveled by gondola and you will never truly get a feel for the city and its architecture until you slide quietly down the canals, pass by the front doors of the houses and institutions, and travel on the original pathways. There is, however, a sneaky way to get a cheap ride just for the experience. There are several points along the Grand Canal where many Venetians need to cross, though there is no bridge. To solve the problem, *gondole* operate a short, cross-canal service. Each trip lasts only a minute or so, but this stand-up style of transportation averages a mere L2000.

For theatrical entertainment, **Commedia in Campo**, a classical Venetian type of theater, operates outdoors in various *campi* throughout the city; performance locations change every night. Tickets are L30,000, or you can try to sneak a peek through the curtains. Call Teatro Goldoni (tel. 520 75 83) for more information.

The famed **Venice Biennale** (tel. 521 87 11 for public relations), centered in the Giardini di Castello, takes place every odd-numbered year, with a gala exhibit of international modern art. (Admission to all exhibits L16,000, less to see individual bits and pieces.) The **Mostra Internazionale del Cinema** (Venice International Film Festival, tel. 520 03 11) is held annually from late August to early September. Tickets (starting at 30,000) are sold at the Cinema Palace on the Lido (where the main films are screened) and at other locations—some late-night outdoor showings are free. Contact the tourist office with questions about the cinema.

After an absence of several centuries, Venice's famous **Carnevale** was successfully (in a monetary if not entirely festive sense) revived as an annual celebration in 1979. During the ten days preceding Ash Wednesday, masked Venetians and camera-happy tourists jam the streets. Write to the tourist office in December for dates and details, and be sure to make lodging arrangements months in advance. Venice's next most colorful festival is the **Festa del Redentore**, originally held to celebrate the end of the plague (third Sun. in July). The Church of Il Redentore is connected with Zattere by a boat-bridge for the day, and a magnificent round of fireworks shoots off between 11pm and midnight on the Saturday night before. On the first Sunday in September, Venice stages its classic **regata storica,** a gondola race down the Grand Canal, preceded by a procession of decorated gondolas. The religious **Festa della Salute** takes place on November 21 at Santa Maria della Salute, with another pontoon bridge constructed, this time over the Grand Canal. Again, the festival originated as a celebration of the end of the plague.

If **shopping** is your bag, a few caveats are in order. Do not make purchases in P. San Marco or around the Rialto bridge. Not only do shops outside these areas boast products of better quality and selection, they also charge about half the price. Venetian glass is best bought toward the Accademia bridge from San Marco, and between the Rialto and the station in Cannaregio, though for fun you may want to look in the showroom at the glass-blowers' factory behind the Basilica of San Marco. The map accompanying the Rolling Venice lists many shops offering reductions to card-holders. For the most concentrated and varied selections of Venetian glass and lace, trips to the nearby islands of Murano and Burano, respectively, are in order. *Vaporetto* #52 (L3000) serves Murano while #12 (L4000) serves both Murano and Burano. Both boats leave from the Fondamente Nuove stop.

Nightlife

Although many places shut down around midnight, there are quite a few good places to go before or after the witching hour. The principal after-midnight strip is Fondamenta della Misericordia in Cannaregio, just past the "Ghetto." From Lista di Spagna, cross the first main bridge, turn left on Fondamenta di Cannaregio, and look for the underpass to your right and signs pointing to the main square of the Ghetto Nuovo. Go to the square, walk straight on the bridge over the large canal, and take a right down the Fondamenta. Continue walking parallel with the canal for a few blocks, and you should be in the center of the action. (In general, keep your eyes open for the numerous clubs, especially in the S. Marco area.) But Venice's selection of nightclubs is paltry, not to mention a meat-market. Respectable Venetians go to Mestre and the mainland when they want to party and most people seem to prefer mingling and dancing in the city's streets. Try **El Souk** (tel. 520 03 71), a swanky place in Calle Contarini Corfù, 1056/A, near the Accademia. (Open Fri.-Wed. 6pm-4am. Cover L18,000 includes first drink.) For a taste of history, swagger over to **Harry's Bar,** favored hangout of "Ernesto" Hemingway and real men ever since. On Calle Vallaresso, in front of the San Marco *vaporetto* stop and across the bridge from the tourist office. (Drinks L8000. Service 20%. Open Tues.-Sun. 10:30am-11pm.) Beyond this, the Lido is your best choice—hit **Nuova Acropoli** (tel. 526 04 66), at Lungomare Guglielmo Marconi (go right after you hit the beach). (Open in the off-season only, Fri. and Sat., cover L12,000-20,000.) Also check out **Al Pugni** (see Food: Dorsoduro page 348).

Paradiso Perduto, Fondamenta della Misericordia, 2540 (tel. 72 05 81). Bar, jazz club, and restaurant. Well-known among locals and natives, this place is young and hip. Dark setting with *caffè*-type paintings adorning the walls, and long wooden tables lit by candlelight. Outdoor seating by the canal. Live jazz and salsa on Sun. Typical Venetian fish dishes. Open 7:30am-late (depending on the night and the crowd). Closed Wed., Jan. 6-20, and August 1-5.

Iguana, Fondamenta della Misericordia, 2515 (tel. 71 67 22) Cannaregio. Also at Fondamenta delle Zitelle, 68 (tel. 523 00 04), just down from the hostel on Giudecca. Yes, there is Mexican food in Italy, and it's good. A favorite hangout for Venetian students. Entrees L7000-15,000. Open Thurs.-Tues. 10:30am-3pm and 7pm-1am. Rolling Venice: 10% lunch discount plus free *aperitif.*

Devil's Forest, San Marco, 5185 (tel 520 06 23). On Calle Stagneri off Campo S. Bartolomeo and near the Rialto bridge. Upscale English pub atmosphere with stout, ale and lager on tap, afternoon teas, cold snacks, and diverse crowds. Drinks about L5500. Open Tues.-Sun. 8am-midnight.

Haig's Bar, San Marco, 2477 (tel. 523 23 68) in Campo S. Maria del Giglio, not too far from the P. San Marco. Exit on the far end of the *piazza* across from the *basilica.* Travel straight on Sal. S. Moisè past the AmEx office, cross 2 bridges and look for the bar next to a restaurant of the same name. A small, elegant indoor bar with patio seating outside in the *campo.* Frequented by locals, visitors, gondoliers, and business-types. Drinks L4000-10,000. Open Thurs.-Tues. 10:30am-2am.

■■■ PADUA (PADOVA)

It took the prosperous Roman city of Padua over five centuries to recover from the Lombardic invasion of 602 AD. At that point its rulers declared independence from Byzantine and Lombard control, and Padua wasted no time becoming one of the intellectual hubs of Europe. The "Bo" was founded in 1222, and is second in seniority only to Bologna among Italy's universities. Luminaries such as Dante, Petrarch, Galileo, and Copernicus all contributed to the collective genius, while the visual arts flourished; Florentines Giotto and Donatello beautified the town, as did local talent Mantegna. Today Padua bustles with students, and its wealth is reflected in the many boutiques and shops lining the *piazze.*

ORIENTATION AND PRACTICAL INFORMATION

Padua's location on the Venice-Milan and Venice-Bologna train lines, as well as the availability of intercity buses, makes the city a convenient destination on almost any northern Italian itinerary. The train station is at the northern edge of town, just outside the 16th-century walls. A 10-minute walk down the Corso del Popolo—which becomes **Corso Garibaldi**—will take you into the modern, commercial heart of town. Another 10 minutes will bring you to the **Basilica del Santo,** the cathedral of Padua's patron saint, St. Anthony. **ACAP** city buses #3, 8, and 18 (L1200) will take you directly downtown. For L5000, you can purchase a 24-hr. ticket valid for all urban lines.

Tourist Office: in the Museo Civico (tel. 875 11 53). Accommodations information and bus schedules for villas outside Padua, but no accommodations service. English spoken, helpful staff. Pick up a map and a copy of the entertainment bro-

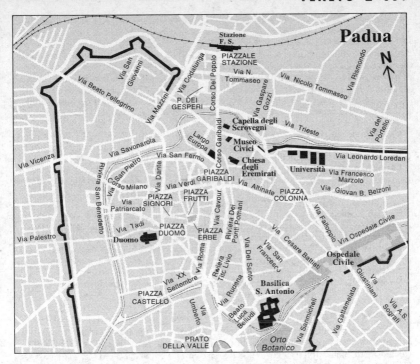

chure, *Padova Today,* or *Padova Welcome* (the office's own comprehensive city guide) for free. Open Tues.-Sun. 9am-7pm. A second office in the **train station** (tel. 875 20 77) is open Mon.-Sat. 9am-7:30pm, Sun. 8:30am-12:30pm. The **seasonal office** at the far end of the Prato della Valle (tel. 875 30 87) is open Mar.-Oct. Tues.-Sat. 9:30am-12:30pm and 1:30-4:30pm, Sun. 9am-noon.

Police: Via Santa Chiara (tel. 83 31 11). **Tourist Police: Ufficio Stranieri** (Foreigners' Office), Riviera Ruzzante, 13 (tel. 66 16 00). English interpreters available Mon.-Fri. 10am-12:30pm.

Post Office: Corso Garibaldi, 25 (tel. 820 85 17). Fax service and *fermo posta.* Open Mon.-Fri. 8:15am-7:30pm, Sat. 8:15am-12:30pm. At the **train station:** Open Mon.-Fri. 8:15am-1pm. **Postal Code:** 35100.

Telephones: Telecom, Riviera dei Ponti Romani, 40 (tel. 66 60 88), in the passageway by Caffè Pedrocchi. Open daily 9am-noon and 3:30-6:45pm. Still closed for remodeling in 1995. Also at Corso Garibaldi, 33, open daily 8am-9:15pm. **Telephone Code:** 049.

Budget Travel: CTS, Via Santa Sofia, 94/96 (tel. 875 17 19), at Via Gabelli. Student IDs and travel information. BIJ and other train tickets. English spoken. Open Mon.-Fri. 9:30am-12:30pm and 4:30-7pm.

Currency Exchange: Banco Antoniana, Via VIII Febbraio, 5 (tel. 83 91 11). The best rates and no commission. **Central branch** located behind Caffè Pedrocchi, in the center of town. Open Mon.-Fri. 8:20am-1:20pm and 2:35-3:35pm. Also at Piazzale Stazione, 7 (tel. 875 10 50).

American Express: Tiare Viaggi, Via Risorgimento, 20 (tel. 66 61 33), near P. Insurrezione. No currency exchange. Open Mon.-Fri. 9am-1pm and 3-7pm, Sat. 10am-noon.

Trains: P. Stazione (tel. 875 18 00), in the northern part of town at the head of Corso del Popolo, the continuation of Corso Garibaldi. To: Venice (every 15min., 30min., L3400); Verona (every hr., 1½hr., L7200); Milan (every hr., 2½hr., L19,000); Bologna (every 30min., 1½hr., L9800). Open daily 7:20am-7pm. **Luggage Storage:** L1500. Open daily 4:40 am-1:30am.

Buses: ATP, Via Triest, 42 (tel. 820 68 33; fax 820 68 14), near P. Boschetti, 5min. from the train station. To: Bassano del Grappa (every 30min., 1¼hr., L5100); Vicenza (every 30min., ½hr., L4800); Venice (every 30min., ¾hr., L4300). Buses operate roughly between the hours of 6am-9pm. Office open Mon.-Thurs. 8:30am-1pm and 2-5:30pm, Fri. 8:30am-1pm.

Car Rental: Europcar, P. Stazione, 6 (tel. 360 94). Offers *Treno più Auto* rates (special rates available upon presentation of a train ticket to Padua). About L150,000 per day, L620,000 per week.

Laundromat: Fastclean, Via Ognissanti, 6 (tel. 77 57 59), near the *portello* and the *segretaria* of the university. Take bus #7, 9, or 15. Self-service. 1-4kg L10,000; 4-7kg L12,000. Soap L600 (use that useless L50 piece!). Dryer L1500. Open Mon.-Fri. 9:30am-11:30am and 3:30-6:30pm, Sat. 9:30am-12:30pm.

English Bookstore: Draghi Libreria Internazionale, Via Cavour, 17-19 (tel. 876 03 05). A large selection of classics (including the *Let's Go* series). Open Mon.-Sat. 8:30am-12:30pm and 3:30-7:30pm.

Swimming Pool: Take bus M to Hotel Cristallo. Walk up Via Roma to Camping Montegro Hoterme. Open Mon.-Sat. 9am-11pm. (L15,000 general admission, children under 9 L8000.)

Emergencies: tel. 113 or 112. **Hospital: Ospedale Civile,** Via Giustiniani, 2 (tel. 821 11 11), off Via San Francesco. Emergency service (tel. 807 23 99).

ACCOMMODATIONS AND CAMPING

Cheap lodgings abound in Padua, but tend to fill up quickly. If you can't get into the places listed below, try any of the hotels near **Piazza del Santo,** or call the **APT** (local tourist board; tel. 875 20 77) or the **provincial tourist board** (tel. 820 15 54) for private rooms in a local home. For summer housing options at the university call or write to **Centro Universitario,** Via Zabarella, 82 (tel. 65 42 99), or **Cattolici Popolari,** c/o Palazzo del Bó (tel. 828 31 11 ext. 399). In summer, start your search as early as 7am.

Ostello Città di Padova (HI), Via Aleardi, 30 (tel. 875 22 19; fax 65 42 10), off Via Camposampiero. Take bus #3, 8, 12, or 18 from the station. From bus #3 or 8, get off when you cross the bridge or when you first glimpse the white statues on the Prato della Valle. Walk back towards the bridge and turn left on Via Memmo. Pass the church; Via Aleardi is on the right. From bus #12 or 18, get off at Via Cavolletto and walk up along Via Manin. Turn left to get to Via Aleardi. Quiet location with large, immaculate, crowded rooms. English spoken. Flexible 5-day max. stay. Open daily 8-9:30am and 6-11pm. Register and drop off your stuff anytime Mon.-Fri. Curfew 11pm. L18,000 per person, hot showers and breakfast included, L16,000 if you stay more than 3 nights. If out-of-the-way castles suit your imagination, consider staying at the hostel in **Montagnana** (see page 363).

Albergo Verdi, Via Dondi dall'Orologio, 7 (tel. 875 57 44). Walk under the clock tower at the end of P. dei Signori and turn right at the end of the row of trees. Large rooms in the center of town. Singles L37,000. Doubles L48,000. Reserve 2-3 days ahead in summer.

Casa della Famiglia (ACISJF), Via Nino Bixio, 4 (tel. 875 15 54), off P. Stazione. Leave the station, cross the street, and walk toward Hotel Monaco; it's on a small street to your left. Women under 29 only. The good sisters reserve the right to turn away "undesirables." Curfew 10:30pm. Modern and tidy doubles, triples, and quads about L20,000 per person. Study and a kitchen open for use at night.

Hotel Riviera, Via Rudena, 12 (tel. 66 54 13), near the corner of V. Rudena and Riviera Businello. Spacious, clean rooms close to the basilica of St. Anthony. Singles L37,000, with bath L50,000. Doubles L48,000, with bath L70,000. Small restaurant downstairs.

Albergo Pavia, Via del Papalava, 11 (tel. 66 15 58). Take Via Roma from P. delle Erbe, turn right on Via Marsala, and left on Via del Papalava. Right down the street from the Pace sign. Rooms in front of the garden have wooden floors; rooms in back have been recently renovated. Rooftop clotheslines—the management will let you have a corner for your laundry. Kitchen facilities, eating areas, and parking space available. Singles L37,000. Doubles L48,000.

Camping: Montegrotto Terme, Via Roma, 123/125 (tel. 79 34 00 or 79 33 32). A 15km bus ride from Padua. Take the ACAP bus "M." Stop at the Hotel Cristallo and turn left; Via Roma is the street at the first stoplight. Walk up Via Roma for about 1km, following the signs to Padova. Friendly, accommodating staff. English and German spoken. Tennis, disco, and restaurants in the vicinity. Prices depend on the season, and range up to L10,500 per adult. Open March-early Nov.

FOOD

Markets are held on both sides of the Palazzo della Ragione. During the academic year, student *mense* pop up all over town, so ask around. There's a convenient supermarket downtown, across from Caffè Pedrocchi: **PAM,** on Via Cavour in P. della Garzeria (open Mon.-Tues. and Thurs.–Sat. 8:30am-7:30pm, Wed. 8:30am-noon). You can sample a glass from the nearby Colli Euganei winery district, or try the sparkling *lambruschi* of Emilia Romagna. Two of the most distinctive whites are produced by **Trattoria da Nane della Giulia,** Via Santa Sofia, 1, off Via San Francesco (open Tues.-Sat. 11:30am-2:30pm and 6pm-midnight, Mon. 6pm-midnight), and **Spaccio Vini Carpanese,** Via del Santo, 44 (tel. 305 81; open Mon.-Sat. 9-11:30am and 4-6pm). Delicious wines run L2000-4500 per glass.

Mensa Universitaria, Via San Francesco, 122 (tel. 66 09 03). The most pleasant and convenient *mensa. Menù* L13,000. Open Mon.-Sat. 11:45am-2:30pm and 6:45-9pm, Sun. 11:45am-2:30pm. Check here for info on the other *mensas'* schedules. If this one is closed, try the *mensa* on Via Marzolo, 4, near Via Morgagni.

Brek (tel. 875 37 88), in the corner of the *piazza* off Via VIII Febbraio, across from Caffè Pedrocchi. Self-service restaurant, upscale appearance, and prices to rival the university *mensa's. Primi* L3800-4500, *secondi* L6100-7200. *Menù* L12,000. Look out for these restaurants in other towns as well. (Open Sat.-Thurs. 11:30am-3pm and 6:30-10:30pm.)

Al Pero, Via Santa Lucia, 72 (tel. 365 61), near Via Dante. Bustling neighborhood eatery with fantastic food and entertaining waiters. To visit Veneto without tasting *polenta* is a sin, so be virtuous and order the *salamini arrosti con polenta* (small roasted sausages with *polenta,* L5000). *Primi* L4000-5000, *secondi* L5000-6500. Cover L1500. (Open Mon.-Sat. noon-2:30pm and 7:30-9:30pm.)

Pizzeria Al Borgo, Via Luca Belludi, 56, a street right across from the *basilica* (tel. 875 88 57). A wide variety of large, yummy pizzas and all within the vicinity of saintly grace. Traditional pizzas L5000-10,500. More creative pizzas 10,000 and up. Cover L2000. (Open Wed.-Mon. noon-3pm and 7pm-1am.)

Alexander Bar, Via San Francesco, 38 (tel. 65 28 84), off Via del Santo. One hundred beers and about sixty types of *panini* (L3000-5500). Open late (Mon.-Sat. 8:30am-2am), so you can take your time deciding.

Lunanuova, Via G. Barbarigo, 12 (tel. 875 89 07), in the *zona duomo.* Vegetarian restaurant complete with comfortable, quiet setting, mellow jazz, and political bulletin boards as well as an array of books and pamphlets on veggie vacations in Italy. The restaurant features brown bread—a rarity in Italy. Lunch and dinner selections from L15,000-20,000. For beverages, choose between beer, wine, fruit juice, and herbal tea. Cover L2000. (Open Tues.-Sat. 12:30-2:30pm and 7:30pm-midnight. Closed Mon.)

SIGHTS

You can buy a **ticket** good at most of the museums of Padua for L15,000 (L10,000 for students and groups), available at any of the following sights and valid for one year: Cappella degli Scrovegni, Museo Civico, Orto Botanico, Palazzo della Ragione, Battistero del Duomo, and the Oratorio di San Giorgio.

Despite four centuries of Venetian dominance, Padua preserves its distinct civic identity, taking pride in its renowned artwork and revered university. The **Cappella degli Scrovegni** (a.k.a. the **Arena Chapel**) alone merits a pilgrimage to Padua. Not just another in the long and often tedious string of Italian chapels, the Scrovegni is a must-see. It contains Giotto's breathtaking floor-to-ceiling fresco cycle, easy to understand and awesome to behold. Executed over the course of three years between 1303 and 1306, these 36 perfectly preserved panels illustrate the lives of Mary and Jesus and comprise one of the most influential works of art from this period. (Open Apr.-Sept. daily 9am-7pm; Oct.-March Tues.-Sun. 9am-6pm. Admission L10,000, students L7000, school groups L5000 per person. Tickets must be bought at the Museo Civico and are good for both the chapel and museum.) The adjoining **Museo Civico** houses an art gallery with Giorgione's *Leda and the Swan* and a Giotto crucifix.

Next door, the **Church of the Eremitani** boasts an imposing exterior and a beautifully carved wooden ceiling that was successfully restored after a devastating 1944 bombing. Unfortunately, Andrea Mantegna's cycle of frescoes —which once rivaled Giotto's masterpiece—was almost entirely lost. Several photos of the WWII destruction are displayed in the front left corner of the church. The restoration appears miraculous after you've seen how much of the church was blown away. (Open Mon.-Sat. 8:15am-noon and Sun. 9am-noon and 3:30-6:30pm; Oct.-March Mon.-Sat. 8:15am-noon and Sun. 9am-noon and 3:30-5:30pm. Free.)

A complex of buildings on P. del Santo pays homage to Il Santo, (Padua's patron St. Anthony). The 14th-century **Basilica di Sant'Antonio** (tel. 66 39 44), where the saint is entombed, is a medieval architectural oddity, a fantastically absurd conglomeration of eight domes, a pair of octagonal campaniles, and some supporting minarets. Tourists seeking everything from lost love to lost limbs keep the church perpetually crowded. You can see the Saint's jawbone and well-preserved tongue in the center arch of a chapel at the back of the church, directly opposite the main entrance. The jawbone sits behind glass in the "head" of the saint's gold bust, and the tongue is kept in a fancy gold case beneath the jawbone. The body parts and the brilliant frescoed arches in the interior provide an odd backdrop to Donatello's bronze sculptures on the high altar. These seven statues are watched over by the artist's *Crucifixion*. The **Tomb of Saint Antony** is to your left when you stand in front of the altar, and is the final destination for the thousands of pilgrims that visit the Basilica each year. A permanent exhibition, "Mostre Antoniane," details the life of the saint and the work of the monks in the attached monastery. It's a visual and audio display à la Epcot Center, both interesting and free. The audio from the speakers is in Italian but special headsets from the front desk provide simultaneous English translation. The show lasts about 20 minutes and is open in summer only from 9am-12:30pm and 3-7pm. From inside the church, follow the green and orange "Mostre Antoniane" signs through the courtyard to the entrance. (*Basilica* open daily 6:30am-7:45pm.)

The adjoining **Oratorio di San Giorgio** houses examples of Giotto-school frescoes, as does the **Scuola del Santo** (tel. 875 52 35) which includes three by the young Titian. (Both open daily 9am-12:30pm and 2:30-7pm, Oct.-Jan. 9am-12:30pm, Feb.-March 9am-12:30pm and 2:30-4:30pm. L3000 for both.)

In the center of P. del Santo sits Donatello's pioneering bronze equestrian statue of **Gattamelata** ("Calico Cat"), a mercenary general remembered for his agility and ferocity in all fields. In true Renaissance spirit, Donatello modeled the statue after the Roman equestrian statue of Marcus Aurelius at the Campidoglio in Rome. Only a block away lies the peaceful **Orto Botanico** (tel. 65 66 14), the oldest botanical garden in the world with an educational purpose (est. 1545). The palm tree planted in 1585 can still be seen in the garden. (Open Mon.-Sat. 9am-1pm and 3-6pm, Sun. 9am-1pm; Nov.-March Mon.-Sat. 9am-1pm. Admission L6000, students free.)

The **Palazzo della Ragione,** built in 1218 (with external *loggias* and a keel-shaped roof added in 1306), marks the city center. (Open Tues.-Sun., 9am-7pm; off-season 9am-1pm and 3-6pm. Admission L7000; special exhibits L10,000, students L7000.)

The **Duomo** in P. Duomo (tel. 66 28 14) was erected between the 16th and 18th centuries. Reportedly, Michelangelo participated in the design. The *Battistero* next door was built in the 12th century, but retouched in the 13th. Inside you will find yet another significant cycle of religious frescoes. (Open Tues.-Sun. 9:30am-12:30pm and 3-6pm. Admission L3000, students L2000.)

The **university** campus is scattered throughout the city but it centers on Palazzo Bò (tel. 828 31 11). (In Venetian dialect *bò* means steer or castrated bull; the word derives from the sign of the inn that formerly occupied the *palazzo's* site.) The **teatro anatomico** (1594) was the first of its kind in Europe and hosted the likes of Vesalius and Englishman William Harvey, who discovered the circulation of blood. Almost all Venetian noblemen received their mandatory instruction in law and public policy in the **Great Hall,** and the "chair of Galileo" is preserved in the **Sala dei Quaranta,** where the physicist used to lecture. **Caffè Pedrocchi** (tel. 876 25 76), across the street, was the headquarters for 19th-century liberals who supported Giuseppe Mazzini. When it was first built, the *caffè's* famous neoclassical façade had no doors and was open around the clock—every university student was entitled to a free newspaper and a glass of water. The battle between students and Austrian police here in February 1848 was a turning point in the Risorgimento. Capture the spirit for the price of a *cappuccino* (L4000; open Tues.-Sun. 7:30am-1am).

ENTERTAINMENT

Padua's nightlife is elusive. To get the inside scoop on the goings on of the collegiate crowd, keep your eyes peeled for posters around the university. The evening *passeggiata* takes place in P. Garibaldi and up Via Cavour. The *caffè* here and in nearby P. delle Frutta come to life at night. You may also want to check out **Lucifer Young,** Via Altinate, 89 (tel. 875 22 51), near the Chiesa di S. Sofia and the University. A hip bar in 3-D whose decorator took his or her lessons from the lowest circle in the Divine Comedy. Mostly drinks (there's a wicked house brew) and some food. (Open Mon.-Tues. and Thurs.-Fri. at 7pm, Sat.-Sun. at 6pm.)

Check the posters around Palazzo Bò or pick up a copy of the newspaper *Il Mattino* for concert and film listings. In July the city organizes the **Cinema Città Estate,** a film series presented in the Arena Romana. Call the tourist office (tel. 875 20 77) or the Assessorato di Turismo (tel. 820 15 30) for further information. On February 8, Padua celebrates the **Festa della Matricola,** in which students and professors take the day off from classes, wear ancient academic costumes, and play practical jokes on each other. On the third Sunday of each month an **antique market** assembles in the Prato della Valle. And on the thirteenth of June, Padua remembers the death of its patron Sant'Antonio (who died June 13, 1231) with a **procession** of the Saint's statue and jawbone through the city, beginning at the Basilica. Padua is packed with pilgrims for the event.

■ NEAR PADUA

The **Colli Euganei** (Eugan Hills), southwest of Padua, offer a feast for the senses. Padua's tourist office has pamphlets suggesting various itineraries. The volcanic hills are rich not only in soil and hot mineral springs, but in extraordinary accommodations as well. Contact the **Agriturismo** office at Via Martiri della Libertà, 9 (tel. 66 16 55) in Padua for information about staying on a real, working farm. Most of the participating farms offer a bed in a double or triple for about L28,000, including breakfast and showers. If you've always dreamed of life in a castle, realize your aspirations with a night at the **Youth Hostel (HI)** in **Montagnana.** The town lies just outside of the *colli*, an hour by bus from either Vicenza or Padua (round-trip L10,200). The hostel (tel. (0429) 81 07 62) offers 70 beds within the Rocca degli Alberi. For L14,000, enjoy a soft bed and hot showers under the auspices of a warm-hearted management. The Montagnana **tourist office** is located in P. Maggiore (tel. (0429) 813 20). Open Mon. and Wed.-Sat. 10am-noon and 4-6pm.

■■■ TREVISO

Treviso means "three faces," and, while the name may be without historical significance, it seems particularly well-suited to this provincial capital. The tourism industry promotes the first two faces, *città d'acqua* (city of water) and *città dipinta* (painted city). On the water side, rivulets from the Sile River flow through town, disappearing only to resurface where least expected, and as for the paint, the frescoed façades of the buildings that line the city streets still display hints of their former glory. The third face of Treviso needs no glossy brochures to catch the eye: Treviso is rolling in dough. Benetton was born here, though there are only four official stores in town. For those who wish to buy their B's from the source, a warning: buy big, for Treviso is also the birthplace of that most dastardly of desserts: *tiramisù*. Since Treviso's affluence keeps bargains at bay, the town is best seen as a daytrip from Venice or Padua.

ORIENTATION AND PRACTICAL INFORMATION

Treviso lies a half-hour inland from Venice. The historic center is contained within the old city walls which are bordered alternately on the inside and outside—sometimes both—by flowing water. **Via Roma** is the entrance to town, and a curving street that changes names at each bend on its way to **P. dei Signori,** the center of Treviso. Pedestrian-dominated **Via Calmaggiore** leads to the *duomo.*

Tourist Office: Via Toniolo, 41 (tel. 54 76 32; fax 54 13 97). Via Roma becomes Corso del Popolo as you cross the Fiume Sile; take this to P. della Borsa, easily identified by the face-off of rival banks. Via Toniolo is to the right. *Treviso Incontri* is a day-by-day listing of current exhibitions and performances. There's also info galore on the Ville Venete (see below, page 369). English spoken. Open Mon.-Fri. 8:30am-12:30pm and 3-6pm, Sat. 8:30am-noon.

Police: Questura: (tel. 59 91).

Post Office: P. Vittoria, 1 (tel. 59 72 07). Stamps and *fermo posta* at #1. Open daily 8:15am-7:30pm. **Postal Code:** 31050.

Telephones: Telecom, Via Calmaggiore, 34, off P. dei Signori. Open Mon.-Fri. 9am-12:30pm and 4-7:30 pm. **Telephone Code:** 0422.

Trains: P. Duca d'Aosta (tel. 54 13 52), at the southern end of town. Treviso lies on the Venice-Udine line. To: Venice (every 30min., 30min., L2700); Udine (every 30min., 1½hr., L9800); Milan (every hr., 3½hr., L20,800). **Luggage Storage:** L1500. Open daily 6am-8pm.

Buses: Lungo Sile Mattei, 21 (tel. 41 22 22), to the left just before Corso del Popolo crosses the river. Comprehensive service throughout Veneto and to the villas. To: Padua (every 30min., L4800); Vicenza (every hr., 1 hr., L6300); Bassano (9 per day, L5500); Asolo (every hr., L4200).

Emergencies: tel. 113. **Hospital: Unit Sanitaria Locale,** tel. 32 21. Take bus #1. **Ambulance:** 118.

ACCOMMODATIONS AND FOOD

Unfortunately for the budget traveler Treviso's wealthy climate has spawned a number of hotels (singles, L60,000) but few cheaper budget accommodations; consider Treviso as a day trip. Treviso is famous for its *ciliegie* (cherries), *radicchio* (red chicory lettuce), and *tiramisù,* a heavenly creation of espresso-and-liquor-soaked cake topped with sweet cream cheese. Cherries peak in June, *radicchio* in December (and *tiramisù* is always yummy). If *primi* and *secondi* seem to be merely an inconvenient delay, begin with dessert at **Nascimben,** Via XX Settembre, 3, the local espresso-and–pastry pit stop (tel. 15 12 91, open Tues.-Sun. 7am-2am, *tiramisù* L2500). For your basics, shop at **Pam Supermarket,** P. Borso, 18 (tel. 539 13) in the corner of the *piazza* behind Banca Nazionale del Lavoro. (Open Mon.-Tues. and Thurs.-Sat. 8:30am-1pm and 3-7:30pm, Wed. 8:30am-1pm.) Pizzeria, bar, and **Ristorante da Max** (tel. 54 59 74) on Via Paris Bordone, 11, is downtown and dirt cheap. The booth and tile atmosphere is a welcome novelty for upscale Treviso. Good pizza for L4500-11,000. (*Primi* L7000, *secondi* L7500-9000. *Menù* L15,000. Cover L1500. Open Sat.-Thurs. 10:30am-3pm and 6pm-midnight.) **All'Oca Bianca,** Vicolo della Torre, 7 (tel. 54 18 50), on a side street off central Via Calmaggiore, is a casual *trattoria* in the thick of things. Try any of the fish dishes. (*Primi* L8000, *secondi* and fish L8000-12,000. Cover L2000. Open Thurs.-Mon. 8am-4pm and 6pm-midnight, Tues. 8am-4pm. AmEx, MC, Visa.)

SIGHTS

The **Palazzo dei Trecento** (tel. 54 17 16), which abuts P. dei Signori, loudly asserts Treviso's successful reemergence from a 1944 air raid (on Good Friday) which demolished half the town. Climb the stairs on the outer wall and look for the clearly marked signs underfoot which mark the pre-bomb extension of the walls. Post-war reconstruction and new building blend with the original townscape, and spiraling prosperity allows the city to devote its resources to endless restoration. (Open Mon-Sat. 8:30am-12:30pm. Free.)

Back in P. dei Signori, you can join in Via Calmaggiore's endless *passeggiata* and walk beneath the arcades to the seven-domed, patchwork-style **duomo.** The **Cappella Malchiostro** was inserted in 1519 and contains frescoes by Pordenone and Titian's *Annunciation.* It's a strange combination considering the two artists were sworn enemies. (Open weekdays 7:30am-noon and 3:30-7pm; Sun. 7:30am-1pm and 3:30-8pm.) From P. del Duomo, Via Risorgimento leads to the large Dominican church of **San Nicolò** on Via San Nicola. The mammoth, 14th-century brick structure sports a triple apse, along with some frescoed saints by Tommaso da Modena. (Open in summer Mon.-Fri. 8am-noon and 3:30-7pm; in winter Mon.-Fri. 9am-noon and 3-5:30pm. Free.)

The **Museo Civico** at Borgo Cavour, 22 (tel. 513 37) houses Titian's *Sperone Speroni* and Lorenzo Lotto's *Portrait of a Dominican,* conveniently hung in the same room. The ground floor protects Treviso's archaeological finds, most impressive among which are the 5th-century BC bronze discs from Montebelluna. (Museum open Tues.-Sat. 9am-noon and 2-5pm, Sun. 9am-noon. Admission L3000.)

■■■ BASSANO DEL GRAPPA

At the foot of Monte Grappa, Bassano del Grappa is a hideaway for many Italian and Austrian tourists. Visit Bassano for the *grappa* brandy, mushrooms, wrought iron, pottery, and the emblematic wooden bridge over Ponte degli Alpini. Oh, and the *grappa.* Locals claim that Bassano's greatest asset is its proximity to the mountains, but they're wrong: Bassano's greatest assets are the spectacular views that the city provides from its bridges. Did we mention the *grappa?*

ORIENTATION AND PRACTICAL INFORMATION

The majority of historical and interesting areas lie between the train station and the **Fiume Brenta.** From the station take Via Chilesotti (straight ahead) to find the downtown area. The center is split between **Piazza Garibaldi** and **Piazza Libertà,** only one-half block apart. Walk across the Ponte degli Alpini to the other side of Bassano, which has many small shops, restaurants, and charming *vicoli.*

Tourist Office: Largo Corona d'Italia, 35 (tel. 52 43 51; fax 52 53 01). From the station, walk down Via Chilesotti, across the larger Viale delle Fosse, and through the gap in the stone wall to the new office complex. The tourist office is the

older, detached building to the right. The monthly, trilingual *Bassano Mese* features hotel listings, restaurants, practical information, and a town map. Bikers of all sorts (motorized and not) will benefit from *Bici e Vai*, an itinerary-packed brochure of the nearby towns. Open Mon.-Fri. 9am-12:30pm and 3-6:45pm.
Police: Via Cá Rezzonico (tel. 22 84 91, or 112 for emergencies).
Post Office: tel. 22 111, on Via XI Febbraio, near the *duomo* (take Via Marinali off P. Libertà all the way to the post office; the street will run into XI Febbraio). Open Mon.-Fri. 8:15am-7:45pm, Sat. 8:15am-6:30pm. **Postal Code:** 36061.
Telephones: Caffè Danieli, P. Garibaldi (tel. 293 22). Open Thurs.-Mon. 7am-9pm and Tues. 7am-noon. **Telephone Code:** 0424.
Trains: at the end of Via Chilesotti (tel. 52 50 34), a couple blocks from the historic center. Ticket counter open daily 5:10am-9pm. To: Padua (14 per day, 1hr., L4200); Venice (16 per day, 1hr., L5700); Trent (9 per day, 2hr., L8000); Vicenza via Cittadella (9 per day, 2hr., L3400). **Luggage Storage:** L1500. Open daily 6:30am-8:40pm.
Buses: in P. Trento (tel. 25 025). As you come up Via Chilesotti, turn left on Viale delle Fosse. A few different bus companies service the surrounding towns: **Autoline Rossi** (tel. 32 150) and **F.T.V.** (tel. 30 850). To: Vicenza (every 30min., L4800); Asiago (5 per day, L5600); Maróstica (every hr., L1900); Thiene (every hr., L3800). **La Marca Line** (tel. in Treviso (0422) 41 22 22). To: Treviso (L5500), Masèr (L3300), and Asolo. Buy tickets at Bar Trevisani in P. Trento.
Hiking: Club Alpino Italiano (tel. 52 93 40; fax 52 93 41), on Via Colomba, 1/B. Hiking and mountain information. Open Tues. and Fri. 9-10:30pm, Wed. 5-7pm.
Late-Night Pharmacy: Consult "Bassano Mese" for the most current list.
Emergencies: tel. 113. **Hospital: Ospedale Civile,** Viale delle Fosse, 43 (tel. 88 82 52). **Night and emergency medical care** (tel. 88 82 57). **Ambulance:** (tel. 52 31 94).

ACCOMMODATIONS AND FOOD

Budget hotels are a rare breed in Bassano. Reserve ahead or consider accommodations elsewhere.

Instituto Cremona, Via Chini, 6 (tel. 52 20 32), past the main post office on Via Emiliani. This school-turned-hostel offers bargain-basement rates. 5-day max. stay. Check in 7-9:30am and 6-10pm. No daytime lockout. Curfew 11pm. L15,000 per night, L18,000 with breakfast. Open late June-early Sept., Mon.-Fri.
Albergo Nuovo Mondo, Via Vittorelli, 45 (tel. 52 20 10) the first street on your right as you enter P. Garibaldi. Clean, spacious rooms in the historical center. Call ahead during the summer months. Singles L27,000-37,000 without bath. Doubles L50,000-60,000 without bath, L60,000-77,000 with bath. AmEx, MC, Visa.

The town's most spirited claim to fame is *grappa*, a steamroller of a liquor distilled from the seeds and skins of grapes. For authenticity, buy a bottle from the **Nardini** distillery by the Ponte degli Alpini. On the tamer side, Bassano is also famous for its white asparagus. Depending on the season, this and other produce can be purchased at the **open-air market** on Thurs. and Sat. 8am-1pm in P. Garibaldi. For cooked food on the run, try the gourmet, deli-style fare at **Venzo** on Via da Ponte (open Thurs.-Tues. 8:30am-1pm and 3:30-7:30pm, 4-8pm; during the summer also Wed. 8:30am-1pm; MC, Visa).

Ottone Birraria, Via Matteotti, 50 (tel. 22 206). Pictures of everything from track runners to autumn in Vermont line the walls of this beautifully decorated eatery. The food is sumptuous, the staff is lovely, and the prices are great (a large coke only costs L2000). Don't miss it! From Hungarian goulash (L12,500) to hot sandwiches (L6000-8000). Pasta L8000. Cover L2500. Open Wed.-Mon. 9:30am-3:30pm and 6:30pm-1:30am. Closed Mon. evening. MC, Visa.
Al Saraceno, Via Museo, 60 (tel. 225 13). A favorite local hangout with seafood specialties and an impressive pizza repertoire. *Primi* L6000-8000, *secondi* L6000-

14,000. Pizza L5000-9000. *Menù* L18,000. Cover L2000. Open Tues.-Sun. 10am-2:30pm and 5:30pm-1am. AmEx, MC, Visa.
Ristorante China Town, Vale delle Fosse,13 (tel.52 42 55). Authentic food, beautifully decorated, and loved by the locals. Pastas (L3500-7000), meat dishes (L6500-11,000). Cover L2000. MC, Visa.

SIGHTS AND ENTERTAINMENT

Bassano's charm is epitomized by the small **Ponte degli Alpini,** a covered wooden bridge dating from 1209 and redesigned by Palladio (1568-70) to resemble a fleet of ships (whether it does is another question). The bridge is named for the Alpine soldiers who died fighting the Austrians and Germans during World War I. The **Museo Civico** in P. Garibaldi (tel. 52 22 35) houses masterpieces by Jacopo da Bassano (1517-1592), including the *Flight into Egypt* and *St. Valentine Baptizing St. Lucilla.* (Open Tues.-Sat. 9am-12:30pm and 3:30-6:30pm, Sun. 3:30-6:30pm. Admission L5000, groups over 20 L2500 per person.)

Next door stands the Romanesque-Gothic church of **San Francesco,** completed in the early 14th century. The spacious interior unfortunately shows few traces of the original frescoes, but the *Madonna and Child* by Lorenzo Martinelli beneath the arches of the entrance has recently been restored.

■■■ VICENZA

This quiet provincial city has one of the highest average incomes in Italy, thanks to a recent boom in high-tech manufacturing and the town's many goldsmiths. What you will mostly see, however, are the stunning *piazze*, many or which were designed by Palladio, and Renaissance interpretations of the classical Roman style. There's no denying it: Vicenza is a gorgeous place to visit.

ORIENTATION AND PRACTICAL INFORMATION

Vicenza lies in the heart of Veneto. The train station is in the southern part of town. **AIM** city buses #1 and #7 run to the center of town and **P. Matteotti** (L1300). Next to the train station is the intercity **FTV** bus station. To walk into town, orient yourself with a glance at the helpful map outside the station and set out on Viale Roma. Take a right on **Corso Palladio** (the central street). P. Matteotti is at the other end, 10 minutes away.

Tourist Office: P. Matteotti, 12 (tel. 32 08 54), next to the Teatro Olimpico. Offers helpful brochures and a city map of wheelchair-accessible facilities. English spoken. Open Mon.-Sat. 9am-12:30pm and 2:30-6pm, Sun. 8:30am-12:30pm.
Police: Via Muggia, 2 (tel. 50 77 00).
Post Office: Contrà Garibaldi (tel. 32 24 88), between the *duomo* and P. Signori. Open Mon.-Fri. 8am-7:30pm, Sat. 8am-1pm. **Postal Code:** 36100.
Telephones: Telecom, P. Giuseppe Giustu, 8 (tel. 99 01 11), off Corso SS. Felice e Fortunato. Open daily 9am-12:30pm and 3:30-7pm. From 7pm-1am, go to Ristorante La Taverna, P. dei Signori, 47 (tel. 54 73 26). **Telephone Code:** 0444.
Budget Travel: AVIT, Viale Roma, 17 (tel. 54 56 77), before you reach the supermarket PAM. BIJ and Transalpino tickets. Avis and Hertz rental cars. Open Mon.-Fri. 9am-1pm and 3-7pm, Sat. 9:30am-12:30pm. English spoken.
Trains: P. Stazione (tel. 32 50 45), at the end of Viale Roma. To: Venice (every 30min., 1hr., L5700); Padua (every 30min., 30min., L3400); Milan (every 30min., 2-3hr., L15,500); Verona (every 30min., 30min., L5000). **Luggage Storage:** L1500, open daily 7am-9pm.
Buses: FTV, Viale Milano, 7 (tel. 54 43 33), to the left as you exit the train station. To: Bassano (every hr., L4800); Asiago (every hr., L6500); Padua (every 30min., L4800); Thiene (every30min., L4800); Schio (every 30min., L3800); Montagnana (3 per day, L5600). All buses run approx. 6am-9:30pm. Office open 7am-8pm.
Car Rental: Avis, Viale Milano, 88 (tel. 32 16 22; fax 32 62 61). Car rental with credit card, age 23 and older. For the best rates reserve from home at the "Tour

Europe" rate. Around L151,000 per day, L200,000 per weekend, and L600,000 per week, all with unlimited mileage. Open 8am-12:30pm and 3-7pm, Sat. 8am-12:30pm.
Swimming Pool: Piscina Comunale, Via Ferrarin (tel. 92 47 31). Open Mon.-Fri. 10am-6:30pm, Sat. 9am-6:30pm, Sun. 9am-7pm. Admission L7000, under 18 L5000. Bathing cap required.
Emergencies: tel. 113. **Medical Emergency/Ambulance:** tel. 118 or 51 42 22 (for Croce Rossa). **Hospital: Ospedale Civile,** Viale Rodolfi, 8 (tel. 99 31 11). **Night and weekend doctor:** tel. 99 34 70.

ACCOMMODATIONS AND CAMPING

You guessed it: Italy's richest town is not the leader in budget accommodations. The fact that many establishments close for vacation in August, and most are packed in September during the annual architecture course, doesn't help. Consider the youth hostels in Padua or Verona if you don't want to splurge.

Albergo Due Mori, Contrà Do Rode, 26 (tel. 32 18 86; fax 32 61 27), around the corner from Hotel Vicenza. Sparkling, newly furnished rooms. Singles L50,000, with bath L56,000. Doubles L60,000, with bath L75,000. Breakfast L8000.
Hotel Vicenza, Stradella dei Nodari, 517 (tel. 32 15 12), off P. Signori in the alley across from Ristorante Garibaldi. Meticulously scrubbed and centrally located. Friendly management who may store your luggage after check-out. Singles L45,000, with bath L60,000. Doubles L65,000, with bath L85,000.
Hotel Italia, Via Risorgimento, 3 (tel. 32 10 43 or 56 58 51), take a right on Viale Venezia, the busy street that runs of the station. Recently renovated rooms with pastel-tiled baths. Restaurant downstairs. Singles L50,000. Doubles L80,000.
Camping: Campeggio Vicenza, Strada Pelosa, 241 (tel. 58 23 11), take Corso Padova out of town; Strada Pelosa is on the right. Impossible to reach without a car. L7500 per person, L8500 per tent, with car L17,500.

FOOD

Produce is marketed outdoors every day in P. delle Erbe behind the Basilica, and on Tuesday and Thursday mornings you can hunt for food among the bizarre clothes sold in the central *piazza*. Thursday's market is the biggie, winding throughout the town. Cheese, chicken, and fish tend to proliferate in P. del Duomo. For more staid shopping, turn to **Supermercato PAM,** Viale Roma, 1 (During summer open Mon.-Fri. 8:30am-7:30pm, Sat. and Sun. 8:30am-1pm and 3-7:30pm, Wed. 8:30am-1pm.).

Righetti, P. del Duomo, 3 (tel. 54 31 35), with another entrance at Contrà Fontana, 6. Self-service with reasonable fare and great ambience, including outdoor seating. *Primi* L4500, *secondi* L6500, cover L500. Open Sept.-late July Mon.-Fri. noon-2:30pm and 7-10pm; bar open 9pm-midnight.
Al Bersagliere, Contrà Pescaria, 11 (tel. 32 35 07), off P. Erbe. Small, with terrific owners, low prices, and great food. *Primi* L6000-7000, *secondi* L8000-12,000, cover L1000. Open Mon.-Sat. 8:30am-11pm.

SIGHTS AND ENTERTAINMENT

The town center, **Piazza dei Signori,** was the town's forum when Vicenza was Roman and the town's showpiece when it was Venetian. Palladio's treatment of the **basilica** (tel. 32 36 81) first made the young architect famous. In 1546, Palladio's patron, the wealthy Giovan Giorgio Trissino, agreed to fund his proposal to shore up the collapsing **Palazzo della Ragione,** a project that had frustrated some of the foremost architects of the day. The ingenious variation of pilaster widths in the twin *loggie* masks the irregular Gothic structure beneath. Look at the **Torre di Piazza** next door to get an idea of the basilica's former appearance. (Basilica open Tues.-Sat. 9:30am-noon and 2:30-5pm, Sun. 9:30am-noon. Free.) Across the piazza, the **Loggia del Capitano** illustrates a later Palladian style. Palladio left the façade unfinished at his death, having completed only the three bays and the four sets of gigantic columns. The two symbolic columns of Venice round out the *piazza*. Behind the Loggia del Capitano, the **Palazzo del Comune** faces **Corso Palladio,** Vicenza's main street. Vincenzo Scamozzi's precise design for the *palazzo* demonstrates a much sharper interpretation of classical architecture than that embodied in the buildings of Palladio, his mentor.

Contrà Vescovado leads out of the *piazza* next to Palazzo Porto-Breganze to the **duomo,** a large Gothic structure in brick with a graceful apse and a Palladian cupola. The **Casa Pigafetta** on nearby Via Pigafetta shows that Palladio wasn't the only architect to influence Vicenza; this unique early Renaissance house successfully fuses Gothic, Spanish, and classical styles.

At the far end of Corso Palladio, Palladio built the villa-like **Palazzo Chiericati,** which now houses the well-stocked **Museo Civico** (tel. 32 13 48). The collection in the first-floor *pinacoteca* includes some of Bassano's best endeavors, works by Bartolomeo Montagna (notably *Madonna Enthroned),* a Memling *Crucifixion,* Tintoretto's *Miracle of St. Augustine,* and a rare, refined *Madonna* by Cima da Conegliano. (Open Mon.-Sat. 9am-12:30pm and 2:15-5pm, Sun. 9:30am-12:30pm and 2-7pm. Admission L3000, students with teachers L1000, free on Sundays. You can also buy an all-day ticket (L9000) good for the Museo Civico, the Teatro Olimpico, and several other local museums.) The nearby **Teatro Olimpico** (tel. 32 37 81) embodies the same classicism cultivated by the 16th-century *palazzo*-building patrons. The city hosts productions here every year June through September, with both local and imported talent. (Open Mon.-Sat. 9am-12:30pm and 2:15-5pm, Sun. 9:30am-12:30pm and 2-7pm; slightly shorter hours Oct.-early June. Admission L5000, or buy the all-day ticket—see above).

Manifestazioni 1996, available at the tourist office, will guide those in search of high culture. Besides the performances in the **Teatro Olimpico** (tel. 32 37 81; Admission L20,000-45,000, students L15,000-25,000), there is the summer concert series **Concerti in Villa.** Check with the tourist office for the foreign film series.

■ NEAR VICENZA

Though most of the Palladian villas scattered through the Veneto are a pain to get to (see Ville Venete below), there are a few great villas close to town. The **Villa La Rotonda** (also called Villa Capra; tel. 32 17 93; walk from town or take bus #8 or #13 from near the station) is considered one of the most magnificent architectural achievements ever. This villa was a model for buildings in France, England, and the U.S., most notably Jefferson's Monticello. (Interior open March 15-Oct. 15 Wed. only. Exterior open Tues.-Thurs. 10am-noon and 3-6pm. Admission L5000, to the exterior L3000.) Palladio's unfinished **Villa Thiene** (tel. 35 60 53 or 35 65 93) is stately and a bit forlorn, remaining aloof despite the encroaching suburbs of Quinto Vicentino. (Open Mon., Wed., and Fri. 10am-12:30pm; Tues. and Thurs. 10am-12:30pm and 6-7pm. Free.)

VILLE VENETE

Venetian expansion to the mainland began in the early 15th century and provided infinite opportunity for Palladio's talents. As the wealth of Venice accumulated and its maritime supremacy faded, its nobles began to turn their attention to the acquisition of real estate on the mainland. The Venetian Senate stipulated that they build villas rather than castles to preclude any possibility of becoming independent warlords. The architectural consequences were stunning: Veneto is now home to hundreds of the most splendid villas in Europe.

Although villas abound in the Veneto, they are difficult to reach, have unpredictable schedules, and often allow tours of their exteriors only. Phone ahead or contact the **APT** in Vicenza on Via Gazzolle, 1 (tel. (0444) 39 91 11). The affable staff has mountains of well-written booklets on the villas. The tourist offices in Vicenza and Treviso provide good literature on Palladio's works, but they have written information only on the villas in their immediate provinces. Check in local bookstores for more complete guides to the *Ville,* in English and Italian.

The bus from Vicenza to Bassano stops at Thiene. Here, change buses for the tiny village of **Lugo** to see two famous Palladian villas at close range (5 per day, 2 on Sun., L3400). The simple **Villa Godi-Valmarana** (a.k.a. "Malinveri," tel. (0445) 86 05 61) was the architect's first. (Grounds open March-Nov. Tues., Sat.-Sun., and holidays 2-6pm. Interior, by prior appointment only. Admission L4000.) A few yards up the street is the more elegant and expansive **Villa Piovene** (tel. (0445) 86 14 81). The villa may be viewed only from the outside; for a close look, pay L3000 to enter the wonderful park around it. (Open daily 2:30-7pm.) Seven kilometers to the east of Asolo (near Vicenza) lies the most famous of the villas, the **Villa Barbaro-Volpi,** at Masèr, constructed in 1560 by Palladio. Wander to the base of the hill to see the exquisite circular temple that Palladio built for the owners. (Interior open Tues., Sat.-Sun., and holidays 3-6pm; Oct.-May Tue., Sat.-Sun., and holidays 2-5pm. Admission L6000. Call (0423) 56 50 02 for more information.) Masèr is an easy bus trip from Bassano (6 per day, L3000). Conclude your immersion in Palladian architecture with a train ride from Castelfranco to Fanzolo (on the Padua-Belluno line). Visit **Villa Emo** (tel. (0423) 48 70 40), considered along with Masèr to be one of the most characteristic Palladian villas; the interior frescoes here balance well with the architecture. (Open Feb.1 to mid-Dec. Sat. 3-6pm, Sun. and holidays 3-7pm. Admission L5000, groups L4000.)

■■■ VERONA

With its rose-colored streets and pastel houses overlooking majestic bridge views, the city of Verona is no less romantic today than it was in Shakespeare's *Romeo and Juliet.* During its formative years as a Roman colony, Verona was an important crossroads, and the remarkably well-preserved remains are tangible evidence of the colony's preeminence. Statuesque remains and opulent *palazzi* adorn Verona, whose mixture of past and present manifests itself best in the celebrated summer opera season held in the Arena, an amphitheater of epic proportions erected in 100 AD. Today Verona is a busy metropolis best seen by wandering through its *vicoli* (alleys); the views from the bridges are more romantic and breathtaking than the city's tragic love story.

ORIENTATION AND PRACTICAL INFORMATION

The heart of Verona lies between the **Arena** and **Piazza delle Erbe**. From the center, **Corso Porta Nuova** is the artery that leads south to the bus and train stations. Most of the scenic portions of town are contained within the lazy loop of the **Adige River**. Piazza Brà is a 20-min. walk up Corso Porto Nuova from the train station, or a ride aboard **AMT** bus #11, 12, 13, or 72. Bus tickets (L1300) are available from all *tabacchi* in the station. Day passes (L4000) are also available.

Tourist Office: Via Leoncino, 61 (tel. 59 28 28), in Piazza Brà, on the left side of the large yellow building with columns. English spoken, and they will help you find a room. Open Mon.-Sat. 8am-8pm. Another branch in the **train station**. Open Mon.-Sat. 9am-7pm. **Youth Info Center:** Corso Porto Borsari, 17 (tel. 801 07 95 or 59 07 56). Open Mon. 3-6pm, Tues. 10am-1pm, Wed. and Fri. 10am-1pm and 3-6pm. Friendly, helpful staff. English spoken. **Hotel Booking Office:** Via Patuzzi, 5 (tel. 800 98 44; fax 800 93 72). Open Mon.-Fri. 9am-7pm.

Police: Questura, tel. 59 67 77. **Ufficio Stranieri:** Lungoadige Porta Vittoria (tel. 809 05 05). Interpreter available, Mon.-Fri. 8:30am-12:30pm.

Post Office: P. Poste (tel. 800 39 98), also known as P. Viviani, follow Via Cairoli off P. delle Erbe. Stamps and *fermo posta* at windows #13, 14, and 16. Open Mon.-Sat. 8:15am-7:30pm. **Postal Code:** 37100.

Telephones: Telecom, Via Leoncino, 55, near the tourist office. Open Mon.-Sat. 9am-1pm and 3:30-7:30pm. 24-hr. phone bank. **Telephone Code:** 045.

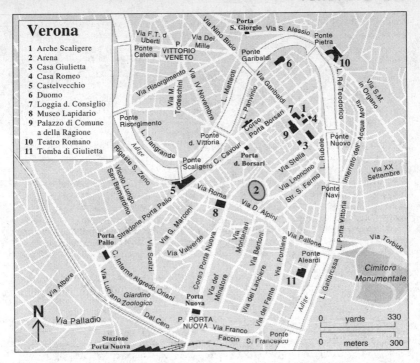

Verona

1 Arche Scaligere
2 Arena
3 Casa Giulietta
4 Casa Romeo
5 Castelvecchio
6 Duomo
7 Loggia d. Consiglio
8 Museo Lapidario
9 Palazzo di Comune
  a della Ragione
10 Teatro Romano
11 Tomba di Giulietta

Budget Travel: CIT, P. Brà, 2A (tel. 59 17 88). Open Mon.-Fri. 9am-1pm and 3-7pm, Sat. 9am-1pm. English spoken. **Centro Turistico Giovanile,** Via Seminario, 10 (tel. 800 45 92), off Via Carducci, the first left after Via Interrato dell'Acqua Morta, on the 3rd floor. Open Mon.-Fri. 9am-1pm and 3-6pm. **CTS,** Largo Pescheria Vecchia, 9/A (tel. 803 09 51), near the Scaligeri tombs. Open Mon.-Fri. 9am-12:30pm and 3:30-7pm.

Currency Exchange: Cassa di Risparmio, P. Brà, centrally located on the corner of Via Roma. Open Mon. Fri. 8:20am-1:20pm and 2:35-4:05pm. Also at the **train station.** Open 7am-9pm, rates better elsewhere.

American Express: Fabretto Viaggi, Corso Porta Nuova, 11 (tel. 800 90 40), two blocks from P. Brà, across from McDonald's. Sells traveler's checks ($US) and changes them without charging commission. Holds client mail (postal code: 37122) Open Mon.-Fri. 8:30am-7:30pm, Sat. 9-12pm.

Trains: P. XXV Aprile (tel. 59 06 88), linked with P. Brà by Corso Porta Nuova. To: Venice (every hr., 2hr., L9800); Milan (every hr., 2hr., L11,700); Bologna (every hr., 2hr., L9800); Trent (every hr., 1hr., L8000); and Rome (6 per day, 6hr., L40,500). **Luggage Storage:** L1500. Open 24 hrs.

Buses: APT, P. XXV Aprile (tel. 800 41 29). To: Riva del Garda (every hr. 7:45am-6:45pm, L9000); Sirmione (every hr., L4600); Brescia (every hr., L9500); Montagnana (3 per day, L7000). Ticket window open daily 6am-8:30pm.

Taxis: tel. 53 26 66, 6am-midnight.

Car Rental: Hertz (tel. 800 08 32), at the train station. Starting at L149,000 per day. Open Mon.-Fri. 8am-noon and 3-7pm, Sat. 8am-noon.

Bike Rental: Paolo Bellomi, Via degli Alpini (tel. 5049 01), off P. Brà, on the sidewalk. L7000 per hr., L20,000 per day. Open daily 9:30am-10pm, off-season 10am-7pm, subject to the weather.

English Bookstore: The Bookshop, Via Interatto dell'Acqua Morta, 3A (tel. 800 76 14), near Ponte Navi. Many classics (including *Let's Go*) and a small selection of German books. Open Mon. 3:30-7:30pm, Tues.-Fri. 9:15am-12:30pm and 3:30-7:30pm, Sat. 9:15am-12:30pm.

Pharmacy: tel. 192. Call this number to find out how late the pharmacies are open. **Emergencies:** tel. 113. **Hospital: Ospedale Civile Maggiore,** Borgo Trento, P. Stefani (tel. 807 11 11). **Ambulance:** 58 22 22.

ACCOMMODATIONS AND CAMPING

Make reservations during the opera season of July and August.

Ostello Verona (HI), Salita Fontana del Ferro, 15 (tel. 59 03 60; fax 800 91 27). From behind the Arena, walk straight up V. Anfiteatro (becomes Via Stella and then Via Nizza) and across Ponte Nuovo. Continue on V. Carducci and turn left on V. Interrato dell'Acqua Morta. Walk to P. Isolo (at the end of the old gray bus station), turn right, and follow the yellow signs. From the station (platform "F") take bus #72 or night bus #90 to P. Isolo. With its friendly, English-speaking staff, spacious, clean rooms, and beautiful views, Ostello Verona is one of Europe's most beautiful and well-run hostels. 5-day max. stay. Rooms open at 5pm, but arrive earlier to register and drop off your stuff. Curfew 11:30pm, with special provisions for opera-goers. L16,000 per person, including hot showers, breakfast, and sheets. Ample dinners (L12,000); vegetarian options if notified in advance. You can also **camp** in the villa's garden (L8000 per person, all inclusive; L6000 without tent). 220 beds. Reservations are only accepted from groups and families.

Casa della Giovane (ACISJF), Via Pigna, 7 (tel. 59 68 80). From P. delle Erbe, walk up Corso S. Anastasia and turn onto Vicolo Due Mori (3rd left). Walk to the end of the *vicolo,* then continue straight on Via Augusto Verità. The arched double door at the end of the street is the entrance. Women only. Beautiful, spacious rooms in the historic center of town. Curfew 11:00pm. If you have opera tickets, the owner will let you back in after the show for an extra L3000. Single room L30,000. Bed in a double or triple L20,000.

Locanda Catullo, Vicolo Catullo, 1 (tel. 800 27 86). Walk along Via Mazzini until you reach 40. Turn onto Via Catullo (a left if you're walking north along Via Mazzini) and then make a right onto Vicolo Catullo. These newly renovated rooms can be very hard to get in July and August. 2-day min. stay. Singles L38,000. Doubles L60,000, with bath L80,000.

Campeggio Romeo e Giulietta, Via Bresciana, 54 (tel. 851 02 43), on the road to Peschiera de Garda. Take the blue APT bus to Brescia from train station (L9500). Alert bus driver that you're going to the campground (last bus from Verona 8pm). Hot showers, plenty of space, store, and pool, but no romantic balconies. Check in 8am-11pm. L6900 for one person without a car, L17,300 for one person with a car, L6500 per additional person. Meals not included. Closed Dec.-Feb.

Hotel Armando, Via Dietro Pallone, 1 (tel. 800 02 06), off Via Pallone. Small rooms, some with TV. Singles with bath L60,000. Doubles L80,000, with bath L100,000. Breakfast L8000. Open Jun-Sept.

FOOD

Verona is famous for its wines: *soave* (dry white), *valpolicella,* and *bardolino* (both red). The vendors in Piazza Isolo offer better prices than those in Piazza delle Erbe. For a large sampling, try **Oreste dal Zovo,** Via S. Marco in Foro, 7/5 (tel. 803 43 69), off Corso Porta Borsari. The congenial owner has shelves of every wine imaginable. The selections are numerous and include *grappa* from a mini-barrel. One can crunch on microscopic snacks (L500-1000) or small *panini* (L2000). (Open Mon.-Sun. 8am-8pm.) For eating essentials at reasonable prices go to **METÁ SUPERNE-GOZI** (tel. 800 67 80), Via XX Settembre, 81. (Open Thurs.-Tues. 8:30-12am.)

VERONA

In The Center

Trattoria Fontanina, Piazzetta Chiavica, 5 (tel. 803 11 33), down the street from the tombs of the Scaligeri. Streetside terrace and pleasant atmosphere. *Primi* L8000, *secondi* L13,000. Cover L1500. Service 12%. Open Wed.-Sun. 12-2pm and 7-10pm, Mon. noon-2pm.

Trattoria Al Pompiere, Vicolo Regina d'Ungheria, 5 (tel. 803 05 37), the first right off Via Cappello from P. delle Erbe. Quiet, but tends to gather afternoon tourists from P. delle Erbe. *Primi* L6500-8000, *secondi* L12,000-15,000. *Menù* L23,000. Cover L3000. Open Mon.-Sun. 1:30-10pm. AmEx, MC, Visa.

Across the River

Unless the gravitational tug of the Arena proves overwhelming, head for the university quarter when in search of sustenance.

Trattoria Al Cacciatore, Via Seminario, 4 (tel. 59 42 91), left of Via Carducci just past Via Interrato dell'Acqua Morta. A genuine neighborhood joint. Come rub elbows with locals, and enjoy delicious food at low prices. *Primi* L4000-7000, *secondi* L8000-14,000. *Menù* L16,000. Cover L2000. Open Mon.-Sat. 10:30am-3pm and 6-11:30pm.

Nuovo Grottina, Via Interrato dell'Acqua Morta, 38 (tel. 803 01 52), off Via Carducci by Ponte Nuovo. Popular with students during the school year, and priced to stay that way. Pizza L5500-10,000. *Primi* L5000-8000, *secondi* L6000-16,000. *Menù* L15,000. Cover L1000. Open Fri.-Wed. 9:30am-2:30pm and 6pm-1am.

Trattoria dal Ropeton, Via San Giovanni in Valle, 46 (tel. 803 00 40), below the youth hostel. Very authentic, very popular, and very hard to get at the courtyard tables. Lots o' delicious food for low prices. If you're lucky, one of the waiters will entertain you with his singing. *Primi* L9000, *secondi* L14,000. Cover indoors L1500, courtyard 2500. Open Wed.-Mon. 12:30-3pm and 7:30-11pm.

Il Grillo Parlante, Vicolo Seghe San Tommaso, 10 (tel. 59 11 56), from P. Isolo, walk around the left side of the old bus station and turn left at the bright yellow building. Make another left when you reach Vicolo Seghe San Tomaso. Verona's vegetarian hotspot has a devoted clientele. *Primi* L7500, *secondi* L8000. Cover L2500. Open Fri.-Sun. and Tues.-Wed. noon-2pm and 7:30-10pm, Thurs. noon-2pm.

SIGHTS

The majestic pink **Arena** (tel. 800 32 04) in P. Brà dates back to 100 AD, and among Roman amphitheaters it is surpassed in size only by the one at Capua and the Colosseum in Rome. The Arena's superb condition testifies to Verona's municipal pride. (Open Tues.-Sun. 8am-6:30pm, in opera season 8am 1:30pm. Admission L6000, students L1500.)

From P. Brà, Via Mazzini takes you into **Piazza delle Erbe,** the former Roman Forum. The center of the *piazza* holds the Madonna Verona fountain, installed by Cansignorio della Scala in 1368. At the far end rises the 1523 column of St. Mark (topped by a winged lion), a symbol of four centuries of Venetian domination. The **Gardello Tower,** built in 1370, stands between the imposing Baroque **Palazzo Maffei** and two buildings with frescoed façades and spacious terraces that Verona's first families, the Scaligeri (della Scala) and the Mazzanti, once called home. In the center of the piazza, almost hidden by fruit vendors' awnings, stands the **Berlina**— during medieval times, convicts were tied to the marble structure to be pelted with rotten fruit.

The **Arco della Costa,** called the "Arch of the Rib" for the whale rib hung from it, separates P. delle Erbe from **Piazza dei Signori.** Local legend says that the rib will fall on the first person to pass under the arch who has never told a lie (hmph. Some incentive to be honest!). Witness to the visits of popes and kings, the rib has hung securely in place for 1000 years. The delicate **Loggia del Consiglio** (1493), built in the Venetian Renaissance style, stands adjacent to the *prefettura.* The grey **Palazzo della Ragione** stands on the corner. This densely knit brick and marble ensemble was the seat of thedella Scala dynasty for centuries. The della Scala was a violent and dogged family, as their names suggest: Cangrande (Big Dog), succeeded by Mastino II (The Mastiff), and then Cansignorio (Head Dog). Yet, like many of their brutish peers, the della Scala were also sensitive patrons of the arts. Dante passed many months here as the guest of Cangrande and eventually dedicated his *Paradiso* to the powerful warlord.

Through the arch at the far end of P. dei Signori lie the peculiar outdoor **Tombs of the Scaligeri,** further testimony to the Scala family temperament. The **Casa di Romeo,** long the home of the Montecchi family (model for the Montagues), has slowly deteriorated into a disappointing coffee bar (around the corner from P. dei Signori at Via Arche Scaligori, 2). At Casa Capuletti, Via Cappello, 23, more commonly known as **Casa di Giulietta** (tel. 803 43 03), you will find a tall, ivy-covered wall next to a balcony where you can wait your turn in line to spot your Romeo among the trinket stands. If you're wondering, the feuding dal Capellos (Capulets) never lived here. (Open Tues.-Sun. 8am-6:30pm. Admission L5000, students L1500.)

At the other end of P. delle Erbe, Corso Sant'Anastasia leads to the Gothic **Basilica of Sant'Anastasia**. Walk in and be awed by the magnificent art throughout the interior. Don't miss Pisanello's *St. George Freeing the Princess* (in the Giusti Chapel in the left transept), considered one of his best paintings, and the frescoes by Altichiero and Turone. Walk down Via Duomo from the basilica to the **duomo,** decorated with medieval sculpture by local stone carvers. The first chapel on the left features Titian's ethereal *Assumption of the Virgin*. The **Biblioteca Capitolare** (tel. 59 65 16), the oldest library in Europe, maintains a priceless medieval manuscript collection that scholars won't want to miss. (Cathedral open daily 7am-noon and 3-7pm. Library open Mon., Wed., and Sat. 9:30am-12:30pm; Tues. and Fri. 9:30am-12:30pm and 4-6pm. Free.)

Over the Roman Ponte Pietra (across the Adige) the recently uncovered **Teatro Romano** (tel. 800 03 60) now provides a venue for Shakespearean plays. See Entertainment for more info. The theater was built during the early Roman Empire at the foot of what today is called St. Peter's Hill. It affords a wonderful view of Verona, especially in the evening. (Open Tues.-Sun. 8am-1:30pm. Admission L5000.)

At the bottom of the hill, Via Interatto dell'Acqua Morta leads to the 15th-century **Church of Santa Maria in Organo.** Although Sammicheli made a significant contribution to the façade, the most delicate inlay work was completed by Giovanni da Verona. Behind the church beckons the **Giardino Giusti** (tel. 803 40 29), a delightful 18th-century garden. (Open daily 8am-8pm. Admission L5000, students L2000.)

The della Scala fortress, the **Castelvecchio** (tel. 59 47 34, at the end of Via Roma from P. Brà), was carefully reconstructed after devastation during World War II. The many-leveled interior is decked out with walkways, parapets, and an extensive collection of sculptures and paintings including Pisanello's *Madonna and Child,* Luca di Leyda's *Crucifixion,* and works by Andrea Mantegna, Francesco Morone, Tintoretto, and Tiepolo. (Open Tues.-Sun. 8am-6pm. Admission L5000, students L1500.)

The church of **San Zeno Maggiore,** upstream from the Castelvecchio, is one of the finest examples of Italian Romanesque architecture. Built and expanded upon from the 10th to 12th centuries, the massive brick church of Verona's patron saint surpasses its more central counterparts in artistic wealth. The 17th-century sculpted bronze doors sparked a craze throughout Italy. The interior structure is notable for its wooden "ship's keel" ceiling and the spacious crypt area. The two-story apse contains a Renaissance altarpiece by Mantegna. (Open daily 8am-noon and 3-7pm.)

If you're staying at Ostello Verona, try not to miss the **Museo Africano,** Vicolo Pozzo, 1 (tel. 22 418). The museum is run by the religious missionary started by Fr. Camboni. There are missionary workers throughout Africa, and the museum celebrates the ancient and cherished traditions, arts, and relics of African peoples. The nun at the door is extremely welcoming, and a detailed guide of all the rich work is available in English. The museum is free and wheelchair accessible.

ENTERTAINMENT

Verona has parlayed the romance of its pervasive rosy marble and vast Roman Arena into the city's premier cultural event, an **opera and ballet extravaganza** in July and August. Prices start at L15,000 for unreserved gallery seats. *Jazz Italia* and *Praga Sinfonietta* prices start at L10,000. For more information, call 59 01 09 or 59 07 26, or go directly to arch #8 or #9 to make a reservation or a purchase. If you opt for general admission seating, be prepared to encounter crowds of operaholics who camp out up to two hours before the gates open.

The Teatro Romano stages Shakespeare productions (in Italian) every summer. (Tickets start at L72,000. Reserve ahead at arch #18. Open in season Mon.-Sat. 10:30am-1pm and 4-7pm. For information call 807 72 19, for reservations 59 00 89.) *Verona for You* (available at the tourist office) lists current exhibits and events.

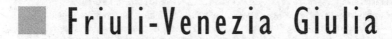

Friuli-Venezia Giulia

Overshadowed by the touristed cities of Veneto and the mountains of Trentino-Alto Adige, Friuli-Venezia Giulia has traditionally received less than its fair share of recognition. Triest has been a long-standing exception to this rule, and today increasing numbers of beach-goers flock to the least expensive resorts on the Adriatic. The area towns owe their charm to their small size; they offer an untainted slice of the local life and culture that is otherwise missed in Italy's larger cities.

Friuli-Venezia Giulia was once a number of distinct provinces, as its name suggests. From the 6th to 15th centuries the local clergy unified and maintained autonomy from the church and other states. The entire region was then appropriated by the Venetian Republic, only to be reabsorbed, Venetians and all, into Austria-Hungary. The present region is the product of a postwar union between Udine, Pordenone, Gorizia, and Triest. The historical differences between these provinces, and the area's vulnerability to Eastern forces given its marginal geographic location in the north of Italy, combine to give Friuli-Venezia Giulia a hybrid character and culture. The mix of political intrigue and coffee-culture elegance brought by the Austro-Hungarian Empire attracted various intellectuals to turn-of-the-century Friuli: James Joyce lived in Triest for 12 years, during which he wrote the bulk of *Ulysses;* Ernest Hemingway's *A Farewell to Arms* draws part of its plot from the region's role in World War I; Freud and Rilke both worked and wrote here. The mixture of Slovenian, Friulian, and Italian peoples has produced an indigenous literary tradition of its own, which includes Italo Svevo and the poet Umberto Saba.

The Tagliamento and Natisone River Valleys shelter fertile farmlands, and local dialect and hearty culinary traditions are the legacy of the society's peasant origins. The Carnian Alps to the north and the Julian Alps to the east present copious opportunities for hiking, rock-climbing, and skiing, and provide an alternative climate to the beaches of the southern coast.

■ ■ ■ TRIEST (TRIESTE)

The unofficial capital of Friuli-Venezia Giulia lies at the end of a narrow strip of land sandwiched between Slovenia and the Adriatic. Given its strategically placed harbor and proximity to Austrian and former Yugoslavian borders, Triest has been a bone of contention over the centuries. Even as an independent city during the 9th-15th centuries, and Venice's main rival in the Adriatic until Venice overtook it, Triest was always coveted by the Austrians. Austria finally got its crack at a real Adriatic port in the post-Napoleonic real estate market and proceeded to rip the medieval heart from Triest, replacing it with Neoclassical bombast. The Hapsburgs' equally heavy-

TRIEST

handed style of government succeeded in turning the mostly Italian population into fervent *irredentisti* clamoring for the return of the vaguely Italian province to Italy. They emerged victorious in 1918 when Italian troops occupied the Friuli, but unification only brought more trouble: Mussolini's thicket of fascist statuary provided an appropriate counterpoint to the Austro-Hungarian architecture, while his policies of cultural chauvinism offended anyone not already alienated by the Hapsburg rulers.

Today, evidence of Triest's multinational history lingers in the numerous buildings and monuments of Hapsburg origin and the Slavic nuances in the local cuisine. The city's Italian identity, on the other hand, is vehemently asserted by the persistence of fascist and anti-Slav parties, and more tangibly in the formidable Piazza Unità d'Italia, the largest *piazza* in Italy. The cumulative product of these conflicting forces is a cosmopolitan hub of transportation, a logical departure point for travelers to Eastern Europe.

ORIENTATION AND PRACTICAL INFORMATION

Triest is a direct train ride from Venice or Udine, and several trains and buses cross over daily to neighboring Slovenia and Croatia. Less frequent ferry service runs the length of the Istrian Peninsula. The gray, industrialized quays catering to ferries and fishermen taper off into Triest's equivalent of a beach—a stretch of tiered concrete, populated with bronzed bodies, that runs 7km from the edge of town out to the castle at Miramare. Moving inland one encounters **Piazza Oberdan,** which opens onto the ever-busy **Via Carducci.** Shoppers pack the fashion-oriented streets that intersect with this central artery near P. Goldoni. The artistically inclined can head to the pride and glory of Triest, **Piazza Unità d'Italia,** which looks out to the harbor. Public transportation runs throughout the city, and most buses stop in the immediate vicinity of the train station.

Tourist Office: In the train station (tel. 42 01 82), to the right before exiting the station. Copious information on Triest including a list of *manifestazioni* (cultural events) occasionally encompassing international programs as well. Ask about staying at private homes; it's cheaper. English spoken. Open Mon.-Fri. 9am-7pm, Sat. 8:30am-1:30pm.

Police: Via del Teatro Romano (tel. 379 01), off Corso Italia.

Post Office: P. Vittorio Veneto, 1 (tel. 36 67 42), along Via Roma, the 2nd right off Via Ghega coming from the train station. *Fermo posta* at counter #21. Fax downstairs. Open Mon.-Sat. 8am-7:30pm. **Postal Code:** 34100.

Telephones: Telecom, Via Pascoli, 9. Open Mon.-Fri. 8:30am-12:30pm and 4-7pm. Phonebooths throughout town open 24 hrs. **Telephone Code:** 040.

Budget Travel: CTS, P. Dalmazia, 3 (tel. 36 18 79). Agency for air and train tickets plus a variety of other vacation information. Open Mon.-Fri. 9am-1pm and 1:30-7pm. **Aurora Viaggia,** Via Milano, 20 (tel. 63 02 61), 1 block from Via Carducci. Information on transportation and lodging in the former Yugoslavian territory. Open Mon.-Fri. 9am-12:30pm and 4-7pm, Sat. 9am-noon.

Consulates: The **U.S.** no longer has a consulate here, but it does have an honorary representative at Via Roma, 15 (tel. 66 01 77). Ask for Sig. Bearz. Otherwise try the consulate in Milan. **U.K.,** Vicolo delle Ville, 16 (tel. 30 28 84), available Tues. and Fri. 9am-12:30pm. The closest **Canadian** and **Australian** consulates are in Milan. **New Zealand** citizens should contact their embassy in Rome. To check on the current state of visa requirements for travel eastward, contact the **Slovenian** consulate, Via S. Giorgio, 1 (tel. 30 78 55), or **Croatia** in Rome, Via Santi Cosma e Damiano, 26 (tel. 33 25 02 42).

Currency Exchange: Banca d'America e d'Italia, Via Roma, 7 (tel. 63 19 25). Cash advances on Visa cards. Open Mon.-Fri. 8:20am-1:20pm and 2:35-3:50pm. Also try **Assomar Cambio** in the bus station in P. della Libertà (tel. 42 53 07). Open daily 7:30am-8pm. No commission.

Trains: P. della Libertà (tel. 41 82 07), down Via Cavour from the quays. Info office open daily 8:30am-12:30pm and 3:30-6:30pm. To: Udine (15 per day, 1½hr., L7200); Venice (16 per day, 2hr., L13,600); Milan (1 per day, 5½-7½hr., L33,400);

Ljubljana (6 per day, 3½hr., L16,000); Budapest (1 or more per day, L75,000).
Luggage Storage: L1500. Open daily 5am-midnight.
Buses: Corso Cavour (tel. 336 03 00), in the fringe of P. della Libertà near the train
station. To: Udine (8 per day, L6200); Rijeka/Fiume (2 per day, L13,600). **Luggage Storage:** L1500. Open daily 6:20am-8pm. There are also several smaller
lines that run throughout the region. Check at the station.
Ferries: Agemar Viaggi, P. Duca degli Abruzzi, 1/A (tel. 36 37 37; fax 77 723), by
the waterfront next to the canal. Will arrange trips with **Adriatica di Navigazione** and provide the latest visa requirements for entering the former Yugoslavia.
To: Grado (1hr., L10,000); Lignano (1¼hr., L11,500); Rovigno (3hr., L30,000);
Pirano (1½hr., L15,000). Office open Mon.-Fri. 8:30am-1pm and 3-7:30pm.
Public Transportation: ACT, Via d'Alviano, 15 (tel. 779 51). Open Mon.-Fri. 9am-1pm. Ticket for travel within the city L1400 from any *tabacchi.*
Taxis: tel. 545 33 or 30 77 30.
Rental Cars: Hertz, in the bus station, P. della Libertà (tel. 42 21 22; fax 41 89 46).
Open Mon.-Fri. 8:30am-12:30pm and 3-6:30pm, Sat. 8:30am-12:30pm. Another
Hertz office at the airport (tel. 77 70 25). **Avis,** also in the bus station (tel. 77 70
85). Open Mon.-Fri. 8am-12:30pm and 3:30-7pm, Sat. 8am-noon. Rates at both
places around L150,000 per day.
Laundromat: Via Ginnastica, 36 (tel. 36 74 14). Roughly L15,000 per load. Open
Tues.-Fri. 8am-1pm and 3:30-7pm, Sat. 8am-1pm.
Swimming Pool: Piscina Comunale "Bruno Bianchi," Riva Gulli, 3 (tel. 30 60
24), along the waterfront. Indoor. Open Oct.-July Mon.-Sat. noon-3pm, Sun. 9am-1pm. Admission L5000. Lockers L1500.
English Bookstore: Libreria Cappeli, Corso Italia, 12B (tel. 63 04 14). English
books (in the back right corner) and travel guides. Open Tues.-Sat. 8:30am-12:30pm and 3:30-7:30pm. AmEx, Visa.
Late-Night Pharmacies: tel. 192. Insert 3 telephone tokens for a listing.
Emergencies: tel. 113. **Hospital: Ospedale Maggiore,** P. dell'Ospedale (tel. 77
61), up Via Tarabocchia from Via Carducci. **Ambulance:** tel. 118.

ACCOMMODATIONS AND CAMPING

Watch out for weekdays, when companies often fill up the smaller *pensioni* with
workers. Consult the tourist office, which leaves a helpful list of Triest's hotels and
pensioni taped to the door for those who arrive after hours.

Ostello Tegeste (HI), Viale Miramare, 331 (tel. 22 41 02). The hostel is on the seaside, just down from the castle Miramare, about 6km from the city center. From
the station take bus #36 (L1100; across the street as you exit). Get off the bus just
before it starts heading up the hill; if in doubt, ask the driver. Walk along the
waterfront toward the hostel (look for the yellow signs). Modern hostel with garden, bar, and gorgeous views of the sea. Live bands play here periodically; other
times loud, recorded American music fills the air. Average of 4 bunks per room.
Personal lockers with locks provided free of charge. HI members only. Registration noon-11:30pm. Checkout 9:30am. Lockout 9:30am-noon. Curfew 11:30pm.
L17,000 includes hot showers and breakfast. Also serves lunch and dinner (*menù*
L13,000, though you can eat 1 or 2 courses for less). Reserve ahead.
Centrale, Via Ponchielli, 1 (tel. 63 94 82). Centrally located, as the name suggests,
right off the canal. Spacious, clean rooms. Singles L35,000, with shower L40,000,
with toilet L55,000. Doubles L55,000, with shower L60,000, with bath L75,000.
Triples L75,000. Showers L3000.
Julia, Via XXX Ottobre, 5 (tel. 37 00 45), up 2 flights. Big, well-lit rooms with sink.
Newly renovated. Singles L35,000. Doubles L55,000.
Centro, Via Roma, 13 (tel. 63 44 08 or 37 11 16). Centrally located. Quiet hotel
with standard rooms. Singles L30,000. Doubles L60,000. Triples L81,000.
Valeria, Via Nazionale, 156 (tel. 21 12 04). Located in Opicina, this hotel offers
clean rooms in a peaceful suburb of Triest. From P. Oberdan take the tram to
Opicina (every 20min. 6am-midnight). Singles L30,000. Doubles L50,000.
Camping Obelisco, Strada Nuova Opicina, 37 (tel. 21 16 55 or 21 27 44), is 7km
from Triest in Opicina, a suburb on the rocky *corso*—a sparsely beautiful place to

camp for those not umbilically attached to the beach. Take the tram from P. Oberdan (L1400), and get off at the "Obelisco" stop; follow the yellow signs to the camp. Nice facilities with bar and tranquility. L4000-5000 per person, L2500-4500 per tent (depending on size), light L2000-3000, car L2500-3500.

FOOD

Many dishes in Triest's restaurants have Eastern European overtones (usually Hungarian) and are often loaded with paprika. The city is renowned for its fish; try *sardoni in savor* (large sardines marinated in oil and garlic). Monday is a non-day in Triest: most shops and restaurants close. To fend for yourself, visit one of the several **alimentari** on Via Carducci or try **Supercoop** on Via Palestrina, 3, at Via Francesco (open Mon. and Wed. 8am-1pm, Tues. and Thurs.-Sat. 8am-1pm and 5-7:30pm). If you're near the waterfront, go to **Supermercato Despar** across from the public pool (open Mon.-Fri. 8:30am-1:30pm and Tues. and Thurs.-Fri. 4:30-7:30pm, Sat. 8:30am-7:30pm). While in town, sample a bottle of *Terrano del Carso,* a dry red wine with a low alcohol content that has been valued for its therapeutic properties since the days of ancient Rome. For unadulterated grapes, stroll through the open-air **market** in P. Ponterosso, by the canal. (Open Tues.-Sat. 8am-5:30pm.)

> **Brek,** Via San Francesco, 10 (tel. 73 26 51). Self-service restaurant. Economical, efficient, and tasty. Everything is *alla carta* so pick and choose between fresh fruit, wine, pasta, and more. *Primi* L3500-4100, *secondi* L7200. IYHF card: 10% discount. Open Sat.-Thurs. 11:30am-2:30pm and 6:30-10pm (daily May 1-Sept. 30).
>
> **Paninoteca Da Livio,** Via della Ginnastica, 3/B (tel. 63 64 46), inland off Via Carducci. Small, smoky shop boasts monster *panini* (L2500-7000) and dozens of brands of beer. Usually crowded. Open Mon.-Sat. 9am-3pm and 5-10pm. Closed last week of June and first week of July.
>
> **Pizzeria Barattolo,** P. Sant'Antonio, 2 (tel. 64 14 80), along the canal. Amazing pizza (L6000-13,000). Also bar and *tavola calda* offerings. Open Tues.-Sun. 8am-1am. AmEx, MC, Visa.

SIGHTS

In honor of the Hapsburg empress, 19th-century Viennese urban planners carved out a large chunk of Triest to create Borgo Teresiano, a district of straight avenues bordering the waterfront and the canal. Facing the canal from the south is the district's one beautiful church, the Serbian Orthodox **San Spiridione.** (Open daily 9-11:30am. Free.) The **Municipio** at the head of **Piazza dell'Unità d'Italia** is a monument whose ornate design complements the largest *piazza* in Italy. The *piazza* itself is a huge space with beautifully designed buildings on all sides and an allegorical fountain with statues representing four continents. Enjoy a waterfront view from any of the *caffè* in the area.

The 15th-century Venetian **Castle of San Giusto** presides over **Capitoline Hill,** the city's historic center. You can take bus #24 (L1400) from the station to the last stop at the fortress and ascend the hill via the daunting **Scala dei Giganti** (Steps of the Giants—all 265 of them) rising from P. Goldoni. It offers a great view of the sea and downtown Triest, and is a prime sunset-watching spot if the *bora* winds don't blow you away. Within the walls is a huge outdoor theater where film festivals are held in July and August (pick up a copy of *Triest '96, Eventi Luglio-Agosto* at the tourist office). Directly below are the remains of the old Roman city center, and across the street is the restored **Cathedral of San Giusto.** Its irregular plan is due to its origin as two churches built simultaneously from the 5th through 11th centuries, one dedicated to San Giusto, the other to Santa Maria Assunta. Inside are two splendid mosaics in the chapels directly to the left and right of the altar. Walk around the ramparts of the castle (open daily 8am-7pm), or peek into the museum, which has temporary exhibits in addition to a permanent collection of weaponry (tel. 31 36 36; open Tues.-Sun. 9am-1pm. Admission L2000).

Down the other side of the hill past the *duomo* lies the eclectic **Museo di Storia de Arte** and **Orto Lapidario** (Museum of History and Art and Rock Garden; tel. 37

05 00 or 30 86 86) at Via Cattedrale, 15, in P. Cattedrale. The museum provides archaeological documentation of the history of Triest during and preceding its Roman years, and boasts a growing collection of Egyptian art and artifacts from south Italy. (Open Tues.-Sun. 9am-1pm. Admission L3000, students L1500.) Descending the hill toward the ruins of the *Teatro Romano* you end up only a few short blocks from P. Unità d'Italia. The **Teatro Romano** on Via del Teatro Romano off Corso Italia was built under the auspices of Trajan (first century AD). Originally gladiatorial contests were held here; later, spectators enjoyed the passion and the blood in the form of Greek tragedies.

An excellent collection of drawings and a less impressive selection of paintings by Tiepolo, Veneziano, and others has been moved from the Capitoline Hill to an elegant 18th-century villa at Largo Papa Giovanni XXIII, 1, which is now the **Museo Sartorio** (tel. 30 14 79). The museum is easily reached by walking a short distance from the center along the quays. (Open Tues.-Sun. 9am-1pm. Admission L3000.)

ENTERTAINMENT

The regular opera season of the **Teatro Verdi** runs November to May, but a six-week operetta season is held in June and July. Purchase tickets or phone for reservations at P. Verdi, 1 (tel. 36 78 16; open Tues.-Sun. 9am-noon and 4-7pm; seats from L10,000). Inquire at travel agency **UTAT-Galleria Prolti** for info on all performances (tel. 63 00 63).

Caffè Tommaseo, Riva III Novembre, 5 (tel. 36 67 65 or 36 72 36), in P. Tommaseo along the canal (closed on Mon.), and **Caffè San Marco,** Via Battisti, 18 (tel. 37 13 73), preserve the city's turn-of-the-century coffee culture (the latter frequently offers live musical performances). (Open Thurs.-Tues. 7am-2am.) Coffee in Triest is an art form, thanks to the influence of the Viennese. It comes to you on a silver platter, with a glass of water and, if you're lucky, a few sweet pastries (typically L4000-6000). The liveliest *passeggiata* takes place along Viale XX Settembre, a cool and largely traffic-free and *caffè*-lined avenue—a good place to relax in the shade.

■ NEAR TRIEST

West of Triest you can sunbathe along the rocky coast and visit the **Castello Miramare** (tel. 22 41 43), the gorgeous castle of Archduke Maximilian of Austria, who ordered its construction in the middle of the 19th century. It was rumored that anyone spending the night here would come to a bad end, a belief helped along by the decision of Archduke Ferdinand to spend the night here on the way to his assassination at Sarajevo. Poised on a high promontory over the gulf, Miramare's white turrets are easily visible from the Capitoline Hill in Triest or from the train on the journey through the *corso;* its extensive parks are open to the public at no cost. To reach Miramare, take bus #36 (30min., L1100), get off at the hostel stop (see above), and walk along the water. (Castle museum open daily 9am-6pm. Admission L8000, with a tour in Italian. English tours L22,000.) Fortunately, each room has a description and history provided in English. In July and August, a series of **sound and light shows** transform Miramare into a high-tech playground. (Shows Tues., Thurs., and Sat. at 9:30pm and 10:45pm. The show is in English. Admission L9000. Call the tourist office for more info.)

Near the castle, a **marine park** (tel. 22 41 47) sponsored by the World Wildlife Fund conducts several programs throughout the year, including guided introductions to the coast's marine life. The park itself is the area marked by buoys off shore surrounding Castle Miramare. Swimming is not allowed here without a guide. Guided water tours (both snorkeling and scuba) are offered. (Open Wed. and Fri. Admission L29,000, children L18,000. In Italian. Call the office to make reservations, which are required. Office open Mon.-Fri. 9am-7pm, Sat. 9am-5pm. You can also rent snorkel, fins, and mask together for L27,000 or separately.)

About 15km from Triest in Opicina, you'll find the **Grotta Gigante** (tel. 32 73 12), the world's largest accessible cave. Staircases wind in and around the 90m-high interior, which the brochure claims could hold the whole of St. Peter's. (Open Tues.-Sat. 9am-noon and 2-7pm, Nov.-Feb. 10am-noon and 2:30-4:30pm.) Transportation from P. Oberdan. (Admission L9000.) You can also take bus #45 (5 per day, L1600).

The more alcoholically-savvy can walk the famous and beautiful **Terrano wine-routes.** (Terrano is a local wine of the region.) The route begins in Opicina and goes to Vispogliano. Restaurants with regional specialties line the route and welcome tourists to dine. For more information on the wine-route, contact the tourist office.

■■■ AQUILEIA AND PALMANOVA

AQUILEIA

Aquileia was founded in 181 BC on the banks of the now-defunct Natisone-Torre River. Between 200 and 452 AD it flourished as the Roman capital of the region, serving as the gateway to the Eastern Empire and as the principal trading port of the Adriatic. The Patriarchate of Aquileia was established in 313, but as the Huns and Lombards descended to sack the city in the 5th and 6th centuries, the Patriarch fled to Grado and then moved on to Cividale del Friuli. Aquileia finally regained control in 1019, and in celebration rebuilt its great *basilica*. From this point on the Patriarchate successfully defied the popes until the port silted up and malaria set in. The disgruntled Patriarch moved on to Udine and dwindled into an archbishop, leaving behind a perfect open-air museum of Roman and early Christian art, the most important archaeological remains in north Italy.

Aquileia can be reached by bus from Udine (16 per day, 1hr., L4100), and local buses travel to Cervignano, a train station on the Triest-Venice line (every 30min., L1400). The **tourist office** (tel. (0431) 91 087; open daily 2:30-6pm, April-Oct. Fri.-Wed. 9am-1pm and 4-6pm) is a block from the bus stop in P. Capitolo.

Across the *piazza* from the tourist office stands Aquileia's **basilica.** The *basilica* is a tribute to the town's artistic heritage, offering a sampling of artwork from across the centuries. The floor, a remnant of the original church, is a 4th-century mosaic of unequalled magnitude, animating over 700 square meters with geometric designs and realistic bestial depictions. The 9th-century crypt beneath the altar holds several 12th-century frescoes illustrating the trials of Aquileia's early Christians and scenes from the life of Christ. In the *Cripta degli Scavi*, to the left upon entering, excavation has uncovered three distinct layers of flooring, providing vivid evidence of the building's varied history. (*Basilica* open daily 8:30am-7pm; in winter 8am-12:30pm and 3-6pm. Crypt open Mon.-Sat. 9am-3pm, Sun. 9am-1pm. Admission L3000.)

Yellow signs and clearly delineated tourist maps make it easy to find the various ruins, but the cypress-lined alley behind the *basilica* runs parallel to the once-glorious **Roman harbor** and is a pleasant alternative to Via Augusta as a path to the **forum.** Continue from there to the **Museo Paleocristiano** (tel. 91 11 30), where displays explain the transition from classical paganism to Christianity and moss covers the ubiquitous mosaics. (Open Tues.-Sat. 9am-6:30pm, Sun. 9am-1pm and 2-6:30pm, Mon. 9am-2pm; in winter Mon.-Sat. 9am-2pm, Sun. 9am-1pm. Free.)

A lack of budget accommodations almost makes Aquileia a mandatory daytrip; if you must stay, try **Camping Aquileia,** Via Gemina, 10 (tel. 910 42; in winter 910 37), up the street from the forum, a shady spot with a swimming pool. (Adults L7000, under 12 L4400. Tent sites L9000-12,000, bungalows for 2 L50,000-60,000. Open May 15-Sept. 15.) The **Desparo Supermarket** on the Udine end of Via Augusta is a penny-pincher's salvation (open Tues.-Sat. 8am-1pm and 4pm-midnight, Sun. 8am-1pm), and the **Trattoria Augusta** upstairs serves a decent *menù* for L16,000 (open Tues.-Sun. 9am-3pm and 5pm-midnight).

PALMANOVA

Palmanova, a town girded by a nine-sided Venetian fortress, lies between Udine and Aquileia on the bus route to Grado (16 per day, 20min., L2500). With a hexagonal central *piazza* and six main streets radiating out to the ramparts, Palmanova is an exceptionally well preserved example of Renaissance military planning. It is also a charming, small town with *trattorie* and shops. A nice daytrip from Triest or Udine, Palmanova serves as a great way to witness local Italian life far away from the hordes. The **tourist office,** Borso Udine, 4/C (tel. (0432) 92 91 06) is on the ground floor of the **Museo Civico,** which displays manuscripts and artifacts documenting Palmanova's military history. (Both open Tues.-Sun. 10am-noon.)

■■■ UDINE

Come to Udine and congratulate yourself on your unorthodox itinerary. Udine is not riddled with tourists, and yet it is an unexpectedly captivating town. Its *piazze* are beautifully designed and the town itself is filled with interesting historical sites. In addition to Italian, natives speak some German, some Serbo-Croatian, and the old *Friulàn* dialect, an obscure relative of equally obscure Swiss Romansch. The linguistic intermingling of Central European, Balkan, and Italian influences typifies the exotic composite of Udinese life. Given its turbulent history—conquered by Venice in 1420, appropriated by Austria in the late 18th century, and heavily bombed during WWII—Udine is fortunate to have escaped with its landmarks intact.

As a more disturbing legacy of WWII, Udine had the only concentration camp in Italy, which occupied a converted rice factory. Naturally, this fact cannot be found in any of the tourist brochures. The park on Viale della Vittoria, on your right as you head out of the city center, stands as an understated reminder of Udine's past.

The present town is notable primarily for its graceful Gothic and Renaissance architecture, and for works of the Rococo pioneer Giambattista Tiepolo. Udine today is filled with shoppers who stream through the small, attractive streets. The local attractions are not that of Florence, but the city serves as a comfortable base for those who want to explore Friuli-Venezia Giulia.

ORIENTATION AND PRACTICAL INFORMATION

Udine's train and bus stations are both on Viale Europa Unita in the south part of town. All bus lines pass the train station, but only buses #1, 3, and 8 run from Viale Europa Unita to the center of town, by the **P. della Libertà** and **Castle Hill.** You can also make the 15-minute walk: from the station, go right to Piazzale D'Annunzio, then turn left under the arches to Via Aquileia. Continue up Via Veneto to P. Libertà.

Tourist Office: P. 1° Maggio, 7 (tel. 29 59 72). From P. della Libertà, turn right onto Via Manin and left onto P. 1° Maggio; then look for the pink-arched façade, or take bus #2, 7, or 10 to P. 1° Maggio. Wonderful maps, copious information. Itineraries for visiting the town are on the town map and in *Udine and its Environs.* English spoken. Open Mon.-Sat. 9am-1pm and 3-6pm.

Police: Via Prefettura, 16 (tel. 50 28 41).

Post Office: Via Veneto, 42 (tel. 50 19 93). *Fermo posta* and stamps through the right door at desk #6. Fax at window #3. Open Mon.-Sat. 8:15am-7:40pm. Also a smaller **branch** at Via Roma, 25, straight ahead from the train station. Open Mon.-Fri. 8:10am-1:15pm, Sat. 8:05am-1pm. **Postal Code:** 33100.

Telephones: Telecom, Via Savorgnana, 13 (tel. 27 81), off P. Duomo. Open Mon.-Fri. 9am-12:30pm and 4-7:30pm. Also in the train station. **Telephone Code:** 0432.

Currency Exchange: Banco Ambrosiana Veneto, Via Vittorio Veneto, 21 (tel. 51 74 11), off P. della Libertà. Has the best rates in town. Open Mon.-Fri. 8:20am-1:20pm and 2:35-4:05pm.

Trains: on Viale Europa Unita (tel. 50 36 56). **Information** office open 7am-9pm. Trains to: Venice (22 per day, 2hr., L11,700); Triest (19 per day, 1½hr., L7200); Milan (4 per day, 5hr., L29,800); Vienna (6 per day, 7hr., L86,000). **Luggage storage:** L1500. Open daily 7:30am-10:30pm.

Buses: on Viale Europa Unita (tel. 20 39 41), 1 block to the right of the train station as you exit. Walk through the lifeless station and turn left when you see the bus parking garage. There you'll find **Autolinea Ferrari** (tel. 50 40 12). Service to Triest (9 per day, 1hr., L6200); Lignano (17 per day, 1hr., L6200); Venice (1 per day, 2hr., L10,200); Grado (16 per day, 1hr., L4500); Cividale (24 per day, 30min., L2400); Palmanova (23 per day, 40min., L2400); Aquileia (18 per day, 1½hr., L4500). Bus line offices housed in the "Pullman Bar" next door (tel. 50 24 63).

Mountain Information: the bulletin board of the **Club Alpino Italiano,** inside city hall on Via B. Odorico, 3 (tel. 50 42 90). Info on upcoming trips and skiing. For info on hikes within Friuli-Venezia Giulia, contact **Gruppo Attività ed Informazione Ambientali,** Via Monterotondo, 22 (tel. 60 18 92). **Società Alpina Friulana,** Via Odorico, 3. Open Mon.-Sat. 5-7:15pm, Thurs. 9-11pm. Alpine info and excursions.

Swimming Pool: Piscina Comunale, Via Ampezzo, 4 (tel. 269 67 or 269 29), near P. Diacono. Indoor pool open Sept.-May; outdoor June-Aug. Open Mon.-Sat. 10am-7pm, Sun. noon-7pm. L6000. Bathing cap required.

Late Night Pharmacy: tel. 192.

Emergencies: tel. 113. **Medical Emergency:** tel. 118. **Hospital: Ospedale Civile** (tel. 55 21), in P. Santa Maria della Misericordia. Take bus #1 north to the last stop.

ACCOMMODATIONS

The good news is that the large map outside the train station is clearly marked with the locations of Udine's hotels, some of which are real bargains. The bad news is that local workers probably snagged the best spots long ago. Many single rooms are booked by the month. In June and July students taking exams also vie for vacancies.

Suite Inn, Via di Toppo, 25 (tel. 50 16 83). Take bus #1 or #3 from the station, get off at Via Gemona or Piazzale Osoppo, and walk up Via di Toppo. Sweet proprietor is eager to please. Cozy sitting room with TV and piano. Beautiful, spacious rooms. Singles L35,000, with bath L60,000. Doubles L60,000, with bath L80,000. Triples L110,000. Breakfast L7000.

Locanda Piccolo Friuli, Via Magrini, 11 (tel./fax 50 78 17). From P. Garibaldi take Via Brenari to Via Poscolle and continue on Vicolo Gorgo. More expensive, but worth it: a beautiful old building with antique fixtures. Creaky wood floor, big sitting room, and frescoes complete the atmosphere. Singles with bath L50,000. Doubles with bath L70,000. L20,000 per extra bed. Breakfast L8000.

Al Vecchio Tram, Via Brenari, 32 (tel. 50 25 16). Just off P. Garibaldi. Elegant staircase and large rooms. Bar downstairs. Singles L30,000. Doubles L55,000.

Locanda Da Arturo, Via Pracchiuso, 75 (tel. 29 90 70). Take bus #4 from the station, get off at P. Oberdan, and walk down Via Pracchiuso on the far side of the *piazza.* Quiet, with only a few rooms. Restaurant downstairs (*menù* L20,000). Singles L25,000. Doubles L45,000. Reserve ahead. Closed either July or Aug.

FOOD

An array of Italian, Austrian, and Slovene, Udinese cuisine tends more toward the hearty than the *haute.* A typical regional specialty is *brovada e museto,* a stew made of marinated turnips and boiled sausage. Shop for produce weekday mornings in the **open-air market** at P. Matteotti near P. della Libertà, or head for Via Redipuglia or P. 1° Maggio on Saturdays between 8am and 1pm. Buy staples at the **Despar Supermarket,** at Viale Volontari della Libertà, 6, off P. Osoppo. (Open Mon. and Wed. 8:30am-1pm, Tues., Thurs., and Fri. 8:30am-1pm and 4-7pm, Sat. 8:30am-7pm.) Also try **Lavoratore Supermercati,** Via Stringher, 10, down from the *duomo.* (Open Mon. and Wed. 9am-1:30pm, Tues. and Thurs.-Sat. 9am-1:30pm and 4-7:30pm.) Cheap *pizzerie* and *trattorie* cluster around Via Pracchiuso, including **Pizzamania,** Via Pracchiuso, 63. (Slices and takeout only. Open Tues.-Sat. 10am-1:30pm and 4-9pm, Sun. 4-9pm.)

Zenit, Via Prefettura, 15. A cross between a '50s diner and a pre-school cafeteria but reasonable as a self-service place. Popular with local businesspeople. *Primi* L4300-6500. *Secondi* L6500-7500. Cover L500. Open Mon.-Sat. 11:45am-2:30pm.

Ristorante/Pizzeria Ai Portici, Via Veneto, 8 (tel. 50 89 75), under the arcade before P. della Libertà. Pizza for L6000-10,000 is reasonable, given the chic ambience. *Primi* L6000-9000. *Secondi* L7000-25,000. *Menù* L16,000. Cover L1500. Open Wed.-Mon. 9am-midnight or 1am.

SIGHTS AND ENTERTAINMENT

The heart of Udine is **Piazza della Libertà,** an elegantly elevated square. Along its higher side runs the Renaissance **Arcade of San Giovanni.** The two symbolic columns of Venice in the *piazza* commemorate the conquest of Udine by the Venetian Republic; across the *piazza* stands the delicate, candy-striped **Loggia del Lionello,** another architectural reminder of the conquerors' presence in Udine. Originally built in 1448, the beloved *loggia* was severely damaged by a fire in 1876, but reconstructed shortly thereafter by popular demand.

The rugged **Arco Bollani** (1556, designed by Palladio) (tel. 50 18 24), in the corner near the clock tower, allows you through the walls enclosing the **Chiesa di Santa Maria** and the **castello** of the Venetian governors. The *castello* is home to the **Museo Civico,** which exhibits a myriad of notable frescoes including a frieze and several *putti* by Giambattista Tiepolo. (Open Tues.-Sat. 9:30am-12:30pm and 3-6pm, Sun.-Mon. 9:30am-12:30pm. Admission L4000, students L2000.)

In P. del Duomo, 50m from the more hectic P. della Libertà, stands the Roman-Gothic **duomo,** with several Tiepolos on display in the Baroque interior (the first, second, and fourth altars on the right side). There is a small **museum** (tel. 50 68 30) in the squat brick *campanile,* which is comprised of two chapels with 14th-century frescoes by Vitale da Bologna. (Museum closed for renovation in 1995.) Udine has been called the city of Tiepolo, and some of this Baroque painter's finest works adorn the **Oratorio della Purità** (tel. 50 68 30), across from the *duomo.* The *Assumption* frescoed on the ceiling (1759) and the *Immaculate Conception* of the altarpiece represent Tiepolo's world of light, air, and awe. (Ask the cathedral sacristan to let you in. Tip expected.)

A sizeable sampling of earlier Tiepolo frescoes is housed in the **Palazzo Arcivescovile** (tel. 50 43 14), P. Patriarcato, 1, at the head of Via Ungheria. Here, from 1726 through 1730, Tiepolo executed an extensive series of Old Testament scenes. (Closed for restoration in 1995.) Several blocks south from P. della Libertà along Via Stringher, off P. XX Settembre, stands the **Chiesa di San Francesco.** This architectural gem of the early Renaissance is considered Udine's most beautiful church. Unfortunately, it opens only for exhibitions.

There are also a number of interesting museums, including an excellent **Gallery of Modern Art** at P. P. Diacono, 21 (tel. 29 58 91), on the ring road that circles the old city. The museum transports you to the idiosyncratic worlds of De Kooning, Lichtenstein, Chagall, Picasso, and every major 20th-century Italian artist. (Open Tues.-Sat. 9:30am-12:30pm and 3-6pm, Sun. 9:30am-12:30pm. Admission L4000, students L2000.) The **Friulian Museum of Popular Arts and Traditions,** Via Viola, 3 (tel. 50 78 61), northeast of the P. XXVI Luglio, exhibits a collection of regional costumes and folk art. (Closed for restoration in 1995.)

■■■ CIVIDALE DEL FRIULI

At the far edge of Italy and unknown to most travelers, sleepy Cividale saw its glory days come and go during the darkest of the Dark Ages. In the 6th century, land-hungry Lombards seized what was then *Forum Iulii* and made the vanquished Roman trading center the capital of the first Lombard duchy. By the 8th century, the Patriarch of Aquileia had grabbed a piece of the action, setting off a building frenzy. Since then things have been generally quiet, despite devastating earthquakes that have twice toppled the city's monuments. Cividale thus remains the only place in Italy to see magnificent medieval art from the least known century of Italian history.

This tiny town can easily be seen in an afternoon. No need for a map—just wander through the ancient portal and follow the yellow metal or natural wood signs past the restaurants, shops, and *caffè* to the historical points of interest.

CIVIDALE DEL FIULI

Orientation and Practical Information Cividale is easily reached by train from Udine, which lies at the end of a *locale* line that connects the two cities (every hr., 20min., round-trip L4000). The **train** and Rosina **bus** stations (tel. 63 10 46; open Mon.-Fri. 8:30am-12:30pm, Sat. 8:30am-1pm) open onto Viale Libertà and are a brief walk from the **center**. (Bus to Udine L2400.) From the train station head directly onto Via Marconi, turning left through the **Porta Arsenale Veneto** when the street ends. Bear right in P. Dante, then left onto Largo Boiano. **Tourist office** at Corso Paolino (tel. 73 13 98). Extremely helpful staff. (Open Mon.-Fri. 9am-1pm and 3-6pm, Sat. 9am-1pm.) You'll find the **post office**, at Aquileia, 10 (tel. 73 11 57), going toward the Ponte del Diavolo. Also has an exchange service that accepts traveler's checks. (Open Mon.-Fri. 8:30am-5:30pm and Sat. 8:30am-1pm. Exchange open Mon.-Fri. 8:30am-4:30pm.) The **postal code** is 33043. The **telephone code** is 0432. In case of **emergency**, call 113, or seek out the **police** on P. A. Diaz (tel. 73 14 29). The **hospital (Ospedale Civile)** is in P. dell'Ospedale (tel. 70 81).

Accommodations and Food Accommodations are certainly not Cividale's forte. The two-star **Al Pomo d'Oro,** P. S. Giovanni (tel. 73 14 89), is a lovely old building in the medieval quarter with a restaurant downstairs. (Singles with bath for L55,000, doubles with bath for L85,000; breakfast included. AmEx, MC, Visa.) The specialties of the area are *gubana* (a fig and prune-filled pastry laced with *grappa*) and *Picolit,* a pricey dessert wine rarely sold outside of the Natisone Valley. Most bars stock pre-packaged *gubana,* but for fresh mouth-watering sweets, look for the "Gubana Cividalese" sign on your right as you near the **Ponte del Diavolo,** located at Corso D'Aquileia, 16. P. Diacono hosts Cividale's **open-air market** every Saturday from 8am to 1pm. The management of **Antica Trattoria Dominissini,** Stretta Stellini, 18 (tel. 73 37 63), serves up *cucina friulana* in the shadow of **Chiesa S. Francesco.** Ask to sit outside in the vine-roofed area with a view of the church's tower. (*Primi* L6000, *secondi* L5000-12,000. Cover L2000. Open Sun.-Fri. 8:30am-3pm and 5-11pm.) A favorite with the locals, particularly for its local cuisine, is the **Bar Al Campanile,** Via G. B. Candotti, 4 (tel. 73 24 67), right off the *duomo.* Specialties include *prosciutto al salto* (L5000). (Open Tues.-Sun. 7am-11pm.)

Sights and Entertainment Built and expanded upon over the centuries, Cividale's *duomo* (tel. 73 11 44) is an odd melange of architectural styles. Most of the credit is given to Pietro Lombardo, who completed the bulk of the construction in 1528 (directly on your left as you leave the tourist office; open 9:30am-noon and 3-7pm, winter 9:30-noon and 3-6pm). Walk to the far end of the *duomo* to view the 12th-century silver **altarpiece of Pellegrino II,** with its 25 saints and pair of archangels. Move on to the Renaissance **sarcophagus of Patriarch Nicolò Donato,** located to the left of the entrance. Annexed to the *duomo* is the **Museo Cristiano.** This free display includes the **Baptistery of Callisto,** a wonderfully sculpted piece of architecture commissioned by the first Aquileian patriarch to move to Cividale. More significantly, the museum houses the **Altar of Ratchis,** a delicately carved work from 749 AD, one of the few surviving masterpieces of the Middle Ages. (Open Mon.-Sat. 9:30am-noon and 3-7pm, Sun. 3-7pm. Museum also open Sun. 9am-noon. Both free.)

The greatest Italian work of the 8th century can be found downhill at the **Tempietto Longobardo** (tel. 70 08 67), built on the remains of Roman homes (follow the signs). Although the "little temple" suffered greatly from the earthquakes of 1222 and 1976, exhaustive efforts have restored a famous sextet of 8th-century stucco figures to their original form. The beautiful 14th-century wooden stalls partially compensate for the loss of the original frescoes. Another bonus is the spectacular view of river and mountains, obtained from the entrance overlooking the rocky riverbed. (The Tempietto is open daily in summer 10am-1pm and 3:30-6:30pm; in winter mornings only. Admission L2000, students L1000.) The lush countryside rolls into the distance, and on a high vista sits the picturesque **Castelmonte Stara Gora.** For a similarly stunning view, try the **Ponte del Diavolo,** an impressive stone bridge of indeterminate age. For a better look at the bridge itself, descend the stairs to the water on the far side. Local legend has it that the devil himself threw down the great stone in the center of the river on which the bridge was built.

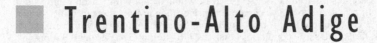

Trentino-Alto Adige

"Grüss Gott!" Travelers to Italy's northern reaches often hear this and fear they have stumbled into Austria. And they have in all but name; the influence of Austrian culture exceeds that of Italian in much of the region. Trentino in the south is predominantly Italian-speaking, while Südtirol (South Tirol) in the north is largely German-speaking and encompasses most of the mountain region known as the Dolomites. Long an integral part of the Holy Roman Empire, the provinces were conquered by Napoleon only to pass into the hands of the Austro-Hungarian Empire. At the end of World War I, however, Trentino and the Südtirol fell under Italian rule. Germany curtailed Mussolini's brutal efforts to Italianize the Südtirol during the 1920s, but not before Mussolini had given every German name in the region an Italian equivalent.

The intermingling of Austrian and Italian traditions permeates everything from art to cuisine. North of Bolzano, you may get better service by trying to speak German; in Trent, Italian is the ticket.

■■■ DOLOMITES (DOLOMITI, DOLOMITEN)

Stunning limestone spires shoot skyward from green fields and pine forests. These amazing peaks—fantastic for hiking, skiing, and rock-climbing—start west of Trent and extend north and east to the Austrian frontier. Finding accommodations in the Dolomites is easy: there are hundreds of alpine huts and many rooms in private homes advertised by the *zimmer/camere* signs. Pick up the complete *Südtirol Hotel Guide,* free at the provincial office in Bolzano and in local tourist offices. These offices also provide listings of campgrounds in the region, but travelers camp almost anywhere. The **SAD** (Società Automobilistica Dolomiti) deploys a team of **buses** that covers virtually every paved road in the area with surprising frequency.

HIKING

Even the least bold can become avid Dolomitists. The terrain varies from wide, gentle trails to vertical cliffs. **Alpine huts** (*rifugi*) abound, making journeys into the mountains easier and safer. All huts are clearly marked on the *Kompass Wanderkarte,* the best map of the region, available at most newsstands and bookstores. Huts generally operate from late June through early October, but at higher altitudes the hut season is often shorter. The provincial tourist offices in Trent and Bolzano supply information in English on their respective provinces. The Alpine desk of the office in Bolzano is run by Dr. Hannsjörg Hager, a noted Alpinist who speaks English and can help you pick a suitable route, making sure the huts are open before you get into the mountains. Hut prices were unavailable for 1996, but in 1995 averaged about L15,000 per dormitory cot and L21,000 per bed. All offered a *menù* for roughly L13,000. (Expect an increase from these listed prices.) Bring your own food if possible, and pick up information about winter walking paths from the tourist office. Also, look for books by author and veteran hiker Gillian Price, among them *Walking in the Dolomites*, *Classic Climbs in the Dolomites*, and *Walking in the Central Italian Alps: Vinschgau, Ortler, Adamello and their Parks*. All are published by Cicerone Press, 2 Police Square, Milnthorpe, Cumbria, LA7 7PY, United Kingdom (tel. (053) 956 20 69; fax (053) 956 34 17). For further information about

Trentino huts, contact the SAT at Via Manci, 57 (tel. 98 18 71 or 98 64 62), in Trent (open Mon.-Fri. 8am-noon and 3-7pm).

SKIING

The Dolomites offer immensely popular downhill skiing with usually sunny skies and light powdery snow. The **regional tourist office** in **Bolzano** (tel. (0471) 99 38 09) is a good source of information. For more specific information concerning prices, deals, and snow conditions contact **Club Alpino** (See Essentials: Camping). Major ski centers near Bolzano include **Alta Venosta** (around Lake Resia) and **Colle Isarco;** near Trent, **Folgaria, Brentonico, Madonna di Campiglio,** and **Monte Bondone** (especially close to the city); near Bressanone, **Val d'Isarco,** the **Zona dello Sciliar,** and **Val Gardena;** and near Corvara, **Alta Badia.**

One of the cheapest and most convenient ways to enjoy a skiing holiday in the Dolomites is to get a **settimana bianca** (white week) package deal from any CTS or CIT office. Prices start around L500,000 and include a week's room and board and ski passes. If you want to travel the region by bus or car, or if you're planning to stay in the region of interlocking trails around the Gruppo Sella, consider purchasing the **Superski Dolomiti** pass, good on all 464 cablecars and lifts in the Dolomite area (around L45,000 per day, L245,000 per week, with discounts for senior citizens and children under 14.)

■■■ TRENT (TRENTO, TRIENT)

The strategic significance of Trent, located inside of the Alpine threshold yet connected back to the Veneto by a long, deep valley, made the city an important gateway. The Romans created two imperial roads through Trent. During the centuries to follow, fortress-like castles proliferated in the region, which can still be seen and enjoyed today. Cultural and physical ownership of the city itself was contested in the 19th century, but was settled once and for all at the end of World War I when Trent became an Italian city. The city is made up of several, lovely, frescoed *piazze,* the most famous of which is the Piazza del Duomo. What truly makes the city unique are its ever-apparent contrasts: those between the ancient castles and newly built housing complexes, and between the city itself and the awesome mountains that surround it. These mountains are a skier's or mountain hiker's dream come true. Trent is also an ideal departure point for the Lago di Guarda area.

ORIENTATION AND PRACTICAL INFORMATION

Behind Trent's train station flows the **Adige River;** in front are the **public gardens.** A right turn on Via Pozzo will take you past a helpful signboard map at the corner of the garden to Via Orfane which becomes **Via Cavour** and leads to **P. del Duomo.** An earlier left on Via Roma leads in the direction of the **Castello del Buonconsiglio.** All of Trent's *piazze* are within close walking distance of each other, which makes navigating the city quite easy.

> **Tourist Office: Azienda Autonoma** (City Tourist Office), Via Alfieri, 4 (tel. 98 38 80; fax 98 45 08). From the station walk through the park and follow Via Alfieri to the right. Friendly, English speaking staff. Open Mon.-Sat. 9am-noon and 3-6pm, Sun. 10am-noon; Sept.-June Mon.-Fri. 9am-noon and 3-6pm, Sat. 9am-noon. **APT del Trentino** (Regional Tourist Office), Corso III Novembre, 132 (tel. 91 44 44; fax 39 00 05), a 15-min. walk on the continuation of Via S. Vigilio from behind the *duomo.* Open Mon.-Fri. 8:30am-12:30pm and 2:30-6pm, Sat. 9am-noon.
> **Police:** tel. 112. **Questura,** P. Mostra (tel. 98 61 13).
> **Post Office:** Via Calepina, 16 (tel. 98 72 70), at P. Vittoria. Open Mon.-Fri. 8:10am-7:30pm, Sat. 8:10am-1pm. Another office to the left from the train station on Via Dogana has the same hours. **Postal Code:** 38100.

Telephones: Telecom Italia SPA, Via Torre Verde, 11 (tel. 23 40 40). Open Tues.- Sat. 8:30am-12:30pm and 3-7pm, Mon. 3-7pm. Phones also on Via Belenzani, 30. Open daily 8:30am-9pm. **Telephone Code:** 0461.
Budget Travel: CTS, Via Cavour, 21 (tel. and fax 98 15 33), near P. del Duomo. Student IDs, plane and train tickets, Transalpino tickets, and occasional organized outings. English spoken. Open Mon.-Fri. 9:30am-12:30pm and 2:30-6:30pm.
Trains: (tel. 23 45 45) To: Verona (every hr., 1hr., L8000); Bolzano (every hr., 45min., L5000); Bologna (11 per day, 3hrs., L16,450); Venice (7 per day, 3hrs., L17,150). **Luggage Storage:** L1500. Closed 1:40-3:40am.
Buses: Atesina, Via G. Marconi, 3 (tel. 82 10 00), next to the train station. To Riva del Garda (every hr., 1hr., L4800). Extensive local service. Ask for schedules at the information booth in the station.
Cableways: Funivia Trento-Sardagna, Via Lung'Adige Monte Grappa (tel. 23 21 54). Up and over the tracks; past the bus terminal take a right on busy Cavalcavia San Lorenzo, and you'll find the Funivia on the other side. This lift gets you onto Mt. Bondone, specifically to Sardagna (every 30min., daily 8am-8pm, L1500).
Hiking Equipment: Rigoni Sport, P. Battisti, 30/31 (tel. 98 12 39). Open Tues.- Sun. 9:10am-noon and 3-7pm, Mon. 3-7pm. **Mountain Shop,** Via Buonarotti, 4 (tel. 82 42 58), near the campground. Less expensive. Open Mon.-Sun. 9:15am-noon and 3-7pm.
English Bookstore: Libreria Disertori, Via M. Diaz, 11 (tel. 98 14 55), near P. Battisti. Open Tues.-Sat. 9am-noon and 3:30-7pm, Mon. 3:30-7pm. MC, Visa.
Medical: tel. 118. **Civic:** tel 113. **Hospital: Ospedale Santa Chiara,** Largo Medaglie d'Oro (tel. 90 31 11), past the swimming pool and up Via Orsi. **Alpine Emergency: CAI-SAT hotline,** tel. 23 31 66. The **fire station,** tel. 115, can also reach alpine help.

ACCOMMODATIONS

Trent has plenty of rooms for rent except in August, when private rooms are impossible to find without reservations. Check with the tourist office about *Agriturismo.*

Ostello Giovane Europa (HI), Via Manzoni, 17 (tel. 23 45 67), a continuation of Via Torre Verde. Hotel turned hostel. One- to six-person rooms. Bar and TV. Check-in from 7:15am, Lockout 9am-5:30pm. Curfew midnight. L15,000 per person; breakfast included. Lunch and dinner for groups only (L12,000). Closed for renovation in 1995; check with the tourist office for more up-to-date info.
Hotel Venezia, P. Duomo, 45 (tel. 23 41 14). Clean, spacious rooms, some with a view of the *duomo.* High quality and fair prices. Singles L37,000, with bath L53,000. Doubles L58,000, with bath L78,000. Breakfast L10,000. MC, Visa.
Al Cavallino Bianco, Via Cavour, 29 (tel. 23 15 42), down the street from the *duomo.* Clean, airy rooms, but the main draw is the lifelike paint job in the living room—you'll feel like you're sitting in a sunny field. Singles L35,000, with bath L50,000. Doubles L57,000, with bath L78,000. Triples with bath L100,000. Closed in Dec. and June 16-26. AmEx, MC, Visa.

FOOD

The **market** in P. Lodron behind the *duomo* does its thing every morning from 8am to noon and occasional afternoons. **Open-air markets** spring up on Thursday in Vie Maffei, Prati, Esterle, Torrione, and Borsieri, as well as P. d'Arogno. Budget buys await at **Supermarket Orvea,** Via Belenzani, 49 (tel. 98 17 37; open Mon.-Fri 8:30am-12:30pm and 3:15-7:15pm, Sat. 8:30am-12:30pm; if you crave Coca-Cola, buy it here at a bargain price) and at **Supermarket Poli,** near the station at the corner of Via Roma and Via delle Orfane (tel. 98 50 63, open Mon.-Fri. 8:30am-12:30pm and 3:10-7:10pm, Sat. 8:30am-12:30pm).

Pizzeria Duomo, P. Duomo, 22 (tel. 98 42 86). Choose from a variety of large, delicious pizzas. Local joint that is very popular with the university students. Pizzas start at L5500. Cover L1500. Open Sun.-Fri noon-2pm and 6-10:30pm.

La Cantinota, Via S. Marco, 24 (tel. 23 85 27 or 23 85 61), at the other end of Via Manci from Via Roma. Everything, including the red carpet, is rolled out for you here. Enjoy the delicious cuisine and humor the management by dropping by the piano bar after dessert. *Risotto* for at least 2 people L9000; *wurstel alla griglia* (grilled sausage) L9000. Cover L2000. Open Fri.-Wed. noon-3pm and 7-11pm. Piano bar open 7:30pm-2:30am. Closed July.

Ristorante/Pizzeria Chistè, Via delle Orne, 4 (tel. 98 18 46), off Via Belenzani near the *duomo*. Serves huge portions that are popular with the locals. *Primi* about L8000-L15,000. Pasta about L8000. Cover L1200. Open Tues.-Sun. noon-2pm and 6:30-11pm. Closed Aug.

SIGHTS AND ENTERTAINMENT

The pointed dome of Trent's Gothic-Romanesque **duomo,** also known as the **Cathedral of Saint Vigilio,** rises in modest emulation of the looming Alps. The famed Council's decrees were delivered in front of the huge cross in the Chapel of the Holy Crucifix. (Open daily 6:30am-noon and 2:30-8pm.) The remains of a 6th-century Paleo-Christian *basilica* were recently uncovered beneath the *duomo*. Admission to this underground church is included in the admission to the **Museo Diocesano,** P. Duomo, 18 (tel. 23 44 19). (Open Mon.-Sat. 9:30am-12:30pm and 2:30-6pm. Admission L5000, students L1000.) Take a right at the end of Via Belenzani onto Via Roma to get to the **Castello del Buonconsiglio,** Trent's other main sight. Once the home of the bishop-prince who governed Trent, the castle was incorporated into the city walls. The castle also houses the **Museo Provinciale d'Arte.** (Castle and museum tel. 23 37 70. Open Tues.-Sun. 10am-7pm. Admission L6000, under 18 and over 60 L2000.)

If you arrive in the summer, try to catch a play or performance at one of the private castles (admission free-L10,000). Check with the tourist office for information.

■ MOUNTAINS NEAR TRENT

Monte Bondone rises majestically over Trent and begs for pleasant daytrips and overnight excursions. Check with the tourist office (tel. 94 71 28, fax 94 71 88) in **Vaneze,** halfway up the mountain, about accommodations, ski lifts, and maps. **Ski School Monte Bondone** (tel. 94 82 11) gives lessons and rents equipment. Pick up a map at the tourist office in Trent, and then catch the cable car from Ponte di San Lorenzo, between the train tracks and the river, to **Sardagna,** a great picnic spot (every 30min., daily 7am-6:30pm, L1500; in Trent tel. 91 03 32 or 38 10 00). From there, a 10- to 12-km hike takes you to the **Mezavia Campground** (tel. 94 81 78; L5000 per person, L7000 per tent; open June to mid-Sept.).

■ ■ ■ BOLZANO (BOZEN)

Bolzano encourages peaceful relations among its youth with mandatory instruction in both Italian and German, but the disproportionately large number of fair, rosy-cheeked bilinguals reveals the city's true Austrian tendencies. If you listen, you'll hear natives and tourists speaking German; if you look around, you'll think you're in a Bavarian town. Though P. Walther serves as the center of the city, walk through the back alleyways of Bolzano and discover the magic that the locals see all the time. Bolzano is a combination of spacious *Plätze/piazze* and arcaded alleys that present a friendly face to the mountain-bound traveler.

ORIENTATION AND PRACTICAL INFORMATION

Bolzano's historic center rests in the hollow of the converging Isarco and Talvera rivers, and is linked by bridge to the more modern, industrial sectors to the west. The main *piazze* are within close walking distance of one another and serve as guides as one navigates the town. A brief walk up **Via Stazione** from the train station, or **Via Alto Adige** if you've arrived by bus, leads to **P. Walther.**

Tourist Office: For Bolzano only, P. Walther, 8 (tel. 97 56 56 or 97 06 60; fax 98 01 28). Lists of every accommodations option, including *agriturismo*. *Walks and Hikes* suggests nearby hikes of varying lengths and difficulty. *Manifestazioni* includes several pages of tourist-oriented phone numbers. English spoken. Open Mon.-Fri. 8:30am-6pm, Sat. 9am-12:30pm. **Provincial Tourist Office for South Tyrol,** P. Parrocchia, 11 (tel. 99 38 08), just down from P. Walther, across from the *duomo*. A must for those setting out for the mountains. Friendly staff; English spoken. Open Mon.-Fri. 9am-noon and 2-5pm.

Police: tel. 94 76 11.

Post Office: Via della Posta, 1 (tel. 97 94 52), by the *duomo*. Open Mon.-Fri. 8:15am-5:15pm, Sat. 8:15am-12:45pm. **Postal Code:** 39100.

Telephones: Telecom, P. Parrocchia, 17, to the left of the post office. Office open Mon.-Sat. 8:30am-12:30pm and 3-7pm. Booths open daily 7:30am-10pm. **ASST,** Via Roma, 36/M, across the river near P. Adriano. Open Mon.-Sat. 8am-8pm. **Telephone Code:** 0471.

Budget Travel: CIT, P. Walther, 11 (tel. 97 85 16). Transalpino tickets and skiing packages. English spoken. Open Mon.-Fri. 8:30am-12:30pm and 3-6:30pm, Sat. 9am-12:30pm.

Currency Exchange: Banca Nazionale del Lavoro, in P. Walther at the end of Via Stazione, right next door to the Bolzano tourist office. Best rates, Visa services. Open Tues.-Fri. 8:20am-1:20 pm and 3-4:30pm, Mon. 8:20am-1:20pm.

Trains: P. Stazione (tel. 97 42 92). To: Trent (14 per day, ¾hr., L5000); Verona (27 per day, 1¼hr , L11,700); Merano (every 45min., 45min., L3400); Milan (2 per day (though more frequent if you change at Trent), 4hr., L22,600). Information open Mon.-Sat. 7am-8pm, Sun. 9am-1pm and 2:30-5:30pm. **Luggage Storage:** L1500. Open 24hrs.

Buses: SAD buses, Via Perathoner, 4 (tel. 45 01 11; fax 97 00 42), between the train station and P. Walther. To: Alpe di Siusi (13 per day, 1½hr., L5000); Collalbo (5 per day, 50min., L2600); Cortina d'Ampezzo (4 per day, 3½hr., L15,000); Merano (13 per day, 1hr., L4000); Brunico (about 6 per week and 6 per weekend, 1¾hr., L8400). Less frequent service on weekends. For information, call 460 47. **Local buses: ACT,** Via Conchpelli, 60 (tel. 97 12 59). Bus service extends throughout the city. All lines stop in P. Walther.

Cableways: 3 cableways, located at the edges of Bolzano, will whisk you 1000m or more up and over the city to the nearest trailhead. To Colle (Kohlern): take the world's oldest cableway, the Funivia del Colle (or as the locals call it, the Kohlerer Seilbahn; tel. 97 85 45), departing from Via Campiglio (Kampillerstraße). Every hr. on the hr. To Renon (Ritten): take the Funivia del Renon (tel. 97 84 79) departing from Via Renon (5-min. walk from train station). Round-trip L7500. To Salto high plateaus take Funivia S. Genesio (Jeneseiner Seilbahn; tel. 97 84 36) on Via Sarentino, the farthest from the station. Cross the Talvera river. Tickets around L3000, round-trip L5200. Bike (L5600) and pet (L2000) transport possible

Car Rental: Avis, P. Verdi, 18 (tel. 97 14 67). Open Mon.-Fri. 8am noon and 3-7pm, Sat. 8am-noon.

Bike Rental: Via Stazione, near P. Walther. Borrow a bike for 4hr. by leaving a L10,000 deposit and ID information. Intercity cruisers, not mountain-worthy.

Camping Equipment: Sportler, Via dei Portici/Laubengasse, 37/A (tel. 97 40 33). Expensive, extensive selection. Open Mon.-Fri. 9am-12:15pm and 3-7pm, 1st Sat. of the month 9am-12:30pm and 2:30-6pm. You may get a better deal down the street at **Sport Reinstaller,** Via Portici, 23. Open daily 8:30am-noon and 3-7pm.

Laundromat: Lavanderia Automatica Westinghouse, P. Matteotti, 3 (tel. 91 44 46), across the river off Via Torino. Wash your own clothes for the price of a good dinner (L17,000). Open Mon.-Fri. 8am-noon and 2:30-7pm.

Swimming Pool: Piscina Coperta, Viale Triest (tel. 91 10 00), across the river. Indoor pool. Admission L5300. Bathing cap required. Open Oct.-June Tues.-Fri. 12:30-2:30pm and 7-9pm, Sat. 4-6pm and 6:30-8:30pm.

Emergency: tel. 113. **Medical Emergency:** tel. 90 83 30. **Hospital: Ospedale Regionale San Maurizio,** Via Lorenz Böhler (tel. 90 81 11). **Medical Assistance: White Cross,** tel. 27 44 44.

BOLZANO

ACCOMMODATIONS AND CAMPING

Bolzano has many budget deals in the spring and fall; in summer and winter, you'll be hard-pressed to find anything affordable. Given the magnificent surroundings, it is almost a pity to stay in the city; the romantic and luxuriant possibilities on the mountainside often run cheaper than their city counterparts. Try the mountain options or ask about the *agriturismo* program at the tourist office.

Pensione Reiseggerhof, Sta. Maddalena di Sotto, 24 (tel. 97 86 94), uphill from Weinstube. Here's your chance to live like they do on *Lifestyles of the Rich and Famous,* at budget rates. Doubles L32,000 per person. Breakfast included.

Schwarze Katz, Sta. Maddalena di Sotto, 2 (tel. 97 54 17). Not feeling too excited about the steep uphill hike with pack? Then look to your left. You have arrived at hotel "Black Cat," a family-run, friendly place with rooms and a garden restaurant popular with locals. L30,000 per person, with bath L35,000.

Croce Bianca, P. del Grano (Kornplatz), 3 (tel. 97 75 52). Spacious, old-style rooms. Its central location makes rooms scarce in the summer and winter. Make reservations. Singles L34,000. Doubles L54,000, with bath L70,000.

Camping: Moosbauer, Via San Maurizio, 83 (tel. 91 84 92). Take bus #10A or 10B from the station (last bus at 8:30pm). Get off at the hospital stop, then walk down San Maurizio 1km. L8500 per person, L7000 for tent, L16,000 for car space and tent. Showers included.

FOOD

Rindsgulasch is a delicious beef stew, *Speck* is tasty smoked bacon, and *Knödel* (dumplings) come in dozens of rib-sticking varieties. Fall spotlights the local vineyards with the week-long Südtiroler Törgelen tasting spree. Festive P. delle Erbe (Obstplatz) has an all-day produce **market** every day but Sunday, and two **Despar supermarkets** (tel. 97 45 37) thrive at Via della Rena, 40 (open Mon.-Fri. 8:30am-12:30pm and 3:30-7:30pm, Sat. 8am-12:30pm and 3:30-6:30pm, 1st Sat. of the month 8am-1pm), and Via dei Bottai, 29 (open Mon.-Fri. 8:30am-7:30pm for the summer). For baked goods, try the delectable selections at **Panificio/Backerei Lemayr,** Via Goethe, 17 (open Mon.-Fri. 6:30am-12:30pm and 3:30-7:15pm, Sat. 6:30am-1pm). If you arrive in July, try one of Via dei Bottai's many eating options.

Restaurant Weisses Rössl, Via dei Bottai/Bindergasse, 6 (tel. 97 32 67), the continuation of Via Laurin and Via dei Grappoli, at the end of Via dei Portici. A cheap place with Austrian atmosphere. Nearly 100 regional and Italian dishes. Daily *menù* (L10,000-15,000). Open Aug.-June Mon.-Fri. 7am-1am, Sat. 7am-3pm.

Spaghetti Express, Via Goethe, 20 (tel. 97 53 35). A noisy, fun place with a young crowd. Try any of the umpteen kinds of pasta (L8500-11,000); the dish with crabmeat, *risotto,* cream, and brandy is great. Cover L1500. Open Mon.-Sat. noon-2:15pm and 6-10pm.

SIGHTS AND ENTERTAINMENT

Piazza Walther is altogether clean and attractive—even the McDonald's on the corner is tasteful. It is dominated by the Gothic **duomo** and its delicate, lace-like tower. (Open Mon.-Fri. 9:30am-noon and 2-6pm, Sat. 9:30am-noon.) The **Church of the Francescani** rests in a peaceful garden off P. Erbe. (Open daily 6am-noon and 2:30-6pm.) The firetowers of the **Castel Mareccio** (tel. 97 66 15), on Passeggiata Lungo Talvera, are later additions. (Open Mon.-Sat. 10am-noon and 3-6pm.)

The bike-borrowing option is the best way to visit the castles that cluster in the nearby valleys. **Castello Mareccio,** closest to the center, has a core structure which dates back to the 13th century. A 15-minute bike ride up Via Weggerstein to Via S. Antonio will take you past **Castello Roncolo (Runkelstein Castle)** (tel. 98 02 00), the most impressive of the lot. Guided tours of the frescoed rooms are available for groups, preferably by reservation. (Open Mar.-Nov. Tues.-Sat. 10am-5pm. Admission L1000.) For breezy mountain views and a pleasant *passeggiata,* stroll along the far side of the Talvera River (just across Ponte Talvera).

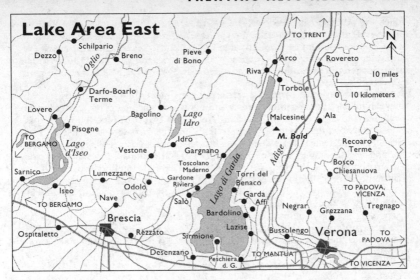

Lake Area East

■■■ LAKE GARDA
(LAGO DI GARDA)

Garda is the grandest and most popular of the Italian lakes, thanks to its breezy summer and mild winter. Overlooked in favor of its western neighbors in the last century, it now boasts a more contemporary air. Of the lake's major towns, three in particular warrant a visit: Riva for its seclusion, reasonable prices, and splendid swimming; Gardone Riviera for the morbidly fascinating villa of Gabriele D'Annunzio; and Sirmione for its extensive Roman ruins and beautifully situated medieval castle. If you're coming from Verona, consider a daytrip to the tiny but stunning bay at **Punta San Vigilio** (just past Garda) for swimming, sunning, and picnicking.

Desenzano lies on the Milan-Venice train line, two hours from Venice, 25 minutes from Verona and Brescia, and one hour from Milan. Once you're there, it's easy to get to the lake towns by buses, hydrofoils, and ferries. Check the schedules carefully and plan ahead, as buses and ferries stop running early in the evening. For shorter trips, take the ferry—it's cheaper than the hydrofoil and you can sit on deck. **Campgrounds** surround the lake but are concentrated between Desenzano and Salò. Unofficial camping is discouraged. Many private residences rent rooms (mostly doubles) in Lake Garda's larger towns. Get a list of these from the tourist office.

SIRMIONE

Alas, shrewd developers realized the potential of what Catullus once lauded as the "jewel of peninsulae and islands." The Space Boat Disco has landed just offshore, and the expansive (and expensive) Garda Village is forthcoming, bringing with it a swarm of tourists from all over the world. In the off-season, however, the crowds thin out, revealing cypress and olive groves.

Practical Information Buses run to Sirmione every hour from Brescia and Verona (1hr., L5400 and L4600 respectively), and every half hour from Desenzano, the closest train station (½hr., L2100). The ride down the peninsula's central artery concludes in Sirmione on Viale Marconi, next to the **tourist office** in the disk-shaped building at #2 (tel. 91 61 14), where you can arm yourself with maps and accommodations information. (Open in summer daily 9am-12:30pm and 3-6pm; in winter Mon.-Fri. 9am-12:30pm and 3-6pm, Sat. 9am-12:30pm.) In the same building you will find the new **hotel booking office** (open daily 12:30-3pm and 6-10pm).

Bikes can be rented at Green Walk, Via Verona, 47 (tel. 990 40 34), or on Via XXV Aprile (L5000 per hr., L25,000 per day; proper ID required; no age restriction, but small children should be accompanied by an adult). **Postal code:** 25019. **Telephone code** (Sirmione and Desenzano): 030. In **emergencies,** dial 113. For **medical emergencies or ambulance,** call toll-free 167 82 10 49.

Accommodations and Food Sirmione is best visited on a daytrip. If you arrive in July or August without a reservation, plan on sleeping in the lake. **Albergo Grifone,** at Via Bocchio, 5, off Via Dente (tel. 91 60 14; fax 91 65 48) boasts a spectacular view and the cheapest prices in the *centro storico*. (Singles L50,000. Doubles L73,000. All with bath.) There are cheaper options available if you don't mind walking several kilometers from the center. Ask at the tourist office. **Sirmioncino,** Via Sirmioncino, 9 (tel. 91 90 45), in Colombare behind Hotel Benaco, usually has camping space. (L19,000 per person, L9000 per tent, per site. Open Mar. 15-Oct. 15.) Lugana boasts two campgrounds: **Il Tiglio** (tel. 990 40 09) and **Lugana Marina** (tel. 91 91 73), both open April-Oct.

Food prices drop marginally outside the castle's immediate vicinity. If the inescapable waterfront views have you craving seafood, the **Ristorante/Pizzeria del Pescatore** does the trick at Via Piana, 20 (tel. 91 62 16). Pizza around L8000, *primi* from L7000, *secondi* from L10,000. Service 15%. (Open daily 11:30am-3pm and 6:30-11pm.) Sirmione's **market,** Piazzale Montebaldo, operates on Fridays from 7:30am to 12:30pm.

Sights and Entertainment Marking the central *piazza* is the conspicuous **Rocca Scaligera,** built in the 13th century. You can roam around the interior and climb the lofty towers for the equally lofty sum of L8000. (Open daily in summer 9am-6pm; in winter 9am-1pm.) At the far end of the peninsula, the **Grotto di Catullo** offers the ruins of a Roman villa and bath complex. (Open in summer Tues.-Sun. 9am-6pm; in winter 9am-4pm. Admission L8000.) Between the ramparts and the ruins lie two clean and quiet public beaches and the **Church of San Pietro in Mavino.** The hilltop house of worship was originally constructed in the 9th century, and now sports handsome interior frescoes dating from the 13th century.

GARDONE RIVIERA

Formerly the playground of the rich and famous, Gardone Riviera is now home to Lake Garda's most famous sight, Gabriele D'Annunzio's villa **Il Vittoriale.** In summer the town experiences a crush of German tourists in search of the perfect tan. Still, the crowds can be avoided in the hills behind Gardone, threaded with walking paths, where aging lemon groves scent the air.

Practical Information The **tourist office** is at Corso Repubblica, 35 (tel. 203 47), in the center of Gardone Sotto. When you get off the boat, turn left onto the corso. Pamphlets are few, but the amiable staff fills in the gaps. Ask for the map of nearby walks. Information on rooms, but no reservations. (Open Mon.-Sat. 9am-12:30pm and 4-7pm; in winter Mon.-Fri. 9am-12:30pm and 3-6pm, Sat. 9am-12:30pm.) The **post office,** at Via Roma, 8 (tel. 208 62), is open Mon.-Fri. 8:10am-1:30pm, Sat. 8:30-11:40am. **Postal Code:** 25083. **Telephone Code:** 0365. **Buses** (tel. 210 61) run to and from Brescia (every 30min., 1hr., L4800), Desenzano (6 per day, 30min., L3600), Milan (2 per day, 3hr., L14,300), and Riva (3 per day, 1¼hr., L4600). In case of **emergency,** call 113 or 112; for **police** call 406 40. For **medical assistance,** call 403 61 nights and holidays. For **ambulance,** call 167 82 10 49.

Accommodations and Food Gardone is best seen as a daytrip. Rooms are expensive and breakfast is often automatically included. If you must stay, the views from **Pensione Hohl,** Via dei Colli, 4 (tel. 201 60), are well worth the price (singles L45,000, doubles L80,000; breakfast included). **Trattoria Ristoro,** Via Triest, 16 (tel. 209 86), about halfway up the hill, is a good buy. *Primi* from L7500, *secondi* L12,000. *Menù* (from L20,000). (Open Fri.-Wed. 10:30am-3pm and 6-11pm.)

Sights and Entertainment Above Gardone sprawls the playground of Gabriele D'Annunzio (1863-1938), the poet, novelist, and latter-day Casanova. Parked in the garden is the prow of the battleship *Puglia,* the emblem of D'Annunzio's popularity. After World War I, he raised an army of poetry lovers and steamed across the Adriatic to retake Fiume from infant Yugoslavia. But even Mussolini found D'Annunzio's ultra-nationalist squawking embarrassing, and in 1925 he presented the poet with a lovely rural villa in an attempt to keep him quiet. D'Annunzio regularly went into debt to stuff his house with the most expensive and useless bric-a-brac available. The fascist rummage-sale effect is most pronounced in his bathroom, which is strewn with 2000 bizarre objects and fixtures. The *Sala del Mappamondo* contains a huge globe on which to dream dreams of global conquest, while the *Sala del Lebbroso* houses the cradle/coffin in which D'Annunzio contemplated death and the surrounding leopard skins.

The Vittoriale is up the hill from Gardone, best reached along Via Roma and Via dei Colli. Visit the house early—before the crowds arrive. Taped tours of the house play in German, English, French, and Italian. (Open Tues.-Sun. 9am-12:30pm and 2-6pm; in winter 9am-12:30pm and 2:30-5:30pm. Admission L7000 to grounds, L15,000 for both grounds and house.) To recover from the perversity, visit the **botanical gardens** laid around a stately villa halfway up the hill to Il Vittoriale. (Open March-Oct. daily 8:30am-7pm. Admission L4000.)

The **Fondazione "al Vittoriale"** (tel. 201 30 for info, 215 51 for ticket info) puts on a summer program of plays, concerts, and dance in the outdoor **Teatro del Vittoriale,** located surprise!—in the Vittoriale itself (mid-July to early Aug., cheapest seats about L20,000).

RIVA DEL GARDA

On Lake Garda's northernmost point, Riva is a glorious meeting of mountain and water. This refreshing lakeside town is a retreat from the normal tourist grind of churches, palaces, and castles—a vacation for those on vacation. With mixed Austrian and Italian heritage, Riva appeals to both nationalities and nature-lovers from all over the world. Join the colorful windsurfers at play in Riva's steady breezes, or explore the drier options of nearby hiking trails.

Practical Information Riva is easily reached by **bus** from Trent (8 per day, 1hr., L5000), and buses run frequently to and from the closest train station at Roverto (20min., L3000). The Roverto Sud exit of the Brennero Autobahn is only 15km away. The **tourist office,** Giardini di Porta Orientale (tel. 55 44 44), is to the left of the castle as you face the water. The electric board out front will help you locate hotel vacancies, and hiking maps are posted in back. Ask for a schedule of events on Riva and other nearby lake towns. (Open Mon.-Sat. 9am-noon and 3:15-7pm. Sun. 10am-noon and 4-7pm.) A **post office** is located on Viale S. Francesco, 26 (tel. 55 23 46). There you can send mail, buy traveler's checks, and cash traveler's checks. Open Mon.-Fri. 8:15am-7:45pm and Sat. 8:15am-7:45pm except last Sat. of the month open 8:15am-noon. Riva's **telephone code** is 0464 and its **postal code** is 38066. **Bike rental** is at Cicli Pederzolli, Viale Canella, 14 (tel. 55 18 30), near the Chiesa dell'Inviolata. L15,000 per day, mountain bikes L20,000. Call one day ahead to have a bike waiting at your hotel when you arrive. The **hospital** is inland from the center on Largo Inviolata (tel. 55 40 04).

Accommodations and Camping Riva is one of Lake Garda's few affordable destinations. While an off-season visit takes less planning, July and August trips demand reservations many months ahead of time. The recently renovated **Ostello Benacus (HI),** P. Cavour, 9 (tel. 55 49 11; fax 55 65 54), is next to the church in the center of town. Reception is open 8-10am and 6pm-midnight, but the happy proprietor never stays away for long and the daytime lock-out is not enforced. HI members given precedence over non-members. (L17,000 per person, includes hot showers and breakfast. Be sure to have your own sleepsack.) In summer advance reservations (with 30% deposit) are recommended. (Open March-mid-Nov.) The **Garni Carla,** Via Negrelli, 2 (tel. 55 21 40; fax 55 52 97), has sparkling rooms, cool balconies, and a lovely garden. From the Church of the Inviolata walk up Viale dei Tigli, turn left on Via Rosmini, then right onto Via Negrelli. (Singles with bath L42,000. Doubles with bath L74,000.) The **Locanda La Montanara,** Via Montanara, 20 (tel. 55 48 57), is very central. (Singles L27,000. Doubles with bath L54,000. Breakfast L6000. Half- and full-pension provided in cozy downstairs *trattoria*. Reserve at least a month ahead for summer. Open mid-March-Dec.) The **camping** option is **Bavaria,** Viale Rovereto, 100 (tel. 55 25 24), on the road toward Torbole. An excellent location right on the water, with a *pizzeria* on the premises. Filled with die-hard windsurfing families. (L8000 per person, L10,000 for a parking space. Hot showers L1500. Open April-Oct.)

Food A large **open-air market** comes to Riva every other Wednesday on Vie Dante, Prati, and Pilati, while the **Orveo supermarket** inland from the tourist office is open on a more regular basis. (Open Mon.-Sat. 8:30am-8:30pm, Sun. 8am-noon. Slightly shorter hours Oct.-May). **Alimar SRL,** P. Cavour, 6 (tel. 55 49 11), is next to the hostel and provides the usual *mensa* combo of institutional appearances and good prices. (*Primi* L5000, *secondi* with side-dish L8500, *menù* L13,000. Cover L1000. Open Mon.-Fri. noon-2pm and 7:30-8pm, Sat. 11am-3pm.) A less institutional choice is the **Birreria Spaten,** Via Maffei, 7 (tel. 55 36 70). Wonderful, large portions, and the Bavarian furniture and German-speaking waitresses will make you feel as though you are in *The Sound of Music*. (Pizza begins at L6500, *primi* at L7000, *secondi* L6000-17000. Cover included. Open daily 10:30am-3pm and 5:30pm-midnight, off-season Tues.-Sun. only.)

Sights and Entertainment The thing to do in Riva is windsurf. Before heading out to see the "sights," head to **Bavaria** (tel. 55 60 77), where you can rent all necessary equipment. (L20,000 per hour, L35,000 per half day (4 hrs.), L40,000 per day, all equipment, bodysuit and shoes. 5-day lesson and rental package (all-inclusive) L280,000.) Before you hit the lake to windsurf, look out at the gorgeous view of the blue-green water contrasted with the mountains that surround it. Riva is a nature-lover's delight. More than just a water sports resort, Riva also has a 12th-century **Rocca** (castle), surrounded by water and graced by a small shady park. Also worth a visit is the Austrian-influenced **Church of the Inviolata** (1611), up Viale Roma, across the street from the hospital. For an excursion from Riva visit **Cascata Varone** (3km away), a 100-m. waterfall surrounded by a breathtaking natural gorge. Buses to Varone from Riva are few and oddly timed, but you can always hike or rent a bike. **Musica Riva** (July 16-29) is an internationally known festival of performances by well-known young musicians. (Ask at the tourist office for a program. Admission varies from free to L15,000.) Look out for the **IX Annual Rustico Medioevo,** a gala festival celebrating medieval dance and folklore. The festival runs from August 5-15. For those of you who are interested in more current musical forms, Riva's **Annual International Jazz and Folklore Festival** takes place June 21-25. The best lake view and people-watching are found along the beachfront path, a 20-minute stroll along the water to the left from the tourist office.

■ Emilia Romagna

Go to Florence, Venice, and Rome to sightsee. Come to Emilia Romagna to eat. Italy's wealthiest wheat- and dairy-producing region covers the fertile plains of the Po river valley and fosters the finest culinary traditions on the Italian Peninsula. Plan to go over budget in Emilia Romagna, as you gorge on Parmesan cheese and *prosciutto*, Bolognese fresh pasta and *mortadella*, and Ferrarese *salama* and *grana* cheese. Complement these with the respectable selection of regional wines, including reds like the sparkling *lambrusco* from Parma and *sangiovese* from Romagna.

Though the Romans originally settled this region, most of the ruins you see are remnants of medieval structures. Developed as autonomous *comuni* during this time, the towns later fell under the rule of great Renaissance families whose names still adorn every *palazzo* and *piazza* in the region. In the 19th century the Italian Socialist movement was born here, and the area remains a stronghold of the left.

Emilia Romagna looks different from the rest of Italy. Muted yellows and browns predominate, and the farm buildings are low, square, and flat-roofed. The uninterrupted plains seem to stretch forever, and the illusion of distance is magnified by the cold gray fog of winter—replaced in summer by a silver haze and stifling heat that make distant towns shimmer. A naturalistic spirit runs through the local architecture; cathedrals' arches seem to have grown into their places, and carved columns resemble ivy-clad trees.

■■■ BOLOGNA

Bologna is my first name.

> #### Four Types of Bologna
>
> With a forkful of *tortellini* in hand and Oscar Mayer in mind, call her *"La Grassa"* (the fat one); as you admire the architecture, call her *"La Turrita"* (the turreted one); or simply call her *"La Dotta"* (the learned one) because of the university that enriched the minds of Dante, Petrarch, Tasso, and Copernicus—the oldest in Europe. But whatever you do, *don't* call her "Baloney."

ORIENTATION AND PRACTICAL INFORMATION

At the heart of north Italy, Bologna is the hub for rail lines to all major Italian cities, and to the Tyrrhenian and Adriatic coasts. Buses #25 and 30 run between the train station and the historical center at P. Maggiore (tickets L1300 at most *tabacchi* and newsstands). On the north edge of P. Maggiore is Piazza del Nettuno. From here, **Via Ugo Bassi** runs west, **Via dell'Indipendenza** runs north, back toward the train station, and **Via Rizzoli** runs west to **Piazza Porta Ravegnana,** site of the two towers. After dark, women should take the bus instead of walking to the town center.

Let's Go: Italy tries to help you by including the **map grid coordinates** of our Bologna listings whenever possible.

Tourist Office: Main office in Palazzo Comunale, P. Maggiore, 6 (C3; tel. 23 96 60), on the right side of the *piazza* as you face the *basilica*. Modern, genial, and efficient. Computer terminal "Tutto Bologna" has tons of info in English (branch terminals pervade the city). Open Mon.-Sat. 9am-7pm, Sun. 9am-12:30pm. A less helpful branch in the **train station** (C-D1; tel. 24 65 41), near the main exit to the street. Stop for the free map and to book a room with no charge. Open Mon.-Sat. 9am-12:30pm and 2:30-6:30pm. Another well-stocked **branch office** at the airport, near international arrivals (tel. 38 17 22). Open Mon.-Sat. 9am-1pm.
Police: P. Galileo, 7 (C3; tel. 23 33 33). **Tourist Police:** tel. 33 74 73 or 33 74 75.

Post Office: P. Minghetti (tel. 22 35 98), southeast of P. Maggiore, off Via Farini. *Fermo posta* at #18, stamps at #16. Open Mon.-Fri. 8:15am-6:30pm, Sat. 8:15am-12:20pm. **Postal Code:** 40100.

Telephones: Telecom, P. VIII Agosto, 24, off Via dell'Indipendenza. Open 8am-10pm. Also at the train station (C-D1). **Telephone Code:** 051.

Budget Travel: Centro Turistico Studentesco (CTS), Largo Respighi 2/F (E2-3; tel. 26 18 02 or 23 73 07), off Via Zamboni (temporary location while renovating). Open Mon.-Fri. 9:30am-12:30pm and 2:30-6pm. Closed the last week of July and the 1st week of Aug. **University Viaggi,** Via Zamboni, 16/E (tel. 22 85 84 or 23 62 55). Open Mon.-Fri. 9am-1pm and 2:30-6:30pm; closed 2 weeks in Aug. Both issue BIJ tickets and HI cards. Big discounts on sea and air travel.

Currency Exchange: Banca d'America e d'Italia, Via Marconi, 13 (C2-3; tel. 33 64 11). ATM, MC, and Visa services. Open Mon.-Fri. 8:20am-1:20pm and 2:45-3:45pm.

Flights: Aeroporto G. Marconi (tel. 31 15 78 or 31 22 59), at Borgo Panigale northwest of the town center. Take blue (suburban) bus #91 from the station. European flights. Many charters available.

Trains: Information tel. 24 64 90. Open 8am-8pm. The harried staff rarely answers the phone, but is very helpful in person; or try the tourist office in P. Maggiore (C3), and pick up free copies of any national train schedule. Trains to: Florence (every 30min., 1½hr., L13,200); Venice (every hr., 2½hr., L13,600); Milan (every hr., 3hr., L17,200); Rome (every hr., 3½hr., L48,000).

Buses: ATC buses for nearby cities depart from the terminal on the far side of P. XX Settembre (D1; tel. 24 83 74). Walk left from the train station. Bologna's efficient urban buses, also run by ATC (tel. 35 01 11), get crowded in early afternoon and evening. Inner-city tickets cost L1300 and are valid for 1hr. after they are punched on board. Strict fine for evaders.

Taxis: (tel. 37 27 27, 37 37 50, or 37 47 18). L7000 for the first 2km, L1400 for each additional km.

Laundromat: Self-Service Acqua Lavasecco, Via Todaro, 4 (D2; tel. 24 07 40), street parallel to Via Irnerio. Coin-operated. L13,000 per load. Open Mon.-Fri. 8am-7pm, Sat. 8:30am-1pm.

Public Baths: Diurno, P. Re Enzo, 1/B (D3), in the building in the center of P. Maggiore, to Neptune's left. Showers, shampoo, and towels L10,000. Bathrooms L1000. Open Mon.-Fri. 8:30am-12:30pm and 3:30-7pm, Sat. 8:30am-noon.

English Bookstore: Feltrinelli International, Via Zamboni, 7 (tel. 26 80 70). Browse with the university students. Large selection of contemporary books and travel guides, including our personal favorite. Open Mon.-Sat. 9am-7:30pm.

Late-Night Pharmacy: at the train station (C-D1; tel. 24 66 03) and at P. Maggiore, 6 (C3; tel. 23 85 09) in the center. Open Mon.-Sat. 7:30am-11pm, Sun. 8am-10pm.

Emergencies: tel. 113. **Medical Emergency:** tel. 33 33 33. **Hospital:** Ospedale Policlinico Sant'Orsola-Malpighi, Via Massarenti, 9 (F3; tel. 636 31 11).

ACCOMMODATIONS

Prices are high and rooms scarce due to the glut of students and business travelers. The situation improves very slightly in January, July, and August. But don't despair: Bologna has an affordable youth hostel.

Ostello Di San Sisto (HI), Via Viadagola, 5 and 14 (tel./fax 50 18 10); English spoken. In the Località di San Sisto 6km northeast of the center of town, off Via San Donato. Ask at the tourist office for the map with directions. Catch bus #93 from Via Irnerio/Via dei Mille (heading away from P. dei Martiri) which cuts across Via dell'Indipendenza 3 blocks from the train station. (Mon.-Sat. every 30min., last bus at 8:15pm.) Get off at the first stop after the Q8. Cross the street and walk up Via Viadagola to the hostel. On Sun. you must take bus #20B, which heads from the town center toward the station. Get off at the 1st stop after the bus leaves Via San Donato, and walk the 2km to the hostel. A villa among green pastures. New, clean, and well-designed. Open 7-9am and 5-11:30pm. Lockout 9am-5pm; you can't even drop off your bag during these hours. L17,000 per person, non-members L22,000. Breakfast and hot showers included. Dinner 8pm, L12,000.

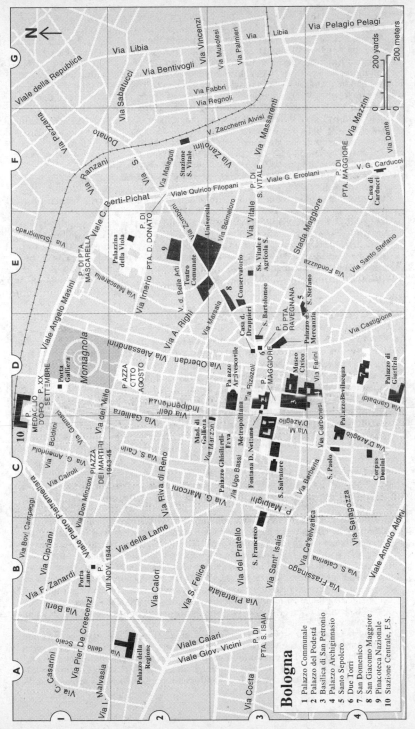

Bologna

1 Palazzo Communale
2 Palazzo del Podestà
3 Basilica di San Petronio
4 Palazzo Archiginnasio
5 Santo Sepolcro
6 Due Torri
7 San Giacomo Maggiore
8 Pinacoteca Nazionale
9 San Domenico
10 Stazione Centrale, F.S.

Albergo Panorama, Via Livraghi, 1 (C3; tel. 22 18 02 or 22 72 05). The 3rd left off V. Ugo Bassi from P. Maggiore; take the elevator to the 4th floor. True to its name, this hotel has large rooms with views of the hills behind Bologna. Friendly management. Singles L50,000. Doubles L75,000. Triples L105,000. Quads L120,000.

Albergo Minerva, Via de' Monari, 3 (C-D2-3; tel. 23 96 52), the 5th left off Via dell'Indipendenza from P. Maggiore. Nice, breezy rooms in a central location. Singles L35,000. Doubles L75,000, with bath L100,000. Triples L90,000.

Albergo Apollo, Via Drapperie, 5 (D3; tel. 22 39 55; fax 23 79 04). Take the 2nd right off Via Orefici from P. Maggiore. Clean white rooms with plenty of space. Couldn't be closer to the center of town. Singles L46,000. Doubles L75,000, with bath L98,000. Closed in Aug.

Pensione Marconi, Via Marconi, 22 (C2-3; tel. 26 28 32). Bear right from the station onto Via Amendola, which becomes Via Marconi. Spotless rooms. Desk monitored all night. Singles L42,000. Doubles L68,000, with bath L85,000.

Protezione della Giovane, Via Santo Stefano, 45 (tel. 22 55 73), just past Via Rialto from the two towers, up the grand staircase in the back. Women only. Beautiful, clean rooms, but they're often filled with students in the winter. Bring your own toilet paper. Curfew 10:30pm. L20,000 per person.

Albergo Il Guercino, Via L. Serra, 7 (tel./fax 36 98 93). Turn left out of the station and go left over the tracks on Via Matteotti. Turn left on Via Tiarini and then immediately right on Via Serra. Away from the busy city center. The young, friendly, English-speaking owner has recently renovated his hotel. Expensive, but worth every *lira*. Midnight curfew. Singles L60,000, with bath L80,000. Doubles L90,000, with bath L120,000. AmEx, MC, Visa.

FOOD

Bologna's cuisine centers on fresh hand-made egg pasta in all shapes and sizes. The best of the stuffed pastas are *tortellini*, bursting with ground meat, and *tortelloni*, made with *ricotta* and spinach. Don't miss Bologna's namesake dish, *spaghetti alla Bolognese*, pasta with a hefty meat and tomato sauce. Bologna is also renowned for salamis and hams of all kinds, including (surprise!) "bologna," known locally as *mortadella*, which is nothing like the American processed product.

Restaurants cluster on side streets only minutes away from the town center; the areas around Via Augusto Righi and Via Piella, as well as the neighborhood of Via Saragozza, are especially good for cheap, traditional *trattorie*. **Mercato Ugo Bassi,** Via Ugo Bassi, 27 (C3), a vast indoor market, sells produce, cheeses, and meats. (Open Mon.-Wed. 7am-1:15pm and 5-7pm, Fri. 7am-1:15pm and 4:30-7:30pm, Thurs. and Sat. 7am-1:15pm.) Or shop Bologna's **outdoor market** in Via Pescherie Vecchie, off P. Maggiore (same hours). You'll find the large, American-style **Supermarket Coop** off Via dei Mille at P. Martiri (C1; open Tues.-Sat. 8am-7:30pm and Mon. 2:30-8pm). Near the university is **Superconad supermarket,** Via della Bella Arti, 31/C (E2). (Open Fri.-Wed. 8:30am-7:30pm, Thurs. 8:30am-1pm. MC, Visa.)

Mensa Universitaria Irnerio, Via Zamboni, 47 (E2), where Via Zamboni meets Via delle Belle Arti. Pick out what you want and show the cashier your ID—amazingly inexpensive for students. Local students are usually eager to meet foreigners; strike up a conversation while waiting. A bulletin board inside lists jobs and apartments. Open Tues.-Fri. 11:45am-3pm and 7-10pm, Sat.-Sun. 11:45am-3pm.

Lazzarini, Via Clavature, 1 (D3; tel. 23 63 29), off P. Maggiore. Snack bar with an exquisite self-service restaurant upstairs. The menu changes daily, but look for the *tortellini alla panna* (L6000). Other pasta dishes L4000-8000. *Secondi* L4000-7500. Restaurant open Mon.-Sat. 11:45am-3pm. Snack bar open Mon.-Sat. 7:30am-8pm. AmEx, MC, Visa.

Ristorante Clorofilla, Strada Maggiore, 64 (tel. 23 53 43). The name sounds like throat medicine, but the food is innovative, healthy, and almost exclusively vegetarian. Bulletin board is the communication center for local environmental and social action groups. Try one of the imaginative salads (L6000-12,000) or hot dishes (L6000-9500). Desserts L2000-4000. Cover L1500. Also sells soy milk

(L2000 per liter) and a handful of other veggie products. Open Sept.-July Mon.-Sat. 12:15-3pm and 6pm-midnight. In winter, tea served 4-7pm.

Antica Trattoria Roberto Spiga, Via Broccaindosso, 21/A (E-F3; tel. 23 00 63). A modest, miraculous Bolognese relic: one room, a couple of servers, and hearty food. Complete meals L19,000 with wine or water. *Primi* L8000, *secondi* L12,000. Cover L2000. Open Sept.-July Mon.-Sat. noon-2pm and 7-10pm.

Trattoria Da Maro, Via Broccaindosso, 71/D (E-F3; tel. 22 73 04), off Strada Maggiore. Students and locals gather here to lunch on satisfying plates of *tagliatelle* or *tortellini* (L8000) and any of the standard *secondi* (L9000-12,000). *Menù* L19,000. Cover L1500. Open Mon.-Sat. noon-3pm and 8-10:15pm.

Oggi Si Vola, Via Urbana, 7/E (C4; tel. 58 53 08). Student-chic macro-heaven. Entirely macrobiotic, a rarity in Italy. Cheerful and homey interior with an open kitchen. Miso soup and such macrofaves as grilled vegetables, L10,000. Open Mon.-Fri. 12:30-2:30pm and 8-10:30pm, Sat. 8-11pm.

Pizzeria La Mamma "Self Service," Via Zamboni, 16. A hangout frequented by boisterous university and military students (10% discount with student ID). Table service also available. Delicious pizza L4500-8500. *Primi* L7000-9000, *secondi* L8000-15,000. *Menù* L13,000. Cover L3000. Wine starts at L2500 per glass. Open daily noon-2:30pm and 7-10pm. Karaoke on Sun. 8pm-2:30am.

Trattoria Da Danio, Via S. Felice, 50 (C2-3; tel. 55 52 02). A short walk up V. San Felice off V. Ugo Bassi rewards you with a large, appetizing menu at this humble, authentic *trattoria*. *Primi* L7000-12,000, *secondi* L6000-18,000. *Menù* L13,500. Cover L3000. Open Mon. Sat. noon-2:30pm and 7:30-10pm. AmEx, MC, Visa

SIGHTS

Bologna's most remarkable sight is the endless series of porticoed buildings throughout the city. During the 14th century, porticoes offered a solution to the housing crisis of a growing city; buildings expanded into the street while leaving room for mounted riders to pass underneath. The building frenzy lasted several centuries, resulting in a mix of Gothic, Renaissance, and Baroque styles.

The tranquil expanse of **Piazza Maggiore,** the heart of the city, reflects both Bologna's historical wealth, exhibited in its collection of tidy monuments, and its modern-day prosperity. The **Basilica di San Petronio,** designed by Antonio da Vincenzo (1390), was built to over-awe. The Bolognese originally planned (like many cocky Italian towns) to make their *basilica* larger than St. Peter's in Rome, but the jealous Church ordered that the funds be used instead to build the nearby Palazzo Archiginnasio. The marble façade of the *duomo*, displaying the town's heraldic red and white, extends to the magnificent central portal. Jacopo della Quercia (1367-1438) carved the now-eroded marble *Virgin and Child* and the expressive Old and New Testament reliefs. The cavernous Gothic interior has played host to such historic events as meetings of the Council of Trent (when not meeting in Trent) and the 1530 ceremony in which Pope Clement VII gave Italy to the German king Charles V. According to legend, the pomp and pageantry of the exercises here drove a disgusted Martin Luther to reform Germany. The zodiacal sundial is the largest in Italy—it measures hours, days, and months when the sun shines through the ceiling opening onto the floor. (Open daily 7:30am-7pm.)

Behind San Petronio, through one of Bologna's busiest porticoes, visit the **Palazzo Archiginnasio** (tel. 23 64 88), formerly a university building, covered with memorials to and crests of notable scholars. It now houses the town library; there's an old anatomical theater upstairs; ask the *portiere* to open it. Shattered during the bombing of 1944, the theater was subsequently reconstructed from thousands of rubbly bits. (Open Mon.-Sat. 9am-1pm. Free.)

Piazza del Nettuno adjoins P. Maggiore. The famous 16th-century bronze *Neptune and Attendants* statue and fountain, the work of Giambologna, grace the square. Affectionately called "The Giant" by town citizens, Neptune reigns over the seas and a collection of extremely erotic sirens and water-babies. To the right, a clock tower, a beautiful terra-cotta *Madonna* by Nicolò dell'Arca, and a Menganti bronze statue of Pope Gregory XIV punctuate the large brick block of the **Palazzo**

BOLOGNA

Comunale. (Open Tues.-Sat. 9am-2pm, Sun. 9am-12:30pm. Free.) The Romanesque **Palazzo del Podestà,** across the *piazza* (facing San Petronio), was remodeled by Fioravanti's son Aristotle, who later designed Moscow's Kremlin.

Via Rizzoli leads from P. Nettuno to **Piazza Porta Ravegnana,** where seven streets converge in Bologna's medieval quarter. The two towers here are the emblem of the city. Of the 200 towers built in the 12th and 13th centuries by aristocratic Bolognese families, only a dozen or so remain. Legend has it that the two principal families of Bologna, the Asinelli and the Garisendi, competed to build the tallest and best-looking tower. The Garisendi plunged into the construction of their tower without suitably reinforcing the foundation. It sank on one side and the upper portion fell off; all that remains is the leaning section. The Asinelli were more cautious and built their tower to a sleek 97m (number four on the list of tallest Italian towers—after Cremona, Siena, and Venice, just to keep score). Reality tells a simpler, if less dramatic, story: land movement botched an attempt to build an observation tower for the civic defense system (the lower, tilting tower), so the city started again and found greater success nearby. Climb the **Torre degli Asinelli** for an amazing view of the city; the arches of Lorraine ogli Estara are particularly breathtaking. (Open daily 9am-6pm; in winter, 9am-5pm. Admission L3000.)

Going down Via Zamboni to P. Verdi, one enters the **Zona Universitaria,** Europe's oldest university campus (founded 900 years ago). Keep your eyes peeled, though, or you might miss it. Only the signs over the doors let you know that these are the ancient halls of the learned—the buildings at first don't appear to be affiliated with a university. The political posters plastered everywhere reflect the idealistic bent of Bologna's college crowd and the town's position as the seat of the Italian Communist Party. If you're in town in June, look for the traditionally vulgar posters lampooning the lives of graduating students.

Back at the two towers, the Strada Maggiore leads east past the **Basilica of San Bartolomeo.** Stop here and see the exquisite *Madonna* by Guido Reni in the left transept before proceeding to the **Church of Santa Maria dei Servi** (tel. 22 68 07; open daily 6:30-11:45am and 3:30-7:45pm), a remarkably intact Gothic church. Inside, columns alternate with octagonal pillars to support a unique combination of ogival arches and ribbed vaulting. In a left-hand chapel behind the altar hangs Cimabue's great *Maestà.* Giovanni Antonio Montorsoli, a pupil of Michelangelo, executed the exquisite Renaissance altar.

Via Santo Stefano leads from the two towers past the pointed arches of the portico of the **Palazzo di Mercanzia,** opening onto the triangular **Piazza Santo Stefano.** The **basilica's** four interlocking Romanesque churches are all that remain of the original seven. The most spectacular church, the round **Chiesa del San Sepolcro,** is the center of the group. San Petronio, patron saint of Bologna, lies here, buried under the pulpit. In the courtyard in the rear is the **Basin of Pilate**—the governor supposedly absolved himself of responsibility for Christ's death in this bath-size tub. Flanking San Sepolcro is the oldest church in the group, the **Church of SS. Vitale e Agricola.** Its arched interior incorporates bits of Roman temples, capitals, and columns. A labyrinth of little chapels opens off the side of "Pilate's courtyard," and in the back you'll come upon the dark **Church of the Trinity.** You can skip the small religious museum on the top story with a good conscience. (Open daily 9am-noon and 3:30-7pm. Admission L2500.)

From P. Maggiore, follow Via dell'Archiginnasio to Via Farini and then Via Garibaldi to the **Church of San Domenico.** San Domenico, founder of the Dominican order, is buried here. Nicolò dell'Arca earned his nickname for his work on the saint's tomb, or "ark." His statues rival the Michelangelos in the tomb and the softly modeled 13th-century reliefs by Nicola Pisano. To tell whose work is whose, consult the informative schema hanging near the entrance to the chapel. Look for Filippo Lippi's *Visit of St. Catherine* at the end of the right aisle.

The **Church of San Giacomo Maggiore** in P. Rossini is a successful melange of the Romanesque and Gothic styles. The edifice was designed in the late 13th-century, when the Dominican and Franciscan brotherhoods, who favored the Gothic design, began to influence the aristocratic clergy, adherents of the Romanesque style. The adjoining Romanesque **Oratorio di Santa Cecilia** (ask the sacristan to let you in through the back of the church) presents a cycle of Renaissance frescoes by Amico Aspertini. Behind, in the ambulatory, is the **Bentivoglio Chapel,** commissioned by 15th-century tyrants of Bologna.

The **Museo Civico Archeologico,** Via Archiginnasio, 2 (tel. 23 38 49), has innumerable Roman inscriptions and Bronze and Stone Age tools on display along with various artistic antiquities. (Open Tues.-Fri. 9am-2pm, Sat.-Sun. 9am-1pm and 3:30-7pm. Admission L5000, students L2500.)

The **Pinacoteca Nazionale,** Via delle Belle Arti, 56 (tel. 22 32 32), ranks among Italy's best galleries. Follow the progress of Bolognese artists from primitivism to Mannerism and beyond. Bolognese artists may have missed the boat on the Renaissance, but the Pinacoteca doesn't. The first section contains a Giotto altarpiece, and the Renaissance wing contains Raphael's *Ecstasy of Santa Cecilia,* Perugino's *Madonna in Glory,* Guido Reni's *Madonna,* and Parmigianino's *Madonna di Santa Margherita.* One room holds great works by the three Carracci, Bolognese natives who helped spark the Baroque revolution. (Open Tues.-Sat. 9am-2pm, Sun. 9am-1pm. Admission L8000.)

The **Museo Civico Medioevale e del Rinascimento** (tel. 22 89 12) is in the 15th-century Palazzo Ghisilardi Fava at Via Manzoni, 4. In addition to a number of exquisite curios, it contains a superb collection of the sculpted tombs of medieval Bolognese professors, typically showing the professor reading to students. The diligent students are shown dozing, daydreaming, and gossiping. The "Stone of Peace" depicts the Virgin and Child flanked by kneeling students who came to terms with the *comune* in 1321 after protesting the execution of a fellow student. (Open Mon.-Fri. 9am-2pm, Sat.-Sun. 9am-1pm and 3:30-7pm. Admission L5000, students L2500.)

The *piazzola,* a large and diverse **open-air market,** takes place on P. VIII Agosto (Sept.-July Fri.-Sat. 8am-2pm). Literature buffs may want to investigate the **museum and house of Giosuè Carducci,** P. Carducci, 5 (tel. 34 75 92), to see the poet's works and sundry possessions. (Under renovation in 1995. Call the tourist office for current info.)

ENTERTAINMENT

Bologna Spettacolo News, available at the tourist office (free) or any newsstand (L1000), has all the info you need about upcoming concerts and music festivals, whether they be 17th-century chamber music or 20th-century love-ins. The city sponsors daily **open-air discos** in July and August in Parco Nord, on the outskirts of the city. Take bus #30 from Via Marconi or the train station (after 8:30pm take #25A) and ask the driver when the last bus back is (usually around 12:30am). The action starts at about 10pm; admission is free. Bologna's newest nighttime summer entertainment is the city-sponsored **Bologna Sogna** (Bologna Dreams) series, which features shows and concerts at *palazzi* and museums around town through July and August. Ask the tourist office for a schedule of events.

During the academic year, current **English-language movies** are screened every Monday at **L'Adriano,** Via S. Felice, 52 (tel. 55 51 27; L8000). Bologna's tremendous university population makes for lively nighttime diversion during the academic year as well. Try one of the many *osterie* and bars in the university district, particularly along Via delle Belle Arti or P. Verdi. Also check out the upscale **Cantina Bentivoglio** at Via Mascarella, 4/B, for jazz. (Wines start at L8000 per bottle, pasta L8000-12,000. Open Tues.-Sun. 8pm-2am.) **Cassero,** a gay bar, is located in the Porta Saragozza at the end of Via Saragozza, a popular part of town. Mostly men, some women. (Open daily 10pm-2am.)

■■■ FERRARA

Ferrara earned its laurels as the home turf of the Este dynasty from 1208 to 1598. Between murdering sundry relatives, these sensitive rulers proved themselves some of the most enlightened (and bloodthirsty) patrons of their age. Their court and university attracted Petrarch, Ariosto, Tasso, Mantegna, and Titian, among others. Ercole I's early 16th-century city plan broke new ground with its spacious, harmonious design, and the modern theater (with curtains, stage, and seated audience) was invented here. But the balding dukes eventually went heirless, and Ferrara succumbed to two and a half centuries of cruel neglect. Today, Ferrara is a town of contrasts: modern shops and boutiques share their space with ancient *palazzi*. Ferrara is a wonderful place to enjoy art as well as the immense friendliness of the locals.

ORIENTATION AND PRACTICAL INFORMATION

Ferrara is on the Bologna-Venice train line. When you walk out of the train station, turn left and then right on **Viale Cavour,** which leads to the Castello Estense at the center of town (1km). Buses #1, 2, and 9 also travel this route.

Tourist Office: Corso Giovecca (the extension of Viale Cavour next to a church), 21 (tel. 20 93 70; fax 21 22 66). Well-stocked. Exceptionally knowledgable folk eager to discuss everything from local politics to your dining preferences. Open Mon.-Sat. 8:30am-7pm, Sun. 2:30-5:30pm. Another **branch** on Viale Kennedy, 2 (tel. 76 57 28) has slightly shorter hours.

Police: Corso Ercole I d'Este, 26 (tel. 20 75 55), off Largo Castello. **Ufficio Stranieri:** assistance in English, tel. 269 44. **Post Office:** Viale Cavour, 27 (tel. 345 04), 1 block toward the train station from the *castello.* Open Mon.-Fri. 8am-7:30pm, Sat. 8am-1pm. *Fermo posta* at window #7. **Postal Code:** 44100.

Telephones: Telecom, Largo Castello, 30 (tel. 497 91), off Viale Cavour at the *castello.* Open Mon.-Sat. 8am-8pm. On Sun. and from midnight to 8am, try **Hotel Ripagrande,** Via Ripagrande, 21 (tel. 76 52 50). **Telephone Code:** 0532.

Trains: Information, tel. 77 03 40; open Mon.-Sat. 8:30am-noon and 3-7pm. To Bologna (33 per day, 40min., L4200); Venice (24 per day, 1½hr., L9800); Ravenna (14 per day, 1hr., L6500); Padova (every hr., 1h., L6800). **Luggage storage:** L1500. Open daily 8am-8pm.

Buses: ACFT, tel. 472 68 and **GGFP,** tel. 20 52 35. Main terminal on Via Rampari San Paolo. Open 9:30am-11:30pm. Most buses can also be taken from the train station (buy tickets at the booth next to the kiosk to your left from the trains). To Ferrara's beaches (12 per day, 1hr., L8200). Buses to Modena depart from the train station (11 per day, 1½hr.-2hr., L8200).

Emergencies: tel. 113. **Hospital: Ospedale Sant'Anna,** Corso Giovecca, 203 (tel. 29 51 11).

ACCOMMODATIONS AND CAMPING

Ferrara's decent budget accommodations are likely to be full. Reserve at least a day or two in advance if possible.

Albergo San Paolo, Via Baluardi, 9 (tel. 76 20 40). Walk down Corso Porta Reno from the *duomo* and turn left on Via Baluardi. Ferrara's best option. New rooms in a quiet, central location. Singles L45,000, with bath L65,000. Doubles L65,000, with bath L85,000. Reservations advised.

Albergo Nazionale, Corso Porta Reno, 32 (tel. 20 96 04), on a busy street between the Chiesa di San Paolo and the *duomo.* Clean rooms with telephone. Friendly manager knows everything about America. Singles with bath L50,000. Doubles with bath L85,000. Rooms fill quickly: reserve 4 days ahead July-Sept.

Camping: Estense, Via Gramicia, 5 (tel. 75 23 96). Take bus #11. L6000 per person, L4800 per child. Open Easter-Oct.

FOOD

Ferrara produces an enticing array of local specialties. Don't miss the chance to gorge on *cappelletti,* delicious triangular meat *ravioli* served in a broth, or *cappellacci,* stuffed with squash and parmesan cheese and served in a light sauce of butter and sage. The gastronomic symbol of the city is its robust *salama da sugo,* an aged, ball-shaped sausage of meats soaked with wine, served hot in its own juices. The traditional Ferrarese dessert consists of a chunk of luscious *pampepato*, a chocolate-covered almond and fruit cake. **Negozio Moccia,** Via degli Spadari, 19 (tel. 353 75), sells the renowned *pampepato Estense* brand in ½-kg (L8150) and 1-kg (L13,850) sizes. (Open Mon.-Sat. 9am-1pm and 4:30-8pm.) For picnic goodies, stop by the **Mercato Comunale,** Via Mercato, off Via Garibaldi next to the *duomo* (open Sat.-Thurs. 7am-1:30pm, Fri. 7am-1:30pm and 4:30-7:30pm), or **Supermarket Conad,** Corso Garibaldi, 51/53 (open Mon.-Wed. and Fri.-Sat. 8:30am-7:30pm, Thurs. 8:30am-1pm). **All shops in Ferrara close on Thursday afternoon.**

Trattoria da Giacomino, Via Garibaldi, 135 (tel. 20 56 44). Rumored to be the best place in town. *Primi* L5000-6000, *secondi* L5000-9000. Cover L2500. Open Sept.-July Sun.-Fri. noon-2pm and 5:30-10pm.

Trattoria Da Noemi, Via Ragno, 31/A (tel. 76 17 15), off Corso Porta Reno. The smells of Ferrarese cooking have wafted out of this *trattoria* for over 30 years. The *salamina* (L8000) is as succulent as ever, and a plate of the homemade *gnocchi* (L7000) makes a divine dinner. A veranda stretches out back. *Secondi* L8000. Cover L2500. Open Wed.-Mon. noon-2:30pm and 6:30-10pm.

Osteria Al Brindisi, Via G. degli Adelardi, 9/B (tel. 20 91 42). The oldest *osteria* in Italy. Recently blessed by a full-fledged cardinal, so you can dig in without fear. Copernicus and Cellini did. No joke. Try delicious sandwiches (L5000) paired with one of the 600 varieties of wine (L1000-6500 per glass). Open Tues.-Fri. and Sun. 8:30am-8:30pm and Sat. 8:30am-midnight.

SIGHTS

Those on an extensive tour of Ferrara's museums may wish to purchase a **biglietto cumulativo** (L20,000, good for one week) available from and valid at the Palazzo Schifanoia, the Palazzina di Marfisa d'Este, all of the Palazzo Massari museums, and several other municipal museums. Ticket for Museo Schifanoia, Palazzina di Marfisa d'Este, and Civico Lapidario L8000, students L4000. Ticket for Museo Boldini and Museo d'Arte Moderna L6000, students L4000.

Towered, turreted, and moated, the awesome **Castello Estense** (tel. 29 92 79) stands precisely in the center of town. Corso della Giovecca lies along the former route of the moat's feeder canal, separating the medieval section of town from that planned by the d'Este's architect, Biagio Rossetti. The Salone dei Giochi and the surrounding rooms retain rich frescoes on their ceilings, the best of which are in the Loggetta degli Aranci. The Lombardesque **Cappella di Renata di Francia** (Chapel of Renée of France) seems a bit out of place—as Renée herself, a Protestant married to a Catholic, must have felt. Parisina, the wife of Duke Nicolò d'Este III, was killed with her lover, the Duke's natural son Ugolino, in the damp prison underneath. This domestic spat beneath the castle's surface of unruffled elegance inspired Browning to pen "My Last Duchess." (Open Tues.-Sun. 9:30am-5:30pm. Admission L10,000, groups over 20 L8000, student groups L4000. Entrance inside the courtyard.)

Walk down Corso Martiri della Libertà to P. Cattedrale and the **duomo.** Alongside the church under the double arcade, little shops and vendors operate much as they did in the Middle Ages. Reshaped by every noble with designs on Ferrara, the cathedral and the castle remain the effective center of town. The tall slender arches and terra-cotta that ornament the apse were also designed by Rossetti; Alberti (1404-1484) executed the pink *campanile* covered with Estense seals and crests. Notice the *faux* rose windows in the left and right portions of the façade. (Church open Mon.-Sat. 7:30am-noon and 3-6:30pm, Sun. 7:30am-1pm and 4-7:30pm.) Upstairs, in the **Museo della Cattedrale** (tel. 20 23 92), reside the best pieces: Cosmè Tura's 15th-century *San Giorgio* and *Annunciation* from the Ferrarese school, and Jacopo della Quercia's *Madonna della Melagrana.* (Museum open Mon.-Sat. 10am-noon and 3-5pm. Free.)

From behind the *duomo,* turn left and then right on Via Voltapaletto, which becomes Via Savonarola. At #30 is the **Casa Romei** (tel. 403 41), the 15th-century dwelling of a Ferrarese merchant, filled with some of the most beautifully decorated rooms of the period. The museum displays statues and frescoes salvaged from destroyed churches in Ferrara. (Open Mon.-Fri. 8:30am-2pm, Sat.-Sun. 8:30am-5pm. Admission 4000.) Continue on Via Savonarola, turn right at Via Madama, and take the first left. Only the carved door of the **Palazzo Schifanoia,** Via Scandiana, 23 (tel. 641 78), hints at the wealth of frescoes inside. The magnificent frescoes in the Saloni dci Mesi offer one of the most accurate and vivid depictions of 15th-century courtly life. (Open Mon.-Fri. 8:30am-2pm, Sat.-Sun. 8:30am-5pm. Admission L6000, over 60 L3000. Second Sun. and Mon. of the month free.)

Cross the street from the *palazzo,* find Via Mellone (to your right), and continue until you reach Via XX Settembre. The **Palazzo Ludovico II Moro,** Via XX Settembre, 124, features a courtyard designed by Rossetti. Inside, the **Museo Archeologico Nazionale** (tel. 662 99) houses extensive finds from the Greco-Roman city of Spina and an outstanding collection of Athenian vases. (Closed for restoration in 1995.)

Returning to the Palazzo Schifanoia and Via Madama, continue straight until you reach Corso Giovecca, Ferrara's boring main drag. Turn right to find the recently restored **Palazzina di Marfisa d'Este,** Corso Giovecca, 170 (tel. 20 74 50), a splendid palace in miniature. (Open Mon.-Sun. 9am-12:30pm and 3-6pm. Admission L3000, second Sun. and Mon. of the month free.)

From the Castello Estense, cross the main road onto Corso Ercole I d'Este. At the corner of Corso Rossetti lies the **Palazzo dei Diamanti,** which outshines all other ducal residences. Inside, the **Pinacoteca Nazionale** (tel. 20 58 44) contains the best work of the Ferrarese school. Most impressive are the *Passing of the Virgin* (1508) by Carpaccio and the incredibly overworked *Massacre of the Innocents* by Garofalo. (Open Tues.-Sun. 9am-2pm. Admission L8000, student groups free.)

Turn right onto Corso Porta Mare to find the **Palazzo Massari** museum complex at #9. The Museo Civico d'Arte Moderna (tel. 20 69 14) includes the **Collezione Boldini,** filled with paintings by the 19th-century Italian painter Giovanni Boldini. Often the museum also mounts special exhibits by well-known contemporary Italian and European artists. The **Museo Documentario della Metafisica** (tel. 20 69 14) documents the inception of metaphysical art in a collection of works by Giorgio de Chirico, Carlo Carrà, Tino Puenté, and Giorgio Morandi, Italy's greatest 20th-century painters. Other museums in Palazzo Massari include the **Museo Ferrarese dell'Ottocento,** which houses a hodgepodge of 19th-century Italian paintings, and the tiny **Galleria della Fotografia** and **Galleria Civica,** both of which display local work. (All museums in the complex open daily 9:30am-1pm and 3:30-7pm. Admission L8000, first Sun. and Mon. of the month free.)

Continue on Corso Porta Mare and turn left on Via Vigne to reach the **Cimitero Ebraico** (Jewish cemetery). Here the Finzi and Contini lie buried, along with most of Ferrara's 19th- and 20th-century Jewish community. Ring the bell and the custodian will let you in. Look for the monument to Ferrarese Jews murdered at Auschwitz.

ENTERTAINMENT

Each year on the last Sunday of May, Ferrara re-creates the ancient **Palio di San Giorgio.** This event, dating from the 13th century, is a lively procession of delegates from the city's eight *contrade* (districts) followed by a series of four races in P. Ariostea: the boy race, the girl race, the donkey race, and finally, the great horse race. The flag-waving ceremony of the eight *contrade* takes place two weeks earlier in P. del Municipio. In July and August, Ferrara hosts **Ferrara Estate,** a music and theater festival that brings diverse performances to the city's *piazze* (contact the tourist office for specific info). During the summer, local bands play next to the *duomo* for free.

■■■ MODENA

It is fitting that Modena is the hometown of Luciano Pavarotti—operatic tenor virtuoso and avid eater—as well as of Ferrari and Maserati factories. Like all three, Modena purrs with prosperity. Conquered by the Romans in the 3rd century BC,

MODENA

the city owed its early prominence to its location; the region's principal road, Via Emilia, ran through the heart of this town. Modena is best visited as an excursion from Bologna or Parma, or as a stopover between the two.

ORIENTATION AND PRACTICAL INFORMATION

Modena lies roughly midway between Parma and Bologna. From the train station, take bus #7 or 11 (L1100) to **Piazza Grande** and the center of town. The alternative is a walk that takes you left on Via Crispi, right down Corso Emanuele, right around the Palazzo Ducale, and finally to **Via Emilia** (Modena's main street) and the Piazza by way of Via Battisti. But beware: Via Emilia goes through several name changes: from Via Emilia Ovest on the west side of the center to Via Emilia in the center, and then to Via Emilia Est on the east.

Tourist Office: Via Scudari, 8 (tel. 22 66 60; fax 20 66 59). From P. Grande, walk right on Via Emilia and turn right on Via Scudari. In the same office as the **Informa Giovani,** (tel. 20 65 83), which is both more helpful and more friendly. Geared specifically to young people. The office also keeps bulletin boards with job and housing notices. Both open Mon.-Tues. and Thurs.-Sat. 10:30am-12:30pm and 4-7pm.

Police: Foreign Dept., Viale Rimembranze, 14 (tel. 41 04 14) or **town policemen,** Viale Amendola, 152 (tel. 34 28 28).

Post Office: Via Emilia, 86 (tel. 23 02 83). Open Mon.-Sat. 8:15am-7:40pm. **Postal Code:** 41100.

Telephones: Telecom, Via Università, 21, off Corso Canalgrande. Office open Mon.-Fri. 8:30am-12:30pm and 2:30-5:30pm. Phone booths open daily 6am-midnight. Also at Via Farini, 26, off Via Emilia. Same hours. **Telephone Code:** 059.

Budget Travel: Hersa Viaggi, Via Emilia Est, 429 (tel. 37 28 63). Somewhat out of the center, offers information and numerous student discounts. Open Mon.-Fri. 8am-12:30pm and 3-7pm, Sat. 8am-12:30pm. Also try **Agenzia Viaggiatori Iter,** Via S. Carlo, 5 (tel. 24 11 46); from P. Grande, take a right on Via Emilia and another right on Via S. Carlo. Similar discount services. Open Mon.-Sat. 9am-7pm.

Currency Exchange: Credito Italiano, Via Emilia, 102 (tel. 41 21 11). On the corner across from Via Scudari and the tourist office.

Trains: P. Dante Alighieri (tel. 21 02 26 or 22 31 01). To: Bologna (every hr., ½hr., L3400); Parma (every 30min., 30min., L5000); and Milan (about every hour, 2hr., L15,500). **Luggage Storage:** L1500. Open 6:35am-12:20pm and 1:50-8:25pm.

Buses: ATCM, Via Fabriani (tel. 30 88 01), off Viale Monte Kosica, which leads to the right from the train station. Take the center street at the circle. Bus #7 to Ferrara (every hr., L8200), bus #2 to Maranello (every 1-2hr., L3500).

Bike Rental: at the train station. L1000 per hr. for first 2hr., L500 per hr. thereafter. Open 6:35am-12:20pm and 1:50-8:25pm.

Late-Night Pharmacy: Farmacia Comunale at Via Emilia Est, 416 (tel. 36 00 91), which is only closed 12:30-3:30pm.

Emergencies: tel. 113 or 115. **Hospital: Ospedale Civile,** Piazzale San Agostino, tel. 20 51 11. **Pronto Soccorso:** tel. 22 22 08. **Ambulance: Red Cross,** tel. 23 75 70.

ACCOMMODATIONS AND CAMPING

Most businesses close on Thursday afternoons.

Locanda Sole, Via Malatesta, 45 (tel. 21 42 45), off Via Emilia at P. Muratori, west of P. Grande. Only 100m from town center. Cool, airy, basic rooms catering to students. English spoken. Singles L30,000. Doubles L50,000. Expect prices to go up as they get TVs in each of the rooms. Showers included. Closed first three weeks in Aug.

Albergo del Pozzo, Via del Pozzo, 72/A (tel. 36 03 50), slightly east of town center. Take bus #7 east and get off at Via del Pozzo. Adequate but often full; call 2-3 days ahead. Singles L32,000. Doubles L35,000-50,000, with bath L50,000-65,000.

Camping: International Camping Modena, Via Cave Ramo, 111 (tel. 33 22 52), in Località Bruciata. Take bus #19 (to Rubiera) west from the station for about 10min. to within ½km of the site. Buses run from 6:20am-7:50pm. L4000 per person, L1300 per tent. Open March 15-Oct.

FOOD

Thanks to the low plains area around the rich Po river basin, inhabitants of Modena and its environs till some of the most fertile soil on the Italian peninsula. Modena, like nearby gastronomic centers Bologna and Parma, produces unsurpassed *prosciutto crudo* and the sparkling *lambrusco* red wine. Modena's own claim to culinary fame derives from the curiously tame but fragrant and full-bodied balsamic vinegar that Modenese sprinkle liberally over salads, vegetables, and even fruit. Balsamic vinegar can be aged for decades, and the finest vinegars can do damage upwards of L100,000 per bottle. Top off a meal with the local *vignola* cherries, considered some of the tastiest in Italy.

Stock your picnic basket at the **Mercato al Minuto Commestibili,** a few steps down Via Albinelli from Piazza XX Settembre. Locals come to this community food bazaar to haggle over prices of everything from bread to snails. (Open Tues.-Sat.6:30am-2pm, Sun. only in the morning; also Sat. afternoons Sept.-May 5-7pm.) To watch local Modenese society in action, drop into **Bar Molinari,** Via Emilia, 153 (tel. 22 23 57), next to STANDA, immediately before lunch and dinner or in the evening. Small pastries run L1200, large ones (all you'll need for lunch) L3200. Try the delicate *torta Elizia.* (Open daily 7am-12:30am.)

Trattoria Da Omer, Via Torre, 33 (tel. 21 80 50), off Via Emilia across from P. Torre. Look for the hand-painted sign among the jewelry and fur stores; Via Torre's entrance is almost hidden. Chef Omer is the saving grace of Modena with his reasonably priced, meticulously prepared delicacies. *Tortellini fiocco di neve,* filled with fresh cheeses and seasoned with butter and sage, is pasta at its prime for L10,000. Zesty vegetable buffet from L3000 and L10,000. Cover L3000. A/C. Open Mon.-Sat. 12:30-2:30pm and 7:30-10pm. MC, Visa.

Mensa Il Chiostro, Via San Gemignano, 3 (tel. 23 04 30). From Via Emilia, turn right on Via San Carlo, which becomes Via Canalino. Via San Gemignano is on your left. This self-service restaurant is located in the courtyard of an antique cloister. *Primi* L3000, *secondi* L5000. Cover L1050. Open Mon.-Fri. 11:45am-2:30pm, Sat. noon-2pm.

L'Aragosta, Via Emilia, 192 (tel. 22 22 75). A/C, but you can also dine outside under a big white tent. Pizzas L6000-10,000; cover (for pizza) L3000. *Primi* L8000-10,000. *Secondi* L14,000-22,000. Try the *scaloppina all'aceto balsamico* (veal in balsamic sauce, L14,000). Cover L1300. Open Tues.-Sun. 12:15-3pm and 6:30pm-1am. AmEx, MC, Visa.

SIGHTS

One of the best-preserved Romanesque cathedrals in Italy, Modena's **duomo,** in P. Grande, dates from the early 12th century. Its patron, the Marchioness Matilda of Canossa, held a fiefdom that backed the Holy Roman Emperor. As a result, the stylistic innovations on the religious buildings sponsored by the Marchioness often bore political significance. The *duomo* also houses a somewhat gruesome relic of patron saint San Gimignano—his arm, encased in silver, takes to the streets in a religious procession on January 31. The sculptor Wiligelmo and his school decorated most of the *duomo* with stylized carvings that draw on local, Roman, Biblical, and even Celtic themes. Carvings around the doors depict scenes from the Old Testament and San Gimignano's travels to Asia. (*Duomo* open daily July-Aug. 6:30am-12:30pm and 3:30-7pm, Sept.-June 7am-12:30pm.)

Looming high over the *duomo* is the 95m **Ghirlandina Tower,** Modena's symbol. Built in the late 13th century, it incorporates both Gothic and Romanesque elements. A memorial to those who died fighting the Nazis and Fascists during World

War II has been added to the base. (Open Mon.-Fri., Sun. and holidays 10am-1pm and 3-7pm. Admission L2000.)

The **Palazzo dei Musei,** in Largo Sant'Agostino at the western side of Via Emilia, contains both the **Biblioteca Estense** (Este Library, tel. 22 22 48 or 22 27 42) and a picture gallery. The library's collection of masterpieces includes a 1501 Portuguese map of the world and a 1481 copy of Dante's *Divine Comedy.* Don't miss the **Bible of Borso d'Este,** a 1200-page tome partially illustrated by Taddeo Crivelli, a 15th-century Emilian painter. (Open Mon.-Thurs. 9am-7pm, Fri.-Sat. 9am-1:40pm. Free.)

The **Galleria Estense** (tel. 22 21 45 or 23 50 04), on the floor above the library, is a well-stocked and meticulously organized collection. The long gallery on the right after you enter begins with earthy Emilian primitives and peaks in Cosmè Tura's *St. Anthony of Padua.* Beyond, an excellent Flemish section features Joos van Cleve's *Virgin and Child with St. Anne.* The Mannerist and Baroque galleries which follow contain some Venetian works by Tintoretto and El Greco, as well as Velàzquez's famous portrait of Francesco I d'Este. (Open Tues., Fri.-Sat. 9am-7pm, Wed.-Thurs. 9am-2pm, Sun. 9am-1pm. Admission L8000, under 18 and over 60 free.) On the second floor of the **Palazzo dei Musei,** discover the newly restored **Archaeological Museum,** which focuses on topics such as Florentine paper-making, early electromagnetic experiments, and paleolithic stone tools. (Open Tues.-Sat. 9am-noon, Tues. and Sat. also 4-7pm, Sun. 10am-1pm and 4-7pm. Admission L3000, under 18 and over 60 free.)

Modena's real claim to international fame is the **Ferrari** automobile. The factory is located southwest of Modena in **Maranello.** (See above Buses for information on buses to Maranello.) After the Maranello stop, there are buses heading straight to the factory. Though you're not allowed to sniff around the inner workings of this top-secret complex, you can view a truly astounding display of antique and modern Ferrari cars, Formula One racers, and trophies at the nearby **Galleria Ferrari,** the company museum, Via Dino Ferrari, 43 (tel. 64 93 15). To reach the museum from the Ferrari factory stop, continue along the road in the same direction as the bus for about 200 yards, and then screech a right at the sign that says Galleria Ferrari; the museum is located in an oversized glass-and-steel structure on the left, about 100 yards down the street. More than twenty Ferraris are on display; fantasize over the stately antiques of yesteryear or the flashy turbos of the 90s. (Open Thurs., Sat., and Sun. 10:30am-1pm and 4-7pm. Admission L2000, under 7 and over 60 free.)

If you're more of a food fan than a Ferrari freak, consider a visit to one of the many local foundations specializing in typical food products. The **Consorzio del Prosciutto di Modena** is at Viale Corassori, 72 (tel. 34 34 64). For wine-tasting possibilities, contact the **Consorzio Tutela del Lambrusco di Modena,** Via Schedoni, 41 (tel. 23 50 05). Queries regarding the native *vignola* cherries can be directed to the **Consorzio della Cigliegia Tipica di Vignola,** Via Barozzi, 2, in the hamlet of Savignano sul Panaro (tel. 77 36 45). For information on local balsamic vinegar production, call the **Consorzio Produttori di Aceto Balsamico** at the Chamber of Commerce, Via Ganaceto, 134 (tel. 20 82 98), and ask for Signor Costanzini.

If you're really on a hell-bent pilgrimage, you can find **Pavarotti's house,** the big villa hidden more or less at the corner of Stradello Chiesa and Via Giardini. But don't get your hopes up to hear Luciano belting out "La donna è mobile" from his balcony—he's known to be a recluse. On another note, the weekly **market** is close by *casa Pavarotti* in the Parco Novi Sad (held Mon. 7:30am-1:30pm). There is also a market in Piazza XX Settembre (open Mon.-Sat. 8:30am-12:30pm and 3:30-7:30pm; closed Thurs. afternoon).

ENTERTAINMENT

For one week—usually falling sometime around the end of June and the beginning of July—the **Settimana Estense** livens up Modena with special exhibits, art shows, street vendors, and nights when residents dress up in Renaissance garb for an authentic *corteo storico* (historic parade). During July and August, the city sponsors a summer music, ballet, and theater series called **Sipario In Piazza.** You might even

happen on a performance by Pavarotti. Contact the Ufficio Sipario in Palazzo Comunale, Piazza Grande (tel. 20 64 60; open Mon.-Sat. 10am-12:30pm and 4-7pm) for
information and tickets (L15,000-30,000). Winter brings **opera** to Modena's **Teatro
Comunale,** Corso Canal Grande, 85 (tel. 22 56 63). On the fourth weekend of every
month, the city puts on the **Fiera d'Antiquariato** at the Ex Ippodromo park northwest of the town center (take bus #7), a boisterous celebration of food, wine, and
local customs. To experience Modenese life in the fast lane, check out the list of **discos** at the tourist office or at Informa Giovani. (Unfortunately, the discos are outside
the city limits and fairly hard to reach without a car.)

■■■ PARMA

Parma's place in the international limelight derives not from its splendid history or
culture but from the dedication with which *i Parmigiani* (people from Parma) craft
their incomparable delicacies. Parmesan specialties include a sweet and buttery-
smooth *prosciutto crudo,* the sharp and crumbly *parmigiano* (Parmesan) cheese,
and a bright sparkling red wine called *lambrusco.*

The city's market-town prosperity has long financed robust cultural activity: here
16th-century Mannerist painting came to full bloom under Il Parmigianino, while
Giuseppe Verdi became so enamored of the local countryside that he remained in
Parma to compose his greatest music. Stendhal, then an unknown French function-
ary, made the city the setting of his 1839 novel *The Charterhouse of Parma.* Twentieth-century Parma has given the world *maestro* Arturo Toscanini. Today, it
cultivates an air of mannered elegance, recalling the refinement of the 19th century.
The town is blanketed in tranquility, overtrafficked by neither cars nor tourists.

ORIENTATION AND PRACTICAL INFORMATION

Parma lies about 200km northwest of Bologna, conveniently served by the Bologna-
Milan train line. The historical center lies on the eastern side of the **Torrente Parma**
(in summer it's no torrent, but a dry riverbed). Walk left from the station to **Via
Garibaldi,** then right 1km to the town center. Turn left on Via della Repubblica to
reach **Piazza Garibaldi,** people-watching site extraordinaire. The main streets
branch off this *piazza,* with **Via Mazzini** running west, **Via della Repubblica**
extending east, **Strada Cavour** heading north toward the *duomo,* and **Strada Farini**
branching south in the direction of the **Cittadella,** the park that houses Parma's
youth hostel and the *Lunapark* carnival in spring and summer.

Tourist Office: P. del Duomo, 5 (tel. 23 47 35). From the station, walk left and turn
right down Via Garibaldi, then make a left onto Strada Pisacane. Info on all nearby
towns, but not necessarily in English. Ask for the *Informagiovani* newsletter, full
of everything from daytrip advice to job listings (in Italian). Don't despair: English
is spoken. Open Mon.-Fri. 9am-12:30pm and 3-5pm, Sat. 9am-12:30pm. Also try
the **Informagiovani** office itself, Viale Toscanini, 2/a (tel. 21 87 49). Open Mon.-
Tues. and Thurs.-Fri. 11am-1pm and 3:30-5:30pm, Sat. 11am-1pm.

Police: Questura, Borgo della Posta (tel. 23 88 88).

Post Office: Via Melloni, 4/C (tel. 23 75 54) between Via Garibaldi and Strada
Cavour, near the *duomo.* Open Mon.-Sat. 8:15am-6:40pm. Also a **branch** across
the street from the station, at Via Verdi, 25 (tel. 20 64 39). Open Mon.-Fri. 8am-
noon. **Postal Code:** 43100.

Telephones: Telecom (SIP), (tel. 26 51), underground in P. Garibaldi in the front
of the city hall. Looks like the entrance to a subway. Self-service phones. Beware:
loud and chaotic at night. Open daily 7:30am-midnight. **Telephone Code:** 0521.

Currency Exchange: Credito Romagnolo, Via Mazzini, 8/A (tel. 28 10 74). Open
Mon.-Fri. 8:50am-1:20pm and 3-4:30pm, Sat. 8:20-11:50am. Try the **train station**
as a last resort. *Cash only.*

Trains: P. Carlo Alberto della Chiesa (tel. 77 11 18, rarely answered). To: Milan
(every hour, 1½hr., L11,700); Bologna (every 30min., 1hr., L7200); Florence

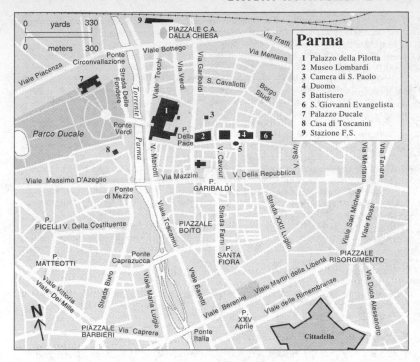

Parma

1 Palazzo della Pilotta
2 Museo Lombardi
3 Camera di S. Paolo
4 Duomo
5 Battistero
6 S. Giovanni Evangelista
7 Palazzo Ducale
8 Casa di Toscanini
9 Stazione F.S.

(7per day, 2¾hr., L15,500 but ask about alternative routes). **Luggage Storage:** L1500. Open 6:30am-1:30pm and 2:50-8:30pm.

Buses: (tel. 21 41), on Viale P. Toschi before the Ponte Verdi. Automated self-service. More convenient than trains to provincial towns. To: Colorno (9 per day, L2500); Fontanellato (6 per day, L3600); Torrechiara (L3600); Busseto (8 per day, L5800); Bardi (4 per day, L6600); Montechiarugolo (L2500).

Taxis: tel. 20 69 29 (general number).

English Bookstore: Feltrinelli, Via della Repubblica, 2 (tel. 23 74 92), on the corner of P. Garibaldi. A whole wall of choices including Toni Morrison. Open Mon.-Fri. 9am-7:30pm, Sat. 9am-1pm and 3:30-7:30pm.

Pharmacy: Farmacia Guareschi, Strada Farini, 5 (tel. 28 22 40). Open 8:30am-12:30pm and 3:30-7:30pm. For night service, there's the **Farmacia Costa,** Via Emilia Est, 67/g (tel. 426 85). Open 7:30pm-8:30am. Take Strada della Repubblica, which becomes Emilia Est. Look for an archway.

Emergencies: tel. 113. **Hospital: Ospedale Maggiore,** Via Gramsci, 14 (tel. 99 11 11 or 25 91 11), over the river past the *Palazzo Ducale.* **Ambulance:** tel. 118.

First Aid: tel. 28 58 30.

ACCOMMODATIONS AND CAMPING

Ostello Cittadella (HI), Via Passo Buole (tel. 96 14 34). From the station, take bus #9 (Ask the driver if he's going toward the *ostello,* last bus 8pm; L1300). Get off after about 15min., when the bus turns left on Via Martiri della Liberazione. Follow Via Liberazione two blocks and turn right onto Via Passo Buole. At the end of Via Passo Buole, go into the large white portico surrounded by ancient walls, and look for the hostel on your left. From P. Garibaldi, take bus #2 or 6. Hostel occupies a 15th-century fortress. Spacious, 6-bed rooms and luxurious hot showers. Three-day max. stay. Lockout 9:30am-5pm. Strictly enforced curfew 11pm. L13,000 per person. HI members only, but sometimes accepts student ID.

Casa della Giovane, Via del Conservatorio, 11 (tel. 28 32 29). From Via Mazzini, turn left on Via Oberdan; Via del Conservatorio winds around to your right. Women only. An upbeat, young atmosphere with beautiful rooms, sturdy furniture, and polished wood floors. Free use of washing machine. Curfew varies with season; usually 10:30pm. Half pension L28,000 per person for women under 25, L18,000 for room only. Women over 25 (exceptional cases only) L34,000 for half-pension, L22,000 for room only. Breakfast and afternoon snack included. Dining room is open to women daily 12:30-2:30pm (full meal L10,000).

Albergo Croce di Malta, Borgo Palmia, 8 (tel. 23 36 43), off Strada Farini, next to an old church. Peaceful rooms kept sparkling. Singles L40,000. Doubles L60,000. A lovely **restaurant** downstairs with typical Parmesan food. *Primi* from L8000, *secondi* from L15,000. Cover L5000. Open Mon.-Sat. 9am-3pm and 7-11pm. AmEx, MC, Visa. May be closed for renovations in 1996; call ahead.

Locanda Lazzaro, Borgo XX Marzo, 14 (tel 20 89 44), off Via della Repubblica. No sign, but upstairs from the restaurant of the same name. Eight homey rooms. Singles L38,000, with bath L42,000. Doubles with bath L65,000. Am Ex, MC, Visa.

Albergo Leon d'Oro, Viale Fratti, 4 (tel. 77 31 82), off Via Garibaldi. From the station, go 2 blocks left. Attractive rooms (no baths) and convenient to the center. Singles L45,000. Doubles L55,000. Make sure to call ahead for a reservation. **Restaurant** downstairs open Mon.-Fri. noon-2pm and 7:30-9:30pm with *primi* around L10,000 and a L2500 cover. Open Sept.-July.

Camping: at the Ostello Cittadella (above). The only campground near Parma. Has electrical outlets and a public park nearby. Three-day max. stay. L8000 per person, L6500 per tent. Open Apr.-Oct. 30.

FOOD

The cuisine of Parma is unequaled and wonderfully affordable. Native *parmigiano* cheese, *prosciutto,* and an abundance of local sausage varieties fill the windows of the numerous *salumerie* along Via Garibaldi. *Lambrusco* is the wine of choice. When exported, this sparkling red loses its natural fizz, so carbon dioxide is added—this is your chance for the real thing. An **open-air market** can be found at P. Ghiaia, off Viale Mariotti past Palazzo Pilotta (open daily 8am-1pm and 3-7pm). Shop for basics at **Supermarket 2B,** Via XXII Luglio, 27/C (tel. 28 13 82). (Open Mon.-Wed. and Fri.-Sat. 8:30am-1pm and 4:30-8pm, Thurs. 8:30am-1pm.)

Trattoria Corrieri, Via Conservatorio, 1 (tel. 23 44 26). From Via Mazzini, go left on Via Oberdan; Via del Conservatorio winds to your right. Whitewashed arches, brick columns, red and white tablecloths, and hanging salami and cheeses await you. Devour traditional *tortelli di zucca* (ravioli stuffed with sweet squash in a cheese sauce, L7000) or try the *tris,* a mix of *tortelli* with *asparagi* and *erbette* (greens) for L8000. *Lambrusco* wines L9500 per *carafe.* Cover L3000. Open Mon.-Sat. noon-2:30pm and 7:30-10:30pm. AmEx, MC, Visa.

Le Sorelle Pichi, Strada Farini, 27 (tel. 23 35 38). Near P. Garibaldi. Open for lunch only. A traditional *salumeria* that hides one of the best *trattorie* in town in the back. Seems to be a well-kept local secret. Menu changes daily: *primi* L9000, *secondi* L10,000-12,000. Cover L3000. *Trattoria* open Mon.-Sat. noon-3pm. *Salumeria* open 8:30am-1pm and 4-7pm for picnic fixings.

Mensa Universitaria di Parma, Vicolo Grossardi, 4 (tel. 21 36 32) in a huge gray building on your way to the John F. Kennedy public garden, on the opposite side of the *torrente* from the *centro storico.* Cross the bridge from Via Mazzini to the other side, now the Via Azeglio. Vicolo Grossardi hides to your right at the arcade. On the first floor. Full meal only L7500 for students (flashing your ISIC works), L12,000 for non-students. Open Mon.-Fri. noon-2pm and 7-9pm, Sat. noon-2pm. Closed Aug. and 2-3 weeks in Dec.

Pizzeria La Duchessa, P. Garibaldi (tel. 23 59 62). An excellent *trattoria* with a grand variety of pizza as well. Large outdoor dining area is great for people-watching in the evening. Be prepared to wait for a seat. Pastas average L8500, pizza L6500-11,500, and *secondi* from L9000. Try the *tortelli alla parmigiana* (ravioli with spinach, butter, and *grana* and *ricotta* cheeses) for L9000. Half liter of wine L5000. Open Tues.-Sun. 10:30am-2:30pm and 7pm-1am. MC, Visa.

Cluny Bar, (tel. 28 41 44) at the corner of Via Cavour and P. Garibaldi. Very centrally located, this is where locals come for Parma's best *gelato*. A good-sized cone will cost you L1200. Open Mon.-Sat. 7am-midnight. Say hello to the English-speaking New Yorker behind the bar.

SIGHTS AND ENTERTAINMENT

Parma's *duomo* and baptistery repose in **Piazza Duomo** amidst the calm magnificence of the entire city (though restoration of both buildings currently dispels both calm and majesty). Masterpieces fill the 11th-century Romanesque **duomo** (tel. 23 58 86). The interior houses the *Descent from the Cross* bas-relief by master Benedetto Antelami in the south transept, and the *Episcopal Throne* supported by piers in the apse. In the cupola Correggio's *Virgin* rises to a gold heaven in a spiral of white robes, pink *putti,* and blue sky. (Open daily 9am-noon and 3-7pm.)

The **baptistery** (tel. 23 58 86), in pink and white marble, was built over a period of time spanning from Romanesque to Gothic. Through the beautifully sculpted portals by Antelami, the interior showcases stunning 13th-century frescoes. (Open daily 9am-12:30pm and 3-6pm. Admission L3000, students L500.)

Behind the *duomo* in P. San Giovanni is the **Church of San Giovanni Evangelista** (tel. 23 55 92), with a Correggio-frescoed cupola. Along the left nave over the first, second, and fourth chapels are frescoes by Parmigianino. (Open daily 6:30am-noon and 3:30-8pm. Free.)

Back toward the river on Strada al Duomo, turn right on Strada Cavour, then take a quick left-right to reach Correggio's fresco **Camera S. Paolo** (tel. 23 33 09), in the small courtyard behind the gate that opens off Via M. Melloni (actually out the back door of the post office). (Open daily 9am-7:30pm before June, 9am-1:45pm after June. Free.) From the Camera, cross Via Garibaldi and P. Marconi to find the gigantic complex of the **Palazzo della Pilotta.** Constructed in 1602, the palace expresses the authoritarian ambitions of the Farnese dukes. The Farnese built two new clusters, the Pilotta Palace and the **Cittadella** (now a park), in an attempt to unify the city. Today it houses several museums, the most important being the **Galleria Nazionale** (tel. 23 33 09). Enter the gallery through the **Farnese Theater,** (1615) an imitation of Palladio's Teatro Olimpico in Vicenza, but much larger than the original. The theater also houses an extraordinary art collection in the gallery that includes works by Correggio and Parmigianino. Leonardo da Vinci's *Testa di una Fanciulla* (Head of a Young Girl), all of Dosso Dossi's work, and the *Pietà* by Cima da Conegliano are here as well. (Gallery open daily 9am-1:45pm. Admission L12,000, includes theater. Theater open daily 9am-7:30pm before June, 9am-1:45pm after June.) Also in the Palazzo della Pilotta, the sizable **Museo Archeologico Nazionale** (tel. 23 37 18) displays coins, bronzes, and sculptures of Greek, Etruscan, Roman, and Egyptian origin. Visits to the museum can be made only with advance notice, so contact the tourist office. (Open Tues.-Sun. 9am-1:30pm. Admission L4000.)

Outside the *duomo* district a French flavor lingers, the aftertaste of Gallic influences of the 16th to 18th centuries. The **Museo Glauco Lombardi,** in the Palazzo di Riserva at Via Garibaldi, 15 (tel. 23 37 27), has a collection of period pieces devoted to Parma during the reign of Marie-Louise. (Open Tues.-Sat. 9:30am-12:30pm and 4-6pm, Sun. 9:30am-1pm; Oct.-Mar. Tues.-Sat. 9:30am-12:30pm and 3-5pm, Sun. 9:30am-1pm. Free.) Unfortunately, many of the French *palazzi* were blasted to pieces during the war, but enough of the older buildings survive to convey the sophistication depicted by Stendhal.

To remedy cultural overload, retreat to the green flourish of the Baroque **Ducal Park,** located west of the Pilotta Palace over the Ponte Verdi bridge. (Open 7am-midnight; Dec.-Jan. 7:30am-5:30pm.) South of the park on Borgo Rodolfo Tanzi, the birthplace of **Arturo Toscanini** (1867-1957), conductor *extraordinaire,* now houses a small museum with memorabilia from the *maestro's* life. (Tel. 28 54 99. Open Tues.-Sat. 10am-1pm and 3-6pm, Sun. 10am-1pm. Free.)

Observe the complex production processes of either *Parmigiano* cheese or *prosciutto di Parma* by contacting the **Consortio di Parmigiano,** Via Gramsci, 26/A (tel. 29 27 00), or the **Consortio di Prosciutto,** Via M. Dell'Arpa, 8/B (tel. 24 39 87). They'll provide a guided tour of the facilities and a free sample at the end.

The city of Parma sponsors a summer music festival, **Concerti Nei Chiostri,** featuring classical music in the area's churches and cloisters. (Call 28 32 24 for information 5-7pm. Tickets available at the door L23,000; under 18 L18,000.) You can also contact the tourist office for info, and ask for their brochure listing the local summer concerts and festivals, including starlit concerts in neighboring castles. Make sure to see the premier **opera house** of Parma, the **Teatro di Reggio,** (tel. 21 89 10) next to P. della Pace. Check with the tourist office for prices of cheaper standing-room tickets during Oct.-May. Just visiting is free.

■ NEAR PARMA

Enthusiasts and students of Italian architecture and opera will be pleased by the offerings of the cities and towns around Parma. No composer embodies the Italian soul better than opera giant Giuseppe Verdi, whose native hamlet of **Roncole Verdi** rests on the Parma plain 3½km outside the city of **Busseto** (from Parma 15 buses daily to Roncole and Busseto, 30min., call general info line above for prices). To see where this son of a poor innkeeper received his earliest inspiration, visit the house and museum at **Verdi's birth site** (tel. (0524) 924 87 or 92 23 39) in Roncole. In Busseto proper, within the walls of the ancient **Rocca,** you'll find the famous **Teatro Verdi,** opened in 1868 (and, unfortunately, closed now for renovations). Three kilometers away from Busseto (on the same bus) lies the **Villa Sant'Agata** (tel. (0524) 83 02 10), Verdi's residence during sabbaticals from his work in Milan. Fed up with Busseto's infamous gossips regarding his choice to "live in sin" with his premier *diva,* he decided to place his home in Sant'Agata, right where the province of Parma ends and that of Piacenza begins. Parts of this mansion are open to the public and remain unaltered from the time of his death in 1901. (Open Apr.-Oct. Tues.-Sun. 9-11:40am and 3-6:40pm. Admission L5000, groups L4000, groups of students L1000. Call ahead for reservations.)

■■■ PIACENZA

Tucked into the distant northwest corner of Emilia Romagna, almost bordering on Piemonte, Piacenza eschews a tourist economy to embrace home-grown prosperity. True to its name, this town is pleasantness incarnate. Piacenza houses several noteworthy monuments of the Renaissance and Middle Ages, and makes a convenient stopover on your way to Parma or Bologna.

Orientation and Practical Information Piacenza lies on the main rail line between Milan (L6500) and Bologna (L11,700), as well as on a secondary line that connects to Turin (L15,500) through Alessandria. From the station, located in **Piazzale Marconi,** walk along the left side of the park on Viale delle Mille, and take a right on Via Alberoni at the far side of the park. Bear right onto Via Roma and go left onto Corso Cavour, which leads directly to the **Piazza dei Cavalli.** The **tourist office** in Piazzetta Mercatini, 10 (tel. 32 93 24), tucked in on the left of the Gothic palace off P. Cavalli, distributes a map full of useful information (in English) on hostels and sights. English spoken. (Open Mon.-Wed. and Fri.-Sat. 9am-12:30pm and 4-6:30pm, Thurs. 9am-12:30pm.) Piacenza's **post office** is at Via San Antonio, 38-40 (tel. 32 06 98); the **postal code** is 29100. The **Telecom office** (tel. 54 41 11) is at Via Vittorio Emanuele, 118, but for phone booths try P. Cavalli or Via Garibaldi. **Telephone code:** 0523. The many banks in the center (except the Banca d'Italia) all have **currency exchange** services, as does the post office. The **train station** information line is 32 06 37. **Taxis** can be reached at 32 38 53, 32 22 36, or 75 47 22. For medical emergencies, call the **hospital** at 30 11 11, or the **Red Cross,** tel. 32 47 87. **Ambulance:** tel. 118. The **outdoor market** is held every Wed. and Sat. in P. Duomo and P. dei Cavalli in the *centro storico.*

Accommodations and Food The most convenient lodging option is the **Hotel Moderno,** Via Tibini, 31 (tel. 38 50 41 or 32 92 96; fax 38 44 38). Just walk along the left side of the park, directly onto Via Tibini. True to its name, it offers cheerfully modern rooms with new, sturdy furniture and well-scrubbed bathrooms. (Singles L45,000, with bath L55,000. Doubles L58,000, with bath L70,000.) Another option, only a few blocks away, is **Hotel Corona,** Via Roma, 141 (tel. 32 09 48) above a **pizzeria** (pizza from L6000). From the train station, follow Viale delle Mille along the left side of the park to a right on Via Roma. Singles L35,000. Doubles L50,000. Half pension L48,000, full pension L55,000. AmEx, MC, Visa. As in any Italian town, specialty shops selling meats, cheeses, bread, and fruit are omnipresent. An especially good place to try is **Via Calzolai,** near the center. Local specialties include *tortelli,* filled with spinach and *ricotta,* and *pisarei e fasö,* a hearty bean-and-pea soup. Or head away from the station to **Osteria Del Trentino** (tel. 32 42 60), Via del Castello, 71, off P. Borgo, a charming restaurant where you can eat indoors or out back in the leafy garden. *Primi* average L8000, *secondi* L12,000. (Cover L2500. Open Mon.-Sat. noon-3pm and 8pm-midnight. AmEx, MC, Visa.)

Sights The entire *centro storico* is off-limits to automobile traffic, making it a haven for pedestrians. The central square, **Piazza dei Cavalli,** is named for the two massive 17th-century equestrian statues by Francesco Mochi. Even though the statues were intended as tributes to their riders, Duke Rannucio I and his father Duke Alessandro Farnese, the horses seem to dominate their masters. The true masterpiece of the *piazza,* however, is the gothic **Palazzo del Comune,** now called **Il Gotico.** The building was constructed in 1280, when Piacenza was a leading member of the Lombard League (a powerful trading group of city-states in northern Italy). From P. dei Cavalli, follow **Via XX Settembre** to the **duomo,** constructed between 1122 and 1233, with its unpretentious, three-aisle nave. The crypt, a maze of thin columns, is one of the most beautiful and spookiest in Italy—grab a friend's hand when you visit. (*Duomo* open daily 8am-noon and 3-6pm.)

The **Palazzo Farnese,** in P. Cittadella at the opposite end of Corso Cavour from P. dei Cavalli, houses the **Museo Civico,** which comprises both the **Museo delle Carrozze** and the **Museo del Risorgimento** (tel. 282 70 or 269 81), containing, among other things, a Botticelli fresco depicting Christ's birth. (Open Mon., Wed., Fri. 9am-12:30pm, Thurs., Sat., and Sun. 9am-12:30pm and 3:30-5:30pm. Admission L4500, under 18 and over 60 L3000. For only the Museo delle Carrozze or the Museo del Risorgimento, under 18 and over 60 L2500 or L1000.) The **Galleria Ricci Oddi,** Via Sirio, 13 (tel. 207 42), south of P. Sant'Antonino, exhibits a collection of contemporary and modern art, including works by Klimt and A. Bocchi.

■■■ RAVENNA

Ravenna's moment of geopolitical superstardom came and went 14 centuries ago, when Justinian and Theodora, rulers of the Byzantine Empire, made Ravenna the headquarters for their attempt to restore order to the anarchic west. Although they were unsuccessful, Ravenna remained the seat of the Exarchs of Byzantine Italy for two centuries; the artistic legacy of the period remains, including the most important examples of Byzantine art outside Istanbul. Today, Ravenna is an attractive town that draws tourists to famed mosaics and pilgrims to Dante's tomb. It's a charming city that makes a nice base for exploration of the Emilia-Romagna region as well as the beaches along the Adriatic coast.

RAVENNA

ORIENTATION AND PRACTICAL INFORMATION

Visit Ravenna as a daytrip from Bologna via Castelbolognese or Ferrara. The train station sits at the east end of town in P. Farini. **Viale Farini** leads from the station straight into Via Diaz, which runs to **P. del Popolo,** the center of town.

Tourist Office, Via Salara, 8 (tel. 354 04). From the train station, take Viale Farini to P. del Popolo. Then take Via Muratori to P. XX Settembre, go right on Via Matteotti, follow it to its end, go left on Via Cavour, and take the 1st right. Useful maps and accommodations info. Open Mon.-Sat. 9am-1pm and 3-6pm, Sun. 9amnoon; in winter closed Sun. **Video Info** around the corner on San Vitale. **Branch office** outside the train station to your left. Also rents **bikes** at L2000 per hour, L15,000 per day. Open Mon.-Sat. 6:15am-8:20pm.

Police: tel. 112 (emergencies) or 33 333, in P. del Popolo, 26.

Post Office: P. Garibaldi, 1, off Via Diaz before P. del Popolo. Open Mon.-Fri. 8:15am-7pm, Sat. 8:15am-12:50pm. *Fermo posta* at #1. **Postal Code:** 48100.

Telephones: Telecom, Via Rasponi, 22, off P. XX Settembre. Very helpful staff. Open Mon.-Fri. 8:30am-12:30pm and 2:30-5:30pm (daily 8am-11pm for self-service booths). 8pm-8am, try **Albergo Diana,** Via Rossi, 4. **Telephone Code:** 0544.

Budget Travel: CTS, Via Mazzini, 11 (tel. 399 33). Friendly office. English spoken. ISIC and HI cards sold. Discount airfares. Open Mon.-Fri. 9:30am-12:30pm and 3:30-7:30pm, Sat. 9am-12:30pm.

Currency Exchange: Via Diaz is lined with banks. Most open Mon.-Fri. 8:20am-1:20pm and 2:45-3:45pm, Sat. 8:20-11:20am. Also at the post office.

Trains: In Piazza Ferini. To: Bologna (5 trains per day, 1¼ hr., L6700), Ferrara (9 per day, 45min., L6000). At Ferrara, change for Venice (3hr., L17,800). Change at Faenza for Florence, (3hr., L14,400).

Buses: ATR (regional) and **ATM** (municipal) buses depart from outside the train station for the coast and beach towns of Marina di Ravenna (L1600), Lido di Classe (L3600), etc. Buy tickets at the ATM booth across the *piazza* from the station (L1200 for most towns)—get a return ticket too, as they're difficult to find in the suburbs. Office hours Mon.-Sat. 6:30am-8:30pm, Sun. 7am-8pm (slightly shorter hours in winter).

Public Toilets: Via Pasolini, 20, off Via Cavour. Super-modern and disinfected after every use. L400. Another at P. Baracca, and a third upstairs to your left as you enter the Mercato Coperto in P. Costa.

Emergencies: tel. 113. **Hospital: Santa Maria delle Croci,** Via Missiroli, 10 (tel. 40 91 11). **Medical Assistance:** tel. 330 11.

ACCOMMODATIONS

Most of Ravenna's inexpensive accommodations lie near major transportation lines, and are thus quite noisy. Except during the tanning months of July and August, consider a hotel or campground in one of the quiet beach towns nearby.

Ostello Dante (HI), Via Nicolodi, 12 (tel. 42 04 05 or 97 36 98). Take bus #1 from Viale Pallavicini, left of the station (last bus shortly after 9pm, L1200). A clean, simple hostel in the eastern suburbs with 172 beds. Hot showers 6-9pm only. 6-bed rooms. Reception open 7-9:30am and 4-11:30pm. Curfew 11:30pm. L16,000 per person. Showers and breakfast included. Fine dinner L14,000. Bike rental L10,000 per day (for guests only).

Hotel Ravenna, Viale Marconcelli, 12 (tel. 21 22 04; fax 21 20 77), to the right as you exit the station. Neat, vintage 1960s rooms with matching furniture. Singles L38,000, with bath L50,000. Doubles L60,000, with bath L75,000. MC, Visa.

Albergo Al Giaciglio, Via Rocca Brancaleone, 42 (tel. 394 03). Walk along Viale Farini, then right across P. Mameli. All rooms carpeted and clean. Singles L30,000, with bath L35,000. Doubles L43,000, with bath L55,000. Triple L75,000, with bath L85,000. Breakfast in rooms without bath L3500. Closed 2 weeks in Dec. MC, Visa. Prices executed to rise in 1996.

FOOD

Those looking for tasty local fare will find disappointment in Ravenna. If you're staying at the hostel, you may want to go for the L14,000 dinner or L6000 plate of spaghetti. Hostelers also benefit from the adjacent bargain **supermarket**. (Open Mon.-Wed. and Fri.-Sat. 8am-1pm and 3:30-8pm, Thurs. 8am-1pm.) The busy **Mercato Coperto** occupies P. Andrea Costa, up Via IV Novembre from P. del Popolo (open Mon.-Sat. 7am-2pm and Fri. 4:30-7:30pm).

Bizantino, in P. Andrea Costa, inside the Mercato Coperto. Self-service restaurant with stylish, iron-detailed interior. *Primi* L4000-6000, *secondi* L3000-7000. Full meals L14,000. Cover L500. Open Mon.-Fri. 11:45am-3pm.

Mensa Il Duomo Self-Service, Via Oberdan, 8 (tel. 21 36 88), off P. del Duomo. Well-prepared self-service. Popular; come early. Pasta L3500. Full meals L12,000. Wine L1000 per glass. Cover L1500. Open Sept.-July Mon.-Fri. 11:40am-2:30pm.

Ristorante/Pizzeria Guidarello, Via Gessi, 7, off P. Arcivescovado, beside the *duomo.* A huge place with surprisingly good food—the only real *trattoria* in town. Try the *Fantasia della Casa,* 3 differently prepared meats with mixed veggies, a complete meal at L15,000. *Primi* L4500-8500, *secondi* L6000-15,000. Cover L2500. Open daily noon-2:15pm and 7-9pm. The exact same fare is available at the owner's other restaurant, **Galleria da Renato** (tel. 236 80), around the corner at Via Mentana, 31. Same hours, but closed on Sun. MC, Visa.

SIGHTS AND ENTERTAINMENT

If you're staying in Ravenna, or dutifully making the rounds on the church-mosaic-museum circuit, consider buying a cumulative ticket of the city sights (L9000, students L7000). The ticket is available and valid at the Basilica di San Vitale, the Basilica of Sant'Appolinare, Mausoleum of Galla Placidia, Battistero Neoniano, Museo Arcivescovile, and Basilica dello Spirito Santo.

Inside and out, the 6th-century **Basilica di San Vitale,** Via San Vitale, 17 (take Via Argentario off Via Cavour), is a sight to behold. Restoration of the imposing ancient structure is nearing completion. An open courtyard overgrown with greenery leads to the awe-inspiring interior, where brilliant mosaics depict scenes from the Bible. The courts of the Emperor Justinian and his wife Theodora stand in formal Byzantine splendor; Christ, seated in the dome, rests on a sphere of blue so vivid it belies its 1400 years. (Open daily 9am-7pm. Admission L5000.) The oldest and most interesting mosaics in the city cover the interior of the **Mausoleum of Galla Placidia,** behind the basilica. The coin box for illumination is outside. (Open daily 9am-7pm; entrance included with admission to the basilica.)

Through the gate between San Vitale and the mausoleum, in the cloisters of a one-time convent attached to the church, lies the sprawling **Museo Nazionale,** Via Fiandrini (tel. 344 24), with collections from a wide range of periods: Roman, early Christian, Byzantine, and medieval. (Open Tues.-Sun. 8:30am-7:30pm. Admission L6000, EU citizens under 18 and over 60 free.)

The **duomo** (tel. 391 96), due south in P. Duomo, is the fusion of everything Baroque. (Open daily 7:30am-noon and 3:30-6:30pm.) In the **Battistero Neoniano,** next door on Via Battistero (tel. 336 96), some poorly restored mosaics in Hellenistic-Roman style reside on the lower level, with three levels of 5th-century mosaics above. (Church open daily 7am-noon and 3:30-6pm. Baptistery open daily 9am-7pm. Admission L4000.)

A small but precious collection of mosaics from the *duomo* is on display in the **Museo Arcivescovile,** nearby in P. Arcivescovado. While you're there, check out the mosaic chapel and the Throne of Maximilian, perhaps the best piece of ivory carving in the Christian world and the zenith of Ravennine sculpture. (Open daily 9am-7pm. Admission L4000.) Compare the mosaics in the orthodox Battistero Neoniano with those in the **Battistero degli Ariani,** on Via degli Ariani off Via Diaz, which was used by the Arians, a sect condemned as heretics for doubting the Trinity. (Open 9am-7pm.) For still more mosaics, continue to the **Church of Sant'Apol-**

RIMINI

linare in **Classe** (tel. 47 30 04), a 6th-century *basilica* 5km south of the city (bus #4 or 44, every 30min. from the train station, L1200). The classical style yields to Byzantine depictions of angels and apostles on the heavily decorated triumphal arch. (Open Mon.-Fri. 9am-12:30pm and 2-7pm, Sat. and Sun. 2-5pm. Admission L4000.)

For those who grow weary of Ravenna's mosaics, the **remains of Dante Alighieri** (1265-1321), located at the end of Via Dante Alighieri, will satiate any morbid curiosity. (Open daily 9am-noon and 2-5pm, but sometimes left open during the lunch hour. Free.) There is also a **Dante Museum,** Via Dante Alighieri, 4 (tel. 336 67), whose Dante library is 18,000 volumes strong. (Open Tues.-Sun. 9am-noon. Admission L3000, free on Sundays and holidays.)

Every Sunday in summer, a **flea market** (books, antiques, etc.) appears in P. Garibaldi, in front of the post office. From the last week in June to the last week in August, the Church of S. Francesco sponsors **Ravenna in Festival,** featuring operas, concerts, folk music, and drama. The festival culminates in the **concerti d'organo,** a series of organ recitals held in San Vitale. Contact **Teatro Alighieri,** Via Mariani, 2 (tel. 325 77), for programs and information. In winter, opera and ballet animate the Teatro Alighieri. An annual **Dante Festival** during the second week in September brings Hell to Ravenna with exhibits, readings, and performances. This festival is also given under the auspices of the Church of S. Francesco (tel. 332 56).

■■■ RIMINI

One face of Rimini, sporting sunglasses and a dark tan, gazes toward the sea, a bohemian Miami Beach with a shortage of bikini tops and an excess of *discoteche*. Its other face sighs nostalgically toward the inland historic center, an alluring jumble of medieval streets dominated by the Malatesta Temple. In summer, Rimini is the most populated tanning spot on the mid-Adriatic coast, and the city's nightlife is the liveliest in the area. Yet it is also populated by those seeking tranquility by the sea. Rimini is a great spot for families as well as those in search of a hot nightlife.

ORIENTATION AND PRACTICAL INFORMATION

Rimini is a major stop on the Bologna-Lecce train line and its airport has service to many European cities (mostly charters). To get to the beach from the station on foot (15min.), walk right from the station along Piazzale C. Battisti, turn right again into the tunnel when you see the yellow arrow indicating *al mare,* then follow **Via Principe Amadeo.** By bus, take #10 or 11. Buy tickets (L1300, L4500 per day) at the kiosk in front of the station or at *tabacchi.* To reach the historic center of town, take **Via Dante Alighieri** from the station (5min.).

Tourist Offices: IAT, Via Dante Alighieri, 86 (tel. 513 31 or 514 80), across the *piazza* from the train station. Friendly, English-speaking staff. Be sure to pick up *Book Istantaneo,* an excellent all-purpose guide to Rimini, particularly the beach scene. Open daily 8am-8pm. **Branch office,** P. dell'Indipendenza, 6 (tel. 245 11), at the sea next to the Cassa di Risparmio di Rimini. Open daily 8am-8pm; off-season 8am-2pm. **Hotel Reservations-Adria** in the train station (tel. 39 05 30) will phone to find rooms. Free. Open daily 8am-8pm.

Police: Corso d'Augusto, 192 (tel. 510 00).

Post Office: Corso Augusto, 8 (tel. 78 16 87), near the Arch of Augustus off P. Tre Martiri. *Fermo posta* at #10. Open Mon.-Sat. 8:10am-7:10pm. Also at the beach, Viale Mantegazza at Viale Vespucci. Open Mon.-Fri. 8:15am-1:30pm, Sat. 8:15am-noon. Also at Via Roma, 64, open Mon.-Fri. 8:30am-7pm. **Postal Code:** 47037.

Telephones: Telecom, P. Ferrari, 22, in the Galleria Fabbri off Via Tempio Matestiano, which intersects with Via IV Novembre. Open daily 8am-10pm. Other branches, Viale Carducci, 30 and Viale Triest, 1, open daily 8am-11pm. Or try any of the bars along the beach or near the station. **Telephone Code:** 0541.

Budget Travel: CTS, Cooptur Viaggi, Via Oberdan, 35 (tel. 247 81; fax 235 56), off Via Dante Alighieri. Buy *Transalpino* tickets here. English spoken. Open Mon.-Fri. 9am-12:30pm and 3:30-7pm, Sat. 9:30am-noon.

Airport: Miramare Civil Airport, Via Flaminia (tel. 37 31 32). Mostly charter flights. Rates vary. Check with Cooptur (under Budget Travel, above).
Trains: Piazzale C. Battisti and Via Dante (tel. 535 12). Trains to Bologna (14 per day, 1½hr., L9800) and Milan (15 per day, 3hr., L26,200). Periodic trains to Rome (L27,800). Trains every hr. to Ravenna (1hr., L4200).
Buses: TRAM intercity bus station at Viale Roma at P. Clementini (tel. 39 04 44; fax 39 08 26), a few hundred meters from the station. To many inland towns and San Marino (11 per day, 1hr., L4000). Many buses leave from the train station, where you can buy tickets in the orange booth.
Car Rental: Hertz, Viale Triest, 16/A (tel. 531 10). Near the beach off Viale Vespucci. L690,000 per week or L130,000 per day with unlimited mileage, including tax. Open Mon.-Sat. 8:30am-1pm and 3-8pm, Sun. 8:30am-1pm. Also an office at the airport (tel. 37 51 08).
Laundry: Lavanderia Self-Service. Via Vespucci, 137, just off Via Tripoli (tel. 39 14 90). Very new, sparkling clean, and offers instructions in English. L6000 wash, L6000 dry, L1200 detergent. Open daily 7am-11pm; in winter 7am-10pm.
Emergencies: tel. 113. **Hospital: Ospedale Infermi,** Via Settembrini, 2 (tel. 70 51 11). English-speaking doctors. **Medical Assistance:** on the beach at the end of Viale Gounod, beyond Viale Pascoli. Free walk-in clinic for tourists. Open in summer daily 9:30am-noon and 3:30-7pm. **24-hour medic and ambulance:** 38 70 01. **Red Cross:** Via Savonarola, 6 (tel. 266 12), near the canal.

ACCOMMODATIONS AND CAMPING

During high season (the last week of June through Aug.), your best chance of finding a room is through the tourist or accommodations offices. Reserve in advance by phone to avoid hassles. Rimini's hotel seasons are divided into high (last week in July and the first 3 weeks in August), shoulder (first 3 weeks in July and the last week in August), and low (all other times) and listed in that order when possible.

Ostello Urland (HI), Via Flaminia, 300 (tel. 37 32 16), by the airport, 25min. away on bus #9 (L1800). Get off at Via Stokholm (ask bus driver) and follow the signs. Lockout 9am-5pm. Curfew 11pm. L14,000 per person. Non-HI members pay an additional L5000. Breakfast included. Dinners L10,000, pasta only L4000. Call ahead. Open May-mid-July and mid-Aug.-Sept.
Albergo Filadelphia, Via Pola, 25 (tel. 236 79). Clean rooms, soft beds, and an owner with a soft spot for Americans and *Let's Go* travelers. L35,000/30,000/25,000 per person. Reduced for extended stays. Reservations help.
Hotel Pigalle, Via Ugo Foscolo, 7 (tel. 39 10 54). Clean and classy hotel on a quiet street. Jazz posters, a peaceful terrace, and young and snazzy staff. All rooms with bath. Singles: L60,000/L55,000/L50,000. Doubles: L130,000/L100,000/L90,000. Breakfast included. Full pension required in Aug. Open mid-June to mid-Sept.
Pensione Mille Fiori, Via Pola, 42 (tel. 256 17), down the street from currency exchange. Large rooms, all with bath. Singles and doubles (per person): L56,000/45,000/36,000. Make reservations July and Aug. Full pension required in Aug. Open Easter-Sept.
Hotel Cardellini, Via Dante, 50 (tel. 264 12; fax 543 74), 100m from the train station, but very respectable. This 2-star offers 63 tidy rooms with big beds, high ceilings, and TV at 1-star prices. Very helpful English-speaking manager. Singles L48,000/35,000, with bath L69,000/L49,000. Doubles L69,000/L52,000, with bath L110,000/L74,000. Extra beds 35% more. Breakfast L9000. AmEx, MC, Visa.
Camping: Maximum (tel. 37 26 02 or 37 02 71). Take bus #10 or 11 to stop #33 ("Miramare"). July 6-Aug. 24: L10,000 per person, L7800 per child, L18,000 per tent. May 14-July 5 and Aug. 25-Sept.: L4400 per person, L4000 per child, L7000 or L10,000 per tent. Also try **Italia** (tel. 73 28 82) with campsites and bungalows, at Via Toscanella, 112 in Viserba di Rimini, 1½km north of Rimini. From the train station take bus #4 directly to the campsite. L10,500 per adult, L8000 per child, L12,000 per tent.

FOOD

Rimini's seaside swarms with sterile cut-purse eateries. Fortunately, you can survive on the resort's delicious snacks. Look in the center of town for affordable full meals. For brown-baggers, Rimini's **covered market,** between Via Castelfidardo and the Tempio, provides an array of foodstuffs. (Open Mon., Wed., and Fri.-Sat. 7:15am-1pm and 5-7:30pm, Tues. and Thurs. 7:15am-1pm.) The **rosticceria,** in the market, offers cheap seafood and delicious *piadina.* Closer to the beach is the **STANDA Supermarket,** Via Vespucci, 133 (open Mon.-Sat. 8:30am-11pm, Sun. 9am-11pm, MC, Visa), or **Margherita supermarket,** Viale Triest, 34. (Open Mon.-Wed. and Fri. 7:30am-1pm and 5-8pm, Thurs. 7:30am-1pm.)

Mensa Dopolavoro Ferroviario, Viale Roma, 70 (tel. 553 88). Near the train station, to the left off Via Dante and down a driveway. Food is fresh and service friendly. *Primi* L4100, *secondi* L6100, *menù* L12,000. Menu changes daily. Open Mon.-Sat. 11am-3pm and 6-10pm.

Ristorante/Pizzeria Pic Nic, Via Tempio Malatestiano, 30 (tel. 219 16), off Via IV Novembre at the *tempio.* Huge buffet overflowing with gourmet specialties. *Primi* L7000-9000, *secondi* from L7500. Mozzarella blankets the homemade *lasagne al forno* (L7000). Try the *pizza bianco verde,* a fire-baked cheese and herb delight (L8000). Cover L2000. Open Wed.-Mon. noon-3pm and 7pm-1am.

Gelateria Nuovo Fiore, Viale Vespucci, 7 (tel. 236 02), and a 2nd location at Viale Vespucci, 85. Endless flavor selection. Cones L2000-4000. House *aperitivo* L4000. Open March-Oct. daily 8am-3am; Jan.-Feb. Sat.-Sun. 8am-3am.

SIGHTS

Any tour of Rimini's historic center should begin with the Renaissance **Tempio Malatestiano** on Via IV Novembre (tel. 511 30). The church was originally constructed in Franciscan Gothic style; however, in the 1440s the ruling Sigismondo Malatesta ("Sigmund Headache") modestly transformed the church into a classical monument to himself and his fourth wife, the lovely Isotta. Ironically, Sigismondo Malatesta was canonized to hell by the papacy (a privilege unique in history) as a heretic guilty of "murder, violation, adultery, incest, sacrilege, perjury so dissolute that he raped his daughters and sons-in-law and as a boy often acted as the female partner in shameful loves, and later forced men to act as women." But Siggy was also a soldier and patriot who ruled Rimini at its height (1417-1468) and employed such artists as Piero della Francesca and Leon Battista Alberti, who designed the exterior of the new church.

Alberti modeled the front of the temple after the Roman Arch of Augustus, which still stands at the gates of Rimini (see below). The two front arches, originally intended to hold the sarcophagi of Sigismondo and Isotta, are now filled with limestone. The large single-aisled interior and wooden-trussed roof recall the temple's original Franciscan design space. The sprightly sculptures and reliefs in almost every chapel are the creations of Agostino di Duccio. (Open daily 7am-noon and 3-7pm.)

A short distance from the temple, **Piazza Tre Martiri,** named after three partisans hanged by the Fascists in 1944, forms the ramshackle, noisy city center on the site of the Roman forum. The most striking vestige of Rimini's former glory is the **Arch of Augustus,** at the end of Corso d'Augusto. The oldest Roman triumphal arch (27 BC), it blends the architectural elements of arch, column, and medallion.

Rimini's medieval center and favorite hangout, **Piazza Cavour,** off Corso d'Augusto, contains one of the oddest ensembles of buildings in Italy. The tall Renaissance arcade of the **Palazzo Garampi** contrasts dramatically with the adjoining fortress-like **Palazzo dell'Arengo** (1207) and the smaller **Palazzo del Podestà** (1334). Between the first two buildings is an Italian version of Brussels's famous *le pisseur.* Perpendicular to the Municipal building, the pink brick **Teatro Comunale** (1857), an auditorium destroyed by a bomb in WWII, completes a second side of the square. On the third side, a motley collection of shops, bars, and offices surround the Renaissance entrance to the **fish market.** Four stone dolphins in the corners of the market once filled the small canals (still visible under the benches) with water used to clean the fish. In addition, two curious sculptures pose in the center of the *piazza:* an eccentric, moss-encrusted fountain (1543), engraved with an inscription recalling the presence of Leonardo da Vinci, and a seated, sumptuously garbed Pope Paul V (1614) brandishing ferocious eagles.

Also worth seeing is the old fortress, **Rocca Malatestiana,** built by Sigismondo between 1437 and 1446 (behind the Communal Theater). Inside is the new **Museo Dinz Rialto** (tel. 239 22), a museum of ethnology with educational exhibits on aboriginal cultures, focusing on Africa and Polynesia. (Open Mon.-Sat. 8am-1pm; Fri.-Sat. also 4-6pm. Admission L4000, children/students L2000.) One noteworthy church is the **Church of Sant'Agostino;** its choir holds a great cycle of Gothic frescoes. The **Museo Civico,** Via Gambalunga, 27 (tel. 70 43 25), displays a collection of Roman mosaics and early Italian paintings, highlighted by Giovanni Bellini's *Dead Christ with Four Angels.* (Museum open Tues.-Sun. 8:30am-1pm and 3:30-8:30pm; Sept.-June Mon.-Sat. 8am-1pm. Admission L4000, children/students L2000.)

ENTERTAINMENT

Don't be too flattered by Rimini's roving photographers offering "modeling deals"—attractive as you may be, it's actually a ploy aimed to get tourists to buy photos. A picture may be worth a thousand words, but it's not worth your *lire*...

Rimini is notorious throughout Europe for its sleazy pickup scene. *Passeggiata* is a euphemism for the wild cruising you can witness nightly along the *lungomare* spanning **Viale Amerigo Vespucci** and **Viale Regina Elena.** The *discoteche* in Rimini are among the largest and most dazzling on the continent, and there are literally hundreds to choose from. Rimini has instituted a **Blue** and **Red Line** bus service (L3000 per night, L12,000 per week) that runs from mid-July to August for carless disco-goers. The blue line originates at the station and travels between the beach towns nearby (2-5:30am, every 40min.) and the red line originates in P. Kennedy (10pm-5am, every hr.) and runs to all the clubs within Rimini. Also in P. Kennedy is the "Night Office," an information service located in a double-decker bus, open nightly in the summer from 9pm to 3am.

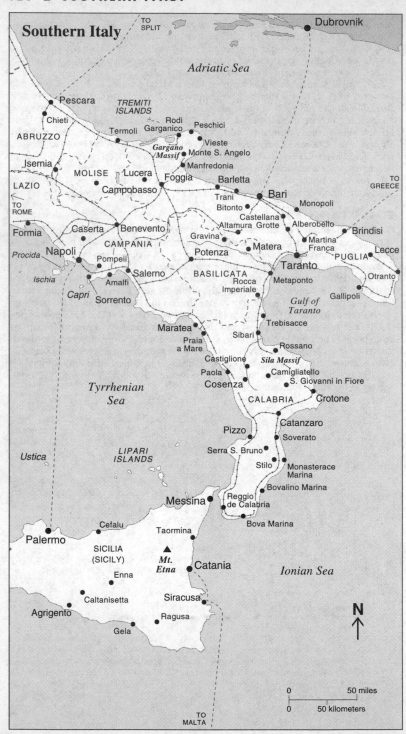

Southern Italy

TO
SPLIT

Adriatic Sea

Dubrovnik

Pescara

TREMITI
ISLANDS

Chieti

Rodi
Garganico

Peschici

ABRUZZO

Termoli

Vieste

*Gargano
Massif*

Monte S. Angelo

Isernia

Manfredonia

MOLISE

Lucera

Foggia

Barletta

TO
GREECE

LAZIO

Campobasso

Trani

Bari

TO
ROME

Bitonto

Monopoli

Formia

Caserta

Benevento

Castellana
Grotte

Alberobello

CAMPANIA

Altamura

Martina
Franca

Brindisi

Procida

Napoli

Pompeii

Gravina

Matera

PUGLIA

Lecce

Ischia

Potenza

BASILICATA

Taranto

Otranto

Capri

Salerno

Amalfi

Rocca
Imperiale

Metaponto

Gallipoli

Sorrento

*Gulf of
Taranto*

Maratea

Trebisacce

Praia
a Mare

Sibari

*Tyrrhenian
Sea*

Castiglione

Sila Massif

Rossano

Paola

Camigliatello

Cosenza

S. Giovanni in Fiore

CALABRIA

Crotone

Pizzo

Catanzaro

*LIPARI
ISLANDS*

Soverato

Serra S. Bruno

Ustica

Stilo

Monasterace
Marina

Bovalino Marina

Messina

Reggio
de Calabria

Palermo

Cefalu

Taormina

Bova Marina

SICILIA
(SICILY)

▲
*Mt.
Etna*

Catania

Ionian Sea

Enna

Caltanisetta

Siracusa

Agrigento

Ragusa

Gela

N
↑

| 0 | | 50 miles |
| 0 | | 50 kilometers |

TO
MALTA

SOUTHERN ITALY

◼ Campania

In the shadow of Mount Vesuvius, the fertile crescent of Campania cradles the Bay of Naples and the larger Gulf of Salerno. Looking out from Naples, the region's chief port and capital, Charles Dickens observed, "The fairest country in the world is spread about us." Justly famous for its rising cliffs and lush vegetation, the pleasure-island of Cápri draws wallets both thick and thin. For a less-touristed island adventure, head for Procida and Ischia. If you're more historically inclined, step back through the centuries with a visit to the archaeological sites of Pompeii and Herculaneum. Or escape the crowds in some out-of-the-way towns of the stunning Amalfi Coast, or at the temple ruins in Paestum.

◼◼◼ NAPLES (NAPOLI)

Don't believe everything you hear about Naples; it's *not* that bad. True, the markets are mile-long hordes of crazed shoppers and shouting merchants, traffic jams follow one after the other like recurring nightmares, stoplights are regarded as optional, and mopeds race down the sidewalk almost as often as down the street. But somehow Neapolitans thrive on this chaos. The city has a vitality that can be seen at the street markets off Piazza Dante and tasted in the world's best pizza. Superb art and archaeological museums and wonderful Renaissance and baroque churches reward your patience with Naples' rough edges. In 1994 Naples hosted G7, a meeting of the world's seven industrialized nations. Not only did the city clean itself up for its guests, but it also saw itself for the first time as a proud player in the modern world.

GETTING IN AND OUT OF NAPLES

> Hitching in and around Naples is extremely risky.

Naples is southern Italy's transportation hub: frequent **trains** from the Stazione Centrale connect the city to Italy's other major cities, including the port of Brindisi on the Rome-Lecce line (where the ferries to Greece accept Eurailpasses). **Ferries and hydrofoils** run from Naples' Molo Beverello to the islands of Cápri, Ischia, and Procida. The tourist office brochure *Qui Napoli* and the newspaper *Il Mattino* both carry up-to-date ferry schedules. There are also connections to Sardinia and Sicily. Hydrofoils (Alilauro and SNAV) leave the port of Mergellina for the islands and Sorrento. Ferry schedules and prices change constantly, so it's best to check ahead. At both ports, large signs clearly show the departures of the several lines.

Ferries: Companies' prices differ minimally; those listed apply in high season.
   Caremar (tel. 761 36 88), ticket office on Molo Beverello open daily 6am-11pm. Hydrofoils and ferries To: **Cápri,** 4 per day, 70min., L8800; **Ischia,** 9 per day, 70min., L8800; **Procida,** 6 per day, 1hr., L7500. Less frequent in off-season.
   Siremar Lines (tel. 761 36 88), tickets at Molo Angioino next door to Molo Beverello (open Mon.-Sat. 8:30am-1:30pm and 2:30-5:30pm; also open daily 5:30-9pm to buy tickets for that day). Ferries leave at 9pm from the Molo Angioino at the Stazione Marittima Thurs.-Tues.; June 1-15 Mon., Thurs., and Sat.; Sept. 25-May 31 Tues. and Fri. To: **Stromboli** (8hr., L72,300), **Lipari** (12hr., L70,000),

and **Vulcano** (13hr., L60,700). Fares quoted are June-Sept.; at other times they will be somewhat lower.

Tirrenia Lines (tel. 761 36 88 or 720 15 13), at Molo Angioino, Stazione Marittima. Ticket office open Mon.-Sat. 8:30am-1:30pm and 2:30-7pm; also open daily 5:30-8pm to buy tickets for that day. To: **Palermo** at 8pm (11hr., L69,100). L2000 port tax on entering and leaving Palermo; **Cagliari** Oct.-May Thurs. at 7:15pm, June-Sept. at 5:30pm (16hr., L65,000).

Trains: Information (tel. 553 41 88); phone lines are usually busy. Ticket prices and schedules in English and Italian. Also **information booths** and *Digiplan* machines at Stazione Centrale. Telephone service and info booths open daily 7am-9pm. To: Milan (8hr.; L61,800, express L83,700), Rome (1-2 per hr.; 2½hr.; L17,200), Syracuse (9hr.; L51,200, express L70,600), Brindisi (6½hr., L29,800).

Flights: Aeroporto Capodichino, Viale Umberto Maddalena (tel. 709 28 00, departures 780 32 35, arrivals 780 30 49), NW of the city. Take bus #14 from P. Garibaldi in the city center, or call for info on the airport shuttle (tel. 531 17 06). A taxi from P. Dante should be L25,000 with L1500 airport surcharge. Connections to all major Italian and European cities. **Alitalia,** Via Medina, 41/42 (tel. 542 51 11), off P. Municipio. Open Mon.-Fri. 8:45am-5:30pm. **TWA,** Via Partenope, 23 (tel. 764 58 28). Doesn't handle flights from Naples, but covers Rome and other airports. Open Mon.-Fri. 9am-5:30pm. **British Airways,** in the airport (tel. 780 30 87) and Via Partenope, 31 (tel. 764 55 50). Daily flights to London. Open Mon.-Fri. 9am-1pm and 2-5:30pm.

TRANSPORTATION WITHIN NAPLES

Taxis: (tel. 556 44 44), no English spoken. Be sure to take only taxis with meters. L4000 plus L100 per 100m or 25sec. (Minimum L6000.) Sun. and holidays L2000 supplement; 10pm-7am L3000 supplement. L500 per piece of luggage. To the airport should be about L25,000 with a L1500 airport surcharge.

Car Rental: Avis, at Stazione Centrale (tel. 28 40 41). Open Mon.-Fri. 8am-1pm and 3-7:30pm, Sat. 8:30am-1pm and 4-6pm. A small car that fits 5 tightly will be about L151,000 per day, L600,000 per week. **Hertz,** P. Garibaldi, 69 (tel. 20 62 28) rents small cars at L111,000 per day and L550,000 per week. Open Mon.-Fri. 8am-1pm and 2-7pm, Sat. 8am-noon.

Public transportation: The system in Naples has been standardized so that one ticket is valid for all modes of transport: bus, train, *metropolitana*, and funiculars up to the hills (the Vomero area). Tickets are available in 2 types, 1 valid for1½hr. (L1200), and the other for the entire day (L4000). City buses congregate in P. Garibaldi outside the train station, and all stops have signs indicating their routes and destinations. To cover long distances (i.e., from Mergellina to the station), use the efficient and cool subway, tram #4. Three high-speed **local trains** head to the outlying suburbs and towns: the **Circumvesuviana** (tel. 779 24 44), to Herculaneum, Pompeii, and Sorrento; the **Cumana** (tel. 551 33 28) to Pozzuoli and Baia; and the **Circumflegrea** (tel. 551 33 28) to Cuma. The Circumvesuviana starts at the Stazione Centrale (one floor underground), while the other two begin at the Montesanto station by the subway stop.

Buses #150 and 104: From P. Garibaldi to the center of the city, P. Municipio, and onward to the bay (Riviera di Chiaia) and Mergellina (for the youth hostel and Pozzuoli).

Trams #1 and 4: From the station to Mergellina. Stops at the Molo Beverello port. Hop on in front of the Garibaldi statue near Stazione Centrale.

Metropolitana: The subway system is convenient from the train station to points west: P. Cavour (Museo Nazionale), Montesanto (*Cumana, Circumflegrea,* funicular), P. Amedeo (funicular to Vomero), Mergellina, and Pozzuoli. Go to platform #4, 1 floor underground, at Stazione Centrale.

Funiculars: connecting the lower city to the Vomero and S. Martino. **Centrale,** the most frequently used, from P. Fugo on Via Roma/Toledo; **Montesanto** from P. Montesanto; **Chiai** from P. Amedeo. They run Mon.-Sat. every 15min. 7am-10pm, Sun. reduced service 8am-7pm.

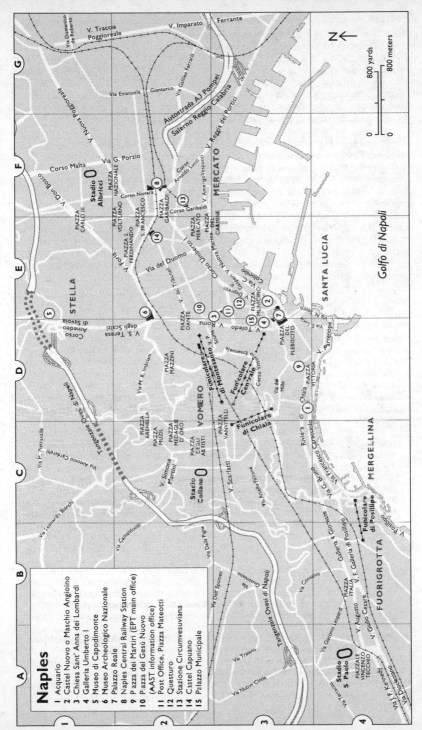

Naples

1 Acquario
2 Castel Nuovo o Maschio Angioino
3 Chiesa Sant' Anna dei Lombardi
4 Galleria Umberto I
5 Museo di Capodimonte
6 Museo Archeologico Nazionale
7 Palazzo Reale
8 Naples Central Railway Station
9 Pazza dei Martiri, Piazza Mateotti
10 Pazza del Gesù Nuovo
    (AAST Information office)
11 Post Office, Piazza Mateotti
12 Questuro
13 Stazione Circumvesuviana
14 Castel Capuano
15 Palazzo Municipale

800 yards
800 meters

Golfo di Napoli

NAPLES

CRIME

Neapolitans' vivacity and unruliness often seem to transform the city into an anarchical landscape of haggling market crowds, hell-bent motor vehicles, and volatile youngsters known as *scugnizzi*. Like its *scugnizzi*, Naples possesses an unkempt and dangerous charm that is often difficult to appreciate, especially for those who fall prey to *lo scippo* (petty thievery). Naples is neither more dangerous nor more crime-ridden than most other large European cities, but don't make yourself a target for crime: follow common sense safety rules warranted by large cities, and review the Safety and Security (page 20) and Women Travelers (page 33) sections.

ORIENTATION AND PRACTICAL INFORMATION

Immense **Piazza Garibaldi**, on the east side of Naples, contains the central train station and the major city bus terminal. Broad, tree-lined **Corso Umberto I** leads southwest from P. Garibaldi, ending at **P. Bovio.** From here Via Depretis branches to the left, leading to P. Municipio and nearby **P. del Plebiscito,** an area of stately buildings and statues. On the water at the foot of P. Municipio lie **Molo Beverello** and the **Stazione Marittima,** the point of departure for ferries. Turn right from P. del Plebiscito and go up **Via Toledo** (also called **Via Roma**) through the old quarter and to **Piazza Dante,** the **university district,** and Spaccanapoli (literally "splitting Naples"), a straight, narrow street whose name changes every few blocks. Lined with palaces and churches, Spaccanapoli follows the course of the ancient Roman road through the middle of historic Naples. (Be careful you don't get yourself *spaccato* by the hordes of youngsters on mopeds who use this alley as a racecourse.) Along the coast past P. Plebiscito, you'll find the **Santa Lucia** and **Mergellina** districts and the public gardens, **Villa Comunale.** Farther west are the most scenic areas of Naples: hillside **Via Posillipo** (older than the old quarter), **Via Petrarca** winding up above Mergellina, and **Via Manzoni** running along the crest of the ridge. A park crowns the cliffs of panoramic **Capo di Posillipo.** The hilltop **Vomero** district above Santa Lucia commands a view of Mount Vesuvius to the east, historic Naples below, and the Campi Flegrei (Phlegraean Fields) to the west. The Vomero can be reached by funicular from Via Roma/Toledo or the Montesanto station (northwest of P. Dante).

If you plan to be in town for a few days, either invest in a detailed city map from a *tabacchi* (about L6000) or pick up either of the two available tourist maps from a tourist office.

Tourist Offices: EPT, at the central train station (tel. 26 87 79). Helpful, almost to a fault—you'll have to wait as they exhaustively help the people in front of you. They'll also call hotels and ferries. Pick up a map and the indispensable guide *Qui Napoli,* featuring everything from train schedules to entertainment listings (in English and Italian). English spoken. Open Mon.-Sat. 8am-8pm. **Main office,** P. Martiri, 58, Scala B, 2nd floor (tel. 40 53 11), inside Ferragamo's *palazzo.* Take bus #150. Open Mon.-Fri. 8:30am-2:30pm. Also at Stazione Mergellina (tel. 761 21 02) and the airport (tel. 780 57 61). In theory open Mon.-Fri. 8:30am-2pm and 5-7:30pm. **AAST,** P. Gesù Nuovo (tel. 552 33 28). Take bus #185 up Via Roma toward P. Dante, get off at Via Capitelli, and follow it to the *piazza*—right in front of the Chiesa del Gesù Nuovo. Helpful and professional. Open Mon.-Sat. 9am-7pm, Sun. 9am-2pm. **Other offices** at Castel dell'Ovo (tel. 764 56 88) and the Palazzo Reale (tel. 41 87 44), both open daily 9am-2pm. For specific info on arts and entertainment, check out the *Posto Unico,* a poster/calendar covering theaters, restaurants, and clubs. **Qui Napoli Computer Information,** with multilingual terminals located throughout the city in public buildings and sights, offers tourist info and more.

Police: tel. 794 11 11. English speakers always available. **Ufficio Stranieri,** at the Questura, Via Medina, 75, off Via Diaz, helps with passport problems.

Post Office: P. Matteotti (tel. 551 14 56), on Via Diaz, which runs between P. Bovio and Via Toledo. *Fermo posta* L250 per letter retrieved. Offers special *EMS Servizi Postacelere,* which delivers packages anywhere in the world in 3 days (from L46,000 for packages up to ½kg). Open Mon.-Fri. 8:15am-7:15pm (EMS

only until 6pm), Sat. 8:15am-noon. Also at Galleria Umberto, 21 (tel. 552 34 67), and Stazione Centrale (tel. 553 41 21); both open same hours. **Postal Code:** 80100 (for *fermo posta* at P. Matteotti).
Telephones: ASST, at Via Depretis, 40, on the street off P. Bovio at the end of Corso Umberto; open 24 hrs. **Telecom (SIP),** at Via Petronio, 16, off Via N. Sauro on the water in Santa Lucia. Cards only. Open Mon.-Fri. 9am-noon and 4-7:30pm. Via Depretis office has the shortest lines. **Telephone Code:** 081.
Budget Travel: CTS, Via De Gasperi, 35 (tel. 552 00 74), near P. Bovio. Student travel information, ISIC/FIYTO cards, and booking service. Open Mon.-Fri. 9:30am-1pm and 3-6pm, Sat. 9:30am-noon. **Eurostudy Travel,** Via Mezzocannone, 119 (tel. 552 09 47; fax 551 16 42). Open Mon.-Fri. 9:30am-1:30pm and 3-6pm. **CIT,** P. Municipio, 72 (tel. 552 54 26), and at the Stazione Marittima (tel. 552 29 60). The city's most complete travel agency. Open Mon.-Fri. 9am-1pm and 2:30-6pm. For ferry reservations to Greece, go to **Travel and Holidays,** Via Santa Lucia, 141 (tel. 764 01 29), near P. Plebiscito. Take bus #150 from P. Garibaldi. Open Mon.-Fri. 9am-1:30pm and 3-6:30pm, Sat. 9am-1:30pm. **Italian Youth Hostel Organization (Associazione Alberghi Italiani per la Gioventù),** Salita della Grotta, 23 (tel. 761 23 46). An excellent resource for info on youth hostels and special HI and Transalpino plane, train, and ferry discounts. HI cards L30,000. Open Mon.-Fri. 9am-1pm and 3-6pm.
U.S. Consulate: (tel. 583 81 11 or 761 43 03; 24-hr. emergency tel. (0337) 79 32 84), on P. della Repubblica (sometimes called "P. Principedi Napoli" on maps) at the west end of the Villa Comunale. Passport and consular services. Open Mon.-Fri. 8am-noon; open 2-4pm for emergencies only. Bring proof of citizenship.
Currency Exchange: The few banks willing to change money are slow and charge L3000 commissions. Banks' main offices offer the most efficient transactions. Closest to the train station is **Banca Nazionale del Lavoro,** P. Garibaldi (tel. 799 71 13), at the corner of Corso Umberto. Open for exchange Mon.-Fri. 8:30am-1:30pm and 2:45-4pm. You can also exchange in Stazione Centrale, which has long hours but bad rates. Open daily 8am-1:30pm and 2:30-8pm.
American Express: The closest office is in Sorrento (tel. (081) 807 30 88).
English Bookstore: Feltrinelli, Via S. T. d'Aquino, 70 (tel. 552 14 36). Turn off Via Roma/Toledo onto Via Ponte di Tappia at the Motta restaurant. The store is 20m ahead on the left. An extensive selection, including yours truly. Open Mon.-Fri. 9am-8pm, Sat. 9am-1:30pm. **Universal Books,** Rione Sirignano, 1 (tel. 66 32 17), upstairs on the 1st floor, off Villa Comunale. Multilingual. Open Mon.-Fri. 9am-1pm and 4-7pm, Sat. 9am-1pm.
Luggage Storage: follow signs on ground floor of the train station. L1500 per piece per day. Open 24 hrs.
Late-Night Pharmacy: tel. 26 88 81, at Stazione Centrale in front of the Ferrovie dello Stato ticket windows. Open Mon.-Fri. 24 hrs. For Sat.-Sun., one pharmacy in the area stays open 24 hrs.; call 192 for a recording of the rotation (in Italian).
Emergencies: tel. 113. **Medical Assistance: Ambulance,** tel. 752 06 96. **Psychiatric First Aid:** tel. 743 43 43.

ACCOMMODATIONS

When you arrive at the central train station, hotel-hawkers will invariably approach you. If you do need to stay near the train station, and all you want is a cheap bed for the night, following one of them may be the easiest route. If you're planning to stay more than one night, however, seek out accommodations farther away from the station in a nicer section of town.

There are better alternatives in the area around the **university,** between P. Dante and the *duomo.* Hotels here cater primarily to students and offer well-furnished, clean rooms at low prices, though it's hard to find a room when school is in session. The **Mergellina** area at the far end of the waterfront (served by subway and trolley) has outstanding views of Vesuvius and Cápri, but hotels and restaurants range in price from expensive to exorbitant.

Some advice: although Naples has some fantastic lodging at great prices, be cautious when renting a room. Always agree on the price *before* you unpack your bags, never give up your passport before seeing your room, and be alert for shower charges, obligatory breakfasts, and the like. When selecting a place to stay, check for double-locked doors and door buzzers. The **ACISJF**, at the Stazione Centrale near the EPT (tel. 28 19 93), helps women find safe and inexpensive rooms. (Open Mon., Wed., Thurs. 3-7pm, Tues., Fri., Sat. 9:30am-1pm and 3-7pm.) Phone numbers are posted at the booth (or try tel. 40 41 28). For additional information on accommodations for women only, contact the **American Women's Club** (tel. 575 00 40). If you have a serious complaint, call the tourist office's **hotline:** 40 62 89. (English spoken.) For info on **camping,** check out some of the smaller towns in the Bay of Naples area, among them Pozzuoli (page 436) and Pompeii (page 445).

Ostello Mergellina (HI), Salita della Grotta, 23 (tel./fax 761 23 46). Take the *Metropolitana* to Mergellina and make 2 sharp rights onto Via Piedigrotta. Walk under the overpass and follow the signs up to your right (*before* you get to the tunnel), or tag behind the kid with the backpack. A 15-min. walk from the subway, and not far from the waterfront and hydrofoil port. Well-maintained 2-, 4-, and 6-person rooms, all with bath. Though there are 200 beds, it's best to reserve in July-Aug. Lockout 9:30am-4pm. Check-out 9am. Curfew 12:30am. L18,000 per person. Breakfast, sheets, and shower included. Private doubles L40,000. Self-service cafeteria downstairs offers à la carte items and full meals for L12,000.

Pensione Teresita, Via Santa Lucia, 90 (tel. 764 01 05). Take bus #106, 128, or 150 from P. Garibaldi. Cozy and secure inside. All rooms with TV, fridge, and telephone. Hall toilets and showers. Singles L35,000. Doubles L55,000.

Near Piazza Dante and Vomero

Take bus #185, CS, or CD from the train station to the bargain rooms around P. Dante. The area makes a great base for exploration of the historic quarter, although tourists should be cautious when wandering the narrow alleys alone or at night. To reach the chic Vomero, catch the *metro* to Montesanto and take the funicular up.

Soggiorno Imperia, P. Miraglia, 386 (tel. 45 93 47). From P. Dante, walk east through the arch to the left of the clock tower. Continue on Via San Pietro a Maiella, to the right of Pizzeria Bellini. Walk through P. Miraglia and look for two large gray doors on the right side of the narrow street. A 4-floor climb to bright, clean rooms in a 16th-century *palazzo*. Young, friendly management accustomed to working with students. English spoken. Singles L30,000, doubles L45,000. Call 1 or 2 days in advance during July-Aug. and at Easter.

Albergo Duomo, Via Duomo, 228 (tel. 26 59 88), near Via S. Biagio. Spacious white-and-baby-blue-trimmed rooms, all with TV and bath. Immaculate. Curfew 1-2am. Singles L60,000. Doubles L80,000. Triples L100,000. Quads L120,000.

Soggiorno Sansevero, P. San Domenica Maggiore, 9 (tel. 551 59 49), in Palazzo Sansevero. A small but charming hotel with large, attractive rooms, each named for a location or monument around Naples and decorated with a painting of that area. Prices for *Let's Go* users: singles with common bath L30,000-40,000; doubles L50,000, with bath L60,000; the luxurious room with bath and fridge L80,000. Extra beds L15,000. Breakfast included.

Albergo Orchidea, Corso Umberto, 7 (tel. 551 07 21), scala B, on the 5th floor (bring a L50 coin for the elevator). Take bus # 150, 152, or 104 from P. Garibaldi to P. Bovio. On this noisy but safe *piazza* (the police station is around the corner) you'll find dazzling, high-ceilinged rooms with small balconies and great views. All rooms with private shower. Singles L60,000. Doubles L80,000. Triples L120,000. Quads L140,000. Prices lower Oct.-June.

Pensione Margherita, Via Cimarosa, 29 (tel. 556 70 44 and 578 28 52), on the 5th floor (bring a L50 coin for the elevator), in the Vomero outside the Centrale funicular station and downhill from the Montesanto station. Charges the lowest prices in this posh residential district. Well-kept rooms, some with terrace. The area gets noisy at night when Naples' drug-hippie crowd comes out to play. Curfew midnight. Singles L45,450. Doubles L80,800. Extra bed L28,280. Breakfast and showers (in hall shower) included (towel L1000).

Near Piazza Garibaldi

Although many hotels in the Piazza Garibaldi are worthy of your disdain, others are clean, safe, and even plush. Use caution and common sense when picking a hotel in this area.

Casanova Hotel, Via Venezia, 2 (tel./fax 26 82 87). Take Via Milano off P. Garibaldi and turn left at its end. Airy, clean rooms, knowledgable management, and a rooftop terrace with bar service. Some rooms with TV, fridge, and phone. Prices for *Let's Go* users: singles L22,000, with bath L30,000; doubles L42,000, with bath L55,000; triples with bath L75,000; quads with bath L80,000. Breakfast L4500. AmEx, MC, Visa.

Hotel Ginevra, Via Genova, 116 (tel. 28 32 10). Turn right immediately as you exit the station. Walk 2 blocks up Corso Novara, and take the 2nd right onto Via Genova. Pleasant, bright rooms and friendly management. (Call from the station at night and Alfredo will pick you up.) English spoken. Singles L36,000. Doubles L60,000, with bath and TV L70,000. Triples L80,000, with bath and TV L95,000. 10% discount with *Let's Go*. Breakfast L5000. Laundry service L8000 per load. AmEx, MC, Visa.

Hotel Ideal, P. Garibaldi, 99 (tel./fax 26 92 37), to the left of the station. Elegant, well-furnished rooms with TV and phone; modern and secure. English spoken. Prices with *Let's Go:* singles L35,000, with bath L45,000; doubles L50,000, with bath L65,000; triples with bath L75,000. Breakfast included. AmEx, MC, Visa.

Hotel Prati, Via Rosaroll, 4 (tel. 554 18 02; fax 26 88 98). From the far end of P. Garibaldi take Corso Garibaldi to the right to P. Principe Umberto. Well-decorated, once-elegant rooms with mini-balconies, phones, wooden dressers, tiled bathrooms, fridges, and color TVs. English spoken. Prices for *Let's Go* users: singles with bath L70,000, doubles with bath L90,000. L30,000 per additional person. Breakfast included. Lunch or dinner L22,000. Major credit cards and traveler's checks accepted.

Albergo Zara, Via Firenze, 81 (tel. 28 71 25; fax 26 82 87). From the train station, turn right onto Via Torino, then take the 1st left. Clean, old rooms, some with decorative ceilings. Cozy TV room. Singles, doubles, and triples L25,000 per person, with shower L30,000.

FOOD

Pizza, that world-famous concoction of crust, tomatoes, and cheese, was a Neapolitan invention. The unique combination of the skill of the *pizzaiolo* (pizza chef), sweet local tomatoes, fresh mozzarella cheese, extra-light dough, and a wood-burning oven yields an exquisite pie. Stands throughout the city sell slices of pizza fresh out of the oven for about L1000—they're popular late-morning snacks. (Try the stands around P. Capuana and P. Mercato, to the north and south of the train station.) Naples' most venerable (though not oldest) *pizzeria* is **Antica Pizzeria Da Michele,** Via Cesare Sersale, 1/3 (tel. 553 92 04), to the right off Corso Umberto not far from the train station. They only make the two most traditional types of pizza, *marinara* (tomato, garlic, oregano, and oil, L3000) and *margherita* (tomato, mozzarella cheese, and basil, L3500). (Open Sept.-mid-Aug. Mon.-Sat. 8am-11pm.)

Neapolitans love **seafood.** Fortunately for them, they do it well. Try the *cozze* (mussels) of the gulf in soup or with lemon, or savor *vongole* (clams) of all varieties, including razor clams and their more expensive second cousin, the *ostrica* (oyster). *Aragosta* (crawfish) is sweeter than lobster, and *polipi* (octopus) is one of the cheapest (and chewiest) sources of protein around. The city's most notable wines are *lacrime christi* ("Christ's tear"), which usually accompanies seafood, and the red *gragnano.*

Spaghetti, now an Italian staple, was first boiled in the pots of Neapolitan kitchens—and don't mumble any nonsense about Marco Polo and China to the Neapolitans if you want to stay on their good side. Today, Naples' most famous pasta dishes are the savory *spaghetti alle vongole* (with clams) and *alle cozze* (with mussels); both are served in their shells atop the pasta.

Naples' most beloved pastry is *sfogliatella*, filled with sweetened *ricotta* cheese, orange rind, and candied fruit. It comes in two forms, *riccia*, a flaky-crusted variety, and *frolla*, a softer, crumbly counterpart. The city's foremost *sfogliatella* producer is **Pintauro**, Via Roma/Toledo, 275 (tel. 41 73 39), near the Centrale funicular station, a tiny bakery that has been around since 1785. It sells both varieties, piping hot, for L1600 each. (Open May-July Mon.-Sat. 8:30am-7:30pm, Sept.-April Wed.-Mon. 8:30am-7:30pm.)

Have fun at Neapolitan **markets**. On **Via Soprammuro**, off P. Garibaldi, you can create your own repast from the street market's edible grab bag. (Open Mon.-Sat. 8am-1:30pm.)

The Via to Margheritaville

Pizza Margherita will be the most common pizza variety you'll see in Italy; sadly for you, it has nothing to do with tequila or Jimmy Buffet. This culinary tradition originated when the queen of Italy, Queen Margherita, visited Naples around the turn of the century. To honor her, a local *pizzaiolo* made her a pizza with tomato sauce, mozzarella, and basil—red, white, and green, the three colors of the Italian flag. *Buon appetito!*

Near Piazza Dante

The historic center around P. Dante, served by buses #185 and CD, shelters some of the city's most delightful *trattorie* and *pizzerie*. Amidst its narrow, winding streets hide gastronomical treats found only in Naples. You'll find some of the cheapest eats on Via dei Tribunali.

Pizzeria Sorbillo, Via Tribunali, 35. A tiny, hole-in-the-wall restaurant, and a testimony to Neapolitan pizza-making culture. The cheapest pizza in the area (from L3500). In summer, try your pizza with *filetto* (fresh tomato chunks) for L1000 extra. Beer L2000. Open Mon-Sat. 12:30-3pm and 7-11pm.

Le Bistrot dell'Università, Via Sedile di Porto, 51 (off Via Mezzocannone near P. Bovio). Relaxed, informal atmosphere draws a college crowd. You'll be hard pressed to beat their L11,000 lunch *menù* (excludes drinks). *Primi* from L4000. Open for lunch Sept. to mid-Aug. Mon.-Fri. noon-4pm. Sept.-June also open Wed.-Sun. 7-11pm with Colombian fare.

Pizzeria Port'Alba, Via Port'Alba, 18 (tel. 45 97 13), inside the Port'Alba arch on the left side of the P. Dante clock tower. Established in 1830, this is the oldest *pizzeria* in Italy. Try the *Port'Alba* with *frutti di mare* (L10,000), or the pungent *pugliese* (with strong onions, L8000). Cover for *pizzeria* L2000, for restaurant L2500. Service 15%. Open Thurs.-Tues. 9am-2am.

Trattoria Fratelli Prigiobbo, Via Portacarrese, 96 (tel. 40 76 92). From P. Dante, turn right off Via Roma at the Motta restaurant and walk 2 blocks. Dirt-cheap seafood *secondi* like roasted *calamari* (L6000). *Primi,* including *gnocchi alla mozzarella,* around L4000. Also has pizza (L4000-5000). Wine L2000 for a half-bottle. Open Sept.-early Aug. Mon.-Sat. 9am-midnight.

Gelateria Della Scimmia, P. della Carità, 4 (tel. 552 02 72). The bronze monkey that hangs on the storefront has come to symbolize superior ice cream and desserts. Try the *formetta,* an ice-cream sandwich with thin, crispy wafers—you pick the flavors (L2000). Cones L2500-4000. Open Thurs.-Tues. 10am-midnight.

Piazza Amedeo and Santa Lucia

Piazza Amedeo, with its own *metropolitana* stop, is a favorite hangout of Naples' chic youth. Along its scenic avenues, just north of the Villa Comunale park, you'll find several trendy *caffè* and pubs. Restaurant prices are high, but you can explore the streets for great finds.

Osteria Canterbury, Via Ascensione, 6 (tel. 41 35 84). Take Via Vittoria Colonna off P. Amedeo, make the 1st right down a flight of stairs, then turn right and immediately left. The best affordable meals in the area. The elegant interior, with lots of wood and fresh flowers, prepares your senses for a delicious meal. Devour the pilgrims' favorite *penne di casa Canterbury* (pasta with eggplant, cheese, and tomato sauce, L6000 in the afternoon, L9000 at night). Cover L2000. Service 12%. Open Sept.-July Mon.-Sat. 1-3:30pm and 8:30pm-midnight. AmEx, Visa.

Pizzeria Trianon da Ciro, Via Parco Margherita, 27 (tel. 41 46 78), off P. Amedeo. This stylish and modern place caters to a snobby crowd but has gained a popular following for its tasty large pizzas (L5500-10,500). *Pizza Trianon* is their hallmark, with 4 sections piled with eggplant, *prosciutto, ricotta,* peppers, and mushrooms (L10,500). Service 15%. Open Mon.-Sat. 10am-3pm and 6pm-1am, Sun. 6pm-1am. Reservations may be necessary Sat. nights. All credit cards accepted.

Mergellina

Take tram #4 or the subway to **Mergellina** (4th stop from P. Garibaldi, the 1st after the tunnel), southwest of P. Amedeo on the waterfront. It's an excellent area for informal but hearty Neapolitan dining. **Piazza Sannazzaro,** in the center of Mergellina, is famous for its many *trattorie,* which serve the beloved local *zuppa di cozze.* Via Piedigrotta and the surrounding streets also present affordable alternatives.

Pizzeria Da Pasqualino, P. Sannazzaro, 79 (tel. 68 15 24). Outdoor tables and amazing pizza (L4000-10,000). Terrific seafood and fried snacks. What's hot, Italian, mussel-bound, and will really spice up your evening? The *cozze impepata* (mussels in pepper broth, L8000) of course! Wine L3000 per bottle. Cover and service included. Open Nov.-Sept. Wed.-Mon. noon-midnight.

Vomero

A cable car up to Vomero brings you to the city's favorite culinary enclave. Restaurants are generally more expensive, but **Via Bernini** and **Via Kerbaker,** both off Via Scarlatti near the funicular stations, offer some reasonable *trattorie.*

Trattoria La Pentolaccia, Via Kerbaker, 124 (tel. 556 71 34). Enter around the corner at P. Durante, 1. A local favorite. Excellent house wines L4000 per liter. Go for the house fish specialty, *farfalle salmone* (L6000). Small but varied menu changes daily. If you liked Thumper in *Bambi,* you'll love him *alla cacciatore,* (L6500), Bunny-lovers can bottle for the *pasta e fagioli,* L4500. Cover L500. Open Mon.-Sat. 12:30-3pm and 8-11:30pm.

Trattoria da Sica, Via Bernini, 17 (tel. 556 75 20). Family-run with traditional Neapolitan fare like *vermicelli alla puttanesca* (pasta with tomatoes, olives, and capers, L6000). A local hangout. Excellent wines from L4000 per bottle. Cover L1000. Service 12%. Open Oct.-Aug. Fri.-Wed. noon-3:30pm and 8pm-midnight.

Osteria Donna Teresa, Via Kerbaker, 58 (tel. 556 70 70). Wonderfully homey atmosphere. Try the excellent *pasta al forno* (baked pasta, L8000). The specialty is *spaghetti alle vongole* (L10,000). *Menù* L18,000. Wines L3000 per bottle. Open Sept.-July Mon.-Sat. noon-3:30pm and 8pm-midnight.

Near Piazza Garibaldi

Tourist-ridden, expensive, and mediocre restaurants dominate P. Garibaldi. Fortunately, high-quality low-cost meals can be found on the side streets just off the *piazza.* These areas become seedy at night, so eat early.

Trattoria Da Maria, Via Genova, 115 (tel. 28 27 11), the 2nd right off Corso Novara. In a city where tradition, simplicity, and hospitality come first, Papà Riccio and his family have kept their small, unrefined *trattoria* true to the Neapolitan style. All pasta L5000-6000. The popular favorite is *penne "sciuè sciuè"* (L5000). *Secondi* from L6000. Local wines L5000-8000. Open Mon.-Sat. noon-3:30pm and 6:30-10pm. Closed Aug. 15-30.

Pizzeria Trianon da Ciro, Via Pietro Colletta, 44/46 (tel. 553 94 26), near Antica Pizzeria da Michele. From P. Garibaldi, follow Corso Umberto, take a right 200m down on Via Egizaca a Forcella, then a left at the 1st *piazza.* With marble tables and wood-burning ovens, this ancient *pizzeria* (the big sister of the one off P.

Amedeo) is just as famous as Da Michele down the street, and many prefer its larger and more innovative selections (such as *8-gusti*, a pizza divided into 8 differently flavored sections, L12,500). Pizzas L5500-12,500. Service 15%. Open Mon.-Sat. 10am-4pm and 6pm-midnight, Sun. 6-11:30pm.

Avellinese da Peppino, Via Silvio Spaventa, 31 (tel. 26 42 83). From the train station, take the 3rd left on P. Garibaldi. In a well-lit area. Locals and tourists dine at the outdoor tables, lured by tasty seafood dishes like *spaghetti alle vongole* (L7000). *Gragnano* wine L3000 per bottle. *Menù* L18,000, cover and wine included. Cover L1000. Service 10%. Open daily 11am-midnight.

Le Brace, Via Silvio Spaventa, 14 (tel. 26 12 60). Across the street from da Peppino. Another great option in a ramshackle neighborhood, hearty and inexpensive. *Primi* around L6000, *secondi* around L8000. Pizza 12" around, served all day, from L4500. Cover L1500. Service 13%. Open Mon.-Sat. noon-midnight.

SIGHTS

Although much of Naples is beautiful, interesting, and friendly, first-time visitors to the city are often deceived and disheartened by the unpleasant region around the train station. **Piazza Garibaldi,** locally known as the "Zona Vasta," is a confusing conglomeration of hotels, small bars, parked cars, buses, vendors, and black-market dealers. Naples' main artery, **Corso Umberto,** leading away from the *piazza,* is an impressive boulevard lined with beautiful cast-iron street lamps and 19th-century buildings that transforms into a transvestite strip at night. A couple of detours lead off the *corso* into the interesting alleys of old Naples.

Corso Umberto ends in **Piazza Bovio** at the 17th-century **Fountain of Neptune,** with a view over P. Municipio of the massive **Castel Nuovo.** Charles of Anjou built the castle in the 13th century to replace the waterfront Castel dell'Ovo, which was too susceptible to attack. The finely modeled central panel of the remarkable double-tiered **Laurana Arch** (1467), adorns the entrance and portrays King Alfonso I in his chariot. It is one of the earliest examples of Renaissance sculpture in the city, built to commemorate Alfonso's 1443 arrival in Naples.

Continue away from the station past P. Municipio to **Piazza del Plebiscito,** the most regal square in the city. It separates religion, as embodied in the neoclassical **Church of San Francesco di Paola** (1816-1831), from the state, the **Royal Palace** (1600-1602) on the opposite side. The church displays a dome modeled after Rome's Pantheon. (Open daily 7am-noon and 4-5:30pm.) On the second floor, the former royal apartments now house the **Palace Museum** (tel. 41 38 88) and the plush 18th-century **Court Theater.** Many of the rooms are decorated with tapestries, and the palace houses an impressive collection of Romantic paintings. (Palace and museum open Tues.-Sun. 9am-1pm, Sat. and Sun. also 4-7:30pm. Admission L8000.) In summer the palace holds occasional concerts; tickets begin at L4000.

Next to the palace presides the **Teatro San Carlo,** the most distinguished opera theater in Italy after Milan's La Scala. Its gray and white neoclassical façade dates from an 1816 rebuilding. Unfortunately, the theater itself is closed to the public except for shows. The ticket office is open Tuesday to Sunday 10am-1pm and 4:30-6pm when there is a performance. Opera season runs October to June; the cheapest tickets are L15,000, but this section is often sold out to season ticket holders. (Ticket office tel. 797 23 31, theater tel. 797 21 11.) Also neighboring the *palazzo* is the **Galleria Umberto,** a four-story arcade of shops and offices constructed between 1887 and 1890 in imitation of Milan's Galleria Emanuele.

Spaccanapoli (Historic Naples)

Beginning to the side of P. del Plebiscito and stretching through the heart of the city's historic district is **Via Roma,** first called Via Toledo by the Spanish and still occasionally labeled that way. At the corner of the small and busy P. Trieste e Trento, off P. Plebiscito, rests the Jesuit **Church of San Ferdinando** (1622). Inside, a lectern, fonts, and chairs bear the emblem of the king of Spain, and a Ribera painting of Sant'Antonio is tucked away in the sacristy. (Church open daily 8am-12:30pm and 4:30-7pm.)

From the church, walk up the street, angling to your right through P. Carità to reach P. Monteoliveto, where you'll encounter the unassuming **Church of Sant'Anna dei Lombardi**, a museum of Renaissance sculpture. Its most noted work, Guido Mazzoni's *Pietà* (1492), sits in the chapel at the end of the right transept. In the Piccolomini Chapel, to the left of the entrance, note the beautiful monument to Maria d'Aragona by Antonio Rossellino and Benedetto da Maiano. (Open daily 7:15am-1pm.) Walking up Calata Trinità Maggiore from the church, you'll reach **Piazza Gesù Nuovo.** On one side of the *piazza* stands the **Church of Il Gesù Nuovo,** erected between 1584 and 1601, with a dark pyramid-grid façade taken from a 15th-century Renaissance palace. Colored marble and typically florid Neapolitan frescoes adorn the light interior. (Open daily 7:30am-1pm and 4-7:30pm.)

On the other side of the square rises the **Church of Santa Chiara** (1310), one of the principal monuments of medieval Naples. It was rebuilt in the Gothic style after being destroyed by World War II bombings. The large, single-aisled apseless interior is literally littered with medieval sarcophagi and tombs. Behind the main altar stands the impressive multi-tiered tomb of Robert I of Anjou, who died in 1343. As you exit the church, head to the right to enter the **Convent of the Clarisse,** an oasis of serenity amidst Naples' chaos. Vine-covered walkways crisscross the courtyard bordered by columns and benches. (Church open daily 8am-12:30pm and 4:30-7:30pm. Cloister open Mon.-Sat. 8:30am-12:30pm and 4-6:30pm, Sun. 8:30am-12:30pm.)

Take Via Benedetta Croce off P. Gesù Nuovo to the **Church of San Domenico Maggiore.** A 14th century church with a 19th-century Gothic interior, San Domenico combines two styles: the pointed arches, windows, and the vaulted side aisles are Gothic, but the color and texture of the decor are strictly Neapolitan Baroque. The 13th-century painting that spoke to St. Thomas Aquinas, a resident of the church's adjoining monastery, hangs in the Chapel of the Crucifix (on the right side of the altar in the nave). (Open daily 8am-12:30pm and 4:30-7pm.)

Hidden on Via De Sanctis, a small side street off the upper corner of P. San Domenico Maggiore, is the **Cappella di San Severo.** The chapel, now a private museum, features several magnificent marble sculptures, including the Veiled Christ by Sammartino. Downstairs, check out the two truly grisly 18th-century corpses, one of them an obviously pregnant woman. One legend claims that the alchemist Prince Raimondo of the San Severos, who built the chapel, killed his wife and her lover by injecting them with a poisonous elixir that happened to preserve their veins, arteries, and vital organs. (Open Mon. and Wed.-Sat. 10am-5pm, Tues. and Sun. 10am-1:30pm. Admission a steep L6000, students L2000.)

Via Benedetto Croce, Via San Biagio dei Librai, and Via Vicaria Vecchia are just three of the names **Spaccanapoli** takes as it follows the course of the old Roman Decumanus Maximus. This is the heart of the old city, a narrow way enclosed by tall tenements and decaying *palazzi*. On Via San Biagio dei Librai alone lie the Renaissance **Palazzo Sant'Angelo** (#121), **Monte di Pietà** (Banco di Napoli, #114), and **Palazzo Marigliano** (#37). The street widens at intervals to accommodate churches and monuments. Via San Biagio ends at Via del Duomo, where you'll find the 18th-century **Church of San Giorgio Maggiore.** In the vestibule of its warm yellow interior stand the antique columns and walls of a 5th-century Paleo-Christian structure. Diagonally across from the church rises the beautiful Renaissance **Palazzo Cuomo** (1464-90). You can enter the foyers of most of these private palaces Monday through Friday roughly 9am to 2pm.

One block uphill, to the left on V. Duomo, runs **Via dei Tribunali,** possibly the most representative of all Neapolitan streets. Try to avoid getting run over in the tiny alley as cars and scooters race between palaces, churches, and *pizzerie,* while black-market cigarette dealers peddle their wares from roadside fruit crates (offering discounts to local priests and *carabinieri*). Take refuge from this mayhem just as Petrarch sought shelter from a terrible storm inside the 13th-century **Church of San Lorenzo Maggiore** on P. San Gaetano, to the left on V. dei Tribunali from V. Duomo. Boccaccio first met Fiammetta here in 1334, and recent excavations have revealed Greek and Roman ruins along with the tombs of Catherine of Austria and

Robert of Artois. (Excavations open Mon.-Sat. 9am-12:30pm. Free.) Grab a bite across the street at Pizzeria Di Matteo, a favorite hangout of students and Bill Clinton; as pictures lining the walls attest, he came here during his visit for the G7 conference in 1994. (Open Mon.-Sat. noon-3pm and 7pm-1am.)

Continuing down V. Tribunali past the Neapolitan Baroque **Church of San Paolo Maggiore,** built on the ruins of a 9th-century church that had, in its turn, been built on the ruins of a Roman Dioscuri temple, you will come to **Piazza Bellini** and the open excavations of the ancient Greek city walls, uncovered underneath the *piazza.* The revered shops of Naples' traditional artisans line Spaccanapoli and the surrounding alleys. Off the *piazza* of the church of San Domenico Maggiore at **Calace Strumenti Musicali,** Vico San Domenico Maggiore, 9 (up the stairs on the left of the courtyard on the 1st floor), mandolins, guitars, and other instruments are still crafted by hand with techniques passed down through the generations. (Open Mon.-Sat. 8:30am-6:30pm.) **Scultura Sacra Lebro,** Via San Gregorio Armeno, 41, a family operation, is one of the last to produce hand-carved and painted religious statues. (Open Mon.-Fri. 9am-1:30pm and 4-7:30pm, Sat. 9am-1:30pm.) The most endearing shop in Old Naples may be the tiny **Ospedale delle Bambole** (doll hospital), Via San Biagio dei Librai, 81 (tel. 20 30 67), near Via Duomo, founded in 1899. The mirthful shopkeeper is perfectly suited to his merciful calling. (Open Mon.-Fri. 10:30am-1:30pm and 4:30-8pm, Sat. 10:30am-1pm. Closed 3 weeks in Aug.)

Unlike the cathedrals of other Italian cities, Naples' **duomo** loiters on an obscure *piazza* (on Via Duomo, to the left from Via San Biagio). The church began as a 4th-century Paleo-Christian *basilica* and was rebuilt and consecrated in 1315. Although the façade is late 19th-century neo-Gothic, the cathedral retains its original doors. A baroque veneer covers the Gothic outlines of all the pointed arches in the interior, except in the two chapels decorated with 14th-century frescoes. Halfway down the left side, enter the **Church of Santa Restituita,** the first Christian *basilica* of Naples. Built in the 4th century, it preserves its ancient forms in the nave's columns and in a 5th-century baptistery (the oldest in the West), whose dome is decorated with a blue and green fresco (the entrance to the baptistery lies at the end of the right aisle). A beautiful 17th-century bronze grille protects the baroque **Chapel of San Gennaro.** Reputedly, relics of St. Januarius stopped lava from Mount Vesuvius at the gates of the city. A silver reliquary is stowed behind the high altar, bearing the head of the saint and two vials of his coagulated blood. According to legend, disaster will strike the city if the blood fails to liquefy at appointed times (the first Sat. of May, Sept. 19, and Dec. 16), when boisterous and confident crowds jam the *duomo.* Beneath the *duomo,* excavations have exposed remarkable vestiges of Naples' past; you can wander the remarkably intact Greek and Roman roads that run under the modern city. (Enter through Santa Restituita. L4000 ticket also allows entrance into the baptistery.) You can call for a special tour of the excavations (tel. 44 90 97; ask for Signor Amerigo). (Cathedral open daily 8am-12:30pm and 5-7pm. Santa Restituita and the excavations open Mon.-Sat. 9am-noon and 5-6pm, Sun. 11-11:45am.)

Continue up Via Duomo and turn left at Piazza Cavour to visit the must-see **Museo Archeologico Nazionale** (tel. 44 01 66), a world-class museum that houses many of the astonishing treasures of Pompeii and Herculaneum. Since few pieces are adequately labeled, you should pick up an English guidebook at the souvenir shop (L10,000), or leave your passport at the information desk and borrow a copy of the museum's own guide (available in English). You enter the exhibits through a main hall crammed with massive statues that foreshadow the tremendous sculptures of the Farnese collection, stored in the rooms to the right. The **Farnese Hercules** presents the tiny-headed hero at a rare moment of repose in his otherwise busy life, while the **Farnese Bull,** the largest known ancient sculpture, captures the uncontrollable power of the bull as it tramples Dirce (her punishment for mistreating Antiope, who stands by looking somewhat bemused). Upstairs on the mezzanine level, you'll find subtle, intricate mosaics from Pompeii, some of them made of *tesserae* (squares) so small you'd swear the work was a painting rather than a mosaic. Don't miss the fantastic marine life scenes, the tender *Portrait of a Woman,* and the famous wall-size **Alexander Mosaic,** which portrays a young and fearless Alexander routing a terrified army of Persians under the Great King Darius. Also check out the mind-blowing collection of paintings, small statues, and busts. The top floor houses an extensive collection of ancient ceramics—die-hard vase-painting fans should definitely pay a visit. Unfortunately, many of the museum's exhibits close at inconvenient times (i.e., when you want to see them). Groups are often allowed to visit the closed exhibits; check at the info desk about tours leaving at 10:30am, 11:30am, and 12:30pm. (Open daily 9am-7pm; Nov. 16-Aug. 14 Mon.-Sat. 9am-2pm, Sun. 9am-1pm. Admission L12,000.)

Santa Lucia and Mergellina

Walk along the bay in the late afternoon or early evening to see the Villa Comunale fill with locals taking their *passeggiata*. Via Sauro, in the Santa Lucia section, is the traditional place to watch the sunset. The 12th-century **Castel dell'Ovo** (Egg Castle; open for exhibits only), a massive Norman structure of yellow brick and incongruously converging angles, stands on the promontory of the port of Santa Lucia, dividing the bay into two parts. The nearby seaside rocks are loaded with sunbathers. To the west lies the **Villa Comunale,** a waterfront park dotted with sycamores and palms and graced by sculptures, fountains, and an **aquarium** (tel. 583 31 11). The oldest in Europe, this zoological institute features a collection of 200 species of fish and marine fauna native to the Bay of Naples. (Open June-Sept. Tues.-Sat. 9am-6pm, Sun. 10am-6pm; Oct.-May Tues.-Sat. 9am-5pm, Sun. 9am-2pm. Admission L3000.) A streetcar runs along the Riviera di Chiaia, where at #200 you'll find the **Villa Pignatelli,** one of the few verdant villa grounds left in the city.

At the foot of the hills of Posillipo, **Mergellina** affords the most celebrated view in Naples: climb Via Petrarca for a postcard-perfect panorama.

Vomero and the Hills

The breezy calm of the hillside residential district of Vomero is an antidote to the frantic pace of the rest of Naples. A full morning, or perhaps two, should be reserved for visiting Vomero's important historical sights, the Villa Floridiana and the Monastery of St. Martin. Funiculars to this area leave from Via Roma/Toledo across from the Galleria, from P. Amedeo, and from P. Montesanto.

The **Villa Floridiana** (entrance at Via Cimarosa, 77) crowns a knoll notable for its camellias, pine trees, and terrace overlooking the bay. The villa itself, a graceful white neoclassical mansion (1817-19), houses the **Duca di Martina Museum** (tel. 578 84 18), which contains porcelain, ivory, china, pottery, and a small group of 17th-century Neapolitan paintings. Surrounding the villa is a tranquil park. (Museum open Tues.-Sun. 9am-2pm. Admission L4000; under 18 and over 60 free. Park open daily 9am-1hr. before sunset—typically 7pm in summer and 4pm in winter. Free.)

The huge Carthusian **Certosa di San Martino** (Monastery of St. Martin) rises from a spur of the Vomero hill near Castel Sant'Elmo. Erected in the 14th century, it was remodeled during the Renaissance and Baroque periods. It now houses the **Museo Nazionale di San Martino** (tel. 578 17 69), documenting the art, history, and life of Naples from the 16th century to the present. (Open Tues.-Sun. 9am-2pm. Admission L8000; under 18 and over 60 free.) The **Castel Sant'Elmo,** begun in 1349 under the Anjou reign, provides a remarkable view from its ramparts. (Open Tues.-Sat. 9am-2pm, Sun. 9am-1pm. Free.)

The **Museo e Gallerie di Capodimonte** (tel. 744 13 07) occupy a restored 18th-century palace set in the sylvan hills north of the National Museum. Masterpieces and kitsch compete for attention along the walls; the former are usually on the second floor, the latter on the first. Among the many works are Massacio's *Crucifixion,* Filippino Lippi's *Annunciation and Saints,* Raphael's portrait of Pope Leo X and two cardinals, Michelangelo's stunning drawing of *Three Soldiers,* and two superb Breughels—*The Allegory of the Blind* and *The Misanthrope.* The museum may be temporarily closed; call before you trek out. (Open Tues.-Sat. 9am-2pm, Sun. 9am-1pm. Admission L12,000; under 18 and over 60 free.) Take bus #110 or 127 from

Stazione Centrale, #22 or 23 from P. del Plebiscito, or #160 or 161 from P. Dante. (Gardens around museum open daily 7:30am-8pm; off-season 7:30am-5 or 6:30pm.)

Down Via Capodimonte from the museum, head into the **Chiesa della Madonna del Buon Consiglio,** which Neapolitans refer to as "Little St. Peter's." Inside, in the third chapel on the left (the Chapel to the Duchesses of Aosta), resides a smaller (but still sizeable) copy of Michelangelo's *Pietà.* Outside under the portico sits a copy of his *Moses.* Outside the church, enter the 2nd-century **Catacombe di San Gennaro** (tel. 741 80 71), noted for their frescoed early Christian chapels. (Guided tours daily at 9:30am, 10:15am, 11am, and 11:45am. Admission L5000.)

ENTERTAINMENT

The monthly *Qui Napoli* and the weekly poster *Posto Unico,* both available at the tourist office, provide excellent info on happenings in Naples. Most of *Qui Napoli* is translated into English, including brief descriptions of the city's major sites and tour listings. *Posto Unico* publishes lists of films, *discoteche,* and clubs (in Italian).

Once famous as never-ending parties, Naples' religious festivals have become times of sales and shopping sprees. The city celebrates the **Festa di San Gennaro,** patron saint of Naples, on September 19. The festivals of **Madonna del Carmine** (July 16) and the **Assunta** (Aug. 15) culminate in spectacular fireworks displays. During Christmas, hundreds of crèches *(presepi)* decorate the city, and on Easter the town hosts a large parade.

Most of Naples slumbers at night, except for the Sunday evening *passeggiata,* when the Villa Comunale along the bay fills with folks taking in the cool air. The young elite strut their new threads around **Piazza Amedeo.** Via Posillipo beckons those who savor the smell of the sea (take bus #140 from P. del Gesù) and Via Petrarca is ideal for a romantic stroll (take bus #C21 at P. Plebiscito). Or join legions of amorous couples at the scenic park at Capo di Posillipo (take bus #140 to the end). While strolling Via Posillipo, sample an ice cream from **Bilancione,** Via Posillipo, 398/B (tel. 769 19 23), near P. San Luigi. It's a Neapolitan tradition. (Open Sept.-July Thurs.-Tues. 10am-11pm.)

Naples' nighttime hotspots include **Piazza di Spagna,** Via Petrarca, 101 (tel. 575 48 82); **Chez Moi,** Parco Margherita, 13 (tel. 40 75 26; take the *metro* to P. Amedeo); and the larger **KissKiss,** Via Sgambati, 47 (tel. 546 65 66), in Vomero. A respectable crowd frequents all three. They feature dancing Friday through Sunday starting at 10pm and charge a L15,000-20,000 cover. (KissKiss puckers up during the week as well. All open Sept.-July.) Ask around to get the latest on the club scene. **'A Canzuncella,** P. Santa Maria La Nova, 18 (tel. 551 90 18), plays Neapolitan music, while **Airone,** V. Petrarca, 123 (tel. 575 01 75), and its piano bar play host to a more mature clientele. Although Naples has no exclusively gay or lesbian clubs, **Bar Marotta,** on P. Vittoria, is a favorite local hangout, and **Arci Gay** (tel. 551 82 93) has free advice on nighttime hotspots and gay and lesbian nights at local clubs.

If you find the discos too pricey, check out **Piazza Bellini,** which closes to traffic on summer evenings. *Caffè* and bars set out tables, and young people fill the *piazza.* You don't even need to order a costly drink (beer L5000 and up) to sit down.

SHOPPING

Throughout the city, and particularly in the **Duchesca** region off Via Mancini near P. Garibaldi and the **Pignasecca** region off P. Carità, street markets peddle belts, radios, shoes, and other inexpensive items. Never buy electronic products here—even brand-name packages have been known to contain only bricks. As in all crowded areas in Naples, hold on tight to your valuables on Pignasecca's streets. (Markets are generally open Mon.-Sat. 9am-sunset; many close Tues. at 2pm.)

For those who feel more comfortable window-shopping at fancy stores, the main shopping districts center around **Corso Umberto, Via Roma/Toledo, Via Chiaia** near P. Trieste e Trento, and **Via dei Mille** in the Santa Lucia region. The most modern and expensive shopping district is in the hills of Vomero along perpendicular

Via Scarlatti and Via Luca Giordano. Two affordable clothing chains that sell contemporary Italian casual wear are Wiscky & Coca and Omonimo.

■■■ INLAND FROM NAPLES

CASERTA

There is little reason to visit Caserta, or rather, one very large reason: the magnificent **Palazzo Reale** (Royal Palace; tel. 32 14 00), locally referred to as the "Reggia." Upon leaving the train station (45min. from Naples, L3400), you will be unable to miss the palace, smack dab in front of your face. Commissioned by the Bourbon King Charles III to imitate Versailles, the enormous building has 1200 rooms, 1790 windows, and 34 staircases. Frescoes and intricate marble floors adorn the Royal Apartments. Pass through the three libraries with original manuscripts, and you will come to the *presepe,* an immense Nativity scene set in an Italian market. (Open July-Oct. Mon.-Sat. 9am-7pm, Sun. 9am-2pm. closes 1:30pm in off-season. Admission L8000.) Behind the Reggia are the vast **palace gardens.** If you like to frolic barefoot in the grass, this is the place to do it (but don't let the caretakers catch you): three km of lush green lawns, fountains, sculptures, and carefully pruned trees culminate in a 75-m man-made waterfall. If you don't feel like attempting the long walk, take the bus (L1500) or a romantic horse-and-buggy ride (price varies). Pack a lunch and a bottle of water, especially if you plan to walk. (Gardens open daily 9am-1hr. before sunset. Admission L4000.) If you happen to be around on July 26, catch the **Festa Sant'Anna,** when music and fireworks light up the town. The beginning of September brings concerts to Caserta Vecchia in a festival known as **Settembre al Borgo:** 20 nights of theater, comedy, music, and dancing.

If you're too tired after touring the palace to visit the gardens (or vice versa), stay at **Albergo Limone,** Via Verdi, 52 (tel. 44 35 04), to the right as you exist the train station. Rooms are clean and modern. (Singles with bath L40,000. Doubles L50,000, with bath L65,000. Triples L90,000.) Hungry after a long stroll in the park? **Farina R&V,** Via S. Giovanni, 7 (tel. 32 61 38), off Corso Trieste, offers *primi* for L3000-4000 and a complete lunch for L13,000. (Open Mon.-Sat. 8am-8pm.) **Tavola Calda Il Corso,** Corso Trieste, 221 (tel. 35 58 59), serves full meals with drink for about L18,000. (Open Mon.-Sat. 10am-midnight.) Caserta's **EPT** offices are located at Corso Trieste, 37 (tel. 32 11 37), at the corner of P. Dante, and in the Palazzo Reale (tel. 32 22 33). Pick up a brochure on the Palace. (Open Mon.-Fri. 8am-3:30pm.) Caserta's **postal code** is 81100; its **telephone code** is 0823. The **post office** is on Viale Ellittico, to the left of P. Carlo III in front of the train station. Telecom (SIP) **telephones** are at Via Roma, 53. **Avis Rent-a-Car** is in the train station (tel. 44 37 56). (Open Mon.-Fri. 9am-1pm and 2-6pm, Sat. 9am-2pm.)

BENEVENTO

According to legend, this town was first called *Maleventum* (Bad Wind), but after the Romans defeated Pyrrhus here in 275 BC, they decided it might be a "good wind" (*Benevento*) after all. Traces of the Roman Empire include **Trajan's Arch,** constructed in 114 AD and decorated with fine bas-relief, and the huge **Roman theater** from the 2nd century BC—one of the largest in Italy (admission L2000). The Church of S. Sofia (762), with an attached monastery, has been transformed into the **Museo del Sannio.** Displays include a large collection of archaeological remains from the area that date as far back as the Iron Age. (Open Tues.-Sun. 9am-1pm. Free.) Benevento can be reached by train from either Caserta or Naples. From the train station, head left on Viale Principe di Napoli, over the bridge, and left again on Corso Garibaldi (a 10-min. walk, or bus #1 (L800)). The EPT **tourist office** (tel. 254 24) hides in the far corner of P. Roma off C. Garibaldi. The office houses an amazing store of info on the town's monuments and on a few other cities as far away as Bologna. (Open Mon.-Sat. 8am-2pm and 4:30-8pm.) Benevento's **postal code** is 82100; the **telephone code** is 0824.

POZZUOLI

Albergo della Corte hides at P. Piano di Corte, 11 (tel. 548 19). Off C. Garibaldi, follow the narrow V. Bartolomeo Camerario (across from Banca di Roma). Luxurious and newly renovated rooms are L45,000 for singles and L70,000 for doubles, all with bath. Discounts for groups or extended stays. Near Trajan's Arch, **Ristorante e Pizzeria Traiano,** Via Manicotti, 48 (tel. 250 13), has scrumptious meals for about L22,000. (Open Wed.-Mon. 8am-1am.) Before returning to Naples, be sure to sample Benevento's *Strega* liqueur, appropriately named after the legendary powerful witches of ancient Benevento. The recipe is a centuries-old secret.

The surrounding countryside of steep hills, farms, and vineyards is similarly enchanting. Visit the village of **Montesarchio**, with its 15th-century castle, or **Sant'Agata dei Goti** and its Romanesque cathedral. (The bus terminal is on Viale dei Rettori.)

BAY OF NAPLES: CAMPI FLEGREI

The Bay of Naples originally served as a strategic trading port for the Greeks, who associated its westerly peninsula with the underworld. Hades didn't scare them off, however; the area is covered with imposing monuments from the earliest Greek colonies in Italy. The volcanic lakes and bubbling mud baths of the Phlegrean (Burning) Fields were later transformed into posh Roman baths: spas for Italy's elite. You can still visit the baths at Baia or see the area's impressive ruins at Cuma (Cumae)—though it might be more fun to swim at a local beach. Since the sights of the fields are spread widely throughout the area, you should allow a full day to see them.

■■■ POZZUOLI

Although somewhat shabby and neglected since an earthquake in 1980, **Pozzuoli** has several ancient ruins worth seeing. It is also the most convenient jumping-off point for the islands of Procida and Ischia, and home to the only good camping near Naples. The town is serviced by subway from Naples' Stazione Centrale (line #4, L1200) and by the Ferrovia Cumana train from Montesanto in Naples (southwest of P. Dante, L2000). The Ferrovia Cumana station is conveniently located on the port, while the *metropolitana* subway station is a 10-minute walk away. To get to the **port** from the subway, take Via Solfatara down a series of hairpin turns, then turn right on Corso della Repubblica and again on Via Cosenza. Grab a map and info on local sights at Pozzuoli's **tourist office,** Piazza Matteotti, 1A (tel. (081) 526 66 39), where V. Solfatara and C. della Repubblica intersect under a bridge (ignore signs pointing to the administrative office). (Open Mon.-Fri. 9am-2pm; English spoken.) **Traghetti Pozzuoli** (run by the parent company Linee Lauro) runs the most frequent ferry line to Ischia (18 per day in summer, 1½hr., L6500). **Procida Lines** runs (of course) to Procida (6 per day in summer, 1hr., L3500). Buy tickets at the *biglietteria marittima* on the port (tel. 526 77 36).

Pozzuoli's **camping** is the best in the area. Large and well-maintained, with a swimming pool, restaurant, and easy access to the Solfatara Crater, **Camping Vulcano Solfatara** (tel. 526 74 13), up Via Solfatara past the *metro* stop, is the closest to town. (During summer months, L10,500 per person, L6500 per tent; 2-person bungalows L70,000, 4-person bungalows L96,000. Open April-Oct.) If you prefer to stay in town and don't feel like another return to Naples, stay in one of the four rooms at **Il Capitano,** V. Lungomare Colombo 13 (tel. 526 22 83). (Doubles without bath L70,000. AmEx.) For cheap picnicking, stop at the **fruit market** on the port (open 7am-1pm). Or if you like seafood, grab a full meal at **La Lampara,** also on the port at Via dell'Emperio, 10 (tel. 526 37 62). Its well-prepared fish dishes (L10,000 and up) and pizza (L5000-13,000) are served at outdoor tables by the bay. (Open Thurs.-Tues. 12:30pm-1am. Visa.) On a hot day try the refreshing drink with a kick, *birra con menta* (beer with mint extract).

Pozzuoli's **Anfiteatro Flavio,** built under Vespasian from 69 to 79 AD, stands on Via Solfatara downhill from the subway station. Its unusually well preserved underground galleries and arenas display the complicated mechanics necessary for raising and lowering animal cages. (Open daily 9am-2hr. before sunset. Admission L4000.) The **Tempio di Serapide,** on the port, was not a temple at all, but an ancient city market that just happened to enclose a statue of the god Serapis. A strange form of volcanic activity, bradyseism, which causes slow earthquakes that can raise or lower the entire region by several feet over the course of a few months, has intermittently submerged, shaken, and lifted this site. With its puddles of water and eerie, half-submerged pillars, the marketplace looks like a miniature Atlantis just risen from the sea. From Via Solfatara, to the right of the subway station, snag any of the city buses going uphill to get to the still-active **Solfatara Crater.** Alternately, walk the easy (20min.) route uphill from the *metro* station to see the steaming fissures and bubbling mud. (Open 9am-1hr. before sunset. Admission L5500.)

■■■ BAIA AND CUMA

BAIA

By way of the Ferrovia Cumana (L2000 from Naples or Pozzuoli) or from any of the SEPSA bus stops located throughout Pozzuoli (L1500 by bus), take the 20-minute ride to **Baia,** known in ancient times as a hotbed of hedonism. Today, this untouristed *parco archeologico* replaces the frustration of Pompeii's crowds and locked rooms with some honest-to-goodness exploring. See the ruins of past glory at the recently excavated **Roman baths** (tel. (081) 868 75 92), one of the few extant ancient buildings where you can climb stairs to the second and even third floors. In one hall you'll see a misdirected tree growing down from the ceiling; two halls to the right rises the largest of the domes (22m in diameter). The floor is submerged in water, creating an eerie echo chamber that causes sounds to reverberate for several seconds. (Baths open daily 9am-2hr. before sunset (6:20pm in June, 3pm in Jan. Admission L4000.) A bit to the north is **Lake Averno,** a spooky haunt that Homer and Virgil described as the entrance to Hades. The castle off the point contains the **Archaeological Museum of the Campi Flegrei** (tel./fax 523 37 97), with sculpture and ruins from the area and a collection of ancient plaster casts of lost Greek sculpture. (Open Mon.-Sat. 9am-1hr. before sunset, Sun. 8am-2pm. Free.)

CUMA

Take the bus from Baia (every 20min., L1000 on the Napoli-Torregaveta line) or the Circumflegrea train from Naples (L2500) to **Cuma,** one of the most impressive sites in the Campi Flegrei. Cuma was the earliest Greek colony on the Italian mainland (founded in the 8th century BC), and the mother of Pozzuoli, Naples, and many cities of the Magna Graecia. Its highlight is the **Antro della Sibilla,** a long cave-gallery built for the Cumaean Sibyl, the most famous oracle west of Greece. In this great hallway, used as a pizza oven prior to its rediscovery in 1932, devotees (including the hero Aeneas) awaited the Sibyl's prophecies. Ascend the acropolis to the ruined **Temple of Jove** (take the steep stairs that tunnel up through the rock) which rewards the climb with a view of the curving coast. You may be able to sneak into the huge gallery underneath the promontory; it leads past subterranean cisterns to other ruins farther inland. The whole sprawling site requires at least an hour's visit. Bring a flashlight. (Open daily 9am-2hr. before sunset. Admission L4000.)

BAY OF NAPLES: ISLANDS

Lingering off the shores of the Bay of Naples, the pleasure islands of **Cápri, Ischia,** and **Procida** beckon the culture-weary traveler with the promise of beautiful natural

CÁPRI

sights and a variety of first-rate accommodations. Large **ferries** *(traghetti)* and **hydrofoils** *(aliscafi)* leave daily from Naples' Molo Beverello at the end of P. Municipio. (Take bus #150 or tram #1 or 4 from Naples' *stazione centrale.*) You can also head for the islands from Naples' Mergellina port or from ports in Sorrento and Pozzuoli (Cápri is not accessible from Pozzuoli, however). The route via Pozzuoli, accessible on Naples' Ferrovia Cumana (L2000), probably involves the least hassle for jaunts to Ischia and Procida.

■■■ CÁPRI

The Roman emperor Augustus fell in love with this fantastic island's beauty in 29 BC and swapped its more fertile neighbor, Ischia, for it. His successor Tiberius passed his last decade here in wild imperial debauchery, leaving several villas around the island. Today's visitors may seek a certain debauchery too, but in Cápri most seem content to pay top *lira* for mass boat excursions to the renowned Blue Grotto, and to gawk at the rich and famous in Cápri's town center, Piazza Umberto I. You might consider renting a moped on the mainland and bringing it to Cápri or Ischia on the ferry, since distances between sights, ports, and hotels are great. **Be sure to wear a helmet when riding a moped:** drivers in Cápri are kamikaze, and traffic rules are enforced. Those without death wishes will be well served by the efficient bus service.

For a more peaceful stay, get out of the port area; the island's remote areas are spectacular. **Anacapri,** literally "over Cápri," sits high on a plateau of **Monte Solaro** (589m). It is less frequented by daytrippers, and qualifies as a budget version of paradise, with many affordable lodging options. Due to the ever-present English- and German-speaking crowds, most residents of the island are trilingual and usually prefer to speak in English than to wait for your attempts at Italian.

ORIENTATION AND PRACTICAL INFORMATION

Most ferries dock at **Marina Grande** on the north side of the island, from which the **funicular** runs to **Piazza Umberto** in the town of Cápri (every 15min. 6:30am-9:20pm, L1500). Buses leave from town to **Marina Piccola** (on the south shore) and **Anacapri** (every 15min. 6:30am-1:40am, L1500). Expensive clothing stores and pastry shops crowd the narrow streets that radiate off Piazza Umberto. **Via Roma,** to the right, leads to Anacapri after winding up the mountain. The bus to Anacapri also follows this route and drops you in **Piazza Vittoria. Via Giuseppe Orlandi,** running in both directions from the *piazza,* leads to the cheapest and best establishments.

Tourist Office: in Cápri, at the end of the dock at Marina Grande (tel. 837 06 34). Open Mon.-Sat. 8:30am-8:30pm, Sun. 8:30am-2:30pm. Also in P. Umberto, under the clock (tel. 837 06 86). Open Mon.-Sat. 8:30am-8:30pm, Sun. 8:30am-2:30pm in the summer. In Anacapri, information office is at Via Orlandi, 19/A (tel. 837 15 24), off the main *piazza,* to the right as you get off the bus. Open Mon.-Sat. 8:30am-8:30pm, Sun. 10am-1pm; Nov.-May 9am-3pm.

Police: Via Roma (tel. 837 72 45). They'll connect you with an English speaker.

Post Office: central office in Cápri on Via Roma (tel. 837 72 40), a couple of blocks downhill from P. Umberto. Open Mon.-Sat. 8:15am-7:20pm. **Changes money** at the best rate in town. Mon.-Fri. 8:15am-6pm, Sat. 8:15am-1pm. L2000 commission, L5000 for sums over L100,000. Another office in Anacapri at Viale de Tommaso, 4 (tel. 837 10 15). Open Mon.-Fri. 8:15am-1:30pm, Sat. 8:15am-noon. **Postal code:** 80073.

Telephones: Telecom (SIP) (tel. 837 55 50), behind the funicular stop in Cápri. Open daily 9am-1pm and 3-11pm; Oct.-June 9am-1pm and 3-8pm. Public phones in Anacapri at P. Vittoria, 4 (tel. 837 33 77). Open daily 8am-10pm; Oct.-Feb. 9am-1pm and 3-8pm; March-May 8am-9pm. **Telephone code:** 081.

Currency Exchange: Cambio, Via Roma, 33 (tel. 837 07 85), across from the main bus stop in Cápri. Open daily 9am-9pm. Also at P. Vittoria, 2 (tel. 837 31 46),

in the center of Anacapri. Open March-Nov. daily 8am-6pm. Worse rates than at the post office but no commission at either location.
Buses: tel. 837 04 20. In Cápri, buses depart from Via Roma for Anacapri, Marina Piccola, and points in between. In Anacapri, buses depart from P. Barile off Via Orlandi for the Grotta Azzurra (Blue Grotto), the *faro* (lighthouse), and other points nearby. There's also a direct bus line between Marina Grande and P. Vittoria in Anacapri. Buses cost L1500 per ride; tickets available at *tabacchi* shops.
Ferries: Caremar runs ferries from Naples' Beverello port to Cápri (8 per day, 6:30am-7:40pm, last return 6pm, L8800) and from Sorrento (5 per day, 7:55am-7:40pm, last return 6:45pm, L5300). **Linee Lauro's** hydrofoil runs to and from Ischia once daily (L18,000).
Luggage Storage: Caremar ticket office (tel. 837 07 00) in Marina Grande, L2000 per bag. Also at the funicular in Cápri (L1500 per bag) and in Piazza Vittoria in Anacapri (L2000 per bag). Open daily 7am-7pm.
Public Toilets and Showers: (tel. 837 33 77), at the funicular in Cápri (L300) and at P. Vittoria, 5 in Anacapri (L300, showers L3000).
Swimming Pool: Bagni Nettuno, Via Grotta Azzurra, 46 (tel. 837 13 62), above the Blue Grotto in Anacapri. Take the bus from Anacapri center. Full use of outdoor pool, private beach, reclining chair, shower, and changing room in scenic cliffside surroundings for a special *Let's Go* price of L8000 per day (regularly L16,000). Open mid-March to mid-Nov. daily 9am-7pm.
Emergencies: tel. 113. **Hospital: Ospedale Capilupi**, Via Provinciale Anacapri (tel. 837 00 14 or 837 87 62), between Cápri and Anacapri. **Hospital Emergency First Aid:** tel. 837 81 49. For minor medical assistance in summer, call the **Guardia Medica Turistica** in Cápri (tel. 837 10 12).

ACCOMMODATIONS

Call in advance and confirm reservations—Anacapri is your best bet. It's possible to find impromptu vacancies in July, but not in August. Makeshift camping is illegal; heavy fines are strictly imposed. Don't be put off by the inconvenience: you won't want to miss this natural splendor.

Anacapri

Villa Eva, Via La Fabbrica, 8 (tel. 837 15 49; fax 837 20 40). Set high among the gardens and trees, this is the perfect vacation setting. A scenic 30-min. walk from the Grotta Azzurra and a 10-min. walk from P. Vittoria. Call from the port and the warm-hearted Mamma Eva or her husband Vincenzo will pick you up. Vincenzo built the beautiful rooms, bar, and swimming pool himself. They also provide a barbecue for your use. L25,000 per person. Private doubles L60,000, in low season L50,000. Group discounts. Call a few days in advance to confirm your reservations, especially in Aug. English spoken.
Hotel Caesar Augustus, Via Orlandi, 4 (tel. 837 14 21), another 100m past Hotel Lorelcy. It's difficult to dispute their claim to "most beautiful view in the world." Once the most expensive luxury hotel on the island, it still retains much of the luxury without the cost. All rooms with terrace and bath. L35,000 per person (July-Aug. L40,000) upon mention of *Let's Go*. Open Easter-Oct.
Il Girasole, Via Linciano, 47 (tel./fax 837 23 51). A great place for students and backpackers; comfortable terrace and adequate rooms. The management loves *Let's Go* and will probably ask you to send us a letter. Call from Marina Grande and they'll pick you up. Singles L35,000. Doubles L60,000. Triples L75,000. Quads L90,000. AmEx, MC, Visa.
Hotel Loreley, Via G. Orlandi, 16 (tel. 837 14 40; fax 837 13 99), 100m back toward Cápri from Piazza Vittoria. Large, bright rooms with baths. Singles L40,000, July-Aug. L80,000. Doubles L80,000, July-Aug. L130,000. Breakfast L5000. Open April-Oct. AmEx, MC, Visa.

Cápri Town

Pensione Quattro Stagioni, Via Marina Piccola, 1 (tel. 837 00 41). From P. Umberto, walk downhill 5min. on Via Roma. Turn left at the 3-pronged fork in the road and look for the 2nd gate on the left. Though hot in summer, the cozy

CÁPRI

flower-filled rooms are spotless and have sensational views. All rooms with bath. Prices for *Let's Go* users: singles L80,000; doubles L140,000. Breakfast included. 10-15% discounts Sun.-Fri. and during low season. Half-pension required in Aug., L100,000. Open March 15-Oct.

FOOD

Caprese food is as glorious as the panoramas from the island's cliffs. Savor the local *mozzarella* on its own, or with tomatoes, oil, and basil in a dish known as *insalata caprese*—considered by many the best summer meal in the world. The *ravioli alla caprese* is hand-stuffed with the tastiest of local cheeses. Don't miss the *torta di mandorla* (chocolate almond cake). Accompany meals with the local red and white wines, which bear the *Tiberio* label. Restaurants often serve *Cápri DOC,* a light white wine. If restaurant prices make you gasp, buy food from one of the groceries instead. Take the right prong of the fork at the end of Via Roma to reach **Supermercato STANDA** (open daily 8:30am-1:30pm and 4-8pm; July-Aug. 8:30am-1:30pm and 5-9pm). Ask at your hotel for local low-cost restaurants, but don't expect to pay less than L25,000 for a full meal.

Anacapri

Ristorante Il Cucciolo, Nuova Trav. Veterino, 50 (tel. 837 19 17). A preview of paradise, this restaurant is a wonderful stop on a walk back from the Grotta Azzurra and a must for guests at Villa Eva (only 5min. away). Follow the signs from the bus stop for Villa Damecuta. The fish is fresh, the herbs come straight from the garden, and everything is served on a terrace with expansive views of the bay. The *ravioli caprese* (L8000) and *agnolotti* (pasta stuffed with spinach and *ricotta*, L8500) are delicious. Cover L2600. Open March 15-Oct. 20 Wed.-Mon. noon-3pm and 7pm-midnight.

Trattoria Il Solitario, Via Orlandi, 96 (though the tile says #54; tel. 837 13 82), 5min. from P. Vittoria. An amazingly tranquil, ivy-covered hideaway. *Cannelloni alla caprese* L8000, homemade pasta L8000, salads L3500. Cover L2500. *Menù* L15,000. Open daily 12:15-3pm and 7pm-midnight; Sept. 21-June 19 closed Mon.

La Quercia, Via Migliara, 46 (tel. 837 37 20). Walk up the path to the left of the chairlift to Mt. Solaro. The restaurant is halfway on the 30-min. walk to the panoramic view from Belvedere Migliara. Near Il Girasole. Supreme view and divine seafood at reasonable prices. Open Wed.-Mon. noon-3pm and 7pm-midnight.

Pizzeria Aumm Aumm, Via Caprile, 2D (tel. 837 20 61). Lively crowd and excellent service. Wood-burning brick-oven pizza (L7000-14,000). Open 7pm-1am.

Cápri Town

Buca di Bacco, Via Longano, 35 (tel. 837 07 23), off P. Umberto I. Elegant yet affordable. *Pennette alla bacco* (L8000) is the specialty. Also pizza at night L7000-12,000. Cover L2000. Service 12%. Open Dec.-Oct. Thurs.-Tues. noon-2:30pm and 7-11pm. AmEx, MC, Visa.

Moscardino, Via Roma, 28 (tel. 837 06 87). Limited but excellent selection; maritime setting. Cover L2500. Service 11%. Open Tues.-Sun. 11am-3pm and 7pm-1am. AmEx, MC, Visa.

SIGHTS AND ENTERTAINMENT

There is no question about it: visitors to Cápri must see **Grotta Azzurra** (Blue Grotto). Light enters the cavern through a hole in the rock beneath the water, causing the whole grotto to glow a fantastic neon blue. Unfortunately, visiting the grotto is expensive if you want to stay dry: L15,000 plus tip for boat "tours" barely long enough to let your eyes adjust. Thousands of tourists each week find it worth the cost, but locals and the more intrepid visitors say the most impressive way to visit is to swim when the boats stop running (before 9am or after 6pm). Visitors who try this go with friends (for safety). You can get to the grotto by motorboat from Marina Grande (about L10,000) or by bus from Anacapri.

Leaving every day from Marina Grande at 9am, **boat tours** show you Cápri's coast from the most impressive vantage point for L18,000. There are several rock and pebble **beaches** around the island. Take a boat from the port (L8000) or descend north between vineyards from P. Umberto to **Bagni di Tiberio,** a bathing area amidst the ruins of an imperial villa. A bus or a 10-min. walk down the path (to the left where Via Roma splits into three) brings you to Marina Piccola, a gorgeous seaside stretch on the southern coast. Cavort in the clear water among immense lava rocks or rent a **kayak** or a **motor boat** (L8000 and L30,000 per hour respectively). Call Bagni le Sirene (tel. 837 02 21) for more info.

If you prefer the **mountains** to the sea, take Via Longano from P. Umberto in Cápri center and then make the trek up to the left on Via Tiberio to Villa Jovis (1hr.). This is the Roman emperor Tiberius's ruined but still magnificent **pleasure dome.** Legend has it that Tiberius tossed those who displeased him over the precipice; *Let's Go* advises walking down. (Open daily 9am-1hr. before sunset. Admission L4000.) The view of Cápri from the nearby chapel **Santa Maria del Soccorso** is unrivalled. On the descent along the path, a short detour takes you to the **Arco Naturale,** a majestic stone arch, off Via Matermania on the eastern cliffs. On a clear day you can see as far as Paestum through the weathered arch. The *belvedere* (beautiful view) from **Punta Cannone** shows off the dramatic cliffs of the southern coast. Cápri's tourist office offers suggested walking itineraries to see the less-touristed parts of the island.

Until the completion of the cliffhanging roadway a few decades ago, only a narrow Phoenician staircase joined **Anacapri** to the lower town. Upstairs from Piazza Vittoria and to the left (past Cápri's Beauty Farm) you'll find **Villa San Michele.** The lifelong work of Swedish author and physician Axel Munthe, it was built earlier this century on the site of one of Emperor Tiberius' villas. Henry James called it "the most fantastic beauty, poetry, and inutility that I have ever seen clustered together." The villa houses remarkable classical sculptures retrieved from Cápri's sea bottom where they were hurled after Tiberius' death, allegedly by the ghosts of his victims. (Open in summer 9am-6pm; winter 10am-3pm. Admission L5000.)

From P. Vittoria in Anacapri, take the 12-min. chairlift (round-trip L7000) to the top of **Monte Solaro.** (Open 9:30am-1hr. before sunset.) The view from the top is terrific: on a clear day, you can see the Apennines to the east and the mountains of Calabria to the south. A bus from the central *piazza* leads to the **faro,** Italy's second-tallest lighthouse, where you can snorkel, tan, or leap from volcanic rocks along with countless Italians. Call the Cápri Diving Club (tel. 837 14 40) for **scuba** lessons or to rent equipment. To reach the most inexpensive (but still expensive) tourist **shopping** on Cápri, follow the yellowish brick road of Via Orlandi off P. Vittoria.

Nighttime action doesn't come cheap either. The largest club in Anacapri is **Zeus,** Via Orlandi, 21 (tel. 837 11 69). Admission is L30,000, but passes from local hotels, including the ones we list, slash L10,000 (women often get in free). If you're looking for live music, try the nearby **Underground,** Via Orlandi, 259 (tel. 837 25 23).

■ ■ ■ ISCHIA

Across the bay from overrun Cápri, larger, less glamorous Ischia (EES-kee-yah) displays a variety of landscapes, including beautiful beaches, natural hot springs, ruins, forests, vineyards, lemon groves, and a once-active volcano. According to Greco-Roman mythology, the island is home to the giant Typhoeus, who responded to Jupiter's scorn with the fury of volcanoes; now he seems content to heat the hot springs of the many exclusive spas.

ORIENTATION AND PRACTICAL INFORMATION

The bus (route 1) follows the coast in a counterclockwise direction, passing most of the island's towns and points of interest. From **Ischia Porto** (an almost perfectly circular port formed by the crater of an extinct volcano) you come to **Casamicciola Terme,** with its overcrowded beach, and then to **Lacco Ameno**—the oldest Greek settlement in the western Mediterranean, now known for the island's cleanest boardwalk. The bus heads on to **Forio,** the hippest area on Ischia thanks to its tree-lined streets and popular bars.

Tourist Office: (tel. (081) 99 11 46; fax 98 19 04), at the mid-point of the main port. Open Mon.-Sat. 8am–8pm. Some English spoken. Has listings of local tours and can help with accommodations.

Buses: SEPSA, in P. Trieste, the main departure point (just off Ischia Porto). Buses leave every 30min. 5am-midnight; one-way (L1200). Morning (L2500), afternoon (L2800), and full-day (L4000) tickets are valid to destinations all over the island.

Ferries: Caremar (tel. 99 17 81) and **Linee Lauro** (tel. 837 75 77) have main offices right by the tourist office. Caremar is generally less expensive. Ferries to Ischia from: Naples (almost every hour 8am-7pm, L8800) and Pozzuoli (3 per day, L6500); Procida (8 per day, L3400). Linee Lauro runs from Sorrento to Ischia (L14,000) and connects the island to Cápri with a hydrofoil once daily (L18,000).

ACCOMMODATIONS

Hotels in Ischia run the gamut from reasonable to exorbitant. Most *pensioni* are in Forio; stay in Ischia Porto only if you don't mind the noise at night. By late July and August rooms are hard to come by without reservations made at least one month in advance. Few hotels offer singles, and since rooms are in such high demand, some hotel owners may not rent rooms for just one night. There are several good camping options to make the island easier on your money belt.

Forio

Pensione Di Lustro, Via Filippo di Lustro, 9 (tel. 99 71 63). Close to the beach. At first you might think you've mistakenly stumbled into botanical gardens—the central courtyard and stairs overflow with tropical plants. Large terrace provides gorgeous views. Truman Capote slept here in '68. *Let's Go* price: doubles with bath L80,000 in June; prices higher July-Aug. and lower in off-season.

Hotel Villa Franca and **Baia Verde,** Strada Statale 270, #183 (tel. 98 74 20; fax 98 70 81). Take bus #1, 1-bar, or C.S. from Ischia Porto and get off at the stop for the San Francesco beach. Two hotels with the same prices and the same management. Good for families. Well-kept rooms, many with terrace. A pretty patio, and 3 swimming pools: 2 cold mineral baths and 1 thermal bath. A 15-min. walk from the beach. English spoken. All rooms with bath. Singles L45,000. Doubles L80,000. Breakfast included. Half pension L55,000 for singles, L100,000 for doubles. Open March-Oct.

Casamicciola Terme

Pensione Quisisana, P. Bagni, 34 (tel. 99 45 20). Take bus #3 from the port to the *piazza*. Comfortable, family-run establishment with well-kept rooms. A 15-min. walk from the beach. Curfew midnight. Doubles with bath L56,000-64,000. In Aug. obligatory full pension L58,000-64,000 per person, depending on the room. Extra bed L20,000. Open May-Oct.

Ischia Porto

Il Crostolo, Via Cossa, 32 (tel. 99 10 94). From the bus station at P. Trieste, ascend the street and take a right at the top. Charming owner. Large terrace. All rooms newly renovated, with bath. L40,000 per person, L30,000 in off-season. Half pension required in July (L60,000) and Aug. (L70,000).

Albergo A. Macri, Via Iasolino, 96 (tel. 99 26 03), in a side street on the right as you come into the port, near the *traghetti* dock. Modern rooms far from the beaches. *Let's Go* prices: Singles L30,000, with bath L35,000. Doubles L55,000, with bath L65,000. L5000 more per person mid-July to mid-Aug.

Camping

The most economical source of accommodations. Two delightful campgrounds lie near Ischia Porto. Prices below are for high season.

ISCHIA

Eurocamping dei Pini, Via delle Ginestre, 28 (tel. 98 20 69), the quieter of the 2 camping sites, and a 10-min. walk from the port. Take Via del Porto onto Via Alfredo de Luca, walk uphill and take a right on Via delle Terme, where you will see the arrow indicating camping. L12,000 per person, L7000 per tent. 2-person bungalows with bath and kitchen facilities L65,000 (reserve ahead). The tent site is more scenic than the bungalow site. Open year-round.
Camping Internazionale, Via M. Mazzella (tel. 99 14 49), a 15-min. walk from the port. Take Via Alfredo de Luca from Via del Porto and bear right onto Via M. Mazzella at P. degli Eroi. (There are 2 Via Mazzellas, Michele and Leonardo, that run parallel.) Luxuriant foliage and tranquil surroundings. L14,000 per person, L10,000 per tent. Immaculate 2-person bungalows with bath L75,000, L15,000 per additional person. Bathless bungalows slightly cheaper. Open May-Oct.15.

FOOD

Ischia has numerous outdoor eateries and *alimentari,* and plenty of fruit vendors. **Emiddio,** at Via Porto, 30, is located right on the docks at Ischia Porto. Their *ravioli alla panna* (L6000) reign supreme. Other *primi* go for L4000-9000. (Open daily noon-3pm and 7pm-midnight. Cover L1500. AmEx, MC, Visa.) Or try **Ristorante Zelluso,** Via Parodi, 41 (tel. 99 46 27), to the left as you enter Casamicciola; look for the white sign and walk down the alley. The outdoor section is great for families or large groups. (Scrumptious pizza L6000. Cover L2000. Service 10%. AmEx.)

SIGHTS

Most visitors to Ischia go to the beach at **Citara** (get off at the Hotel Imperial bus stop past Forio), but for something new try **Sorceto** (on the far side of the island) which features relaxing hot springs. Beautifully situated and somewhat remote, the beach provides cliffs and boulders to lounge on as you soak your aching feet (for healthy skin, try rubbing the light green porous rocks together to form a lather). Reach the beach by boat-taxi from the Sant'Angelo port (L5000 per person; ask for a group discount and remember to arrange for your pick-up) or take the 15-min. walk down from the Panza bus stop. Those ready for more hiking should take the CD or CS bus to Fontana and head for the peak of **Mt. Epomeo** (788m); the view extends from Terracina to Cápri.

For those weary of beaching, Ischia's scattered sights provide a reprieve from the sun and surf. Near Ischia Porto, the **Castello d'Ischia** (1441), built by the King of Spain on the site of a 5th-century BC Greek fortress and destroyed repeatedly over the years, is situated on a little island of its own (Ischia Ponte), connected to Ischia by a 15th-century footbridge. The **cathedral,** mostly destroyed by WWII bombing, displays a unique mix of Roman and baroque styles. Below, the **crypt** houses wonderfully colorful 14th-century frescoes by the school of Giotto. The **nuns' cemetery,** which belonged to the Poor Clares from the 16th through 18th centuries, is somewhat ghastly; when nuns died, the order propped up the decomposing bodies on stone thrones as a constant (and fragrant) reminder to the other nuns of their own mortality. The castle also features an exposition room with changing modern art exhibits. (Open daily 9am-sunset. Admission L8000.) Take bus #7 to Ischia Ponte.

The church of **Santa Restituta** houses the ruins of Lacco Ameno's ancient villas dating back to the 8th century BC. In a cross-section of soil you can see a record of the island's numerous civilizations. (Open Mon.-Fri. 9:30am-noon and 5-7pm, Sat.-Sun. 9:30am-noon.) Also check out the 14th-century church **Santa Maria di Loreto,** with red, blue, white, and gold marble pillars. For some dancing, head to the clubs **Valentino** (L5000) and **Charly** (L20,000), out on Via Roma from Ischia Porto, or to the outdoor club **Castello** (L25,000) in the castle at Ischia Ponte.

■■■ PROCIDA

A small island of fisherfolk and farmers, Procida prefers to remain a spectator to its neighbors' summertime transformation into country clubs. The island compensates for its less dramatic scenery with its colorful and chaotic local culture. **Caremar, Linee Lauro,** and **Aliscafi SNAV** run **ferries** to the island from Naples (40min., L8000), Ischia (15min., L3400), and Pozzuoli (35min., L4000). **Hydrofoils** are L5100 to Ischia and L12,600 to Naples. The AAST **Tourist Office** (tel. (081) 810 19 68) is on Via Roma by the ferry ticket offices to the far right of the main port. They have a useful but old map of the island (L3000) and can help you find an apartment for L30,000-60,000 a night for two people. (Open daily 9am-1pm and 4:30-8pm.) Short stays are difficult to accommodate. The **ETP Residences office,** Via Principe Umberto, 1 (tel. 896 90 67), can also help you find an apartment. In August reservations and a minimum stay of 1-2 weeks are required.

Buses (L1000 in *tabacchi* shops, L1200 on the bus) serve the island with three principal routes, all starting at the main port, the northernmost point of the island. The buses leave every 20 minutes from 7am to midnight. One route takes you to the west coast: **Ciraccio** and **Pozzo Vecchio,** the most tranquil beaches on the island. A second route covers the middle and south regions of the island, bringing you past the hotels and campgrounds and stopping at the port of **Chiaiolella,** the site of the beach of the same name and the liveliest restaurants. You can walk or take the third bus route to the **Abbazia Arcangelo San Michele** (St. Michael's Abbey) on the easternmost and highest hilltop in Procida (open daily 9am-noon and 4-7pm). On the way up you'll see the medieval walls of **Terra Murata** (the old city) on Via San Michele just below the monastery. The abbey's pastel yellow façade, redone in 1890, belies the interior, where you'll find ornate 15th-century gold and lead frescoes, and bleeding Christ figures (tel. 896 76 12; open mornings and after 5:30pm). On the way down, check out the crowds to the left on **Chiaia,** the island's most popular beach; stop to admire the Pantheon-domed **Santuario Mariano** and its 1810 façade on Piazza dei Martiri. From Chiaiolella, you can cross the footbridge to the islet of **Vivara,** a wildlife sanctuary and breeding ground for the rabbits *Procidani* cook up in their famous stew. To see those bunnies on your plate, try **Ristorante Pizzeria Da Michele** in Chiaiolella, Via Marino Chiaiolella, 21 (tel. 896 74 22). Watch the nightlife heat up over a tasty dish of spaghetti with mussels (L8000). Open daily 8am-2am (closes at 8pm in winter). For dessert, ask at any bar for the refreshing lemon liquor *(limoncello)* made from Procidan lemons.

If you dislike lemons, don't spend the night: it's hard to find a hotel here that isn't surrounded by lemon groves and private gardens. **Eldorado,** Via Vittorio Emanuele, 228 (tel. 896 80 05), is a prime example. Its six choice rooms have vaulted, decorative ceilings. (Singles with bath L30,000. Doubles L50,000, with bath L55,000. Prices L10,000 higher July-Aug.) **Pensione Savoia,** Via Lavadera, 32 (tel. 896 76 16), has eight large rooms and a comfortable terrace. Behind the hotel stretches a garden of lemon trees, grapevines, flowers, and a chicken coop. (Singles L30,000, in summer L35,000. Doubles L55,000, in summer L60,000. In Aug. full pension required, L68,000.) **Hotel Riviera,** Giovanni da Procida, 36 (tel. 896 71 97; fax 896 76 11), is larger but no less friendly (and still surrounded by lemons). All rooms with bath, phone, and breakfast; some also have a view of the sea. (Singles L40,000. Doubles 80,000. Full pension required July-Aug., L95,000. Discounts in off-season and for longer stays. Open April-Sept.) Pitch your tent at the well-maintained and colorful **La Caravella** on Via IV Novembre (tel. 896 92 30). (L9000 per person, L7000 per small tent, L10,000 per large tent. Bar on grounds.) For bungalows, try **Graziella,** on Via Salette (tel. 896 77 47) on the beach. Take the bus to P. Urno and walk 500m to Spiaggia Ciraccio. (Four-person bungalows L60,000, July-Aug. L90,000.)

BAY OF NAPLES: VESUVIUS

■■■ POMPEII

Stand at the bottom of the great market-place of Pompeii, and look up at the silent streets … over the broken houses with their inmost sanctuaries open to the day, away to Mount Vesuvius, bright and snowy in the peaceful distance; and lose all count of time, and heed of other things, in the strange and melancholy sensation of seeing the Destroyed and Destroyer making this quiet picture in the sun.

—Charles Dickens, Pictures from Italy

On August 24, 79 AD, life in the prosperous Roman city of Pompeii came to a sudden halt. Mount Vesuvius' fit of towering flames, suffocating black clouds, and seething lava buried the city—stately temples, patrician villas, massive theaters, and all—under more than 20 feet of volcanic ash. Except for the few lucky ones who dropped everything and ran at the first tremors of catastrophe, the inhabitants of Pompeii suffered a nasty live burial. Perhaps the most ghastly—and evocative—relics of the town's untimely death are the "frozen people": plaster casts made from the impressions of the victims' bodies in the hardened ash, preserving their last contortions and expressions of horror. The excavation of Pompeii is an ongoing project: from the first unearthings in 1748 through current digs, every decade has brought to light new finds that provide the clearest and most vivid picture of daily life in the Roman era.

Practical Information The quickest route to Pompeii (25km south of Naples) is the **Circumvesuviana train** line from Naples' Stazione Centrale (toward Sorrento, 35min., L2700, Eurailpasses valid). Get off at the Pompeii-Villa dei Misteri stop just outside the west entry (ignore the inconvenient Pompeii Santuario stop). An alternative is the less frequent state train, leaving from the main track at the station, which stops at Pompeii en route to Salerno (7 per day 7:10am-1:15pm, L2500). The FS train station is a 5-minute walk to the east entrance, straight on Via Sacra, then left in front of the *santuario* onto Via Roma.

To get to the **site** of Pompeii, head downhill from the Villa dei Misteri station and take your first left. The **tourist office** is at Via Sacra, 1 (tel. (081) 850 72 55), on the way to the ruins from the FS train station. Follow the road to the right of the Circumvesuviana stop to the branch office at the bottom of the hill. Pick up a free map and the informative pamphlet *Notizario Turistico Regionale*. (Both offices open Mon.-Fri. 8:30am-3:30pm. Via Sacra office also open Sat. 8am-noon.)

Accommodations and Food Unless you wish to tour Pompeii extensively, there is no reason to stay overnight in the dull, modern city. If you decide to, however, the **Motel Villa dei Misteri,** Via Villa dei Misteri, 11 (tel. 861 35 93), uphill from the Circumvesuviana station, is a wonderful option, with comfortable, clean, modern rooms and a terrific pool. A/C available. (Doubles with bath L75,000; extra bed L15,000. Full pension L75,000.) **Soggiorno Pace,** Via Sacra, 29 (tel. 863 60 25), has large, quiet rooms with common bath and a peaceful garden. (L20,000 per person.) **Pensione Minerva,** Via Roma, 137 (tel. 863 25 87), near the east entrance to the site, rents doubles for L55,000 and triples for L70,000. (Rooms with showers are L5000 more.) The cheapest alternative is to stay at one of the local campgrounds, which are all near the ruins. Unfortunately, they tend to be somewhat ruined themselves. **Camping Zeus** (tel. 861 53 20), outside the Villa dei Misteri Circumvesuviana stop, is convenient and respectable (L6000 per person, L4000 per large tent, L3000 per small tent). Not far away, on Via Plinio, the main road that runs from the ruins, **Camping Pompeii** (tel. 862 25 82; fax 850 27 72), with the same ownership and prices as Zeus, has attractive bungalows for L50,000 for two people and L80,000 for four. If you're desperate you can sack out on the floor of its indoor lobby for L6000 per night. These places are eager for customers, so you can usually bargain them down at least 25%.

Stock up at the **GS Supermarket,** Via Statale, km. 24, on the main road between the east and west entrances to the archaeological site. Take advantage of the good prices and air-conditioning. (Open Mon.-Sat. 8am-8:30pm; closes Thurs. 2pm.) A good alternative to the local McDonald's, **La Vinicola,** Via Roma, 29, tempts with a pleasant outdoor courtyard and abundant *gnocchi con mozzarella* (potato dumplings with tomato and cheese, L5000). Also try the *zuppa di cozze* for L5000. (Cover L1500. Service 15%. Open daily 10am-midnight.) More expensive but equally tasty meals are found at the **Trattoria Pizzeria dei Platani,** Via Colle San Bartolomeo, 8 (tel. 863 39 73), down the street from the Museo Vesuviano. *Cannelloni* is L7000, and the *menù* is L18,000. (Cover L1500. Open daily 9:30am-10pm.)

Sights A comprehensive walk through Pompeii will probably take four or five hours; pack a lunch and a water bottle, as the cafeteria is hideously expensive. **Guided tours** are expensive as well, but are probably the best way to savor the gory details of life and death in the first century AD. Call **GATA Tours** (tel. 861 56 61; fax 536 85 77) or **Assotouring** (tel. 862 25 60) for info. The tour guides have gotten wise to freeloaders, and go beyond evil stares to actually yelling at offenders. If a tour is too rich for your blood, consider buying the informative *How to Visit Pompeii* (ed. Bonechi) for L8000, available outside all site entrances.

The west entrance leads past the Antiquarium (permanently closed since the 1980 earthquake) to the **Forum,** surrounded by a colonnade that retains a portion of what was once a second tier. Once dotted with numerous statues of emperors and gods, this was the commercial, civic, and religious center of the city. Showcases along the west side display some of the gruesome body-casts of the volcano's victims. To the right rises the **Temple of Jupiter,** mostly destroyed by an earthquake that struck 17 years before the city's bad luck got worse; to the left is the **Temple of Apollo,** with statues of Apollo and Diana (these are copies; the originals are in Naples) and a column topped by a sundial. To the left of the temple is the **basilica,** or law-court, whose walls are decorated with stucco to imitate marble. On the opposite long side of the forum, to the left of the **Building of Eumachia** (note the carved doorframe of animals and insects hiding in scroll-like plants), the **Temple of Vespasian** houses a delicate frieze depicting the preparation for a sacrifice.

Follow the Forum north by the cafeteria and enter the **Forum Baths** to the left on Via di Terme. Parts of the body casts here have chipped away to reveal the teeth and bones underneath. Decorating the rooms to the right are remarkable terra-cotta figures. Exit to the right, and on the left opens the **House of the Faun,** where a small bronze of a dancing faun and the spectacular Alexander Mosaic (now in Naples) were found. Before the door, the word *Have* ("welcome") is inscribed in a mosaic. Continue to the left on Via della Fortuna and turn left on Vico di Vetti to see the **House of the Vettii,** home to some of the most vivid frescoes in Pompeii. In the vestibule is a depiction of Priapus (the god of fertility) displaying his colossal member; in ancient times phalli were believed to scare off evil spirits, but now they seem only to invite hordes of tittering tourists.

Walk back on Vico di Vetti and continue on Vico del Lupanare, where there is a small **brothel** with several bed-stalls. Above each of the stalls a pornographic painting depicts with unabashed precision the specialty of its occupant (or so archaeologists fantasize). Continue down the street to the main avenue, Via dell'Abbondanza. The **Stabian Baths,** privately owned and therefore fancier than the Forum Baths (just think: ritzy spa vs. YMCA), lie to the left. The separate men's and women's sides each included a dressing room, cold baths *(frigidaria),* warm baths *(tepidaria),* and hot or steam baths *(caldaria).* Via dei Teatri across the street leads to a huge complex consisting of the **Great Theater,** constructed in the first half of the 2nd century BC, and the **Little Theater,** built later for music and dance concerts. North of the theaters stands the **Temple of Isis,** Pompeii's monument to the Egyp-

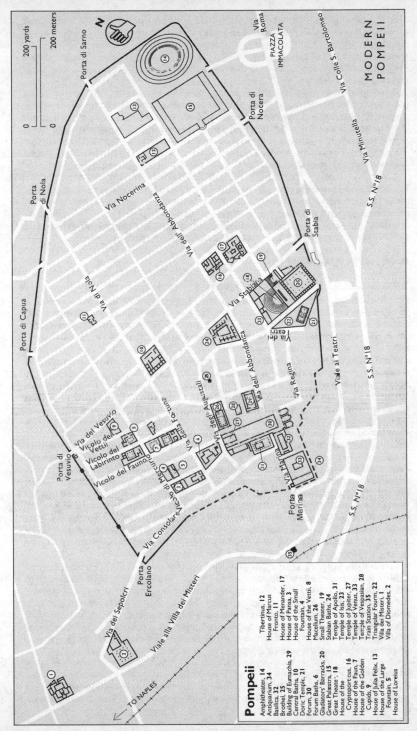

POMPEII

MODERN
POMPEII

PIAZZA
IMMACOLATA

Pompeii

Amphitheater, 14
Antiquarium, 34
Basilica, 32
Brothel, 25
Building of Eumachia, 29
Central Baths, 10
Doric Temple, 21
Forum Baths, 6
Forum, 30
Gladiators' Barracks, 20
Great Palaestra, 15
Great Theater, 18
House of the
    Cryptoporticus, 16
House of Julia Felix, 13
House of the Faun, 7
House of the Golden
    Cupids, 9
House of the Large
    Fountain, 5
House of Loreius

Tiberinus, 12
House of Marcus
    Fronto, 11
House of Menander, 17
House of Pansa, 3
House of the Small
    Fountain, 4
House of the Vettii, 8
Macellum, 26
Small Theater, 19
Stabian Baths, 24
Temple of Apollo, 31
Temple of Isis, 23
Temple of Jupiter, 27
Temple of Venus, 33
Temple of Vespasian, 28
Train Station, 35
Triangular Fourm, 22
Villa dei Misteri, 1
Villa of Diomedes, 2

TO NAPLES

tian fertility goddess. Exit the temple to the right and pass two fine houses, the **House of Secundus** and the **House of Menander** (so named because a painting of the comic poet hangs on the wall, not because he actually lived there). At the end of the street, turn left to return to the main road. The Romans believed that crossroads were particularly vulnerable to evil spirits, so they built altars (like the one here) designed to ward them off.

Turn right down Via dell'Abbondanza and note the red writing on the walls. You'll see everything from political campaign slogans to declarations of love— apparently graffiti hasn't changed much in 2000 years. At the end of the street rest the **House of Tiburtinus** and the **House of Venus,** sprawling complexes with wonderful frescoes and gardens replanted according to modern knowledge of ancient horticulture. The nearby **amphitheater** (80 BC), the oldest in the world still standing, held 12,000 spectators, and the **Great Palestra** was a gym complete with pool.

Complete your day with a visit to the **Villa of the Mysteries,** outside the main complex and 10min. up the hill from the Circumvesuviana station. A renowned cycle of paintings (in the room directly to the right of the entrance) depicts an initiation into the cult of Dionysus. You don't need a separate ticket, but you can't return to the central site after leaving it. (Entrances to Pompeii open 9am-1hr. before sunset (June-July 8pm, Nov.-Dec. 3:45pm). Admission L12,000.)

■ NEAR POMPEII

ERCOLANO (HERCULANEUM)

Neatly excavated and impressively intact, the remains of the Roman town of Herculaneum (modern Ercolano) hardly deserve the term "ruins." Once a wealthy residential enclave on the Roman coast road, Herculaneum does not evoke the same sense of tragedy that Pompeii does—all but a handful of its inhabitants escaped the ravages of Vesuvius. In a much less disorienting (and less crowded) tour than those offered in Pompeii, you can wind your way through the 15 or so houses and baths that are now open to the public. There are no colossal buildings, temples, or off-color frescoes to excite your imagination here, but the houses, with their fresh interior decoration, attest to the cultural development of this affluent community. Two-thousand-year-old frescoes, furniture, mosaics, small sculptures, and even wood paneling seem as vital as the day they were made, preserved by a mud avalanche that tumbled off the volcano on a cushion of gas. Fortunately, since the town remained unexcavated until this century, few of its treasures were carted off by rich nobles and, in contrast to Pompeii, most of its frescoes and mosaics are intact and on the walls, not in museums. The **House of Deer** (so named for a statue of a deer being savagely attacked by greyhounds) is one of the more alluring villas. Probably big partiers, the owners had a statue of a *Satyr with a Wineskin* and an all-too-recognizable statue of the town's namesake Hercules in a drunken stupor trying to relieve himself. The **baths,** with their largely intact warm and hot rooms and giant vaulted swimming pool, evoke images of past opulence. **The House of the Mosaic of Neptune and Amphitrite,** which belonged to a rich shop owner, is famous for its mosaic depicting—well, take a guess.

To get to Ercolano, take any Circumvesuviana train toward Pompeii from Naples' central train station to the Ercolano stop (15min., L1800). Walk 500m downhill to the **ticket office.** (Open daily 9am-1hr. before sunset (June-July 8pm, Dec. 2:45pm). Admission L12,000.) Before entering, consider purchasing the little blue *Istituto Poligrafico dello Stato* guide to Herculaneum, with an excellent map, reliable text, and some beautifully clear black-and-white illustrations (L10,000). Be forewarned that the neighborhood surrounding the site can be less than savory at times; solo travelers and women should be on guard.

MT. VESUVIUS

Take a peek inside the only active volcano on the European continent. **SITA** buses run from Ercolano up to the crater of Vesuvius (6 per day, last return 4:30pm, L2000 each way), but once there you must be accompanied by a guide (L5000). Hikers can take the orange city bus #5 (L1800 each way) to the base of the mountain and climb from there; bring plenty of water and wear decent shoes. Experts say the trip is safe—the last eruption was March 31, 1944.

■■■ SORRENTO

The men of Odysseus' crew shielded their ears from the spellbinding song of the Sirens, who inhabited Sorrento's peninsula. If the Sirens still exist, chances are they chant in English and German to camera-laden foreigners. Nevertheless, poised between Naples, Cápri, and the Amalfi Coast, Sorrento offers many inexpensive accommodations and makes a convenient base for the daytripper.

ORIENTATION AND PRACTICAL INFORMATION

A short throughway leads you from the train and bus station to Piazza Angelina Lauro and **Corso Italia,** Sorrento's main street. Fifty meters to the left lies **Piazza Tasso,** the center of town. Past P. Tasso, you come to the **old quarter** and the **cathedral.** From P. Tasso, Via de Maio on your left (facing the sea), and a stairway straight ahead lead to the **port.**

Tourist Office: Via L. De Maio, 35 (tel. 807 40 33). **Do not follow the signs labeled "Tourist Information."** From P. Tasso, take V. de Maio through P. Sant'Antonio and continue to the right toward the port; the office is to the right within the Circolo del Forestiere complex, in the room on the left as you enter the building. Helpful English-speaking staff with maps, accommodations service, and info on cultural events. Grab a free copy of *Surrentum*, the monthly tourist magazine. Open Mon.-Sat. 8:30am-2pm and 4-7pm, Oct.-March Mon.-Sat. 8:30am-2pm and 3:45-6:15pm.

Police: Vico 3° Rota, (tel. 807 30 88), a left off Corso Italia 1 block after Viale Nizza, to the right of the station. Ask for the English-speaking foreigners' office (*Ufficio Stranieri*).

Post Office: Corso Italia, 210T-U (tel. 878 16 36), near P. Lauro. Open Mon.-Sat. 8:15am-7:20pm. **Exchange money** at the best rates in town 8:15am-5:30pm (commission L2000, L5000 for sums over L100,000). **Postal code:** 80067.

Telephones: Telecom (SIP), P. Tasso, 37 (tel. 878 24 00), leave the train station and turn right immediately before you come to the *piazza.* Open daily 9am-1pm and 4-10pm. **Telephone code:** 081.

Currency Exchange: Exchange desks can be found along Corso Italia and in the old quarter, 9am-9pm. Worse rates than the post office, but no commission.

American Express: Acampara Travel, P. Angelina Lauro, 12 (tel. 807 30 88). Open daily 9am-1pm and 3-9pm; Oct.-June Mon.-Fri. 9am-1pm and 3:30-7pm. Currency exchange only on weekday mornings.

Buses: SITA (tel. 878 27 08). Blue buses depart for towns on the Amalfi Coast from the Circumvesuviana station. Approx. every hr. 6:30am-9:45pm to and from Positano (L2000), Praiano (L2700), Amalfi (L3400), and Salerno (L6100). From Amalfi, change buses and pay an additional L1500 to go to Atrani, Ravello, or Scala. Buy all SITA tickets at bars and *tabacchi,* and validate them when you board the bus. **CITAL** runs to Rome at 6am or 5:30pm (L23,000). The bus to Sorrento from Rome leaves at 3pm from the Tiburtina station. **Local orange buses** leave from P. Tasso every 20-30min. for the port, Punta del Capo, and other regions of the city (L1000 within city, L1500 outside).

Ferries: the cheapest route to Cápri. Descend the stairs at P. Tasso. **Caremar** (tel. 807 30 77; fax 807 24 79) is the least expensive and runs most frequently. Boats leave daily at 8, 10am, 2:45, 5:45, and 7:45pm (less frequently in winter); 1hr.; L5300. **Alilauro hydrofoils** (tel. 807 30 24) take 15min. for the crossing (L8000), and run every hr. 8:20am-4:45pm. Hydrofoils also to Ischia (L15,000) and Naples (L13,000).

Trains: Circumvesuviana, to Naples, passing Pompeii and Torre Annunziata, (2 per hr. 4am-11pm; L3900).

Car and Moped Rental: Sorrento Rent-A-Car, Corso Italia, 210/A (tel. 878 13 86). This is the only moped rental place from Sorrento to Salerno. Mopeds L45,000 per day, L260,000 per week. Also rents Vespa 125s (for 2 people), L70,000 per day, L380,000 per week. Helmet and insurance included. Passport, credit card, and driver's license required.

Laundromat: Terlizzi, Corso Italia, 30 (tel. 878 11 85), in the old quarter. Coin-op (L15,000 wash and dry) and dry-cleaning.

Emergencies: tel. 113. **Hospital: Ospedale Santa Maria Misericordia,** Corso Italia (tel. 533 11 11). English speakers on hand.

ACCOMMODATIONS AND CAMPING

The numerous lodging options make up for Sorrento's dearth of sights. Reservations, however, are still a good idea in July and August. Some Sorrento hotels allegedly charge more than their official prices. If you feel you're being overcharged, ask to see the official price list; after the fact, you can write a letter to the EPT and perhaps eventually get a refund. **Prices listed below are for high season.**

Hotel Elios, Via Capo, 33 (tel. 878 18 12). Halfway to the Punta del Capo; take the bus from P. Tasso (L1500). Clean rooms, colorful bedspreads, and paintings. Tranquil area. Prices for *Let's Go* users: singles L35,000, doubles L60,000.

Hotel Loreley et Londres, Via Califano, 2 (tel. 807 31 87). Take Via Capasso past the youth hostel to the waterfront. The Sorrento hotel you've dreamed of, with views of cliffs and sea. Worth the price. Doubles with bath, including breakfast on a delightful terrace, L100,000. Half pension (L85,000) required in Aug.

Hotel Savoia, Via Fuorimura, 48 (tel. 878 25 11), on the street off the right hand of the statue in P. Tasso. The best bet if you're arriving in the summer without reservations. Friendly English-speaking management. Singles with bath L60,000. Doubles L80,000. Breakfast L8000, for 2 people L15,000.

Hotel City, Corso Italia, 221 (tel. 877 22 10), left on Corso Italia from the station. A bit noisy at night. Money exchange, tickets for ferries and excursions, small bar. Comfy doubles with bath (some with garden patios) L80,000. Extra bed L15,000. Singles (available Oct.-June) L50,000. Breakfast L5000.

Camping: Nube d'Argento, Via del Capo, 21 (tel. 878 13 44). From the station, follow Corso Italia past P. Tasso until it becomes Via del Capo. It's a 25-min. walk, so you may want to take the bus from P. Tasso (L1500). An ideal location by the ocean, with a swimming pool, hot showers, market, and restaurant. Check-out noon. L12,000 per person, L6000 per tent, L12,000 per large tent. Two-person bungalows L70,000. **Villaggio Verde,** Via Cesarano, 12 (tel. 807 32 58; fax 807 30 28). From P. Tasso take bus #2 (L1500) or turn left on Via Fuorimura. Follow this road (it turns into brick Via Atigliana) for 15 min. and turn left at the Napoli sign. L9500 per person, L8500 per tent. Two-person bungalows L100,000, 4-person bungalows L140,000.

FOOD

Sorrento is famous for its *gnocchi,* potato dumplings smothered in a zesty tomato sauce and mozzarella cheese. Also popular are the local *cannelloni,* stuffed with cheese and herbs, and *Nocillo,* a dark liqueur made from the hefty local walnuts. Unfortunately, many of the affordable restaurants in Sorrento cater to the Germans with *Würstel* and to the British with fish and chips. With a little effort you can avoid the menus written in English and find traditional fare in and around the city center. Otherwise, **Supermercato STANDA,** at Corso Italia, 221, is an even less expensive option (open Mon.-Wed. and Fri.-Sat. 8:30am-12:55pm and 5-8:55pm, Thurs. 8:30am-12:55pm). From P. Tasso, follow Via San Cesareo until it turns into Via Fuoro, where you will find fresh fruit, fish, or bargain shoes sold at a variety of **market stands.** (Go in the morning for the best deals.)

Ristorante e Pizzeria Giardiniello, Via Accademia, 7 (tel. 878 46 16). Take the 2nd left off Via Giuliani, which runs off Corso Italia at the cathedral. Mamma Luisa does all the cooking in this large family-run establishment. Her *gnocchi* transcend poetry (L6000). Try the *bocconcini al Giardiniello,* tiny pizza-like pastries with *prosciutto* and mushrooms (L7000 for 10). Cover L1500. Open daily 10:30am-3pm and 7pm-2am; Oct.-May Wed.-Mon. 10:30am-3pm and 7-2pm. MC, Visa.

Ristorante Sant'Antonino, Via Santa Maria delle Grazie, 6 (tel. 877 12 00), off P. Sant'Antonino, near the tourist office. Popular with locals and tourists. *Farfalle con zucchine* (butterfly-shaped pasta with zucchini, L8000) and famed *gnocchi alla sorrentina* (L8000). *Menù* from L18,000. Long wine list. Open Feb.-Nov. daily noon-3pm and 7pm-midnight. AmEx, MC, Visa.

Ristorante-Pizzeria Il Mulino, Via Fuorimura, 7 (tel. 878 12 16; fax 807 28 99), off P. Tasso. Try the heavenly *canneloni alla Mulino* (L8500), or the *impepata di cozze* (mussels; L10,000). Pizza L6000-10,000. No cover. Open daily noon-4pm and 7:30-11pm. MC, Visa.

Snack Bar 2000, Largo Sedil Dominova (tel. 878 13 51), off a *piazza* on Via Cesareo in the old quarter. An Anglicized hangout that dominates the tiny square with its outdoor tables. Open daily 9am-11pm.

Gigino Pizza a Metro, Via Nicotera, 11, at Vico Equense (tel. 879 84 26), a 10-min. train ride from Sorrento. Take the Circumvesuviana to the Vico Equense stop, go left as you exit the station, and follow the winding road uphill to its end at P. Umberto. Finally, take a left on Via Roma and another left on Via Nicotera. This is unofficially the world's largest *pizzeria,* a massive 2-story facility with monstrous wood-burning ovens that cook *pizza a metro* (1m-long pizza; from L28,000). A meter will feed at least 5 starving tourists; starving Italians, however, are likely to eat elsewhere. Cover L1000. Service 13%. Open daily noon-1am.

SIGHTS AND ENTERTAINMENT

The westerly orientation of the beaches makes sunset swims truly memorable. For a free swim, take the bus all the way to **Punta del Capo** and walk ten minutes down the footpath to the right. On the coast you will also see the remains of the ancient Roman **Villa di Pollio.** The ruins aren't worth visiting unless you take a dip in the beautiful cove or farther out on the point. Nearby lies **Sant'Agata** (9km by SITA bus from the train station, L1500), a tiny city perched high in the hills. Known as the "city on the two gulfs," its majestic height is a great vantage point from which to see both the Bay of Naples and the Gulf of Salerno. The city's church, the **Chiesa di Sant'Agata,** boasts a 13th-century mother-of-pearl altar.

Jazz and classical music are performed about every other night throughout July and August at the outdoor atrium of the **Chiostro di San Francesco,** near the Villa Comunale on the water. (Showtime 9pm. Admission L20,000, students L12,000, some shows half-price.) Free events from July through September take place in the Villa Comunale, the Chiostro di San Francesco, and the town's two ports. Get a list at the tourist office. From November to March, the Sorrento Tourist Board organizes **Sorrento Inverno,** a free entertainment program that includes movies, concerts, local folklore exhibits, and guided tours of the town.

The area around P. Tasso heats up and gets down after dark. People swarm the streets, look out over the bay, and careen around on mopeds. The outdoor **Blue Mare Club** on Punta del Capo is as beautiful as you want your *discoteca* to be (open in summer only). And even the winter stays hot at the imaginatively named **The Club,** held in the Bar Fauno in Piazza Tasso.

AMALFI COAST

Many people choose the Amalfi Coast as the place to come and relax after doing some serious European country-hopping; they usually leave more than satisfied. The bold, arresting bluffs and tiny towns nestled into steep coastal ravines merit every superlative that tourist brochures heap upon them. A warm, calm sea, delicious seafood, and sumptuous fruits temper this harsh southern shore which divides the Bay of Naples from the Gulf of Salerno. Taste the fresh peaches, yellow plums, sweet figs, and lemons in every form imaginable.

The coast is accessible by SITA buses leaving Sorrento and Salerno every two hours, ferry and Circumvesuviana (the Meta stop) service from Naples on a less regular basis, and daily CITAL buses from Rome. If you're prone to sea-sickness, take the ferry between towns (really); they're faster, steadier, and less harrowing than the blue SITA buses, although those with a stronger stomach shouldn't miss the roller-coaster bus ride and its spectacular views. If you don't mind a little danger in your life, rent a moped or scooter and stop at any gorgeous place that strikes your fancy. (Leave extra luggage at the train station.) But be warned: the Amalfi Coast is not the place to learn how to ride a moped. For less life-threatening options and great walking tour suggestions, read Julian Tippet's *Walks from Amalfi*.

■ ■ ■ POSITANO

While Positano looks as if it might slip into the sea, and the roof of the house in front of you makes a great patio, it's still an ideal place to bask in coastal Italian culture. The slow pace of life results from the ever-present threat of a precipitous plunge; go slow and enjoy yourself.

Orientation and Practical Information Positano is 35 minutes from Sorrento by SITA bus. Get off at the Bar Internazionale stop and either walk down the winding stairway to the village (affectionately referred to as the "Thousand Steps") or take the local orange bus, which makes its rounds every 30 minutes on the town's only street open to traffic (L1000). When leaving, buy tickets in advance from the **Bar Internazionale** for trips to Sorrento, the Amalfi Coast, and Naples; if you're heading for Rome, buy tickets on the CITAL bus (departs 6:45am, L23,000). The terse but well-informed **tourist office** is at Via del Saracino, 4 (tel. 87 50 67). Facing the town from the port, walk to the left up Via Giovanni and take a right immediately before the arch. Pick up a map and the info-packed pamphlet *A Guest in Positano.* (Open Mon.-Fri. 8:30am-2pm, Sat. 8:30am-noon.) A row of ten **SIP telephones** is located directly behind the tourist office on Via Giovanni. The **telephone code** for Positano is 089. A **pharmacy** is located at Via dei Mulini (tel. 87 58 63). The **emergency number** is 113; the **police** are at Chiesa Nuova (tel. 87 52 77). Numerous **ferry** companies provide extensive service; buy tickets at the *biglietteria marittima* on the port. To: Cápri (morning only; L10,000), Amalfi (5 per day; L6000), and Salerno (5 per day; L7500). **Alilauro hydrofoils** run to Cápri (3 per day; L13,000) and down the coast (Amalfi L7000, Salerno L13,000). There is also limited service to Sorrento and Naples. Small companies on Marina Grande will take you on a boat tour of Cápri's coast and the Blue Grotto (9am; L27,000 per person), or ferry a group of four to a nearby yet secluded beach (L30,000). Call 87 50 32 for info.

Accommodations and Food Homer's Sirens allegedly inhabited the three Isole dei Galli off Positano's beach. If you too feel the pull of the Sirens' call, try one of the many *pensioni* in the area. (Reserve early in summer.) **Casa Guadagno,** Via Fornillo, 22 (tel. 87 50 42), earns praise for pampering its patrons with spotless rooms, beautifully tiled floors, and sublime views (as well as heating in winter). Call ahead, as the 10 rooms with bath are often reserved early. (Doubles L75,000/ 80,000. Breakfast included.) To get there, take the local bus down from Bar Internazionale and ask to be let off by the hotel. Follow the signs and take the left fork. Next door, **Villa Maria Luisa,** Via Fornillo, 40 (tel. 87 50 23), has bright rooms and the jolliest owner in Italy. (All rooms with bath. Singles L40,000. Doubles L80,000. Extra bed L25,000.) Just down the street from the hotels, **Il Saraceno D'Oro,** Via Pasitea, 254 (tel. 87 53 90), serves cheap, great pizza to go from L4000. If you sit down, pizzas start at L7000; *spaghetti alla Saracena,* bathed in a sauce of tomatoes, tuna, mushrooms, and peppers, is L7000. Pizza evenings only. Cover L2000. (Open daily 12:30-2:30pm and 7:30-11:30pm.) At the top of the hill toward Montepertuso rests

Il Ritrovo, Via Montepertuso, 53 (tel. 81 13 36). Try the *penne al ritrovo* (L7000), with mushrooms, tomatoes, and sausage, or the *grigliata di carne* (L12,000), a sampling of fresh meats. *Menù* L20,000-25,000. (Open daily noon-3pm and 7:30pm-midnight.) If you're heading to Praiano, consider stopping first at **La Taverna del Leone,** Via Laurito, 43 (tel. 87 54 74), on the main road. Enjoy strawberries, pears, peaches, and even walnuts filled with sorbet (L3500 per 100g)—or get a full meal. (Cover L2000. Open daily 1-4pm and 7pm-midnight. Oct.-April closed Tues. AmEx, MC, Visa.) Remember to have another ticket handy so you can hop back on the bus!

Sights   Spiraling upwards from Marina Grande, Positano's grey but attractive beach, **Via dei Mulini,** is a study in tourism, with its many boutiques and well-dressed foreigners. For more traditional sight-seeing, however, the 17th-century church of **Santa Maria Assunta,** located in P. Flavio Gioia, crowns the memorable Positano landscape with a beautiful tiled dome. Hop the bus from Piazza dei Mulini on the port (or from Bar Internazionale; L1000) or hike the 45-minute trail to **Montepertuso,** a high cliff pierced by a large *pertuso* (hole). On the way, stop at the locals' favorite freshwater spring, at the foot of a small Madonna. From the port, take one of many boating itineraries from **L'Uomo e il Mare** (tel. 87 54 75); you can take a personalized tour of the coast or go night fishing for squid (call for prices). On August 15, Positano puts on a **fireworks** display over the sea in celebration of its patron saint, Santa Maria Assunta.

■ NEAR POSITANO: PRAIANO ~ *The bar was here*

Six kilometers down the coast (25min. by bus due to the winding road; L1500), Praiano provides wonderful and inexpensive accommodations, including the only camping on the coast. It makes a wonderful mealtime trip that avoids the expensive restaurants of nearby touristed towns.

On the road from Positano, next to the church with the blue and gold domes, is the restaurant **San Gennaro,** Via San Gennaro, 75 (tel. (089) 87 42 93). Try the titillating tastes of their *spaghetti alla puttanesca* (made quickly and dished up hot; L6000), or their clam and mussel sauté (L8000). In the evenings, pizza starts at L5500. (Open daily noon-3pm and 7pm-midnight.) Once in Praiano, enjoy the panorama from the excellent campground-hotel **La Tranquillità,** Via Roma, 10 (tel. (089) 87 40 84), located on the road to Amalfi (ask the bus driver to stop at the Ristorante Continental/La Tranquillità). The rooms offer the coast's most awe-inspiring views of the surrounding caves, castles, gorges, and sea, while the spotless campsite sits atop precipitous cliffs. A long stairway takes you down to a stone dock and the beautiful green water. (Camping L30,000 per person. Clean, new bungalows with bath: singles L50,000, doubles L80,000. Breakfast included. Open Easter-Nov.) Don't leave the coast without savoring a meal at the open-air **Ristorante Continental,** above La Tranquillità. It's the place to go for fresh mountain air, endless views, and exquisite food. *Primi* L7000-11,000, *secondi* L9000-15,000, and local wine runs L6000 per bottle, but *Let's Go* bearers receive a 15% discount. (Cover L2000. Open Easter-Nov. daily noon-3pm and 8pm-midnight.) There's another marvelous beach up the road toward Positano but you must be willing to descend 400 steps (keep the return trip in mind). Alternate accommodations may be found at **La Perla,** Via Miglina, 2 (tel. 87 40 52), located 200m towards Amalfi from La Tranquillità on the main road. (Singles L40,000. Doubles L70,000. All rooms with bath. AmEx, MC.)

Around the bend from Praiano as you walk towards Amalfi you'll find a ramp down to **Marina di Praia,** a 400-year-old fishing village tucked in a tiny ravine. If you turn right on the path along the water you'll come to **Africana,** a nightclub that draws young crowds from all along the coast (tel. 87 40 42; open June-Sept.). The **Grotto dello Smeraldo** lies halfway between Praia and Amalfi; the SITA bus will drop you off at the elevator entrance to the grotto. The cave's green water isn't as stunning as Cápri's azure equivalent, but the multilingual guides try to make up for

A M A L F I

it with silly tricks like spotting Lincoln's and Mussolini's profiles in the rock formations. (Admission L5000. Open 9am-5pm; Oct.-April 10am-4pm.)

■■■ AMALFI

Amalfi was the first Sea Republic of Italy, and has been a bustling seaside town since
Roman times. Amalfi was also home to Flavio Gioja, inventor of the compass, and
the point of origin of the "Tabula de Amalpha," a code of laws that governed the sea
until 1570. After the Norman conquest and the earthquake of 1343, Amalfi fell from
its maritime pre-eminence, but today it has the life, noise, and chaos of a city many
times its size. Fortunately, the tourist crunch isn't as intense as that in Sorrento, and
the milieu is far more enchanting. Known as the "pearl of the coast," Amalfi attracts
the travel-weary with the promise of strolls on bayside promenades, coffee in the
intimate *piazza* in front of the cathedral, and forays into the high hills of the surrounding coast.

ORIENTATION AND PRACTICAL INFORMATION

Buses stop in **P. Flavio Gioia.** Note the statue of the *piazza*'s namesake, which
shows him looking at his newly invented compass. Head away from the water and
pass through the white, arched portal into **Piazza del Duomo.** The main street is
Via Lorenzo d'Amalfi, leading uphill from the *piazza*.

Tourist Office: Corso delle Repubbliche Marinare, 27 (tel. 87 11 07; fax 87 26 19).
   On the water toward Salerno from the bus stop. Friendly staff has limited info; ask
   for the city pamphlet, hotel list, and map. Open Mon.-Sat. 8am-1:30pm.
Police: Carabinieri, Via Casamare, 19 (tel. 87 10 22).
Post Office: Corso delle Repubbliche Marinare, 35 (tel. 87 13 30), next to the tour-
   ist office. Open Mon.-Fri. 8:15am-6pm, Sat. 8:15am-1pm. **Postal Code:** 84011.
Telephones: In the courtyard by the tourist office. Open daily 8am-8pm. **Tele-
   phone Code:** 089.
Buses: P. Flavio Gioia (tel. 87 10 09), on the waterfront. Blue SITA buses leave reg-
   ularly for Sorrento (L3400), Positano (L2000), and Salerno (L2700); local orange
   buses leave every hr. for Ravello and Scala (L1500). Buy tickets at the **Travel
   Tourist** office at P. Flavio Gioia, 1.
Ferries: several companies sail from the port to the right of P. Flavio Gioia. Get up-
   to-date ferry info (prices change frequently) and buy tickets at the Travel Tourist
   office. **Gabbiano** propels from June to Sept. to: Cápri (3 per day; L11,000) and
   Salerno (4 per day; L5000). **Alilauro** runs 3 hydrofoils a day from Salerno to Cápri
   (L11,000) via Amalfi and Positano (L6000) (only 2 per day Oct.-June).
Luggage Storage: Piazza Gioia, 1. L3000 per bag. This office also has many maps
   and pamphlets unavailable at the tourist office. Open daily 8am-9:30pm.
Boat Rental: Raffaele Florio (tel. 87 21 47), on the port by the restaurant Lo
   Smeraldino. Luxurious 4-person boats L25,000 per hour. Farther down the street,
   Lido Delle Sirene, Piazzale dei Protontini (tel. 87 14 89), rents boats for L70,000
   per 2 hrs.
Emergencies: tel. 112. **Guardia Medica:** Piazza Municipio, 4 (tel. 87 27 85), to the
   right of the tourist office. Open 24 hrs.

ACCOMMODATIONS

Staying in Amalfi is expensive. Accommodations fill in August, so reserve at least
one month in advance. The best bargain is A'Scalinatella, a stone's throw away in
the less crowded village of Atrani.

Hotel Lidomare, Via Piccolomini, 9 (tel. 87 13 32), through the passageway
   across from the *duomo*. Take a left up the stairs, then cross the *piazzetta*. Terrific
   rooms in a 700-year-old house. All rooms with bath, TV, and telephone, and some
   with A/C. Antique lounge with color TV and piano. Run by a dynamic duo. Singles
   L60,000. Doubles L100,000. Prices L10,000 less in low season. Breakfast included.

✓ **Hotel Amalfi,** Via dei Pastai, 3 (tel. 87 24 40; fax 87 22 50), to the left off Via Lorenzo as you go uphill. A 3-star establishment with immaculate rooms, attentive management, terraces, and citrus gardens. All rooms with bath. English spoken. Singles L60,000. Doubles L50,000. Breakfast L5000. These are special *Let's Go* prices, so be sure to mention the book. Greater discounts in low season.

Pensione Proto, Salita dei Curiali, 4 (tel. 87 10 03). Take Via Lorenzo d'Amalfi from P. Duomo and go right into the tiny alley by the sign for the Church of Maria Addolorata. Comfy but run-down rooms. English spoken. Rooms L35,000 per person; discounts for extended stays. Discounts for hotel guests at La Shahrazad.

—CARMELA — 130

FOOD

Via Lorenzo d'Amalfi is paved with gold: golden bottles of *limoncello,* a lemon liqueur that has become the specialty of the Amalfi Coast. In every shape and size, on racks, on shelves, and in baskets, bottles of this tart but delicious beverage— served ice-cold—line the street. Try some along with *passolini,* a regional specialty of plump raisins wrapped in lemon leaves (but don't eat the leaves).

✓ **Trattoria La Perla,** Salita Truglio, 3 (tel. 87 14 40), around the corner from the Hotel Amalfi. Elegant but moderately priced. Terrific seafood. Try the bounteous *excellent spaghetti al profumo di mare* (spaghetti with seafood, L10,000) or the *menù* for L20,000. Open daily noon-3:30pm and 7pm-midnight; Oct.-May closed Tues.

Shahrazad Club (tel. 87 33 80), on Via dei Prefetturi, 10m to the left of the cathedral, up the stairs. The omelettes (L4000) are made with fresh eggs from the proprietor's chickens. In the evenings the downstairs becomes a piano bar where the multi-lingual owner tickles the ivories. Open daily 10am-midnight.

Bar-Gelateria Royal, Via Lorenzo d'Amalfi, 10 (tel. 87 19 82), near the *duomo.* Fancy setting, not fancy prices. The excellent hand-churned ice cream here is possibly Amalfi's best, though you may have to sample a lot to be sure. Their specialty is the *pastiera napoletana,* with bits of Neapolitan Easter fruitcake. Cones L2000-3000. Open daily 11am-2am; Oct.-May closed Mon.

SIGHTS

The 9th-century **duomo** imparts grace, elegance, and dignity to the Piazza del Duomo. Rebuilt in the 19th century according to the original medieval plan, the cathedral features a startling façade of varied geometric designs typical of the Arab-Norman style, but very unusual in Italy. The exceptional **bronze doors,** crafted in Constantinople in 1066, started a bronze-door craze that reached all the way to Rome. Downstairs, the crypt houses **the remains of St. Andrew (except half of his head,** which the Pope kindly donated to St. Andrew's church in Patras, Greece; the back half is in the altar here) and a bronze statue of the apostle. (Cathedral open daily 7am-1:30pm and 3-8pm. Appropriate dress required.) To the left of the church the **Chiostro Paradiso** (Cloister of Paradise), a 13th-century cemetery, has become a graveyard for miscellaneous column, statue, and sarcophagus fragments, while its museum houses mosaics, sculptures, and the church's treasures. Its Arabic arches create a romantic setting for piano and vocal concerts on Friday nights from July through September. Tickets are L5000. (Cloister open daily 9am-1:30pm and 3-8pm. Admission L3000 for cloister, museum, and tomb; multi-lingual guides available.)

The old 9th-century **arsenal** on the waterfront by the entrance to the city contains relics of and info on Amalfi's former maritime glory. Continue up the street to the ceramic workshop **Ceramiche Giovanna Fusco,** Via delle Cartiere, 22, where you can see pottery made before your very eyes. (Open Jan. 7-Aug. 17 and Aug. 26-Dec. 22, Mon.-Sat. 9am-1pm and 3-6pm.) Just before the workshop, several yellow signs point to a path that leads up to one of the treasures of Amalfi, the **Valle dei Mulini** (Valley of the Mills). Hike along a stream bed by the old paper mills for a pastoral view of lemon groves and rocky mountains. On the way, stop by the **Museo della Carta,** dedicated to the history and art of paper. (Open Tues.-Thurs. and Sat.-Sun. 9am-1pm. Free.) On June 26 and 27 the town celebrates its patron Sant'Andrea;

among much pomp and circumstance, a horde of men runs a solid metal statue of the saint up the cathedral's numerous stairs, leaving behind a shining trail of sweat.

■ NEAR AMALFI: ATRANI

If you stay in Amalfi, your first excursion should be to **Atrani**, a quiet beachside town of 1200 inhabitants just around the bend from Amalfi (1 bus stop, L1500). The pebble beach here is the perfect place to float in the warm water and admire the stunning backdrop of mountains. From Amalfi, walk five minutes along the waterfront toward Salerno. Either pass directly through the tunnel, or just before you arrive at the tunnel, descend the stairs that pass through the Ristorante Zaccaria to the water. Cross the parking lot and under the arch into the town's only *piazza*, **Piazza Umberto I**. Atrani's main street, **Via dei Dogi**, heads up through the **Valley of the Dragons**, named for the torrent of water and mist (like smoke from a dragon) that runs through the town and out to sea every winter. The investiture of some of Amalfi's doges took place in the town's **Church of San Salvatore dei Birento**, which faces you as you enter the town's main archway. Although the church has been remodeled, the 11th-century Byzantine bronze doors are still intact. Thirteenth-century **Santa Maria Maddalena** with its tiled cupola and gorgeous view of the coast is also worth a visit.

One of the cheapest places on the coast, **A' Scalinatella**, P. Umberto, 12 (tel. 87 19 30), is Atrani's best budget accommodation. The congenial family that manages this quasi-hostel caters to students and budget travelers. (L20,000 for bed and shower, one-time sheets fee of L5000, washing machine L7000. Private rooms available. Curfew midnight.) Lodgers here can partake of discounts at **Ristorante La Piazzetta** (see below): either a free *primo*, or the *menù* for L11,000. As you climb up the main street (Via dei Dogi) from the port, clean **public toilets** are on the left, and **phones** are on the right. **Ristorante La Piazzetta**, P. Umberto I (tel. 87 14 92), offers a *menù* for L16,000. Try the grilled fish or spaghetti with *frutti di mare* (when available). (Open daily 7-11pm.) **Le Arcate**, on the waterfront, offers a full *menù* including a sampling of seafood *antipasti;* a full meal will cost around L30,000. (Open June-Sept. daily, Oct.-May Tues.-Sun. 12:30-3:30pm and 7:30pm-midnight. AmEx, MC, Visa.)

■■■ RAVELLO

Ravello is an ideal spot for an afternoon stroll, a good read, or quiet contemplation. The town has retained the medieval beauty and landscaping prized by Boccaccio, who dedicated part of the *Decameron* to it, and by Wagner, who made it the setting for the second act of *Parsifal*. Whether or not you sense yourself on the brink of creative genius, it's worth the journey up the mountain. The bus ride is easier, but you can hike the 7km up from Amalfi for the most spectacular views.

Orientation and Practical Information Ravello is a short bus ride from Amalfi (7am-10pm, every hr., L1500). From the bus stop, walk through the tunnel to **Piazza Vescovado,** the town's center and nighttime hang-out. The English-speaking **tourist office,** at P. Vescovado, 13 (tel. (089) 85 70 96; fax 85 79 77), to the left of the cathedral, has helpful brochures, maps, and up-to-date accommodations information. (Open Mon.-Sat. 8am-8pm; Oct.-April Mon.-Sat. 8am-7pm.) To the left of the tourist office sits the **post office** (open Mon.-Sat. 8:15am-1:30pm). The **postal code** is 84010. Next along the street you will find the **pharmacy.**

Accommodations and Food Two affordable options are available if you're planning to spend the night. The dramatically situated **Hotel Villa Amore,** Via dei Fusco, 5 (tel./fax 85 71 35), en route to Villa Cimbrone, has cute tidy rooms and a garden overlooking cliffs and the sea. (All rooms with bath and balcony. Singles L45,000/55,000. Doubles L88,000/98,000. July-Aug. half-pension required at

L80,000. MC, Visa.) Up the street to the left of the tourist office, **Albergo Toro,** Viale Wagner, 3 (tel. 85 72 11), lends pleasant, comfortable rooms on an oleander-filled side street, and has a pretty covered terrace. (All rooms with bath. Singles L56,000. Doubles L85,000; June-Sept. L10,000 more. Breakfast included. July-Aug. half-pension required at L85,000. AmEx, MC, Visa.) Several **alimentari** and assorted specialty food shops line Via Roma off P. Vescovado. For a sit-down meal try **La Colonna** at Via Roma, 20 (tel. 85 78 76). The affable young owner Alfonso speaks English and is well-known throughout the town for his delectable fish and homemade pasta. (Open daily noon-2pm and 7-11pm. Nov.-May closed Tues.) At **Cumpà Cosino,** Via Roma, 44/46 (tel. 85 71 56), you can savor a variety of local specialties with an *assaggio di primi* (L15,000), which will stuff you with all of the available pasta dishes. Although many wines savored around the globe are decanted under a Ravello label, actual wine from the area is neither common nor commercially available; make friends in the town if you hope to try some.

Sights and Entertainment The beautiful churches, ivy-covered walls, and meandering gardens of **Villa Rufolo,** 360m above the sea, led Wagner to transports of ecstasy. A medieval tower with beautiful Norman-Saracen vaulting and statues representing the four seasons serves as the entry to the famous Moorish cloister. (Enter through the arch toward the bus stop from P. Vescovado. Open daily 9:30am-1pm. Afternoon hours: June-Sept. 3-7:30pm, Oct.-March 2-4:30pm, April 2-5:30pm, May 2-6pm. Admission L4000, under 12 L2000.)

Outside Ravello's **duomo** on P. Vescovado you can see the Amalfi coast's third set of spectacular bronze doors (not to be outdone by the neighbors, Ravello modeled these 12th-century doors on Amalfi's). Inside, a simple nave arcade of antique columns sets off two pulpits decorated with fantastic mosaics. To the left of the altar stands the chapel of San Pantaleone, patron of the town. Walk behind the painting to see his "unleakable" blood preserved in a cracked vessel. (San Pantaleone was beheaded at Nicomedia on July 27, 290 AD.) Every year on this date the city holds a **festival** and the saint's blood reputedly liquefies. Open daily 9am-1pm and 3-7pm, Oct.-May 9am-1pm and 2-5pm.) Next to the cathedral is the newly opened **museo.** (Open daily 9am-7:30pm; Oct.-April. 9am-5pm. Admission L2000.)

Follow the signposts for **Villa Cimbrone** on the small road passing to the right of Villa Rufolo. Floral walkways and gardens are the prelude to some of the most magnificent views on all the Amalfi coast. (Admission L5000.) Walking back to the town center, you'll pass the **Chiostro di San Francesco,** which exhibits **Italian modern art** throughout the summer.

Ravello's numerous **classical music festivals** (held the weeks of New Year's Day, Easter, and during parts of June, July, and September) host internationally renowned musicians. Concerts draw crowds to the cathedral and the gardens of Villa Rufolo. Tickets run from L20,000, and may be purchased at the tourist office.

■ NEAR RAVELLO: MINORI

Minori was once Amalfi's arsenal and as such suffered attacks from all of the bigger port's enemies. In these more settled times, however, the city is better known for its lemons, exported all over the world, and for its beaches and family atmosphere. Those on an antiquity-kick may want to check out the **Roman villa** with frescoes and black and white mosaics. (Open daily 9am-7pm. Free.) The **beach,** the closest this coast gets to real sand, is a favorite place for locals to knock around a volleyball.

The coastal SITA bus (L1500 from Amalfi or Atrani) stops right on the boardwalk. The Pro Loco **tourist office** at P. Umberto I, 18 (tel. (089) 87 70 87 or 87 76 07), is often out of pamphlets, but willing to help as much as possible. (Open Mon.-Sat. 9am-noon and 4-8pm.) **Public toilets** can be found at the heart of the city, where Via San Pietro splits off from Corso Vittorio Emanuele III.

For a place to stay, homey and inexpensive **Albergo Cápri,** Via Lama, 19 (tel. 87 74 17; on the third floor) is a good bet. Take the road through Church San Trofi-

SALERNO

mena's bell tower. (Doubles L50,000, with bath L54,000. June-Sept. L6000 more. Extra bed 15% more.) The **Caporal Hotel,** Via Nazionale (tel. 87 74 08), provides some of the finer amenities, like a phone in each room. (Singles with bath L70,000. Doubles with bath L100,000. Half-pension L85,000. Oct.-May L10,000-20,000 less. AmEx, MC, Visa.) For a satisfying meal, try **La Botte,** Via S. Maria Vetrano, 15 (tel. 87 78 93). Savor splendid *scialetelli con frutti* (L9500) at the outdoor tables. (Pizza L6000-8000. Cover L2000. Open daily noon-3:30pm and 7pm-1am. AmEx, Visa.)

■■■ SALERNO

After serving as the capital of the Norman Empire from 1077 to 1127 and housing Europe's first medical school, Salerno was almost completely destroyed by the bombings of World War II. The big-city atmosphere and postwar buildings are a shock to the system of a traveler accustomed to peaceful coastal villages; nevertheless, inexpensive food and accommodations make Salerno an excellent base for exploring the area. Extensive train and bus connections facilitate transit to Calabria and provide for daytrips to Paestum, the Amalfi Coast, and Pompeii.

ORIENTATION AND PRACTICAL INFORMATION

From the train station on **P. Vittorio Veneto,** the expansive and remarkably clean **Corso Vittorio Emanuele** veers off to the right (closed to traffic). A 15-minute walk brings you to Via dei Mercanti and the **old quarter,** the most interesting and vivacious part of the city. Alternatively, continue straight on **Via Mauro** from the train station, cross Corso Garibaldi and come to **Piazza della Concordia** on the waterfront. **Lungomare Trieste** runs along the coast, and **Via Roma** heads off to the right from the *lungomare*.

Tourist Office: EPT, on P. Veneto (tel. 23 14 32), to the right as you leave the train station. Limited info on the Amalfi Coast. Pick up a copy of the essential guide *MEMO,* complete with hotel, restaurant, club, and special events listings. English spoken. Open Mon.-Sat. 9am-2pm and 3-8pm.

Police: tel. 113.

Post Office: Corso Garibaldi, 203 (tel. 22 99 70). Open Mon.-Sat. 8:30am-5:30pm. **Branch office** at P. Veneto (tel. 22 99 98), to the right as you leave the train station. Open Mon.-Fri. 8:15am-1:30pm, Sat. 8:15am-12:10pm. **Postal Code:** 84100.

Telephones: Telecom (SIP), Corso Garibaldi, 31/32, set in from the street to the left as you leave the train station. Open Sun.-Fri. 9:30am-1pm and 2-5:30pm. **Telephone Code:** 089.

Budget Travel: CTS, Piazza A. Santelmo, 7 (tel. 72 19 75). From Lungomare Trieste, take bus #6, 8, or 11 south about 2km to the intersection with V. Mantegna at Bar Marconi; follow V. Mantegna to P. Santelmo. Open Mon.-Fri. 9am-1pm and 4:30-7:30pm.

Trains: P. Veneto (tel. 25 22 00). Trains depart every hr. 6am-9:30pm to Pompeii (40min., L2000) and Naples (1hr., L5100). 3 trains daily to Paestum on the Salerno-Reggio di Calabria line (45min., L4200). Information office, first door to the right outside the station, open daily 7am-9pm. **Luggage Storage:** Follow the signs in the station to the huge warehouse. Bags and bikes L1500 per day.

Buses: SITA, Via Irno, 2-4 (tel. 79 50 21). Information office open Mon.-Sat. 8am-1pm and 4:30-8pm. Buses to Naples (every 10-15min. 6am-9pm, L5000) leave from Corso Garibaldi outside SITA office. Buses for the Amalfi coast depart from P. della Concordia to: Amalfi (frequent buses 6am-10:30pm, L2700); Sorrento (9 per day 6am-7pm, L6100) with stops at the coastal towns of Praiano (L3400) and Positano (L4200). Buses run less frequently Sun. **ATACS** (tel. 22 58 99) city bus #41 leaves regularly from outside the train station to Pompeii (every 20min. 6:05am-10:10pm, 30min., L3400). Several bus lines run from P. Concordia to Paestum (1hr., direction "Agropoli," L4300).

Ferries: departures from P. della Concordia or Molo Manfredi (Molo is a 15-min. walk to the right while facing the port at P. della Concordia). A good alternative if the careening bus ride along the Amalfi Coast scares you. Check the *MEMO* guide at the port for current departure times and prices; to: **Amalfi** (L4000) and **Positano** (L7500) 6-9 ferries daily in summer, fewer in winter; **Cápri** (L12,000) 3-5 daily in summer. Hydrofoils take half the time but run less frequently (3 daily in summer). To: **Amalfi** (L7000), **Positano** (L13,000), and **Cápri** (L17,000). **Emergencies:** tel. 113. **Hospital: S. Lenardo** tel. 67 11 11. **Medical Assistance:** tel. 33 99 99.

ACCOMMODATIONS

Several options can make your stopover in Salerno inexpensive. Establishments fill rapidly in late July and August, so arrive early in the morning to secure a place.

Ostello della Gioventù "Irno" (HI), Via Luigi Guercia, 112 (tel. 79 02 51). Exit the train station and turn left on Via Torrione, which runs along the tracks. After about 300m you'll come to Via Mobilio, which will take you left under the tracks. The second stairway on the right, about 300m ahead, leads up to Via Luigi Guercia. Clean rooms, hot showers, kitchen facilities, TV room, and kind management. Curfew 12:30am. Lock-out 10:30am-5:00pm. L15,000 per person, L2000 for sheets. Ask at desk for a list of eateries that offer discounts to hostel clientele.

Albergo Santa Rosa, Corso Vittorio Emanuele, 14 (tel. 22 53 46), off the *piazza* in front of the train station. Clean, bright, and reasonably priced. English spoken. Curfew midnight. Common bathrooms. Singles L40,000. Doubles L60,000. Prices lower Jan.-May.

Hotel Salerno, Via Vicinanza, 42 (tel. 22 42 11), the first left off Corso Emanuele. The furniture was new in the 50s and hasn't died yet. Phones in the rooms and TV lounge. Singles L35,000, with bath L55,000. Doubles L65,000, with bath L75,000.

Hotel Cinzo, C. Vittorio Emanuele, 74 (tel. 23 27 73). Large, airy rooms, all doubles with common bathrooms (L50,000).

FOOD

Salerno serves up typical Campanian culinary delights, including *pasta e fagioli* (pasta and bean soup) and all sorts of seafood, and even adds some unusual specialties like *milza* (spleen). Nearby Battipaglia produces the famous *mozzarella alla buffala,* fresh cheese made from water buffalo milk. Shop cheap at **Supermercato STANDA,** Corso Vittorio Emanuele, 228, near the old quarter (open Mon.-Fri. 9am-1pm and 4:30-8:30pm, closed Sat. afternoon and Sun.). Or, nearer the youth hostel, try **Di Luccio,** Via Mobilio, 62 (open Mon.-Sat. 7am-9:30pm).

Trattoria-Pizzeria Da "Sasà" La Casereccia, Via Diaz, 42 (tel. 22 03 30), to the right, 300m down Corso V. Emanuele from the train station. A lot of fun for those who *parlano* a little *italiano*. There's no menu—it all depends on what's fresh. Full meal L15,000-20,000. Open Sat.-Thurs. noon-3pm and 8-11:30pm.

Hosteria Il Brigante, Via F. Linguiti, 4 (tel. 22 65 92), near the cathedral. Follow C. Vittorio Emanuele to Via dei Mercanti and turn right on Via del Duomo, going through the gate to the left, just past the cathedral. Try the *pasta alla Sangiovannara,* or with zucchini and scampi. Full meals from L15,000. Open Tues.-Sun. 8:30pm-midnight. AmEx.

Pizzeria Del Vicolo della Neve, Vicolo della Neve, 24 (tel. 22 57 05). From Via dei Mercanti, take your first left after Via Duomo. In the old city, this piece of Salerno's history hasn't changed since its opening 500 years ago. Full meal from L20,000. Cover L2000. Service 12%. Open Thurs.-Tues. 8pm-3am.

Ristorante Il Caminetto, Via Roma, 232 (tel. 22 96 14). Near the AAST tourist office. A family-run restaurant with low prices. Savor *risotto alla pescatore,* a delicious mix of rice and seafood, for only L8000. Pizzas L5000-7000. Cover L2000. Service 12%. Open Thurs.-Tues. noon-3:30pm and 7pm-midnight. AmEx, Visa.

SIGHTS AND ENTERTAINMENT

Meandering through Via dei Mercanti and its tiny side-streets, you can get a feel for the hustle and bustle of life in the Middle Ages. Turn right on Via Duomo to see the

cathedral, begun in 845 AD and rebuilt 200 years later by Norman leader Robert Guiscard. The atrium has an ancient pool surrounded by columns taken from Paestum, while the crypt houses the **holy tooth** of the city's patron saint, San Matteo. In the attached museum you can see the fine work of medieval ivory-carvers from Amalfi. (Cathedral open daily 10am-noon and 4-6:30pm; museums open daily 9am-1pm and 4-7pm.) In the nearby Largo Casavecchia, the **Museo della Ceramica** exhibits local ceramic art. (Open Mon.-Sat. 9am-1pm, Thurs. also 4-7pm. Free.)

Turn left off Via Mercanti and stroll along the waterfront on the **seawall.** Once there, revel in the divine Amalfi coastline and the sights and sounds of the nearby fishing harbor. The hamlet of **Vietri sul Mare** is home both to hundreds of ceramic artisans and to the closest beach to Salerno (take the SITA bus toward Sorrento, 15min., L1500). The other nearby option—Paestum's strand—is farther away, but its stretches of white sand beat the rocky beaches of the Amalfi Coast.

For a view of Salerno's majestic surroundings (though there is actually little to see *inside* the castle), take bus #19 from Teatro Verdi (at the far end of Via Roma) to the medieval **Castello di Arechi** (tel. 22 72 37), which dates from the 8th century. (Open Mon.-Fri. 9am-1pm. Free. Buy bus tickets at bars and *tabacchi,* L1500 per half day, L2500 per full day.) Back at city level, visit Salerno's **medieval quarter.** It was once the capital of the Norman empire (1077-1127) and home to Europe's oldest medical school (9th-century texts were already calling it ancient).

Don't miss the evening *passeggiata,* when the *lungomare* overflows with people strolling and enjoying ice cream. From June through August, an **arts festival** features free concerts and theater in the atrium of the cathedral and at the city's stadium. Salerno also hosts several **international film festivals** from June through October at Cinema Capitol in the city center (admission free-L6000). In July, experience both "hot" and "cool" at the international **blues festival** (buy tickets at the stadium; weekly passes L35,000).

The area around Salerno rocks with **discos,** but be warned: prices are steep without passes (women can often get in free, but take that as its own warning). From June through September the nighttime hotspot is the renowned **Fuenti** (tel. 26 14 77), located in Cetara, 4km west of Salerno. Situated on the coastal cliffs, it features three full floors of open-air dancing (open Sat.-Sun. 10pm-4am). In the winter, Salerno lives it up at **Living,** Via Gelsi Rossi (tel. 79 92 01), near the hostel (open Oct.-May Thurs.-Fri. 8:30pm-2am, Sat. 9:30pm-3am, and Sun. 6:30pm-3am). The cheapest way to get into these clubs is to look for free passes handed out at random. Also check the magazine *MEMO* (at the tourist office and some local bars) for special events and more club listings, including those outside Salerno.

■■■ PAESTUM

Not far from the Roman ruins of Pompeii and Herculaneum, the Greek temples of Paestum are among the best-preserved in the Italian peninsula, rivaling even those of Agrigento in Sicily. Greek colonists from Sybaris founded Paestum as Poseidonia in the 7th century BC, and the city quickly became a flourishing commercial center, prospering from extended trade with people to the north. After a period of Lucanian (native Italian) control in the 5th century BC, Poseidonia eventually passed to the Romans in 273 BC and became Paestum. For a time, Paestum minted its own coins, but when the Appian Way was extended from Rome to Brindisi, the city was bypassed by trade. Plagued by malaria and pirates, Paestum's last inhabitants abandoned the city in the 9th century AD.

Orientation and Practical Information Buses from Salerno (every 30min., 6am-8pm, L4300) let you off on **Via Magna Graecia,** the main modern road; ask to stop at the ruins *(gli scavi)* or at your hotel and save yourself a walk. Be sure to check return bus times in advance. If you catch one of the infrequent **trains** (5 per day from Salerno, L3900), head straight out of the station and through Porta Sirena, the most intact of the ancient city gates; a short walk brings you to V. Magna

Graecia. The last bus back to Salerno passes by at 7:30pm, and the last train at
8:10pm. Another option is to take the bus to nearby Agropoli (L1800), which allows
for many other train connections. In July and August, Paestum hosts its own international festival of music, drama, and dance. For a program and info, contact the **tourist office** at P. Basilica 151-153 (tel. (0828) 81 10 16; open Mon.-Sat. 8am-2pm.)
Cointur is not located in Paestum, but can help with reservations over the phone
(tel. 72 47 47; some English spoken).

Accommodations and Food Paestum makes a great daytrip from Salerno,
but if you want to spend the night, **Albergo delle Rose,** Via Magna Graecia, 193 (tel.
81 10 70), is a relatively inexpensive option with luxurious rooms. (Singles L40,000.
Doubles L80,000. Prices L5000-10,000 lower Oct.-April.) A 10-minute walk on Via
Principe di Piemonte to the right past the ruins and toward the coast will bring you
to numerous **campsites. Apollo** (tel. 81 11 78) provides a soccer field, bar, and *discoteca*. (L5500 per person, L11,500 per tent. Four-person bungalows L60,000.
Open May-Sept.) **Dei Pini** (tel. 81 10 86) also keeps you well-fed, with a *pizzeria,*
bar, and food store on-site. English spoken. (L8000 per person, L24,000 per tent.
Oct.-May L5000 per person, L15,000 per tent. Open year-round.) Restaurants in
Paestum are scarce. With outdoor seating under a large tent that looks like something from the stereotypical deserts of Arabia, **Oasi,** on V. Magna Graecia (100m to
the left of the museum; tel. 81 19 35), serves full meals (about L20,000) during the
day and pizzas in the evening (from L5000). Cover L1500. Service 15%. (Open Jan.-
Sept. daily and Oct.-Nov. Wed.-Sun. noon-3pm and 7pm-midnight.)

Sights The ancient Greeks built Paestum on a north-south axis, marked by the
still-paved Via Sacra. (Looking at the ruins from the modern V. Magna Graecia,
which runs parallel to Via Sacra, north is to your right.) Most guided tours start from
the Porta Giustizia, at the southern end of Via Sacra—quiet types can sometimes join
without paying the steep rates.

Paestum's three **Doric temples** rank among the best-preserved in the world.
Amazingly, they were built without any mortar or other cement; the bronze clamps
were added only later as protection against earthquakes. To imagine the buildings as
they originally stood, picture a roof of terra-cotta tiles supported by wooden beams.
All the stone you see now was covered in stucco and painted, in some places to look
like marble, in others with bright reds and blues. For a more detailed discussion of
the history, architecture, and archaeology of the temples and the site, look for *Paestum: Guide to the Excavations and Archaeological Museum* (ed. Matonti; available in any of the roadside shops, L6000).

When first uncovered, the three temples were quickly misnamed. Recent excavations have enlightened archaeologists about which gods the temples actually honored, but the old names stuck anyway. The southernmost temple, the so called
basilica, is the oldest, dating to the second half of the 6th century BC. Its unusual
plan, including a main interior section (*naos*) split in two by a single row of columns down the middle, has led archaeologists to theorize that the temple may have
been dedicated to two gods (Zeus and Hera) instead of just one. The next temple to
the north, the **Temple of Poseidon** (actually dedicated to Hera), was built 100 years
after the "basilica," in the middle of the 5th century BC. While the squat, squishy columns of the "basilica" look like overgrown mushrooms, the Temple of Poseidon
incorporates many of the same dimensions and optical refinements that made the
Parthenon in Athens famous. A little farther up on the temple, you can make out
some small **lions' heads;** when it rained, water from the gutters came pouring out of
their mouths. The third major Doric temple, the again-misnamed **Temple of Ceres,**
is not in line with the other two; it lies off to the north of the Forum. The temple
was built around 500 BC (placing its construction date exactly between those of the
other two temples) and was dedicated to Athena. It was transformed into a church
in the early Middle Ages and abandoned in the 9th century.

Continuing north on Via Sacra, you come to the Roman **Forum,** even larger than the one at Pompeii. The Romans leveled all the older structures at the center of the city to make room for this proto-*piazza,* the commercial and political arena of Paestum. To the right, a large, shallow pit marks the site of the pool in the ancient **gymnasium.** East of the gymnasium lies half of the Roman **amphitheater** (the rest is buried under the modern road). Because the going rate for lions was so high in Paestum, gladiators faced off against angry mastiffs.

The **museum** on the other side of V. Magna Graecia houses an interesting collection of ancient sculpture and paintings found in the area. Those well versed in mythology can play guessing-games with sculptural panels from a temple dedicated to Hera found 9km to the north of Paestum. According to legend, the temple was founded by Jason and the Argonauts. Also of note are the paintings from the famous **Tomb of the Diver,** rare examples of Greek murals. (Archaeological site open 9am-1hr. before sunset; ticket offices close 1 hr. earlier. Museum open 9am-7pm. L8000 admits you to both ruins and museum.)

After visiting the ruins, you may want to go worship the sun at the **beach** 2km to the east. The golden sand stretches for miles—unfortunately, much (but not all) of it is owned by resorts that require you to rent a chair for the day. Ask around for the *spiaggia pubblica* for a free dip in the Mediterranean.

■ Apulia (Puglia)

Welcome to hard-core *Italia,* where the sun's scorching rays and the people's intense passions continually threaten to bring things to a boil. Conversations, complete with elaborate hand gestures, quickly progress from pleasant joking to yelling and (sometimes) back again. Some travelers interpret the southerners' mercurial passions as rudeness, but you'll have a better understanding (and a better time) if you try to see them as part of an uninhibited zest for life. Unfortunately, a legacy of *machismo* persists which women may find threatening, especially in large cities. In public, the best tactic for dissuading persistent, obnoxious behavior is to ignore it.

The heel of Italy's boot, Apulia has been prized throughout the centuries for its fertile plains and numerous natural ports. The ancient Greeks flourished here, and the Romans controlled the region as a vital trade route to the East along the Appian Way. With the Middle Ages came an onslaught of invaders whose influences created a conglomerate culture. Modern Apulia, having served its time on "skid row," is regaining its prominence as the richest and most educated region in southern Italy. In its interior, remote medieval villages and whitewashed, cone-roofed *trulli* houses dot a cave-ridden plain; along the shore, ports have a distinctly Middle Eastern air.

Apulia is as accessible to contemporary tourists as it was to ancient invaders. Direct train lines run from Naples to Bari and from Bologna to Lecce; rail service is supplemented within the region by the private Ferrovie Bari-Nord, Ferrovie Del Sud-Est, Ferrovie del Gargano, and Ferrovie Calabro-Lucane lines. (Eurailpass and *cartaverde* not valid on these lines.) The transportation hubs of Foggia, Brindisi, and Taranto are perhaps best viewed from the station as you make your connections; base yourself in Bari or Lecce instead.

THE GARGANO MASSIF

The Gargano Massif once ranked among the most popular pilgrimage destinations in Europe: the Archangel Michael was said to have appeared in a cave here in the 5th century, and in ancient times the same cavern was occupied by a respected oracle. In these more secular times, the peninsula is renowned for the 65km of beaches on the north and east coasts, some of the best in continental Italy. The inland is covered by the **Foresta Umbra,** which abruptly gives way to classic Mediterranean terrain on the southern half. The Gargano is succumbing to the twin blights of southern coastal areas—smokestacks and beach umbrellas—so visit the region soon, before it becomes an industrial tract interrupted by the occasional seaside town.

Siponto

Three km southwest of Manfredonia, the ancient city of Siponto was abandoned after a 12th-century earthquake and plague. The sole survivor is the remarkable **Church of Santa Maria di Siponto,** which stands in a grove of pines amidst modest pre-Roman ruins. The church was built during the 11th century in Puglian-Romanesque style, though the blind arcade shows strong Pisan influence and the square plan and cupola also point to Byzantine roots. Siponto is the next-to-last stop on the Foggia-Manfredonia train line.

■■■ BARI

Bari, the capital of Apulia, makes an amusing and inexpensive base for exploring the region and a pleasant departure point for Greece. The city's transformation into a backpacker's haven is mostly due to the efforts of the dedicated workers of the "Stop-Over in Bari" program, who do everything they can think of to make your stay entertaining, interesting, and cheap (see below). Bari was once a cornerstone of several empires because of its port and central location. It was a major stronghold of Byzantine power in southern Italy and later an important point of departure for the Crusades. The modern city splits into a new city, laid out on a well-organized grid of wide streets, and the small and increasingly poor old city. Hold purses and cameras tightly, wear money belts inside your clothes, and try not to let the widespread petty thievery diminish your enjoyment of the city's great seafood and hopping nightlife.

THE "STOP-OVER IN BARI" PROGRAM

Ten years ago, local government and grass roots organizations came up with a unique idea to make Bari a mecca for backpackers from all over. They designed the "Stop-Over in Bari" program and inaugurated a free campsite to entice those heading to Greece to stop and enjoy all Bari has to offer. Between **mid-June** and **mid-September,** Stop-Over can be of immeasurable assistance to non-resident travelers under 30. Although older visitors are not eligible for Stop-Over's freebies, they should still stop by the offices for the most complete and up-to-date info on Bari.

Outside the central train station parks a raucously-painted double-decker **bus** with a large "Stop-Over in Bari" sign above. Relax while the multilingual staff kindly provides you with every piece of info you could possibly need about Bari, ferries, and more. Another **info booth** is inside the **Stazione Marittima** (open Mon.-Sat. 8:30am-8:30pm, Sun. 9am-6pm). Stop-Over's **main office** at Via Dante Alighieri, 111 (tel. 521 45 38; fax 521 18 22) has more detailed information on sights and events, and provides free luggage storage (open Mon.-Sat. 8:30am-8:30pm and Sun. 9am-6pm).

Pick up a daily Stop-Over **newsletter** for info on discounted restaurants, supermarkets, shops, museums, and cultural events. For free accommodations take bus #5 (last departure 11pm, but be there no later than 10:45pm) or #3/ (a longer route) to Pineta San Francesco, a **campground** with bar, free showers, and more free luggage storage. They'll provide a tent if you don't have your own. All city buses are free as long as you are under 30 and a non-resident of Bari; just flash your passport or the special card that they'll give you at the campground. Be aware that buses to the campground are infrequent.

If the rustic showers and bathrooms at the Pineta frighten you, or you simply want a more luxurious sojourn, take advantage of Stop-Over's **Package** (starting July 1), which puts you up in apartment rooms for two nights for a mere L30,000 (L15,000 per additional night). You'll be housed with college students in residential neighborhoods safer than those in which Bari's *pensioni* cluster. (Call (080) 521 45 38 or fax 521 18 22 to reserve.)

Stop-Over also offers various events and seminars (such as pizza-making) throughout the summer at the campground Pineta S. Francesco. (All events free.) Tour Bari for free using their **bicycles** and **skateboards** but don't leave them unattended since you don't get a lock. There are also two free weekly **concerts** and occasional events throughout the summer, as well as free copies of an English edition of Luca Conti's *Inter-Rail Man,* a funny and detailed guide to railpass travel from a personal perspective. The **summer hotline** is 577 23 49 (at the Pineta).

FERRIES

Getting to Greece from Bari is cheaper and more appealing than going by way of the highly industrial Brindisi (unless you have a Eurail or InterRail pass). Ferries go to **Corfu** (10hr.), **Igoumenitsa** (12hr.), and **Patras** (19hr.). There are no discounts for Eurailpasses or *cartaverde,* but most lines offer special student rates and a 10% discount on round-trip tickets (Poseidon discounts 20%). The following are ferry companies with their destinations; the lowest prices (deck class) for each are shown. The high season varies slightly from company to company, year to year, and place to place (ah, l'Italia!), but is generally from the first week of July to the last week of August. Tickets and info can be obtained directly at the **Stazione Marittima** or at the offices listed below. **You must check in at the Stazione Marittima two hours before departure.** After check-in, a police booth will check your passport. **OTE,** the travel agency connected with Stop-Over (open year-round, even after Stop-Over is over; see Budget Travel, below), also has ferry and ticket info.

Poseidon Lines, c/o Morfimare, Corso de Tullio, 36/40 (tel. 521 00 22; fax 521 12 04). Box 11-12 at the port. To: **Patras** (L60,000, high season L75,000; students L45,000, high season L60,000); **Igoumenitsa** (L45,000/L65,000; students L35,000/L50,000). Departures to both sites Tues. and Thurs. 9pm, Sat. 7pm, and Sun. 11pm; in Aug. Mon., Wed., and Sat. 7pm, and Fri. 10am. From Greece, Poseidon ferries head to **Cyprus** and **Israel.**

Ventouris Ferries, c/o Pan Travel, Stazione Marittima Box 9-10 (tel./fax 521 87 83). To: **Patras** and **Cefalonia** (L65,000/L85,000; students L60,000/L75,000; departs daily at 8:30pm or 6pm; check schedules); **Corfu** and **Igoumenitsa** (L45,000/L65,000; students L35,000/L60,000). To Corfu in June on scattered days, July-Sept. daily. To **Igoumenitsa** Feb.-June and Oct.-Dec. on scattered days, July-Sept. daily. Departs 8:30pm.

Marlines, c/o P. Lorusso & Co, Car Ferry Terminal Box 3-4 (tel. 521 76 99; fax 521 77 34). To: **Patras** (L62,000/L77,000; return ticket L56,000/L69,000); **Corfu** and **Igoumenitsa** (L46,000/L72,000; return ticket L41,000/L65,000). April 1-Dec. 21 departures for Corfu and Igoumenitsa daily at 9pm. June 24-Aug. 5 departures for Patras Sat. 8pm and Wed. 9pm, Aug. 10-Sept. 14 Sat. 9pm and Tues. 8pm.

ORIENTATION AND PRACTICAL INFORMATION

Via Sparano leads straight from the train station two blocks to **Piazza Umberto,** the main square in town. Farther along Via Sparano, the streets are lined with unique stores and fancy boutiques, providing some of the city's best window shopping. At the end of V. Sparano is **Corso Vittorio Emanuele II** and the edge of the old city. Those attempting the long walk to the **port** should skirt the old city's hopelessly winding streets by turning left on Corso Emanuele II and right at Piazza della Libertà onto Via Giuseppe Massari. Walk around the castle and follow the coast to the right. For a more leisurely stroll, turn right off V. Sparano onto Corso Emanuele II; this takes you past **Corso Cavour** to **Piazza Eroi del Mare,** a favorite nighttime hangout for many of the city's youths.

Tourist Office: Stop-Over should satisfy your every need, but just in case, there's **EPT,** P. Aldo Moro, 33A (tel. 524 22 44), to the right as you leave the station. Regional and local maps of Apulia. English spoken, sort of. Open Mon.-Sat. 9am-1pm and 4-8pm; in winter Mon.-Sat. 9am-1pm.

Police: tel. 113. **Carabinieri:** tel. 112.

BARI

Post Office: P. Battisti (tel. 521 03 81), behind the university. From P. Umberto, take a left on Via Crisanzio, then the 1st right on Via Cairoli. Open Mon.-Fri. 8:20am-8pm, Sat. 8:20am-1pm. **Postal Code:** 70100.

Telephones: Telecom (Iritel), to the right of the station. Open daily 8am-9:45pm. **Telephone Code:** 080.

Budget Travel: OTE, Via Dante, 111 (tel. 521 45 38). From the station, walk 1 block past P. Umberto and to the left. Info on student discount travel from the people who run Stop-Over. Open Mon.-Sat. 8:30am-8:30pm, Sun. 9am-6pm.

Currency Exchange: at the information desk in the F.S. train station (open daily 7am-8:45pm), or at the **Automobile Club Italiano** at the ferry terminal (only when boats are arriving or departing).

American Express: Morfimare, Corso de Tullio, 36/40 (tel. 521 00 22), near the port. Open Mon.-Fri. 9am-12:30pm and 3:30-6:30pm.

Trains: F.S. train station in P. Aldo Moro (tel. 521 68 01). Bari lies on train lines from Rome (6 per day, 8hr., L37,000) and Milan (15 per day, 10hr., L65,400). Frequent trains connect Bari with Apulia's larger towns: Foggia (1½hr., L9800), Taranto (2hr., L9800), Brindisi (2hr., L9800), and Lecce (2½hr., L11,700). The station is also home to several private lines, including the **Ferrovie del Sud-Est** (tel. 558 32 22; to Castellana Grotte, Alberobello, and Martina Franca), on the last track of the central station, the **Bari-Nord** (tel. 521 47 14; to Bitonto, Barletta, Andria, and Ruvo di Puglia), and the **Ferrovie Apulo-Lucane** (tel. 572 52 22; to Matera in Basilicata), both to the left as you exit the main station. Eurail and *cartaverde* are only good on F.S.

English Bookstore: Feltrinelli Bookstore, Via Dante, 91 (tel. 521 96 77), a half-block from Stop-Over's main office. A decent collection of classics. Open Mon.-Fri. 9am-1pm and 4-8pm, Sat. 9am-1pm.

Emergencies: tel. 113. **Ambulance:** tel. 522 15 14 or 504 40 40.

ACCOMMODATIONS

If you are over 30 or it's summer, Bari offers few inexpensive options for lodging. Be sure to call ahead during the summer months, as the hotels fill up quickly.

Pensione Fiorini, Via Imbriani, 69 (tel. 554 07 88), several blocks down Via Dante from the Stop-Over office. Rooms have high ceilings and balconies, but few have private baths. Friendly management loves foreign tourists. Small singles L25,000. Doubles L48,000, with bath L58,000.

Pensione Giulia, Via Crisanzio, 12 (tel. 521 66 30; fax 521 82 71). From the station, turn left just before P. Umberto. Clean, spacious, and recently remodeled rooms. Singles L45,000, with bath L65,000. Doubles L70,000, with bath L80,000. Triples L95,000, with bath L108,000. Quads L136,000. All credit cards accepted.

Pensione Romeo, Via Crisanzio, 12 (tel. 523 72 53). Downstairs from Pensione Giulia. Hm. Small singles L35,000, with bath L45,000. Doubles with bath L70,000.

Ostello del Levante (HI), Palese Marina, Lungomare Massaro, 33 (tel. 530 02 82). Take the train to the Bari-Palese stop (L1000) or bus #1 from Corso Cavour to Palese and walk to the beach. The hostel resides in safer territory outside the city. It doubles as a home for the mentally handicapped, so watch which column you check when you register. 6 beds per room. Lockout 9am-5pm. Curfew 11pm. L19,000 per day, L14,000 with HI card. Breakfast included.

FOOD

As much as the city seems to cater to Greece-bound tourists, it is nevertheless incredibly easy to find a good, authentic, Apulian menu for a reasonable price. Take advantage of the many colorful **markets** like the daily vegetable frenzy in P. del Ferrarese. If you're not staying in town, stop by **Supermercato Vito Caldarulo,** V. de Giosa, 97 (tel. 524 74 85), three streets to the right of P. Umberto I while facing away from the station, and grab a snack; it will undoubtedly be cheaper and tastier than food bought on the ferry. (Open Mon.-Sat. 8am-1pm and 5-8:30pm.)

Vini e Cucina Da Nicola, Strada Vallisa, 23, in the old city. Take a right off Via Sparano onto Corso Emanuele. From P. IV Novembre, enter the old city on your left; the restaurant will be on your left. Inexpensive dining at its best. Don't let the mostly male clientele and no-frills service frighten you off. No menu, dishes change daily, and the *calamari* (if available) is exquisite. *Menù* L11,000. Open Mon.-Sat. noon-3pm and 7pm-midnight.

Taverna Verde, Largo Adua, 18/19 (tel. 54 03 09), on a triangular *piazza* on the *lungomare;* off Corso Cavour (parallel to Via Sparano and two blocks to the right), turn right on Via Cognetti. Black-tie service at black-t-shirt prices. *Orecchiette alla barese* (the regional pasta speciality) L7000. Local wine L3000 per bottle. Cover L2500. Open Mon.-Sat. noon-3pm and 8-11pm. AmEx, MC, Visa.

Osteria delle Travi, Largo Chiurlia, 12, at the end of Via Sparano. Turn left through the arches at the entrance to the old city. Support the *Mezzogiorno* (southern Italy) in this charming stone cellar by ordering such local specialties as pasta with arugula or *ricotta e braciola* (stuffed horsemeat). Full meals L17,000 without drinks. Other prices vary. Open daily 12:30-3pm and 7:30-10:30pm.

El Pedro Self-Service, Via Piccinni, 152 (tel. 521 12 94), off Via Sparano; go left 1 block before Corso Emanuele. Not a Mexican restaurant, but a great cafeteria serving authentic Apulian specialties, different every day. Complete meal with drink about L16,000. Open for lunch only Mon.-Sat. noon-3pm.

SIGHTS

A strategic port on the Italian coast, Bari has always been a primary point of attack for invading armies. To help deter and defend against encroaching troops, Bari's citizens built the old city as a labyrinth. Residents could hide in the narrow, twisting passageways or use them to ambush those less familiar with the streets, but thieves learned to use the maze of the old city to their advantage—and it can become a nightmare for the careless tourist. **Do not venture alone into the old city, especially at night.** Avoid flashy watches and jewelry; keep valuables in front, inside pockets; and hold purses, bags, and cameras tightly where thieves cannot grab them. Stick to the larger streets, use a map, and don't make yourself a target for crime.

Still, don't let petty criminals scare you off entirely, since the old city is of immense historic interest and well worth visiting. On the outskirts of the old city, right in front of the cathedral, the **Castello Svevo** (Swabian Castle) evokes the grandeur and power of three different periods. The Norman Ruggiero II began the structure with the castle proper and four keeps. It was then rearranged by Frederick II (1230-1240) into a trapezoid with two of the towers still standing in the interior. The pointed door and beautiful mullioned windows in the north, toward the sea, were constructed in this period. Finally, Isabel of Aragon and Sona Sforza reorganized the internal court and added the bulwarks and angular keeps (16th century). Almost all of the castle is closed for the excavation of a recently discovered **Roman city** on the site. You can, however, admire plasters of Apulian sculpture of the 11th-16th centuries in the **Gypsoteca** (open daily 9am-1:30pm and 3:30-7pm; admission L4000, under 19 and over 59 free).

Enter the **old city** behind the castle, and follow P. Massari to P. Federico II di Svevia. Turn right at P. Odegitria, which leads to the **cathedral.** Begun at the end of the 12th century during the peaceful years of Norman rule, the cathedral displays a typically austere Romanesque façade, somewhat modified by baroque decorations around the doors. Its interior is a fine example of Romanesque architecture, with a choir and chapel protruding from the nave. (Open daily 8am-noon and 4-7pm.)

Yes, Virginia, there is a **Santa Claus,** and he's dead. His remains were stolen from Asia Minor by 60 Baresi sailors in 1087—they don't call Bari *scippolandia* (petty thieves' land) for nothing. The victorious sailors refused to hand over the saint to the local clergy, saying they had vowed to construct a special temple for the remains. From the cathedral, follow V. Crociate north to Santa's final (?) resting place, the **Church of San Nicola,** completed in the 12th century (though by the Catholic Church and not by the sailors). The church's spartan appearance is better suited to a fortress; in fact, the tower on the right survives from a Byzantine castle that originally occupied the site. Inside, an historical mish-mash awaits. An 11th-century epis-copal throne hides behind the high altar, and elaborate 17th-century paintings adorn the ceiling. The crypt, with its windows of translucent marble, houses the remains of St. Nicholas beside a beautiful silver reliquary. To the left as you enter is a Greek Orthodox shrine, built for pilgrims visiting from the east. On the back wall are several panels painted in the 17th century to depict the saint's accomplish-ments, among them the resurrection of three children who were sliced to bits and plunged into a barrel of brine by a nasty butcher. (Open daily 8am-noon and 3:30-7pm, except during mass.)

Follow Lungomare Augusto from behind the church, along the sea to the right to the next gate, at P. Mercantile, the site of a colorful morning **market.** The *piazza* lies under the open porch and clock tower of the **Sedile,** the medieval meeting place of local councils. Continuing farther along the *lungomare* you will come first to the innumerable fish markets at P. Eroi del Mare, then on to **Molo San Nicola** (San Nicola's Wharf). The gray-and-white towered building in the distance, the **Palazzo della Provincia** on Lungomare N. Sauro (tel. 541 24 21), houses the **Pina-coteca Provinciale** on its top floor. The museum displays paintings by Veronese, Tintoretto, and Bellini. Ask to see the works of Francesco Netti, Bari's most acclaimed artist and possibly Italy's most impressive Impressionist painter. (Open Tues.-Sat. 9am-1pm and 4-7pm, Sun. 9am-1pm. Free.)

Whence and Wherefore the Red Pillar?

In St. Nicholas's crypt, to the far right, sits a red alabaster pillar that originally stood among those still in place in the crypt. Legend holds that he brought this pillar from Myra, and a 17th-century painting in the back depicts angels helping him lift it. Now iron bars protect it from devout visitors who would chip it to keep as relics. But traditional beliefs about the pillar seem rather dubious in light of the fact that St. Nick *never once set foot in Italy.* Thus, we are left with sev-eral unresolved and pressing questions—who brought the pillar here? and why? How old is it? And was it carried by angels or eight tiny reindeer?

ENTERTAINMENT

Bari rivals Naples as the south's cultural nucleus. Stop-Over has the latest news on events and ever-changing hotspots, and sponsors everything from recycling work-shops and kite festivals to comic-strip shows. Unfortunately, one of the most renowned theaters in Italy, the **Teatro Petruzzelli,** was almost completely destroyed in a fire in October of 1991 and is closed indefinitely. **Teatro Piccinni** (tel. 521 37 17) offers a concert season in the spring. In summer, occasional con-certs are held in the *castello.* Entertainment listings crowd *Ecco Bari,* the tourist office's entertainment guide, and the *Bari Sera* section of *La Gazzetta del Mezzo-giorno* (the local newspaper).

Reiff, Largo Adua, serves American food and has live music. (Open Tues.-Sun. 8pm-2am.) **Kanthos,** on Via XXIV Maggio, plays live country, jazz, and blues on Tues. and Wed. (Open Mon.-Sat. 8:30pm-1:30am.) For dancing, try grooving to the English/American/Italian disco beat at **Arena,** Via Tridente, 15/21. (Open Tues.-Sun. 8pm-1:30am.) For coffee and sweets (and colorful caricatures of the owner by a local artist), head to **Caffè Tazza d'Oro,** across from El Pedro Self-Service on Via Pic-ciuni. (Open daily 9am-10pm.) Or grab a pint at **Pellicano,** an English-type pub at Via Quarto, 10. A cool place to chill on a hot summer evening is the always-crowded P. Eroi del Mare on the waterfront, a popular hangout for the local youth.

The great commercial event of the year, the **Levante Fair,** runs for 10 days in mid-Sept. The largest fair in southern Italy, it displays goods from all over the world in the huge fairgrounds by the municipal stadium, off Lungomare Starita.

■ NEAR BARI

The numerous train lines that radiate from Bari make daytripping easy and affordable. The nearby towns arrange themselves in several groups along these tracks: Barletta and Trani to the northwest along the coast; Bitonto, Ruvo di Puglia, and Castel del Monte to the west; Altamura and Gravina in Puglia on the way to Matera; Castellana Grotte, Alberobello, and Martina Franca to the south on the way to Taranto; and Polignano a Mare, Egnazia, and Ostuni to the southeast on the way to Brindisi.

BITONTO

For a potent dose of Apulian-Romanesque architecture, take the half-hour train ride from the Bari-Nord station to Bitonto (every hr., last return 10:20pm, L2000 round-trip). When you arrive, a 1-km walk down Via Matteotti and a right turn deposit you in the medieval quarter. Many signs with detailed maps will help direct you around town. Bitonto's glorious **cathedral** stands in the medieval quarter; it was constructed between the 12th and 13th centuries from golden stone in loose emulation of the Church of San Nicola in Bari. Majestic side arches enhance the church's compact form, while sculptured lions, griffins, and bas-relief New Testament scenes enliven the main portal. Inside, windows illuminate a finely carved wooden ceiling (a late 19th-century reproduction of the original design), and a splendid pulpit crowns the nave (1229). The **crypt** rests on 30 columns salvaged from a Roman temple. Their capitals were the gifts of 30 members of the city's medieval nobility. Excavations of the floor have revealed a mosaic with the design of a griffin.

For more info try the local **Biblioteca** (library), at Via dei Mercanti, 52. (Open Mon.-Fri. 9am-1pm, Tues. and Thurs. also 4-7pm.) The **Centro Ricerche Storia e Arte Bitontine,** Via Ferrante Aporti (tel. 874 52 94), can also provide maps and historical documents on Bitonto. (Open in the afternoons, except when closed.) Finally, the local **police** offer tours of the city; they also have keys to some of the buildings. It's better to call ahead (tel. 951 10 14; no English spoken). For food shopping there are numerous **supermarkets** in town, including several on Via Matteotti as you come from the train station. Restaurants are scarce and can be expensive.

RUVO DI PUGLIA

Midway between Bari and Barletta on the Bari-Nord line (from Bari 40min., last return 10:20pm, L3400), Ruvo di Puglia began as a Greek colony in about the 8th century BC and reached the pinnacle of its influence four to five centuries later. Ruvo later passed into Roman hands; in 463 AD those fun-loving Goths destroyed the town in a fit of good-humored mayhem. The three-naved Apulian-Romanesque **cathedral,** begun in the 13th century and restored several times from the 16th through 19th centuries, was the high point of the town's gradual rebuilding process. Much of the exterior ornamentation is original; the man on the throne on the façade is believed to be Federico II, prolific builder of local *castelli.* To the right of the cathedral stands the resolute **campanile,** built more than 1000 years ago. The **Jatta Museum,** to the right of the cathedral, contains a collection of over 2000 classical and later-era terra-cotta vases. (Open Mon.-Thurs. and Sun. 9am-1pm., Fri.-Sat. 9am-1pm and 4-7:30pm. Free.) To get to the *centro storico* from the station, turn right and then onto Corso Duca della Vittoria; follow the signs that lead to the wooded *piazza.*

CASTEL DEL MONTE

Situated halfway between the Murge and the sea, Castel del Monte stands as a monument to a world of fantasy and chivalry, as well as to what a creative king can do with his money. Frederick II built it around 1240 without defensive structures or strategic purpose. Scholars hypothesize it may have been constructed to house the legendary Holy Grail, but realistically speaking, it was probably an astronomical observatory. The recurrence of octets in the design (8 perfectly proportioned walls, 8 stone towers, 8 rooms on each floor) symbolize the power of the crown and show the Arab influences in the Imperial court. The grounds are always open, but you can only visit the inside of the castle on Sunday mornings. From Bari take the 6:50am Bari-Nord train to Andria (1hr., round-trip L8400) and catch the morning bus toward Spinazzola; check with the bus company for the last return time. Food is expensive in Castel del Monte: bring a picnic.

CASTELLANA GROTTE

Take a Sud-Est train from Bari toward Alberobello to reach Castellana Grotte, home to Italy's finest caverns (1hr. from Bari, 40min. from Alverobello; L8400 round-trip; last return to Bari 7pm, to Alberobello 7:08pm). Since the town was named after the caves, the new train station by the cave entrance has the redundant name Grotte di Castellana Grotte. The town is a 2-km hike away. The cave tours (in slow Italian) enter from an enormous pit called La Grave, which, despite its beauty, was used as a garbage dump until the rest of the caverns were discovered in 1938. The real highlight waits at the end of the tunnel—the Caverna Bianca (White Cavern), a landscape of stalactites. In the summer of 1995 only partial tours of the caverns were offered, but the management expects to reopen the full tour in the summer of 1996. Tours leave every hr. 8:30am-12:30pm and 2:30-6:30pm and cost L15,000. For more information, call (080) 896 55 11.

■■■ THE HIGH MURGE

ALTAMURA

Trains on the **Ferrovia Appulo-Lucane** line from Bari to Matera cross gently rolling hills to the quiet town of **Altamura** (frequent departures from Bari, 6:05am-8:14pm, round-trip L5500; from Matera, round-trip L3200). Although one of the largest cities in the Murge region, the old town has managed to retain its tranquility. From the FAL train station, go right, through the underpass, and straight uphill on Via Regina Margherita for 1km. A portal through the old city wall leads to Corso Federico II di Svevia. On the left down Corso Federico you can see the petite **Church of San Nicolò of the Greeks,** a simple church serving the Greek Ortho dox community. A bit farther down towers the *campanile* of the **cathedral.** The finely carved portal depicts the Last Supper and two weepy lions. The façade's two towers reveal northern European influences. Inside, look for the treasury and women's gallery. The Pro Loco **tourist office** is in P. della Repubblica on C. Federico before you come to the cathedral and, for reasons beyond our control, has no phone number.

As you continue up C. Frederico, over the crest of the hill on the left rises the tiled dome of the **Liceo Cagnazzi,** which houses the town archives and library. Just past the school is the **Hotel Svevla,** Via Matera, 2a (tel. (080) 871 17 42; fax 871 26 77), the least expensive hotel in Altamura (which isn't saying much). Large, bright rooms come with phone, TV, and bath; most singles run L75,000 and doubles L105,000, but some older, still-pretty-nice rooms are available for less (singles L60,000; doubles L80,000). **"Lo Sfizzietto" Il Rè della Griglia** (tel. 84 10 53) serves tasty calzones (L4000), pizzas (L4500), *menù* (L12,000) and other regal fare at Via La Maggiore, 2—look for the sign off Corso Frederico, 30m from the gate. (Open Tues.-Sun.10am-3pm and 7pm-midnight.) A **supermarket** STANDA sits on Via Vittorio Veneto, 4 (tel. 84 25 52), to the right off Via Margherita immediately before the gate. (Open Mon. 5-9pm, Tues.-Sat. 9am-1pm and 5-9pm.)

GRAVINA IN PUGLIA

Gravina in Puglia seems even more rustic and tranquil than Altamura until you discover the oddities on the side of town that most natives avoid. To get there, take a Gravina train (FAL lines) from Altamura (10 per day, 6am-10pm, 10min., L1600). To the right of the station as you exit stands the church of the **Madonna delle Grazie,** with an eagle sprawled across its façade. (Bad aim or artistic license? You decide.)

The big bird is the symbol of the Orsini clan, a powerful Roman family who, among other things, spawned a number of popes. From here take the underpass to the far side of the tracks and walk right to the train station. Go straight onto Corso Aldo Moro, continuing on Via Vittorio Veneto past the **Palazzo di Città.** About 300m up Via Veneto, at the intersection with Via del Museo, a faded blue sign points toward the **Museo Ettore Pomarci Santomasi,** Via del Museo, 20 (tel. 85 10 21), which exhibits archaeological finds from the area. (Open Mon.-Fri. 9am-noon, Sat. 9-11am. Admission L5000. Hour-long tours leave on the half-hour.)

From Via Veneto, turn left onto Via Cassese and walk until Piazza della Repubblica. Several eerie sights await at the end of Via Matteotti to the right. In P. Domenico, pray that your sins aren't too bad, because **Purgatory Church** on the right would be a very creepy place to spend eternity (closed for renovations; in Italian time, this could very well mean eternity). The two skeletons on the portal are supported by bears, which were also Orsini mascots. To the left of the church and right of the **Biblioteca** (1743) lies a street leading to the **Basilica,** an immense four-aisled edifice. Back and to the left of the Biblioteca, a narrow path runs through a particularly decrepit section of town. At the bottom lies the entrance to **the area superstitiously avoided by all locals.** Ravines and vestiges of cave dwellings give new meaning to the name *gravina*. Some of the vestiges take the form of bones, which now rattle around in the **Grotto-Church of San Michele.** The gate to the grotto area and church stays locked, but pay a few hundred *lire* to one of the kids nearby to summon the caretaker. Do this as well for the **Church of San Vito Vecchio** on the right towards the top of the hill. It's not hard to see why the whole area is riddled with superstition.

■■■ TRULLI DISTRICT

Hundreds of unusual, cone-shaped dwellings, known as *trulli,* cluster in the **Valley of Itria,** between Bari and Taranto. There are many stories surrounding the origin of the *trulli*. Here's the tourist office version: the first recorded *trulli* were around in the 1400s, but the peculiar buildings did not take their current, mortarless form until 1654. Sometime that year, the local Court heard of an impending royal inspection and ordered the *trulli*—considered substandard living conditions and thus illegal—razed to the ground. After the inspection, the foresighted Court ordered the buildings rebuilt, this time without mortar so that they could be dismantled in case of another royal visit to the farming community. The *trulli* have been incorporated into modern life as residences, restaurants, and tourist-infested boutiques.

ALBEROBELLO

The greatest concentration of *trulli* is in Alberobello, 1½hr. south of Bari on the Ferrovie del Sud-Est train line to Taranto (15 per day, fewer on Sun., more on school days, L5700 from Bari, Locorotondo L1500, Martina Franca L2000). From the train station, bear left and take Via Mazzini, which becomes Via Garibaldi, to the P. del Popolo. A left turn from the *piazza* will take you to **Largo Martellota,** the commercial center of the small town, and continuing across it will bring you to the **Monti region,** the thick of the *trulli* zone. With more than 1000 *trulli*, a *trullo* church, and the Trullo Siamese, the area would look just like a gnome city—or possibly Hobbiton—were it not crawling with tourists. Beware the limpid-eyed souls who beg you to "visit" the interior of their *trullo*. Many a *trullo* has become a gift shop; even where signs read *Ingresso Libero* (Free Entrance) you will be expected to buy at least a postcard. Be sure to bring sunglasses if the day is bright, as the white *trulli* are blinding in the sun.

You can pick up an info booklet (with a marginally useful map) from the **Pro Loco Tourist Office,** Corso Vittorio Emanuele, 15 (tel. 72 19 16; open Mon.-Fri. 9:30am-noon and 5-8pm), just off P. del Popolo. Alberobello's **phone code** is 080. The **postal code** is 70011. Bear left at the church at the end of C. Vittorio Emanuele, then make a quick right. Straight ahead is the **Trullo Sovrano,** or Sovereign Trullo.

This mammoth two-story structure, the only *real* two-story *trullo,* was built in the 19th century as headquarters for a religious confraternity and *carbonari* sect.

Eating and sleeping in Alberobello can be expensive; it's less costly to visit the *trulli* as a Bari-based daytrip. For those determined to spend the night here, though, **Hotel Airone,** Via Coldilana, 30 (tel. 932 28 04; fax 932 28 03), to the right from the station and a right just before the hospital, is a great three-star alternative to sleeping in the street. New and modern; the hotel's friendly management offers a quiet lounge, a bar, and telephones in the rooms. (Singles L40,000. Breakfast L5000.) **Gli Ulivi,** Contrada Popoleto, 15 (tel. 932 37 96), on V. Cavour, off V. Mazzini (follow it around to the left under the overpass, then take the first right); has excellent food and quality service; a full meal can cost under L22,000. Splurge and try the *antipasto* of the house (L12,000), or save some *lire* and *mangia* pizza (L4000-7000).

■■■ BARLETTA

Barletta's star attraction has its origin in a five-century old battle. On the first or second Sunday of September, the city (amidst crowds of French and Italian tourists) reenacts the *Disfida* (challenge)—a battle when 13 Italians battled 13 Frenchmen in defense of their chivalric honor. In celebration of the Italian victory, each year the city comes alive with medieval pageantry as the Barlettans don colorful helmets, crests, and elegant costumes. The city is also home to Romanesque churches, a castle built by Frederick II, and an immense, ancient bronze statue.

Orientation and Practical Information The historic quarter of Barletta and most of its interesting sights lie along Corso G. Garibaldi and Corso Vittorio Emanuele. From the train station, walk straight ahead across the *piazza* and down Viale Giannone to C. Garibaldi. Turn right, and C. Emanuele heads off to the left for about 200m. Barletta is 15min. north of Trani on the Bologna-Lecce train line (from Bari 1hr., L5000; from Bologna, 6hr., L44,100). For more info, the AST **tourist office,** Via D'Aragona, 95 (tel. (0883) 33 13 31), offers maps and literature. From C. Emanuele, turn right and walk one block on C. Garibaldi. V. D'Aragona, unmarked, is to the left, on the left side of Piazza Caduti in Guerra. (Open Mon.-Sat. 8am-2pm.)

Accommodations and Food The only budget accommodations are at **Pensione Prezioso,** Via Teatini, 11 (tel. 52 00 46), just off Piazza del Plebiscito. From the train station, walk straight down Via Giannone through Piazza Aldo Moro and straight ahead on Via da Cordova until you reach the gardens of Piazza del Plebiscito. Rooms are small but quiet. (Singles L30,000, doubles L60,000; all without bath.) Inexpensive restaurants are as scarce as budget hotels. On the same *piazza,* **Pizzeria Dai Saraceni,** Piazza del Plebiscito, 65 (tel. 51 71 00), offers complete meals for L22,000. Try their tasty *pizza ai Saraceni* (with ham, artichokes, olives, and capers, L6500). (Cover L2000. Service 20%. Open Tues.-Sun. noon-3pm and 7:30pm-1am.) From Corso Emanuele, 1 block past Piazza Caduti in Guerra, and 1 block to the left on Via Barletta is **Supermarket DOK,** Via G. de Nittis. (Open Mon.-Sat. 8:30am-1:30pm and 4:30-7:30pm.) What the city lacks in restaurants it makes up for in fresh seafood, sold on virtually every corner in the area around V. da Cordova.

Sights The 12th-century **Church of San Sepolcro** graces the center of town on Corso Vittorio Emanuele at Corso Garibaldi. The façade preserves remnants of an original porch, a pointed doorway, and two blind arches. The only decorations remaining in the recently restored church interior are the large 13th-century baptismal font to the left of the entrance, the 16th-century Byzantine-style Madonna at the end of the right aisle, and pieces of frescoes adorning the walls. (Open in summer Mon.-Sat. 9:30am-noon and 6:30-9pm, in winter 9:30am-noon and 5:30-8:30pm.) On a low podium next to the church towers the 5-m **Colosso.** This 4th-century bronze statue from Constantinople represents a Byzantine emperor—possibly Valentinian I—holding the cross and globe, symbols of the two realms of his power. As the

Venetians were hauling home the loot from the Fourth Crusade, a shipwreck sent the Colosso to Barletta's shore. It was then dismembered by friars who melted its bronze limbs for use as church bells. The limbs you see were fashioned in the 15th century. Walk down Corso Emanuele to see the refreshingly austere and eccentric architecture of the 11th-century **Church of San Giacomo** at C. Emanuele, 143.

Return to Corso Garibaldi, turn left, and venture into the old town. About a block before the *duomo*, 10m off C. Garibaldi on Via Cialdini, is the **Cantina Della Sfida,** where the fabled confrontation of the knights took place. The *cantina* itself is simply the basement of a Gothic palace; note the huge stone cistern in the back. Via del Duomo veers off to the right where Corso Garibaldi ends and brings you to the enormous **castle** (tel. 57 86 20). The fortress, first a Saracen outpost, was subsequently enlarged by the Normans and rebuilt by Frederick II. The final and most substantial change was done by Carl V (1532-1600). (Open Tues.-Sun. 9am-1pm and 4-7pm, Oct.-April 9am-1pm and 3-4pm. Admission L3500, under 14 L1000. Half-hour guided tour, available in English.) The castle now houses the **Museo** and **Pinacoteca** (picture gallery) with an impressive collection of works by the local Giuseppe de Nittis, but both are now closed indefinitely (open only for research).

During the summer, check out **Margherita di Savoia** (take the bus from Via Manfredi, off of P. del Plebiscito; L1000 one-way) for kilometers of beautiful beaches and clear blue water. Unfortunately most of the beach is private, but for about L15,000 you can rent a whole package (umbrella, chair, bed, and freshwater showers). It's best to shop at a supermarket before going.

■ NEAR BARLETTA: TRANI

Situated between Bari and Barletta on the F.S. train line, Trani welcomes visitors with its peaceful gardens and scenic old city. The town curls around a small bay, with the historic quarter stretched along the waterfront and the gardens resting on the right arm. Trani's jewel, an 11th-century **cathedral,** stands tall on the water's edge at the tip of a small promontory on the left arm, with the imposing 13th-century **Castello Svevo** lurking nearby. Across the *piazza* from the train station at Via Cavour, 140, is the **tourist office** (tel. (0883) 58 88 25; fax 58 88 30; open Mon.-Fri. 8:30am-12:30pm and 3:30-5:30pm, Sat. 8:30am-12:30pm), while down Via Cavour, in the Piazza della Repubblica, you'll find an AAST **tourist booth** (tel. 432 95) which gives out a great map and recommends restaurants and hotels (same hours as the other office). From Piazza della Repubblica continue straight on Via Cavour to Piazza Plebiscito and the lush seaside **public gardens,** or head left on Via Pagano through Piazza Mazzini and turn right on Via Beltrani, continuing through the old city to the cathedral. Hold onto your valuables as you walk through this section. If you go right off Via Beltrani onto Via Sinagoga you'll eventually stumble upon a 13th-century **synagogue,** historically one of four in what was the Jewish Quarter. The building was later converted into the **Church of Santamaria Scolanova** and is now closed to the public. As you walk back to the town center from the cathedral, follow the coast to the right and you'll pass the 18th-century baroque **Church of Santa Teresa** and the 12th-century **Church of Ognissanti,** built by the Knights Templar, with a beautiful front portal.

To extend a daytrip, check into **Albergo Lucy**, Piazza Plebiscito, 11 (tel. 410 22), a 17th-century *palazzo* with huge rooms and elegant, high ceilings. (Doubles L70,000. Triples L90,000. Quads L120,000. All rooms with bath.) For a picture-perfect morning view of the sunrise on the Adriatic try **Hotel Regio,** P. Archivo, 2 (tel. 58 45 27; fax 58 65 68), just next to the cathedral. (Singles L50,000. Doubles L85,000. Breakfast L5000. Extra beds 35% more. All rooms with bath and phone. MC, Visa.) Good, affordable food abounds in Trani. A block off the midpoint of the port at Via Zanardelli, 17, **La Vite** (tel. 412 75) serves up Greek specialties and tea— with 90 different choices, it's got the widest selection in all of Italy. Enjoy plentiful plates of the day to the snapping beat of early jazz. *Menù* L20,000. (Open Mon. and Wed.-Sat. noon-3pm and 5pm-1am, Sun. 5pm-1am.) **Pizzeria Al Faro,** on the port just around the corner, offers good food and exceptional service, with pizzas L7000-L9000 and a broad selection of *antipasti* and other dishes. Cover L3000. (Open daily noon-2:30pm and 7:30-11pm.)

■ ■ ■ BRINDISI

American and British backpackers, ferry offices, and the port are what most visitors see of Brindisi, lingering here just long enough to catch a ferry from Greece. In recent years, the town has developed much of its economy around the ferry indus-try; it takes only a glance at the backpackers lining the streets in front of restaurants advertising "Tourist Menu" in English to realize the extent to which Brindisi depends on tourists. Unfortunately, the city has little to offer travelers other than cheap Eurail passage to Greece; although the narrow medieval alleys and flowered 19th-century streets remain from a bygone era, they are sadly obscured and over-shadowed by the by-products of a busy port. Come here, if anyplace, to get away from old-world charm.

FERRIES

Brindisi is Italy's major departure point for ferries to Greece. The fact that InterRail and Eurail discounts are only valid through Brindisi explains the port's chaos, yet the discounts themselves help make up for it. There is regular service to: **Corfu** (10hr.), **Igoumenitsa** (12hr.), **Patras** (20hr.), and **Cefalonia** (Hellenic Mediterranean Lines, 16½hr.). From Patras, bus service (4hr., L30,000; buy tickets at the *stazione marit-tima)* and train service (railpasses valid) will take you to **Athens**. Most ferries leave in the evening, and many tourists choose to arrive in the morning and buy tickets early. **Be warned: robberies on overnight trains are relatively common, and rumors of train cars being gassed are common.**

Numerous companies large and small serve Brindisi, each with different fares and rebates. The cheapest option will always be deck class, which is fine in summer—sleeping horizontally outside is often more comfortable than spending the night in an airline-type seat in a smoke-filled room. But be sure to bring warm clothes and a sleeping bag other times of the year. **Adriatica,** Via Regina Margherita, 13 (tel. 52 38 25; fax 56 03 32), near the *stazione marittima,* and **Hellenic Mediterranean Lines,** Corso Garibaldi, 8 (tel. 52 85 31; fax 52 68 72), have high regular prices but offer **Eurailpass** holders free deck passage (space-available basis—you could get bumped by a paying passenger). You still must pay the L10,000 port tax, and June 10 to Sept. 30 there's a L19,000 supplementary fee (not including port tax).

InterRail and Eurailpass holders should go directly to the main offices listed above to get their tickets—many travel agencies try to double talk their way to your money with commission-based services. Those without railpasses should seriously consider leaving from **Bari,** a larger city with many tourist facilities and inexpensive lodging and food, or **Otranto,** a beautiful small town to the south. From either of these ports, departures may be both cheaper and less crowded (see page 464 or page 480, respectively). For those intent on leaving from Brindisi, Hellenic Mediterranean Lines often offers discounts of up to 50% for their "bargain" fares: L45,000/L74,000 (high season). In particular, they discount their 9am departures (Aug.-Sept. only) for Corfu and Igoumenitsa. **Fragline ferries,** C. Garibaldi, 88 (tel. 56 82 32; fax 52 48 37), also has special reduced-day fares beginning at L28,000. Call ahead to find out which fares are reduced. **Ventouris,** Via F. Consiglio, 55 (tel. 52 48 69; fax 52 84 46), has few reduced fares but low regular fares. To: Igoumenitsa (L33,000/L38,000) and to Patras (L45,000/L65,000; students L40,000/L50,000).

With all companies, buying a **round-trip ticket** saves 10-20%. For groups of at least 10, there are reductions of approximately 10% on one-way and 20% on round-trip tickets. Bicycles travel free; motorcycles are about L25,000.

When you buy your ticket, you must pay the obligatory port tax (L10,000), and the office will give you a boarding card, which must be stamped at the police station one flight up at the maritime station. On the same floor you'll find **public showers**

(L3000) and a waiting lounge. You lose your reservation on most lines if you don't **check in at least two hours before departure.** Allow plenty of time for late trains and the 1-km walk from the train station to the ferry station. From mid-July to mid-August, it may be worth the effort to purchase ferry reservations at line offices or travel agents in other cities before you get to Brindisi.

ORIENTATION AND PRACTICAL INFORMATION

Brindisi is generally unsafe and crime-ridden; women should beware in the evenings. Lone backpackers are considered particularly easy targets; store your pack or stick to populated areas. Be particularly wary at night.

All that ferrygoers need to know about Brindisi is that **Corso Umberto** runs straight out from the train station and passes through **Piazza Cairoli** with its large, ugly fountain. Veer left as you pass through Piazza del Popolo and Piazza della Vittoria onto **Corso Garibaldi,** which leads to **Piazza Vittorio Emanuele** and the *stazione marittima.* **Via Regina Margherita** runs from the left at P. Vittorio Emanuele, past several more ferry offices.

Tourist Office: EPT, V. Regina Margherita, 5 (tel. 52 19 44), 1 block to the side of P. Vittorio Emanuele. Helpful staff speaks English well, but the city is lacking in tourist itineraries and pamphlets. Open Mon.-Sat. 9am-1pm and 4:30-7pm.

Police: tel. 113.

Post Office: P. Vittoria, 10 (tel. 52 39 56). Open Mon.-Sat. 8:15am-7:40pm. **Postal Code:** 72100.

Telephones: Telecom (SIP), Via XX Settembre, 6; from the train station turn left on Via S. Lorenzo off Corso Umberto, and then take the 2nd left. Full service on international calls. Open Mon.-Fri. 9:15am-12:50pm and 3:30-6:30pm. **Telephone Code:** 0831.

Currency Exchange: Banca Nazionale del Lavoro, Via Santi, 11, uphill from P. Vittoria (open Mon.-Fri. 8:20am-1:35pm and 2:35-4pm). Avoid the poor rates at the *stazione marittima;* change money at one of the many outfits lining Corso Umberto and Corso Garibaldi, all of which offer direct U.S.-Greek conversions. Few places in Brindisi offer good rates, and many charge commission.

Trains: P. Crispi. Both **FS** and **Ferrovie del Sud-Est.** From: Naples (one IC at 4:30pm (6hr., L47,900), less expensive but a longer ride if you change trains); Rome (via Barletta, 4 per day, 7hr., L47,700); Milan (via Ancona and Bologna, 4 per day, 12hr., L72,400). To: Bari (frequent departures, 1½hr., L9000); Taranto (every hr., 1¼hr., L5700); Lecce (frequent departures, 30min., L3400). **Luggage storage:** open daily 7am-11pm; L1500 per bag. Also available at the port (open daily 8am-10pm; L1500 per bag.)

Buses: Ferrovie del Sud-Est, at the train station (tel. 52 59 91), handles buses throughout Apulia. **Marozzi,** c/o Agestea, V. Regina Margherita, 8 (tel. 52 16 84), wheels to Rome at 11am or 10pm (7½hr., L49,000), while **Miccolis,** c/o Agenzia Marittima Perrino, C. Garibaldi, 109 (tel./fax 56 06 78), roams to Naples at 5:55am, 2:50, and 5:55pm (5hr. L40,000).

Public Showers: by the waiting lounge, 1 flight up at the *stazione marittima.* Surprisingly clean. Showers L3000, toilets L500. Open daily 6am-midnight.

Emergencies: tel. 113. **Hospital: Ospedale di Summa,** P. Antonio (tel. 20 42). **Ambulance:** tel. 52 14 10 or 22 20 78.

ACCOMMODATIONS

Not many people choose to stay the night in Brindisi. Hotel rooms are expensive and hard to find, and young backpackers often end up on top of a backpack in one of the *piazze* along C. Garibaldi—a miserable and dangerous experience.

Ostello della Gioventù "Brindisi," 3km away in Casale (tel. 41 31 23). Take bus #3 or 4 from the train center (L800). Although a youth hostel, it will often accept older guests during off-season. Clean rooms, but you may want to shower at the *stazione marittima.* Open 7am-midnight, no daytime lockout. L18,000 per person, sheets included. Breakfast L3000. Full pension L40,000.

Hotel/Pensione Altair, Via Tunisi, 4 (tel./fax 52 49 11), off Corso Garibaldi near the *stazione maritima.* Spacious, modern rooms and relatively safe. Singles L30,000, with bath L50,000. Doubles L40,000, with bath L60,000.

FOOD

A wonderful **open-air market,** off Corso Umberto on Via Battisti, sells fresh fruit by the metric ton. (Open Mon.-Sat. 7am-1pm.) Pizza and *focaccia* are made in huge sheets and sold by weight. **Supermarket Sidis,** Corso Garibaldi, 106, is well stocked but crowded with Greece-bound backpackers. (Open Fri.-Wed. 8am-1pm and 4:30-8:30pm, Thurs. 8am-1pm.) Avoid the restaurants on the main drag; often, advertised "tourist menus" have small portions and are hardly worth the "extra-low" price. Better options lie on nearby side-streets.

Spaghetti House Osteria Cucina Casalinga, Via Mazzini, 57, from the train station take the 2nd left off Corso Umberto onto Via Bruno. Delicious fare and a proprietor who loves *Let's Go* readers. Try the *spaghetti alle Ulive,* L4500. Full meal of pasta, beverage, and bread about L7000. Cover L500. Open daily 9am-9pm; Sept.-June closed Sun.

Ristorante La Forchetta, Via Mazzini, 13. Walk down the street 2 blocks from the Spaghetti House, or turn left at P. Cairoli while facing the port and make a quick right. Pizzas (L4000-8000) and a small selection of other dishes. Full meal L10,000. Open daily noon-3pm and 8-11pm.

Trattoria L'Angoletto, Via Pergola, 3 (tel. 52 50 29), 200m up Corso Garibaldi from the port. Pleasant, elegant outdoor eating. Pizza L5000-9000. Open Wed.-Mon. 9am-midnight.

Trattoria da Emilia Spaghetti House, Vico dei Raimondo, 11. From the train station, turn left on Via San Lorenzo 2 blocks before P. della Vittoria. A selection of fresh pastas; L7000 includes salad, beverages, bread, and cover if you bring your *Let's Go.* Open daily 9am-10pm. Ring bell next door if the owner isn't there.

SIGHTS AND ENTERTAINMENT

Facing the port, turn left on V. Regina Margherita. A block down, on the stairs facing the water you will find a terminal **column** of the Appian way. If you look closely, you'll see a marble capital graced by the sculpted figures of Jove, Neptune, Mars, and eight tritons. The column's twin, once on the base next to the column, now stands in Lecce. Via Colonne runs from behind the column to P. Duomo. Here lies the **cathedral** (11th-century, rebuilt in the 18th) where Frederick II wed Jerusalem's Yolande. Next door is the **Archaeological Museum** (tel. 22 14 01), which houses Attic vases and some ancient sculpture (open Mon.-Sat. 8:30am-1:30pm, Tues. also 3:30-6pm; free). Continue across P. Duomo and down Via Tarantini to the **Cloister of San Benedetto,** whose peaceful courtyard is just the place to read a book while you wait for your ferry.

Across this arm of the bay from the column rises another monument. In the somewhat odd form of a 52m-high rudder, the **Marinaio d'Italia** (1933) celebrates the sailors of Italy. Hop over on one of the red and white **Casale** ferries that leave every 15min. from Banchina Montenegro, to the left as you face the water (10min., L800). Three km inland on the rudder side of the port lies the church of **Santa Maria del Casale.** The pride of Brindisi, this multicolored, elaborately adorned building is reminiscent of Byzantine design but also incorporates Gothic ornamentation. If you're stuck overnight around the first week in July, you can party at the **Festa dell'Unità.** The **P.C.I.** (Italian Communist Party) subverts the minds of capitalism-weary *Brindisini* with nightly dancing, movies, music, and even a fashion show. (Most events are free and take place in Via Grandi.)

■ NEAR BRINDISI

EGNAZIA, POLIGNANO, AND BEACHES

Mid-way between Bari and Brindisi on the coast lie the ruins of Egnazia. This former Messapian city was famed for its pottery, which characteristically superimposed yellow, purple, and white designs on a glossy black background. You can view examples of these wares at the **archaeological museum** (tel. (080) 72 90 56). (Museum and archaeological zone open daily 8:30am-1:30pm and 2:30-6:30pm. Admission L4000. Museum wheelchair accessible.) Egnazia served as a Greek port (under the name of Gnathia) and later as a Roman stronghold. The ruins of the port are the most extensive Roman remains in Apulia; unfortunately, they're mostly underwater and are currently being studied by underwater archaeologists. What you can see along the water are curious rectangular pools which are in fact the remains of tombs cut into the rocky coast. Within the archaeological park, the ruins of the **forum**, the **acropolis**, and the residential section stand only a few feet high, making a visit seem like a walk through two-dimensional floor plans. Most of the fabulous **mosaics** were moved to the museum and restored. Across Via Traiana, which ran roughly parallel to the Appian Way but along the coast, lie two early Christian **basilicas** built between the 4th and 6th centuries AD.

Travel to Egnazia by way of **Fasano**, 50min. from Bari by train (every hr., L5000) and 45min. from Brindisi (almost every hr., L5000)—the train stop for Egnazia actually leaves you several miles from the ruins. From the Fasano station take the bus to the center (about every 30min., L1000; buy 4 tickets at the *tabacchi* shop). The last stop is the central bus station; catch the bus to *scavi di Egnazia* (in the direction of "Savelletri," using the 2nd bus ticket here and the last 2 to return to Fasano station; departures to *scavi* every 2hr. 7:10am- 7:10pm except 3:10pm; bus returns 10min. after each departure time). You can get great picnic fare two blocks uphill from the Fasano bus station at **Furleo,** Via San Francesco, 33 (open Fri.-Wed. 7:30am-5pm). Fasano's wild things come out to play at **Zoosafari**, where lions, crocodiles, and the like roam uncaged (tel. (080) 71 30 55 for information).

Several picturesque towns and beautiful beaches punctuate the stretch between Bari and Fasano. **Polignano** (30min. from Bari, L3200) graces the nearby steep cliffs with its tranquil old town. Head down **Viale dell Rimembranze** from the station (street name changes to Via Fani and then Via Neapolis) to P. Aldo Moro. In the far corner the Arco Marchesale leads into the old city. If you've got a hankering for hiking, follow the road over the bridge to the left of the gate and make your way down the coast past the ports. As you cross the bridge look over on the left, where a tiny footbridge marks the path of the ancient Via Traiana. A 4-km walk brings you to the 9th-century abbey **Abbazia di San Vito**. The elegant arches and domed nave were added in the 16th century.

Work on that tan at **Cozze,** the beach closest to Bari (30min., L2900). Or, the more frequent connections to **Monopoli** and its sandy beach (instead of Cozze's pebbles) may make the slightly longer trip worthwhile (45min. from Bari, L4900).

OSTUNI

Rising out of a landscape of sea, red earth, and olive trees, the *città bianca* (white city) of Ostuni appears completely ethereal from afar. The walls of the *centro storico* are kept blindingly white, partly as protection from the elements, but primarily to maintain the town's traditional status as "The White Queen." From the train station (Ostuni is 1½hr. from Bari (L6500) and 30min. from Brindisi (L3400)) take the shuttle bus to **Piazza della Libertà** (Mon.-Sat. on the hr. and ½-hr., Sun. on the hr. L800). For a divine view of the old city, climb Corso Vittorio Emanuele for five minutes and peer off the scenic terrace. Return to the *piazza* and climb Via Cattedrale up through the center of the old town. The play of light and shadows on the labyrinthine passageways is a photographer's dream. Standing out from the white background, the golden hue of sandstone marks Ostuni's historic buildings. **The Convento Delle Monacelle** (Convent of the Little Nuns) on Via Cattredrale sports a baroque façade and is topped by a blue-, yellow-, and white-tiled dome of Moorish inspiration. Crowning Ostuni's hill, the **cathedral** (1437) stands as the last Byzantine building erected in southern Italy. Don't forget to wander through the city's side streets; as you descend on Via Cattedrale, turn left on Via B. Continelli, where you'll find the modest **Chiesa di San Giacomo di Compostella,** a family chapel founded in 1423. On August 26th and 27th Ostuni celebrates St. Oronzo with the **Cavalcata,** a parade of costumed horses and riders.

Ostuni's AAST **tourist office** at C. Mazzini, 6 (tel. (0831) 30 12 68), near where Via Cattedrale juts off, provides assistance and a great booklet: *Ostuni, the white queen of olive trees.* (Open late June-Aug. Mon.-Sat. 9am-12:30pm and 4:30-8pm.) During the rest of the year go to the administrative office at Via V. Continelli, 47 (tel. 30 37 75; open Mon.-Sat. 8am-2pm) down Via Roma to Via Pepe. Ostuni's delights do not require more than a daytrip—avoid the steep prices at local hotels. For refueling and a change of color, go to the kitschy **Osteria del Tempo Perso,** Via G. Tanzarella, 47 (tel. 30 33 20), in the old city behind the cathedral. The plentiful *antipasto* smorgasbord (L12,000) will satisfy you with its sampling of local dishes. (Open Mon.-Sat. 5:30pm-12:30am, Sun. and holidays noon-3pm and 8pm-midnight.)

■■■ LECCE

A hidden pearl in the oyster of Italian tourism, Lecce is where Italians go when foreign tourists invade Florence. Lecce has an astounding collection of well preserved 15th-, 16th-, and 17th-century palaces, scads of Roman ruins, and an impressive number of Baroque and rococo churches. A cosmopolitan succession of conquerors—Cretans, Romans, Saracens, Swabians, and more—passed through here, but the city's modern form was defined under the sway of Hapsburg Spain in the 16th and 17th centuries. Merchants, aristocrats, and the religious orders of the Counter-Reformation competed to display their wealth, thereby creating the examples of the Leccese Baroque that we see today.

The "Florence of the Baroque" is an ideal starting point for a tour of the Salento Peninsula, Italy's high heel. While the University of Lecce's student scene ensures the presence of nighttime activities, your days will be occupied with visits to local castles, strolls through century-old olive groves, and tours of the many archaeological sites and ruins dating back thousands of years.

ORIENTATION AND PRACTICAL INFORMATION

The southeastern terminus of the state railway system, Lecce lies some 35km south and inland of Brindisi. Many streets in Lecce lack signs, but it's a pleasant place to lose yourself. A enjoyable 10-min. walk takes you to **Piazza Sant'Oronzo,** the main square: from the station, take **Viale Quarta,** cross **Viale Gallipoli,** and continue on Via Cairoli which winds through the historic district and becomes **Via Paladini.** Turn right onto **Via Vittoria Emanuele;** P. Sant'Oronzo is ahead past a few churches while **Via Libertini** and the **Piazza del Duomo** are on the left.

Tourist Office: EPT and **AAST** (tel. 31 64 61). They are moving this year, so call ahead. Helpful, informed, and somewhat English-speaking.
Police: Viale Otranto (tel. 31 53 42 or 113).
Post Office: in Piazzetta Libertini (tel. 30 30 00), behind the castle from P. Sant'Oronzo. Open Mon.-Sat. 8:15am-7:30pm. **Postal Code:** 73100.
Telephones: Telecom (SIP), Via Oberdan, 13d (tel. 31 42 99). From the post office, cross Viale Cavalloti and walk straight on Via 47° Rgt. Fanteria for 6 blocks. Open daily 7am-10pm. **Telephone Code:** 0832.
Budget Travel: CTS, Via Palmieri, 91 (tel. 30 18 62). From P. Sant'Oronzo, take Via Emanuele and turn right on Via Palmieri. Flight and train info, tickets. Open Mon.-Fri. 9am-1pm and 4:30-8pm, Sat. 9am-1pm.
Trains: in P. Stazione, about 1km from the town center. Buses #1, 2, 3, 13, 14, and 15 run from the train station to the center of town (buy tickets at newsstand,

L1000). 25 trains per day run to Brindisi (30min., L3400). **F.S.** (tel. 30 10 16) travels north to Taranto (change at Brindisi, 8 per day, 2hr., L9800) and to Bari (frequent departures, L11,700). The provincial **Ferrovie del Sud-Est** (tel. 34 76 34) runs down the Salento Peninsula to Gallipoli (8 per day, 1hr., L8000 round-trip) and Otranto (change at Maglie, 4 or 5 per day, 1½hr., L6000 round-trip).
Buses: Sud-Est, Via Boito (tel. 34 76 34), easily accessible by urban bus #7 (L1000) from the train station. To: Otranto (2 per day, 1½hr., L6000); Gallipoli (5 per day, 1hr., L4000); Taranto (2 per day, 1½hr., L7500); and other Apulian destinations. **STP,** Via Adua (tel. 30 28 73), heads to the smaller cities of the Salento Peninsula. From the train station, walk left on Viale Gallipoli and turn right at its end.
Emergencies: tel. 113. **Hospital: Ospedale Vito Fazzi,** P. Bottazzi (tel. 68 51). **Ambulance:** tel. 68 54 03 or 63 54 11.

ACCOMMODATIONS AND CAMPING

Unfortunately, inexpensive lodging in Lecce is difficult to find. Consider visiting on a day trip from Gallipoli, or try bartering with hotel owners on room prices.

Grand Hotel, Viale Quarta, 28 (tel. 30 94 05; fax 30 98 91), half a block in front of the station. Clean if institutional rooms. Singles L40,000, with bath and breakfast L60,000. Doubles L65,000, with bath, breakfast, telephone, and TV L110,000.
Hotel Cappello, Via Montegrappa, 4 (tel. 30 88 81; fax 30 98 91). From the station, take the 1st left off Viale Quarta onto Via Don Bosco and follow the signs. Nice and modern, but be prepared for a rude awakening by the morning trains. All rooms with bath, telephone, TV, and fan. Singles L50,000. Doubles L85,000. Triples L110,000. Quads L130,000.
Camping: Torre Rinalda (tel. 65 21 61), 3km from the beach. Local discounts on food and entertainment included in high season. Take bus #18 to Litoranea. July 7-Aug. 26 L9500 per person, L10,000 per tent, L5000 per car. Off-season L5700 per person, L4500 per tent, L3000 per car.

FOOD

Regional specialties range from the hearty *cicerietria* (chickpeas and pasta) and *rustici* (mozzarella and tomato wrapped in a delicate pastry shell) to *confettoni* (chocolate candies made from a top-secret recipe at De Matteis Oronzo—see below). Buy picnic supplies at **Salumeria Loiacono,** Via Fazzi, 11, in P. Sant'Oronzo, a century-old cheese store. The indoor food **market** next to the post office provides a chance to haggle. (Open Mon.-Fri. 5am-1pm, Sat. 5am-1pm and 4-8pm.)

Pizzeria Carlo V, Piazzetta Ignazio Falconieri, 1 (tel. 24 35 09), off Via Palmieri near Piazza del Duomo. Try pizza with *mascarpone* and *spek* (sweet cream cheese and bacon, L7000) or one of the daily specials (from L8000). Pizza from L5000. Cover L2000. Open Tues.-Sun. 7-11:30pm.
Ai Tre Ghiottoni, Via Dalmazio Birago, 7 (tel. 24 79 07), down Via Libertini and through Porta Rudiae. Snack on *rustico*, or feast on *risotto* with asparagus and roast squid (each L8000). *Menù* L20,000. Open daily 8am-11pm.
Ristorante-Pizzeria Da Claudio, Via Cavour, 11 (tel. 24 95 29), parallel to Viale Lo Re, to the right as you approach the castle. A menu with a table of contents. Complete dinner L20,000 (including cover). Pasta from L7000. Meat dishes L5000-8000. Pizza L3500-5000. The excellent house red wine is L3000 per liter. Cover L1500. Open Thurs.-Tues. noon-2:30pm and 7-11pm.
La Puccia, Viale Leopardi (tel. 39 09 01). Take Via Trinchese from P. Sant'Oronzo to Viale Japigia which becomes Viale Leopardi. This is the place to try *puccia*, a local bread heavily stuffed with your choice of ingredients (L5000). Open daily 9am-1am; Sept.-June closed Wed. AmEx.
De Matteis Oronzo, Via Marconi, 61 (tel. 30 28 00), near the castle. Come here for *confettoni* or their *cotognata leccese*, heavenly dried fig candies so delicious they're specially ordered by the Pope. Look for His picture.

SIGHTS AND ENTERTAINMENT

Unfortunately, recent restoration projects have artificially whitened the naturally golden stone of local buildings. While this process seems to heighten the play of light on the curved façades of some Baroque buildings, it has left much of the ornamentation difficult to see. In particular, delicate rococo carvings and inscriptions have suffered. The moral: if it's Baroque, don't fix it.

For those with a one-church limit, the definite place to hit is the **Church of Santa Croce** (1548-1646)—the supreme expression of Leccese Baroque. From P. Sant'Oronzo, head down Via Templari and brace yourself for the intricacy and extravagance of the church's façade, where menacing dragons and swooping hawks mingle with merry angels and grave saints. Most of the area's accomplished architects contributed their efforts to this church at some time or another; Gabriele Riccardi drafted the original design, and his disciples completed the church after his death. Inside, instead of the sculpture and painting found in many Baroque buildings, two simple rows of Corinthian columns support plain white walls. A wonderfully animated altar (1614) by F. A. Zimbalo adorns the chapel to the left of the apse. (Open daily 9am-7:30pm.) To the left of Santa Croce rises the **Palazzo Celestini.** Giuseppe Zimbalo—nicknamed "Lo Zingarello"—designed the lower half of the façade, while his pupil, Giuseppe Cino, worked on the upper portion. Diagonally across the street sprawls the Florentine-style **Palazzo Adorni** (under restoration; view both from the street outside).

Lecce has a seemingly endless supply of superb churches. Return to P. Sant'Oronzo and take a right down Via Emanuele to the exquisite **Piazza del Duomo,** blindingly white due to recent restorations. In front looms the **cathedral,** founded in 1114 but "Zingarelloed" between 1659 and 1670. The interior dates mostly from the 18th century, with the exception of two Leccese altars. (Open daily 8-11am and 4:30-7:30pm.) Attached to the right of the cathedral, the **Palazzo Vescovile** (Bishop's Palace), with its open portico, has been remodeled several times since its original construction in 1632. The porticoes held shops in the days when an annual fair took place in the *piazza*. Farther to the right, you'll encounter the **seminary** (1709), flamboyantly designed by Cino. The final component of the *piazza*, the **campanile** (1682), contributes a more restrained elegance.

A stroll down Via Libertini to the left takes you to the phantasmagorically complicated **Church of San Giovanni Battista (Church of the Rosary),** Lo Zingarello's last work. Here, the Baroque movement seems to lose its handle on reality as the finely carved trees, birds, and angels almost overflow the tiny alley where the church stands. Walk back up Via Libertini and turn left on Via Palmieri (across from P. Duomo); a 5-min. walk brings you to the **Arco di Trionfo**, erected in 1548 in honor of Charles V, whose coat of arms adorns the front. Located in an ancient cemetery beyond the arch, the **Church of SS. Nicolò e Cataldo** was founded in 1180 by the Normans and modified in 1716 by Cino. Note the Arabic influences, especially in the portal. Small mausoleums of every conceivable style cluster around the narrow paths of the cemetery next door.

A few hints remain of Lecce's Roman past. The **Column of Sant'Oronzo,** towering in front of the tourist office, is one of the two that once marked the termination of the Appian Way in Brindisi; now a statue of the saint tops the column. Also in Piazza Sant'Oronzo lies a partially-excavated 2nd-century AD **amphitheater.** If you ask to speak to the Foreign Office of the Credito Popolare Salentino bank next door, they'll kindly take you down to their basement, where several more arches of the amphitheater were uncovered during the bank's construction.

On Viale Gallipoli near the station, you'll find the urbane **Museo Provinciale,** housing figurines, rare ceramic pottery, and a collection of 4th-century BC inscriptions. (Open Mon.-Sat. 9am-1:30pm and 2:30-7:30pm, Sun. and holidays 9am-1:30pm. Free. Wheelchair accessible, but the ramps are steep.) The **pinacoteca** on

O
T
R
A
N
T
O

Via Imperatore Adriano, 79 (Convento S. Antonio), has a collection of 17th- and 18th-century religious paintings. (Open Mon.-Fri. 9am-noon and 4:30-7pm. Free.)

This quiet city comes alive in July and August. **Estate Musicale Leccese** (July 1-Aug. 15) is a festival of music and dance. Ask at the EPT for *Calendario Manifestazioni 1996,* which describes seasonal goings-on in the whole province. Many of the *piazze* in the old quarter fill with local youths after dark. Pop by Piazzetta del Duca d'Atena, or sing a few notes at the **Karaoke Club,** Via Palmieri, 56 (tel. 33 12 56). Food L8000-13,000, but drinks can be more (L5000-*200,000!*). Shake your booty at **Corto Maltese,** Via Giusti, 13 (open Wed.-Mon 9pm-2am). For current info on nighttime hotspots and musical and theater events, pick up a copy of *Notes-Appunti dal Salento* from the tourist office or at local bars and clubs.

SALENTO PENINSULA

Foreign tourists often overlook Italy's high heel, home to beautiful sandy beaches on two seas, hidden grottoes, medieval fortresses, and some of Italy's oldest and best-preserved art and architecture. With cultural roots stretching back past the Greeks, the peninsula is worthy of exploration, however you choose to transport yourself. Rove the enchantingly varied coastline or venture inland and sample wine and olives from the villages.

■■■ OTRANTO

Otranto is a spectacular starting point for a tour of the Adriatic Coast (from Lecce, 7 trains per day, 6:30am-4:30pm, 1½hr., L3200; change at Maglie). If you have some time in town, though, don't miss Otranto's **cathedral.** When the Ottoman Turks conquered Otranto in 1480 with the hopes of invading Italy, the town's 800 initial survivors opted to join their comrades in death rather than side with the Turks; their skulls are now behind glass in the cathedral. (Cathedral open daily 8am-noon and 3-5pm.) The **crypt** houses a melange of 42 columns pilfered from Greek, Roman, and Arab sites. The cathedral itself is paved with a phenomenal 11th-century mosaic of the Tree of Life. The mosaic—visited by Dante as he wrote the Divine Comedy—extends the entire length of the nave and depicts religious, mythological, and historical figures, from King Arthur to Alexander the Great. (And that's just the "A"s.)

Orientation and Practical Information From the train station, turn right at the circle and bear left down the hill on **Via Pantaleone,** named after the artist of the cathedral's mosaic. Ignore all the signs pointing right; go through the stoplight and come to Lungomare d'Otranto, the beach, and the pale green water. Walk three blocks to the right to **Piazza de Donno,** and to the left, down Via Vittorio Emanuele II, you'll see the entrance to the old town. Turn right on **Via Basilica** to come to the cathedral and the tourist office, or continue straight on Corso Garibaldi, which leads to Piazza del Popolo; from there a path takes you up to the Church of San Pietro. (Otranto's **tourist office,** at Via Basilica, 8 (tel. (0836) 80 14 36), rests at the foot of the cathedral. Open Mon.-Sat. 8am-2pm.) To get to the **post office,** turn right at the stoplight on Via Pantaleone and look on your left; the office is at the corner of Via Paolo and Via Eula. **Postal code:** 73028. A small, quiet, and simple port and low prices make Otranto a good departure point for **ferries** to Corfu and Igoumenitsa (Greece) and Valona (Albania). **Rainbow Lines** (tel. 80 10 05); call for specific info. Buy tickets at the **port,** a 10-min. walk from Piazza de Donno (up the hill of Via San Francesco and left on Via del Porto at the bottom).

Accommodations and Food Lodging in Otranto can be expensive and difficult to find during high season, but you might try a room in a local home; check with the tourist office for current info. Many of Otranto's hotels have obligatory half-pension on the order of L80,000 per person in August. **Pensione de Plancia,** Via Porto Craulo (tel. 80 12 17), has good prices and a great location right across the northern beach of Otranto. (Doubles with bath L80,000; half-pension (L80,000) required July-Aug.) The **Albania Hotel** and its large, white rooms with bath, TV, telephone, and A/C, sit off Piazza de Donno on Via S. Francesco (tel. 80 11 83). (Singles L55,000, doubles L80,000. Half-pension (L75,000 per person) required July-Aug. AmEx, MC, Visa.) The **Hotel Bellavista,** Via Vittorio Emanuele, 18 (tel. 80 10 58), has the best view in town and a high-class attitude to match. Half-pension required in July (L65,000 per person) and August (L78,000 per person). The rest of the year, singles L50,000, doubles L87,000. (Breakfast included. All rooms with bath.) The **market** by Piazza de Donno sells fruit, vegetables, meat, and fish (open Mon.-Sat. 7am-1pm and 5-9pm), while **Taverna del Leone Marino,** Corso Garibaldi, 7, offers sit-down fare at respectable prices: L20,000 will net you a feast of fresh fish and a plate of pasta. (Open daily noon-3pm and 7-11pm. Closed Nov.)

Sights and Entertainment Take C. Garibaldi to P. del Popolo and follow the signs to the Byzantine **Church of San Pietro,** the town's oldest church. In contrast to the town's massive cathedral, this humble building in a tiny *piazza* seems to be hiding from the public. Built in the 8th century, the church's intimate interior is brightened by red, pink, and blue mosaics of the Garden of Eden. Overlooking the town is the 16th-century **Aragonese castle,** complete with imposing city walls and a newly excavated moat (note the street-level line on the castle wall showing where the moat had been filled in for centuries). In August, Otranto welcomes tourists with a feast in honor of the martyrs. On September 4, the town celebrates again with the **Festa della Madonna dell' Altomare.** Venture a few miles north of Otranto to **Torre dell' Orso,** a beach cradled in pine woods at the end of a beautiful inlet. A bemused Madonna sits at the **Grotta della Poesia,** a small pool of clear water enclosed by low cliffs and a natural bridge, while a few meters away rests another grotto, covered in religious inscriptions from the Messapic through Roman eras. The coast south of Otranto is more rugged than the sandy beaches to the north, bordered by limestone cliffs and dotted with flat-roofed homes. If you have a car, toodle down to **Porto Badisco,** legendary landing point of Aeneas and today a stunningly beautiful swimming hole. Farther south, take a bath at **Santa Cesarea Terme,** famous for its thermal springs. The **tourist office** gathers dust at Via Roma, 209 (tel. (0836) 94 40 43). Six km south of here is the **Zinzulusa Grotto** (L5000), filled with stalactites and stalagmites (*zinzuli* in the local dialect). Two Ferrovie del Sud-Est buses run daily to Santa Cesarea Terme from Via Adua in Lecce.

■■■ GALLIPOLI

Electricity nearly killed Gallipoli (*not* the Gallipoli of World War I fame in Turkey), but fish and tourism are bringing it back. As a wealthy resort town in the 1600s, Gallipoli's palaces were sumptuous homes for the rich; through the centuries they were preserved in their elegant states until the advent of electric light destroyed their town's oil-based economy. Fortunately, a recovering economy coupled with extensive building restorations has returned the town to its original splendor. To reach the old city from the train station, walk on Viale Borvio and turn right on **Corso Roma,** the main street of the modern quarter. Cross the bridge to reach the old city, a tiny island with only the one road connecting it to the mainland. Near the bridge on the shore opposite the castle is the **Piazza Fontana Greca** and its odd fountain. Built by the Greeks and originally just the part that now forms the fountain's base (with the water spouts), the fountain was first altered by the Romans; the ornate top section was built in the 16th century.

The Pro Loco **tourist office,** C. Roma, 225 (tel. 47 62 02), near P. Fontana Greca, has limited info on local accommodations and prices. Ask for *agriturismo* options or call 20 22 95; in winter 281 04. (Open Mon.-Sat. 10am-noon; July-Aug. 10am-noon and 5-7pm, Sun 10am-noon.) The **post office** is on P. Imbriani (open Mon.-Fri.

8:30am-5:30pm, Sat. 8:30am-1pm). **Postal code:** 73014. **Telephone code:** 0833. The **Seminary** (tel. 26 43 94, evenings preferred) on Via de Pace in Gallipoli just before the cathedral, offers what may be the best inexpensive lodging south of Bari. A well-preserved *palazzo* with private rooms and hostel-style lodgings. Clean, hot showers and a kitchen available; sheets not provided. L15,000 per person. Call ahead. **Pensione Al Pescatore,** Riviera C. Colombo, 39 (tel./fax 26 36 56), to the right as you cross the bridge, has a special *Let's Go* price of L50,000 for singles and L90,000 for doubles. Large, elegant rooms with TV, phone, and bath. (L10,000 more in July. Half-pension required in Aug. at L90,000 per person. AmEx, MC, Visa.) **Baia de Gallipoli** (tel. 26 69 06), about 3km from town, charges L9000 per person, L7200 per tent, L95,000 per two-bed bungalow. (Open June-Sept.) Exquisite homemade sauces make the pizza at **La Tonnara,** Via Garibaldi, 7 (tel. 26 44 17), some of the best in Puglia. Across from the cathedral. (Open daily noon-3pm and 7:30-11pm.)

Stretching along Gallipoli's northern coast are two beautiful beaches, **Santa Maria al Bagno** and **Santa Caterina** (buses leave from P. Fontana Greca several times daily during July and Aug., L1500). To the south, take the beach road to Lido San Giovanni and its pebbly sand beach (entrance L2500), or continue down Lungomare Galileo Galilei to the free Baia Verde (a 10-min. walk from town). Agenzia de Luca, C. Roma, 217 (tel. 26 42 43; fax 26 38 41), offers **glass-bottom boat tours** and **sailboat excursions** (up to eight people, open Mon.-Fri. 9am-noon and 4:30-8pm, Sat. 9am-1pm; English spoken).

■■■ TARANTO

Named for Taras, son of the sea-god Neptune, Taranto was supposedly founded by outcast Spartans in 706 BC; archaeological evidence, however, shows that the site was occupied as early as the second millennium BC. For some time the most important city of Magna Graecia, Taranto was a trading port and center of philosophical thought. Today, the only remnants of its former glory are scattered stones almost totally obscured by concrete highways and parking lots. Even the old city is losing out to the modern, industrial new city, as more and more residents move out and let once-beautiful *palazzi* fall to ruin. The waterfront is a desolate shambles, flanked by a naval base and, to the north, postwar smokestacks churning out steel.

Orientation and Practical Information Trains depart frequently from Piazza Duca d'Aosta to: Brindisi (1½hr., L5700) and Bari (1½hr., around L9800). **Buses** run to: Bari (4 per day, 2hr., L8500), Matera (5 per day, 1¾hr., L9800), and Naples (3 per day, 4hr., L31,000). For more local traveling, you can get a city bus full-day pass for L2500. Taranto is sandwiched on a peninsula between two seas, the Mare Piccolo and the Mare Grande. The **old city** rests in the center, on a small island joined by bridges to the **new city** in the southeast and the port area and train station to the north. **Be careful of pickpockets in the old city during the day; avoid it altogether at night.** Grab a map of the city from the information booth in the station, and walk to **Piazza Garibaldi,** Taranto's main square. The EPT **tourist office,** Corso Umberto, 113 (tel. 453 43 92), in the new city, is well-equipped. Genial staff provides help with accommodations. English spoken. Open Mon.-Fri. 9am-1pm and 5-7pm, Sat. 9:30-11:30am. The **post office** is on Lungomare Vittorio Emanuele II (tel. 43 59 51). Open Mon.-Sat. 8:15am-7:30pm. **Postal code:** 74100. **Telephone code:** 099. For **emergencies** call 113 (police, tel. 112).

Accommodations and Food Unlike most other Apulian cities, Taranto is not lacking in cheap, comfortable lodgings. Most hotels line the brightly lit streets of the new city and the end of the well-traveled *Lungomare* in the old city, but exercise caution throughout Taranto at night. **Albergo Pisani,** Via Cavour, 43 (tel. 453 40 87), across the bridge in the new city off P. Garibaldi, is a bright, new place in town. (Singles L38,000, with bath L46,000. Doubles L73,000, with bath L88,000.) **Albergo Sorrentino,** P. Fontana, 7 (tel. 471 83 90 or 470 74 56), has large, once-elegant rooms just over the bridge as you go from the port area to the old city. (Singles L25,000. Doubles L40,000, with bath L50,000.) **Albergo Rivera,** Via Campania, 203 (tel. 735 32 74), is on the outskirts of town. Take the "Circolare Rossa" bus (L800) from Via Regina Margherita (on Piazza Garibaldi) and get off at Via Campania (15min.). Contemporary, comfortable rooms. (Singles L35,000. Doubles L55,000.)

Taranto's economic problems have left it with one great advantage over more-touristed towns: seafood is good, plentiful, and inexpensive. Try *cozze* (mussels) in basil and olive oil (but avoid anything raw). The new city is full of inexpensive restaurants, and the *menù* is often as varied as the regular menu. Grab your daily bread at **Supermercato STANDA** in P. Immacolata (open Mon.-Fri. 9am-1pm and 4:30-8:30pm, Sat. 9am-1pm) or at the daily **market,** in the *piazza* just across the bridge into the old city (open daily 7am-1:30pm). **Trattoria Gatto Rosso da Rino,** Via Cavour, 2 (tel. 452 98 75), off P. Garibaldi specializes in seafood. The *spaghetti mare misto* (mixed sea pasta) is a primo *primo* (L6000), as are the *tubetti alle cozze* (tubular pasta with mussels, L6000). Cover L1500. (Open Tues.-Sun. noon-3pm and 7-11pm.) **Ristorante Basile al Ristoro,** Via Pitagora, 76 (tel. 452 62 40). Their spaghetti with *pesto* makes you want to kiss the cook (L6000, kiss extra). Offerings vary with the season. *Primi* from L6000, *secondi* from L7000. *Menù* L20,000. (Open Sun.-Fri. noon-3pm and 8-11pm. MC, Visa.) **Gesù Cristo,** Piazza Ramellini, 8 (tel. 452 64 66), is in the new city, a 15-min. walk from P. Garibaldi (or take bus #8). Like their namesake, they feed the crowds with a seemingly endless supply of fresh fish (around L12,000). Plate of oysters L8000. (Open noon-3pm and 7pm-1am.)

Sights and Entertainment The most telling testimony to Taranto's former importance resides within the excellent **National Museum** (tel. 453 21 12), in Piazza Garibaldi. This museum's collection of Magna Graecian art now rivals those of Reggio and Naples as the best in Italy; its terra-cotta figure collection is the world's largest. The collection also includes sculpture and mosaics, imported and local pottery, jewelry, coins, and prehistoric materials. (Open Mon.-Sat. 9am-1:30pm and 3-7pm, Sun. 9am-1:30pm; Oct.-May 9am-2pm. Admission L8000.) The old city is what remains of a Byzantine village built after Saracen invaders razed the original city to the ground. Walk through the astoundingly desolate landscape, and marvel that such decay also harbors a remarkable **cathedral,** built in the 10th century and rebuilt in 1713. The church was originally a Greek cross; the Latin arm was added in 1170. The Byzantine exterior walls and cupola are still visible at the sides. As you approach the chancel look for remains of the original mosaic under your feet (hint: there are camels). Take the stairs down to the **crypt** with 13th-century frescoes. Before leaving the cathedral, peek into the **San Cataldo Chapel,** whose multicolored, intricate marble designs exemplify the Leccese Baroque influence. Locals may not admit it, but the statue inside is not solid silver; it's a ceramic reproduction made after the silver original was stolen. (Open daily 8am-noon and 4-8pm.)

Every night from about 6 to 11pm, the entire stretch of **Via d'Aquino** throngs with scoping crowds. The action centers on **Piazza Garibaldi,** where you can also hear the navy band accompany the lowering of the flag at sundown. Taranto's **Holy Week Festival** draws crowds from around the country. In a ceremony rooted in medieval Spanish ritual, men don masks, long white robes, and pointed hoods and parade a cart through the streets on a pilgrimage to the Holy Sepulchres in Taranto's churches. The festivities begin the Sunday before Easter; call the tourist office for more information. On May 10, the city celebrates the **Festa di San Cataldo** with a procession of boats that escorts the statue of San Cataldo around the harbor and a stirring display of fireworks.

MATERA

■ Basilicata

Basilicata is a region with more farm animals than people. Infertile soil and few natural resources mean that the region is one of the poorest areas in Italy. But the tourist industry is slowly bringing life to the area, making Basilicata a more and more desirable stopover; the beaches are less crowded than Apulian beach resorts, and remain clean and beautiful. Even if you're just passing through the area, don't miss the breathtaking sights of Matera.

■■■ MATERA

A few decades ago, Matera represented the quintessence of Italian poverty, its primary residential area consisting of houses built over caves (sassi). The government forced the citizens to abandon their unsafe and unsanitary houses in 1952, but since 1986 when the law was changed, many of the ancient rock-hewn houses have been restored and are occupied once again. Although strikingly beautiful and oddly captivating, Matera has not yet become a major tourist center and is a fine day trip or weekend stopover for anyone seeking to avoid the summertime crowds.

ORIENTATION AND PRACTICAL INFORMATION

From the train and bus stations at **Piazza Matteotti,** head down Via Roma to **Piazza V. Veneto,** the heart of the city. Climb Via del Beccherie (off P. Veneto to the right of Banco di Napoli) to **Piazza Duomo** in the *sassi*. The small paths, steep stairs, and labyrinthine passages would give even the Minotaur a headache, so take a map. Any map. No good maps exist for the *sassi* (construction and destruction continually close and reopen paths), but a bad one is better than none; try the freebie from the tourist office. **Don't ignore the warning signs: *crollo* means collapse, and many of the old buildings just might.**

> **Tourist Office: APT,** Via de Viti de Marco, 9 (tel. 33 19 83; fax 33 34 52). From the station, walk down Via Roma and take your 2nd left. Maps and pamphlets in English; English spoken. Open Mon.-Sat. 8:30am-2pm and 4:30-7pm. **Cooperativa Amici del Turista,** P. San Pietro Caveoso (tel. 31 01 13), in the *sassi,* and **Cooperativa Amici dei Sassi,** P. Sedile (tel. 33 10 11), halfway up V. Beccherie, provide detailed L6000 maps and free advice on exploring the *sassi*. Open daily 9:30am-1pm; Oct.-Feb. erratic morning hours.
> **Police:** tel. 33 42 22.
> **Post Office:** on Via del Corso (tel. 33 18 22), off P. Veneto. Open Mon.-Sat. 8:15am-7:40pm. **Postal Code:** 75100.
> **Telephones: Telecom (SIP),** Via del Corso, 5 (tel. 24 21), off P. Veneto. Open Mon.-Fri. 9am-12:30pm and 2:30-6pm. **Telephone Code:** 0835.
> **Trains:** There are four stations in Matera; Centrale is, not surprisingly, the main one. **Ferrovie Appulo-Lucane** (tel. 38 70 94). Runs from Bari, through Altamura, and on to Matera, leaving Bari every hour or so (1½hr.; L6500 to Matera Centrale).
> **Buses: SITA** buses (tel. 33 28 62) head to Matera from Taranto (P. Castello; 4 per day, 2hr., L7500) and from Metaponto (5 per day, 1½hr., L5000). For tickets or info on SITA buses from Matera, go to the company office at the top of Via Roma. **Grassani** buses (tel. 72 14 43) wheel over from Potenza twice per day (1½hr., L9800; buy tickets on the bus; service reduced Sundays and holidays).
> **Emergencies:** tel. 113. **Ambulance:** tel. 33 35 21. **Hospital:** on Via Lanera, tel. 33 41 81. **Tourist Aid:** Via Gattini 47b, tel. 33 67 48.

ACCOMMODATIONS

Many choose to visit Matera as a day trip from Taranto or Bari. If the picturesque hillsides strike your fancy, or you didn't get to finish exploring the *sassi,* it's possible to find a reasonably priced room if you arrive early in the day. You're best off making reservations a few days in advance.

Albergo Roma, Via Roma, 62 (tel. 33 39 12), by the tourist office. Friendly, clean, and conveniently located. Fills up fast during festival period (late June to early July). Singles L35,000. Doubles L50,000, with bath L55,000. Extra bed L15,000.
De Nicola, Via Nazionale, 158 (tel. 38 51 11). Follow Viale A. Moro from P. Matteotti to Via Anunzia Tella on the left, which becomes Via Nazionale. A bit of a hike from the station, but might still have a room late in the day. You can also get there on one of the orange city buses (#1, 2, or 6; about L1000). Modern rooms, some with bath. TV, telephone. Singles L50,000-63,000. Doubles L96,000.

FOOD

While in Matera, try some of the local specialties: *favetta con cicore* (a soup of beans, celery, chicory, and croutons, all mixed in olive oil), or *frittata di spaghetti* (pasta with anchovies, eggs, bread crumbs, garlic, and oil). Experience true Materan grit by gnawing on *pane di grano duro;* made of extra-hard wheat, this bread stays fresh almost as long as Twinkies. Almost. **Panificio Perrone,** Via dei Sarlis, 6 (tel. 33 44 11), off Via Lucana, sells both this and more normal bread. They also sell a variety of sweets, including tasty *biscotti al vino* (cookies baked with wine). (Open Mon.-Sat. 6am-2pm and 4-9pm; closed Thurs. afternoon.) The daily fruit **market** is between Via Lucana and Via A. Persio, near P. Veneto. (Open Mon.-Sat. 7am-1pm.) Down the block from the tourist office sits **Supermercato Divella,** Via Spine Bianche, 6. (Open Mon.-Sat. 8:30am-1:30pm and 5-8:30pm, closed Thurs. evenings.)

Ristorante Pizzeria Il Terrazzino, Vico San Giuseppe, 7 (tel 33 25 03), off P. Veneto to the left of the Banco di Napoli. Savor local delicacies in a cave dug into the cliffs or on the outdoor terrace that offers a perfect view of the *sassi.* Try hand-made pasta like *cavatelli alla boscaiola,* with a sauce of tomatoes, mushrooms, and *prosciutto* (L8000). Pizzas L5500-12,000. Local wine L5000 per bottle. Cover L2000, L1000 for pizza. Service 10%. Open Wed.-Mon. noon-3pm and 7pm midnight, Tues. noon-4pm (June-mid-Sept. only).
Trattoria Lucana, Via Lucana, 48 (tel. 33 61 17), off Via Roma. Begin with the *orecchiette alla materana* (ear-shaped pasta with tomatoes and fresh veggies, L7000), and continue with the *bocconcini alla lucana* (thinly sliced veal with mushrooms, L12,000), their specialty. Cover L2000. Service 10%. MC, Visa. Open Mon.-Sat. 12:30-3pm and 8-10pm Closed early Sept.

SIGHTS

Before venturing to the *sassi,* take a quick peek in the 13th-century **Church of San Giovanni Battista** on Via San Biagio off P. Veneto. Much of the church is preserved in near original condition; even time has not been unkind to the interior. Moved by its harmonious blend of arches, vaults, and columns, some proclaim it one of the most beautiful churches in Italy.

Enter the heart of the *sassi* zone from P. Veneto by climbing Via delle Beccherie. From Piazza Sedile, Via Duomo leads, yessiree, to the **duomo** in P. del Duomo. The cathedral (1268-70) is a fine Puglian-Romanesque construction with reaching naves, projecting moldings, rose windows, and richly carved portals. Inside, the 15th-century carved choir stalls compete with the stunning 16th-century **Cappella dell'Annunziata** for your attention. (Under partial renovation. Officially open daily 9am-noon, but often unlocked until 7 or 8pm.)

From P. Sedile two well-marked paths, **Itinerari Turistici,** head to the *sassi* in the valleys **Sasso Caveoso** (to the right) and **Sasso Barisano** (to the left). Of obscure origin, the *sassi* come in several types. The oldest and crudest are simply niches in the rock lining Sasso Barisano (across the canyon formed by the Gravina River), inhabited around 7000 years ago. The second type includes the carved nooks around Sasso Caveoso dating from around 2000 BC. Over the centuries, homes have been built around these, now mostly abandoned. Third are the more elaborately carved homes in the rock around Via Buozzi (stemming from Via Madonna delle Virtù near the *duomo);* these are around 1000 years old. Although the *sassi* were almost completely evacuated after the new city was erected, and most of the 6th-century *chiese rupestri* (rock churches) remain unmodified, young couples have been renovating and jazzing up many of the ancient homes. In addition, the more than 120 churches still display remnants of 12th- through 16th-century Byzantine frescoes.

From the scenic balcony on Via Madonna delle Virtù, wind through Sasso Caveoso to the right and you will arrive at the **Churches of San Pietro Caveoso, Santa Maria d'Idris,** and **Santa Lucia alle Malve.** The Church of San Pietro Caveoso is currently closed to the public, but access is still permitted to the two other churches, both of which preserve beautiful 11th-century Byzantine frescoes painted on the caves. (No regular hours, but try asking the caretaker to let you in and provide a brief tour (tip him about L2000).) A nearby cave is furnished as it was when ten people and two horses shared its two small rooms. (Open daily 9am-2pm and 3-8pm; reduced hours in winter; L2000.) As you roam the Sasso Caveoso, you'll be approached by children offering "tours." You are better off going with the *Amici dei Sassi* or *del Turista,* listed above. Organized tours are L40,000 for up to 4 people; they are more expensive, but worth the extra cost. Up Via Buozzi from the Church of San Pietro, the **Museo Nazionale Domenico Ridola,** Via Ridola, 24 (tel. 31 12 39), houses an excellent, boldly displayed prehistoric and early classical collection, all in a former 17th-century monastery. (Open Tues.-Sat. 9am-2pm, Sun. 9am-1pm. Admission L6000.)

ENTERTAINMENT

Matera lets loose during the **Festival of Santa Maria della Bruna,** held during the last week of June and first week of July and accompanied by numerous musical and sporting events. The festival reaches its climax on July 2, when a procession of shepherds leaves the *duomo* at dawn, and a cart holding a Madonna follows at dusk, illuminated by thousands of small lights. The ornate cart rumbles along Via XX Settembre, while warriors in medieval costume and clergy on horseback march solemnly alongside. At the end of the procession, everyone participates in the *Assalto al Carro,* in which relic-hungry spectators tear apart the cart after the Madonna and other valuables have been removed to safety.

■■■ METAPONTO

Metaponto beaches are clean, beautiful, and less crowded with foreigners than many beach resorts in Southern Italy. It's still not paradise, however; while the waters are worth a swim, the town is known as an expanding beach community. Be prepared for high-priced hotels lining the waterfront and large umbrellas for rent everywhere. In any case, the sparkling sea and nearby Greek ruins make a great daytrip from Taranto or Matera.

Orientation and Practical Information Metaponto is an important **train junction** on the Taranto-Reggio line (16 per day to Taranto, 1hr., L4200; 5 per day to Reggio, 6hr., L33,400), with a connection to Naples by way of Potenza (5hr., L20,800). **Bus** service connects the Metaponto station with Matera (8 per day, 7am-8pm; in winter 5 per day, 7am-5:30pm; L5000). The SITA bus from Matera alternates with the Chiruzzi line for approx. hourly service between the three small areas that comprise Metaponto (L1500): **Lido** (with beach and hotels), **Scalo** (the train station), and **Borgo** (the museum and archaeological sites). To hike from the station to the hotels in the Lido district (2km), walk straight 50km from the station to the highway, **Viale Jonio,** then turn right and follow it up the overpass, continuing straight past the campgrounds to the beach area. If you turn right on the highway from the station and continue straight across, you get to the Borgo (500m); if you turn right at the sign for the Temple of Apollo, you will arrive at the Greek ruins; a left turn leads straight to the museum.

The Lido is a small area with **Piazza Nord** in the center (this is where the bus drops you off). From Via Jonio, take the middle fork at the first intersection; the Piazza is straight ahead. Here the **bank** changes traveler's checks (L5000 commission; open Mon.-Fri. 8:20am-1:20pm and 3:30-4:30pm, Sat. 8:20am-1:20pm), and you can rent **bikes** (L3000 per hr., L6000 per hr. for tandems). Across P. Nord and a few meters straight along Viale delle Nimfe is Piazzale Lido and the volunteer-run **tourist office** (open daily June-Sept., 8am-noon and 3-8pm). The **post office** is by the Archaeological Museum (open Mon.-Sat. 8:30am-5:30pm). Metaponto's **postal code** is 75010; the **telephone code** is 0835.

Accommodations and Food To get to the **Hotel Oasi,** Via Olimpia, 12 (tel. 74 19 30), from Piazza Nord, bear right on the tree-lined avenue with signs for parking. Take your third right and look for a red gate on your left. Doubles with bath and balcony are L50,000. Full pension required July-Aug. (L65,000). A pleasant alternative is the **Hotel Kennedy,** Viale Jonio (tel. 74 19 60), at the first intersection. Gorgeous doubles with balconies and bath go for L60,000. One person can use a double for L50,000. (Extra bed L20,000. Half-pension generally required July 15-31 (L55,000) and Aug. (L65,000).) **Camping** is the most economical option (if you plan to hang out for a few days). **Camping Magna Grecia,** Via Lido, 1 (tel. 74 18 55), lies 500m off Via Ionio from the strand. (Aug. 1-20 L10,000 per person, L10,000 per tent, L3500 for electricity, L4000 per parking space; prices lower at other times.) With all the comforts of home and/or Disneyland, Magna Grecia's tennis courts, swimming pool, game rooms, disco, and bars will keep you occupied if you don't want to take their shuttle to the beach. The *pizzeria* **Coop Tur,** Viale delle Sirene, 12, sits to the left of the tourist office. They bring a tasty meal (about L10,000) to your beachside table. (Open June-mid-Sept. daily noon-2:30pm and 7pm-1am.)

Sights After enjoying the clear water and fine sand of Metaponto's **beach,** rent a bike (or walk or catch the bus) to the **Archaeological Museum.** (Tel. 74 53 27; for directions see Orientation and Practical Information above. Open daily 9am-7pm. Admission L4000, under 18 and over 60 free.) The museum displays ancient jewelry, vases, and figurines that explain the archaeological and historical significance of the ruins at the nearby Parco Archeologico. At the turnoff to the museum, take a right instead of a left; 500m leads to the scanty ruins of the Doric **Temple of Apollo Licius** and a **Greek Theater.** It's another 5km (turn right toward Taranto after 3km) to the **Tavole Palatine,** the well-preserved ruins of a Greek temple of Hera. The famous Greek triangle-lover Pythagoras taught here until his death in 479 BC.

Calabria

The region of Calabria comprises the southern part of Italy, from boot-tip to arch. Calabria began with the ancient Greeks and the rich towns of **Sibari** and **Locri;** legions of Byzantines, Saracens, Normans, and Aragonese followed, leaving behind their own marks on the region's population and cities. The coming of the World Wars also marked the formation of organized crime—the 'ndrangbeta—which caused thousands of Calabrians to leave their homes in search of a better life. Today the effects of the "crime-families" are felt less here than they are in the rest of Italy; the mob, along with many others, seems to have given up on Calabria.

Calabria remains far less organized for tourism than most regions, with limited, inconvenient transportation and few affordable accommodations. Of its four major towns, only two warrant visits. Set in the heart of the Sila Massif, a huge granite plateau (1100-1700m), **Cosenza** appeals to visitors for its environs and its picturesque old town. Near the southern tip of Calabria is **Reggio di Calabria,** a dynamic place whose superb archaeological museum houses the famous Bronze Warriors from Riace. On a venture north along the sandy but bleak beaches of the Ionian Coast, visit **Gerace,** a little-touristed town that preserves numerous Byzantine monuments.

■■■ TYRRHENIAN COAST

PRAIA A MARE

Farther up the coast lies **Praia a Mare,** a small but lively beach town (train station Praja; from Naples 2½hr., L17,200; from Reggio 3hr., L20,800). Straight ahead from the station sits the Pro Loco **tourist office,** Via Polo, 15 (tel. 77 70 30). Helpful staff speaks some English. (Open Mon.-Sat. 9am-12:30pm and 5:30-9:30pm.) If you follow Via Stazione (which turns into Via Polo) from the station, you'll quickly arrive at the long stretch of sandy beach. A 15-min. walk to the left brings you to **Spiaggia di Fiuzzi,** a beautiful area where the imposing island, Isola di Dino, looms in front of you, with a 13th-century Norman castle on the left. Those who missed or loved Cápri's Blue Grotto should take a tour of Dino's many caves, one of which displays the same eerie luminescence. Boats leave from the beach in front of the island between 9 and 10am (about L12,000 per person; tel. (0985) 77 92 75 for info). Or rent a canoe and explore the coast at a more leisurely pace (one-seater L8000 per hr., 2-seater L15,000 per hr.). Inland from Spiaggia Fiuzzi, a water park called **Aqua Fans** (tel. 77 94 04) sends you down giant flumes, waterfalls, and a lazy river for L20,000. Back in town proper, you can take a break from the sun in the **Santuario Madonna della Grotta,** a peaceful chapel set in a mountain cave. From the station, take your second left on the main strip, Via Giugni. After 100m, turn left on Via della Grotta and bear right at all forks.

If you've been waiting for a relatively safe place to experiment with a scooter or moped, Praia is a good bet. **Noleggio Praia 90,** Via Cilea, 27 (tel. 734 55), rents 1-person scooters (L80,000 per day, L250,000 per week). You need to present your passport and stay at a local hotel (5min. from the station; turn right on Via Longo, left on Via Verga, and then left on Via Cilea). Clean, cozy rooms at the cheapest rates in town are at **Pensione La Piedigrotta,** Via Maiorana, 6 (tel. 721 92), on the way to the Santuario Madonna della Grotta. When you see the chapel above, the hotel will be on your right. (Singles L30,000, with bath L35,000. Doubles L45,000, with bath L55,000.) Ask for a room on the side away from the train tracks, since trains rumble by all night. On the waterfront to the left of Via Polo, you'll see the restaurant **Riviera,** Piazza Sturzo, 2 (tel. 732 79), beautifully situated for sunset dinners. Pizza from L4500, *primi* from L6000, and *secondi* from L8000.

MARATEA

Just over the border into the Basilicata region, this collection of secluded beaches makes for a great daytrip from Praia a Mare. To get there, ride a scooter along a gorgeous, winding road, or take the train (8 per day, last return 10:20pm; L2000). Compared to Praia, Maratea is more tranquil, relaxing, and expensive; on Sundays, crowds pack both sites. To head for smaller beaches, from the Marina, catch a boat from Spiaggia Macarro (L14,000). You can also rent **canoes** (one-seater L10,000, 2-seater L14,000). Grab a bite to eat on a peaceful patio outdoors at **El Sol,** Via Santa Venere, 151 (tel. (0973) 87 69 28). From the station, follow the road to the highway, turn right, and wind down through town toward the beach. A good selection of pizza (L4000-8000). Cover L2000. (Open daily noon-3pm and 7:30-11pm.) Lodging is fairly expensive, but **Hotel Settebello** (tel. 87 74 88) is an attractive option; walk out of your L60,000 double right onto the beach. All rooms with bath, telephone, and A/C. Half-pension required in July (L85,000) and Aug. (L95,000). Reserve ahead. Open Easter-Oct. One bus in the morning and two in the late afternoon roll to Maratea Castrocucco, site of **Camping Maratea** (tel. 87 90 97). The main AAST **tourist office** is on Via Santa Venere (tel. 87 69 08), with colorful booklets on the area and its surroundings plus helpful listings of hotels and prices. (Open June.-Sept.

daily 9am-1pm 3:30-8pm; Sept.-May 9am-1pm and 3:30-6:30pm.) The **post office** at the port can also be of some help to tourists (open Mon.-Sat. 8am-2pm and 3-9pm, Sun. 9am-12:30pm and 5-8pm).

■■■ COSENZA

Set on seven lush hills, Cosenza bears marks of both the past and the present: a flat urban metropolis bustles on one side of the Busento River, and on the other, an old city shares a hill with a castle built by Frederick II. Besides offering opportunities to shop in glitzy stores and walk along historic cobblestone paths, Cosenza's greatest attribute is its location, which makes it the perfect base for hiking in the Sila Massif.

ORIENTATION AND PRACTICAL INFORMATION

Getting around Cosenza is rather easy, once you realize there are two bus stations and two train stations. From the **new station (Cosenza)**, trains service the western coast; from the **old station (Cosenza Centrale)**, trains service the eastern coast or the arch of the boot. One block away from Cosenza Centrale stretches **Corso Mazzini**, a main thoroughfare which runs parallel to the tracks of Cosenza Centrale and connects the small bus station with the large one at P. Fera. To reach C. Mazzini, exit the old station, follow the walkway, turn right out of the station entrance, and left at the next street. The next street you cross is C. Mazzini. Once on C. Mazzini with your back to the old train station, the old town is to your left, and the central bus station and Telecom are to your right.

Tourist Office: APT (tel. 48 26 40), at the new train station. Maps, hotel listings, and info on the Sila. English spoken. Open Mon.-Sat. 8am-8pm. There are two others in town, one on **Via Rossi** opposite the rotary (tel. 39 05 95; open Mon.-Fri. 8am-8pm) and one on **C. Mazzini**, 92 (tel. 278 21 or 274 85; fax 278 21; open Mon.-Fri. 8am-2pm) that's easier to reach.

Police: Questura (tel. 360 01).

Post Office: (tel. 264 35 or 268 08), on Via Vittorio Veneto at the end of Via Piave off Corso Mazzini. Open Mon.-Sat. 8:15am-7:30pm. **Postal Code:** 87100.

Telephones: Telecom (SIP), Via dell'Autostazione, above the central bus station. Open daily 8:10am-8pm. At other times, try **Croce Bianca**, Via Beato Angelo d'Acri, 29. **Telephone Code:** 0984.

Trains: (tel. 48 15 21/22/23/24). The **Cosenza station** is on Via Popilia at the *superstrada*. Trains to Paola, on the Rome-Reggio di Calabria coastal line (over 20 per day, 20min., L2400), and Metaponto (5 per day, change at Sibari, 3hr., L8800). A "shuttle" train connects the two stations (every 20 min. 7am-12:30am, L1000), as does bus #5 (every 15min. 6am-12:30am, L1000). From **Cosenza Centrale** (off P. Matteotti), trains depart for Camigliatello, San Giovanni, and other cities in the Sila. **Cosenza Monaco, Cosenza Campanella, and Cosenza Casali** are three other stations in and near the city.

Buses: At the new train station or off P. Fera, at the opposite end of Corso Mazzini from the old train station. L1000 one way. Get schedules at the information booths in the new train station (tel. 48 26 40). Gate #5 for Catanzaro, #14 for the Tyrrhenian coast. Snack bar open 24 hrs. Buses run erratically Sun. and holidays.

Emergencies: tel. 113. **Ambulance: Croce Azzurra Associazione Volontaria** (tel. 725 55). **Hospital: Ospedale Civile dell'Annunziata** (tel. 68 11), on Via Felice Migliori. On weekends, call 318 31.

ACCOMMODATIONS AND FOOD

The most affordable lodgings cluster around the old station, just a few blocks from the old city—a quarter blessed with good *pensione* and cursed with evil tourist traps like expensive craft stores and *caffè*. Family-run **Albergo Bruno**, Corso Mazzini, 27 (just one block from the train station, tel. 738 89), offers recently renovated bathrooms, spacious rooms, and free use of the kitchen, pool table, TV room, and musical instruments (guitar, piano, drum set). Singles L35,000, with bath

THE SILA MASSIF

L50,000. Doubles L55,000, with bath L70,000. Triples L75,000, with bath L90,000. Quad L90,000, with bath L100,000. The best **camping** in the area is at the Sila Massif (see below, page 490) and in the seaside towns of **Scalea** and **Marina di Belvedere** (at least 4 buses per day to each location 6:35am-6pm, 1¼hr., L3000-5000). Two sites on Scalea's Tyrrhenian waterfront are **Camping il Gabbiano** (tel. (0985) 205 63), with beach bungalows and free hot showers (L8000 per person, L9000 per tent; open mid-June-mid-Sept.), and **Campeggio Moby Dick** (tel. (0985) 202 78), well-organized with sporting activities (soccer, beach volleyball, tennis, and ping-pong) and a club. L15,000 per person, L15,900 per tent. Free hot showers and beach bungalows. Open June-Sept. While staying here, pay a visit to another beautiful beach up north, **S. Nicole.**

Cosenza's best dishes are prepared *ai funghi* (with fresh mushrooms from the forests of the Sila). Pasta lovers should proceed to **Trattoria Peppino,** P. Crispi, 3 (tel. 732 17), reached by turning right just before the Mario Martire bridge (two blocks from the old train station towards the old city), walking one block and bearing right. Full meals with drink go for L15,000. (Open Mon.-Sat. 10am-10pm.) For a good cup of coffee and a savory pastry after climbing to the cathedral, try the **Gran Caffè Renzelli,** "the historical location of Cosenza," at Corso Telesio, 46 (tel. 268 14); take a left after crossing M. Martire Bridge. Or do it yourself at **Supermercato STANDA,** C. Mazzini, 98 (tel. 746 32), in the basement of the department store. Open Mon.-Fri. 9am-1pm and 4:30-8:30pm, Sat. 9am-1pm.

SIGHTS AND ENTERTAINMENT

All historic sights of interest in Cosenza lie in the old city across the shallow **Busento River** from the old train station. Follow C. Mazzini to its end (left with your back to Cosenza Centrale), cross the *piazza*, turn left, and then quickly right. Cross the Mario Martin bridge, turn left onto Corso Telesio, and climb uphill to the Romanesque **cathedral** built in the mid-12th century. The winding streets are lined with abandoned shops, wood-workers, fruit stands, and clotheslines. Keep your head up and your mouth closed—there's no telling what will be tossed from the medieval windows. Once in the cathedral, note the mural of the *Madonna and Child* (1863) on the right side. The city's prized possession—the tiny, ornate **Byzantine Cross** donated by Frederick II—adorns the *Arcivescovato* near the cathedral. The colorful artifact bears a Christ and mourning Madonna on the left arm, a supplicating St. John the Evangelist on the right, and the archangel Michael above. A 12th-century **Norman Castle** built by Frederick II lies at the top of this hill, upon the city's highest point. The castle itself is not open to the public, but the view at the top is well worth the long uphill hike on cobblestone roads. For more information call the *Teatro Comunale* (tel. 741 65) or the tourist office.

■■■ THE SILA MASSIF

Located in the heart of Calabria is the **Sila Massif,** an elevated 2000sq.km. of pristine wilderness consisting of three main zones: La Greca, the area to the north; La Grande, the central area; and La Piccola, a coastal area. These areas constitute one of Italy's last mountain chains still covered with virgin forest. To reach **Camigliatello** from Cosenza, you can take either a bus (7 per day, 45min., L2800) or a train (2 per day, 1½hr., L2500 one-way). Though slower, train travel should not be missed: from Cosenza Centrale, trains no more than 20m in length inch their way up and through the mountains, accessing incredible views. You'll be awed by the feats of engineering required to build the route.

CAMIGLIATELLO

The first major stop you'll come to on the train line from Cosenza is Camigliatello, a small, alpine town with fairytale streets and the area's best base for exploration. Upon arrival you should confer with the hiking experts at Pro Loco **tourist office** (tel. 57 80 91), on Via Roma, 5, 100 yds. away from the train station to your right;

ask for their useful map of the Sila. (Open Mon.-Sat. 9am-12pm and 3:30-6pm.) Look next door for brochures and maps of the region. The office at the **Parco Nazionale** sells maps of hiking trails, but the brave can try two interesting hikes from Camigliatello's *castro.* The first involves walking (1½hr.) to **Lago Cecita,** one of five major lakes in the region, sharing a border with the **Parco Nazionale.** Following the signs in front of the station, keep walking until you reach the small pine forest; several dirt roads then branch from the highway, leading ultimately to Cecita's shores. A second, more demanding hike is the three-hour climb to the top of the highest peak in the Sila, **Monte Botte Donato** (1930m). To get there, follow the highway toward Cosenza for about 4km and take the left turn at the *Fago del Soldato* intersection. As you begin climbing, bear left—you'll come to a ski lift—climb below it until you reach an unmarked road. Turn left onto the road and you'll eventually reach the summit. On a clear day, you can see both the Tyrrhenian and Ionian Seas from the peak. Less adventurous souls can visit the nearby pine forest (be sure to bring bugspray) or just savor the fresh mountain air.

Pro Loco can help with lodging inquiries, or you can walk down Via Roma or Via del Turismo and look for yourself (from Via Roma, take the street that forks in front of the Post Office). Or try **La Baita,** Via Roma, 99 (tel. 57 81 97), to the right as you exit the station. Fresh and clean. (Singles with bath L35,000. Doubles with bath L80,000. Triples with bath L93,000. Special weekly rates for couples; call for more info. AmEx, MC, Visa.) **Hotel Mancuso,** Via del Turismo, 51 (tel. 57 80 02), is on your right as you exit the station. Requires full pension in high season at L80,000 for pleasant rooms with baths. Curfew midnight. All rooms with bath. (Off-season singles L35,000. Doubles L80,000. Triples L105,000. Quads L130,000. Mandatory full pension in Aug. and Dec. L80,000.) For campers, **La Fattoria** (tel. 57 83 64) lies about 3km from Camigliatello on the road to Lago Cecita. The nicer **Villaggio Lago Arvo** (tel. 53 70 90) awaits on the banks of Lago Arvo in Lorica, 37km from Camigliatello, but is inaccessible by public transportation. Your best bet is to take the bus or train toward San Giovanni in Fiore and get off at Silvana Mansio, which is 15km from Lorica. (Campsite open May-Sept.) For assistance in Lorica, try the Pro Loco **tourist office** (tel. 53 70 69) on Via Nazionale. There is a **post office** (tel. 57 80 76) at the intersection of Via del Turismo and Via Roma (walk uphill on V. Roma, office on left). Open Mon.-Fri. 8:15am-1:30pm, Sat. 8:15am-12:10pm. The **bank** (tel. 57 80 27), the Cassa di Risparmio de Calabria e de Lucania, is also on Via Roma, 61. Open Mon.-Fri 8:20am-1:20pm and 2:35-3:20pm. **Telephone code:** 0984 (Lorica also).

While in Camigliatello, picnic on the local specialties—cheeses, cured meats, and marinated mushrooms. The main drag overflows with *salumerie* that can provide you with sandwich supplies, as well as family-owned restaurants offering regional delicacies. **Ristorante "La Stragola,"** Via Roma, 160 (tel. 57 83 16), near the train station on the left-hand side (look for the wagon wheel), offers complete meals including beverages for L25,000. (AmEx, Visa.) **Ristorante Pizzeria al Buongustaio,** Via del Turismo, 34 (tel. 57 81 54). Look for a red sign snuggled within a row of pine trees (two quick rights off Via Roma at the sign for the Hotel Meranda). Share a romantic pizza (only in Italy would pizza be emotional). *Menù* L25,000.

If exploring on foot isn't your thing, check to see if there are bike trips organized with the tourist office. Amazing **skiing** conditions draw downhill diehards from Christmas until mid-March. Camigliatello's **Tasso Ski Trail** (tel. 57 81 36), on Monte Curcio, is about 3km from town, up Via Roma and left at Hotel Tasso. Hop a ride in summer for memorable views. Lift runs daily 8:30am-6:30pm. Round-trip L5000. Ask at the tourist office for rental information.

■■■ REGGIO DI CALABRIA

After a devastating earthquake in 1908, Reggio was completely rebuilt. It now brims with designer stores and lacks an old-world charm, but presents a good picture of modern Italy and its culture. For history buffs, there is the National Museum which

REGGIO DI CALABRIA

houses the famous bronze figures that recall Calabria's ancient glory as part of Magna Graecia.

ORIENTATION AND PRACTICAL INFORMATION

Most travel in Reggio is along **Corso Garibaldi,** connecting Stazione Centrale in the south with Stazione Lido in the north. With your back to S. Centrale, walk straight through P. Garibaldi; the road on the other side of the *piazza* is C. Garibaldi. City buses continuously traverse the route (L1000), though it is only 1½km from S. Centrale to S. Lido.

Tourist Office: APT booth (tel. 271 20), at the central train station. Useful maps and directions. "Here is spoken English." Open Mon.-Sat. 8am-2pm and 2:30-8pm. Two other booths with similar hours at the **airport** (tel. 64 32 91) and at the **main office** on Via Roma, 3 (tel. 211 71). Another **APT office** is at Corso Garibaldi, 329 (tel. 89 20 12). English spoken. Open Mon.-Fri. 7:45am-7:45pm.
Police: (tel. 530 04), on Via S. Caterina, in the northern end of town near the port.
Post Office: Via Miraglia, 14 (tel. 81 21 52), near P. Italia. Open Mon.-Fri. 8:15am-7pm, Sat. 8:15am-1:30pm. **Postal Code:** 89100.
Telephones: Telecom (SIP), Corso Vittorio Emanuele, 110 (tel. 89 75 79). Behind the post office, outside. Open 8am-10pm. **Telephone code:** 0965.
Currency exchange: Banca Nazionale del Lavoro, Corso Garibaldi (tel. 85 17 16). Open Mon.-Fri 8:30am-1:20pm, 2:45-4pm. Or at the **FS** info booth inside the station (7am-9pm).
Airport: Svincolo Aeroporto, (tel. 64 22 32), 5km south of town. Catch orange bus #113, 114, or 115 from P. Garibaldi outside S. Centrale (L1000). Service to all major cities in Italy.
Trains: Reggio has two train stations. All trains stop at **Stazione Centrale,** P. Garibaldi (tel. 89 81 23), at the southern end of town. The much less frequented (albeit more convenient) **Stazione Lido** sits at the northern end of town off Via Zerbi and near the museum, port, and beaches. Reggio is linked to most major cities, including Rome (15 per day, 7hr., L55,000, *rapido* L82,000) and Naples (20 per day, 5hr., L38,600, *rapido* L62,000).
Ferries: Several ferries cross the strait to Messina in Sicily, but a greater number of ferries and all trains make the crossing from the nearby city of **Villa San Giovanni** (30min. north by train, L1600). **Caronte** lines have the most frequent and fastest service (once you're in Villa S. Giovanni, follow the signs to the private ferry services). Nevertheless, three companies do provide service from Messina to Sicily. **Ferrovie dello Stato** (tel. 89 81 23), at the port five blocks to the left of Stazione Lido (facing away from the sea), accepts all InterRail, Eurail, and kilometric tickets for the Sicily crossing. **Tirrenia,** Via B. Buozzi, 31 (tel. 89 40 03), sits off Via III Settembre, three blocks from the Lido station. (Ticket office open Mon.-Fri. 8:30am-1pm and 4-7pm.) **SNAV** (tel. 295 68), next to Ferrovie dello Stato, specializes in hydrofoil service.
Villa San Giovanni-Messina: Ferrovie (tel. 75 82 41 or 75 14 13) ferries 3:20am-4:45pm (14 per day, 35min., L1800).
Reggio-Messina: Ferrovie (tel. 89 79 57) ferries 7:15am-8:45pm (17 per day, 20min., L4000). **SNAV** (tel. 295 68) hydrofoils Mon.-Fri. 7:15am-8:40pm (24 per day, Sat. 18 per day, 20min., L5000 one way).
Reggio-Lipari Islands: SNAV hydrofoil (2-4 trips per day, L32,300 to Vulcano, L51,500 to Alicudi).
Luggage Storage: at both Centrale and Lido stations (L1500). Open 24 hrs.
Emergencies: tel. 113. **Medical Assistance:** tel. 34 71 06. **Hospital: Ospedale Riuniti,** tel. 34 71 11, on Via Melacrino.

ACCOMMODATIONS

Staying in Reggio often means parting with a lot of money. Hotel quality is notably low and campgrounds are distant from the city center.

Pensione S. Bernadetta, Corso Garibaldi, 585 (tel. 89 45 00), right across P. Garibaldi from the central train station all the way up on the 5th floor. You get what you pay for. Singles L20,000. Doubles L40,000.

Albergo Noel, Viale Genoese Zerbi, 13 (tel. 33 00 44 or 89 09 65), a few blocks north of Stazione Lido. With the sea behind you, turn left as you exit the station. Great location. Decent restaurant. All rooms with bath and TV. Singles L45,000. Doubles L60,000. Triples L75,000. Credit cards accepted. Reserve for June-Sept.

Hotel Diana, Via Diego Vitrioli, 12 (tel. 89 15 22), can be seen from Corso Garibaldi, halfway between Stazione Centrale and Stazione Lido. Look for large signs. All rooms with bath and telephone. Singles L38,000. Doubles L83,000. Triples L112,000. If staying in Aug., reservations recommended 1 month in advance.

FOOD

Reggio's chefs feel most at home making *spaghetti alla calabrese* (noodles dressed in a potent pimento sauce), *capocollo* ham (salami spiced with local hot peppers), and *pesce spada* (swordfish caught off neighboring Bagnara Calabra). At Corso Garibaldi, 107, towards the S. Lido end, a **STANDA supermarket** (tel. 283 10) supplies the basics. (Open Mon., Wed.-Sat. 8:30am-1pm, 4:45-8:15pm, Tues. 8am-1pm.) There is also an **A&O supermarket** (tel. 33 02 59) at Corso Garibaldi, 587, right under the pensione and across from the train station. (Open Mon.-Sat. 8am-3pm.)

La Pignata, Via Demetrio Tripepi, 122 (tel. 278 41), up Via Giutecca from Corso Garibaldi near the Telecom. An elegant *pizzeria*-restaurant with carved wooden ceilings and nude panel-paintings inside. *Maccheroni calabresi* L7000. *Bruschette* (toasted bread with garlic and a spicy red sauce), L2000. Cover L3000. Open Mon.-Sat. 12:30-3pm and 7:30-10:30pm. AmEx, MC, Visa.

Cordon Bleu, Via Corso Garibaldi, 203 (tel. 33 24 47), close to the museum, modern, and chic. *Calamari* (L8000) and assorted pastries (L1000-2000) are especially tasty. Wine L4000 per bottle. Cover L1000. Open for "real food" Thurs.-Tues. 10:30am-midnight. **Another location** on Via Emanuele III, 39 (tel. 89 11 61), where you can eat in a lush garden and listen to piano accompaniment. Same hours, same prices, more food.

Ristorante Bonaccorso, Via Cesare Battisti, 8 (from the central station, one block down Via N. Bixio with your back to the station). The proprietor moonlights as an artist, so ask him for a tour of his work displayed throughout the restaurant. Pizza L6000-8000; double price for "gigantic pizza." Cover L2000. Open Tues.-Sun. noon-3pm and 7:30-11pm. AmEx, MC, Visa.

SIGHTS AND ENTERTAINMENT

If you're passing through Reggio, you might as well spend the day by the sea. The **lungomare,** a pleasant park overlooking the water and the rugged Sicilian coast, stretches from one end of Reggio to the other. While you're at it, don't miss the **Museo Nazionale,** P. de Nava, 26 (tel. 81 22 55) on Corso Garibaldi near the Stazione Lido, which documents the history of Magna Graecia with material from excavations in Calabria and underwater treasure-hunts off the coast. Notable are the works in the upstairs gallery by southern Italian artist Antonello da Messina and a set of dramatic Greek tablets from the 5th and 6th centuries BC which tell the stories of Persephone, Castor and Pollux, and Achilles and Agamemnon. The masterpieces of the museum are the **Bronzi di Riace,** two monumental bronze Greek statues found off the coast of Riace, Calabria, in 1972, and preserved for over 2000 years in the gentle waters of the Ionian. After painstaking restoration, the statues were identified as Greek originals and dated to the mid-5th century BC, the Golden Age of Greek sculpture. (Open Tue.-Sat. 9am-1pm and 3:30-7:30pm, Sun.-Mon. 9am-1pm.) Calabrians finish off the summer with the **celebration of the Madonna della Consolazione.** The festival lasts four days in mid-September and concludes with fireworks. Call the tourist office for more specific information.

■ NEAR REGGIO

Scilla and **Bágnara Calabra,** two picturesque fishing villages, lie about 30km from Reggio along the Tyrrhenian coast. The beach resort of Scilla sits above the famous rock which, according to Homer, hid a ship-devouring female monster with six heads and twelve feet. With tall green mountains ending in soft blue waters, Scilla today offers beautiful views and relaxing beaches. Scilla is accessible from Reggio by train (8 per day, ½hr., L5400 round-trip) or by bus (12 per day, last bus 9:00pm, L2500), and is well worth the trip. If you do stay in Scilla, try to get one of the rooms in the **Pensione Le Sirene,** Via Nazionale, 57 (tel. (0965) 75 40 19 or 75 41 21). Just one block from the beach (1 block back from the *lungomare*), Le Sirene offers shady, communal terraces that overlook the sea and cool rooms with ceiling fans and showers. Curfew midnight. (Singles L38,000. Doubles L60,000. Triples L75,000. Breakfast L4000. Reservations recommended June-Aug.)

The cheapest meals around are at **Pizzeria San Francesco** on the beach (tel. (0965) 75 46 91). Pizza runs L5000-10,000. (Open Thurs.-Tues. 7pm-1am.) Walk 10 minutes toward the castle from the beach to relax with a drink at **Vertigine,** P. San Rocco, 14. Outdoor seats feature great views of the ocean and the castle. (Drinks from L1500. Cover L2000, service 10%. Open daily noon-3pm and 7pm-midnight.)

The summer night spot is the open disco created under the arch of a bridge by the *superstrada*. **Il Ponte** offers giant screen video music. Before you dance the night away, be sure to visit the **Church of Maria S.S. Immacolata,** right next to the castle. Inside, you'll enjoy 14 bronze sculptures depicting the Crucifixion, as well as an awe-inspiring altar-painting. (Open 8-11am and 3-7pm.)

Bagnara Calabra, 8km north of Scilla (L1500 one-way by train), is a typical Tyrrhenian fishing village with crumbling buildings and swordfishing boats bobbing offshore. The road north of town offers a view of Sicily and the Lipari Islands. Bring a picnic, as local prices tend to be astronomical. **A&O Discount Supermarket,** Via Garibaldi, 127, offers a cheap haven. (Open Mon., Wed.-Sat. 8am-1pm and 4:15-8:15pm.) **Ristorante La Torre,** Piazza Cesare Battista, 11 (tel. 37 17 09) has no set menu; they serve what they catch. Expect to pay about L15,000 for a delicious plate of fresh swordfish; prices fall as the season progresses. English spoken.

Aspromonte, a bump Calabria developed after kicking Sicily, presides over southern Calabria in pine-and-birch-covered glory, and awaits those who can't get to the Sila for their nature break. To reach the center of the area, take one of nine daily blue buses (#127 or 128) in front of Reggio's central train station to **Gamberie** (L4000). Here visitors enjoy a fabulous view of Sicily and the straits of Messina from the heights of **Puntone di Scirocco** (1660m), accessible by chairlift. Hop a train to the beach at **Melito di Porto Salvo** on the southern tip of the Italian peninsula. It's one of the area's nicest swimming locales. (15 per day, 11 on Sun., 30min., L2500).

■■■ THE IONIAN COAST

The starkly beautiful beaches which stretch between Reggio di Calabria and Metaponto are sparsely populated with Italian and German tourists and rarely frequented by anyone else. The beaches offer both a cool dip in the Ionion Sea as well as a beautiful contrast to the mountains in the distance. If a strip of sand is all you desire, consider hopping on a train from either Reggio di Calabria or Crotone and getting off when the scenery looks inviting. **Soverato** (130km from Reggio, L9000) offers one of the most expansive, scenic, and popular strips; the beaches at **Bovalino Marina, Palizzi,** and **Brancaleone** are closer and almost as agreeable. All travelers should be forewarned that trains traversing the Ionian coast often have erratic schedules and multiple connections; give yourself ample time to get where you want to go.

CROTONE

Behind the factory façade of Calabria's most industrial city there remain a few glimpses of history. Crotone's dual nature is surprisingly appealing: the eastern half (the new town) is centered along the main drag, **Via Vittorio Veneto,** which extends from the town's central square, **Piazza Pitagora,** to Crotone's eastern limits. The other half of Crotone, the Old City, is a cluster of interconnected old buildings wrapped around a hill. Exploring this historical section without a map may leave you lost forever in a maze of narrow alleyways, but be sure to visit the **cathedral** (one block from the main square Piazza Pitagora) and the 16th-century **Castle of Carlo V** on Via Risorgimento (castle open Mon.-Fri. 9am-1pm, Tues. and Thurs. 9am-1pm and 4:30-6:30pm; free).

As with the rest of Calabria, Crotone has limited budget offerings. Right off Piazza Pitagora is **Albergo Italia,** Piazza Vittoria, 12 (tel. 239 10). Don't come for the 70s deco and tepid showers, but for the price and location. Curfew 11:30pm. (Singles L30,000, with shower L35,000. Doubles L50,000, with shower L60,000. Triples L30,000 per person.) **Pensione Europa,** Via Ruffo, 44 (tel. 240 69), second right off Via Nicoletta, provides singles with bath for L30,000, doubles L50,000. Once you work up an appetite (and if your wallet can stand it), stop in at **Al Mio Ristorante,** Via M. Nicoletta, 8-10 (tel. 217 36; open daily 9am-3pm and 7pm-midnight). This place specializes in seafood and will whip up a delicious *menù* for L20,000. Look for the giant wooden spoon and fork on the wall inside, as well as the autographs of famous Italians. Another option is **Pizzeria Piranha**, Via XXV Aprile, 13-15 (tel. 242 73). Devour a *rotonda pizza* (L22,000, feeds 3-4) and watch the shop's mascots devour left-overs. If you're shopping for provisions, avoid the overpriced STANDA and go for the family-run shops throughout the city.

Trains run to Crotone from Rome; more locally, **buses** run from Camigliatello (1-2 per day, 1hr., L5800) to Piazza Pitagora. **Tourist office** on Via Torino, 148 (tel. 231 85) off Via Vittorio Veneto. Open daily 8am-2pm. **Telephones** on Via M. Nicoletta, 11 (tel. 238 52) open 8:30am-10:30pm. **Telephone Code:** 0962. **Post Office** on Via Tedeschi (tel. 224 43) open 8:15am-1:30pm.

LOCRI AND GERACE

The town of **Locri** (80km from Reggio, L7000; L11,200 from Crotone) is not where you want to spend your time; head for the shore or the mountains. Locri is the most organized of the several towns along this coast, but only has one hotel, **Hotel Orientale**, Via Tropoli, 33 (tel. (0964) 202 61). The beach is Locri's main attraction; the best restaurants are situated along the pebbly shoreline.

From the train station, a quick right will bring you to the doors of **Paolo lervase Supermarket,** Via R. Margherita, 65 (tel. (0964) 204 64; open Mon.-Sat. 7:30am-1pm, 4-9pm). Continue down this road until you come to an intersection where you can see the beach to your right. Heading to the beach (crossing the railroad tracks) brings you to **Bar Eros,** Via Lungomare (tel. 299 18), offering arcade games, pool tables, and foosball, as well as a great rooftop view. Open 24 hrs. In the summer, Locri meets at **La Playa,** Via Lungomare (tel. (0964) 21 431). (Disco right off the beach and *menù* for L16,000. Open 9am-4am or later, depending on the crowd.)

Locri is a good starting point for wilderness lovers. Take the bus from the train station to **Cimina,** and start your hike up on **Monte Trepitó.** For information about Gerace and Locri, consult the **tourist office** in Locri, Via Fiume, 1 (tel. (0964) 296 00). To get there, follow Via G. Matteotti toward the library (#160) and park/maze off Via Umberto; Via Fiume is a small street to your left. (Open Mon.-Sat. 8am-8pm.)

To get to the taciturn town of **Gerace,** 10km inland from Locri and high above the Calabrian countryside, grab a bus from in front of Locri's train station (roughly L1500 each way). Gerace's heart and a point of pride for the region is the **cathedral,** Calabria's largest. The structure's imperial crypt is supported by 26 ancient Greek columns pilfered from Locri. From the crypt, climb the stairs into a Romanesque interior of the grandest proportions. Outside the main portal of the cathedral, down the street to the left is the town's historic center, **Largo delle Tre Chiese.** The **Castle of Roberto il Guiscardo** is currently being renovated, but the trek up to Gerace's pinnacle is still worth it for the best view in southeastern Calabria.

SICILY (SICILIA)

"Without Sicily, Italy cannot be fully understood. It is here one finds the key to all things."

—J.W. Goethe

Throughout the ages, every great nearby civilization has at one time turned its attention toward Sicily, the largest island in the Mediterranean, transforming its landscape and people but never conquering its independent spirit. The Greeks, Romans, Arabs, Normans, and Aragonese have all held Sicily—usually with the support of an invading army. While this series of hostile takeovers may have angered Sicilians at the time, it's now a lure for the modern traveler. Each wave of conquerors has left its own imprint upon the island, offering the 20th-century visitor a fascinating and diverse cultural landscape. Today, Sicily is invaded only by tourists eager to take in its legacy of over three millennia. Nonetheless, the island's inhabitants hold on to their traditions, a testament to their resilience during centuries of occupation, creation, and destruction.

The history of Sicily began with Greek colonialism in the mid-8th century BC, when a group of Corinthian settlers founded Syracuse. In the 6th and 5th centuries BC, the Greek city-states of Sicily were among the most powerful and populous in the Mediterranean. A succession of external struggles with the Carthaginians and internal conflicts among the various cities occupied Sicilians from the late 5th century until 211 BC, when the Roman capture of Syracuse (and defeat of Carthage) brought the entire island under Roman control. In the 9th century AD, Sicily became a Muslim outpost second in importance only to Spain. It later served as the seat of the Norman court, and subsequently became the pawn of Renaissance dynasties. The next phase of Sicilian history was one of harsh Aragonese rule; the Bourbons' shortsighted agricultural policies exhausted the rich volcanic soil and reduced much of the Sicilian interior to a parched wasteland. In 1860, Garibaldi and his "redshirts" defeated the Bourbon troops and declared the island "liberated," though in fact it became a part of the Kingdom of Italy. Even that juncture was superficial; cultural, economic, and geographical conditions meant that the island of Sicily was a long way from assimilation into Italy.

The bloodshed of Sicilian political life has been matched by the cruelty of Mother Nature. To Giuseppe Lampedusa, Sicily's prince-turned-writer, it was a "landscape which knows no mean between sensuous sag and hellish drought." The Sicilian countryside is dominated by sheer, rock-strewn crags, rendering much of the land non-arable. Much of what can be cultivated has been converted to olive, citrus and almond groves. Geographically, Sicily is dominated by Europe's highest volcano, Mt. Etna (which the locals simply call "the mountain"). The island's position at the edge of the European geologic plate has resulted in a succession of seismic and volcanic catastrophes that have periodically snuffed out the lives of its inhabitants. Those not destroyed seem to have drawn strength from survival; the fruits of Sicily's artistic and intellectual heritage range from Selinunte's stark ancient grandeur to Noto's baroque frivolity, from the irrefutable logic of Pythagoras to the wry irrationalities of Pirandello. Not all have chosen to remain in its harsh territory, however. In the late 19th and early 20th centuries, hundreds of thousands of Sicilians left the island in favor of the promised lands of the United States and Argentina.

Modern Sicily bears the scars of its history quietly, and speeds into the future. Locals install condom-vending machines in front of medieval cathedrals and raise petrochemical refineries beside Greek acropolises. Thousands of immigrants arrive from North Africa each year. Most recently, Sicilians have decided to eliminate the "tradition" of Mafia control; more and more Sicilians are expressing their frustration with continued mob activity and the perceived inertia of a government that has had

SICILY

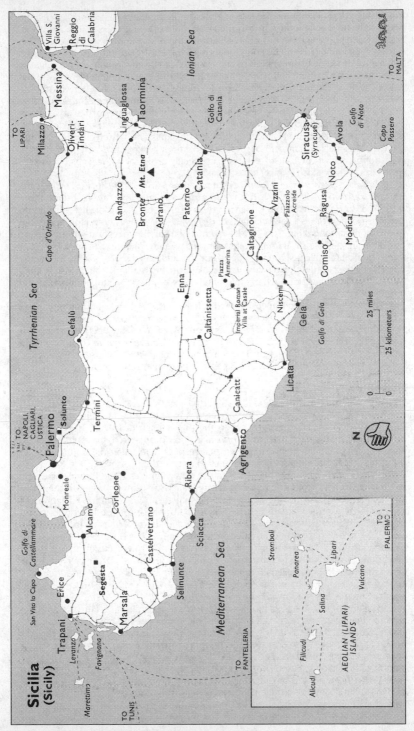

Sicilia
(Sicily)

Villa S. Giovanni
Reggio di Calabria
Messina
Ionian Sea
TO MALTA
Oliveri-Tindari
Linguaglossa
Taormina
Milazzo
TO LIPARI
Golfo di Catania
Golfo di Noto
Capo Passero
Avola
Siracusa (Syracuse)
Noto
Randazzo
Mt. Etna
Bronte
Adrano
Paterno
Catania
Vizzini
Palazzolo Acreide
Ragusa
Modica
Comiso
Caltagirone
Piazza Armerina
Imperial Roman Villa at Casale
Niscemi
Enna
Caltanissetta
Gela
Golfo di Gela
Licata
Capo d'Orlando
Tyrrhenian Sea
Cefalù
Canicatti
Agrigento
Termini
Solunto
Palermo
TO NAPOLI, CAGLIARI, USTICA
Monreale
Corleone
Ribera
Sciacca
Selinunte
Castelvetrano
Alcamo
Segesta
Marsala
Erice
Trapani
Levanzo
Favignana
Marettimo
San Vito lo Capo
Golfo di Castellammare
TO TUNIS
TO PANTELLERIA
Mediterranean Sea

25 miles
25 kilometers

N

Stromboli
Panarea
Salina
Filicudi
Alicudi
Lipari
Vulcano
AEOLIAN (LIPARI) ISLANDS
TO PALERMO

limited success in stemming the tide of violence. Recent demonstrations against the Mafia have brought thousands into the streets, demanding an end to corruption. Unfortunately, change is not likely to happen quickly; the number of defendants currently awaiting trial will fill courtrooms until the end of the century. (See below.)

Because of Sicilian immigration to the United States, and to some extent because of the welcomed American invasion in 1942, *Statunitensi* (particularly *Sicilo-Americani)* receive an exceptionally warm welcome. Women, however, should be aware that male attention in Sicily is often aggressive and unceasing, and those unequipped with the extensive lexicon of Sicilian cut-downs are particularly susceptible. Cases of physical harassment and assault are relatively few (by American standards), but, unfortunately, petty crime is rampant. The larger cities (Palermo, Catania, Messina, and Trapani) are notorious for their pickpockets and purse-snatchers, and their downtown districts can be especially unsafe at night. Travel in groups if you can, or stay close to busy areas.

In summer, Sicily swelters for weeks at a time (35-45°C/100-120°F). The burning African *scirocco* winds can scorch your vacation in July and August. In addition, haze and random fires often obscure vistas in the summer months. Spring and autumn are ideal times to visit the island. Holy Week in Sicily is noted for its colorful processions, among them Good Friday in Enna, where marchers don white, hooded costumes in the Spanish tradition. For complete details, pick up the booklet *Easter in Sicily,* available at most tourist offices. For the traditional tour of Sicily, follow the coast; for a tour of traditional Sicily, venture into the heartland. If you do visit in summer, follow local custom: eat a big lunch, take a two-hour nap, and enjoy the island in the cool early evenings.

As for the local fare, Sicilians pride themselves on the goodness of their raw ingredients. Specialties include pasta with sardines, *frutta martorana* (sugar candies), swordfish, green peppers, *panellas, arancini al riso* (Sicilian riceballs with meat fillings), *cannoli,* and *cassata* (rich ice cream). The *melanzane* (eggplant) and *pomodori* (tomatoes) of the island are some of the best you'll find in all of Italy, and try eating *gelato* like the natives do—in a *brioche* (sweet pastry bun).

THE MAFIA

Non-Sicilians have a Hollywood-influenced vision of the Mafia: pin-striped suits, machine guns, horse-heads, and the Godfather. In reality, the Mafia in Sicily is very different. For starters, *Mafiosi* refer to themselves as *uomini d'onore* (men of honor). Don't laugh: the system of *mafia* is in a complicated and rigid structure based on hierarchical relationships, mutual respect, and territorial boundaries. At the head of a family is the person we refer to as the "don," or rather, the Representative. (This man represents his family to the other families.) The Representative is aided by anywhere from one to a cabinetful of Advisors; lower down on the chain are *capodecine* (heads of ten) who manage groups of *soldati* (soldiers). Even lower are the local youths who aren't true *mafiosi,* but work for the local don in the hopes of someday becoming *mafiosi.* Mafia families control an established area of action, be it a neighborhood in Palermo or the entire city of Catania. Women are excluded from the Mafia system; mothers and wives are prized family members but considered too talkative to participate in secret operations. Contrary to popular belief, women and non-Mafia children were once immune from the blood feuds of Mafia interaction; only in recent years have dons seen fit to assassinate the innocent, much to the dismay of more "traditional" *mafiosi.*

The system of *mafia* has its roots in the *latifondi* (agricultural estates) of rural Sicily. Land managers and salaried militiamen (read: landlords and bouncers) were necessary to defend the land and the people from robbers, and out of this class grew the *mafia. Mafiosi* were powerful because people owed them favors; they were strong because they supported each other; and they were feared because they did not hesitate to kill offenders. Some *mafiosi* today claim that they descend from a group called *I Beati Paoli,* a Robin-Hood like secret society that protected the poor and dispensed "true" justice to the inhabitants of Palermo in the 19th century. While the

Mafia suffered under Fascist-era purges, Allied support toward the end of World War II helped get the organization back on its feet. Since the mid-80s, the Italian government has seriously tried to curtail Mafia influence, with inconclusive results. Among Sicilians (especially the *Palermitani),* one thing is certain: they've had enough. Present and increasingly vocal, opposition to the mafia continues to grow.

While you're traveling through Sicily or (southern Italy for that matter), avoid mentioning "the Mafia." Whereas some Sicilians will be pleased to talk about the changing tide of opinion against the Mafia, you're more likely to get one of two responses: locals who don't want to talk about the Mafia will deny that it exists, while others will immediately cease being friendly. While chowing down in Cosenza, our researcher Sandrine mentioned the word "Mafia" in conversation and was treated to the abrupt silence and direct stares of a nearby tableful of men. *Uomini d'onore* of today dislike the term "Mafia" and its derivatives; they refer to their system as *Cosa Nostra* or "our thing." Unfortunately, over the course of the last half-century, Mafia activities have expanded to include national politics, drug-smuggling, and, most recently, the assassination of high-profile judges. "Their thing" has expanded to become a serious problem for Italy and the world at large.

One final note: be aware that "Mafia" refers only to *Sicilian* organized crime; the *Camorra* in Naples and the *'ndrangheta* of Calabria are separate, mutually disdainful networks.

TRANSPORTATION

Flights from all major Italian cities service Palermo and Catania. The easiest way to reach Sicily from Rome is a train-ferry combination to Messina (from Rome via Reggio di Calabria, L72,300). **Tirrenia,** in Palermo (tel. (091) 33 33 00), the largest private ferry service in Italy, is the most extensive and reliable, although you should still expect considerable delays; **Grandi-Traghetti** (tel. (091) 58 79 39) offers better off-season rates to Palermo from Genoa and Livorno. Prices and schedules vary according to specific dates; approximations are given below. Listings are for Tirrenia lines unless otherwise stated.

Reggio di Calabria-Messina: 17 per day on the state railroad ferry *(Ferrovie Statale;* tel. (090) 67 55 82; 6am-8:40pm, 20min., L4000) or take the hydrofoil from the same terminal at the Reggio port (20 per day, L5000).

Villa San Giovanni-Messina: 32 per day (around the clock) on the state railroad ferry (L2200).

Genoa-Palermo (24hr.): **Grandi-Traghetti Lines** Tues. 8pm, Thurs. midnight, L94,000-120,000. **Tirrenia Lines** From: Genoa (Sept. 12-July 20 Tues., Thurs., Sat. at noon; July 21-Sept. 20 at 5pm); Palermo (Sept. 12-July 19 Wed., Fri. at 4pm; July 20-Sept. 11 at 11am). L109,7000.

Naples-Palermo (11hr.): From: Napoli (daily at 8:00pm); Palermo (Nov.-July daily at 8pm, Aug.-Oct. daily at 10pm). L69,100.

Cagliari-Palermo (14hr.): From: Cagliari (Fri. at 7pm); Palermo (Sat. at 7pm). L60,000.

Livorno-Palermo (19hr.): **Grandi-Traghetti** Tues., Thurs., and Sat. 8pm (L94,000-120,000).

Cagliari-Trapani (11hr.): From: Cagliari (Sun. 7pm); Trapani (Tues. 9pm). L60,000.

Trapani-Tunis: From: Trapani (Mon. at 9am; 7½hr.); Tunis (Mon.at 8pm; 10½hr.). L92,000.

Trains in Sicily only partially deserve their reputation for tardiness; even the diminutive *Elettromotrici* are reasonably reliable and convenient. Two major bus companies, the private, air-conditioned, and punctual **SAIS,** and the public, often steamy **AST,** serve many of the destinations that are inaccessible by train. There's no central transportation authority in Sicily, so check in every city and with every driver for the bus schedules to your next destination. Give yourself a few extra hours to get where you're going, especially if you're heading for isolated ruins, and if you hear the word *sciopero*, head home—it means that there's a strike.

Hitchhiking is difficult on long hauls; hitchers reputedly have better luck near the turn-offs to roads for short, specific trips. **Hitchhiking in Sicily is extremely risky—Let's Go does not recommend it. Driving** in Sicily isn't that safe either. You'll need an International Driver's Permit (available at AAA; see *Documents and Formalities* in the *Essentials* section, page 7), a rental car, and nerves of steel. Travelers (drivers and pedestrians alike) should be aware that most Italians drive without regard to lanes, safe driving distance, or impending doom. And Sicilians seem to be particularly fond of using their car horns, an annoying tendency that may save your life. **Pedestrians** should note that simple tasks like crossing the street can become a real challenge here. One strategy is to follow other people across, using them as a buffer between you and the speeding cars. Another alternative is to treat oncoming traffic as if it were a charging rhinoceros: make eye contact and pray to the local saint. Italians waste no space on streets, which are usually just wide enough for a car to pass through. Make your mother happy—look both ways before crossing.

THE NORTHERN COAST

■■■ MESSINA

History has handed Messina (pop. 400,000) misfortune after misfortune. Initially founded in 730 BC and named "Zancle," the city was captured and renamed Messene by Anaxilas, the tyrant of Reggio, in 493 BC. A century later, the Carthaginians came and razed the site. Thereafter, the city fell into the hands of everyone from the Marmertines to the Normans to Richard the Lionheart. The city grew to prosperity under Norman rule and burgeoned as a Crusader port, remaining a proud bastion at the periphery of European civilization for 600 years.

Since the 17th century, however, Messina hasn't had as much luck. After rebelling against Spanish rule in the late 1600s, the city lost its special privileges and shrank to one-eighth of its former size. It went on to be devastated by plague in 1743, demolished by an earthquake in 1783, bombarded from the sea in 1848, struck by cholera in 1854, slammed by more earthquakes in 1894 and 1908 (the latter killing 70,000 of a population of 170,000), and flattened by both Allied and Axis bombs during World War II. What is left is a city that has struggled time and again to rebuild itself, and now seems to have taken a few too many blows to get up off the canvas. Buildings in Messina generally date back no more than several decades, and nearly all appear to have been hastily constructed; even the cathedral, rebuilt twice in this century alone, is essentially new. A sense of impermanence hangs about, as if Messina's inhabitants know that yet another disaster will soon prove their efforts futile.

Messina is the main point of entry into Sicily from the mainland, so you will probably have to pass through here. Although no city is without its virtues (the fruit stalls in Piazza Carducci near the university sell juicy blood-oranges for less than L200 apiece), you'll probably want to move on as soon as possible, if only because your money is much better spent elsewhere in Sicily. Messina has all of the costs of a place like Taormina, and only a fraction of the charm.

ORIENTATION AND PRACTICAL INFORMATION

Major transportation routes and tourist offices cluster around the train station at P. della Repubblica. Right in front of the train station runs **Via G. la Farina;** on the left (with your back to the station) **Via Tommaso Cannizzaro** leads to the center of town, meeting **Viale S. Martino** (the city's main drag) at **Piazza Cairoli.** Cross Via Farina from the station and to the right lies **Via I Settembre** which crosses **Corso**

MESSINA

Garibaldi and ends at **Piazza del Duomo.** Corso Garibaldi runs along the harbor to both the hydrofoil dock and Corso Cavour.

> Women should not walk alone in Messina at night, and *no one* should roam the streets near the train station or the harbor after 10pm. Stay near the more populated streets around the *duomo* and the university. Be wary of those pickpockets and purse-snatchers, and keep your money in a secure place.

Tourist Office: APT, (tel. 67 42 36) outside the Central Station to the right in P. della Repubblica, offers a deluge of maps and information on Messina and the Lipari Islands. English spoken. Open Mon.-Sat. 8:15am-7pm. **Ufficio Informazioni Comunali,** (tel. 67 29 44) next door to the APT. Replete with materials and maps on Messina, the Lipari Islands, Taormina, and other areas within the province of Messina. Open Mon.-Sat. 8:30am-1pm. **AAST,** P. Cairoli, 45 (tel. 293 35 41 or 293 35 42). Open mornings only.

Police: tel. 112. **Pronto Intervento:** tel. 555 55. **Carabinieri:** tel. 449 30.

Post Office: at P. Antonello, off Corso Cavour near the *duomo* (tel. 77 41 90). *Fermo posta* at window #12. Open Mon.-Fri. 8:15am-6:30pm, Sat. 8:30-1pm. **Postal Code:** 98122.

Telephones: ASST, on your right from the train station. Open daily 8am-7:45pm. **Telephone Code:** 090.

Currency Exchange: Cambio/Ufficio Informazioni (tel. 67 52 34 or 67 52 35), just inside the train station. Good rates plus information on trains and buses.

Trains: at P. della Repubblica (tel. 67 52 34). To: Palermo (12 per day, 5:30am-8:05pm, 3½hr., L17,800); Syracuse (11 per day, 5:45am-8:10pm, 3hr., L14,400); Rome (5 per day, 11:05am-12:15am, 10hr., L72,300); Milazzo, the main port for the Lipari Islands (10 per day, 5:30am-8:15pm, 40min., L3700). **Luggage Storage: Deposito Bagagli:** L1500 per bag for 24 hrs. Open 24hrs.

Buses: SAIS, at P. della Repubblica, 46 (tel. 77 19 14), to the left of the train station. To: Taormina (15 per day, 1½hr., L5100) and Catania (24 per day, 1½hr., L9500); Rome (1 per day at 9:30pm, 10hr., L60,000, under 27 L50,000). **Giuntabus** (tel. 67 37 82 or 67 57 49), in the town center, on Via Terranova, 8. To Milazzo (14 per day 6am-6:15pm, 40min., L5500 one-way, L8000 round-trip).

Ferries: Stazione Marittima, same building as train station, on the water, 300m to the right of P. della Repubblica. To Reggio (17 per day, 20min., L4000). **Hydrofoils: SNAV** (tel. 36 40 40, 36 77 75 for reservations; fax 36 40 45), a blue, one-story building on Corso Vittorio Emanuele II, 1km north of train station off Corso Garibaldi. To the Lipari Islands (4-5 per day June 1-Sept. 30, 2hr., L30,000-50,000). Save L10,000 by taking the train to Milazzo and catching the ferry there.

Public Transportation: ATM buses leave from P. della Repubblica and go into town. Purchase tickets (L700; L2000 for all-day bus pass) at any *tabacchi* or newsstand. Detailed bus info on the signs with yellow borders outside the station.

Lost Property: at the **Municipio di Messina** (tel. 777 01), where Via Vettovaglie hits the harbor (to the right from P. della Repubblica). Open Mon.-Sat. 9am-noon. Ask for **oggetti smarriti.**

Late-Night Pharmacy: tel. 192. All pharmacies are open during the day 8:30am-1pm and 4:30-8pm. After that, they are on a rotation with least two open during the night and on weekends; check with the tourist office for a list. The pharmacy **LoJacono** (tel. 67 20 18), at Corso Garibaldi, 69, is close to the center of town.

Emergencies: tel. 113. **Hospital: Ospedale R. Margherita,** Via Libertà (tel. 36 51 or 36 54 54); **Policlinico Universitario,** Messina-Gazzi (tel. 22 11, nights and weekends 67 50 48).

ACCOMMODATIONS AND CAMPING

Some smaller establishments are wary of foreign backpackers; check your bags at the station while searching for a place to stay.

Hotel Monza, Viale San Martino, 63 (tel./fax 67 37 55), at Via Cannizzaro. Leafy lobby welcomes you to comfortable, modern rooms. Singles L40,000, with bath L55,000. Doubles L68,000, with bath L110,000. Triples L89,000. Visa, MC.

Hotel Touring, Via Scotto, 17 (tel. 293 88 51). Exit the train station, go under the overpass, and turn right (hotel is 100m away). Hallways of mirrors and faux-marble lead into stark rooms. Convenient for travelers stranded between trains. Singles L40,000, with bath L50,000. Doubles L60,000, with bath and TV L100,000.

Camping: Il Peloritano (tel. 84 40 57). Take bus #28 from the station to the small town of Rodia-Tarantonio. Make sure to stock up on food before you go. Showers available. L5000 per person per tent. Open mid-May-Oct.

FOOD

Relatively inexpensive restaurants and *trattorie* crowd the area around Via Risorgimento, reached by following Via Cannizzaro (see *Orientation* above) one block after P. Cairoli. In summer, try the legendary *pesce spada* (swordfish) direct from the Straits of Messina, delectable enough to earn Homer's mention in the *Odyssey*. On Via S. Cecilia, eight blocks from P. Maurolico down Via C. Battisti, there is an outdoor **market** (open daily 6am-2pm).

Osteria del Campanile, Via Loggia dei Mercanti, 9 (tel. 71 14 18), behind the *duomo* and right next to the post office. Look for the yellow awning. Complete meals start at L18,000, but there's much to be had. Cover L2000. Open Tues.-Sun. noon-3pm and 7:30pm-midnight. AmEx.

Safari Sandwich, Via G. Venezian, 83 (tel. 67 59 89). Branches off from P. Duomo. Good for a quick fix while on safari at the cathedral. Sandwich L5000. *Ziti* L3500. TV and music upstairs in winter. Open Thurs.-Tues. 8am-midnight.

Supermarket: STANDA, P. Cairoli Isolato, 222 (tel. 292 77 30). Go into the main entrance of the STANDA department store, take a right, and go down the stairs. Although it's cheaper to buy fruit and vegetables from street vendors, STANDA is your best bet for everything else. Open Mon. 4:10-8pm, Tues.-Sat. 9am-8pm.

SIGHTS

Messina has seen many monuments built over its long history, and it has also seen most of them crumble to the ground. It is a city undergoing a constant facelift; many sights are currently shrouded in scaffolding and large white tents.

The **Piazza del Duomo's** wide open spaces and large flagstones provide some Renaissance relief from the asphalt hustle and bustle of the rest of Messina. The *piazza* contains the 12th-century **duomo** (open 8am-12:30pm and 4-7pm, currently under restoration) and the squat **Church of SS. Annunziata dei Catalaní** from the same period. The cathedral's stark exterior features an ornate portal portraying the Archangel Gabriel and the Madonna with saints. In front of the church is the **Fontana di Orione** (circa 1547, also under restoration), the work of Michelangelo's pupil Angelo Montorsoli, where lazy nudes recline on a richly embellished base. The clock tower houses what is supposedly the world's largest astronomical clock. The Grim Reaper keeps time until the grand spectacle at noon, when a mechanical procession of animals, angels, and legendary figures re-enacts the local legend of the Madonna della Lettera, patron saint of the city. A **festival** in her honor takes over the town every June 3; another festival, the **Ferragosto Messinese,** takes place Aug. 14-15, featuring the 150,000-strong "Procession of the Giants."

Just down the road from the hydrofoil port on Viale della Libertà is the **Museo Regionale** (tel. 36 12 92). Founded in 1806 with five private collections, it was adopted by the state in 1904 as a repository for the furnishings, valuables, and works of art recovered from churches and civic buildings after the 1894 earthquake. Today it includes a collection of Renaissance and Baroque masterpieces, among them *The Polyptych of the Rosary* (1473) by local hero Antonello da Messina, an Andrea della Robbia terra-cotta of the Virgin and Child, and Caravaggio's *The Adoration of the Shepherds* (1608) and *Resurrection of Lazarus* (1609). Take bus #8 from the station or P. Duomo and get off at P. Museo (20min.); walk part of the way back to view the harbor's sickle-shaped form, which led the original Greek settlers to name the colony "Zancle" (the Greek word for scythe). (Museum open Mon., Wed., and Fri. 9am-1:30pm; Tues., Thurs., and Sat. 4-6:30pm; Sun. 9am-12:30pm.) If all of Messina seems closed for renovation, take solace with the fish in the **Acquario Comunale,** Villa Mazzini (tel. 488 97; open 9am-2pm).

Messina is not renowned for its beaches. Still, the route traveled by bus #8 through the ramshackle fishing villages provides some great waterfront scenery (departs from the train station, L700; L2000 for an all-day unlimited bus pass). Get off at whichever stop catches your eye, or wait until the **Lungolago** (20min. from the station at Messina). This is literally a "long lake," lined with *caffè* and palm trees, and overlooked by crumbling villas.

■■■ AEOLIAN ISLANDS (ISOLE EOLIE)

Set in the sparkling Mediterranean, the **Aeolian** (or **Lipari**) **Islands** are all places of remarkable beauty. The breezy islands are renowned for their fiery volcanoes and long rocky beaches. The archipelago comprises one of the last areas of unspoiled seashore in Italy and has only recently been discovered. Food and accommodations are more expensive than elsewhere in Sicily; prices peak in the August high season, for which you'd better make reservations on the main islands no later than May. Fortunately, Lipari has a youth hostel. Of the seven isles, visit Lipari for a well-equipped tourist center, a castle, and easily navigable vistas; Vulcano for bubbling mud baths and a sulfurous crater; Stromboli for luxuriant vegetation and a restless volcano; Panarea for inlets and a more elite clientele; Salina for grottoes and pilgrims; Filicudi for winding trails and coastal rock formations; and Alicudi for a rare dose of solitude. The telephone code for the islands is 090.

Dealt an Unfortunate Blow

The **Aeolian** (or **Lipari**) **Islands** are mentioned in Homer's *Odyssey* as the domain of Aeolus, King of the Winds. According to this tale, Aeolus gave Odysseus a bag of winds to help quicken his return trip. His sailors—not the brightest of seafarers—ignored Aeolus' warning and opened the bag, blowing themselves right back to the islands. Hey, at least they weren't all turned into pigs. (D'oh!)

GETTING THERE

The archipelago lies off the Sicilian coast, north of **Milazzo,** the principal and least expensive embarkation point (on the Messina-Palermo train line; 18 per day 5.30am-8.13pm, 1hr. from Messina, L3900; 4hr. from Palermo, L13,800). **Giuntabus,** Via Terranova, 8 (tel. (090) 67 37 82 or 67 57 49) also services the town. (14 per day from Messina 6am-6:15pm, 4 on Sun., 45min., L5500; also daily from Catania airport June-Sept., L20,000.) The bus is more convenient than the train; it takes you directly from Messina to Milazzo seaport. **Ferries** leave much less frequently from **Naples'** Molo Beverello port. Hydrofoils (about twice the ferry price) run regularly in late July and August from **Messina, Naples, Cefalù, Palermo,** and **Reggio di Calabria.**

To get to the port in Milazzo from the train station, take the orange bus in front of the station. Get your ticket at the bar (L600) and ask to get off at the ferries (*traghetti*). If you're up for a long walk, cross Piazza Marconi from in front of the train station and bear left on Via XX Luglio. You'll hit the port 1km later, as Via XX Luglio becomes Via dei Mille and then, as it curves to the right hugging the port, Via Luigi Rizzo. Ferry offices can be found on **Via dei Mille,** while *aliscafi* (hydrofoils) and their owners repose on **Via Rizzo.**

Siremar and **Navigazione Generale Italiana (NGI)** operate reliable **ferries** out of Milazzo. Siremar also services several smaller islands and Naples (tel. (081) 551 21 12 in Naples). For **hydrofoil** (*aliscafi*) services to the islands, go to Siremar or **SNAV.** Pick up hydrofoil and ferry schedules in every port (ask for *un orario generale*). Schedules and prices tend to vary from season to season, so always call ahead to check. Frequencies listed are for June through September. Unless stated, prices are the same for both lines. Connections can be made between any stops in a line.

SNAV: in Milazzo: Via dei Mille, 32 (tel. 928 45 09 or 928 78 21). In Lipari: tel. 981 24 48. In Messina: tel. 36 40 44.

Siremar: in Milazzo: tel. 928 63 81 or 922 18 12; fax 928 60 20; open 7 days, 5am-7pm. In Lipari: tel. 981 22 00.

Navigazione Generale Italiana: in Milazzo: Via dei Mille, 26 (tel./fax 928 34 15 or tel. 928 40 91). In Lipari: Via Ten. Mariano Amendola, 14 (tel. 981 19 55). In Vulcano: Molo di Levante (tel. 985 24 01). In Salina: P. Santa Marina (tel. 984 30 03 or 984 30 78).

Ferries: Milazzo-Vulcano-Lipari-Salina: To Vulcano (1½hr., L10,200); Lipari (2hr., L11,600); Salina (3hr., L14,700). **Siremar:** 4-6 daily at 7am-6:30pm (Salina 7am-2:30pm). **NGI:** 2-4 daily at 6:30am-10pm.

Milazzo-Panarea-Stromboli via Vulcano and Lipari: To Panarea (3¼hr., L13,400) and Stromboli (5hr., L18,500). **Siremar:** 1 per day 7am (2:30pm Thurs.) **NGI:** 1 per Thurs. at 6:30am.

Milazzo-Filicudi-Alicudi via Vulcano, Salina, and Lipari: To Filicudi (4½hr., L20,100) and Alicudi (5½hr., L22,300). **Siremar:** 1 daily at 7am (2:30pm Thurs.). **NGI:** 1 daily Sat. at 6:30am.

The increasingly popular **hydrofoils** *(aliscafi)* run twice as often as ferries do, for twice the price and in half the time. From May 15 to October 15, SNAV runs to Lipari from Messina (4 per day 7:05am-6:30pm, L31,400) and Reggio di Calabria (5 per day, L33,700). Cabins are air-conditioned, although it's never quite as strong as one might hope. Frequencies listed below are for June through September; off-season schedules are more erratic, with as few as a third of the number of trips. Connections can be made between any two points in a route unless otherwise noted.

Milazzo-Vulcano-Lipari-Salina: To: Vulcano (35min., L18,400), Lipari (55min., L19,700), Salina (80min., L22,800). **Siremar:** 6-12 daily, 7:05am-7:00pm (7:05am-6:00pm for Salina). **SNAV:** 6 daily 7:30am-7:30pm.

Milazzo-Panarea-Stromboli via Vulcano and Lipari: To Panarea (1¾hr., L23,700), Stromboli (2½hr., L28,700). **Siremar:** 4 daily, 6:15am-3:00pm. **SNAV:** 2 daily at 10:30am and 4pm.

Milazzo-Filicudi-Alicudi via Vulcano and Lipari: To Filicudi (2hr., L31,100), Alicudi (2½hr., L38,300). **Siremar:** 1 daily 7am or 2:30pm, Thurs. 7am and 2:30pm; Alicudi 7am only. **SNAV:** 1 daily at 7:35am, plus another Mon.-Wed. and Sat. at 1:40pm.

■ LIPARI

...a floating island, a wall of bronze and splendid smooth sheer cliffs.
—Homer

Lipari is the largest and most beautiful of the islands off the coast of Sicily. In the town of the same name, pastel-colored houses dot a small promontory crowned by the walls of a medieval *castello,* the site of an ancient Greek acropolis. Although placid in appearance, Lipari bustles with summer activities from folk festivals to discos. The town's best beaches, **Spiaggia Bianca** and **Spiaggia Porticello,** are easily reached by bus. Lipari is an ideal base for daytrips to the neighboring six islands and their splendid beaches.

ORIENTATION AND PRACTICAL INFORMATION

The looming *castello* sits at the heart of the town, with the ferry dock to the right and the hydrofoil landing just to the left as you approach by sea. From Piazza Ugo di Sant'Onofrio in front of the hydrofoil dock, **Via Garibaldi** runs around the base of the *castello* to Piazza Mazzini, shadowing the ferry dock. Farther inland the main street, **Corso Vittorio Emanuele,** runs parallel to the harbor.

Tourist Office: Corso Vittorio Emanuele, 202 (tel. 988 00 95), up the street from the ferry dock. Useful free handouts. English spoken. Open Mon.-Fri. 8am-2pm and 4:30-7:30pm, Sat. 8am-2pm. Open July-Aug. weeknights until 10pm.

Police: tel. 112. **Carabinieri:** tel. 981 13 33.

Post Office: Corso Vittorio Emanuele, 207 (tel. 981 13 79), one block up from the tourist office, in the building that looks like two stacked steam-pipes. *Fermo posta.* Open Mon.-Fri. 8:30am-1:30pm, Sat. 8:30am-1pm. The **postal code** for Lipari is 98055, for Canneto-Lipari 98052, and for the rest of the islands 98050.

Telephones: Telecom (SIP) (tel. 981 12 63), in Boutique Ruggiero (with the yellow awning) on Via Maurolico, off Corso Vittorio Emanuele. Open Mon.-Sat. 8:30am-12:45pm and 4:30-8:45pm, Sun. 9am-12:45pm. At other times use the Hotel Augustus, Via Ausonia, the first right off Corso Vittorio Emanuele from the port. Open daily 9am-11pm. **Telephone Code for the Islands:** 090.

Currency Exchange: Banca del Sud (tel. 981 13 47) and **B.A.E.,** both on Corso Vittorio Emanuele. AmEx checks accepted. Open Mon.-Fri. 8:30am-3:30pm. Other exchanges will change money at rip-off rates, but are always available in an emergency. Compare rates with exchange available at the post office (cash only).

Public Transportation: Autobus Urso Gugliemo, Via Cappuccini (tel. 981 12 62 or 981 10 26). Ticket office open 9am-1pm; tickets can also be bought on the bus. To Quattrocchi (8 per day, L1500), Aquacalda (7 per day, L2000), Quattropani (8 per day, L2000), and Canneto (10 per day, L1500).

Taxis: Corso Vittorio Emanuele (tel. 981 11 10) or Marina Corta (tel. 981 11 95).

Bike/Moped Rental: Foti Roberto, Via F. Crispi, 31 (tel. 981 23 52 or 981 25 87), on the beach to the right of the ferry port. Bicycles L5000/hr., L20,000/day. Mopeds and scooters L30,000/2hr., L45,000/day. They ask for a L100,000 deposit and your passport number. Open Easter-Oct. 15 daily 9am-6pm.

Public Showers: Salone Doccie, at the barbershop of the Fratelli Acquaro, Corso Vittorio Emanuele, 261, across from Officina Fonti motor service near the ferry dock. Hot showers L5000. Open Mon.-Sat. 9am-noon and 4-8:30pm.

Pharmacy: Farmacia Internazionale, Corso Vittorio Emanuele, 128 (tel. 981 15 83). English-speaking doctor sometimes on duty. Open Mon.-Sat. 9am-1pm and 5-9pm. MC, Visa.

Emergencies: tel. 113. **Medical Emergency:** tel. 988 52 26. **Night Emergency:** tel. 981 10 10. **Hospital:** tel. 988 51. **Night doctor** available for housecalls (tel. 988 52 26).

ACCOMMODATIONS AND CAMPING

As you ply the port or walk around, locals will ask if you are looking for *affitta camere* (private rooms and apartments). These are often the best bargains but prices vary according to demand; proprietors ask for higher prices earlier in the day, then lower the costs later if their rooms haven't filled up. Try bargaining, but expect to pay at least L15,000 per person from September to June; start at L25,000 in August. Inquiring at local shops (try the bait-and-tackle store on Via Garibaldi near the hydrofoil dock) is often a useful route for finding *affitta camere.*

Lipari is invaded by more and more tourists as the summer progresses, and reaches full capacity in August. Hotels fill almost instantaneously and owners raise their prices by as much as 25%. Make reservations as far in advance as possible.

Ostello Lipari (HI), Via Castello, 17 (tel. 981 15 40, off season 981 25 27), 120 beds, on the hill within the walls of the fortress, next to the cathedral, 300m from port ferry. Strict management sternly enforces midnight curfew. Nevertheless, it's probably the best deal on the islands. Their sign warns to you keep an eye on your valuables. Reception open daily 7:30-9am and 6pm-midnight, downstairs only noon-2pm (to check in luggage). L11,000 per person. Cold showers only. Sheets and blankets free. Kitchen facilities (L500 extra for use). Breakfast L3000. Lunch and dinner each L10,000-14,000 only if enough demand (book them in the morning). HI card required when near capacity. Reservations recommended in July and Aug. Open Mar.-Oct.

Locanda Salina, Via Garibaldi, 18 (tel. 981 23 32), a few steps up from the hydrofoil port. Beautiful rooms overlooking the water. Communal terrace with great view. Singles L35,000. Doubles L60,000. Reserve several days in advance for June, weeks ahead for Aug.

Hotel Europeo, Corso Vittorio Emanuele, 98 (tel. 981 15 89). Great location on the bustling *corso*. Singles L40,000, with bath L45,000. Doubles L70,000, with bath L80,000. Showers L2000. Reserve early for June-Aug.

Camping: Baia Unci (tel. 981 19 09 or 981 25 27; fax 981 17 15), 2km from Lipari at the entrance to the hamlet of Canneto. This small, shady expanse has amiable management and a cheap self-service restaurant (roasted swordfish a bargain at L11,000). L11,500 per person, tent included. Open Mar. 15-Oct. 15. Restaurant open daily noon-2pm and 7pm-midnight.

FOOD

Try any dish with the island's famous *capperi* (capers), and follow it up with the indigenous, extremely sweet *Malvasia* dessert wine. Unfortunately, eating cheaply on Lipari is something of a challenge. The **Upim Supermercato d'Anieri Bartolo** (tel. 981 15 87), Corso Vittorio Emanuele, 212, stocks the basics. (Open Mon.-Sat. 8am-3:20pm and 4-11pm. AmEx, MC, Visa.) The *alimentari* lining Corso Vittorio Emanuele are generally open seven days a week.

Trattoria d'Oro, Via Umberto I, 28 (tel. 981 13 04 or 988 00 61). Look for the red and white sign pointing off Corso Vittorio Emanuele. Packed with locals. The *menù* is an especially good buy (L17,000). Try the *polpo all'insalata* (marinated octopus salad, L10,000) or the *ravioli di pesce spada* (swordfish ravioli, L12,000). Open daily 11:30am-3:30pm and 6:30pm-2am. AmEx, MC, Visa.

Il Galeone, Corso Vittorio Emanuele, 220 (tel. 981 14 63 or 981 26 35). Good piz-zas and a handy location, close to the ferry docking site. Tempts with 32 types of pizza (L7000-12,000). Open daily 8am-midnight, Oct.-May Thurs.-Tues. 8pm-mid-night (pizza available only after 7pm). MC, Visa.

Moby Dick, Via T.M. Amendola (tel. 981 18 76), right on the ferry port. *Menù* L17,000. Very good *spaghetti libarota* (with basil, capers, green olives and anchovies) for L9000, and *macaroni* "Moby Dick" (with cream, mushrooms, ham, and nutmeg) for L9000. No cover. Open 5:30am-2am.

Trattoria A Sfiziusa, Via Roma, 29 (tel. 981 12 16), 100m from the hydrofoil dock. They make a mean pasta, but beware of frozen *calamari*. *Primi* L6000-9000, *secondi* L11,000-25,000. Best bet is the *menù* at L17,000. Open daily noon-2:30pm and 7pm-midnight; closed Fri. in winter. Amex, Visa.

Pasticceria Subba, Corso Vittorio Emanuele, 92 (tel. 981 13 52). If you still have room after dinner, try anything from this *pasticceria*, named one of Italy's best by a popular magazine. Dante fans should go for the *paradiso*, a lemon-stuffed dumpling topped with almonds. Open Thurs.-Tues. 7am-2am.

SIGHTS AND ENTERTAINMENT

Lipari Town

A medieval **castello** crowns the town; within its walls stand four churches and a **duomo** which contains an 18th-century silver statue of San Bartolomeo (above the high altar) and a 16th-century Madonna (in the right transept). The ruins opposite the cathedral in the *parco archeologico* reveal layers of civilization dating back to at least 1700 BC. Many of the artifacts found here decorate the exterior of the superb **Museo Archeologico Eoliano,** which occupies the two buildings flanking the cathedral. (Open Mon.-Fri. 9am-2pm and 4-7pm; no entrance 30min. before closing time.) Inside the museum is the *serione geologico-vulcanologica,* an exposition of the volcanic history of the islands. The fortress holds a small archaeological park, and a neoclassical amphitheater (worth a visit just for the incredible view of Lipari town and the ocean) hosts events during July's riotous **Festival delle Isole Eolie.** (Open Mon.-Sat. 9am-7pm.) A walk around the island or town is a treat in and of itself. The twilight view of the Marina Lunga from near the *municipo* is unbelievably picturesque (right at the base of the *castello* entrance—look for the illuminated cross on the far peak). Even better—for both your eyes and your camera—take a sunset **ferry ride** to the islands.

As the sun sets and breezes blow in off the water, squeeze into your spandex and bop over to the **Discoteca Turmalin** (tel. 981 15 88), right on the waterfront, outside the castle walls and to the right as you exit. Even if you don't dig your date, you can enjoy the view while you dance. (Cover L12,000. Open daily 10am-2am, Sept.-June Sat. 10am-2am.) For a dose of American pop culture, visit the **Megaton Bar** at Via XXIV Maggio, 51 (tel. 981 26 19), across from the disco. Enjoy big-screen TV (showing international stations via satellite) and loud music while sampling a variety of teas, beers, sandwiches, and cocktails. (Open daily 9:30am-3am and 6pm 'til they're danced out.) Another alternative is **Ritrovo Eolclub**, Via Troncoa, 11 (tel. (0330) 69 52 97), an entertainment-complex fantasy with billiards (L9000 per hr.), foosball, air hockey, ping-pong tables, a card-playing room (L3000 per night), large-screen TV, video games, juke box, and a "kiddie park." (Open 5pm-2am. From the ferry port, take a right off Vittorio Emanuele; it's 20m down the road.) In a blowout party to mark the end of the summer tourist season, Lipari goes crazy with a colorful procession, fireworks, and other **festivities** on August 24—the day of the cathedral's patron saint, St. Bartholomew.

Around the Island

Lipari is known for its beaches and hillside panoramas. Go all out—rent a moped or a bike and take a day to tour the island (but keep your wits about you—the roads are narrow and the cars zip by). Work your way counterclockwise from Lipari's marina, where you'll first stop at **Canneto**, a small town fronted by a rocky beach. To get to the **Spiaggia Bianca** (White Beach) north of Canneto, take the waterfront road to the "No Camping" sign, then walk up the stairs of Via Marina Garibaldi and bear right down the narrow, cobblestoned path along the water's edge for one-third of a kilometer. There's good swimming all along this area. The beach is the spot for topless (and sometimes bottomless) sunbathing. Protect your delicate flesh, though—the pebbles are sharp and the sun is hot. From Canneto center, explore the secluded sandy coves flanking Spiaggia Bianca by renting one of the rafts, kayaks, or canoes that line the beach at Via M. Garibaldi (L6000-8000 per hour, L25,000-35,000 per day). Buses leave the Esso station at Lipari's ferry port for Canneto 10 times per day (16 per day in July and Sept., 21 per day in Aug.; L1500).

Just a few kilometers north of Canneto lies **Pomiciazzo**, where dozens of pumice mines line the road. On clear days, spectacular views of Salina, Panarea, and Stromboli adorn the horizon. Travel a few kilometers north and you're at **Porticello**, where you can bathe at the foot of the pumice mines while small flecks of the stone float on the sea's surface. As you dive beneath the waves for polished black obsidian, note the red and black veins (pumice and obsidian) that stretch from the beach into the seabed.

After passing through Acquacalda (nobody likes to be in "hot water"), the island's northernmost city, you'll see signs for the **Duomo de Chisea Barca**, right on the border of **Quattropani**. Head up the slope toward the church and check out some of the homes lodged in the obsidian hills. After a series of twists, turns, and some *very* steep inclines you'll finally reach the church and be granted a vista only those of saintly stature deserve.

Traveling south, across the island from Lipari town, you'll pass through **Varesana**, where the road splits: one route leads to **M.S. Angelo** (dominating the center of the island; follow signs for **Pirrera**) and the other runs to **Pianoconte**, where lava-coated battle gear has been unearthed. After this fork, the next stop on the main road is **Quattrocchi** (Four-Eyes), so called for its view of the four headlands that lie off the island's coast. If you make it to the Quattrocchi Belvedere (4km from Lipari, but a heady climb), you receive in return a noble vista of Lipari's *castello*, Vulcano, and the *Faraglione*, a series of monoliths rising from the sea between Vulcano and Lipari. South of Quattrocchi sits **Monte Guardia**, home to UNESCO's **Geophysical Observatory** (not open to the public) and a close-up view of Vulcano.

From July 1 to Sept. 30 only, you can catch a "Bus Tour of the Isle of Lipari" (daily at 9:30am, 11:30am, and 5:00pm, L5000). The other alternative is to grab **boats** from the hydrofoil port in Lipari and tour around Lipari and its neighboring islands. Excursions are run by **SEN** (Società Eolie di Navigazione) Corso Vittorio Emanuele, 247 (tel. 981 23 41; fax 981 20 55), next to the hydrofoil port, which conducts tours of Salina and Lipari (Mon.-Thurs. 10am, return 6:15pm, L35,000); Alicudi and Filicudi (Fri. at 9am, return 8:30pm, L50,000); Panarea (Tue., Wed., Fri.-Sun. at 10am, return 1pm, L30,000); Stromboli (Tues., Wed., Sat., Sun. at 3pm, return 11:15pm, L45,000); and Vulcano (Thurs. at 9am, return 1pm, L20,000). If these prices are too high, try privately contracting a fishing boat for a personalized excursion. Bargain for a decent price—about L12,000 per person per hour is reasonable. Consult the **NGI** office, Via Ten. M. Amendola (tel. 981 19 55), near the ferry port, for other ways to experience the islands.

■ VULCANO

Stretch out and immerse yourself; the hand of the god Vulcan will hold you gently, transforming thoughts into bubbles of music and culture.
—a signpost in Vulcano

The psychedelic sensations promised by these words may elude you, but if you are seeking an escape from the crowds of Lipari, this island could be worth a visit. Climb up to the sulfurous crater; take a dip in the bubbling sea or sink deeply into the therapeutic mud. But beware: some geologists think the gurgling volcano may explode within the next twenty years. For now, the great crater lies dormant at the island's center. Easy access from Lipari (by hydrofoil, L4000; by ferry, L2400) and the density of sulfur in the air make Vulcano an excellent daytrip.

The island's history, not surprisingly, has always been tied to its volcano. Frequently mentioned in historical accounts (among them Aristotle's and Thucydides'), the island was believed to be the primary residence of Hephaestus (Vulcan), god of fire and blacksmiths. Medieval lore took the crater to be the entrance to Hell. Today Vulcano continues to simmer, huffing and puffing sulphur but not blowing anything down—yet. Vulcano is a summer island; if you get here before June or after September, most restaurants will be closed and it will be tough to find a place to stay. (A larger island like Lipari is more convenient in the off-season.)

ORIENTATION AND PRACTICAL INFORMATION

Ferries and hydrofoils dock at **Porto di Levante,** on the eastern side of the isthmus between **Il Cardo** (the mountain to the left as you approach the port) and the Vulcanello peninsula (to the right). **Porto di Ponente,** along with **Spiaggia Sabbie Nere** (Black Sands Beach—one of the few smooth ones on the Aeolian Islands), lies across the isthmus on the west side of the island. Vulcano has no street signs, so it will often take more than an address to find what you're looking for. Don't be afraid to ask for directions, even if you don't speak Italian (the old men who sit outside the bar at the port are especially happy to oblige). From the dock at P. di Levante, **Via Provinciale** curves to the left (toward the volcano), and **Via Porto Levante** to the right leads into the center of town. After 200m Via Porto Levante bears to the left and turns into Via Lentia; a bit farther on you'll hit **Via Porto Ponente,** which leads to the right down to the port of the same name.

> **Tourist Office: AAST,** Via Porto di Levante (tel. 985 20 28; July-Aug. only). For information on **rented rooms** *(affitta camere),* call 985 22 15. Otherwise, get info from the Lipari tourist office, listed above.
> **Police:** tel. 985 21 10.
> **Post Office:** on the other side of the island in the hamlet of Vulcano Piano, on Via Piano (tel. 985 20 49). Open Mon.-Fri. 8am-1:30pm, Sat. 8am-11:20am.
> **Currency Exchange: Vulcan Tours,** Porto di Levante (tel. 985 22 15).

Buses: Scaffidi Tindaro (tel. 985 20 94) runs 8 per day from the port to Vulcano Piano (9am-6pm, L2000).
Ferries: to Milazzo (6 per day, L9900, and Lipari (5 per day, L2400). **Hydrofoils** to Milazzo (10 per day, L18,500) and Lipari (10 per day, L4000).
Taxis: tel. 985 22 73.
Boat, Auto, Scooter, and Bicycle Rentals: Porticciolo di Ponente (tel. 985 24 77) and **Pino Marturano** (tel. 985 24 19).
Pharmacy: Farmacia Bonarrigo, Via Faualauoro, 1 (tel. 985 22 44). Open daily 9am-1pm and 5-9pm. **Medical Emergencies:** tel. 985 22 20.

ACCOMMODATIONS AND CAMPING

Keep in mind that all of Vulcano reeks with pervasive sulfur vapors—the island's accommodations are no exception. Staying here overnight is both expensive and unwarranted, but, if you *must* stay, try looking for unofficial *affitta camere.*

Residence Lanterna Blù, Via Lentia, 58 (tel. 985 21 78). Rents cozy apartments for longer stays. Each with tiny kitchen, bath, A/C, and private terrace shaded by flowering vines. Two-person apartments May-June L60,000; July and Sept. L70,000; August L100,000. Extra bed L20,000. One-time fee of L18,000 charged for cleaning the apartment at the end of your stay. Open Jan. 16-Dec. 14.
Togo Bungalows, at the far end of Via Lentia (tel. 985 21 28). Small, run-down but comfortable 4-person bungalows with stoves. Lockers for valuables. L30,000 per person, MUCH more during peak season.
Pensione La Giara, Via Provinciale, 18 (tel. 985 22 29), on the way to the crater from the hydrofoil port. They use a daunting bell-curve to work out how much to charge for rooms: L29,000 (Apr.-May), L35,000 (June), L45,000 (July), L64,000 (Aug.), L42,000 (Sept.), L25,000 (Oct.). Breakfast included.
Camping: Campeggio Togo Togo (tel. 985 23 03), 800m from the port in the Vulcanello area behind the Sabbie Nere beach. Large and conveniently located. Rudimentary facilities. L10,000 per person, L10,000 per tent. Open June-Sept.

FOOD

The **general store Tridial Market** (tel. 985 22 22) is located off Via P. Levante. (Open daily 8am-1:30pm and 4-8pm.) **Panificio Alongi,** Via Mercalli, 28, is one of the island's best bakeries. To get there, hook a left on Via P. Levante from Via Provinciale as you're heading away from the port. You can always grab a quick munchie at the vegetable stand directly across the street from the mud bath.

Ristorante Il Castello, Vulcano Porto (tel. 985 21 17). Tall ceiling and a patio enhance the bargain dining. Self-service lunch L14,000, noon-2pm. Dinner menu L20,000-25,000, 8pm-1am.
Ristorante al Cratere, Via Provinciale, 31 (tel. 985 20 45), just past the entrance to the path to the crater. Great food that won't dissolve your budget. *Fettuccine fresche al cratere* (with eggplant, zucchini, *pesto,* and baked *ricotta,* L8000) and aromatic grilled swordfish (L14,000). Excellent imported beer (from L3000). Open daily 9am-4pm and 6pm-midnight.
Il Sestante-Ritrovo Remigio, Via Porto Levante (tel. 985 20 85), right on the port. Hot and cold sandwiches, *gelato,* and probably the widest selection of tasty desserts on the Lipari Isles. *Tiramisú* (L3000), *cassata* (L4000), *cannoli* (L2000), and an awesome selection of marzipan fruits. Proprietor Tony speaks perfect English. Piano bar and dancing July 1-Sept.10. Open 6am-3am.
Ristorante Il Palmento, Via Porto Levante (tel. 985 25 52). A volcanic luau. Pizza from L8000-14,000. Open noon-4pm and 6:30pm-midnight. MC, Visa.
Taverna del Marinaio, Via Favaloro (tel. 985 24 26), just across from Tridial Market. Pizzas from L7000. Or be a little daring and order their specialty *"spaghetti alla riccio"* (with sea urchin) for L15,000. *Menù* L25,000. Cover L1500. Open noon-3:30pm and 7pm-whenever. AmEx, MC, Visa.

SIGHTS

One way to begin your visit to Vulcano is to tackle the one-hour hike to the **Gran Cratere** (Great Crater) along the snaking footpath beside the crater's fumaroles. Be warned: between 11am and 3pm the sun transforms the side of the volcano into a furnace, so head out in the early morning or late afternoon. Make sure you have sunscreen, a hat, plenty of water, and good climbing shoes. The climb is challenging; there are some fairly steep inclines, but it's worth it. On a clear day, you'll be able to see all the other islands from the top. But don't inhale: the sulfur smoke spouting from the volcano is saturated with toxins. To get to the path from the port, follow Via Piano for 200m and look for the *"cratere"* signs.

Just up Via Provinciale from the port sits the **Laghetto di Fanghi** (mud pool) to your right, a bubbling pit where hundreds of zealots come to spread the allegedly therapeutic glop all over their bodies. You can't miss the smell. If you have no dermatological crises, or simply would rather not bathe in dirt, wade in the nearby waters of the **acquacalda** just behind the *laghetto*. Here, underwater volcanic outlets make the sea percolate like a jacuzzi; don't scald your feet! For cooler pleasures, visit the crowded beach and crystal-clear waters of Sabbie Nere, just down the road from the *acquacalda* (follow the signs off Via Ponente through the black sand). Those wanting to enjoy themselves a little further out to sea can hire boats (from L90,000 per day) from **Centro Nautico Baia di Levante** (tel. 63 48 57), on the beach facing the port. (Open May-Oct. 9am-6pm.)

A **bus** runs from the pier to **Volcano Piano** on the other side of the island. There's little to do except visit the skeleton of the **Church of Saint Angelo**, admire the vistas, and savor the aroma of sun-ripened ginger. In the opposite direction from the pier lies **Vulcanello**, with a peninsula all to itself. Like its bigger (and more interesting) sibling across the way, it comes complete with noxious fumes; on the other hand, the colors of the rocks along the way help to compensate for the odor.

■ STROMBOLI

Viewed from Lipari or Vulcano, the island of Stromboli looks like a giant iceberg jutting out of the water. Upon closer inspection you'll see that the opposite is true: Stromboli is a volcano, and an active one at that. In a different sense, Stromboli town (pop. 370) lies dormant until the bustling summer tourist season. Foreigners converge on the island from mid-June to early September, making cheap accommodations almost impossible to find—don't plan on staying unless you camp overnight. In the slow off-season, either *pensioni* are closed or their owners are reluctant to rent rooms for fewer than three nights at a time. If you can manage it, see Stromboli on a day trip out of Lipari.

Two towns cling to the volcano's slopes. Minuscule **Ginostra** huddles in the southern corner, essentially cut off from the rest of the island. On the opposite side, the adjoining villages of Piscità, Ficogrande, San Vincenzo, and Scari have fused to comprise Stromboli town on the island's northeast corner. The **Church of San Vincenzo** rises above the town and is replete with Rodinesque sculptures of the Holy Trinity. From the ferry and hydrofoil dock, Via Roma leads up the hill to the church at Piazza Vincenzo. **Corso Vittorio Emanuele,** dipping and turning from P. Vincenzo to the edge of town, is as close as Stromboli comes to having a main drag. Via Filzi and Via Nunziante branch off of the *corso* to the right; both meet up with Via Marina (which originates at the ferry dock) at the black sand beach of **Ficogrande** (big fig). From here 2km in the distance rises **Strombolicchio,** a gigantic rock with a small lighthouse perched on its rim. The ravages of the sea have eroded the rock from 56m high to a mere 42m in the past 100 years alone. **Boats** for hire make their way out to the base of Strombolicchio (L12,500-20,000), from which one can climb the stairs (reinforced with concrete in the 1920s).

Practical Information Stromboli's **post office** (tel. 98 60 27) lies on Via Roma (open Mon.-Fri. 8:05am-1:30pm, Sat. 8:05-11:20am). **Siremar** runs **boat** and hydrofoil services to: Lipari (hydrofoil only, 3 daily, 8:10am-4pm, L23,700); Panarea (3 daily, 8:10am-4pm, L11,900); Salina (3 daily, 9:45am-5:10pm); and Vulcano (3 daily, 7:25am-3pm, L27,700). The **ferry** from Lipari runs L13,900. **Change money** at Le Isole d'Italia (on Via Roma; tel. 98 62 74), a travel agency. (Open Mon.-Sat. in summer 10am-12:30pm and 5-8pm.) The town **pharmacy** is also on Via Roma (tel. 98 60 79; open 9am-1pm and 5-9pm, Sept.-June 14 9am-noon and 4-8pm). For **medical emergencies** call 98 60 97 or go to the Guardia Medica on the Ficogrande side of the church; for **police** call 98 60 21.

Accommodations Hotels on Stromboli are booked solid for August by the previous winter. In other months, **Pensione la Nassa** (tel. 98 60 33) is a good bet (on Via Fabio Filzi just 20m before the beach at Ficogrande as you depart from the port). Open June-Sept. **Pensione Roma,** Via Roma, 15, next to Ristorante da Luciano (tel. 98 60 88) and owned by the Ristorante's proprietor, is five minutes from the ferry dock up on Via Roma, almost at the top of the hill to the right. Barter for rooms, starting around L25,000 per person.) Farther past the church, **Locanda Stella,** Via F. Filzi, 14 (tel. 98 60 20) offers warm doubles and triples. (Obligatory half-pension L40,000 per person including breakfast. Open June-Aug.) **Villa Petrusa,** Via V. Emanuele, 13 (tel. 98 60 45; fax 98 61 26), has singles for L35,000 and doubles for L60,000 from Aug. 30 to July 15; from July 16 to Aug. 31 they charge obligatory half-pension at L90,000 per person. **Affitta camere** are available for extended periods of time. Inquire at bars, stores, or the tourist office.

Food The best deals can be had at the **Duval Market** (tel. 98 60 52), to the left off Via Roma right before the church. (Open daily 8:30am-1pm and 5-9pm. AmEx, MC, Visa.) On a breezy terrace overlooking the sea you'll find **La Lampara** at Via Vittorio Emanuele, 27 (tel. 98 60 09), between the church and Via Nunziante. Grilled swordfish (L12,000) and pizzas (L8000-12,000) are quite filling. Try the heavenly *tiramisù* (L5000), possibly the best on the Aeolian Isles. (Open end of May-Oct. daily noon-2pm and 6pm-1am.) **Ristorante da Luciano,** Via Roma, 15 (tel. 98 60 88), provides you with a tremendous view of the beach, the sea, and Strombolicchio hulking in the distance (L7000-13,000 for *frutti di mare*; service charge L1500 per person). Just 100m from the port on Via Roma (#34) is the *rosticceria* **La Trattola** (tel. 98 60 46 or 98 61 27). Pizza runs L6000-12,000. Ask for the "Stromboli pizza"—actually shaped like the volcano. (Open daily in summer 8:30am-11pm.)

Sights Società Navigazione Pippo (tel. 98 61 35) runs an evening **boat trip** from Stromboli to see the molten crimson trail of the *Sciara del Fuoco* ("Trail of Fire," which unfortunately only streams down once every 15 years). Boats leave the port at 10pm and return at 11pm (L15,000). They also operate daily tours of the island (10:10am-1:10pm and 3:10-6:10pm, L20,000 per person). **Pino and Stefano,** another boat rental/tour service, will take you anywhere around the island you wish to go (tel./fax 98 60 03 or tel. 98 61 94).

> Let's Go does not recommend, advocate, or otherwise take responsibility for anyone hiking the volcano, but hopes that if you do, you'll be smart about it. A red triangle with a black vertical bar means "danger."

An ordinance passed in 1990 made hiking the volcano officially illegal, but it hasn't seemed to stop people. If such criminality doesn't suit you, look into a trip with the **Guide Alpine Autorizzate** (tel. 98 62 63), the island's authorized guides. If it does, then ignore the large warning signs and head up. Travelers often stash their bags at the Villa Petrusa (see above). Hikers should take sturdy shoes, a flashlight, snacks, warm clothes for the exposed summit (sleeping bag is a real bonus), and *at least* 2 liters of water; otherwise, pack as light as possible. The hike takes about three hours up and two down. Reaching the summit around dusk—one really can't see anything but smoke during the day—allows adventurers to camp out and see the brilliant lava bursts by night.

To hike to the volcano, follow Corso Vittorio Emanuele (from P. Vincenzo) a good kilometer or so until a large warning sign and a fork in the road appear; bear to the left. When a secluded stretch of beach comes into view, the path turns upward and (after 400m) cuts between two white houses, the last structures hikers see except for the bar/*ristorante* L'Osservatorio a little farther on. Take only the well-trodden shortcuts—anything else will lead to a maze of thick brambles and reeds. Halfway up the slope is the island's best view of the **Sciara del Fuoco** and a glimpse of the crater. Finally, the trail degenerates into a scramble of volcanic rock and ash; follow the red, orange, and white striped rock markings. The warning signs at the top ridge are sincere: years ago a photographer fell to her death in search of a closer shot. Avoid climbing with heavy loads or in the dark, since the last part gets steep. For an overnight trip, hikers should bring a sturdy food bag, plastic to place between themselves and the wet sand, warm clothing, and foul weather gear for the frigid fogs that envelop the peak.

■ OTHER ISLANDS

The remaining three *Eolie* provide an uncrowded detour from the ordinary, whether you're in the mood for a rural fishing village or an overindulgent resort.

SALINA

A verdant paradise and the second-largest isle, **Salina** is renowned for the rock formations at Semaforo di Pollara and Punta Lingua, and for some of the best *Malvasia* wine around. Salina is relatively uncorrupted by tourism; its beaches are uncrowded, and its sleepy character intact, but there's talk going around that it is going to be the next Cápri. As it is, hotel prices are high, making Salina a better day trip than destination. From Lipari, Salina is accessible by Siremar, **hydrofoil** (7 per day, 1hr., L10,500) and **ferry** (3 per day, L5400). Salina's main port, where both the ferries and hydrofoils dock, is the **Porto Santa Marina.** Unless otherwise noted, the listings for food and accommodations that follow are all located in the small settlement that rises above Santa Marina's docks. From the port, Via Lunga Mare heads to the right toward **Malfa** and **Pollara,** site of the last eruption on the island some 12,000 years ago. Pollara is also a geological wonder: a verdant half-submerged crater with a town tucked in just before the land hits the water. From Malfa a road cuts through the center of the island through Valdichiesa and down the slopes of Rinella, where some of the hydrofoils dock. The town of **Lingua,** famed for its clear water, lies just south of **Santa Marina,** 3km to the left on Via L. Marel. From Lingua and Valdichiesa, paths extend to the peak of **M. Fossa delle Felci,** which towers an impressive 962m above the island. If you show up on August 15 for the Feast of the Assumption of the Virgin, you'll be surrounded by pilgrims en route to the **Sanctuary of the Madonna del Terzito,** nestled in Valdichiesa and dating back to the early 1600s. **Buses** run frequently (10 per day) to any of these towns from the port; consult the schedule posted outside the SNAV ticket office next to the docks (approx. L1200 per town). Get a round-trip ticket (L5500) for a great tour of the island. The patient driver might even stop for picture-taking.

Pensione Mamma Santina, Via Sanità, 40 (tel. 984 30 54), has singles for L35,000 and doubles for L55,000 (with bath L60,000 March-June; July-Sept. obligatory half-pension L70,000). Mamma Santina's is a long, steep walk through narrow streets, but worth the climb. To get there from the port, walk up into town and take a right on the first cross street you see, Via Risorgimento; after about 250m, a sign for Mamma Santina's will point out the way. Via Sanità is a narrow path woven into the hill. **Villa Orchidea,** on Via Roma, 161, in Malfa (tel./fax 984 40 79), is run by a friendly Australian woman. (Doubles with bath L100,000-130,000 depending on the season.) Take the bus or *aliscafo* to Rinella for Salina's only true budget accommodations: **Camping Tre Pini** (tel. 980 91 55) charges L10,000 per person, L12,000 per tent (open Mar.-Oct.), with market, bar, restaurant, and TV; located by the sea. **Ristorante da Franco** (tel. 984 32 87) is a long haul, but there's no better view on all of Salina. Follow signs from the top of Via Risorgimento. Homegrown *antipasti* and *primi* are L8000-L12,000. *Macaroni Siciliano* is yummy and filling (L8000). (Open daily noon-3pm and 8pm-midnight; July-Aug. 8pm-midnight.) **Mamma Santina** (tel. 984 30 54) also runs a small eatery, especially convenient if you're staying there for the night. The *menù* goes for L28,000, wine included. (Dinner only 8-11pm.) The cheapest way to eat, as usual, is the cold lunch route; try any *alimentare* or market you find on Via Risorgimento.

Posta Telegrafo is at Via Risorgimento, 130, and is open Mon.-Sat. 8am-1:20pm. The **post office** is on Via Marina Garibaldi (tel. 984 30 28). The **postal code** is 98050. **Police** in Salina are at 984 30 19. There is a cluster of **SIP telephones** down by the port, and a **bank** next door where you can change your money (open summer only; the only year-round bank is down the road 7km in Malfa). The **Farmacia Comunale** (tel. 984 30 98) sits at the bottom of Via Risorgimento, 111, ready to help (Tues.-Fri. 9am-1pm and 5:30-8:30pm, Mon. 5-8pm).

FILICUDI

West of Lipari, **Filicudi** presents an array of volcanic rock formations and the enchanting **Grotto del Bue Marino** (Grotto of the Monk Seal) on the side opposite the port (accessible only by boat, roughly L15,000 per person). Heading to the right up the hill of **Montepalmieri** as you arrive at the port brings you rapidly to the rocky terraces of **Fossa Felci** (774m) and the island's **post office** (tel. 988 99 43). Adjacent to the post office (and located in the same building) is the **Pensione La Canna,** Via Rosa, 43 (tel. 988 99 56; fax 988 96 71). (July-Aug. doubles L75,000, full pension L90,000; off-season doubles with bath L70,000; full pension L80,000. Visa.) As you head further up to the town of **Valdichiesa** with its rapidly deteriorating church (note its precariously balanced bell tower), paths run around to the western edge of the Fossa and down to **Pecorini,** home to a set of ancient Greek inscriptions. The island's one paved road carries you back to the port from here, as the peninsula **Capo Graziano** reaches into the sea from the right. **La Canna,** an impressive rock spike (71m high, 9m wide), points up from the sea a kilometer from Filicudi's west coast. It's easily visible if you take the footpath around the Fossa; otherwise rent a boat (L15,000-20,000) or grab a ferry to **Alicudi** (Siremar L5400), which will pass right by the suggestive Rock. The **police** are at tel. 988 99 42.

ALICUDI

On the westernmost fringes of the Aeolian islands sits isolated **Alicudi,** the estranged cousin of Filicudi. At 5 sq. km, it is little more than a speck in the sea. With one telephone, a hotel, 120 inhabitants, no paved roads, and recently-installed electricity (Feb. 91), Alicudi is just the place to go if you're headed nowhere in particular. Left of the port, make your way over the stones to untouristed **Tonna.** The **Albergo Ericusa** (tel. 988 99 02; fax 988 96 71) is the only place on the island and *very* expensive; half-pension runs at L85,000 and full pension at L98,000. (Open June-Sept., but call before you come—it's a looong way back to civilization.) Full pension is advisable; food is expensive here, too.

■■■ CEFALÙ

Cefalù was once a quiet fishing village, but now the fishermen have opened up shops and restaurants to accommodate the visitors drawn by its beaches, pleasant streets, and mixed-bag architecture. Hotels fill up during the summer, and the prospects of finding an inexpensive *pensione* are fairly dismal even in the off-season. Visit Cefalù as a stopover or daytrip from Palermo, only an hour away by train. You can easily tour the town in half a day and still have time for a swim, either in the crowded waters right below town or at the beaches a short bus ride away.

CEFALÙ

ORIENTATION AND PRACTICAL INFORMATION

Via A. Moro leads to the right from the station into town. At the first big intersection, **Via Roma** runs off to the left and into Cefalù's modern quarter. To get to the **old city,** continue on Via Moro as it turns into Via Matteotti and then (at P. Garibaldi) into Corso Ruggero. **Via Lungomare** runs the length of Cefalù's main beach before it passes into the old city as **Corso Vittorio Emanuele.**

> **Tourist Office:** Corso Ruggero, 77 (tel. 210 50; fax 223 86), in the old city. English spoken. Staff helps with accommodations and stocks a city map. If you don't see anyone, check in back. Open Mon.-Fri. 8am-2pm and 4-7pm, Sat. 8am-2pm.
> **Police:** tel. 113
> **Post Office:** Via Vazzana (tel. 215 28), off Via Roma. Open Mon.-Fri. 8:10am-5:30pm, Sat. 8:10am-1:20pm. **Postal Code:** 90015.
> **Telephones: Agenzia San Mauro,** Via Vazzana, 7 (tel. 234 43). In front of the *lungomare.* Open Mon.-Sat. 9am-1pm and 4-7:30pm. **Telephone Code:** 0921.
> **Currency Exchange: Banca S. Angelo,** near the station at the corner of V. Giglio and V. Roma. Open Mon-Fri. 8:30am-1:30pm. For 24-hr. access, try the change machine by the **Banca di Sicilia** in P. Garibaldi.
> **Trains: Stazione F.F.S.S.,** off Via Gramsci (tel. 225 06). To Messina (17 daily, 2½hr., L13,600), Milazzo (6 daily, 3hr., L11,700), Palermo (14 per weekday, 1hr., L5700), and Termine Imerese (every hr., 30min., L3200).
> **Buses: SAIS,** to Castelbuono and Geraci. **SPISA,** Via Umberto I, 28 (tel. 243 01), up to the right from P. Garibaldi. Inquire at the Bar Musotto (SPISA leaves from here and from the station); their buses serve all local towns for under L2000.
> **Pharmacy:** Dr. V. Baltaglia, Via Roma, 13 (tel. 217 89). Open 8:30am-1pm and 4:30-8:30pm.
> **Emergencies:** tel. 113. **Hospital:** Via A. Moro (tel. 211 21). **Nighttime Medical Emergency:** tel. 236 23.

ACCOMMODATIONS AND CAMPING

Cefalù's hotels cater primarily to deep-pocketed northern Europeans, but there are some cheap diamonds among the coal. An alternative is camping out and saving your moola for a sunset dinner by the sea.

> **Pensione delle Rose,** Via Acca, 2 (tel. 218 85). Turn right on Via A. Moro from the station. At the first stoplight, turn right onto Via Mazzini and continue up the hill until it turns right again on Via Umberto, which becomes Via Gibilmanna. Make a final right at the *pensione* sign, walk past the apartment complex, and left up the flowered-vine pathway. Attractive rooms with spectacular views of the town. Doubles L45,000 with bath L66,000. Oct.-May doubles L40,000 with bath L50,000 (includes breakfast). Half pension L65,000. Full pension L80,000. MC, Visa.
> **Locanda Cangelosi,** Via Umberto I, 26 (tel. 215 91), off P. Garibaldi. *The* budget shack. Only 4 rooms, so call in advance for the cheapest cot in the old city. Singles L35,000. Doubles L55,000. Three-min. hot showers L2000. Oct.-May singles L25,000, doubles L30,000.
> **Pensione La Giara,** Via Veterani, 40 (tel. 215 62; fax 225 18), off Corso Ruggero, a block from the beach. Comfortable rooms with balconies; community terrace offers a gorgeous view. In Aug. half-pension required. July-Aug. singles L45,000-50,000; doubles L94,000-98,000. During the rest of the year, prices are lower, but you must stay a full week. Restaurant downstairs. AmEx.
> **Camping: Costa Ponente,** Località Ogliastrillo (tel. (0921) 200 85), 3km west at Contrada Ogliastrillo (a 45-min. walk or a short ride on the Cefalù-Lascari bus, L2000). Swimming pool and tennis court. L7800 per person, L6500 per small tent, L9000 per large tent; Sept.-June L6800 per person, L5500 per small tent, L8000 per large tent. Nearby **Camping Sanfilippo,** Località Ogliastrillo (tel. 201 84) charges L7300 per person, L6000 per small tent, L8500 per large tent. Both campgrounds run markets in the summer, but you're probably better off stocking up at the STANDA in the center of Cefalù (see below).

FOOD

Affordable restaurants cluster around Corso Ruggero and Via Vittorio Emanuele, and many fine *pizzerie* converge on Via C. O. di Bordonaro and the *lungomare*. Shop for basics at **STANDA,** Via Vazzana (tel. 245 00) near the post office. (Open 8:30am-1pm and 5-8:30pm.) The smaller **Galla' Santo (GS) Market** lies on Via Roma, 27 (tel. 214 31), near the train station. (Open 8:30am-1:30pm and 4:30-8pm.)

Pizzeria "da NINO," Via Lungomare, 11 (tel. 225 82) to the right down the *lungomare*. Low prices, outdoor dining, and a seaside view make it worth the tourist crowd. Simple entrees like *pizza margherita* (L5000) or *spaghetti al pomodoro* (L5000) are the best deals. June-Sept. noon-3pm and 7-11pm. AmEx, MC, Visa.

L'Antica Carte, Cortele Pepe, 7 (tel. 232 28), off Corso Ruggero to the left, past the *duomo* as you head toward the sea. Eat outdoors in a tiny courtyard under a grapevine, or indoors in the air-conditioned basement. Fabulous seafood, *primi* (L7000-10,000), and pizza (L6000-11,000). *Menù* L20,000. Open daily noon-3pm and 7pm until they decide to close. AmEx, MC, Visa.

White Horse Restaurant, Via Roma, 106 (tel. 201 37). A standard joint with plaid table cloths. Pizzas from L5000. Open 7:30pm-midnight. AmEx, MC, Visa.

Pasticceria Pietro Serio, Via G. Giglio, 29 (tel. 222 93), the first left off Via Moro from the train station. A classy *caffè* offering old-style chic and fantastic *gelato*, only a few paces from the station. Open 7am-1pm and 3-10pm.

SIGHTS AND ENTERTAINMENT

Throughout the old city, you can catch a glimpse of history in the Arab windows, the Saracen walkways, and the medieval archways. In P. Duomo off Corso Ruggero you'll find Cefalù's austere, 11th-century Norman **cathedral,** supposedly erected by Roger II in gratitude for divine protection from a shipwreck. The golden stone and solidity of the square-tower echo the monumentality of the Rocca behind it. Inside, 16 Byzantine and Roman columns support superb capitals, as well as elegant horseshoe arches that exemplify the Saracen influence on Norman architecture in Sicily. The bright Byzantine mosaics, dated to 1148, depict angels, the famous **Christ Pantocrates mosaic** (one of three in Sicily) giving his blessing, the Madonna, and the Apostles. (Open daily 9am-noon and 3:30-7pm. Proper dress required—shoulders and knees should be covered.)

Opposite the cathedral, the private **Museo Mandralisca,** Via Mandralisca, 13 (tel. 215 47), houses a small collection of paintings, Greek ceramics, Arab pottery, antique money, stuffed birds, and Antonello da Messina's *Ritratto di Ignoto* ("Portrait of an Unknown Man," 1470-1472), the face featured on most Sicilian tourist brochures. Note how the eyes seem to follow you wherever you go. (Hours vary according to season; best bet is 9:30am-12:30pm and 4-6pm. Admission L4000.)

At the end of Via XXV Novembre on Via Vittorio Emanuele (hugging the beach) is the curious semi-subterranean 16th-century **lavatoio medievale** (medieval laundromat). Don't drink the water coming from its fountains, and try your best not to inhale the noxious fumes spewed from the ancient tubs.

For a bird's-eye view of the city, make the half-hour haul up the **Rocca** by way of the Salita Saraceni, which begins near P. Garibaldi off Corso Ruggero. Follow the brown signs for *"pedonale Rocca."* On the mountain, walkways lined with ancient stone walls lead to the **Tempio di Diana** (Temple of Diana). Dating back to the 4th century BC, it was first used for sea-cult worship and later as a defensive outpost.

From July to September, Cefalù hosts the **Incontri d'Estate,** which features classical, contemporary, and Sicilian folk music, as well as opera, in outdoor concerts. The Sicilian Symphony Orchestra is a featured performer at these concerts. Shows are moved to the *duomo* from August 4 to 6 to accommodate the **Fiesta di San Salvatore** (in honor of Cefalù's patron saint), celebrated with a rousing display of fireworks and marching bands. Cefalù's best beaches, **Spiaggia Mazzaforno** and **Spiaggia Settefrati,** are located west of town on SPISA's Cefalù-Lascari bus line.

■ NEAR CEFALÙ: THE RUINS OF TYNDARIS

Seventy-five km east of Cefalù and just 15km west of Milazzo lies **Tindari**, site of the ruins of **Tyndaris**. Dating from the 4th century BC, the Greek settlement was founded high on a hill as a fortification against enemy attacks. Politically, Tyndaris chose wisely, siding with Rome in the Punic Wars and supplying ships for the expedition that destroyed Carthage in 146 BC. However, an earthquake in 365 AD destroyed the city, and the Arabs mopped up the remains in 836. Unearthed only in the mid-1900s, the ruins are now home to a museum, several archaeological curiosities, olive groves, and spectacular views of the Aeolian Isles.

The first sight you'll see upon climbing the hill to the ancient site is the **Santuario di Tindari**, erected less than 30 years ago for the **Madonna Nera** (Black Madonna). Local legend has it that a statue of this eastern madonna washed up on the shores of Tindari hundreds of years ago. The current sanctuary stands on the site where the first church in her name once stood. Across from the entrance to the sanctuary, a path leads to the heart of the ruins, including the **basilica** and **agora**. The **theater** perches 125m farther down, cut into the hill with an impressive panorama of the surrounding seascape. The **museum**, adjacent to the theater, has a series of knick-knacks uncovered from the site as well as some drawings illustrating what life was like in the ancient town. Just in front of the museum proceeds the main street of the town, the **decumanus**. Follow it to the right as you exit the museum; it will curve past the base of the *basilica* and lead you to **Casa Romana,** an old Roman house replete with intricate mosaics. All around the site stand bits and pieces of the city's walls as well as the original city gate on the main road en route to the *santuario*. If you have the chance, drop by Tindari to see **Greek drama** in the theater; the tourist office in Cefalù has listings of current plays and performance times.

Before you head to Tindari, check with a tourist office about bus times and prices. Above all, be sure to double-check when buses are returning; Tindari is no mecca and you can readily find yourself stranded there late in the day. The ruins are also accessible by taking the train to Oliveri-Tindari and making the 40-min. hike up the hill. Follow your first right out of the station until the street ends; bear left under the highway and then right past a grove of lemon trees. When you come to a green gate, go left (following the white arrows). Finally, bear right when the path forks.

■■■ PALERMO

Sicily's capital Palermo, although known for many things, is above all else a crossroads of Mediterranean cultures. First a Phoenecian city named "Ziz," then held under Roman and Byzantine sway, Palermo blossomed under Saracen (831-1071) and Norman (1072-1194) rule and emerged as one of Europe's most prominent cities. Hohenstaufen, Angevin, Aragonese, and Bourbon overlords followed. In modern times, Palermo has earned notoriety of a less lofty sort: it is considered to be the cradle of Italian organized crime (for more information see The Mafia, page 498). Don't expect to see any drive-by shootings, however; to the unaware traveler, organized crime is nonexistent. Although the ongoing battle of intimidation and assassination continues to make headlines and coffee-shop conversation, petty thievery and drive-by snatchings are far more likely to trouble a traveler. Palermo, population 700,000, has areas of both fantastic beauty and appalling poverty. Be cautious, especially as you stray farther from the center of this fascinating patchwork city.

ORIENTATION AND PRACTICAL INFORMATION

Palermo and its crescent-shaped harbor lie at the end of a fertile basin called the **Conca d'Oro** (Golden Conch). To the north, 610m of Monte Pellegrino's limestone mass separate the city from **Mondello,** its beautiful beach. As you exit the front of the station onto P. Giulio Césare, **Via Roma** runs straight into Palermo. Ten blocks from the station, Via Roma is intersected by **Corso Vittorio Emanuele,** leading from the sea toward the mountains, and 10 blocks after that by **Via Cavour,** run-

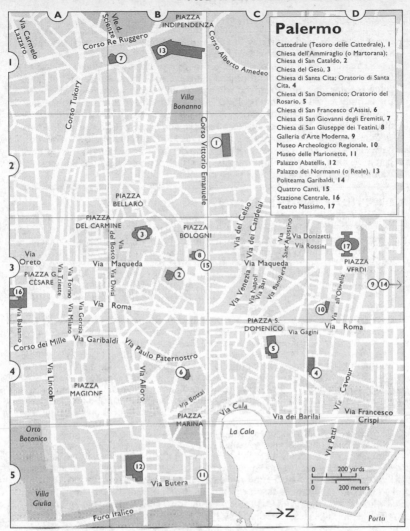

Palermo

Cattedrale (Tesoro delle Cattedrale), 1
Chiesa dell'Ammiraglio (o Martorana);
Chiesa di San Cataldo, 2
Chiesa del Gesù, 3
Chiesa di Santa Cita; Oratorio di Santa
Cita, 4
Chiesa di San Domenico; Oratorio del
Rosario, 5
Chiesa di San Francesco d'Assisi, 6
Chiesa di San Giovanni degli Eremiti, 7
Chiesa di San Giuseppe dei Teatini, 8
Galleria d'Arte Moderna, 9
Museo Archeologico Regionale, 10
Museo delle Marionette, 11
Palazzo Abatellis, 12
Palazzo dei Normani (o Reale), 13
Politeama Garibaldi, 14
Quattro Canti, 15
Stazione Centrale, 16
Teatro Massimo, 17

ning parallel to Corso Vittorio Emanuele. One block to the left of Via Roma as you exit the station lies **Via Maqueda,** paralleling Via Roma through its intersection with Corso Vittorio Emanuele at P. Verdi all the way to the Teatro Mássimo at Via Cavour. At this point it transforms into **Via Ruggero Séttimo,** and at Via E. Amari (in **Piazza Castelnuovo**) it changes again into **Viale della Libertà.**

Behind the once-grand *palazzi* lining the main avenues you'll find a maze of alleys and courtyards. These vestiges of historic Palermo contrast with the grid of the modern quarter west of P. Castelnuovo. Shop at food markets off Via Roma on Via Divisi, and between the Palazzo dei Normani and the station at P. Ballarò; for clothing, try Via Bandiera near the Church of San Domenico. Ritzier shops strut their stuff along Via Roma, Via Maqueda, and Viale della Libertà. With the exception of restaurants, just about everything in Palermo closes from noon to 3pm and again around 8pm.

Don't let crime ruin your stay in Palermo. Pickpockets and moped-mounted, strap-cutting bag-snatchers will get you if you fail to take precautions. Keep wallets in moneybelts or neck pouches, *not* in front pockets or handbags. Leave all bags, valuables, watches, and other expensive jewelry at your hotel; if your room is not secure, however, you will have to choose between two evils. Avoid the dark, deserted back streets of old Palermo at night; stick instead to the fancier, more modern (and therefore safer) sections of the city. The Via P. di Belmonte (between Via Roma and Via Maqueda, one block before P. Castelnuovo) is a good choice; so is the popular beach at Mondello (see below). The area between Via Roma, Corso Vittorio Emanuele, and the water (to the right as you're leaving the station), known as "La Cala," is notorious for being unsafe. Women simply should not carry purses.

PRACTICAL INFORMATION

Tourist Office: P. Castelnuovo, 34 (tel. 58 38 47), 2km up Via Maqueda (turn right onto V. Maqueda from the station) or take bus #101 or 107 going toward Teatro Politeama; the office is in the building with the huge SICILCASSA sign. Open Mon-Fri. 8am-8pm and Sat. 8am-2pm. Also in the **train station** (tel. 616 59 14). Open Mon.-Fri. 8am-8pm. English spoken. Both offer detailed info on Palermo (maps and brochures) and other places of interest such as Cefalù, Monreale, and Ustica. The booth at the **airport** (tel. 59 16 98) is open daily 8am-8pm. Yet another tourist booth (the tourist police) can be found at the **port** (tel. 586 68 30).

Police: tel. 112.

Post Office: Via Roma, 322 (tel. 160), by the Museo Archeologico, 2 blocks from Via Cavour. Open Mon.-Sat. 8:15am-7:30pm for letters, 8:15am-1:20pm for packages. *Fermo posta* at window #6. **Postal Code:** 90100.

Telephones: ASST, Via Lincoln, across from the train station. Open 24 hrs. **Telecom,** in P. Ungheria, to the left off V. R. Settimo past Teatro Massimo. Open Mon.-Sat. 8am-1pm and 4-8pm, Sun. 8am-noon and 4-5:30pm. **Telephone Code:** 091.

Budget Travel: CTS, Via Garzilli, 28/G (tel. 32 57 52). Take Via Maqueda to P. Castelnuovo; go one block past P. Castelnuovo on Via Libertà and turn left on Via Carducci. Two blocks farther you'll hit Via Garzilli; the office is on your right. Harried but efficient. Open Mon.-Fri. 9am-1pm and 4-8pm, Sat. 9am-1pm.

Consulate: U.S., via G. B. Vaccarini, 1 (tel. 34 35 32 or 30 78 13), off Viale della Libertà. Take bus #28 from V. della Libertà. Open Mon.-Fri. 8am-12:30pm and 3-5pm. Emergencies only. **U.K.,** Via C. Cavour, 117 (tel. 58 25 33); **Australian** citizens should contact their embassy in Rome (tel. (06) 83 27 21), as should **Canadians** (tel. (06) 440 30 28) and **New Zealanders** (tel. (06) 440 29 28).

Currency Exchange: Banks open Mon.-Fri. 8:20am-1:20pm. Train station "information window" changes money 8am-8pm. Cash only 7:40am-1pm and 2-8pm.

American Express: G. Ruggieri and Figli, Via E. Amari, 40 (tel. 58 71 44). Follow Via E. Amari from P. Castelnuovo toward the water. Very busy. Open Mon.-Fri. 9am-1pm and 4-7:30pm, Sat. 9am-1pm. Regarding card theft: tel. (06) 722 82.

Flights: Cinisi-Punta Raisi (tel. 59 16 91 for domestic info; tel. 59 12 95 for international info), 20km west of Palermo. Public buses connect the airport to P. R. Settimo in front of the Politeama (every 30min., L4500). Taxis charge at least L60,000 for the same route.

Trains: P. G. Césare (tel. 616 18 06), on the eastern side of town. To Milan (L120,400), Rome (L83,200), Naples (L67,300). **Luggage Storage: Deposito Bagagli,** L1500 per bag for 24 hrs. Open 6am-10pm.

Buses: Cuffaro, Via Paolo Balsamo, 13 (tel. 616 15 10), to the right as you exit the station. **Autoservizi Segesta,** Via Balsamo, 26 (tel. 616 79 19), has over 20 daily departures direct to Trapani (1¾hr., L11,000). **SAIS,** Via Balsamo, 16 (tel. 616 60 28). To Catania (16 daily, 2½hr., L16,000), continuing to Syracuse (L5200 more).

Ferries: Tirrenia (tel. 602 12 35), in Palazzina Stella Maris within the port. Entry to port off Via Francesco Crispi. Open Mon.-Sat. 8:30am-1pm and 2:15-8pm, Sun. 9am-12:30pm and 4-8pm. **Grandi Traghetti,** Via M. Stabile, 57 (tel. 58 78 02; fax

58 96 29). Open Sun.-Fri. 8:30am-5pm. **Siremar,** Via Francesco Crispi, 118 (tel. 58 24 03). Open 8:30am-1pm and 4-6:30pm. Siremar has daily ferries to Ustica (Mon.-Sat. at 9am, Sun. at 8:15am, 2hr. 20min., L16,700) as well as hydrofoils three times daily in July and Aug. (at 10:30am, 3:30pm and 7pm, 1¼hr., L28,500). **SNAV:** (tel. 32 42 55). Tirrenia and Grandi Traghetti serve more distant ports: Tunisia, South America, Northern Europe.

Public Transportation: orange **City Buses (AMAT)** (tel. 22 23 98). L1000 for a 1-hr. ticket, L3000 for a 1-day pass. Buy tickets from coin-operated machines inside buses (exact change only), from *tabacchi,* or at the bus depot. The main terminal is in front of the train station.

Lost and Found: Palazzo del Municipio, P. Pretoria (tel. 33 93 30), off Via Maqueda near Via Vittorio Emanuele. Open daily 8:30am-1:30pm. The **train station** also has its own lost and found office (open 8am-8pm).

Gay Men's Resource Center: Arci-Gay, Via Trapani, 3 (tel. 32 49 17 or 32 49 18). Information on events. Open Mon.-Fri. 9:30-11:30pm.

Late-Night Pharmacy: Lo Cascio, Via Roma, 1 (tel. 616 21 17), near the train station. Open Mon.-Fri. 24 hrs., Sat.-Sun. 8pm-9am. Consult tourist office for seasonal openings.

Emergencies: tel. 113. **Hospital: Civico Regional e Generale,** Via Lazzaro (tel. 48 45 44). **Medical Emergency:** tel. 666 11 11. **Road Assistance:** 116.

ACCOMMODATIONS AND CAMPING

Finding a decent and inexpensive place to stay is a breeze. A vast array of *alberghi* blesses **Via Roma** and **Via Maqueda** (look up for the signs), but women especially should avoid the eastern part of town by the train station after dark.

Albergo Orientale, Via Maqueda, 26 (tel. 616 57 27), just 100m from the station. Simple rooms maintained by a nurturing family. Come for the surreal experience of meandering through the halls of this gloriously run-down 17th-century *palazzo* with painted ceilings. Singles L25,000. Doubles L40,000, with bath L50,000. The only triple (with bath) has a balcony E.M. Forster would have died for (L60,000).

Hotel Cortese, Via Scarparelli, 16 (tel. 33 17 22). From the train station, walk 10min. down Via Maqueda to Via dell'Universita; look for the sign to the left. Turn left and go another 200m. Probably the nicest hotel in its price range despite its not-so-safe location. Impeccable, modern rooms with new furniture. A perk: June 15-Sept. 15 you get free tickets to the beach—sun umbrellas and cabanas included. Huge market right next door. Singles L25,000, with shower L30,000. Doubles L45,000, with shower L55,000. All rooms with TV. Hall showers free. Half or full pension available. AmEx, MC, Visa.

Albergo Castiglia, Via Gorizia, 8 (tel./fax 617 23 41), the 3rd right off Via Roma when coming from the train station. Simple, clean, and well-lit. Great location near station. A steal at L30,000 for a single and L55,000 for a double.

Albergo Cavour, Via Manzoni, 11 (tel. 616 27 59), on the 5th floor. From P. G. Césare in front of the station, hang a right on Via Lincoln; Via Manzoni is the first street on your left. Large rooms, classic wood-paneled elevator. Singles L30,000. Doubles L40,000. Showers L3000.

Hotel Ariston, Via M. Stabile, 139 (tel. 33 24 34), in the busy part of town far from the station. Take Via Roma 3 blocks past Via Cavour or take bus #102 and get off before Via E. Amari. Spotless, modern rooms overlook a small courtyard. Singles L32,000, with bath L42,000. Doubles (all with TV) L45,000, with bath L55,000.

Albergo Letizia, Via Bottai, 30 (tel. 58 91 10), from Via Roma head toward the water on Corso Vittorio Emanuele. Via Bottai is the 8th street on your right, just before the entrance to P. Marina. Spacious rooms with high ceilings, but it's a little out of the way. Singles L35,000, with shower L45,000. Doubles L60,000, with shower L70,000. Extra bed: 35% extra. AmEx.

Petit Hotel, Via Principe di Belmonte, 84 (tel. 32 36 16), to the left off Via Roma 2 blocks before Via E. Amari as you head from the station. Quiet, clean, and in a relatively safe neighborhood crowded with posh *caffè*. Drop by Frankie's place downstairs (Bar Fiore) for a late-night snack. Singles L35,000, with shower L40,000, doubles L60,000, with shower L65,000. AmEx.

Camping: Trinacria, Via Barcarello (tel. 53 05 90), at Sferracavallo by the sea. Take bus #28 from Teatro Mássimo. L5500 per person and per tent. Also at Sferracavallo is **Campeggio dell'Ulivo,** Via Pegaso (tel. 53 30 21). L7000 per person, tent included.

FOOD

Palermo is famous for its *pasta con le sarde* (with sardines and fennel) and *rigatoni alla palermitana* (with a sauce of meat and peas). The most popular seafood is swordfish, either plain (*pesce spada*) or rolled and stuffed (*involtini di pesce spada*). Eggplant comes in every shade of purple, in forms ranging from slender to stout. At certain stands in the markets you can get octopus simmered to order (snack portion about L1500). Also try *panelle,* tasty fried balls of chick pea flour sliced and sandwiched. For the pinnacle of local cuisine, have *spaghetti al broccoli affogati alla palermitana,* spaghetti combined with spicy fried broccoli. And, of course, don't forget to partake of the heady local wines.

The **STANDA supermarket** has outlets at Viale della Libertà, 30 (tel. 33 16 21), in the northern end of town past Piazza Castelnuovo, at Via R. Séttimo, 18/22 (tel. 58 60 19), and on Via Roma, 59 (tel. 616 90 43). (All three open daily 9am-1pm and 4-8pm. Closed Mon. mornings and Wed. afternoons.)

Bar Fiore, Via Principe di Belmonte, 84 (tel. 33 25 39), left off Via Roma near the Teatro Politeama. A cheap and decent eatery in this otherwise expensive pedestrian mall. If you have a whole meal, jovial owner Frank, Palermo's greatest extrovert, will treat you to a glass of *zibbibbo,* an Olympian ambrosia that Bacchus brought to Palermo. Try his superb *frullata,* the Italian milkshake (L4000), or munch on a slice of pizza (L2500). Delicious *granita al limone.* Discounts for groups carrying *Let's Go.* (Frank's a big fan.) Open daily 7am-midnight.
Hostaria al Duar 2, Via E. Amari, 92 (tel. 32 16 78), off Via Roma as you angle toward the port. Award-winning Italian and North African fare. Experience Tunisia's finest with the *Completo Tunisio* (L15,000, food, drink, and cover included) or the more traditionally Italian (and spicy) *penne all'arrabiata.* Cover L1200. Service 10%. Open Thurs.-Tues. 10am-3pm and 7pm-midnight. AmEx, MC, Visa.
Ristorane Pizzeria al 59, Piazza Verdi, 59 (tel. 58 31 39), a few short blocks from the Politeama. Hidden behind the jungle-like exterior of this posh restaurant is a gurgling fountain and some of the best pizza in Palermo. *Primi* L9000-10,000. Pizza under L10,000. Cover L2000. Service 15%. Open Thurs.-Tues. 7pm-1am (pizza only served 7-10). AmEx, MC, Visa.
Antica Focacceria S. Francesco, Via Alessandra Paternostro, 58, off Corso Vittorio Emanuele across from the Church of S. Francesco on the *piazza.* A 161-year-old *pizzeria:* dark wood, cast iron, and aged cacophony. Pizza about L2000 per slice. *Arancino,* a fried-rice-and-meat ball, costs L2000. Open Tues.-Fri. 9:30am-10pm, Sat.-Sun. 9:30am-midnight.
Trattoria dei Vespri, P. Sta. Croce dei Vespri, 6/A (tel. 617 16 31), two blocks south of Corso Vittorio Emanuele. Turn right on Via Cagliari off Via Roma a few blocks away from the station. A gourmet oasis in the midst of the dark old city. *Primi* L9000-11,000. *Menù* L25,000. The *pesce spada arrosto* (roasted swordfish) is unbeatable (L12,000). Service 10%. Open Mon.-Sat. 8:30pm-1am.
Osteria Lo Bianco, Via E. Amari, 104 (tel. 58 58 16), off Via Roma as you head towards the port. Local crowds wipe the sweat from their brows between each delectable bite. If you're lucky they'll have some *pesce spada* (swordfish, L9000). Sample local wines from the stainless steel barrels perched safely overhead (L3000 per liter). Open Mon.-Sat. noon-3pm and 7-11pm.
Au Domino, Via P. di Belmonte. A small *caffè,* popular on weekends. Crepes from L5000-7000. International coffee, too. Open Tues.-Sun. 5pm-2:30am.

SIGHTS

After ancient glory followed by seven centuries of neglect, Palermo is an incongruous mix of the splendid and the shabby. The bizarre sight of Palermo's half-crumbled, soot-blackened, 16th-century *palazzi* startles visitors accustomed to the cleaner historic districts of northern Italy. In the past several years, however, efforts have slowly begun to clean, rebuild, and reopen structures like the magnificent Teatro Massimo, closed for over 20 years due to water damage and Mafia-induced lethargy. Peek into random courtyards on your path to find the *cortili* for which the city is famous. For a glimpse of Palermo's ravaged splendor, climb the red marble staircase to the top floor of Via Maqueda, 26 (across from the Orfeo cinema).

From Quattro Canti to San Giovanni degli Eremiti

The intersection of Corso Vittorio Emanuele and Via Maqueda forms the **Quattro Canti**, where each corner celebrates a season, a king of Spain, and one of the city's patron saints. The Canti date from the early 17th century, when Sicily was under Spanish rule. Next to the statue of Philip III in the Quattro Canti, the dismal gray façade of the **Church of San Giuseppe dei Teatini** (1612) belies its "as much as you can put on the walls without tearing them down" Baroque interior. Don't miss such details as the upside-down angels supporting the fonts at the entrance, or the frieze of children playing musical instruments on the wall of the south transept. (Open daily 7:30am-noon and 6:30-8:15pm.)

Farther down Via Maqueda and to the left as you approach the station, **Piazza Bellini** embraces the **Church of San Cataldo** (1154), a Norman building whose red domes and arches give it the air of a mosque. **La Martorana**, or, more properly, **Santa Maria dell'Ammiraglio** (built for an admiral of the Norman king Roger II), shares San Cataldo's leafy platform. Baroque additions partially conceal its 12th-century structure. The Byzantine mosaics inside are 12th-century equivalents of celebrity photos: here's Roger I with Jesus, there's George the Admiral with the Mother of God. (Both open Mon.-Sat. 8:30am-1pm and 3:30-7pm, Sun. 8:30am-1pm.)

To the right across Via Maqueda from P. Bellini, **Via Ponticello** winds through a crowded neighborhood to the **Chiesa del Gesù** (or Casa Professa, built 1363-1564). Look for its green mosaic dome. The stucco conceals a dazzling, multicolored marble interior and an almost Dalí-like depiction of the Last Judgment. Standing in Il Gesù's courtyard, you can see traces of American bombing during World War II. The **Quartiere dell'Albergheria**, the inner core of the city, never quite recovered from the war's destruction—as evinced by the numerous shattered buildings, including the one next to the church. (Church open daily 7am-noon and 5-6:30pm.)

Farther along Via Ponticello, one of Palermo's two main open-air **markets** extends from **Piazza Ballarò** to the **Church of the Carmine**. This 17th-century *chiesa* has a mosaic dome that is all emerald fans and gold swirls—it looks like a cross between a Ming vase and a parlor room teacup. This area, replete with narrow streets and hidden gardens, warrants exploration.

Venturing from the Quattro Canti onto **Corso Vittorio Emanuele**, heading away from the harbor, you will pass the dilapidated *palazzi* of the **Piazza Bologni** to the left before confronting the striking exuberance of Palermo's **cattedrale** up on the right. Begun by the Normans in 1185, it absorbed elements of every architectural style from the 13th through 18th centuries, though the best exterior elements are the original Norman towers and the three-apsed grandeur of the eastern side. Inside, the chapels on the left contain six royal tombs (four canopied and two set in the wall) of Norman kings and Hohenstaufen emperors dating from the 12th to 14th centuries. The *tesoro* (treasury), to the right of the apse, contains a dazzling array of sacerdotal vestments from the 16th and 17th centuries as well as episcopal rings, chalices, and croziers. (Open daily 7am-7pm. L1000 to see the treasure, the crypts, and chiseled *sarcophagi* hosting various saints and city patrons.) The *cattedrale* is connected by the flying buttresses to the former Archbishop's palace (1460).

Set behind a tropical garden near the church on Corso Emanuele, the **Palazzo dei Normanni** (entrance in back) contains the **Cappella Palatina** (1132-40). Built by Roger II, it exhibits a fantastic fusion of styles—a carved wooden stalactite ceiling, a cycle of golden Byzantine mosaics rivaled only by those of Ravenna and Istanbul, and marble walls with geometric designs. In the apse, an enormous Christ looms above a 19th-century mosaic of the Virgin. Before leaving, visit the **Sala di Ruggero**

(King Roger's Hall, one floor above the Palatina), a room adorned with mosaics in flora and fauna motifs. Because the *palazzo* is now the seat of the Sicilian Parliament, you must wait at the desk for an escort. (Palace open Mon. and Fri.-Sat. 9am-noon unless Parliament is in session. Chapel open Mon.-Fri. 9am-noon and 3-5pm, Sat.-Sun. 9-10am and noon-1pm. Chapel closed Sunday and holiday afternoons.)

Perhaps the most romantic spot in Palermo is the garden and cloister of the **Church of San Giovanni degli Eremiti** (St. John of the Hermits), at Via dei Benedettini, 3. With courtyard fountains and bougainvillea vines, this paradise offers a haven of gazebos and stone archways. As you exit the Cappella Palatina, follow the castle walls around to the right to Piazza della Pinta; V. dei Benedettini is to the right. To get there from the station, take bus #9. Built in 1132 by fanciful Arab architects, it is topped by pink domes. Beside the church a tropical garden shades 13th-century cloisters. (Open daily 9am-1pm.)

The Fountain of Shame

Piazza Pretoria, (up Via Maqueda from the station) features a 16th-century fountain originally intended for a Florentine *villa*. The fountain features, among other unpublishable things, **nude men and women half-heartedly attempting to cover their genitalia** and (gasp!) eyeing one another suggestively. The *Palermitani* were so shocked when it was unveiled that they nicknamed the sculpture "the fountain of shame." Decide for yourself whether or not you can handle it.

From the Church of San Francesco to the Villa Giulia

The churches and palaces east of Via Roma toward the old port (La Cala) lie in a maze of tiny, serpentine streets. The 13th-century **Church of San Francesco d'Assisi** on Via Paternostro (off Corso Vittorio Emanuele about five blocks from Via Roma and to the right as you head to the harbor), features an intricate rose window and a zigzag design common to many churches in the area. The restored Gothic interior was augmented by side chapels in the 14th and 15th centuries and adorned with Renaissance and Baroque accessories. (Open daily 7-11am and 4-6pm.)

The **Oratory of San Lorenzo,** just a few doors down Via Imacolatella (to the left as you face the church of San Francesco), was decorated by the master of stucco, Giacomo Serpotta (1656-1732). This monochrome stucco has a hard finish that looks like carved stone when looked at from afar. Caravaggio's last known work, *The Nativity* (1609), was stolen from the altar in 1969—hence the seven locks on the oratory door. The inlaid mother-of-pearl benches are too impressive to sit on. (Open erratically; the oratory is maintained by an elderly neighbor in her spare time. To enter, ring at #5, and be prepared to make a L3000 *offerta*.)

The **Giardino Garibaldi,** a park several blocks further toward the sea on Corso Vittorio Emanuele, is replete with royal palms, fig trees, and giant banyans. The two fig trees are the oldest and most distinctive: they grow wildly, each with over 100 separate trunks sprouting from the ground that fuse into three or four main arteries. Follow signs from P. Marina to the **Museo delle Marionette,** which showcases Sicily's proud tradition of puppetry as well as collections of puppets from India, England, and the Congo. (Open Mon.-Sat. 9am-1pm; Mon., Wed., and Fri. also 4-7pm. Puppet shows on request. Admission L5000, students L2000.) Signs in Piazza Marina also point towards the part-Gothic, part-Renaissance **Palazzo Abatellis** (1495), which houses one of Sicily's superb regional galleries. Upstairs, an entire room is devoted to painter Antonello da Messina (1430-1479), Sicily's number-one son. Works by Leandro Bassano (1557-1622), Vincenzo da Pavia, and Leonard Macaluss round out the Sicilian fans. (Open Mon.-Sat. 9am-1:30pm; Tues., Thurs., and Fri. also 2-7:30pm; Sun. and holidays 9am-12:30pm. Admission L2000.)

Down Foro Italico to the east is a **small amusement park,** which opens every day in the late afternoon when the Sicilian sun has gotten cool enough. Farther down, on Foro Umberto I along the harbor, **Villa Giulia** has an eclectic garden, which harbors a little something for everyone: band shells, playgrounds, menageries, sculpture, floral gardens, and cenotaphs.

From the Church of San Matteo to the Museo Archeologico

Most of Palermo's other noteworthy sights lie along **Via Roma** north of Corso Vittorio Emanuele as you walk away from the station. The Baroque **Church of San Matteo** (on Corso Vittorio Emanuele) conceals an ornate marble interior and four statues by Serpotta in the pilasters of the dome. (Open daily 8am-noon and 4-7pm.) On Via Roma to the right, just a block from its intersection with Corso Vittorio Emanuele (again as you move away from the station), is the 12th-century **Church of Sant'Antonio,** revamped in the 14th and 19th centuries. You can still see the original structure in the square frame and the columns of the chancel. (Open Mon.-Sat. 8am-noon and 6:30-8:15pm, Sun. 7:30am-1pm.) Just past the intersection, on Via Vucciria off Corso Vittorio Emanuele, is another **market.** Dozens of varieties of fish, seafood, fruits and vegetables, including six-foot zucchini, tantalize the palate and the eye. (Open 8am-8pm; closed Wed.)

The **Church of San Domenico** fronts the *piazza* of the same name on Via Roma (to the right with the station behind you). Rebuilt in 1640, the church is Sicily's Pantheon, containing tombs of distinguished citizens. The **Oratorio del Rosario,** behind San Domenico on Via dei Bambinai (ring at #16), houses a famous altarpiece by Van Dyck, *Madonna of the Rosary with St. Dominique and the Patroness of Palermo* (1628). (Both open 7:30am-noon.)

Via Meli extends from Piazza San Domenico and leads—wow!—to Piazza Meli. By bearing left on Via dei Bambinai, through Piazza Valverde, and onto Via Squarcialupo, you'll find the **Church of Santa Cita** to your left on V. Valverde. The exterior was damaged during the war, but a rose window remains, lighting the interior with baroque color and texture. The marble arches on the east wall of the choir and the sarcophagus in the second chapel on the left remain from the original Renaissance structure. The **Oratorio di Santa Cita,** behind the church (ring at Via Valverde, 3), is decorated with Serpotta's *Virtues,* reliefs of New Testament scenes, and, on the short wall near the entrance, a depiction of the Battle of Lepanto, where Cervantes lost a hand. (Both open 8-11am and 4-5:30pm.)

The **Museo Archeologico Regionale** awaits you at P. Olivella, 4 (tel. 662 02 20; fax 611 07 40), left on Via Bara two blocks before Via Roma hits Via Cavour as you head away from the station. This museum occupies a 17th-century convent and displays a remarkable collection in two beautiful courtyards. See the building for its *cortile.* In the bronze collection is the *Ram of Syracuse* (Greek, 3rd century BC), renowned for its realism. (Open Mon.-Sat. 9am-1:45pm, Tues. and Fri. also open 3-5:45pm, Sun. and holidays 9am-12:45pm. Admission L2000.)

Other Sights

Across Via Maqueda from the Archaeological Museum, the **Teatro Massimo,** constructed between 1875 and 1897 in a robust neoclassical style, is the largest indoor stage in Europe after the Paris Opera House. The Massimo has been undergoing reconstruction since 1985; the projected completion date is in 2010 (or maybe 3010, given the Sicilian track-record). The exiled opera and symphony perform in the **Politeama Garibaldi** (farther up Via Maqueda, which becomes Via Ruggero Settima), a huge circular theater built in 1874. The entrance is a triumphal arch crowned by a bronze chariot and four horses. The theater also houses the **Galleria d'Arte Moderna.** (Theater performances Jan.-late May and mid-July-Aug. Admission from L30,000. Gallery open Tues.-Sun. 9am-1pm and 3-6pm. Admission L5000.)

The **Convento dei Cappuccini,** on Via Cappuccini (tel. 21 21 77), welcomes amateur paleontologists and the morbidly fascinated into its **catacombs;** 8000 bodies—some mummified and intact, all sorted by profession—inhabit lengthy subterranean corridors. Don't miss the baby girl—she's so well-preserved that she looks alive. (Open daily 9am-1pm and 4-6pm; tours offered intermittently by friars. Free,

NEAR PALERMO

but *offerta* expected.) Take bus #109 from Stazione Centrale to P. Indipendenza, and walk the rest of the way; or take bus #124 from Politeama.

Monte Pellegrino, an isolated mass of limestone rising from the sea, is Palermo's principal natural landmark, separating the city from the beach at Mondello. Near its summit, the **Santuario di Santa Rosalia** marks the site where Rosalia, a young Norman princess, sought ascetic seclusion. Her bones were discovered in 1624 and brought to Palermo, where they vanquished a raging plague. The present sanctuary is built over the cave where she performed her ablutions; its trickling waters are said to have miraculous powers. The summit of Monte Pellegrino (a half-hour climb from the sanctuary) offers a gorgeous view of Palermo, Conca d'Oro, and on a clear day, the Lipari Islands and Mount Etna. Take bus #812 from Politeama.

ENTERTAINMENT

Palermo shuts down at night. After about 9 or 10pm, there is virtually nothing to do—and just as well, since walking any later is not a particularly wise idea. Crowds of young *Palermitani* pass the summer nights on the *lido* of **Mondello.** Take bus #101 or 107 to the end and then #614 to Mondello. In summer, express bus #6 ("Beallo") also runs to Mondello, beginning at the train station and stopping along Via della Libertà. The bar and disco at **Villa Boscogrande,** Via Tomm. Natale, 91 (tel. 24 11 79), the gorgeous *palazzo* where director Lucino Visconti filmed *The Leopard,* attract a posh crowd. Take bus #806 from Piazza Sturzo, or try **Mondello Palace,** Via Ppe. di Scalla (tel. 450 01), on the cape beyond Monte Pellegrino.

The major summer event in Palermo takes place at the **Teatro di Verdura Villa Castelnuovo.** From the first week of July through the first week of August, an international festival of ballet, jazz, and classical music jams in this open-air seaside theater. For tickets and information, contact the **Politeama Garibaldi,** P. Ruggero Séttimo (tel. 605 33 15; open Tues.-Sat. 10am-1pm and 5-7pm, Sun. 10am-1pm), across from the tourist office. The **Festa di Santa Rosalia,** held July 10-15, gives the city an excuse to shed its usual sobriety and go on a binge of music and merriment.

Palermo resorts to two other beaches aside from the Lido at Mondello. **Sferracavallo** is a roomier but rockier beach (take bus #101 or 107 from Politeama to Piazza de Gasperri, and then #616 to the beach), while **Addaura** entertains the young Palermitan jet-set crowd in summer (bus #833 from Piazza Sturzo).

For more in-depth information on cultural events and nightlife, pick up a copy of *Un Mese a Palermo,* a monthly brochure in Italian, available at any APT office.

■ NEAR PALERMO

MONREALE

About 10km southwest of Palermo lies the golden city of **Monreale** and its magnificent Norman-Saracen **duomo,** Santa Maria La Nuova (c. 1174). At the time of its construction, this cathedral was the biggest in Europe. The church's incredible medieval mosaics supposedly inspired Jacques Cartier to name his Canadian city Montreal. The Old and New Testaments are depicted in 130 panels against a brilliant gold background, over which a massive Christ Pantocrator (Ruler of All) presides. To read this brilliant Bible, start at the upper right-hand corner of the main chapel with the Creation and work your way back to the present under Christ Pantocrator, where Virgin and Child sit with attendant angels (L500 to light up mosaics). The **tesoro,** off the transept, is housed in one of the most raucously Rococo chapels in Italy (admission L2500). Outside, circle around to see the Arab-style inlay behind the apse and a spectacular view of the *Conca d'Oro* below. Then step in to see the intricate arches and multicolored inlay of the **cloister,** renowned for the capitals of its colonnade (228 paired columns in all, each one unique). Considered to be the richest collection of Sicilian sculpture anywhere, the capitals run the gamut of styles: Greco-Roman, Saracen, Norman, Romanesque, Gothic, and various combinations thereof. In the corner by the lesser colonnade and its fountain, look for the capital depicting William II offering the Cathedral of Monreale to the Virgin. Be sure to climb up to the **roof** (access from inside the cathedral; look for the sign) and look down on the central apse. Two doors down from the cloister is the entrance to a series of quiet **gardens** which look out over Palermo and its sprawling expanse. (Cathedral open daily 8am-12:15pm and 3:30-6:15pm. Cloister opening times for July-Sept. Mon-Fri. 9am-7pm; Sat.-Sun. 9am-1pm; Oct.-June ask at cathedral. Admission to cloister L2000, to roof L2000.)

Bus #389 leaves for Monreale from Palermo's Piazza Indipendenza (you can take bus #109 from the station to Piazza Indipendenza), and takes you directly to Piazza V. Emanuele. When you hop off the bus, the *duomo* is to the right; Via Roma runs uphill to the right. **Tourist information** (tel. 656 42 70) resides in the building to the left of the church. Surrounding the *duomo* in the *piazza* lie an assorted array of *pizzerie*, pastry shops, and restaurants. Take your pick, then sit and observe the festivities; the locals celebrate as many as three weddings in the *duomo* per day.

USTICA

The volcanic island of **Ustica** lies within reach of Palermo, 36 miles off the coast. Settled first by our friends the Phoenicians, then by pirates and exiled convicts, this marine reserve features prime snorkeling and grotto-hopping opportunities. Inquire at the Palermo tourist office for further details. **Siremar** runs ferries and hydrofoils out to the island (see Palermo Orientation and Practical Information: Ferries).

THE WESTERN COAST

■■■ TRAPANI

Trapani is not your typical Italian city. Surrounded by the ocean on three sides, Trapani stays cool under even the hottest Mediterranean sun. Its residents display a combination of Sicilian candor and North African effusiveness that has earned Trapani the designation of "Sicily's friendliest city." While its sights are not at the top of most tourists' itineraries, it makes a perfect base for expeditions to the beaches of the western coast, the ruins of monumental Greek temples, and the breathtaking mountain-town of Erice. If you're in Trapani for more than a few hours, the town's churches, fashioned with a mix of European and African influences, merit more than just a hurried glance.

FERRIES

Ferries and *aliscafi* (hydrofoils) leave Trapani for the Egadi Islands (Levanzo, Favignana, and Marettimo) and Tunisia. Both leave from the docks off Via Ammiraglio Staiti, which runs the length of the port just south of Corso Italia. Tickets for ferries are available from **Siremar,** Via Ammiraglio Saiti, 61 (tel. 54 05 15; open Mon.-Fri. 6am-2pm, 4-6pm and 9pm-midnight; Sat. 6am-2pm, 4-5pm and 9pm-midnight; Sun. 6am-2pm). Siremar has its hydrofoil ticket office (tel. 277 80) right on the docks, as does **Alilauro** (tel. 240 73). These open up at least a half-hour before each hydrofoil departs. The following departure times are for mid-June through mid-September only; prices are the same on all lines. Keep in mind that inter-island ferries are somewhat less than reliable.

Trapani-Favignana: 6 per day (7am-2pm, 1-1½hr., L4600). 10 hydrofoils per day (7am-7:15pm, 20min., L9600).
Trapani-Levanzo: 4 per day (7am-2pm, 1-1½hr., L4600). 11 hydrofoils per day (7am-7:15pm, 20min., L9200).
Trapani-Marettimo: 1 per day at 9am (2½hr., L10,400). Two hydrofoils per day (8:15am-6:15pm, 1hr., L20,600).
Trapani-Pantelleria: Ferries depart daily at 9am and midnight (4½hr., L35,100). (Siremar only.)

Trapani-Tunis (Tunisia): Tirrenia runs a ferry every Mon. at 9am (9hr., L87,200); **Alimar** runs Wed. at 11am and Fri. at 10pm (L78,000). Tickets for both lines are available at **Sudovest Viaggi** (tel. 271 01), located 50m back from the port.

ORIENTATION AND PRACTICAL INFORMATION

Trapani sits on a peninsula, two hours west of Palermo by train (L11,700). An express bus makes the trip in two hours, rolling from Via Paolo Balsamo, 26, near the train station in Palermo, to P. Garibaldi in Trapani (L13,500). Trains run from Marsala (13 per day, 45min., L4200). From Agrigento, **S. Lumia** (tel. 204 14) runs four buses per day from P. Garibaldi (behind the movie theater, near the post office; 6:20am-2:10pm, L14,500). To get your bearings, take a look at the city map posted on the wall of the train station, near the ticket office. **Via Osorio** starts a little to the left of the station; turn left at the end, and the first right is **Corso Italia**. At the end of Corso Italia sits **Piazza S. Agostino,** and beyond the *piazza,* Trapani's main thoroughfare **Corso Vittorio Emanuele** cuts through the old city to the tip of the peninsula and intersects **Via Roma,** which spans the peninsula. The old town lies directly in front of the train station; the new town is behind it.

Tourist Office: P. Saturno (tel. 290 00). Take Via Osorio from the Mobil sign, turn left at the end, and then go right onto Corso Italia all the way to the *piazzetta.* Armfuls of handouts. English spoken. Open Mon.-Sat. 8am-2pm and 3-8pm, Sun. 9am-noon. **Information booth** at airport open for incoming flights. **APT main office,** Via Vito Sorba, 15 (tel. 270 77; fax 294 30), four blocks behind the station to the right. Open Mon.-Sat. 8am-2pm; might supply free tour guides for large groups, but not that helpful to individual tourists.

Police: Via Orlandini, 19 (tel. 271 22). **Municipal Police:** tel. 212 91.

Post Office: P. Vittorio Veneto (tel. 87 30 38 or 291 28), up Via Osorio and then right on Via XXX Gennaio. Open Mon.-Fri. 8am-5pm. **Postal Code:** 91100.

Telephones: Telecom, Via Scontrino, near the station. Open Mon.-Sat. 9am-1pm and 4-8pm, Sun. 9am-12:30pm and 4:30-8pm. **Telephone Code:** 0923.

Currency Exchange: in the train station. Open Mon.-Sat. 7am-noon and 3:30-5:30pm.

Flights: V. Florio Airport (tel. 84 12 22), 16km outside the city in Birgi en route to Marsala. Buses leave 1hr. before flight time from outside **Salvo Viaggi,** Corso Italia, 52/56 (tel. 54 54 11).

Trains: at P. Stazione (tel. 280 71 or 280 81). Office open Mon.-Sat. 5:40am-8:20pm and Sun. 5:45am-7:50pm.

Buses: AST (tel. 210 21) buses to Erice leave from P. Malta (Montalto), to the left of the train station (Mon.-Sat. 12 per day, 6:45am-9:30pm, Sun. 5 per day, 9am-6:15pm; L2500, round-trip L4300). Catch the return bus in Erice on Via Pepoli (Mon.-Sat. 7:30am-10:15pm; Sun. 10am-7:15pm). **SAV,** the orange city bus, can be taken all over town for L700. Tickets can be bought at most *tabacchi.*

Luggage Storage: at the train station, L1500 per piece. Open 7:12am-9:12pm.

Emergencies: tel. 113. **Hospital: Ospedale Sant'Antonio Abate,** Via Cosenza, very far from town (tel. 80 94 50).

ACCOMMODATIONS AND CAMPING

The cheaper hotels can be found toward the end of the peninsula, in the heart of the old city. Don't let the youth hostel sign outside of the train station lure you; it's 12km from town and frequently overbooked.

Pensione Messina, Corso Vittorio Emanuele, 71 (tel. 211 98), on a Renaissance courtyard just a few blocks from P. S. Agostino. Big rooms, firm beds, pink bathroom. Run by a friendly, slightly rambunctious family. Closes at midnight. Singles L18,000/20,000. Doubles L35,000/40,000. Breakfast L3000. Showers L2000.

Albergo Moderno, Via Genovese, 20 (tel. 212 47). Turn right off Corso Vittorio Emanuele (heading away from P. S. Agostino) onto Via Roma, then take a left on Via Genovese. Trapani's oldest hotel. Quiet, clean rooms, all with a nautical theme. Singles L25,000, with bath L40,000. Doubles L40,000, with bath L52,000. Triples L54,000, with bath L70,000.

Albergo Maccotta, Via degli Argentieri, 4 (tel. 284 18), behind the tourist office on P. Saturno. Quiet location and pleasant, airy rooms. Singles L30,000, with bath L40,000. Doubles L50,000, with bath L70,000. MC, Visa.

Albergo Nuovo Russo, Via Tintori, 4 (tel. 221 66; fax 266 23), off Corso V. Emanuele to the left. Six floors of wooden furniture, long carpets, and soft armchairs. You can live it up in this 3-star hotel at a low price, as long as you don't mind not having your own bathroom. All rooms have telephones; free TV upon request. English spoken. Singles L38,000, with bath L63,000. Doubles L70,000, with bath L100,000. Breakfast L5000. A/C L5000. Reserve one month ahead for Aug.

Camping: Capo San Vito and Castellamare del Golfo, on the opposite side of the cape, harbor most of the nearby campgrounds (buses daily to Castellamare at 12:30pm and 2:30pm, 1½hr., round-trip L6400). **Near Capo San Vito: Camping La Fata,** Via Mattarella (tel. 97 21 33), charges L7000 per person, L6500 per small tent, L11,500 per large tent. **Camping Soleado,** Via della Secca (tel. 97 26 88), charges L7500 per person, L7000 per small tent and L10,000 per large tent. Both open year-round. **Near Castellamare del Golfo: Baia di Guidaloca** (tel. 560 22); **Lu Baruni** (tel. 391 33); **Nausicaa** (tel. 315 18); and the cheapest, **Ciauli** (tel. 318 33), which charges L5500 per person, L5500 per small tent, L7500 per large tent. The other places charge about L1500 more. All open June-Sept., except Lu Baruni, which is open year-round.

FOOD

Take your money to the **open-air market** in P. Mercato di Pesce (at the end of Via Torrearsa), and stock up on seafood. (Open Mon.-Sat. 8am-1pm.) This market is such an institution that the *piazza* was named after it. Pick up essentials at the supermarket **Margherita,** Via San Domenico, 32, between the port and the train station. (Open Mon.-Sat. 8am-1:30pm and 5-8pm.) Trapani is known for its sardines and its *couscous con pesce*. Also try a *biscotto coi fichi*, the Italian fig-newton; all of the bakeries along Corso V. Emanuele stock them for about L400 each. For a closed-air market, stop by the **mini-Standa** Via Liberta, 12 (tel. 211 14), right by the open-air market, on the 3rd floor. (Open 9am-1pm and 4:30-8pm.)

Pizzeria Calvino, Via Nasi, 77 (tel. 214 64), one block off Corso Vittorio Emanuele as you're headed toward the port. All of Trapani comes here for take-out pizza (small L5500) before soccer games. Savor *lasagne al forno* (L6000). Cover L3000. Sit-down or take out. Open Tues.-Sun. noon-2pm and 5:30pm-1am.

Pizzeria Mediterranea, Corso Vittorio Emanuele, 195 (tel. 54 71 76). Wide range of delectable choices. Try the *pizza origanata* (L6000) with tomatoes, garlic, oregano, anchovies, and *pecorino* cheese. Small L5000-6000, large L15,000-16,000. Service 20%. Open Fri.-Wed. 9am-1pm and 6pm-midnight.

Ristorante da Bettina, Via San Francesco d'Assisi, 69 (tel. 200 50), near the port at Via Serisso. A classy, Arab atmosphere with a bubbling fountain, large ceiling fan, and soft classical music. Pricey, but worth it. Try their specialty *couscous con pesce* (L9000). Open Tues.-Sun. noon-4pm and 7pm-1am. AmEx.

Trattoria da Salvatore, Via Nunzio Nasi, 19, around the corner from Albergo Russo. Good food, but be wary of pushy waiters. *Couscous* L6500, *bucatino con sarde* L6000. Open Mon.-Sat. 9am-3pm and 7-11pm. AmEx.

SIGHTS AND ENTERTAINMENT

You can tour most of Trapani's major sights in one fun-filled afternoon. Begin one block off Corso Italia on Via S. Elisabetta, where the Gothic-Renaissance **Church of Santa Maria** displays a beautiful marble canopy which shelters a della Robbia sculpture. Farther up Corso Italia you'll hit Piazza S. Agostino, which runs right into Piazzetta Saturno by way of Via S. Agostino, where the buildings begin to get older and more ornate. Here you'll find the façade of the former **Church of Sant'Agostino** (14th century), which preserves a Gothic portal and rose window. The **Fountain of Saturn,** a triple-tiered basin supported by sirens, dates from the late 16th century.

The main street of the old city, **Corso Vittorio Emanuele II,** around the corner, is lined with elaborate façades. At one end, the 17th-century **Palazzo Seratorio** houses temporary art exhibits on its main floor; the **Collegio dei Gesuiti** (1636) contains an 18th-century carved-walnut cupboard; and the **cattedrale** displays a striking green-tiled dome and pink stucco walls. Down a small street to the left on Via Giglio, the tiny Baroque **Chiesa del Purgatorio,** Via San Francesco d'Assisi (tel. 213 21), sports a free-standing sculpture and a small emerald dome outside, and a group of 20 incomprehensible wooden statues inside. This collection, called *I Misteri* (The Mysteries), is carried in a procession around the town on Good Friday. At this time, their bearers call out, asking if anyone knows whose they are or what they're used for. No one ever does, so they are returned to the church for another year. Their identities have been a mystery for over 600 years (and will probably remain so for 600 more). (Open Tues. 10am-noon, Fri. 10am-noon and 4-7pm.)

Viale Regina Elena runs along the port to **Viale Duca l'Acosta,** where fishermen dry and mend their nets. Trapani used to be supported by its tuna market; these fishermen are the last in the line of Trapani's rich tuna heritage. For a treat, get up at the crack of dawn, head down to see the fishermen do their stuff, and continue up to the tip of the city to see the sunrise at the **Torre di Ligny,** which doubles as a **Museo di Preistoria** (tel. 223 00. Open 9am-1pm and 4-8pm. Admission L2000.) From the Torre you can take Via Libertà past the fish market at Piazza Mercato de Pesce to **Via Garibaldi,** whose cream-colored *palazzi* are rivalled only by those of Córso V. Emanuele.

Farther out in the new section of town, visit the **Museo Nazionale Pepoli** (tel. 55 32 69; fax 53 54 44). (It's a grueling walk; buses to the museum are run by **SAU** and they leave from Via G. Fardella, 2 blocks to the right of the station—take bus #1 or 10, L700.) The museum's magnificent baroque staircase leads to a collection of local sculpture, painting, coral carvings, and folk-art figurines. (Open Tues.-Sat. 9am-1pm; Tues. and Thurs.-Fri. also 3-6pm; Sun. 9am-12:30pm. Admission L2000, Sun. free.)

Trapani sponsors an annual festival of opera, ballet, and drama, **Luglio Musicale Trapanese** (tel. 229 34), which attracts troupes from abroad. It takes place in an open-air theater in the city park, the Villa Margherita, during the last three weeks of July. (Shows begin at 9pm. Admission from L15,000.) **Settimana dell'Egadi,** in late May, greets the new crop of tourists with music, food, and archaeological tours.

At night the young and the restless populate the beer gardens in P. XVIII Novembre or the *gelaterie* along Via Turetta, but only until 9pm, when the entire town seems to pass out.

■ NEAR TRAPANI

SAN VITO LO CAPO

The gentle shores of San Vito lo Capo (sometimes known as Capo San Vito) present an immense, sandy beach and a vast selection of *gelaterie*. Although it's a major resort for northerners, the town remains inexpensive, genuine, clean, and an ideal place to relax for a day. Rent a bicycle carriage at the Ditta Russo Anna, Via Nino Bixio, 14, and practice your Italian driving skills by careening down the sidewalks: leering men=50 points (tandem bikes L10,000 per hr.). For more seclusion, drive 12km, or make the bus connection through Castellamare to Guida Loca, to the **Riserva dello Zingaro,** a nature preserve whose pastoral, cow-lined trails lead to crystalline coves and a grotto that could serve as the entrance to Dante's Underworld. Buses to San Vito leave from the Trapani *autostazione* at P. Malta (Mon.-Fri. 8 per day 7am-8pm, Sun. 4 per day, 8:30am-7pm, 1¼hr., L4400 one way, L7300 round-trip). The last bus back to Trapani on weekdays leaves at 8:15pm (Sun. return trips from 10am-8:15pm). For more on the Zingaro nature reserve, ask for information (in English) at the Trapani tourist office. And if you're so inclined to stay, look for **Sabbia d'Oro,** Via Santuario, 49 (tel. 97 25 08), just off the beachfront in San Vito lo Capo. In an impeccable, great location, and a bargain for the area. Singles L35,000. Doubles L50,000. Sept.-June, singles with breakfast L26,000. The same management runs **Pensione Ocean View** (tel. 97 26 13) in the same building. Less opulent rooms. L19,500 per person, L22,500 with bath. AmEx. There are many camping options in the area (see Trapani: Accommodations and Camping, page 526).

ERICE

Erice soars 750m above sea level only a short distance from the coast. Once the biggest town in the area (Trapani was merely Erice's port), Erice's mountain slopes could not support any more houses, so the *Ericiani* began to develop the nearby harbor. In ancient times, Erice was one of Sicily's most revered sites. As such, the city has been the mythical home to several goddesses of fertility: first the Elymian Astarte, then the Greek Aphrodite and the Roman Venus. Both the city itself and the vistas it affords are a visual delight. The outer walls date back to the 16th century BC, and the town is virtually unchanged from medieval times. There are a number of worthwhile sights, particularly the **Norman castle,** with its medieval towers (adorned with TV broadcast aerials in typical Sicilian fashion), and the lush adjoining "Balio" **gardens.** There is also a 14th-century **duomo** with a 13th-century bell tower which was first a watch-tower, and then a prison, before being transformed for its present use. One of the greatest pleasures of visiting Erice is strolling the cool cobblestone streets, savoring the well-preserved buildings and the awe-inspiring panoramic views of the coast (occasionally reaching all the way to Tunisia).

The **tourist office** (AAST) awaits you at Via C. A. Pepoli, 11, on the hill near the bus stop (tel. (0923) 86 93 88 or 86 91 73; open Mon.-Sat. 8am-2pm and 4-7pm; Sun. (summer only) 8am-2pm). The **bus** from Trapani leaves from P. Malta (Montalto). (Mon.-Sat. 12 per day, 6:45am-9:30pm.; Sun. 5 per day 9am-6:15pm. Last bus back weekdays at 10:15pm, Sun. at 7:15pm, 45min., L4300 round-trip.) Since hotel prices tend to be as lofty as the altitude, Erice is best seen on a daytrip from Trapani. If you're stuck, the cheapest place is the **Edelweiss,** Cortile P. Vincenzo, 9 (tel. 86 91 58; singles with bath L100,000, doubles L130,000; includes breakfast). Although cheap food is hard to find in Erice, try your luck at the **Caffè S. Rocco,** Via G.F. Guarnotta, 23 (tel. 86 93 37). Just down the block, the **Antica Pasticceria del Convento,** Via Guarnotta, 66 (tel. 86 90 05), makes sinfully good sweets for the nuns and the public alike. L18,000 buys a kilo, enough to earn four people an afternoon in purgatory. (Open daily 10:30am-1pm and 3-9pm.)

SEGESTA

Segesta, with its unusual ruins set in the most dramatic of landscapes, is a must-see for anyone exploring western Sicily. The unfinished monumental **temple,** dating to the 5th century BC, provides a rare glimpse of a work in progress (as opposed to a finished building that has crumbled with age). Its incomplete state has taught archaeologists a great deal about how ancient temples were constructed and what optical and physical refinements the ancients used. Try, for example, the not-so-famous "hat trick"—if you place a hat on one corner of the temple steps, and look at it at eye level along the long side of the temple, the hat will disappear from view. This bending of the steps actually has the effect of making the steps look straight. There is also a majestic **theater,** where the ancient Elymi (a native Sicilian people and the inhabitants of Segesta) went to see (in all probability, Greek) plays.

Segesta, having been razed and rebuilt five times in its less-than-illustrious history, is finally here to stay. From mid-July until the first week of August during odd-numbered years, classical plays (and Indian and Japanese theater too) are performed in the ancient theater. Special buses leave P. Politeama in Palermo (1¾hr. before showtime) and P. Marina in Trapani (1hr. before showtime). Buy the L15,000-25,000 tickets from a travel agent in Palermo or Trapani. To reach the theater, walk up the road from the *bar* (20min.). For those allergic to hiking, an air-conditioned bus will take you to the top (every 30min. from 9:30am-6pm; L2000 round trip). **Buses** to Segesta from other towns are run by **Autoservizi Tarantola** (tel. 310 20), leaving Trapani Mon.-Sat. at 8am, 10am, noon, and 2pm; returning at 11am, 1:10pm, 3:45pm, and 6:20pm (L4000, round-trip L6700).

EGADI ISLANDS

■■■ EGADI ISLANDS (ISOLE EGADI)

The mid-afternoon summer sun is far kinder to the Egadi Islands than to their scorched neighbor, Sicily. Cats lounge on the terraces of whitewashed houses soothed by the warm massage of the *scirocco* (sea breeze). You might want to bypass Favignana, tourist trap and home to the remnants of the archipelago's tuna trade, and head straight for the outlying islands of Marettimo and Levanzo. Connected by sporadic ferry and hydrofoil service (both between islands and between the islands and Trapani; see Trapani, Ferries page 525). These rough and barren islands—strewn with bushes, wildflowers, and lost sheep—offer archaeological wonders, sea grottoes, and hiking trails with incredible views.

FAVIGNANA

Favignana, the biggest of the three islands and the closest to Trapani, got its name from the *favonio*, or "zephyr," the warm, westerly winds which blow its way. Industrial and gritty Favignana has a large military camp and a beach, the Lido Burrone, 3km across the island from the main harbor. Rent a bike (L5000 per day) and pedal to one of Italy's hidden treasures, an old quarry by the sea called the **Bue Marino** (Elephant Seal). A small number of overpriced *pensioni* and distant campgrounds await on Favignana; for more reasonable accommodations, hop on the hydrofoil to Marettimo or Levanzo. When hunger strikes, raid the *alimentari* and *pizzerie* on Corso V. Emanuele. **Alilauro,** Molo San Leonardo (tel. (0923) 92 16 05), has a hydrofoil service from Favignana to the other islands: to Levanzo (4-6 per day, 7:55am-7:15pm, off-season 7:55am-6:05pm, L3900); to Marettimo (1 per day in high season only, 6:05pm, L11,000) and back to Trapani (6 per day, 7:55am-7:15pm, in low season 7:55am-5:05pm, L9100). These are the published times, but true to Italian form, they are not always reliable.

LEVANZO

The prehistoric cave art in the **Cava del Genovese,** about an hour on foot from the port, is only visible on a guided tour (in Italian only). *Signore* Castiglione's son can be found at the Siremar office above the dock (or call him at (0923) 92 40 32) and will lead you to the cave in a small boat for L15,000. The Paleolithic incisions and ocra-grease paintings show both early fishing trade and dance (the bug look-alikes are actually women dancing). The Neolithic paintings of animals that no longer inhabit the islands illuminate the geological history of the archipelago. The island also offers a number of secluded beaches and grottoes for swimming. Levanzo lacks a bus system and a tourist office, so pick a road and start walking. Though no accommodations on the Egadi Islands are cheap, Levanzo is your best bet if you refuse to stay on the mainland. There are only two *pensioni* on the island: **Albergo Paradiso** (tel. 92 40 80) with newly renovated rooms overlooking the sea (singles L35,000, doubles L60,000; Sept.-June singles L30,000, doubles L55,000), and the **Albergo dei Fenici** (tel. 92 40 83), right behind the Paradiso, with a large terrace and an even better view, a common room with TV, and airy hallways (singles L40,000; doubles L67,000). Pick up groceries or bring food from Favignana or Trapani. Sundown draws locals, travelers, and resident expats to the seaside *caffè,* **Bar Arcobaleno,** where an evening of cards and a warm North African breeze can easily stretch one *cappuccino* (L1500) into four. (Open until everyone decides to go to bed.)

MARETTIMO

Marettimo, the most remote of the Egadi Islands, offers the most remote atmosphere and the Pizzo Falcone (884m) is the highest point on the islands. Newly established hiking trails take you up and down the rocky cliffs of the island, and on clear days, the view stretches as far as Tunisia. A handful of *caffè, gelaterie,* and the **Torrente Trattoria,** on P. Umberto across from the Siremar office, vend sandwiches and *gelato.* If you like Marettimo enough to stay overnight, ask at the Torrente about renting a room in a private house for L20,000-25,000 per night. (There are no official accommodations on the island.) **Alilauro** offers ferry services to Trapani (via Levanzo and Favignana): one per day in high season only, 6:45pm, L18,200. (**Siremar** runs to Trapani: three per day, 6:50am-4:05pm, L18,200.)

■■■ MARSALA

When the island-city of Mozia was destroyed at the hands of the Syracusans in 397 BC, the survivors fled to the mainland of Cape Lilybeo and founded what is now **Marsala.** (The Arabs renamed *Lilybaeum* "Mars-Alí," "port of Alí.") These days, most Italians know the city as home to the famous Marsala wine. Although Marsala is best visited in passing on your way to the enigmatic Mozia, the city's museums and archaeological sites offer a telling glimpse into the past.

From the train station, Via Roma is a straight shot into Marsala's historic center, changing into **Via XI Maggio** at P. Matteotti. Following Via XI Maggio will land you in front of the 18th-century **Palazzo Comunale** and the Baroque **duomo,** which stand in **Piazza della Repubblica.** A variety of sculpture from the 16th-century school of Gagini decorates the church's vast interior. Behind the *duomo* at Via Garraffa, 57, the **Museo degli Arazzi** contains eight elaborate 16th-century Flemish tapestries illustrating Titus' war against the Jews. (Explanations in English and Italian. Open daily 9am-1pm and 4-6pm. Admission L1000.) At the end of Via XI Maggio lies P. della Vittoria, separating the city from the sea. To the right is the entrance to Marsala's *zona archeologica*; to the left is the **Museo Baglio Anselmi** (tel. 95 25 35), which houses the remains of a 35-m Carthaginian warship believed to have sunk during the Battle of the Egadi Islands, which ended the First Punic War in 241 BC. (Open Mon.-Sat. 9am-2pm, Sun. 9am-1pm; Wed., Sat., and Sun. also 3-6pm).

The nearby **Villa Romana** (Roman Tenement), one of the few excavated buildings in the vast archaeological zone, further documents Marsala's ancient past. (Open upon request at the Museo Lilybeo.) The small 5th-century **Church of San Giovanni,** next to the museum, covers the **Grotto della Sibilla,** a cave where a mythical Sibyl proclaimed her oracles. Check out the remnants of mosaics that speckle the floor. (Church open 9am-2pm and 3-6pm.)

To witness the production of Marsala wine, take a free tour of the **Cantina Florio** facilities, located on Lungomare Mediterraneo just past Via S. Lipari, to the left behind the train station. (Open to the public Mon.-Fri. 9am-noon and 3-6pm.) Marsala's **Pro Loco,** at Via Garibaldi, 45 (tel. 71 40 97), off Via XI Maggio, will direct you to other Marsala distillers (ask them about Azienda Agricola Montalto, which features a wine-making museum and some great wines) and help find accommodations. (Open Mon.-Sat. 8am-1pm and 4-7pm.) **Trattoria da Pino,** Via San Lorenzo, 25 (tel. 71 56 52), offers a L16,000 *menù.* To get there from P. Repubblica, head away from the station on Via XI Maggio and bear left on Via Curatolo, which eventually becomes Via San Lorenzo. (Open Mon.-Sat. 7pm-midnight. AmEx.) Nearby at Via San Lorenzo, 8, an unmarked **bakery** sells fresh, warm bread at L1100 a loaf (get there before noon). For those on a shoe-string budget, make your way over to **STANDA,** Via Cammareri Scurtil, 10 (open 9am-1pm and 5-9pm). The cheapest hotel in town is the **Garden,** Via Gambini, 36 (tel. 98 23 20); follow signs from the right of the train station. Still pricey, but has gorgeous marbled hallways, chandeliers, and spic 'n' span rooms. (Singles L40,000, with bath L45,000. Doubles L60,000, with bath L80,000.)

■ NEAR MARSALA

MOZIA

Mozia (now known as San Pantaleo) was the scene of a monumental naval battle in which Dionysius of Syracuse annihilated the Carthaginian Himilco in 397 BC with the aid of that new super-weapon, the catapult. The near-deserted islet lies 8km north of Marsala, across a thin strait traversed by a rickety little boat; a boatman will come and pick you up when he sees you waiting on the dock (Mon.-Sat. 9am-6pm, L3000; Oct.-Mar. boat runs in morning only; tel. 96 81 87). Remains of the original child-sacrificing inhabitants (they switched to animals around 5 BC) are limited to the fenced-in *tophet* (sacrificial area) and the dry dock on the other end of the tiny island. Many of the island's archaeological finds are displayed in the tiny museum at the port, including a 5th-century BC Greek statue entitled "Youth of Mozia." (Closed for repair in 1995.) A walk around the cactus-studded island will show you the ancient fortifications, dating to 600 BC. The island itself may be a disappointment, but the salt flats and windmills, characteristic of the region, are worth the bus trip. To get to Marsala from Trapani, take a **bus** from P. Malta (5 per day, departs 6:50am-2pm, returns 7:05am-2:10pm, L3700 each way). The bus company Municipilizatta (tel. 95 11 05), in Marsala, runs 12 buses a day to and from Mozia, leaving from P. del Popolo. (Bus #11 departs 7am-6pm, returns 7:55am-6:45pm, L1500.) The boat to Mozia leaves from a pier at the end of the road where this bus will let you off.

SELINUNTE

A magnificent jumble of ruins atop a plateau overlooking the Mediterranean, Selinunte awes with its immensity and desolation. Founded in the 7th century BC by the citizens of Megara Hyblaea, the city's fortunes took a decided downturn after 409 BC, when the place was sacked by Segesta and Carthage; it was finally destroyed by its own (Carthaginian) people in 241 BC in anticipation of a Roman attack. Selinunte remains shrouded in an air of mystical isolation that justifies the title given it by the Arabs: "the place of the idols." (Open 9am-6pm. Admission L1000.) About a kilometer inland, the enormous half-quarried drums for unbuilt columns lie abandoned in a stone outcropping.

Getting to Selinunte can be a challenge. From Palermo, Trapani, or Marsala, take the bus or train to **Castelvetrano.** If you're lucky, you'll catch the 2pm bus that leaves straight from Castelvetrano's train station for Selinunte (L1700). If not, blue buses leave for Selinunte from Castelvetrano's bus station (5 per day Mon.-Sat. 7:15am-5pm, Sun. 9am-7:15pm). To get there, follow Via Minghetti up the hill from the left of the train station. Make a left at the top onto Via Vittorio Emanuele; when this street comes to an end, go to the right through P. Garibaldi. P. San Giovanni is just beyond. If you miss the bus to Selinunte, **Hotel Zeus,** Castelvetrano's cheapest hotel, is up the hill from the station at Via Veneto, 6 (tel. (0924) 90 55 66; fax 90 55 65; singles L45,000, doubles L80,000). Cheaper stays (and more pleasing countryside) can be found in Selinunte. For a wonderful family-run establishment, head for **Il Pescatore,** at Via S.P. 13n, 31 (tel. 463 03), where clean rooms, a view of the monuments, and a great host await you. (Singles L20,000-25,000, doubles L40,000-45,000.) **Costa d'Avorio,** Via Ventinove, 10 (tel. 462 07), has singles for L25,000, with bath L30,000, doubles for L40,000, with bath L50,000, and half-pension for L55,000. Down the road from the ruins is **Camping Athena,** whose L14,000 *menù* and after-dinner guitar and singing is a must. (Open 7pm-whenever the singing stops.) If you're desperate, see if the staff at **Pro Loco** in P. Garibaldi (see directions above) can help. (Open Mon.-Sat. 8am-1pm and 4-8pm; no phone.) They can provide you with the phone numbers of Selinunte's *affitta camere*.

THE SOUTHERN COAST

■■■ AGRIGENTO

The Greek poet Pindar once lauded Agrigento as "Man's Finest City," and in spite of some serious competition, Agrigento still holds the title. Founded by Greek colonists in the 6th century BC, the city itself sits on a mountain ridge, looming protec-

AGRIGENTO

tively over its famous Valley of the Temples. The *centro storico* is a cobblestone web of welcoming streets, where butcher shops and Gucci boutiques sit comfortably side by side. The city has tree-lined Parisian-style avenues and squares, plus 4km of golden beach thrown in for good measure. Luigi Pirandello, winner of the 1934 Nobel Prize in Literature, was born here—something no Agrigentan will let you forget. Add to all this the fact that the city boasts some of the world's best preserved classical Greek architecture, and maybe you'll side with Pindar after all.

ORIENTATION AND PRACTICAL INFORMATION

Agrigento marks the midpoint of Sicily's southern coast. The transportation terminals, along with a park in P. Moro, divide the medieval from modern cities. Trains from Palermo and Catania arrive at the station in **Piazza Marconi**. **Viale della Vittoria** is the arrow-straight boulevard that leads to the train station, then veers uphill to the right, ending in **Piazza Vittorio Emanuele**. The staircase leading up from P. Marconi brings you to one edge of **Piazzale Moro**. The cobblestoned **Via Atenea**, the old city's main drag, begins nearby. Along it you'll find most of the town's shops and restaurants.

Tourist Office: AAST, Via Empedocle, 73 (tel. 203 91). Enthusiastic staff that doesn't speak English. Good handouts. Open Mon.- Sat. 9am-1:45pm and 4-7pm.

Police: P. Moro (tel. 59 63 22).

Post Office: P. Vittorio Emanuele (tel. 59 51 50), with great fascist "worker style" mosaics out front. Full services (including telegraphs and **currency exchange**) open Mon.-Fri. 8:10am-1:20pm. Basic services (letters, stamps, packages) Mon.-Sat. 8:10am-7:40pm. **Postal Code:** 92100.

Telephones: Telecom (SIP), Via Atenea, 96. Open daily 8am-8pm. **Telephone Code:** 0922.

Trains: run from the station to Palermo (11 per day, 8 on Sun., 1½hr., L10,900) and Catania via Caltanissetta and Enna (4 per day, 3hr., L14,400 to Catania; 2hr., L9200 to Enna). Ticket office open 6:10am-3:10pm and 4:10-8:10pm.

Buses: gather up the hill past P. Vittorio Emanuele, in P. Roselli, an otherwise empty lot. (Note the map of the city posted in the bus station.) From Trapani, **Autoservizi Lumia** (tel. 204 14) runs four buses per day to Agrigento (departures from Trapani's P. Garibaldi; 4hr., L15,200, round-trip L25,900). From Marsala, take the train to Castelvetrano (15 per day, 1hr., L3700), and then one of four daily buses to Agrigento (L9600) via Selinunte and Ribera. From Ragusa, take an **AST** bus (tel. 62 12 49; in Agrigento tel. 51 10 17) to Gela, where you can switch to a **Licata** bus (in Agrigento tel. 296 92) to Agrigento. **Autoservizi Cuffaro** (tel. 91 63 49) makes six trips per day to and from Palermo's P. Balsamo (7am-6:30pm, 2¼hr., L10,200; L27,000 roundtrip). Finally, **SAIS** buses (tel. 59 52 60; ticket and info office down the hill from P. Roselli) serve Catania (5 per day, 2½hr., L16,000; L27,000 roundtrip).

Ferries: Siremar, Porto Empedocle (tel. 63 66 85). Take a bus from the train station (at least 1 per hr., L2000). To the **Pelagie Islands,** Linosa (L39,000) and Lampedusa (L55,600), one departure per day at midnight, arriving Linosa at 5:45am, Lampedusa at 8:15am, and Linosa at 10:15am. Tickets at the Siremar office in the port. Get there at least an hour before departure.

Public Transportation: Most orange TUA city buses depart from the train station. #1, 2, 3, and 4 run to the Valley of Temples, #10 to San Leone (Agrigento's beach), and #11 to Luigi Pirandello's house. Buy tickets (L1000) at any *tabacchi*.

Emergencies: tel. 113. **Hospital: Ospedale Civile San Giovanni di Dio** (tel. 49 21 11; emergencies tel. 40 13 44), off P. S. Giuseppe on Via Atenea.

ACCOMMODATIONS AND CAMPING

Hotel Concordia, Via San Francesco, 11 (tel. 59 62 66), above an active market square near the train station. Take Via Pirandello from the top of the steps that lead into P. Moro. Tiny but tidy rooms. Avoid the dingy basement shower. Singles L25,000, with bath L35,000. Doubles L50,000, with bath L60,000. All rooms with bath have TVs.

Hotel Bella Napoli, P. Lena, 6 (tel./fax 204 35 or tel. 205 92), off Via Bac Bac, which leads uphill from the high end of Via Atenea. Simple, clean rooms are adequately furnished. Rooftop terrace overlooks the valley. Singles L25,000, with bath L40,000. Doubles L55,000, with bath L70,000. Triple L85,000. AmEx.

Hotel Belvedere, Via San Vito, 20 (tel. 200 51), at the top of the stairs which begin by the Restaurant Kalos, opposite P. Moro. The modern rooms are dark, clean, and quiet. A two-star establishment, for whatever that's worth. Singles L35,000, with bath L60,000. Doubles L55,000, with bath L80,000. Breakfast L4000.

Camping: Fairly expensive and far from the city. Beautiful beach fronts, but check with the tourist office before heading out (bus service is sporadic), and bring your own food or face high market prices. Occasional #10 buses to San Leone come out this far (a zone called "Le Dune"); otherwise you'll have to hike the 3km from the center of S. Leone (face the beach and walk to the left). **Internazionale Nettuno** (tel. 41 62 68). L7500 per person, L7000 per small tent. Open year-round.

FOOD

There are a couple of small fruit and vegetable stands in front of the Hotel Concordia (open Mon.-Sat. mornings). Agrigento's **STANDA** doesn't stock food, so your best bet is one of the small *alimentari* lining Via Pirandello or Via Atenea. Indulge a sweet tooth at the candy stalls along Via della Vittoria (open all day and well into the evening). The specialty is *torrone,* a heavy, creamy, nut-filled toffee. The "market" by the soccer field consists of a bunch of stalls selling cheap clothes.

Trattoria Atenea, Via Ficani, 12 (tel. 202 47), the 4th right off Via Atenea from P. Moro, has a quiet courtyard. Two-course lunch L15,000; dinner *menù* L12,000. Extensive seafood offerings. *Calamari* (squid) and *gamberi* (shrimp) are L9000. The house specialty is *grigliata mista di pesce* (mixed grilled fish, L9000). All pasta L5000. Wine L4000 per liter. Open Mon.-Sat. noon-3pm and 7pm-midnight.

Paninoteca Manhattan, Salita M. Angeli, 9 (tel. 59 66 95), up the steps to the right off Via Atenea near P. Moro. Creative Italian sandwiches with creative American names. The "Rockfeller" combines tuna, pepper, lettuce, *insalata russa,* tabasco, and a healthy dose of whiskey (L4000). Spaghetti from L6000. *Menù* L18,000. Innumerable brands of beer L4000. Open Mon.-Sat. 8am-3pm and 7pm-midnight.

Trattoria Black Horse, Via Celauro, 8 (tel. 232 23), off Via Atenea. An interesting family-run establishment. If you're lucky, you might even get to overhear the chef singing Verdi. *Tronchetto dello chef (*a thick lasagna packed with peas, ham, and meat sauce, L6500) is the specialty. *Menù* L13,000. Cover L2500; service 10%. Open Mon.-Sat. noon-3pm and 7-11pm. AmEx, MC, Visa.

Ristorante Pizzeria La Corte degli Sfirzii, C. Contarini, 3 (tel. 59 55 20), in the Cortile (garden) Contarini off Via Atenea. Fine food. Go for the *pizza menù,* your choice of pizza, *insalata mista,* and wine or beer, including cover and service (L14,000). Regular *menù* L18,000. During the summer, ask to be seated in the private garden in the back. Open Thurs.-Tues. noon-3pm and 7:30pm-2am. MC, Visa.

Trattoria de Paris, Piazza Lena, 7 (tel. 254 13). Conveniently located next to the Hotel Bella Napoli. No croissants here, but some genuinely tasty Italian dishes. *Cavatelli in cartoccio* (we don't know what it is either, L8000) is their specialty. Service 10%. Open daily noon-3pm and 7:30-11pm. AmEx, MC, Visa.

Trattoria La Forchetta, P. San Francesco (tel. 59 62 66), off Via Atenea, next to Hotel Concordia. Authentic Agrigentan cuisine in a restful setting. Excellent *calamari fritti* (fried squid). Service 10%. Open Mon.-Sat. 12:30-3pm and 8-11pm.

Ingenito Alimentari, Via Atenea, 319. This labyrinthine mini-supermarket caters to all of your gastronomical needs. Open Mon.-Sat. 8am-2pm and 5-11pm.

SIGHTS AND ENTERTAINMENT

Valle dei Templi

Agrigento's star attraction is the **Valle dei Templi** (Valley of the Temples), a couple of kilometers down the hill from the modern city. Take bus #1, 2, 3, or 4 from the train station (last bus back at 9:45pm; L1000) and ask to be dropped off at the *Quar-*

tiere Ellenistico-Romano (Hellenistic-Roman Quarter). Walk to the **Museo Nazionale Archeologico di San Nicola** to orient yourself. The museum contains a notable collection of artifacts, especially Greek vases from Agrigento and the rest of central Sicily. (Open Mon.-Sat. 9am-1pm, Tues. and Fri. open till 5pm. Free.) The adjacent **Church of San Nicola,** a small 13th-century Romanesque-Gothic church on the site of a Greek sanctuary, preserves Roman sarcophagi with reliefs depicting the death of Phaedra (second chapel on the right). Unfortunately, the church is only opened for weddings. Walking one km down the busy road in front of the museum will bring you to a dirt lot, a snack bar, lots of tour buses, and the Valley of the Temples.

With the exception of the Temples of Concord and of Juno, the structures here were destroyed by a combination of earthquakes and early Christian anti-paganism. In the site adjacent to the parking lot are the ruins of the **Tempio di Giove Olimpico.** Had its construction not been halted by the Carthaginian sack of the city in 406-405 BC, it would have been one of the largest Greek temples ever built. Now little is left; most of the temple's stone was carted away in the 18th century to build a jetty at nearby Porto Empedocle. The temple's 38 18m columns were supported by 8m *telemones*—sculpted human figures standing in as supporting columns. A reconstructed telamon lies alongside the ruins. Further along in the same area, the four columns supporting an entablature represent the piecemeal effort to rebuild the 5th-century BC **Tempio di Castore e Polluce** (Castor and Pollux). Across from the parking lot are the few remaining columns of the **Tempio di Ercole** (Heracles), the oldest temple (6th century BC) here.

Uphill from the Temple of Hercules looms the **Tempio della Concordia,** one of the most well-preserved (34 columns!) Greek temples in the world. Erected in the mid-5th century BC out of limestone (now weathered golden), it owes its remarkable preservation to early sanctification as a Christian church by the then-Bishop of Agrigento San Gregorio delle Rape (St. Gregory of the Turnips). The niches in the interior walls originally created for Christian worship are still visible. The **Tempio di Giunone** (Juno) dates from the same period as the Temple of Concord. Though nowhere near as well-preserved, it offers a great view from the top of the hill.

In Agrigento

The most interesting building in medieval Agrigento is the small, 11th-century Norman **Church of Santa Maria dei Greci,** which occupies the site of a 5th-century BC Doric temple. (Follow the signs up the hill from the top of Via Bac Bac off Via Atenea.) Part of the wooden Norman ceiling remains, as well as a portion of the 14th-century Byzantine frescoes and the Greek columns of the original temple. Look for the secret tunnel, which you can enter from the courtyard. It preserves the stylobate (the platform beneath the columns) and the six stumps of the ancient temple. (If closed, call 59 54 79.)

The **Chiesa del Purgatorio** (Church of Purgatory) in P. Purgatorio off Via Atenea houses eight statues representing the Virtues. To the left of the church, underneath a sleeping lion, is the entrance to a network of underground channels and reservoirs built by the Greeks in the 5th century BC (closed for restoration in 1995). Wandering behind the church on Via Fodera will lead you to **Santo Spirito,** a complex containing a chapel, charterhouse, and refectory (now used as a library), founded by Cistercian nuns at the end of the 13th century. The church displays beautiful stucco work (1693-1695) by Serpotta, illustrating scenes from Christ's life; ring the bell on the church door to enter.

For a change of pace, visit the birthplace of playwright **Luigi Pirandello** in P. Kaos. Take bus #11 to this small museum of books and notes. (Open Mon.-Fri. 9am-1hr. before sunset; Sat.-Sun. 9am-1pm. Free.) The **Settimana Pirandelliana,** a weeklong outdoor festival of plays, operas, and ballets in P. Kaos, happens in late July and early August (tickets L10,000-20,000; ask at the tourist office or call 263 33 for info).

The first Sunday of February brings the **Almond Blossom Festival,** an international folk event in the Valley of the Temples. In early July, townsfolk throw bread to the effigy of St. Calogero in gratitude for curing the city of a yeast epidemic. **San**

Leone, 4km from Agrigento (take bus #10), is laden with splendid stretches of beach. Beginning in the early evening, *ragazzi* gather in front of the beach-side **Aster** game room/*pizzeria* to strut their stuff and sing along to the music pouring out of the *caffè* (open noon-midnight). The last bus to Agrigento leaves at 9:45pm.

■ NEAR AGRIGENTO: SCIACCA

Sciacca (SHAH-kah) is well known throughout Italy as the site of thermal-mineral baths. The area's bubbling mud and steaming sulfuric water were enough to frighten the locals 4000 years ago, but today's inhabitants have adopted a more capitalistic approach; the facilities at the **Terme di Sciacca** (immediately to your left as you get off the bus) would do even the Sultan of Brunei proud. While most of the services offered by this therapeutic facility are a bit out of the budget traveler's reach (sulfuric bath L18,000, vapor caves L30,000, massage L18,000), the town still has plenty to offer. The **Church of St. Agostino** (build in 1753, Via Padre G. Cusmano) is a squat, stone building with an impressive portal and bell tower. Walk a short way up Via Valverde to the **Church of Santa Maria delle Giummare,** with its courtyard altar sunken into an outdoor cave. Stroll up Via Conte Luna to the impressive **Castle of Conti Luna** (1380). In the center of the old city lies Piazza G. Noceto. Look for the free-standing 14th-century **tower.**

The best of all that Sciacca has to offer can probably be seen on a daytrip. If you wish to spend the night, however, cheap lodgings can be found at the **Pensione Buenos Aires,** Via Triolo, 11 (tel. 218 37), close to the *comune* in the historic center. In addition to the ceramic dolls in the lobby, you'll find pleasantly affordable rooms (singles L25,000, doubles L50,000; half pension: add L15,000 per person; full pension: add L20,000). Closer to the bus stop is **La Paloma Blanca,** Via Figuli, 5 (tel. 256 67), across the street from Terme di Sciacca. (Singles L42,000, doubles L72,000. Breakfast L3000. MC, Visa.) If you're hungry, the best deal can be found at the **Ristorante Miramare,** Piazza Scandaliato, 6 (tel. 260 50). True to its name, the restaurant has a great view of the port and water. Pizza from L7000, *menù* L20,000.

Sciacca can be reached by **bus** from Agrigento's Piazza Roselli. Busline **Lumia,** Via Pindaro (tel. (0922) 204 14), will make the trip for L6800 (Mon.-Sat., 8 per day, L11,500 roundtrip). The **tourist office AAST,** Corso Vittorio Emanuele, 84 (tel. 211 82), should be able to answer any tourist questions. Public **telephones** can be found at Via Roma, 38 (tel. 210 62). **Telephone code:** 0925), while the **post office** is on P. Rossi (tel. 22 30 00). **Emergency assistance** is on Via Figuli (tel. 234 99). The **Carabinieri** can be reached at tel. 210 10 and 210 60.

■ ■ ■ ENNA

This mountaintop city just might be Sicily's best-kept secret. Soaring above the poorest and only landlocked province in Sicily, Enna invites you to view the life of the island's interior. Ennans are prone to modesty and self-deprecation, and coastal Sicilians view them with a condescending eye, a combination which has kept Enna out of the Sicilian touristic limelight for years. But Enna is a cool, animated city with numerous *piazze* offering panoramas of the surrounding countryside. Ennans like to point out that theirs is a city of true tranquility, and the only provincial capital without a Mafia presence. The town has been a popular military base throughout history, passing from the hands of its original inhabitants through Greek, Roman, Arab, Norman, Lombard, and Bourbon rule. The only vestiges of this past are a huge medieval castle, a Lombard tower, and a curiously remodeled cathedral.

ORIENTATION AND PRACTICAL INFORMATION

Enna, located at the center of the island, is known as the "navel of Sicily." It is easily accessible by bus (from Catania and Palermo) and train (from Catania). See listings below. To get to the center of Enna from the bus depot, turn right onto Viale Diaz in front of the station and then take another right onto the downward sloping Corso

Sicilia; walk until Via Sant'Agata branches off to the right. This runs directly into **Via Roma,** Enna's main strip, at P. Matteotti. Via Roma then leads past **Piazza Vittorio Emanuele** and up to the **Castello di Lombardia** on the left; to the right it winds through a residential and shopping district, eventually coming to an end in the vicinity of the **Torre di Federico II.**

Tourist Office: AAPIT, Via Roma, 413 (tel. 52 82 88). One of Sicily's best. Extremely informative and well organized. Pick up the fine map of Enna. Open Mon.-Sat. 9am-1pm. **ASST,** P. Colajanni, 6 (tel. 261 19 or 50 08 75), 100m up from AAPIT and to the right. Smaller, but also well organized. Open Tues.-Fri. 8am-2pm and 4:30-7:30pm (winter 4-7pm), Mon. and Sat. 8am-2pm.
Police: tel. 112. **Carabinieri:** Corso Sicilia, 57 (tel. 50 12 67).
Post Office: Via Volta, 1 (tel. 50 09 50). Take a left off Via Roma just before the AAPIT, and walk to the right behind the building labeled "Provincia." Open Mon.-Fri. 8:10am-5:30pm, Sat. 8:10am-1:20pm. **Postal Code:** 94100.
Telephones: Enna has plenty of telephone booths scattered around the city, or try **Albergo Sicilia,** P. Colajanni. **Telephone Code:** 0935.
Currency Exchange: Banks along Via Roma, between P. Vittorio Emanuele and P. Umberto I. You can also change money at the post office (8:10am-5pm).
Trains: From: Catania (12 per day, 1hr., L7200) and Palermo (7 per day, 2hr., L12,700), but Enna's train station is 5km downhill from the center of town. Fortunately there are 11 buses per day connecting the station to the city center (schedule posted in the train station, L1500).
Buses: SAIS, Viale Diaz (tel. 50 09 02), a few blocks outside the city center. Open daily 6am-2pm and 3:15-8:30pm. From Palermo or Catania: voyaging from the south requires transfers at either Caltanissetta (Mon.-Sat., 4 per day, 1hr., L4000) or Gela (2 per day, 1hr., L8600). Buses leave Catania from the train station (7 per day, 3 on Sun., 1¼hr., L8000), and Palermo from Via P. Balsamo, 16 (3 per day, 2 on Sun., 2hr., L11,000). From Enna, buses to: Caltanisetta (4 per day, L4000), Catania (7 per day, 3 on Sun., L8000), and Palermo (4 per day, L11,000).
Emergencies: tel. 113. **Hospital: Ospedale Umberto I,** tel. 451 11. **Guardia Medica:** tel. 454 89. **Ambulance:** tel. 219 33.

ACCOMMODATIONS AND FOOD

Enna is expensive; don't sleep here if you can help it. If an overnight stay is inevitable, however, the town's only hotel is the **Hotel Sicilia,** P. Colajanni, 7 (tel. 50 08 50), on Via Roma past the AAPIT office. This modern building is posh and clean, with a great view, phone, hairdryer, and TV in every room. (Singles L80,000. Doubles L150,000. Triples L200,000. All-you-can-eat breakfast included. All rooms with shower. AmEx, MC, Visa.) If there are no vacancies at the hotel, or too many vacancies in your wallet, head down the mountain to the smaller (and cheaper) town of Pergusa (see Near Enna, page 538).

Enna's most famous food is its *piacentino* cheese: sharp, spicy, and available at **Centro Formaggi** on Via Mercato Sant'Antonio, 33 (tel. 50 07 29). Just follow your nose to P. Umberto, off Via Roma. (Open 7:30am-1pm and 5-8:30pm.) There's also a **TOPS Discount Alimentare,** up the steps behind the bus station. **Ristorante La Fontana** at Via Volturo, 6 (tel. 254 65), is well known for its Sicilian cuisine. The specialty is *risotto all'Ennese* (with tomatoes, mushrooms and olives, L7000). Also good is the *cavatelli alla Siciliana* (tomato, eggplant, mushrooms, and hot peppers, L7000). (*Menù* L20,000. Cover L2000, service 15%. Open daily 9am-4pm and 7:30pm-midnight. AmEx, MC, Visa.) **Tiffany Ristorante-Pizzeria** Via Roma, 467 (tel. 50 13 68), offers typical Sicilian cuisine and pizza (from L5000) a few steps from the *duomo* (Open Fri.-Wed. 11am-4pm and 7pm-2am. AmEx, MC, Visa.)

SIGHTS AND ENTERTAINMENT

Via Roma ascends through the old city, leading to the **cathedral.** Founded in 1307 and renovated in the 16th century, it has a slender Baroque façade. The polygonal transepts, the apses, and the south door remain from the original medieval structure. Behind the cathedral, the small **Museo Alessi** (tel. 240 72) displays the *duomo's* treasures and some Greco-Roman artifacts and medieval paintings. (Open Tues.-Sun. 9am-1pm and 3:30-7pm. Free.) Across Piazza Mazzini from the *duomo* is the nearby **Museo Varisano** (tel. 247 20), which exhibits pottery shards and figurines. (Open daily 9am-6:30pm. Free.)

The **Castello di Lombardia** (tel. 50 09 62), constructed on a 5000-year-old foundation at the eastern end of town, was built by Frederick II to maintain control of the center of the island. Six of the original 20 towers remain. One of the three courtyards is now used as an open-air theater. The castle offers a thrilling view of the characteristic Sicilian landscape. (Open daily 9am-6pm.) The **Torre di Federico II,** an octagonal lookout with excellently preserved Gothic vaulting, rises 24m at the opposite edge of the city, surrounded by the city's **public garden.** (Garden open daily 9am-8pm. Free.) A secret tunnel once connected the tower with the Castello di Lombardia. To get to the tower, walk along Via Roma past the Upim department store (away from P. Vittorio Emmanuele). Via Roma eventually turns into Via della Libertà. Turn left onto Viale 4 Novembre to reach the foot of the public gardens.

One of Enna's largest festivals is the **Festa della Madonna.** Held on July 2, it is marked by the incessant popping of firecrackers and the eating of renowned *mastazzoli* (apple cookies). Parties also accompany the feasts of **Saint Anna** on the last Sunday in July and **Saint Valverde** on the last Sunday in August. Enna's most renowned festival, however, is its Easter **Holy Week.** Different groups and religious orders don unique costumes for the Holy Week parade, the *"Processione del Venerdì Santo,"* revealing the Spanish influence once quite strong in Sicily.

Down the hill at the **Autodromo di Pergusa,** processions are of another (faster) sort. Pergusa's racetrack hosts international Gran Prix auto races year-round. The most important ones take place between June and October (for info, call 256 60 for the *Ente Autodromo di Pergusa* in Enna, Piazza V. Emanuele, 24, or the Secretary of the Autodromo in Pergusa at tel. 54 10 69).

■ NEAR ENNA

PERGUSA

Enna's lack of cheap hotels is compensated for by its proximity to the wondrous village of Pergusa. What this tiny haven lacks in size (Pergusa could be called a "one-horse town" if it had even that), it makes up in charisma. You can't walk down Via Nazionale (the main drag) twice without being recognized by the locals who sit on the roadside eating *gelato.* Pergusa provides the perfect nightcap to a day spent wandering the streets of Enna. It can be reached from Enna proper by **bus #4,** which makes the 7-km trip from the bus station and from Via Roma just below P. Vittorio Emanuele (L600). Buses leave every 1½ to 2 hours, but can be erratic. **AST buses** also make the trip (5 per day, L4600). To stay in Pergusa, search out the **Miralogo,** Contrada da Staglio (tel. 54 12 72), right before the entrance to the town. With soft towels, cheery bedspreads, and telephones in every room, Miralogo is a pleasant stay (singles L40,000; doubles L60,000; all rooms with bath). Breakfast L3000.

Pergusa might be the place to head for dinner from Enna. The **Proserpina,** Via Nazionale, 8 (tel. 54 10 31), is the local favorite. Although the specialty is seafood, the cheap pizzas (from L4000) are superb. *Menù* L17,000. Ask to sit in the courtyard out back. (Open 9:30am-4pm and 7pm-1am. AmEx.) Pack a lunch at the **mini-market** at Via Nazionale, 16 (tel. 54 11 88), and picnic in the pine-forest **Parchi Attrezzati** (on the far side of the course). (Market open 6:30am-2:30pm and 4-10pm.)

The **post office** can be found at Via Nazionale, 125 (tel. 54 15 12), as can the **pharmacy** of Dr. Persico (tel. 54 13 59; open 9am-1pm and 5-9pm). For emergencies, contact the **Carabinieri** (tel. 54 10 26).

PIAZZA ARMERINA AND VILLA ROMANA DEL CASALE

The golden Baroque buildings of **Piazza Armerina** rise gracefully on three knolls overlooking the Ennese countryside. Nearby is the **Villa Romana del Casale,** an ancient Roman country house that preserves some of the ancient world's finest mosaics, a must-see for anyone within a 100-mile radius.

Orientation and Practical Information Piazza Armerina is a 45-minute **bus** ride from Enna (7 per day, 3 on Sun. and holidays; L3700, round-trip L6100). Buses also run directly from Piazza Armerina to Palermo, Catania, and Syracuse. To reach Ragusa on the way east or south, take a bus to the petrochemical wasteland of Gela (several per day, 1hr., L4600). From Gela, the best option is the train (7 per day, 1½hr., L5700). Be sure to allow time to catch the last bus out (around 4pm), or you'll find yourself stranded. In general, buses in Piazza Armerina gather in **Piazza Generale Cascino,** which sits on the new city's principal street, Via Generale Muscarà. The streets to follow to get to the old city (an easy walk) are well indicated by a yellow sign at the edge of P. Cascino. City **tourist info,** Via Cavour, 15 (tel. 68 02 01; fax 68 45 65), is marked from Piazza Garibaldi in the *centro.* (Open Mon.-Sat. 8am-2pm.) **Pharmacy: Quattrino,** P. Garibaldi, 31 (tel. 68 00 44), on the way to the *duomo.* (Open 9am-1pm and 4-8pm.) **Carabinieri:** tel. 68 20 14. **Hospital: Ospedale Chiello,** tel. 98 11 11. **Pronto Intervento:** tel. 113. **Telephone code:** 0935.

Accommodations and Food Piazza Armerina has few inexpensive accommodations, but if you're stuck, try the **Hotel Villa Romana,** Piazza Alcide de Gasperi, 18 (tel./fax 68 29 11), at the bottom of Via Roma, which begins in P. Garibaldi (Singles with bath L60,000. Doubles with bath L90,000. Triple L105,000.) They also offer some budget rooms with common bathrooms and showers. (Singles L25,000-45,000; doubles L50,000; breakfast L10,000.) Unfortunately, these go fast and there are very few to begin with. Out by the turn-off for the mosaics (4km outside the city), the **Trattoria La Ruota** (tel. 68 05 42) also runs an informal **campground.** The owners are helpful, the food yummy, and the price negotiable (L2000-4000 per person; bring your own tent). Catch the bus from Piazza Armerina to Villa Romana and ask the bus driver to let you off at the *trattoria.* **Picnics** are generally the best eating option in Piazza Armerina. **Supermercato Gemma** on Via Gen. Muscarà, 22 (tel. 68 20 70), a few blocks from the buses, offers good deals and friendly service. (Open Mon.-Sat. 8am-1pm and 4-8pm.) If the urge for restaurant fare is simply too strong to resist, head for **Pepito** at Via Roma, 140 (tel. 827 37); right next to the Hotel Villa Romana. Pizza (in the evening only) from L4500. Cover L2000. (Open noon-3:30pm and 7-11pm. AmEx, MC, Visa.)

Sights and Entertainment The *villa* lies 5½km southwest of town. Be sure to pick up a guide (along with a map) at the tourist office in Enna or Piazza Amerina—it will help you find your way around and discover what's what. The *villa* was probably a hunting lodge of Maximanius Heraclius, co-emperor with Diocletian at the turn of the 4th century AD. Occupied until the Arab period, sacked in 1160, and buried by a landslide soon after, it remained undiscovered until 1916. The *villa* houses 40 rooms of incredibly vivid **mosaics,** the largest and most intact of their kind in the world. They range through every conceivable kind of theme: chariot races, big-game hunts, pudgy Cupids fishing, Ulysses blinding the Cyclops, and even the Ancient Sicilian Bikini Team: the bizarre **Sala delle 10 Ragazze** (Room of the Ten Maidens) portrays a group of women in skimpy outfits playing catch, lifting weights, and crowning themselves with garlands. The so-called **Cubicolo Scena Erotica,** near the exit to the villa, is hardly a big deal—you've seen much steamier on *Melrose Place.* Other mosaics not to miss are the stunning **Ambulacrum of the Great Hunt,** with the gorgeous personification of Africa in the right-hand exedra, the **Diaeta of Arion,** with the hero Arion riding on a dolphin, and the **Vestibule of Polyphemus.** From May 1 to September 6 buses (L500) shuttle back and forth between the villa and Piazza Armerina. (Departures on the hour, 9-11am and 4-6pm; buses return on the ½hr., 9:30-11:30am and 4:30-6:30pm.) Flag the bus down as it rolls past the Hotel Villa Romana (see below), or catch it at Piazza Generale Cascino. (Villa open daily 9am-1hr. before sunset. Admission L2000; under 18 and over 60

RAGUSA

free.) If you're really taken by the mosaics, ask for info about some of the other nearby ancient *ville*, such **Morgantina, Ardone,** and **Nicosia.**

Piazze filled with pine, eucalyptus, poplar, and cedar trees punctuate Piazza Armerina's narrow medieval streets. In the center is **P. Garibaldi,** with several 18th-century buildings. The **duomo** (1627) at the summit of the town peers down with its imposing Baroque façade (17th-18th c.) and a 15th-century Gothic-Sicilian belfry. Inside, revel in the refreshing white and pale-blue interior. The painted crucifix and the Madonna in the chapel to the left both date from the 15th century. Above the high altar, a baroque tabernacle contains a Byzantine icon of the *Madonna della Vittoria,* a gift of Pope Nicholas II. It is carried in procession during the **Feast of the Assumption** (August 15). The Feast of the Assumption is preceded on August 13-14 by the **Palio dei Normanni,** a costumed horse race commemorating the presentation of the key to the city to the Norman Count Roger III.

■■■ RAGUSA

The provincial capital of Ragusa has quietly avoided the frenetic pace of other Sicilian cities, simultaneously managing to escape inclusion on most tourist itineraries. The city has grown uphill from its beginnings at **Ragusa Ibla,** so that walking the streets is tantamount to following an architectural timeline. The old city begins with a well-preserved Baroque center, constructed 300 years ago after the town was completely destroyed by an earthquake, then winds up and down the hills toward a frenzy of construction in the new city, near the station. Along the way, the city evolves from an orderly grid of cement offices into a chaotic weave of terraced alleys, and displays examples of all of the intervening stylistic periods. The citizens seem to acknowledge the break between the new and old town: the young hang out in the former, while their elders congregate in the latter. Though the Ragusan pace of life is somewhere between comatose and dead, the old city will reward the dedicated street-wanderer with architectural treasures and near-perfect solitude.

ORIENTATION AND PRACTICAL INFORMATION

The train and bus stations are in P. del Popolo and nearby P. Gramsci, respectively. To reach the city center from these adjacent *piazze,* hang a left as you exit either station onto **Viale Emanuele Lena,** and follow it through P. Libertà and over the Ponte Senatore F. Pennavaria, the northernmost of three bridges crossing the Vallata Santa. The road over the bridge becomes **Via Roma,** which ends at the other side of town. **Corso Italia,** off Via Roma, leads downhill for several blocks, changes into Via 24 Maggio, and ends at the **Chiesa di Santa Maria delle Scale.** From here, stairs and roads zig-zag the rest of the way down the hill to **Ragusa Ibla.**

> **Tourist Office: AAPIT,** Via Capitano Bocchieri, 33 (tel. 62 14 21), in Ragusa Ibla; signposted in P. del Duomo. **Ufficio d'Informazione,** Via Collodi (tel. 65 33 00), has similar handouts and location. Both offices provide brochures and city maps, as well as info on nearby beaches and sights. Both open Mon.-Sat. 8am-2pm.
>
> **Police:** tel. 62 34 00 or 112.
>
> **Post Office:** P. Matteotti (tel. 62 40 43), two blocks down Corso Italia from Via Roma. Open Mon.-Sat. 8am-7:30pm. The post office also changes money 7am-1:20pm. **Postal Code:** 97100.
>
> **Telephones: Telecom,** V. Maiorana, on the city side of Ponte Vecchio (the middle bridge). Open Mon.-Sat. 9am-12:30pm and 4:30-8pm. **Telephone Code:** 0932.
>
> **Currency Exchange: Banks** on Via Lena and Via Roma. Outside of banking hours, try **Ragusana Viaggi** (tel. 65 43 31) on Via Lena near the bus station. Open Mon.-Fri. 9am-12:45pm and 4-7:30pm, Sat. 9am-1pm.
>
> **Trains:** From: Syracuse (5 per day, 2¼hr., L8800). There are also five per day from Gela (1½hr., L5700). One or two trains per day make the trip from Agrigento (4hr., L13,800) or Palermo (L22,000).
>
> **Buses: AST** (tel. 62 12 49), in P. Gramsci. Schedules posted on side of building bordering the depot. Buy tickets on bus. **ETNA** to Catania (10 per day, 6 on Sun.;

3hr.; L8900). A ticket office and schedule is located in the GranBar, across from P. Gramsci. AST buses run regularly from Syracuse's Piazzale Marconi (Mon.-Sat. 8 per day, 2 on Sun., 3hr., L7500). From Gela, a connection can be made to Agrigento (4 per day, 1½hr., L9600). From Enna, take the bus to Gela (1½hr., L8600) and then the train (1½hr., L5700). Or you can take the bus to Ragusa—it's L900 more, but Ragusa's train and bus stations are relatively close, and in the case of a *sciopero,* it's a good alternative. To: Siracusa (7 per day), Catania (5 per day), and Palermo (3 per day).

Emergencies: tel. 113. **Hospital: Ospedale Civile,** right across from the train station on Via Leonardo da Vinci (tel. 62 14 10 during the day; tel. 62 39 46 for nighttime and holiday emergencies). **Ambulance: Ambulanza Croce Bianca,** Via L. da Vinci, 29 (tel. 65 26 60). 24-hr. service.

ACCOMMODATIONS AND CAMPING

Hotel San Giovanni, Via Transpontino, 3 (tel. 62 10 13), off the center bridge on the station side. A quiet, clean hotel with great beds and marble bathrooms. TV in every room. Singles L33,000, with bath L50,000. Doubles L48,000, with bath L80,000. Prices include breakfast. AmEx, MC, Visa

Hotel Jonio, Via Risorgimento, 49 (tel. 62 43 22). Closest to the train station; walk down Viale Sicilia from P. del Popolo. Darker than the San Giovanni, but the showers are strong and hot. A TV in every room, and a map of Ragusa on the wall in the lobby. Singles L34,000, with bath L58,000. Doubles L56,000, with bath L89,000. Breakfast L7000. AmEx, MC, Visa.

Camping: Ragusa's campgrounds are at Marina, 20km to the south. Tumino buses (tel. 62 31 84) run regularly from P. Gramsci in Ragusa to P. Duca degli Abruzzi in Marina (30min., L2900, round-trip L4900). **Baia del Sole,** Lungomare Andrea Doria (tel. 23 98 44). L6000 per person, L6000 per small tent, L9000 per large tent, L7000 per person with sleeping bag. **Campeggio Internazionale,** Via Duilio (tel. 23 91 18), runs L7000 per person, L7000 per small tent, L10,000 per large tent. Oct.-May prices drop by L500-1000. Buy supplies at SMA in Ragusa before heading out (see below).

FOOD

While in Ragusa, make a point to try some *panatigghie,* thin pastries filled with cocoa, cinnamon, and ground meat. Unfortunately, they aren't cheap, and neither are the *trattorie* where they're sold. If you're low on cash, visit the immense **SMA Supermarket** on Viale Sicilia, downhill to the right from the train station. (Open Mon. Tues., Thurs., and Sat. 8:30am-2pm and 5-9pm; Wed. 8:30am-1:30pm; and Fri. 8:30am-8pm. AmEx.)

Pizzeria La Grotta, Via G. Cartia (tel. 25 57 95), the 2nd right off Via Roma at the red sign. A back-alley joint with melt-in-your-mouth pizza (L2000 per slice) and *calzoni* (L2000). Open Thurs.-Tues. 6am-2pm and 5pm-midnight.

La Valle, Via Risorgimento, 70 (tel. 22 93 41). From the station, take a right onto Viale Sicilia, then walk downhill past the gas station. *The* place young Ragusans recommend, though on the pricey side. Picture menu shows off their wide variety of pizza L6000-8000. Pasta L5500-8000. *Secondi* L9000-16,000. Cover L2500. Open Sat.-Thurs. noon-3pm and 7:30pm-midnight. AmEx, MC, Visa.

Caffè Trieste, Corso Italia, 76 (tel. 62 10 61), across from the post office. Superior Sicilian pastries (L1500-2000) and perfect iced *espresso* (L1700). Their specialty is *focaccia* (L2500). No seats, just pit-stop consumption. Open Mon.-Sat. 6am-10pm or earlier, depending on business.

Pub Shaker, at the beginning of Lungomare Mediterraneo, is the resort's most animated eatery and serves a variety of *panini,* including the oddly stuffed *tropicale* (with *prosciutto,* pineapple, lettuce, and mustard). Open daily 7pm-4am.

SIGHTS AND ENTERTAINMENT

Judge Ragusa and Ibla by their exteriors—church interiors rarely match their elaborate Baroque façades. The many side streets delight with their ornamented doorways. The upper town boasts an **Archaeology Museum** (tel. 62 29 63) that lies one floor down and in back of the STANDA off Via Roma, with artifacts from the nearby Syracusan colony of Camarina. Go down the stairs to the ground level under the bridge, turn right, walk up the road a few steps, and take another right. If you see graffiti along the way, you're on the right path. (Open Mon.-Sat. 9am-2pm and 3-6:30pm, Sun. 9am-1pm and 3-6:30pm. Winter afternoon hours are 3-5:30pm. Free.) Via Santa Anna, your first right off Via Roma, is crossed by **Via della Frecce** and **Via dei Vespri,** two small streets lined with some of Ragusa's most charming homes.

To get to Ragusa Ibla, you can take the #3 city bus (L600, tickets in *tabacchi*), which leave every hour on the half-hour from in front of the train station at P. del Popolo, and every hour on the hour from Via Roma. The bus ride is fairly long; a prettier and quicker alternative is to make the steep 10-min. walk from the Chiesa di Santa Maria delle Scale, at the very bottom of Corso Italia (Via 24 Maggio).

The stairs at Santa Maria offer a stellar view of Ragusa Ibla, crowned by a monastery and the 18th-century dome of **San Giorgio.** (Proper dress required: no shorts, tank tops, or mini-skirts.) Descend under the roadway to P. Repubblica, at the bottom of 200m of tricky staircases. The road to the right circumscribes the town, passing abandoned monasteries and a lush valley of farmland. On the way, try to spot the humorous balcony carvings. You will eventually come to the beautiful **P. del Duomo di San Giorgio,** at the top of the city. Corso 25 Aprile runs downhill from the bottom of this *piazza* and ends at the **Giardino Ibleo,** home to two churches and walks shaded by palm trees. Below the entrance to the gardens is the **Portale di San Giorgio,** one of the few 14th-century structures to survive the 1693 earthquake. An **antique market** takes place the last Sunday of each month at Giardino Ibleo.

In summer, any citizen who owns a swimsuit spends the weekend at **Marina di Ragusa,** a drab resort strip. Autolinee Tumino (tel. 62 31 84) runs 14 buses per day to Marina (last departure 8:30pm; last return 10pm; L2900, round-trip L4900). A complete schedule is posted in the Polleria Giarrosto in Marina's P. Duca degli Abruzzi. In the same *piazza,* savor Marina's best **gelato** at Delle Rose, where the scoops are so enormous they give you *two* cones.

THE EASTERN COAST

■■■ SYRACUSE (SIRACUSA)

The most beautiful and noble of the Greek cities.
—Titus Livius (Livy), on Syracuse

If you were visiting Sicily in ancient times, Syracuse would have been *the* principal attraction. Founded by the Greeks in 734 BC on the island of Ortigia, the town grew quickly, swelling over the 40m strait that separated it from *terra firma,* and extending into a much larger and even more prosperous development (Neapolis) on the mainland. From the 6th to 3rd centuries BC, Syracuse was arguably the greatest city in the world, cultivating such luminaries as Theocritus, Archimedes, and the great Greek lyric poet, Pindar. The city also boasts the creation of both the world's largest theater and the first known cookbook. That, however, was in antiquity—today's *Siracusani* can only lament their city's millennia-long decline. Some say the city began to slide in 668 AD, when the bathing emperor Constans was bludgeoned to death with a soap dish. Others set the fatal date at 211 BC: Syracuse just hasn't been the same since being sacked by the Romans. On the bright side (for modern tourists, that is), the Roman sack was not without the benefits of cultural diffusion. Indeed, today Syracuse combines the classical romance of Rome with a vacation island climate. Perhaps the city can no longer claim to be the center of the civilized world, but the busy *caffè* and businesses of Ortigia, the latter-day *palazzi* of Neapolis, and the extensive archaeological remains are well worth seeing.

ORIENTATION AND PRACTICAL INFORMATION

Syracuse rests on and off the southeastern coast of Sicily. Most of the historic city is on the island of **Ortigia,** which is connected to the mainland by two bridges. The principal bridge leads to **Corso Umberto** on the mainland, which runs through **Piazzale Marconi,** the main bus terminal. Coming from the train station, the first left off this Piazzale (Via Catania) leads to **Corso Gelone,** cutting through the modern city and out towards the **archaeological park.** The other important street off P. Marconi is **Via Francesco Crispi,** which leads to the train station.

Tourist Office: APT, Via San Sebastiano, 43 (tel. 677 10). Take a right onto Viale Teocrito at the end of Corso Gelone; the office is down a street to the left (near the catacombs). It's a 15-min. walk from the bus and train stations, but they have maps, brochures, and speak just enough English to get by. Open Mon.-Sat. 9am-1pm and 3-6:30pm. Also try **AAT** at Via Maestranza, 33 (tel. 652 01), near P. Archimede in Ortigia. Open Mon.-Sat. 9am-1pm.

Police: Via S. Sebastiano (tel. 46 35 66).

Post Offices: P. delle Poste, 15 (tel. 684 16), left after you cross the bridge to Ortigia. The larger one (tel. 669 95) holds *fermo posta.* Open Mon.-Sat. 8:15am-7:40pm. The smaller office across the street (tel. 689 73) will change money Mon.-Fri. 8:30am-5:30pm, Sat. 8:30am-1pm. **Postal Code:** 96100.

Telephones: Telecom (SIP) is now located on Via Teracati (near the Motel Agip), a hell of a long walk past the end of Corso Gelone. Open daily 8am-8pm. Better to try the Bar Belcaffè Tamanaco, P. Marconi, 19, or else make do with street phones. There are also phones in many of Syracuse's hotels, as well as a cluster in front of the train station. **Telephone Code:** 0931.

Currency Exchange: The city has plenty of **banks,** especially in Ortigia. Also try the ticket office in the train station, where the rates are just as good as the banks'. Open 7am-8:30pm. The smaller post office in P. delle Poste handles transactions.

Trains: Via Francesco Crispi, midway between the old city and the archaeological park. To: Catania (12 per day, 1½hr., L6700); Taormina (11 per day, 2hr., L10,900); Messina (9 per day, 3hr., L14,400); Ragusa (6 per day, 3hr., L9200); Noto (10 per day, L3200).

Buses: SAIS ticket office at Via Trieste, 28 (tel. 667 10). To: Catania (12 per day, 3 on Sun., 1¼hr., L6100, L10,300 round-trip); Palermo (5 per day, 1 on Sun., 4hr., L20,000, round-trip L30,000); and Noto (11 per day, 3 on Sun., 1hr., L3700, round-trip L6100). **AST** ticket office (tel. 46 27 11), next door to the post office in Ortigia. To: Catania (14 per day, 7 on Sun., L10,300); Noto (14 per day, 4 on Sun., L6100); and Piazza Armerina (7am, 3hr., L11,700; round trip L19,500); Ragusa (6 per day, 2 on Sun., L7500; round trip L12,700). Catch the buses at Piazzale Marconi, where you can buy bus tickets (AST and SAIS) from the newsstand located behind the *fermata* sign. **City buses** leave from Piazza della Poste.

Bookstore: Il Libraio, Via Catania, 13 (tel. 46 44 20), has multi-lingual books as well as the occasional tourist guide. Open Mon.-Sat. 8:30am-1pm and 4-8pm.

Emergencies: tel. 113. **Hospital:** Via Testaferrata (tel. 685 55). **Late-Night Emergencies: Guardia Medica,** on Via Reno just a block from the station (tel. 225 55). **Pharmacy:** La Madonnina, Corso Gelone, 1 (tel. 664 28). Open 8:30am-1pm and 4:30-8pm.

ACCOMMODATIONS AND CAMPING

Syracuse offers plenty of cheap accommodations in the new city and by the train station, but, if you'd prefer seashells and cobblestones, a room in charismatic Ortigia is well worth the expense. Be wary of the area around the station at night.

Pensione Bel Sit, Via Oglio, 5 (tel. 602 45; signposted off Corso Gelone), is close to the train station. Modern and basic, with white rooms and personable proprietors. Singles L30,000, with bath L35,000. Doubles L40,000, with bath L50,000. Reserve one week ahead in Aug.

Albergo Aretusa, Via F. Crispi, 73 (tel. 242 11), right outside the train station. Worth the higher prices; spacious rooms and friendly management. English spoken. Singles L38,000, with bath L45,000. Doubles L55,000, with bath L60,000.

Hotel Centrale, Corso Umberto, 141 (tel./fax 605 28); follow signs from the train station. If your train from Rome gets in at 1am, this is just the place to tide you over until the daylight hours. Modern and clean. Singles L25,000. Double L40,000. Showers included.

Camping: Fontane Bianche, Viale dei Lidi, 476 (tel. 79 03 56), near the beach of the same name. Take bus #21 or 22 (L600) from the post office. 20km from Syracuse. L7000 per person, L7000 per small tent, L10,000 per large tent, L5000 per sleeping bag. Open May-Oct. Buy basics at a Syracuse supermarket before you go.

FOOD

Pizza is about the only budget option in Syracuse other than the **market** on Via Trento, near the Temple of Apollo. (Open Mon.-Sat. 7am-early afternoon.) For staples, try the **Supermercato Linguanti,** Corso Umberto, 174 (tel. 46 29 24), across from the Hotel Centrale just a block from the station. (Open Mon.-Sat. 7:30am-1pm and 3:30-8pm.) You can also try the **Supermercato SMA** on Corso Gerone, 33 (open 8:30am-1pm and 4:30-8pm). After your meal, head for the pastry shop of **Corrado Costanzo,** Via Silvio Spaventa, 7-9 (tel. 83 52 43), near the new *municipio*, where you can enjoy marzipan, nougat, almond sweets, and quince jam. Ice cream lovers will dig the specialty flavors: jasmine, rose, and tangerine. (Open daily 8am-2pm and 4pm-midnight; in winter closes at 10pm.)

Spaghetteria do Scugghiu, Via D. Sciná, 11, off P. Archimede. An ancient Syracusan institution. Eighteen delicious types of spaghetti, all L6000. Try the *spaghetti a modo nostro* (L6000) for a special treat. Liter of wine L5000. *Secondi* L8000-12,000. Cover L1500. Open Tues.-Sun. noon-3pm and 7pm-midnight.

Trattoria Paolina, Via F. Crispi, 14 (tel. 70 23 21), up from P. Marconi. No tourists in sight; just you, the old men who sit outside, and the warbling array of birds in the cage near the front door. *Primi* L4000-5000. *Secondi* L8000-9000. *Menù* L20,000. Open Mon.-Sat. 11am-3pm and 7-10pm, Sun. 11am-3pm.

Trattoria la Foglia, Via Capodieci, 29 (tel. 662 33), at the far end of Ortigia, near the Fontana Aretusa. Sicily's chic-est vegetarian restaurant has been favorably reviewed by, among others, the *New York Times.* Expensive. Pasta L15,000 and up; full meals L30,000-40,000. Cover L3000. Open daily 10:30am-3:30pm and 6:30-11pm, closed Tues. during winter. AmEx, MC, Visa.

Ristorante Cartagine, Via Catania, 19 (tel. 222 03). Italian cuisine with seafood specialties. Cheap pizza menu from L4000-8000. James Bond fans should go for the "007 Pizza" (wurstel, mushroom, egg, ham, and olives). *Menù* L20,000. Open noon-3:30pm and 6pm-midnight; pizza served only in evenings. AmEx, MC, Visa.

SIGHTS

The historic sights are concentrated in two areas a few km apart: the enclosed archaeological park in the north part of town, and the island of Ortigia.

Ortigia

From the main approach to the island, Corso Umberto, cross over the bridge into Ortigia and you'll find yourself in a breezy island refuge, with no sign of the sweltering mainland. The ruins of two Greek temples and several Gothic and Renaissance churches and palaces are sprinkled along the winding streets of the island. Just after the bridge to Ortigia are the ruins of the **Temple of Apollo,** the oldest peripteral (with columns running all the way around it) Doric temple in Sicily (c. 575 BC). All that remain are two columns supporting a piece of entablature and parts of the *cella* wall enclosed in a fence. The lawns surrounding the ruins are in much better shape.

Up Corso Matteotti to the right is **Piazza Archimede,** the principal square of the old city. The partially moss-covered **Fountain of Diana** spits forth a gurgling trickle of water amidst its whinnying horses and fish-riders. The 15th-century **Palazzo Lanzo** (#6) is graced by original Gothic windows and a beautiful 14th-century Catalàn staircase in the courtyard. Down Via dei Montalto, a small passageway capped by a tiny portal leads to a fantastic external view of the **Palazzo Montalto** (1397), the fanciest of the Gothic palaces in town, with triple windows set in pointed arches decorated Arabic-style.

The **duomo** (P. del Duomo) is one of Italy's most extraordinary buildings. More than 2300 years separate the 18th-century baroque façade from the attached 5th-century BC **Temple of Athena,** and the intervening centuries made their own additions. The cumulative effect is the representation of every period of Italian architecture. Once admired by Cicero, the temple was converted to a three-aisled Christian *basilica* in the 7th century. The columns were embedded in a solid wall, and arches were carved out of the interior (as in Agrigento's Temple of Concord). Of the 34 original columns, 26 remain, not only on the sides but also in the entrance and in the Byzantine chapel at the end of the north aisle. The 16th-century wooden ceiling is inscribed with an excerpt from a papal bull issued by Leo X in 1517 asserting the importance of the church. The *duomo* is open to the public (daily 7am-1pm and 4-8pm). Electronic audio-visual info booths (L400) give mini-lectures on the cathedral.

P. del Duomo, in front of the cathedral, is lined with fragrant oleander trees and elegant *palazzi*. At #24, the graceful façade of the **Palazzo Benevantano,** reconstructed in 1788, conceals a serpentine balcony. At the far end of the square, wiggly columns frame the entrance to the church of **Santa Lucia alla Badia** (1695-1703; open only during church services). Santa Lucia, martyred at the hands of Christian-hating emperor Diocletian in the 3rd century AD, is Syracuse's patron saint.

From the *piazza*, wander down Via Picherale to the ancient **Fonte Aretusa,** a "miraculous" freshwater spring by the sea. Legend has it that the nymph Arethusa escaped from her admirer Alpheus through a tunnel and was transformed into this fountain by the goddess Diana; Alpheus was transformed into the eponymous river in Greece that supposedly feeds this spring via Arethusa's getaway tunnel. Bring some *pane* to feed the ducks and swans that revel in the fresh water. Steps lead from here to the **Foro Vittorio Emanuele,** a tree-lined walk along the harbor.

Walk back into the city from the fountain along Via del Capodieci to reach the opulent **Galleria di Palazzo Bellomo** (#16; tel. 695 11). This 14th- to 15th-century *palazzo* is a treasure trove of all kinds of art: from ornate Sicilian carriages to Byzantine Bible scenes to wax crèches depicting the birth of Christ. Paintings of note are *The Annunciation* by Antonello da Messina, and the gigantic *Burial of Santa Lucia* (1608) by Caravaggio. (Museum open Mon.-Sat. 9am-2pm, Sun. 9am-1pm. No entrance 30min. before close. Admission L2000, under 18 and over 60 free.)

Archaeological Park

Syracuse's larger monuments are in or near the **Archaeological Park** (tel. 662 06) on the north side of town. Follow Corso Gelone until it is intersected by Viale Teocrito; the entrance to the park is down Via Augusto to the left. (Open daily 9am-6pm, winter 9am-3pm. Admission L2000.) The **Greek theater** was originally scooped out of solid rock, with a trapezoidal orchestra, around 475 BC; not long afterwards, the Greek playwright Aeschylus produced his *Persians* here. The orchestra was made semi-circular in 335 BC and enlarged in the 3rd century BC; at 138m in diameter, the theater is among the largest of its type and age known today. The *cavea*, or auditorium, originally had 59 rows of seats (now 42) in nine wedges, seating up to 15,000 people. You can still distinguish the three divisions of the theater—the *cavea*, the semi-circular orchestra pit, and the rectangular stage, which had a two-story permanent set with niches and colonnades. Classical Greek plays are now staged in the theater every other year (see Entertainment below, page 546).

The **Paradise Quarry,** outside the entrance to the Greek theater, is a flowered area in front of the chalk cliffs, with two large grottoes: the **Orecchio di Dionigi** (Ear of Dionysius) and the **Grotta dei Cordari** (Cordmakers' Cave). While the latter is temporarily closed to the public, the former is an artificial grotto of cathedral proportions (65m long, 5-11m wide, 23m high). Its name derives from its resemblance to a giant earlobe and its exceptional acoustics. According to legend, the tyrant Dionysius placed his prisoners here so he could eavesdrop on their conversations.

Exiting the theater/quarry area, you'll come to a fence through which you can see the **Altar of Hieron II** (241-215 BC), which was used for public sacrifices. At 198m by 23m, it is the largest altar known. Walk up the hill and enter the other gate to get to the **Roman amphitheater,** constructed in the 2nd century AD. A stage is occasionally set up in the amphitheater for dance and drama performances; contact the tourist office for more info. As you exit the park, follow the perimeter from the outside (keep the green fence on your left), and make a left onto Via E. Romagnoli to find the **tomb of Archimedes,** which sits behind a fence on a busy street corner. The tomb is dug entirely out of rock, even down to the triangular portico and crude columns at its entrance.

The **Catacombe di San Giovanni,** a few blocks away down Viale Teocrito, are extensive, sporadically frescoed catacombs dug between 315 and 360 AD. Take care not to get lost; one obviously weary traveler reported that a minotaur lurks in the depths of these dark and winding passages. Outside the catacombs lie the ruins of a building said to be the first Christian church in Sicily. The 4th-century **crypt of San Marziano** (the first bishop of Syracuse) lies below the ruins, also home to some hauntingly faded frescoes, complete with Latin inscriptions. (Open Mar. 15-Nov. 14 9am-1pm and 3-6pm; 9am-1pm the rest of the year. Admission L2000, under 10 L1000.) The entire city is rumored to rest on a labyrinth of similar underground galleries, some running all the way to Catania, dug to provide refuge from invaders.

Down Viale Teocrito from the park, on the grounds of the Villa Landolina, the three-year-old **Museo Archeologico Regionale Paolo Orsi,** Viale Teocito, 66 (tel. 46 60 22), displays one of the world's best collections of Greek artifacts. Its holdings consist of a myriad of clay figurines, fossils, and elephant skeletons, and a collection of Greek vases that'll make your head spin. The museum's *pièce de résistance* is the headless statue of "Venus Anadiomene." (Open Tues.-Sat. and 1st and 3rd Sun. of each month 9am-1pm. Admission L2000, under 18 and over 60 free.) Behind the Paolo Orsi, spend a few minutes at the **Museo del Papilo,** Viale Teocrito, 66 (tel. 616 16). With beautiful papyrus products, air-conditioning, and great bathrooms, this museum is a respite for the weary traveler. (Open Mon.-Sat. 9am-1pm and 3-6pm. Free.) Across from the museum is Syracuse's newest monument, the space-age **Santuario della Madonna delle Lacrime** (tel. 640 77). The sanctuary was built to commemorate the period in 1953 when a statue of the Madonna cried for four days on end. The statue's tears were accompanied by several "miracles," and the spot has been a favorite with pilgrims ever since. The sanctuary can be viewed from any part of the city, so if you don't visit it, it will haunt you no matter which way you turn. (Open daily 10:45am-noon and 5-6pm.)

ENTERTAINMENT

Every even-numbered year, **Greek classical drama** is performed in the spectacular setting of the Greek Theater during May and June. The cheapest seats cost L15,000-20,000; ask for details at the APT office. July and August bring all kinds of music and theater to the Roman amphitheater. (Admission L7000-25,000.)

Beachcombers can bus the 18km from Syracuse to **Fontane Bianche** (bus #21 or 22; L600), a crescent-shaped, silken beach frequented by a jet-set crowd. A smaller, less spectacular beach, more popular with the locals, is **Arenella,** 8km from the city (bus #23 from Piazza della Poste, Mon.-Sat. every 45min., Sun. every 1½hr., L600).

Natives rate Ortigia nightlife a *"niente"* (nothin'), but don't give up so easily. Much tax money has been spent on lighting the monuments, and the tiny island becomes a nightly stage for the *passeggiata.* The prime place to promenade is along the port in the **Foro Vittorio Emanuele.** After 8pm, a sea of *Siracusani* mills around by the water, taking breaks in the *caffè,* admiring the trinkets for sale, or gawking at the foreign luxury yachts docked nearby. The APT tourist office organizes an evening boat tour of the port, walking tours of Ortiga by night, and a day trip to Pantalica Necropolis (each L5000 per person). During the summer, boogie at the **Discoteca Speak-Easy** on Via Alberto Mario, 1 (tel. 46 14 33), a left off Via Catania, a few streets down from Piazzale Marconi.

■ NEAR SYRACUSE

In a river gorge about 30km northwest of Syracuse near Sortino, the eerie neolithic necropolis at **Pantalica** merits a visit. The gouged-out sockets of more than one thousand tombs stare out from looming cliffs. Bring a flashlight. Pantalica is most easily accessible by car, but you can take a bus from Syracuse to Sortino and walk the remaining 6km; or call up Zuccalà (tel. 46 42 98), who run half-day tours from Syracuse for L35,000 per person.

NOTO

After suffering complete destruction in a 1693 earthquake, **Noto,** 32km southwest of Syracuse, was rebuilt in Baroque opulence by the wealthy Landolino family. A cascade of palaces and churches, some set atop monumental staircases and others behind tropical gardens, glitters along **Corso Vittorio Emanuele,** which begins as you follow Viale Marconi right above Noto's **Giardini Pubblici** (Public Gardens) through the **Porta Reale** (1838). The APT **tourist office,** P. XVI Maggio (tel. 83 67 44), on Corso Vittorio Emanuele, provides a free map of the most beautiful buildings. (English spoken. Open Tues.-Fri. 8am-2pm and 4-7pm; Mon. 8am-2pm.) The office is located just behind the Fontana d'Ercole (1757). While proud Noto lavishes care on its 18th-century edifices, its Romanesque, Gothic, and modern structures languish in acute disrepair. The first site you reach as you approach the city center from Corso V. Emanuele is the **Chiesa di S. Francesco all'Immacolata** (1704). (Open daily 7:30am-noon and 4-8pm.) The town's most noteworthy sight is the **duomo,** a few blocks before the tourist office. Construction of the cathedral was begun immediately following the earthquake of 1693. Note that it bears the mark "S.P.Q.N." above the huge bronze door, Noto's twist on *senatus populusque romanus*. Inside, you'll be captivated by 12 frescoes of saints glaring down at you from the *duomo's* ceiling. (Open daily 8am-noon and 4-8pm. Dress appropriately.)

Noto is best seen as a daytrip from Syracuse. If you choose to stay over, try the clean and pleasant (if far away) **Albergo Stella,** Via F. Maiore, 44 (tel. 83 56 95). (Singles L30,000. Doubles L50,000, with bath L60,000. Showers L2000.) **Trattoria del Carmine,** Via Ducezio, 9 (tel. 83 87 05), the second right off Via S. La Rosa downhill from P. XVI Maggio, serves home-cooked *ravioli di ricotta* (L5000). *Primi* L5000, *secondi* L9000-13,000. Try the *antipasto rustico* for L3000 (cheese, olives, mushrooms, and dried tomatoes). (Open daily noon-4pm and 7:30pm-midnight; closed Mon. in winter. AmEx, MC, Visa.) Eggplant is a specialty at **Trattoria al Buco,** Via Zanardelli, 1 (tel. 83 81 42), the first left off Corso Vittorio Emanuele after the Porto Reale. Try the *tagliatelle alla melanzane* (egg noodles with eggplant) for L5000. *Menù* L15,000. Cover L1000. The owners also offer *affitte camere* at L60,000 for a double with bath and use of kitchen. (Open daily 10am-3:30pm and 7-10pm.)

SAIS and AST **buses** leave from Syracuse in a steady stream from 5:40am to 7:50pm (26 per day, 7 on Sun., 1hr., L6300 round-trip); the last bus heads back at 9:15pm (7:15pm on Sun.). Noto can also be reached by train (10 per day, 30min., L3200), but it's a 20-minute walk uphill to town from the station. Fine beaches are only 7km away at **Marina di Noto;** buses leave from the Giardini Pubblici (July-Aug. Mon.-Sat. 4 per day, rest of year 2 per day, L1200).

■■■ CATANIA

Catanians claim their city prepares them for every surprise that the rest of the world has to offer. The metropolis is certainly intimidating, with its chaotic traffic, immense, collapsing housing projects, and unfortunate status as Italy's most crime-ridden city. Beneath the squalid veneer of its sooty *palazzi,* however, Catania

CATANIA

reveals an intriguing urban mosaic. This ancient city has been leveled (often by the nearby volcano) and rebuilt many times since its initial founding as a Greek colony in 729 BC; its present appearance dates from reconstruction following the monstrous 1693 earthquake, after which G. B. Vaccarini embellished the city with sumptuous Baroque buildings. Walls of dark volcanic stone lend a characteristic pall to the historic quarters, matched by gray concrete elsewhere. In spite of what you've been told, the city is not merely a den of thieves, but a metropolis with a complex and interesting architectural history.

ORIENTATION AND PRACTICAL INFORMATION

Catania lies between Messina and Syracuse on Sicily's eastern coast. The main street, **Via Etnea,** runs north from P. del Duomo to P. Gioeni, but there is little of interest beyond P. Cavour. From the train station, cross the *piazza* and turn right on the first main street that runs in front of the *piazza*, **Corso Martiri della Libertà.** This becomes bank-laden **Corso Sicilia,** and intersects Via Etnea. From here, budget accommodations and boutiques await to your right; to the left are the **duomo, Via Vittorio Emanuele II** running to the water, and P. dei Martiri.

While Catania is notorious for its crime, it is nevertheless conquerable by the cautious traveler. Don't let crime spoil Catania for you; be particularly wary of anything which might be intended as a distraction: a (staged) fight, someone pointing out a stain on your clothes, even an intentional fender-bender to get you out of your car. Be cautious walking around the city, especially at night; single women should be particularly careful. Leave expensive watches or jewelry somewhere safe (in your hotel, *if secure*), and don't be afraid to make a scene if you feel threatened. Check the General Introduction sections on Safety and Security (page 20) and Women Travelers (page 33) for further important information.

Tourist Offices: AAPIT, Largo Paisiello, 5 (tel. 31 21 24 or 31 77 20), up the hill on Via Pacini, off Via Etnea near the post office. Maps, guides, and cultural information. Open Mon.-Fri. 9am-1pm and 4-7pm, Sat. 9am-1pm. **Branch office** (tel. 53 18 02), in the train station on the tracks. **Airport branch** office, (tel. 34 19 00). Both branches open Mon.-Sat. 8:30am-1pm and 2:15-7:30pm.

Police: tel. 112 or 31 77 33.

Post Office: Via Etnea, 215 (tel. 31 15 06), in the big building next to the Villa Bellini Gardens. Open Mon.-Sat. 8:15am-7:40pm. **Postal Code:** 95100.

Telephones: Telecom (SIP), Corso Sicilia, 67 (tel. 49 01 11). Open Tues.-Sat. 9am-1pm and 4-7pm, Mon. 4-7pm. **Telephone Code:** 095.

Budget Travel: CTS, Via Garofalo, 3 (tel. 715 04 34), up the hill from the intersection of Via Etnea and Corso Sicilia. Student travel information. Open Mon.-Fri. 9:30am-1pm and 4:30-7pm, plus Sat. 9:30am-12:30pm in summer.

Currency Exchange: Banks near the intersection of Via Etnea and Corso Sicilia, or else the **Ufficio Informazioni** near the ticket office in the train station. English spoken. Open 7am-8pm. The post office will change money for you Mon.-Sat. 8:15am-1pm.

American Express: La Duca Viaggi, Via Etnea, 65 (tel. 31 61 55). Cardholders can get emergency cash, pay monthly AmEx bills here, and have incoming mail held for up to one month. Also a good place to inquire about ferries to Malta. Open Mon.-Fri. 9am-1pm and 4-7:30pm, Sat. 9am-noon.

Flights: Fontanarossa (tel. 34 53 67). Take bus #24 from the train station. Daily flights to Malta with **Air Malta,** Via Ventimiglia, 117 (tel. 53 99 83), where Corso Sicilia turns into Corso Martiri della Libertà.

Trains: P. Papa Giovanni XXIII (tel. 53 16 25). To: Syracuse (18 per day, 1¾hr., L6700, *rapido* L11,200); Messina (every hr., 2hr., L7400); Enna (11 per day, 1½hr., L6700); Palermo (5 per day, 4hr., L17,800); Taormina-Giardini Naxos (every hr., 1½hr., L3900). Information window open 7am-9pm.

Buses: Inter-urban buses arrive in front of the train station. **SAIS,** Via D'Amico, 181 (tel. 53 61 68), in the right corner of the *piazza* as you exit the train station. Open 6am-9pm. To: Messina (8 per day, 1½hr., L9500); Taormina (15 per day, 1½hr., L5100); Syracuse (8 per day, 1½hr., L6100); Enna (7 per day, 1¼hr., L8000); Palermo (22 per day, 3hr., L16,000); Agrigento (7 per day, 3hr., L16,000). In the same offices, **ETNA** (tel. 53 27 16) takes you from the train station to Piazza Armerina (7 per day, 2hr., L8600) and Ragusa (10 per day, L8900). **AST,** Via Luigi Sturzo, 220 (tel. 28 12 80), in the left corner of the same *piazza*. Open 6am-7pm. In addition to local routes, service to Syracuse (13 per day, 1½hr., L6100). All bus services are reduced considerably on Sun.

Public Transportation: AMT. From Via Etnea, headed towards the *duomo*, buses #29 and 36 to the central train station; bus D (June-Sept. only) to the beach. From the train station, bus #24 goes to the airport; bus #27 to the beach. Buy tickets (valid 1½hr.; L1300, round trip L2000) at *tabacchi* or newsstands. If you're caught without one, you'll suffer a fine of a cool 60 times the ticket price.

Ferries: To Malta: **Marangolo Viaggi** on Via Vittorio Veneto (tel. 37 66 51). Open Mon.-Sat. 9am-1pm and 3:30-7pm. Student fares from L120,000.

Late-Night Pharmacy: Crocerossa, Via Etnea, 274 (tel. 31 70 53).

Emergencies: tel. 113. **Hospital:** Via Vittorio Emanuele, off Via Plebiscito (tel. 32 65 33). **Guardia Medica:** tel. 726 26 00 (night-time and holidays). **Ambulance: Pronto Soccorso Ambulanze** tel. 49 77 77.

ACCOMMODATIONS

As always, reservations are a good idea in August.

Pensione Gresi, Via Pacini, 28 (tel. 32 27 09), off Via Etnea near Villa Bellini and the post office. Don't let the charred doors on the 1st floor discourage you; the *pensione* on the 3rd floor is *molto pulito*. Rooms have carved ceilings, gorgeous bathrooms, and antique furniture. Singles L35,000, with bath L50,000. Doubles L55,000, with bath L70,000. Breakfast L7000.

Pensione Ferrara, Via Umberto, 66 (tel. 31 60 00; fax 31 30 60), off Via Etnea just a few blocks from Via Pacini. Randomly furnished rooms with high ceilings. Balconies and 3rd floor breezes keep things cool. Singles L34,000, with bath L42,000. Doubles L55,000, with bath L68,000.

Pensione Südland, Via Etnea, 270 (tel. 31 24 94 or 31 13 43), across from the post office. Immense and elegant, though rather noisy and often full. Singles L35,000, with bath L47,000. Doubles L52,000, with bath L66,000. Breakfast L5000.

Pensione Rubens, Via Etnea, 196 (tel. 31 70 73). Clean rooms of Rubenesque proportions. Feed the fish in the lobby tank. Singles L34,000. Doubles L50,000. Triples L60,000.

FOOD

Don't leave Catania without trying their famous eggplant-and-*ricotta* spaghetti, named after Catanese composer Vincenzo Bellini's well-known opera (and TV's favorite barroom regular) *Norma*. Also keep an eye out for another Catanese favorite, extremely small *masculini* (fresh anchovies, not men). A sprawling **market** extends from the end of Via Pacini (off Via Etnea) all the way to Corso Sicilia (open Mon.-Sat. early morning-2pm). Another market, almost as big, can be found on Via Pardo, off P. del Duomo; the main attraction is fish, but there are foods of all kinds. The **SMA Supermarket** lurks at Corso Sicilia, 50. (Open Mon.-Tues. and Thurs.-Fri. 8:30am-1pm and 4-8pm; Wed. 8:30am-1pm. MC, Visa.)

Trattoria la Paglia, Via Pardo, 23 (tel. 34 68 38), across from the *duomo* behind the fountain near the fish market. *Primi* from L6000. Try *insalata di polpo* (octopus salad, L7000). *Menù* L20,000-25,000. Cover L1000. Area not recommended for single women at night. Open Mon.-Sat. 8am-midnight.

Trattoria Casalinga, Via Biondi, 19 (tel. 31 13 19), 3rd left off Via Antonio di Sangiuliano, which is to the right of Via Etnea as you walk from the *duomo*. The menu changes daily, but they're always happy to do the classic *norma* (L8000). *Menù* L20,000-25,000. Cover L1500. Open Mon.-Sat. noon-3:30pm.

Ristorante Rapido, Via F. Corridoni, 17, near the Bellini Garden. A good, cheap eatery. *Primi* from L4500. *Menù* L12,000. Cover L1000. Open Mon.-Sat. noon-3pm and 6:30-10pm.

CATANIA

Trattoria Calabrese, Via Penninello, 34 (tel. 32 24 61), off Via Etnea near the Roman amphitheater. *Pasta alla Norma* L6000. *Menù* L15,000-20,000. Open Mon.-Sat. 8am-10pm, sometimes on Sun.

Cineseria, Via Umberto, 180 (tel. 31 00 38), serves Chinese food—a nice break from pasta. *Primi* from L5000. Cover L1000. Open Mon.-Sat. noon-3pm and 6-11pm. [Come on, guys—when in Rome, don't eat ramen. -Ed.]

Gastronomy G. Conte, Via Etnea, 158 (tel. 31 23 99). Centrally located. An excellent eatery. *Pizzette* and other *tavola calda* snacks L1800-2000. Counters only, so come early. Take-out service. Open Mon.-Sat. 5:30am-midnight.

SIGHTS

At the center of Catania's **Piazza del Duomo,** Vaccarini's lava-built **Fontana dell'Elefante** (Elephant Fountain, 1736) boasts a unique anatomical feature. Vaccarini, true to reality, carved his elephant (the symbol of the city) without visible testicles. When the statue was unveiled, horrified Catanian men concluded that this was a slur on their virility and demanded corrective measures; Vaccarini's acquiescence was, um, monumental. Residents pledge that visitors may attain citizenship by smooching the elephant's massive tush, but the altitude of the pachyderm's backside precludes such aspirations. Stand behind the cool fountain on the rear end of the square for a good view of the **cathedral,** introduced by an open space at its side, allowing for the full play of Baroque regalia. The other buildings on the square (the 18th-century Palazzo del Municipio on the left, the former Seminario dei Chierici on the right) are striped black and white to mirror the side of the *duomo.*

The church interior, with a Baroque barrel-vaulted nave and domed side aisles, once looked quite different, as 1950s restoration work revealed. Stumps of old columns were found, as well as the tall pointed arches of the original three apses. The two transept chapels have exquisitely paneled Renaissance frames (1545). One of them, the Norman **Cappella della Madonna** (right), also preserves a beautiful Roman sarcophagus and a 15th-century statue of the Virgin. You can see the body of Catania's beloved priest, the Beato Cardinale Dusmet, lit up by fluorescent lights 25 ft. from the chapel, his bony (quite literally) fingers sticking out of the vestments. To the right as you come through the main entrance is **Bellini's tomb,** guarded by a marble angel. The words and music inscribed above are from *Sonnambula,* one of the composer's four principal works. Proper dress is required for entry to the *duomo.*

Up the hill from P. del Duomo at Via Vittorio Emanuele 266, is the entrance to the **Greco-Roman Theater** (415 BC). Behind the theater (entrance around back) is the similar but smaller **Odeon.** Mt. Etna's 1669 eruption coated the marble of both theaters in lava. (Open daily 9am-1hr. before sunset. Free.) In mid-July, **Catania Musica Estate** takes place on a stage set up in the Odeon; inquire at AAPIT.

Up Via Etnea the **Bellini Gardens,** complete with serpentine walkways and a miniature duck pond, offer a lush refuge against Mt. Etna's backdrop. A few blocks before the gardens, at the intersection of Via Etnea and Corso Sicilia, are the ruins of a 2nd-century **Roman amphitheater,** just below street level. The more recent inscription reads: "For me, Christ made the city of Catania sublime."

Beware the Animal Spirits!

Catanians believe that animal spirits inhabit the city's many animal fountains, and that anyone who falls asleep by such a fountain will lose their soul to the resident animal spirit and never wake up. Sweet dreams!

ENTERTAINMENT

The **Teatro Bellini** (tel. 31 20 20) is the city's principal theater for opera and concerts. The opera and symphony seasons begin in October. Symphonies run until January (tickets from L6000); operas until June (from L13,000). From July to September, the city and province host performances (mostly in the Odeon) of music, theater, and dance. All events are free and schedules are plastered about town. The AAPIT is very active culturally and puts out a free monthly bulletin (*Lapis*) on **nightlife** in Catania: movies, concerts, and festivals.

La Plaja is a pleasant but crowded beach within view of a nearby power-plant (take bus #27 or D, June-Sept. only). Farther away from Catania's port, **La Scogliera** is a better choice, with a clear bathing area spread out beside igneous cliffs (bus #34 from P. Duomo, 30min.).

■ NEAR CATANIA: MOUNT ETNA

Mt. Etna is one of the world's largest active volcanoes and, at 3350m, is the largest and highest in Europe. The Greek poet Hesiod envisioned Etna as the home of Typhon, the last monster conceived by Earth to fight the gods before the dawn of the human race. If so, Typhon remains restless; a 1985 eruption destroyed much of the tourist station near the summit. Etna blew its top again in 1992, unsettling residents of some of the towns along its slopes.

The **trains** of Ferrovia Circumetnea circumnavigate the volcano's base, stopping at the local villages of Adrano, Randazzo, and Giarre. From Catania, use **Stazione Borgo,** Via Caronda, 350 (tel. 541 24); Via Caronda is the street that forks off Via Etnea to the right just after the Bellini Gardens. At this station, you can hop on a train that runs along Etna's entire inland perimeter, finishing near the coast at Giarre-Riposto (3 per day, last one leaves Catania at 11:05am, 3½ hr., L7500). From Giarre-Riposto you can make connections onto the national railway and get back to Catania (or go on to Taormina) in less than an hour. If you'd like to do some real hands-on exploring, an AST **bus** leaves from Catania's central train station at 8:15am for **Rifugio Sapienza,** making a 10-minute rest stop at Nicolosi (where you can fill up your picnic basket), and returns at 4:15pm (round-trip L6700). From Sapienza (1900m), you can hike up to **Torre del Filosofo** (The Philosopher's Tower; 2920m) and back in about five hours. From here, about all you can see are the looming peaks of Etna's craters and rising steam. The hike is difficult because the ashy, pebbly terrain slips underfoot; it's like climbing up a beach at a 35° angle. The other option is the (expensive) cable-car service that runs to 2500m and is then supplemented by 4x4s up to 2920m (9am-4pm, last down 4:30pm; one-way to 2500m L14,200, round-trip L25,700; one-way to 2920m L25,700, round-trip L45,000; children under 10 half-price; closed if winds are high).

From the Philosopher's Tower it is possible to hike another two hours to the **craters** themselves (roughly 1hr. to return). While the view is incredible, it may not be to die for; in fact, the trail is so difficult and the volcanic activity so unpredictable that all guided tours have been suspended. **A few years ago 11 tourists died when one of the craters erupted unexpectedly.** If you choose to brave the hike, take the necessary precautions—tell someone you are going up, make the trip with a partner, and carry sunscreen and water. However you choose to get up the volcano, you're in for a thrill; the hardened lava, huge boulders, and craters are unearthly. Bring sweaters and windbreakers; winds are ferocious, and even in mid-July pockets of snow sometimes remain. On the way down from the Tower, be sure to check out the **Valle de Bove,** Etna's original crater. If you are going up by jeep, don't worry: the driver will stop to let you look.

Stock up on food before you leave, or explore the numerous eateries around the volcano's base; as a last resort the self-service cafeteria at the tourist station serves decent pizzas (L2000) and pasta (L7000). **CIT,** Corso Umberto, 101 (tel. (0942) 233 01), and **SAT,** Corso Umberto, 73 (tel. 246 53), in Catania, offer pricey package tours to Etna. Trips to 1900m start at L30,000 per person; to the Philosopher's Tower L65,000.

■ ■ ■ TAORMINA

The story goes that Neptune shipwrecked a boat full of Greeks off the eastern coast of Sicily in the 8th century BC, and only one sailor survived to crawl ashore. He was

TAORMINA

so inspired by the beautiful scenery that he decided to found a city, and Taormina (or, as it was called then, Tauromenium) was born. Historians, however, will tell you that the Carthaginians founded Tauromenium at the turn of the 4th century BC, only to have it wrested away almost immediately by the Greek tyrant Dionysius. You choose your favorite version; regardless of its origin, Taormina is and has always been a city of unsurpassable beauty—a cliff-top city of mansions, pine trees, and purple flowers, with a hazy-blue coastline stretching out below.

ORIENTATION AND PRACTICAL INFORMATION

The easiest way to get to Taormina is by **bus** from Messina or Catania. Although **trains** from Catania and Messina are more frequent, the train station is located far below Taormina, and access to the city depends on buses which make the run uphill every 15 to 75 minutes until 10:20pm (L2500). Taormina's main streets are closed to cars, and the town's small size makes it the ideal place to walk anywhere. From the bus depot, take a left up Via Pirandello to **Corso Umberto I**, the main drag, which runs the length of the town. Innumerable stepped side streets branch from the *corso*. Via Naumachia leads downhill to **Via Bagnoli Croci,** which continues on to the public gardens. The four principal *piazze* are along Corso Umberto I.

Tourist Office: P. Santa Caterina (tel. 232 43; fax 249 41), in Palazzo Corvaia off Corso Umberto at P. Vittorio Emanuele. Helpful and well-organized, if they slow down enough to notice you. Will help with your accommodations search (difficult in Aug.). English spoken. Excellent city map. Open Mon.-Sat. 8am-2pm and 4-7pm. Tentatively open Sun. July-Aug.

Police: tel. 112 (also tel. 232 32; fax 231 05).

Post Office: P. S. Antonio (tel. 230 10; fax 212 42), at the top of Corso Umberto I near the hospital. Open Mon.-Sat. 8:30am-6:40pm, Sun. 8:30am-1:40pm. **Postal Code:** 98039.

Telephones: Telecom (SIP), Via San Pancrazio, 6 (tel. 246 69), at the top of Via Pirandello in the Avis office. Open Mon.-Sat. 8am-1pm and 3-8pm, Sun. 9am-1pm. **Telephone Code:** 0942.

Currency Exchange: Cambio Valuta, Corso Umberto, 224, right before P. S. Antonio. Open Mon.-Sat. 9am-1pm and 4-8pm. Also, hordes of other places on the *corso*. The ticket office in the bus depot (open early morning until 7pm) will exchange cash only. The train station will change money daily 5:40am-9:40pm.

American Express: La Duca Viaggi, Via Don Bosco, 39 (tel. 62 52 55), right on P. IX Aprile. Cash advances, traveler's check refunds; will hold mail for one month. Open Mon.-Fri. 9am-1pm and 4-7:30pm, Sat. 9am-noon.

Trains: (tel. 510 26 or 515 11). At the bottom of the hill, halfway between Taormina and neighboring Giardini-Naxos. To/from: Catania (29 per day, 45min., L3900), Messina (30 per day, 50min., L3900), Enna (L10,900), Palermo (L21,100), and Agrigento (L17,800).

Buses: SAIS (tel. 62 53 01). To Catania (11 per day, L5100), Messina (13 per day, L5100), and local destinations. Also, **CIT** offers "Etna Tramonto," a sunset trip up the volcano (June-Oct. Mon. and Wed., L65,000 per person).

Car Rental: Avis, Via San Pancrazio, 6 (tel. 230 41). Open Mon.-Sat. 8:30am-12:30pm and 4:30-8pm, Sun. drop-off only 9am-noon. AmEx, MC, Visa.

Moped Rental: Sicily on Wheels, Via Bagnoli Croci, 90 (tel. 62 56 57). Scooters L18,000 per day, L110,000 per week. Vespa 2-seaters L26,000 per day, L180,000 per week. Must be over 15. Open daily 8am-12:30pm and 4-8pm. Also try **California,** (tel. 237 69) next door, which has similar prices.

English Bookstore: Libreria Interpress, Corso Umberto, 37 (tel. 249 89). Look for the awning that says "Book Shop." Also carries books in Spanish, French, and German. Open Mon.-Sat. 8:30am-1pm and 4-8:30pm, Sun. 8:30am-1pm.

Emergencies: tel. 113. **Medical Emergency: Guardia Medica,** tel. 62 54 19. **Hospital: Ospedale San Vincenzo** (tel. 231 49), in P. San Vincenzo.

ACCOMMODATIONS AND CAMPING

Reservations are a must in August; a call ahead in July will also save you much grief. The following *pensioni* usually have vacancies in the off-season, but most will not accept phone reservations from late June through September. If you are determined to stay overnight in summer, have the tourist office book a room for you. Additional accommodations are available in the nearby towns of Mazzarò, Spisone, and Giardini-Naxos, but bus service to these areas stops around 9pm; the only alternative for the first two is a long hike down steep trails. To avoid high prices and the massive rush of tourists, your best bet is to visit Taormina in June or early July.

Pensione Svizzera, Via Pirandello, 26 (tel. 237 90; fax 62 59 06), between the bus station and the town center. A little expensive, but well worth every *lira*. The rose-colored building looks out over the magnificent coastline. Kept so neat, even the Swiss would be impressed. All rooms have bath; include breakfast. English spoken. Singles L50,000. Doubles L80,000. Triples L108,000. Open March-Nov. Usually booked in Aug.; telephone reservations recommended. MC, Visa.

Villa Pompei, Via Bagnoli Croci, 88 (tel. 238 12), across from the public gardens. You can see the flowers from the rooms. Run by sweet, caring sisters. Singles L35,000. Doubles L52,000, with bath L60,000. Extra bed L15,000. Reservations for June-Sept. required a month in advance with deposit.

Inn Piero, Via Pirandello, 20 (tel. 231 39), near the base of Corso Umberto. Tidy, recently renovated rooms. All with shower. Call ahead to arrange Wed. arrival, they're closed. Singles L40,000. Doubles L63,000. AmEx, MC, Visa.

Locanda Diana, Via G. Di Giovanni, 6 (tel. 238 98), if you're stuck, try this *locanda* for cheap prices and a great location. Singles L30,000. Doubles L40,000. All rooms with bath.

Camping: Campeggio San Leo, Via Nazionale (tel. 246 58), on the cape 200m up the hill from the train station, can be reached by any bus from Taormina that passes the station on its route (L1500). L7000 per person, L8000 per small tent, L10,000 per large tent. **Eurocamping Marmaruca** (tel. 366 76), 5km from Taormina in the Letojanni area. Marmaruca is accessible by buses from Taormina headed in the direction of Messina (L1500). L5600 per person, L4500 per small tent, L7700 per large tent. Both places have food stores within 500m.

FOOD

Cheap eateries are few and far between; avoid everything off Corso Umberto I. Even buying bread, cheese, and fruit can be expensive unless you try the **Supermercato STANDA,** Via Apollo Arcageta, 49 (tel. 237 81), at the end of Corso Umberto, one block up from the post office. (Open Mon.-Sat. 8:30am-1pm and 5-9pm.)

Trattoria da Nino, Via Pirandello, 37 (tel. 212 65), between the buses and the town center. The sign says "Stop, you have found the best home-made cooking and pasta in Taormina." It may very well be correct. *Primi* from L5500. Open daily noon-3:30pm and 8:30-11:30pm; closed Fri. in winter. AmEx, MC, Visa.

San Pancrazio, P. San Pancrazio, 3 (tel. 231 84), at the end of Via Pirandello. Outdoor tables, plenty of company, and a great location. Pizza L8500. *Cannelloni alla Siciliana* L7000. Cover L1500. Open Wed.-Mon. noon-3pm and 7-11pm. AmEx, MC, Visa.

Trattoria da Giorgio, Via Cappucini, 1 (tel. 248 93). Typical Sicilian cuisine without the cover or service charges. *Primi* from L6000. "Any type of pizza you so desire" for L6000-8000. Open Mon.-Sat. 6am-midnight. AmEx, MC, Visa.

Café L'Arco, Via C. Patricio, 26 (tel. 211 21), uphill from the start of Corso Umberto. The young clientele doesn't wait for the savory pastries to cool. The *cipolline* is stuffed with *mozzarella, prosciutto,* tomatoes, and onions (L2500). Pizza from L4000; *menù* L16,000. Karaoke! Take-out available. Open Tues.-Sun. 9am-1.30pm and 5:30-11pm.

SIGHTS AND ENTERTAINMENT

Goethe thought the 3rd-century **Greek Theater** in Taormina commanded one of the most beautiful views in the world; see if *you* would sell your soul for the panorama. (Open daily 9am-7pm. Admission L2000, under 18 or over 60 free.) To get there, walk up Via Teatro Greco, off Corso Umberto I at P. Vittorio Emanuele. As you exit the theater, the grand Timeo Hotel is on your left: this was Taormina's first hotel. Descend Via di Giovanni and follow the signs to the *Villa Comunale*, a beautiful **park** complete with benches sunken into flowered hedges and a gorgeous view of Giardini-Naxos below. The park also houses—of all things—an old-fashioned submarine. (Open 8am-8pm.)

On the other side of P. Vittorio Emanuele, behind the tourist office, is the **Roman Odeon,** a small theater now partly covered by the Church of Santa Caterina next door. A ways up Corso Umberto, P. del Duomo showcases Taormina's 13th-century **duomo,** rebuilt during the Renaissance. (Open when the Monsignor "wants it to be open," but try the morning or early evening hours.) The Gothic interior shelters paintings by Messinese artists and a fine alabaster statue of the Virgin. A walk along Via Circonvallazione, which runs parallel to and above Corso Umberto, leads you to a small set of steep stairs that snake up the mountainside to the **castello,** which provides you with Taormina's finest view.

In the summer, the city hosts **Taormina Arte,** an international festival of theater, music, and film (late July-Sept.). Most performances are in the Greek Theater or in the public gardens. (Admission L7000-50,000. For info call 211 42, visit the outdoor offices in P. Vittorio Emanuele, or inquire at the tourist office.) Taormina is home to a number of overpriced, uneventful **discotheche.** This sort of nightlife concentrates in nearby Giardini-Naxos (see below). One worthwhile nightspot in Taormina is **Tout Va,** Via Pirandello, 70 (tel. 238 24; fax 238 25), an open-air club with great views, although it's a tiring half-hour trek from town. (Cover from L15,000. Open in summer daily 10pm-3:30am.) **Le Perroquet** (tel. 244 62), on Via Roma and P. S. Domenico de Guzman (walk downhill from P. IX Aprile), is a popular **gay club.** (Cover L15,000. Open daily July 15-Sept. 15.)

■ NEAR TAORMINA

Taormina's closest and most popular beach is the Lido Mazzarò below town. Down the road to the right and 100m off the coast is the tiny **Isola Bella,** a national nature preserve. The *lido* is accessible by the cable car from Via Pirandello in Taormina (every 15min.; L2000 one-way, L2500 after 8pm). (Open Mon.-Sat. 8am-1:30am, Sun. 9am-1:30am.) Huge lines form for the return trip at "rush hour" from 5 to 7pm. Some of the nearby towns—**Castelmola** in particular—are also scenic, and a short bus ride out of town. While in Taormina, don't miss the **Gole Alcantara,** a nearby haven of gorgeous gorges, freezing waterfalls, and crystal rapids. SAIS runs one bus there and back a day (leaves 9:15am, returns 2:20pm; L4200). The water is so cold that you may want to rent a rubber suit from the Gole Alcantara office (tel. 98 50 10) for L10,000. L3000 will get you into the "water park." Remember to bring a towel, sunscreen, a change of clothes, and a pair of shoes in which you don't mind climbing rapids. If you're looking for a cheap place to stay outside of town, the **Albergo Moderno,** Via Nazionale, 36 (tel. 510 17), is right across the street from the train station midway between Taormina and Giardini-Naxos. (Singles L30,000-40,000, doubles L40,000-50,000.)

■ ■ ■ GIARDINI-NAXOS

Giardini-Naxos was the site of the first Greek colony in Sicily (734 BC). In its heyday, the city (then called Naxos) had about 10,000 inhabitants. The region's beauty allowed the Naxians to live the good life—that is, until they took the wrong side in the big Athenian-Syracusan conflicts of the late 5th century BC and were destroyed by Syracuse in 403BC. Nonetheless, the citizens of Syracuse have cause to be jealous

GIARDINI-NAXOS

today; with its gorgeous beach, active nightlife, and rich historical tradition, Giardini is a must-see for anyone touring eastern Sicily.

Practical Information Only 5km away from Taormina, the township of Giardini shares the same train station with its sister city. **SAIS** buses run from Giardini to the train station to Taormina in a continuous daily flow (36 buses per day) from 5:30am to 10pm (L1500 one-way, L2500 round-trip). The **AAST** tourist office, Via Tysandros, 54 (tel. (0942) 510 10; fax 528 48), along the beach, is open Mon.-Fri. 8:30am-2pm and 4-7pm in the winter (summer afternoons 4:30-7:30pm). English and French spoken. There is a **post office** at Via Erice, 1 (tel. 510 90). In an **emergency**, call the **Ospedale Civico** at tel. 57 91; the **Carabinieri** are at tel. 516 66.

Accommodations and Food Hotels in Giardini are often filled in August—either make reservations in advance or visit at any other time. The **Hotel Villa Mora,** Via Naxos, 47 (tel. 518 39), is a real Sicilian treat. The charming family who runs the hotel has stocked it with an outstanding medley of furnishings, including TVs. Cool off in the evenings at the attached seafront Mediterranean bar. (Off-season singles from L45,000, doubles from L75,000. Breakfast L6000.) Prices rise significantly in August, when half (L80,000) or full (L95,000) pension is mandatory. A little bit down the road is the clean and miraculously skinny **Hotel Costa Azzurra,** Via Naxos, 35 (tel. 514 58. Off-season singles L35,000, doubles L55,000. Late July-Aug. singles L45,000, doubles L70,000. Half pension L60,000; full L75,000. MC, Visa.) In the **Pensione Otello,** Via Tysandros, 62 (tel. 510 09), all rooms have either bath or shower and a balcony overlooking the sea. (Singles from L35,000, doubles from L70,000. Breakfast included; restaurant and bar on premises.) For **camping,** try **Maretna** on Via Pietralunga (tel. 527 94), a cheap alternative to the beachfront hotels. (Campsites from L5000.)

Cheap food can be bought at the **Supermercado Saglimbeni Giovanni,** Via Vittorio Emanuele, 184 (tel. 526 85. Open 8:30am-1:30pm and 5-9pm.) **Calypso,** Via IV Novembre, 267 (tel. 512 89), is right on the seafront. Pizza from L4000, and pasta from L5000. *Menù* L18,000. (Open 11am-3pm and 7-11pm. AmEx, MC, Visa.) Before or after eating, check out Piazza XXIV Maggio, characterized by its pointy, red church, **Chiesa Maria S.S. Immacolata. La Sirena,** at Via Schisò, 36 (tel. 518 52), is next to the archaeological museum at the far end of town. Pizza from L5000. Cover L1000. (Open daily noon-3pm and 8-11pm. AmEx, MC, Visa.) Seafood is the house specialty at **Angelina,** Via Calcide Eubea, 2 (tel. 514 77). *Primi* from L6000. (Open daily 7am-4am; closed Wed. in winter. AmEx, MC, Visa.)

Sights and Entertainment Recent excavations in the **archaeological park** have revealed the outlines of the city walls, built with monstrous irregular blocks of solidified lava. This sounds promising, but the remains are so scant that they're unlikely to interest anyone who isn't a Ph.D. candidate in archaeology. (Open daily 2-7pm. Free.) The **archaeology museum** (tel. 510 01); on the Capo Schisò peninsula on the other side of Giardini, shows further evidence of the city's earliest inhabitants, including an inscribed ceramic cup (the earliest example of a written document from the colony. Open daily 9am-2pm and 3-7pm; closed Mon. afternoons. Free.) At the tip of Capo Schiso is a **Nike statue** (the goddess, not the shoe), as well as a great view of Giardini's beaches with Taormina sitting in the background.

At night, Giardini turns into a hip youth hangout. Most of the city's *gioventù* head over to **Mister Roll,** Via Jannuzzo, 31 (tel. 65 30 87). This *pizzeria*/sandwich joint doubles as a karaoke bar. (Open daily in summer from 8pm "till the last person leaves." Closed Mon. in winter.) When you're done eating, consider heading over to the **Marabu** *discoteca/ristorante/pianobar,* at Ctr. Scavi Naxos (tel. 518 10).

SARDINIA (SARDEGNA)

Sardinia is the perfect antidote to Italy-overdose. When you're fed up with all the Botticellis and Brunelleschis, when you'd trade all the Gucci in the world for a single Gap, when the sight of one more church interior will surely send you screaming into the path of the nearest speeding Fiat, come to Sardinia to recover from all that refinement. Inspired by the island's harsh, mountainous terrain and rustic, undeveloped villages, D. H. Lawrence proclaimed it "not a bit like the rest of Italy." Although parts of the northern coast have sprouted the concrete condominiums of the modern tourist industry, much of Sardinia persists in its gorgeously untamed state. The mysterious ruins, the wild horses and pink flamingos, the wind-carved rock formations, and the deserted beaches all provide happy evidence that Lawrence's assessment still holds true today.

An old Sardinian legend says that when God finished making the world, he had a handful of dirt left over, which he threw into the Mediterranean and stepped on, thus creating Sardinia. Other curious landscaping phenomena took place over 3500 years ago; the island is dotted with *nuraghi*, monuments to ancient civilizations constructed around the 2nd millennium BC. The cone-shaped fortified tower-houses were built of huge blocks of stone without the aid of mortar, and over 7000 of them survive today. The same civilization erected bird-shaped **Giants' Tombs** to house its collective dead and forged amusingly detailed figurines to bury with them.

The first recorded invaders of Sardinia were the seafaring Phoenicians, followed by the Carthaginians. It was the methodical and business-minded Romans, however, who turned the island into an agricultural colony. After both the Vandals and the Moors weakened Rome's hold, a local independent government grew up in its place. By 900 AD, the island had been divided into four sovereign kingdoms called *giudicati* and run by representational government. Sardinia's period of democratic self-rule lasted only until the 13th century, when foreign invasions began once again. The Pisans, the Aragonese, and the newly-united Spanish all succeeded in conquering the island. Even Napoleon tried (but failed) to take Sardinia in 1793 in an offensive launched from Corsica. Vittorio Emanuele, who became king of Italy in 1861, began his campaign to unify Italy from Sardinia (helped by its favorite son Giuseppe Garibaldi) and made it part of the whole. Mussolini did much for the island and its transport networks and is still fondly remembered by many. In 1948, the island gained back some of its ancient independence when the Italian government granted it autonomous administration.

Well into this century, the economy of Sardinia still depended exclusively on agriculture. Only decades ago, *padroni* (landlords) still held the land, and poor farmers toiled under a system akin to serfdom. Due to the growing influence of the Italian Communist Party (both its founder, Antonio Gramsci, and its late Secretary General, Enrico Berlinguer, were Sardinians), much of the land is now owned by those who work it, although large sections of Sardinia's scenic coastline have fallen into the hands of foreign speculators. Yet, despite an Italian campaign to promote the island as a vacation destination, the tourist industry is not uniformly developed; many of the island's attractions remain virtually inaccessible without a car.

GETTING THERE

The cheapest way to go is *posta ponte* (deck class) from Civitavecchia to Olbia (usually around L30,000). Beware the summer tourist rush (late July and August) and the strong possibility of strikes when planning your trip to Sardinia. If you plan on traveling at the height of the season, reserve two weeks prior to departure. Prices listed below are for *poltrone* (reserved reclining chairs). *Posta ponte* fares are often available only when all the *poltrone* are taken. **Tirrenia** operates the most ferries and offers the cheapest fares, but long delays occasionally mar the service. During the

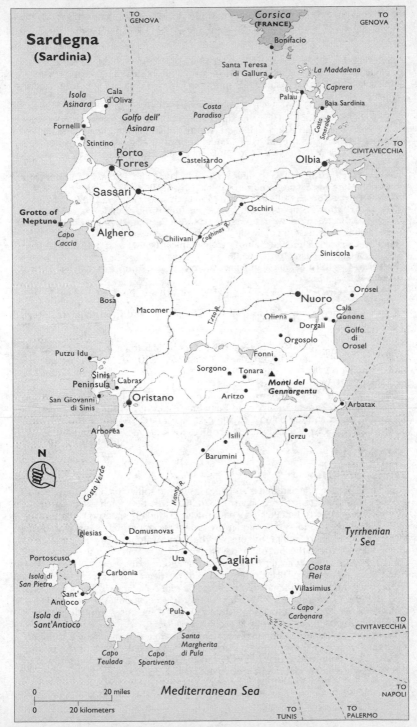

months of June-Sept., there are often extra ferries when the demand is great; the times listed below are the regular schedule. Tickets can be purchased at many travel agencies in Italy and the U.S. In Italy, look for Tirrenia signs outside travel agencies.

Civitavecchia-Olbia: daily both ways at 11pm (8hr., L33,900). There is also a **Ferrovie dello Stato** connection to Golfo Aranci, near Olbia (4 per day, 8hr.).

Civitavecchia-Cagliari: daily at 6:30pm from Civitavecchia and 6pm from Cagliari (13hr., L64,000).

Civitavecchia-Arbatax: Wed. and Fri. from Civitavecchia at 6:30pm. (11hr.) Departs Arbatax for Civitavecchia Sun. midnight. Additional service from Arbatax: Summer: Tues. 8pm, Thurs. midnight, winter Wed. midnight (8½hr., L52,000).

Genoa-Olbia: daily at 6pm from Genoa, at 5pm in Aug. Daily at 8:30pm from Olbia. In Oct.-May, service from Olbia runs only Tues., Thurs., Sat. at 8:30pm (13hr., L70,000).

Genoa-Cagliari: mid-June to mid-Sept. only. Tues. and Thurs. at 4:45pm from Genoa. Mon. and Sat. at 3pm from Cagliari (21hr., L94,000).

Genoa-Porto Torres: daily at 7:30pm from both cities (12½hr., L70,000).

Genoa-Arbatax: Fri. at 6pm from Genoa, mid-July through mid-Sept. at 7pm. Seasonal service Mon. or Wed. From Arbatax, Sat. at 2pm, in Aug. at 4pm (19hr., L72,000).

Naples-Cagliari: Thurs. at 5:30pm from Naples. Oct.-May at 7:15pm. Wed. at 6:30pm from Cagliari (16hr., L65,000).

Palermo-Cagliari: Sat. at 7pm from Palermo. Fri. at 7pm from Cagliari (14hr., L60,000).

Trapani-Cagliari: Tues. at 9pm from Trapani. Sun. at 7pm from Cagliari (11hr., L60,000).

Tunis-Cagliari: Mon. at 8pm from Tunis. Sun. at 7pm from Cagliari (22hr., L107,000).

Tirrenia offices are found in **Civitavecchia,** Stazione Marittima (tel. (0766) 288 01/02/03); **Genoa,** Stazione Marittima, Ponte Colombo (tel. (010) 275 80 41); **Palermo,** Calata Marinai d'Italia (tel. (091) 33 33 00); **Livorno,** Carlo Laviosa, Via Cairoli, 49 (tel. (0586) 89 03 32); and **Rome,** Via Bissolati, 41 (tel. (06) 675 462 04).

Flights also link Olbia, Alghero, and Cagliari to most major Italian cities, as well as to Paris, Geneva, Zurich, Munich, and Frankfurt. Flights are faster, but the chaos of an Italian airport and the pain of paying exorbitant fares should discourage most budget travelers. Check with local travel offices for schedules, fares, and discounts.

ONCE THERE

Transportation

Public transportation in Sardinia is an inexpensive but somewhat inefficient way to see the island. Buses tend to miss many of Sardinia's treasures, such as campgrounds next to Roman ruins or hidden coves with private bathing in spectacular natural settings. Instead they go to its cities and more crowded campgrounds. It is possible to plan a decent itinerary around the bus schedule, but watch out: if you get stuck in the middle or (worse) the end of the day in a town you're ready to escape, you may end up spending the night there. The two main bus companies are ARST and PANI. **ARST** links almost every village on the island to the nearest big town. Its service is oriented toward local residents; the bus stops on request at any cluster of houses as well as at the planned stops. **PANI,** by contrast, connects only the major cities— Cagliari, Sassari, Oristano, and Nuoro—and although some buses stop at one or two intervening towns, many only stop at their destination.

Train service has improved in recent years and remains significantly less expensive than buses. For those not in a hurry, they can provide vistas of the unique beauty of the countryside that highway travel sacrifices. They are often timed to meet ferries arriving from or departing to the mainland and stop in the port.

The most prized destinations simply cannot be reached without a car. **Car rental** rates have recently come within the range of many budget travelers. One good, possible Sardinian holiday combines a rented car with stays at the many campgrounds set in magnificent natural settings. The best car rental deals will be found in larger cities, and many agencies offer special weekend deals. Prices otherwise range from L50,000-155,000 per day. **Mopeds** are another option, starting at L25,000 per day; finding rental outlets, however, is a challenge. **Bikes** seem to be an enticing option, but unless you have the leg muscles of an Olympian, Sardinia's mountainous terrain will reduce you to a hiker with a two-wheeled backpack. Anyone traveling alone should think twice about bicycling in some of the less populated inland areas south of Nuoro; women are especially cautioned. Also, women should never go on hikes alone in the countryside. **Hitchhiking in Sardinia can be very dangerous, particularly for women—even when traveling in pairs.**

Accommodations and Food

Virtually all growth in Sardinia's rapidly expanding vacation industry has occurred in the luxury sector. Most cities lack an adequate selection of moderately priced accommodations. Consult the local tourist office, and ask for the semi-reliable and comprehensive *Annuario Alberghi* which lists prices for all hotels, *pensioni,* and official campsites on the island. You can usually find a decent single in town for about L30,000, but during peak season single travelers will probably have to scrounge for roommates. Rooms are scarce in August. The two **youth hostels** (in Alghero and Porto Torres) provide an inexpensive but unreliable alternative, as they often fill up or shut down unexpectedly. Both lie near the beach and have crowded but airy rooms. **Camping** outside official campsites is illegal, but discreetly practiced nonetheless. **Agriturismo** is an excellent alternative to *pensioni;* tourists live on farms in the countryside and eat dinners with their host families, but a car is almost always necessary to reach these rural destinations (bed and breakfast approximately L25,000, half pension L45,000, full pension L50,000). Ask the tourist office for a list of participating farms in the area, or contact one of the two agencies that run *agriturismo* centers in Sardinia. They will make reservations without the usual booking fee generally required for the summer months. If you write early enough they will send you a complete directory of their *agriturismo* locations in Sardinia, complete with photos: **Terra Nostra,** Associazione Sarda per l'Agriturismo, Via Sassari, 3, 09123 Cagliari (tel. (Tues. and Thurs. only) (070) 66 83 67).

For those interested in an alternative vacation with forays into pristine natural settings, Sardinia has much to offer. Over 50% of Italy's endangered species is found here. A battle is currently engaged between various wildlife federations and the Italian government in order to establish more sanctuaries that will protect these species from the constant encroachment of the tourist industry (and local shepherds) into their habitat. **Hiking and trekking** have become increasingly popular as guides from various cooperatives lead groups along shepherds' paths in the golden hills of the interior. Most local tourist agencies have info on local trekking adventures, or contact Ignazio Porcedda, an English speaker who arranges excursions in Sardinia with **Guide Ambientali Escursionistiche GAE,** Cooperativa Turistica "Sinis" Campeggio Nurapolis 09070 Narbolia (Oristano), (tel. (0783) 522 83). Sardinians have raised beautiful horses for centuries. **Horse-lovers** can design their own riding adventures by contacting one of the local centers (ask at the tourist office).

Sardinia's **cuisine,** like its terrain, is rustic and rugged. The typical bread here, called *pane carasau* or *carta da musica,* is thin and crisp, perfect for shepherds (and hikers) who have no local bakery in sight but still want fresh bread. A menu often includes hearty dishes like *sa fregula* (pasta in broth with saffron), *malloreddus* (dumplings with saffron), or *culurgiones* (ravioli stuffed with cheese and beet roots, covered with tomato sauce, lamb, and sausage). The most celebrated dishes are a vegetarian's nightmare: grilled pigs or goats, *cordula* (lamb entrails), and pork cooked in lamb's stomach. Fish and shellfish abound on the island and are often served in novel ways (even on pizza). Don't leave the island without sampling such distinctive local specialties as *pane frattau,* a thin bread covered with eggs, cheese, and tomato sauce, and *sebada,* a delicious dough stuffed with sweet cheese, sugar, and honey. One infamous product of Sardinian shepherds is *formaggio con vermi* (cheese with worms living inside), considered a delicacy but, thankfully, rare. Look for daily outdoor markets in older neighborhoods, where you can get fresh bread, fruit, and goat and sheep cheese. In the summer months local fruits such as apricots, peaches, and nectarines provide succulent picnic fare. The local honey spread on bread makes an excellent breakfast—Sardinian bee pollen is an unusual and inexpensive delicacy you shouldn't miss. The local wines, often sweet and strong, warrant a taste or two (or more). Try *vernaccia d'Oristano* (with a heady almond aftertaste) with fish, or the robust *cannonau di Sardegna* with meat.

■■■ CAGLIARI

Cagliari earns the superlatives among Sardinian cities: it is the island's capital, its largest metropolis, the chief port, and one of the best destinations on the island. The city's streets twist and turn around Roman ruins, Spanish churches, and medieval citadels. Pink flamingos gather in the lakes on the edge of town, as locals and tourists gather on Cagliari's nearby beaches. Founded by and raised to prosperity under the Carthaginians, Cagliari passed through the hands of numerous Roman, Spanish, and Pisan conquerors. The city's present disposition, however, seems influenced more by the sun and pleasant climate than by its tumultuous history. From Cagliari, you can make daytrips to the *nuraghic* ruins near Barumini, the Phoenician-Roman city of Nora, and the Costa del Sud beaches.

ORIENTATION AND PRACTICAL INFORMATION

Via Roma hugs the harbor on one side and sports many outdoor *caffè* beneath its arcades on the other; whether you arrive by train, boat, or bus, it will be right in front of you. At Via Roma's western end, **Piazza Matteotti** houses the train station, the ARST station, and the tourist office. To the east, it terminates in **Piazza Deffenu, Piazza Amendola,** and the PANI station. Across from Piazza Matteotti, broad **Largo Carlo Felice** climbs up the steep hill that leads to the *castello* (castle) and the historic center of town.

> **Tourist Office,** P. Matteotti (tel. 66 92 55 or 66 49 23). Look for the weirdly shaped cubicle in the park in front of the train and bus station. Sporadic hours, but when there, the multi-lingual staff offers lots of information on the local sights. Open in summer Mon.-Fri. 8am-8pm, Sat. 8am-2pm; in winter Mon.-Sat. 8am-2pm. For more reliable help, try the office at **Via Mameli,** 97 (tel. toll free 167 01 31 53; open daily in summer 8am-8pm, in winter 9am-7pm).
> **Police: Questura,** Via Amat, 9 (tel. 602 71).
> **Post Office:** P. del Carmine (tel. 66 83 56), near P. Matteotti. *Fermo posta* L300 per letter. Open Mon.-Sat. 8am-7:20pm, but some services close at 1pm. Will change AmEx cheques. **Postal code:** 09100.
> **Telephones: Telecom (SIP),** Via Angioy, 4, off P. Matteotti. Open daily 8am-9:45pm. **Faxes** sent L2000 per page. **Telephone Code:** 070.
> **Budget Travel: CTS,** Via Cesare Balbo, 4 (tel. 48 82 60). Information on discounts and travel packages for students. Sells HI cards. Open Mon.-Fri. 9am-1:30pm and 4-7:30pm, Sat. 9am-1:30pm. **Associazione Italiana Studenti Sardi: Memo Travel,** Via Pitzolo, 1/A (tel. 40 09 07). General travel information. Open Mon.-Fri. 9am-1pm and 4:30-8pm, Sat. 9am-1pm.
> **Currency Exchange:** In the train station at the information desk. Convenient, but poor rates. Open Mon.-Sat. 7:30am-7:25pm. For more *lire* for your money try any of the many banks that line Largo Carlo Felice. Open Mon.-Fri. 8am-1pm.
> **Airport:** in the village of **Elmas** (tel. 24 01 11, 24 00 47, or 24 01 69). Free ARST buses for ticketholders run between the airport and the city terminal at P. Matteotti (20min.) before each flight.

Trains: Ferrovie dello Stato P. Matteotti (tel. 65 62 93). Multi-lingual info. Open Mon.-Sat. 7am-10pm, and convenient ticket machines all the time. To: Olbia (3 per day, 4hr., L22,600); Porto Torres (2 per day, 4hr., L22,600); Sassari (2 per day, 3hr., L20,800), and Oristano (9 per day, 1½hr., L8000). **Ferrovie Complimentarie della Sardegna** (tel. 49 13 04), P. della Repubblica. A private railroad with supplementary (or complimentary?) services around the island.

Buses: PANI, P. Darsena, 4 (tel. 65 23 26), on the corner of Via Roma and Viale Regina Margherita; look for the big red PANI sign. To: Sassari (7 per day, 3½hr., L23,000-26,000); Oristano (5 per day, 1½hr., L11,800); and Nuoro (4 per day, 3½hr., L21,000). Open Mon.-Sat. 9am-2pm and 5-7pm, Sun. 1-2pm and 5:15-6:15pm. **ARST,** P. Matteotti, 6 (tel. 65 72 36), serves local towns, including Pula (every hr.) and Teulada (every hr.). Open Mon.-Fri. 4:30am-9:35pm, Sat.-Sun. 5:50am-9pm.

Ferries: Tirrenia, at the Stazione Marittima (tel. 66 60 65). Service to Genoa (L81,000), Civitavecchia (L54,000), Palermo (L46,000), and Tunis (L107,500). Open Mon.-Fri. 9am-1pm and 4-7pm. For port info, call 66 33 28, Italian only.

Public Transportation: (tel. 290 727) for info in Italian. Orange APT buses run in the city and beyond. All lines depart from P. Matteotti; buy tickets inside the ARST station at the newsstand (day pass, unlimited rides, L3800). Buses #7 and 8 go up to the *castello*, and Bus P goes to the beach at Il Poetto.

Car Rental: Ruvioli, Via dei Mille, 11 (tel. 65 89 55). Minimum age 18. Major credit card (recommended) or L500,000 deposit. L100,000 per day. L150,000 per weekend. L486,000 per week. Reserve one week in advance. Another branch location at the airport (tel. 24 02 23). Open Mon.-Sat. 8:30am-1pm and 3:30-8pm. **Avis,** at the airport or the train station (tel. 66 81 28). Min. age 23. From L150,000 per day. Open Mon.-Fri. 8:30am-1pm and 4-7pm, Sat. 8:30am-1pm. Also try **Hertz,** at the airport (tel. 24 00 37) or at the ARST station (tel. 66 81 05).

Laundry: Lavanderia Erica, Via Ospedale, 109. Up the hill toward the Roman amphitheater, and across the street from the hospital. Bus #8 will bring you there. Self-service L7000 for 5kg, L2000 for 5min. of drying time. Open daily 8am-10pm.

Pharmacy: Farmacia Dr. Spano, Via Roma, 99 (tel. 65 56 83). Open Mon.-Sat. 9am-1pm and 4:30-10:10pm.

Emergencies: tel. 113. **Hospital:** military hospital on Via Ospedale, 46 (tel. 66 57 55), by the Chiesa di San Michele. Near Il Poetto, try **Ospedale Marino,** Viale Poetto, 12 (tel. 37 36 73). **First Aid:** tel. 267.

ACCOMMODATIONS

Cagliari has an ample stock of inexpensive places to stay, but there is fierce competition year-round: university students from September until mid-July, tourists from July to mid-September. Ask the tourist office in P. Matteotti for help.

Albergo Firenze, Corso Vittorio Emanuele, 50 (tel. 65 36 78 or 65 52 22), off Largo Carlo Felice, on the 3rd floor. Sweet proprietress rents immense rooms with imposing furniture and welcomes you into her very Italian home. The walls are covered in paintings and sketches by her mother, her guests, and other notable persons. Singles L33,000. Doubles L42,000. Pets allowed.

Pensione Vittoria, Via Roma, 75 (tel. 65 79 70), next to the movie theater. An elegant family-run *pensione*—one of the best in Cagliari—with cavernous, majestic rooms, mosaic floors, beautiful furnishings, and views of the sea. Singles L45,000, with bath L55,000. Doubles L75,000, with bath L85,000.

Hotel La Terrazza, Via Santa Margherita, 21 (tel. 66 86 52; fax 66 08 63), the street to the left at the top of Piazza Jenne (at the top of Largo Carlo Felice). A bit of a walk, but you'll be rewarded with a friendly staff and clean rooms on a quiet street. The newly remodelled rooms offer huge beds. Close to the *centro storico*. Singles L40,000, with bath L60,000. Doubles L70,000, with bath L80,000.

Locanda Las Palmas, Via Sardegna, 14 (tel. 65 16 79). Simply decorated, small rooms in an excellent location. Singles L30,000. Doubles L42,000/45,000.

FOOD

For basic picnic fare and a bevy of cheap restaurants, head to **Via Sardegna,** where many small shops provide fruit, cheese, and bread. Try **Panetteria Mura,** Via Sardegna, 40, a small market and a heavenly bakery. Also offers soy milk and other hard-to-find protein products. (Open Mon.-Sat. 7:40am-1:30pm and 4:30-8:30pm.) On Sundays, explore the **food market** on the far side of the stadium in Borgo Sant' Elia. Fresh fruit and seafood reward the careful shopper and fearless bargainer.

Trattoria Lilicu, Via Sardegna, 78 (tel. 65 29 70). Established 80 years ago and still run by the same family, this *trattoria* resides in a single ancient room with wooden beams on the ceiling and tapestries on the walls. A wild boar's head greets you as you enter. Open Mon.-Sat. noon-3pm and 8-11pm.

Da Bruno, Via Cavour, 17 (tel. 653 54). True Sardinian cuisine in a warm, hospitable atmosphere. Try the *malloreddus alla Campidanese* (traditional corn-flour dumplings with saffron and *pecorino* cheese, L7000) and the *porchetto sardo* (roast pork with Sardinian seasoning, L12,000). Tourist menu L20,000. Open Tues.-Sun. 12:30-2:30pm and 7:30-11pm. MC, Visa.

Trattoria Gennargentu, Via Sardegna, 60 (tel. 65 82 47). A *salumeria* and a restaurant. Join the locals for an *etto* of *calamari arrosto* (roasted squid, L5000) or simply *ravioli* (L5000). The wine list is as long as the menu. Open 6am-2:55pm and 7-10:55pm. AmEx, MC, Visa.

Ristorante Pizzeria Downtown, P. Jenne, 18, at the top of Largo Carlo Felice. Fill up after an exhausting climb to the *castello* with their *menù* (L15,000), including *riso nero,* shrimp, and *tiramisù.* Open daily noon-2:30pm and 8-10:30pm.

Antica Hostaria, Via Cavour, 60. One of Cagliari's reputedly best restaurants is not wholly outside the budget traveler's reach. Though founded in 1852, this beautiful restaurant maintains a turn-of-the-century, art nouveau decor. Elegantly serves *malloreddus* (L10,000), along with more *haute* fare like veal in a *vernaccia* sauce (L13,000). Open Mon.-Sat. noon-2:30pm, 8-10:30pm. All credit cards accepted.

SIGHTS

The conspicuous pink towers of the **Bastione di San Remy** mark the division between the modern port and the cramped medieval quarter on the hill above. Climb up the double stairway at **Piazza Costituzione** for a spectacular view of the Golfo degli Angeli, flamingos, the marshes to the west, and the "Devil's Saddle," a rock formation set amidst the mountains surrounding Cagliari. Narrow steps behind the *bastione* lead to medieval Cagliari, where wrought-iron balconies overflow with flowers. The alarmingly narrow streets wind their way up the hill to the **duomo,** a charming exemplar of Pisan geometry refinished in the Romanesque style of the Pisa cathedral. The pulpits at the entrance, depicting scenes from the New Testament, are the work of Guglielmo Pisano, as are the four wrestling lions at the base of the 12th-century altar. Before leaving, glance below at the **sanctuary** carved into the island rock in 1618. The colorful marble inlays, many of which depict Sardinian saints with sharp objects protruding from their bodies, cover the 292 niches containing the relics of early Christian martyrs.

The **Torre di San Pancrazio** crowns the hill on P. Indipendenza, and its mate, the **Torre dell'Elefante,** lies below on Via Università. Erected at the beginning of the 14th century, they once guarded Cagliari's castle. Pass under the Torre di San Pancrazio to the **Arsenale,** from whose lofty towers you can admire the cityscape. There you will find the **Cittadella dei Musei,** a modern complex of research museums, including the **National Archaeological Museum.** The collection holds Phoenician ceramics and Roman glass, but most impressive are the many detailed, Gumby-like figurines culled from nearby *nuraghi,* in poses of everyday *nuraghi* life. Some descriptions are in (poor) English. (Open daily 9am-7pm. Admission L4000, under 18 and over 65 free.) The same complex also houses the **National Painting Museum of Cagliari,** which, despite its name, holds ceramics (mostly 16th century) and religious paintings lifted from nearby churches. Except for one painting by Pietro Cavaro in which Mary Magdalene looks like she's about to bite Christ's foot, the museum is largely uninteresting. From time to time, however, it mounts temporary exhibitions of internationally known artists. (Open daily 9am-7pm. Free.) Both museums are wheelchair accessible

To the right of P. Arsenale from the museums are more lovely views of the city and sea. Viale Buon Camino leads to the **Roman amphitheater,** one of the most significant Roman ruins in Sardinia. The 2nd-century BC theater follows the natural outcrop of the rock. Check out the underground store rooms where the animals were kept for the shows. (Open daily 9am-1pm and 3-5pm. Free.) Continue down Via San Ignazio da Laconi to the university **botanical gardens** with over 500 species of plants. (Open Mon.-Sat. 8:30am-8pm. Admission L1000, children L500.)

ENTERTAINMENT

Merchants converge on the terraces of the Bastione di San Remy for a **flea market** on Sunday mornings. Sift through used clothes, toys, and assorted junk. Because of strict zoning laws, there are no *discoteche* in Cagliari itself. A young crowd hangs out at **Oblomov** on Corso Emanuele, 75, but if you gotta dance, get outta town. Nearby **Assemini** is home to several clubs, including **K2, Woodstock,** and the gargantuan **Eurogarden.** All open at 11pm and are closed Mon. Bus #9 from P. Matteotti goes to Assemini, but you'll need a taxi to get back. If you have a car or moped at your disposal, enjoy a night at the beach with the locals—quite a happening scene.

During the first four days of May, Sardinians flock to Cagliari for the stupendous **Festival of Sant'Efisio,** faithfully honoring a deserter from Diocletian's army who saved the island from the plague but couldn't save himself from a beheading. A costumed procession escorts his effigy from the capital down the coast to the small church that bears his name. From July to September, the city hosts an **arts festival.** The amphitheater comes alive with concerts, operas, and classic plays, and outdoor movies are shown at the Marina Piccola, off Spiaggia del Poetto.

■ NEAR CAGLIARI

BEACHES

Il Poetto, Cagliari's most popular stretch of pure white sand and emerald-sapphire water, spans 10km from the massive Sella del Diavolo (Devil's Saddle) to the Margine Rosso (Red Bluff); behind it are the salt-water **Stagno di Molentargius** (Ponds of Molentargius), a popular flamingo hangout. City buses P, PQ, and PF cart natives and tourists alike *alla mare* (20min., L1300; tickets must be bought beforehand at the newsstand or the green bus kiosk in P. Matteotti). Once you see the beach from the bus, wait a few stops to avoid the crowded areas. For more private sunning and swimming, head for **Cala Mosca,** a smaller, less-crowded beach surrounded by dirt paths leading to isolated coves. To get there, take city bus #5/12 to Stadio Amsicora (ask the driver or look out the window to your left) and then city bus #11 to the beach. It takes a bit longer to reach than Il Poetto, but is well worth the trip.

DAY TRIPS

The ruins of **Barumini,** an agricultural village in the rolling countryside, lies 60km north of Cagliari and 1km west of the Nuraghi of Su Nuraxi. (Open daily 8am-dusk.) These ruins constitute the biggest and best-preserved complex of *nuraghi* in Sardinia. Set atop a hill, the village is constructed of huge, rough-hewn blocks in an intricate layout, vividly illustrating the defensive nature of this civilization. The only direct service from Cagliari to Barumini is the daily ARST bus at 2pm (1hr. 30min., L7500). Buses return to Cagliari only in the morning, so if you want get back in the evening, take the FS bus at 6:30pm (L3500) to San Luri. Once in San Luri, go to the FS train station to catch the commuter train to Cagliari at 7:10pm (L4500).

The tiny village of **Uta** (20km west of Cagliari) shelters the Church of Santa Maria, one of the island's most notable Romanesque buildings. Built around 1140, the church is a deft fusion of French and Pisan architectural styles. Nine ARST buses per day commute from Cagliari (40min., L2700).

Ruins and beaches provide relief from Cagliari in nearby **Pula.** ARST buses will get you to Pula (every hr., ½hr., L3700) where you can see the treasures of nearby Nora displayed in the archaeological museum. (Open May-Sept. 9am-8pm, Oct.-April 9am-noon and 2-5pm. Admission L4000.) From the museum you can catch the bus to the ruins (May-Sept.; or a 25min. walk along Via Nora; follow the signs). The city of **Nora,** reputedly the oldest city in Sardinia, was settled by Phoenicians (circa 850 BC) who coveted its strategic location at the end of a high, narrow peninsula on the Mediterranean. The prosperous town passed through the hands of the Carthaginians and the Romans, and was finally abandoned in the 8th century after too many pirate raids. Today Nora overlooks emerald waters in one of the most serene spots in southern Sardinia. Explore the remains of Punic temples, patrician homes, and a remarkably well-preserved Roman theater, or take a short walk up to the watchtower for a breathtaking view of the site and the coastline. For those with a knowledge of Italian, a free guided tour will fill in the historical gaps. Otherwise the guidebooks in English (L10,000) offer more pictures than explanations. All signs are in Italian. (Open daily May-Sept. 9am-8pm, Sept.-April 9am-noon and 2-5pm. Free.) Another option from Pula is the glittering beach of **Santa Margherita** (buses every hr., 30min., L1100). The hotels in S. Margherita are geared to those in their golden years with gold in their pockets, but the beaches are uncrowded and beautiful.

NUORO PROVINCE

Most guidebooks would have you believe that Nuoro is the last bastion of true Sardinian culture. If that's the case, then the traditional Sardinian dress is Benetton and folk music is techno. Although many of the province's inland towns are quite isolated, it is only the older women who wear the typical black dress draped with a Spanish *fazzolletti* (shawl); in a generation or so this custom may disappear as well. Nuoro is a modern capital that makes an excellent base for exploring the rich archaeological treasures and beautiful, rugged countryside nearby. Unfortunately, you'll need a car to reach many of the region's most intriguing locales.

■■■ NUORO

ORIENTATION AND PRACTICAL INFORMATION

If you arrive by ARST bus, turn left off the little side street where you've been dropped, and you'll be facing the train station and the ARST ticket counter. Turn right onto Via Lamarmora and follow it to **Piazza delle Grazie.** From there, if you turn left and follow Via IV Novembre up the hill, you'll come to **Piazza Italia,** where the tourist office is located. Or cross Piazza della Grazie and keep going straight up **Corso Garibaldi,** a pedestrian walkway, to reach Nuoro's main square, **Piazza Vittorio Emanuele,** and beyond it, the *duomo.* Bus #4 makes the same trip from the station and saves you a good 15- to 20min. walk, while buses #5, 6, and 7 all end up at Piazza Vittorio Emanuele after various trajectories.

Tourist Office: P. Italia, 19 (tel. 300 83). Armed with an array of booklets and brochures, the staff is eager to evoke Nuoro's past. English spoken. Usually open Mon.-Fri. 8am-2pm, Tues.-Wed. 3:30-6:30pm; summer also Sat.-Sun. 9am-1pm. If they're closed, try upstairs in the same building, 4th floor.

Post Office: P. Crispi, 8 (tel. 302 78), off Via Dante. Open Mon.-Sat. 8am-7:40pm. **Postal Code:** 08100.

Telephones: Telecom (SIP), Via Brigata Sassari, 6, at P. d'Italia one block from the tourist office. Open Mon.-Sat. 8:30am-12:30pm and 3-7pm, Sun. 8am-1pm.

Public telephones available in the office annex. Open Mon.-Sat. 8:30am-7pm.
Telephone Code: 0784.
Trains and Buses: The **train and ARST** station is located on the corner of Via
Lamarmora and Via Stazione. Train to Cagliari (1 per day, 4hr., L18,500). ARST
buses to Oliena (L1500), Orgosolo (L2500), and Cagliari (L19,500). The **PANI** station (what there is of it) lies on Via B. Sassari, 15 (tel. 368 56), which you can
reach by walking up Via Stazione and following it around to the right. Buses to
Sassari (6 per day, L13,000), to Oristano and Cagliari (4 per day, L16,000 and
L28,000 respectively). Municipal buses cost L1200 per ride. Buy tickets beforehand in the *tabacchi* in the station, or in the *pizzeria* in the southwest corner of
the station. Bus #4 runs from Piazza Vittorio Emanuele to the station every 20
min. **Luggage Storage:** at the station. Ask at the ticket counter. L1500 per day.
Car Rental: Autonoleggio Maggiore, Via Convento, 32 (tel. 304 61). Open Mon.-
Sat. 8am-1pm and 4-7pm.
Emergencies: tel. 113. **Ambulance/Medical Emergency:** tel. 363 02. Volunteer
ambulance service only.

ACCOMMODATIONS

Inexpensive hotels are few and far between in Nuoro, and the campgrounds are
quite far away in neighboring towns. If you are unable to find accommodations
here, consider staying in Orgosolo or Oliena, where rooms tend to be available.

Il Portico, Via Mons. Bua (tel. 375 35), to the right off the end of P. Vittorio Emanuele. Airy, clean rooms with private showers and baths and a rustic decor. Management runs a great **restaurant** below. Definitely reserve ahead; they're usually
full. Singles L35,000. Doubles L50,000.
Mini Hotel, Via Brofferio, 13 (tel. 331 59), off Via Roma. Tidy rooms with tiled
floors and flowered bedspreads. Bathrooms are gargantuan. Some rooms with
flower-filled balconies. Singles L57,000. Doubles L72,000. Triples L97,000. All
rooms with bath. Family-run, so curfew is 11pm.
Hotel Grillo, Via Mons. Melas, 14 (tel. 386 78), off Via Manzoni. Follow the signs
from Piazza delle Grazie. Rooms decorated in earth tones, with perks: TV and
hairdryer. All rooms with bath. Breakfast in the restaurant downstairs L6000. Singles L65,000. Doubles L87,000. AmEx, Visa.

FOOD

Cheap restaurants are scarce. Try a bar on Corso Garibaldi or P. Vittorio Emanuele
for a sandwich. For more substantial provisions head to the **supermarket** on Via
Manzoni, next to the Alitalia office. (Open Mon.-Fri. 8am-2pm and 5-8pm, Sat. 8am-
2pm.) For fresh fruit, cheese, and meat, explore the enclosed **market** at P. Mameli,
20, off Via Manzoni. (Open Mon.-Tues. and Thurs.-Sat. 8am-1pm and 4:30-7pm,
Wed. 8am-1pm.) Across the street and uphill from the ARST station awaits the **Ippo
Mercato** (open daily 9am-2pm, 5-8pm); look for the smiling pink hippo.

Pizzeria del Diavolo, Via Dante, 10, near the post office. A variety of sinfully good
pizzas (L2000 a slice), *panini,* and fresh *focaccia* bread. This is where locals
come for take-out. Open Mon.-Sat. 9am-2pm and 5-9:30pm.
Il Portico, Via M. Bua (tel. 331 59), off the north end of P. Vittorio Emanuele. Connected to the hotel, this restaurant draws families with its enormous pizzas
(L7000), luscious pastas (L9000), and salads. Desserts include pie and the fresh
fruit in season. Friendly staff understands sign language. Cover L2000 for pizza,
L2500 for everything else. Open Tues.-Sun. noon-2:30pm and 8-10:30pm.

SIGHTS AND SEASONAL EVENTS

Nuoro is home to a few small treasures. Ethnography buffs enjoy the **Museo della
Vita e delle Tradizioni Popolari Sarde** (Museum of Sardinian Life and Popular Traditions), Via Mereu, 56. Masks, traditional costumes, and a good deal of sheep wool
recall the days when the land, the men, and the sheep interacted more closely. (Oct.
-June 14 open Tues.-Sat. 9am-1pm and 3-7pm, Sun. 9am-1pm; June 15-Sept. 30 open

daily 9am-7pm. Admission L3000, under 18 and over 60 free.) On Via Grazia Deledda lies the **home of Grazia Deledda** (the winner of the 1926 Nobel Prize for Literature), now a museum celebrating her life. (Open Oct.-June 14 9am-1pm and 3-7pm, Sun. 9am-1pm; June 15-Sept. 30 open daily 9am-7pm. Admission L3000. Combined ticket for both museums L5000.)

For a picnic, take the orange APT bus from P. Vittorio Emanuele up to **Monte Ortobene** (3 per day, L1200), or hike up the hillside (about 6 km; follow the signs, be aware of cars, and if you're alone, don't venture into the side paths). At the peak lies a shady park where a bronze statue of Christ the Redeemer overlooks the neighboring hamlets. From the bus stop on Monte Ortobene, walk 20m down the road to get a good view of colossal **Monte Corrasi,** which dwarfs the neighboring town of **Oliena.** Nuoro still celebrates one folkloric festival, the **Sagra del Redentore,** on the last two Sundays of August. Nuoro's natives claim that while in other parts of Sardinia such rites exist to placate tourists, here they are *proprio sentiti* (truly felt). Named for a local writer, the surreal **Piazza Sebastiano Satto** lies off Via Roma and Corso Garibaldi. Imitating the Sardinian megaliths, the *piazza* sprouts huge pillars of rock with alcoves cut into them, each cradling statuettes that tell Satto's story.

■ NEAR NUORO

OLIENA

Oliena lies sheltered by the rocky terrain of Monte Corrasi. Catch the ARST bus from Nuoro (4 per day, L1700) to this undeveloped heartland village where black-clad women attend mass daily and old men cluster in the *piazze* for hours on end to discuss whatever it is old men discuss. There are several churches in Oliena; the most inspiring, **Santa Croce** on Via Grazia Deledda, is still largely intact and well worth a visit. The stone exterior is surrounded by flowers, and the interior contains an ancient wooden tabernacle with an eerily realistic wooden sculpture of Christ's body in a coffin (used during the rites of Saints' Week). Ask the **Pro Loco** (tourist office; tel. (0784) 28 87 77) for the keys to visit; to reach the office, continue straight on Via Vittorio Emanuele II after the bus drops you off at the little white chapel, and take the large stairway to your left. The office is in the middle of a flight of stairs on your right. No map of the city exists, but you can get directions here. (Open daily 9am-1pm and 3:30-7:30pm.)

Ci Kappa, on Via Martin Luther King (tel. (0784) 28 87 33) is a famous bar, restaurant, and hotel, with a view onto Corso Vittorio Emanuele II and the mountain. The rooms are modern and comfortable, and all have private baths. (Singles L45,00. Doubles L65,000.) For an inexpensive, alternative accommodation, check with the Terranostra agency for available *agriturismo* rooms.

ORGOSOLO

Penetrating the province south of Oliena is problematic due to the paucity of public transportation. **ARST** buses run round-trip at inconvenient hours. One remote town easily accessible from Nuoro is **Orgosolo;** the trip is a twisting tour (40min., L2700) through rugged green mountains with vineyards clinging to their sides. The area's bloody history of *banditismo* (banditry) was made famous throughout Italy by the 1963 *The Bandits of Orgosolo;* the film is immortalized by a mural in the town. The outer edges of the town are quite modern, with pastel-colored apartment buildings, on-going construction, and occasional busloads of students, yet the winding streets of the *centro* still feel untouched by the outskirts' developments. Welcome additions to Orgosolo's buildings include bright, Picasso-esque murals depicting society's ills, from commercialism to fascism to American imperialism. A local teacher initiated the painting in the 1960s after studying art in Latin America.

If you can't tear yourself away from the murals or the mountain views, or if you decide to hike in the surrounding hills and need a place to stay in Orgosolo, follow the signs to the **Hotel Sa'e Jana,** Via E. Lussu (tel. (0784) 40 24 37), across town from the ARST bus stop. This family-run hotel has a rustic atmosphere despite its small new disco. Good, simple food is offered at low prices in the **restaurant** downstairs. Ask the proprietor about his tri-weekly "peasant" feasts accompanied by traditional Sardinian folk songs. (Singles L40,000. Doubles L70,000. Most rooms with bath.) In the center of town lies the **Petit Hotel,** Via Mannu, 9 (tel. (0784) 40 20 09), off Corso Repubblica. Sardinian crafts decorate the entryway; impeccable rooms and hospitable staff welcome you to Orgosolo. (Singles L35,000. Doubles L55,000. All rooms with bath.) If you miss the last bus back to Nuoro and are tempted to hitch after dark, reconsider—**hitchhiking is not safe here.** *Bandito* activity occasionally resurfaces in the countryside, though it is usually not directed at tourists but reserved for the locals. Women should not walk alone in the countryside here.

CALA GONONE

Just over one hour east of Nuoro by ARST bus (3 per day via Dorgali, L5000) lies **Cala Gonone,** the gateway to several spectacular beaches and caves. Take the steps through the wooded area when you get off the bus. The **beaches** at Cala Gonone are pebbly and crowded. A walk or ride down the dirt road along the coast rewards the effort with sandier, less-populated beaches. Boats leave four times per day, more often in July and August (L15,000), for the stunning **Grotta del Bue Marino** (Cave of the Monk Seal), one of the last haunts of this elusive creature. The seals rarely appear during the day, though, and the cave itself is the main attraction. Nearly 1km of caverns, stalactites, and lakes is illuminated. Unfortunately, stampeding crowds and the locked gate isolating the glowing *grotto* mar the experience. Just down the coast lies the vast beach of **Cala Luna.** Encircled by marshes and caverns, the beach is accessible only by boat (L11,500, combined *grotto*/Cala Luna ticket L25,000). Boats also run to the more remote and equally breathtaking beaches of **Cala Sistre** (L17,000), and **Cala Mariolu** (L24,000), both accessible only by boat. **Consortto Marittimo Transport** has monopolized the boat transport market to beaches. Call for reservations (tel. (0784) 93 305). **Cala Osal** is accessible only by car.

Cala Gonone recognizes its allure to wealthy tourists, so budget accommodations are hard to come by. Try the convenient **Albergo Gabbiano** at P. Porto, in the port (tel. 93 130). Rooms overlook the water. (Singles L45,000-65,000. Doubles L60,000-70,000.) Also enjoy the newly renovated **Piccolo Hotel,** Via Colomba, 32 (tel. 93 232). The gracious proprietor lends elegant, immaculate rooms with balconies overlooking a quiet garden. (Singles with bath L40,000-60,000. Doubles with bath L75,000-99,000, with possible mandatory summer pension L99,000 per person.) A large, well-equipped, and expensive **campground** on Via Collodi (tel. 931 65), across from the city park, charges L18,500 per person (Jul.-Aug. L22,000). Shower included. (Open April-Sept.)

The stunning mountains and scruffy hills that separate Nuoro from Cagliari hide towns of varying degrees of quaintness. One beautiful village is **Aritzo,** on the ARST bus line and near Gennargentu mountain (2000m high). The **Hotel Castello,** Corso Umberto (tel. 62 92 66) is pretty and modern. All rooms have fantastic views of the surrounding countryside. Singles with bath L45,000. Doubles with bath L60,000.

ORISTANO PROVINCE

The province of Oristano sustains a quiet life, keeping the beauty of the Sinis Peninsula beaches and ruins to itself. During prehistoric times, the mineral wealth of the region attracted settlers from the *nuraghic* civilization, who left stone monuments as evidence of their presence here. The capital town of Oristano saw the height of its independent splendor in the 14th century when the princess Eleanora d'Arborea led the natives in their last stages of resistance to mainland invaders. Oristano's provincial, agricultural feel sets it apart from the more touristed towns in Sardinia.

ORISTANO

■■■ ORISTANO

ORIENTATION AND PRACTICAL INFORMATION

Piazza Roma is the center of town. From the train station, follow **Via Vittorio Veneto,** the street furthest to the right as you exit the station, straight to **Piazza Mariano,** then take **Via Mazzini** to Piazza Roma (a 20min. walk). The ARST station and tourist office are located at the south end of Via Cagliari. There is a large map outside the ARST station. To get to P. Roma from there, follow **Via Emanuele** from nearby **Piazza Mannu.** From the PANI station (located on Via Lombardia on the other side of town—north of P. Roma) head toward Via Tirso. Make a right and then a quick left onto Via Cagliari. When you come to Via Tharros, turn left; this will take you directly into the square.

Tourist Office: Via Cagliari, 278 (tel. 731 91 or 741 91), 6th floor, near P. Mannu across from the ARST station. Helpful, well-informed staff with info on the town and region. Open Mon. and Thurs.-Fri. 8am-2pm, Tues.-Wed. 8am-2pm and 4-8pm. **Pro Loco,** Via Vittorio Emanuele, 8. Independent tourist office with information on Oristano only. Open Mon.-Fri. 9am-noon and 5-8pm, Sat. 9am-noon.

Post Office: For *fermo posta,* Via Liguria, 60, (tel. 21 17 78) near the PANI station. L300 for pick-up. (Open 8:15am-1pm and 2-8pm.) **Postal Code:** 09170.

Telephones: Telecom, P. Eleanora d'Arborea, 40, opposite the Church of San Francesco. Open Mon.-Fri. 9am-1pm and 4-7:30pm, Sat. 9am-1pm. **Telephone Code:** 0783.

Trains: P. Ungheria (tel. 722 70), about 1km from the town center. To: Sassari (5 per day, 3hr., L13,500); Olbia (6 per day, 4hr., L15,000); and Cagliari (10 per day, 1hr., L8000).

Buses: PANI, Via Lombardia, 30 (tel. 212 68), at a bar. Three buses leave daily to: Cagliari (8:55am, 4:10pm, and 9:35pm, 1½hr., L10,800); Nuoro (7am, 3:30pm, and 7:50pm, 2hr., L10,800); Sassari (7am, 3:30pm, and 7:50 pm, 2¼hr., L13,200). **ARST,** Via Cagliari (tel. 780 01), connects local routes and runs 2 slower buses to Cagliari (7:10am and 2:10pm, 1¾hr., L10,700).

Taxi: at the train station, some at P. Roma (tel. 702 80) during the day.

Emergencies: tel. 113. **Ambulance/Medical Emergency:** tel. 782 22. **Main hospital,** Via Fondazione Rockefeller (tel. 742 61). **First Aid:** tel. 743 33.

ACCOMMODATIONS AND CAMPING

The hotel scene here is extremely limited. Oristano caters more to travelers on their way to the beaches; competition is low, keeping prices high. Check the tourist office for *agriturismo* options; these will be less expensive but farther away.

Piccolo Hotel, Via Martignano, 19 (tel. 715 00). From the tourist office, take a left at P. Mannu, and the first right onto Via G. Angioy. Via Martignano is the first left after the curve. Probably the best budget option you'll find in town. Friendly owner, clean rooms, and firm beds make up for what lacks in interior design. All rooms with bath, many with balconies. Singles L60,000. Doubles L90,000.

I.S.A., P. Mariano, 50 (tel. 36 01 01). If the Piccolo is full, this is one of the few other reasonable options in town. The lobby is carpeted in purple velour with elevators, gleaming glass panes, and silver surfaces everywhere. Holiday Inn-ish feel. Singles L65,000. Doubles L90,000.

Hotel Ca. Ma., Via Veneto, 119, (tel. 743 74) near the train station. Modern and sterile; browns, grays, and puces abound. All rooms with bath. Singles L70,000. Doubles L96,000.

Camping: Marina di Torregrande, Via Stella Maris (tel. 22 228), 100m out of Torre Grande on the road to Oristano (7km). Facilities galore, but packed in summer. L6000 per person, L10,000 per tent. Open May-Sept. There are also bungalows available for rent. They house up to 4 and are a bargain at around L80,000 (off season L50,000).

FOOD

You can buy the basics as well as special *Sardi* products for rock-bottom prices at the **Euro-Drink market,** P. Roma, 22. (Open Mon.-Sat. 8:15am-1pm and 5-8pm.) The **STANDA supermarket** is at the corner of Via Diaz and Via Cavour. (Open Mon.-Fri. 8:30am-1pm and 4:30-8pm, Sat. 8:30am-1pm.)

La Torre, P. Roma, 52 (tel. 707 84). Packed with families of locals, serves up *Sardi* fare (try the *gnocchi all'orgosolese*) as well as standard *pizza margherita.* Restaurant open noon-3pm and 7-10:30pm. *Pizzeria* open 6:30-11pm.

Trattoria del Teatro, Via Parpaglia, 13, off P. Roma. All the basics, done up right. Open Mon.-Sat. noon-2:30pm, 8-10:30pm. AmEx.

Mike and Maty, Via Veneto, 109, near the train station. Small hand-held pizzas wrapped up like *gyros* (L2000) as well as standard sizes (starting L5000). One of the few places in town open on Sunday. Open Fri.-Wed. noon-10:30pm.

SIGHTS AND ENTERTAINMENT

Piazza Roma is dominated by the 13th-century **Tower of St. Mariano II.** On summer evenings, young *Oristanesi* rock and ramble through the *piazza* and the adjoining **Corso Umberto.** The pastel **Church of San Francesco** (1838) stands at the end of Via de Castro, at P. E. d'Arborca. The sacristy of this Pantheon-inspired building contains a 16th-century polyptych of *St. Francis Receiving the Stigmata* and Nino Pisano's 14th-century statue of San Basilio. The main sanctuary displays a wooden crucifix carved by Nicodemo—a simple cross on which the emaciated and tortured body of Christ is draped (typical of 14th-century German art, left altar)— and a balustrade formed from fragments of an 11th-century pulpit (right transept).

Down Via E. d'Arborea from P. E. d'Arborea is the **duomo,** a delightful blend of styles. Originally constructed by Lombard artists in the 13th century, it was completely renovated in the 18th. In addition to the Gothic windows and medieval multi-colored bell tower, the cathedral holds Baroque paintings, some neo-classical architecture, stained glass, and an animated sculpture of St. Michael. The **Antiquarium Arborense,** Via Parpaglia, 37, near P. Eleonora, shelters a small but fascinating collection of artifacts from the Nuraghic, Punic, and Roman eras unearthed at Tharros. (Open Tues.-Sun. 9:30am-1pm, 4:30-7pm. Admission L4000.) Three km out of town on the road to Cagliari is the 12th-century **Basilica of Santa Giusta,** typically Sardinian in its synthesis of Lombard and Pisan influences. The sculpted façade depicts two lions dismembering and devouring a deer. Set against this macabre backdrop is a tremendous square cross of dark blocks. The interior is stark, so as not to distract earnest churchgoers.

On the last Sunday of *Carnevale* and the following Tuesday (usually in March; inquire at the tourist office), inhabitants of Oristano don their best traditional finery and celebrate the **Sartiglia.** The main event started in the 16th century and is best described as star-jousting: masked horsemen try to pierce six-inch metal stars with their swords as they gallop down the street. Those who pierce many stars bring *Fortuna* (good luck) upon the next harvest. Away from the stampeding people and horses, the **Malu Entu Adventure Team** offers scuba-diving classes and expeditions, rents canoes and sailing boats, and leads guided hikes and mountain bike tours. It's based in the town of **Cuglieri,** 45km from Oristano (tel. (0785) 38 352).

■■■ SINIS PENINSULA AND THE COSTA VERDE

The coastal areas surrounding Oristano offer everything that the better-known resorts do—except the concrete and crowds.

In the southernmost tip of the peninsula, 17km west of Oristano, lie the ruins of the ancient Phoenician port of **Tharros.** Much of the city remains submerged, but excavations have revealed Punic fortifications, a Roman temple dedicated to Demeter, a paleo-Christian baptistry, and a Punic shrine. There's even a medieval watch-

ALGHERO

tower atop the hill. Nearby lie serene beaches, where crystal-clear water laps at the shore. An easy bike ride (it's all flat) or an even easier drive from Oristano will make up for the patchy ARST bus service (Sept.-June 3 buses per day, July-Aug. 6 buses, 40min., L4800 round-trip). On the way to Tharros you'll pass two pagan-shrines-turned-churches: **San Salvatore,** near Cabras, was built above a pagan temple whose Roman deities (Venus, Cupid, and Hercules) are still visible on an underground wall. (Ask the curate to show you. No fixed hours, but don't come at lunchtime.) **San Giovanni in Sinis,** a part-pagan, part-Christian shrine dating from the 5th century seems, in structure and spirit, to be a distant ancestor of Oristano's Santa Giusta. During the 1960s San Salvatore was converted into a Mexican-American "Old West" village for several spaghetti westerns.

If you're tired of sight-seeing, sprawl on the beaches or check out the village of **San Giovanni di Sinis.** Two beaches, **Putzu Idu** and **Cala Saline,** lie 15 km north of San Giovanni on the peninsula. Beautiful, white-sanded, and uncrowded, they're worth a swim or even a few quiet days of lolling. Three villages lie in close proximity on this remote corner of the peninsula. The only affordable accommodation is **Hotel "Su Pallosu,"** Via Sa Margosa, 2, in Marina di S. Vero Milis (tel. (0783) 580 21). (Singles L40,000-60,000. Doubles L70,000-90,000.) The local fishing community frequents the bar. You can find cheap food, live music, and a friendly gathering every night at **Club Tomoka;** ask at the hotel for directions. To get to Putzu Idu from Oristano, take the ARST bus (direction: Barátili or San Pietro) and get off at Riola (25min.). Walk down Via Roma until the street ends at Via Umberto, and turn right. Wait for the connecting bus a few meters down the street, across from the motorcycle repair shop. The connecting bus (use the same ticket) will be marked "Cala Saline"; take it for another 8km (10-15min.) right to the beach. Bus schedules change seasonally, but plan to get up early. Walk a few kilometers south along the coast to see the stunning cliffs at **Capo sa Starraggia.** Approximately 7km south, the lovely cliffs and white beach of **Is Arustas** await the hardy hiker; the less ambitious can take an ARST bus directly to Is Arutas (same line as San Giovanni, L3500).

About 35km south of Oristano, the **Costa Verde** stretches nearly 40km, a happy mingling of sandy coves and scintillating ocean. Yet apart from the two coastal towns of Porto Palma and Marina di Arbus (where there is a rudimentary campsite), there are few locals to speak of, and even fewer travelers. ARST buses take you part of the way to Arbus (*not* Marina di Arbus or Diane) at 8:10am, 2:15pm, and 5:45pm (1½hr., L6000) but you'll have to fend for yourself from there.

NORTHWEST SARDINIA

■■■ ALGHERO

Don't be surprised to find yourself strolling by the sea at sunset, thinking of former romances and lovers lost; in Alghero the smell of burning wood, the echo of cobblestone streets, and the caress of a cool sea breeze are bound to induce romantic nostalgia. Local residents have never quite freed themselves from the past. Taken over by Pere I of Aragon in the 14th century, Algherese today still speak a melodious Catalàn dialect. In fact, the town has earned the nickname "Little Barcelona of Sardinia."

ORIENTATION AND PRACTICAL INFORMATION

Arriving by ARST or FS bus, you will be dropped off at the corner of Via Catalogna and Via Cagliari, one block from the port. The tourist office, located in **Piazza Porta Terra,** lies diagonally across the small park, toward the towers of the **centro storico.** From the train station, follow **Via Don Minzoni** until it turns into **Via Garibaldi** along the waterfront. The old city will be on your left. City buses AF and AP run from the train station to the port.

Tourist Office: P. Porta Terra, 9 (tel. 97 90 54; fax 97 48 81), near the bus stop on your right as you walk toward the old city from the park. The most organized office in Sardinia, if not Italy. Cheerful, helpful staff speaks English, French, and German (and some Italian—just kidding) and offers an indexed street map, tours of the city, and day trips to local villages. Open May-July and Sept. Mon.-Sat. 8am-8pm; in Aug. also open Sun. 9am-noon; Oct.-April Mon.-Sat. 8am-2pm.

Police: P. della Mercede, 4 (tel. 113).

Post Office: Via XX Settembre, 108 (tel. 97 93 09). Open Mon.-Sat. 10am-7:30pm, *fermo posta* 10am-1:20pm. **Branch Offices,** Via Carducci, 35 (tel. 97 42 15) and Via Carbonia, 20 (tel. 95 03 17). **Postal Code:** 07041.

Telephones: booths at P. Sulis and throughout town. **Telephone code:** 079.

Currency Exchange: Banca Nazionale del Lavoro, across from the tourist office. Has a 24-hr. automatic exchange machine (bills only, no traveler's checks). Also changes money inside, like most banks. Open Mon.-Fri. 8:20am-1pm.

Trains: at Via Don Minzoni (tel. 95 07 85), in the northern part of the city. Take the AP or AF city bus from the stop 1 block north of the tourist office (every 20min.), or stroll 1km along the port. Open daily 5:30am-9:30pm. If you buy your ticket at the **FS booth** at the port, you can ride the city bus to the station for free. To Sassari (11 per day, 40min., L3200).

Buses: ARST (information tel. 26 00 48) and **FS** (tel. 95 01 79) buses depart from Via Catalogna. Buy tickets for either line at the stand in the park. To Sassari (18 per day, 1hr., L4500-4800), Bosa (4 per day, 1½hr., L6900), and Porto Torres (5 per day, 1hr., L4800).

Public Transportation: Orange city buses begin their routes every 20 min. and cost L1100 per trip. (Book of 12 tickets L11,000.) Line AF travels between Fertilia and the port, line AP goes to the train station, and line AO runs to the Lido and hospital. All three begin service around 7:15am and the last run leaves at 9:30pm.

Taxis: P. Porta Terra (tel. 97 53 96), across from the tourist office.

Car Rental: Budget, at the airport in Fertilia (tel. 93 51 67). **Avis,** at the airport (tel. 93 50 64). **Autonolotaxi Farris Carlo,** Via Mazzini, 44 (tel. 97 85 51). Rates start at L55,000 plus L450 per kilometer. Minimum age 22.

Bike/Moped Rental: Cycloexpress di Tomaso Tilocca, Via Garibaldi, at the harbor (tel. 97 65 92). Bikes L12,000 per day, mountain bikes L18,000 per day, tandem bikes L20,000 per day. Mopeds L25,000 per day. Scooters L50,000 per day. Insurance included. Ask for their English-language brochure with a complete listing of prices and restrictions. Another location on Banchine Porto. Open Mon.-Sat. 8:30am-1pm and 4-8:30pm, Sun. 8:30am-noon.

Horse Rental: Club Ippico Capuano (tel. 97 81 98). 3km from Alghero. L25,000 per hour to rent a horse (often more reliable than Italian cars). Special guided excursions for an afternoon—reservations recommended 2-3 days in advance. They will pick you up in Alghero for a charge of L5000 per person.

Public Baths: stalls at the port, next to the train office. Coin-accessed toilets and showers. Toilets L200. Showers L1000.

Pharmacy: Farmacia Mugoni, Via Sassari, 8, across from the market. Open Tues.-Sun. 9am-1pm and 4:30-8:30pm.

Emergencies: tel. 113. **Medical Emergency:** V. I Maggio (tel. 95 06 13). Open 8pm-8am. **Hospital: Ospedale Civile,** Regione la Pietraia (tel. 99 62 00), a few blocks north of the train station on V. Don Minzoni. **Ambulance:** tel. 97 66 34.

ACCOMMODATIONS AND CAMPING

Prices escalate and rooms vanish in July and August. Unless you've made a reservation far in advance or are willing to pay for half-pension, which doesn't come cheap, consider radiating your search from the center of town; many hotels line the beach on the way to Fertilia. Or inquire at the tourist office for *agriturismo* opportunities.

Ostello dei Giuliani (HI), Via Zara, 3 (tel. 93 03 53), 7km from Alghero in Fertilia—great for getting to the beach. Take the yellow AF city bus from Via La Marmora next to the train station (every hr., 15min., L1100). ARST buses around the corner also go there. Curfew 10pm. L14,000 per person. Showers L2500. Breakfast L3000. Scrumptious lunches and dinners L12,000. (Meals served July and

ALGHERO

Aug. only.) *Always* reserved to capacity in July and August, but call and ask about cancellations. Open April 15-Oct. 15.

Hotel San Francesco, Via Machin, 2 (tel. 98 03 30). With your back to the tourist office, walk straight and take the 2nd right. Simple but comfortable rooms in the church cloister, all with swell bathrooms and prayers by Saint Francis over the beds to ensure sweet dreams. Breakfast included, and you can have it on the cloister's patio. Occasional concerts. Reserve ahead in summer. Singles L40,000/50,000. Doubles L65,000/85,000. MC, Visa.

Pensione Normandie, Via Mattei, 6 (tel. 97 53 02), a 15-min. walk from the port. From Via Cagliari (which turns into Via Papa Giovanni XXIII), turn right on Via Mattei. Decent, nondescript rooms in a family-run place. The cheapest in town, but there's not much around. Singles L27,000. Doubles L50,000.

Hotel San Guian, Via G.M. Angioy, 2 (tel. 95 12 22). Across from the beach. Bright rooms with firm beds and the cleanest of bathrooms. Singles L50,000/70,000. Doubles L88,000/100,000. Breakfast included. AmEx, MC, Visa.

Camping: Calik (tel. 93 01 11), 6km away, beyond the bridge into Fertilia. Large and crowded, 50m from the beach. L10,000/14,000 per person. Open June-Nov. **La Mariposa** (tel. 95 03 60), Via Lido, 3km away on the Alghero-Fertilia road and near the beach. Packed in summer. L10,000/16,500 per person, L7000 per car. Open June-Oct.

FOOD

Two blocks up from the tourist office, at the corner of Via Cagliari and Via Mazzini, a **market** offers the freshest in Sardinian produce (open Tues.-Sun. 7am-1pm). Every Wednesday, crowds engulf the open air market on Via de Gasperi. Take the special bus, marked "Linea Mercato," from Via Cagliari. Cheese-lovers should not miss the pungent **Casa de Formaggio,** at Via Mazzini, 43, which makes and ages a delicious *pecorino*. (Open Tues.-Sun. 7:30am-1pm and 4-8pm.) Specialty stores in **Piazza Civica** sell traditional Sardinian fare, including eucalyptus honey and the marmalade-filled pastries called *tilicus*. Some of these stores also carry soy-based products for vegetarians. Beware of the Algherese *menu turistico*; most cost L25,000 and consist of little more than spaghetti with tomato sauce and the unavoidable fried calamari.

Ristorante La Muraglia, Bastioni Marco Polo, 7 (tel. 97 50 02). Hands-down winner in the "Have a Stunning View of the Sea to Go With Your Spaghetti" sweepstakes. The food is not as good as the view, but if you're sitting at one of their outdoor tables, you probably won't notice. Pizzas from L6000. AmEx, MC, Visa. Open Mon.-Sat. 11am-3pm and 6:30pm-1am.

Ristorante La Piconia, Via Principe Umberto, 27 (tel. 987 001). A cozy tunnel of a restaurant, with a wood-burning fire at one end and heavy wood tables at the other (coincidence?). Enjoy their *spaghetti al nero* (L9000) or crispy pizzas (L7000-9000). Open Tues.-Sun. noon-3pm and 7pm-midnight. AmEx, Visa.

Jamaica Inn, Via Principe Umberto, 57 (tel. 97 41 10). A pub/restaurant that draws locals for the beer selection (including Guinness) and tasty *panini* (L6000). Also serves up burgers and fries. Pasta from L8000-10,000. Open Tues.-Sun. 7pm-3am.

SIGHTS AND ENTERTAINMENT

A leisurely walk through the *centro storico* reveals tiny alleyways, half-hidden churches, and the ancient town walls. Don't miss the fantastic views of the sea along Bastioni Marco Polo. From P. Sulis, Via Carlo Alberto takes you to the **Church of San Francesco,** whose heavy Neoclassical façade conceals a gracious Gothic presbytery. Although built in the 14th century, the church was partially rebuilt in the 16th; the different colored stones show where the original left off and the renovation began. In July and August, the classical music of the **Estate Musicale Internazionale** (Summer Music Festival), sponsored by the tourist office, fills the cloisters. Schedules and tickets are available from the office in the cloister of the church. Brown and green shutters complement the beige walls along nearby medieval **Via Principe Umberto.** At #7 you'll find the **Casa Doria,** with its beautiful 16th-century façade, built by the powerful Doria clan of Genoa who fortified the fishing village of

Alghero in the 11th century. Down the street you can get the most interesting view of the cathedral—the backside. Begun in 1552, the cathedral took 178 years to build, resulting in a motley Gothic-Catalàn-Renaissance façade. Rebuilt in the 19th century, the church retains its striking Gothic choirs and *campanile*.

There are three strategically located medieval **towers** in Alghero. **Torre del Portal,** on Piazza Porta Terra, was one of two access routes to the fortified Catalàn city, complete with a drawbridge and (at the time) an artificial moat. **Torre de l'Espero Reial,** in Piazza Sulis, a prison in the 18th century, is a circular fortification with a grand view of the ocean. The **Torre de Sant Jaume** is commonly known as the **Torre dels Cutxos** (Dog's Tower) since it served as a 15th-century dog pound.

Those who prefer to see fish in water rather than on their plate can check out the local underwater population at the **Mare Nostrum Aquarium,** Via XX Settembre, 1 (tel. 97 83 33), across from the old city. (Open daily June-Sept. 10am-1pm and 5-11pm; Oct.-May 5pm-10pm. Admission L8000, students L4000.)

In addition to the Jamaica Inn (see above), the **Zebra Bar,** Via Barcelonetta, 15 (tel. 97 76 33) attracts cool, young Algherese for cocktails and conversation. Closed Sunday. Down on the waterfront, at Lungomare Valencia, **Bar de Trò** takes full advantage of its location on a picturesque bend in the bay, and offers live music nightly. Open 8pm-1am. **Rhapsody in Blues,** Via Garibaldi, 53 (tel. 98 45 22) on the waterfront serves up yummy crepes. (Open 8pm until the dawn.)

■ NEAR ALGHERO

The **Grotte di Nettuno** (tel. 94 65 40) is a vast natural wonder, an eerie cavern-complex of dagger-like stalactites and stalagmites. The caves delve into Capo Caccia, a steep promontory which projects from Porto Conte (25km by land from Alghero, 15km by sea). (Groups admitted hourly 9am-6pm; Oct.-April 9am-2pm. Admission L10,000; under 12 L6000.) Boats leave Alghero's Bastione della Maddalena hourly on the hour at **Compagnie Navisarda** (tel. 97 55 99; round-trip 2½hr., L14,000, under 12 L8000). The SFS bus combs the beautiful coast (leaving at 9:15am, 2:50pm, and 5:15pm, returning at noon, 3:45pm, and 6pm; 1hr.; one way L3000, round-trip L5700). Mopeds can reach the *grotte* in 30 minutes. Once there, descend the memorable 654 steps that plunge between massive white cliffs all the way to the sea. If you're on moped, stop at the **beaches of Porto Conte** and exquisite **Capo Caccia,** as well as the **Nuraghe di Palmavera** (10km out of Alghero), where an intriguing central tower dates from 1500 BC. (Open April-Oct. daily 9am-1pm and 3-7pm. Admission L3500.) Price includes a guided tour. Call ahead for a language other than Italian (tel. 98 07 50). If you've rented a moped for the whole day, ride 10km toward Porto Torres to the **Necropolis of Anghelu Ruju,** the largest in Sardinia, a group of 38 tombs built around 3000 BC by the local fishing tribes. You can also take the ARST bus from Alghero (departures at 7:05am, 1:45pm, and 4:35pm; L1500).

BOSA

Clinging to the hills above the mouth of the Temo, Sardinia's only navigable river, Bosa maintains the quiet charm of a small town. The *centro storico* along the river and the beach of Bosa Marina have so far escaped the onslaught of tour buses, and the town itself, with pastel buildings, narrow streets, and no stoplights, seems unaware of its appeal. Enjoy it while you can. Climb to reach the **Castello Malespina,** built in the 14th century by the family of the same name. Only the ramparts remain, but the view of the ocean, river, and town are stunning. Bosa's **duomo,** Chiesa Santa Maria Immacolata, is an amalgam of 13th- and 14th-century styles, though the interior is pure baroque. The **Church of San Antonio** sits quietly on the other side of the river; you might pass it by for its plain cream and brown exterior. A walk across the river from the *centro storico* leads to the **beach** of Bosa Marina, as well as to the medieval **watchtower.** A walk along the seaside offers the hiker cliffs and the less energetic with a paved stretch of several kilometers.

A youth hostel is in the works for Bosa Marina, but until it opens, try **Albergo Su Pischedda,** Via Roma (tel. 37 30 65), near the beach. Doubles L45,000, with bath L50,000. Closer to the *centro storico* try **Albergo Perry Clan,** Viale Alghero, 3 (tel. 37 30 74; fax 37 52 63). Pink and brown rooms, all with bath. Singles L30,000. Doubles L60,000. Grab a pizza in air-conditioned **La Margherita,** Via Parpaglia (tel. 37 37 23). MC, Visa. When your sweet tooth acts up, head to **Caffè Chelo** on Corso Emanuele, 62 (tel. 37 30 92). (Open Tues.-Sun. 7am-midnight.) A young crowd frequents the **Caffetteria-Gelateria Pirino,** Viale Giovanni XXIII, 10 (Open 7am-11pm).

ARST **buses** connect Bosa to Alghero (2-3 per day, 1hr, L4000), Macomer (2-3 per day, 1 hr, L4000 with connections to Oristano, Nuoro, and Cagliari), and Sassari (2hr, L10,800). Buses stop either in Bosa Marina on the ocean side of the river with easy access to the beaches, or in the *centro storico* (it's a 15min. walk between the two). The **tourist office,** Corso Emanuele, 73, is temporarily closed; try your luck with their hours when you get there. A **post office** hides at the dead end of Via G. Pischedda (tel. 37 31 39). (Open Mon.-Fri 8:30am-5:30pm and Sat. 8:15am-12:45pm.) It also **exchanges** traveler's checks. **Telephone code:** 0785.

■■■ SASSARI

Sardinia's second-largest city sits atop a limestone plateau, where its founders sought refuge from the foreign invaders and malaria epidemics common to coastal territory. Today Sassari is an important petrochemical center, with modern suburbs surrounding its compact medieval core. In the capital of Italy's largest province, Sassarians enjoy the highest standard of living in Sardinia. The grandiose 18th-century Piazza d'Italia and several wide boulevards lend Sassari an air of continental pretension. But the pleasant, old-fashioned character of the city manifests itself in the evening gathering of Sassarians, young and old, in Piazza d'Italia.

ORIENTATION AND PRACTICAL INFORMATION

All roads radiate from the newly restored **Piazza d'Italia.** As you stand facing the Banco di Napoli in the *piazza,* **Via Roma** and the **PANI station** are on your left. **Emiciclo Garibaldi** and the **ARST station** are straight ahead, with the leafy **Piazza Castello** behind it. The main shopping street, **Corso Vittorio Emanuele,** and the **train station** (down a little further) are on your right. The towns of Alghero and Porto Torres are located 37km southwest and 18.5km northwest, respectively.

Tourist Office: Viale Umberto, 72 (tel. 23 35 34). One block up and two blocks to the right of Piazza d'Italia, on the ground floor of a nondescript office building. Free maps. Open Mon.-Fri. 8am-2pm and 4-6pm. Sat. (summer only) 8am-noon.

Police: Via Coppino, 1 (tel. 23 23 43).

Post Office: Via Brigata Sassari, 13 (tel. 23 21 78), off P. Castello. *Fermo posta,* fax. Open Mon.-Fri. 8:15am-7:40pm. Money and some other services not available after 1pm. **Postal code:** 07100.

Telephones: Telecom (SIP), Viale Italia, 7/A. Open Mon.-Fri. 9am-1pm and 4-7:30pm. **Telephone Code:** 079.

Budget Travel: CTS, Via Costa, 48 (tel. 23 45 85), off Viale B. Sassari. Open Mon.-Fri. 9:30am-1pm and 4:30-7pm, Sat. 9:30am-noon.

Currency Exchange: Banca Commerciale Italia, Piazza d'Italia, 23. Open Mon.-Fri. 8:20am-1:35pm and 3:15-4:45pm or anywhere along Corso Emanuele.

Flights: 28km south, near Alghera Fertilia. Free ARST buses leave for the airport from the station 1¼hr. before departures. Both domestic and international flights. **Airport Information:** tel. 93 50 33.

Trains: P. Stazione (tel. 26 03 62), 1 block from P. Sant'Antonio. To: Olbia (9 per day, 2hr., L9200); Oristano (5 per day, 2¾hr., L11,000); Cagliari (4 per day, 3½hr., L19,300); Alghero (10 per day, 40min., L3600). Ask for a complete schedule at the tourist office. Take the #8 bus from the station to avoid the long uphill trek to Piazza d'Italia. Buy tickets in the newsstand at the station (L1100). **Luggage Storage:** Open 6:30am-8:30pm, L1500.

Buses: PANI, Via Bellieni, 25 (tel. 23 69 83 or 23 47 82), 1 block from P. d'Italia. To: Cagliari (6:35am, 9:30am, 2pm, and 7:15pm, 4hr., L26,000; nonstop at 6am, 2:15pm, and 6pm, 3¼hr.); Nuoro (6 per day, 2½hr., L13,000); Oristano (4 per day, 2¼hr., L12,500). Open Mon.-Sat. 5:30-6:30am, 9:15am-2:15pm, and 5:30-7:15pm. Ask at the desk for a schedule of local buses. **ARST,** Emiciclo Garibaldi, 23 (tel. 26 00 06). Serves most local routes. **FS,** tickets in the bar next door at #26 (tel. 24 13 01). Runs buses to Alghero (10 per day, 1½hr., L4800), Porto Torres (L2200), Castelsardo (L3700), and Torrelba (L4300). Open Mon.-Sat. 7am-1:30pm and 2-8pm. **Luggage Storage ARST:** L2000. Open Mon.-Sat. 10am-4:30pm.
Taxi: at Emiciclo Garibaldi (tel. 234 630).
Car Rental: Avis, Via Mazzini, 2 (tel. 23 55 47). From L150,000 per day. Minimum age 23. **Hertz,** Corso Vico, 5 (tel. 23 21 84). Open Mon.-Fri. 8:30am-1:30pm and 3:30-7pm. L155,000 per day, L705,000 per week. Minimum age 24.
All-Night Pharmacy: Simon, Via Brigata Sassari, 2 (tel. 23 32 38). Open Mon.-Fri. 9am-1pm and 5pm-9am. Posts a weekly list of pharmacies open Sunday.
Emergencies: tel. 113. **Medical Emergency: Ospedale Civile,** Via de Nicola, off Via Costa (tel. 22 05 00). **First Aid:** tel. 22 06 21.

ACCOMMODATIONS

Unless you want to stay near chemical plants or pay big bucks, rooms in Sassari are few and far between. For information on camping, see Platamona page 576.

Pensione Famiglia, Viale Umberto, 65 (tel. 23 95 43). A large establishment comprised of massive rooms filled with equally massive furniture. Reminiscent of a European hospital, though not quite as sterile—flies seem to congregate in the entryway. Singles L25,000. Doubles L30,000.
Hotel Giusy, P. Sant'Angelo, 21 (tel. 23 33 27). Near the train station. Very clean, modern, and professional, though some rooms are noisy due to the busy streets. All rooms with private bath. Singles L48,000. Doubles L65,000.

FOOD

A wide selection of *pizzerie* lines **Corso Emanuele.** Any student ID allows you to eat at the **University Mensa,** Via Padre Manzella, 2 (tel. 21 91 11), off P. Gramsci. A basic, filling meal is yours for L7000, but you might be able to get a student outside to sell you a ticket for about L1000. (Open Mon.-Sat. 12:30-2:20pm and 7:30-9pm.) The large, enclosed **market** occupies P. Mercato, down Via Rosello from Via Vittorio Emanuele. (Open Mon.-Fri. 8am-1pm and 5-8pm, Sat. 8am-1pm.) The **STANDA supermarket** is on Viale Italia at Via Sardegna. (Open Mon.-Fri. 8:45am-1pm and 4:30-8:15pm, Sat. 9am-1pm.) Or try the well-stocked minimarket (tel. 26 02 13), to the left as you exit the station (open Mon.-Fri. 8am-1pm and 5-8pm, Sat. 8am-1pm). Vegetarians will find soy products, raw nuts, and other protein products at the *alimentari* at Via Brigita Sassari, 56. Many Japanese products can be found here as well. (Open Mon.-Fri. 8am-1pm and 5-7:30pm, Sat. 8am-1pm.)

Trattoria Da Peppina, Vicolo Pigozzi, 1 (tel. 23 61 46), off Corso Emanuele. A small, simple place filled with locals. Reservations recommended. Vegetarians beware: all the sauces have meat in them. *Primi* L5000-9000, *secondi* L8000-12,000. Open Mon.-Sat. noon-3pm and 7-10pm.
Pizzeria Al Corso, Corso Emanuele, 148 (tel. 23 42 10). Perhaps the island's best pizza, twirled and loaded with cheese before your very eyes, and toasted to perfection in a wood-burning oven (L4500-9500). Even the plain mozzarella *margherita* will send your tastebuds into orbit. Pasta, meat dishes, dessert served as well. Cover for pizza L1500, otherwise L2000. Open Tues.-Sun. 7pm-1am.
Bar-Trattoria Gennargenta, Via Università, 53. Popular with local students. Friendly staff. Dark interior, but the food is hearty and filling. The student *menù* includes *primo, secondo, contorno,* fruit, wine, and coffee for L18,000.

NEAR SASSARI

SIGHTS AND SEASONAL EVENTS

The **Museo Giovanni Antonio Sanna,** Via Roma, 64 (tel. 27 22 03), houses reconstructed *nuraghi,* Sardinian paintings, traditional costumes, and a pleasant garden. The graceful Roman statues and mosaics are a treat. Listen for the Sardinian pipe music played in the ethnographic section. (Open Mon.-Sat. 9am-2pm, Sun. 9am-1pm, 2nd Wed. of each month 4:30-7:30pm. Admission L4000.) Sassari's duomo, the **Cathedral of San Nicolò,** is a 13th-century Romanesque structure with a 17th-century Spanish colonial baroque façade (dubbed "an immense flower of stone" by Elio Vittorini). Entry is not allowed, however. The **Church of Santa Maria di Betlem,** near the train station, is another hybrid: displaying Islamic influences, its 14th-century Gothic vaults also shelter elegant Baroque altars, and the adjacent cloister preserves a bronze-spigoted medieval fountain. (Open 10am-6pm.)

The lavish **Sardinian Cavalcade,** held on the second-to-last Sunday in May, is Sardinia's most notable folk festival. The festivities include a morning procession of costumed emissaries from dozens of villages all over Sardinia, an afternoon *Palio* (horse race), and an evening song-and-dance show. **I Candelieri,** the festival of the candlesticks (great wooden columns in the shape of enormous tapers), takes place on Assumption Day (August 14), when the *Gremi,* or farmers' guilds, parade giant replicas of candles and matches through the streets. The festival dates back to the 17th-century, when people reasoned that a lack of candle offerings to the Virgin had caused the latest plague.

■ NEAR SASSARI

Castelsardo's striking location on a lofty promontory and its proximity to sandy beaches make it a popular stop along Costa Paradiso. Only 34km northwest of Sassari, it is also a convenient daytrip (10 ARST buses per day, L3500). The hilltop town offers a few cultural sights, including the castle of the town's name, a museum, and a late-Gothic **cathedral** (shamelessly replastered in drab stucco), which shelters an impressive 15th-century painting of the *Madonna with Angels.* There are no rooms in the old town. Try **Pensione Pinna,** Lungomare Anglona, 7 (tel. (079) 47 01 68), across the street from the harbor. Ask for a room on the second floor with a view of the sea. (Singles L40,000. Doubles L50,000-68,000, with bath L60,000-78,000.)

Some easily accessible *nuraghi* await you 30km south of Sassari—most notably **Nuraghi Santu Antine** at **Torralba.** Some of the most interesting prehistoric architecture in the western Mediterranean can be found just off this road. The central tower dates from the 9th century BC and the fortifications surrounding it from the 7th. (Site open daily 8:30am-8:15pm.) The must-see **Museum of the Valley of the Nuraghi** at Via Carlo Felice, 97 (tel. 84 72 98), in Torralba, provides information on the *nuraghi,* next to excavated relics. (Open Tues.-Sun. 9am-1pm and 3-8pm. Admission L4000, under 18 free.) The Torralba **train station** (on the Cagliari-Sassari line) lies 1km from the monument, and PANI and ARST buses also run to the town (4km from the site, L4000).

The most convenient **beach** from Sassari is found in **Platamona,** a long white expanse of sand where the locals go on weekends. Take the orange city bus labelled "Via Budi Budi" (chant it on the ride for added fun) from Via Torse Tonda in the middle of the public gardens (every 40min., 30min., L4000 round-trip). Buy tickets at the **FS Office,** 28 Emiciclo Garibaldi. This bus also goes to the best place to stay near Sassari, if you have camping gear: the **International Cristina Camping Village,** Platamona (tel. 31 02 30). Get off the bus when you see the large sign on your right. It's a decent campground, perhaps a bit crowded with trailers, but featuring its own beautiful beach that makes it a worthy stopover. (Camping L12,000 per person; bungalows for 5, L59,000-71,000.)

NORTHERN COAST

The northern shore of Sardinia is its most crowded, and most likely to be confused with Miami Beach. It includes the Emerald Coast (Costa Smeralda), Sardinia's greatest casualty of the Eurotourist deluge, and Santa Teresa di Gallura, a coastal retreat which in July and August harbors more vacationing Germans than Italians. Still, the scenery here is stunning, with white cliffs jutting into truly turquoise water and strange rock formations carved by the strong winds. Timing is everything: come in high season only if you're prepared to pay loads of *lire* for a room.

■■■ STINTINO

Stintino, 24km northwest of Porto Torres on the Capo del Falcone, *was* a legitimate fishing village, but has recently been swallowed up in the ever-spreading tourist trade. The winter population of fewer than 1000 swells to almost 20,000 in summer. Much of Stintino's transformation can be attributed to the stunning beauty of **Spiaggia di Pelosa,** a beach 4km outside town, whose sparkling waters glisten against the bone-dry **Isola Asinara,** an island penal colony. An easy 500-m wade through thigh-deep water takes you to a tiny islet and its marooned 18th-century **Aragonese tower;** a great day trip to the best beach near Sassari. Buses run to and from Sassari (4 per day, 1hr., L4700). Don't miss the last bus, as impromptu camping is nearly impossible and hotels cater to European tourists with *very* flexible budgets. If you're desperate, try **Albergho Silvestrino** at Via Sassari, 12 (tel. 52 30 07; singles L45,000-50,000/65,000, doubles L70,000-80,000/85,000-110,000).

■■■ SANTA TERESA DI GALLURA

Perched on Sardinia's northwest tip, Santa Teresa di Gallura is a perky, pastel beach town. The gentle sound of the waves lapping at the cliffs and beaches can be nearly hypnotic. The main scene here is the family vacation, making Santa Teresa a bit sleepy in the evening. From the small, immaculate **Rena Bianca** beach, you can actually see Corsica across the hazy waters. This beach also has some of the biggest waves in Sardinia, perfect for riding to the shore.

ORIENTATION

Turn right from where the ARST or FS bus stops and walk uphill toward the church. There, at **P. San Vittorio,** turn right to arrive at **P. Vittorio Emanuele.** The **tourist office** is at #1, up the stairs. To get to the beach, walk down the opposite side of the *piazza.* A dirt path leads away from the beach up the hill. At the fork, the lower path leads to **Isola Municca,** a stadium-like islet with high rocks that surround a field of grass. The higher trail twists between magnificent granite formations and offers an excellent view of Corsica and Capo Testa, especially in the morning. Follow the hill to reach the isthmus connecting **Capo Testa** with the mainland. Otherwise, go back into town and take Via Capo Testa (3km) or the ARST bus from the post office mornings and afternoons. There are beaches on both sides of the isthmus. From Capo Testa's lighthouse, you can walk down to a secluded series of scenic coves. Paths lead south through the spectacular granite quarries of the **Valle della Luna.**

PRACTICAL INFORMATION

Santa Teresa's Azienda **tourist office,** P. Vittorio Emanuele, 24 (tel. 75 41 27), can assist you with accommodations and has dozens of pamphlets advertising local services, such as boat, moped, and horse rentals. (Open daily 8:30am-1pm and 3:30-8pm; Oct.-May Mon.-Sat. 8:30am-1pm and 4:30-7pm.) From Santa Teresa, daily **ferries** sail to Bonifacio in Corsica (3 per day, 1hr., L15,000, French visa required). Both **Tirrenia** (tel. 75 41 56) and **Navarma** (tel. 75 52 70) have staff offices at the tiny port. If you wish to cross into French waters yourself, rent a sailboat or motorboat from **Circolo Nautico Capo Testa** (tel. 75 54 56) on the isthmus, which also runs a scuba-diving school (Open May 15-Oct.15 daily 8am-8pm). Alternatively, explore *terra firma* by renting a horse at **Centro Ippico Ruoni** (tel. 75 15 90), 5km out of town in Ruoni or at the **Scuola di Turismo Equestre** (tel. 65 16 40) in nearby Marazzino, which leads guided treks on horses (L25,000/L30,000 per hour). Bike and moped rentals are available from **GULP,** Via Nazionale, 58 (tel. 75 56 89). Mountain bikes go for L23,000 per day, and scooters start at L45,000. (Open Mon.-Fri. 9am-1pm and 4-7:30pm, Sat. 9am-1pm.) All-day (9:30am-5pm) boat excursions to the archipelago islands are available, complete with lunch and horse ride for L70,000. Reserve two days ahead from **ONDA,** Via Carlo Alberto, 9 (tel. 75 41 49). **ARST buses** travel to Olbia (5 per day, 1½hr., L6700), Sassari (2 per day, 3hr., L14,700), and Palau (40min., L3200) from Via Eleonora d'Arborea, adjacent to the post office off Via Nazionale. Tickets can be purchased at the Black and White Bar across from the station on Via Nazionale. **Telephone code:** 0789.

ACCOMMODATIONS AND CAMPING

Though there are cheap hotels in Santa Teresa, they are often full in July, and *always* full in August. Reserve far in advance during the high season. Many demand half pension.

Pensione Scano, Via Lazio, 4 (tel. 75 44 47), near the center of town, on the way to Capo Testa. Clean, with blond wood furniture, on a quiet street. Singles L30,000/35,000. Doubles L60,000/70,000. Half pension L75,000. MC, Visa.

Hotel Belvedere, P. della Libertà (tel. 75 41 60), one block from P. Vittorio Emanuele, overlooking the sea. Firm beds and huge windows. Many rooms with television, all with bath. Singles L50,000-55,000/60,000-65,000. Doubles L70,000/100,000. AmEx, MC, Visa.

Hotel del Porto, Via del Porto, 20 (tel. 75 41 54). Get off at the ARST port stop or turn from Via Nazionale onto Via del Porto and follow it to the port. Large, almost elegant rooms with views of the water and the Sardinian countryside. Friendly manager willing to answer questions about walks and beaches. Singles L30,000/40,000, with bath L40,000/45,000. Doubles L55,000/65,000, with bath L75,000/90,000. AmEx, MC, Visa.

Camping: Arcobaleno (tel. 75 20 40), 10km from Porto Pozzo. L15,000 per person, including tent and car. Open June-Sept. Also **Gallura** (tel. 75 55 80), Loc. Li-Lucianeddi, 1½km from town. Near the beach, but big and likely to have openings. L11,000-17,000 per person, depending on season. Open May 15-Sept. 30.

FOOD

Most local restaurants are astronomically expensive. For hearty low-cost basics, *alimentari,* fruit and vegetable markets, and delis are easy to find on Via Aniscara off P. Vittorio Emanuele (open during regular business hours). There is also an open-air market by the bus station on Thursday mornings.

Papa Satan, Via La Marmora, 20/22. No phone. Look for the sign off Via Nazionale. Wacky white stucco booths on the back patio. Wood-burning ovens. Try the devilishly good *spaghetti alla Papa Satan* (L12,000). Open daily noon-2:30pm and 7pm-midnight.

Gastronomia Artigiane del Corso, Via XX Settembre (tel. 75 57 25). *Menù* includes tasty *primo, secondo,* and *contorno* for L1500. Or just grab some of their pre-prepared food, like roasted eggplant or various seafood salads, for a picnic.

■■■ PALAU

Palau's most famous attraction is a rock. Carved by the wind to resemble a bear, it is featured in nearly every brochure on Sardinia. If that doesn't draw you, the nearby beaches will. Palau is a comparatively sleepy beach town whose main industry seems to be shuttling passengers across the bay to the island of La Maddalena. More beaches await there, as well as a nature preserve and an American military base.

Orientation and Practical Information Palau is basically a one-street town. ARST buses drop you at the port end of Via Nazionale. The **tourist office** at Via Nazionale, 94 (tel. 70 95 70), lies uphill at the other end and can give you information on how to get to several nearby beaches. (Open Mon.-Sat. 8am-1pm and 3-8pm.) **Ferries** for La Maddalena depart every hour. Buy tickets (summer 4:30am-midnight, 15min., L4000) inside the port terminal. Nine **buses** per day travel to Santa Theresa (L3200) and 10 per day go to Olbia (L4700). If you're too tired to walk to the beach, **rent a car** from Hertz at the Agenzia Viaggi Aquarius (open 9am-12:30pm and 4:30-8pm) or call a **taxi** (tel. 70 92 66).

Accommodations and Food The only real budget hotel is the **Albergo Serra,** Via Nazionale, 17 (tel. 70 95 19), which has bright, clean rooms overlooking the street. Singles L40,000/50,000. Doubles L55,000/60,000, with bath L60,000/65,000. There are several **campgrounds** near Palau. The closest is **Acapulco,** Loc. Punta Palau (tel. 70 94 97), L14,000/18,000 per person. Some bungalows available for L25,000/35,000 per person. (Open June 1-Oct. 15.) **La Uva Fragola,** serves pizzas and a variety of salads (including octopus) and is open daily from 10am-2am for those late-night tentacle cravings; it's on P. Vittorio Emanuele, right off Via Nazionale (tel. 70 87 65). **Ristorante Robertino** dishes out a flavorful spaghetti with scallops or *zuppa marinara* for L12,000. (Open Tues.-Sun. 12:30-3:30pm and 6:30-9:30pm. DC, MC, Visa.)

■■■ OLBIA

Most visitors stop in Olbia on their way to other Sardinian spots on the mainland. With a single, unremarkable medieval church and nary a beach in sight, the city's main draw is its convenient ferry connecting Sardinia to Corsica and the rest of Italy. Still, as port towns go, it's actually pleasant. Lounge for a while in one of the convivial outdoor *caffè* that line Olbia's leafy Piazza Margherita—there are many worse ways to spend an evening.

ORIENTATION AND PRACTICAL INFORMATION

Ferries arriving at the port are greeted by blue ARST buses to other cities and a train timed to meet incoming passengers. The cluster of buildings to the right as you disembark houses a bar, newsstand, and televisions to entertain stranded travelers. To reach Olbia's centro, take the waiting train to the first stop: tickets can be purchased on board. (For those who can handle a bit more travel, the train continues on to Sassari.) To get to the tourist office, walk directly from the train station up Via Pala until it intersects with Corso Umberto; the ARST station will be about 200m to your right. Turn left and continue past Piazza Margherita on your right until you reach Via Catello Piro (also on your right), where you will find the tourist office. It's likely that your boat will arrive long before business hours, but don't despair—relax and revive yourself at one of several caffè along Corso Umberto. Sip espresso and enjoy cream-filled pastries with other weary travelers waiting for Olbia to come to life.

Tourist Office: Via Catello Piro, 1 (tel. 214 53), off Corso Umberto. Look for the mod white building. Ask for the map of Olbia, the *Annuario Alberghi* (a list of prices for almost every hotel in the Sassari province), or one of the numerous guides in Italian and English highlighting Sardinia's coasts, archaeological sites, and "trekking adventures." Open Mon.-Fri. 8am-2pm and 3:30-6pm, Sat.-Sun. 9am-noon. High season Mon.-Sat. 8am-2pm and 3:30-6pm. Sun. 9am-noon.
Post Office: on Via Acquedotto (tel. 222 51), 2 blocks off P. Matteotti. Open Mon.-Sat. 8:30am-7pm. **Postal code:** 07026.

Telephones: Public phones are available in the Piazza Margherita. Open 8am-10pm. Buy phone cards at one of the *tabacchi* on Corso Umberto or Piazza Margherita. **Telephone code:** 0789.

Currency Exchange: mediocre rates at the Tirrenia window inside the ferry station, or try Banco di Sardegna, Corso Umberto, across from P. Margherita. Open Mon.-Fri. 8:40am-1:20pm.

American Express: Avitur, Corso Umberto, 139 (tel. 243 27). Check cashing and mail service for cardholders on weekday mornings. **Those without cards cannot cash personal checks or buy traveler's checks here.** Friendly English-speaking staff. Open Mon.-Fri. 9am-1pm and 4-7pm, Sat. 9am-1pm.

Trains: Via Pala, off Corso Umberto by the bus station (tel. 224 77). Before ferry departures, trains (originating in Sassari) run from the station to the port. Trains to: Cagliari (9 per day, L23,000); Sassari (9 per day, L10,000); and Golfo Aranci (10 per day, L3200). **Luggage storage:** open 6:10am-1:10pm and 1:30-7:10pm.

Buses: ARST, Corso Umberto, 168 (tel. 211 97), at the far end away from the water (actually just a place for the buses to pull in). Buy tickets at the Snack Bar Papagallo to the right of the station. Open Mon.-Sat. 9:30am-10pm. To: Nuoro (4 per day, L11,600); Arzachena (10 per day, L3200); Santa Teresa di Gallura (5 per day, L6900); Palau (L4500). Schedule posted in station. Waiting room open 4am-1am. Local rides L1200-1300; buy tickets on board from coin-only machines.

Ferries: Tirrenia, Corso Umberto, 17/19 (tel. 285 33 or 286 33). Service to Civitavecchia and Genoa. Open Mon.-Sat. 8:30am-1:30pm and 4:30-6pm. **Port office** (tel. 246 91) open when ferries are running—check 1½hr. in advance for schedule changes. **Linea dei Golfi** (tel. 221 26), in the port office, runs lines to Piombino (the port for Elba, at 7:30pm) and Livorno in Tuscany (7am).

24-Hour Taxi: Via B. Sassari, 20 (tel. 310 39).

Car Rental: All agencies are well represented. **Budget** (tel. 696 05); **Avis** at the airport or in town at Via Genova, 67 (tel. 224 20); **Hertz** (tel 212 74). In town there's also **Gallura**, Viale Aldo Moro, (tel. 515 18). Rates start around L70,000 per day plus VAT and optional insurance. Mopeds too, starting at L35,000.

Pharmacy: Farmacia Lupacciolu, Corso Umberto, 134 (tel. 213 10), at the corner of Via Porto Romano. Open Mon.4:30-10pm, Tues.-Sat. 9am-1pm and 4:30-10pm. Check local paper "La Nuova Sardegna" to find out which pharmacy in town is open on Sunday.

Emergencies: tel. 113. **Hospital: Ospedale Civile,** Via Aldo Moro (tel. 522 00 or 522 01). Some English spoken. **Medical Assistance: Guardia Medica** Via Fern, 4 (tel. 224 91), near the Church of San Simplicio. For evening and weekend assistance: open Sat. 2pm-Mon. 8am, Tues.-Fri. 8pm-8am.

ACCOMMODATIONS

Both hotels listed here also have restaurants.

Albergo Terranova, Via Garibaldi, 3 (tel. 223 95), off P. Margherita. Stark furniture, but the friendly staff and geranium-bedecked balconies add some Sardinian warmth. Cheap, clean, and centrally located. Singles L25,000/35,000. Doubles L50,000/60,000. Breakfast L8000. Half pension L50,000/60,000 per person; full pension L65,000/75,000.

Hotel Minerva, Via Mazzini, 6, (tel. 211 90), first right off Corso Umberto as you head from P. Margherita towards the water. The management is friendly, the rooms bright and airy, and the lobby amusingly eclectic. Singles 32,000/40,000, with bath L35,000/43,000. Doubles L50,000/55,000, with bath L60,000/65,000. Breakfast starts at L4000 (just coffee).

FOOD

Dining in Olbia can be either inexpensive and bland or very expensive and delicious. For self-service bargains, shop at the **Mercato Civico** on Via Acquedotto (open Mon.-Sat. 7:30am-1pm and 4:30-8pm), or at the **STANDA Supermarket** at Corso Umberto, 156 (open Mon.-Sat. 9am-1pm and 4-8pm). Vegetarians can stock up on soy milk and other supplies here.

Pizzeria il Portico, Via Olbia, 5 (first left as you enter the Piazza Margherita). This tiny pizzeria serves up huge slices of the traditional pizza, but also *focaccia* (flat bread) with chicken cutlets, meats, and your choice of topping (try the roasted eggplant). Cheese slice L2000, sandwiches starting at L8000. Coke machine inside. Open daily noon-midnight.

Ristorante Terranova, beside Hotel Minerva. Though some of the seafood dishes are expensive, good-sized pizzas start at L7000. Other entrees range L7000-L15,000. A big lunchtime hit with the locals. Open Sun.-Fri. noon-2:30pm and 7pm-10:30pm.

SIGHTS IN AND NEAR OLBIA

A walk along the water in Olbia affords a hazy blue vision of Sardinian peaks and blue coasts, a welcome invitation or a fond farewell. Nearly all traces of Olbia's Greek, Roman, and medieval past have disappeared; the one exception is the 12th-century **Church of San Simplicio** behind the train station. Built in the Pisan-Romanesque style, the structure features a bold, imposing façade of off-white granite. Inside, Cyclopean faces leer from the tops of stone pillars.

Excursions from Olbia include trips to **S'Abe,** an archaeological site (6 km away) and the "Giant's Tombs" (prehistoric burial grounds with megaliths) of **Su Monte,** on the road to **Castello Pedrese,** a 14th-century fortress. If you're on the bus to Nuoro, not far out of Olbia you'll pass the surrealistic **Isola Tavolara,** an immense prism of rock protruding 450m out of the sea. Five buses per day run to **San Teodoro,** 30km from Olbia (L3000), where a long, luxurious beach eases into ultra-marine water. Especially in July and August, you'll be walking on a carpet of tourists, but go ahead—it's worth it. Stay at **Albergo L'Esagono** (tel. (0784) 86 57 83), a complex of red clay buildings right on the beach, off Via Cala d'Ambra (doubles L80,000; full pension required in August for L95,000 per person). Less posh is **Albergo La Palma,** Via del Tirreno (tel. (0784) 86 59 62). Singles L38,000/44,000. Doubles L70,000/77,000. All rooms with bath. Prices and pensions rise in August; L92,000 for half pension. Up the road is the Cala d'Ambra **campground** (tel. (0784) 86 56 50) with satisfactory facilities (L11,000/13,000 per person, tent included; reservations strongly recommended during the summer).

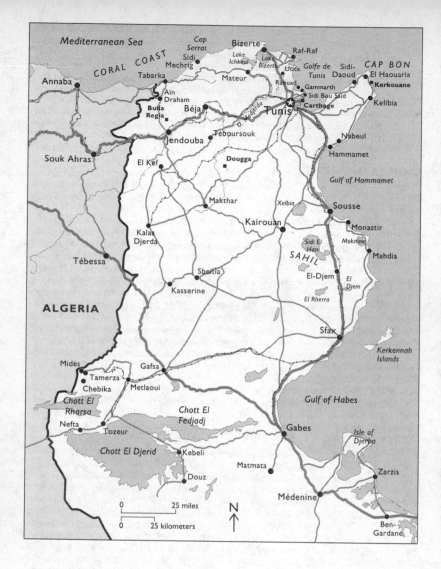

TUNISIA

Tunisia's appeal to visitors is, quite literally, legendary: Odysseus's crew preferred to remain here and eat the local fruit. Were it not for some serious divine prodding, Aeneas would never have founded Rome, so enamored was he with Carthage and Queen Dido. Mythology has given Tunisia some ringing endorsements—and the heroes never even got past the coast. Even today most visitors content themselves with the country's popular beaches; package tourists fly into Cap Bon and Jerba, spend two weeks frolicking in the surf, and leave without ever venturing farther.

This is a pity for them but a boon for the independent traveler (a relatively rare specimen in Tunisia). Despite its small size, Tunisia possesses an enormous potential for varied adventure and discovery. The capital, Tunisia's physical embodiment of its efforts at Westernization and secularization, is only three hours away from Kairouan, one of Islam's holiest cities and testimony to the country's profound faith. The green fields of the Tell, which once filled the granaries of ancient Rome, still possess imperial remnants in Dougga and Bulla Regia guaranteed to fascinate even those who had their fill of ruins in Italy. Rome's former cities crumbled despite their fertile surroundings, but just 200km away, Bedouin continue to live in oases surrounded by the inhospitable Sahara Desert.

Tunisia's national character demonstrates a diversity to the point of schizophrenia, yet it remains a stable and prosperous state—remarkable given its neighbors. With friendly people, affordable prices, and an infrastructure just rough enough to make for a good story back home, Tunisia will amply reward the visitor willing to step out of the air-conditioned tour buses and interact with this, the most accessible Arab state from Italy.

Though the Tunisian government welcomes tourism, the country's self-portrayal as open and democratic has been repeatedly questioned over the past decade. Amnesty International and the Lawyers Committee for Human Rights have published reports implicating the government in the violation of numerous human rights, including the right to a fair trial and freedom from arbitrary arrest and torture. Tunisians under closest watch include defense lawyers and persons accused of disseminating minority political ideas or aiding an unauthorized political organization. Primarily, but not exclusively, the government has targeted Islamic opposition groups. For more info, contact Amnesty International at (212) 544-0200, or the Lawyers Committee for Human Rights at (212) 629-6170.

ESSENTIALS

■■■ PLANNING YOUR TRIP

Most of the information contained in the Italy Essentials Section also applies to Tunisia. The following addenda should supplement what you already know.

The **Tunisian National Tourist Office (ONTT)** is a good source of info and brochures about the country and its regions. The country's central tourist office is at 1, av. Mohammed V, 1002 Tunis (tel. 34 10 77; fax 35 09 97). Another good place for assistance is the **Agence Tunisienne de Communication Extérieure** (tel. (01) 34 58 66; fax 35 34 45), Av. Jean Jaurès, 1001 Tunis. In the U.S., write or call the **Embassy of Tunisia,** Cultural Section in Charge of Tourism, 1515 Mass. Ave. NW, Washington, DC 20005 (tel. (202) 862-1850; fax 862-1858). The ONTT in the U.K. is at 77a, Wigmore St., London W1H 9LJ (tel. ±44 (0171) 224 55 98; fax 224 40 53). In Italy, contact the office at Via Sicilia, 50 (tel. +39 (06) 482 19 09; fax 482 17 55), 00187 Rome. For the U.S. State Department's *Background Notes* on Tunisia, write to the **Superintendent of Documents,** U.S. Government Printing Office, Washington, DC 20402. Major Tunisian cities also operate a local tourist office called the **Syndicat d'Initiative,** referred to in listings as the "Syndicat."

No visa is required of American and Canadian citizens to enter Tunisia for up to four months, or of U.K. citizens for up to three months. Australians, New Zealanders, and South Africans must obtain a visa before departure from the nearest Tunisian consulate (do this at least 1-3 weeks before you leave).

MONEY MATTERS

US $1 = 0.71 dinar (D)
CDN $1 = 0.53D
UK £1 = 1.11D
IR £1 = 1.13D
AUS $1 = 0.53D
NZ $1 = 0.47D
SA R = 0.20D

1D = US $1.40
1D = CDN $1.90
1D = UK £0.90
1D = IR £0.88
1D = AUS $1.90
1D = NZ $2.14
1D = SA R5.12

The *dinar* (D) consists of 1000 millimes (ml). Sums are generally written with periods: 14.300 means 14 *dinars*, 300 millimes. Amounts under 5D are frequently expressed in thousands of millimes. Change is often scarce, so hang on to it, especially the precious 100ml pieces used in pay phones. **Save your exchange receipts:** with them, only 30% of what you originally change can be reconverted, up to a maximum of 100D (without them, you can't reconvert any currency at all). It is illegal to import or export Tunisian currency.

Banks are generally open for exchange in summer Mon.-Fri. 8-11am and in winter Mon.-Thurs. 8-11am and 2-4pm, Fri. 8-11am and 1:30-3pm. During **Ramadan** (see Festivals and Holidays, page 593), banks are open Mon.-Fri. 8-11:30am and 1-2:30pm. **STB** is the largest bank in Tunisia and unlike other banks, which are more selective, will cash any major brand of **traveler's checks** (300-500ml commission per check is standard). **Post offices** will only exchange hard currency. Find **ATMs** at a bank in every major town, but their receipts will not help you when you want to reconvert *dinars*. They also tend not to be connected to international networks. A few large hotels and all airports provide exchange services outside regular hours.

HEALTH

Two of the health concerns outlined in the Italy Essentials: Health section (page 22) merit special attention by the tourist in Tunisia: **diarrhea** and **heatstroke.** Always wear a sun hat to prevent heatstroke and carry plenty of bottled water, especially in the desert (for some additional advice on desert survival see below). Finally, be sure that, along with sunscreen, your medical kit includes Imodium, chewable Pepto Bismol, or Kaopectate tablets.

No matter how many precautions a visitor takes, a visit to Tunisia is a gastrointestinal gamble; unfamiliar **cooties** exist everywhere. How safe you want to be depends on how much inconvenience you are willing to stand. Many travelers drink local water and are fine, but the cautious should stick to **bottled water.** Remember, **avoiding tap water** entails declining ice cubes, glasses still wet from washing, and worst of all, the thirst-quenching *citronade* found in every *pâtisserie.* Even brushing your teeth poses some risk. Other sensible precautions include selecting produce that can be peeled, or washing it thoroughly with *bottled* water. Don't eat creamy pastries or any food that has been standing out. Although sandwiches and salads in restaurants are generally fine, if you want to play it safe, stick to cooked vegetables. Perhaps the best precaution you can take is to **wash your hands before eating, like your mother told you** to do. If diarrhea persists beyond a couple of days, don't hesitate to seek out a Tunisian doctor. If the diarrhea is a sign of something more serious, waiting until you get home could be dangerous.

The **vaccinations** recommended for travelers to Tunisia are hepatitis, gamma globulin, tetanus, and typhoid—consult your doctor for specifics.

Desert Survival

Summer temperatures soar in the Sahara. The body loses four liters or more of liquid per day—**drink a liter of water every hour and a half or so,** even if you're not thirsty. Thirst is the first sign of dehydration, which comes on rapidly. **Drinking enormous quantities of water after the fact is not effective—in fact, it's dangerous to do so in high temperatures.** If you're using sweet beverages, dilute them with water to avoid over-reacting to high sugar content—even orange juice should be diluted at least by 50%. Alcohol and coffee cause dehydration; better not to indulge, but if you do, compensate with a lot of water. For long-term stays, a high-quality beverage with potassium compounds and glucose, such as ERG (an industrial-strength Gatorade), will help keep your strength up.

Light-colored, porous long sleeves and trousers reflect the sun's heat, and therefore keep you cooler and protect you from harmful rays. Wearing a sweaty shirt, though uncomfortable, will prevent dehydration more effectively than removing it will. Thick-soled shoes and two pairs of socks can help to keep feet comfortable on a hike in the summer, when the sand can register a scorching 150-200°F. Make sure to carry sunglasses with 100% UV protection, sunscreen of sufficient strength (even if you don't usually burn), and a hat. **Always keep your head covered**—you can buy a wide-brimmed straw hat on the street for about 4D. A bandana or towel dipped in water and wrapped around the head might add protection and relief. Temperatures fluctuate unpredictably, so consider bringing a sweater or jacket. In winter, temperatures in the Sahara approach freezing point, and it occasionally snows.

SAFETY AND SECURITY

Tunisia's nationwide **emergency phone number** is 197.

Tourists to Tunisia should encounter few problems if they take care to understand their surroundings. For general information on safety while traveling, see the Italy Essentials: Safety and Security section (page 20).

Urban areas in which extra caution is in order are the **souks** (market streets) and the **medinas** (old cities). The maze-like medinas vary in size and intricacy, but don't rely solely on the tourist office maps to guide you through them. Extreme caution should be used at night in most medinas. Never go alone, and when in doubt, ask your hotel proprietor or hostel manager for advice and directions before venturing out. Carry sums of over 10 or 15D in a moneybelt or neck pouch, and be especially careful to keep any valuables or money on you at all times; theft, while less frequent here than in Italy, still occurs even in "upscale" hotels When purchasing anything, keep your money securely in hand or belt until you have agreed on a price. Pay with small bills and request them when you exchange money.

Some tourists have had problems with **con artists who claim to be guides.** Someone may offer to show you around a city or give you directions, and later turn around and demand compensation for being your "guide." In general, if there's something you don't want and won't pay for, make this absolutely clear right up front. Always negotiate a price for services *beforehand*.

Security forces are ubiquitous in the country; the uniforms differ, but to Tunisians they are *kif kif* (all the same). Tunisians try to avoid contact with them, but in general the **police** (blue uniforms) and **garde national** (khaki) are polite and nonconfrontational. The police generally work in the cities and handle crimes like petty theft. The *garde national* generally patrol the roads, frequently stopping vehicles. **Carry your passport with you at all times.** Make sure your visa is updated and be prepared to explain your presence if you are not in an obvious tourist town.

In contrast to much of North Africa, Tunisia has very harsh laws regarding the possession or use of drugs. **Do not attempt to bring drugs in, take them out, buy them, or use them.** Don't even talk to dealers—some drug dealers might be narcs, and even if they're not, you would not want to be caught in a compromising position—Tunisian law allows for guilt by association.

WOMEN TRAVELERS

Unlike more fundamentalist Muslim countries, women in Tunisia experience a good deal of freedom. In 1956, President Bourguiba presented his Code of Personal Status for Women, making Tunisia the first Arab nation to outlaw polygamy and to advance women's rights significantly. Nonetheless, women travelers from Western countries have been known to encounter trouble simply because they are Western.

The West has only itself to blame: Tunisians arrive at their conceptions through a steady cinematic diet consisting mainly of kung fu and offerings of the "Convent School Girls Act Naughty" type. The belief that all Western women are "easy" has not disappeared, and some verbal harassment is inevitable. Women travelers to Tunisia should make an effort to travel in a group which includes men, and to dress conservatively and modestly. These warnings are especially important when traveling in the south or in the interior, although incidents have been known to happen in Tunis and the north as well.

LANGUAGE

As in any country, attempts at the native language evoke an enthusiastic response (and discourage merchants and guides looking for easy tourist meat). Here are a few handy **Arabic phrases:** *salaam aleikum* (generally abbreviated to *salaam*; "hello"*),* *ayee/aa* ("yes"), *la* ("no"), *shokran* ("thank you"), *samahanee* ("excuse me"), *min fadlak*(to a man)*/fadlik*(to a woman) ("please"), *saiyay* ("enough"), *la bes* ("how are you?"), *la bes hamdullah* (reply to *la bes*), *bi' as-salaama* (good-bye), *shwaya* ("a little"—a response to the inevitable "Do you speak Arabic?"), *insh'Alla* ("God willing"), *kif kif* ("it's all the same"), and two effective rebuffs for hustlers: *imshee* ("go away"), and *shooma!* ("for shame!"). Older people (50+) are particularly impressed if you address them as *"El Hadj,"* a courtesy title that politely assumes they've made the pilgrimage to Mecca.

Tunisians communicate with their hands, and two **hand gestures** in particular are good to know. Waving an open hand with the palm facing down seems dismissive to Westerners (like someone is shooing you away), but in Tunisia it means "come here" or "follow me." Holding the tips of all five fingers together pointing skyward means "wait" or "be patient." Shaking this gesture means, um, just about anything.

Although Arabic is the official language of Tunisia, all Tunisian secondary school students study **French,** and most people who commonly deal with tourists speak a smattering of English and German as well. French is common among educated Tunisians even in the interior. Some useful words and phrases are: *bonjour* (bohn-ZHOOR; "hello"), *excusez-moi* (ess-KOO-zay MWAH; "excuse me"), *parlez-vous anglais, Madame/Monsieur* (PAHR-lay voo an-GLAY, mah-DAHM/muh-SYUR; "do you speak English, ma'am/sir?"), *combien* (kohm-BYEN; "how much?"), *je voudrais* (ZHUH voo-DRAY; "I would like"), *où est/sont* (OO AY/SOHN; "where is/are?"), and *je ne comprends pas* (ZHUH nuh kohm-prahn PAH; "I don't understand").

GETTING THERE

Ferry or plane tickets to destinations abroad (i.e. home) can only be bought with *dinars* that have been purchased with hard currency. You'll have to produce the exchange receipt when buying the ticket, and keep a copy when moving through customs. Bear in mind that the money exchanged for this reason does *not* count toward the 30% of the *dinars* you can re-exchange.

By Plane

There are no direct flights between North America and Tunisia. North Americans should fly to London or Rome, and then make their way to Tunis by plane, train, or boat (from Italy, fares for flights are often comparable to those for ferries). **Tunis Air** flies from most major European and North African cities and offers a confusing array of round-trip deals. Flights to London cost about 175D, but a charter company will reduce that by about 50%. Tunis Air flights to and from France are about the same price. Flights between Tunis and Marseille cost around 189D.

By Boat

As far back as 204 BC, boatloads of visitors were coming from Italy to present-day Tunisia; it's still one of the best ways to get there. Try calling **Tirrenia** (tel. (0923) 218 96 in Trapani) for ferry information:

Trapani-Tunis (7½hr.): June-Sept., Easter, and Dec. 25: chair L92,000; off-season L77,000. Departures from Trapani Mon. 9am, arrival 4:30pm; from Tunis Mon. 8pm; arrives Tues. 6:30am.

Alimar (tel. (0923) 271 01): departures from Trapani Wed. 11am and Fri. 10pm; from Tunis (May-June only) Sat. 1pm. (L78,000).

Cagliari-Tunis: chair June-Sept., Easter, and Dec. 25: chair L107,000; off-season L99,500. Departures from Cagliari Sun. 7pm (21½hr.); from Tunis Mon. 8pm (36hr.).

Report for all ferries leaving the port of La Goulette (a 15-min. ride on the TGM commuter train from downtown Tunis; get off at Vieille Goulette) **two hours in advance,** or you'll miss the boat. During the last two weeks of August, book tickets well in advance—all boats from Tunisia are packed with Europe-bound migrant workers. To buy a ferry ticket, you must show your bank receipt for the purchase of *dinars* and obtain a *Bons de Passage* from the bank itself—a minor but requisite bureaucratic hassle. You can buy tickets from all major travel agents. In the late summer crunch, fight it out at the crowded **Tirrenia ticket office,** 126, rue de Yougoslavie, 1000 RP, Tunis (tel. (01) 24 28 01).

All boat lines are supervised by the **Compagnie Tunisienne de Navigation (CTN),** which provides information and runs ticket offices at 5, rue Dag Hammarskjold in Tunis (tel. 24 28 01; fax 24 29 99), at La Goulette (tel. (01) 73 51 11; fax 73 13 04), at Ponte Colombo (Gare Maritime) in Genoa (tel. ±39 (010) 269 81), and at Rione Sirignano, 2, in Naples (tel. ±39 (081) 761 36 88).

On arrival, you will have to fill out a detailed **customs** declaration, although it is unlikely that you will have any of the items asked about (refrigerators, firearms, etc.).

■■■ ONCE THERE

GETTING AROUND

By Train

A major **train** line runs south from Tunis to Sousse, and then splits into an east line through Sfax ending in Gabes and a west line to Tozeur and Gafsa. Another line runs west through Jendouba to the Algerian border and splits into northwest branches ending in Bizerte and Tabarka. Although trains are infrequent, they're comfortable and have A/C. Second-class prices compete with the cost of other modes of transportation. For info, contact **Société Nationale de Chemins de Fer Tunisienne (SNCFT)** at the train station (Gare Tunis-Ville) in pl. de Barcelone (1000 RP, Tunis), between rue de Hollande and av. de Carthage at 67 av. Farhat Hached (tel. (01) 24 99 99). Get a train schedule for all of Tunisia at the info booth in the Tunis station.

By Bus

Buses are the most common form of intercity transit. They are inexpensive and convenient, but crowded. Schedules change frequently and service can be painfully slow, especially in rural areas. Try to board at the terminal (*gare routière*)—this increases your chance of finding a seat and may get you onto an express, air-conditioned coach (*confort*). In any given city there are at least two bus companies, generally occupying the same terminal (Sfax is a notable exception). The "national line," the **Société de Transports Rural et Interurbain (SNTRI)** runs the intercity and international routes; their service is faster and more comfortable. All large towns have a **regional bus company** with the acronym **"SRT"** in the title, which runs throughout the locale and to the nearest cities. Each company has its own window and schedules are always in Arabic, so be prepared to ask around to find the next departure time. An old man generally sits at the bus lot's entrance charging "*droit d'entrée,*" an official hustle that will leave you about 50ml poorer. Within Tunis itself, the **Société National des Transports (SNT;** tel. (01) 49 24 56) operates

ONCE THERE

buses between the city and its suburbs. The **Société du Métro-Léger du Tunis (SMLT),** av. Muhammad V, Tunis (tel. (01) 78 44 33), operates the light rail system.

By Louage

Tunisia has a well-developed network of intercity taxis, or **louages.** These are without a doubt the most convenient form of transportation, as they are faster and more comfortable than buses and much more frequent than trains. Most towns have at least one, if not two, *louage* "stations," usually vacant lots near the bus station. *Louages* are usually white Peugeot station wagons with a red or blue stripe around the side. The small placard displayed on the roof does not necessarily indicate where the *louage* is headed, just where it has been registered. The driver waits for at least five to fill the car, then takes off like a bat out of Gabes for the destination. For most routes this will only require a five to ten minute wait. If your destination is more obscure (a small town or a ruin), the driver may charge you extra for the unfilled seats; don't fall for this unless you're sure that there is no one else headed that way. Most drivers have regular routes with fixed prices (although these are only displayed in Arabic). Use the rate of **2.500D per person per hour** as a general yardstick to determine the correct fare. If you feel you're being overcharged, though, use your fellow passengers as a reference. Tunisian *louage* riders know the going rate; don't ever pay more than what another rider has paid for the same trip.

In the rural regions, **camionettes** take up where the *louages* leave off. Generally pick-up trucks, they shuttle from village to village, charging a pittance for a ride in the back. They are neither comfortable nor very safe, but the experience possesses a certain adventurous appeal—and it sure beats walking.

By Car

A **private car** is indispensable for touring the Sahara, where public transportation is scarce. You must be at least 21 and have a valid international driver's license (see Italy Essentials: "International Driver's Permit" on page 14). Although there are cheaper local places, it's advisable to rent from a reliable international agency. **Budget,** 12, rue d'Autriche, Tunis (tel. (01) 79 60 25) has the cheapest rates. A Renault Super 5 costs 25D per day plus 250ml per km and a 17% tax. Week-long rentals with unlimited mileage cost 400D. Both **Hertz** (tel. (01) 79 02 11) and **Avis** (tel. (01) 78 05 93) have offices throughout Tunis. Ask to inspect the car before you sign.

Before undertaking any desert expeditions with your own vehicle, **make sure that your car has been recently serviced and is in good running condition.** Carry water for drinking and for the radiator, and make sure your car is equipped with a spare tire and necessary tools. Five gallons of water is recommended for each vehicle. For trips off major roads, a board and shovel are useful in case your car gets stuck in sand; shove the board under a tire to gain traction. **Stay with your vehicle if it breaks down:** it's easier to spot than a person. In the most nightmarish scenario—being stranded in extreme heat with little or no water—find whatever shade you can, drench yourself with (but don't drink) cooled radiator water to fight dehydration, burn motor oil in a hubcap to send smoke signals, and if you must move, do so only at night. If you see the temperature gauge climbing while driving, turn off the air conditioning. If an overheating warning light comes on, stop and wait about a half hour before trying again. Never pour water over the engine to cool it; you can crack the engine block. Leave in the early morning or after midday to avoid the most oppressive heat, and tote plenty of water (buying it later will cost you plenty).

By Thumb

Let's Go does not recommend hitchhiking as a means of transportation.

Hitchhiking is illegal in Tunisia, but many foreigners find it fairly easy. **Women should never hitch alone in Tunisia.** Keep in mind that many Tunisians consider hitching tantamount to freeloading and may request a contribution. Hitching doesn't save a great deal of money, since public transportation is so cheap, but it does save time and if you get stranded (quite possible), it might be your only hope.

ACCOMMODATIONS

Two groups administer Tunisia's **hostels**. The government Ministry of Culture runs about 30 of these, known as **Maisons des Jeunes** and basically designed to house soccer teams. They tend to be large, functional, and clean, with all the charm of a locker room, and charge a flat 4D per night. While convenient to the local stadium, they are often far from the center of town. Not all are safe for women. The HI-administered **Auberges de Jeunesse,** of which there are over 30 (including three in Tunis and three in Nabuel), are much less institutional in character and most have completed or are in the midst of undergoing renovations to conform to HI standards. They are some of the best budget accommodations in Tunisia. The HI affiliate in Tunisia is the **Association Tunisienne des Auberges de Jeunesse,** 10, Rue Ali Bach Hamba, BP 320-1015 Tunis RP (tel. (01) 35 22 77; fax 35 21 72).

The ONTT classifies **hotels** on a zero- to four-star scale and provides listings of all official hotels. Budget travelers should stick with the unrated (3-10D per person), one-star (8-16D per person), and two-star (12-22D per person) establishments. Prices plummet during the off season (Sept.-June), particularly along the coast. The cheapest hotels lurk in the medinas, but don't expect more than a bed and primitive communal plumbing. The rooms are often crowded with beds, and hotels may force tourists to pay for all of them, occupied or not. Women may not feel comfortable (or safe) in many of these hotels. Even classified hotels rarely have hot water during the summer, and remember to **BYOTP** (toilet paper, that is).

Organized **camping** hasn't yet come of age in Tunisia, except in the south, where it may be your only option. Nevertheless, a handful of campgrounds do exist. As for unofficial camping, the ONTT guide states, "You can pitch your tent where you wish on beaches and in parks after having first obtained permission from the property owner or from the nearest Police or National Guard station." It can be hard to get such permission, or even to find the right people to ask. In a pinch, most youth hostels will allow camping on their grounds for 500ml-2D per person, including use of the facilities. Public beaches are the most popular places for setting up camp. Freelance camping can be dangerous, though—think twice before pitching your tent (especially given the low cost of regular accommodations). **Never camp alone.** Once again, bring your own toilet paper.

Tunisia's **electric current** runs at 220v AC.

FOOD

It is easy to eat very well and very cheaply in Tunisia. Be prepared to eat much **couscous,** the North African staple of steamed semolina served with whatever else the cook feels like including: generally potatoes, veggies, fish or meat, and a sauce. *Pommes de terre* **(potatoes)** and haricots **(beans)** make up the other starch dishes, generally served in a spicy tomato sauce. **Meat dishes** (lamb, beef, or liver) are grilled and served as *brochettes* or *mechoui*. They usually come with fries and salad. Ubiquitous *rotisseries* serve inexpensive portions of chicken roasted on a spit. **Fish** along the coast is excellent, although the cheaper places generally fry rather than grill; *calamar* (squid) and *poulpe* (octopus) are a specialty. *Kamounia* combines meat, beef, or a strange falafel-like substance with a cumin sauce. *Merguez* is a spicy sausage often included in *ojja*, a tomato and pepper stew with scrambled egg. *Tajine*, a Tunisian specialty, can be a meat stew with pot-luck ingredients, but more often it's a *quiche*-like substance that may or may not contain meat.

The Tunisian national appetizer, **brik** ("bringer of coronary occlusions") is nothing so much as a fried egg wrapped in a wonton. Messy, greasy, and delicious, it must be tried once. *Salade tunisien* is finely chopped cucumbers, tomatoes, and onions (perhaps with tuna), but for a more genuine **Tunisian salad,** sample some *mechouia*, a spicy mass of mashed roasted peppers served in a lake of olive oil. **Tunisian soup,** *chorba*, varies considerably but generally contains a spicy tomato base and a meat stock. Satisfy your sweet tooth with *kab el ghazal* ("gazelles' hooves," almond-filled pastry with a distinctive shape) or *makroudh* (date-stuffed biscuits soaked in honey, a specialty of Kairouan). And in Tunisia, no better (or sweeter) dessert exists than **fruit,** of which the country produces an absolutely orgiastic selection. Cactus fruit (prickly pears) is one specialty, sold at stands and costing 50ml a bud (great for sick tummies). When in season, dates from the southern oases are another obvious choice. No trip is complete, though, without sampling most of the range, which includes figs, melon, strawberries, oranges, and plums.

Vegetarians have it tough in Tunisia, an unashamedly carnivorous nation. The very concept of vegetarianism confuses most Tunisians, who view meat as essential to nearly every dish. *Couscous aux legumes* can be a lifesaver, but bear in mind that the cook may have simply picked (most of) the chunks of meat out of the sauce. The same goes for any other dish that you order *sans viande*. However, every town has a **produce market,** and all but the smallest towns have **supermarkets** ("Monoprix" or "Magasin General") which sell pasta and yogurt.

Tunisian restaurants can be divided into two categories: those that are holes in the wall and those that are not. Both types serve nearly identical menus, but the former are cheaper and quicker, while the latter pay more attention to aesthetics and probably hygiene as well. Tunisian cooking involves a great deal of preparation—restaurants often run out of certain dishes toward the end of the day, so arriving on the early end of lunch or dinner hours for the best food selection.

There are other **drink options** in Tunisia besides the bottles of swimming-pool-flavored water. *Citronade*, a concoction of whole lemons, sugar, and water (from the tap; be careful!), can kill the meanest thirst. Fresh orange juice is common and *pâtisseries* often serve other juices consisting of blended fruit and milk. *Thé verit* is a very acidic version of tea, steeped with mint, heavily sugared, and often served with almonds or pine nuts. Coffee in any form is excellent. Despite Islam's prohibition, **alcohol** is consumed in abundance. You will almost inevitably be approached by Tunisians on Friday asking you to buy some wine or beer for them, since stores only serve tourists on this day. *Celtia,* the local brew, makes Budweiser look offensively strong (1.300D per bottle). Tunisia produces its own wine as well; red wines tend to be on the heavy side, but *gris de Tunisie* and *Koudiat,* both rosés, achieve favorable reviews. Tunisian liquor deserves some mention (and caution). *Thibarine* is a sweet date liqueur, while *boukha* is a skull-popping distillation of figs. **Bars,** outside resort hotels, are generally seedy, all-male, and dedicated to serious heavy drinking. Male tourists will find them intimidating; females will find them frightening.

First you take a blindfolded camel...

How *do* Berbers make olives into oil? To begin, the olives are pressed by a stone wheel turned by a blindfolded camel. The resulting mush is then placed in flat palm containers and thoroughly squashed by a heavy oak trunk. Finally, the oil is stored until it ferments. What goes around comes around, and the chunky remainder becomes camel food. For info on touring olive presses, see page 619.

KEEPING IN TOUCH

The country code for Tunisia is 216. Tunisian **telephones** take 100ml coins; one coin is enough for local calls and at least six are needed to call anywhere else in the country. Unused coins will be returned. (You do not need the code to dial locally. Make sure to include the zero when calling another region.) Certain rural areas can be reached only with the operator's assistance (tel. 15).

Although **post offices** (**PTT**, for *Poste, Téléphone, & Télégraphe*) usually have telephones, their hours are not always convenient, especially for calls to North America. Ubiquitous **taxiphones,** pay-phone banks with an attendant dispensing change, generally have later hours. Tunisia has no direct dial service, so **calling cards** are useless here. To make matters worse, **collect calls** have been "temporarily" suspended. Sorry, but you'll have to suck up the cost of calling abroad yourself, or arrange for someone to call you at a local address. International calls can be placed from almost any phone; obtain a bunch of *dinars* (calls to the U.S. cost 2.400D per minute) and dial direct (00—country code—area/city code—phone number).

Letters to the U.S. and Canada weighing up to 20g cost 500ml; postcards are 400ml. Letters to Europe are 450ml; postcards are 350ml. PTT offices are generally open Mon.-Fri. 8am-noon and 3-6pm, Sat. 8am-noon; in winter Mon.-Sat. 7:30am-1:30pm. Ramadan hours are usually 8am-3pm. Allow at least three weeks for mail sent from Tunis to the U.S., and two weeks for European addresses; allow 10 days for US mail to reach Tunisia, and five days for European mail. To have a post office retain your mail for you, your mailing address should include your name, the words *"poste restante,"* and the post office at which you will pick up your mail. Send **telegrams** and **faxes** from telephone offices or post offices. (Stamps are also sold at newsstands and tobacconists.)

BARGAINING

If you come to Tunisia, be prepared to bargain; asking prices are about ten times the actual value. If you really intend to buy, avoid mingling with tour groups, and shop late in the day when salespeople are anxious to unload their wares. Never appear interested when examining potential purchases: declare that you've done your shopping already; claim student status. Refuse, turn your back, and walk away; the price will decrease substantially. Above all, **never allow a price to escape your lips, unless you intend to pay it.** Never go shopping with a guide; s/he will collect at least 30% in commission. It is often possible to **barter** in Tunisia. American cigarettes, cheap digital watches, jeans, and t-shirts with English printing on them are particularly coveted in Tunisia—consider bringing cheap Western paraphernalia to trade.

HOSPITALITY

In the not unlikely event you are invited to a Tunisian home (especially common in rural areas), here are some tips: Remove shoes and socks before entering. You'll almost certainly be offered food, which is generally eaten from a communal dish by scooping it up with bread using the right hand (takes practice). As the guest, you eat what's directly in front of you, but the host may also push a particularly "good" morsel in your direction and you'll be expected to eat it. Bear in mind that the "best" cuts of meat in Tunisia are the ones with the most fat. Not to eat it, however, may insult your host. You're expected by tradition to **bring a gift.** Don't think of it as payment for services rendered—it's more of a thank-you gesture. Tea is a traditional offering, but few travelers carry it in their day pack. Kids love chewing gum or pens. In poor rural areas a package of Band-Aids or aspirin, both rare and expensive, will be immensely appreciated. If there are English speakers or students in the household, an old paperback will be happily accepted. If you have a camera, your hosts will enthusiastically pose for a picture. Send a copy through the mail (the ritual of exchanging addresses will take place with even passing acquaintances) as an expression of gratitude, and keep one as an excellent memento.

■■■ LIFE AND TIMES

HISTORY AND POLITICS

Tunisia has long treasured its physical and ideological openness. Centuries of immigration and empire-fortification as well as various foreign influences have left their mark on this tiny nation, which today belongs as much to the Mediterranean as to the Maghreb (North Africa).

The earliest archaeological evidence of settlement in Tunisia dates from about 750 BC, but legend attributes the founding of **Carthage** to the Phoenician Queen

Dido in 814 BC. By the 6th century BC, already prosperous from coastal and North African trade, the city had become a major power in the Mediterranean. When both Carthage and Rome intervened in Sicily, the two empires went to war with one another in a series of conflicts known as the **Punic Wars,** comparable in relative size and scope to the World Wars of our century. Of the three wars, the second was the most spectacular and devastating. **Hannibal,** the Carthaginian general, led an army that included 370 elephants over the Alps in order to surprise the Romans from the north, and trounced the Romans at Lake Trasimeno and Cannae. Nevertheless, the clever Roman leader **Fabius Cunctator** ("the delayer") prevailed over Hannibal in the end. (Subsequent Italian governments appear to have hung onto this delaying concept, though without the same fortuitous outcome.) The Second Punic War ended with a Roman victory in 201 BC, but the influential Roman senator Cato the Censor made *Carthago delenda est* ("Carthage must be destroyed") his cry, and eventually people listened. Perhaps to shut him up, the Romans declared the Third Punic War, which permanently settled the conflict in their favor in 146 BC.

Despite the Romans' attempt to prevent Carthaginian resurgence by sowing the city site with salt, Carthage soon flourished as a provincial capital. Tunisia was Rome's primary African granary; the richness of its archaeological remains attests to the colony's wealth. Like much of the Roman Empire, it was sacked by the Vandals and reconquered by the **Byzantine Empire.** The region was overrun in 698 AD and, soon after Arab expansion had begun to weaken the Byzantine hold over the Middle East, it was incorporated into the Arab **Abassid Empire** centered in Baghdad. The four dynasties that ruled Tunisia established the Islamic faith locally and built the medinas at the center of present-day Tunisian cities.

In the late 16th century, the **Ottoman Turks** seized the area, but within a century yielded to the **Beys,** a dynasty of Turkish origin. Under these rulers, Tunisia acquired its current name and borders. When they weren't cavorting in their Bardo Palace, the Beys supervised the adoption of the 1861 constitution—the first in any Arab country—and pushed Tunisia toward Westernization. The latter efforts led to economic dislocation and allowed European nations to "manage" Tunisia's economy.

After invading Tunisia in 1881, the **French** did a great deal to organize and develop the country; they also seized all the best land for their own settlers. Their lasting legacy is the Tunisian civil service, one of the best in the developing world. Although French rule remained relatively liberal in Tunisia, a nationalist consciousness developed among the intelligentsia, who formed the reformist **Destour Party** shortly after WWI. They were soon superseded by a new generation of young agitators led by a lawyer named **Habib Bourguiba,** who split and formed the more radical **Neo-Destour party.** Bourguiba, whom the French jailed before he escaped into exile, returned triumphantly in 1955 to negotiate Tunisia's relatively painless transition to independence, which came on March 20, 1956. A year later he deposed the last Bey, then the titular head of state, and became President-for-Life.

A pragmatist, Bourguiba encouraged the French to stay, to the benefit of Tunisia's economy. **Social reforms** were introduced, including equal rights for women, liability reform, and greater, more equitable educational opportunities. By the last decade of Bourguiba's reign, however, Tunisia was in financial turmoil and a state of civil unrest. After 31 years in office, the elderly Bourguiba was deposed in a bloodless coup on November 7, 1987. He is currently 90 years old and retired from politics, but his influence is still strongly felt and his face continues to adorn the currency. He was replaced by **President Aine el Abidine ben Madj Hamita Ben Ali.** General Ben Ali has attempted to reverse the economic decline with new programs and active pursuit of Middle Eastern unity. The constitution implemented in 1988 limits Presidential service to two terms of five years each. However, there is good reason to doubt that President Ben Ali will step down in 1998. Ali reportedly won the 1993 elections by a suspicious 99.91% of the vote, but then again, two of his opponents were serving time in jail.

FESTIVALS AND HOLIDAYS

Islam is the primary cultural force molding Tunisian life; the major celebration each year is **Ramadan,** the Muslim month of fasting that comes at different times of the Gregorian year, depending on the lunar calendar (Jan. 21-Mar. 1 in 1996). Ramadan affects all aspects of daily life. Shops and services close down for the afternoon. Muslims are forbidden to eat, drink, or smoke between sunrise and sunset. After sunset, streets swell with people, shops and businesses re-open, and the festivities continue well past midnight. The end of Ramadan is marked by Id al-Fitr, a three-day celebration during which all commercial activity comes to a standstill. In rural areas and smaller towns, restaurants and cafés close for the day.

Southern Tunisia regularly hosts national festivals, which invariably include camel fights as well as such less raucous forms of traditional culture as folkloric presentations and parades. Public holidays include: **January 1** (New Year's Day); **March 20-21** (Independence); **April 9** (Martyr's day); **May 1** (Labor Day); **July 25** (Republic Day); and **November 7** (Anniversary of Ben Ali's takeover).

GULF OF TUNIS

■ ■ ■ TUNIS

Travel literature would label Tunisia "cosmopolitan," a code word for "more Westernized than we'd really like it to be." Some of the responsibility lies with the French Protectorate, whose architectural stamp remains all over its *nouvelle ville.* Even after independence, Tunisia continues to embrace Western culture not only for its attractive lifestyle, but also because of the importance of the nation's worldwide image as a "liberal" Arab state. Tunis, the center of political and commercial power as well as a tenth of the country's population, spearheads this effort.

Originally named Thunes, the city survived the destruction of nearby Carthage to become a prominent outpost under the Roman and Byzantine empires. By the 13th century it had matured into a bastion of Islam. Under the Hafsid Dynasty, the city was made the capital of Tunisia in place of Kairouan by virtue of its favorable location for trade. As the Islamic world's first "university town," it also acquired a reputation for liberal ideas and progressive ways which survives today. The Ottomans swept in during the 16th century, but their power soon waned; European merchants acquired increasing influence on the beylical government of the Sick Man of Europe, and France occupied it as part of its "Protectorate" in 1881. Bourguiba kept Tunis as the nation's capital upon independence in 1956, and the city continues to have an overwhelming influence on the life of the nation. So while the travel brochures take visitors elsewhere to see the "real Tunisia," it is actually Tunis that embodies the ambitious reality of the nation—acceptance as a member of the "developed world." The historically and romantically minded will find many splendid reminders of the past (particularly in the famous Bardo museum and nearby Carthage), but visitors would be remiss in failing to acknowledge this Westernization as a vital part of Tunisia's present.

ORIENTATION AND PRACTICAL INFORMATION

The new center of Tunis was laid out by the French, with predictable results. This *ville nouvelle* meets the medina at the gate **Bab Bhar** in the **place de la Victoire.** From here, **avenue de France** extends eastward and, not coincidentally, becomes **avenue Habib Bourguiba** at the **place de l'Independance.** This thoroughfare is the Tunisian version of the Champs Elysée, which begins at the southbound bus station. Avenue Bourguiba is intersected by the major north-south artery, **avenue de Carthage,** which becomes **avenue de Paris** and then **avenue de la Liberté** as it proceeds north to the **Parc du Belvédère.** The **Métro,** Tunis' trolley system, has a major junction in front of the station. It's generally only useful in getting to the museum (see sights below) and **Tunis Marine**, the central TGM station. This commuter rail serves Carthage, Sidi Bou Said, and La Goulette, where ferries dock.

Tourist Office: ONTT Reception Office (tel. 34 10 77), pl. d'Afrique at av. Bourguiba and av. Mohammed V. Far away and not too helpful. Many brochures, little information, even less English. Ask for a map of the city and hope it isn't in Arabic. Open Mon.-Sat. 8am-6pm; Sun 8am-noon. A better bet is the ONTT branch offices at the **train station** (same hours), which offers good maps of both Tunis and Tunisia, as well as train and bus schedules. There is a booth on the 2nd floor of the Tunis-Carthage **airport** as well.

Police: tel. 197.

Post Office: 30, av. Charles de Gaulle, (tel. 65 01 21), off av. de France. Afternoon services limited. *Poste restante* at window #8 (180ml per letter). Open Mon.-Fri. 7:30am-1pm and 5-7pm, Sat. 7:30am-1pm, Sun. 9-11am; Sept.-June open Mon. 8am-6pm. Sun. 9-11am. Ramadan open Mon.-Sat. 8:15am-3:45pm, Sun. 9-11am.

Telephones: PTT, 29, rue Gamal Abdel Nasser, on the opposite side of the block from the post office. In the process of being fitted with telecard phones. Send **telegrams** from here or the post office. Open 24 hrs. 24-hr. payphones also in the underpass at av. de Paris/av. du Ghana intersection. **Telephone Code:** 01.

Budget Travel: Sotutour-Stav, 2, rue de Sparte (tel. 24 70 48), off av. de Paris. *May* be helpful if you need a cheap flight in a hurry; sells ISICs too. Open Mon.-Sat. 8:30am-12:30pm and 2:30-8pm.

Embassies: U.S., 144, av. de la Liberté (tel. 78 25 66). **Canada,** rue du Sénégal (tel. 79 80 04). **U.K.,** 5, pl. de la Victoire (tel. 34 14 44), at the entrance to the medina. Also the only service for citizens of **Australia** and **New Zealand.** For a visa—required of U.S. and Canadian citizens staying longer than 3 months, and of any Australian citizens—bring 7.500D to the consulate at 136, av. de la Liberté (tel. 28 00 55). The embassy of **Italy** is at 37, rue G. Abdennasser (tel. 34 18 11).

Currency Exchange: any of the **banks** along av. H. Bourguiba. They're all open Mon.-Fri. 8am-noon. Some close and re-open later (from 4:30-6pm) while others remain open until 4pm. The airport kiosk claims to be open all the time.

American Express: Carthage Tours, 59, av. Habib Bourguiba (tel. 35 49 93; fax 35 27 40). No banking services. Emergency check cashing for cardholders only; others can only report lost or stolen traveler's checks here. Open Mon.-Fri. 8am-noon and 2-6pm, Sat. 8am-noon.

Flights: Tunis-Carthage International Airport (tel. 23 60 00). Take bus #35 from av. Bourguiba to the airport (*aérodrome*) and back (about 400ml, taxi 2D). Note: the TGM "Aéroport" stop is actually a beach named Aéroport—not the airport. Tunis Air office at 48, av. Habib Bourguiba (tel. 77 01 00; fax 28 81 00).

Trains: SNCFT Tunis Ville Station, pl. de Barcelone (tel. 24 44 40), between rue de Hollande and av. de Carthage. The new Métro connects this station to the TGM station. To: Hammamet and Nabeul (2.200D); Sousse (4.600D); Sfax (7.550D); Gabes (10.950D); Bizerte (2.400D). **Commuter Trains: TGM,** at the foot of av. Bourguiba. Carthage-La Marsa via La Goulette and Sidi Bou Said. Speedy, frequent tram service 5am-midnight. To Carthage and La Marsa 450ml.

Buses: City buses at av. Dr. Habib Thameur at **Jardin Thameur** before av. de Paris; also next to the **TGM Tunis-Marine Station.** Buses also stop at pl. de Barcelone, in front of the Tunis-Ville train station and along av. Bourguiba. Fare 150ml and up, depending on distance traveled. Both intercity bus stations have nearby **Métro** stops. **Bab Saadoun** (tel. 56 22 99). From pl. de la Victoire take rue Mongi Slim to pl. Bab Souka, then rue Bal Saadoun in the same direction. Serves Bizerte, Tabarka, and Le Kef. **Bab El Fellah** (tel. 49 52 55), down the road from the train station, serves the rest of the country: Nabeul (2.250D), Kelibia (2.400D), Kairouan (4.000D), Sousse (4.200D), Gabes (9.200D), and Sfax (6.500D). **Louages** also depart from outside the stations.

Ferries: La Goulette (tel. 27 50 00). Take the TGM train to Vieille Goulette, 1km from the port. Ferry tickets at any of the travel agencies along av. Bourguiba. Arrive at least 2hr. before departure.

TUNIS

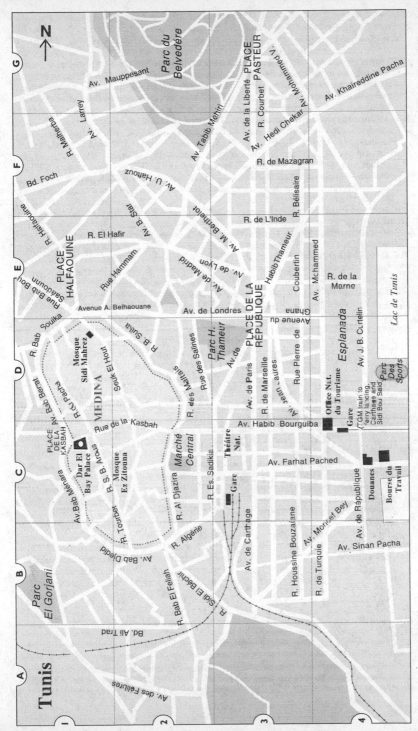

Tunis

Taxis: (tel. 78 33 11 or 28 22 11). Always metered. Three passengers is the usual maximum. 50% surcharge after 9pm. To airport: about 2D.

Car Rental: Europcar, 17, av. Habib Bourguiba (tel. 34 03 03 or 28 22 11). The cheapest. Renault Super 5s cost 230D per 3 days, 480D per week. Open daily 8am-12:30pm and 2-7pm. **Hertz,** 29, av. Bourguiba (tel. 24 85 59), or at the airport (tel. 23 60 00). **Avis,** in the lobby of the Hotel Africa (tel. 78 05 93). It is illegal for a rental car to carry more than 5 people including the driver. Always have passports ready for security checks. You must be 21 to rent and drive, and have had a license for more than 1 year.

Luggage storage: at the train station. 2D per 24 hrs. Open 24 hrs.

Laundromat: There are no coin-operated laundromats in Tunisia, but some dry cleaners take laundry by the kilo. Try **Laverie,** 15, rue d'Allemagne, across from the produce market (5.600D per basket). Open Mon.-Sat. 7am-6:30pm.

Swimming Pool: in the **Parc du Belvédère,** at the end of av. de la Liberté. Open July-Sept. 10am-5pm. 500ml. Take bus #5, 28, or 38 from av. Bourguiba.

Late-Night Pharmacy: 43, av. Bourguiba (tel. 25 25 07), or 20, av. de la Liberté (tel. 24 35 20). Open until 10am.

Hospital: Hôpital Charles Nicolle (tel. 66 30 10), bd. du IX Avril 1938 at rue Paul Bourde.

Emergencies: tel. 190 or 34 12 50. **Medical Emergency:** tel. 34 12 50.

ACCOMMODATIONS

Finding a budget hotel in Tunis is generally no problem except in the height of summer; the problem is finding one that seems safe. Think twice before staying in the cheapest hotels (anything under 4D) or in the medina. If you exercise the same precautions you would in any major city, however, you should not have a problem.

Auberge de Jeunesse (HI), 25, rue Saida Ajoula (tel. 56 78 50). From pl. de la Victoire, take rue de la Kasbah about 400m. Take the 7th right and walk another 100m. A notable exception to the medina rule. Huge and feline-filled. Modern toilets and hot showers. English-speaking warden serves up amazing lunch and dinner feasts (3D, breakfast 1D). Laundry on Tues. and Fri. 500ml per piece. Bicycle rental 8D per day. Lockout 10am-4pm. 3.500D per person. Members only.

Medina Hotel, pl. de la Victoire (tel. 25 50 56) to the right of the square above the Café Medina. Convenient (on the medina's edge) and easy to find. Rooms are bare but clean. Doubles 10D, triples 13D, quads 16D. Hot shower 1D.

Hotel Hammami, 1, pl. Bab Carthagène (tel. 26 04 51). From av. de France hang a right along rue Mongi Slim, which skirts the medina walls. Bear left through the square facing the Anglican Church. A classic medina hotel. Everyone washes at communal basins; women should think twice about staying here. Singles 2.500D, doubles 4.500D, triples 6D. No shower but there's a nearby *hammam*.

Hotel Bristol, 30, rue Mohammed el Aziz Taj, (tel. 24 48 36), off av. de Carthage behind the Café de Paris. Clean, cheap cubbyholes. Singles 4D. Doubles 6D. Triples 9D. Quads 11D. Breakfast 900ml.

Hotel Cirta, 42, rue Charles de Gaulle (tel. 24 15 82), across from the Agriculture. The tiny but tidy rooms have big windows, but provide little light in the night. Singles 6D. Doubles 10D. Triples 13D. Quads 15D. Showers (cold in summer) 1D.

Hotel Commodor, 17, rue d'Allemagne (tel. 24 49 41), 2nd right off av. Charles de Gaulle from av. de France. A cut above the rest, and not much more expensive. Polished wood lobby, pleasant tea salon, and spotless rooms. Singles 9D, with bath 13D. Doubles 17D with bath 20.500D. The showers along the corridor cost 1.700D, so spring for the bath.

FOOD

It's strange that a city with such a cosmopolitan air should offer such limited dining options. Non-Tunisian cuisine tends toward the mediocre, with the unsurprising exception of French food (*not* Italian). Still, one can dine well and cheaply here. Many places are dirty, and the clean places are often overpriced. The stand-up *rôtisseries* and sandwich shops off av. Bourguiba and av. de la Liberté are often dirty *and* overpriced. The farther away from av. Bourguiba you go, the less you'll have to pay, and usually the places are cleaner. Those on a budget can survive on the hot snacks sold at most *pâtisseries:* mini-pizzas, hot anchovy rolls, tuna rolls, and meat pies (about 350ml). Peruse the stalls of the comprehensive **central market,** on rue Charles de Gaulle between rue d'Allemagne and av. d'Espagne (open daily 6am-2pm). **Monoprix,** a large supermarket with stores off av. Bourguiba on rue Charles de Gaulle and on rue de la Liberté at rue du Koweit, also stocks a selection of inexpensive edibles and useful toiletries. (Open daily 9am-1pm and 3-7:30pm.)

Restaurant Carcassonne, 8, av. de Carthage (tel. 25 67 68). *Brasserie*-type place that's very popular with both tourists and locals. Vegetarians should try the *tagine* (a bit like quiche, 1.600D). Solid, 4-course *menu* a super-bargain at 3.100D. Open daily 8am-10pm.

Pâtisserie Le Prince, 5, rue Ibn Khaldoun, just off av. Bourguiba (look for the obnoxious "Fast Food" sign). One of the few reasonable stand-up sandwich shops. Massive, greasy *chaourma* sandwich and fries 1.200D. Open Mon.-Sat. 6am-10:30pm.

Restaurant Des Palmiers, 11, rue d'Egypte (tel. 28 54 07), off av. de la Liberté. Well worth the 15-min. walk from av. Bourguiba. Tunisian dishes are fresh and served quickly. Try the *meloukya,* a delicious meat dish which looks extremely unappetizing (1.750D). The lamb *couscous* is also excellent (1.900D). Open Mon.-Sat. noon-10:30pm. Closed mornings during Ramadan.

M'Rabet (tel. 26 17 29), at the center of the medina in Souk Et-Trouk. The 300-year old building contains the sarcophagi of an Ottoman sheik, his servant, and his daughter, M'Rabet. A very cool place to indulge in a *chicha* (2D) or Turkish coffee (700ml). Upstairs is a restaurant with a reputation for the best Tunisian food around (entrees 7-9D). Sept.-June, it puts on an "Oriental show" (i.e. belly dancers) for diners for 5D. Open Mon.-Sat. noon-3pm and 8pm-midnight.

Chez nous, 5, rue Marseille (tel. 24 30 43) just off av. Bourguiba. Tries hard for that Parisian *brasserie* effect: *pommes frites,* haughty waiters, and photos of obscure French celebrity-patrons. Uninspiring *menu* (9D), but the seafood is divine. A place to try Tunisian wine (8-10D). Open noon-2:30pm and 7-10:30pm. MC, Visa.

SIGHTS

The New City (Nouvelle Ville)

French-built modern Tunis is best seen as you stroll up **av. Habib Bourguiba;** the boulevard spreads nearly 70m. Along the way, you can also stock up on flowers and such Tunisian souvenirs as Levis 501 T-shirts and Michael Jackson bootlegs. The **place d'Afrique,** at the intersection of av. Muhammed V, was once occupied by an equestrian statue of Bourguiba. That statue now resides in front of La Goulette, and in its place stands a four-legged clock tower. The site has been officially renamed **place du 7 Novembre 1987,** commemorating the recent *coup d'état* of Pres. Ben Ali, whose likeness is plastered everywhere in somewhat Orwellian fashion.

Without a doubt the most interesting, if not aesthetically pleasing, aspects of the new city are the examples of **French Colonial architecture.** These public buildings were designed to convey a grand sense of European culture adapted to the North African environs. The virginal-white buildings are aptly described as "wedding cake" architecture. The **National Theater,** with its simple, classical motifs, emanates a somewhat patronizing air two blocks from pl. de l'Indépendance. The theater, however, pales in comparison to the **cathedral** facing the square. The 1882 structure is a weird mixture of Romanesque and Islamic styles; its rounded edges and unsubtle statues belong to a cartoon rather than a place of worship. The **French Embassy,** understated in comparison, is ironically the only institution of the three to have had a serious impact on Tunisian life as the executive seat of the Protectorate.

Medina

Until the advent of European colonialism, the entire city of Tunis was contained within the medina's fortified walls. These protected a self-sufficient system of commercial, domestic, and religious institutions, each with its place within the maze of streets. At its best, the medina of Tunis is an evocative remnant of this exquisitely orchestrated society. At its worst, it is a dispensary of oriental kitsch and photo-ops. At its liveliest, however, the medina is a commercial area integral to modern Tunis—a flea market-*cum*-shopping mall where residents bargain for jeans, deodorant, and Ace of Base albums. Whatever your motivations, the medina is a great place to wander. Take a left or a right down some small alley and you'll find yourself on a side street where the signs are only in Arabic. **Be careful however: exploring the medina by day is less risky than at night, when it's unsafe for anyone.** On av. Bourguiba and by the mosque, young men claiming to be students may offer either to guide you around the sights (they will expect payment) or to accompany you to the grossly over-priced artisan shops (they will receive a commission). Also, beware of merchants who drag you upstairs to see their "terraces" and then request an outrageous fee for the privilege of having entered their shop.

Maps of the medina are available at the ONTT office, or study the tile rendering of the old city outside the Great Mosque, as well as other strategic locations. From pl. de la Victoire, two main streets lead to the Great Mosque and the heart of the medina. The package tours barge through **rue Jamaa ez Zitouna** (on the left), the place to go for stuffed toy camels and chintzy brass plates. **Rue de la Kasbah** (on the right) is equally congested with locals shopping for everything *but* souvenirs.

Rue de la Kasbah passes two prime examples of Ottoman-influenced architecture. The first is the **Hammouda Pacha Mosque,** whose octagonal minaret is an instinctively Turkish feature that became dominant in the 17th century. Strangely enough, the façade's ornamentation is actually derived from European Renaissance style; the mosque's patron was an Italian convert in the Ottoman civil service. This mosque's predecessor is a bit further down the street: the **Youssef Dey Mosque** was built in 1616, the first example of the Turkish attempt to spruce up Tunis.

Souk el Bey is the name of the street heading left by the Youssef Dey Mosque. Another quick left hits **Souk des Chechias,** named for the crimson skullcaps crafted from luxuriously heavy felt. Once *de rigeur* throughout the Islamic world and Tunis' primary industry, the craft is now almost extinct—although the caps are still worn by some older men. The **Dar el Bey,** straight ahead on Souk el Bey houses the Ministry of Foreign Affairs. A left here places you on **Souk el-Trouk,** with vendors selling just about anything: cheap sandals, dried fruit, circumcision outfits...

The **Jemaa Zitouna,** the city's great mosque, presides at the end of this *souk* and at the center of the medina. The mosque was the site of an Islamic university with origins predating its educational institution counterparts by far. The **minaret** is a dignified, classically proportioned tower—the product of the Moroccan-based Almohad Empire of the 13th century—much in contrast with the gaudy Ottoman style. For a price, you can have a look at the courtyard, whose columns were recycled from various Roman sites. Each teacher had his own column from which he would regularly instruct. The prayer hall is off-limits to non-Muslims; take this into consideration before paying admission. (Open daily 8am-noon. Admission 1.500D.)

The covered market along the Great Mosque's walls is the **Souk el Attarine** (Perfume Souk), where aggressive vendors tout inexpensive Chanel knock-offs. **Souk el-Blag-Djia,** a market with all sorts of shoes (some fresh from the factory, others made on the premises), becomes tiny rue el-Jelloud. Where you see the sign "el-Jelloud," take a left into a cul-de-sac (Impasse Echemmahra). At the far end, you can ring the doorbell at #9 and ask to visit the small, elegant 17th-century **Tomb of Princess Aziza,** now a private residence. The princess had a charitable reputation, and established a dowry fund in order to allow poor girls to get married.

Walking back up Souk el-Attarine and turning left at the Great Mosque's minaret puts you on Souk des Femmes. Take the first right onto Souk el-Lefta, where smooth dealers roll out beautiful carpets. (If you're reading this book, you probably can't afford one.) Many of the larger emporiums have intricately tiled terraces from which you can see the rooftops of the *souks* and the surrounding medina. The most famous is that of the **Palais d'Orient,** the large bazaar at #58 Souk el-Leffa. Their enameled terrace dates from the 15th century; its view is featured on hundreds of postcards. (Free.) Souk des Femmes becomes Rue Tourbet el-Bey, which predictably leads toward the **Tourbet el-Bey.** Built in the 18th century, it houses the tombs of several members of the Husaynid dynasty amidst rather excessive stucco work. The sacrophagi seem skinny to non-Muslims because the dead are traditionally buried on their side facing Mecca to await Judgement Day (open daily 8:30am-6:30pm; admission 1.500D). From here follow the green tourist signs to the **Dar Ben Abdallah** (Museum of Arts and Traditions). The museum, housed in a fine old palace, depicts traditional Tunisian domestic life (using rather frightening mannequins). The displays of household goods are excellent, illustrating how any sort of object can be imbued with the Islamic sense of style. **A museum annex** is also devoted to traditional industries, most importantly *chechia*-making. Unfortunately, exhibit descriptions are only in French and Arabic. (Open Tues.-Sun. 9:30am-4:30pm. Admission 1.500D, 1D to take photos.)

Just down the street from the museum you'll find the **Mosquée des Teinturiers**—dyers' mosque, built in 1716. Although closed to non-believers, the mosque is worth seeing for its fancifully colored eaves in red, green, and yellow. A mosque was an essential part of each quarter within the medina, which were generally based on specific trade and manufacturing activities. (Worshippers would go to the local mosque for daily prayers, and the Grand Mosque on Fridays.) Other institutions found in these communities were (are) a *hammam,* a well or fountain, and a bakery. Of course, the *souks* were also nearby; in this case the dyer's stalls, **Souk des Teinturiers,** run past their mosque along rue des Teinturiers. Continue toward rue Jamaa Zitouna to complete the circuit of the medina center.

The Bardo Museum

While a trip to North Africa generally means escape from the endless "must-see" museums of Europe, Tunis offers no better diversion than the **Bardo Museum,** home to one of the world's finest collections of ancient art. The Bardo is most renowned for its Roman mosaics; the finest works have been transported here from various archaeological sites throughout the country and more than compensate for the uninspiring ruins at Carthage and other sites. Both the size of the collection and of the visiting tour groups overwhelm the visitor, but a little persistence and patience will allow you to avoid the latter and appreciate the best of the former.

The ground floor starts with a cross-shaped baptistery in the **Paleochristian Room,** which features brightly colored mosaic tombstones with sour-faced icons and Latin admonitions. Around the corner to the right in the **Room of Baal Hammon,** ritual slabs illustrate the Carthaginian procedure for sacrificing children to their dark goddess, Tanit (read the explanation to find out how). Room VI exhibits artifacts from **Bulla Regia,** highlighted by twice-life-size statues of Roman gods and a mosaic of Perseus and Andromeda. The palace's second floor displays the major attractions. The mosaics are not only important as works of art but as documents depicting the daily life of their epoch. They are grouped in rooms by origin. Room IX **(Carthage),** the central exhibition hall, is a courtyard with a Turkish twist, used by the bey's harem. Now it houses sculpture and mosaics excavated at Carthage. The **Hadrumetum Room** is decorated below by an immense mosaic from Sousse, the *Triumph of Neptune,* while the walls above are a backdrop for three semi-circular works depicting rural houses and a 4th-century piece entitled *Mosaïque du Seigneur Julius.* The adjacent Room XI contains a superbly preserved *Neptune in his Chariot.* Across from this the **Virgilius Room** devotes almost all its space to the exhibition of a single, small mosaic of the poet himself with Muses gazing admiringly at him from each side. High school Latin scholars can have some fun (finally) by trying to guess which verse of the *Aeneid* Virgil is holding in his lap. Room XXVII displays finds from **Dougga,** including a celebrated mosaic that depicts *Ulysses and the*

Sirens, the latter quite homely and the former frightened nonetheless. Complete your odyssey at the **Uthina Room,** where a wall-mounted mosaic depicts the love-lorn and disfigured Orpheus enchanting the beasts with his music. Orpheus' facelift was probably the work of the 5th-century vandals, who also had a field day on the statuary downstairs. (Open Tues.-Sun., 9:30am-4:30pm; during Ramadan until 4pm. Admission 4D; 1D extra take photos.) Take bus #4 from av. Habib Thameur, just by the cathedral, to the Bardo stop (400ml). The museum is a short walk down the road to the right. Alternatively, take a cab (2D) to avoid public transportation.

■ NEAR TUNIS: CARTHAGE AND SIDI BOU SAID

Tunis boasts some easy daytrips. Efficient TGM commuter trains make **Carthage** (30min., 550ml) and **Sidi Bou Said** (35min., 550ml), easy, quick rides. Trains come every 15 minutes or so. Be warned; weekend trains tend to be infrequent and *very* crowded. The spectacular 30km beach of **Raouad** begins just past **Gammarth,** but both these towns (and La Marsa as well) are now overrun tourist nightmares. The beaches of **Cap Bon** make for excellent daytrips as well. Indeed, because of the country's size, consider stuffing a few days' worth of underwear in a day pack, leaving your backpack at Tunis Care, and heading into the country.

CARTHAGE

Any visitor expecting to see magnificent reminders of Carthage's legendary history will be disappointed; the few remains are surrounded by an air of stupendous medi-ocrity, and there is, of course, little trace of the Punic Empire that once rivaled Rome for Mediterranean supremacy. The few remains are surrounded by an air of stupen-dous mediocrity; modern Carthage is essentially an overpriced suburb of Tunis. Still, anyone with the barest sense of history and a little imagination cannot help but be impressed by the momentous aura of the site where Aeneas and Dido trysted, Han-nibal launched his campaign across the Alps, and St. Augustine preached.

The city's origins are attributed to the Phoenician Queen Dido, whose unfortu-nate affair with the founder of Rome is described in Virgil's *Aeneid.* Little historical information is known of the citizens of this Punic city except that they were phe-nomenal traders and had a habit of pissing off everyone whom they met. The Romans finally put a stop to all this in 146 BC; contemporary accounts describe the complete immolation of the city in loving detail. As Rome's power in Africa grew, Carthage was refounded as the provincial capital, and thrived and declined with the Empire's fortunes, finally falling to vandals in 429.

The ruins are scattered over a wide area that coincides with the stops of the TGM train line. Successive stops are close together and can be traversed easily on foot. If you're short on stamina or time, get off at the **Carthage-Byrsa** station, visit the Tophet and the Punic Ports, then get back on the TGM to **Carthage-Hannibal** and visit the Roman baths. The nearby **beaches** of the Bay of Tunis offer a refreshing alternative to yet another ruin. Buy a ticket for all Carthage sites at either the Carthage Museum, the Roman baths, or the Amphitheatre and Tophet Roman baths. (Admission 4D, photos 2D; fend off guides or use up some loose change.)

Carthage-Byrsa

Though most of the uncovered ruins of Carthage date to the Roman era, evidence of the original Punic settlement has been discovered here in the form of a cemetery. At the site of the **Tophet** (also called the **Sanctuary of Tanit**) bushes conceal stones shaped like the planks of picket fences, engraved with a deceptively innocuous design: a circle atop a rectangle that balances on a triangle. The pictogram repre-sents the figure of the bloodthirsty goddess Tanit, who demanded the sacrifice of first-born 12- and 14-year-olds in time of hardship. Each stone mourns one of the 1200 children who were sacrificed here. (Open daily 7am-6pm.) To reach the

Tophet, facing the direction in which you came, head left towards the sea, then take a right onto rue Hannibal.

Almost nothing remains of what was the world's greatest harbor in its time, but determined archaeologists have reconstructed the contours of the original **Punic Ports.** Inside the "Antiquarium" (the custodian will unlock it for you) are detailed models of the military port from the Punic and Roman periods. (Site open daily 7am-6pm.) To reach either site, walk toward the large palm tree until you see a small lake. From here, the Tophet is your first right (rue Hannibal) and the Punic Ports are further on, around the lake to your left.

Carthage-Hannibal

The **National Museum of Carthage** occupies the site where an immense Roman temple once stood; bits of marble columns and statues saturate the surrounding gardens. Inside are only a few Punic funerary steles and two expressive 4th-century sarcophagi of Italian Carrara marble—an indication of the city's former wealth. (Open daily 8am-7pm.) To reach the museum from the station, follow the palm-lined avenue up to its crest, and just as it's about to slope down again, take a left up a narrow dirt path. The most substantial rubble of Carthage lies in the village of Hannibal. From the station, walk towards the water and turn left on rue Septime Sévère to find the 2nd-century Roman **Baths of Antoninus**—the single most impressive ruin in Carthage. Once rivaling Rome's Baths of Caracalla in size, the baths were gradually destroyed by villagers who used the site as a quarry. Unfortunately, you can't enter this forest of humpbacked pediments and fallen pillars. Back near the entrance, you'll discover a tiny underground Christian chapel, whose floor is patterned with an ornithological mosaic. (Open daily 8:30am-7pm; off-season 8:30am-5pm.)

Head farther up the road, cross beneath the railway tracks, and follow the signs to the **Roman Villas** and **Archaeological Gardens,** where you'll find two Byzantine churches and a Punic necropolis. The guides will tell you that the elegant villa was Hannibal's Palace; they refuse to admit that Hannibal wasn't Roman and died 400 years before the villa was built. Over the hill lies the well-preserved 3rd-century **Odeon.** (Open daily 8am-7pm.) From the station, cross the tracks and go uphill to reach the remnants of the Roman **amphitheater.** Another 2km ahead, the scrupulously restored **Theater of Carthage** provides the backdrop for the **Festival of Carthage** (July to mid-Aug.). For info, contact the tourist office in Tunis or see the schedule in *La Presse*. From the Archaeological Gardens the road leading away from the coast leads to some uninteresting **cisterns.** A right on this road, however, leads to the **American Cemetery.** The immaculate grass and stars seem out of place in the context of ancient Carthage or modern Tunis, but their presence is most appropriate. The cemetery holds the remains of 2,840 servicemen (only 39% of the men who died in North Africa), while a wall bears the names of the 3,724 whose bodies were never recovered. A large mural depicts the North African campaign, on which the caretaker may elaborate (open Mon.-Sat. 8am-6pm, Sun. 9am-6pm).

SIDI BOU SAID

After getting sweaty and sandy in Carthage, the village of Sidi Bou Said (10 min. farther down the TGM line, return service to Tunis until midnight) is the perfect spot to rejuvenate. The streets are smooth cobblestone, the houses are freshly painted blue and white, and purple flowers and century plants spill out of wall-top gardens. It is, of course, packed with tourists, but things calm down by the evening. Decorative detail is one secret of the town's charm: look for carved doorknockers, brightly painted metal window grilles, and wooden window boxes thick with flowers. Of course, no eye for detail is necessary to appreciate the cliffs and sea views.

From the TGM station, proceed to the right and turn left at the police station. Walk up the hill to the tiny **town square.** Follow rue Sidi Bou-Fares from the main square, turn left, and hike up the hill; a small tip will persuade the guardian to let you climb the **minaret.** Or continue from the square until you see the steep flight of 254 stairs to the right; these descend to the small **beach.** Before 10am or after 9pm, travelers can ask around the port about working on one of the fishing boats that ply the sea all night and return at dawn. Travelers who can spare several days may even get paid. Aspiring fishers should choose their fishing boat with discretion.

The only budget accommodation is the truly excellent **Hotel Sidi Bou-Fares,** up the hill from the main square at #15 (tel. 74 00 91). The neat rooms have thick walls and the courtyard has an immense apricot tree to ensure midday coolness. There are only eight rooms, and the hotel is extremely popular, so call ahead. (Singles 12.500D. Doubles 22D. Triples with bath 30D. Breakfast included.) If you're lucky enough to have a room at the Boufares, take advantage of the excellent lunches and dinners served here for 7D, the best deal in town. **Restaurant Chergui,** off the main square (tel. 74 09 87), is also an attractive dining option. Try the *couscous poulet* for 4D, or the *tagine de fromage* (a meatless quiche) for 4D; all is served in a beautiful, breezy courtyard with a nice view. For dessert you must try the *bambolini,* fried dough swamped in sugar (250ml), sold at stands near the beach. In the cool evenings, the cafés quickly fill up with people busy being beautiful. The **Café des Nattes,** near Hotel Boufares, has the best pedigree; Cervantes, de Beauvoir, and Klee all sipped and quipped here. The nicest establishment by far is the **Café Sidi Chabane,** with its irregular tiers and delicate teas.

CAP BON PENINSULA

Stretching northeast toward Sicily, Cap Bon touches the Gulf of Tunis on one side and the Gulf of Hammamet on the other. The cape's hillsides, rich with olive and orange groves, and its shimmering sea provide welcome relief from both the scorching heat of the south and the wearying bustle of Tunis. Cap Bon was ancient Carthage's supplier of limestone; now its major purpose is tourism. Vacationing Europeans crowd the peninsula's fine beaches and fill its azure waters on the beach towns of Kelibia, Hammamet and Nabeul. Frequent and packed buses link the villages of the peninsula with Tunis and each other. Inexpensive hotels are rare, but staying at hostels will help salvage your budget.

■■■ NABEUL

After some consideration, the local tourist board decided *not* to adopt the slogan "Nabeul: At Least We're Not Hammamet." While the beaches of Nabeul are not as spectacular, they are also not hidden by a carpet of sunbathing tourists. Nabeul does possess its fair share of resort hotels and daytrippers looking to buy the famous local ceramics. But you'll have no trouble finding a few idyllic and unpopulated stretches of beach (including the one in front of the youth hostel). The number of tourists peaks on Fridays for the town's **camel market** (although how visitors plan to get their dromedary friends through customs is somewhat unclear).

Orientation and Practical Information Trains from Tunis (7 per day, 1½hr., 3.100D), arrive in place du 7 Novembre, near the tree growing out of a massive ceramic vase. Across the street and to the right is a small **museum** of Carthaginian and Roman artifacts (open Tues.-Sun. 8am-1pm and 4-7pm. Admission 1D). There is a **Syndicat** next door but it's poorly stocked and rarely helpful (open Tues.-Sun. 9am-1pm and 3-7pm). Better try the **ONTT,** at Taïeb Mehiri (tel. 28 68 00), where they speak English and have maps. Head one block from the station, and take a right on av. Taïeb Mehiri. Proceed almost to the beach; it's on your right. (Open July-Aug. 7:30am-1:30pm, Sept.-June 8:30am-1pm and 3-5:45pm.) The **bus and louage station** (excepting Cap Bon *louages*) is located on av. Habib Thameur, the town's main street. Buses leave every half-hour for Tunis (1½hr., 2.750D) and every hour for Kelibia (45min., 1.850D). Both services stop at 6pm. *Louages* to Tunis (3D) leave from the bus station, while Kelibia *louages* (1.850D) leave from the station an av. Hached. A right from the av. Habib Thameur station brings you to an intersection with av. Bourguiba, which leads down to a potted tree and the **beach.** Av. Thameur becomes av. Farhat Hached; the **Cap Bon louage station** is on the right 500m further down. Head left on av. Bourguiba for the **post office;** head right for the **police station** (tel. 28 54 74). (Post office open Mon.-Sat. 8am-6pm.) **Telephone code:** 02.

Accommodations and Food The **HI Youth hostel** (tel. 28 55 42) is the best reason to come to Nabeul. While *Full Metal Jacket* could have been filmed in the barracks-like dormitories (the warden is hoping to build a new hostel by 1996), the location on the beach is marvelous. Half (6.500D) or full (9.500D) pension is required, but don't gripe; the simple, delicious meals are the best deal in town. HI membership required. Back in town, the **Pension Les Roses,** rue Sidi Abdel Kader (tel. 28 55 70) off av. Hached, has cheery, clean rooms with hot water, towels, and soap. Small and popular, so call ahead. (8D per person, shower 500ml). The touristed **Hotel les Jasmins** (tel. 28 53 43) is 2km from the bus station, down the Hammamet Road; it's the only campsite in town (1.900D per person, 1.300D per car, 2D per shower). If you're not eating at the youth hostel, there are few cheap, decent eateries. **Restaurant de la Jeunesse,** 76 av. Farhat Hached, serves decent *brochettes* or couscous for 3D (open daily 9am-9pm). A picnic on the beach is always attractive; pick up the supplies at the **central market** behind the bus station.

■■■ KELIBIA

It is an inexplicable miracle that the largest group of visitors to Kelibia are the students at the Tunisian School of Fishery; the 6th-century Byzantine fortress overlooking the port recalls a time when the town was much more coveted by foreigners. The breeze that greets you as you arrive will lure you to the pristine sands of **El-Mansourah** (2km north), perhaps Cap Bon's finest beach. The hotels here are few and may stretch the budget, but the tranquil location is certainly worth it. Should you think differently, Kelibia and its environs are an easy daytrip from Nabeul.

Orientation and Practical Information Arriving by either bus or *louage,* you will be deposited in Kelibia town, a dusty, modern place noteworthy only for its 10 mosques, all with varied minarets. To get to the more attractive seaside section (2.5km away), head right, with the arches of the bus station behind you. Walk until you come to a large street with a flower-laden divide, where you should turn right; you'll pass the **supermarket** on your left. At the fork in the road bear left onto **av. des Martyrs** (there's a sign for Kelibia Plage). Catch a cab (350-450ml), walk a couple of blocks to the bus stop (every 30min., only in July and August), or hike. Fourteen **buses** per day leave Tunis for Kelibia from the SNT station at Baba Aliwa (2½hr., 3.700D). Twelve buses per day run to and from Nabeul (1½hr., 1.850D); a *louage* costs about the same.

Accommodations and Food The best value is the **Hotel Florida** (tel. 29 62 48), next to a tourist hotel off av. des Martyrs. It's a bit pricey, but it's right on the sand and has a great view of the Borj. The best values are the motel-like bungalows with tourists and showers. (Singles 15.500D, doubles 24D, breakfast included.) Back in town, **Pension Anis,** av. Erriadii (tel. 27 31 28), is spotless and well managed. Bear right from the end of rue Khaldoun; it's a block down on the left. (Singles 14.500D, doubles 23D; breakfast and hot showers included.) Free-lance **camping** is often tolerated along Mansourah beach and the long stretches of deserted beach further north. Check with any possible owner of the site or the police, and be sure to consider safety. The two hotels above also have the best **restaurants** in town. The Anis serves spaghetti with a divine seafood sauce (5.500D), while Florida serves its *menu* (5D, go with the fish) on a terrace overlooking the sea. (Anis open daily noon-3pm and 7-10pm. Florida open daily 12:30-3:30pm and 7pm-midnight.) The Florida also runs a relaxed **bar** where seafarers swap stories over cold Celtia (1.250D). A little farther down the road, around to the right as the road to El-Mansourah splits off to the left, is the **Cafe Sidi El-Bahri.** Stop in, sit on a terrace overlooking the sea, and sample some of the most marvelous *chocolat chaud* you'll ever taste (500ml).

Sights The remarkably intact **Borj** (fortress) sits between Kelibia and Mansourah. Along with the fort at Hammamet, it controlled the eastern portion of the Cap Bon peninsula. Little remains of the original 4th-century BC walls; most of the present battlements were added by the Romans and Byzantines in the subsequent centuries. In the 16th and 17th centuries, the Spanish wrested control of the fort and built the crenellations atop the walls. It was later occupied by the Turks and then the French. The anti-aircraft gun emplacements are American adornments; the fort's Axis occupants came under attack by Allied aircraft. The fort is generally open all day during the summer, depending on the local occupant and guardian. The road that winds around the base of the fort leads to **El-Mansourah** and its ivory **beaches** 2km away. There's no public transportation, but it's a quick, breezy walk by beach cottages and farmland. No signs point you towards the beach; just follow one of the sandy paths that lead to the blue water.

■ NEAR KELIBIA

EL HAOUARIA

El Haouaria is on the map only because it is home to one of the most unusual sites in all of Tunisia: the **Grottoes Romaines** (Roman Caves), a labyrinth of underground pyramids carved out of the limestone rock along the shore. You can explore the grottoes yourself; though there are quite a few, the path between them is simple and a local guide (no matter what he tells you) just won't be necessary. The oddly shaped rock formation in the first cave is called "Le Dromadaire," and with a little squinting and a lot of acid, the lump really does resemble a camel. A series of other man-made grottoes is linked to this first one, most of which are pyramidal with holes at the top to admit sunlight. Both the Carthaginians and the Romans quarried stone for their cities here; the site's **guardian** spins a tale of slaves spending decades in the tiny caverns. When you tire of the solitude, join the packs of El Haouarian boys who take advantage of the caves and rock formations to plunge into the Mediterranean. (Grottoes open daily 8am-7pm; admission 1D, photo permit 1D.)

Buses to El Haouaria depart daily from Tunis's Gare Routière du Nord (near the Bab Saadoun), itself a bus trip on the #3 from the center of town (5 per day, 2¼hr., 4.300D; check return times with the driver). Service is much more frequent to and from nearby Kelibia (every hour), and **louages** are constantly heading there and back (1D by bus or *louage*). To reach the caves themselves, walk straight through town along av. Bourguiba and then head 1.5km past the end of town and toward the shore. You'll come to a café patio with a thatched roof; the rocks slope down to the sea from here. The entrance to the "camel" cave is a short distance to the right.

SAHEL

The **Sahel** (seashore) bulges through eastern Tunisia, from the Cap Bon peninsula south along the Mediterranean to Sfax. This region was the base of the independence movement of the 1930s and has been the country's richest area since Independence in 1956. Arabs arriving in the 7th century took advantage of its beautiful, wide beaches, and its residents have long benefitted from some of Tunisia's highest rainfall and prime soil, making the Sahel a leading exporter of olives. While the northern city of Sousse swells its massive medina with package-tour visitors, the southern city of Sfax has industrialized with nary a tourist in mind. Monastir, the birthplace of former president Bourguiba, offers only the inflated trappings of a personality cult. Down the coast, the origin of the Fatimid dynasty lies in the ancient port of Mahdia. Inland, Tunisia's most sacred mosque reposes in Kairouan, while at sleepy El Jem a Roman amphitheater bears witness to a great and cruel civilization.

■■■ SOUSSE

Sousse handles its status as an obvious tourist attraction gracefully, remaining clean, inexpensive, and generally agreeable. Its central location on the Sahel made it an important site long before anyone invented the tour-bus wheel. Starting in the 3rd century BC, various groups fought bloody battles to give the city the name of their choice: Hadrumetum under the Romans, Hunsericopolis under the Vandals, Justinopolis under the Byzantines, and Sousse under the Aghlabid Arabs. In recent years the city has grown and prospered, not at all hurt by the fact that President Ben Ali is the local boy who made good.

Orientation and Practical Information Pedestrians, buses, cars, and a ridiculous "Noddy Train" compete for space in the central place Farhat Hached, also the entrance to the medina. The **post office** (tel. 22 47 50) and **night pharmacy** (tel. 22 47 95) are located on av. de la République, which branches off pl. Farhat. Most everything else is located on av. Bourguiba. This includes the Monoprix **supermarket** (open daily 8:30am-12:30pm and 3:30-7:30pm), the **police station** (tel. 22 55 66), and numerous **banks.** (Most open for changing money Mon.-Fri. 8-11:30am and 2-5pm, Sat.-Sun 9am-noon.) Around the corner from the Monoprix, on rue du Caire, is a **telephone** office, where you can pay in cash at the desk for international calls (open daily 7am-11pm). **Telephone code:** 03. Just at the start of av. Bourguiba by the square is the **tourist office of the gods,** 1, av. Bourguiba (tel. 22 51 57). The English-speaking staff has maps, cultural event schedules, and fares and times for trains and buses—and even serves tea. (Open Mon.-Sat. 7:30am-1:30pm and 3-6pm, Sun. 9am-noon and 3-6pm.) One hundred meters left of p. Farhat Hached sits the **central train station.** (From Tunis: 11 per day, 2½hr., 4.600D; Nabeul: 8 per day, 2-3hr., 3.550D, change at Bir Bou Regba.) Trains to Mahdia and Monastir use the **Sousse Bab Jedid** station located near the port, 200m past pl. Farhat Hached. (To Monastir: 16 per day, 30min., 750ml. To Mahdia: 8 per day, 1hr., 2D. Fewer trains to both cities on Sun.) **Buses and louages** to local destinations congregate to the left of the medina entrance. (Buses to: Sfax, 5 per day, 4.960D; El Jem, 5 per day, 2.500D; Mahdia, every hr., 2.300D.) Buses to Tunis (6 per day, 5.600D) and Kairouan (11 per day, 2.390D) leave from the station to the right of the medina entrance.

Accommodations and Food As you enter the medina, you'll find **Hotel de Paris,** 15, rue Rempart Nord (tel. 22 05 64), on the right, just inside. Each clean room features a bed, a sink, and little else. (Singles 8D. Doubles 14D. Shower 500ml.) Trade the sink for a desk, and you have the rooms at **Hotel Ghabes,** rue de Paris (tel. 22 69 77). To get there, turn right by the Hotel Medina and follow the signs. The shower, separated from the corridor by a curtain, isn't very private. (Singles 6D. Doubles 10D. Only cold showers in summer, 500ml.) Right next to the Great Mosque, the **Hotel Medina** (tel. 22 17 22), puts on a luxurious display for its German package tourists. It has plenty of rooms, so it's a good fallback. (Prices vary according to season: singles 10-15D, none in high season; doubles 18-24D. Showers and breakfast included.) Eating out in Sousse is generally expensive. As a rule, avoid any place on av. Bourguiba or pl. Farhat Hached. An exception to this rule is the **Restaurant Sidi-Yahia,** at the Medina's entrance (look for the beige and black awning with Arabic writing). It's a touristy location, but the clientele is strictly Tunisian (others are perhaps scared by the none-too-clean floor). Most entrees here are *spicy* and under 1.500D. The best snack option in town is the **unnamed juice stand,** just off av. Bourguiba (2nd right from the pl. Farhat Hached). The stand sells fresh fruit juice (600ml., essentially whole strawberries and melons puréed in an industrial blender) and Middle Eastern pastries (400ml). There's a mellow **bar** at the Hotel Medina where locals and Germans mingle, especially during soccer season.

MAHDIA

Sights The Aghlabids were a possessive bunch, and they built a citadel that has withstood the attacks of time as well as the armies of Europe and the rural Berber interior. Access to the medina was made easier in 1943, when the Allies bombed a big hole in the walls near the place des Martyrs. Most striking are the remarkably preserved outer walls, which protected a social and commercial system designed to be self-sufficient in times of siege. The medina's **Ribat,** an 8th-century fortress-within-a-fortress, embodies a time when war was an act of piety as much as a political tool. The coastal *ribats* served as "fighting sanctuaries," wherein a special class of warrior-monks called *murabatin* divided their time between prayer and smiting Christians. You can climb the **tower** for a good view of the area. The tower served as a link in the chain of beacons that could send messages form Egypt to Morocco overnight. (Open May-Sept. Tues.-Sun. 8am-5pm, Oct.-April Tues.-Sun. 8:30am-3:30pm. Admission 1D, photo permit 1D.) Even the **Grand Mosque,** from the same era, has a defensive, military feel to it; the lack of a minaret emphasizes the building's low lines. As always, the prayer hall is closed to non-Muslims, but the simple, elegant courtyard is open to all visitors. (Open 9am-1pm. Admission 500ml.) Outside the medina walls is a small but worthwhile **Museum of Antiquities,** with one of the best collections of mosaics outside of the Bardo Museum in Tunis. To get there, head uphill from the main entrance to the medina and walk about a kilometer along blvd. Maréchal Tito. The museum is just beyond the point where the army and police barracks guard each other from across the street. (Open Tues.-Sun. 8am-noon and 3-7pm. Admission 1D, photo permit 1D.)

■■■ MAHDIA

Package tours overlook Mahdia's strengths. This has historically been the case: Mahdia's easily defended peninsula attracted little attention until the 10th century, when one of the more colorful heretics in Islamic history made it his capital. Obaidallah Said claimed descent from the Prophet through Fatima and led a Shi'ite faction to Cape Africa in order to establish a new stronghold. Calling himself "the Mahdi" (the final prophet of Islam), Obaidallah and his Fatimid descendants launched several campaigns to conquer the Arab world, making it to Egypt in 961 AD. Under the Fatimids, Mahdia eclipsed even Kairouan in importance, but its status declined after their downfall. The Spanish, who took it from the pirate Dragut in 1550, couldn't be bothered with it and blew up the fortifications before leaving four years later. Modern-day tourist hordes in Sousse and Monastir mercifully overlook Mahdia, but someday this will change; sooner or later, resort hotels will exploit the 17km of beautiful beaches nearby. For now, Mahdia remains untouristed, quiet, and endearing.

Orientation and Practical Information Upon arrival by bus or train, walk with the water to your right until you see a large square with the Banque de Tunisie on the far side. Up the street to your left is the massive stone entryway, or **Skifa Bub Zaouïa,** to the **medina.** Farther along the water is the squat Obeidite **Mosque;** the easily recognizable **Borj** (fortress) is 200m past the mosque, on the tip of the peninsula. The medina's narrow main street, **rue Oubad Allah el-Mahdi** (street signs in Arabic) originates at the Skifa and passes through **place du Caire** and **place Kadi Noamene,** thus hitting all three of the old city's focal points.

Just inside the Skifa, the **Syndicat Tamarind** occupies the first building on the street (tel. 68 10 98). The English-speaking official will give you a brochure with a fuzzy map of the peninsula. (Open Mon.-Sat. 7:30am-1pm and 3-6pm.) Near the Banque de Tunisie you'll find a **pharmacy** ("pharmacie de nuit"; tel. 68 14 90), which is open all night, and international **telephones** (open daily 7:30am-1:30pm and 3:30-10:30pm). **Telephone code:** 03. **Avenue Habib Bourguiba** starts outside the Skifa and is the new city's main artery; along it you'll find most **banks** and travel agents. A **police station** sits at #71 (tel. 68 10 99). Next door is the Magasin General **supermarket.** (Open Tues.-Sat. 8am-12:30pm and 2:45-7pm, Sun. 8am-12:30pm.) Down the road there's a **post office** on the left (tel. 68 17 14; open Mon.-Sat. 8am-

MAHDIA

6pm, Sun. 9-11am; July-Aug. Mon.-Sat. 7:30am-2pm; Sun. 9-11am). **Buses** depart from the port area for: Monastir (10 per day, 1hr., 1.900D), Sousse (14 per day, 1¾hr., 2.300D), and El Jem (6 per day, 1hr., 1.700D). **Louages** are a more convenient option to and from Mahdia, as service is frequent and competitively priced to Sousse (2.250D), and El Jem (1.500D). *Louages* leave from the Esso station next to the port, two blocks from the Skifa across from the **train station.** Eleven metro trains per day leave for Monastir (1hr., 1.360D), and continue to Sousse's Bab Jedid station (1½hr., 1.875D), along the port a few blocks from pl. Hached.

Accommodations and Food The paucity of visitors to Mahdia means few budget accommodations, but those that do exist are clean and affordable. One of the best bargains in Tunisia is the cozy **Hotel Jazira,** 36, rue Ibn Fourat (tel. 68 16 29). To get there from rue el-Mahdi, turn left at pl. du Caire and walk to the sea. This family-run establishment boasts new mattresses, crisp white linen, and a sublime ocean view (7D per person, hot showers included; reserve in advance). If you have little money, or the Jazira has no rooms, head for the **Maison des Jeunes** (tel. 68 15 59), up the street heading away from the Esso station. It's as institutional as the rest of them, but also clean and cheap (4D per person). **Hotel Rand,** 20, av. Taïeb Mehiri (tel. 68 05 25), is a more distant choice in more ways than one, but it's the only other reasonably priced Mahdia hotel. The *en suite* rooms have seen better days. To get there take av. Bourguiba away from the medina and turn left at the "Clinique de Plan Familial" sign. (Singles 11.500D. Doubles 22D. Breakfast included.)

Mahdia's handful of restaurants clusters in the port area. Evenings in the medina revolve around cozy **place du Caire,** where outdoor café tables brim with locals. You may not notice the Arabic sign for **Restaurant Medina,** (tel. 806 07), but the waiter's Salvador Dalí moustache is hard to miss. Located in the market building behind the Banque de Tunisie, the restaurant serves spicy fare at mild prices. Try the couscous *au poisson* (2.500D). (Open daily 7am-11pm.) The cheapest place to eat in Mahdia is **Restaurant El Moez;** bear right on the street entering the medina to Skifa's right. The menu changes every day, but there's usually a filling dish of spicy macaroni (1.700ml). Open daily 10am-9pm. The **market** near the bus stop and behind the Banque de Tunisie sells fresh produce beside newly killed chickens.

Sights and Entertainment The **Skifa Bab Zouila** ("Dark Entrance") is the gateway to the medina, and a logical place to start a tour of Mahdia. It's actually a replica of the gate blown up by the Spanish: the Mahdi had no illusions regarding his popularity amongst the neighbors, and the original Skifa was the sole opening in a wall which essentially sealed the peninsula off from the rest of the country. The passageway was once protected by a complex series of gates designed to pen attackers into easily dispatchable groups. Even today, overactive imaginations are apt to grow nervous progressing through the dark 44m stretch.

Nowadays, the medina is fairly benign to visitors. The **place du Caire,** down rue el-Mahdi from the Skifa, is a comfortable place for a drink, with the glazed tiles of the **Moustapha Hamza Mosque** as a backdrop. Neighboring streets offer a pleasant area in which to wander. You'll hear the constant rattling of dozens of **textile looms** running in the village; ask a sweaty worker to show you how the looms function. The **Obeidite Mosque** is Islam's oldest Fatimid mosque. Obeid Allah first erected the structure in 921 AD, but cyclic deterioration and restoration have continued, with the most recent restoration occurring from 1961-65. Despite major reconstructions, the simple linearity of the original Fatimid design has been preserved. Visitors are restricted to the main courtyard, and extremely modest attire is required. (Inquire at the Syndicat for entrance hours, or try the mosque Sat.-Thurs. in late afternoon.)

Continue from the Great Mosque along the medina's waterfront, where you're likely to see young locals diving for octopus. The **fishing port,** Tunisia's busiest, is the scene for intriguing arrivals (human and fish) in the early morning and at dusk. The sizable **Borj el-Kebir** (big fort; 1595) isn't very interesting, but its strategic location provides a view that may be worth the admission. (Open Tues.-Sun. 9am-noon and 2-6pm. Admission 1D, photo permit 1D.) From mid-July to August, the Borj hosts **The Nights of Mahdia,** the equivalent of the International Festival of Sousse, featuring the same shows. Tickets are sold at the gate (2-5D, students half-price).

Farther along the peninsula, hewn out of the rocky shoreline, the 1000-year-old **Fatimid Port** continues to harbor fishing boats. At the tip of windblown Cape Africa, a solitary lighthouse presides over Mahdia's sprawling **cemetery.** After the circuit of the peninsula, continue down the coast toward Monastir and you'll come upon the **municipal beach.** Up the coast toward Sousse, beaches remain unmarred by the debris of resort hotels that litter the coastline to the north.

■ NEAR MAHDIA: EL JEM

The tiny village of El Jem possesses one hotel, two cafés, and a whole lotta **Roman amphitheatre**—the sixth largest in the world. A collection of ramshackle buildings huddles at its feet, and it seems as if the coliseum is all that's saving modern-day El Jem from being swallowed up by the hot Tunisian sands. In its day of course, the arena did not cause, but rather resulted from, the region's prosperity. The original Roman city of Thydrus grew rich on the olive oil trade, so much so that in 238 the residents rebelled against Roman taxes and crowned an old man named Gordian emperor. In true imperial fashion, Gordian constructed the amphitheater to keep his subjects docile. The rebellion soon petered out and, consequently, so did the construction. The mostly completed building is still impressive, reflecting the skill of the Roman engineers responsible for its design. The damage you see is no fault of theirs, but rather of an overzealous government official, who in 1695 ordered artillery fired at the amphitheater in an attempt to flush out a band of tax evaders. The amphitheater held 30,000 spectators and hosted games of all sorts—you can still see the pits in its sandy floor where the beasts and gladiators stretched before games.

On the road south to Sfax (a 10-min. walk from the amphitheater) lies the **Archaeological Museum** and another, smaller amphitheater. The many mosaics found locally illustrate that there was indeed money to be made in olive oil. (Both open daily 7am-7pm. Combined admission 4D, photo permit 1D.) During the last three weeks of July, the arena hosts a series of mediocre Western art and music performances in the **Festival International de Musique Symphonique.** If anything, go just to see the amphitheater lit by hundreds of braziers. (Tickets 10D, but students may be able to finagle a discount just before the 9:30pm showtime.)

The drab main avenue of El Jem bears the predictable name of Bourguiba. At the end opposite the arena and next to the **train station,** you will find El Jem's only hotel; **Hotel Julius** (tel. 69 00 44) is a plush bargain. (Singles 8.500D, doubles 15D. Breakfast and private toilets and showers included.) Fast food joints surround the amphitheater, but better food and bargains await at **Restaurant de Bonheur** (tel. 69 04 21), one block from the hotel down the road to Sfax. In addition to the standard *poulet rôti* (3D), it also serves a delicious omelette with salad and fries (2D; ask for it if it's not on the menu). (Open daily 8am-10pm.)

Facing the coliseum from the train station, you'll see a **police station** (tel. 69 07 00) and a **late-night pharmacy** up the road to the right. Down the same road but to the left, you'll find (all near Restaurant de Bonheur) a **post office** (tel. 69 01 39; open Mon.-Sat. 8am-1:30pm, Sept.-June 8am-noon and 3-6pm), **telephones** (open daily 8am-10pm), and **banks. Telephone code: 03.** El Jem is served by seven trains a day to Sousse and Sfax (both 2.500D). Bus service is infrequent, but there are at least two each afternoon to Sousse and Sfax (2.500D), and to Mahdia (1.100D). *Louages* to Sousse, Sfax, and Mahdia are also available. Both buses and *louages* depart from the square in front of the Hotel Julius, across from the train station.

■ ■ ■ KAIROUAN

For centuries the faithful have made their way across the desert to the most sacred mosque in the Maghreb region—the **Mosque of Sidi Oqba** at **Kairouan,** dedicated to the saint who spread Islam across North Africa. Located on a desolate plain smack in the middle of nowhere, Kairouan is drenched in seasonal rains during the rare moments when it's not baked by the sun. It is a hellacious place for a holy city, and yet Kairouan prospers, a testament to profound faith. The sense of reverence is palpable to even the most casual of tourists who come to view some of Tunisia's most exquisite architecture and decorative art.

After its founding in 670 AD, Kairouan had a rocky first century; the city was captured and pillaged, then captured and pillaged again. Most of the town's major buildings were constructed during the golden age of the Aghlabid dynasty (800-1057), and the city attained a religious and cultural preeminence which it retains to this day. In prestige, Kairouan ranks only behind the Islamic triad of Mecca, Medina, and Jerusalem; popular convention deems seven trips to Kairouan a fulfillment of the **Haj,** the pilgrimage to Mecca required of every Muslim. The city's devout nature (read: "holier than thou") has at times resulted in conflict with the secularizing efforts of the government; citizens fiercely resisted both the outlawing of polygamy and Bourguiba's attempt to dispense with the Ramadan fast (Kairouan pointedly does *not* have a street named after Tunisia's founder). With Kairouan's attention focused east toward Mecca rather than north to Tunis, its Islamic monuments, medina craft shops, and legendary sweetmeat stands possess an exotic appeal to visitors while giving them exposure to the culture of one of the world's great religions.

The Holy Campground for Camels

The founding of Kairouan is literally legendary. Sidi Oqba Ibn Nafi, the warrior-saint who spread Islam across North Africa, established his capital here in 670 AD when a spring suddenly sprouted at his feet, revealing a precious gold chalice that had mysteriously disappeared from Mecca. The spring's water source was linked to the Mecca's well of Zem Zem. For good measure, Oqba banished all scorpions, snakes, and reptiles from the region. Immediately after, the sanctity of the spot was acknowledged, and the city became known by the unassuming name of "Kairawan"—"camping place for camels."

ORIENTATION AND PRACTICAL INFORMATION

Kairouan is sprawling. Most historical sights are spread around the large medina, and services are not conveniently clustered together, but scattered outside the walls of the old city. To make matters worse, Kairouan's residents rarely use street names. Don't get discouraged, however; once you've gotten lost a few times, you'll get a sense of the city and things will improve.

Kairouan's transportation center is far removed and difficult to reach from the heart of the city; it's advisable to grab a taxi, which will take you anywhere in the city for under 700ml. If you insist on walking from the **bus and louage stations,** (next to each other), head left and follow the signs pointing toward "Sousse." Continue for about 15min. until **rue de Gafsa,** where you turn left, and walk along the medina walls until you hit the square in front of **Bab ech Chouhada,** the medina's principal south entrance. **Bab Tounes,** the medina's north gate, links up with Bab ech Chouhada by **av. 7 Novembre,** which continues onward into the newer city. The city limits are loosely defined by **av. de la République,** which runs along Kairouan's north and east perimeter, and **rue Farhat Hached** in the south, which joins av. de la République at **pl. de la Victoire** (marked by a giant pedestal that once supported a statue of Habib Bourguiba).

Note: old and inaccurate maps and pamphlets (i.e. all of them) show av. 7 Novembre as av. Bourguiba (or rue Ali Bel Hovane). In general, Kairouan changes its street names more often than a *Let's Go* researcher does his t-shirt, so be prepared. In addition, both the bus and *louage* stations have moved, so you won't find them on maps either. Happy hunting.

Tourist Office: The **Syndicat** (tel. 22 04 52), **Tourist Information,** and a mysterious **Agence National de Patrimonie (ANP)**, share the same building near the intersection of av. de la République and rue des Aghlabites. From Bab et Tounes, walk past the *louage* station and then straight down the wide rue des Aghlabites; the offices are 1km down, at the end of the road to the right (across from the hospital). Buy the admission ticket to Kairouan's sites from the Syndicat here (admission 4D, photo permit 1D). The ANP gives out a surprisingly well-written brochure and an astonishingly awful map. Offices open Sat.-Thurs. 8am-6pm. You may have to sign a bureaucratic "Petition to the Mayor of Kairouan to see the sites of the city," more amusing than annoying.

Police: tel. 22 04 52 or 197. Offices in the middle of the medina or else off av. de la République near Hotel Splendid.

Post Office: pl. de la Victoire (tel. 225 55), from Bab ech Chouhada, head down av. 7 Novembre and turn right on av. Hached. Open Mon.-Fri. 7:30am-1pm and 5-7pm, Sun. 9-11am; in winter Mon.-Sat. 8am-6pm, Sun. 9-11am.

Telephones: Taxiphones are everywhere, including one 2 blocks from the PTT on the road to Tunis, on the right. Open daily 6:30am-1am. **Telephone Code:** 07.

Currency Exchange: Banks can be found all over, but in particular on the streets that lead from Bab ech Chouhada to av. de la République.

Louages: with your back to Bab Tounes, turn left outside the medina and right onto av. de la République. Continue to the intersection with signs for various cities. Turn left and continue for about 5min. Continuous service to Sousse (2.800D), Tunis (6.850D), and smaller regional towns until about 8pm.

Buses: Gare Routière, a block farther from the *louages,* behind a small shopping complex with a large pharmacy. The **SNTRI** counter is inside and to the left; it serves Tunis (16 per day, 3hr., 6.100D), among other towns. The **regional** companies have a schedule (in Arabic only). They serve Sousse (10 per day, 1½hr., 2.390D), Sfax (3 per day, 2hr., 4.020D), Sbeïtla (4 per day, 2hr., 4.100D), and Le Kef via Makthar (2 per day, 2hr., 3.700D to Makthar; 2hr, 2.150D more to Le Kef).

Taxis: In front of the post office, at Bab ech Chouhada, and at Bab Tounes.

Swimming Pool: at the **Hotel Continental** (tel. 22 11 35), across from the tourist office. Admission 2D.

Late-Night Pharmacy: Pharmacie de Nuit, outside the medina walls. With Bab ech Chouhada behind you, take a right along the walls and then another right at the first 4-way intersection. Open daily 7:30pm-8:30am.

Hospital: across from the tourist office (tel. 22 00 36 or 198).

ACCOMMODATIONS

Pilgrims tend to stay in hostels attached to mosques, hence there is a dearth of budget hotels. Those that do exist are, like the sights, scattered throughout town.

Hotel Marhala, (tel. 22 07 36), Souk el Bey; from Bab ech Chouhada, head onto av. 7 Novembre and turn right into the covered street with the multilingual "Old Market." A converted *medersa* (Koranic school) that approaches adorable. In the medina. 6.500D per person. Showers included. Breakfast 500D. MC, Visa.

Hotel Sabra (tel. 22 02 60), just outside the medina at Bab ech Chouhada. Thirty rooms plus 2 lounges and a panoramic rooftop terrace (a good place to do laundry). Rooms are well lit and the clean showers have *hot* water year-round. 7D per person. Breakfast included.

Hotel Sidi el Bechir (tel. 22 77 45), on route Ouestlia, across from the *louage* station. Pro: it's near the buses and *louages.* Con: it's near the buses and *louages.* Cheap rooms, thin mattresses, modern toilets, and hot showers. 3D per person.

FOOD

There are few bargains for hungry visitors. Many of the cheaper restaurants in Kairouan offer only a fixed-price *menu.* Due to the intense heat and greedy vendors, beverages go for a whopping 600-900ml. (Café Sabra next to the tourist office sells soda for 300ml.) Always inquire about prices before you chow or chug. Your cheapest eating options are the roast chicken places along av. de la République. The

Magasin General (1 block past the pedestrian mall opposite Bab ech Chouhada) is bigger than most Tunisian supermarkets and is an excellent option. (Open Tues.-Sat. 8am-12:30pm and 3:45-7:45pm, Sun. 8am-1pm.) Do not fail to make a pilgrimage to Kairouan's sweet shops for the divine *makroudh* (Tunisian Fig Newtons), small biscuits stuffed with dates and smothered in honey (800ml per kilo).

Restaurant Barrouta, behind the Barrouta well in the medina. The best *menu* around, with salad, couscous, dessert, bottled water, and tea (3.500D). Walk through the kitchen to get to the tables or eat outside. A wonderful, spicy sauce blankets omelettes (2D). Open daily noon-3pm and 6-9pm.

Restaurant La Lanterne (tel. 22 48 86), on pl. de Tunis; head straight out from Bab Tounes. A higher grade of greasy spoon than normal. The cheapest bowl of couscous in town (2D). Open daily 11am-3pm and 5-9pm.

Restaurant Sabra (tel. 22 50 95), next to Hotel Tunisia on rue Farhat Hached; go right from av. 7 Novembre. Clean and pleasant. *menu* 4D. Open 10am-11pm.

SIGHTS

Start walking tours at the tourist office, since you have to go there anyway to buy the **comprehensive ticket** for the monuments. The ticket covers entry into all the sights listed below, unless otherwise noted. The **Aghlabite Pools,** just next door, once acted as cisterns for the city, a rather unpalatable thought given the shallow basins' rancid condition in the summer. Head right along av. de la République to the **Zaouia de Sidi Sahab,** a venerable destination for pilgrims. The mosque houses the Mausoleum of Abou Zama, a companion of Muhammad who carried three hairs of the Prophet's beard with him, thus earning the nickname "the Barber." Flowery blue tiles cover the walls up to eye level, and minutely filigreed gypsum take it from there. A colonnaded corridor and a second, domed foyer are paneled similarly. The final courtyard, surrounded by cells and vessels containing saints' remains, is clad in tiles patterned with buildings and trees. The ability to squeeze through the corner columns reputedly signifies *baruka*, good luck/saintly blessing.

From the *zaouia,* it's a bit of a hike to av. 7 Novembre. The curious and intrepid can work their way through the labyrinthine neighborhoods of the medina. To avoid getting lost, skirt around the old city by way of av. de la République. From Bab ech Chouhada, take the first right to the **Zaouia of Sidi Abid el Ghariani,** where the **marabout** rests serenely in another excellent example of the Andalusian decorative style originated in Moorish Spain. A star attraction for pilgrims and tourists alike is **Bir Barrouta,** a holy well farther along av. 7 Novembre and slightly to the right. Within its narrow confines a blindfolded camel circles endlessly, delivering water from the mystical Meccan source. It is said that a taste of this water will bring you back to Kairouan one day. Just down the side street waits the **Mosque of Thletha Bibane** (The Three Doors), one of the oldest monuments in Kairouan. Though visitors cannot enter, the façade alone, with all its 9th-century calligraphy and floral relief, is worth the detour.

Monuments aside, one of the most delightful aspects of visiting an Arab city as traditional as Kairouan is the potential for endless **wandering through the medina;** *Souks* line the alleys off av. 7 Novembre. On afternoons in the covered **Souk des Tapis,** past Bir Barrouta to the right of av. 7, women auction their famous carpets to merchants from around the country, eager to mark them up a few hundred percent. If you can't afford a Kairouan carpet (i.e. if your camel has not just laid a golden egg), you can purchase a *kessa* (a friction glove used in bathing), for which the city, for some reason, is also famous. Alternatively, try the more ephemeral but delicious *makroudh,* sold from stands lining the avenue.

Despite its unusual peripheral location, the **Great Mosque** functions as the spiritual center of Kairouan and indeed of the entire Maghreb. As usual, non-Muslims can enter the courtyard but not the main prayer room. (Zebra-striped robes provided for those not in proper attire, i.e. knees and shoulders covered.) A tour around the fortified walls and impressive gates is warranted before entering. The solidity of these defenses against the outside walls emphasizes the serene effect of the courtyard's simplicity. As the walls suggest, the mosque is a place of refuge; the call to prayer invites the faithful to "come to security." The fans and water coolers in the prayer hall may clash with the decor, but they are very much in keeping with this spirit of comfort for the faithful. Peer through the carved banana wood door on the right to catch a glimpse of the **mihrab** (prayer niche) and **minbar** (pulpit) brought from Baghdad in 862 AD, two of the oldest examples of luster tile decoration in the world. The 296 columns throughout the prayer hall are topped with Roman, Greek, and Punic capitals collected from all over Tunisia. The odd apparatus in the courtyard's center purifies trapped rainwater before sending it into a 12m-deep cistern below the mosque. The oldest Islamic monument in the Western world, the mosque was erected in 688 and rebuilt in 695. Most of what you see today is 9th-century Aghlabite work that has been renovated and altered over the centuries. Opposite the sanctuary stands **the oldest minaret in the world,** built in 836. Its ponderous appearance hints at a secondary, defensive purpose—note those decorative arrow-slits in the crenellations near the top.

■ NEAR KAIROUAN: ARCHAEOLOGICAL SITES

MAKTHAR

Although one of the least-visited archaeological sites in the country, Makthar features a surprisingly extensive spread of ruins 110km west of Kairouan. This site was once the Carthaginian and (later) Roman city of **Mactaris**. It's not worth a special trip, but makes an excellent stop if you're traveling between Le Kef and Kairouan. The Roman-built **Bab el Ain arch** divides modern Makthar, a small and unremarkable little town, from ancient Mactaris. Just beyond, a three-room **museum** serves as the entrance to the site; inside are a few well-crafted funerary steles and a rare example of **Latin carved in elegant cursive script.** (Open daily 8am-6pm; Oct.-March 9am-noon and 2-5:30pm. Admission 2D, photo permit 1D.) Presiding over the entire site from its center is the 2nd-century **Arch of Trajan.** From a distance the arch appears to stand alone; as you approach you'll catch glimpses of the forum that lies behind it, strewn with fallen columns and broken rock. The **Roman baths,** 200m from the arch, are Makthar's largest ruins. Traces of mosaics remain upon the floor. Makthar is remarkable for possessing the identifiable remnants of another imperial cornerstone, the *schola,* Rome's version of the Boy's Club (privileged young men who studied and socialized together, and acted as an imperial paramilitary group). The *schola*'s basilica is along a path to the right of the Forum. The remnants of other buildings and temples are scattered around the site, which you can inspect virtually undisturbed. One bus leaves daily from Le Kef at 3pm (1½hr., 2.150D). Buses depart opposite the Hotel Restaurant Mactaris. Two buses hit Makthar on the way to Le Kef, so you can take the first and catch the second to move on (depart Kairouan at 1:30pm and 4pm, 2hr., 3.700D, 5.850D to go to Le Kef). **Louages,** farther up the main road, are rather hard to come by, but you might find one going to Le Kef.

SBEÏTLA

Sbeïtla is one of the sites most often photographed by the Tunisian Tourist Office, yet the modern town isn't overly exciting. The Capitoline temple that graces many "Tunisie" posters is the best-preserved building in a complex of ruins that were once the Roman town of Sufetula. Step through history as you walk through Roman, early Christian, and Byzantine ruins dating from the first through 6th centuries AD.

The **origins** of Sufetula remain uncertain, but the Romans appear to have built the town from scratch at the end of the first century AD. The place never attained real prominence, except possibly for a short time in the 7th century. In the year 646, the Patriarch Gregory elected to challenge the Byzantine authorities in Constantinople, proclaiming himself Emperor and making Sbeïtla his capital. He chose poorly—the following year 20,000 Arabs under Abdullah ibn Saad came by and beat the daylights out of Sbeïtla, a blow from which neither Gregory nor Sbeïtla ever really recovered.

On arrival at the bus station, turn right with the train tracks behind you. Walk two blocks, and turn left onto av. Belhaouane. Walk straight 1km until you come to the ruins, nicely heralded by the **Triumphal Arch,** which formerly marked the entrance to the city. A little farther along is the small but well-kept **museum** on the left side of the street and the site entrance on the right. (Ruins and museum open daily 6:30am-7:30pm; Sept.-June 8am-sunset. Museum closed Mon. Combined admission 2D, photo permit 1D.) Enter opposite the museum and disregard anyone attempting to sell you "authentic" Roman coins and statues; turn left and pass the 7th-century **Byzantine Forts.** There are still enough surviving walls and foundations to give a good impression of an imperial town's grid-like structure. Climb inside and explore the **baths,** a staple of Roman colonial life, and stroll through the classical equivalent of a shopping mall. Sbeïtla's citizens could apparently buy all sorts of things; the stone with the **large carved phallus** near the forum was the unsubtle advertisement for a brothel. Step through the **Arch of Antoninus Pius** into the **Forum,** one of the best-preserved examples in the world. The enclosing walls and **Temples to the Capitoline Trinity** architecturally express both civic pride and imperial dominance. Though the three deities normally shared a temple, Sbeïtla nonetheless constructed separate, adjacent temples to the trio of Jupiter, Juno, and Minerva. Exit between the temples and head off for some early (3rd- to 6th-century) **Christian basilicas.** There is a miraculously preserved mosaic baptistery in the **Basilica of Vitalis.**

Three **buses** per day make the trip from the Kairouan bus station to Sbeïtla (1:30-4:30pm, 2hr., 4.200D). Sbeïtla is also connected to the Roman ruins at Makthar (4 buses daily, 8am-2:30pm, 1½hr., 3.500D) from which connections can be made to Tunis and Le Kef. If you find you've missed the last bus back to Kairouan (not at all hard to do) take a **louage** for 4.700D. *Louages* also head to Kasserine (1.500D), with connections to Kairouan and the South.

■■■ SFAX

Despite its status as Tunisia's second-largest city, Sfax has little to offer as a cultural or tourist center. The reason, as any Tunisian will tell you, is that Sfaxians are too busy making money to be bothered with such things—even Sfax's tourist brochure acknowledges the city's reputation for commercial success. Sfax does lack obvious tourist attractions; the massive wall surrounding the medina is the only reminder that Sfax is over 1000 years old, in spite of the banks, businesses, and tall buildings. Even the **Great Mosque,** almost exactly in the center of the medina, leaves something to be desired; you could easily mistake it for a carpet factory or a fish warehouse. However, a day in Sfax while on the way to islands of Kerkennah (read: oblivion) can be far from unpleasant. The **Archaeological Museum** (tel. 22 97 44), despite its small size, has a fine collection displaying everything from Caspian stone tools to Roman wall paintings (and mosaics for those who haven't overdosed at the Bardo). The museum awaits in a domed building on the main thoroughfare of av. Bourguiba, 500m from the train station. (Museum open Mon.-Sat. 8am-1pm and 3-6pm. Admission 1D, photo permit 1D.)

In the medina, the 17th-century Dar Jellouli houses the **Museum of Traditional Costumes** (tel. 22 11 86). To get there, head up the medina's main street, rue Mongi Slim, and take the second right on the rue de la Driba. (Open Mon.-Sat. 8am-1pm and 3-6pm. Admission 1D, photo permit 1D.) The **gardens** to the left of the medina's entryway, shaded by the huge walls of the old city, are a pleasant place to pass time. Cap off the day with some rose-water Turkish coffee at the cool **Café Diwan.** Head left after entering the medina and take the second left (100m in); the café is built into the medina walls. Sfax's main street is—gasp!—**avenue Habib Bourguiba,** heading straight away from the train station. About 250m down on the right, a large square signals the beginning of **blvd. de la République** which crosses av. Bourguiba, and ends at **Bab Diwan,** the medina's main entrance. Rue Mongi Slim begins just inside and to the right.

The **Syndicat** (tel. 22 46 06) is a decorous little kiosk on the right side of av. Bourguiba, 200m from the train station. The office carries a brochure with maps of both Sfax and Kerkennah, as well as a **ferry schedule.** (Supposedly open daily 8:30am-1:30pm. Good luck.) A **police station** (tel. 22 97 00) sits about 100 meters back from the Syndicat, and a **late-night pharmacy** (tel. 22 16 26; open 8pm-8am) can be found at #24, rue Leopold Senghor (branching off the square by the town hall). The **post and telephone office** (tel. 22 47 22; open Mon.-Fri. 7:30am-1pm and 5-7pm, Sat. 7:30am-1pm, Sun. 9-11am; Sept.-June Mon.-Sat. 8am-6pm, Sun. 9-11am) is across from the train station to the right. **Telephone code:** 04. Five **trains** run daily to Tunis (4 hr., 13.100D) via Sousse (2hr., 4D), and three run to Gabes per day (3hr., 4.700D). **Buses** leave for Gabes much more frequently from the SNTRI depot just in front of the train station (2½hr., 5.100D) and to Jerba. The rival SORETRAS bus station is at the other end of av. Bourguiba (1km), and offers service to local cities. **Louages** congregate in front of Bab Diwan.

One of Sfax's virtues is its large number of cheap hotels, particularly in the medina. **Hotel de la Medina,** 53, rue Mongi Slim (tel. 22 03 54), about 100m along rue Mongi Slim on the left, offers clean rooms with sinks and towels (3.500D per person, hot showers 500ml). A number of options line rue Borj Ennar, just off to the right inside Bab Diawan. The **Hotel el-Mokthar** (tel. 22 08 92) is the cheapest of the lot (4D per person), providing a cell-like room with a bed and a ceiling fan. Those uncomfortable in the medina should try the generic **Hotel de la Paix,** 17 rue Alexandre Dumas (tel. 22 14 36). Unlike at the medina hotels, the rooms have furniture and the bathrooms have toilet paper. (Singles 5D, with shower 9D. Doubles 10D, with shower 15D. Corridor showers 1D.) From the train station, head down av. Bourguiba and turn left by the French Consulate. There exist few budget restaurants besides the fast food dives lining blvd. de la République. A notable exception is the **Restaurant Tunisien,** just inside the medina, which serves a fine *couscous aux legumes* for 1D. Buy your produce at the **market** on the other side of the medina, at the end of rue Mongi Slim. **Monoprix** sells the usual canned goods, pasta, and yogurt down the street across from the Syndicat. (Open daily 9am-1pm and 3:30-7:30pm.)

■ NEAR SFAX: KERKENNAH ISLANDS

Though quite close (21km) to Sfax's metropolitan activity, the Kerkennah Isles remain the city's antithesis. In mythology, the lovelorn nymph Circe imprisoned Odysseus here. Ironically, the Arabs disposed of adulterous women on the islands, and Habib Bourguiba did time before making a legendary escape in 1945. These days, the people shunted here are tourists who can't tolerate or afford the developed beach of Hammamet. Voluntary exile on a desert island has its pros and cons. On the up side, underdevelopment offers little to do besides splash around (shallow water hinders swimming) and daydream. On the down side, daydreaming can get old pretty quickly. Because of the dearth of tourism, transportation on the island is irregular and there are few budget restaurants. Still, with the right attitude, Kerkennah makes an ideal location to watch the sun set and shun the rest of the world.

To get to the Isles, catch a **ferry** from the terminal at Sfax (tel. (04) 22 22 16). (Sept.-mid-June, 4 times per day each way, 1¼hr., 570ml). From Sfax at 7:30 and 11:30am, 3 and 6pm. From the islands at 5:30, 9am, 1, and 4:30pm. Mid-June to the end of Aug., the number of ferries is doubled.) You will arrive at the westernmost point in the archipelago, on **Gharbi,** which is connected to **Chergui** (the other major island) by a causeway. Three hotels cluster together in **Sidi Frej,** on Chergui. To get there you can take one of two buses. A mini-bus serves the hotels directly (1D), and a larger one, Kerkennah's only form of transportation, stops near the hotels (600ml) along its route (ask for the *zone touristique*) to **Remla** (870ml), the islands' largest "town," 7km away from the hotels.

The **Hotel Cercina** (tel. (04) 28 12 28; fax 28 12 62) is the cheapest and most charming of the three beach hotels. The friendly, multilingual management will show you to either a simple whitewashed room with a shower (singles 20D, doubles 30D; includes breakfast) or a "bungalow," essentially a hut with beds (singles 17D, doubles 24D; includes breakfast and shower). **Camping** here is also allowed (1-2D per person). An extra 5D gets lunch and dinner at the hotel's excellent **restaurant.** Of the pricey two-star hotels farther down the beach, the **Grand Hotel** (tel. 28 12 65; fax 28 14 85) is significantly better. It's fully equipped, but stretches the definition of budget accommodation. (Singles 34D. Doubles 54D.) The best **restaurant** (and bar), particularly for seafood, is the **Cercina.** If it's available, sample the Kerkennah specialty of *tchich* (octopus soup; 1.500D). Dinner runs about 5D. Those on the cheap can head into Remla and its **Maison des Jeunes** (tel. 28 11 48), which has standard, spartan doubles and triples for 4D a head. (Breakfast 1D, lunch or dinner 4D. Hot shower 500ml, cold free.) The hostel is right by the beach, and rents windsurfing equipment (4D per hr.) and bicycles (3.600D per day, 600ml per hr.). To get there, continue down Remla's main street and follow the signs on the right. The town has a rather meager **supermarket** (open daily 8am-1:30pm and 4-8pm), as well as the islands' **post office, pharmacy** (tel. 28 10 74), and **police station** (tel. 28 10 53). U.I.B. bank will **change money,** as will the hotels in Sidi Frej.

SOUTHERN TUNISIA

Berbers still dwell in caves, Bedouins still herd camels and harvest dates, and 20th-century civilization is still a rare mirage in the vast ocean of sand that is southern Tunisia. A large part of the area is taken up by the great Sahara, which contains small villages huddled close together. Yet the diversity of the desertscape is surprising. The Great Eastern Erg incorporates endless sand dunes alongside the marshy salt flats of Chott el Jerid, the jagged Ksour Mountains, the lunar landscape of Matmata, and the bursts of green foliage in the oases. See Tunisia Essentials: Health: Desert Survival (page 584) for some advice on how to survive when traveling in this region.

■■■ GABES

The principal activity for tourists in Gabes should be moving on as soon as possible. (Gabes's role as transportation hub ensures that you will pass through it on the way to the Sahara or Jerba.) Those with a few hours to kill or who do not plan to visit Tunisia's interior (an absolute crime) can explore the immense 300,000-palm oasis by hiking the shady trails behind the bus station. Other than this, there's not much to see—there are no great mosques (except the one under construction) or museums (except the *souk* that tries to attract customers by calling itself one). The better *souks* are located at the end of av. Bourguiba (away from the Hached-Bourguiba intersection) and are good places to buy a straw hat, the essential Saharan accessory (2.500-6D), before getting out of town.

Orientation and Practical Information The city's two major streets, **avenue Farhat Hached** and **avenue Habib Bourguiba,** intersect to become **avenue Habib Thameur,** which continues on another 500m to the beach. The other important street is **avenue Monji Slim,** which runs parallel to av. Farhat Hached before merging into it. Streets are long and the city is spread out, stretching over 2km from one end of av. Farhat Hached to the other. The **tourist office** is on av. H. Thameur, 300m down from the intersection of avenues Bourguiba and Hached (tel. (05) 27 02 54; open Mon.-Sat. 8am-2pm). Unless you're going to the beach anyway, it's not worth the walk, as the staffers are apt to close up shop and take off for a few days without any advance notice. You can pick up the available literature—a brochure with an extremely vague map and some info on Matmata—at the Hotel Néjib at the Bourguiba-Hached intersection. The **post office,** on av. Bourguiba near the intersection, doubles as a **currency exchange,** but accepts cash only. (Open Mon.-Sat. 8am-1pm and 3-6pm; July-Aug. Mon.-Fri. 7:30am-1pm and 5-7pm, Sat. 1:30-

5:30pm, Sun. 9-11am.) For traveler's checks, try one of the **banks** on av. Bourguiba. **Late-night pharmacy** stays open 8pm-8am, one block to the right of the train station, on av. Monji Slim. A block and a half past the pharmacy, **Magasin General** sells all the pasta, canned goods, and yogurt you'll ever need (open daily 8am-12:30pm and 3-7pm). Gabes has plenty of **international taxiphones** on nearly every block of av. Bourguiba or av. Farhat Hached (open daily 8am-9:30pm). Gabes is also a good place to **rent a car** for the desert. **Hertz** (tel. 27 05 25) is located at the Bourguiba-Hached intersection, and **Avis** (tel. 27 02 10) is a few blocks up av. Bourguiba on the side-street, rue du 9 avril. Be sure to consult with the English-speaking staff about what sort of vehicle is appropriate for the destinations you wish to explore.

The **train station** is on av. Monji Slim; av. Farhat Hached is straight ahead one block. Three air-conditioned trains per day (9:15am, 7:35, and 11:10pm) zoom to Tunis (6½hr., 10.950D), Sousse (4½hr., 6.100D), and Sfax (3hr., 4.700D). The **bus station** sits on the outskirts of town, where av. Hached merges with the road to Sfax (it looks abandoned—go around through the side entrance for signs of life). The destinations and schedules are in Arabic; you'll have to inquire at the counters of the three different companies about the next bus to your destination. Buses run to Jerba (6 per day 7am-3pm, 4hr., 3.850D), Matmata (11 per day 5am-6:30pm, 1hr., 1.670D), Kebili (4 per day 9am-3:30pm, 2hr., 4D), Douz (1 per day at noon, 3hr., 5D), and Tatouine (2 per day, 2½hr., 5.420D). **Louages,** as always more flexible and a bit more expensive, kick up dust just in front of the bus station.

Accommodations and Food The Gabes **youth hostel,** a.k.a. **Centre de Stages et de Vacances (HI)** (tel. 27 02 71), is a bit hard to find, but a great deal. From av. Farhat Hached, to the left of the train station, turn onto rue Sadok Lassoued at Hotel Salama. Continue to the end of the street, turn right (av. Bourguiba), and take an immediate left, plunging straight through the *souk*. The hostel is 200m ahead on the left. Lunches and dinners are 3D, and breakfast (700ml) includes an egg. (Curfew 10pm. Clean doubles and triples 3D per person. Well-shaded camping 2D per person, 500ml per tent. HI members only when the hostel is near capacity.) The hotels near the bus and *louage* stations are generally cheaper and better than those by the Hached-Bourguiba intersection. The best deal is **Hotel Medina** (tel. 27 42 71), just inside the city from the bus station; turn left on rue Ali Jemel. The rooms and toilets are clean, and towels are provided for the free cold showers (6D per person). A bit farther down, **Hotel Ben Nejima,** 66, rue Ali Jemel (tel. 28 22 76) puts on a more upscale veneer and charges accordingly. Berber-style blankets in the whitewashed rooms are a nice touch. (Singles 8.500D. Doubles 12D. Showers 1D.) Gabes fails to overwhelm the traveler with dining options. The newly opened **Restaurant Bagdad,** 177, av. Bourguiba, has clean tablecloths and wooden furniture, although the menu is standard Tunisian grill fare (*brochette* 3D, couscous 1.600D. Open daily 8am-3pm and 6-10:30pm). **Restaurant Boukka Chouka** (tel. 22 03 87) is a meat-and-potatoes kind of place, literally (*pommes de terre à la viande,* 2D. Open daily 7am-11pm). The **produce market** sits with the other *souks* at the end of av. Bourguiba.

■■■ JERBA

Jerba's greatest endorsement is also its oldest; this island claims to be the legendary Land of the Lotus Eaters described in Homer's Odyssey; the friendly residents of Jerba offered Odysseus' crew a taste of the local (addictive) lotus wine, hence the Greeks completely forgot about their journey home. Roughly three millennia later, Jerba still bills itself as a haven of R&R, despite the fact that the rise of Islam has made the famous local product a lot harder to come by. Homer notwithstanding, Jerbans today retain a fiercely independent streak, despite being linked to the mainland by a 7km causeway since the days of Carthage. The island's history cycles through invasion and subsequent rebellion against new overlords, but more recently, Jerba has become increasingly accommodating to invading Europeans; daily direct flights from most continental capitals keep Jerba's 27 luxury hotels and beaches full. Though the island is no longer the mythical paradise it once was, you'd be missing out if you were in southern Tunisia and didn't stop off for a day or two in breezy, leafy Jerba. It's wisest to avoid the string of expensive shoreline hotels and instead stay in **Houmt Souk,** the island's largest city and transportation hub, and explore the beaches and interior from there. **The following listings are for Houmt Souk unless otherwise indicated.**

Orientation and Practical Information Buses run from Gabes (6 per day, 4hr., 4.290D) and depart via Gabes for Sfax (3 per day, 5 hr., 8.730D), Tatouine (2 per day, 3hr., 5.500D), and Tunis (2 per day, 10 hr., 16.620D). **Louages** run slightly more often and gather in front of the bus station. **Tunis Air** also flies once daily to Jerba from Tunis (46.300D).

Av. Bourguiba leads straight from the bus station into Houmt Souk's *centre ville.* The cafés are almost always full, and, if you speak French, it's not unlikely that you will find an audience thrilled to hear tales of adventure (or Michael Jordan). The **Syndicat** (200m down the avenue on your left), is in a nice pavilion; on your right will be the confusing tangle of streets and *souks* where most of the hotels are found. The Syndicat can give you a handout with a map and answer (in English) any questions. (Open Mon.-Sat. 7:30am-1:30pm; Sept.-June Mon.-Thurs. 8:30am-1pm and 3-5:45pm, Fri.-Sat. 8:30am-1pm.) The **post office** (open Mon.-Fri. 7:30am-1pm and 2-5pm, Sat. 7:30am-1pm; in winter Mon.-Thurs. 8am-noon and 3-6pm, Fri.-Sat. 8am-12:30pm) and **telephones** (open daily 7am-7pm) are next to the Syndicat. **Telephone code:** 05. **Banks** line the avenue, and the **American Express** representative can be found at Carthage Tours (tel. 65 03 08) in the nearby Commercial Center. **Car rental** agencies include **Budget,** av. Abdelhamid El Gadhi (tel. 65 34 44) and **Avis,** av. Med. Badra (tel. 65 01 51). The best way to see the island is by **bike** or **moped.** Hotel rates are not cheap; instead, try either of the two "Location de Vélos" shacks on av. Abdelhamid el Cadhi, the main road on the other side of the *souks* (past the two mosques). (Bikes 7D per day, mopeds 25D per day.) Bargain hard and be picky about which bike or moped you get; once you've paid, it's tough to get a refund even if the bike self-destructs. There is a **late-night pharmacy** (tel. 65 07 07; open 8pm-8am) behind the bus station, 100m past the ESSO station. The **police** (tel. 65 05 28) are on call at the top of av. Bourguiba, 50m down from the bus station.

Accommodations and Food The beautiful **Auberge de la Jeunesse (HI),** rue Moncef Bey (tel. 65 06 97), awaits you in an old *fondouk,* a centuries-old inn for traveling merchants. A bed in one of the old cubbyholes surrounding the white-washed courtyard costs 4.500D (breakfast, cold showers, and kitchen use included; ostensibly, members only). Next door, the **Hotel Marhala** (tel. 65 01 46) is also a converted *fondouk.* The tiled rooms (which can be locked from the outside with enormous antique keys) have low beds and straw matting. All rooms are the same price, although only a few possess a private toilet and shower. (Singles 10.500D. Doubles 16D. Breakfast included.) The hostel and Marhala can be reached by walking from the bus and *louage* stations to the crossroads with av. Bourguiba. Take the first right onto av. Mohammed Badra and then left at the large pl. 7 Novembre. Bear left onto rue Moncef Bey and take it through the *souks* to the end (10min.). Making a left and then another after the Marhala brings you to the **Hotel Sables d'Or** (tel. 65 04 23). It's not a *fondouk,* but it does have old-fashioned charm with its white stucco, wood ceilings, and Moroccan knick-knacks. All the rooms have showers and the toilets positively shine. (Singles 10D. Doubles 18D.)

While all the restaurants in Houmt Souk are geared toward tourists, some are much cheaper than others. The cheapest is the nameless **restaurant,** at Habib Bougaffa, 12, off pl. Sidi Abdelkader, which is off pl. Mongi Bali across from the PTT. Their tasty *kammounies* (1.700D) is a bit like falafel in a cumin sauce. (Open daily 6am-10pm.) Other cheap yet decent places are **Restaurant du Palmiers,** 45, rue de Bizerte (open 11am-4pm and 6pm-midnight) and **Restaurant du Sportif** on av. Bourguiba (open 11am-4:30pm and 6:30-10pm). A filling meal at either place is about 4D. **Marché Central** is mostly devoted to souvenir stands, but it does have a small **produce market.** Head under the sign off av. Bourguiba and take the first left.

Sights Near the tourist office, the 13th-century **Borj Ghazi Mustapha** is worth the walk. Another Dragut memento, Houmt Souk's fortress sits on the coast looking out to sea. To get there, walk down av. Bourguiba and bear right at the crossroads. (Open daily 8am-7pm; Oct.-June 9:30am-4:30pm; admission 1D, photo permit 1D. Known to be inexplicably closed at times; even if you can't get in, a walk around the perimeter is worth it.) A small **museum** displays the gaudy local costume (with diagrams detailing the complex process of putting them on) and a traditional pottery factory. It's down at the end of av. Abdel Hamid el Kadhi which sharply lurches to the right. (Open Sat.-Thurs. 8am-noon and 3-6pm; in winter Sat.-Thurs. 9:30am-6:30pm. Admission 2D, photo permit 1D.)

The **beaches** of Jerba are easy to reach by bicycle or bus. The best beaches are along **Sidi Mahares,** the location of the resort hotel ghetto known as the *zone touristique* (bus #11 from the station 1D; taxi 2.500D). **Flamingo Point (Ras el R'mel)** is a sandy peninsula 5km east of Houmt Souk. The birds that give the beach its name flock here during the winter. The least accessible and consequently the most peaceful beaches lie on the **west coast.** The 11km stretch of road (head past Melita and the airport) is easy enough by bike or moped, but there are no taxis returning to Houmt Souk. On a bike ride into the **interior,** you will come across traditional *houch,* fortress-residences with a single window in the *ghorfa* (tower). The historic **El Ghriba Synagogue** stubbornly remains in Erriadh, 6km south of Houmt Souk. Jerba's small but enduring Jewish community claims to be descended from a group that fled Jerusalem in 584 BC, after the fall of Jerusalem to Nebuchadnezzar. The present **synagogue** was built in the 1920s, on the spot where a stone supposedly fell from heaven in the early 6th century BC. The temple is open for viewing during the week and conducts services on the Sabbath (Fri. night and Sat. morning).

■■■ MATMATA

When the makers of *Star Wars* were searching for a setting for a desert planet, they came upon the otherworldly scenery surrounding Matmata, where the scorched terrain of twisted mountains and sprawling craters stretch to the horizon. Nature adds its own special effects at sunset, when the ominous landscape assumes an eerie red glow. Indeed, Jawas and their sand crawlers seem much more appropriate to the surroundings than do the paunchy, pink aliens who emerge from shiny vehicles, take photos, devour couscous, and seal themselves up again in their unique air-conditioned environment. The Hollywood-style, multi-lingual Welcome to Matmata sign on the side of a nearby mountain is an incredible eyesore, and at any given time during the day no fewer than a dozen coaches occupy the small village. However, wait until nightfall: with the moonrise all becomes peaceful. Walk just a kilometer or so along either the Tamezret or Gabes roads and savor some memorable images.

The Berber population has developed a remarkable mode of habitation in which a large central pit is carved in the ground (about 10m deep and 10m wide), while tunnels connect a network of adjoining chambers. The earth naturally insulates against the day's heat and the night's cold. No less impressive are the *jessours,* agricultural terraces, that line the hillsides. The construction of these requires an immense amount of labor, demonstrating the Berbers' willingness to exist in an inhospitable environment in order to preserve their autonomy and identity, which has begun to dissolve only recently. While several "homes" with very large parking lots line the Gabes-Matmata road, most continue to be private residences. Bear in mind that **peering uninvited into a central courtyard is tantamount to peeping through someone's living room window.** Children will inevitably approach you and offer to show you their homes for a few hundred *millemes.* Those uncomfortable with this admittedly exploitative form of tourism can check out the **underground**

hotels and the **museum** behind the PTT (ostensibly open daily 9am-noon and 1:30-5pm; be sure to tip the caretaker).

Orientation and Practical Information Matmata is easily seen as a day-trip from Gabes, but consider an overnight stay: the daylight hours are an endless parade of tour buses deploying battalions of tourists, and the town becomes far more pleasant in the evenings when the buses depart and sunset introduces a cool, serene nightfall. There is also the novelty of staying in Matmata's unique hotels/con-verted pit dwellings, one of which boasts, "Luke Skywalker slept here."

The opening hours of Matmata's **Syndicat** (up the hill from the main bus stop) are haphazard even for a Tunisian tourist office (posted hours: daily 8am-1pm and 3-6pm). If no one's there, try the café across the street. Not much here in the way of literature; the chief service is arranging donkey and camel hire. After hours a bus schedule is posted on the door (show up a good 45min. before the scheduled depar-ture time; drivers tend to be lenient about timing). Next door to the Syndicat, Mat-mata's **post office, telephones,** and **currency exchange** are all in the same building. The telephones are direct-dial; pay after. Currency exchange will change hard cash only and, at last check, were refusing U.S. dollars because "the dollar is too easy to counterfeit." Try anyway. (All three open Mon.-Fri. 7:30am-1:30pm; Sept.-June Mon.-Thurs. 8am-noon and 3-6pm, Fri. 8am-12:30pm.) **There are no banks,** so change traveler's checks in Gabes. **International taxiphones** are across the street by the café. Nine **buses** per day run between Matmata and Gabes (1.650D), leaving Matmata from the pl. 7 Novembre, about 50m farther downhill from the Syndicat. From Gabes, go all the way to "Matmata *ancien*," while *louages* go only as far as "Matmata *nouvelle*," from which *camionettes* make the 15-km connection (600ml).

Accommodations and Food Three of Matmata's hotels are, like the Berber homes, holes in the ground. Due to the natural insulation, they'd be excellent places to sleep through the midday if it weren't for the busloads of gawking tourists. All are marked, within easy reach of the bus stop and the center of town, and include breakfast. The **Marhala** (tel. (05) 23 00 15) is the most expensive, but it has hot showers year-round and the coolest rooms, literally and figuratively. (Singles 8.400D, full pension 15.900D. Doubles 26.800D, full pension 56.800D.) **Hotel les Berberes** (tel. 23 00 24) is cheaper and has the best food of the three; the rooms consist of a couple of beds and a lightbulb. (Singles 5.800D, full pension 11.500D. Doubles 11.200D, full pension 21D.)

Matmata does have one or two restaurant-cafés, but the hotel pension-plans are the best bargains. All of them serve a menu of *brik*, couscous, and dessert. Bring your own drink; the hotels' prices are inflated. The downside to eating lunch at the hotels is that you will join hordes of package tourists. For picnic fare, there are sev-eral small grocery shops that sell bread, yogurt, canned goods, and juice.

May the Force be with You

The hotel Sidi Driss (tel. 23 00 05) was the set for the **Skywalker farm and can-tina** scenes in *Star Wars*. This one-time "wretched hive of scum and villainy" bears no traces of the film, but you can stay here overnight (and the doors lock). (Singles 5.800D, full pension 11.600D. Doubles 11.600D, full pension 23.200D. Showers 2D.) Sit down for a beer, and you can tell your friends you had a frosty mug at the same place Han Solo whacked Greedo. Sorry, no 'droids allowed.

■ NEAR MATMATA

The sleepy subterranean village of **Haddej** remains untouched by mass tourism and George Lucas. Chances are you'll be greeted by a band of local children shouting whatever French they know: "Bonjour! Bonjour! Un stylo!" A few *millemes* or a Bic ballpoint will earn you friends for the day who will show you around. Ask to see one of the community's **olive presses;** the children will explain the multi-stage process in French and may offer you a sample of the oil stored in a subterranean well. (Be advised that a Berber's idea of good olive oil tastes spoiled to Western palates.)

Your young guides will dutifully bring you to the **Marriage Cave,** which used to be the subterranean venue for the ceremony. The many-chambered cave contains kitchens, a room for the bride's preparation, and one for signing the marriage contract. The poor couple would spend the first days of their conjugal bliss in a tiny, windowless chamber while the rest of the village partied outside. One of the best reasons to go to Haddej is the 3-km **mountain pass** that connects it to Matmata and meanders through the most magnificently desolate landscape you could ever wish to travel; walk or hire a donkey through the Syndicat (20D per day). Head along the Gabes road and turn right after the café/craft shop to get to the start of the trail. The trail is fairly easy to follow (head roughly 45° to the Gabes road); by the time it gets complicated you can see Haddej's white buildings. For an alternate route, take one of the Gabes-Matmata buses and get off at Tijma, 5km outside of Matmata; a sign points out the 3-km paved road leading east to Haddej. Getting back is a problem, of course; the options are hitching or waiting for another Gabes-Matmata bus.

Tamezret, 13km to the west of Matmata, is a well-preserved Berber village carved into the cliffs along the side of a mountain. Its stone houses huddle tightly together in defensive Berber style, and are best seen from above. At the top of the town by the steepled building, enjoy a cup of mint tea with almonds at the café (400ml) or clamber onto the roof for a look at the village below. One bus per day runs at noon from Matmata to Tamezret (500ml), supplemented very sporadically by *camionettes* (1D). Even if you don't make it to the village, a hike on the road is worthwhile for the dramatic landscape. Twenty-three km along the bumpy road lies **Toujane,** perched on the edge of a cliff and split in two by a deep gorge. There are no restaurants or cafés here, but children tote small buckets with bottles of lukewarm soft drinks for 300ml. No public transportation is available to Toujane. Arrange to hire a *camionette* and driver for the day (a fair price would be around 20-25D).

■■■ TATAOUINE AND CHENINI

Venturing out south from Gabes, you'll come to the **Berber towns,** on the fringes of inhabited Tunisia. The Berber villages, or *ksour,* have names and styles noticeably different from those in the Arab cities to the north. As often as not, these settlements are located in astoundingly harsh settings, a function of the Berbers' desire to maintain their autonomy. The Berber town defenses, which have fended off Romans, Arabs, and Turks, now open wide for the latest invaders and the much-needed money they bring with them.

TATAOUINE

The most convenient base from which to explore the Berber homelands is **Tataouine,** sometimes also called **Foum Tataouine.** Apart from the **movie theater** on av. Bourguiba, which shows such classics as *Fist Fighter: There's Only One Vanquisher* and *Fist Fighter II: The Second Vanquisher* (500ml), Tataouine does not have much to see or do. Since most visitors consequently blow through town or stay in an air-conditioned resort hotel, foreigners are a welcome novelty in the cafés—a good reason to spend the night. Everything from Islam to Michael Jordan is fair game over *chicha* and tea (albeit mostly in French).

The 125km journey from Gabes south to Tataouine proceeds by way of **Medenine,** itself a Berber city of some interest until the 1960s, when the government bulldozed the entire place. Don't stay in the new, improved Medenine longer than it takes to change buses (Gabes to Medenine, more or less every hr. from 7am, 1½hr., 2.600D). From Medenine take a connecting bus or *louage* to Tataouine (1hr., 1.750D). **Buses** leaving Tataouine include five to Medenine, as well as one direct to Gabes (5:30am, 2½hr., 4.300D) and two to Jerba (6:30am and 10am, 3½hr., 5.500D). From the Tataouine bus station, take a right onto rue 1 Juin. **Louages** leave two blocks from the buses, and rue 1 Juin runs to an odd monument, a whitewashed concrete block sunk into the ground. The first right from the block is av. Farhat Hached, the second av. Bourguiba. Tataouine's **post office** sits under a mountain at the end of av. Bourguiba (open Mon.-Sat. 7am-1:30pm, Sept.-June 8am-6pm). Across the street is a **late-night pharmacy** (open 8pm-8am). One block back toward the center of town and to the right, the **police** are on call (tel. 197). The **telephone office** is across from the Hotel Ennour (open 7am-midnight). **Telephone code:** 08.

Accommodations and food in Tataouine are affordable, and found at the inelegant but inexpensive **Hotel Ennour** (tel. 86 01 31), on av. Bourguiba; it is unmistakable as you enter town. (Dusty rooms 4D per person; showers upon request.) Plates in the restaurant downstairs run 1.500-2.500D. The **Hotel Medina,** rue Habib Mestaoui (tel. 86 09 99), is considerably more uplifting and central (5D per person, showers included; restaurant prices the same as at Ennor). To get there, head right on av. Bourguiba, make a quick left and then another. One good *rotisserie* is **Restaurant El Kaïma,** one block before the post office.

CHENINI

The Berber village of **Chenini** is the most spectacular and accessible of the South's *chorfa* (fortified granary) villages. Like the famous subterranean dwellings of Matmata, towns like this were constructed by the fiercely independent Berbers in response to Arab invasions, and perch precariously on a mountain ridge. The *ghar* (residences) are carved out of the mountain's soft clay, and their steep progression up the mountainside is a formidable sight. Visitors who take a closer look will be rewarded with views of a region awe-inspiring in its desolation; navigate the path from the new mosque down the other side of the mountain and onward to the abandoned **Mosque of the Seven Sleepers** (about 1km). The mosque's informal name refers to seven Christians supposedly buried alive here by the Romans. According to local legend, when Muslim settlers uncovered the site centuries later, the seven woke up as if from a deep sleep. Their bodies had grown while they slept and they died upon converting to Islam. Their enormous tombs remain by the mosque, though the story's credibility is somewhat weakened by the more than seven tombs. Since the mosque is no longer in use, visitors can enter the rather spooky place.

The cheapest way to make the 8km trip to Chenini is to grab a seat in one of the *camionettes* that leave from in front of the Café du Sud on rue 2 Mars in Tataouine, near the post office (1D each way). Departure times are very irregular, but the only other alternative is to charter a *louage*. They'll try to hit you up for 25D, but never pay anything more than 15D round-trip. The ride out to Chenini features some spectacular desert landscape, and for once there's not a telephone wire, souvenir stand, or TV antenna to be seen. You'll be dropped off at the **Relais Chenini,** which serves a standard, fixed-price meal for 5D, and will let you sleep overnight. Below are the **post office** and the town's lone **telephone** (**telephone code:** 08). Be prepared to wait a loooong time for a ride back. If worse comes to worse, the workers at the Relais Chenini drive back to Tataouine around 7pm.

Keep in mind that while Chenini is the most impressive of the Berber villages in the vicinity of Tataouine, it is also the most touristed. Most groups schedule their visits for Mondays and Thursdays (market days), but don't let the crowds daunt you— the steep, rocky hills and the endless views make Chenini worth it. Less-frequented villages include **Guermessa, Ghomrassen,** and **Ksar Hadada.** Getting there (and more importantly, getting back) can be problematic. If you don't have your own wheels, see what you can arrange at the Tatouine *louage* station. Much farther south (78km) lies the town of **Remada.** Beyond Remada, a military pass is required for trans-Saharan expeditions toward Libya or Algeria. **Be warned that Americans are not welcome in Libya or Algeria; be extremely cautious near the borders, as there is a great deal of tension in these areas.**

DOUZ

■■■ DOUZ

Douz looks exactly the way you think an oasis should: a haven of lush, green, date palms surrounded by endless sand dunes. Yet Douz is far more than a piddly pond flanked by some trees and guarded by Omar Sherif; acres and acres of date farms watered by scores of underground springs dominate the horizon as you approach Douz, and the guys dressed like sheiks are merely touting camel rides. Despite its size, Douz remains dwarfed by the vastness of the Great Eastern Erg and Chott deserts. Legend has it that Douz got its name when the French army's 12th battalion bivouacked here in the 19th century—*douze* means "twelve" in French. Modern Douz still has army barracks (don't try to take photos—it's *not* appreciated), but the town is also becoming increasingly touristy. Package travelers tend to remain in the luxury hotels of the oasis, however, so the town proper remains relaxed, friendly, and inexpensive. The sleepy environs wake up considerably in the late fall due to the influx of migrant laborers working the date harvest.

Orientation and Practical Information   Public transportation places Douz within easy reach. Direct **buses** to larger cities are infrequent—there's only one per day to Tozeur (8am, 4D) and Gabes (6:45am, 5.100D), but buses run to nearby Kebili (950ml), where you can make the necessary connections. Departures from place 7 Novembre; if the SNTRI office is closed, try the *patisserie* next door for info. **Louages** line up under a canopy 25m down the street and speed off to Kebili (1.500D) more frequently. Camionettes wait across the street.

The first thing you'll see in Douz is **place du 7 Novembre,** with a statue of a camel and its Bedouin rider. This feeds onto an avenue of the same name that runs along one side of Douz's **market square.** The large road heading to the right (approaching from the Kebili road), **av. Taieb Mehiri,** eventually merges with **av. des Martyrs,** and doubles back to the market square in one direction while continuing to the desert in the other. Down av. Taieb Mehri past the merge with av. des Martyrs, a well-informed English speaker awaits you at the **Syndicat.** (Open Mon.-Thurs. 7:30am-1:30pm and 5-8pm, Fri.-Sat. 8am-1pm; Sept.-June Mon.-Sat. 8:30am-1pm and 3-6pm.) **Camel rides** (5D per hr.) and the like are best arranged at a hotel. The **post office, telephone office,** and *cash only* **currency exchange** are grouped together in the PTT building on av. Taieb Mehri. (Open Mon.-Thurs. 7:30am-1pm; Sept.-June Mon.-Thurs. 8am-noon and 3-6pm, Fri.-Sat. 8am-12:30pm.) **Telephone Code:** 06. Those with **traveler's checks** can choose between Banque du Sud, Douz's only bank (a block up the Kebili road), and the large hotels down av. des Martyrs. Two **pharmacies** trade off late-night responsibilities: there's one near the post office, another on av. Rue 7 Novembre. (Open daily 8am-1pm and 4-8pm.) The **police station** (tel. 49 53 33) is next to the bank.

Accommodations and Food   Regardless of price or location, all hotels in Douz have a thin film of sand. The budget hotels also serve as contact points to meet other travelers, generally young backpackers, heading into the desert. The **Hotel Bel Habib** (tel. 49 51 15), on av. 7 Novembre, has the best deal. Some rooms have balconies overlooking the market square. Take your mattress out on the terrace for a snooze in the fresh air. (5D per person including breakfast and hot showers.) The **Hotel 20 (Vingt) Mars** (tel. 47 02 69) is run by two accommodating and lovable brothers. Take a left from av. Taieb Mehiri after the bus station and follow the signs. (5D per person, showers included.) The **Hotel Splendide** (tel. 49 51 73; to the left behind the *louage* station) doesn't quite live up to its name, but does fine with a setup like the Bel Habib. The owner is proud of the camel rides he arranges for guests. (Rooms 4.500D per person, showers included.) In the oasis, the newly renovated **Hotel Roses des Sables** (tel. 49 54 84; fax 49 53 66) offers perks like A/C, rooms with bath, and a swimming pool—all for a fairly reasonable price. (Singles 11D. Doubles 16D. Breakfast included. Full pension 4D extra per person.) Camping is an option in Douz only if you have your own tent and some trees for shade. **Desert**

Club Camping, on rue des Affections off av. des Martyrs, isn't much more than an empty lot with an overpriced Italian restaurant attached. The 3D (5D per person in a big tent) price is as high as prices at the hotels. Douz possesses a number of cheap restaurants geared for tourists but frequented by locals. **Restaurant Ali Baba** (tel. 47 02 69), one block up the Kebili road, could never seat all forty thieves but serves couscous (2D) in which the owner takes great pride, with good reason. (Open daily 6am-11pm.) **Restaurant Caravan** (tel. 47 04 15), by the bus station, is rather oddly decorated, but the owner is friendly and the *ojja merguez* (1.400D) is a reliable stomach-filler. (Open daily 11am-11pm.)

Sights Douz is generally the staging post for desert adventure, but it does offer a little to the daytripper not planning on heading further south. You can tread through the sands of the highly photogenic **Great Dune,** coincidentally situated near the expensive Hotel Mehari, 2km past the tourist office. The fact that it's essentially a glorified sandbox (constructed by bulldozer) may dampen any buzz brought on by the romantic landscape. An excellent **oasis hike** begins near the entrance to the market on av. des Martyrs. Following the signs for "Desert Club Camping" will bring you to the edge of the oasis. Take a right down the sandy road and into the thick of the palms. This track continues (bear right at the fork) through one kilometer of quiet green before hitting a small paved road. A left here will take you through more oasis, past the Hotel Saharien and the abandoned Hotel Marhala, through a small village, and, finally, out of the oasis. The hike is about 3km, ending with a fantastic desert view at the stadium in the Place du Festival. Vacant 51 weeks of the year, the stadium on the town's outskirts comes to life in late December for Douz's **Festival International du Sahara,** when you can watch Berber tribes play sand hockey with a bran-filled ball, or cheer on fighting camels. Hundreds of tourists saturate the town during that week, and most hotels tack extra *dinars* onto their prices. Several agencies compete to send you into the desert. **Saharan excursions** organize camel rides into the Grand Erg, cooking bread and meat in the sand, and sleeping under the stars in Bedouin-style tents. It's all pretty contrived of course, but the experience is unforgettable. Longer excursions (at least six days) actually follow the annual migratory route of specific tribes. **Abdelmouda Voyages** (tel. 47 05 97), next to the Hotel Roses des Sables, is flexible in arranging tours, with no minimum group size and trips ranging from one day to two weeks (35D per person per day). There's a slight chance of finding less expensive guides through the hotels listed above, and Hotel Zaafrane (see "Near Douz" below) is less expensive.

■ NEAR DOUZ

The smaller oases to the west of Douz attract fewer tourists and offer better views of the Erg. Four buses a day (6:45am-2:30pm, 500ml) run to **Zaafrane,** 10km away along a (somewhat) paved road. Arrange **desert camel rides** (4D per hour) with the **Syndicat** (right by the Douz road), which does little else. The **Hotel Zaafrane** (tel. 49 17 20), farther down and across the road, has decent rooms with A/C as well as a bar and pool, but it's none too cheap. (Singles 16D. Doubles 26D. Breakfast included.) The hotel arranges **desert excursions** for 30D a day. Buses continue across the wasteland to **Es-Sabria** and finally **El-Faouar** (1.500D). Sabria, a tiny village 3km off the main road, is particularly attractive. Tourists remain a novelty and the huge dunes and their fine views are ideal for playing Lawrence of Arabia. If there's no bus heading back, drivers walk back through the oasis to the main road to hitch a ride. El-Faouar itself has little to offer besides its location fairly deep in the desert, making for a fabulous bus ride. Four **buses** per day (6:30am-3:30pm) return from El-Faouar and Es-Sabria via Zaafrane. **Camionettes** serve both towns for the same price as the buses, but with a lot more frequency. **Hitchhiking** from the main road is also a fairly easy option, though *Let's Go* does not recommend it, of course. *Camionettes* are the only way to get to **Nouil** (650ml), another nearby desert village with a small oasis. **Novil Campement** (tel. 47 05 84) has offices on av. Taieb Mehri

TOZEUR

in Douz and offers "hotel-style" accommodation in large Bedouin tents. (8D per person. Half-pension 2.500D extra.)

■■■ TOZEUR

Despite its precarious location on the southwest edge of inhabited Tunisia, Tozeur has done its best to stay in the middle of things. The legendary ascetic Abu Himara ("the man on the donkey") led the forces of the Kharjite sect across the country to lay an ultimately unsuccessful siege on Mahdia, Tunisia's capital at the time. After again siding with the underdog in the Almoravid-Almohad dynastic struggle, Tozeur switched gears and became a regional economic powerhouse, serving as a terminus for the trans-Saharan caravans dealing in wool, dates, and slaves. What with the slave market dwindling and all, Tozeur is now making a play to become the Hammamet of the South. The oasis features a dozen resort hotels lining a *route touristique* and fleets of 4x4s and carpet merchants hungrily awaiting tourists. Don't write off Tozeur either, however; the oasis never fails to impress, the geometric brickwork in the medina is lovely, and excursions to nearby villages reward travelers with some of Tunisia's most spectacular scenery.

Orientation and Practical Information Tozeur's main street is the imaginatively named **Farhat Hached,** heading west to Neft and east to Kebili, where it becomes av. de la Liberté. **Av. Habib Bourguiba,** the main north-south drag, connects with av. Hached at a square featuring yet another odd Tunisian independence monument. As you pass the souvenir shop toward the other end of av. Bourguiba, av. **Abou El Kacem Ech Chabbi,** a.k.a. the **route touristique,** extends to your right.

Buses stop in front of the SNTRI office, which serves Douz via Kebili (1 per day, 2½hr., 4.900D) and Tunis via Kairouan (5 per day, 4hr., 10.500D to Kairouan; 7hr. 15.600 to Tunis). The regional bus company across the street runs six buses to Nefta (30min., 700ml). The **louage station** is a short walk away from av. Bourguiba. The **Syndicat** (tel. 45 00 34), resides in a brick building at the Bourguiba-Hached intersection. The helpful staff speaks English, distributes a map of Douz and Nefta, and arranges camel rides at 20D per half day (open Mon.-Sat. 8am-1pm and 3-6pm). The **ONTT tourist office** (tel. 45 45 03) is a hike down av. Abou El Kacem Ech Chabbi, but can provide encyclopedic info on the entire region. (Open Mon.-Thurs. and Sat. 7:30am-1:30pm and "evenings," about 6-8pm, Fri. and Sun. 8:30am-1pm; Sept.-June Mon.-Thurs. and Sat. 8:30am-1pm and 3-5:45pm, Fri. and Sun. 8:30am-1pm.) A **taxi-phone** station is next to the Syndicat (open 7am-10pm), and **currency exchanges** line both av. Hached and av. Bourguiba. If you have traveler's checks, the best bank to go to is the **STB** at the end of av. Habib Bourguiba. After banking hours try the hotels on the *route touristique,* including the **Warda** (open 8pm-8am). The **post office** (tel. 45 01 30) is just off av. Bourguiba (open Mon.-Sat. 7:30am-1pm; Sept.-June Mon.-Fri. 8am-noon and 3-6pm, Sat. 8am-12:30pm). The **police** (tel. 45 23 43) are 1km away on the Gafsa road; the hospital (tel. 45 04 00) is located in town. In **medical emergencies,** call 198 for help. From the Syndicat head left on av. Hached for 200m to find the **night pharmacy** (tel. 45 44 00). **Telephone code:** 06.

Accommodations and Food Hotels in Tozeur are slightly pricier than their counterparts in other Tunisian cities, but they are good places to meet other travelers who are looking for partners for 4x4 excursions. The laid-back, palm-shaded campground should be your first housing choice. **Campement Beaux Rêves,** on the *route touristique* (tel. 45 12 42), 1km past the ONTT office, features a café with *chicha* and reggae music. (3.500D per person whether you sleep in the open, the palm frond huts, the "Bedouin tent," or your own tent; cold showers included.) To get to Tozeur's hostel, **Maison de Jeunes,** G.P. no. 3 (tel. 45 02 35), turn right onto av. Hached from av. Bourguiba, and bear left (toward Gafsa) at the roundabout. Expect large, loud groups of Tunisians. This is one of the more decrepit of the country's hostels, with an unpleasant toilet/shower room, but the price is a low 3D per person. **Residence Essalem,** is on rue de la Liberté, down av. Hached/liberté toward Kelibia. Though it's not plush by any means, Essalem always has water, most rooms have showers, and the 6D per person includes breakfast. Right on the *route touristique* lies **Résidence Warda,** av Abou El Kacem Ech Chabbi (tel. 45 25 47). Quite a locus for independent travelers, Warda has clean, attractive rooms. The sinks even have plugs! Exchanges currency for 350ml per check. Singles 9.500D, with en suite shower 10,500D. Doubles 14D, with shower 16D. A/C 3D. Breakfast included.

As usual, restaurants here are clones of each other, with a few exceptions. Close to the *route touristique* is the **Restaurant de la Medina,** on av. Bourguiba where the carpet stores begin. This standard hovel serves dishes higher in quality and lower in price than its neighbors. The *chorba* soup (800ml) is spicy, oily, and delicious (though not veggie-friendly). Unusually, they prepare their *ojja* (1.440D) with tuna and not sausage. (Open 10am-midnight.) **Restaurant le Soleil,** av. Abou El Kacem Ach Chabbi (tel. 45 02 20), across from the Warda, is a *brochetterie* with a touch of class. Outdoor dining here is accompanied by the latest hits in *rai* music and rounded off by a complimentary mint tea. The *brochettes* (3D) are on the fatty side, but the parsley-laden *tajine* (2D) is worth a try. (Open noon-3pm and 6-11pm.) Head right from av. Bourguiba to reach **Restaurant du Sud** (tel. 45 08 26), on av. Farhat Hached. The specialty here is cuisine from Sfax, which—like the city itself— isn't much different from that of the rest of Tunisia. Couscous aficionados may notice a difference, but it's just as tasty (2.500D). The *omelette sfaxienne* (1.900D) is stuffed with tomatoes and tuna. (Open daily noon-10pm.)

Sights Tozeur's medina, the **Ouled el-Hadef,** extends to the left as you walk down av. Bourguiba past the Syndicat. Lacking any major monuments, it nonetheless makes for a nice place to stroll. The ornate abstractions of the buildings' brickwork originate in 8th-century Mesopotamia and cannot be found outside Iran except in Tozeur and nearby Nefta. This method of construction serves a practical, as well as ornamental, purpose: the yellowish bricks, handmade from local clay and sand, insulate against the heat much better than other inexpensive building materials. The medina contains a **Museum of Archaeology and Traditional Arts** (tel. 45 00 34) that isn't worth the time; three small rooms present more dust than exhibits. (Open 8am-noon and 3:30-6:30pm; Sept.-June 8am-1pm and 3-5pm. Admission 1D.) The name of Tozeur's park, **Le Paradis,** overstates the case a bit, but a stroll through the flowers and (of course) palm trees is nice enough. From the end of av. Bourguiba, veer right and walk about 500m; there will be a sign to the left. Rent **bikes** at another anonymous "Location de Vélo," on the same road as Le Paradis. (Rickety **bikes** 1D per hr., 5D per day.)

Past the tourist office is the **Dar Cheraït cultural center;** it's unclear which culture this is the center of, but it's certainly not Tunisian. The pastel-colored pseudo-palace incorporates a tea salon, hotel, museum, and "mini-*souk*" into a hyper-real Tunisialand. The centerpiece of this fantasy, and the final insult to Tunisia's cultural identity, is the "1001 Medina Nights," a pre-fabricated, sized-down conception of an "oriental" city with costumed workers mugging for the cameras. For once the brochure does justice to the grotesque entity by billing it as a "spectacle." (Open daily 8pm-midnight. Admission 5D.) The monorail to Space Mountain is still under construction. In fairness, the museum, for all its sugar coating and bright colors, does give a sound introduction to Tunisian crafts and the life of the *pasha* (with predictable emphasis on the harem), and the explanations, unlike in other Tunisian museums, are in English. (Open 7am-midnight. Admission 3D, photo permit 1D.)

A sandy path leads from the left of the cultural center, past a mosque under construction, and into the oasis. The track winds its way along a small stream for another kilometer before it finishes at the **Belvedere,** an impressive collection of rocks and gorges from which you can survey all 2500 acres of palm trees, plus part of the Chott. Men and boys come here to bathe; female swimmers should expect unpleasant commentary

WEST OF TOZEUR

■ WEST OF TOZEUR: NEFTA AND VICINITY

Nefta, 23km west of Tozeur, lies toward the Algerian border. With a deep connection to the charismatic Sufi brotherhoods since the 9th century, the town remains a place of pilgrimage. Nefta is most noteworthy today for the **Corbeille de Nefta**, a natural bowl-shaped slope filled with palms. The site is eye-catching, but the view is marred by an architectural eyesore: the Sahara Palace Hotel. More intriguing structures are the several mosques along the bowl's edge that comprise the **Ridge of Domes**. While the Corbeille is attractive, it's not quite as fabulous as the tourist offices might claim—especially if you've already seen the oases at Douz and Tozeur.

To get to Nefta and the Corbeille, take the bus from Tozeur (850ml); you'll pass the **Syndicat** (tel. (06) 45 71 84) on your way in. The personable, English-speaking staff will answer questions. To reach the rim, take av. Bourguiba until it splits just past the post office, then the unpaved right fork to the first street to the right; keep heading in that direction for about 250m. To enter the Corbeille itself, take the dirt track down. The Corbeille features **open-air baths** with both hot and cold springs, which can get quite crowded. Women generally go in the morning, men in the afternoon. Intruding on the opposite sex is of course most impolite. It's important to remember that while this is Nefta's big tourist attraction, it is (like most oases) just farmland, and as such, private property. Don't be surprised by the scrappy guard-puppies that patrol the area—their bark is a lot worse than their bite.

Ten km down the road past Nefta, the **Sahara** begins in earnest. Except for a small shack or two and the scraggly bushes that grow by the side of the road, there are no signs of life. The desolate terrain serves as an abridged "Tunisian Desert Experience," with the Chott salt flats on one side of the road and rolling dunes on the other. One shack is actually the **Marché des Roses des Sables**, an outdoor market for "sand roses," those gypsum rock formations found in *souks* all over Tunisia. Moving past the market, you can walk out onto the Chott. The location is also a particularly good one for seeing mirages. If you return to the road and walk a kilometer past it into the desert (make sure you can find your way back!), the vegetation will gradually decrease until there's nothing but fine sand and large dunes. (As always, **be sure to bring at least one liter of water per person per hour.**)

Buses, louages, and **camionettes** all pass the Marché on their way to the Algerian border and will be more than happy to leave you stranded for around 1.200D. Since traffic back to Nefta is extremely light, hitchhiking is very difficult; the few cars that do pass are either reluctant to stop or stuffed to the brim with immigrating Algerians. The safest way to see the Marché is to charter a *louage* in Nefta to take you there and back (15D round-trip). Another 24km along the same road is the Algerian frontier; one of the few points of entry is found at **Hazoua. Be warned that a great deal of tension exists between Tunisia and Algeria, and that Americans are not welcomed across the border; be extremely cautious in this area.**

■ EAST OF TOZEUR

The mountains, deserts, and oases surrounding Tozeur constitute some extremely difficult terrain, but they also offer some of the most spectacular scenery in all of Tunisia. The three towns of Chebika, Tamerza, and Mides each possess photogenically ruined buildings as well as unique and marvelous natural features. Unless you enlist the aid of a 4x4 for the day, getting to the towns is a process that is at best laborious and at worst impossible. However, the circuitous routes themselves reward the intrepid (and patient) traveler with magnificent views.

Chebika is the least spectacular, least accessible, and ironically the most touristed of the three oases. The old, abandoned village (there is a modern inhabited one nearby) sits on a rock platform that also has room for about forty Land Rovers. A superfluous but insistent guide will lead you into the twisted foothills to the small cascade that waters the oasis. The top of the mountain is high enough to provide you with an excellent perspective of the surroundings, making Chebika's tiny swatch of brilliant green seem miraculous, flanked as it is by the lifeless desert and salt flats. **Tamerza,** connected by a rough, paved road to Chebika, reveals two waterfalls belonging to hot and cold springs, connected by a 1½-km ravine. The pools below are popular swimming holes for (male) Tunisians. **Mides** manages to surpass the other two with the natural splendor of a gorge that opens like a wound in the landscape. The old Berber village precariously clusters around the sheer walls of this natural defensive position. If you arrived here by 4x4, don't be content with peering into the canyon from the top. Double back about 25m and descend through the dense growth of an easy slope to get to the canyon floor.

The three towns really need to be reached by Land Rover, the vehicle of choice for navigating the treacherous but direct Tozeur-Chebika-Tamera road, which also runs across the mirage-infested Chott Gharsa and through the truly breathtaking mountain passes. Your best option is to hire a 4x4 vehicle and a guide for the day. Get a group together and pile as many people as you can into the car—the cars can seat up to eight passengers. **Hafsi Voyages,** av. Farhat Hached (tel. 45 26 11), offers the best deal, charging flat rates for a Land Rover and driver (80D for half day, 120D for full). Other agencies charge 30D per person for a day-long excursion with a four-person minimum. **Mahari Voyages,** av. Farhat Hached (tel. 42 03 87), handles the large tour groups, but has a couple of English-speaking guides and the largest Land Rover fleet, so usually has extra places (11th-hour bargaining *may* pay off). Try to convince the driver to do the towns in the opposite order (Mides, Tamerza, then Chebika) to avoid the masses.

The stubbornly independent, the extremely cheap, and the slightly masochistic can get to Tamerza using **public transportation,** but it takes about three hours to get there and even more time (and luck) to return. Start with a *louage* from Tozeur to the mining center of **Metlaoui** (2.100D), and take another to **Redeyef** (2D). In Redeyef, ask to be let off near the *camionettes.* In front of the park, small pick-up trucks and the occasional bus make the trip to Tamerza and sometimes to Mides (1D; no buses to Mides). Even if you're lucky enough to get out there, though, it's hell finding a way back. It's possible to persuade a *camionette* driver to take you on a quick tour of both towns for around 10D. From Tamerza, you can hire a **donkey and guide** to negotiate a trail to Mides and walk back through the gorge, a four to five-hr. excursion. The midday heat is brain-scrambling, and transport out of Tamerza dries up by 3:30pm, so if you go this route you'll probably have to spend the night at the over-priced and primitive **Hotel Cascades,** (tel. 45 37 32), which has singles for 13D and doubles for 18D, including breakfast. If you're lucky enough to have your own vehicle, the best route to take is the road to Metlaoui and then to Redeyef. Beyond Redeyef, 25km of paved road leads straight to Tamerza; the turn-off for Mides 5km before Tamerza is bumpy but easily negotiable. You'll have to skip Chebika; the roads from Tamerza are steep and rocky. See Tunisia: Essentials: Getting Around: By Car (page 588) for tips on driving in the desert.)

THE NORTHERN (CORAL) COAST

The north coast of Tunisia is the green part of the country. Thick fields and high forests run along the white beach that makes up the stunning coastline from Tunis to the Algerian border. In fact, the Coral Coast (named for the large reefs found offshore) has a lot more in common with neighboring Sicily (about 200 miles away) than it does with the rest of Tunisia; the principal cities, Bizerte and Tabarka, with their tree-lined streets and red tile-roofed dwellings, only serve to reinforce this impression. Since the north coast is virtually undiscovered by tour groups and hotel complexes, you can come here to escape the crowds of Hammamet and Jerba. This may change soon, however, as the tourist office is very actively promoting Tabarka.

■■■ BIZERTE

Jules Ferry, former prime minister of France and imperialist/colonist pioneer, said, "If I have taken Tunisia, it is to have Bizerte!" While M. Ferry may simply have been a fan of Bizerte's white beaches and pulchritudinous old quarters, more likely than not he was referring to its enormous natural harbor, strategically commanding the Mediterranean bottleneck between Africa and Sicily. The site has been exploited since the time of Carthage, when the canal between the sea and the inland Lake Bizerte was dug. The French Navy couldn't bear to leave such a location upon Tunisian independence in 1956 and continued to hold onto it, despite the fledgling government's objections. The situation came to a head in 1961, when Tunisian forces blockaded the base. The fighting that ensued resulted in 1000 Tunisian casualties and France's withdrawal, and has been immortalized in the town's *Cimetière des Martyrs*. Bizerte's economy continues to revolve around the port, with its shipping and fishing activities; tourism plays second fiddle, despite the charm of the Old Port and the nearby beaches, including Raf Raf, one of the country's best.

ORIENTATION AND PRACTICAL INFORMATION

The compact town center can be perplexing because many roads run diagonally. **Av. Habib Bourguiba** runs the length of the city and separates the *nouvelle ville* from the medina. **Av. de l'Algérie,** which begins at the main **bus station,** cuts through the main square (**pl. 7 Novembre 1987**), crosses av. Bourguiba, and ends in place Slah-Edine Bouchoucha, near **Old Port,** the most beautiful part of town.

Blue-and-orange **buses** depart from the main station for nearby beach towns Ras Jebel (8 per day, 1.490D) and Ghar-el-Melh (3 per day, 1.490D), both about an hour's ride. Buses run to Tunis's Bab Saadoun station (every hr., 1½hr., last bus 7pm, regular 2.340D, *confort* 2.710D). One bus per day goes to Le Kef (6.500D), but leaves from in front of the **train station,** 500m further along the canal (away from the drawbridge). Four slow trains crawl daily to Tunis (3 on Sun., 2.650D). For the same price, *louages* make the same trip in two-thirds the time; they congregate in the shadow of the drawbridge just up from the bus station.

Tourist Office: O.N.T.T., 1, rue de Istamboul (tel. 43 28 97). From the bus station, walk along the water past the bridge and the *louages* and make a left at the sign. Friendly and English-speaking staff is short on info and maps. Open Mon.-Sat. 7:30am-1:30pm; Sept.-June 8:30am-1pm and 3-5:45pm.

Post Office: half a block up from pl. 7 Novembre on av. de l'Algérie (tel. 315 85). Open Mon.-Sat. 8am-6pm, Sun. 9-11am; July-Aug. Mon.-Sat. 7:30am-1:30pm and 5-6pm, Sun. 9-11am.

Telephone office: across the street and around the corner on rue du 1er Mai. Open daily 8am-5pm; July-Aug. 7:30am-1:30pm. **Telephone Code:** 02.

Currency Exchange: Cash only at the post office; if the **banks** on pl. 7 Novembre are closed, you'll have to trek to the **hotels on the Corniche.**

Late-Night Pharmacy: rue Ali Belhaouane, off av. Bourguiba, facing the Old Port. Open nightly 7:30pm-7:30am.

Hospital: rue du 3 Août (tel. 43 14 22).

Police: (tel. 197), on the square between av. Bourguiba and av. 2 Mars 1934.

ACCOMMODATIONS

The expensive resort hotels along the beach are packed with tour groups, and most cheap hotels in town fill in July and August, so arrive early. Though it's 4km south of town (on the road to Tunis), the **Remel Youth Hostel (HI)** (tel. 44 08 04), is the best place if all you want to do is hit the beach. Take "Menzel Jemil" bus #8A or a "Ras Jebel" bus (both 210ml) and ask to get off at Remel Plage (taxi 1.5D). The hostel is due for renovations, but a fine stretch of beach is 100m away. (HI members only. 3D per person. Shower included. Breakfast 1D. Lunch or dinner 3D. Cooking facilities available.) In Bizerte, the cleanest lodgings are at **Hotel Saadi** (tel. 43 75 28), on rue Salah Ben Ali. Head away from the Old Port on av. Bourguiba, take the second right after the uniquely shaped Tunis Air office. Saadi has large windows and a quiet, somewhat removed location. (Singles 6.500D. Doubles 10D. Cold showers on the corridor.) More central is the **Hotel Continental,** 9, rue du 2 Mars 1934 (tel. 43 14 36). As you walk from the main square on av. de l'Algérie, it's the second right after the post office; the sign is broken, so keep your eyes peeled. Beds consist of strips of foam and sheets Every inch is covered with random tiling for a colorful, if aesthetically appalling, effect. (5D per person. Showers included.)

FOOD

A lively covered **market** flourishes near the base of the Old Port. There's a **Monoprix Supermarket** on rue 2 mars 1934. (Open daily 8:30am-12:30pm and 3:30-7:30pm; opens on Sun. at 9am.) From pl. 7 Novembre, walk diagonally on av. Taleb Mahri past the Office National des Pêches in the upper left-hand corner of the square. A number of touristy but reasonable restaurants cluster at the end of av. Bourguiba farthest from the port. On rue 2 Mars, just past Hotel Continental, sits **Restaurant Cuisine Tunisienne,** a greasy spoon. Come for a quick *brik* (350ml) or spicy *ojjo merguez* (1.200D). If you're lucky they'll have couscous (1.500D). (Open daily noon-11pm.) **Restaurant du Bonheur,** 31, av. Thaâlbi (tel. 43 25 72), is off av. Bourguiba. It's clean and the furniture is better-than-average, but the selection is standard. Enormous *menu* (7.500D). Open daily noon-3pm and 7-11pm.

SIGHTS

The collective aroma of coffee and rotten fish wafts through the air around the **Old Port.** By twilight, the normally quiet quays are packed with tables at which café patrons sip tea, admiring their surroundings and each other. Facing the Old Port, **place Slah-Edine Bouchoucha** is ringed with fruit and vegetable stalls, above which rise the twin minarets of the Debaa and Grand Mosques. Two fortresses guard the port's entrance. The larger **kasbah** is a medina within a medina. Built in the 18th century, its crenellated battlements contain an entire residential quarter replete with its own mosque and shops. A cozy café sits on the top level, offering a broad view of the port, the coast, and the medina. Enter at the end of the old port, 100m from the sea. (Open daily 9am-noon and 3-7pm. Admission 400ml.) The **Andalusian Quarter,** with its ancient archways, winding alleys, and nail-studded doors, lies just to the north. The Old Town is best viewed at dusk, when the half light gives its shabbiness a certain romantic aesthetic. Sheep wander the streets chewing hay, and caged parakeets twitter gaily from the shops. On the neighboring hilltop, the 16th-century **Spanish Fort** is now an open-air theater. The fort was actually built by the Turks, and received its name when the Arabs captured it from Don Juan of Austria.

Cap Blanc, which forms Africa's northernmost point, is perhaps the most spectacular sight near Bizerte. To get there, follow av. de la Corniche along the beach and up the coast to the *Radiophare du Cap Blanc* sign, where you turn right. The rough road struggles to the top of **Jebel Nador** (288m), the perfect perch for a glorious sunset view. Below, chalky Cap Blanc protrudes into the sea. To reach its tip, descend the mountain and follow the trail leading off the road. The bike ride is scenic and challenging; count on three hours round-trip. It's even longer to **Lake Ichkenl,** but well worth it, especially if you like birds. The lake, one of only two Wetlands World Heritage sites (the other is the Everglades in Florida), is a rest stop for birds migrating between Africa and Europe. Widgeon, pochard, and the rare white-headed duck all take a break here, sometimes in staggering numbers. Follow their lead, and enjoy the beautiful surroundings.

Two "luxury" beach hotels (4km out along the Corniche), the **Jalta** (tel. 43 11 69) and the **Nadhour** (tel. 43 18 44), monopolize sports and entertainment. Both rent **horses** and **bikes.** The Nadhour also offers **windsurfing** and **tennis.** If you like **waterskiing,** ask at the Jalta's reception desk. Both complexes are too far to walk to from the town: the quickest way to get to either one is by the "La Corniche" #1 bus, (220ml) which departs regularly from av. Bourguiba near the Old Port. The trip also makes a nice bike ride.

■ NEAR BIZERTE: RAF RAF

Along the coast of Bizerte, the mountains at **Raf Raf** plunge into the sea, forming a crescent-shaped beach. The shore immediately in front of the cafés and vacation villas suffocates under a thick covering of Tunisian vacationers and their refuse, but a 1km walk along the shore (facing the sea, head right) brings you to secluded stretches of white sand, the rocky island of Pilav jutting out of the crystal clear waters, and mountains of dark pine forests within 50m of the beach—some of the finest area in the vicinity of Bizerte. Shallow water and strong surf make for good bodysurfing and boogieboarding.

In July and August, there are four **buses** per day direct from Bizerte to "Raf Raf Plage" (1hr., 1.850D); otherwise, take one of the year-round "Ras Jebel" buses to Ras Jebel (8 per day, 1hr., 1.300D), and hop in a *louage* (400ml) to Raf Raf town. The beach is a short walk downhill. You're unlikely to make it back to Bizerte or Tunis after 6:30pm, and staying overnight can be an expensive prospect, especially during summer. On the positive side, the big towels that come with the **Hotel Dalia's** (tel. 44 70 77) rooms serve admirably on the beach. (Singles 20D. Doubles 28D. Don't pay the extra 2D for the "sea view." Breakfast included.)

■■■ TABARKA

Ten km from the Algerian border, Tabarka teeters precariously on the fine line between mellow beach town and tourist-mad resort. Welcoming breezes blow through this town—mercifully removed from the *zone touristique*—which is flanked on one side by a beach and on the other by rocky cliffs. A fortress perches dramatically overhead. Tabarka is as laid back as Nabeul, but more beautiful and upscale; several luxury hotels and an international airport have recently been built.

Orientation and Practical Information Tabarka's biggest street, **av. Habib Bourguiba,** runs from the beginning of town straight to the sea. Halfway there, it opens up into a lush, well-kept park, whose centerpiece is an immense statue of you-know-who with his pet dog. To get to the helpful offices of the **ONTT** (tel. 44 44 91), head right from the **bus and louage stations** along av. Bourguiba, and make the last left before the Tunis-Aïn Draham roundabout. They'll give you a hand-drawn map with important points highlighted. (Open Mon.-Sat. 7:30am-1:30pm; Sept.-June 8:30am-1pm and 3-5:45pm). There's a **post office** at the end of av. Bourguiba, near the beach (open Mon.-Fri. 8am-noon and 3-6pm, Sat. 8am-12:30pm; July-Aug. Mon.-Sat. 7:30am-1:30pm). **Taxiphones** and the two **banks** are found on the main drag, back toward the center of town. **Telephone code:** 08. The **late-night pharmacy** on rue Alzouaoui (off av. Bourguiba near the entrance to town; across from the Hotel Novelly) is on call 8pm-7:30am. **Police** (tel. 197) are at the end of the park closest to the mountains. The town has two **bus** companies. The first, situated at the beginning of av. Bourguiba, is **regional** and runs one morning bus per day to Bizerte, Le Kef, and Jendouba; service is more frequent to nearby Aïn Draham. **SNTRI,** the national company, has seven buses per day to and from Tunis (last bus leaves Tabarka at 3:45pm; *confort* 6.550D, regular 5.800D). Tunis buses depart from rue du Peuple, parallel to av. Bourguiba and close to the Hotel Corail. **Louages** (serving Tunis, Aïn Draham, and Jendouba), originate near the regional bus station.

Accommodations and Food There are only a few hotels in Tabarka, and most of these are pricey and geared toward couples. If you arrive by yourself in high season (July-Aug.), expect to pay the cost of a double room. The cheapest hotels are usually booked solid; call well in advance of your arrival. Only two hotels approach budget standards. The better, **Hotel de la Plage** (tel. 64 40 39) on av. 7 Novembre, near the beach by the Port de Plaisance, has a terrace, wood furniture, and gleaming showers and toilets (10D per person). The other option is the **Hotel Corail,** at 1, rue Tazerka (tel. 64 45 44), off av. Bourguiba between the park and the beach. A fairly clean and spacious hotel; its rooftop terrace is one of the highest in the city. (Single with double bed 15D; showers included.) The best part of town for low-priced, filling meals is rue Farhat Hached, off av. Bourguiba one block down from the park toward the water. **Restaurant El Hana** offers a savory, sizable bowl of couscous for 1.700D (open daily 10am-10pm). For seafood, try the **Hotel de France** (tel. 64 45 77) on av. Bourguiba, which cooks up a *menu* for 6D. (Open noon-4pm and 6pm-midnight.) You can get picnic supplies at the **supermarket** (Magasin General) across from the Bourguiba statue.

Sights Tabarka's most captivating sight is its **Genoese Fort,** an integral part of the city's history. It was built by the Lomellini family, who received the Isle of Tabarka as ransom for the release of the Turkish pirate Dragut (who spent four years rowing a Genoese galley after being captured). Dragut proceeded to prove himself worthy of such a price; after his release, he captured Tripoli, destroyed a Spanish fleet, and conquered Jerba. Meanwhile, Tabarka remained in the hands of the Lomellinis for over 200 years. Tabarka's other notable sight is the cluster of rocks at the end of town, **Les Aiguilles** (The Needles). These huge (20m) natural spires shoot out of the water and are quite striking, particularly at sunset. There is also a museum at **La Basilique,** the site of a French basilica, featuring mosaics. (Admission 1D.)

TELL

"Tell" is an Arabic word for mountain, but don't expect the Alps. Nonetheless, the mild climate and fertile fields of this northern interior region have made it a preferred spot throughout history. Passing through, you'll see sweeping countryside and a range of agriculture including wheat, olives, and hay. Bulla Regia and Dougga, the finest archaeological sites in Tunisia, testify to Tell's five centuries as Rome's primary granary, while the walled city of Le Kef has attracted worshipful Romans, Christians, Muslims, and legions of plundering mercenaries through the centuries.

■■■ LE KEF

Le Kef (also "El Kef") means "The Rock," an appropriate name for a fortress town built atop a craggy mountain strategically overlooking the Tell. While the city considers itself the capital of the western region, it is perhaps resting on its historical laurels; the large town is generally sleepy. The town was settled in prehistoric times and dubbed "Sicca" by the Carthaginians; when the Romans took over they added the title "Veneria" to the name, referring to the city's cult of the love goddess (not to the consequences of recklessly pursuing her impulses). The Romans perpetuated the belief that every year Venus flew between Rome and Le Kef, accompanied by a flock of doves (the ruins of the Temple of Venus are 5km away up a road negotiable only in a 4x4), and even today, Islamic pilgrimages to Kairouan and to Mecca traditionally pass through Le Kef to solicit the doves' blessing. Arab refugees from the Christian *Reconquista* of Spain later settled the town.

Le Kef played an aggressive role in the history of Arab nationalism in the late 50s, when the FLN (a guerilla group fighting for Algerian independence) made the city their headquarters. Le Kef remains a fine place for launching campaigns; explore the Roman ruins of Dougga and Bulla Regia during the day, and return to wander the old town and admire its panoramas in the early evening.

Orientation And Practical Information With hills reminiscent of San Francisco and views that stretch forever, the medina, lurking under the towering *kasbah*, feels like the *centro storico* of an Italian hilltown. The bus and *louage* station lies in the new city, five minutes downhill from the medina—take a right out of the bus lot and up to the top of the hill, turn right again, then take the second left

LE KEF

on rue Ali Belhaouane. This street ends at **place de l'Indépendence;** the medina is up high. **Av. Habib Bourguiba** (the main road to Tunis) begins in pl. de l'Indépendence, and heads uphill and to the right out of town. Frequent *louages* supplement bus service to Jendouba (4 per day, 1hr., 2.100D), Tunis (14 per day, 4hr., 6.300D), Bizerte (1 per day at 7am, 4½hr., 6.650D), and Kairouan (2 per day, 3½hr., 5.850D).

Le Kef's **tourist office** (tel. 22 11 48) is located next to Café du Dinar in pl. de l'Indépendence. Comfortable couches and wooden tables make this unusual office a good place to unwind; Mohamed Tlilli, the friendly and knowledgable volunteer director of the bureau, also heads the *kasbah* restoration effort. Opening times here are irrelevant; try your luck from 9am to 8pm. Also in pl. de l'Indépendance is a **bank** where you can exchange traveler's checks. For other **currency exchange,** not to mention the **post office** *and* the **telephone office,** head to PTT, on the corner of rue Hedi Chaker and rue d'Algérie. Bear left at the fork downhill from the tourist office and walk 2 blocks. (Open Mon.-Sat. 8am-6pm, Sun. 9-11am, July-Aug. Mon.-Sat. 7:30am-2pm.) You'll find more telephones at **Taxiphone** (open daily 6am-midnight); bear right at the fork downhill from the tourist office. **Telephone code:** 08. The **late-night pharmacy** (tel. 22 28 80) sits on the small street that winds upward from pl. de l'Indépendance, 50m from Café du Dinar (open daily 8pm-8am); the **police** (tel. 197) are in a large building up the hill from the bus station.

Accommodations and Food Decent rooms are scarce in Le Kef. The **Hotel de la Source** (tel. 22 42 24), uphill from the tourist office and left on av. Bourguiba, has a magnificent exception, an elaborately tiled and stuccoed chamber fit for a *pasha* (12D, fits up to four people). The other rooms are anticlimactic, with ragged beds and cement-floored showers (6D for one or two people). The **Hotel El Medina,** 18, rue Farhat Hached (tel. 22 32 14), is as bare as any other hotel with this name, but the rooms are clean and freshly painted in tasteful blue and gray (4D per person, hot showers 500ml). If these choices aren't sufficiently posh (or expensive) for you, try the new **Residence Venus** (tel. 22 46 95), on rue Mouldi Khamessi. The rooms are lovely and cool, decorated with prayer rugs and Mickey Mouse lamps, each with private bath. (Singles 14-20D. Doubles 24-28D. Breakfast included.) From the tourist office, head right and follow the signs uphill.

In general, dining options in Le Kef are scarcer than decent rooms. **Restaurant les Ruines** (tel. 22 27 19) distinguishes itself with a large menu and cleanliness. Couscous 1.800D, *mechoui* 3D. (Open daily 8am-10pm.) **Restaurant de l'Afrique** (tel. 22 20 79), on rue Heidi Chaker just below pl. de l'Indépendance, serves tasty *mloukia* and *chakchouka,* along with the main course, generally limited to *brochettes* or *poulet rôti* for 1.800D. (Open daily noon-3pm and 6-10pm.) Twice as expensive but three times as fancy, the **Restaurant Venus** (tel. 22 03 55) serves Tunisian cuisine, with wine if you like. A/C. Entrees 3-4D. (Sketchy opening hours.)

Sights Sightseeing in Le Kef is an informal, slow-paced pleasure. With the exception of the regional museum, none of the sights charge admission, have a regular staff, or keep strict opening hours (though most try to stick to an 8am-noon and 3-7pm schedule). Most places of interest have an old guardian or caretaker; if he's around, you're in luck. Caretakers are invariably friendly and enthusiastic, and will often give you a history lesson along with a tour.

Climb up through the medina from the steps starting to the right of the Hotel de la Source. These will lead you to the foot of the **kasbah** (1601), at the peak of Le Kef's once impregnable rock and featuring a fine view of irrigated plains and the new town. The fortifications, in the midst of extensive restorations, look like they could still put up a good fight, but the Turkish gateway is generally left open during the day. Beneath the *kasbah,* the well-preserved 4th-century **Christian basilica** surrounds an open-air court with massive, oblong columns. During the 8th century, the basilica was converted into a mosque, making it one of the oldest in the country. The restoration crews running rampant throughout the town have removed the structure's minaret in the process of re-Romanizing efforts. The basilica now houses a collection of ancient artifacts, including stelae featuring the stylized, highly un-Classical figures common to Neo-Punic art. The fluted domes and slender minaret of the **Mosque of Sidi Bov Makhlouf** clash with the rocky mass of its imposing neighbors, the *kasbah* and the basilica. The small mosque is a tiny treasure of Andalusian tiling, carving, and stained glass. Inside are the brightly ornamented coffins of several saints. If the caretaker is around, ask him to let you climb the minaret; the view is worth the uncomfortably compact stairway and the pigeons that get in your way.

From the street running alongside the *kasbah,* take the second to last right to get to the **regional museum,** built inside an old mosque and primarily devoted to the customs of the nomads who migrate annually to the Tell. Many of the items displayed as artifacts are still used today. (Open Tues.–Sun. 9am-1pm and 4-7pm, Sept.-June Tues.-Sun. 9:30am-4:30pm. Admission 1D, photo permit 1D). Turn right out of the museum and take the first left to the **Bab Ghedive,** one of the few gateways in Le Kef's extensive set of walls and fortifications. Le Kefians call it **Bab-Ghdar,** or the Gate of Treachery, because of the popular belief that Governor Ghedive opened the gates for the French in 1881. The tourist office historians don't believe a word of it; they point out that the French attacked from Algeria, which is in the opposite direction. Beyond the *bab,* you abruptly step from the city out into a deserted meadow below a steep cliff face. Past the stone walls is a series of holes in the ground (they look like wells) into which you can peer for a glimpse of the **Roman cisterns,** an ancient sewage- and water-processing network that runs under all of Le Kef. If you want to go inside, ask at the tourist office; they'll take you down into another set of cisterns right next to the Hotel de la Source. Across from these cisterns are the ruins of some fourth-century **Roman baths;** nearby lies what are claimed to be the remains of the **Temple of Venus.**

On the street behind Hotel Medina, the **Eglise de Saint Pierre** predates both the French and the Arabs, who call it Dar el-Kous. This 4th-century Roman basilica stands empty now, with but a few columns standing. Two blocks on the left past the Hotel Medina, an unmarked **synagogue** recalls the Jewish community limited by the Turks to this street. Knock on the blue door on rue Markat Karama to see if the caretaker will let you peep inside. For an unusual outdoor excursion you can take a hike up the **Jugurtha's Table,** a huge slab of stone that offers an orgasmic panorama. To get there, take a *louage* from Le Kef to the village of Kalaat Senan (2.200D). A 4-km path leads to a 1500-year-old staircase cut into the mountain; from the top, you can look out over Algeria and the fields of the Tell.

■ NEAR LE KEF: ARCHAEOLOGICAL SITES

BULLA REGIA

While the extensive ruins at Dougga have gained more prestige, the site at Bulla Regia should be on the "to see" list of any traveler, even those who thought they had their fill of Roman monuments in Italy. At first glance, the trip to remote Bulla Regia will hardly seem worth the trouble. But look deeper (literally) and you'll see that Bulla Regia's treasures remain buried beneath the ground, in a series of **underground mansions** and sites. The city was the capital of the Numidian kingdom until the last of the Numidian heirs, Jugurtha, was defeated by the Romans. The town grew in prestige and wealth throughout the 2nd and 3rd centuries, and achieved colony status during the reign of Hadrian (117-138 AD). One plutocrat apparently got the idea that building a villa underground would beat the heat, and others lavishly followed suit. A 7th-century earthquake destroyed most of the above-ground sections of the city, but the underground chambers survive to recall a way of life unique to the empire and preserve **mosaics** of museum quality.

Orientation and Practical Information To reach Bulla Regia, catch one of the four morning **buses** from Le Kef to Jendouba (1½hr., 1.750D); *louages* cost more (2.150D). In Jendouba, all buses and *louages* stop in or near **pl. 7 Novembre 1987.** There are three bus companies in town, providing service to a variety of destinations. Buses also run north to Aïn Draham (1hr., 1.550D) and on to Tabarka (2hr., 2.200D). The last bus to Le Kef is at 3pm; *louages* (2.150D) make the run until mid-afternoon. Buses run every hour or so to and from Tunis, stopping at the SNTRI office (3hr., 2.260D). Walk toward the center of the square and head left onto the Aïn Draham road, which heads in the right direction. If you're lucky, you may catch the blue-and-white **minibus** that runs to and from the site. It leaves from the Fina gas station but only in the morning (about 8-9am), midday, and evening (6-8pm). Otherwise, yellow cabs are the only option. Drivers will demand 2-3D to take you there, but heading back it's 500ml per place if you flag a cab on its way to Jendouba.

Sights Purchase your entrance ticket at the **museum** across the road from the site. (Open daily 8am-7pm, Sept.-March 8am-5pm. Admission 2D; photo permit 1D.) Here, you can wise up on your Bulla Regia history (assuming you read French or Arabic); relics include a chubby-faced, stick-figure representation of the Carthaginian goddess Tanit. The main entrance to the site stands by the extensive 2nd-century **Baths of Julia Memma,** dominated by a massive arch. No one comes here to see them, but the large complex is a fun place to explore. Head along the path to the right, which leads to the **theater.** The galleries remain intact and a mosaic of a bear continues to paw the space in front of the stage. The ruined complex near (to the north of) the theater is the ancient **market** and **forum,** containing a decimated Capitol and temple of Apollo. Take the path leading away from the Capitol until it passes a small pumping station, which continues to exploit the spring that supplied the Roman and Numidian settlements. The path leading left passes the cavernous **Maison de la Pêche** (Fishing Villa), to the right, whose subterranean chambers shelter a clam-shaped fountain and a large mosaic of two fishermen and assorted undersea life: squid, octopi, eels, and catfish. The house served as a tribunal and prison; the judge sat by the underground fountain and sent miscreants into cells behind him. The most elaborate of the underground constructions is located farther along the path in the **Nouvelle Maison de la Chasse** (New Villa of the Hunt). Five entire rooms survive below, surrounding the most beautiful courtyard in Bulla Regia. Graceful Corinthian columns support the underground ceiling, while the blue sky looks down upon the central patio. In the adjacent above-ground rooms to the north, mosaics artfully depict gazelles, birds, and other animals. Another yellow sign points the way to the **Maison d'Amphitrite;** inside is an exquisite mosaic of Venus flanked by Poseidon and other mer-creatures—it's Botticelli's *Birth of Venus* minus the big clam.

DOUGGA

The Roman metropolis of Dougga, the largest and best-preserved ancient site in Tunisia, is everything you expected from Carthage but failed to find. From its temple to its toilets, the ancient city remains almost completely intact; it was inhabited up to a century ago, when a new town was built down the hill for its inhabitants who, it was felt, were distracting the tourists. Framed by pastures, olive trees, and grain fields, and located on a high bluff, Dougga is also the most scenically situated of Tunisia's ruined Roman cities. The site extends over a large area, requiring the better part of a day for a complete tour. Fortunately, the major ruins are concentrated in the small area around the ancient forum.

Orientation and Practical Information You can get to Dougga on the Le Kef-Tunis **bus** line. Just take any of the 16 daily buses from Le Kef to Tunis and ask to be let off at Dougga (1hr., 2.520D). If you're coming from Tunis, there are nearly as many from that direction (2hr., 4.100D). In Dougga town, the road to the ruins is marked and begins at the Mobil station. It's a 3km **hike** to the site; the road is paved but steep in places (250m before the ticket office, a track leads across the field into the ruins; the only thing stopping you from taking it is your conscience). At the entrance of the ruins, a guide will tell you that your visit will be immeasurably poorer without his services. Unless you can agree in advance on a reasonable price

(1-2D), shrug him off. To get home, flag down a bus on the main road headed for Tunis (every hour) or Le Kef (every 1½-2 hrs.). The buses are green and white and run late into the evening. Note that the ruins at Dougga can also be reached by way of **Teboursouk,** a neighboring village also on the Le Kef-Tunis line. The roads are better on that side of the hill, but the walk is twice as long (6km).

Sights The site's main entrance (by the theater) opens onto the Teboursouk road. The Nouvelle Dougga road leads to the "back" of the site (open daily 8am-7pm; admission 2D, photo permit 1D). From here, a path leads to a ruined bath complex; take a left and walk up the hill to the romantically disheveled **Temple of Caelestis,** dedicated to the Latin version of the Carthaginian Tanit. An aqueduct stretches to the east and the **Arch of Alexander Severus** (the last of the "African" emperors). The path running from the arch to the right (west) leads to the ancient city center and the **Capitol of Dougga.** This 2nd-century building deserves its reputation as one of the finest examples of Roman construction in Tunisia. Six slender, fluted columns crowned with a full triangular portico recall the grandeur that was Rome. Inside there's half a marble head of Jupiter, surrounded by a crossword puzzle of fragmented Latin inscriptions (the cellar of this temple has become a storehouse for the extra inscriptions found at the site). Adjacent to the capitol are the **Forum** and the **Plaza of the Twelve Winds,** where the careful eye will discern a circular compass rose carved into the marble pavement. All around the compass' border, the names of the winds are also carved. Two **temples,** one to Mercury and the other to "Augustan Piety," border the plaza, and the **market** extends to the south (downhill). With your back to the Capitol, notice that the path leading to the left ends at a set of stairs that descend into the large **Lycinian baths.** The baths are well preserved, with many of the massive walls and interior colonnades still standing; below, you can step down to the service tunnels. Exiting from the tunnels drops you amongst the residences, more or less in front of the remarkably intact **House of Ulysses.** The place takes its name from a particularly well-preserved mosaic, since moved to the Bardo Museum. Across the street, stairs lead down to the **House of Trifollum.** Dougga's largest building was not a temple or government structure—it was a brothel. Numerous small rooms, about whose functions archaeologists like to speculate, branch off the central courtyard. Next door are the **Cyclops Baths,** replete with ancient toilet seats, where clients probably dropped by to wash up.

One remnant of Carthage survives among the monuments of its conquerors. The pagoda-like tower visible down the hill is the **Lybido-Punic Mausoleum,** built in the 2nd century BC in honor of a Numidian prince. It is about the only significant example of Punic architecture in Tunisia; the Romans didn't leave much standing once they had taken over Carthaginian territory. The structure is distinct in style from its surroundings, but Carthage traditionally possessed little in the way of original artistic style. The mausoleum's columns and pediments demonstrate that Greco-Roman influenced Punic society by other means than invasion.

APPENDICES

Language

Knowing a few basic words and phrases will make your trip much easier, and you'll find that even poor attempts at Italian will be appreciated. Take a phrase book (the *Barron's* book is fairly useful, and *Berlitz* has some handy phrases, though the vocabulary is geared toward business travelers) and practice before you leave. If you can learn only three complete sentences, learn *Parla inglese?* (PAHR-lah een-GLAY-say: Do you speak English?), *Non parlo Italiano* (nohn PAHR-loh ee-tal-YAHN-o: I don't speak Italian), and the always appropriate *Va bene* (vah BEH-neh: It's ok, it's cool, what's up?).

In this section we include a rudimentary introduction to pronunciation, and some useful phrases and vocabulary. There are sections on general information and vocabulary, numbers, time, reservations by phone, transportation and directions, restaurant basics, and emergency and self-defense phrases. For more information on the Italian language, see page 78.

PRONUNCIATION

VOWELS

There are seven vowel sounds in standard Italian. **A, I,** and **U** each have only one pronunciation. **E** and **O** each have two possible pronunciations, one tense and one lax, depending on where the vowel appears in the word, whether or not it's stressed, and regional accent (some accents don't even incorporate this distinction). It's difficult for non-native speakers to predict the quality of vowels, but you may be able to hear the difference, especially with **E.** We illustrate below the *approximate* pronunciation of the vowels, but don't worry too much about **E** and **O.**

a:	*a* as in f*a*ther *(casa)*
e: tense	*ay* as in b*ay* *(sete)*
e: lax	*eh* as in set *(bella)*
i:	*ee* as in cheese *(vino)*
o: tense	*o* as in bone *(sono)*
o: lax	between *o* of bone and *au* of c*au*ght *(zona)*
u:	*oo* as in droop (g*u*sto)

CONSONANTS

Italian consonants won't give you many problems, except for the few quirks noted here. **H** is always silent and **R** is always trilled.

C and G: before **a, o,** or **u, c** and **g** are hard, as in *cat* and *goose* or as in the Italian word *colore* (koh-LOHR-ay), "color," or *gatto* (GAHT-toh), "cat." They soften into **ch** and **j** sounds, respectively, when followed by **i** or **e**, as in the English *cheese* and *jeep* or the Italian *ciao* (CHOW), "good-bye," and *gelato* (djeh-LAH-toh), "ice cream."

CH and GH: h returns **c** and **g** to their "hard" sounds in front of **i** or **e** (see above); making words like, *chianti* (kee-YAHN-tee), the Tuscan wine, and *spaghetti* (spah-GEHT-tee), the pasta.

GN and GLI: pronounce **gn** like the **ni** in *onion*, thus *bagno* ("bath") is "BAHN-yoh." **Gli** is like the **lli** in *million*, so *sbagliato* ("wrong") is said "zbal-YAH-toh."

S and Z: An **s** found between two vowels or followed by the letters **b, d, g, l, m, n r,** and **v** is pronounced as the English **z**; thus *casa* ("house") sounds like "KAH-zah" and *smarrito* ("lost") like "zmahr-REE-toh." A double **s,** an initial **s,** or an **s** followed by any other consonant has the same sound as an English initial **s,** so *sacco* ("bag") is SAHK-koh. **Z** has a **ts** or **dz** sound; thus *stazione* ("station") is pronounced "staht-see-YOH-nay," while *zoo* ("zoo") is pronounced "dzoh" and *mezzo* ("half") is "MEHD-zoh."

SC and SCH: when followed by **a, o,** or **u, sc** is pronounced as **sk,** so *scusi* ("excuse me") yields "SKOO-zee." When followed by an **e** or **i,** the combination is pronounced **sh** as in *sciopero* (SHOH-pair-oh), "strike." **H** returns **c** to its hard sound **(sk)** in front of **i** or **e,** as in *pesche* (PEHS-kay), "peaches," not to be confused with *pesce* (PEH-shay), "fish."

Double consonants: The difference between double and single consonants in Italian is likely to cause problems for English speakers. When you see a double consonant, think about actually pronouncing it twice or holding it for a long time. English phrases like "dumb man" or "bad dog" approximate the sound of a double consonant. Failing to make the distinction can lead to some confusion; for example, *penne all'arrabbiata* is "short pasta in a spicy red sauce," whereas *pene all'arrabbiata* means "penis in a spicy red sauce."

STRESS

In many Italian words, stress falls on the next-to-last syllable. When stress falls on the last syllable, an accent indicates where stress should fall: *città* (cheet-**TAH**) or *perché* (pair-**KAY**). Stress can fall on the third-to-last syllable as well. It's not easy to predict stress, so you'll have to pick this up by listening to Italian speech.

PLURALS

Italians words form their plurals by changing the last vowel. Words that end in an **a** in the singular (usually feminine), end with an **e** in the plural; thus *mela* (MAY-lah), "apple," becomes *mele* (MAY-lay). Words that end with **o** or **e** in the singular take an **i** in the plural: *conto* (KOHN-toh), "bill," is *conti* (KOHN-tee) and *cane* (KAH-neh), "dog," becomes *cani* (KAH-nee). There are several exceptions to these rules; for example, *braccio* becomes *braccia* in the plural. (But don't worry too much about irregular plurals.) Words with final accent, like *città* and *caffè,* and words that end in consonants like *bar* and *sport* do not change in the plural.

■■■ USEFUL PHRASES AND VOCABULARY

GENERAL

Hi/So long (informal)	*Ciao*	chow
Good day/Hello	*Buongiorno*	bwohn JOHR-noh
Good evening	*Buona sera*	BWOH-nah SEH-rah
Good night	*Buona notte*	BWOH-nah NOHT-tay
Goodbye	*Arrivederci/arrivederLa*	ah-ree-veh-DAIR-chee/ah-ree-veh-DAIR-lah
Please	*Per favore/per cortesia/ per piacere*	pair fah-VOH-ray/pair kohr-teh-ZEE-ah/pair pee-ah-CHEH-reh
Thank you	*Grazie*	GRAHT-see-yeh
You're welcome/May I help you/Go right ahead	*Prego*	PRAY-goh
Pardon me.	*Scusi*	SKOO-zee
May I get by?	*Permesso*	pair-MEHS-soh

I'm sorry.	Mi dispiace.	mee dees-PYAH-cheh
Yes/No/Maybe	Sì/No/Forse	see/no/FOHR-say
I don't know	Non lo so	nohn loh soh
I don't speak Italian.	Non parlo italiano.	nohn PAR-loh ee-tahl-YAH-noh
I don't understand	Non capisco	nohn kah-PEES-koh
What does this mean?	Che vuol dire questo?	kay vwohl DEE-reh KWEH-stoh
Is there someone who speaks English?	C'è qualcuno che parla inglese?	cheh kwahl-KOO-noh kay PAR-lah een-GLAY-zay
Could you help me?	Potrebbe aiutarmi?	poh-TREHB-beh ah-yoo-TAHR-mee
Could you repeat that?	Può ripetere?	pwo ri-PEH-teh-reh
Okay/I understand.	Ho capito.	oh kah-PEE-toh
What do I know?	Che ne so io?	keh neh soh EE-oh
I have no idea	Boh.	boh
this/that	questo/quello	KWEH-sto/KWEHL-loh
who	chi	kee
where	dove	DOH-vay
which	quale	KWAH-lay
when	quando	KWAN-doh
what	che/cosa/che cosa	kay/KOH-za/kay KOH-za
why/because	perché	pair-KEH
more/less	più/meno	pyoo/MEH-noh
How do you say...?	Come si dice...?	KOH-may see DEE-chay
What do you call this in Italian?	Come si chiama questo in italiano?	KOH-may see key-YAH-mah KWEH-stoh een ee-tahl-YAH-no
Wow! Holy Cow!	Accidenti!	ah-chee-DEHN-tee
I would like...	Vorrei...	vohr-RAY
Where is...?	Dov'è...?	doh-VAY
How much does it cost?	Quanto costa?	KWAN-toh CO-stah
reduced (price)	ridotto	ree-DOHT-toh
a student discout	uno sconto studentesco	OO-noh SKOHN-toh stoo-dehn-TEHS-koh
the consulate	il consolato	eel kohn-soh-LAH-toh
the station	la stazione	lah staht-see-YO-nay
the grocery store	il negozio di alimentari	eel neh-GOT-syoh di ah-lee mehn-TAH-ree
the hostel	l'ostello	lo-STEHL-lo
the hotel	l'albergo/la pensione	lahl-BAIR-goh/lah pehn-see-OH-neh
the street address	l'indirizzo	leen-dee-REET-soh
the building	l'edificio/il palazzo	leh-dee-FEE-choh/eel pah-LAHT-soh
the church	la chiesa	lah kee-AY-zah
the telephone	il telefono	eel teh-LAY-foh-noh
the sea	il mare	eel MAH-ray
the beach	la spiaggia	la spee-AHJ-jah
the hospital	l'ospedale	los-peh-DAH-leh
open/closed	aperto/chiuso	ah-PAIR-toh/KYOO-zoh
the post office	l'ufficio postale	loo-FEE-choh poh-STAH-lay

the entrance/the exit	*l'ingresso/l'uscita*	leen-GREHS-soh/loo-SHEE-tah
the reservation	*la prenotazione*	lah pray-noh-taht-SYOH-neh
with bath/shower	*con bagno/doccia*	cohn BAHN-yo/DOH-cha
bathroom	*il gabinetto/il bagno/la toletta*	eel gah-bee-NEHT-toh/eel BAHN-yo/ lah toh-LEHT-tah
the towel	*l'asciugamano*	lah-shoo-gah-MAH-noh
the sheets	*le lenzuola*	lay lehnt-SWOH-lah
the blanket	*la coperta*	lah koh-PAIR-tah
heating	*il riscaldamento*	eel ree-skahl-dah-MEN-toh
How much does it cost?	*Quanto costa?*	KWAN-toh CO-stah
Where is...?	*Dov'è...?*	doh-VAY
How much does it cost?	*Quanto costa?*	KWAN-toh CO-stah
Where is...?	*Dov'è...?*	doh-VAY

NUMBERS

1	uno	20	venti
2	due	21	ventuno
3	tre	22	ventidue
4	quattro	30	trenta *thirty*
5	cinque	40	quaranta
6	sei	50	cinquanta
7	sette	60	sessanta
8	otto	70	settanta
9	nove	80	ottanta
10	dieci	90	novanta
11	undici	100	cento
12	dodici	101	centuno
13	tredici	102	centodue
14	quattordici	200	duecento
15	quindici	813	ottocento tredici
16	sedici	1000	mille
17	diciassette	2000	due mila
18	diciotto	million	un millione
19	diciannove	billion	un milliardo

TIME

At what time...?	*A che ora...?*	Ah kay OH-rah
What time is it?	*Che ore sono?*	kay OH-ray SOH-noh
It's 2:30.	*Sono le due e mezzo*	SOH-noh lay DOO-ay eh MEHD-zoh
It's noon.	*È mezzogiorno*	eh mehd-zoh-JOR-noh
It's midnight.	*È mezzanotte*	eh mehd-zah-NOT-teh
tomorrow	*domani*	doh-MAH-nee
today	*oggi*	OHJ-jee
yesterday	*ieri*	ee-YEH-ree
this evening/ tonight	*stasera*	stah-SEH-rah
week	*settimana*	seht-tee-MAH-nah
morning	*mattina*	maht-TEE-nah
afternoon	*pomeriggio*	poh-meh-REEJ-joh
day	*giorno*	JOHR-noh
night	*notte*	NOHT-teh

evening	*sera*	SAIR-ah
soon	*fra poco*	frah POH-koh
right away	*subito*	SOO-bee-toh
now	*adesso/ora*	ah-DEHS-doh/OH-rah
already	*già*	JAH
early (before sched-	*in anticipo*	een ahn-TEE-chee-poh
uled arrival time)		
late (after scheduled	*in ritardo*	een ree-TAHR-doh
arrival time)		
early (in the day)	*presto*	PREH-stoh
late (in the day)	*tardi*	TAHR-dee
weekdays	*i giorni feriali*	ee JOHR-nee feh-ree-AH-lee
Sundays and holidays	*i giorni festivi*	ee JOHR-nee fehs-TEE-vee

Months (*i mesi*) are not capitalized in Italian: *gennaio* (jehn-NAH-yoh), *febbraio* (feb-BRAH-yoh), *marzo* (MART-soh), *aprile* (ah-PREE-lay), *maggio* (MAHJ-joh), *giugno* (JOON-yoh), *luglio* (LOOL-yoh), *agosto* (ah-GOHS-toh), *settembre* (seht-TEHM-bray), *ottobre* (oht-TOH-bray), *novembre* (noh-VEHM-bray), *dicembre* (dee-CHEHM-bray).

Days of the week are not capitalized either: *lunedì* (Monday, loo-neh-DEE), *martedì* (mahr-teh-DEE), *mercoledì* (mayr-coh-leh-DEE), *giovedì* (joh-veh-DEE), *venerdì* (veh-nair-DEE), *sabato* (SAH-bah-toh), *domenica* (doh-MEHN-ee-cah).

RESERVATIONS BY PHONE

Mastery of the following phrases should allow you to get through the process of reserving a room on the telephone.

| Hello? (phone greeting). | *Pronto!* | PROHN-toh |
| Do you speak English? | *Parla inglese?* | PAR-lah een-GLAY-zay |

| Could I reserve a single/ double room with/ without bath for the second of August? | *Potrei prenotare una camera singola/doppia con/senza bagno per il due agosto?* | poh-TRAY pray-no-TAH-ray OO-nah KAH-mch-rah SEEN-goh-lah/DOHP-pyah KOHN/SENT-sah BAHN-yo pair eel DOO-ay ah-GOHS-toh? |

I will arrive at 14:30 (remember, Italians use the 24-hour clock, so add twelve to afternoon /evening arrival times).	*Arriverò alle quattordici e mezzo*	ahr-ree-veh-ROH ahl-lay kwaht-TOHR-dee-chee eh MEHD-zoh
How much is the room?	*Quanto costa la camera?*	KWAHN-toh KOHS-ta lah KAM-eh-rah
Okay, I'll take it.	*Va bene. La prendo.*	vah BEHN-eh. lah PREN-doh

Some replies you might hear are:

Certainly!	*Certo!*	CHAIR-toh
I'm sorry but...	*Mi dispiace, ma...*	mee dees-PYAH-chay, mah...
Nope, we're full.	*No, siamo al completo*	noh, see-YA-moh ahl cohm-PLEH-toh
We don't take telephone reservations.	*Non si fanno prenotazioni per telefono*	nohn see FAHN-noh pray-noh-tat-SYO-nee pair tay-LAY-foh-noh

You must arrive before 2pm.	*Deve arrivare primo delle quattordici*	DAY-vay ahr-ree-VAH-ray PREE-moh deh-leh kwaht-TOHR-dee-chee
You'll have to send a deposit/check.	*Bisogna mandare un acconto/un anticipo/un assegno.*	bee-ZOHN-yah mahn-DAH-reh oon ahk-KOHN-toh/oon ahn-TEE-chee-poh/oon ahs-SAY-nyoh

TRANSPORTATION AND DIRECTIONS

a ticket	*un biglietto*	oon beel-YEHT-toh
a pass (bus)	*una tessera*	OO-nah TEHS-seh-rah
one way	*solo andata*	SOH-loh ahn-DAH-tah
round-trip	*andata e ritorno*	ahn-DAh-tah eh ree-TORH-noh
reduced (price)	*ridotto*	ree-DOHT-toh
a student discount	*uno sconto studentesco*	OO-noh SKOHN-toh stoo-dehn-TEHS-koh
the station	*la stazione*	lah staht-see-YO-nay
the train	*il treno*	eel TRAY-noh
the plane	*l'aereo*	lah-AIR-eh-oh
the (city) bus	*l'autobus*	LAU-toh-boos
the (intercity) bus	*il pullman*	eel POOL-mahn
the car	*la macchina*	lah MAHK-kee-nah
the ferry	*il traghetto*	eel tra-GHEHT-to
the flight	*il volo*	eel VOH-loh
the arrival	*l'arrivo*	lahr-REE-voh
the departure	*la partenza*	lah par-TENT-sah
the track	*il binario*	eel bee-NAH-ree-oh
the terminus (of a bus)	*il capolinea*	eel kah-poh-LEE-neh-ah
the train	*il treno*	eel TRAY-noh
Do you stop at...?	*Ferma a...?*	FAIR-mah ah
What time does the train for ... leave?	*A che ora parte il treno per...?*	ah kay OH-rah PAHR-tay eel TRAY-noh pair
What platform for..?	*Che binario per...?*	kay bee-NAH-ree-oh pair
Is the train late?	*È in ritardo il treno?*	eh een ree-TAHR-doh eel TRAY-no
Where does the bus for ... leave?	*Da dove parte l'autobus per...?*	dh DOH-vay PAHR-tay LAU-toh-boos pair
What time does the...open (close)?	*A che ora si apre (chiude)...?*	a kay OH-rah see AH-pray (KYOO-day)
I'd like a ticket for...	*Vorrei un biglietto per...*	vohr-RAY oon beel-YET-toh pair
near/far	*vicino/lontano*	vee-CHEE-noh/lohn-TAH-noh
Turn left/right.	*Gira a sinistra/destra*	JEE-rah ah see-NEE-strah/DEH-strah
straight ahead	*sempre diritto*	SEHM-pray dee-REET-toh
up/down	*su/giù*	soo/joo
here	*qui/qua*	kwee/kwah
there	*lì/là*	lee/lan
down there at the end	*giù in fondo*	joo een FOHN-doh
strike	*sciopero*	SHOHP-eh-roh

RESTAURANT BASICS

For more Italian food terms, see Essentials: Food, page 61.

knife	*il coltello*	eel kohl-TEHL-loh
fork	*la forchetta*	lah fohr-KAYT-tah
spoon	*il cucchiaio*	eel koo-kee-EYE-oh
napkin	*il tovagliolo*	eel toh-vahl-YOH-loh
plate	*il piatto*	eel PYAT-toh
drinking glass	*il bicchiere*	eel bee-KYAIR-eh
drink	*la bevanda*	lah beh-VAHN-dah
appetizer	*l'antipasto*	lahn-tee-PAHS-toh
first course	*il primo (piatto)*	eel PREE-moh PYAHT-toh
second course	*il secondo (piatto)*	eel seh-KOHN-doh PYAHT-toh
dish	*il contorno*	eel kohn-TOHR-noh
dessert	*il dolce*	eel DOHL-chay
cheese, cheese course	*il formaggio*	eel fohr-MAHJ-joh
breakfast	*(prima) colazione*	PREE-mah koh-laht-SYO-nay
lunch	*il pranzo*	eel PRAHND-zoh
dinner	*la cena*	lah CHAY-nah
waiter/waitress	*cameriere/a*	kah-meh-ree-AIR-ray/rah
cover charge	*il coperto*	eel koh-PAIR-toh
service charge	*il servizio*	eel sehr-VEET-syoh
the tip	*la mancia*	lah MAHN-chah
Is the serivce included?	*È compreso il servizio?*	eh kohm-PREH-zoh eel sehr-VEET-syoh?
bill	*il conto*	eel KOHN-toh
May I have...	*Posso avere...*	POHS-soh ah-VAY-reh
May I pay by credit card?	*Posso pagare con una carta di credito?*	POHS-soh pah-GAH-reh kohn OO-na KAR-ta dee KREH-dee-toh

EMERGENCY AND DEFENSE PHRASES

Wait!	*Aspetta!*	ah-SPEHT-tah
Stop!	*Ferma!*	FAIR-mah
Help!	*Aiuto!*	ah-YOO-toh
You're gross	*Fai schifo*	fy SKEE-foh
Go away!	*Va via! Vattene!*	va VEE-ah/VAHT-teh-neh
Leave me alone	*Lasciami in pace!*	LAH-shah-mee een PAH-cheh
Don't touch me!	*Non mi toccare!*	NOHN mee tohk-KAH-reh
I'll call the police!	*Chiamo la polizia!*	KYAH-moh lah poh-leet-SEE-ah
Could you help me find...?	*Mi potrebbe aiutare a trovare...?*	mee poh-TREHB-beh ah-yoo-TAR-eh ah troh-VAH-reh
I've lost my passport (my money)	*Ho perso il mio passaporto (i miei soldi)*	oh PEHR-soh eel MEE-oh pahs-sah-PORT-oh (ee mee-AY-ee SOHL-dee)
I've been robbed.	*Sono stato derubato.*	SOH-noh STAH-toh deh-roo-BAH-toh

GLOSSARY

■ # Glossary

The following is a partial glossary of Italian, English, and Arabic terms used in this book. Many are artistic, architectural, and historical, but some commonly used terms are included as well.

Abbazia	Also *Badia*, an abbey.
Agriturismo	A program which allows tourists to stay in farmhouses. Depending on the region, the cost of the stay may be offset by laboring on the farm.
Aisle	Sides of a church flanking the nave, separated from it by a series of columns.
Amphora	Large ancient vase, usually used to hold oil or wine.
Apse	A semicircular, domed projection at the altar end of a church.
Atrium	A central court, usually in an ancient Roman house or a Byzantine church.
Bab	Gate (Arabic).
Baldacchino	A stone or bronze canopy supported by columns over the altar of a church.
Basilica	In ancient Rome, a building used for public administration. Early Christians adopted the architectural style, a rectangular building with aisle and apse but no transept, for their churches.
Battistero	A baptistery; (almost always) a separate building near the town's *duomo* where the city's baptisms were performed.
Borgo	A suburb or street leading into a suburb from the center of town (these suburbs are now often just sections of town).
Campanile	A bell tower, usually free-standing.
Camposanto	A cemetery.
Cartoon	A preparatory drawing for a painting or sculpture. Promise.
Caryatid	A column in the shape of a female figure.
Castrum	Ancient Roman military camp. Many Italian cities were originally built on this rectilinear plan with straight streets, the most important of which were the perpendicular *decumanus maximus* and *cardo*.
Cenacolo	The Last Supper (often to be found in the refectory of an abbey or convent).
Chancel	The enclosed space around the altar in a medieval church reserved for clergy and choir; in most Italian churches the space has been opened.
Chicha	Arabic flavored tobacco (honey, cherry, etc.), often smoked in a hookah ("bong").
Chott	A salt lake (Arabic).
Cipollino	Onion marble; marble with veins of green or white.
Cloister	A quadrangle with covered walkways along its edges, usually with a garden in the center.
Comune	The government of a free city of the Middle Ages.
Condottiere	The captain of a mercenary band hired by Italian cities to fight their medieval and Renaissance wars.
Corso	Principal street.
Crenelations	Battlements. Sometimes spelled with two "l"s.
Cupola	A dome.

Diptych	A panel painting in two sections.
Duomo	Cathedral, the official seat of a bishop, and usually the central church of an Italian town.
Exedra	A semicircular recess, at the end of a room or free-standing.
Façade	The front of a building, or any other wall given special architectural treatment.
Fiume	A river.
Forum	In an ancient Roman town, a square containing municipal buildings and/or market space. Smaller towns usually have only one central forum, while large cities, such as Rome, can have several.
Fresco	*Affresco,* a painting made on wet plaster. When it dries, the painting becomes part of the wall.
Frieze	A band of decoration. Architecturally, can also refer to the middle part of an entablature (everything above the columns of a building) between the *architrave* and the *cornice.*
Funicolare	Funicular, a cable railway ascending a mountain.
Ghibelline	One of the two great medieval factions that supported the Holy Roman Emperor (Frederick II when the troubles began) in his struggles against the papacy. Later, distinctions became blurred and being a Ghibelline merely meant that the rival town down the road or the rival family up the street was Guelph. See Guelph.
Giardino	Garden.
Greek Cross	A cross whose arms are of equal length.
Grotesque	1) Ugly. 2) Painted, carved, or stucco decorations of fantastic, distorted human or animal figures, named for the grotto work found in Nero's buried Golden House in Rome. Grotesque elements are a frequent part of Renaissance art.
Guelph	One of two great medieval factions that supported the Pope in his struggles against the Holy Roman Emperor (Frederick II when the troubles began). Later, distinctions became blurred and being a Guelph merely meant that the rival town down the road or the rival family up the street was Ghibelline. See Ghibelline.
Hammam	Turkish-style bath house common in Tunisia (Arabic).
Jemaa	A mosque (Arabic).
Kasbah	A citadel or fort, often used for civic purposes (Arabic).
Latin Cross	A cross whose vertical arm is longer than its horizontal arm.
Loggia	A covered gallery or balcony.
Lungo, Lung-	Literally "along," so that a *lungomare* is a boardwalk or promenade alongside the ocean, and a *lungarno* in Florence is a street running alongside the river Arno.
Lunette	A semi-circular frame in the ceiling or vault of a building that holds a painting or sculpture.
Maestà	The Madonna and Child enthroned in majesty, always accompanied by angels and, in later medieval and Renaissance art, saints.
Mausoleum	A large tomb or stone building with places to entomb the dead above ground.
Medina	The fortified medieval part of an Arabic town.
Mezzogiorno	A nickname for the southern part of Italy.
Nave	The central body of a church.
Opera	The office charged with building a public structure, most often a city's *duomo.*

Pala	A large altarpiece.
Palazzo	An important building of any type, not just a palace.
Palio	A banner. In modern times, has come to mean a horse race in which the neighborhoods of a city compete for a banner.
Panino	Sandwich. Often comes without garnish.
Piazza	A city square. In Venice, the term *campo* (literally field) is usually used instead.
Pietà	A scene of the Virgin, sometimes accompanied, mourning the dead Christ.
Pietra serena	A soft, gray sandstone, easily carved.
Piscina	A pool, or a wash-basin used by a priest before Mass.
Polyptych	A painting made in more than three panels or sections.
Porphyry	Egyptian rock composed of feldspar crystals embedded in a compact base of dark red or purple crystals.
Predella	A step, or, in medieval beds, the low boxes surrounding a bed. The meaning is taken over in painting of altarpieces to signify the small paintings, usually in several sections, beneath the main painting or altarwork.
Pulchritudinous	The longest one-word synonym in this book for beautiful.
Putto	(pl. *putti*) The little nude babies that flit around Renaissance art occasionally, and Baroque art incessantly.
Quatrefoil	A four-lobed design typical of Gothic framing.
Rifugio	(pl. *rifugi*) Type of refuge (alpine huts) scattered all over the Alps and Dolomites which offer beds and meals for hikers.
Salutation	Hi, Mom!
Sciopero	A strike, usually related to public transportation.
Scuola	Modern word for "school," originally the Venetian name for a confraternity.
Settimana Bianca	Literally "white week," special package for a week of skiing which offers a set price for room and board (sometimes the rate includes ski passes—check before making reservations).
Sinopia	A red pigment sketch made on a wall as a preliminary study for a fresco.
Souk	Itinerant weekly market (Arabic).
Stigmata	Miraculous body pains or bleeding that resemble the wounds of the crucified Christ.
Strada	Street.
Telamones	(Also *telamons*) Supporting columns sculpted as male figures (the counterparts of caryatids).
Tessera	1) One of the small (often square) component pieces of a mosaic 2) a bus pass, membership card, or phone card.
Thermae	Ancient Roman baths and, consequently, social centers.
Transept	The individual arms of a cruciform church, or both together.
Travertine	A type of limestone, the chief building material in Rome, ancient and modern. Always light-colored, but sometimes with black speckles.
Triptych	A painting in three panels or parts.
Trompe l'oeil	A painting or other piece or art whose purpose is to trick the viewer, as in a flat ceiling painted so as to appear domed.
Tufa	Along with travertine (see above), the other major non-luxury building material of ancient Rome. A soft stone composed of volcanic ash. *Tufo* in Italian.
Via	Street.
Villa	A country house, usually a large estate with a formal garden.

■ Index

0 3386316319
7 8 10 2 4   Salerno

CONNIE WILLIAMS
2 Stuyvesant Oval
Apt 5G
New York, N.Y. 10009
(212) 460-9250
Come Visit!
_____

Wines: Santa Cristina 1994
        Eleano 1992

OROLOGIO (watch)

2 8   23
2 7   23

Luigi   ⟩ Train from Rome → Salerno
Antonio   / In Navy from Messina

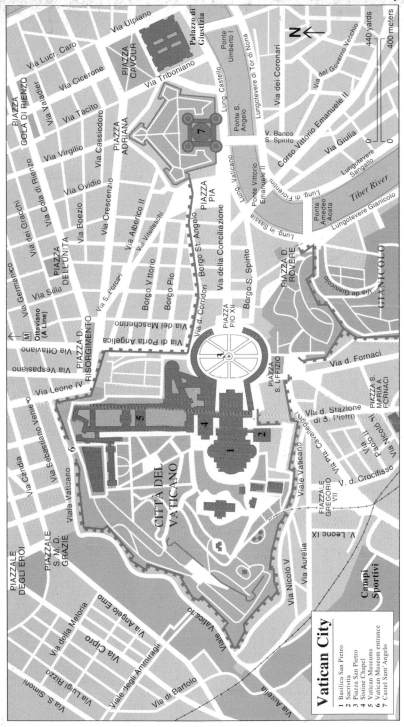

Rome: Vatican City

Vatican City

1 Basilica San Pietro
2 Sacristia
3 Piazza San Pietro
4 Sistine Chapel
5 Vatican Museums
6 Vatican Museum entrance
7 Castel Sant'Angelo

CITTÀ DEL VATICANO

Tiber River

Campi Sportivi

Palazzo di Giustizia

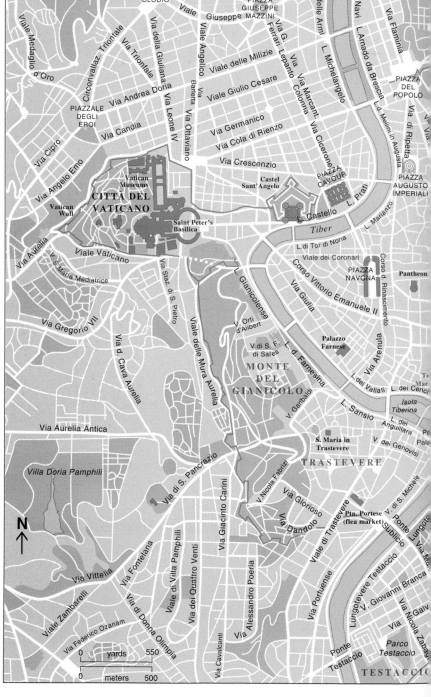

Rome Overview

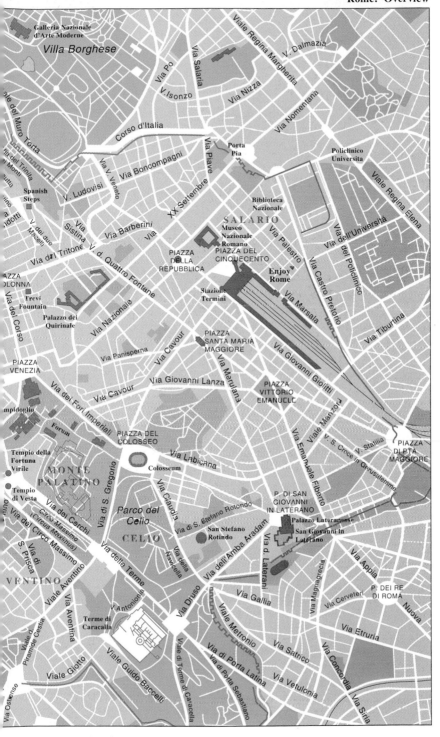

Rome: "Walks"

Walks

1 Piazza del Popolo
2 Ara Pacis
3 Mausoleum of Augustus
4 Palazzo Borghese
5 Spanish Steps
6 Trevi Fountain
7 Vittorio Emanuele Monument
8 Campidoglio
9 Teatro Marcello
10 Isola Tiberina
11 Palazzo Doria Pamphili
12 Church of Santi Apostoli
13 Church of San Marcello
14 Piazza di S. Ignazio
15 Piazza di Pietra
16 Piazza Colonna: Column of Marcus Aurelius
17 Palazzo Chigi
18 Pantheon
19 Giolitti
20 Piazza Minerva
21 Church of Santa Maria Sopra Minerva
22 Church of San Luigi dei Francesi
23 Piazza Navona
24 Church of Sant'Antonio dei Portoghesi
25 Museo Napoleonico
26 Il Gesù
27 Largo Argentina
28 Church of Sant'Andrea delle Valle
29 Palazzo del Cancelleria
30 Chiesa Nuova
31 Piazza Sforza Cesarini
32 Campo dei Fiori
33 Piazza Farnese
34 Piazza della Quercia
35 Monte di Pietà
36 Church of Santissima Trinità dei Pellegrini

VILLA BORGHESE
VILLA MEDICI

v. del Muro Torto
Via del Muro Torto
Via Belvedere
Via Trinità del Monti
Via del Babuino

Spagna

PIAZZA TRINITÀ D. MONTE
PIAZZA DI SPAGNA
Via Propaganda
Via d. Due Macelli
Via Mario de Fiori
Via della Croce
Via della Carozze
Via d. Condotti
Via Borgognona
Via Borgogna
Via Frattina
Via delle Vite
Via della Mercede
PIAZZA S. SILVESTRO
LARGO CHIGI
Via del Tritone

Via Vittorio
Via del Corso
Via Campo Marzo
PIAZZA DEL PARLIAMENTO
Via Prefetti

PIAZZA DEL POPOLO

Via di Ripetta
Via del Vantaggio
Via Brunati
Via Canova
LARGO D. SCHIAVONI
PIAZZA D. AUGUSTO IMPERATORE
Via Tomacelli
Via Borghese
PIAZZA D. PORTO DI RIPETTA
Via della Scrofa
Via Clementino

Via F. di Savoia
Lung. in Augusta
Ponte Cavour

Tiber River
Lung. dei Mellini
Via V. Colonna
Via Ulpiano
Lung. Prati
Ponte Umberto
Via dell'Orso

Via Orsini
PIAZZA D. LIBERTA
Via Feder. Cesi
Ponte Margherita
Via G. Belli
Via P. Cossa
PIAZZA DEI TRIBUNALI

Via Cola di Rienzo
Via E. Q. Visconti
Via Lucr. Caro
Via Cicerone
PIAZZA CAVOUR
Via Triboniano

Via Tacito
Via Cassiodoro
PIAZZA ADRIANA
Lungotevere Castello
Ponte S. Angelo

Via Boezio
Via Ovidio
Castel Sant'Angelo
Via Vaticano
PIAZZA PIA
Ponte Vittorio Emanuele
Lungotevere di Tor di Nona

Via Crescenzio
Via Alberico II
Via Vitelleschi
Via della Conciliazione

MONTE CAPITOLINO

PIAZZA DEI S.S. APOSTOLI

PIAZZA D. PILOTTA

Via della Umiltà

V. Minghetti

Via S. S. Apostoli

Via del Corso

Via Gatta

PZA. DEL COLLEGIO ROMANO

PIAZZA GRAZIOLI

Via del Gesù

PIAZZA VENEZIA

Via del Plebiscito

PIAZZA D. GESÙ

PIAZZA SAN MARCO

V. S. MARCO Marco

Via d'Aracoeli

Via del Teatro di Marcello

V. P.

V. MONTECITORIO

Via V. Seminario

PIAZZA DELLA ROTONDA

Via Santa Chiara

LARGO DI TORRE ARGENTINA

V. di Torre Argentina

Corso Vittorio Emanuele II

PIAZZA CAMPITELLI

Via d. Portico d. Ottavia

Lung. di Pierleoni

Ponte Fabricio

d. Dogana V.

PIAZZA S. EUSTACCHIO

Via d. Barbieri

LARGO ARENU_A

Vic. d. Chiodaroli

Via Arenula

Via Catilana

Via d. Cenci

Lurg. dei Cenci

Corso del Rinascimento

PIAZZA NAVONA

V. dell' Anima

LARGO TEATRO VALLE

PIAZZA SAN PANTALEO

PZA. DEL PARADISO

LARGO DEI PALLARO

Via dei Chiavari

LGO. DEI LIBRARI

Via dei Pettinari

Ponte Garibaldi

PIAZZA G. G. BELLI

Lungotevere dei Vallati

Via dei Coronari

Via del Governo Vecchio

PIAZZA S. SIMEONE

Via Maschelone

Via d. Farnesi

PIAZZA V. PALLOTTI

Ponte Sisto

Lungotevere Sanzio

Via del Moro

PIAZZA DEI CORONARI

Corso Vittorio Emanuele II

Via del Monserrato

Via Giulia

Lungotevere dei Tebaldi

Tiber River

V. a S. Dorotea

PIAZZA DI SANT' EGIDIO

Via d. Mattonato

LARGO PEROSI

Ponte Mazzini

Lungotevere della Farnesina

Via della Lungara

Via Corsini

Via S. Francesco di Sales

Via Gambaldi

Ponte Principe Amadeo

PIAZZA D. ROVERE

Lungotevere di Fiorentini

Via

Lungotevere Sangallo

Tiber River

Lungotevere Gianicolense

Via delle Mantellate

Via di Riari

PARCO GIANICOLENSE

N

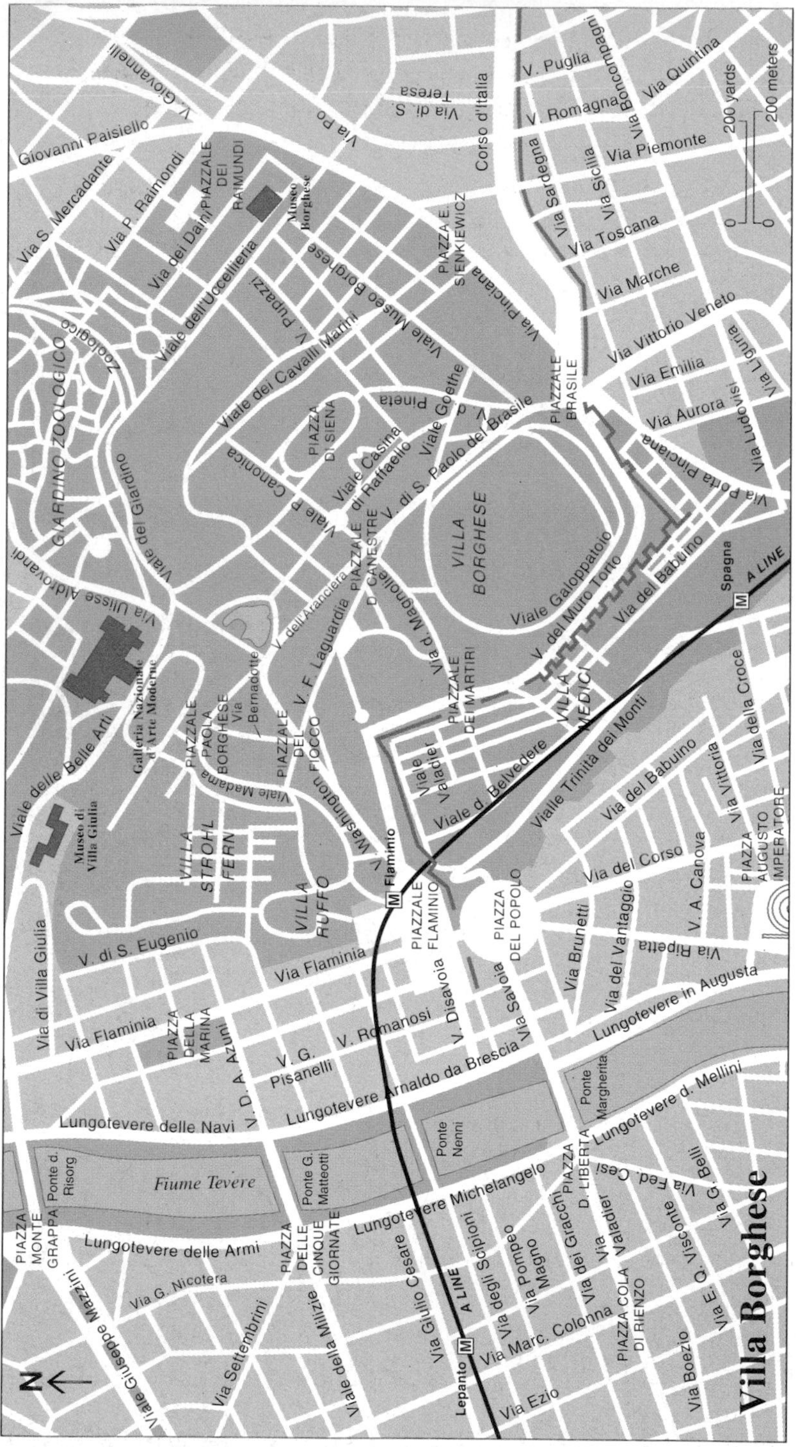
Villa Borghese
N
200 yards
200 meters
GIARDINO ZOOLOGICO
VILLA BORGHESE
VILLA STROHL FERN
VILLA RUFFO
VILLA MEDICI
Museo Borghese
Galleria Nazionale d'Arte Moderne
Museo di Villa Giulia
Fiume Tevere
PIAZZALE DEI RAIMUNDI
PIAZZA DI SIENA
PIAZZA E. SIENKIEWICZ
PIAZZALE BRASILE
PIAZZALE D. CANESTRE
PIAZZALE DEI MARTIRI
PIAZZALE PAOLA BORGHESE
PIAZZALE DEL FIOCCO
PIAZZALE FLAMINIO
PIAZZA DEL POPOLO
PIAZZA DELLA MARINA
PIAZZA AUGUSTO IMPERATORE
PIAZZA MONTE GRAPPA
PIAZZA DELLE CINQUE GIORNATE
PIAZZA D. LIBERTA
PIAZZA COLA DI RIENZO
Ponte d. Risorg.
Ponte G. Matteotti
Ponte Nenni
Ponte Margherita
Flaminio
Spagna
Lepanto
A LINE
Via Giovanni Paisiello
V. Giovannelli
Via S. Mercadante
Via P. Raimondi
Via dei Daini
Viale dell'Uccelliera
Zoologico
Via Ulisse Aldrovandi
Viale del Giardino
Viale delle Belle Arti
Via di Villa Giulia
V. di S. Eugenio
Via Flaminia
Viale Madama
Via Bernadotte
V. dell'Aranciera
V. F. Laguardia
V. Washington
Viale dei Cavalli Marini
V. Pupazzi
Viale Museo Borghese
Viale P. Canonica
Viale Casina di Raffaello
Viale Goethe
V. d. Pineta
V. di S. Paolo del Brasile
Via d. Magnolie
Viale Galoppatoio
V. del Muro Torto
Viale Valadier
Viale d. Belvedere
Via Pinciana
Via Po
Via di S. Teresa
Corso d'Italia
V. Puglia
V. Romagna
Via Boncompagni
Via Quintina
Via Piemonte
Via Sardegna
Via Sicilia
Via Toscana
Via Marche
Via Vittorio Veneto
Via Emilia
Via Aurora
Via Liguria
Via Ludovisi
Via Porta Pinciana
Via del Babuino
Viale Trinità dei Monti
Via della Croce
Via Vittoria
Via del Corso
V. A. Canova
Via Ripetta
Via Brunetti
Via del Vantaggio
Lungotevere in Augusta
Via Savoia
V. Disavoia
V. Romanosi
V. G. Pisanelli
V. D. A. Azuni
Lungotevere Arnaldo da Brescia
Lungotevere delle Navi
Lungotevere d. Mellini
Lungotevere Michelangelo
Lungotevere delle Armi
Via Fed. Cesi
Via G. Belli
Via Giulio Cesare
Via degli Scipioni
Via Pompeo Magno
Via dei Gracchi
Via Valadier
Via Marc. Colonna
Via E. Q. Visconte
Via Boezio
Via Ezio
Via G. Nicotera
Viale Giuseppe Mazzini
Via Settembrini
Viale della Milizie